Telecommunications, Broadcasting and the Internet: EU Competition Law and Regulation

AUSTRALIA
Law Book Co.
Sydney

CANADA and USA
Carswell
Toronto

HONG KONG
Sweet & Maxwell Asia

NEW ZEALAND
Brookers
Wellington

SINGAPORE and MALAYSIA
Sweet & Maxwell Asia
Singapore and Kuala Lumpur

Telecommunications, Broadcasting and the Internet: EU Competition Law and Regulation

2nd edition

L.J.H.F. Garzaniti

THOMSON
™
SWEET & MAXWELL

Published in 2003 by
Sweet & Maxwell Limited of
100 Avenue Road, London NW3 3PF
(http://www.sweetandmaxwell.co.uk)
Typeset by Advance Typesetting Limited, Oxon
Printed and bound in Great Britain by
Athenaeum Press Ltd., Gateshead

A CIP catalogue record for this book is available from the British Library

ISBN 0 421 851406

Foreword

One of the key achievements of competition policy in the European Union has been the liberalisation of the telecommunications sector. The opening up of national markets to competition has ensured that consumers and the economy as a whole have benefited from the development and availability of new communication services and products at competitive prices. The liberalisation of the EU telecommunications market has been successful and has contributed to an accelerated growth rate, reduced tariffs and market entry by a considerable number of new entrants. This has led to significant benefits for consumers in terms of better quality and choice, and lower prices.

The liberalisation process in the European Union is the result of the close interaction between sector-specific regulation and the application of the EC Treaty's competition rules. Finding the appropriate relationship and balance between the two has been and remains a delicate balancing exercise. Sector-specific regulation has played a particularly important role in the process of liberalisation. It has ensured the establishment of effective competition through facilitating significant market entry by new operators and the control of the dominant former incumbent operators. Although this approach has been successful, we are not yet at the stage of liberalisation where we can forgo sector-specific regulation altogether and rely exclusively on the competition rules: the sector is still in a transition phase and many markets either are not yet effectively competitive or (as with the local loop infrastructure) may never become so. The majority of European incumbent operators still have a dominant position on the main infrastructure and services markets, most notably at the local loop level. There are continuing bottlenecks in the provision of network access to end users and there remains a clear need to actively encourage the emergence of competitive alternative local access infrastructure.

As the full objectives of the 1998 liberalisation package have not yet been totally achieved, sector-specific regulation must be maintained for the time being. However, its application needed to be adjusted so that it is more consistent with the principles of competition law, thereby preparing the sector for a time when markets are fully competitive, sector-specific regulation can be phased out and the competition rules alone will be applicable. There was also a need to adjust sector-specific regulation to ensure that it remained effective as a result of the ongoing convergence of telecommunications, broadcasting, media and internet services.

To meet this changing environment, the Commission proposed a "New Regulatory Framework" for electronic communications, which was adopted by the Council and the European Parliament in March 2002 and entered into force on July 24, 2003. This has introduced more flexible legislation for the communications sector, which will allow regulation to evolve with technological developments and changes in the market. To take account of the process of convergence, the New Regulatory Framework will apply to all transmission networks regardless of the type of information conveyed. Moreover, it allows sector-specific regulation to be rolled back, thereby removing regulatory obligations on operators, once a market is competitive.

The implementation of the New Regulatory Framework will further develop the relationship between the competition rules and sector-specific regulation by aligning the concept of significant market power, the threshold for regulatory intervention, with the competition law concept of dominance.

The publication of the second edition of this book coincides with the entry into force of the New Regulatory Framework. Its publication is therefore particularly timely and appropriate. As with the first edition, one of the interesting and novel aspects of this second edition of Laurent Garzaniti's book remains that it covers not only the EU regulatory framework applicable to traditional telecommunications activities, but also covers broadcasting and the internet. This approach therefore naturally takes on board the ongoing process of convergence and the "technology neutral" nature of the New Regulatory Framework. This new edition, like the first one, is not limited merely to describing the New Regulatory Framework, but also reviews in detail the application of competition law in this sector and examines thoroughly the decision-making practice of the European Commission and the case law of the European courts. This unique aspect of the book undoubtedly contributed to the success of the first edition and I am confident that the second edition will continue to serve as a reference guide for all those involved in applying EU competition law and regulation in the communications sector.

Karel Van Miert

Preface

The aim of this book is primarily to serve as a reference guide and research tool for legal practitioners involved in the application of EU competition law and regulation in the telecommunications, broadcasting and internet sectors. It therefore focuses on describing the regulatory regime and reviewing the relevant case law as thoroughly as possible from a practical perspective. For instance, particular attention has been given to describing the available remedies in case of infringement of the applicable rules. In light of the increased importance of competition law in these sectors, the competition rules are described in great detail. In this context, the practice of the European Commission and the case law of the European Court of Justice and the Court of First Instance have been systematically described.

Since the first edition of this book was published in April 2000, the telecommunications legislative environment has radically changed. The second edition of this book thus represents more than a mere update of the previous edition. The regulatory part of the book was substantially redrafted to take into account the recently adopted EU telecoms package. The internet has also seen a number of recent developments that needed to be reflected. This new edition also takes into account the large number of competition cases and merger decisions which have been adopted over the last few years, whilst the chapter on state aids has been significantly developed to introduce recent legislative changes, as well as a number of recent judgments and decisions. The book covers publicly available materials up to June 2003. However, a number of later developments were able to be incorporated at the proof stage.

I wish to express my thanks to a number of people from Freshfields Bruckhaus Deringer who have helped me on this project. This second edition has been very much a collective work.

The main responsibility for revising and updating the different chapters lies with: Chapter 1 (Electronic Communications): Francesco Liberatore; Chapter 2 (Broadcasting): Blanca Montejo and Yael Ginzburg; Chapter 3 (Internet): Brandon Johnson; Chapter 4 (Overview of EU Competition Rules): Bénédicte Claes; Chapter 5 (Market Definition in the Telecoms Sector): Francesco Liberatore; Chapter 6 (Market Conduct): Andreas von Bonin; Chapter 7 (State Aid Rules): Kirsten Elsner; Chapter 8 (Mergers and Acquisitions, Joint Ventures): Michael Rosenthal; Chapter 9 (Interaction between the Competition Rules and Sector-Specific Regulation): Andreas von Bonin; Appendices: Francesco Liberatore, Mary Michelle O'Connor, Nathalie Fairburn and Elizabeth-Ann Staton.

I wish to express particular gratitude to Matthew O'Regan, who reviewed meticulously the entire book. His comments and suggestions have been very valuable in significantly improving the work. Thanks to Nathalie Fairburn and Francesco Liberatore for their assistance in co-ordinating and reviewing the various contributions. I would also like to thank Liliana Trillo Diaz and Dominic Ziegenhahn for their research assistance. I also thank Inna Toure, Clemens Heusch and Mary Michelle O'Connor for checking the references and citations and Michele Parker, Patricia Graham and Alexis Gerratt for their secretarial support. I am also grateful to my publisher Sweet & Maxwell for their support.

Preface

Finally, I would like to express very special thanks to my wife Clare, for her continued support, patience and tolerance throughout the revision of this book. I told her after the first edition "never again", and I feel like saying that again this time; however, I fear that I have probably lost any credibility with her in this respect by now.

Laurent Garzaniti

Table of Contents

Contents

7 Application of State Aid Rules

8 Mergers and Acquisitions, Joint Ventures and other Alliances

Contents

Table of Cases

TABLE OF EUROPEAN CASES

Cases before the European Court of Justice

Table of Cases

Cases before the Court of First Instance

Cases before the European Commission

Cases before the EFTA Court

TABLE OF NATIONAL CASES

Table of European Treaties

Table of European Secondary Legislation

Regulations

Decisions

List of Abbreviations

API	Application Programme Interface
ASO	Address Supporting Organisation
ATM	Asynchronous Transfer Mode
CCITT	Consultative Committee on International Telegraphy and Telephony
CDS	Content Delivery Service
CEN	European Standards Committee
CENELEC	European Electrotechnical Standards Committee
CEPT	European Conference of Postal and Telecommunications Administrations
CI	Common Interface
CPP	Calling Party Pays
CSS	Contents Scramble System
C.M.L.R.	Common Market Law Review
C.T.L.R.	Computer & Telecommunications Law Review
DARPA	Defence Advanced Research Project Agency
DBS	Digital Broadcasting Service
DCS	Digital Communications System
DECT	Digital European Cordless Telecommunications
DES	Data Encryption Standard
DNS	Domain Name System
DNSO	Domain Name Supporting Organisation
DRM	Digital Rights Management
DSL	Digital Subscriber Line
DTE	Data Terminal Equipment
DTH	Direct-to-Home
DTT	Digital Terrestrial Television
DVB	Digital Video Broadcasting
E.C.L.R.	European Competition Law Review
ECTRA	European Committee on Telecommunications Regulatory Affairs
EDI	Electronic Data Interchange
ENF	European Numbering Forum

E.L.R.	European Law Review
EPG	Electronic Programme Guide
ERC	European Radio Communications Committee
ERG	European Regulators Group
ERMES	European Digital Radio-Messaging System
ERO	European Radio Communications Office
ETNS	European Telephone Numbering Space
ETO	European Telecommunications Office
ETSI	European Telecommunications Standards Institute
EuR	Europarecht, legal journal
FCC	Federal Communications Commission
FDC	Fully Distributed Cost Method
FL-LRAIC	Forward-Looking Long-Run Average Incremental Costs
FTC	Federal Trade Commission
FTTH	Fibre-to-the-Home
GATS	General Agreement on Trade and Services
GCTS	Global Corporate Telecommunications Service
GPRS	General Packet Radio Service
GSM	General System for Mobile
GTC	Global Telecommunications Services
GTS	Global Telecommunications System
IANA	Internet Assigned Numbers Authority
IAP	Internet Access Provider
IC	Incremental Cost
ICANN	Internet Corporation for Assigned Names and Numbers
I.C.C.	Interstate Commerce Commission Reports
ICS	International Carrier Service
IDD	International Direct Dial
iDTV	Interactive Digital TV
IOT	Inter-Operator Tariff
IP	Internet Protocol
IPLC	International Private Leased Circuit
ISDN	Integrated Services Digital Network
ISI	Information Sciences Institute
ISP	Internet Service Provider
ISR	International Simple Resale
ISS	Information Society Service

ITU	International Telecommunication Union
J.N.I.	Journal of Network Industries
KTS	Key Telephone Systems
LAN	Local Area Network
MDNS	Managed Data Network Service
MFN	Most Favoured Nation
MHP	Multi Home Platform
MPEG	Moving Picture Experts Group
MVNO	Mobile Virtual Network Operator
NCA	National Competition Authority
NRA	National Regulatory Authority
NSF	National Science Foundation
OFCOM	Office of Communications
ONP	Open Network Provision
OS	Operating System
PABX	Private Automatic Branch Exchange
PBX	Private Branch Exchange
PSDS	Packet Switched Data Service
PSO	Protocol Supporting Organisation
PSPDN	Packet Switched Public Data Network
PSTN	Public Switched Telephone Network
RAM	Random Access Memory
R.I.W.	Recht der Internationalen Wirtschaft
RR	Radio Regulations
SAC	Stand Alone Cost
SCMS	Serial Copyright Management System
SDH	Synchronous Digital Hierarchy
SMATV	Satellite Mast Antenna Television
SMP	Significant Market Power
SMS	Short Messaging Service
SNG	Satellite News Gathering Service
S-PCS	Satellite Personal Communications Service
SRS	Shared Registration System
STIRA	Standard International Roaming Agreement
TLD	Top-Level Domain
T.M.R.	Telekommunikations und Medienrecht
TTP	Trusted Third Party

TVRO	Television Receive-Only Equipment
UDRP	Uniform Domain Name Dispute Resolution Procedure
UMTS	Universal Mobile Telecommunications System
URL	Uniform Resource Locator
USAT	Ultra Small Aperture Terminal
USO	Universal Service Obligation
VANS	Value-Added Network Service
VoIP	Voice over the Internet
VPN	Virtual Private Network
VSAT	Very Small Aperture Terminal
WAP	Wireless Application Protocol
W-LAN	Wireless Local Area Network
WLL	Wireless Local Loop
WRC	World Radio Conference
WTO	World Trade Organisation

Part I: Regulatory Issues

Part I will review the EU regulatory framework applying to electronic communications transmission networks and services (Chapter I). The EU initiatives to regulate the broadcasting sector (Chapter II), as well as the internet will also be discussed (Chapter III).

Chapter I

The EU Regulatory Framework
Applicable to Electronic Communications

Chapter I describes the EU regulatory framework applicable to electronic communications.[1] It will first explain the background to the regulatory initiatives of the European Union (EU) in the early to mid-1990s that culminated in the 1998 full liberalisation of the provision of electronic communications services and networks in the Member States (Section A). It will then review the new EU regulatory regime that is applicable from July 2003 to electronic communications and will focus, in particular, on the following subjects: the concept of significant market power and the harmonisation mechanisms introduced for the purposes of *ex ante* regulation (Section B); the liberalisation of electronic communications services and market access (Section C); network provision (Section D); satellite communications (Section E); access and interconnection (Section F); tariffs (Section G); universal service (Section H); directory services (Section I); data protection and information security (Section J); the application of the EU public and utilities procurement rules in the telecommunications sector (Section K); and telecommunications equipment (Section L). Section M discusses the various remedies that are available for businesses if national regulatory measures are infringed. Given the early stage of the implementation of the new regulatory package at national level, this book will focus on the review of the provisions of the new EU directives and accompanying measures, with only limited reference to national implementing laws, when available. Finally, Section N explains the application of the EU regulatory framework to non-EU businesses.

A. Background to the EU Regulatory Initiatives

1–001 The EU Regulatory Framework for Electronic Communications contains the principles that are applicable to the establishment and operation of electronic communications networks and services and associated facilities and services across Europe (hereinafter the "New Regulatory Framework"). It provides the basis for all national communications legislation in the Member States. The New Regulatory Framework constitutes the completion of a process of liberalisation and harmonisation initiated by the Commission in 1987 with the adoption of the Green Paper on Telecommunications.[2] At that time, the EU telecommunications market was still characterised by

---

[1] "Electronic communications" means telecommunications, datacommunications and sound radio.
[2] *Towards a dynamic European economy: Green Paper on the development of the common market for telecommunications services and equipment* ("1987 Green Paper"), COM(87) 290 final, July 30, 1987. For a comprehensive review of the historical context of the EU Telecommunications Regulatory Framework, see

the presence of state-owned monopoly operators in all Member States (with the exception of the United Kingdom, which had partially liberalised its telecommunications market in 1983), which did not face competition in the major aspects of their activities. The technological development of the sector (in particular digitalisation) dramatically and very rapidly changed the sector's economic context. It became apparent that unless markets were deregulated and new competitive forces were introduced on the market, the required investment to develop the technology would not be made, with the risk that consumers would not benefit to the fullest extent from this technological revolution.[3] The Commission also considered that, unless an effort was made at the EU level to adopt an adequate regulatory framework to support the development of the telecommunications market, Europe would have been left behind its trading partners.[4]

1–002 In order to create a more competitive environment for telecommunications services and equipment, the 1987 Green Paper proposed a three-pronged action: (i) the liberalisation of the supply of telecommunications services and equipment; (ii) the establishment of harmonised and open access conditions to telecommunications networks; and (iii) the application of the EC Treaty's competition rules to incumbent telecommunications operators.[5] Liberalisation, harmonisation and application of competition rules are the three pillars of the liberalisation of the telecommunications sector.

1–003 Liberalisation — The objective of liberalisation is to abolish monopolies and other special rights enjoyed by incumbent operators and to remove legal barriers to entry for new players. Article 86(3) of the EC Treaty (*ex* Article 90(3))[6] empowers the Commission to adopt general legislative measures to ensure that Member States comply with the EC Treaty, in particular the competition rules. Article 86(3) is an effective legislative tool since it permits the Commission to adopt measures relatively rapidly as there is no need to involve the Council and the Parliament, although in practice the Commission did consult the Member States and the European Parliament in adopting the liberalisation directives.[7] To achieve that objective, the Commission has adopted a number of so-called "liberalisation" directives under Article 86(3).

1–004 The liberalisation of the EC telecommunications market was a gradual process, starting with telecommunications equipment and value-added telecommunications services. These were opened to competition as a result, respectively, of the so-called "Telecoms Terminal Equipment

---

Larouche, "Broad Lines of EC Telecommunications Regulations" in *State Monopolies in the European Union and Beyond* (Kluwer, 2000).

[3] 1987 Green Paper, para.1–001, n.2, above, pp.1–3.

[4] Larouche, para.1–001, n.2, p.3.

[5] See Géradin, "L'Ouverture à la Concurrence des Entreprises de Réseau — Analyse des Principaux Enjeux du processus de Libéralisation" in *Cahiers de Droit Européen* (1999), p.15.

[6] A considerable number of articles of the EC Treaty were renumbered as a result of the entry into force of the Treaty of Amsterdam on May 1, 1999.

[7] The use of Art.86(3) as the legal basis for the adoption by the Commission of directives in the telecommunications sector was challenged by some Member States. In a landmark ruling on March 19, 1991, the European Court of Justice confirmed the main elements of the Commission's policy, including the right of the Commission to abolish all special and exclusive rights in the telecommunications sector and the appropriateness of Art.86(3) as a legal instrument on which to base such action. See Joined Cases 188–190/80, *France, Italy and UK v Commission* [1982] E.C.R. 2545; see also Case C–202/88 *France v Commission (Competition in the markets in telecommunications terminal equipment)* [1991] I E.C.R. 1223.

Directive" in 1988[8] and the "Services Directive" in 1990.[9] The liberalisation process was then extended, through successive amendments to the Services Directive, to satellite networks in 1994,[10] cable networks in 1995,[11] mobile telephony[12] and alternative infrastructure[13] in 1996, and finally public voice telephony services and networks as of January 1, 1998.[14] As part of the New Regulatory Framework, these directives were consolidated into a single piece of legislation, the so-called "Liberalisation Directive".[15] The graduation in the pace of liberalisation, in particular the temporary maintenance of incumbent operators' exclusive and special rights to supply public voice telephony services and to operate networks, was justified by the need to preserve the financial stability of incumbent operators and their capacity to provide universal service, which the Member States considered could have been threatened by a sudden opening of the entire market to full competition. Until full liberalisation of telecommunications markets in 1998, there was thus a distinction between "reserved services", *i.e.* services such as public voice telephony that continued to be provided by incumbent operators under exclusive or special rights, and "non-reserved" services, *i.e.* the liberalised services.[16] This distinction ceased to have any relevance following the full liberalisation of the EU telecommunications sector on January 1, 1998.

1–005   One essential aspect of the liberalisation process was the separation of the regulatory and operational functions of the incumbent national telecommunications operators, which were generally performed by the same body. The continued exercise of regulatory functions by the incumbent was considered a major obstacle to the introduction of competition, as it entailed the inherent risk of discrimination against new entrants in favour of the incumbent's operations. Accordingly, the liberalisation directives required the Member States to create independent national regulatory authorities ("NRAs") that would be responsible for matters such as licensing, the allocation of frequencies and the granting of type-approval to terminal equipment, as well as other regulatory functions.[17]

1–006   Harmonisation — Liberalisation has moved in step with the harmonisation of national regulatory rules, which is its necessary complement. Harmonisation aims at setting out equivalent

---

[8] Commission Directive 88/301 of May 16, 1988 on competition in the markets in telecommunications terminal equipment, O.J. 1988 L131/73.

[9] Commission Directive 90/388 of June 28, 1990 on competition in the markets for telecommunications services (Services Directive), O.J. 1990 L192/10.

[10] Commission Directive 94/46 of October 13, 1994 amending Directive 88/301 and Directive 90/388 in particular with regard to satellite communications (Satellite Directive), O.J. 1994 L268/15.

[11] Commission Directive 95/51 of October 18, 1995 amending Directive 90/388 with regard to the abolition of restrictions in the use of cable TV networks for the provision of already liberalised telecommunications services (Cable Directive), O.J. 1995 L256/49.

[12] Commission Directive 96/2 of January 16, 1996 amending Directive 90/388 with a view to opening up the mobile and personal communications market to competition (Mobile Directive), O.J. 1996 L20/59.

[13] Commission Directive 96/19 of March 13, 1996 amending Directive 90/388 with regard to the implementation of full competition in telecommunications markets (Full Competition Directive), O.J. 1996 L74/13.

[14] *ibid.*

[15] Commission Directive 2002/77 of September 16, 2002 on competition in the markets for electronic communications networks and services, O.J. 2002 L249/21.

[16] On the difficulty of defining the boundary between reserved and non-reserved services, see Larouche, para.1–001, n.2, pp.8–9.

[17] For a comprehensive discussion of the role of the NRAs, see, below, para.1–041 *et seq.*

regulatory systems in all Member States to ensure that undertakings can compete on equal terms and benefit fully from the liberalisation of the market. Harmonisation has been achieved through a series of directives adopted under Article 95 of the EC Treaty (*ex* Article 100a), which enables the Council and the European Parliament, upon a proposal from the Commission, to adopt legislative measures aimed at the establishment and functioning of the internal market by harmonising the various laws of the Member States. The adoption of directives under Article 95 requires a cumbersome and lengthy legislative process, the so-called co-decision procedure (pursuant to Article 251 of the EC Treaty, *ex* Article 189b), involving the Commission, the Parliament and the Council.[18] The process of harmonisation started with the adoption in 1990 of the ONP Framework Directive,[19] which set out common rules for open access to, and use of, public services and networks and principles for setting tariffs for such services and networks (the so-called "Open Network Principles"). The ONP Framework Directive was supplemented by a series of subsequent harmonisation directives implementing ONP principles in specific areas, including leased lines in 1992,[20] voice telephony in 1995,[21] licences[22] and interconnection[23] in 1997, and universal service in 1998.[24] Article 95 was also used for the adoption in 2002 of the set of directives which form the New Regulatory Framework and replace these earlier directives.

1–007 Competition rules — The effective application of the EC Treaty's competition rules is essential to achieve the full benefits of the liberalisation required by the sector-specific regulation summarised above and contained in the New Regulatory Framework directives. In particular, these rules ensure that the liberalisation process is not undermined by unilateral or co-ordinated market conduct and concentrations protecting market players from competition. The application of the EC Treaty's competition rules in the telecommunications sector is reviewed in Part II of this book.

1–008 New Regulatory Framework — Building on the original liberalisation and harmonisation directives, on March 7, 2002, the European Parliament and the Council adopted the New Regulatory Framework, which repeals the existing EU services and ONP directives. The New Regulatory Framework extends its scope to all types of electronic communications infrastructures and associated services (without prejudice to existing regulations in respect of broadcast content and

---

[18] For an explanation of the co-decision procedure, see Weatherill & Beaumont, *EC Law* (Penguin, 3rd ed., 1999), pp.122–126.

[19] Directive 90/387 of June 28, 1990 on the establishment of the internal market for telecommunications services through the implementation of open network provision (ONP Framework Directive), O.J. 1990 L192/1. The ONP Framework Directive was amended in 1997 by Directive 97/51, for the purpose of adaptation to a competitive environment in telecommunications, O.J. 1997 L295/23.

[20] Directive 92/44 of June 5, 1992 on the application of open network provision to leased lines (ONP Leased Lines Directive), O.J. 1992 L165/27.

[21] Directive 95/62 of December 13, 1995 on the application of open network provision to voice telephony, O.J. 1995 L321/6.

[22] Directive 97/13 of April 10, 1997 on a common framework for general authorisations and individual licences in the field of telecommunications services (ONP Licensing Directive), O.J. 1997 L117/15.

[23] Directive 97/33 of June 30, 1997 on interconnection in telecommunications with regard to ensuring universal service and interoperability through application of open network provision principles (ONP Interconnection Directive), O.J. 1997 L199/32.

[24] Directive 98/10 of February 26, 1998 on the application of open network provision to voice telephony and on universal service for telecommunications in a competitive environment (ONP Voice Telephony Directive), O.J. 1998 L101/24.

telecommunications equipment, which fall outside the reform). The New Regulatory Framework consists of a set of directives and other legal measures, designed towards:

(i) the adoption of competition law-based sector-specific regulation — the New Regulatory Framework indeed adjusts *ex ante* regulation to concepts of EU competition law, in order to better harmonise the application of sector-specific regulation and competition rules, given their complementary nature and objectives;

(ii) the harmonisation of national regulatory systems — the New Regulatory Framework provides Member States' regulatory authorities with a set of objectives and regulatory tools that are to be applied consistently across the EU under the Commission's guidance and supervision;

(iii) the gradual phasing out of sector-specific regulation — the New Regulatory Framework allows for specific regulatory measures to be rolled back once markets have become competitive, thereafter making competition rules the prime instrument of regulation;

(iv) ensuring flexibility to allow for adjustment to take account of industry convergence — the New Regulatory Framework covers all electronic communications networks and services, irrespective of their means of transmission and regardless of the type of information conveyed. However, content continues to be regulated separately under other EU and national rules.

B. The New Regulatory Framework for Electronic Communications

1–009 The 1998 telecommunications liberalisation and harmonisation package successfully created the conditions for effective competition in the telecommunications sector during the transition from monopoly to open markets. Building on this progress, on March 7, 2002, the European Parliament and the Council adopted the New Regulatory Framework. This overhauls the existing legislation in response to market and technological developments in the converged communications environment. The New Regulatory Framework simplifies and reduces the number of existing legal measures from 28 to eight, with the aim of gradually phasing out sector-specific regulation as electronic communications markets become subject to effective competition.[25]

1–010 Principles of the New Regulatory Framework — The principles underlying the New Regulatory Framework are: (i) a set of clearly defined policy objectives (*e.g.* the promotion of competition and consumer protection as well as the completion of the internal market in electronic communications); (ii) *ex ante* regulation to be limited to the minimum necessary to meet those objectives; (iii) a balanced approach towards the need for legal certainty and flexibility; (iv) technological neutrality; (v) fostering the use of general authorisations (except

---

[25] Directive 2002/21 of March 7, 2002 on a common regulatory framework for electronic communications networks and services, O.J. 2002 L108/33 ("Framework Directive"), Recital 27.

for the use of scarce resources, such as radio frequencies and numbers); (vi) a common EU-wide approach to radio spectrum management; (vii) an extension of the definition and scope of universal service; and (viii) the introduction of mechanisms for its periodic review.[26]

1–011   Road map — The New Regulatory Framework comprises a series of directives and other legal measures, which were conceived and adopted as a single package. It consists of a general framework directive, the directive on a common regulatory framework for electronic communications networks and services ("Framework Directive")[27] which lays down the foundations for the other measures, and four specific directives:

   (i)   the directive on the authorisation of electronic communications networks and services ("Authorisation Directive")[28];

   (ii) the directive on access to and interconnection of electronic communications networks and associated facilities ("Access Directive")[29];

   (iii) the directive on universal service and users' rights relating to electronic communications networks and services ("Universal Service Directive")[30]; and

   (iv) the directive on the processing of personal data and the protection of privacy in the electronic communications sector ("E-Privacy Directive").[31]

The package also includes the decision on a regulatory framework for radio spectrum policy ("Radio Spectrum Decision").[32]

1–012   The New Regulatory Framework is completed by the Commission directive on competition in the markets for electronic communications services ("Liberalisation Directive").[33] This consolidates the provisions of the Services Directive and its subsequent amendments,[34] maintaining in force only the provisions of these directives that are considered to be still relevant. In addition, as part of the process of implementing the provisions of the New Regulatory Package by the Member States, the Commission has issued a series of accompanying measures, such as guidelines and recommendations, which aim to provide guidance to the NRAs in their application of the rules of

---

[26] *ibid.*, Art.8.

[27] *ibid.*

[28] Directive 2002/20 of March 7, 2002 on the authorisation of electronic communications networks and services, O.J. 2002 L108/21.

[29] Directive 2002/19 of March 7, 2002 on access to, and interconnection of, electronic communications networks and associated facilities, O.J. 2002 L108/7.

[30] Directive 2002/22 of March 7, 2002 on universal service and users' rights relating to electronic communications networks and services, O.J. 2002 L108/51.

[31] Directive 2002/58 of July 12, 2002 concerning the processing of personal data and the protection of privacy in the electronic communications sector, O.J. 2002 L201/37.

[32] Decision 676/2002 of March 7, 2002 on a regulatory framework for radio spectrum policy in the European Community, O.J. 2002 L108/1.

[33] Cited at para.1–004, n.15, above.

[34] See para.1–004, n.9, above.

the New Regulatory Framework. The two main measures for the purposes of implementing the New Regulatory Framework are:

(i) the Commission's guidelines on market analysis and the assessment of significant market power ("SMP Guidelines")[35];

(ii) the Commission's recommendation on relevant product and service markets within the electronic communications sector susceptible to *ex ante* regulation ("Recommendation on the Relevant Markets").[36]

These are both discussed in more detail later in this chapter.

1–013 Scope of the New Regulatory Framework — Article 2 of the Framework Directive contains the key definitions for the application of the New Regulatory Framework: (i) "electronic communications networks"[37]; (ii) "electronic communications services"[38]; and (iii) "associated facilities".[39] These definitions cover all services provided over satellite and terrestrial networks, including both fixed and wireless networks, the public switched telephone network, data networks that use the internet protocol (IP), cable television networks, and other radio and television broadcast networks. The aim of the framework is not to let any network have a competitive advantage over any other.

1–014 *Technology-neutral framework* — The principle of technological neutrality underlies the New Regulatory Framework and is reflected in the definitions. This is fundamental to the achievement of policy objectives and the application of regulatory principles in an environment where

[35] Commission Guidelines of July 11, 2002 on market analysis and the assessment of significant market power under the Community regulatory framework for electronic communications networks and services, O.J. 2002 C165/06.

[36] Commission Recommendation of February 11, 2003 on the relevant product and service markets within the electronic communications sector susceptible to *ex ante* regulation in accordance with Directive 2002/21 of the European Parliament and of the Council on a common regulatory framework for electronic communications networks and services, O.J. 2003 L114/45.

[37] "Electronic communications networks" means "transmission systems and, where applicable, switching or routing equipment and other resources which permit the conveyance of signals by wire, by radio, by optical or by other electromagnetic means, including satellite networks, fixed (circuit and packet-switched, including Internet) and mobile terrestrial networks, electricity cable systems, to the extent that they are used for the purpose of transmitting signals, networks used for radio and television broadcasting, and cable television networks, irrespective of the type of information conveyed".

[38] "Electronic communications services" means a "service normally provided for remuneration which consists wholly or mainly in the conveyance of signals on electronic communications networks, including telecommunications services and transmission services in networks used for broadcasting, but exclude services providing, or exercising editorial control over, content transmitted using electronic communications networks and services; it does not include information society services which do not consist wholly or mainly in the conveyance of signals on electronic communications networks". "Information Society Services" is defined in Art.1 of Directive 98/34: see para.1–015, n.43, below.

[39] "Associated facilities" means "those facilities associated with an electronic communications network and/or an electronic communications services which enable and/or support the provision of services via that network and/or service". This includes all conditional access systems, thus including those for digital TV as well as analogue and non-audiovisual services, and electronic programming guides.

telecommunications, broadcasting and computer services are converging. The traditional regulatory regimes for the broadcasting and telecommunications sectors did not take into account the convergence of networks and services and different technologies. Definitional boundaries between telecommunications and broadcasting were established in a pre-converged environment where specific networks were associated with the delivery of specific types of message or signal. For example, telecommunications services were defined as

> "services whose provision consists wholly or partially in the transmission and routing of signals on telecommunications networks, with the exception of radio and television broadcasting services".[40]

This definition, which determined the application of sector-specific telecommunications regulation, was based on the nature of the network used to transmit the service, rather than the nature of the service. With convergence, this definition was no longer appropriate since it ignored the effects of network convergence. Under the traditional definitions, similar services would have been subject to different regulatory regimes depending on the network on which they were carried. The new definitions of electronic communications networks and services take convergence into account and ensure that sector-specific regulation applies to any network or service by which signals can be transmitted, regardless of the type of information conveyed.

1–015 *Exclusion of content* — The Framework Directive continues to differentiate between the regulation of the transmission of broadcasts and the regulation of content.[41] Regulation of the content of television programmes continues to fall under the so-called "Television without Frontiers Directive",[42] which will be discussed in Chapter II. Similarly, financial services and certain information society services,[43] which do not consist wholly or mainly in the conveyance of signals on electronic communications networks, fall outside the scope of the Framework Directive and continue to be regulated under the "E-Commerce Directive",[44] which will be discussed in Chapter III. The interpretation of the key definitions contained in the Framework Directive is

---

[40] ONP Framework Directive, para.1–006, n.19, above, Art.2.

[41] Framework Directive, para.1–009, n.25, above, Art.2(3).

[42] Directive 89/552 of October 3, 1999 on the co-ordination of certain provisions laid down by law, regulation or administrative action in Member States concerning the pursuit of television broadcasting activities, O.J. 1989 L298/23, as amended by Directive 97/36, O.J. 1997 L202/60.

[43] "Information Society Service" is defined in Art.1 of Directive 98/34 of the European Parliament and the Council of June 22, 1998, laying down a procedure for the provision of information in the field of technical standards and regulations and of rules of information society services, O.J. 1998, L204/37, as amended by Directive 98/48, O.J. 1998 L217/18 (the so-called "Transparency Directive"), as "any service normally provided for remuneration, at a distance, by electronic means and at the individual request of a recipient of services". This definition spans a wide range of economic activities which take place online, and which are provided at request. Most of these activities are not within the scope of the Framework Directive, because they do not consist wholly or mainly in the conveyance of signals on electronic communications networks, *e.g.* web-based content services. However, the Recitals to the Framework Directive specifically state that electronic communications services, such as access to the internet, fall within the scope of the New Regulatory Framework.

[44] Directive 2000/31 of June 8, 2000 on certain legal aspects of information society services, in particular electronic commerce in the internal market, O.J. 2000 L178/1.

therefore crucial for the applicability of the provisions of the New Regulatory Framework with respect to content providers seeking access to electronic communications networks.[45]

1–016 Timeframe for national implementation measures — Member States had 15 months from the date of publication of the directives comprising the New Regulatory Framework, *i.e.* April 24, 2002, to implement them into national law, *i.e.* until July 25, 2003 (with the exception of the E-Privacy Directive which was published only on July 31, 2002, with a subsequent delay of the implementation deadline until October 31, 2003).

1–017 Implementation of *ex ante* regulation — NRAs have primary responsibility for the implementation of the provisions of the New Regulatory Framework. In doing so, NRAs are required to carry out a number of specific functions: (i) to define the relevant markets in the communications sector, and in particular the geographic scope of those identified by the Commission Recommendation on the Relevant Markets; (ii) to analyse these markets to assess whether they are competitive or not, *i.e.* whether there is any operator with significant market power[46]; and, finally, (iii) to withdraw or amend existing sector-specific regulations imposed under the previous regime, depending on whether the markets are found to be competitive or not, or to impose new obligations in accordance with the Access Directive and the Universal Service Directive. In doing so, NRAs must act in pursuit of the policy objectives set out in the Framework Directive, which are: (i) the promotion of an open and competitive market for electronic communications networks, services and associated facilities; (ii) the development of the internal market; and (iii) the promotion of the interests of European citizens.[47]

1–018 Significant Market Power (SMP) — The Framework Directive re-defines the notion of Significant Market Power ("SMP"). SMP is the key concept used in determining those operators on whom NRAs can impose sector-specific obligations in order to guarantee effective competition. The new definition of SMP is based on the competition law concept of market dominance, contained in Article 82 of the EC Treaty, as interpreted by the Commission and the European Court of Justice.[48] Under Article 14 of the Framework Directive, an undertaking shall be deemed to have SMP if, either individually or jointly with others, it enjoys a position equivalent to dominance, that is to say a position of economic strength affording it the power to behave to an appreciable extent independently of competitors, customers and ultimately consumers. This definition encompasses the concepts of single and collective dominance, as well as the leveraging of market power on closely related markets.[49]

---

[45] See Section F, para.1–144, below.

[46] On the concept of significant market power, see para.1–018, below.

[47] Framework Directive, para.1–009, n.25, Art.8.

[48] Case 27/76, *United Brands Company and United Brands Continentaal BV v Commission* [1978] E.C.R. 207. On the concept of dominance under EC competition rules, see also para.6–014 *et seq.*, below.

[49] Art.14(3) of the Framework Directive, para.1–009, n.25, states that "*where an undertaking has significant market power on a specific market, it may also be deemed to have significant market power on a closely related market, where the links between the two markets are such as to allow the market power held in one market to be leveraged into the other market, thereby strengthening the market power of the undertaking*". For a comprehensive description of this provision, see para.1–038, below.

1–019 Transition from the 1998 Regulatory Framework to the New Regulatory Framework — Under the 1998 Regulatory Framework, the concept of SMP was defined by use of a market share threshold: it was a rebuttal presumption that an operator with 25 per cent or more of the relevant market (being interconnection or public-switched telephone service or mobile service) had SMP, although an NRA could determine the existence of SMP at lower or higher market shares).[50] The reasoning behind such a low threshold was the need to have a straightforward tool to restrain the incumbent operators' market power, which was the primary policy objective in the early days of the EU's telecommunications liberalisation process. This arbitrary presumption of market power was, however, criticised as being inconsistent with the principles of competition law and resulted in obligations being imposed that were greater than those that could be imposed under Article 82 of the EC Treaty (as a market share of 25 per cent would generally not be considered sufficient to give market dominance within the meaning of Article 82). Under the 1998 Regulatory Framework, *ex ante* regulation was imposed on the basis of a set of legal presumptions, regardless of any detailed market analysis that would be undertaken as part of a competition law assessment. Under the New Regulatory Framework, *ex ante* regulation must be applied in the light of a market analysis, which NRAs must conduct in accordance with competition law concepts. Under the 1998 Regulatory Framework, several activities in market areas of the telecommunications sector were subject to *ex ante* regulation, including network access, interconnection, leased lines offering, tariffs setting, costs accounting.[51] These activities were identified in the applicable directives, but were not always economic "markets" within the meaning of competition law and practice. Annex I of the Framework Directive therefore contains a list of the activities to be included in the initial version of the Commission Recommendation on the Relevant Markets.[52] In order to allow a smooth transition from the 1998 Regulatory Framework to the New Regulatory Framework, the existing obligations imposed by NRAs on operators determined under the previous regime to have SMP will continue to apply until NRAs have decided that such operators no longer have SMP, in the light of their market analyses.[53]

1–020 Relevant markets — The Framework Directive is based on the premise that there is a need for *ex ante* obligations in certain circumstances, in order to ensure the development of a competitive market.[54] At the same time, the Framework Directive provides that *ex ante* regulation should be rolled back (*i.e.* reduced or removed completely) when market conditions indicate that it is no longer needed, with competition law becoming the primary means of regulation.[55] The first step to be carried out by the NRAs is thus to define the relevant markets, and then identify which have the characteristics which justify the imposition of *ex ante* regulation.[56]

---

[50] See Art.4(3) of the ONP Interconnection Directive, para.1–006, n.23. To date there have been a few exceptions to the 25 per cent market share test, *e.g.* the Irish NRA refused to find SMP for a mobile operator with a market share above 25 per cent. The latest list of SMP operators notified under the regime of the ONP Interconnection Directive was published on December 20, 2002, in O.J. 2002 C320/4.

[51] See Arts 4, 7 and 8 of the ONP Interconnection Directive, para.1–006, n.23, above; Art.16 of the ONP Voice Telephony Directive, para.1–006, n.21; and Arts 4, 5, 6 and 10 of the ONP Leased Lines Directive, para.1–006, n.20.

[52] See para.1–024, below.

[53] Framework Directive, para.1–009, n.25, Art.27.

[54] *ibid.*, Recital 25.

[55] *ibid.*, Recital 27.

[56] *ibid.*, Art.15(1).

1–021 *Market definition for the purposes of* ex ante *regulation* — NRAs are required to define the relevant markets in accordance with the SMP Guidelines and the Commission's Recommendation on the Relevant Markets.[57] These documents adopt the same methodologies used to define markets for the purposes of competition law,[58] *i.e.* assessing whether demand-side and supply-side substitution and actual and/or potential competition will constrain the competitive behaviour of market participants. For this reason, these documents, together with the relevant Commission Notices,[59] are also discussed in Chapter V. In practice, however, it can be expected that in most instances the exercise of defining the relevant markets by the NRAs will be limited to the definition of the geographic scope of the product markets indicated by the Commission in its Recommendation on the Relevant Markets.[60] In the electronic communications sector, the geographical scope of the relevant market has traditionally been determined by reference to two main criteria: (i) the area covered by the operator's network; and (ii) the existence of legal and other regulatory instruments that may limit competition from other geographic areas.[61]

1–022 *Commission Recommendation on the Relevant Markets for the purpose of* ex ante *regulation* — Once the relevant markets have been defined, NRAs are required to identify those markets that have characteristics that may be such as to justify the imposition of *ex ante* regulation. In doing so, NRAs must take the utmost account of the Commission's Recommendation on the Relevant Markets.

1–023 *Criteria for identifying markets to be subject to* ex ante *regulation* — The Recommendation on Relevant Markets identifies three criteria that are to be applied cumulatively in identifying the relevant markets for the purposes of *ex ante* regulation:

- the presence of high and non-transitory barriers to entry, including both structural[62] and regulatory[63] barriers[64];

[57] *ibid.*, Art.15(2).

[58] *ibid.*, Art.15(3).

[59] See para.5–002 *et seq.*, below.

[60] Framework Directive, para.1–009, n.25, Art.15(3).

[61] For a more comprehensive analysis of the definition of the geographic dimension of the relevant markets under competition law, see para.5–017, below.

[62] See Recommendation on the Relevant Markets, para.1–012, n.36, Recital 11. A structural barrier to entry exists when the state of technology, and its associated cost structure, as well as the level of demand, are such that they create asymmetric conditions of competition between incumbents and new entrants, so as to impede or prevent market entry by the latter. For example, high structural barriers may exist in markets characterised by substantial economies of scale, scope and density and high sunk costs. Such barriers can still be identified with respect to the widespread deployment and/or provision of local access networks to fixed locations.

[63] *ibid.*, Recital 12. Legal and regulatory barriers are not based on economic conditions, but result from legislative, administrative or other State measures that have a direct effect on the conditions of entry and/or the position of operators on the relevant market. One example is the legal limit in all Member States on the number of undertakings that have access to radio spectrum, owing to its scarcity. A regulatory barrier may exist when entry into a particular market is rendered non-viable as a result of regulatory requirements, particularly where this situation is expected to persist for the foreseeable future. For example, the retail tariffs set by NRAs for access to the public telephone network at a fixed location or address may fail to cover the forward-looking incremental costs for the provision of such services. In this way, new entry into the market for local access services would be deterred as the new entrant could not profitably compete with the incumbent: tariff rebalancing is considered in para.1–199 *et seq.*, below.

[64] Recommendation on the Relevant Markets, para.1–012, n.36, Recitals 9 and 10.

- the dynamic characteristics of the markets considered (for example, considering whether market shares may change over time, prices may fall over time, such that market power may exist only because of the incumbent's "first mover" advantage)[65]; and

- the sufficiency of competition law by itself (absent *ex ante* regulation) to address competitive concerns.[66]

The fact that *ex ante* regulation must be complementary to the application of competition law in addressing persistent market failures should thus be seen as the decisive criterion for the application of *ex ante* regulation.[67] *Ex ante* regulation would constitute an appropriate complement to competition law in circumstances where the application of competition law would not adequately address the market failures concerned. Such circumstances would, for example, include situations where the compliance requirements for regulatory intervention to redress a market failure are extensive (*e.g.* the need for detailed accounting for regulatory purposes, the identification and assessment of costs, monitoring of terms and conditions including technical parameters, etc.) or where frequent and/or timely intervention is indispensable (*e.g.* the need to set specific tariffs on a regular basis).[68] Competition law cannot easily be applied on an *ex ante* basis: it is more appropriate for *ex post* regulation. Such an assessment would need to include a preliminary assessment by the NRA of the problem affecting a defined market. Market definition and market analysis for the purpose of *ex ante* regulation must therefore be considered in parallel by the NRAs and, to the maximum possible extent, in co-operation with the national competition authorities. It goes without saying, however, that the identification of the markets for *ex ante* sector-specific regulation is without prejudice to the relevant markets that may be defined in specific cases under competition law.[69] This is even more true because of the presence of the requirement to consider whether the application of competition law would be sufficient when NRAs identify the markets that are to be subject to *ex ante* regulation; this is self-evidently absent when defining markets for competition law purposes. In principle, this means that the relevant markets defined by competition authorities in

---

[65] *ibid.*, Recital 14.

[66] *ibid.*, Recital 15.

[67] The fact that these criteria must be considered cumulatively should mean that in the absence of any of them, the market should not be included in the Recommendation on the Relevant Markets and should not be subject to *ex ante* regulation. But this conclusion would lead to the illogical situation where recourse to *ex ante* measures would be denied, even if competition law was not sufficient to remedy a particular problem, should the other two criteria be met. Indeed, there might be the need in certain cases to define a relevant market to address competition concerns by means of *ex ante* regulation, even where there are low barriers to entry and strong dynamic market factors are present, because the application of competition law alone had proved not to be sufficient to address those concerns. It might therefore be appropriate to adopt a different approach in the application of these criteria that is more consistent with the objectives of the Framework Directive set out in Art.8. In addition, from a policy perspective, the Commission itself has indicated that an overall assessment of the sufficiency of the application of competition law should be adopted (Public Hearing on the Draft Recommendation on the Relevant Markets, Brussels, July 3, 2002). Available at: *http://www.europa.eu.int/ information_society/topics/telecoms/regulatory/publicconsult/index_en.htm.*

[68] On the issue of the relationship between sector-specific regulation and competition law, see Chap.IX.

[69] Under competition law, it is established law that the Commission is not bound by a market definition adopted in a previous decision, even where the same parties are involved: Joined Cases T–125 and 127/97, *The Coca-Cola Company and Coca-Cola Enterprises Inc. v Commission* [2000] I E.C.R. 1733.

the telecommunications sector may not necessarily be relevant markets for the purpose of *ex ante* regulation and *vice versa*.

1–024 *Relevant markets included in the initial version of the Recommendation* — The activities that the Commission is to include in the initial version of the Recommendation are set out in Annex I of the Framework Directive. The Recommendation indicates how these activities are linked to the corresponding competition law markets set out in the Annex to the Recommendation. The starting point of the examination of markets for the purpose of market definition is a characterisation of the retail markets, followed by a description of the related wholesale markets. Retail markets should, in principle, be examined in a way that is independent of the network or infrastructure being used to provide the services, in accordance with the principle of technological neutrality that underlies the New Regulatory Framework.

1–025 In examining retail and wholesale markets for the purpose of the Recommendation, the Commission has made a general division between services provided at fixed locations and those provided to non-fixed locations (*i.e.* mobile communications). The Commission has also made a general distinction between voice services and non-voice (*e.g.* data) services. These distinctions, however, do not imply that these services constitute separate product markets. Furthermore, at wholesale level, the distinction between voice and data services may not be so easy to make; for example, a network may carry both voice and non-voice services. However, the Commission has considered that, at retail level, demand substitution between voice and data services is not at present sufficiently developed; they are therefore dealt with separately in the Recommendation.

1–026 The following 18 markets have been included in the Annex to the initial version of the Recommendation, in order to reflect the market areas contained in the Annex I to the Framework Directive:

- the *provision of public telephone services at fixed locations, i.e.* the provision of a connection or access to the public telephone network for the purpose of making and/or receiving telephone calls and related services, including internet service provision, which corresponds:

  o at the retail level, to the markets for (i) access to the public telephone network at a fixed location (or address) for residential and (ii) for non-residential (*i.e.* business) customers; (iii) publicly available local and/or national telephone services provided at a fixed location (or address) for residential and (iv) non-residential (*i.e.* business) customers; (v) publicly available international telephone services provided at a fixed location (or address) for residential and (vi) non-residential (*i.e.* business) customers; and

  o at the wholesale level, to the markets for (i) call origination (originating access or interconnection) or capacity (on all networks serving a fixed location); (ii) call termination on individual networks; and (iii) transit services or call conveyance in the fixed public telephone network[70];

---

[70] The main elements to produce or supply retail telephone services are call origination, call conveyance of varying kinds (transmission, transit interconnection, etc.) and call termination. Call conveyance or transit

- the *provision of access to data and related services at fixed locations*, which corresponds:

   o at the retail level, to the same markets for the provision of telephone services at fixed locations, described above; and

   o at the wholesale level, to the markets for (i) wholesale unbundled access (including shared access) to metallic loops and sub-loops for the purpose of providing broadband internet and voice services; (ii) wholesale broadband access, including "bit-stream" access that permits transmission of broadband data in both directions over the incumbent's PSTN, and other wholesale access provided over other infrastructures (*e.g.* cable networks), if and when they are able to offer facilities equivalent to bit-stream, for the purpose of providing broadband services[71]; and (iii) call origination on the public telephone network at a fixed location[72];

- the *provision of dedicated connections and capacity (leased lines)*, which corresponds:

   o at the retail level, to the markets for the provision of (i) retail leased lines in the minimum harmonised set,[73] the conditions of which are specified by the Universal Service Directive; and

   o at the wholesale level, to the markets for (i) wholesale local or terminating segments of leased lines; and (ii) the trunk segments of leased lines[74];

interconnection involves transmission and/or switching or routing. For an undertaking providing services to a limited number of end-users, an alternative to using wholesale call conveyance services could be to use inter-connected leased lines or dedicated trunk capacity. As call conveyance typically includes switching or routing, it is however considered to be a separate wholesale market from the leased lines market (see Explanatory Memorandum to the Recommendation on the Relevant Markets, available at: *http://www.europa.eu.int/ information_society/topics/telecoms/regulatory/maindocs/index_en.htm#directives*).

[71] For the purpose of the Recommendation, "bit-stream" is a service which depends in part on the PSTN and may include other networks such as the ATM network. The wider formulation given to this market than in previous drafts of the Recommendation allows NRAs to include in this market cable networks and other alternative infrastructures, such as satellite and wireless broadband access, where they consider that such infrastructures are substitutable from a supply-side perspective with bit-stream access, according to competition law (on the issue of market definition under competition law, see Chap. V).

[72] Whilst the relevant wholesale market for call origination fulfils the criteria to warrant identification in the Recommendation on the Relevant Markets, wholesale call termination does not. Indeed, the Commission considers that internet service providers (ISPs) have a wide choice of terminating operators and that there is evidence of ISPs switching terminating operators.

[73] The leased lines in the minimum harmonised set are identified in the List of Standards that the Commission is required to adopt in accordance with Art. 17 of the Framework Directive. The list of standards is not generally mandatory for Member States to adopt. However, adoption of the minimum harmonised set of leased lines in the Commission's List of Standards is mandatory by virtue of Art. 18 of the Universal Service Directive. For a discussion of the work of the Commission on the List of Standards, see further para. 1–166. In any event, where the Commission considers that interoperability is at issue, it can make any of the standards contained in the list mandatory, following public consultation with all interested parties, according to Art. 17(3) of the Framework Directive.

[74] In its Explanatory Memorandum to the Recommendation on the relevant markets, para. 1–026, n. 70, the Commission indicated that it is possible to distinguish separate wholesale leased lines markets for the terminating segments of a leased lines circuit (sometimes called local tails or local segments) and the trunk segments. Additional market segmentation would also be possible between high and low capacity leased lines, taking account of the bandwidth used, for example where there are constraints with respect to supply

- the *provision of services provided at non-fixed locations, i.e.* mobile communications, which corresponds only to the:

  o wholesale markets for (i) access and call origination on public telephone networks[75]; and (ii) voice call termination on individual mobile networks[76]; and (iii) the national market for international roaming services on public mobile telephone networks,[77] as retail mobile communications markets are deemed to be competitive, and thus no market is included for the purposes of *ex ante* regulation; and

- the markets relating to *broadcasting transmission services*, which correspond only to the markets for:

  o wholesale broadcasting transmission services and distribution networks in so far as they provide the means to deliver broadcast content to end-users.

Indeed, services providing or exercising control over content transmitted using electronic communications networks and services (*i.e.* retail broadcasting services) fall outside the definition of "electronic communication services" under the Framework Directive.[78] Consequently, the provision of retail broadcasting services to end-users (*i.e.* consumers) falls outside its scope and no retail market is identified for the purposes of the Recommendation. This means that, in practice, the retail broadcasting markets can thus only be subject to competition law. In order to provide subscription (or pay) broadcasting or interactive services to end-users, the broadcasting undertaking that supplies such services typically needs access to ancillary technical broadcasting services, such as conditional access systems, electronic programme guides and associated facilities, on one or more transmission networks. However, no wholesale market for conditional access systems is

substitution in providing bandwidth in excess of 2 Megabit/sec capacity. However, further segmentation is obviously subject to the procedure under Art.7 of the Framework Directive, see para.1–048, below.

[75] The Commission considers this market to be still subject to entry barriers owing to the scarcity of spectrum and the subsequent regulatory barriers to obtaining spectrum. However, in its Explanatory Memorandum to the Recommendation on the Relevant Markets, para.1–026, n.70, above, the Commission acknowledged that a number of undertakings have overcome this barrier, for example, Mobile Virtual Network Operators (MVNOs) — which can be described with a certain amount of simplification as operators without a mobile network who provide services to their own subscribers (in certain cases controlled by their own SIM cards) via other mobile operators' radio networks, by means of roaming agreements or through indirect access arrangements (wholesale call origination) and that this market might tend over time towards effective competition.

[76] The issue of high call termination charges on mobile networks has been dealt with both at the national and EU levels by NRAs, National Competition Authorities and the Commission. In brief, because of the "calling party pays" principle, there is considered to be a lack of competitive constraint in this area, in particular with respect to fixed-to-mobile calls. As regards the Commission's investigations under the EU competition rules, see Chap.VI.

[77] As stated by the Commission in its Explanatory Memorandum to the Recommendation on the Relevant Markets, para.1–026, n.70, above, there are incentives for mobile network operators (in addition to mobile service providers) to negotiate lower-priced wholesale agreements for roaming if it means that they can generate more traffic on their networks or attract and retain end-users. On the basis of this consideration, and depending on the evolution of these markets at national level, it is possible that future revisions of the Recommendation might not include this market.

[78] Framework Directive, para.1–009, n.25, Art.2.

included in the Recommendation, because open access obligations would apply in any event to all operators of such systems, regardless of any market analysis, by virtue of the provisions of the Access Directive.[79]

1–027 *Review of markets for the purposes of* ex ante *regulation* — In the rapidly evolving markets of the electronic communications industry, proper market definitions can change more rapidly than in other sectors. Because of this, the New Regulatory Framework provides for the periodic re-assessment of market definitions, both by the Commission when revising its Recommendation on the Relevant Markets, and subsequently by the NRAs, when defining the geographical scope of these markets.[80] In summary, whether an electronic communications market continues to be identified by subsequent versions of the Recommendation on the Relevant Markets as justifying possible *ex ante* regulation would depend on: (i) the continued persistence of high barriers to entry; (ii) a measurement of the dynamic state of competitiveness; and (iii) the sufficiency of the application of competition law alone (absent *ex ante* regulation) to address persistent market failures.[81] The Commission has indicated that a market could also be removed from the Recommendation once there is evidence of sustainable and effective competition in that market within the EU, provided that the emergence of effective competition in the market is not due to the existence of existing *ex ante* regulatory obligations.[82]

1–028 The market for "voice call termination" services on individual mobile networks is explicitly stated by Annex I of the Framework Directive as the market for "call termination onto individual mobile telephone networks". The inclusion of the word "voice" in the Recommendation clearly excludes SMS, but would also seem to exclude data services (such as certain non-voice global packet switched radio services (GPRS) and third generation (UMTS) mobile services) within this market.[83] The Commission has, however, stated that the development of third generation mobile networks is likely to change the way mobile services, including voice telephony, are tariffed and sold. Voice services might be priced in a way that resembles the approach used in packet data

[79] Access Directive, para.1–011, n.29, Arts 5 and 6, in conjunction with Annex I. The obligation to provide conditional access services applies only to the benefit of broadcasters and not to other operators. In the case of cable operators, for instance, access could only be mandated in respect of network operators who are found to have SMP on the relevant market. In this case, it should be considered that the relevant issue for undertakings seeking access to ancillary technical broadcasting services, *i.e.* conditional access systems, is considered to be the ability to deliver to, or negotiate access to, sufficient end-users to sustain viable business. Hence, if switching costs for a substantial proportion of users between alternative delivery platforms were sufficiently high, it might be argued that the relevant market is that for ancillary technical broadcasting services on a given delivery platform carrying a large number of subscribers and to which cable operators need access. On conditional access systems, see further para.1–171 and para.2–065 *et seq.*

[80] Framework Directive, para.1–009, n.25, Arts 15 and 16. According to Recital 21 of the Recommendation on the Relevant Markets, para.1–012, n.36, the first date for the review of the markets identified in Annex I should be no later than June 30, 2004.

[81] Recommendation on the Relevant Markets, para.1–012, n.36, Recital 16.

[82] *ibid.*, Recital 14. In addition, if regulatory obligations on an undertaking have already been imposed, the fact that effective competition may have been restored in the relevant market as a result of the obligations imposed would not in itself mean that that undertaking no longer enjoys a dominant position and that it should no longer continue to be designated as having SMP.

[83] See, however, para.1–039, discussing the concept of leveraging of market power between different clearly related markets in the context of emerging markets.

networks, where receivers as well as senders pay for part of the communication. Such a development would clearly modify the incentives for anti-competitive behaviour, *e.g.* setting excessive termination charges, even with respect to traditional voice mobile telephony services. If these developments were to occur, this would arguably lead to the exclusion of the mobile call termination market from future versions of the Recommendation.

1–029 *Identification of other markets for the purposes of* ex ante *regulation* — When NRAs consider that the definition of different relevant product markets is justified by national circumstances, they must communicate their decision to the other NRAs and the Commission. The Commission retains the power to withdraw or amend such a decision.[84] There may be a number of ways in which market definitions at national level might differ from the markets identified in the Recommendation. For example, an NRA may need to introduce further segmentation at national level in order to better deal with a situation of market power in that specific segment of the market, or to combine two or more markets that were defined separately by the Recommendation, for reasons relating to national circumstances. The Recommendation already includes a non-exhaustive list of possible segmentations of the markets, as identified in Annex I to the Framework Directive.

1–030 *Transnational markets* — In addition to the markets indicated by the Recommendation, the Commission may decide to adopt a binding decision defining transnational markets, *i.e.* markets that are cross-border in nature, where such markets are found to meet the three criteria for being considered eligible for *ex ante* regulation.[85] The Commission will have to consult the NRAs and the Communications Committee before adopting such a decision.[86] If such a decision is adopted, NRAs will clearly need to co-operate with each other in assessing the presence of any operators with SMP in a transnational market, using one of the EU-wide fora established in accordance with the provisions of the New Regulatory Framework, *e.g.* the European Regulators Group (ERG).[87]

1–031 **Assessment of SMP** — Once the relevant product and geographic markets have been established, the next step for the imposition of *ex ante* regulatory obligations on one or more operators is the assessment of whether these operators have SMP, so as to justify the imposition of specific regulatory obligations. In doing so, NRAs must act in accordance with the SMP Guidelines.[88] The SMP Guidelines summarise the existing case law under EC competition rules on single and collective dominance, as well as the leveraging of market power. The New Regulatory

---

[84] Framework Directive, para.1–009, n.25, Art.7. Furthermore, Recital 17 of the Recommendation on the Relevant Markets para.1–012, n.36, states that: "*[NRAs] may identify markets that differ from those of the Recommendation, provided they act in accordance with Article 7 of the Framework Directive*". For a more comprehensive analysis of the procedure under Art.7 of the Framework Directive, see para.1–047 *et seq.*

[85] Framework Directive, para.1–009, n.25, Art.15(4). See para.1–023, above.

[86] *ibid.*, Art.22(3), under which the Communications Committee is established. The Communications Committee works as the interface of the Commission with the NRAs for issues concerning the implementation of the New Regulatory Framework. For a discussion of the duties and the powers of the Committee, see below para.1–175.

[87] *ibid.*, Recitals 10 and 27, as confirmed by the SMP Guidelines, para.1–012, n.35, at para.122. On the ERG, see further para.1–046, below.

[88] *ibid.*, Art.16.

Framework requires an assessment of dominance on an *ex ante* basis. Under Article 82 of the EC Treaty, dominance is traditionally decided on an *ex post* basis — *i.e.* by analysing past behaviour. Because past behaviour cannot be considered in an *ex ante* assessment, a determination of SMP will mean a substantial amount of projection and assumptions by the NRA on likely future market developments. This will make the task of the NRAs even more complex, as their analysis will have to be carried out more along the lines of a merger control analysis, which is also forward-looking.[89] It is for this reason that Member States are required to ensure that such analysis is carried out, where appropriate, in collaboration with national competition authorities, which have more experience in undertaking this forward-looking analysis.[90]

1–032 Single-firm dominance — The traditional form of dominance is single-firm dominance. In the SMP Guidelines, the Commission states that in an *ex ante* regulatory environment, market power is essentially measured by reference to the power of the undertaking concerned to raise prices by restricting output without incurring a significant loss of sales or revenues. However, the Commission explicitly states, in line with its common practice, that the market power of an undertaking can be significantly constrained by the existence of potential competitors, provided they are credible market entrants.[91]

1–033 *Market shares* — Market shares are often used as a rough indication of market power, but are not conclusive. According to the Commission's decision-making practice, under both Article 82 and the EC Merger Control Regulation, an undertaking would normally need to have a market share of more than 40 per cent in order to be dominant in the relevant market. A market share of over 50 per cent raises a rebuttable presumption of dominance,[92] whilst one of less than 25 per cent is rebuttably presumed not to confer dominance.[93] According to the SMP guidelines, it is for the NRAs to decide which are the most appropriate parameters for measuring market share. The Commission points out that retail revenues, call minutes or number of fixed telephone lines or subscribers of public telephone network operators are possible criteria for measuring the market shares of undertakings active in telecommunications markets. However, the Commission indicates that where the relevant market is an interconnection market, a more realistic measurement parameter would be the revenues accrued for terminating calls to customers on fixed or mobile networks, as appropriate. According to the Commission, this is an appropriate approach because the use of revenues (rather than, for example, call minutes) takes into account the fact that individual call minutes can have different values and provides a measure of market power that reflects both the number of customers and network coverage. For the same reasons, the Commission indicates that

---

[89] See Council Regulation No.4064/89, as amended by the Council Regulation 1310/97 of June 30, 1997 (the "Merger Control Regulation").

[90] Framework Directive, Art.16(1), see para.1–009, n.25, above.

[91] SMP Guidelines, para.1–012, n.35, at para.74.

[92] Case C–62/86 *AKZO Chemie BV v Commission* [1991] I E.C.R. 3359, at para.60.

[93] The Commission has consistently never based the finding of a dominant position upon a threshold below 25 per cent market share. Furthermore, the Commission has only once found a firm to be dominant with a market share of less than 40 per cent in an Art.82 case: decision on *Virgin/British Airways,* O.J. 2000 L30/1, (2000) 4 C.M.L.R. 999, where British Airways was found to be dominant in the market for the procurement of travel agency services, where its market share was 39.7 per cent. However, no such a precedent exists in the telecommunications sector.

the use of revenue for terminating calls to customers for mobile networks may be the most appropriate means to measure the market presence of mobile network operators.

1–034   *Other criteria for assessing dominance* — The SMP Guidelines stress that the existence of dominance cannot be established on the sole basis of large market shares.[94] NRAs are required to undertake a thorough and overall analysis of the economic characteristics of the relevant market. The following criteria (amongst others)[95] can be used alone or in combination to measure the ability of an undertaking to behave to an appreciable extent independently of competitors, customers and consumers: (i) a lack of actual potential competition; (ii) high barriers to market entry[96]; (iii) an absence of, or low, countervailing buyer power; and (iv) economies of scale and scope.

1–035   Joint or collective dominance — Article 14(2) of the Framework Directive clearly states that two or more companies that are jointly or collectively dominant in a relevant market should each be considered as having SMP. This follows the approach under Article 82 of the EC Treaty[97] and the Merger Control Regulation[98] to identify situations of joint or collective dominance. The Commission has indicated that it would consider two or more undertakings to be in a collective dominant position when they had substantially the same position *vis-à-vis* their customers and competitors, as a single company has if it is dominant, provided that no effective competition exists between them.[99] However, the concept of joint and collective dominance is relatively new in the

[94] *ibid.*, para.78.
[95] The SMP Guidelines, para.1–012, n.35, explicitly state that criteria other than those listed in that document may be considered when assessing the state of effective competition on a particular relevant market. For that reason, NRAs may consider other criteria that they consider to be relevant, but they are required to state their reasons for doing so and submit them to public consultation. See for example, Oftel's market review guidelines: criteria for the assessment of significant market power, August 5, 2002, available at: *www.oftel.gov.uk*. See also ERG Working Paper on the SMP concept for the New Regulatory Framework, ERG (03) 09 Rev 02, May 2003, available at *www.erg.eu.int*. The ERG Working Paper clarifies the common understanding of the NRAs on single and collective dominance, on the basis of the criteria given in the SMP Guidelines; and it also discusses some further indicators which, although as such cannot justify a finding of dominance, can nevertheless provide some useful information for the assessment of SMP: *i.e.* (i) evidence of previous anti-competitive behaviour and collusion; (ii) rate of growth in geographic/service coverage by competitors (*i.e.*, another way to measure market entry); (iii) existence of standards and conventions; (iv) customers' ability to access and use information; (v) price trends; (vi) existence of infrastructure-based competition (which is an indicator of sustainable competition, thus excluding SMP); and (vii) international benchmarking in comparable economies.
[96] See SMP Guidelines, para.1–012, n.35, at para.80, where the Commission states that barriers to entry are often high in the electronic communications sector because of existing legislative and other regulatory requirements, which may limit the provision of services, but also, in some instances, the market power of incumbent operators. Furthermore, the Commission indicates that barriers to entry exist where entry into the market requires large investments and the programming of capacities over a long time in order to be profitable. However, the Commission stresses that high barriers to entry may become less relevant with regard to markets characterised by ongoing technological progress. In such markets, where competitive constraints may come from innovative threats from potential competitors that are not currently on the market, the competitive assessment should be based on a prospective, forward-looking approach. For a discussion of the emerging market theory, see also para.1–039 below in this chapter.
[97] Cases T–68/89 *Societá Italiana Vetro v Commission*, [1992] II E.C.R. 547, paras 357–369.
[98] Case T–102/96, *Gencor v Commission*, [1999] II E.C.R. 753.
[99] SMP Guidelines, para.1–012, n.35, para.87. On the application of the concept of collective dominance in competition law cases, see para.6–025 *et seq.*

European context and one that is still developing. Based on two milestone judgments of the European Courts,[1] the Commission has developed a checklist of criteria that are relevant in assessing collective dominance. These criteria are summarised in Annex II of the Framework Directive and repeated in the SMP Guidelines. NRAs are required to use such criteria in their assessment, as well as applying the SMP Guidelines.[2]

1–036 According to the SMP Guidelines, NRAs are required to analyse whether the characteristics of the market makes it conducive to tacit co-ordination and whether such a form of co-ordination is sustainable; that is (i) whether any of the duopolists or oligopolists has the ability and incentive to deviate from the co-ordinated outcomes, considering the ability and incentives of the non-deviators to retaliate; and (ii) whether customers, fringe competitors and/or potential entrants have the ability and incentive to challenge any anti-competitive co-ordinated conduct by the duopolists or oligopolists.

1–037 *Checklist of indicators of joint or collective dominance* — Together with the traditional criteria for the assessment of dominance, indicators of joint or collective dominance include: (i) a small number of market players; (ii) a high level of market concentration; (iii) the maturity of the market; (iv) the similarity of cost structures and market shares; (v) the homogeneity of demand; (vi) the existence of informal or other links between the market players; and (vii) retaliatory mechanisms to punish the "cheaters". Annex II of the Framework Directive expressly states that the above list is by no means exhaustive and that the criteria are not cumulative. It is clear from this list that the assessment of joint or collective dominance requires a complex, in-depth analysis on a case-by-case basis that cannot be performed mechanically. In the SMP Guidelines, the Commission also refers to a number of decisions adopted under the Merger Control Regulation in the telecommunications sector, in which the Commission examined whether any of the notified concentrations could give rise to a finding of collective dominance. Those decisions are discussed in Chapter VIII.[3] It should also be noted that Annex II of the Framework Directive states that the criteria used to establish joint or collective dominance set out in the SMP Guidelines are without prejudice to the case law of the European Court of Justice.[4]

---

[1] Joined Cases C–395 and 396 *Compagnie Maritime Belge SA and Dafia-Lines A/S v Commission* [2000] I E.C.R. 1365 and Case T–102/96 *Gencor Ltd v Commission* [1999] II E.C.R. 753.

[2] Framework Directive, para.1–009, n.25, Art.13(2).

[3] Contrary to the initial draft, the final SMP Guidelines do not mention the Commission Working Document on the initial findings of the sector inquiry into mobile roaming charges that it adopted on December 13, 2000 available at: *http://www.europa.eu.int/comm/competition/antitrust/others/sector_inquiries/roaming/working_document_on_initial_results.pdf*. However, attention should be paid to this document as regards the issue of collective dominance in the mobile sector. In the roaming inquiry, the Commission is investigating retail and wholesale roaming offerings, in particular pricing. The Commission has expressed concerns that roaming charges are too high and that the national markets for international roaming are conducive to (tacit) collusion: see para.6–012, below.

[4] In Case T–342/99 *Airtours v Commission* [2002] II E.C.R. 2585, the Court of First Instance (CFI) annulled the contested Commission decision on the grounds that the Commission erred in facts and law in its competitive assessment of collective dominance (see also para.6–025, below). In this judgment, the CFI held that a determination of a situation of collective dominance requires three conditions to be met: (i) there should be sufficient market transparency to enable market players to be aware of the conduct of their competitors and consequently allow them to adopt the same policy; (ii) collective dominance should be sustainable over time, which implies the existence of a retaliatory mechanism in the market; (iii) existing competitors that are

1–038   Leveraging of market power into neighbouring markets — Article 14(3) of the Framework Directive makes clear that an undertaking may possess SMP if it is dominant in a specific market and possesses the ability to leverage that market power onto a closely related neighbouring market. This provision is intended to address situations such as those that gave rise to the European Court of Justice's judgment in the *Tetra Pak II* case,[5] where a dominant undertaking was found to have infringed Article 82 by leveraging its market power on a market so as to distort competition on a neighbouring market. In the SMP Guidelines, the Commission refers to the fact that close links between the two markets should be present. This is often the case with telecommunications markets, where vertically integrated firms are active both on the infrastructure markets and on downstream services markets. However, in practice, if an undertaking has been designated as having SMP on an upstream market, NRAs will be in a position to prevent any likely spillover or leveraging effects on downstream markets by imposing on that undertaking any of the obligations provided for in the Access Directive.

1–039   *Leveraging on emerging markets* — It is questionable whether the application of this leveraging theory should not be applied in cases of leveraging from a regulated market into an emerging non-regulated market. In such cases, the Commission seems to be of the opinion that such conduct should only be assessed under competition law and that *ex ante* regulation is not appropriate in such cases.[6] For example, if an incumbent operator in a traditional second generation mobile market is alleged to be capable of leveraging market power into the market for third generation mobile services, an argument could be made that the relevant market for such services, if any, should be considered as an emerging market and that there is no need to regulate on any *ex ante* basis. The same argument would arguably apply with respect to narrowband and broadband internet access services. In competition law cases, the Commission has concluded that

not part of the oligopoly, potential competitors, as well as customers, should not be able to jeopardise the expected results of a common policy adopted by the oligopolists in the market. The *Airtours* judgment also provides useful insights into the application of the so-called "collective-dominance" checklist and in particular the level of proof required to establish collective dominance. As regards the number of market participants, the CFI denied that the risk of collective dominance would occur in a market (the UK market for short-haul foreign package holidays) where the number of large market participants would be reduced from four to three. Expanding on the above mentioned criteria, the CFI indicated that, as regards the existence of deterrent (or retaliation) mechanisms to secure unity within the oligopoly, the analysis should be threefold: (i) the members must be able to detect a deviation; (ii) the retaliation must be quick and sufficiently effective; and (iii) the retaliation must not harm the retaliators too much so as to make retaliation economically unrealistic. Finally, the judgment implies that, in order to counter a potential collective dominance situation, customers are no longer required to be able to exert buying power, but only have the ability to trade-off between sellers, *i.e.* by reacting to a price increase, which would result should the undertakings restrict capacity. Whilst the criteria as mentioned in Annex II of the Framework Directive and repeated in the SMP Guidelines remain relevant for the application of the concept of collective dominance by the NRAs, as the Guidelines are without prejudice to evolving case law, NRAs should arguably take the *Airtours* judgment and any subsequent judgments into consideration when making their assessment.

[5] Case C–333/94 P *Tetra Pak International SA v Commission* [1996] I E.C.R. 5951 ("Tetra Pak II"). See also para.6–026.

[6] The Commission at n.92 of the SMP Guidelines, para.1–012, n.35, clarifies that Art.14(3) of the Framework Directive is not intended to apply in relation to market power leveraged from a regulated market into an emerging non-regulated market. In such cases, according to the Commission, any abusive conduct in the emerging market would normally be dealt with under Art.82 of the EC Treaty.

emerging markets are characterised by rapid shifts in market shares and fierce innovation-driven potential competition, as a result of which even high market shares should not necessarily be viewed as indicators of market power.[7] It goes without saying that the emerging market theory is also relevant as regards the assessment of single and collective dominance.[8]

1–040 Imposition, maintenance and withdrawal of *ex ante* regulatory obligations — After having defined the relevant market and identified operators that possess SMP, the final decision to be taken by the NRAs is the imposition, maintenance, amendment or withdrawal of any *ex ante* regulatory obligation. When imposing remedies, NRAs must choose regulatory obligations, which are appropriate and based on the nature of the problem identified, proportionate and justified in the light of the objectives laid down in the Framework Directive (*e.g.* maximising benefits for users, ensuring no distortion or restriction of competition, encouraging efficient investment in infrastructure and promoting innovation, and encouraging efficient use and management of radio frequencies and numbering resources). The notion of effective competition means that if the NRA has not identified any undertaking as possessing SMP on the relevant market because there is effective competition, it is not possible to impose *ex ante* specific regulatory obligations on any operator.[9] However, this general principle has a number of defined exceptions, where obligations similar to those that can be imposed on operators with SMP may also be imposed on operators that do not have SMP. The applicable provisions are analysed under Section F.

1–041 National Regulatory Authorities — NRAs are primarily responsible for the implementation of the provisions of the New Regulatory Framework. Member States must ensure that their NRAs are competent for the tasks assigned under the New Regulatory Framework and that they act in an impartial and transparent manner.[10]

1–042 *Responsibilities of the NRA* — The separation of commercial and regulatory functions has now been implemented in all Member States, which have all created independent regulators. The Framework Directive includes provisions to strengthen the independence and the impartiality of NRAs. In particular, NRAs must be legally distinct and functionally independent from all operators providing electronic communications networks, equipment or services. Member States that retain ownership or control of undertakings that operate electronic communications networks and/or provide services, must ensure the structural separation of their NRAs' regulatory functions from

---

[7] See Case IV/M.1908, *Alcatel/Newbridge Networks*, Commission Decision of May 19, 2000, concerning a concentration in the market for DSL equipment, which was found to be emerging and rapidly growing. The Commission found it very difficult to obtain accurate market shares, and different parties' estimations of market sizes and market shares differed widely. More recently, in Case IV/37.462, *Identrus*, Commission Decision of August 1, 2001, the Commission concluded that market share figures available for the cross-border regional market of the provision of electronic trust services by Certification Authorities were unreliable and held that the emerging and evolving nature of the seamless services market and the large traffic volume of large business customers constituted evidence of such unreliability. This reasoning has also been applied in other industrial sectors, such as the graphic arts, film and offset printing plates sector and the medical imaging sector.

[8] See Case IV/M.1332, *Thomson/Lucas*, Commission Decision of December 31, 1998, concerning a joint venture to enter the emerging market for adaptive cruise control (ACC) systems, where the Commission concluded that the existence of a collective dominant position was thought to be less likely on a new market.

[9] Framework Directive, para.1–009, n.25, Art.16(3).

[10] *ibid.*, Arts 3(1) and 3(3).

the State's activities as a shareholder.[11] Member States must publish in an accessible form the tasks to be undertaken by the NRAs. Member States are furthermore responsible for ensuring that the NRAs exercise their powers impartially and transparently. Where a Member State assigns its tasks to more than one body, it must ensure, where appropriate, consultation and co-operation between those authorities[12] and between those authorities and national authorities entrusted with the implementation of competition law[13] and consumer protection law.[14]

1–043 *NRAs' powers of investigation* — Member States are required to ensure that NRAs have the necessary resources in terms of number and quality of the staff, and have the power to collect the information they consider necessary in order to assess market power in a given market as required by the Framework Directive.[15] To this end, operators are required by the terms of their general authorisation to supply the information necessary for NRAs to conduct their market analysis,[16] and, in general, to provide all the information necessary for NRAs to ensure conformity with EC law.[17] NRAs are required to state the reasons justifying requests for information. They may impose financial penalties on undertakings that fail to provide information, if they are given this power under national law.[18] NRAs are required to co-operate with national competition authorities (NCAs) in their assessment of the competitiveness of the relevant markets, but they remain legally responsible for conducting such analysis.[19] They must publish all information received that would contribute to an open and competitive market. However, the confidentiality of sensitive commercial information must always be ensured.[20]

---

[11] *ibid.*, Art.3(2).

[12] For example, with respect to the granting of rights of way, Art.9 of the Authorisation Directive, para.1–011, n.28, requires NRAs to issue, upon request of concerned undertakings, a standardised declaration confirming the undertaking's entitlement to apply for the relevant rights of way, granted under a general authorisation, in order to facilitate the exercise of those rights at other levels of government.

[13] NRAs are required to co-operate with national competition authorities in the exercise of assessing the competitiveness of the relevant markets, in order to verify the existence of any operator that possesses SMP: see Framework Directive, para.1–009, n.25, Art.16(1).

[14] *ibid.*, Art.3(4).

[15] Art.16(1) of the Framework Directive requires NRAs to conduct an analysis of the relevant markets identified in the Recommendation on the Relevant Markets, para.1–012, n.36, and any subsequent Decision that the Commission may adopt on transnational markets as soon as possible after their adoption or any subsequent update. The NRA's conclusion of the analysis of each relevant market, together with the proposed regulatory measures to the telecommunications operator(s) with SMP, must be published, following a period of public consultation on the draft conclusion.

[16] Authorisation Directive, para.1–011, n.28, Art.11.

[17] Framework Directive, para.1–009, n.25, Art.5.

[18] Authorisation Directive, para.1–011, n.28, Art.10(4).

[19] Art.3(5) of the Framework Directive, para.1–009, n.25, requires NRAs and NCAs to provide each other with the information necessary for the application of the regulatory framework, and the receiving authority must ensure the same level of confidentiality as the originating authority. NCAs should therefore provide NRAs with all relevant information obtained using the former's investigatory and enforcement powers, including confidential information. This provision also implies that evidence of dominance in a given relevant market, which was used in former investigations under competition rules, could be used for a finding of SMP in that same market.

[20] *ibid.*, Art.5(4), read in conjunction with SMP Guidelines, para.1–012, n.35, at para.137. The requirement of ensuring the confidentiality of sensitive information applies to all the circumstances in which the NRAs receive the information, *i.e.* by enforcement of their investigatory powers, directly from the concerned operators, and by other national authorities. In particular, information that is considered confidential by the

1–044   Consultation, co-ordination and transparency mechanisms — In order to ensure a consistent application of the provisions of the New Regulatory Framework in the different Member States, in particular given the wide margin of discretion left to NRAs, the Framework Directive includes a set of consultation and transparency mechanisms. Certain decisions that NRAs may take are subject to these mechanisms, including those which: (i) define the relevant markets for the purposes of an SMP analysis; (ii) assess whether an operator possesses SMP in those markets; (iii) impose, amend or withdraw any *ex ante* regulatory obligations; and (iv) any other measure, which may have an effect on trade between Member States (for example, licensing procedures for communications services that are cross-border in nature). The Framework Directive provides for three types of mechanisms, which are described below.

1–045   *Consultation mechanism* — When NRAs intend to impose measures to apply the relevant provisions of the directives comprising the New Regulatory Framework and/or national measures that implement these directives, they must give interested parties, including operators active in the concerned relevant market, an opportunity to comment on the draft measure within a reasonable period.[21] This period should normally be not less than two months.[22] NRAs are required to publish their national consultation procedures. A single information point through which all ongoing consultations can be accessed should be established in each Member State. NRAs must publish the results of public consultations without prejudice to requirements of EU and national law protecting the confidentiality of business secrets.[23]

1–046   *Co-ordination mechanism* — Under Article 7(2) of the Framework Directive, NRAs have a general duty of co-operation with each other and with the Commission in a transparent manner to ensure the consistent application of the directives comprising the New Regulatory Framework. In particular, they are required to seek agreement on the types of instruments and remedies that are best suited to address particular types of situation in the market place. Pursuant to Recital 36 of the Framework Directive, the Commission has set up the ERG for electronic communications networks and services. The ERG will act as a forum for NRAs and will have advisory co-operation and co-ordination powers.[24]

1–047   *Transparency mechanism* — In addition to the consultation and co-ordination mechanisms explained above, NRAs are required to notify the Commission and other NRAs of any draft

NCA should only be exchanged with the NRA where such exchange is necessary for the application of the provisions of the regulatory framework. The information exchanged should be limited to that which is relevant and proportionate to the purpose of such exchange. See SMP Guidelines, at para.137.

[21] *ibid.*, Art.6(1).

[22] According to para.145 of the SMP Guidelines, para.1–012, n.35, NRAs' decisions should not be delayed excessively as this can impede the development of the market. For decisions relating to the existence and designation of undertakings with SMP, the Commission considers that a period of two months would be reasonable for the public consultation. Different periods could be used in some cases, if this is justified. Conversely, where the NRA proposes to adopt an SMP decision on the basis of the results of an earlier decision that has been subject to public consultation, the consultation period for the decision may well be shorter than two months.

[23] Framework Directive, para.1–009, n.25, Art.6.

[24] See Commission Decision of July 29, 2002, establishing the European Regulators Group for Electronic Communications Networks and Services, O.J. 2002 L200/38. For further information on the work of the ERG, see *http://erg.eu.int*.

measure that concerns the definition of the relevant markets, the designation of an operator as possessing SMP, the imposition of a specific remedy other than those listed in the Access and Universal Service Directives (even in those limited cases where a prior SMP designation is not required), or otherwise affects trade between Member States (hereinafter "Draft Measures"). The other NRAs and the Commission have a one-month period (which may not be extended) to review the Draft Measures and submit their comments to the relevant NRA.[25]

1–048 If the Commission indicates that a Draft Measure would create a barrier to the functioning of the internal market, or expresses serious doubts as to the compatibility of the Draft Measure with EU law (in particular the objectives referred to in Article 8 of the Framework Directive), the NRAs are required to suspend the adoption of the concerned Draft Measure for a period of two months. This period may not be extended. Within this period the Commission may adopt a decision requiring the relevant NRA to amend or withdraw its Draft Measure. The Commission's decision must include a detailed and objective analysis of the reasons why the Commission considers that the Draft Measure should not be adopted, together with specific proposals for amending it to make it compatible with EU law.[26]

1–049 The Recommendation on the Relevant Markets and the SMP Guidelines are not legally binding on NRAs. However, the NRAs are required to take the utmost account of these measures, in making their decisions. The veto power granted to the Commission under the transparency mechanism gives it a direct legal tool to enforce its decision, the Recommendation and the SMP Guidelines if NRAs do not implement them correctly.[27] The transparency mechanism applies only to those cases where an NRA has taken the initiative to regulate a specific issue. It does not grant the Commission the power to force an NRA to regulate when it has failed to take the initiative to adopt a sector-specific regulation to address a specific situation of market failure. This might lead to the situation, where, should similar situations of market failure exist in two Member States, and one of the NRAs concerned does not define that market for *ex ante* regulation purposes, or designate any operator as possessing SMP, or impose sector-specific regulation, the Commission would not have any legal means within the provision of Article 7(4) of the Framework Directive to force that NRA to act. In such a situation, the Commission might only be able to exercise political pressure on that NRA, in the context of the consultation mechanisms provided by Article 6 of the Framework Directive. Should the NRA continue to fail to act, it seems that the only possibility for the Commission would be to initiate a proceeding under Article 226 of the EC Treaty against the Member State in question, for failure to implement a directive properly (see also Section M, below).

1–050 *Urgent cases* — The mechanisms described above may not apply in cases of urgency. In order to safeguard competition and protect the interests of users, NRAs may adopt proportionate

---

[25] Framework Directive, para.1–009, n.25, Art.7(3) and Recital 38; and Access Directive, para.1–011, n.29, Art.8(4).

[26] *ibid.*, Art.7(4). See flowchart in App.1. It must be noted that the Commission does not have such a veto power in relation to NRAs' decisions to impose a remedy upon an SMP operator, provided that this remedy is listed in the Access and Universal Services Directives.

[27] Such considerations are of particular relevance with respect to the question of whether such measures are susceptible to judicial review under general EU law. Although it is settled law that a private party may not challenge the Recommendation or the Guidelines directly (as they are not legally binding), it remains to be seen whether their content might be indirectly challenged via judicial review of the Commission decision adopted under Art.7(4) of the Framework Directive or indeed of any NRA decision adopted in reliance on them.

and provisional measures, without having first consulted interested parties, other NRAs or the Commission. However, in such cases the NRA must communicate without delay such provisional measures to the other NRAs and the Commission, which is ultimately required to assess their proportionality against the policy objectives set out in Article 8 of the Framework Directive. If the NRA wishes to make its provisional measures permanent, it must follow the normal consultation procedure described above.[28]

1–051 Adoption of a final decision — Once an NRA has, following the application of the transparency mechanism required by Article 7(2) of the Framework Directive, adopted a final decision, the NRA is required to notify the Commission of (i) the names of the undertakings designated as possessing SMP, and (ii) the obligations imposed on them. The Commission will then report to the Communications Committee as appropriate. Likewise, NRAs must publish the names of the designated undertakings and keep this information updated.[29]

C. Electronic Communications Services

1–052 Electronic communications services are now fully liberalised within the EU. The liberalisation process started with the so-called "value-added" or "enhanced" services (*e.g.* email, voice mail, online information and database services, electronic data interchange ("EDI"), audio and video-conferencing, traveller services, enhanced facsimile services, code and protocol conversion, online information and data processing services). It was only extended subsequently and gradually, first to mobile, and later to fixed, voice telephony services. Although the same regulatory regime is now applicable to all these services, until recently public voice telephony services remained subject to a higher level of regulatory intervention than value-added services.[30] Furthermore, value-added and voice telephony are still considered separately for the purposes of *ex ante* regulation with respect to the definition of the relevant markets under the Commission Recommendation on the Relevant Markets.[31] Therefore, the provisions of the New Regulatory Framework are arguably likely to have a different impact on operators providing these different types of service. In this section a distinction is therefore made between these two categories of service.

1. Regulatory Framework for Value-Added Services

1–053 It could not be argued, as it was done for voice telephony at the end of the 1980s, that the monopoly of incumbent operators to provide value-added services needed to be further maintained in order to preserve their ability to provide universal service.[32] On the contrary, it was perceived

---

[28] Framework Directive, para.1–009, n.25, Arts 7(3) and 7(4).

[29] Universal Service Directive, para.1–011, n.30, Art.36(2) and the Access Directive, para.1–011, n.29, Art.15(2), as clarified in paras 155 and 156 of the SMP Guidelines, para.1–012, n.35.

[30] See Garzaniti, *Telecommunications, Broadcasting and the Internet: E.U. Competition Law and Regulation* (Sweet & Maxwell, 1st ed., 2000), p.11.

[31] See above, para.1–025.

[32] The maintenance of special and exclusive rights in relation to value-added services was considered a breach of Arts 82 and 86 in conjunction with Art.49 of the EC Treaty (freedom to provide services). Also, special and exclusive rights for such services prevented competitors from accessing the market, limited consumer choice and enabled incumbent operators to bundle network services with unconnected services, in violation of Arts 82

that the liberalisation and entry of new players on those markets were essential to ensure the development of the sector and the availability of advanced telecommunications services to European customers.[33]

(a) Liberalisation of Value-Added Services

1–054   The so-called Commission "Liberalisation Directive" consolidates the provisions of the existing "Services Directive" which initiated the opening to competition of the telecommunications services market in 1990 and was subsequently amended as more services were liberalised in the run-up to the introduction of full competition in 1998. The Liberalisation Directive was adopted under Article 86(3).

1–055   Abolition of monopoly rights to provide value-added services — The Liberalisation Directive requires the removal of special and exclusive rights[34] granted by Member States to incumbent communications operators. In addition, it extends this requirement for the establishment and/or the provision of electronic communications networks, and the supply of electronic communications services to the public.[35]

1–056   Types of services covered — The Liberalisation Directive refers to "electronic communications services and networks" rather than the previously used term "telecommunications services and networks". These new definitions take account of the convergence of the information technology, media and telecommunications industries over the last years, by bringing together under one single definition all electronic communications services and/or networks involved in the transmission of electronic magnetic signals (*i.e.* fixed, mobile, cable television, satellite networks). Therefore, the Liberalisation Directive requires Member States to abolish all exclusive or special rights also with respect to operators of broadcast transmission networks,[36] such as cable television and satellite operators.[37]

---

and 86(1). The need to preserve universal network provision could not justify a derogation under Art.86(2), Arts 49 or 82 since the liberalisation of added-value services could not reasonably be considered as threatening the financial resources of incumbent operators and their ability to provide universal service.

[33] See 1987 Green Paper, para.1–001, n.2.

[34] According to Arts 1(5) and (4) of the Liberalisation Directive, para.1–012, n.33, "exclusive rights" means the rights that are granted by a Member State to one undertaking through any legislative, regulatory or administrative instrument, reserving to it the right to provide an electronic communications service or to undertake an electronic communications activity within a geographic area. "Special rights" means the rights that are granted by a Member State to a limited number of undertakings through any legislative, regulatory or administrative instrument which, within a given geographical area: (a) designates or limits to two or more the number of such undertakings authorised to provide an electronic communications service or undertake an electronic communications activity, otherwise than according to objective, proportional and non-discriminatory criteria; or (b) confers on undertakings, otherwise than according to such criteria, legal or regulatory advantages which substantially affect the ability of any other undertaking to provide the same electronic communications service or to undertake the same electronic communications activity in the same geographical area under substantially equivalent conditions.

[35] Liberalisation Directive, para.1–012, n.33, Art.2(1).

[36] This is, however, without prejudice to rights corresponding to *"must carry"* obligations imposed by national legislation (see further, para.2–063).

[37] See para.1–120 *et seq.*

1–057 **Processing of signals** — Member States must abolish all restrictions on the processing of signals before and after their transmission via the networks established by the providers themselves, over infrastructure provided by third parties, or by means of sharing networks, other facilities or sites.[38] Specific conditions may, however, be imposed on the provision of the electronic communications services by operators on a given market.

1–058 **Vertically integrated undertakings** — Article 3 of the Liberalisation Directive requires Member States to ensure that vertically integrated "dominant" public undertakings owning a public telecommunications network do not discriminate in favour of their own retail activities.[39] The use of the word "dominant" in Article 3 does not necessarily correspond to the concept of SMP. Rather, it should arguably be interpreted as a reference to the incumbent former monopolist operators, who previously enjoyed exclusive or special rights (now abolished). It is unclear whether such a non-discrimination obligation could be used *per se* as a basis for the imposition of any specific structural or accounting separation obligations. However, such an interpretation would seem to be too extreme. It would be difficult to justify the imposition of structural separation on the basis of the principle of non-discrimination alone, in view of the lack of explicit reference in Article 3 to the possibility for NRAs to impose structural separation obligations.[40] As regards accounting separation, the Access Directive provides that if a public communications network operator is designated as having SMP, it could be required to keep separate financial accounts for its different activities, in order to ensure detection by the NRA of unfair cross-subsidisation or discriminating practices.[41] However, these provisions of the Access Directive fall short of allowing for the possibility of NRAs requiring structural separation, even on operators with SMP.[42] It would

---

[38] Liberalisation Directive, para.1–012, n.33, Art.2(3).

[39] *ibid.*, Art.3.

[40] In some cases in the communications sector considered by the Commission, under the Merger Control Regulation, the parties involved to a notified concentration have sometimes had to accept structural separation obligations as a condition for obtaining approval from the Commission, *e.g.* see the recent *Telia/Sonera* decision, discussed at para.8–129 *et seq.*, where structural separation obligations were imposed requiring legal separation of the parties' fixed and mobile networks and services both in Finland and Sweden as a condition for clearance for the merger, in order for the Commission to remedy foreclosure concerns raised by the notified concentration. Strictly speaking, the onus to offer commitments is on the parties, and it is not for the Commission to impose the remedies *ex officio*. However, in practice, it is difficult to ignore the fact that the Commission plays an important role in the remedies process. The issue of structural separation has also been considered in proceedings at the national level. Many competitors to the national incumbent operators often claim that an *ex ante* requirement for structural separation of the incumbent's activities at the wholesale and retail levels is a necessary precondition for the take-up of new services provided using the fixed telephone networks, such as broadband internet services. For example, see Case A/285, *Infostrada/Telecom Italia-Technologies ADSL*, in Boll. 16–17/2001 (available at *www.agcom.it*), where the Italian national competition authority endorsed these views in one of the recitals of its decision, but finally did not impose structural separation obligations *ex post*.

[41] Access Directive, para.1–011, n.29, Art.11.

[42] The only case in which structural separation may be imposed is set out in the Framework Directive, which permits the NRAs to impose structural separation obligations on companies that enjoy monopoly rights in other sectors and, at the same time, are also active in the provision of electronic communications services directly or through subsidiaries. In this case, structural separation may be imposed to prevent unfair cross-subsidisation from the monopoly activity. This obligation may be imposed even if the operator does not have SMP in a relevant communications market. See on this point, more extensively, para.1–081 later in this chapter.

therefore appear to be very difficult to justify Article 3 of the Liberalisation Directive alone as a sufficient legal basis for the imposition of structural separation obligations, without the risk of undermining the *rationale* behind other provisions of the New Regulatory Framework.

1–059 Separation of regulatory and commercial activities — Member States are required to ensure that the type approvals and mandatory specifications, the allocation of frequencies and numbers, and the surveillance of usage conditions and any other regulatory functions, are entrusted to a body that is independent from operators of electronic communications network and/or services.[43] This structural separation requirement applies also to public or local authorities that retain ownership or control of operators as regards the granting of rights to install facilities on, over or under public or private land.[44] The separation of commercial and regulatory functions has now been implemented in all Member States, where NRAs have been created. The Framework Directive has introduced provisions to strengthen the independence of NRAs, by requiring in particular the structural separation of the ownership and regulatory activities of Member States that still hold interests in incumbent operators.[45]

(b) Licensing of Electronic Communications Services

1–060 The legal framework laying down the conditions under which electronic communications services may be provided is set out in the so-called "Authorisation Directive".[46] Under the Authorisation Directive, electronic communications services may in principle be provided either without any authorisation or on the basis of a general authorisation.[47] Indeed, the use of individual authorisations must be limited only to those circumstances where the applicant needs to be given access to scarce resources (*i.e.* numbers or frequencies). In principle, an individual licence is no longer required for voice telephony services or in situations when the provider is subject to particular obligations (*e.g.* universal service) or enjoys particular rights (*e.g.* rights of way). Thus, in practice, any undertaking active on the market for the provision of public and non-public electronic communications services can provide these services either without authorisation or subject only to obtaining a general authorisation. The provision of voice telephony services, however, requires access to numbers and, when provided over wireless networks, to frequencies. Providers of voice telephony services may therefore in certain circumstances still be subject to the requirement to obtain an individual authorisation (as discussed below at paragraph 1–082).

1–061 General authorisations — The granting of a general authorisation does not require an explicit decision by the NRA prior to the start of the provision of an electronic communications network or service, whilst the granting of an individual licence does require an explicit decision

---

[43] At the time of adoption of the Services Directive in 1990, incumbent telecommunications operators generally carried out operational and regulatory functions. Although in all Member States this is reported to no longer be the case, such a provision is maintained under the Liberalisation Directive, Art.9.

[44] Framework Directive, para.1–009, n.25, Art.11(2).

[45] See also para.1–042, above.

[46] For an overview/road map of the New Regulatory Framework, see para.1–011, above.

[47] The Authorisation Directive refers to the definition of electronic communications services in the Framework Directive where the term is defined as services the provision of which consists wholly or partly in the transmission and routing of signals on electronic communications networks, with the exception of content. See para.1–013 *et seq.*, above.

prior to the start of operation, and in addition may either give specific rights to, or impose specific obligations on, the licensee. There are two types of general authorisation: (i) those not requiring registration with the NRA; and (ii) those that require notification by the service provider to the NRA. Subject to making any necessary notifications, an operator may avail of a general authorisation if it meets the conditions that are laid down for that authorisation.[48] Under a general authorisation, an operator may be granted: (i) the right to commence the activities covered by the general authorisation; (ii) rights to apply for access to public or private land to install facilities (rights of way or way leaves)[49]; (iii) the right to negotiate and, where applicable, obtain inter-connection with other providers; and (iv) the opportunity to be designated by the NRA as a provider of different elements of universal service.[50]

1–062   Procedures for the granting of general authorisations — If any undertaking meets the conditions attached to a general authorisation, it is entitled to provide the relevant communications services or networks, without requiring a decision.[51] However, Member States may require undertakings to notify the NRA of their intention to provide the relevant services and/or networks, as well as the information relating to the service or network concerned that is necessary for the NRA to ensure compliance with the applicable conditions. Such a notification should not involve more than a declaration of the undertaking's intention to commence the provision of the service and/ or network and the submission of information that is necessary to identify the provider, in order to allow the NRA to keep a register or list of undertakings operating under the relevant general authorisation.[52] Contrary to the previous regime, an explicit decision by the NRA is therefore not necessary before the operator may exercise the rights provided by the authorisation. Information concerning the procedures relating to general authorisations must be published in an appropriate manner, so as to provide easy access to that information.[53]

1–063   Conditions that may be attached to a general authorisation — NRAs may only attach conditions to a general authorisation where this is justified and complies with the principles of

---

[48] See para.1–063, below.

[49] Art.9 of the Authorisation Directive requires NRAs, upon request of any operator, to issue a standardised declaration, within one week from the request, where it confirms that the undertaking has submitted a notification/declaration for the purposes of a general authorisation, and details the circumstances under which any undertaking providing electronic communications networks or services under the general authorisation has the right to apply for rights to install facilities, negotiate interconnection, and/or obtain access or inter-connection in order to facilitate the exercise of those rights, for instance, at other levels of government or in relation to other undertakings (see in this regard also *ibid.*, Art.15(2), which requires Member States to create a user-friendly overview of information on procedures and conditions on rights to install facilities, including information on the relevant levels of government and the responsible authorities). Where appropriate, such declarations may also be issued as an automatic reply following the notification by the concerned applicant.

[50] *ibid.*, Art.4.

[51] *ibid.*, Art.3(1).

[52] According to Art.3(3), *ibid.*, this information must be limited to that which is necessary for the iden-tification of the provider, such as its company registration number, its address and a contact person, a short description of the network or service to be provided, and an estimated date for starting the activity. However, this provision is without prejudice to the extensive information that operators are required to provide to the NRA under the conditions of the general authorisation, once obtained, in order to allow the NRA to conduct its market analysis for the purposes of imposing *ex ante* regulation: see Art.11, *ibid.*

[53] *ibid.*, Art.15.

non-discrimination, proportionality and transparency. The Authorisation Directive provides that Part A of the Annex to the Authorisation Directive sets out an exhaustive list of conditions that may be imposed on general authorisations, as follows:

(i) conditions relating to financial contributions to the provision of universal service;

(ii) conditions relating to administrative charges;

(iii) conditions relating to the interconnection of networks and the interoperability of services;

(iv) conditions relating to the efficient use of numbering capacity;

(v) conditions relating to the execution of infrastructure works in accordance with environmental and town and country planning requirements;

(vi) conditions relating to "*must carry*" requirements;

(vii) conditions relating to the processing of personal data and the protection of privacy;

(viii) conditions relating to consumer protection as well as special arrangements for the disabled;

(ix) restrictions in relation to the transmission of illegal or harmful content;

(x) conditions regarding the provision of information required for the NRAs' market analysis for the purposes of *ex ante* regulation, as well as the verification of compliance with applicable conditions and for statistical purposes;

(xi) conditions relating to legal interception by the competent national authorities intended to prevent anti-competitive behaviour;

(xii) conditions relating to provision of emergency services, *i.e.* the terms of use during major disasters to ensure communications between emergency services and authorities and broadcasts to the general public;

(xiii) conditions relating to the protection of users and subscribers to limit the exposure to electromagnetic fields caused by sites or antennas;

(xiv) access obligations other than those imposed under the Access and Universal Service Directives (discussed, below, in Section F);

(xv) maintenance of the integrity of public communications networks;

(xvi) arrangements for the security of public networks against unauthorised access to their data;

(xvii) conditions for the use of radio frequencies where such use is not made subject to the granting of individual rights; and

(xviii) measures designed to ensure compliance with the standards and specifications that the Commission may introduce in order to ensure interoperability between network interfaces.[54]

---

[54] Framework Directive, para.1–009, n.25, Art.17; see also para.1–173, below.

Specific *ex ante* obligations which may be imposed on operators designated as possessing SMP (and in the exceptional cases where such obligations may be imposed on operators without SMP)[55] must not be included in the rights and obligations contained in general authorisations and must be imposed separately. In order to achieve transparency for undertakings, NRAs must set out the criteria and procedures for imposing such specific obligations in the general authorisation.[56]

1–064 Measures that NRAs may take for non-compliance with the conditions attached to a general authorisation — Where an undertaking does not comply with the conditions attached to a general authorisation, the NRA must inform the undertaking in question and may impose specific measures to ensure compliance. Such measures must, however, be proportionate to the infringement. Only in serious or urgent cases may the NRA prevent the concerned undertaking from operating under the general authorisation. In principle, the undertaking must always be given the opportunity to state its views on the NRA's finding of an infringement of the general authorisation and remedy any breach within one month from the intervention by the NRA. The NRA must adopt a reasoned decision within two months of its initial intervention. The final decision must be communicated to the undertaking concerned within one week of its adoption. Member States must provide the undertaking with a right of appeal before a body that is independent of the NRA.[57]

1–065 Fees and charges for general authorisations — Fees imposed on undertakings for a general authorisation may only cover the administrative costs incurred in the issue, management, control and enforcement of the applicable general authorisation scheme. These fees must be imposed in an objective, transparent and proportionate manner which minimises additional administrative costs and attendant charges; and published in an appropriate and sufficiently detailed manner, so as to be readily accessible. For this purpose, NRAs must publish an annual report showing the total sum of charges collected and the administrative costs incurred, in order to allow verification that the two figures are consistent.[58]

---

[55] See para.1–150 *et seq.*

[56] Authorisation Directive, Art.6(2).

[57] *ibid.*, Art.10.

[58] *ibid.*, Recital 30 and Art.12. Systems for administrative charges should not distort competition or create barriers to market entry. Under a general authorisation system, it is not possible to attribute administrative costs and hence charges to individual undertakings, except for the granting to specific undertakings of rights to use numbers or radio frequencies and rights to install facilities on land. Any applicable administrative charges should be in line with the principles of a general authorisation system. Recital 31 of the Authorisation Directive indicates that a turnover-related charge may be appropriate, except when administrative charges are very low, where a charge combining a flat rate basis with a turnover-related element could also be appropriate. However, the European Court of Justice has recently found that Italy had infringed the provisions of the previous ONP Licensing Directive, para.1–006, n.22, Arts 6 and 11, by imposing financial charges on licence holders, calculated on the basis of their turnover. In its judgement, the Court held that such a charge considerably increases the fees and charges which Member States are expressly authorised to impose under the Directive and creates significant obstacles to the freedom to provide telecommunications services: see Joined Cases C-292 and 293/01 *Albacom SpA and Infostrada SpA v Ministero del Tesoro and Ministero delle Comunicazioni* (not yet reported). Arts 6 and 11 of the ONP Licensing Directive have been repealed by the provisions of the Authorisation Directive (in particular, Arts 6 and 12), but their substance has not changed. Hence, although this ruling stems from the implementation of the previous ONP Licensing Directive, the principle established by the Court remains valid for the interpretation of the provisions of the Authorisation Directive.

1–066   One-stop shopping procedure — Operators of electronic communications services providing services across the EU must notify the NRA in each country in which they operate, when this is required under a general authorisation regime or when, owing to the nature of the service or network, they are required to obtain an individual authorisation. However, as in so far as general authorisations are concerned, because notification is no longer necessarily a prerequisite to commencing the activity, any new entrant on a national market for the provision of electronic communications networks and services that fulfils the conditions laid down in Annex, Part A to the Authorisation Directive, is entitled to commence that activity in that Member State. The Authorisation Directive provides a general framework for the provision of electronic communications networks and services across the EU that, once national regimes are harmonised in accordance with the new provisions, would in practice make the need for a one-stop-shopping procedure less relevant. This is not the case, however, for the grant of individual rights to use frequencies and/or numbers, although, as will be discussed further below, Member States must respect strict time limits for the granting of these rights[59] and the attached conditions cannot be duplicated.[60] In this regard, it should also be noted that NRAs are required to make information concerning the usage of such frequencies publicly available to all interested parties, including other NRAs.[61]

1–067   *One-stop shopping procedure within the European Telecommunications Office* — A limited one-stop-shopping procedure was set up within the framework of the European Telecommunications Office (ETO), which was created in 1994 within the framework of the European Committee on Telecommunications Regulatory Affairs (ECTRA), a committee of CEPT. This one-stop-shopping procedure is not available, however, for voice telephony, telex, mobile radio services, satellite services and broadcasting services. Under this procedure, a service provider wishing to provide a telecommunications service (other than those mentioned above) in more than one CEPT country can submit an application form to the ETO with all the relevant information. The ETO will review the application, determine the right procedure for each country and, within five days, send the application, when necessary, to the NRAs of the countries concerned. The NRAs have to grant the relevant licence within six weeks of receiving the completed application form from the ETO. The ETO then collects the responses of all the NRAs involved and compiles a single document summarising the results of the one-stop-shopping procedure and attaching the licences granted by the NRAs. The entire process should not take longer than nine weeks. The one-stop-shopping procedure provided by the ETO can be used in the following countries: Belgium, Denmark, Finland, France, Germany, Greece, Hungary, Ireland, Italy, Luxembourg, the Netherlands, Norway, Portugal, Spain, Sweden, Switzerland and the United Kingdom.[62]

---

[59] Authorisation Directive, para.1–011, n.28, Art.5(3), which provides that a decision on usage rights must be taken within six weeks from the date of application in the case of radio frequencies, and three weeks in the case of numbers.

[60] *ibid.*, Art.6(4). See para.1–083 *et seq.*

[61] *ibid.*, Art.15. In addition, the general duty on NRAs to exchange information with other NRAs under Art.7(2) of the Framework Directive may also include information on those operators who have already been granted an individual right of use in a Member State, as long as this is with the aim of consolidating the internal market for electronic communications.

[62] For more information, see *www.eto.dk/oss.htm.*

2. Regulatory Framework for Public Voice Telephony Services

1–068 Despite the development of new communications services (such as data and broadband internet access), voice telephony remains the largest single telecommunications market and is likely to remain so in the near future.[63] The introduction of competition into a sector that was long dominated by public monopolies and characterised by a structure of high tariffs, has been the primary objective of the European institutions. This section will review the following: (i) liberalisation of mobile and fixed telephony services and networks; (ii) licensing; (iii) numbering schemes; and (iv) harmonisation of technical standards and the allocation of frequencies.

(a) Liberalisation of Public Voice Telephony Services

1–069 Despite the earlier liberalisation of value-added communications services, the provision of voice telephony services was not liberalised across the EU until 1998. Indeed, for a long time it was argued by some Member States that the granting of exclusive or special rights to incumbent operators was necessary to preserve their financial viability and therefore ensure the continued universal provision of voice telephony services.[64] However, technological and market developments in the 1980s and 1990s made the liberalisation of this sector indispensable.[65] The introduction of full competition was necessary to ensure that the required investment was made in networks and services to enable users to benefit from state-of-the-art voice telephony services.

Mobile voice telephony services

1–070 Liberalisation of voice telephony services started with mobile telephony. Mobile tele-communications networks initially developed within the EU on purely national lines with, at one time in the 1980s, five different analogue systems being established. In addition, the provision of mobile telephony was usually reserved to national telecommunications operators. The development of this market on a pan-European basis involved three steps: (i) the harmonisation of standards for mobile networks and terminals; (ii) the allocation and availability of suitable frequencies on a Community-wide basis; and (iii) the removal of all restrictions on the provision of mobile services by independent service providers.[66] The third condition is reviewed in this section, while the two first conditions are covered later in this chapter.[67]

1–071 Mobile services — The basis for the liberalisation of the mobile sector was the so-called "Mobile Directive". The Mobile Directive amended the Services Directive to open up the mobile and personal communications market to competition.[68] The Mobile Directive was repealed by

---

[63] Even with the introduction of broadband services, analysts have predicted that during the first years following the launch of these new services, voice telephony will remain the major source of revenue for tele-communications operators, whether fixed or mobile.

[64] 1987 Green Paper, para.1–002, n.2, p.34.

[65] Council Resolution of July 22, 1993 on the review of the situation in the telecommunications sector and the need for further development of that market, O.J. 1993 C213/1.

[66] Towards the Personal Communications Environment: Green Paper on a common approach to mobile and personal communications in the European Union, COM(94) 145 final, April 27, 1994.

[67] See para.1–102 *et seq.*, below.

[68] See para.1–004, n.12, above.

the Liberalisation Directive, which is also a directive adopted by the Commission pursuant to Article 86(3) of the EC Treaty.[69] The Liberalisation Directive retains the principle, contained in the Mobile Directive, that restrictions on the number of undertakings authorised to provide mobile or personal communication services infringe Articles 86 and 49 of the EC Treaty, where the restriction is not justified under a specific provision of the EC Treaty or on the basis of the need to ensure the efficient use of radio spectrum and to avoid harmful interference.[70] Moreover, in the Mobile Directive the Commission stated that the granting of exclusive rights in relation to mobile communications to organisations that already enjoyed a dominant position in the fixed network, had the effect of extending that dominant position and was incompatible with Articles 86 and 82 (*ex* Article 86) of the EC Treaty.

1–072 *Abolition of all exclusive and special rights* — The Liberalisation Directive requires Member States (where they have not already done so) to abolish all exclusive and special rights in the provision of mobile and personal communications services. Mobile and personal communications services are defined as services (other than satellite services) whose provision consists, wholly or partly, in the establishment of radio communications to a mobile user, and makes use wholly or partly of mobile and personal communications systems. For the purposes of the directives comprising the New Regulatory Framework, mobile and personal communications services fall under the definition of publicly available electronic communications services.[71] Owing to limited frequency spectrum, the number of mobile operators in a Member State will inevitably be limited. However, provided that rights of use of radio frequencies are granted according to objective, non-discriminatory and transparent procedures, this does not constitute the granting of special rights.[72]

1–073 *Licensing* — The Liberalisation Directive contains specific provisions on the granting of rights for the use of frequencies.[73]

1–074 *Access to radio frequencies* — Member States must designate radio frequencies for electronic communications services, including mobile and personal communications services, on the basis of objective criteria. The procedures for the designation of such frequencies must be transparent and published.[74]

1–075 *Access to infrastructure* — The Mobile Directive required Member States to abolish all restrictions on electronic communications services providers, including mobile operators, establishing their own infrastructure, using infrastructure provided by third parties, or sharing infrastructure.[75] As a result of the liberalisation of cable and other alternative networks, mobile operators could therefore collaborate with the operators of alternative infrastructure (such as cable and utility

---

[69] See para.1–004.

[70] Liberalisation Directive, para.1–012, n.33, Recital 12.

[71] *ibid.*, Art.1 and Framework Directive, para.1–009, n.25, Art.2.

[72] This conclusion is confirmed by Recital 12 of the Notice by the Commission concerning a draft directive on competition in the markets for electronic communications of March 27, 2001 (O.J. 2001 C96/02).

[73] See para.1–083 *et seq.*

[74] Liberalisation Directive, para.1–012, n.33, Art.4(2).

[75] Mobile Directive, para.1–004, n.13, Art.2(3). This is now required by the Liberalisation Directive, para.1–012, n.33, Art.2(3).

networks) for the use of their networks for bulk carriage of the mobile operator's traffic and would no longer be required to use the infrastructure of the incumbent telecommunications operator.[76]

1–076 *Access and interconnection* — The Mobile Directive required restrictions on direct interconnection between mobile operators and between fixed and mobile operators to be abolished.[77] In the past, restrictions on direct interconnection between mobile operators obliged mobile operators to interconnect and transit calls to another mobile operator via the network of the incumbent national operator, which was both restrictive and more expensive than direct interconnection. It also strengthened the position of incumbents on the fixed networks market. Mobile operators are also able to enter into so-called "roaming agreements", which are agreements between operators of mobile services that enable mobile users connected to one network to use their handsets on other operators' networks, whether in the same Member State, or in other Member States. Unlike under the original ONP Interconnection Directive, under the Access Directive, roaming falls within the definition of access that another operator can demand, upon request.[78]

1–077 *Vertically integrated undertakings* — Under the regime put in place by the Authorisation Directive, one operator may provide both fixed and mobile services and/or networks under the same general authorisation. This might create a competitive advantage for a vertically integrated incumbent fixed operator that also has a mobile subsidiary. Arguably, where Member States decide to include the conditions for usage of radio frequencies in a general authorisation for mobile and personal communications systems, the Liberalisation Directive requires that the conditions for the use of such frequencies must ensure that vertically integrated public network operators do not discriminate in favour of their own mobile businesses. In practice, the conditions attached to the authorisation may also include, in justified cases, an obligation on the undertaking's fixed business to provide interconnection on non-discriminatory activity terms, to the extent that is necessary to ensure end-to-end connectivity.[79] It goes without saying that specific access and interconnection obligations may be imposed upon a vertically integrated operator that has been designated as possessing SMP.

---

[76] For instance, one of the activities of Wind, a joint venture company between ENEL, the principal electricity provider in Italy, France Télécom and Deutsche Telekom, is the provision of mobile services using ENEL's network. This pattern is likely to increase with the traffic produced by third generation mobiles.

[77] Mobile Directive, para.1–004, n.12, Art.2(3). This provision is now contained in Art.3(1) of the Access Directive, para.1–011, n.29, which also provides that the undertaking requesting access or interconnection does not need to be authorised to operate in the Member State where access or interconnection is requested, if it is not providing services and does not operate a network in that Member State.

[78] See Section F, para.1–144. For a review of roaming agreements under EC Competition rules, see para.6–012, below.

[79] Liberalisation Directive, para.1–012, n.33, Art.3. This interpretation is supported by the wording of Art.3 in the initial proposal presented by the Commission (see Notice by the Commission concerning a draft directive on competition in the markets for electronic communications services, para.1–072, n.72, above), but the initial wording of Art.3 was subsequently changed, so that as adopted, Art.3 is broader than the initial proposal and does not apply exclusively to mobile operators, but to all "dominant" vertically integrated public undertakings. For a broader discussion of this provision, see para.1–058, above.

Fixed voice telephony services

1–078 The Liberalisation Directive — Fixed voice telephony services were liberalised from January 1, 1998 as a result of the Full Competition Directive,[80] which amended the Services Directive. This opened up the provision of public voice telephony services and networks to full competition. With effect from July 25, 2003, the Full Competition Directive has been repealed and consolidated by the Liberalisation Directive.[81]

1–079 *Abolition of all exclusive and special rights* — The Full Competition Directive required Member States to abolish (where they had not already done so) all exclusive and special rights for the provision of public voice telephony services.[82] Voice telephony means the commercial provision for the public of the direct transport and switching of speech in real time between public switched network termination points, enabling any user to use equipment connected to such a network termination point in order to communicate with another network termination point.[83] Voice telephony is therefore an electronic communications service within the meaning of the Framework Directive and for the purposes of the Liberalisation Directive.

1–080 The Commission expected that the abolition of exclusive and special rights for the provision of voice telephony services and networks would enable incumbent operators present in one Member State to enter the voice telephony market in other Member States.[84] The development of competition in voice telephony services required the liberalisation of the underlying infra-structure, *i.e.* the possibility for voice telephony operators to establish their own infrastructure or to use alternative infrastructure provided by the other operators to provide services. There are now numerous suppliers of voice telephony services in all Member States, who use either their own infrastructure and/or that of other operators, although the incumbents remain the leading players in each Member State.

1–081 *Provision of voice telephony services and networks by operators with monopoly rights in other sectors* — As a result of the liberalisation of the electronic communications market, under-takings with special or exclusive rights in sectors other than electronic communications (for example other utilities, railways and motorways) have been able to enter the electronic commu-nications market. In order to allow the monitoring of possible anti-competitive cross-subsidies between the activities for which these undertakings enjoy special or exclusive rights and their communications activities, Member States are required to ensure that these undertakings keep separate financial accounts for their activities associated with the provision of electronic networks and services, so that all costs and relevant elements associated with such activities can be identified including fixed assets and structural costs. As an alternative, the Framework Directive permits Member States to impose structural separation obligations instead of accounting separation.[85]

---

[80] See para.1–004, n.13, above.

[81] Liberalisation Directive, para.1–012, n.33, Art.10.

[82] Full Competition Directive, para.1–004, n.13, Art.2, now contained in the Liberalisation Directive, para.1–012, n.33, Arts 1 and 2(1). For a discussion of the definition of exclusive and special rights, see above, para.1–055, n.34.

[83] Services Directive, above, para.1–004, n.9, Art.2(e).
Full Competition Directive, para.1–004, n.13, Recital 6.

[85] Framework Directive, para.1–009, n.25, Art.13(1)(a) and (b).

Such measures are intended to prevent operators with special or exclusive rights in other sectors from potentially having a competitive advantage in the provision of electronic communications services, including emerging services such as internet broadband, by using revenues from their monopoly activities to cross-subsidise their communications activities. If such undertakings have an annual turnover from their electronic communications activities of less than €50 million, Member States may choose not to apply these accounting or structural separation obligations.[86]

(b) Licensing of Public Voice Telephony Services

1–082   Under the New Regulatory Framework, public voice telephony and mobile services are considered as electronic communications services and, in principle, their provision should therefore no longer be subject to the granting of an individual licence. However, where this is necessary, Member States are to grant individual rights to use radio frequencies and numbers. In doing so, NRAs must not impose undue burdens on operators, whether through licensing conditions or through procedures. The legal framework for the licensing of fixed and mobile voice telephony services is contained in the Authorisation Directive.

1–083   Requirement for individual rights to use numbers and/or frequencies — The rights to use numbers and/or frequencies should, in principle, be included in a general authorisation.[87] Member States may, however, subject the provision of electronic communications services, including voice telephony, to the granting of individual rights of use if this is necessary to allow efficient access to, and use of, radio frequencies and/or numbers where there is a scarcity of supply of frequencies and/ or numbers.[88] This implies that the provision of fixed voice telephony services and networks does not normally require an individual right of use. Individual rights of use should be used only for ensuring the efficient use of numbers, including short codes, from the national numbering plan.[89] As regards mobile voice telephony services and networks, where possible, in particular where the risk of harmful interference is negligible, conditions for the use of radio frequencies should be included in a general authorisation. Otherwise, a separate individual right of use may be required, given that frequencies are a scarce resource.

1–084   Provision of voice telephony services over the internet — On December 22, 2000, the Commission published a Communication that clarified the conditions under which voice services provided over the internet protocol ("VoIP") may be treated as public voice telephony for the purposes of EU

---

[86] *ibid.*, Art.13(2).

[87] Authorisation Directive, para.1–011, n.28, Art.5(1).

[88] Authorisation Directive, para.1–011, n.28, Art.5(2).

[89] An individual right of use would always be required in the case of the allocation of so-called "golden numbers", which are numbers of exceptional economic value, because they are scarce resources in nature. In the case of golden numbers, Art.5(3) of the Authorisation Directive, para.1–011, n.28, requires Member States that wish to limit the number of such usage rights by virtue of a competitive or comparative selection procedure, to follow the consultation process under Art.6 of the Framework Directive, para.1–009, n.25. For a more comprehensive analysis of the cases and procedures where Member States may limit the number of individual usage rights, see para.1–087. For the consultation procedure under Art.6 of the Framework Directive, see para.1–044 *et seq.*

telecommunications law.[90] According to this Communication, VoIP would be considered as a public voice telephony service, and therefore regulated as such, when: (i) it is offered commercially; (ii) it is provided to the public; (iii) it is provided to and from public switched network termination points; and (iv) it involves direct transport and switching of speech in real time, in particular at the same level of reliability and speech quality as that produced by public switched telecoms networks. ETSI has since confirmed that state-of-the-art VoIP meets these quality standards.[91] Under the Framework Directive, in conjunction with the Authorisation Directive, however, and regardless of whether or not VoIP now meets the quality standards indicated by the Commission in its Communication, VoIP is considered to be an electronic communications service for the purposes of the New Regulatory Framework.[92] It can therefore continue to be provided either without authorisation or on the basis of a general authorisation.

1–085 Procedures for the granting of individual rights of use — Individual usage rights must be granted through open, non-discriminatory and transparent procedures within reasonable time limits.[93] NRAs must inform applicants of their decision as soon as possible, but no more than three weeks after receiving an application in the case of numbers that have been allocated within the national numbering plan, and six weeks in the case of radio frequencies. NRAs may only extend the time limit for numbers up to six weeks in the case of numbers of exceptional economic value (so-called "golden numbers"), after consultation with the interested parties, and in objectively justified cases.[94] They may extend the time limit for the allocation of frequencies to up to eight months if a comparative bidding procedure is adopted.[95] The procedures for granting individual rights of use must be published in an appropriate manner, so as to be readily accessible.[96] Any undertaking that meets the conditions laid down by the Member State must be granted an individual licence, unless the number of available frequencies or numbers exceeds that of the number of applicants. As with general authorisations, operators must provide the NRAs with all information that is proportionate and justified for: (i) the imposition of universal service obligations; (ii) market analyses for the imposition of conditions applied to operators having SMP; (iii) conditions concerning ownership; (iv) conditions regarding the provision of information required for the verification of compliance with applicable conditions and for statistical purposes; and (v) conditions to prevent anti-competitive behaviour.[97] Where such information has already been provided for the purposes of a general authorisation in the same Member State, it would not appear to be proportionate for an applicant to be asked to provide the same information again.

---

[90] Commission Communication of December 22, 2000 on the status of voice on the internet under Community law, and in particular, under Directive 90/388, O.J. 2000 C369/3, updating previous Commission Notice of January 10, 1998 concerning the status of voice communications on the internet under Community law, and, in particular, pursuant to Directive 90/388, O.J. 1998 C6/4. See also para.3–017, below.

[91] ETSI VoIP Quality Report, April 15–24, 2002, available at *www.etsi.org/plugtests/04 History/2002_voipsqa.htm*.

[92] Framework Directive, para.1–009, n.25, Art.2 and Authorisation Directive, para.1–011, n.28, Art.2.

[93] *ibid.*, Art.5(2), and Liberalisation Directive, para.1–012, n.33, Art.4(2).

[94] Authorisation Directive, para.1–009, n.25, Arts 5(3) and (4).

[95] *ibid.*, Art.7(4).

[96] Liberalisation Directive, para.1–012, n.33, Art.4(2).

[97] Authorisation Directive, para.1–011, n.28, Art.11.

1–086 Conditions attached to individual rights of use — In addition to the conditions that can be attached to a general authorisation,[98] the only conditions which may be attached to individual usage rights, where justified and in accordance with the principle of proportionality, are those listed in Part B (for radio frequencies) and Part C (for numbers) of the Annex to the Authorisation Directive. These include:

(i) the designation of the service or type of network or technology for which the rights to use the frequency have been granted, including, where applicable, the exclusive use of a frequency for the transmission of specific content or specific audiovisual services;

(ii) conditions relating to the efficient use of numbering capacity;

(iii) conditions regarding number portability requirements;

(iv) conditions regarding the efficient management of radio frequencies;

(v) technical and operational conditions that are necessary for the avoidance of harmful interference and for the limitation of exposure of the general public to electromagnetic fields, where such conditions are different from those imposed by generally applicable environmental and town and country planning law or the conditions contained in a general authorisation;

(vi) a maximum duration for the usage right;

(vii) requirements relating to the quality, availability and permanence of a service or network;

(viii) usage fees;

(ix) any commitments which the undertaking obtaining the usage right has made in the course of a competitive or comparative selection procedure;

(x) conditions imposing obligations under relevant international agreements relating to the use of frequencies or numbers; and

(xi) conditions for the transfer of the usage right to third parties.[99]

Member States may amend the conditions attached to an individual usage right only in objectively justified cases and in an appropriate manner. Member States must give appropriate notice of their intention to amend the conditions and enable interested parties to express their views on the proposed amendments.[1]

1–087 Member States may limit the number of individual usage rights — Member States may limit the number of individual usage rights that are available only to the extent required to ensure the efficient use of radio frequencies or, for a limited time, if necessary to make available sufficient

[98] *ibid.*, Art.6(4) requires that Member States must not duplicate the conditions of the general authorisation where they grant licences to radio frequencies or numbers.
[99] Framework Directive, para.1–009, n.25, Art.9(3) and (4) which provide for the possibility and the procedures to introduce secondary spectrum trading. For a more comprehensive analysis see para.1–088, below.
[1] Authorisation Directive, para.1–011, n.28, Art.14.

numbers in accordance with EU law (or in the case of "golden numbers").[2] Member States must use objective, transparent, non-discriminatory and proportionate selection criteria in awarding individual rights of use. Competitive selection procedures may be used.[3] Any decision to limit the number of individual usage rights must be published. Member States must give all interested parties, including end-users and consumers, the opportunity to comment on the draft decision within a reasonable period.[4] Any limitation would, however, be without prejudice to the right of the licensee to transfer its number or frequencies, provided that such a possibility is available and the right to use the numbers or frequencies is not granted *intuitu personae*, that is where the specific characteristics of the applicant are relevant in making the allocation (for example, where, in competitive selection procedures, specific conditions that depend on the capabilities of the applicants are attached to the allocation of radio frequencies, *e.g.* certain network coverage requirements).[5]

1–088 Spectrum trading and transfer of right to use frequencies — Spectrum trading covers a range of possibilities, from the straightforward transfer of an assigned block of spectrum with no change of use, to the sharing of blocks of assigned spectrum with a change of use. So far, spectrum trading has not been permitted in the EU, but under the Framework Directive, Member States may (but are not obliged to) introduce provisions to allow undertakings to transfer rights to use radio frequencies, after notifying the responsible NRA.[6] Where the use of frequencies has been harmonised at the EU level,[7] any such transfer must not result in a change of use of that radio frequency. A number of Member States have already announced that, in the near future, they may implement provisions allowing spectrum to be divided and re-sold by those who have acquired it (*e.g.* the UK and Italy).[8]

1–089 Specific licensing conditions for mobile telephony — Member States cannot restrict the use of distinct technologies (*i.e.* GSM 900, DCS 1800/GSM 1800, DECT digital services) to specific frequencies where multi-standard equipment is available. Any restrictions on current licensees extending their services by using other technologies (for example, GSM 900 operators extending

---

[2] Liberalisation Directive, para.1–012, n.33, Art.4(1).

[3] Authorisation Directive, para.1–011, n.28, Art.7(3) and (4).

[4] Authorisation Directive, para.1–011, n.28, Art.7(1), read in conjunction with the Framework Directive, para.1–009, n.25, Art.6.

[5] Framework Directive, para.1–009, n.25, Art.9(4).

[6] *ibid.*

[7] Radio Spectrum Decision, para.1–011, n.32, Art.4(2), (3), (4) and (5). Under the Radio Spectrum Decision, the Commission, in co-ordination with the Radio Spectrum Committee, and the CEPT (in so far as matters that fall within its remit are concerned), may adopt technical implementing measures to harmonise the allocation and use of frequencies across the EU. In doing so, the Commission may, where appropriate, authorise transitional periods and/or spectrum sharing arrangements.

[8] During a public workshop on September 17, 2002 to present and discuss a study carried out for the Commission by McKinsey ("Comparative Assessment of the Licensing Regimes for 3G Mobile Communications in the European Union and their impact on the Mobile Communications Sector", available at: *http:// www.europa.eu.int/information_society/topics/telecoms/radiospec/doc/pdf/mobiles/mckinsey_study/final_report. pdf*), the Commission announced the preparation of guidelines to help NRAs and mobile operators to implement radio spectrum trading arrangements, within the context of the Radio Spectrum Policy Group. For a discussion of the Radio Spectrum Policy Group, see para.1–109, below.

into DCS 1800, or GSM 900/1800 into GPRS[9]) must therefore be removed.[10] However, Member States may limit the use of a given frequency exclusively to a specific technology where this is considered necessary to ensure its efficient use, *i.e.* to avoid harmful interference or for the transmission of specific content and audiovisual services, see para.1–105 below. In light of the general principle of technological neutrality that underlined the New Regulatory Framework, this provision (which is an exception to this principle) should be interpreted restrictively. Specific licensing conditions would, however, be possible where a competitive bidding procedure is necessary, or if the individual usage right is allocated *intuitu personae*.

1–090   Measures that NRAs may take for non-compliance with the conditions attached to individual usage rights — Where the beneficiary of an individual right of use does not comply with the conditions attached to it, the NRA may take, in an appropriate manner, specific measures to ensure compliance. In certain cases, the use of an allocated frequency and/or number may even be revoked. The undertaking concerned must, in principle, be given the opportunity to state its views on the NRA's position that it has infringed the conditions and to remedy any breach within one month from the intervention of the NRA. The NRA may take immediate action in the event of harmful interference between an electronic communications network using radio frequencies and other technical systems. The NRA must adopt a reasoned decision within two months of its initial intervention. The final decision must be communicated to the undertaking concerned within one week of its adoption. Member States must provide the undertaking with a right of appeal before a body that is independent of the NRA.[11]

1–091   Licensing fees and charges — Fees imposed on undertakings as part of the authorisation or licensing procedures may only cover the administrative costs incurred in the issue, management, control and enforcement of the applicable authorisations or licences.[12] However, this cost-based requirement is not applicable where scarce resources are allocated (rights to use numbers or frequencies). In such cases, NRAs may impose charges that reflect the need to ensure the optimal use of these resources.[13] Although these charges must be objectively justified, non-discriminatory, transparent and take into account the need to foster the development of innovative services and competition, this provision enables NRAs to impose substantial charges for allocation of frequencies.[14]

---

[9] GPRS means General Packet Radio Service, and is also referred to as "2.5G mobile". GPRS consists of an upgrade of current GSM networks in order to offer an "always on" function (packet-switched mode), which allows for data transfer at rates that are faster than on GSM networks, but slower than on the future 3G networks. On the issue of the transition towards 3G, see, below para.1–114 *et seq.*

[10] This conclusion follows from the combination of Art.6(1) of the Authorisation Directive, para.1–011, n.28, which prohibits Member States attaching specific conditions to authorisations or licences other than those listed in Annex, Part B, and Art.17 of the same directive, which requires Member States to adapt existing licences to the New Regulatory Framework.

[11] Authorisation Directive, para.1–011, n.28, Art.10.

[12] *ibid.*, Art.12. In general, Member States are prevented from imposing financial charges on licence holders, which are calculated on the basis of their turnover: see Joined Cases C-292 and 293/01 *Albacom SpA and Infostrada SpA v Ministero del Tesoro and Ministero delle Comunicazioni*, above, discussed at para.1–065, n.58.

[13] *ibid.*, Art.13.

[14] See the Commission's decisions in *Omnitel* and *Second Spanish GSM Licence*, at para.6–060 *et seq.*, below, where the substantial level of the fees levied on the new mobile operator was not an issue, but the discriminatory nature of the fees was found to infringe EU competition law. More recently, many operators objected to the high fees paid for the award of the first round of third generation mobile licences (UMTS). However, at the

1–092 Existing authorisations and licences — Member States must ensure that all general authorisations and individual licences that have been awarded since the entry into force of the Licensing Directive in May 27, 1997, conform to the requirements of the Authorisation Directive. This had to be done by July 25, 2003.[15] Where this would result in a reduction of the rights or extension of the obligations imposed under existing licences or authorisations, Member States may extend the validity of such rights and obligations for a further nine months. In other cases, such as where the abolition of a condition regarding access to another network would create excessive difficulties for the undertakings that have benefited from mandated access, because the alternative of negotiating new agreements on reasonable commercial terms is not immediately available, Member States may make to the Commission a reasoned request for a temporary extension. The Commission must take a decision within six months of receipt of the application for an extension.

1–093 One-stop shopping licensing procedure — Under the licensing regime contained in the Licensing Directive, operators of mobile or fixed telephony services providing services in more than one Member State needed to obtain individual licences in each Member State in which they operated. The Authorisation Directive has introduced a simplified framework for the licensing of such operations. However, the management of scarce resources (frequencies and numbering) remains under the exclusive competence of the Member States. In practice, in so far as services that require access to scarce resources are concerned, an application for obtaining the applicable usage right is still required in each Member State.

1–094 The harmonisation of radio frequencies[16] and numbering resources[17] within the EU is envisaged in the New Regulatory Framework. Accordingly, the Commission, in collaboration with the NRAs, may put in place appropriate technical implementing measures on these matters. However, as regards radio spectrum, such technical management measures may include the harmonisation and allocation of radio spectrum, but do not cover allocation and licensing procedures, nor the decision of whether to use competitive selection procedures for the allocation of radio frequencies.[18] This is without prejudice to CEPT's continuing mandate to establish a one-stop

---

time of writing, no formal complaint has yet been lodged and it is unlikely that any complaint will succeed. For a discussion of the first round of UMTS licences, see para.1–112 *et seq.*

[15] Authorisation Directive, para.1–011, n.28, Art.17.

[16] Radio Spectrum Decision, para.1–011, n.32, Art.2. At the time of writing, the Commission announced that it will publish a number of studies on this issue. For instance, on June 25, 2003, the Radio Spectrum Policy unit of the Commission Information Society Directorate General published a call for tender for a study entitled "information on the allocation, availability and use of radio spectrum in the Community", which is available online at: *http://www.europa.eu.int/information_society/topics/telecoms/regulatory/studies/index_en.htm.*

[17] Framework Directive, para.1–009, n.25, Art.10(4). See also Study for the Commission on the "Policy implications of convergence in the field of naming, numbering and addressing". The study provides a broad orientation into some key issues, such: as (i) the strategic value of converged naming, numbering and addressing schemes; (ii) the role of the traditional organisations for the management of these key resources in converged networks; and (iii) the extent of industry self-regulation in this area of regulation. Further information is available at: *http://www.europa.eu.int/information_society/topics/telecoms/regulatory/studies/documents/nna_final_15sept.pdf.*

[18] See Radio Spectrum Decision, para.1–011, n.32, Recital 11.

shopping procedure for the authorisation of services, which by their nature are cross-border, such as third generation mobile services (UMTS) and satellite broadcasting.[19]

(c) Numbering

1–095 Telephone numbers, like frequencies, are a limited resource. The availability of sufficient individual telephone numbers and an appropriate numbering system is an essential requirement for effective competition in telecommunications markets. Regulatory intervention is needed to ensure that this limited resource is used effectively. The regulatory framework applying to numbering is found mainly in the Framework, Access and Universal Service Directives. As far as the granting of rights to use numbers is concerned, the relevant provisions of the Authorisation Directive have already been covered in paragraph 1–085 above.

1–096 **Availability of numbers** — Member States must ensure the provision of adequate numbers and numbering ranges for all publicly available electronic communications services. They must also give NRAs the power to control national numbering plans, in order to guarantee that this is done independently from organisations providing electronic communications networks or services.[20] NRAs must ensure that the procedures for allocating individual numbers are transparent, equitable and timely and that the allocation is carried out in an objective, transparent and non-discriminatory manner. An organisation that is allocated a range of numbers must avoid undue discrimination in the number sequences used to give access to the services of other electronic communications operators.

1–097 **Carrier selection and carrier pre-selection** — In a multi-operator environment, users must be able to access the operators of their choice simply and cheaply, even where this operator does not provide a direct line into the customer's premises. This is particularly important given the limited competition in the provision of "local loop" networks. As a result, the NRAs are required to impose call-by-call carrier selection[21] and carrier pre-selection[22] obligations on operators of public electronic communications networks that have SMP.[23] This applies equally to operators of fixed networks and to mobile operators. NRAs must ensure that the pricing of the interconnection services needed for the provision of carrier pre-selection facilities is cost-orientated and that direct charges to consumers, if any, do not act as a disincentive to the use of carrier selection and pre-selection services.

---

[19] Radio Spectrum Decision, para.1–011, n.32, Recital 24. Should CEPT be able to agree on a one-stop-shopping procedure, the Commission could then mandate it under the procedure established by the Radio Spectrum Decision, Art.2.

[20] Framework Directive, para.1–009, n.25, Art.10. This provision, however, does not confer any responsibility on NRAs in the field of internet naming and addressing.

[21] Call-by-call carrier selection is an easy-access method of carrier selection, whereby the default carrier is the local access provider, but the customer may choose another operator for a specific long distance or international call by dialling a prefix.

[22] Carrier pre-selection is an equal access method for carrier selection that allows the customer to select its own default carrier for long distance and international services, while retaining the option of selecting a different provider on a call-by-call basis.

[23] Universal Service Directive, para.1–011, n.30, Art.19. On the concept of SMP and the related market analysis, see para.1–018 *et seq.*

1–098 Number portability — The need to change telephone numbers when changing network provider has been identified as an important deterrent to business and residential users changing operators. Accordingly, the Universal Service Directive requires that number portability (*i.e.* the possibility for a subscriber to keep his telephone number while changing operator, type of service or location) in fixed and mobile[24] networks be available throughout the EU. Operators are required to offer number portability, regardless of any designation of SMP.[25] Number portability is only required at a specific location for geographic numbers,[26] but at any location for non-geographic numbers.[27]

1–099 Common emergency calls number and international telephony access code — Numbers for accessing emergency services and for making international calls have been harmonised throughout the EU. All Member States use the number "112" as the single European emergency calls number[28] and the "00" code as the standard international telephone access code.[29] Member States must ensure that all users with a connection to the public telephone networks (fixed and mobile) can access emergency services, at no charge, using the number "112".[30] Undertakings which operate public telephone networks must make caller location information available to the authorities handling emergency calls, to the extent that it is technically feasible, for calls to the single European emergency number "112". The provision of caller location information assists in identifying the location from which an emergency call was made. A Commission Recommendation has clarified how the requirement of making available caller location information should be implemented at national level in detail. According to this Commission Recommendation, Member States should draw up national rules to require that public fixed and mobile network operators: (i) put in place, where technically feasible, network systems which automatically forward information on the location of any caller making an emergency call within the EU towards public safety answering points; (ii) provide location information in a non-discriminatory manner, in particular as regards the quality of location information provided on their own subscribers' emergency calls as opposed to other users' emergency calls (*e.g.* in the case of fixed networks, other users may include users of public pay phones; and in the case of mobile networks, roamers or visited users); (iii) send together

---

[24] Contrary to the requirements of the ONP Interconnection Directive on number portability, which imposed number portability obligations only on fixed operators, the Universal Service Directive requires all operators, including mobile network operators, to ensure number portability. However, such number portability is not required between fixed and mobile networks.

[25] Universal Service Directive, para.1–011, n.30, Art.30.

[26] A geographic number is a number from the national numbering plan where part of its digit structure contains geographic significance (*e.g.* local area code) used for routing calls to the physical location of the network termination point of the subscriber to whom the number has been assigned.

[27] Non-geographic numbers are (national) number ranges that do not identify a specific geographic location. Such numbers include mobile numbers, and free-phone, local rate, national rate and premium rate services. Member States must ensure that end-users located in other Member States can access non-geographic numbers within their territory where this is technically feasible, except where the subscriber to which a non-geographic number has been assigned has chosen for commercial reasons to receive calls only from calling parties located in specific geographic areas.

[28] Council Decision 91/396 of July 29, 1991 on the introduction of a single European emergency call number, O.J. 1991 L217/31. The "112" is used in addition to any national emergency numbers.

[29] Universal Service Directive, para.1–011, n.30, Art.27.

[30] *ibid.*, Art.26. Likewise, Member States must ensure that it is possible to make emergency calls from public pay telephones using the number "112", free of charge and without having to use coins or cards.

with any caller location information an identification of the network on which the call originates; (iv) keep sources of caller location information, including address information, accurate and up-to-date; (v) provide public safety answering points and emergency services with the capability of renewing the location information through a call back functionality ("pulling") for the purpose of handling the emergency; (vi) use a common open interface standard to facilitate data transfer, and in particular the common data transfer protocol adopted by the EU standardization body ETSI, where available. In addition, fixed public telephone network operators should make available installation address of the line from which the emergency call is made. This Recommendation has no binding effect on Member States. However, if such a system is implemented at national level, it might result in additional costs for fixed and mobile public network operators. The Commission has therefore encouraged Member States to minimise the overall cost of implementation, through increased cooperation and the development of common solutions in dialogue with the concerned operators.[31]

1–100   National numbering plans and European telephony numbering space — The possible restructuring of national numbering plans on a common basis has also been considered at the EU level. The Framework Directive empowers the Commission to adopt the appropriate implementing measures on this matter following "comitology" procedure.[32] This also applies to the development of a European numbering plan. Measures for the creation of a European Telephony Numbering Space (ETNS) on the basis of the "388" country code have already been adopted. Accordingly, numbers similar to "800" numbers in the United States would enable pan-European services such as freephone services and teleshopping to use the same prefix throughout Europe. In order to ensure connection of calls to the ETNS, public telephone networks providers must ensure that calls bearing the "388" prefix are directly or indirectly interconnected to the ETNS in accordance with the applicable provisions of the Access Directive.[33]

1–101   The role of CEPT — Many aspects of numbering are dealt with in the framework of the CEPT, in order to ensure wider consultation and consensus within the industry in a Europe-wide context. A Memorandum of Understanding and Framework Contract have been entered into

---

[31] See Commission Recommendation of July 25, 2003 on the processing of caller location information in electronic communication networks, for the purpose of location-enhanced emergency call services, O.J. 2003 L189/49; and Commission Press Release IP/03/1122 of July 25, 2003.

[32] Framework Directive, para.1–009, n.25, Art.10(4). The "comitology" procedure is specified in Council Decision 1999/468 of June 28, 1999 laying down the procedures for the exercise of implementing powers conferred to the Commission, O.J. 1999 L184/23. The term "comitology" refers to the delegation of implementing powers by the Council to the Commission for the adoption of EU legislation. According to the comitology procedure, representatives of the Member States, acting through committees called "comitology committees", assist the Commission in the execution of the implementing powers conferred on it. The objective of the Comitology Decision is twofold: (i) to harmonise and simplify the various existing comitology procedures; and (ii) to provide the European Parliament with extended monitoring powers on the Commission's use of its implementing powers. The Comitology Decision lays down three different procedures for the exercise of implementing powers conferred on the Commission: (i) advisory; (ii) management; and (iii) a regulatory procedure. It also sets out the criteria for determining the relevant procedure, based on the purpose that comitology intends to fulfil in a specific case: see the Final Report of the Committee of Wise Men on the Regulation of European Securities Markets (the so-called "Lamfalussy Report", February 15, 2001 available at: *http://www.europa.eu.int/comm/internal_market/en/finances/general/lamfalussyen.pdf*), p.113 *et seq.*

[33] Universal Service Directive, para.1–011, n.30, Recital 37.

between the Commission, the CEPT European Committee for Telecommunications Regulatory Affairs ("ECTRA") and the ETO that has been set up under ECTRA. Under the framework contract, the Commission can entrust funded work to the ETO in the area of numbering. In parallel, the European Numbering Forum ("ENF") was established as an open forum for discussing and co-ordinating numbering matters in Europe. Under the Framework Directive, Member States are under a duty to co-ordinate their position in such international fora in order to ensure the full global interoperability of services within the common market.[34]

(d) Harmonisation of Technical Standards and Allocation of Frequencies for Mobile Systems

1–102 The primary goal of the Commission in the mobile sector was to facilitate the development of mobile communications systems, to permit users to use mobile services whilst moving throughout the EU. Accordingly, to achieve this goal, the liberalisation of the mobile sector had to be accompanied by two types of initiative. First, the allocation and availability of suitable frequencies for mobile systems had to be ensured on an EU-wide basis. Second, a set of basic standards had to be established for mobile networks and services, so that a mobile user could access networks and services across the EU.

Allocation of Frequencies for Mobile Systems

1–103 Principles governing the allocation of frequencies — The allocation of frequencies is a matter for NRAs to decide under national law. However, such an allocation must be made in conformity with EU law, and in particular, the Liberalisation Directive[35] and the Authorisation Directive.[36] These provide that only the lack of sufficient spectrum can justify limiting the number of licences that can be granted, where this is justified under the principle of proportionality. Moreover, as a result of Article 4 of the Liberalisation Directive, Member States must ensure effective competition between mobile operators and therefore must allocate frequencies in a way that will allow effective competition between operators. For example, an inadequate allocation of frequencies could result in increasing operators' costs thereby affecting, especially for new entrants, their ability to compete in the market. Member States must therefore identify the most appropriate allocation procedure in their specific national context on the basis of a thorough evaluation of market requirement.[37]

1–104 EU measures concerning the allocation of frequencies for mobile services — The promotion of mobile services at the EU level was initiated by ensuring the availability of common frequency bands that would be allocated by each Member State, thereby ensuring pan-European operation. For this purpose, the Council adopted directives reserving frequency spectrum for the co-ordinated introduction of pan-European cellular digital land-based mobile communications (Global System for Mobile communications, or GSM), digital radio paging (European digital

---

[34] Framework Directive, para.1–009, n.25, Art.5(5).
[35] Liberalisation Directive, para.1–012, n.33, Art.4.
[36] Authorisation Directive, para.1–011, n.28, Art.5(5).
[37] For example, as regards licensing fees, see Authorisation Directive, para.1–011, n.28, Recital 31.

radio-messaging system, or ERMES), and digital European cordless telecommunications (DECT).[38] The reserved spectrum identified at that time was based on a model where voice services were considered to be the major source of traffic, and only limited data rate services were envisaged at that time. With the introduction of third generation mobile and wireless communications systems (UMTS or 3G),[39] and the increasing possibility for converging applications and the interworking of 3G systems with second generation GSM systems, the existing requirements for the allocation of radio spectrum frequencies for exploiting specific technologies no longer meet market demand. The Authorisation Directive and the Radio Spectrum Decision contain provisions for facilitating a more flexible harmonised approach for the availability and allocation of frequencies.

1–105   Spectrum "re-farming" process for radio — Under the Authorisation Directive, the allocation of a given frequency exclusively for exploiting a specific technology is permitted only where this is necessary in order to ensure the efficient use of that frequency, *i.e.* to avoid harmful interference in the transmission of specific broadcast services, but not mobile communications.[40] Accordingly, the Council Directives regarding GSM, paging, and DECT systems seem to have been in practice repealed by the Authorisation Directive. It follows that Member States may reallocate frequencies spectrum currently allocated under the strict requirements of the previous legislation, in order to maximise the efficient use of frequencies.[41] Following broad consultations conducted at the international level within the framework of the World Radiocommunications Conferences (WRC),[42]

---

[38] Council Directive 87/372 of June 25, 1987 on the frequency bands to be reserved for the co-ordinated introduction of public pan-European cellular digital land-based mobile communications (GSM) in the Community (the "GSM Frequencies Directive"), O.J. 1987 L196/85; Council Directive 90/544 of October 9, 1990 on the frequency bands designated for the co-ordinated introduction of pan-European land-based public radio paging (ERMES) in the Community (the "Paging Frequencies Directive"), O.J. 1990 L310/28; Council Directive 91/287 of June 3, 1991 on the frequency bands designated for the co-ordinated introduction of digital European cordless telecommunications (DECT), O.J. 1991 L144/45 (the "DECT Frequencies Directive").

[39] Decision 128/1999 of December 14, 1998 on the co-ordinated introduction of a third generation of the mobile and wireless communications system (UMTS) in the Community ("UMTS Decision"), O.J. 1999 L17/1.

[40] Authorisation Directive, para.1–011, n.28, Art.6(1) in conjunction with Annex, Part B(1).

[41] The recent history of Blu, the fourth Italian GSM mobile operator, is a good example of the interaction between the old and new rules as regards the re-farming process of frequencies previously allocated under individual licences. Further to a concentration whereby Pirelli and Edizione Holding acquired joint control of Telecom Italia (Commission Decision *Pirelli/Edizone Holding/Telecom Italia* discussed at para.8–117 *et seq.*) approved by the Commission on September 20, 2001, Edizione Holding was required to sell its stake in Blu to a suitable purchaser possessing the necessary technical and financial resources for developing its activities. This was to prevent the new owners of TIM, the largest mobile telephone operator in Italy, from also controlling Blu. In the absence of a suitable purchaser for Edizone's stake in Blu and general difficulties between Blu's shareholders, Edizone was unable to fulfill its commitments. After prolonged discussions, the Commission finally allowed the break-up of Blu's assets. As regards the frequencies allocated to Blu, the Italian Minister of Communications undertook, following a request by the Commission, to re-allocate Blu's UMTS frequencies in a non-discriminatory manner as part of a planned process of re-allocation of the entire frequency spectrum. Blu's 2G frequencies were to be allocated to the other Italian GSM operators immediately. See further below, para.8–120.

[42] The WRC is an international forum in which member countries meet to revise an international treaty, known as the Radio Regulations, lay down the allocation of frequencies for over 40 radio-communications services and specify the technical, operational and regulatory conditions for the use of the radio frequency spectrum and satellite orbits. The WRC is held every two to three years with the purpose of reaching consensus on changes to the Radio Regulations. Some landmark decisions were made at the last WRC in 2000, when the WRC concluded that extra spectrum was needed on the basis of three main considerations: (i) the number of

as well as at the EU level,[43] a general consensus developed that, given the rapid growth of mobile telephony, the existing frequency bands would not be sufficient to meet future demand and that there would be a need to use the GSM extension bands, *i.e.* 880–890 MHz and 925–935 MHz.[44] In addition, the expected increase in traffic that would be generated by the use of third generation systems would require the allocation of further radio spectrum between 2005 and 2010.[45] The Commission stated that Member States should identify the timeframe needed to free up unused spectrum that is currently "reserved" for other uses.[46] This resulted in a European Common Proposal to the WRC to secure 160 MHz of additional spectrum for third generation mobiles, which was subsequently accepted by WRC–2000. The Radio Spectrum Decision and the Authorisation Directive set the legal framework for Member States to do so in a harmonised manner.

1–106 Co-ordination of frequencies at the EU level — The co-ordination of frequencies is undertaken at the EU level within the framework of the so-called Radio Spectrum Decision.[47] The aim of the Decision is to establish an EU policy and legal framework for ensuring the co-ordination of policy and, where appropriate, harmonised conditions with regard to radio spectrum[48] availability and the efficient use of the radio spectrum required for the establishment and functioning of the internal market in areas such as electronic communications, transport and research and development.[49]

mobile users was expected to reach an estimated 2 billion worldwide by 2010; (ii) the rapid growth of mobile data services, mobile e-commerce, wireless internet access and mobile video-based services; and (iii) the need to secure common spectrum worldwide for global roaming and cheaper handsets. Available at: *http://www.europa.eu.int/information_society/topics/telecoms/radiospec/radio/world_radiocomm_conf/text_en.htm.*

[43] Commission Communication of November 10, 1999 on Next Steps in Radio Spectrum Policy: Results of the Public Consultation on the Green Papers; COM(99) 538 final.

[44] Communication from the Commission on the implementation and functioning of the mobile communications frequency directives (the "Communication on Mobile Frequencies"), COM(98) 559 final, p.9.

[45] Communication from the Commission on the strategy and policy orientations with regard to the further development of mobile and wireless communications (UMTS) (the "UMTS Communication"), COM(97) 513 final, pp.21–22. At the international level, WRC members have committed to make unused radio spectrum available for commercial use within the bandwidth above 1 GHz, which was reserved to military bodies (the band 806–960 MHz): see Resolution [COM5/25] (WRC–2000) available at: *www.itu.int/newsarchive/wrc2000/IMT_2000/Res_COM5-25.html*; frequency bands for the terrestrial component of IMT-2000 below 1 GHz — and within the bandwidth below 1 GHz, which is currently assigned to a variety of services (the bands 1710–1885 MHz for mobile systems, and 2500–2690 MHz for satellite systems): Resolution [COM5/26] (WRC–2000) available at: *www.itu.int/newsarchive/wrc2000/IMT_2000/Res_COM5-26.html*; and use of additional frequency bands for the satellite component of IMT-2000 — at the latest by 2005: Resolution [COM5/24] (WRC–2000) available at: *www.itu.int/newsarchive/wrc2000/IMT_2000/Res_COM5-24.html* and additional information on WRC–2000 can be found at: *www.itu.int/newsarchive/wrc2000.*

[46] UMTS Communication, para.1–105, n.45, p.10.

[47] For background information see also Communication of Next Steps in Radio Spectrum Policy, para.1–105, n.43, and Green Paper of December 9, 1998 on Radio Spectrum Policy in the context of European Community policies such as telecommunications, broadcasting, transport and R&D, COM(98) 596 final available at: *www.europa.eu.int/ISPO/infosoc/telecompolicy/en/sgp.doc.*

[48] Radio spectrum for the purpose of the Radio Spectrum Decision includes radio waves in frequencies between 9 kHz and 3000 GHz; radio waves are electromagnetic waves propagated in space without artificial guide.

[49] Radio Spectrum Decision, para.1–011, n.32, Art.1.

1–107   The scope of the Radio Spectrum Decision includes: (i) the effective implementation of radio spectrum policy in the EU, through the establishment of a Radio Spectrum Committee to assist the Commission in adopting appropriate mandatory technical implementing measures[50]; (ii) the co-ordinated and timely provision of information concerning the allocation, availability and use of radio spectrum in the EU from the competent national authorities and operators themselves, provided that confidentiality is respected; and (iii) the effective co-ordination of EU interests in international negotiations where radio spectrum use affects EU policies. With regard to the EU's participation in international negotiations, the Commission should consult the European Parliament and the Council with a view to obtaining a mandate from the Member States on the Community's policy objectives to be achieved and on the position to be taken by the Member States at the international level.

1–108   For the development of technical implementing measures that fall within the remit of CEPT,[51] the Commission must issue mandates to CEPT, setting out the tasks to be performed and the related timetable. For example, CEPT was given four mandates, mainly to harmonise the use of frequencies for UMTS.[52] Under the previous directives, compliance with the results of work of the CEPT were voluntary for Member States and the Commission had to incorporate them into a specific legislative act, in order to make them binding across the EU. However, under the Radio Spectrum Decision, the Commission may directly require the Member States to apply the results of the work carried out by CEPT and set the deadline for their implementation by the Member States. If the Commission, or any of the Member States, considers the work of the CEPT to be unsatisfactory, the Commission can itself adopt the measures that it considers to be necessary to achieve the EU's policy objectives.

---

[50] *ibid.,* Recital 11. Radio spectrum technical management includes the harmonisation and allocation of radio spectrum. This harmonisation should reflect the requirements of general policy principles identified at EU level. Radio spectrum technical management does not cover procedures for the allocation, assignment and licensing of frequencies, nor decisions on whether to use competitive selection procedures for the allocation of radio frequencies. The allocation of frequencies through the grant of usage rights falls within the scope of the Authorisation Directive, para.1–011, n.28.

[51] On the role of CEPT, see para.1–101, above. The actions of CEPT and its European Radio Communications Committee (ERC) has led to the setting up of the European Radio Communications Office (ERO) in Copenhagen. A number of so-called Work Requirements have been submitted to the ERC/ERO, focusing in particular on the designation of harmonised European frequency bands for DCS 1800 services, the TETRA radio system, Terrestrial Digital Audio Broadcasting, Satellite Personal Communications Services (S-PCS) and the Universal Mobile Telecommunications System (UMTS).

[52] See UMTS Decision, para.1–104, n.39, Art.5. The four mandates to CEPT's ERC were aimed at: (i) harmonising the use of the radio frequency bands 1900–1980, 2010–2025 and 2110–2170 MHz (the so-called "core band") for terrestrial 3G services to allow for the use of such bands by January 1, 2002, in accordance with market demand; (ii) drawing the spectrum plan for the use of the core band, as a basis for a common approach of national administrations to licensing 3G services to be operated in the core band; (iii) making available between 2005 and 2010 additional frequencies, which are currently reserved for military purposes, for the provision of commercial 3G applications, as identified by the WRC in 2000; and (iv) adopting a first set of harmonising measures necessary to ensure that such additional frequencies are available for the provision of 3G services. The first three mandates resulted in three ERC Decisions: respectively, ERC Decision (97)07; Decision (00)01; and Decision (99)25; while the work under the last mandate is currently being finalised, at the time of writing. In its Eighth Report on the Implementation of the Telecommunications Regulatory Package (COM(02) 695 final) (hereinafter, the "Eighth Implementation Report"), available at: *http://www. europa.eu.int/information_society/topics/telecoms/implementation/annual_report/8threport/finalreport/com2002_ 0695en01.pdf*, the Commission found that all Member States have complied with these ERC Decisions, and

1–109 In these cases, and for any other matters that fall outside the remit of the CEPT,[53] the Decision created a Radio Spectrum Committee to assist the Commission in the elaboration of binding implementing measures laying down harmonised conditions for the availability and efficient use of radio spectrum.[54] Moreover, the Commission has established a Radio Spectrum Policy Group with consultative powers. This comprises high-level governmental experts from the Member States and high-level representatives from the Commission.[55] CEPT is an observer of the Group. The Group may invite other persons to attend meetings as appropriate: NRAs, national competition authorities, market participants, users and consumer groups.[56] The Group assists and advises the Commission on radio spectrum policy issues, on co-ordination of policy approaches and, where appropriate, on harmonised conditions with regard to the availability and efficient use of radio spectra necessary for the establishment and functioning of the internal market. The Group should not, however, interfere with the work of the Committee.[57]

EU Harmonisation of Technical Standards for Mobile Systems

1–110 The harmonisation of technical standards was necessary to remove technical trade barriers and therefore assist in the achievement of the liberalisation of the mobile sector. Indeed, technical standards for mobile communications initially developed within the EU mainly on purely national lines, with multiple different analogue systems.

1–111 GSM — It is the adoption of the GSM standard that permitted the development of a pan-European mobile communications system. GSM has now become *de facto* the world standard (other than perhaps in the United States and Japan) and has helped European industry (both at the equipment and network operation levels) to establish a strong global presence in mobile communications. The GSM standard was developed initially within the framework of CEPT and subsequently within ETSI. The GSM standard that was selected from amongst a number of proposals from various countries and manufacturers is based on a narrowband design based on Time Division Multiplex Access ("TDMA") technology.[58] All technical details of the GSM standard were laid down between the period 1988 and 1991 within the framework of ETSI.

1–112 UMTS — On January 29, 1998 ETSI adopted the technology for the successor to GSM, the Universal Mobile Telecommunications System ("UMTS").[59] Following a consideration of

have adopted proposals for the necessary legislative changes to their current national regimes for radio spectrum use.

[53] In particular, under Art.4(5) of the Radio Spectrum Decision, para.1–011, n.32, a transitional period and/or radio spectrum sharing arrangement in a Member State may be approved, subject to the Commission's prior approval.

[54] *ibid.*, para.1–011, n.32, Art.4.

[55] Commission Decision 2002/622 of July 26, 2002, establishing a Radio Spectrum Policy Group, O.J. 2002 L198/49.

[56] *ibid.*, Arts 3, 4 and 5.

[57] *ibid.*, Art.2.

[58] For the background to the adoption of the GSM standard, see Bekkers and Liotard, "European Standards for Mobile Communications" (1999) E.I.P.R. 110–126.

[59] Art.6 of the UMTS Decision, para.1–104, n.39, provides that the Commission must take all necessary measures, where appropriate in co-operation with ETSI, to promote a common and open standard for the provision of compatible UMTS services in Europe.

several different systems, a system was adopted that contains elements of two of the systems considered by ETSI, the "Alpha" W-CDMA design and the TD-CDMA design.[60] UMTS will offer mobile telephone users new possibilities, in particular, multimedia capability with wide area mobility and efficient access to the internet, intranet and other internet protocol (IP) based services. To ensure international acceptance of the standard chosen for UMTS, the EU negotiated agreements with other international agencies, such as the International Telecommunications Union (ITU).[61] After initial objections by the United States to the adoption of these standards,[62] some US operators have chosen the route GSM1900-EDGE, which allows migration towards UMTS. In addition, after the initial postponement for the allocation of further frequencies, a positive conclusion was reached on July 26, 2002, when the US Federal Communications Commission decided to allocate 90 MHz of available radio spectrum for third generation mobile services. The adoption of a common technical standard is only one of the conditions necessary to ensure the success of UMTS. Predictable licensing procedures and the timely availability and allocation of frequencies are also fundamental to the successful launch of third generation mobile services.[63]

1–113 The UMTS Decision sets out the framework for the co-ordinated adoption of technology for third generation mobile services. It requires authorisation regimes to be based on a standardised procedure in accordance with the previous Licensing Directive and to be put in place by January 1, 2000.[64] It also requires that licensing conditions (to be defined by each Member State in accordance with applicable EU law on licensing and interconnection) must ensure the provision of roaming capabilities (*i.e.* subscribers to a service in one country must be able to use their mobile telephones in other Member States). To facilitate roaming capabilities, Member States were required to ensure that UMTS network providers are able to conclude the necessary agreements.[65]

1–114   3G roll-out — All Member States have now granted UMTS licences. A total of 62 UMTS licences have been granted across the EU. Different selection procedures were used to award the

---

[60] This proposal was incorporated in the ITU recommendation defining the IMT-2000, the family of standards for third generation mobiles: see Recommendation Q.1701 (03/99) on a framework for IMT-2000 networks, available at: *www.itu.int/ITU-T/imt-2000/recommendations.html.*

[61] Art.9 of the UMTS Decision, para.1–104, n.39, requires the Commission to take all necessary steps to facilitate the introduction of UMTS services and free circulation of UMTS equipment in third countries. The work pursued in collaboration with the ITU resulted in two recommendations concerning the global circulation of IMT-2000 standards: Recommendation M.1579 on global circulation of IMT-2000 terminals and Recommendation M.1581 on generic unwanted emission characteristics of mobile stations using the terrestrial radio interfaces of IMT-2000, both approved in July 2000, and available at: *www.itu.int/ITU-T/imt-2000/recommendations.html.*

[62] The United States argued that the EU's choice of technical standards for UMTS partitioned the global mobile telecommunications market and prevented United States firms using a different technology from competing in the EU. The US argued that the EU had breached various World Trade Organisation agreements. For more details, see *www.umtsworld.com/industry/usa.htm.*

[63] Commission Communication of June 11, 2002 on the Full Roll-out of Third Generation Mobile Communications COM(02) 301 final ("3G Communication") available at: *http://www.europa.eu.int/eur-lex/en/com/cnc/2002/com2002_0301en01.pdf.*

[64] UMTS Decision, para.1–104, n.39, Art.3.

[65] Art.4(1) of the UMTS Decision, para.1–104, n.39, requires Member States to encourage licensees to negotiate among themselves cross-border roaming agreements to ensure seamless EU-wide service coverage. On the consideration of roaming agreements under EC competition law, see para.6–012, below.

licences: (i) auctions (in Belgium, Denmark, Germany, Greece, the Netherlands, Austria and the United Kingdom); (ii) beauty contests (in Spain, Ireland, France, Luxembourg, Portugal, Finland and Sweden); and (iii) a hybrid of the two (Italy). The timely establishment of selection procedures (by January 1, 2000, with a number of exceptions that have now expired) was essential in order to enable prospective market participants to benefit from a co-ordinated and progressive introduction of commercial third generation mobile services across the EU by January 1, 2002, if they so wished.

1–115 The commercial roll-out of UMTS services has, however, been delayed by several factors.[66] The first round of licences awarded were of varying duration and entered into force at different times. Deployment conditions (in particular, legal coverage requirements[67] and network sharing conditions[68]) also differed considerably between Member States. Therefore, in 2001 the Commission launched a consultation with the Member States to identify the conditions that were necessary to promote the full roll-out of third generation mobile communications.[69] The Commission has drawn the following conclusions from this consultation[70]: (i) in principle, existing licences should not be

[66] In some Member States (such as France, Belgium, Greece, Luxembourg and Ireland) the initial licensing procedures did not succeed in attracting a sufficient number of interested parties to issue all offered licences. This was due to the high fees demanded by Member States and the difficulties caused by the general financial downturn of the telecommunications industry at that time. As a result, part of the amount of the spectrum made available for UMTS services remained unused after the first licensing round. In addition, even where licences were successfully awarded, operators faced a number of unprecedented technical, financial and regulatory issues. See 3G Communication, para.1–112, n.63, above.

[67] Under the legal coverage requirements, each licensee is required to ensure the coverage of a certain percentage of the Member State's territory by a specified date (or dates).

[68] Network infrastructure sharing between operators covers the possibility of sharing the use of transmission sites and base stations. For regulatory purposes, the basic distinction that is relevant in this context is between Radio Access Network (RAN) and the core or backbone network. RAN includes mast/antenna sites, site support cabinets (SSC) and power supply, as well as antennas, combiners and transmissions links. It also covers the so-called "Node B", which are the base stations that receive and send data across frequencies and control a particular network cell, as well as the radio network controllers (RNCs), that each control a number of such Nodes B and that are linked to the core network. The core network is the intelligent part of the network that consists of mobile switching centres (MSC), various support nodes, services platforms, client home location registers and operation and maintenance centres. It is linked to the fixed ISDN (integrated services digital network) and internet networks. Network sharing reduces considerably the costs that would be sustained by each operator if it had to build the network alone. On the status of network sharing agreements, under competition rules, see *Rahmenvertrag T-Mobile Deutschland/VIAG Interkom*, O.J. 2002 C189/22; and related Commission Press Release IP/03/1026 of July 16, 2003; and *BT Cellnet and BT3G/One2One Personal Communications*, O.J. 2002 C214/17 and related Commission Press Release IP/03/589 of April 30, 2003: for more details see para.6–006, below.

[69] Commission Communication of March 20, 2001 on the Introduction of Third Generation Mobile Communications in the European Union: State of Play and the Way Forward, COM(01) 141 final available at: *http://www.europa.eu.int/eur-lex/en/com/cnc/2001/com2001_0141en01.pdf*.

[70] The 3G Communication (see para.1–112, n.63, above) also reviews other aspects of the roll-out of 3G services, such as financial and technical issues. Following this report, the European Committee on Industry and Research of the European Parliament adopted a report on January 23, 2003, detailing the current challenges facing the roll-out of 3G communications. The report, which was drafted by French MEP, Danielle Auroi, reiterates the analysis made in the Commission Communication of June 2002. The report of the European Parliament calls on the Commission to develop a stable regulatory environment for 3G infrastructure, applications and services in Europe. It states that along with a general economic recovery, the mobile market is best served by letting the market drive the process ahead by allowing healthy competition to generate new products which consumers will want to buy. The report also calls on the Commission, Member States and national authorities involved in managing telecommunications infrastructures to launch a process

changed, except in circumstances where the licence conditions have changed unpredictably and in these cases any modification should be proportional, transparent and non-discriminatory[71]; and (ii) the modification of roll-out obligations (such as legal coverage requirements and network sharing conditions) may, however become necessary, for example where equipment is not readily available or authorisations for building and using base stations are difficult to obtain.[72] Any proposal for changing coverage requirements or network sharing conditions should be reasoned, justified and be preceded by public consultation at the national level. The Commission has also encouraged the exchange of information and best practices between the responsible national authorities. It has emphasised that co-ordination at the EU level should be ensured using the mechanisms introduced by the New Regulatory Framework, under the Framework Directive and the Radio Spectrum Decision. The Framework Directive imposes a general duty of consultation between Member States on any matter which may have an impact on the development of the internal market for electronic communications. This includes matters related to UMTS licensing.[73] The Radio Spectrum Decision establishes a general policy and procedural framework for discussing spectrum issues at EU level. The creation, within this framework, of two new bodies, the Radio Spectrum Policy Group and the Radio Spectrum Committee, is intended to ensure that Member States' approaches to spectrum issues are co-ordinated at an early stage.

1–116 Wireless local area networks (W-LANs) — Wireless local area networks (also called "Radio Local Area Network", R-LAN, or "Wi Fi Networks") are data communications systems implemented as an extension or an alternative to a wired local area network within a building or a wider area, such as an airport. Using electromagnetic waves, W-LANs transmit and receive data,

---

of consultation of the health professions, citizens' associations and operators in the sectors. The report stresses the importance of protecting children when they use the internet. The report also focuses on the need to formulate universal technical standards for operators to provide disabled consumers with access to 3G services and applications. The text of the report is available at: *http://www.europarl.eu.int/meetdocs/committees/itre/ 20030122/482385en.pdf*. On the issue of accessibility to, and interoperability of, 3G platforms for EU citizens, see also the Commission Communication on "The remaining barriers to the achievement of widespread access to new services and applications of the Information Society through open platforms in digital television and 3G mobile communications" COM(2003) 410 final of July 9, 2003, available at: *http://www.europa.eu.int/ information_society/topics/telecoms/regulatory/publiconsult/documents/211_29_en.pdf*.

[71] Any changes to licence conditions must follow the requirements of Art.14 of the Authorisation Directive, para.1–011, n.28.

[72] As the Commission indicated in its 3G Communication, para.1–112, n.63, the background to these difficulties lies in public opposition to mobile telecommunications base stations based upon the alleged health risks resulting from electromagnetic emissions by base stations, as well as environmental concerns: indeed, many new masts for third generation mobiles must be erected to ensure adequate coverage levels, as mandated by the licences' requirements. Electromagnetic emissions that are considered to be safe were harmonised at the EU level by Council Recommendation 1999/519 of July 12, 1999, O.J. 1999 L199/59. These levels were confirmed in October 2001 by the Scientific Committee on Toxicity, Ecotoxicity and the Environment. In most Member States, the relevant authorisations for the construction of masts and antennae are granted at the regional or even local level, and applicable procedures and rules vary considerably (*e.g.* construction permit from local authorities). Another difficulty faced by operators is the proof of compliance with emission regulations adopted at national level, as this is not harmonised throughout the EU. National and local planning procedures fall outside of the scope of the New Regulatory Framework, although the Framework Directive encourages public authorities to adopt measures to facilitate co-location and facility sharing (see para.1–172 below). Obtaining the necessary planning authorisations for base stations is proving to be a major obstacle to the roll-out of new base stations for UMTS, as UMTS requires many more base stations than a comparable GSM network.

[73] Framework Directive, para.1–009, n.25, Art.7(2). See para.1–044 *et seq.*, above.

minimising the need for users to have wired connections. Since 1995, W-LANs have gained strong popularity in a number of end-use industries, including the health care, retail, manufacturing, warehousing, and academic sectors, thereby becoming a *de facto* standard. W-LANs are complementary to 3G technology, in light of the applications that might be provided using these two technologies. However, W-LANs can only be used in a defined local area, while 3G offers fully mobile applications throughout a Member State and beyond. W-LAN systems may currently use the 2400.0–2483.5 MHz bands, and they would therefore arguably fall within the category of the so-called 2.5 G networks (together with GPRS).[74] Under the Authorisation Directive, the provision of electronic communications may only be subject to a general authorisation, except for the use of radio frequencies and numbers (which may be subject to the granting of individual rights of use). Wherever possible (in particular where the risk of harmful interference is negligible), the use of radio frequencies should be subject to a general authorisation and not an individual right of use.[75] The 2.4 GHz and 5 GHz bands used for W-LANs cannot be considered as representing access to scarce resources. Where the possibility of interference between users of the 2.4 GHz and 5 GHz bands and between different co-existing W-LAN systems is accepted by the parties involved, Member States should then normally allow the provision of public W-LAN access without authorisation, or if justified, subject to a general authorisation.[76]

D. Network Provision

1–117 Until the 1990s, the setting-up and operation of public electronic communications networks was generally the monopoly of incumbent telecommunications operators. This constituted an additional barrier to entry for new operators on the electronic communications markets. Consequently, it became clear that the only way to ensure effective competition in telecommunications was to liberalise the provision of public networks.[77] The Commission has followed a two-pronged policy in this sector: (i) liberalisation of the establishment and use of alternative infrastructures, beginning with cable television networks and continuing with utilities networks;

---

[74] On GPRS, see also paras 1–089 and 1–115, above.

[75] See para.1–060 *et seq.*

[76] A Commission Recommendation, adopted on March 20, 2003, on the provision of public W-LAN access to public electronic communications networks and services in the European Community, and published in O.J. 2003 L78/12, confirms this conclusion; see also Commission Press Release of March 20, 2003 IP/03/418.

[77] See Green Paper on the liberalisation of telecommunications infrastructure and cable television networks — Part I: Principle and timetable COM(94) 440, October 25, 1994; Green Paper on the liberalisation of telecommunications infrastructure and cable television networks — Part II: A common approach to the provision of infrastructure for telecommunications in the European Union, COM(94) 682, October 25, 1995; Council Resolution 93/C213/01 of December 22, 1994 on the principle and timetable for the liberalisation of telecommunications infrastructure, O.J. 1994 C379/4; European Parliament Resolution of April 7, 1995 on the Green Paper on the liberalisation of telecommunications infrastructure and cable television networks (first part – principle and timetable), O.J. 1995 C109/310; European Parliament Resolution of May 19, 1995 on the Green Paper on the liberalisation of telecommunications infrastructure and cable television networks — Part II: A common approach to the provision of infrastructure for telecommunications in the European Union, O.J. 1995 C151/479; Commission Communication to the Council and European Parliament on the consultation on the Green Paper on the liberalisation of telecommunications infrastructure and cable television networks, COM(95) 158 final, May 3, 1995; Council Resolution of September 18, 1995 on the implementation of the future regulatory framework for telecommunications, O.J. 1995 C258/1.

and (ii) the establishment of a regulatory framework to ensure open access to existing public electronic communications networks and services (discussed at Section F).

1. Liberalisation of Alternative Infrastructures

1–118 Liberalisation of cable television networks — The Liberalisation Directive requires Member States to remove (if they have not already done so) exclusive and special rights for the provision of all electronic communications networks, irrespective of the information conveyed.[78] The Commission started the liberalisation of alternative infrastructures with cable television networks.[79] The Commission considered that cable television networks offered opportunities for the provision of an increasing number of telecommunications services, in addition to the transmission of television broadcasts. It was expected that the use of the transmission capacity of cable networks to provide telecommunications services would have the effect of bringing down prices charged by incumbent telecommunications operators for transmission capacity on their networks, by offering an alternative to their existing public telecommunications networks. Cable television networks are defined as "any wire-based infrastructure approved by a Member State for the delivery or distribution of radio or television signals to the public" and fall under the concept of electronic communications networks.[80] Member States must also allow cable television networks to interconnect with other public electronic communications networks and to interconnect directly with each other (as far as possible within the framework of their broadcasting business).[81]

1–119 Joint provision of telecommunications and cable television networks — The Commission has expressed concern that the joint provision of telecommunications and cable television networks by incumbent telecommunications operators may limit the development of electronic communications and multimedia markets.[82] In particular, the Commission considers that joint ownership of both types of infrastructure may have the effect of reducing the incentive of the incumbent telecommunications operator to undertake the necessary investment to upgrade its cable network to achieve the bi-directional capacity required to supply electronic communications and multimedia services. Indeed, there would be no intrinsic financial benefit in upgrading a cable television network, which would then compete for customers with the core telecommunications business of the incumbent communications operator. As a result, incumbent operators' ownership of both telecommunications and cable television networks within the same geographical market is likely to reduce infrastructure competition by removing an alternative source of access to the local loop.

---

[78] Liberalisation Directive, para.1–012, n.33, Art.2(1).

[79] Cable Directive, para.1–004, n.11, above. Until full liberalisation of telecommunications services on January 1, 1998, cable television networks could not be used to provide voice telephony services. This Directive has been repealed and consolidated by the Liberalisation Directive.

[80] Liberalisation Directive, para.1–012, n.33, Art.1.

[81] Access Directive, para.1–011, n.29, Recital 2 and Art.3 in conjunction with Framework Directive, para.1–009, n.25, Art.2 and Authorisation Directive, para.1–011, n.28, Recital 20. On the applicable regulatory framework for access to, and interconnection of, electronic communications networks, see Section F, para.1–144.

[82] Commission Communication concerning the review under competition rules of the joint provision of telecommunications and cable television networks by a single operator and the abolition of restrictions on the provision of cable television capacity over telecommunications networks (the so-called "Cable Review"), O.J. 1998 C71/4.

This in turn may restrict competition in electronic communications services such as voice telephony and broadband interactive services.

1–120 Measures adopted by the Commission — The Commission has adopted several measures to address the concerns it has raised regarding incumbent operators operating both telecommunications and cable networks. Its first measure was the Cable Directive, which has been repealed and consolidated by the Liberalisation Directive. The Liberalisation Directive requires the structural separation of cable television and telecommunications networks when they are both operated by the same incumbent operator.[83] In practice, this means that incumbent operators are required to operate their cable television and public communications networks through different subsidiaries, although they can continue to control both companies. This obligation, however, only applies if the incumbent operator: (i) is controlled by the State or benefits from special rights[84]; (ii) is dominant in a substantial part of the common market in the provision of public telecommunications networks and public voice telephony services; and (iii) operates a cable television network established under special or exclusive right in the same geographic area.[85] The Liberalisation Directive provides that the Commission may withdraw this structural separation requirement in those Member States where there is sufficient competition in the provision of local loop infrastructures and services,[86] following the implementation of the unbundling requirements of the Regulation on the unbundled access to the local loop.[87]

1–121 At the time of the Cable Review, the Commission made clear its intention to apply the EC Treaty's competition rules, on a case-by-case basis, to prevent anti-competitive effects of continuing ownership of cable television networks by incumbent operators. Where it is the only means to allow the creation of a competitive market, the Commission will also "impose" the divestment of cable television networks by incumbent telecommunications operators. The Commission applied this policy in the *BiB* case where it required BT to divest its remaining interest in cable networks in the United Kingdom as a condition for clearance to the transaction.[88] Likewise, in *Telia/Telenor*, the Commission cleared a merger between the two incumbent operators in Norway and Sweden only after they both had committed to divest their cable television interests.[89]

1–122 Restrictions on the use of telecommunications networks to provide cable television capacity — The regulatory framework adopted in the 1990s did not specifically prohibit Member States from restricting the use of telecommunications networks to provide cable television services. Certain Member States did impose dual restrictions: for example in the United Kingdom, BT was prohibited from using its public telecommunications network to transmit broadcast signals. This was done in order to protect the fledgling UK cable sector. The definition of "electronic

---

[83] Liberation Directive, para.1–012, n.33, Art.8.

[84] For the definition of "special rights", see above para.1–055, n.34.

[85] Liberalisation Directive, para.1–012, n.33, Art.8(1).

[86] *ibid.*, Art.8.3.

[87] For a discussion of this Regulation, see para.1–160 *et seq.*, below.

[88] *British Interactive Broadcasting (Open)*, Commission Decision of September 15, 1999, O.J. 1999, L312/1; for an analysis of the case, see para.8–346 *et seq.*

[89] Case M.1439, *Telia/Telenor*, Commission Decision of October 13, 2001, O.J. 2001 L40/1. For an analysis of the case, see para.8–097 *et seq.*

communications networks" contained in the Liberalisation Directive implies that Member States must not restrict the use of an electronic communications network to prevent it being used for the transmission of television signals.[90]

1–123 Such restriction may also infringe other EC Treaty rules. The reduction of potential cable television transmission capacity that would result from such restrictions, may have severe effects on television broadcasters established in other Member States, as the allocation of capacity available on cable networks is based on the media laws of the Member States, which usually give or have given preference to national providers, for example under specific media rules of "must carry" regulations.[91] At paras 50 and 61 of its Cable Review, the Commission indicated that national laws restricting the use of telecommunications networks to provide cable television capacity may be in breach of Article 86 (*ex* Article 90), in conjunction with Article 49 (*ex* Article 59) of the EC Treaty, which provides for the freedom to provide services across the EU.

1–124 Liberalisation of alternative infrastructures — As a further attempt to create local loop competition and reduce the power of incumbent operators in network provision, Member States are required to abolish (where they have not already done so) any restrictions on the use of alternative infrastructures (such as networks maintained by energy and transportation utilities, internal networks of multi-national corporations or other operators' networks) for the provision of communications services.[92] Accordingly, any provider of communications services may set up its own infrastructure or use third party infrastructure to supply services. A number of railways, electricity networks or other utilities have begun to use their telecommunications to supply services to third parties.

1–125 Liberalisation of public communications networks — Since January 1, 1998, there is complete freedom to set up and operate public communications networks throughout the EU. Member States must ensure that no restriction is imposed or maintained on the provision of electronic communications networks, as well as over infrastructures provided by third parties, and by means of sharing networks, other facilities or sites.[93] The establishment and/or the provision of electronic communications networks is thus subject only to a general authorisation granted on the basis of objective, non-discriminatory, proportionate and transparent criteria.[94] If the owner of such an alternative network is granted special or exclusive rights in another sector and is active in the communications market, Member States must ensure either accounting separation or structural separation between the two activities.[95]

1–126 Rights of way — Providers of public electronic communications networks require access to public and private property to install equipment and cables to build their networks.[96] Member

---

[90] Liberalisation Directive, para.1–012, n.33, Art.2 and Recital 8.
[91] Framework Directive, para.1–009, n.25, Art.13(1)(a).
[92] Liberalisation Directive, para.1–012, n.33, Art.2(1).
[93] *ibid.*, Art.2(3).
[94] *ibid.*, Art.2(4) and Authorisation Directive, para.1–011, n.28, Art.3(2); see, also, above, para.1–061 *et seq.*
[95] Framework Directive, para.1–009, n.25, Art.13. See also para.1–081.
[96] Under the Authorisation Directive, para.1–011, n.28, Art.4, the right to make an application for the necessary rights to install facilities is to be included in the general authorisation. Even before a general authorisation

States must not discriminate between providers of public communications networks[97] in the granting of rights of way. They must consider any application for rights of way on, over or under public or private property for the purpose of providing public and non-public communications networks on the basis of transparent and publicly available procedures, that are applied without discrimination and without delay. In practice, however, the procedures may differ depending on whether or not the applicant is providing a public communications network. In either case, the applicant must be granted the right of appeal before an independent body.[98] Where the protection of the environment or town and country planning objectives means that an operator cannot be granted rights of way, Member States may impose obligations requiring the sharing of facilities or property to ensure that operators have access, on reasonable terms, to the existing ducts or poles of other operators.[99]

E. Satellite Communications

1–127 As satellites are extra-terrestrial and extra-territorial by nature, they are regulated by international treaties. Under these treaties, the regulation of satellite systems is often a matter of national law. However, because of the trans-border nature of satellite communications, there was a need for harmonisation and liberalisation across the EU and therefore a need for regulatory intervention at the level of the EU.[1] This section reviews the interaction of international, EU and national law in the regulation of the various aspects of satellite communications, including: (i) the cross-border provision of satellite terminals; (ii) the launching and operation of satellites; (iii) the provision of satellite services; and (iv) access to and marketing of satellite capacity.

1. Liberalisation of Satellite Equipment

1–128 Member States are required to abolish all special and exclusive rights for the establishment of networks for the provision of satellite services.[2] This prohibition applies to satellite earth station equipment, *i.e.* equipment capable of being used for the transmission and/or the reception

---

is granted, at the request of an undertaking, NRAs must issue a standardised declaration, confirming, where applicable, that the undertaking has submitted a notification for the purposes of receiving a general authorisation, in order to facilitate the exercise of the right to apply to any competent authority for rights of way. The notification is not a prerequisite to commencing activities and exercising the rights granted by the general authorisation. See also *ibid.*, Art.9.

[97] Liberalisation Directive, para.1–012, n.33, Art.8 and Framework Directive, para.1–009, n.25, Art.11(1), which requires Member States to follow the principles of transparency and non-discrimination in attaching conditions to the grant of any right of way, over public or private property.

[98] Framework Directive, para.1–009, n.25, Art.4.

[99] *ibid.*, Art.12(2).

[1] For the background to the EU policy in the satellite sector, see "Towards Europe-wide systems and services: Green Paper on a common approach in the field of satellite communications in the European Community", COM(90) 490, November 20, 1990; Council Resolution of December 19, 1991 on the development of the common market for satellite communications services and equipment, O.J. 1992 C8/1; European Parliament Resolution of January 19, 1993 on a common approach in the field of satellite communications in the European Community, O.J. 1993 C42/30.

[2] Liberalisation Directive, para.1–012, n.33, Art.2(1) and Framework Directive, para.1–009, n.25, Art.2(d).

of radio-communications signals by means of satellites or other space-based systems. It includes products such as very small aperture terminals (VSATs), mobile and transportable satellite earth station equipment, satellite news gathering (SNG) equipment and television receive-only (TVRO) satellite earth station equipment.

2. Launching and Operation of Satellites

1–129   Application of national laws — The launching and operation of satellites is not yet regulated at the EU level, but continues to be governed by Member States' laws, within the framework of international treaties drawn up under the ITU.[3] As a rule, jurisdiction over a satellite system rests with the state from which the satellite network is controlled, although a satellite network may be deemed to be controlled from more that one country.

1–130   Allocation of radio frequencies for satellites — The allocation of radio frequencies and positions in the geo-stationary satellite orbit is co-ordinated within the ITU. The use of frequencies is governed by the Radio Regulations ("RRs"). The RRs include a Table of Frequency Allocations that governs the use of radio frequency bands and lays down rules for co-ordination, notification and registration of frequencies. The RRs are reviewed and revised at the WRC held every two years.[4] Applications for access to radio frequencies and orbital positions need to be made to the relevant state authorities, even for privately owned satellites.

The Commission has adopted several initiatives to ensure a coherent EU approach in discussions within the ITU and the WRC to protect the Community's interests.[5] The co-ordination of frequencies is undertaken at a Europe-wide level within the framework of CEPT.[6] This co-ordination has led to the designation of harmonised European frequency bands for Satellite Personal Communications Services ("S-PCS"). The Radio Spectrum Decision offers a further means of co-ordination of the approach within the EU to frequencies for satellite transmissions issues.

1–131   Licensing of satellite systems — In so far as they involve the use of radio frequency and orbit resources, the establishment and operation of satellite systems is typically subject to an individual licence from the relevant state. A licence may contain a variety of operational, technical, financial and other conditions, including the use of a given frequency exclusively for a specific technology. Under EU law, the conditions that may be attached to rights of use for satellite transmissions are listed in Part B of the Annex to the Authorisation Directive and are the same as those for the granting of rights of use of frequencies. The Authorisation Directive requires

---

[3] The role and function of the ITU, and the rights, obligations and duties of ITU members are governed by its current Constitution and Convention which were adopted at the Additional Plenipotentiary Conference held in Geneva in December 1992 (APC Geneva, 1992 ISB and 92-61-04771-8). See *www.itu.int/aboutitu/overview/conferences.html.*

[4] On the WRC, see para.1–105, above.

[5] Communication COM(97) 91 final of March 5, 1997: "European Union Action Plan: Satellite Communications in the Information Society"; Commission Staff Working Paper: "European Union Action Plan: Satellite Communications in the Information Society", S.E.C. (1999) 250 for a discussion of the latest developments. As regards the EU Satellite Action Plan, see para.1–141, below.

[6] See para.1–101, above.

that: (i) conditions imposed on applicants for rights of use are objectively justified, non-discriminatory, proportionate and transparent; and (ii) NRAs grant such rights of use within a specific timeframe (six weeks under normal circumstances, and eight months if a comparative bidding procedure is used).[7] In so far as satellites are used for other applications (such as television broadcasting and defence), it is arguable that national procedures for the licensing of satellite systems may derogate from the requirements of the Authorisation Directive.[8]

3. Provision of Satellite-Based Services

1–132   Liberalisation of satellite-based services — The Satellite Directive, which has been re-pealed and consolidated in the Liberalisation Directive, required Member States to abolish all exclusive or special rights[9] for the provision of satellite network services (being the establishment and operation of earth stations, including "uplinks" and "downlinks") or satellite communications services (being communications services making use of such facilities).[10]

1–133   Licensing of satellite-based services — The provision of satellite-based services such as VSATs and Satellite News Gathering (SNG) is subject to the Authorisation Directive. The provision of satellite broadcasting services such as Direct-to-Home (DTH) Satellite, Digital Broadcasting Services (DBS) and Digital Audio Radio is also subject to the provisions of this Directive.

1–134   Satellite-based voice telephony services (such as S-PCS) can be provided subject to an individual right of use, if the provision of such services needs access to scarce radio frequencies. The situation is less clear as regards other satellite-based services. To the extent that satellite-based services involve the use of limited radio frequencies, under the Authorisation Directive Member States may make their provision subject to individual rights of use, rather than general authorisations. However, the Authorisation Directive is based upon the principle that general authorisations or no-authorisation regimes are to be used in preference to individual rights of use. Moreover, the Commission has clearly indicated that the provision of a satellite service which only involves the use of a dependent VSAT earth station in a Member State can be subject no more than to a declaration procedure.[11] Accordingly, satellite-based services other than voice telephony should arguably only be subject to a general authorisation regime.[12]

---

[7] See para.1–085 *et seq.*, above.

[8] Art.1(2) of the Framework Directive, para.1–009, n.25, provides that the application of the directives comprising the New Regulatory Framework is without prejudice to the rules adopted by the Member States in accordance with Community law, governing the distribution of audio-visual programmes intended for the general public and the content of such programmes. The application of the New Regulatory Framework is also without prejudice to measures taken by Member States concerning defence and in accordance with public interest requirements recognised by the EC Treaty, in particular Arts 30 and 46, especially in relation to public morality, public security (including the investigation of criminal activities) and public policy.

[9] For a definition of exclusive and special rights, see Art.1 of the Liberalisation Directive, para.1–012, n.33, discussed at para.1–055, above, n.34.

[10] Satellite Directive, para.1–004, n.10, Art.2, now replaced by Art.1(1) and 1(2), in conjunction with Art.2(1) of the Liberalisation Directive, para.1–012, n.33.

[11] See, above, para.1–130, n.5.

[12] See Le Goueff, "Satellite Communications, Market Access in the European Union", (1998) 9 *Computer & Telecoms Law Review* 242, which considers the situation under the Satellite Directive and the Licensing Directive and comes to the same conclusion.

1–135   The Authorisation Directive requires licensing conditions to be objectively justified, non-discriminatory, proportionate and transparent. NRAs are subject to specific deadlines for the granting of an authorisation or/and individual rights of use.[13] Conditions that may be attached to an authorisation or right of use are limited to those listed in Part B of the Annex to the Authorisation Directive. However, these provisions are without prejudice to relevant national content regulation applicable to broadcasters. For example, in several Member States, a (temporary) licence is required for every single event broadcast by an SNG service (such as a sporting or news event). As there is no provision yet for permanent SNG services, this causes substantial costs for communications operators.

1–136   Licensing fee — The Authorisation Directive requires that fees imposed on undertakings for an authorisation or right of use should only cover the administrative costs incurred in the award, management, control and enforcement of the applicable authorisation or right of use.[14] Fees must be proportionate to the work involved and must be published. However, if scarce resources such as frequency spectrum are involved, NRAs may impose charges that reflect the need to ensure the optimal use of these resources. In practice, there remain considerable differences in the licence fees imposed by various Member States in their respective authorisation mechanisms, even when they are being applied to comparable systems and/or services.

1–137   One-stop shopping for satellite services — The Authorisation Directive does not provide for the establishment of a one-stop shopping mechanism procedure for the grant of individual rights of use.[15] However, satellite communications benefit from the one-stop shopping procedure established in 1997 within the framework of the ERO. This covers all aspects related to the licensing of satellite network operators, service providers and subscribers of small fixed earth stations or other mobile terminals. It is expected that in the future this mechanism will be extended to cover fixed, mobile and broadcast satellites.[16]

1–138   Satellite Personal Communications Services (S-PCS) — The EU has taken specific action regarding S-PCS. The S-PCS Decision is intended to facilitate the rapid introduction of compatible satellite personal communications services throughout the EU through the harmonisation of frequency bands and usage conditions attached to general authorisations or rights of use of frequencies, as well as removing the remaining barriers to the free movement of terminal equipment.[17] The creation of conditions for the harmonised introduction of S-PCS services throughout the EU, and beyond, is to be achieved by way of CEPT mandates.[18] Based on the S-PCS Decision, the

---

[13] See, above, para.1–085 *et seq.*

[14] See, above, para.1–065.

[15] See para.1–093.

[16] A table with the current status of implementation of such one-stop shop procedure by national administrations is available from the Commission website at: *www.europa.eu.int/information_society/topics/telecoms/radiospec/satellite/one_stop_shopping/index_en.htm.*

[17] Decision 1215/2000 of the European Parliament and of the Council of May 16, 2000, O.J. 2000 L139/1, extending until December 31, 2003, Decision 710/97 of the European Parliament and of the Council of March 24, 1997 on a co-ordinated authorisation approach in the field of satellite personal communications services in the Community, O.J. 1997 L105/4.

[18] *ibid.*, Art.3(1).

Commission has mandated CEPT to adopt appropriate measures concerning: (i) the harmonised use of frequencies; (ii) the harmonised conditions to be attached to general authorisations or individual rights of use of frequencies; (iii) the free movement of terminal equipment in the Community; and (iv) harmonised authorisation procedures for Low Earth Orbit systems. In particular, the S-PCS Decision enables the Commission, where appropriate and in conjunction with CEPT, to take the steps necessary for the operation of a one-stop shopping procedure for the granting of individual rights of use and notification procedures for general authorisations. The S-PCS Decision provides for the possibility of action at EU level if the Commission or any Member State considers that work within CEPT does not progress at a satisfactory pace.[19]

4. Access to and Marketing of Satellite Capacity

1–139 The Satellite Directive (which has now been repealed and replaced by the Liberalisation Directive) required Member States to abolish restrictions on the provision of space segment capacity to licensed satellite earth-station network operators.[20] They are required to authorise the space segment supplier to check the conformity of the earth stations with technical and operational space segment access conditions itself, rather than reserve such conformity checks to the incumbent telecommunications operator. In addition, since most of the available space segment capacity is offered by international satellite organisations (such as Intelsat, Eutelsat and Inmarsat) that are owned by a number of incumbent operators, both EU and non-EU, Member States that are party to such international satellite organisations are required to communicate information concerning the restrictive practices of such organisations to the Commission at its request and take all necessary measures themselves to ensure compliance with EU rules.[21] This reflects the willingness of the Commission to bring intergovernmental treaty satellite organisations within the scope of the EU regulatory framework, including the EC Treaty's competition rules.[22]

1–140 Intelsat, Eutelsat and Inmarsat have undergone restructuring to transform their operating parts into private companies, possibly to be followed by public offerings of shares.[23] These new companies will be run at arm's length from the current signatories. Public participation in the new companies will dilute the shareholdings of the current signatories and reduce the potential for conflicts of interest between the signatories' role as shareholders and as distributors of the organisation's services.[24]

[19] *ibid.*, Art.3(4).

[20] Liberalisation Directive, para.1–012, n.33, Art.7(1).

[21] *ibid.*, Art.7(2).

[22] This objective, together with the objective of non-discriminatory access to space segment capacity, was first expressed by the Commission in its 1994 "Direct Access" Paper, Communication on Satellite Communications: the Provision of — and Access to — Space Segment Capacity, COM(94) 210 final.

[23] Commission Staff Working Paper: "European Union Action Plan: Satellite Communications in the Information Society", para.1–130, n.5, pp.16–17. For a discussion of the recent developments of the EU Satellite Action Plan, see also para.1–141.

[24] This was the *rationale* behind the Commission's decision to make its approval of the restructuring of Inmarsat conditional upon a public offering taking place within three years of the restructuring. Similar discussions were raised in relation to the Commission's investigation of the restructuring of Intelsat, which was finally approved in January 2001. See para.8–312 *et seq.*

1–141   EU Satellite Action Plan — Since its inception in 1996, the EU's Satellite Action Plan has become a forceful platform for debate on matters such as the regulatory environment, market access for third countries, and R&D-related initiatives. Dialogue with the industry on regulatory issues is supported by regular meetings in Brussels with a group of industry representatives in the SAP/Regulatory Working Group. The Commission organises annual plenary sessions to debate and develop new policies, including: (i) the completion of the internal market for satellite service; (ii) the reinforcement of the EU's position at an international level; and (iii) the reinforcement of EU support for research and development and applications development. In this context, on July 9, 2001, the European Satellite Operators Association was launched by EU satellite operators with the aim of putting forward the position of the satellite communications services industry.[25]

5. Provision of Satellite-Based Services by Non-EU Undertakings

1–142   The WTO Basic Telecommunications Agreement, which entered into force on February 5, 1998,[26] provides for comprehensive market access and national treatment commitments with immediate binding effect. The Agreement's scope includes low earth orbit satellite systems and multimedia satellite systems.[27] Broadcasting services, such as Direct-to-Home (DTH), Digital Broadcasting Services and Digital Audio Radio, are specifically excluded from the scope of the Agreement. The exclusion of digital broadcasting services from the Agreement could have the effect of hampering the commercial viability of internet-based multimedia services provided via satellite, because of the fragmentation of national regulations. Mobile satellite services (S-PCS) are covered by the Agreement, although only a minority of the WTO Members that have signed the Agreement (39, including all Inmarsat signatories) made binding market access commitments in this respect.[28] That said, a new round of negotiations started in 2000, with the aim of extending such commitments to all electronic communications services, thus including digital broadcasting services and mobile satellite systems.[29] The EU's position is based on the New Regulatory Framework, whose provisions have already paved the way towards a technologically neutral regulation, to which all EU Member States are therefore committed.

F. Network Access and Interconnection

1–143   An essential complement to the liberalisation of the provision of infrastructure and services was the establishment of a regulatory framework to ensure open access to existing public telecommunications networks and services operated by incumbent telecommunications operators

---

[25] See Commission Press Release IP/01/975, of July 9, 2001.

[26] See para.1–296 *et seq.*

[27] Although a majority of countries are either not party to the WTO Basic Telecommunications Agreement or have made reservations to the market access commitments in respect of such systems.

[28] The Commission has expressed concerns in relation to the potentially discriminatory or lengthy procedures for access to the necessary frequency bands or for authorisation for new satellite systems in the US market. The Commission was also opposed to the US's legislative plans to link the restructuring of Intelsat and Inmarsat to market entry in the US (see Commission Staff Working Paper: "European Union Action Plan: Satellite Communications in the Information Society", para.1–130, n.5, p.19).

[29] See, below, para.1–304.

and interconnection between networks. The previous regulatory framework put in place measures to regulate the provision of network access and interconnection, in particular by the former monopolists in order to develop the supply of services and equipment throughout the Common Market. This involved considerable regulatory intervention by NRAs. The New Regulatory Framework contains measures that will allow the rolling back of specific regulation of access and interconnection if markets become open and competitive, with *ex ante* intervention being withdrawn in favour of the exclusive application of competition rules. The framework for network access and interconnection is based upon the principle that undertakings that receive requests for access or interconnection to their networks should in principle conclude such agreements on a commercial basis, and negotiate in good faith, without the intervention of the NRAs.[30] However, in those markets where the incumbent operators continue to have a strong market position, there remains a need for *ex ante* regulatory intervention, in order to facilitate the entry of new entrants into the relevant markets and prevent anti-competitive practices (such as refusals to interconnect or excessive interconnection rates). The concept of Open Network Provision (ONP) was contained in the original ONP Framework Directive, whose scope was extended as the EU telecommunications market was progressively liberalised. ONP was used as a tool to ensure access to other operators' networks, in particularly access to the incumbents' networks.[31] The New Regulatory Framework replaces the ONP concept with rules that: (i) give all operators the right to request interconnection with other operators; (ii) impose a duty on operators to negotiate access and interconnection when requested to do so by another operator, including operators established in other Member States; (iii) permit NRAs to impose additional obligations on operators designated as possessing SMP, including transparency, non-discrimination, accounting separation and price controls, and give service providers access to networks.

1. Access Directive

1–144   The Access Directive establishes a regulatory framework containing the general principles relating to the provision of access to, and interconnection of, networks for the provision of electronic communications services. It harmonises the conditions for open and efficient access to, and use of, electronic communications networks and services (whether public or private), at the wholesale level. The Directive establishes rights and obligations for businesses granting or seeking interconnection and/or access to their networks or associated facilities.[32] It sets out objectives for

---

[30] NRAs would only intervene if commercial negotiations fail.

[31] On the concept of ONP, see Garzaniti, *Telecommunications, Broadcasting and the Internet: E.U. Competition Law and Regulation* (Sweet & Maxwell, 1st ed., 2000), pp.31–35. The concept of ONP aims to ensure that access is provided to users, service providers and other network operators on a transparent, non-discriminatory basis and at fair and reasonable costs. According to such principles, an incumbent telecommunications operator could not restrict access to its public network to new entrants, unless one of the limited number of non-economic reasons in the public interest existed, *i.e.* security of network operations, maintenance of network integrity, interoperability of services, protection of data, effective use of spectrum, protection of the environment, town and country planning objectives, avoidance of harmful interference between radio-based telecommunications systems and other space or terrestrial technical systems (the so-called "essential requirements").

[32] The definitions of electronic communications networks, services and associated facilities for the purposes of the Access Directive correspond to those set out in Art.2 of the Framework Directive, para.1–009, n.25

NRAs with regard to access and interconnection, and the interoperability of services, and lays down procedures to ensure that obligations imposed by NRAs on operators designated with SMP are reviewed and withdrawn once the relevant market is effectively competitive.[33]

1–145 Definition of "access" — The definition of "access" in the Access Directive has been broadened and fine-tuned from that contained in the ONP Interconnection Directive, in order to cover the making available of all facilities and/or services for the purpose of providing electronic communications services as defined under the Framework Directive.[34] It covers *inter alia*: (i) access to network elements and associated facilities, such as the local loop and the facilities and services necessary to provide services over the local loop; (ii) access to physical infrastructures, such as buildings, ducts and masts; (iii) access to the relevant software systems including operational access systems; (iv) access to number translation or systems offering equivalent functionality (indeed network operators who control access to their own customers do so on the basis of unique numbers or addresses from a published numbering or addressing range); (v) access to fixed and mobile networks, including for services; (vi) access to conditional access systems for digital television services; and (vii) access to virtual networks.

1–146 Definition of "interconnection" — Interconnection is a particular form of network access. It consists of the linking of the communications networks of the same or different undertakings in order to allow the users of one undertaking to communicate with the users of another undertaking or to access services provided by another undertaking.[35] Interconnection is thus one of the most important elements involved in creating a fully competitive communications market. For new entrants, interconnection, in particular to public switched telephone or mobile networks, and access to the end-users of such networks, is essential for them to enter the market and develop their own network services. Incumbent operators, or others with market power, have an obvious incentive to impede access by new entrants to their networks and to end-users, by either refusing interconnection or charging excessive and/or discriminating prices for interconnection. As a result, because of the strong market position of incumbent operators of fixed public telephone networks

(Access Directive, para.1–011, n.29, Art.2). A public communications network is defined as "an electronic communications network used, in whole or in part, for the provision of publicly available electronic communications services" while an electronic communications network is defined as "transmission systems and, where applicable, switching equipment and other resources which permit the conveyance of signals between defined termination points by wire, by radio, by optical or by other electromagnetic means, including satellite networks, fixed (circuit- and packet-switched, including Internet) and mobile terrestrial networks, electricity cable systems, to the extent that they are used for the purpose of transmitting signals, networks used for radio and television broadcasting, and cable TV networks, irrespective of the type of information conveyed". Electronic communications services are defined as "services whose provision consists wholly or partly in the transmission and routing of signals on electronic communications networks, with the exclusion of services providing or exercising editorial control over content transmitted using electronic communications networks and services; it does not include information society services which do not consist wholly or mainly in the conveyance of signals on electronic communications networks". See also para.1–013 *et seq.*, above.

[33] Access Directive, para.1–011, n.29, Art.1.

[34] *ibid.*, Art.2(a).

[35] *ibid.*, Art.2(b). From the combination of this provision with Art.2 of the Framework Directive, where electronic communications networks are defined, it would seem that the Access Directive, para.1–009, n.25, would, in principle, be applicable also to internet backbone providers for peering or transit agreements. On this issue, see, however, para.3–015 below, for a more extensive review.

(and established mobile operators) and the risk of them engaging in anti-competitive behaviour, it was considered that interconnection could not be left entirely subject to commercial negotiation and that a regulatory framework was needed to ensure regulation of operators with market power. This framework was originally contained in the ONP Interconnection Directive and a modified framework is now contained in the Access Directive.

1–147 Access for content providers — The Access Directive applies only in relation to "electronic communications services", so that, for example, access to a cable network can only be requested by another operator if the cable network provider in question has SMP, and mandated if access is required to provide "electronic communications services". Therefore, electronic communications services covers any transmission services but excludes the provision of content (defined as services providing, or exercising editorial control over content).[36] Accordingly, a broadcaster, because it provides content, cannot rely on the terms of the Access Directive to seek access to a cable network. The broadcaster could only rely on competition law or provisions of national law to obtain access.[37] Article 31 of the Universal Service Directive gives Member States the right to impose, on the basis of clearly defined general interest objectives, proportionate and transparent "*must carry*" obligations on cable television network providers. Television broadcasters may therefore be able to benefit from national "*must carry*" rules (see para.2–063 below). In relation to internet Service Providers (ISPs), a distinction should be made between those that only provide content, *i.e.* web-based services, and those that also provide internet access services.[38] ISPs that provide internet access can rely on the provisions of the Access Directive but undertakings that only provide web-based content cannot, as web-based content services fall outside the scope of the Access Directive.

2. Principles Governing Access and Interconnection

1–148 No restriction on access and interconnection — Member States must ensure that there are no restrictions preventing electronic communications organisations (whether in the same or different Member States) from negotiating access and/or interconnection agreements amongst themselves. Technical and commercial arrangements for access and interconnection should, as a matter of principle, be a matter for agreement between the parties involved, subject to the provisions of the Directive.[39] National measures obliging operators to offer different access and/or interconnection conditions for equivalent services and/or imposing obligations not related to the actual access or interconnection services provided must not be maintained.[40]

[36] *ibid.*

[37] In contrast, it would seem that a textual argument could be made that a cable operator, merely transmitting TV broadcast (and regardless of whether it exercises editorial control over the content transmitted via its cable network or not), could rely on the provisions of the Access Directive to obtain mandatory access to another cable network (having SMP). Indeed, such use of the cable network falls within the meaning of transmission services under Art.2 of the Framework Directive, para.1–009, n.25.

[38] Framework Directive, para.1–009, n.25, Recital 10.

[39] Access Directive, para.1–011, n.29, Art.3(1).

[40] *ibid.*, Art.3(2). This provision is, however, without prejudice to Art.31 of the Universal Service Directive, para.1–011, n.30, (relating to national "*must carry*" regulations) in respect of the transmission of radio and television broadcasts and the Annex to the Authorisation Directive (which lists the conditions which may be imposed under a general authorisation or a usage right); see para.1–063, above. On "*must carry*" rules, see para.2–063 below.

1–149 Rights and obligations with respect to access and interconnection — If this is necessary in order to ensure the provision and inter-operability of services throughout the Community, public communications networks operators have the right and, when requested by other operators with the same rights, an obligation to negotiate access and/or interconnection, for the purpose of providing publicly available electronic communications services.[41] This right is granted to, and this obligation is imposed on, operators of public telephone networks or services, public mobile networks and services, and any other operators transmitting communications services to the public. Information exchanged during such negotiations or during the provision of access or interconnection services must be considered as confidential and cannot be used for any other purposes or be passed to any other party, including other businesses or departments of the recipient for whom possession of such information may confer a competitive advantage.[42] Access and interconnection services must be provided on terms and conditions that are consistent with any obligations imposed by an NRA under Articles 5 to 13 of the Access Directive.[43] Article 5 of the Access Directive imposes general obligations on NRAs to encourage and, where appropriate, ensure adequate access, interconnection and interoperability of services so as to promote efficiency, sustainable competition and maximise benefits for end-users. This may involve imposing obligations on all operators, even if they do not have SMP.[44] Member States must also ensure that NRAs are empowered to intervene on their own initiative where this is justified, or at the request of either party where commercial negotiations have failed to ensure the achievement of the policy objectives of the Framework Directive.[45] The NRA's intervention must be in accordance with Articles 6, 7, 20 and 21 of the Framework Directive, which deal respectively with competition and transparency mechanisms, consolidation of the internal market and the resolution of national and cross-border disputes.[46]

1–150 Obligations on non-SMP operators — In certain circumstances, NRAs may impose obligations on operators that do not have SMP.[47] In doing so, the NRAs must comply with their obligations under Article 6 (consultation and transparency mechanism)[48] and Article 7 (consolidating the internal market for electronic communications)[49] and ensure that conditions and obligations imposed are objective, transparent, proportionate and non-discriminatory.[50] Some of these obligations relate to access to conditional access systems, application programme interfaces and electronic programming guides to ensure accessibility to specified digital radio and TV services.[51] Other obligations may be imposed, where they are necessary to ensure end-to-end connectivity, on undertakings that control access to end-users. These obligations may include, in justified cases, an obligation to interconnect

---

[41] Access Directive, para.1–011, n.29, Art.4(1).

[42] *ibid.*, Art.4(3).

[43] Access Directive, para.1–011, n.29, Art.4.1, last sentence, which states that "*operators shall offer access and interconnection to other undertakings on terms and conditions consistent with obligations imposed by the NRA pursuant to Articles 5, 6, 7 and 8* [of the same Directive]" (emphasis added). Most of these obligations apply only to operators designated with SMP.

[44] Access Directive, para.1–011, n.29, Art.5(1).

[45] *ibid.*, Art.5(4).

[46] See, above, para.1-044 *et seq.*

[47] See para.1–149, above.

[48] See para.1–045, above.

[49] See para.1–047, above.

[50] Access Directive, para.1–011, n.29, Art.5(3).

[51] *ibid.*, Arts 5(1), 5(2) and 6, Annex I.

their networks.[52] In addition, NRAs may impose obligations on non-SMP operators under the provisions of various other directives[53]: (i) obligations requiring co-location and facility sharing where rules relating to environmental protection, health, security or town planning deprive other undertakings of the ability to install their own facilities on, under or over land[54]; (ii) obligations for accounting separation on undertakings providing electronic communications services that enjoy special or exclusive rights in other sectors[55]; (iii) obligations relating to commitments made by an undertaking in the course of a competitive or comparative selection procedure for a right of use of radio frequency (*e.g.* coverage and/or roaming requirements)[56]; (iv) obligations to handle calls to subscribers using specific numbering resources and obligations necessary for the implementation of number portability[57]; (v) obligations based on the relevant provisions of the E-Privacy Directive[58]; and (vi) obligations that can be imposed on operators without SMP in order to comply with the Community's international commitments.[59]

1–151 **End-to-end connectivity** — In markets where there continue to be large differences in negotiating power between undertakings, and where some undertakings rely on infrastructure provided by others for delivery of their services, the Access Directive provides NRAs with the means to impose access obligations on those operators controlling access to end-users,[60] even if they do not possess SMP. Such obligations may include, in justified cases, network interconnection, where this is not already the case, on the basis of objective, transparent, proportionate and non-discriminatory terms.[61]

1–152 **Obligations on SMP operators** — When an NRA decides that an operator has SMP, it must impose upon that operator at least one *ex ante* obligation.[62] In doing so, NRAs are required to choose obligations that are proportionate to the problems to be remedied, in accordance with the objectives set by the Framework Directive.[63] The following obligations may, *inter alia*, be imposed on a company with SMP at wholesale level: (i) obligations under the existing 1998 Framework

[52] *ibid.*, Art.5(1)(a).

[53] *ibid.*, Art.8(3), second indent.

[54] Framework Directive, para.1–009, n.25, Art.12.

[55] *ibid.*, Art.13.

[56] Authorisation Directive, para.1–011, n.28, Condition B(7) of Annex, applied via Art.6(1).

[57] Universal Service Directive, para.1–011, n.30, Arts 27, 28, and 30.

[58] See para.1–232 *et seq.*, below.

[59] This provision should, however, be read against Art.11 of the Liberalisation Directive, para.1–012, n.33, which requires Member States to take all appropriate measures to eliminate any incompatibilities of international treaties with EC competition rules in the field of satellite and satellite-based services provision. For a comprehensive analysis of the impact of this directive on satellite communications, see para.1–139, above.

[60] According to Recital 6 of the Access Directive, control of means of access may entail ownership or control of the physical link to end-users (either fixed or mobile), and/or the ability to change or withdraw the national number or numbers needed to access an end-user's network termination point. This would be the case for example if network operators were to restrict unreasonably end-users' choice for access to internet portals and services.

[61] Access Directive, para.1–011, n.29, Art.5(1)(a) and (3).

[62] Framework Directive, para.1–009, n.25, Art.16(4).

[63] Art.8 of the Framework Directive, para.1–009, n.25, states that the key aim of the New Regulatory Framework is to enhance user and consumer benefits in terms of choice, price and quality by promoting and ensuring effective competition. See para.1–010, above.

(which must be maintained until their appropriateness under the New Regulatory Framework has been determined by the NRA)[64]; (ii) transparency obligations[65]; (iii) non-discrimination obligations[66]; (iv) accounting separation obligations[67]; (v) obligations requiring mandatory access to be granted to specific network facilities, including access to technical interfaces, protocols or other key technologies, as well as interconnection of networks[68]; and (vi) tariff regulation, and obligations that tariffs be cost-oriented and that accounting separation be maintained.[69] The Universal Service Directive sets the obligations which may be imposed at retail level, such as the imposition of: (i) tariff regulation[70]; (ii) provision of the minimum set of leased lines[71]; or (iii) carrier selection and/or pre-selection services.[72] However, regulatory controls at retail level should only be imposed where NRAs consider that the relevant wholesale or related measures would fail to achieve the objective of ensuring effective competition.[73] Where NRAs intend to impose obligations concerning access and interconnection other than those listed in the Access Directive, they must submit a request for Commission approval of their proposed course of action. The Commission must seek the advice of the Communications Committee before adopting any approval decision.[74] Any decision of the NRA to adopt such obligations must be reasoned, and include an explanation of the reasons for the proposed measures and why they are proportionate.[75] This implies that any such measures must be for the achievement of a legitimate aim,[76] and be both necessary and the least burdensome.[77] Therefore, any such measures should reflect competitive conditions in the relevant market and be enforced as closely as practicable to the activities being regulated.

1–153 Obligations under the 1998 Framework — Under the ONP Interconnection Directive, public communications operators designated as having SMP on the basis of the 25 per cent market share test, were required to meet all reasonable requests for access to their networks, including access at points other than the network termination offered to the majority of users.[78] In these cases, the organisation providing access could refuse to provide special network access if there were objective technical difficulties in providing access at the network termination point requested.[79] NRAs are

---

[64] See para.1–153, below.

[65] Access Directive, para.1–011, n.29, Art.9; see para.1–154, below.

[66] *ibid.*, Art.10; see para.1–154, below.

[67] *ibid.*, Art.11; see para.1–155, below.

[68] *ibid.*, Art.12; see para.1–158, below.

[69] *ibid.*, Art.13; see para.1–193, below.

[70] Universal Service Directive, para.1–011, n.30, Art.16.

[71] *ibid.*, Art.18.

[72] *ibid.*, Art.19.

[73] *ibid.*, Recital 26.

[74] See Arts 7(4) and 22, Framework Directive, para.1–009, n.25, as explained by para.116 of the SMP Guidelines, para.1–012, n.35. For a comprehensive analysis of the co-ordination mechanisms under the New Regulatory Framework, see paras 1–044 to 1–051, above.

[75] Framework Directive, para.1–009, n.25, Art.16(4); Access Directive, para.1–011, n.29, Art.8(4); Universal Service Directive, para.1–011, n.30, Art.17(2). See also SMP Guidelines, para.1–012, n.35, para.117.

[76] As defined in Art.8 of the Framework Directive, para.1–009, n.25: see para.1–010, above.

[77] SMP Guidelines, para.1–012, para.118.

[78] ONP Interconnection Directive, para.1–006, n.23, Art.4.

[79] ONP Interconnection Directive, para.1–006, n.23, Art.10; see also Access Directive, para.1–011, n.29, Recital 19, which refers to the Commission Access Notice, cited in para.5–004, n.18, below, and discussed in respect to refusal to provide access, in para.6–043 *et seq.*

required to maintain all obligations[80] that were imposed on public communications operators with SMP under the 1998 regulatory framework until they have conducted their market analysis and made any designations of SMP in accordance with the new concept of SMP applied to the relevant markets indicated in the Recommendation on the Relevant Markets, *e.g.* those relating to voice services at fixed locations of the public telephone network.[81] In the light of such analysis, these obligations may be maintained, withdrawn, or modified in a manner consistent with Article 16 of the Framework Directive including the holding of a period of public consultation in which interested parties must be heard.[82]

1–154 Non-discrimination and transparency — NRAs may impose obligations on operators that have been designated as possessing SMP in order to ensure, *inter alia*, that with respect to access and interconnection services provided by them: (i) they offer access and/or interconnection on a non-discrimination basis[83]; (ii) that they make available all necessary information (including accounting information, technical specifications, network characteristics, terms and conditions for supply and use, and prices) on request to organisations considering interconnection in an unbundled form[84]; (iii) that they publish a reference interconnection offer, which is sufficiently unbundled to ensure that other undertakings pay only for the services that they require[85]; and (iv) that information relating to interconnection and/or access agreements is provided to the relevant NRA and (except those parts dealing with commercial strategy) made publicly available, according to standards set by the NRA.[86]

1–155 Accounting separation — Member States may require organisations that have been designated as possessing SMP to keep separate accounts for each activity, in a format and using a methodology specified by the NRA.[87] This has two principal purposes. The first is to assist the

---

[80] In practice, these obligations were: transparency; non-discrimination; accounting separation; mandatory interconnection of networks, including access at points other than the network termination offered to the majority of end-users; price regulation and cost orientation. See ONP Interconnection Directive, para.1–006, n.23, Arts 4, 6, 7, 8, 11, 12 and 14; ONP Voice Telephony Directive, para.1–006, n.20, Art.16; and Leased Lines Directive, para.1–006, n.20, Arts 7 and 8.

[81] Access Directive, para.1–011, n.29, Art.7(1).

[82] *ibid.*, Art.7; and Framework Directive, para.1–009, n.25, Arts 6 and 16.

[83] Access Directive, para.1–011, n.29, Art.10. In particular, this requires equivalent conditions to be offered to undertakings in equivalent circumstances that are providing equivalent services. It also requires interconnection conditions (including quality) to be the same for the operators as those under which interconnection is provided to the SMP operator's own services, subsidiaries and partners. Different tariffs for different types of interconnection may, however, be set. This provision is without prejudice to Art.3 of the Liberalisation Directive (discussed above in para.1–058), which requires Member States to ensure that vertically integrated public undertakings that are in a dominant position do not discriminate in favour of their own activities, regardless of any SMP designation. This would imply that NRAs may impose non-discrimination obligations on dominant vertically integrated undertakings, even where they are not designated with SMP; and, in this case, competitors may rely on the course of action available under Art.86(3) of the EC Treaty, on which the Liberalisation Directive is based (see, below, para.1–286).

[84] *ibid.*, Art.9(1).

[85] *ibid.*, Art.9(2). The NRA may impose changes to reference offers, in order to give effect to obligations imposed under the Access Directive. See, below, para.1–162 regarding the provision of access to the unbundled local loop, including the reference offer for such service.

[86] *ibid.*, Art.9(1) and (3).

[87] *ibid.*, Art.11. Under Art.13 of the Framework Directive, para.1–009, n.25, accounting separation is also required for organisations which operate public communications networks and/or publicly available electronic

NRA in setting tariffs for access and interconnection. The second is to assist it in deterring undue discrimination and unfair cross-subsidisation from one activity to another. The NRA can request that accounting records are provided to it so that it can verify compliance with obligations of transparency and non-discrimination. These records can include details of payments received from third parties. NRAs may publish such accounting information if this will contribute to an open and competitive market, provided that they respect EU and national rules on protecting commercial confidentiality.[88]

1–156 The Commission has adopted a recommendation relating to the implementation of accounting separation and cost accounting systems that the NRA can require to be put in place by operators designated as possessing SMP (the "Accounting Recommendation").[89] The Accounting Recommendation provides that NRAs require operators with SMP to separate their operating costs, capital employed and revenues into at least the following broad business activities: (i) their core network, which provides a range of wholesale interconnection services, including switching and conveyance of calls, technical services related to the development and maintenance of private networks, and services required to support the development of competition (such as number portability and carrier selection); (ii) their local access network, which provides connections from subscribers to the core network, which includes the costs and capital associated with providing and maintaining these connections; (iii) their retail sales, which includes those activities involving the supply of telephony services to end-users (*i.e.* line rental, leased lines, calls, payphones and the provision of directory information); and (iv) their other activities, including rental, repair and maintenance of customer equipment or interests in non-telecommunications activities.[90]

1–157 NRAs may require operators to provide detailed separate accounts for specific activities within each of the four branches of activity, for example, by making a distinction between fixed and mobile networks and services, cable television and local, national and international calls.[91] The Accounting Recommendation indicates that accounting separation should be undertaken on the basis of cost causation, *i.e.* revenues and costs must be allocated to the relevant services or products.[92] It also indicates that asset valuations be made on a forward-looking basis on the basis of their current value in the ownership of an efficient operator, in accordance with current cost accounting methodology.[93] Finally, the Accounting Recommendation recommends that the accounting information provided by an operator should be made available to interested parties at a sufficient level of detail[94] to enable them to verify that there has been no undue discrimination or

communications services and have special or exclusive rights in any Member State for the provision of services in other sectors, provided they have an annual turnover in electronic communications activities in the Member States of more than €50 million, or such a lower turnover as an NRA may specify. See para.1–081, above.

[88] Access Directive, para.1–011, n.29, Art.11(2).

[89] Commission Recommendation of April 8, 1998 on interconnection in a liberalised telecommunications market (Part 2 — Accounting separation and cost accounting), O.J. 1998 L141/6.

[90] *ibid.*, Art.2.

[91] *ibid.*

[92] *ibid.*, Art.3.

[93] *ibid.*, Art.4. On cost accounting methodologies, see paras 1–182 *et seq.*, below.

[94] *ibid.*

cross-subsidy and to enable the average costs of unbundled access and interconnection services to be identified.[95]

1–158   Access to, and use of, specific network facilities — NRAs may require operators that have been designated as possessing SMP: (i) when requested by third parties, to provide reasonable access to specific network elements and/or facilities, including unbundled access to the terminating segments of leased lines and the local loop; (ii) to negotiate in good faith with undertakings that request access; (iii) not to withdraw access to facilities already granted; (iv) to provide specified services on a wholesale basis for resale by third parties, including the provision of leased line capacity to other suppliers of electronic communications networks or services; (v) to grant open access to technical interfaces, protocols or other key technologies that are indispensable for the interoperability of services or virtual networks; (vi) to provide co-location or other forms of facility sharing, including duct, building or mast sharing; (vii) to provide specified services needed to ensure interoperability of end-to-end services to users, including facilities for intelligent network services or roaming on mobile networks; (viii) to provide access to operational support systems or similar software systems necessary to ensure fair competition in the provision of services; and (ix) to interconnect networks or network facilities.[96] The conditions in which such access is provided must be objective, transparent, proportionate and non-discriminatory.[97] Access must also be provided on a fair, reasonable and timely basis. The purpose of such obligations is to ensure the emergence of a competitive market at the retail level: if organisations with SMP were to refrain from giving such access or to provide it only on terms and conditions that are unreasonable, competing suppliers would not be able to enter the market and provide effective competition. This would be to the detriment of end-users' interests.

1–159   Refusal of access — Once obligations requiring access to be given have been imposed, the operator cannot refuse it for any reason, although it clearly cannot be required to provide types of access that are not within its powers to provide.[98] Operators that have been designated as having SMP must be given the opportunity to comment within a reasonable period on any draft measure proposed by the NRAs.[99] The NRA must take a number of criteria into account in deciding if specific network facilities must be made available to third parties: (i) the economic and technical viability of businesses seeking access to use or install competing facilities (taking into account the rate of development of competition in the market, the nature and type of interconnection and access involved); (ii) the feasibility of providing the proposed access, in relation to the capacity

---

[95] *ibid.*, Art.3.

[96] Access Directive, para.1–011, n.29, Art.12(1).

[97] *ibid.*, Art.5(3).

[98] *ibid.*, Art.12(2).

[99] Framework Directive, para.1–009, n.25, Art.6. According to the SMP Guidelines, para.1–012, n.35, at para.145, the NRAs' decisions should not be delayed excessively as this can impede the development of the market. For the decisions relating to the existence and designation of undertakings with SMP and the contextual imposition of *ex ante* regulation, the Commission considers that a period of two months would be reasonable for the public consultation. Different periods could be used in some cases if justified. Conversely, where a draft SMP decision is proposed on the basis of the results of an earlier consultation, the length of consultation period for these decisions may well be shorter than two months. See also Section B of this chapter, in particular para.1–044, above.

available; (iii) the initial investment by the facility owner, bearing in mind the risks involved in making the investments; (iv) the need to safeguard long-term competition; (v) where appropriate, any relevant intellectual property rights; and (vi) the provision of pan-European services.[1]

1–160   Local Loop Unbundling Regulation — By its very nature, the local loop presents all the characteristics of a national monopoly (an essential facility). New entrants do not have widespread alternative network infrastructures and are unable, with traditional technologies, to match the economies of scale and the coverage of operators designated as having SMP. This results from the fact that these operators rolled out their metallic local access infrastructures over significant periods of time protected by exclusive rights and were able to cross-subsidise investment costs through monopoly rents.[2]

1–161   Under the Access Directive, operators designated as having SMP in the market for wholesale local access, for the purpose of providing broadband internet services, and in particular, in the market segment for the unbundled access (including shared access) to metallic loops and sub-loops, may be required to provide unbundled access to their local access networks.[3] However, this provision is without prejudice to those of the Regulation on unbundling of the local loop (the so-called "LLU Regulation"),[4] which was adopted as part of the previous regulatory regime and which should continue to apply until it is repealed.[5] For the purposes of the LLU Regulation, an operator is rebuttably presumed to have SMP when it has market shares of 25 per cent or more in the market for the provision of fixed public telephone networks and services.[6] It is presently unclear whether the LLU Regulation will be repealed once the New Regulatory Framework and the specific provisions regarding the local loop, embodied in the Access Directive,[7] have been fully implemented at national level. Repeal of the LLU Regulation should require a legislative proposal by the Commission and new legislation adopted by the European Parliament and the Council.

1–162   *Reference offer* — The LLU Regulation requires operators notified as having SMP to publish, from December 31, 2000, and keep updated, a reference offer for access to their local loops and related facilities. This should be sufficiently unbundled, so that the beneficiary does not have to pay for network elements or facilities that are not necessary for the supply of its services. The Annex to the LLU Regulation provides a minimum list of items that are to be included in the reference offer to be published by notified operators. The reference must contain a description of the offer, associated terms and conditions, including charges.[8]

---

[1] Access Directive, para.1–011, n.29, Art.12(2), (a)–(f). This provision clearly includes several elements of the essential facilities doctrine, the latter being discussed more extensively in para.6–043 *et seq.*, below.

[2] On the status of unbundled access to the local loop under EC Treaty competition rules, see paras 6–043 and 6–070, below.

[3] Access Directive, para.1–011, n.29, Art.12(1)(a).

[4] Regulation No.2887/2000 of December 18, 2000 on unbundled access to the local loop, O.J. 2000 L336/4 ("LLU Regulation").

[5] Recital 43 of the Framework Directive, para.1–009, n.25, requires the Commission to monitor the transition from the 1998 regulatory framework to the New Regulatory Framework and "*in particular, at an appropriate time, to bring forward a proposal to repeal the [LLU Regulation]*" (emphasis added).

[6] LLU Regulation, para.1–161, n.4, Art.2(a).

[7] See, above, para.1–158.

[8] LLU Regulation, para.1–161, n.4, Art.3(1).

1–163 *Provision of unbundled access to the local loop* — The LLU Regulation applies only to the "traditional" copper loop, *i.e.* the "last mile" of the narrowband telephone network.[9] It requires notified operators to meet all reasonable requests from third parties that are authorised to provide communications services for unbundled access to that local loop and related facilities (including the provision of collocation facilities, cable connections and relevant information technology systems). This shall include "shared access" which enables competitors to offer broadband services to the consumer over the high-frequency (non-voice) part of the frequency spectrum of the copper line whilst voice telephony continues to be offered by the notified operator over the same line. Access to the local loop must be provided under transparent, fair and non-discriminatory conditions.[10] This includes providing third parties with facilities equal to those provided for the notified operator's own services (or to associated companies) under the same conditions and timescales. Disputes may be referred to the NRA.[11] Charges for access to the local loop must be cost-oriented until such time as the NRA determines that the local access market is sufficiently competitive.[12] Requests for access to the notified operator's local loop may only be refused on the basis of objective criteria, relating to technical feasibility or the need to maintain network integrity. NRAs may also intervene wherever justified to ensure non-discrimination, fair competition, economic efficiency and maximum benefits for users.[13]

1–164 *Control by NRAs* — NRAs must ensure that charges for unbundled access to the local loop fosters fair and sustainable competition.[14] In doing so, NRAs may, at their own initiative, change the terms of the reference offer, including prices, where this is justified.[15] Notified operators must supply the NRAs with all relevant information needed for the implementation of the LLU

---

[9] *ibid.*, Art.2(c), which defines the "local loop" as "the physical twisted metallic pair circuit connecting the network termination point at the subscriber's premises to the main distribution frame or equivalent facility of the fixed public telephone network".

[10] Incumbent operators have argued that they are in compliance with the non-discrimination requirements imposed by the LLU regulation, by granting their competitors the same access conditions that they apply to their downstream arm (at one extreme at the local DSL access multiplexer, or DSLAM, at the other at a national point of presence, or POP). But in its Eighth Implementation Report, above para.1–108, n.52, the Commission found that this may impose heavy transmission costs on a new entrant seeking access, whose network does not have the same geographic coverage and topography of the incumbent's network, or, alternatively, condemn it to the simple role of reseller if it cannot control the quality and data rate supplied to the distant customer connected through the incumbent's network to its POP. In addition, access at the ATM (asynchronous transfer mode) level, *i.e.* the software which enables the organisation of a digital signal in such a way as to allow very high speed transmission of the signal, is necessary to new entrants, along with access at DSLAM and POP where appropriate, in order to allow them to make full use of their network (or alternative network offerings) and to control the technical characteristics of the connection to the end-user. In this regard, it should be recalled that under general EU law it is settled that the non-discrimination principle is not to be applied in a purely formal way, but taking into account its underlying objective, which is to open up the market.

[11] *ibid.*, Art.3(2).

[12] *ibid.*, Arts 3(3) and 4(4).

[13] *ibid.*, Art.4(3).

[14] *ibid.*, Art.4(1). The Commission has the mandate to oversee that the Regulation is applied properly by the NRAs. In its Eighth Implementation Report, para.1–108, n.52, the Commission found that two years after the Regulation had come into force, unbundling of incumbents' local loops in most of the Member States was still not satisfactory.

[15] LLU Regulation, para.1–161, n.4, Art.4(2)(a).

Regulation.[16] NRAs may also intervene wherever justified to ensure non-discrimination, fair competition, economic efficiency and a maximum of benefits for users.[17] Where a dispute arises between the parties involved, for example because access is refused on the basis of alleged technical difficulties or if a third party considers that the terms of access do not meet the requirements of the LLU Regulation, it may be referred to the NRA, which must resolve it in the shortest possible timeframe and in any case within four months.[18]

1–165   Leased lines — The Universal Service Directive aims to ensure availability throughout the EU of good quality publicly available services, including a minimum set of analogue and digital leased lines.[19] The objective of the Access Directive is to eliminate technical restrictions on the interconnection between leased lines and public communications networks. The two directives require Member States to continue to apply obligations for access to, and the provision of, a minimum harmonised set of leased lines, that were imposed by NRAs pursuant to the ONP Leased Lines Directive,[20] until such time as the NRA, following a market analysis, has determined that there is effective competition in the relevant markets for the provision of local dedicated capacity (wholesale local or terminating segments of leased lines) and the minimum harmonised set of leased lines (at the retail level), in accordance with the provision of Article 16 of the Framework Directive.[21]

1–166   *Provision of the minimum harmonised set of leased lines by certain operators with significant market power* — If an NRA, having conducted its market analysis in accordance with Article 16(3) of the Universal Service Directive on the continued appropriateness of the conditions imposed by it under the ONP Leased Lines Directive (as amended), determines that the market for the provision of all or part of the minimum harmonised set of leased lines is not effectively competitive, it must identify undertakings with SMP in respect to that market in all or part of its territory.[22] The designated operator(s) must provide a minimum harmonised set of analogue and

---

[16] *ibid.*, Art.4(2)(b).

[17] *ibid.*, Art.4(3).

[18] *ibid.*, Art.4(5), and the Framework Directive, para.1–009, n.25, Art.20(1). For a comprehensive discussion of the dispute resolution procedures under the Framework Directive, see para.1–176.

[19] See Art.18 of the Universal Service Directive, para.1–011, n.30, which supersedes Art.7 of the ONP Leased Lines Directive, para.1–006, n.20. The Universal Service Directive does not include an explicit definition of "leased lines". Leased lines, however, clearly fall within the category of "associated facilities" that are associatied with electronic communications networks and services, referred to in Art.2(e) of the Framework Directive, para.1–009, n.25. According to Art.2 of the ONP Leased Lines Directive, leased lines are telecommunications facilities that involve the provision of full or partial circuits for the transparent transmission capacity between network termination points and which do not include on-demand switching (*i.e.* switching functions which the user can control as part of the leased line provision). On July 25, 2003, the Commission adopted its first decision setting out the minimum set of leased lines to be made available by incumbent operators under Art.18 of the Universal Service Directive (yet to be published at the time of writing): see Commission Press Release IP/03/1114 of July 25, 2003.

[20] See, above, ONP Leased Lines Directive, para.1–006, n.20.

[21] Universal Service Directive, para.1–011, n.30, Art.16(1)(c), and Access Directive, Art.7(1). For a discussion of the provisions Art.16 of the Framework Directive, para.1–009, n.25, see para.1–174, below. The Commission has stated that in general "following the successful liberalisation of electronic communications, there is now competitive supply of leased lines in the EU. Consequently the need to require provision of these leased line services nationwide in the Member States is decreasing": see Commission Press Release IP/03/1114 of July 25, 2003.

[22] Universal Service Directive, para.1–011, n.30, Art.18(1).

digital leased lines (with capacity) up to 2 Mbit/s with harmonised technical characteristics that are identified in the list of standards published by the Commission on a non-discriminatory, cost-oriented and transparent basis.[23] In accordance with Article 18(2) of the Universal Service Directive, NRAs are required to withdraw the obligations concerning leased lines when the relevant market is effectively competitive.

1–167 *Conditions of access to leased lines* — Operators that have been designated as possessing SMP in the markets of local dedicated capacity (wholesale local or terminating segments, and trunk segments of leased lines) must be required to eliminate restrictions on access to the terminating as well as the trunk segments of leased lines of their networks. Access to leased lines (*i.e.* technical characteristics, tariffs, supply and usage conditions, licensing and declaration requirements, conditions for attachment of terminal equipment) must be provided on the basis of the conditions specified in Annex VII of the Universal Service Directive.[24] These must be based on objective criteria, be transparent, non-discriminatory, guarantee equality of access and be cost-based.[25] In the light of market developments, NRAs may also decide to impose obligations set out in the Access Directive, where this is appropriate to the problem to be remedied. In determining whether an operator has market power, the NRA must take into account the organisation's ability to influence the conditions of the leased lines market, its turnover relative to the size of the market, its access to financial resources and its experience in providing products and services in the market.[26]

1–168 *Transparency and cost-oriented tariffs for leased lines* — Member States must ensure that the tariffs for leased lines provided by operators designated as having SMP follow the basic principles of cost orientation and transparency.[27] In particular, tariffs for leased lines must be independent of the type of application for which the leased lines are used.[28] Under the principle of transparency, tariffs will normally contain an initial connection charge and a periodic rental charge; where tariffs are differentiated this must be indicated.[29] The conditions under which leased

---

[23] See, for example, list of standards and/or specifications for electronic communications networks, services and associated facilities and services, O.J. 2002 C331/32. On the list of standards, see also paras 1–026 and 1–174 in this chapter.

[24] Universal Service Directive, para.1–011, n.30, Art.18(1).

[25] Universal Service Directive, para.1–011, n.30, Art.18(1), Annex VII.

[26] SMP Guidelines, para.1–012, n.35, para.77.

[27] Universal Service Directive, para.1–011, n.30, Art.18(1), and Annex VII, paras 2 and 3.

[28] Although this is not explicitly provided for in the Universal Service Directive, para.1–011, n.30, this was required by Art.10(1)(a) of the ONP Leased Lines Directive, para.1–006, n.20, and pursuant to Art.16(1)(c) of the Universal Service Directive, para.1–011, n.30, and it continues to apply to those operators who were designated as having SMP under the ONP Leased Lines Directive until the responsible NRA decides to withdraw such obligations. It is also part of the general principle of non-discrimination.

[29] The Commission has adopted a recommendation on the pricing of short-distance leased lines, in November 24, 1999 available at *http://www.europa.eu.int/ISPO/infosoc/telecom policy/en/ic-ll-final-en.pdf*. This Recommendation sets price ceilings for the leased lines that incumbent telecommunications companies supply to other operators and which can carry high volumes of voice, data and multimedia traffic. The recommended price ceilings aim to provide guidance to NRAs in imposing tariff regulation. Where an operator is charging more than the recommended price for a leased line, the operator should have to justify the higher cost to the NRA. The NRA can also oblige the operator to reduce its prices. In addition, the Recommendation encourages the unbundling of the local loop and other measures to stimulate competition in local access networks. Moreover, the Commission opened a sectoral inquiry into the provision and pricing of leased lines, which aim to establish whether current commercial practices and prices infringed EC competition rules, in

lines are made available must be published, include the typical delivery period (which is the period counted from the date when the user has made a firm request for a leased line, in which 95 per cent of all leased lines of the same type have been put through to the customers), interconnection in the ordering procedure, the minimum entrant period, the typical repair time and any refund procedure.[30] Operators are also required to put in place cost accounting systems suitable for the implementation of these principles and to submit such information to the Commission on request.[31]

1–169 *Control by NRAs* — NRAs decide, on a case-by-case basis, whether to allow or prohibit measures adopted by public communications operators such as the refusal to provide a leased line, interruption of the provision of leased lines or reduction of the availability of leased lines features for reasons of alleged failure to comply with the usage conditions by users of leased lines.[32] In addition, where NRAs consider that the achieved performance for the provision of the minimum set of leased lines does not meet users' needs, they may define appropriate targets for the supply conditions.[33] The Universal Service Directive gives NRAs the power to specify performance and compliance reporting obligations, thus potentially making the detection of high prices and intentional delay in the provision of local leased lines possible to achieve. Indeed, the powers of investigation of the NRAs have been reinforced under the New Regulatory Framework, and evidence from other proceedings conducted by other NRAs, national competition authorities and the Commission could also be used by NRAs and the Commission in investigating such cases.[34]

1–170 *Non-discrimination* — NRAs must ensure that operators that are subject to the provisions of the Universal Service Directive adhere to the principle of non-discrimination when providing leased lines. These must apply similar conditions in similar circumstances to operators providing similar services (*e.g.* competing value-added service providers) and must provide leased lines to others under the same conditions and of the same quality as they provide for their own services, or those of their subsidiaries or partners.[35]

1–171 Conditional access systems — Where a broadcaster does not have its own transmission network (such as a satellite platform), it needs access to ancillary services in order to provide its services over networks. These ancillary services include some or all conditional access systems, application programme interfaces (API) and electronic programming guides (EPG). Although the

---

particular the prohibition of restrictive practices (Art.81 of the EC Treaty) and abuses of dominant position (Art.82 of the EC Treaty); Commission Press Release IP/99/786, October 22, 1999. This inquiry was closed on December 11, 2002: see Commission Press Release IP/02/1852. See also para.6–005, below.

[30] Universal Service Directive, para.1–011, n.30, Art.18(1) and Annex VII.

[31] *ibid.*

[32] *ibid.*, Art.16(1)(c), and Access Directive, para.1–011, n.29, Art.7(1), in their part where they maintain in force the applicable provisions of the ONP Leased Lines Directive, para.1–006, n.20, but only until the responsible NRA considers they are necessary and appropriate in the light of its market analysis.

[33] Universal Service Directive, para.1–011, n.30, Art.18 and Annex VII (para.3.3).

[34] Framework Directive, para.1–009, n.25, Art.3(5), as explained by SMP Guidelines, at para.136, see para.1–012, n.35, above. In the United States, the practice has emerged of setting up a common database between the requesting party and the leased lines provider, in order to allow the electronic ordering of leased lines, which would arguably be less time-consuming than traditional mailing orders, and would thus ensure a timely provisioning of these facilities, as well as provide immediate evidence of any occurred delay in their provisioning.

[35] *ibid.*, Art.18 and Annex VII(1), para.1.

New Regulatory Framework involves a separation between the regulation of transmission networks and the implementation of audio-visual policy (including the regulation of content), this
does not prejudice NRAs taking account of the links existing between them, in particular in order
to guarantee media pluralism, cultural diversity and consumer protection.[36] The application of the
EC competition rules may not be sufficient to ensure cultural diversity and media pluralism in the
area of digital television, and sector-specific regulation is needed to ensure that a wide variety of
programming and services is available and that end-users can access specific digital broadcasting
services.[37] Therefore, where it is necessary to ensure accessibility to end-users to digital radio
and television broadcasting services, operators must provide access to their APIs and EPGs, on
fair, reasonable and non-discriminatory terms, regardless of whether they have been designated
as possessing SMP.[38] Member States are also required to ensure that in relation to conditional
access services for digital radio and television and viewers within the Community: (i) conditional
access systems have the necessary technical capability for cost-effective transaction allowing the
possibility for full control by local or regional operators of the services using such conditional
access systems; (ii) that technical services are provided to broadcasters on fair, reasonable and non-
discriminatory terms and in accordance with Community competition law to ensure consumers
with decoders have access to digital broadcasts; (iii) that operators keep separate financial accounts
for their conditional access services; and (iv) when granting licences to manufacturers of consumer
equipment, holders of industrial property rights to conditional access products and systems are to
ensure that licences are granted on fair, reasonable and non-discriminatory terms so as not to deter
the inclusion in the same product of common interfaces and means specific to another access
system.[39] Their obligations may be amended in the light of market and technological developments.[40] Member States may allow NRAs to review the conditions to determine if they should be
maintained, amended or withdrawn according to an SMP assessment,[41] provided that conditions
may be amended or withdrawn if an NRA finds (i) that one or more operators do not have SMP on the
relevant market; (ii) that accessibility for end-users to broadcasting service and channels would not be
adversely affected and; (iii) that the prospects for effective competition in retail digital broadcasting
services and conditional access systems would not be adversely affected.[42] Notice of amendment or
withdrawal of conditions must also be given.[43] The provisions of the Access Directive are without
prejudice to national rules as to the presentational aspects of these EPGs and other listing and
navigational facilities.[44]

1–172   Co-location and facility sharing — Agreements for co-location or facility sharing are, in
the first instance, a matter for commercial and technical agreement between the parties concerned.
However, in certain circumstances, NRAs may impose facility and/or property sharing arrangements, including physical co-location, even on operators that have not been designated as
possessing SMP in a relevant market. Before doing so, they must hold an appropriate period of

---

[36] Framework Directive, para.1–009, n.25, Recital 5.
[37] Access Directive, para.1–011, n.29, Recital 10.
[38] *ibid.*, Art.5(1)(b), and Annex I, Pt II. See also para.1–026, above.
[39] Access Directive, para.1–011, n.29, Art.6(1) and Annex I, Pt I.
[40] *ibid.*, Arts 6(2) and 14(3).
[41] *ibid.*, Art.6(3). On the assessment of SMP and the related market analysis, see paras 1–017, *et seq.*, above.
[42] *ibid.*, Art.6(3)(a) and (b).
[43] *ibid.*
[44] *ibid.*, Art.6(4).

public consultation.[45] NRAs are required to encourage the sharing of facilities and property on a voluntary basis.[46] Furthermore, where undertakings are deprived of access to viable alternatives to installing their own facilities on, over or under public property or to use property because of the need to protect the environment, public health, public security or to meet town and country planning objectives, Member States may: (i) impose the sharing of facilities or property (including physical co-location) on an undertaking operating communications networks, regardless of whether it has been designated as possessing SMP; or (ii) take measures to facilitate the co-ordination of public works, in either case after an appropriate period of public consultation.[47] Such sharing and co-location arrangements may include rules for apportioning the costs of facility or property sharing. In the absence of such requirements, incumbent operators who have already installed their networks obtain a competitive advantage over new entrants and may have incentives to limit access by their competitors to these essential facilities, thereby abusing their dominant position.[48] If new entrants are unable to obtain adequate access to property to build their networks, market entry may not occur. This is particularly important in the context of local loop unbundling, when new entrants need access to the incumbent's facilities to install their own broadband equipment. Such compulsory sharing covers physical co-location, and the sharing of assets, buildings, masts, antennae and antennae systems.[49] As regards mobile sites and tower sharing, the Framework Directive recognises that the compulsory sharing of sites may lead to a reduction in the maximum transmitted power levels of each sharing operator, owing to technical and regulatory restrictions associated with public health reasons[50] and that this may in turn lead, in the long term, to the need to build more sites to ensure national coverage, as required by the conditions of mobile operators' rights of usage of frequencies.[51] NRAs must therefore pay particular attention to the issues of public health and environmental protection when taking decisions with respect to mobile site sharing.

1–173 Powers and responsibilities of the NRAs — NRAs must encourage and, where necessary, secure adequate access and interconnection, and interoperability of services in the interests of promoting efficiency, sustainable competition and maximising the benefits of end-users.[52] NRAs must have the power to intervene at their own initiative or, in the absence of agreement between undertakings, at the request of either of the parties involved, in order to achieve the policy objectives of the New Regulatory Framework.[53] NRAs may set *ex ante* general conditions relating to various aspects of access and interconnection, either on operators that have been designated as

---

[45] Although no specific period is laid down for this consultation, it should not be less than two months; this is the period of consultation laid down in Art.6 of the Framework Directive, para.1–009, n.25, which concerns the general consultation and transparency mechanisms applicable when NRAs take action under the directives of the New Regulatory Framework. See also para.1–044, above.

[46] *ibid.*, Art.12(1).

[47] *ibid.*, Art.12(2).

[48] On the application of the essential facilities directive under EU competition law, see para.6–037 *et seq.*

[49] Framework Directive, para.1–009, n.25, Recital 24.

[50] Maximum transmitted power levels are determined for each operator for reasons of public health. *cf.* 3G Communication, discussed at para.1–112, above.

[51] Framework Directive, para.1–009, n.25, Recital 24. On the status of network sharing agreements under competition law, see para.6–006, below. On mobile operators' rights to use frequencies, see para.1–104 *et seq.*

[52] Access Directive, para.1–011, n.29, Art.5(1).

[53] *ibid.*, Art.5(4). The EU's policy objectives are contained in Art.8 of the Framework Directive para.1–009, n.25: see para.1–010, above.

possessing SMP or, in certain circumstances, on operators regardless of any such designation.[54] When imposing obligations, they may lay down technical and operational conditions to be met by the provider and/or the beneficiaries of such access, where necessary to ensure normal operation of the network. Such conditions must be consistent with the list of standards set by the Commission.

1–174   Framework for the adoption of standards for harmonised technical interfaces — The Framework Directive sets out a mechanism whereby a list of European standards for harmonised technical interfaces and/or service features suitable for open network provision is published by the Commission in the *Official Journal of the European Communities*.[55] This list shall serve as a basis for encouraging the harmonised provision of electronic communications networks and services and associated facilities and services. Where necessary, the Commission may, following consultation with the Communications Committee, request that CEN, CENELEC or ETSI draw up appropriate standards.[56] Member States are required to encourage the use of such standards and specifications by operators of electronic communications networks for the provision of services, technical interfaces and/or network functions to ensure the interoperability of services and to improve freedom of choice for end-users.[57] If the Commission has not published a list of standards and/or specifications, Member States must encourage the adoption of standards and/or specifications adopted by the European Standardisation organisations or, if none exist, by the ITU, ISO or IEC.[58] If these standards or specifications are not adequately implemented so that interoperability of services cannot be ensured in one or more Member States, the Commission may make their implementation compulsory by publishing a notice in the *Official Journal of the European Communities* and invite public comment by all parties concerned.[59]

1–175   Communications Committee — The Framework Directive provides for the establishment of the Communications Committee, which replaces the ONP and Licensing Committees instituted under the 1998 regulatory framework. The Communications Committee is composed of delegates of the NRAs and is chaired by the Commission. It has both consultative and regulatory powers.

---

[54] See para.1–150, above.

[55] Framework Directive, para.1–009, n.25, Art.17(1). See also, above, para.1–166, n.23.

[56] *ibid.*

[57] *ibid.*, Art.17(2).

[58] *ibid.*

[59] See Framework Directive, para.1–009, n.25, Art.17(3) and 17(4), and Access Directive, para.1–011, n.29, Recital 19, where they require compliance with Directive 98/34 of June 22, 1998 laying down a procedure for the provision of information in the field of technical standards and regulations, O.J. 1998 L204/37, as amended by the Transparency Directive, para.1–015, n.43, above: see also, on the harmonisation of standards, para.1–282, below. In addition, special provisions exist as regards the implementation of technical standards in the field of digital interactive television services, under Art.18 of the Framework Directive: see para.1–171, above. Member States are required to encourage the use of an open standard API, using the Multi Home Platform (MHP) technical specification, which is included in the Commission list of standards, para.1–165, n.23, above. MHP has been developed by the DVB Project, a technical body within the framework of ETSI. However, the testing of MHP is still ongoing. According to ETSI rules, a technical specification which is approved only by a technical body becomes a standard only when it is approved by all ETSI members. The Commission must review the effect of Art.18 of the Framework Directive after July 2004 (Art.18(3)). It could then make the use of MHP mandatory, if interoperability of APIs was not achieved in one or more Member States. The Commission can make use of the MHP mandatory, using the same Art.17(3) procedure referred to above. For an overview of the general procedure for the creation of standards and technical specifications within the framework of ETSI, see *http://portal.etsi.org/directives/*. See further, below, paras 2–070 and 6–089.

The Committee assists the Commission on matters relating to the implementation of the New Regulatory Framework and consults representatives of operators, consumers, providers, users and consumers.[60] In particular, the Communications Committee needs to be consulted each time that an NRA submits proposals to the Commission concerning: (i) the definition of a relevant market, which is different from those included in the Commission Recommendation on the Relevant Markets, (ii) the designation of operators with SMP; (iii) the imposition of *ex ante* obligations; and (iv) any other matters that may affect trade between Member States.[61]

1–176 Dispute resolution — If commercial negotiations concerning access or interconnection do not lead to an agreement within a reasonable time period and a dispute arises, NRAs must, at the request of either party, take steps to resolve the matter within a maximum period of four months of such a request being made, except in exceptional circumstances. The decision to resolve the dispute must be reasoned and published and shall be binding on the parties.[62] Should organisations that provide public communications networks and/or publicly available services not have interconnected their facilities, NRAs may, as a last resort, require the organisations concerned to interconnect their facilities in order to ensure end-to-end interconnectivity, and they may set the terms of interconnection.[63] In the case of a cross-border dispute, *i.e.* between undertakings operating in different Member States, the NRAs involved must co-ordinate their efforts to resolve the dispute.[64] No timeframe is provided for the resolution of cross-border disputes.[65] The NRAs may jointly decline to resolve the dispute if other mechanisms, such as mediation, exist and would better contribute to resolution of the dispute. If after four months the dispute is not resolved and the dispute has not been brought before the courts, the NRAs shall co-ordinate their efforts to resolve the dispute.[66] The provisions of the Framework Directive for the resolution of disputes by NRAs are without prejudice to the right of a party to bring an action before the courts.[67] Decisions by NRAs to resolve disputes must be subject to appeal before an independent body or a court.[68]

1–177 Interconnection with operators in other Member States — One of the key policy objectives underlying the New Regulatory Framework is the development of an internal market in electronic communications services. Therefore, Member States are required to ensure that there are no restrictions on cross-border interconnection between operators in different Member States.[69] Therefore, operators authorised in one Member State must receive equivalent treatment when seeking access or interconnection services in order to deliver traffic to another Member State. Accordingly, all points of interconnection open to national operators must also be open to operators in other Member States who wish to deliver cross-border traffic, so that access or interconnection for those operators is no longer limited to the international switching centre. An operator in another Member State who merely terminates traffic and who does not provide services

---

[60] Framework Directive, para.1–009, n.25, Art.22.
[61] *ibid.*, Art.7.
[62] *ibid.*, Art.20.
[63] *ibid.*, Art.5(1)(a).
[64] *ibid.*, Art.21(1) and (2).
[65] *ibid.*, Art.21(1).
[66] *ibid.*, Art.21(3).
[67] *ibid.*, Art.20(5).
[68] *ibid.*, Art.4.
[69] Access Directive, Art.3(1).

or operate a network in the receiving Member State must also be able to obtain such a transmission link (*i.e.* a leased line or bulk transmission between the point of interconnection and the border) from an alternative infrastructure provider where available, without needing to be authorised or established in the destination Member State, and without affecting the status of the operator with regard to the terms and conditions for interconnection.[70]

3. Interconnection Pricing

1–178 Importance of interconnection tariffs — Interconnection payments are typically the largest cost item for a new entrant (about 50 per cent of expenditure). Accordingly, interconnection pricing is a key element of market liberalisation. If interconnection tariffs are set too high, new players will not be able to enter the market and the market dominance of incumbent operators could be perpetuated. In contrast, if the interconnection price is set too low, incumbent operators would have reduced incentives to invest in the network, which could have a detrimental impact as regards the introduction of new services (*e.g.* interactive services) that require investment in migrating or expanding their networks.

1–179 Under the 1998 regulatory framework, public communications networks operators with SMP (fixed and mobile) in the market for interconnection were required to apply cost-oriented interconnection charges.[71] The Access Directive provides that organisations designated as having SMP must set their interconnection prices in compliance with the principles of cost-orientation and transparency. An organisation might be designated as possessing SMP if it could sustain excessively high interconnection charges or unfairly low prices (so as to be able to apply a price squeeze) in any of the wholesale markets identified by the NRAs in accordance with their market analyses undertaken to identify SMP operators.[72] The Access Directive requires that SMP operators' interconnection tariffs derive from actual costs, including a reasonable rate of return on investment, taking into account the risks involved.[73] Different charges may be set for different categories of organisation, where, for instance, such differences can be objectively justified on the basis of the type of interconnection provided and do not result in distortion of competition and do not involve any value discrimination in favour of the SMP operator's own services, subsidiaries or partners.[74]

1–180 The general principle underlying the New Regulatory Framework is that where competition and the application of competition law is not sufficient to solve enduring market failures, *ex ante* regulation is necessary.[75] Article 82(2)(a) of the EC Treaty gives, as an example of an abuse, the imposition of unfair purchase or selling prices or other unfair trading conditions. However, past experience of the application of Article 82 has shown that it is not easy to decide whether a price is

---

[70] *ibid.*

[71] ONP Interconnection Directive, para.1–006, n.23, Art.7.

[72] Price squeeze (which is also referred to as "margin squeeze") occurs when a dominant company's own downstream operations could not trade profitably on the basis of the wholesale price charged to its competitors by the upstream operating arm of the dominant company, *cf.* Access Notice, para.5–003, n.18, para.117.

[73] Access Directive, para.1–011, n.29, Art.13(1).

[74] Access Directive, para.1–011, n.29, Art.10.

[75] See para.1–023 *et seq.*, above.

excessive and unfair, that is to say excessive in relation to the economic value of the service provided.[76] For these reasons there has been relatively little examination of excessive prices on the part of the Commission, and the case law of the European Courts is not particularly helpful in this regard either. Nevertheless, in recent years, a number of investigations have been carried out by the Commission, NRAs and national competition authorities into the prices for international roaming and call termination on mobile networks.[77]

1–181   Control by NRAs — The Access Directive states that NRAs may impose upon organisations designated as possessing SMP in the relevant interconnection market, obligations for cost recovery and price controls. Their obligations can include requirements that prices be cost-oriented and for the use of cost accounting systems.[78] NRAs may require interconnection charges to be adjusted if they are not cost-oriented, including retrospective changes.[79] The conditions under which the NRAs can impose such retrospective changes are, however, a matter of national law provided that in doing so, they respect applicable provisions of Community law, including the directives comprising the New Regulatory Framework. When an operator is required to adopt a cost accounting system in order to support price controls, NRAs must also require the publication of the reference interconnection offers, which must contain a description of the undertaking's interconnection offerings (which must be unbundled and broken down into components, such as interconnection points and interfaces, so that the applicant is not required to pay for anything not strictly related to the service requested) and the associated terms and conditions including tariffs. Compliance with the cost accountability obligations must be verified by an independent qualified body and the undertaking must publish an annual statement confirming such compliance.[80] NRAs are entitled to mandate the implementation of a particular cost accounting system and, if they do so, must publish a description of it that shows the main categories under which costs are grouped and the rules used for the allocation of cost.[81] The value of the capital employed by the operator should include appropriate labour and building costs, with adjustments where necessary to reflect the current value of the assets and efficiency of operations.[82] In order to check compliance with an operator's cost orientation obligations, the NRA is entitled to require the operator to justify its prices. The operator must meet the burden of proof that its charges are derived from its actual costs, including a reasonable rate of return.[83] The NRA may, however, use a different accounting method other than that used by the operator concerned in verifying this and in calculating the cost of the provision of access and interconnection services by an efficient operator.[84] Cost justification obligations, therefore, serve to check that obligations for the cost orientation of tariffs are respected. Cost justification therefore requires the use of a pricing methodology or a cost accounting system to check that the cost recovery mechanism used by an operator subject to cost orientation obligations is in line with the EU requirements. Although cost orientation and cost justification may appear to be two different concepts, from a practical perspective, an operator that

---

[76] See, *e.g.* Case 26/75 *General Motors Continental NV v Commission* [1975] E.C.R. 1367.
[77] For a discussion of these investigations, see para.6–012, below.
[78] Access Directive, para.1–011, n.29, Art.13(1).
[79] *ibid.*, Art.13(3).
[80] *ibid.*, Art.13(4).
[81] *ibid.*
[82] *ibid.*, Recital 20.
[83] *ibid.*, Art.13(3).
[84] *ibid.*

is subject to an obligation to provide its services on a cost-oriented basis should always be able to justify the costs on which prices are based, and the cost allocation methodology that it has used. As indicated above, NRA may, where appropriate, require retroactive changes to tariffs that it considers do not meet the requirements that they be cost-oriented, which it will undoubtedly do if it is not satisfied with the cost justification provided by the operator.[85]

1–182 **Costs recovery mechanisms** — The Access Directive does not specify which cost recovery mechanism or pricing methodology should be used. NRAs may therefore impose any cost recovery mechanism, provided that it serves to promote efficiency and sustainable competition and maximise consumer benefits.[86] Arguably, in certain circumstances it will be necessary to adopt different mechanisms or methodologies for different types of network, *i.e.* fixed and mobile or for different types of access or interconnection services. In more sophisticated instances, dynamic adjustments to a "pure" cost model might also be necessary to reflect the actual network topology of the SMP operator.[87] The issue of the cost orientation of tariffs thus presents a number of complex policy and technical issues.[88] In collaboration with independent consultants, the Commission has carried out a number of studies into the calculation and allocation of costs in order to develop guidelines for NRAs on the regulation of tariffs on fixed and mobile networks.[89]

1–183 **Cost methodologies** — Since the entry into force of the ONP Interconnection Directive in 1997, a number of disputes have arisen between incumbent operators (with SMP) and new entrants as to the determination of the price that should be charged for interconnecting the new entrant's network to the incumbent operator's public network. Disputes have usually centred on the appropriate cost methodologies to be used in calculating interconnection costs. Incumbent operators favour methods such as the fully distributed cost method (FDC), which enables them to take into account, in setting the interconnection price, historic costs incurred by them in developing

---

[85] *ibid.*

[86] Access Directive, para.1–011, n.29, Art.13(2).

[87] In a dynamic and inherently risky market, such as the communications sector, economic theory suggests that there is a strong case for consideration of the existing network topology rather than an ideal pre-defined one, for example, because the network is dimensioned in response to forecast demand and to provide a certain level of quality, which cannot be pre-standardised. Suitable adjustments, using a "scorched node" approach to a "bottom-up" model may therefore be needed in order to build a mechanism or methodology that reflects the operators' actual costs. Amongst the various studies on this issue, see the recent study on "The implementation of cost accounting methodologies and accounting separation by telecommunications operators with significant market power", prepared by Andersen Consulting for the Commission, July 3, 2002, available at: *www.europa.eu.int/information_society/topics/telecoms/implementation/index_en.htm*.

[88] In general, and on the basis of experience gained in the application of the 1998 regulatory framework, access and interconnection charges may, for example, cover: (i) the initial implementation of the physical interconnection; (ii) the ongoing use of equipment and resources; (iii) ancillary and supplementary services (*e.g.* access to directory services, operator assistance, data collection, charging and billing); (iv) the conveyance of traffic to and from the interconnected network (*e.g.* the costs of switching and transmission); and (v) a fair share of joint and common costs, including the costs incurred in providing equal access and number portability, and of ensuring essential requirements.

[89] For example, see Europe Economics, "Cost Structures in Mobile Networks and their Relationship to Prices", November 28, 2001. See also Oftel, "Europe Economics' view of costs of mobile networks: Oftel's response", available at: *www.oftel.gov.uk/publications/mobile/ctm_2002* and the Reply of Europe Economics, of July 22, 2002, "Oftel's criticism, on the contents of the report", available at: *www.europe-economics.com*.

their public networks. New entrants, supported by the Commission, consider that the use of such methods may lead to an overstatement of the actual costs of providing interconnection.

1–184 Benchmarking and the use of forward-looking, long-run incremental cost methodologies — In ensuring that any cost recovery mechanism that is mandated by an NRA serves to promote efficiency and benefits to consumers, NRAs may take into account prices available in comparable[90] competitive markets in other Member States.[91] Reference to prices charged in other countries is a practice that has been used by the Commission and the NRAs on numerous occasions,[92] given the difficulties that have been encountered in the adoption of a standard methodology for costs allocation. The use of benchmarking alone can no longer be a substitute for the imposition of a cost methodology, although it can still form part of an NRA's overall analysis as to whether an operator's tariffs are cost-oriented and reasonable.

1–185 The Commission has published a recommendation on interconnection pricing in a liberalised telecommunications market (the "Pricing Recommendation"),[93] which was amended on February 22, 2002,[94] to set the framework for the phasing out of benchmarks for interconnection charges between network operators. The initial purpose of the Pricing Recommendation was to provide NRAs with information on the "best current practice" in the EU for interconnection pricing, until appropriate cost accounting information was made available by operators to allow NRAs to properly check that the principle of cost-orientation was being respected by operators with SMP. The "best current practice" information contained in the Pricing Recommendation was drawn from the experience of the three lowest cost Member States and gave a price range for interconnection charges at the local, metropolitan and national levels within which operators' tariffs should fall. From 2002, the Commission considered that it was no longer necessary, in the light of falling interconnection tariffs, to rely on the best current practice benchmarking approach, and NRAs are now encouraged to use forward-looking, long-run, average incremental costs ("FL-LRAIC") as the basis for assessing whether prices are cost-oriented.[95]

1–186 The use of FL-LRAIC implies employing a cost accounting system that uses activity-based allocation of current costs, rather than historic costs. This methodology allows a network operator (or an NRA) to include in its interconnection charges a proportion of the capital investment that would be needed to adjust network capacity in the long term. A mark-up to the

[90] In previous decisions under competition law rules, the Commission took the position that for international benchmarking, the markets have to be comparable, *cf. DT* case, Press Release IP/96/975 of October 31, 1996.
[91] Access Directive, para.1–011, n.29, Art.13(2).
[92] Access Notice 1998, para.5–004, n.18, and discussed at para.6–029 *et seq.*
[93] Commission Recommendation of January 8, 1998 on interconnection in a liberalised telecommunications market: Part I — Interconnection pricing, O.J. 1998 L73/42, as amended by Commission recommendation of July 29, 1998 on interconnection in a liberalised telecommunications market: Part I — Interconnection pricing (Interconnection Pricing Recommendation), O.J. 1998 L228/30. See also Commission Communication on interconnection pricing in a liberalised telecommunications market (the "Interconnection Pricing Communication"), O.J. 1998 C84/3, which provides further details on the methodology for calculation of the forward-looking long-run average incremental costs of a network.
[94] Commission Recommendation 2002/175 of February 22, 2002, O.J. 2002 L58/56, amending Recommendation 98/195 of July 29, 1998, as last amended by Recommendation 2000/263, on Interconnection in a liberalised telecommunications market ("Part I — Interconnection Pricing").
[95] See Interconnection Pricing Recommendation, para.1–185, n.93, pp.5–6.

FL-LRAIC calculation may be applied to reflect the forward-looking joint and common costs of an efficient operator, as would occur under competitive conditions. An increasing number of countries are now able to calculate per minute interconnection charges on the basis of current estimates of FL-LRAIC for fixed networks. The use of this method allows NRAs to check that the interconnection charges of the incumbent operators are consistent with those charged in competitive markets, and, where this is not the case, to require the operator to justify its charges and, in appropriate cases, to require retrospective changes to interconnection charges.

1–187 There is by now a broad acceptance, in so far as the price regulation of interconnection charges for fixed networks is concerned, of the incremental use of the costs standard in several Member States,[96] and between NRAs at the level of the Independent Regulators Group and the European Regulators Group.[97] The Access Directive does not require the NRAs to use FL-LRAIC cost accounting.[98] The only way for an undertaking to seek to require the use of this methodology would be to resort to dispute resolution procedures before an NRA in the context of a dispute over interconnection tariffs.[99]

1–188 *Fixed-to-mobile termination charges* — The Commission and a number of NRAs have objected to the practice of mobile operators charging higher prices for interconnection of fixed to mobile networks than for fixed to fixed networks.[1] The Commission considers that there is no

[96] In its Eighth Implementation Report, para.1–108, n.52, the Commission found that six Member States already use the LRAIC methodology as cost standard for modelling interconnection costs (Germany, Greece, France, Ireland, the Netherlands for termination charges, and the United Kingdom). Other Member States are currently developing LRAIC models under the supervision of the NRA (Belgium, Denmark, Spain, Italy, Luxembourg). Sweden intends to move to LRAIC from January 2004 only, while Portugal and Finland have not taken any decision yet. The Commission has also indicated that cost accounting and accounting separation in Ireland and the UK can be regarded as best practice in the EU as regards the approach and the methodology used, the detail of the verification carried out by the regulators and the availability of information to third parties.

[97] IRG, "Principles of implementation and best practice regarding FL-LRAIC cost modelling", November 24, 2000; ERG, "Consultation Document: Proposed ERG Common Position regarding FL-LRIC cost modelling", July 30, 2003. The IRG is a non-institutional forum of the NRAs of all the Member States, plus third countries such as Switzerland. Under the New Regulatory Framework, it is unclear what the relationship between this body and the new ERG will be. According to Recital 36 of the Framework Directive, the ERG will have institutional advisory and co-ordination powers. For a discussion of the ERG, see para.1–046, above.

[98] In one of the draft versions of the Access Directive, Recital 14 explicitly recommended the adoption of FL-LRAIC cost modelling, but this was ultimately deleted from the final version of the Directive. There is therefore no binding obligation to adopt an FL-LRAIC methodology when NRAs mandate cost-oriented prices.

[99] In such dispute resolution procedures, the operator would argue that the use of any other methodology, such as FDC, would be inadequate to enforce the provisions and objectives of the Access Directive, in particular, the promotion of efficiency and sustainable competition and the maximisation of consumer benefits. In doing so, the prices charged in comparable competitive countries where FL-LRAIC is used may also be relevant. For a review of the procedural remedies offered to private businesses, see Section M, para.1–289, below.

[1] The issue of mobile termination charges (that is to say, the charge that an operator has to pay to a mobile operator to terminate a call on its network) was first dealt with by the Commission in 1999, in a competition investigation conducted together with the NRAs. The inquiry involved 45 companies. In July 1999 the Commission opened 14 cases where there were indications that termination tariffs were excessive and had thus

justification for the large differences in mobile interconnection charges depending on the type of network on which the call originated. Indeed, the cost of conveying a particular call from an interconnection point to its destination on the terminating fixed network is broadly the same whether the call originates on a mobile network or another fixed network. On the other hand, recent studies conducted for the Commission challenge this conclusion in the case of calls terminating on mobile networks, due to the presence of large common costs for the provision of network coverage.

1–189   There is a general consensus amongst the Commission and NRAs that the lack of competitive constraints on mobile termination rates should be attributed to the adoption of the Calling Party Pays principle.[2] However, mobile operators generally claim that cost regulation (*i.e.* the regulation of their termination charges) is artificial and has the effect of increasing or limiting reductions in their retail charges (*i.e.* line rental and outgoing call rates). In addition, they claim that their tariff structures reflect the application of "Ramsey pricing".[3]

infringed Art.82 of the EC Treaty, but then allowed NRAs to investigate first: Commission Press Release, IP/98/141, of February 10, 1998. Following a complaint made by WorldCom, under Art.82 of the EC Treaty, against 5 mobile operators in the Netherlands, Germany and Sweden, the Commission made a further investigation. The complaint against German operators was withdrawn, as they reduced their termination rates by 50 per cent. In Sweden, the national competition authority is dealing with the issue. In addition, OPTA (the Dutch NRA) on March 28, 2002 required a reduction of 32 per cent in mobile termination rates and required further cuts to be made to levels based on FL-LRAIC in 2003. In the Netherlands, the Commission has alleged that KPN has been abusing its dominant position (Statement of Objections was sent on March 27, 2002; see Commission Press Release, IP/02/483). In its Statement of Objections, the Commission indicated that it considered that KPN had abused its dominant position on the following grounds: (i) discrimination by KPN Mobile on the terms for direct termination in favour of KPN Telecom; (ii) unfair pricing practices amounting to a margin squeeze between KPN Mobile's wholesale termination charges offered to other network operators and the retail prices of KPN Mobile/Telecom for certain mobile/fixed services offered to business customers in the Netherlands; and (iii) (constructive) refusal by KPN Mobile to provide direct interconnection for call termination on its network.

[2] The Calling Party Pays principle (under which the calling party pays the interconnection fee for terminating its call) implies that termination charges for calls into mobile networks do not affect the call receiver's behaviour, that is to say the mobile operator's customer, but only the caller, that is to say the fixed operator's customer. cf. Commission's Seventh Implementation Report COM(01) 706 final, of November 26, 2001 available at: *http://www.europa.eu.int/information_society/topics/telecoms/implementation/annual_report/7report/documents/7report2001.pdf*, where the Commission identified this issue as one of the main areas of concern during 2001.

[3] Ramsey pricing is an efficient way for firms to recover fixed and common costs they incur from producing a range of different goods and/or services using the same equipment (such as a network). Under this principle, the price of each good or service is inversely related to market price elasticity of demand (that is to say, the sensitivity of consumers' purchases to changes of price). Services with a less elastic demand should have a higher price (and margin) than other services with a higher elasticity of demand (*i.e.* for which consumers are more sensitive to changes in price). This implies a smaller reduction in consumption than if the same mark-up was applied to a service which was more price-sensitive. In other words, the operator's common costs are recovered through mark-ups set according to the inverse of the price elasticity of demand for each service or consumer group. This is efficient (given the inability to cover common fixed costs with a government subsidy) because it minimises consumption distortions. Applying this theory to the pricing of mobile telephony services, it could be argued that it is almost certainly inefficient to make subscribers bear the full fixed and common costs (which mainly concern handset costs and also network connection costs), because this would discourage handset take-up, making it impossible for anyone to call those individuals who, because of high handset prices, choose not to connect to a network, impeding the so-called network externality effects. Accordingly, mobile

1–190 The wholesale market for call termination on individual mobile networks has been included in the first version of the Commission Recommendation on the Relevant Markets (for the analysis of the existence of operators with SMP),[4] although with a shorter review period (March 2003) than for the other identified markets. The Commission's stated intention was to re-consider the inclusion of such markets in future updates of the Recommendation, with the first update being scheduled for December 2004. The inclusion of a market in the Recommendation requires NRAs to analyse that market to determine if there are any operators with SMP upon whom *ex ante* regulation should be imposed if the market is found not to be competitive. However, each mobile operator would by definition be dominant in the market for calls terminating on its individual network, as is envisaged by the initial Recommendation. Arguably, NRAs' analyses, when deciding whether mobile operators have SMP and should be subject to *ex ante* measures,[5] should therefore

operators (particularly in the United Kingdom) claim that their termination charges (borne by callers) reflect their setting of prices in accordance with the principle of Ramsey pricing and they might be high because cross-subsidisation between products is a normal and necessary practice in a competitive and dynamic, multi-product market. However, NRAs and national competition authorities have so far rejected these arguments. For instance, in the United Kingdom, following its review of the mobile markets in September 2001, Oftel concluded that mobile termination rates are substantially in excess of cost and there is little incentive on operators to reduce these charges. Oftel had proposed charge caps on future termination rates. The four mobile operators publicly objected to the proposed charge controls. Oftel referred the matter in January 2002 to the UK Competition Commission for a decision on whether regulatory action such as charge controls is in the public interest. The Competition Commission has spent a year on its inquiry and has thoroughly analysed all relevant issues. In its decision of January 22, 2003, the Competition Commission concluded that the absence of a control on termination charges would be against the public interest. The Competition Commission has concluded that: (i) the termination charges of the four mobile operators operate against the public interest; (ii) current termination charges are 30–40 per cent above a fair charge; (iii) consumers pay too much for calls from fixed lines to mobiles and from one mobile network to another; (iv) the high cost of termination deters people from calling mobiles; and (v) those who make more calls to mobiles, either from a fixed line or another network, unfairly subsidise other mobile owners who mainly receive calls or make on-net calls. This is in line with Oftel's conclusions, which were set out in Oftel's original proposal and with the Competition Commission's preliminary views, as expressed in previous hearings and in technical papers. The Competition Commission has also agreed with the key elements of the remedies Oftel put forward. It agreed the need for cost-reflective termination charges and that LRAIC is the best basis for such charges. It finally recommended that: (i) each mobile network operator ("MNO") should reduce the level of the total termination charge by 15 per cent in real terms before July 25, 2003; (ii) O2's and Vodafone's charges should be subject to a further reduction between July 25, 2003 and March 31, 2004 and for each of the two subsequent financial years; and (iii) Orange's and T-Mobile's charges should be reduced by a slightly lower percentage than O2 and Vodafone's charges in each of these subsequent two time periods (the difference represents the Competition Commission's view of the difference between the relevant costs of the operators). Oftel accepted the Competition Commission's conclusion on a one-off cut of 15 per cent by July 2003. The Competition Commission's report is available at: *www.oftel.gov.uk/publications/mobile/2003/cc_1.pdf*. The four MNOs' licences have subsequently been modified by Oftel, as part of the implementation of the New Regulatory Framework, to reflect the Competition Commission's arrangements for the control of their termination charges.

[4] See para.1–026, above.

[5] NRAs must choose a measure that is proportionate to the problem to be remedied: see para.1–151, above. NRAs have so far applied different approaches to reduce mobile termination charges. Under the 1998 regulatory framework, most Member States started preparing regulatory frameworks for the mobile operators with SMP on the interconnection market. In Germany, although no mobile operators were notified as possessing SMP, the framework that RegTP put in place for the fixed SMP operators was potentially applicable to all mobile SMP operators. Most models are currently still at the stage of fully distributed costing using historical costs. The two exceptions are the United Kingdom and Austria, where the NRAs have required

consider: (i) technical possibilities to terminate calls via other networks; (ii) evidence that callers employ alternative means to circumvent high termination charges (*e.g.* call back, call forwarding, SMS messaging); and (iii) evidence that users subscribe to mobile networks on the basis of what it costs others to call them.

1–191 Impact of the Access Directive on international accounting rates — The pricing of international telephony services was based for many years on the so-called accounting rate system. An accounting rate is the charge agreed between the public communications operator in the country where the call originates and the public communications operator in the country where the call terminates for carrying a call duration of one minute from its origin to its destination. Each of the two companies involved receives a share (called the "settlement rate"), usually half, of this accounting rate. The balance of amounts due and owed by each company was then settled periodically. The accounting rate system was broadly intended to cover call termination costs but, in practice, accounting rates failed to come down in line with reductions in the costs of international circuits and were, in most cases, significantly out of proportion to costs.[6] Such imbalances were used by fixed operators to by-pass their calls to mobile networks via third countries, in order to avoid direct interconnection charges and benefit from the international settlement rates (so-called "tromboning" or "re-filing"), which were often lower than the mobile termination rates. However, the Interconnection Directive required Member States to ensure that incumbent operators provided cost-oriented interconnection rates also to operators from other Member States. The Commission, in co-operation with NRAs, has monitored the level of international telephone prices within the EU to ensure that accounting rates were brought in line with costs as required by the ONP Interconnection Directive and in the EC Treaty's competition rules. In practice, this has resulted in the collapse of the traditional settlement rate mechanism, at least within the EU, as well as, in many instances, the practice of "tromboning".[7]

---

mobile operators to use cost models based on modified LRAIC cost structures; whilst cost orientation obligations in the UK are implemented by using price caps that increase over a period of three years, in Austria cost orientation is imposed on the basis of reasonable charges. At the end of 2002, only Finland and Sweden imposed strict cost orientation of tariffs, while six other Member States had established price cap systems or ceiling pricing. Accounting separation is, however, required only in Finland and Denmark.

[6] Operators have found ways to by-pass accounting rates by conveying traffic over international private leased circuits and breaking out directly onto the public telephone network at the other end. This is so-called "International Simple Resale" (ISR). The existence of ISR explains the reluctance of certain countries, notably the United States, to open up their national markets unilaterally to operators of third countries, unless these third countries offer reciprocal market access arrangements. Indeed, if this is not the case, countries that have liberalised their markets could find themselves in a situation in which incoming traffic by-passes the accounting rate, while outgoing traffic is subject to it. See Cave, "Cross-border Interconnection: the Beginning of the End for Settlement Rates?" (July/August 1997) *International Business Lawyer* 303. In order to partly resolve this issue, the Federal Communications Commission (FCC) has adopted the so-called "Benchmark Order", an order instructing US operators to limit payments that they make under settlement rates to benchmark levels set for groups of countries at different stages of economic development. See Spinak, "From International Competitive Carrier to the WTO: A Survey of the FCC's International Telecommunications Policy Initiatives 1985–1998" (1998) 51 *Fed. Comm. L.J.* 11.

[7] With the relevant NRAs, the Commission has reviewed the pricing for international phone calls in Finland, Austria, Portugal, Luxembourg, Ireland, Italy and Greece. It had initially decided to close its investigations in Austria, Finland and Portugal following a substantial decrease in accounting/settlement rates. Its investigation is now concluded in relation to the other Member States too, where the practice of

G. Tariffs

1–192   As with the pricing of any other services, the pricing of communications services is subject to competition law, and in particular to Article 82 of the EC Treaty. Under Article 82, excessive or below-cost pricing may constitute an abuse of a dominant position.[8] Given the historic dominance of incumbent operators in the provision of public voice telephony networks and services and the inability of new entrants to challenge such a position in the short term, when the EC telecommunications market was liberalised, it was recognised that specific *ex ante* regulatory measures were needed, in addition to competition law principles, to ensure that incumbent operators did not adjust their tariffs (*e.g.* for access to and use of their networks) either to prevent competition or to exploit end-users. This regulatory framework included specific provisions in relation to wholesale interconnection pricing, which was reviewed in the previous section (at para.1–178). In addition, other specific measures on tariffs were adopted within the framework of the regulatory package applying to electronic communications retail services.

1. General Principles for Tariffs

1–193   The 1998 framework set out harmonised tariff principles for the pricing of retail communications services and networks by operators with SMP. Under the ONP Framework Directive[9]:

- tariffs must be based on objective criteria and, until such time as effective competition can keep down prices for users, must in principle be cost orientated. NRAs may set aside the requirement for cost orientation where an operator no longer has SMP;

- tariffs must be transparent and must be properly published;

- tariffs must be sufficiently unbundled in accordance with the competition rules of the EC Treaty;

- tariffs must be non-discriminatory and guarantee equality of treatment, except for restrictions which are compatible with Community law. Different tariffs may however be charged, in particular to take into account an excess of traffic during peak periods and a lack of traffic during off-peak periods, provided that the tariff differentials are commercially justifiable and do not conflict with the principles of cost orientation and non-discrimination; and

- any charge for access to network resources or services must comply with the principles set out above and with the competition rules.

These principles are now replaced by the provisions of the Universal Service Directive, as discussed below.

---

tromboning has been prohibited. Tromboning is domestic traffic "re-filed" in a foreign country and brought back as international traffic, thus avoiding high domestic termination rates and benefiting from international settlement rates: see INTUG, "Termination of international calls to mobile networks", available at: *www.intug.net/submissions*.

[8] See para.6–028 *et seq.*

[9] ONP Framework Directive, para.1–006, n.19, Art.3(1) and Annex I, as amended by Directive 97/51.

2. Price Controls on Retail Services

1–194   Under the Universal Service Directive, NRAs may impose regulatory controls on retail services.[10] NRAs must maintain obligations imposed on operators for: (i) retail tariffs for access to, and the use of, the public telephone network under the ONP Framework Directive; (ii) carrier selection and carrier pre-selection under the ONP Interconnection Directive; and (iii) leased lines under the ONP Leased Lines Directive, in each case until the NRA has completed an analysis of the relevant market and determined if these measures should be maintained, amended or withdrawn.[11] If, following such an analysis carried out under the principles set by the Framework Directive, the NRA determines that a given retail market is not effectively competitive and the application of pricing measures at wholesale level would not remedy the issues at the retail level, NRAs may impose proportionate and justified measures, such as: (i) retail price cap measures; (ii) measures to control individual tariffs; (iii) cost-orientation obligations; or (iv) tariffs based on international benchmarking of comparable markets to protect end-users whilst promoting effective competition.[12] NRAs may impose these requirements to prevent undertakings with SMP from charging excessive prices, inhibiting market entry or restricting competition by charging predatory prices, showing undue preference to specific end-users or unreasonably bundling services. The Commission can request NRAs to submit information to it concerning retail price controls, including cost accounting systems.[13] Where NRAs impose retail price controls, they may specify the format and methodology to be used for cost accounting.[14] Retail price controls shall not be imposed if the NRA is satisfied that there is effective competition, or if it concludes that obligations imposed under the Access Directive at wholesale level are also sufficient to address existing competition concerns at retail level.[15]

3. Tariffs for Leased Lines

1–195   The Universal Service Directive sets out specific guidelines regarding the pricing of leased lines.[16] Member States must ensure that operators with SMP in the provision of leased lines follow the basic principles of cost orientation and transparency, at least until there is effective competition in the relevant leased lines market. In particular, tariffs for leased lines must be independent of the type of application which the users of the leased lines implement.

4. Tariffs for Fixed Voice Telephony Services

1–196   The 1998 regulatory framework (in particular the ONP Voice Telephony Directive) contained principles applicable to tariffs for the provision of fixed voice telephony services.[17] Fixed telephony services must be available at affordable and cost-orientated prices, and tariffs for access to, and use of, the public communications network must be independent of the type of application

[10] Universal Service Directive, para.1–011, n.30, Art.17(1).
[11] *ibid.*, Art.16.
[12] *ibid.*, Art.17(2).
[13] *ibid.*, Art.17(3).
[14] *ibid.*, Art.17(4).
[15] *ibid.*, Art.17(1)(b) and (5).
[16] *ibid.*, Art.18. See further, para.1–165 *et seq.*, above.
[17] See, above, ONP Voice Telephony Directive, para.1–006, n.24. See also para.1–197, below.

that the users implement, except to the extent they require different services or facilities. Tariffs for facilities or services that are additional to the provision of a connection to the public communications network and public communication services must be sufficiently unbundled so that the user is not required to pay for facilities which are not necessary for the service requested. Discount schemes must be fully transparent, published and applied in accordance with the principle of non-discrimination. The Universal Service Directive requires Member States to maintain these obligations imposed under the ONP Voice Telephony Directive until NRAs have completed their market analysis to determine if such conditions for retail tariffs should be maintained, amended or withdrawn,[18] in accordance with Articles 15 and 16 of the Framework Directive.[19] NRAs may decide to maintain, amend or withdraw existing obligations or impose new obligations after having conducted a market analysis and holding a period of consultation with the Commission and the other NRAs.[20] Measures may include the imposition of retail price caps or measures to control individual tariffs.[21]

1–197   Tariff principles for the provision of universal service — One of the principles underlying the concept of universal service is that access to fixed telephone networks and fixed telephone services provided by undertakings designated with universal service obligations must be available at affordable prices.[22] The affordability of a service is to be defined by Member States in relation to specific national conditions, in particular national consumer prices and income.[23] They may take account of particular situations and priorities, and adopt special tariff options or packages for users with low income or special social needs in order to ensure that they are not prevented from accessing or using publicly available telephone services.[24] Tariffs for facilities additional to the provision of connection to the public telephone network and access to public telephone services at a fixed location must be sufficiently unbundled so that the user is not required to pay for facilities that are not necessary or not required for the service requested.[25] In order to ensure the control of expenditure by subscribers, designated undertakings must provide certain specified facilities and services.[26] Also, in order to ensure transparency, all operators must publish information specified by the NRAs, including subscription charges, line rental charges and standard tariffs.[27] It is for the NRA to decide what information should be published and how best to inform users.

1–198   With respect to undertakings with SMP in any retail markets, tariffs for access to and use of the public telephone network must follow the basic principles of cost orientation. Affordability may therefore co-exist with the requirement for cost orientation, which has driven the process of tariff rebalancing and general cuts in prices. Operators with SMP may also be subject to specific regulatory controls, including controls on their charges and tariffs, which also acts to protect consumers against excessively high prices in markets that are not effectively competitive.[28]

---

[18] Universal Service Directive, para.1–011, n.30, Arts 17(1)(a), 17(2) and 17(3).
[19] See para.1–019 *et seq.*, above.
[20] Framework Directive, para.1–009, n.25, Arts 7(3)(a), 15 and 16.
[21] Universal Service Directive, para.1–011, n.30, Art.17(2): see para.1–194, above.
[22] *ibid.*, Arts 1(2) and 9(1).
[23] *ibid.*, Art.9(1).
[24] *ibid.*, Art.9(2).
[25] *ibid.*, Art.10(1).
[26] *ibid.*, Art.10(1) and Annex I, Pt A.
[27] *ibid.*, Art.21 and Annex II.
[28] *ibid.*, Art.17. See para.1–194.

NRAs can relax the requirement for cost orientation and implementation of cost accounting systems once the intensity of competition is sufficient to keep prices down.[29]

5. Tariff Rebalancing

1–199 The requirement for tariffs to comply with the principles of cost orientation, including for voice telephony services, raised the issue of "tariff rebalancing", *i.e.* the altering of tariffs for local, national and international calls so that all were cost-oriented, thereby gradually ending the subsidisation of network access charges and local telephone calls by revenues from national and international calls. Tariff imbalances can cause distortions in competition, in particular on the market for local calls, in so far as they remove the incentive for new entrants to enter this market, where prices are artificially low (and probably below cost) as a result of cross-subsidisation. However, tariff imbalances also enabled new entrants to undercut the incumbent's tariffs for national and international calls (which were significantly above cost). The incumbent operator had difficulty in responding, as it had to maintain artificially higher prices for these calls in order to cross-subsidise its regulated below-cost charges for access and local calls (the so-called "cream skimming problem").

1–200 The rebalancing of tariffs was essential in establishing efficient economic conditions for all players and users and is therefore beneficial for competition in the long term. However, in the short term, tariff rebalancing involved incumbents reducing tariffs for prices for national and international calls and generally increasing charges for local calls (particularly during peak periods) and for basic network connection and line rental services. There was therefore a tension between the rebalancing process and the goal of maintaining an affordable telecommunications service for end-users.

1–201 Under the 1998 regulatory framework, Member States were required to ensure that public communications organisations rebalanced their tariffs, taking account of specific market conditions and the need to ensure the affordability of a universal telephone service.[30] In particular, Member States were required to allow public communications organisations to progressively adapt their tariffs that were not in line with costs and which increased the burden of providing a universal service. Because tariff rebalancing could have made fixed voice telephony services less affordable in the short term for certain groups of users, Member States were authorised to adopt special provisions to moderate the effects of tariff rebalancing, such as special tariff packages for disadvantaged users[31] or price caps.[32] Member States were required to complete the tariff rebalancing exercise by January 1, 2000,[33] but not all Member States have met this deadline.[34] When operators

---

[29] *ibid.*, Art.17(5).

[30] Services Directive, para.1–004, n.9, Art.4(c), as amended by the Full Competition Directive, see para.1–004, n.13, above.

[31] For example, targeted tariff schemes designed for low users, the elderly, or those on low incomes, which combine a low initial connection charge, low monthly line rental and a limited number of free or cheap call units each month.

[32] Price caps operate by pegging annual price rises either for the whole telephone service or for specific components (such as rental for residential users) at or below the rate of inflation, or indeed require prices to be gradually reduced by more than the rate of inflation.

[33] Services Directive, para.1–004, n.9, Art.4(c), as amended by Full Competition Directive, para.1–004, n.13.

[34] On August 24, 2001, the Commission sent a reasoned opinion to Spain alleging that the tariffs of Telefónica SA, Spain's incumbent telecommunications operator, for the monthly rental of telephone lines to

were subject to such regulatory constraints that prevented them from completing the process of tariff rebalancing (in particular as regards line rental and local call charges), NRAs put in place, on a temporary basis until the process of tariff rebalancing is completed, access deficit contribution schemes that prevent other operators from benefiting from inefficient by-pass and "cream skimming". Such schemes must be separate from any scheme set up for costing and financing the net costs of universal obligations.[35] Article 27 of the Framework Directive allows NRAs to maintain these obligations until tariff rebalancing is fully achieved in all Member States.

H. Universal Service

1–202   A major principle underlying the liberalisation of the EU's electronic communications sector was that a minimum level of "universal" services should be available to all citizens at an affordable price. In a monopoly environment, public communications operators cross-subsidised less profitable services and customers with the revenues from more profitable ones. Concerns were expressed that in a liberalised and competitive market, those operators would either pass on all the full costs of service provision to these services or customers, or cease to provide them at all. As a result, it was feared that those living in peripheral areas (which are expensive to serve) and/or with special social needs (who generally have limited incomes) may be unable to afford those services or that operators would not be able to afford to continue providing them with service. The necessity of imposing universal service obligations on some or all operators as part of the EU regulatory package was therefore widely accepted although there continues to be considerable controversy over how it should be funded.

1. Scope of Universal Service Obligations

1–203   Defining the scope of the universal service involves a delicate balance between protecting the end-user and promoting competition. If universal service is defined too narrowly, certain citizens may be excluded from participation in important aspects of society that are accessed through communications networks and services. If it is defined too broadly, new players may be deterred from entering the market, with a resulting lack of price competition and product innovation. The specific scope of universal service obligations (USOs) under EC law is specified in the Universal Service Directive.

1–204   Minimum set of services that must be made universally available — All electronic communications users throughout the Community must have access at an affordable price to a

---

its end customers were still not in line with its underlying costs. See Commission Press Release, IP/01/1226, of August 24, 2001.

[35] Communication from the Commission on assessment criteria for national schemes for the costing and financing of universal service in telecommunications and guidelines for the Member States on operation of such schemes ("Communication on Costing and Financing of Universal Service"), November 27, 1996, COM(96) 608 final available at: *http://www.europa.eu.int/ISPO/infosoc/telecompolicy/en/com96608.htm*. Such a scheme was set up in France in the form of a supplementary charge to be added to interconnection charges, to cover access deficit charges. In 2002, this system was condemned by the European Court of Justice: Case C–146/00, see para.1–222, below.

minimum of good quality publicly available services.[36] Such services should be provided through effective competition alone, with regulatory action to ensure such provision if end-users' needs are not met satisfactorily by the market, in accordance with national conditions, without distorting competition.[37] Member States are required to ensure that the minimum set of services is made available throughout their territory, independently of the geographic location of end-users, and must determine the most efficient and appropriate approach for implementing universal service.[38] Measures taken must be objective, transparent, non-discriminatory and proportionate and must seek to minimise market distortions (in particular the provision of services other than under normal commercial conditions).[39] Member States must ensure that all reasonable requests for connection at a fixed location to the public telephone network and for access to publicly available telephone services are met by at least one undertaking.[40] This should cover communications by voice, facsimile or data, including narrowband internet access, taking into account the prevailing technologies used by the majority of subscribers and technological feasibility.[41] In addition, users have a right of entry in publicly available directories, must receive an updated comprehensive directory at least once per year and have access to at least one telephone directory inquiry service covering all listed subscribers.[42] All organisations which assign numbers to subscribers, including mobile operators, must meet all reasonable requests to make available relevant subscriber information in an agreed format on fair, cost-oriented and non-discriminatory terms.[43] Member States must ensure that public pay telephones are provided to meet the reasonable needs of users in terms of both numbers and geographical coverage. It must be possible to make emergency calls from those public pay telephones free of charge and without having to use any means of payment.[44] The Universal Service Directive includes specific measures which are provided to ensure equal access to and affordability of public telephone services, including directory services, for disabled users and users with special needs.[45]

1–205 The USO does not include, at this stage, a requirement to provide leased lines, ISDN services, or broadband networks.[46] The extension of universal obligations to such services may be premature.[47] Extension of the USO to these services in the future is, however, not excluded since

---

[36] Universal Service Directive, para.1–011, n.30, Art.1.

[37] *ibid.*

[38] *ibid.*, Art.3(1) and 3(2).

[39] *ibid.*, Art.3(2).

[40] *ibid.*, Art.4(1), although different undertakings can be designated for different geographical areas or for different networks and service elements of the universal service, as stated at *ibid.*, Recital 9.

[41] *ibid.*, Art.4(2).

[42] *ibid.*, Art.5(1) and (2).

[43] *ibid.*, Art.5(3).

[44] *ibid.*, Art.6. The obligation to require the provision of public payphones may be withdrawn if an NRA is satisfied that public telephones or comparable services are widely available: Art.6(2).

[45] *ibid.*, Art.7.

[46] *ibid.*, Recital 8. The provision of leased lines on a cost-oriented basis is, however, required by Art.18. The recommendations on integrated services digital networks (ISDN) and packet-switched data services (PSDS) have expired and are no longer in force. The last follow-up reports on the implementation of these recommendations indeed indicated that the availability of PSDS and ISDN offerings have reached an appropriate level across the EU.

[47] The Commission identified the following reasons for not extending universal obligations to those services: (i) it could end up making users and households pay for services that they neither need nor use; (ii) the costs

universal service is considered to be a dynamic and evolving concept that must be reviewed regularly in light of market development and users' needs.[48] Member States can decide to extend under national law the scope of the USO in their territory to these or other services, provided however that such additional requirements are not financed from a mandatory contribution from specific undertakings.[49]

1–206 Publication of information on publicly available services — The Universal Service Directive contains a number of provisions concerning the protection of end-users' interests and rights. Organisations providing public communications networks and services must publish adequate and up-to-date information for end-users and consumers on their prices and tariffs, standard terms and conditions with regard to access to and use of public communications networks.[50] The use of interactive guides to enable end-users to make an evaluation of the cost of alternative usage patterns is to be encouraged.[51] Operators must also provide consumers with a contract specifying the services to be provided and the service quality level offered, the time for the initial connection, the types of maintenance service offered, information on prices and tariffs and on how up-to-date information on tariffs and charges can be obtained, the duration of the contract, conditions for terminating or renewing the contract, the compensation and/or refund arrangements for subscribers if the contracted service quality levels are not met and procedures for the settlement of disputes.[52] Subscribers must have the right to withdraw from a contract, without penalty, if the supplier wishes to modify the contract's terms and must be given at least one month's notice of any intended modification.[53] These provisions of the Universal Service Directive are without prejudice to Community rules on consumer protection and national rules in conformity with Community law.[54] NRAs have the power to impose further specific measures, including per call tariff

involved (where these have to be shared with the other operators, *e.g.* through a universal service fund) might deter market entry by those operators, delaying the arrival of the benefits which competition will offer to all users; and (iii) it risks providing or even subsidising services which users may be able to pay for on a normal commercial basis. See Communication of the Commission on universal service for telecommunications in the perspective of a fully liberalised environment: an essential element of the Information Society, March 13, 1996, COM(96) 73 (the "1996 Communication"), p.8 available at: *http://www.europa.eu.int/ISPO/infosoc/telecom policy/en/d8.htm.*

[48] Universal Service Directive, para.1–011, n.30, Art.15; the first review is scheduled by July 25, 2005. To this end, the Commission must submit a report to the European Parliament and the Council regarding the outcome of the review in accordance with Annex V of the Directive. Recital 8 indicates that broadband access could be made part of the USO if this is enjoyed by the majority of users so as to be able to support data rates sufficient for internet access.

[49] *ibid.,* Art.32. For example, in France, access to "Minitel", an online information system, is part of the USO.

[50] *ibid.,* Art.21(1), Annex II set out the information that is to be provided.

[51] *ibid.,* Art.21(2).

[52] *ibid.,* Art.20.

[53] *ibid.,* Art.20(4).

[54] In particular, Directive 97/7 on the protection of consumers in respect of distance contacts, O.J. 1997 L144/19, and 91/13 Directive 2002/65 concerning the distance marketing of consumer financial services and amending Council Directive 90/619 and Directive 97/7 and 98/27 O.J. 2002 L271/16: Universal Service Directive, para.1–011, n.30, Art.20(1).

information, in accordance with the policy objectives of the overall legislative package, which call upon NRAs to maximise consumers' interest.[55]

1–207 Quality of service — Following public consultation,[56] NRAs may set quality targets for designated operators with universal service obligations, at least in respect of the provision of access to the public communications network at a fixed location and for access to services at a fixed location.[57] In addition, they must also monitor compliance by these operators designated with universal service obligations for provision of access at a fixed location, directory inquiry services and directories, public pay telephones and special tariffs or packages for consumers on low incomes or with special social needs, with a set of supply-time and quality-of-service indicators (*e.g.* supply time for initial connection, fault rate per access line, fault repair time, response time for operator or directory services and billing accuracy).[58] NRAs may specify additional quality of service standards in respect of the provision of services to disabled end-users and customers.[59] NRAs must ensure compliance with performance targets and persistent failure by an operator to meet them may result in specific measures being taken in accordance with Article 10 of the Authorisation Directive which can include financial penalties or, for serious and repeated failures, even withdrawal or non-renewal of authorisations.[60]

1–208 Integrity of the network — Member States must ensure the integrity of the fixed public telephone network and, in the event of a catastrophic breakdown or in cases of *force majeure*, the availability of the fixed network and services. Operators providing publicly available telephone services at a fixed location are required to take all reasonable steps to ensure uninterrupted access to emergency services.[61]

1–209 Access restrictions — Under the New Regulatory Framework which aims to minimise *ex ante* intervention in favour of the application of competition rules, NRAs are provided with reserve powers to intervene if the competitive market does not satisfy users' and consumers' demands. Therefore, the Universal Service Directive requires a minimum list of safeguards to be included in contracts between end-users and operators, pursuant to which the user has a direct connection to the public telephone network, including those concerning termination of the service.[62] Outside the scope of contracts with end-users, NRAs may establish specific procedures, that operators of public telephone networks or services provided at a fixed location must follow before taking proportionate, non-discriminatory and published measures such as the service interruption

---

[55] The Universal Service Directive, para.1–011, n.30, does not require a user to be informed about the price of a call immediately afterwards ("advice of duration and charge"), but, at least for the use of mobile networks, the market is already responding to customers' demands in this area.

[56] *ibid.*, Art.33.

[57] *ibid.*, Arts 4 and 11(4).

[58] *ibid.*, Art.11(1) and Annex III. This information must be published by the operators concerned, in a manner specified by the NRA: Art.11(1) and (3).

[59] *ibid.*, Art.11(2).

[60] *ibid.*, Art.11, in conjunction with Annex III.

[61] *ibid.*, Art.23.

[62] *ibid.*, Art.20. No *ex ante* requirements apply to concluding contracts between consumers and other service providers, such as internet service providers, although such contracts would still need to comply with the requirements of Community and national consumer protection laws (see para.1–206, above).

or disconnection in cases of non-payment of bills.[63] The user concerned must always be warned before his service is interrupted or disconnected and if a dispute remains unresolved, must have recourse to out-of-court dispute resolution procedures.[64] Except in cases of fraud, persistent late payment or non-payment, these measures should be confined to the service concerned, where technically feasible. In appropriate cases of non-payment, Member States should allow a period of restricted service, during which only calls not incurring a charge to the subscriber (such as emergency calls and incoming calls) are permitted, before total disconnection is made. NRAs must ensure that these procedures provide for a transparent decision-making process in which due respect is given to the parties (*i.e.* both parties must be given the opportunity to state their case, the decision must be substantiated and notified to the parties promptly, and compensation or reimbursement be granted).

1–210 Additional facilities and services — Under the 1998 framework the provision of additional facilities, such as itemised billing, tone dialling and selective call barring (*i.e.* the facility whereby the subscriber can, on request to the telephone service provider, bar outgoing calls of defined types or to defined types of numbers) was mandatory for operators designated with USO (which often coincided with a designation of SMP).

1–211 Under the Universal Service Directive, all operators operating public telephone networks must make available tone dialling (or dial-tone multi-frequency operation) and calling-line identification, where this is technically feasible and economically viable.[65] This may be waived if such facilities are sufficiently available.[66] Undertakings designated with obligations to provide access at a fixed location, directory inquiry services and directories, public pay telephones and special tariffs and facilities for the disabled or those on low incomes or with special social needs must provide specified facilities and services to enable subscribers to maintain and control expenditure and thereby avoid unwarranted disconnection: (i) itemised billing; (ii) selective call-barring for outgoing calls; (iii) pre-payment systems; and (iv) phased payment of connection fees.[67] Other facilities and services, such as direct dial-in (*i.e.* where users on a private branch exchange (PBX) can be called directly from the fixed public telephone network, without intervention of the PBX switchboard) and call forwarding would now normally be provided where it is commercially attractive for operators to do so. Member States must however ensure that there are no regulatory restrictions to the provision of EU-wide access to directory inquiry services and access to operator and directory services in other Member States.[68]

1–212 Special network access — The importance of access to and use of the public telephone network at a fixed location is such that it should be available to anyone reasonably requesting it. Thus, under the 1998 regulatory framework and in particular the ONP Voice Telephony Directive, NRAs were required to ensure that all organisations providing public telephone networks deal with reasonable requests for access to their networks at network termination points other than the

---

[63] *ibid.*, Art.29(3) and Annex I, Pt A, point (e).
[64] *ibid.*, Art.34: see para.1–287, below.
[65] *ibid.*, Art.29(1) and Annex I, Pt B.
[66] *ibid.*, Art.29(2).
[67] *ibid.*, Art.10(2) and Annex I, Pt A.
[68] *ibid.*, Art.25(2) and (4).

commonly provided network termination points. This provision is carried over into the New Regulatory Framework, until NRAs carry out a review of existing obligations, in order to establish whether to maintain, amend or withdraw them.[69] The obligations may only be limited on a case-by-case basis and on the grounds that there are technically and commercially viable alternatives to the special access requested, and if the requested access is inappropriate in relation to the resources available, *i.e.* lack of capacity, to meet the request.[70] The network termination point represents the boundary for regulatory purposes between the New Regulatory Framework and regulation of telecommunications terminal equipment. Defining the location of the network termination point is the responsibility of the NRA, where necessary on the basis of a proposal submitted by the concerned undertaking.[71]

2. Operators Designated as Being Subject to Universal Service Obligations

1–213 Member States must notify to the Commission the names of the operators that have been designated with the responsibility for guaranteeing the provision of universal service.[72] Member States can designate one or more undertakings with USO and can designate different undertakings for different elements of the universal service and/or different parts of their national territory.[73] Designation must be done using an efficient, objective, transparent and non-discriminatory mechanism whereby no undertaking is *a priori* excluded from being designated.[74] Designation of undertakings must be done so as to ensure the cost-effective provision of universal service.[75] It can be expected that Member States will designate those organisations that possess SMP in the provision of public telephone networks and/or publicly available telephony services at fixed locations. In this respect, given the position of incumbent operators *vis-à-vis* their competitors and their geographic coverage, market shares are still arguably decisive criteria for the determination of dominance.[76] However, NRAs may decide to designate different undertakings to provide some or all elements of the universal service. The restrictions based on technologies for the designation of universal service providers no longer apply.[77] At present, operators of cable, utility or wireless fixed access networks providing fixed voice telephony services are not subject to USO under EU law in relation to the provision of telephony services. When these alternative networks attain regional or national coverage comparable to the fixed public telephone network, Member States could in principle designate those operators as having USO.

---

[69] *ibid.*, Art.16.

[70] Access Directive, para.1–011, n.29, Recital 19.

[71] Arguably, the organisation providing access could refuse to provide special network access, if there are objective technical difficulties in providing access at the termination point requested. The Commission has taken this position in its Access Notice, as detailed in para.6–046, below.

[72] Universal Service Directive, para.1–011, n.30, Art.36.

[73] *ibid.*, Art.8(1).

[74] *ibid.*, Art.8(2).

[75] *ibid.*

[76] SMP Guidelines, para.1–012, n.35, at para.77, where the Commission states that market shares in such markets are to be calculated with reference to retail revenues, call minutes or number of fixed telephone lines.

[77] Universal Service Directive, para.1–011, n.30, Recital 8, which indicates that universal service may be provided by any technical means, including wired and wireless (including cellular wireless networks) technologies, provided they are capable of supporting speech and data communications at a rate sufficient for narrowband (56 kbit/s) internet access.

3. Funding of Universal Service Obligations

1–214   Creation of a scheme to fund universal service — The Universal Service Directive does not impose any requirement on Member States to set up a national scheme for funding the USO. However, where NRAs consider that the USO may represent an unfair burden on the designated operator(s), they must calculate the net costs of providing universal service.[78] If the NRA then concludes that the provision of universal service is an unfair burden on the designated undertaking(s), the Member State shall, upon request by a designated undertaking decide to finance the net cost of universal service provision: (i) directly or indirectly from the public funds, by the introduction of compensation mechanisms; and/or (ii) by setting up a financing scheme to share the burden amongst providers of electronic communications networks services.[79] Given the broad discretionary power of NRAs in this respect, it may be quite difficult for communications operators subject to USO to force the setting up of a funding mechanism and they will in any event need to show that the net costs of universal service represent an unfair burden on them. The question of whether a burden is "unfair" may be difficult to assess, and may involve taking account of designated operators' overall profitability (taking account of the costs of USO), overall cost structures and returns on capital employed.

1–215   Universal service funding mechanisms — When Member States decide to set up national financing schemes to share the burden of USO, they must do so in accordance with specific rules set out in the Universal Service Directive,[80] which gathers into a single piece of legislation the different provisions of the directives comprising the 1998 regulatory framework, in this respect. Funding mechanisms must take the form of either compensation from public funds,[81] and/or a system for sharing net costs between providers of electronic communications networks and services. Supplementary charges levied on interconnection tariffs (*i.e.* access deficit charges) are no longer permitted. When the net cost of providing universal service is shared between providers, it must be administered by the NRA or a body independent of the beneficiaries under the supervision of the NRA.[82] The NRA or the independent body will be responsible for: (i) collecting contributions from operators and service providers liable to contribute to the cost of providing universal service; and (ii) overseeing the transfer of sums due to the operator entitled to receive payment from the fund. NRAs are also responsible for ensuring that the sharing mechanism is implemented in a transparent, non-discriminatory and proportionate manner.[83] Member States may exempt new entrants and smaller operators and service providers, which have not achieved any significant market presence, from making contributions to the financing mechanism.[84] Charges related to the sharing of the cost of providing universal service shall be unbundled and identified separately for each undertaking. Charges shall not be imposed and/or collected from undertakings not providing services in the territory of the relevant Member State.[85]

---

[78] *ibid.*, Art.12(1).
[79] *ibid.*, Art.13(1).
[80] *ibid.*, Art.13(2) and (3).
[81] *ibid.*, Art.13(1)(a).
[82] *ibid.*, Art.13(2).
[83] *ibid.*, and Annex IV, Pt B, which set the guidelines for the calculation of net cost of USO.
[84] *ibid.*, Art.13(3). Member States can set a turnover limit for this purpose.
[85] *ibid.*, Art.13(3).

1–216 When a financing mechanism is set up by a Member State, it must be notified to the Commission, in order to allow an assessment of its compatibility with Community law.[86] Such information would, however, normally be covered under the Commission's yearly review of the implementation of the EU communications legislative package at national level, which is conducted together with the Communications Committee.[87]

1–217 NRAs must publish the principle under which a cost-sharing mechanism will be applied and an annual report on its operation, giving details of the calculated net cost of universal service obligations, the contributions made to the mechanism and any market benefits that may have accrued to the designated undertakings(s).[88]

1–218 Principles underlying the financing of universal service — The Commission has indicated that national schemes for financing universal service must be consistent with certain Community policy objectives. In particular, they must not create barriers to entry and must be neutral, *e.g.* as between particular market players, and different technologies, in order to avoid distorting the pattern of market entry or subsequent investment decisions. Administrative burdens and related costs must be kept to a minimum. Moreover, the operation of universal service funding mechanisms must be based on objective, transparent, proportional and non-discriminatory procedures. In order to achieve minimum market distortion and minimise the impact on end-users, NRAs should try to spread contributions as widely as possible, bearing in mind that new entrants and small operators can be exempted from contributing.[89] In addition, the principle of technological neutrality underlying the New Regulatory Framework would prevent any national provision from imposing additional obligations relating to particular technologies and facilities and/or to set service and coverage targets (*e.g.* for mobile services or for ISDN), outside those already imposed under a usage right of frequencies. This is subject to the power of NRAs to change the scope of universal service to take account of evolving social, commercial and technological conditions, so as to include services that are available to the substantial majority of the population, without artificially promoting one technology over another.[90] Market players cannot be required to contribute to the funding of measures that are not part of the USO; any such measures can only be financed by the Member State in accordance with Community law, in particular the state aid rules.[91]

1–219 Organisations required to contribute to the cost of universal service — National financing schemes must identify those organisations that are required to contribute to the net cost of providing universal service. Arguably, contributions may be required from all public communications providers, including mobile operators and cable operators, or certain specified classes of undertakings in an unbundled non-discriminatory and proportionate manner (*i.e.* in proportion to their usage of public communications networks). New entrants and small operators may be exempted. The impact on end-users must be kept to the minimum.

---

[86] *ibid.*, Art.36.

[87] The latest reports can be accessed via the Commission website: *www.europa.eu.int/information_society/topics/telecoms/implementation/index_en.htm.*

[88] Universal Service Directive, para.1–011, n.30, Art.14.

[89] *ibid.*, Recital 23.

[90] *ibid.*, Recital 25.

[91] *ibid.*, Recital 25. State aid rules are reviewed in Chap.VII of this book.

1–220 Organisations that may benefit from payment from a funding mechanism — Payments from a universal service-funding scheme must be made to organisations subject to USO in a proportionate, non-discriminatory and transparent manner. There is an obvious incentive for designated undertakings to seek to raise the assessed net costs of USO; therefore they must provide accounts and/or other information to justify their net costs, which must be audited or verified by the NRA or an independent body approved by it. These cost calculations and the results of the audit must be published,[92] as must the annual calculated cost of providing universal service.[93] It is therefore clear that the NRA must be satisfied that the undertaking has justified the claimed costs[94] and that it has overall responsibility for verifying the net cost.[95]

1–221 Calculating the cost of universal service — The national financing of the provision of universal service (whether from state funding or through a funding mechanism) may only cover the net costs incurred, *i.e.* the difference between the net cost for an organisation operating with USO and operating without it.[96] The calculation of the costs of providing universal service must be based upon the costs attributable to elements of the identified services, which can only be provided at a loss or provided under cost conditions falling outside normal commercial standards. This category includes service elements such as access to emergency telephone services, provision of public pay telephones and the provision of certain services and equipment for disabled people or people with low incomes or special needs. The costs of universal service also cover costs attributable to specific end-users who, taking into consideration the cost of providing the specified network and service and the revenue generated, can only be served at a loss under cost conditions falling outside normal commercial standards. This includes end-users or groups of end-users who would not be served by a commercial operator who did not have an obligation to provide universal service, for instance because those customers are located in peripheral and low-populated areas. In this regard, national financing schemes must ensure that an operator claiming universal service funding clearly identifies (*e.g.* by way of a declaration) which groups of customers or particular areas it would, absent universal service obligations, refuse to serve or would disconnect.

1–222 The calculation of the net costs of each specific element of universal service must be undertaken separately, and avoid any double counting of costs or any direct or indirect benefits from providing the services. Thus, the calculation must take into account the revenues derived from the provision of universal service and other indirect benefits. "Intangible" benefits must also be taken into account: these can include the value that can be attributed to an operator's brand through being a nationwide operator. Other intangible benefits include "consumer lifecycle" (*i.e.* the ability to serve uneconomic customers who later become economic), ubiquity, brand image and national provision of payphones.[97] The total net cost of universal service provision is the sum of the net costs of providing each element of it, taking account of such intangible benefits that may be generally applicable. The methodology approach should be forward-looking, rather than based on historical

[92] *ibid.*, Art.12(2).
[93] *ibid.*, Art.14(2).
[94] See also *ibid.*, Recital 24.
[95] *ibid.*, Annex IV, Pt A.
[96] *ibid.*, Recital 12, Art.12, Annex IV, Pt A, which contains the guidelines to calculate the net cost of USO.
[97] Oftel, "Universal Service Obligation: A Statement issued by the Director General of Telecommunications", August 30, 2000 at: *www.oftel.gov.uk/publications/consumer/uso0801.htm-3*.

costs. The Commission will be particularly vigilant in ensuring that the financing of universal service is not used to recover costs that are not attributable to universal service.[98] In particular, universal service funding mechanisms may not be used to recover deficits in access revenues that are attributable to unbalanced national tariffs.[99] Likewise, the financing of universal service may not be used to recover costs such as the cost of implementing specific measures required for purposes of public security, the provision of communications services outside the scope of universal service to schools, hospitals or similar institutions, compensation and/or refund payments made to users as a result of failure to meet specified service quality levels and the cost of replacement and/or upgrading telecommunications equipment in the course of normal network modernisation. In addition, no account may be taken in calculating the net cost of universal service provision of providing itemised billing, and other facilities (*e.g.* selective call barring and calling-line identification) where such facilities are provided pursuant to obligations imposed on all voice telephony operators under the Universal Service Directive.

1–223 Community law does not specify what should happen when contributions to financing mechanisms exceed the net cost of USO. It would seem that in such a case, the amount exceeding the effective cost of USO should be restituted *pro rata* to those operators that have contributed to the funding. Any amount in excess of the cost of USO allocated to the incumbent operator would arguably constitute an unlawful state aid in violation of Article 87 (*ex* Article 92) of the EC Treaty.[1] This would also be the case where a Member State chooses to meet the net cost of universal service out of general state revenues,[2] rather than under a funding mechanism.

I. Directory Services

1–224 Directories and associated information services are an essential means of access to public communications services and, traditionally, have always been closely associated with the provision of voice-telephony services and considered one of the basic elements of universal service. Accordingly, it was felt early in the EU liberalisation process that the introduction of a competitive environment in telecommunications services required, on the one hand, an extension of the Community's telecommunications rules to include directories and, on the other hand, the

---

[98] 1996 Communication, para.1–205, n.47, p.7. Further guidance can be found in a recent jurisprudence of the European Court of Justice. On December 6, 2001 the European Court of Justice condemned France for failure to comply with the provisions of the ONP Voice Telephony Directive, para.1–006, n.24, in the Case C–146/00 *Commission v French Republic* [2001] I E.C.R. 9767, on the basis that the French financing scheme set up by Decree 97–475: (i) wrongly required France Telecom's new competitors to contribute to the financing of its universal service in 1997, before the French market was liberalised; (ii) failed to comply with the requirement upon Member States to require national operators to rebalance their tariffs; (iii) included within the net costs of universal service provision costs which should not have been included (namely the costs of supply profitable residential subscribers); and (iv) failed to comply with the requirement for a specific calculation of each component of the net cost of universal service provision in a transparent and published manner, because these components were fixed on a flat-rate basis, such that it was impossible to distinguish between the profitable and unprofitable elements of the net cost calculated.

[99] On tariff rebalancing, see para.1–199 *et seq.*

[1] See para.7–037 *et seq.*

[2] As permitted by Art.13(1)(a) of the Universal Service Directive, para.1–011, n.30.

maintenance of a universal directory and information service accessible to all users at an affordable price.[3]

1–225 Liberalisation — The Services Directive required Member States to abolish all exclusive and special rights with regard to the establishment and provision of directory services, including both the publication of directories and directory inquiry services.[4] These provisions are now contained in the Liberalisation Directive.[5] This should lead to the development of a competitive market in directory inquiry services, including the provision of "value-added" directory services, such as direct connection to the requested number.

1–226 Licensing — Directory services are not electronic communications services within the meaning of the Authorisation Directive.[6] The licensing of directory services by Member States is therefore not subject, as such, to the requirements of the Authorisation Directive.[7] However, in so far as national licensing procedures for directory services would unduly restrict the possibility for operators from other Member States to set up competing directory services, those operators might be able to invoke the freedom of establishment guaranteed by Article 43 (*ex* Article 52) of the EC Treaty to challenge such national licensing procedures before national courts (since Article 43 has direct effect) or the Commission. In this context, it would seem contrary to the principles of the New Regulatory Framework to require new entrants to obtain an individual licence before launching competing directory services; a general authorisation requirement would seem more adequate.

1–227 Access to directory services — Directory information and directory service constitute an essential access tool for publicly available telephone services and form part of the USO.[8] Member States must ensure that at least one comprehensive directory is available (in printed and/or electronic form) and is updated regularly.[9] They must also ensure that all users of publicly available communications services, including users of public pay phones, have access to at least one comprehensive telephone directory inquiry service.[10] These obligations may be imposed upon all operators,[11] to ensure that all end-users have access to directory services regardless of the network to which they are connected.

1–228 In order to enable the provision of directory services, providers of publicly available telephone services must meet all reasonable requests to make available their subscribers' information to providers of directory services in an agreed format on terms that are fair, cost-oriented

---

[3] ONP Voice Telephony Directive, para.1–006, n.24, Art.6.

[4] Services Directive, para.1–004, n.9, Art.4(b), as amended by Full Competition Directive, para.1–004, n.13, above.

[5] Liberalisation Directive, para.1–012, n.33, Art.5.

[6] The Authorisation Directive, para.1–011, n.28, refers to Art.2 of the Framework Directive, para.1–009, n.25, where electronic communications services are defined as "services whose provision consists wholly or partly in the transmission and routing of signals on electronic communications networks". See para.1–013 *et seq.*

[7] See Section C, para.1–052 *et seq.*, above.

[8] Universal Service Directive, para.1–011, n.30, Art.5.

[9] *ibid.*, Art.5(1)(a).

[10] *ibid.*, Art.5(1)(b).

[11] *ibid.*, Recital 34.

and non-discriminatory.[12] The issue of access by new entrants to incumbent operators' raw subscriber data has given rise to a number of disputes. In particular, new entrants have argued that the incumbent operators abuse their dominant positions by either refusing, or charging excessive prices for the supply of information regarding their telephone subscribers. These disputes have necessitated the intervention of NRAs and the Commission to force incumbent operators to supply data and/or reduce the price requested for the information.[13]

1–229 Protection of privacy — Member States must give subscribers the right to have an entry in publicly available directories.[14] Before the details of subscribers who are natural persons are included in a directory (whether printed and/or electronic), they must be informed of this fact and of the possible uses of the electronic version of the directory (*e.g.* reverse searching, by which a subscriber's name and address can be obtained on the basis of a telephone number only).[15] Subscribers must have the right to choose if their details should be included in the directory and, if so, what data shall be included; they must also have the right to verify, correct or withdraw personal data. This must all be free of charge to the subscriber.[16] Member States may also take measures to protect the legitimate interests of subscribers who are natural persons.[17] Personal data contained in printed or electronic directories of subscribers available to the public must be limited to that which is necessary to identify a particular subscriber (*i.e.* name and address), unless the subscriber has given his unambiguous consent to the publication of additional data. Subscribers must be entitled, free of charge, to indicate that their personal data may not be used for any purpose other than for searching for their contact details (*e.g.* direct marketing by telephone, mail, email, automated machine, fax or SMS messaging). The prime explicit consent of the subscriber should be obtained before personal data can be used for such additional purposes or provided to third parties.[18]

1–230 Database protection for directories — Directories are databases and benefit as such from the protection of the Database Directive,[19] as the collection and updating of the subscriber information represents a substantial investment.[20] Directories might also qualify for copyright protection to the extent that they show some originality in the selection and arrangement of their content, as well as for the *sui generis* protection afforded by the Database Directive.

---

[12] *ibid.*, Art.5(3) and Recital 35.

[13] In particular, following a complaint by ITT Promedia, the Commission investigated the prices of Belgacom, the Belgian incumbent operator, for access to subscriber data for the publication of telephone directories. It was alleged that Belgacom's prices were excessive and discriminatory, thereby infringing Art.82 of the EC Treaty. The Commission's investigation was closed following a settlement, pursuant to which Belgacom agreed to a substantial reduction of these prices so that they were cost-oriented and did not contain variable components related to the turnover or profitability of the competing directory publishers, thereby allowing Belgacom to recover its costs plus a reasonable profit margin, but no more. See Commission Press Release, IP/97/292 of April 11, 1997. See also para.6–029.

[14] Universal Service Directive, para.1–011, n.30, Art.5.

[15] E-Privacy Directive, para.1–011, n.31, Art.12(1).

[16] *ibid.*, Art.12(2).

[17] *ibid.*, Art.12(4).

[18] *ibid.*, Art.12(3) and Recitals 39 and 40.

[19] See para.1–249 *et seq.*

[20] See para.1–256 *et seq.*

J. Data Protection and Information Security

1–231   In the "internet era", the evolution of communications and information technology markets has substantially enhanced the possibility of cross-border access to, or transfer of, information, including personal data. This raises substantial legal issues regarding the protection of the confidentiality and integrity of, and the proprietary rights in, such information. These issues particularly include: (i) the protection of privacy in the processing of personal data, in particular in the electronic communications sector; and (ii) the legal protection of databases. It also raises issues regarding information security in the framework of cross-border transfer of data.[21]

1. Protection of Privacy in the Processing of Personal Data

1–232   The successful development of new cross-border communications services based on advanced digital technologies, such as video-on-demand and interactive digital television, is partly dependent on the confidence of users that their privacy is not at risk and on Member States not imposing their own rules that could hinder such developments. It is therefore necessary to adopt specific measures at the EU level to ensure the protection of personal data in the communications sector, thereby contributing to the development of these new services across the EU. Accordingly, the "Telecommunications Data Protection Directive"[22] was adopted in 1997.

1–233   The internet is transforming traditional market structures, and publicly available online information opens new possibilities for users. Moreover, new advanced digital technologies are currently being introduced in public communications networks across the EU. This gives rise to a need for specific requirements concerning the protection of personal data and the privacy of users that take account of these markets developments. Therefore, the E-Privacy Directive was adopted within the New Regulatory Framework, to repeal the Telecommunications Data Protection Directive and to replace it with provisions that take account of such technological developments.[23] The E-Privacy Directive (as was the case with the Telecommunications Data Protection Directive before it) complements the "Framework Data Protection Directive", a generally applicable framework directive on data protection adopted in 1995.[24] This section considers the application of the

---

[21] See para.3–042 *et seq.*

[22] Directive 97/66 concerning the processing of personal data and the protection of privacy in the telecommunications sector, O.J. 1998 L24/1.

[23] E-Privacy Directive, para.1–011, n.31.

[24] Directive 95/46 of the European Parliament and of the Council of October 24, 1995 on the protection of individuals with regard to the processing of personal data and on the free movement of such data, O.J. 1995 L281/31. This directive is based on a Council of Europe Convention for the Protection of Individuals with Regard to Automatic Processing of Personal Data, January 28, 1981. Member States had until October 24, 1998 to implement the Telecommunications Data Protection Directive, para.1–232, n.22 and the Framework Data Protection Directive. Article 33 of the Framework Data Protection Directive requires the Commission to make regular reports on the transposition of the Directive. The first report was however only adopted on May 16, 2003, owing to the delays in the transposition of the Directve into the national laws of the Member States. This first report is based on a broad consultation exercise undertaken during 2002. The report comes to the conclusion that the Directive has broadly achieved its aim of ensuring strong protection for privacy while making it easier for personal data to be moved around the EU. However, the Commission noted that late transposition by the Member States and differences in the ways the Directive is currently applied at national level prevented Europe's economy from getting the full benefit of the Directive. The report proposed a work

EU regulatory framework on data protection to the electronic communications sector, although the impact of the new provisions on internet service providers will be dealt with under Chapter III.[25]

1–234 Scope of application of the E-Privacy Directive — The purpose of the E-Privacy Directive is to ensure an equivalent level of protection, in particular as regards the rights to privacy, with respect to the processing of personal data in the electronic communications sector and to ensure the free movement of such data and of electronic communications equipment and services in the Community.[26] Accordingly, the E-Privacy Directive applies to the processing of data relating to private individuals or legal entities wholly or partly by automatic means and, if by non-automatic means, where the data will be maintained as part of a filing system, in connection with the provision of publicly available communications services and networks in the EU.[27] This would apply to data on, for instance, employees of a communications operator, its customers, suppliers and shareholders. Certain provisions apply only to digital networks and not to analogue networks.[28] Unlike the Framework Data Protection Directive, the E-Privacy Directive also covers the protection of the legitimate interests of legal persons.[29] The E-Privacy Directive particularises and complements the provisions of the Framework Data Protection Directive.[30] It does not apply to activities outside of the scope of the EC Treaty (*e.g.* provisions of the Treaty of the European Union concerning a common foreign and security policy and police and judicial co-operation in criminal matters),[31] nor to public security, defence, state security and activities in areas of criminal law.[32]

1–235 Rules for collecting, processing and transferring data — As a general rule, Member States must ensure that personal data is: (i) processed fairly and lawfully; (ii) collected and processed only for specified, legitimate and explicit purposes; (iii) collected only if it is adequate, relevant and not excessive in relation to the purposes for which it is collected; (iv) accurate and kept up-to-date where necessary; and (v) kept in a form which permits the identification of individuals for no longer than necessary in view of the purposes of the processing.[33] This means that traffic data relating to subscribers and users[34] that is processed and stored by a provider of a public communications

---

plan to reduce those differences, based on cooperation among Member States and between Member States and the Commission: see First Report on the Implementation of the Data Protection Directive 95/46, COM (2003) 265 final; and Commission Press Release IP/03/697, of May 16, 2003.

[25] See para.3–038 *et seq.*

[26] E-Privacy Directive, para.1–011, n.31, Art.1(1).

[27] *ibid.*, Art.3. In contrast to the Framework Data Protection Directive, para.1–233, n.24, the E-Privacy Directive, para.1–011, n.31, specifically applies to legal persons.

[28] *ibid.*, Art.3(2) and (3). Their provisions relate to calling line and connected line identification (Art.8), location data (Art.9) and automatic call forwarding (Art.11).

[29] *ibid.*, Art.1(2).

[30] *ibid.*

[31] Treaty on European Union, Titles V and VI.

[32] E-Privacy Directive, para.1–011, n.31, Art.1(3).

[33] Framework Data Protection Directive, para.1–233, n.24, Arts 6 and 7.

[34] The term "subscriber" is defined as "any natural or legal person who or which is party to a contract with the provider of publicly available electronic communications services for the supply of such services": E-Privacy Directive, para.1–011, n.31, Art.2 and Framework Directive, para.1–009, n.25, Art.2. The term "user" is defined as "any natural or legal person using a publicly available telecommunications service, for private or business purposes, without necessarily having subscribed to this service": E-Privacy Directive, para.1–011, n.31, Art.2.

network or service must, subject to certain exceptions, be erased or made anonymous when it is no longer needed for the purpose of the transmission.[35] However, certain data on subscribers collected for the purpose of subscriber billing and interconnection payments may be processed but only up to the end of the period during which the bill may lawfully be challenged or payment may be pursued.[36] The processing of such stored traffic data must be limited to the necessary data, that is to say only data that are adequate, relevant and not excessive in relation to the billing and interconnection payments purposes (principle of proportionality of the processed data).[37] Furthermore, although the E-Privacy Directive does not specify any time-period up to which traffic data may be lawfully stored, the Commission has indicated that a reasonable interpretation of the Directive is that this period should ordinarily involve a routine storage period for billing of maximum 3–6 months, with the exception of particular cases of dispute where the data may be processed for a longer period.[38] Communications operators may also process data after completion of the transmission for the purpose of marketing their own communications services (including value-added services), provided that the subscriber has given his consent, which may be withdrawn at any time.[39] The processing of traffic data in accordance with these provisions must be restricted to persons acting under the authority of the network and service providers and to what is necessary for the purposes of billing or traffic management, customer inquiries, fraud detection, marketing or providing value-added services.[40] It is also without prejudice to providing traffic data to competent bodies for settling interconnection, billing and other disputes.[41]

1–236 The communication of personal data to third parties is also limited under the E-Privacy Directive. The processing of traffic and billing data must be restricted to persons acting under the authority of the communications operator, handling billing or traffic management, customer

---

[35] *ibid.*, Art.6(1). The exact moment after which traffic data should be erased (except for billing purposes) may depend on the type of service that is provided. For example, for a voice telephony call the transmission will be considered completed as soon as either of the users terminates the connection; while for electronic mail, the transmission is considered completed as soon as the addressee collects the message, typically from the server of his service provider. However, the obligation to erase the traffic data or to make such data anonymous when it is no longer needed for the transmission of a communication or for traffic management purposes is without prejudice to certain procedures specific to the internet, such as the caching in the domain name system of IP addresses or the use of log-in information to control the right of access to networks or services, because they fall outside of the scope of the E-Privacy Directive: E-Privacy Directive, para.1–011, n.31, Recital 28; para.3–038.

[36] *ibid.*, Art.6(2). There is no indication in the directive itself of the data that may be so processed. Arguably such data would include: (i) the number or identification of the subscriber station; (ii) the address of the subscriber and the type of station; (iii) the total number of units to be charged for the accounting period; (iv) the called subscriber number; (v) the type, starting time and duration of the calls made and/or the data volume transmitted; (vi) date of the call/service; and (vii) other information concerning payment such as advance payment, payments by instalments, disconnection and reminders.

[37] See Art.29, Data Protection Working Party, Opinion 1/2003 on the storage of traffic data for billing purposes, January 29, 2003 (12054/EN/WP69), p.6.

[38] *ibid.*, p.7.

[39] E-Privacy Directive, para.1–011, n.31, Art.6(3). In contrast, the Framework Data Protection Directive (Arts 6 and 7) permits processing of the data if the processing is necessary: (i) for the performance of a contract to which the person to whom the data relates is a party; or (ii) for the purposes of the legitimate interest of the data processor or the third party to whom the data are disclosed. The E-Privacy Directive therefore arguably provides for stricter rules in data processing in the electronic communications sector.

[40] *ibid.*, Art.6(5).

[41] *ibid.*, Art.6(6).

inquiries, fraud detection and marketing of the provider's own communications services. An exception to this general rule is the requirement to provide caller location information to emergency service centres responding to "112" calls. The exception is justified because in emergency situations the protection of life and health is more important than the protection of privacy.[42] The question then arises as to whether telecommunications operators may communicate personal data to third parties, as part of their commercial activities. It has been argued that the communication of personal data to third parties is not permissible in the communications sector, even with the customer's consent, to the extent this is not specifically permitted by the E-Privacy Directive.[43] However, in so far as the E-Privacy Directive merely particularises and complements the Framework Data Protection Directive, it seems that the better interpretation is that the provisions of the Framework Data Protection Directive apply in the absence of specific provisions in the E-Privacy Directive. Under the Framework Data Protection Directive, personal data may be disclosed to third parties, provided the persons to whom this data relates have been informed of their right to object to the disclosure of such information and have not objected to the disclosure.[44]

1–237 **Notification requirement** — Data controllers[45] must notify a national supervisory authority, specifically appointed to ensure compliance with national data protection regulations, before carrying out any automatic processing operation and must supply detailed information on the purposes of the processing as well as the data recipients and on the categories of data concerned.[46]

1–238 **The data subject's rights** — The person to whom personal data relates to is called the "data subject" under the Framework Data Protection Directive. Data subjects are entitled to have access to their personal data, to know where the data originated and to have the data corrected or erased if it is incomplete or inaccurate.[47] The data subject's rights in relation to the marketing of the data have been discussed above. Data subjects must have a right of recourse in the event of an infringement of any of these rights.[48]

1–239 **Sensitive data** — The processing of personal data which reveal the data subject's racial or ethnic origin, political, religious or philosophical beliefs, trade union membership, or information concerning his or her health or sex life is prohibited, except if the data subject has given explicit consent to the processing.[49]

---

[42] *ibid.*, Art.6(5) sets out the general rule that personal data, including caller location information may be transferred to others only with the consent of the user concerned. Art.26 of the Universal Service Directive provides for an exception to this general rule, as far as caller location information is concerned: see further para.1–099 above.

[43] The same argument was made as regards the Telecommunications Data Protection Directive, para.1–232, n.22: see Cuny, "Commentaire de la Directive Européenne du 15 décembre 1997 concernant le Traitement des Données à Caractère Personnel et la Protection de la Vie Privée dans le Secteur des Télécommunications" (1998) 2 C.T.L.R. 62.

[44] Framework Data Protection Directive, para.1–233, n.24, Art.14.

[45] A "data controller" is defined as "a natural or legal person who alone or jointly with others determines the purposes and means of processing of personal data", *ibid.*, Art.2(d).

[46] *ibid.*, Arts 18, 19 and 28.

[47] *ibid.*, Arts 10–12.

[48] *ibid.*, Art.14.

[49] E-Privacy Directive, para.1–011, n.31, Art.8.

1–240   Confidentiality and security of communications — Called subscribers must also be able to prevent the presentation of the calling line identification of incoming calls[50] and also to reject incoming calls where the presentation of the calling line identification has been prevented by the calling party,[51] in each case free of charge. Similarly, the called subscriber must be able to prevent the presentation of connected line identification.[52] The obligations also apply to costs to and from non-EU countries.[53] Member States must ensure the confidentiality of communications by means of public communications networks or services. In particular, unauthorised listening, tapping, storage or other kinds of interception or surveillance of communications and related traffic data other than by users and without the consent of the users concerned, must be prohibited by national legislation.[54] Exception to this prohibition may be provided by national legislation for safeguarding national security, defence or public security and for the prevention, investigation, detection and prosecution of criminal offences or of unauthorised use of the telecommunications system, in which case data may be retained for a limited period.[55] Communications may also be recorded, when legally authorised, when this is carried out in the course of a lawful business practice for the purpose of providing evidence of a commercial transaction or any other business communication.[56] This would, for example, cover the recording of a call made to a business call centre, provided that the subscriber is made aware of the recording and its purpose and has a right to refuse it.[57]

1–241   Other measures protecting privacy — The E-Privacy Directive contains a number of other measures concerning the protection of privacy. This involves balancing the rights of subscribers to check the accuracy of the bills received from their telecommunications operator by receiving itemised bills, but this must be reconciled with the rights to privacy of calling users and called subscribers. Therefore, subscribers must have the right to receive non-itemised bills[58] and Member States must therefore ensure that sufficient alternative methods of communications or payments are available to ensure the protection of privacy of subscribers and users if itemised bills are used.[59]

1–242   Digital networks allow further use of called line and calling line identification services. Operators must therefore allow the calling user, using a simple means and free of charge, to prevent the presentation of the calling line identification on a call-by-call and per line basis.[60]

1–243   Unsolicited calls, made without human intervention by way of automated calling systems, facsimile machines, email or other means, such as SMS, for the purposes of direct marketing may only be allowed in respect of subscribers who have given their prior consent.[61] However,

[50] *ibid.*, Art.8(2).
[51] *ibid.*, Art.8(3).
[52] *ibid.*, Art.8(4).
[53] *ibid.*, Art.8(1).
[54] *ibid.*, Art.5.
[55] *ibid.*, Art.15.
[56] *ibid.*, Art.5(2).
[57] *ibid.*, Art.5(3).
[58] *ibid.*, Art.7.
[59] For example, in France and Italy, itemised bills do not comprise, in principle, the last four digits of the number of the called subscriber. Member States may also encourage payment facilities that allow for anonymous or private access to communications services, such as pre-paid calling cards and the use of credit cards. Certain types of number, *e.g.* "helpline" numbers, could also be deleted from itemised bills.
[60] E-Privacy Directive, para.1–011, n.31, Art.8(1).
[61] *ibid.*, Art.13(1).

email addresses may be used for direct marketing by individual or legal persons that supply goods or services if the email address has been obtained in the context of a sale of goods or services and the customer has an opportunity to reject such use, both when the address was collected and on each subsequent occasion that a message is sent.[62] Member States must also ensure than direct marketing is not allowed either without the consent of the subscriber or the subscribers who have indicated a general will not to receive such communication.[63] It is prohibited to disguise or conceal the identity of the sender of emails used for direct marketing purposes.[64]

1–244   Location data other than traffic data — Digital mobile networks can identify the location of a user in order to ensure that the call is completed. This location data may also have other potential uses, for example to provide value-added services that are location-specific. Such location data may be used only where it is made anonymous, or where the users or subscribers have given their consent to the provision of such value-added services.[65] This consent may be withdrawn at any time and for individual connections to the network.[66] The processing of location data may in any event be undertaken only under the authority of the network operator or service provider and only for the purposes of providing the value-added services. An exception to this general rule is the requirement to provide caller location information to emergency service centres responding to "112" calls.[67]

1–245   Remedies for breach of privacy requirements — Under the Framework Data Protection Directive and the E-Privacy Directive, the imposition of remedies for an infringement of a data subject's rights is left to individual Member States. Potential remedies include a broad range of civil and criminal penalties, as well as administrative injunctions and claims for damages against the data controller.[68]

1–246   Transfer of personal data to non-EU countries — Personal data may only be transferred out of the EU to a non-EU country if that country ensures "an adequate level of protection".[69] Adequacy is to be assessed "in light of all the circumstances" surrounding a particular data transfer, including the applicable national laws and sectoral rules (*e.g.* industry codes) in force. Transfers of personal data to non-EU countries which do not ensure an adequate level of protection may, nonetheless, be lawful if one of the following conditions is met: (i) the data subject has given his unambiguous consent to the proposed transfer; (ii) the transfer is necessary for the performance of a contract or the implementation of pre-contractual measures that were requested by the data subject; (iii) the transfer is necessary for the conclusion or performance of a contract concluded in the interest of the data subject between the data controller and a third party; (iv) the transfer is necessary or legally required on important public interest grounds; (v) the transfer is necessary to protect the vital interests of the data subject; (vi) the transfer is made from a public

---

[62] *ibid.*, Art.13(2).
[63] *ibid.*, Art.13(3).
[64] *ibid.*, Art.13(4).
[65] *ibid.*, Art.9(1).
[66] *ibid.*, Art.9(1) and (2).
[67] *ibid.*, Art.9(3). See also para.1–236, n.42 above.
[68] Framework Data Protection Directive, para.1–233, n.24, Arts 22, 23 and 24.
[69] *ibid.*, Arts 25 and 26.

register; or (vii) contractual provisions between the transferor of data in the EU and the recipient of data in the non-EU country ensure the provision of an adequate level of protection.

1–247 The approach chosen in the United States has been to create industry sector-specific codes in order to keep government intervention to a minimum and to establish systems appropriate for different sectors. Particular difficulties have arisen with the transfer of personal data to recipients in the United States, which does not have similar data protection legislation and takes a very different approach to data protection. The Commission had initially determined that the United States did not provide an adequate level of protection on the basis that this "*laissez-faire*" approach did not afford an adequate level of protection for data of EU citizens. After long-lasting negotiations, the EU and the United States decided to resolve the matter by agreeing on a set of "safe harbour" principles, developed by the United States Department of Trade, that followed the principles set out by the Framework Data Protection Directive. United States businesses that receive data from undertakings and persons in the EU and comply with such principles on a voluntary basis can benefit from the freedom to receive data sent from the EU. Mechanisms for assuring compliance with these safe harbour principles may take different forms: (i) compliance with industry-specific data protection programs; (ii) compliance with the requirements of legal or regulatory supervisory authorities; and (iii) by committing to co-operate with data protection authorities located in the EU.

2. Legal Protection of Databases

1–248 In the 1988 Green Paper on Copyright and the Challenge of Technology, the Commission had already indicated the need for better legal protection of databases and for the harmonisation of national rules in the Community.[70] As a result, the Database Directive was adopted on March 11, 1996 to harmonise national laws on the protection for databases.[71] EU Member States were required to implement the Directive into national law by January 1, 1998.

(a) Database Directive

1–249 The Database Directive applies to databases in both electronic and non-electronic form. A database is defined as "a collection of independent works, data or other materials arranged in a systematic or methodical way and individually accessible by electronic or other means".[72] This definition will generally cover all commercially operated databases if they are equipped with a database (administration) system. However, the Directive does not apply to recordings, extracts from audio-visual, cinematographic, literary or musical works, nor to the compilation of a number of recordings of musical performances on one CD, since the Database Directive was not intended to affect the protection granted to phonograms.[73] Multimedia anthologies with musical examples

---

[70] COM(88) 172 final, August 23, 1998.

[71] Directive 96/9 of the European Parliament and of the Council of March 11, 1996 on the legal protection of databases (Database Directive), O.J. 1996 L77/20. For a more detailed review of the Database Directive, see, *e.g.* Lehmann, "The European Database Directive and its Implementation into German Law" (1998) 29 (7) ICC 776–793.

[72] Database Directive, para.1–249, n.71, Art.1(2).

[73] *ibid.*, Recital 17.

can arguably claim database protection.[74] Nor does it apply to computer programs,[75] which are protected under the Computer Software Directive.[76]

The Database Directive establishes a dual regime of protection for databases: copyright protection for the structure of certain databases and a newly created *sui generis* right protecting the content of all databases.

(b) Copyright Protection for Databases

1–250   Conditions of eligibility — Databases shall be protected by copyright if, by reason of the selection or arrangement of their content, they constitute the author's own intellectual creation.[77] No other criteria shall be applied to determine the eligibility for that protection.[78] As a result, to qualify for protection, a database must not have been copied or plagiarised and the selection or arrangement of data must show a minimum of originality. This may mean that the "white pages" of a telephone directory would not qualify for copyright protection, although by contrast, the "yellow pages" may meet these requirements and thus be entitled to such protection.[79]

The protection under the Database Directive applies to the structure of the database and does not extend to the contents of the database and is without prejudice to rights in the contents, including copyright protection, which will continue to be determined by the relevant provisions of national law and any Community measures.[80]

1–251   Beneficiaries of copyright protection for databases — Copyright rests in the author of a work. Authorship of a database belongs to the natural person or group of natural persons who created the database, or, when permitted by national law, to the legal person designated as the right holder by that legislation.[81] In contrast to the Computer Programs Directive,[82] the Database Directive does not provide for the transfer as a matter of law to an employer of the user rights relating to a database protected by copyright that is created by an employee in the execution of his duties or following the instructions given by his employer. However, Member States may provide for such a statutory transfer in their national legislation.[83]

1–252   Scope of copyright protection for databases — The owner of copyright in a database benefits from all the rights generally granted by copyright protection[84]: (i) temporary or permanent reproduction by any means and in any form, in whole or in part; (ii) translation, adoption,

---

[74] Lehmann (see para.1–249, n.71), p.780.
[75] Database Directive, para.1–249, n.71, Art.2(b).
[76] *ibid.*, Art.2(a). Likewise, Directive 91/250 concerning the protection of computer programs (Computer Programes Directive), O.J. 1991 L122/42.
[77] Database Directive, para.1–249, n.71, Art.3.
[78] *ibid.*
[79] Lehmann (see para.1–249, n.71), p.781.
[80] Database Directive, para.1–249, n.71, Art.3(2).
[81] *ibid.*, Art.4(1).
[82] Computer Programs Directive, para.1–249, n.76, Art.2(2).
[83] Database Directive, para.1–249, n.71, Recital 29.
[84] *ibid.*, Art.5.

arrangement or other alteration of the database; (iii) any form of distribution to the public of the database or of copies thereof; (iv) any communication, display or performance to the public; and (v) any reproduction, distribution, communication, display or performance to the public of any translation, adaptation, arrangement or other alteration. Their very broad restricted rights means that they would cover the temporary storage or transfer of a database on another medium, such that even browsing a database on the internet would be subject to the author's consent.[85]

The author's exclusive right to any form of public distribution of a database or copies thereof in a physical form (*e.g.* on a CD-ROM) includes distribution in a non-physical form (*e.g.* online access). EU-wide exhaustion of the distribution right applies only to the first sale of each physical copy of a database: the author's rights are only exhausted to that copy of the database and not the database generally.[86] The transfer of a database or part of it through online access alone should be analysed as the provision of a service with the result that there is no exhaustion of rights.[87] This also applies with regard to a copy of all or part of an online database made by the user of online services with the consent of the right holder. Thus, there is no exhaustion of the distribution right in a database in the case of a permitted downloading and creation of a new copy and the author can prohibit any resale or further distribution of such a copy.[88]

1–253 Limitations on copyright protection — A lawful user of a database (*i.e.* a purchaser or a licensee) does not require the consent of the author for any of the restricted acts reserved to the author if they are necessary for the purposes of access to the contents of the database and normal use of the contents.[89] If the user is permitted to use only part of the database, this exception applies only to that part.[90] Any contractual provisions to the contrary are null and void as a matter of law.[91]

---

[85] Lehmann (see para.1–249, n.71), p.784. That said, these provisions are without prejudice to Directive 2001/29 of the European Parliament and of the Council of May 22, 2001 on the harmonisation of certain aspects of copyright and related rights in the Information Society (also called "Information Society Copyright Directive"), O.J. 2001 L167/10, aimed at harmonising the rights of reproduction, distribution and communication to the public in the context of the Information Society. The Directive stipulates that temporary storage or browsing of any copyrightable content is subject to the author's consent, although it provides for an exception for temporary copies that enable the user to make use of the work, such as "caching". The provisions of the Copyright Directive are reviewed in paras 2–075 and 3–021 *et seq.*

[86] Database Directive, para.1–249, n.71, Art.5(c). The "exhaustion of rights" theory, which results from the case law of the European Court of Justice, stipulates that an intellectual property right cannot be used to prohibit the sale in a Member State of goods which have been marketed in another Member State by the holder of the intellectual property right or with his consent. This theory, which is based on the rules of the EC Treaty on free movement of goods (Art.28, *ex* 30), was developed initially in relation to patents (Case–15/74 *Centrafarm BV et Adriaan de Peijper v Sterling Drug Inc.* [1974] E.C.R. 1147) and has gradually been extended to other intellectual property rights, including copyrights (Case–78/70 *Deutsche Grammophon Gesellschaft mbH v Metro-SB-Großmärkte GmbH & Co. KG.* [1971] E.C.R. 487). For more details on the exhaustion of rights theory, see Bellamy and Child, *Common Market Law of Competition* (Sweet & Maxwell, 5th ed., 2001), paras 8–009 and 8–067.

[87] Database Directive, para.1–249, n.71, Recital 33. See Case–62/79 *SA Compagnie générale pour la diffusion de la télévision, Coditel v Ciné Vog Films (No.1)* [1980] E.C.R. 881 and Case–262/81 *Coditel SA, Compagnie générale pour la diffusion de la télévision v Ciné-Vog Films SA (No.2)* [1982] E.C.R. 3381.

[88] Lehmann (see para.1–249, n.72), p.786.

[89] Database Directive, para.1–249, n.71, Art.6(1).

[90] *ibid.*

[91] *ibid.*, Art.15.

Member States have the option of providing, under national implementing law, for limitations on the exclusive rights of the author in the following cases: (i) unrestricted reproduction for private purposes of a non-electronic database (*i.e.* databases whose elements are not individually accessible with the assistance of electronic means); (ii) where there is use for the sole purpose of illustration for teaching or scientific research, as long as the source is indicated and the extent is no more than justified by the non-commercial purpose to be achieved; (iii) where a database is used for the purposes of public security or for the purposes of an administrative or judicial procedure; and (iv) certain national exceptions to copyright traditionally authorised under national law.[92] These exceptions must not unreasonably prejudice the right holders' legitimate interests or conflict with normal exploitation of the database.[93]

1–254   Term of copyright protection — Copyright in a database provides an EU-wide term of protection of 70 years, from the death of the author.[94] Where the author is a legal entity, the term of protection expires 70 years after the database is lawfully made available to the public.[95]

1–255   Remedies for infringement of copyright in a database — The Directive requires Member States to provide for appropriate remedies for authors to enforce the rights provided under the Database Directive. This gives Member States broad flexibility in this respect[96]; remedies will ordinarily include damages, on account of profits from the infringement and injunctions.

(c) *Sui Generis* Database Right

1–256   Conditions of eligibility — The main innovation of the Database Directive was to introduce a *sui generis* right granting protection to database makers who have made a qualitative and/or quantitative substantial investment in the obtaining, verification or presentation of the contents of a database.[97] The *sui generis* protection applies regardless of whether the database or the content of the database show any of the intellectual creation needed for copyright protection: its purpose is to protect the often considerable human, technical and financial investments made in creating databases. This means, for example, that both the "white pages" and the "yellow pages" of a telephone directory would enjoy *sui generis* protection. The *sui generis* right is a purely economic right aimed at protecting the investment made in obtaining and collecting data.[98] This investment can consist of the deployment of financial resources and/or the expending of time, effort and energy.[99] The *sui generis* right applies independently of the eligibility of the database for copyright protection or other rights and irrespective of the eligibility of the owners for protection in their own right. The protection of databases under the *sui generis* right is also without prejudice to any rights existing in their contents.[1]

[92] *ibid.*, Art.6(2).
[93] *ibid.*, Art.6(3).
[94] Council Directive 93/98 of October 29, 1993 harmonising the term of protection of copyright and certain related rights, O.J. 1993 L290/9.
[95] *ibid.*
[96] Database Directive, para.1–249, n.71, Art.13.
[97] *ibid.*, Art.7(1).
[98] *ibid.*, Recital 39.
[99] *ibid.*, Recital 40.
[1] *ibid.*, Art.7(5).

1–257 Beneficiaries of the *sui generis* protection of databases — The beneficiary of the *sui generis* protection is the "maker" of the database, which is "the person who takes the initiative and the risk of investing".[2] This excludes contractors and employees from the protection. The *sui generis* right may be transferred or granted under contractual licence.[3] The s*ui generis* protection of databases is only available to databases whose makers or right holders are nationals of Member States or persons who have their habitual residence in the Community.[4] It shall also be available to companies and firms formed in accordance with the law of a Member State and having their registered office, central administration or principal place of business within the EU.[5] When such a company or firm has only its registered office in the EU territory, its operation must be genuinely linked on an ongoing basis with the economy of a Member State.[6] The possibility is provided for extending the benefit of the *sui generis* protection to databases made in third countries by way of international agreements concluded by the Council, upon a proposal from the Commission, provided that the term of protection does not exceed that granted to Community nationals, companies and firms.[7] As a result of successive agreements, protection under the *sui generis* right granted by the Database Directive has been extended to citizens and companies of the EEA countries (*i.e.* Norway, Iceland and Liechtenstein) and a number of Central and Eastern European countries.[8] Proposals have been made at international level to adopt a global *sui generis* protection of databases.[9]

1–258 Scope of *sui generis* protection — The scope of the *sui generis* right is somewhat narrower than that of copyright. The holder of the *sui generis* right has the right to prohibit the extraction and/or re-utilisation of the whole or of a qualitatively or quantitatively substantial part of the contents of the database created by him.[10] Extraction is defined as "the permanent or temporary transfer of all or a substantial part of the contents of a database to another medium by any means or in any form"[11]; whilst re-utilisation is defined as "any form of making available to the public all or a substantial part of the contents of a database by the distribution of copies, by renting, by online or other forms of transmission".[12] As discussed above in relation to copyright protection,[13] EU-wide exhaustion of the *sui generis* right can only take place in relation to an individual copy of the database and occurs upon the first sale of that copy (*e.g.* on a CD-ROM).[14] There is no exhaustion of the maker's rights in the case of permitted online access to a database, even if the user is authorised to make a copy for himself. The repeated and systematic extraction and/or re-utilisation of substantial parts of the contents of a database can also be restricted, where there is not a normal exploitation of the database or where exploitation unreasonably prejudices the legitimate interests

---

[2] *ibid.*, Recital 41.
[3] *ibid.*, Art.7(3).
[4] *ibid.*, Art.11(1).
[5] *ibid.*, Art.11(2).
[6] *ibid.*
[7] *ibid.*, Art.11(3).
[8] European Economic Area Agreement (EEA), Art.65(2), Annex XVII.
[9] Lehmann (see para.1–249, n.71), p.778.
[10] Database Directive, para.1–249, n.71, Art.7.
[11] *ibid.*, Art.7(2)(a).
[12] *ibid.*, Art.7(2)(b).
[13] See para.1–250 *et seq.*, above.
[14] Database Directive, para.1–249, n.71, Art.7.

of the maker of the database[15]: this would prevent a database being "abused" by a competitor over a prolonged period.

1–259   Limitations on *sui generis* protection — The maker of a database which is made available to the public in whatever manner may not prevent a lawful user of the database from extracting and/or re-utilising qualitatively or quantitatively insubstantial parts of its content for any purpose.[16] Any contractual provision to the contrary is null and void.[17] This limited user right would, for example, permit the citation of a database without the consent of the maker of the database. The exercise by a user of this right may not conflict with normal exploitation of the database or unreasonably prejudice the legitimate interests of the maker of the database, the holder of copyright and neighbouring rights in the works or subject matter contained in the database.[18]

As with copyright in databases, Member States have the option of providing, under national law, for limitations on the exclusive rights of the maker of the database, the extraction or re-utilisation of a substantial part of a database in the following circumstances, without prior authorisation: (i) extraction for private purposes of a non-electronic database; (ii) extraction for the sole purpose of illustration for teaching or scientific research, as long as the source is indicated and the extent of the extraction is no more than justified by the non-commercial purpose to be achieved; and (iii) extraction and re-utilisation for the purposes of public security or for the purposes of an administrative or judicial procedure.[19]

1–260   Terms of protection — Protection under the *sui generis* right runs from the date of completion of the making of the database and expires 15 years from the first of January of the year following the date of completion.[20] However, any substantial change, evaluated qualitatively or quantitatively, within that period to the content of a database results in a new 15-year term of protection for the *sui generis* right, provided that this involves a substantial new investment.[21] The burden of proof that the criteria exist for concluding that a substantial modification of the contents of a database is to be regarded as a substantial new investment lies with the maker of the database.[22] In practice, this would result in unlimited protection for those databases that are updated (by way of successive additions, deletions or alterations) regularly.

1–261   Remedies for infringement of the *sui generis* right — As with copyright in databases, Member States have broad discretion in determining the adequate remedies to enforce *sui generis* rights.[23] In a number of Member States (*e.g.* Germany), the remedies are identical for infringement of copyright and the *sui generis* right.

---

[15] *ibid.*, Art.7(5).
[16] *ibid.*, Art.8.
[17] *ibid.*, Art.15.
[18] *ibid.*, Art.8(2).
[19] *ibid.*, Art.9.
[20] *ibid.*, Art.10.
[21] *ibid.*
[22] *ibid.*, Recital 54.
[23] *ibid.*, Art.12: see para.1–258, above.

K. Public Procurement in the Telecommunications Sector

1–262 The procurement procedures of most undertakings active in the telecommunications sector were subject until recently to the provisions of the so-called "Utilities Directive".[24] Given the extent of competition in the telecommunications sector, the Commission has however decided to exempt EU telecommunications operators in most Member States from public procurement rules in most national markets. The application of public procurement rules in the telecommunications sector was justified by the pre-liberalisation environment of monopoly operators susceptible to governmental pressure to favour national industry, either because they were controlled by the State or depended on the State for the renewal of their operating licences. In so far as the telecommunications sector was not competitive at that time, it was perceived that those operators were unlikely to resist governmental influence to favour local suppliers and/or would in any event chose local operators for reasons such as technical standards.[25]

1–263 Scope of the Utilities Directive[26] — In principle, the Utilities Directive applies to works, supplies, and service contracts awarded by public authorities or public law bodies, public undertakings (*i.e.* undertakings over which public authorities exercise a dominant influence), and private undertakings enjoying exclusive or special rights,[27] for the provision or operation of public telecommunications networks or services.[28] The Utilities Directive sets out the conditions under which a contracting entity may use a specific award procedure (*i.e.* open, restricted or negotiated procedures),

---

[24] Council Directive 93/38 of June 14, 1993 co-ordinating the procurement procedures of entities operating in the water, energy, transport and telecommunications sectors, O.J. 1993 L199/84, as amended by Directive 98/4 of February 16, 1998, O.J. 1998 L101/1.

[25] See generally *e.g.* Arrowsmith, *The Law of Public and Utilities Procurement* (Sweet & Maxwell, 1996).

[26] *ibid.*, at p.31.

[27] Special or exclusive rights are defined by Art.2(3) of the Utilities Directive, para.1–262, n.24, as rights deriving from authorisations granted by a competent authority of a Member State having as their result the reservation for one or more entities of the exploitation of public telecommunications networks or services. Art.2(3) specifies that rights of way must be considered as exclusive or special rights within the meaning of the Directive. Accordingly, to the extent they enjoy rights of way, private telecommunications operators are in principle subject to the Utilities Directive. It has been argued that this is no longer the case following the judgment of the Court of Justice in the *British Telecom (Leased Lines)* case (Case C–302/94 *R. v Secretary of State for Trade and Industry Ex p. British Telecommunications plc* [1996] E.C.R. 6417). In this case, the Court concluded, in relation to the interpretation of "special or exclusive rights" for the purposes of the ONP Leased Lines Directive, that an entity did not enjoy special or exclusive rights merely because it holds a licence when the ONP licence (i) was granted by the authorities of a Member State to an undertaking or number of undertakings using criteria that are objective, proportionate, and free from discrimination, and (ii) did not substantially affect the ability of the other undertakings to provide or operate telecommunications networks or provide services in the same geographic area under substantially equivalent conditions. Should the interpretation applied in the *British Telecom (Leased Lines)* case be applied to the Utilities Directive, many privately owned telecommunications operators would escape the application of procurement rules: see Arrowsmith, "The Community's Legal Framework on Public Procurement: The Way Forward at Last?" (1999) C.M.L.R. 1–49 at p.32. It does not seem, however, that this interpretation of the concept of "special or exclusive rights" can be applied to the Utilities Directive in light of the clear wording of Art.2(3), which clearly defines a right of way as an exclusive or special right without any qualification. In any event, the exemption of telecommunications services from the procurement rules as a result of Art.8 of the Utilities Directive, as discussed below, has rendered the issue largely irrelevant.

[28] Utilities Directive, para.1–262, n.24, Art.1.

the formalities applying to calls for tenders, as well as the qualification, selection and award process (*i.e.* contracts should be awarded to the candidate offering the lowest price or the most economically advantageous tender, requiring examination of various criteria depending on the contract in question and mentioned in the market notice or specific contract terms).[29] A specific directive (the "Remedies Directive") was also adopted providing for remedies at both the EU and national levels to enforce the procurement rules in the Utilities Directive.[30]

1–264 Exemption from the application of the Utilities Directive in the telecommunications sector — Article 8 of the Utilities Directive gives the Commission the power to exempt from the procurement rules in the Utilities Directives procurement contracts relating to telecommunications services which other undertakings are free to offer in the same geographic area under substantially the same conditions. In the *British Telecom* (Utilities Directive) case, Article 8 was interpreted by the Court as meaning that for the exemption to apply, other entities must not only be authorised to provide the services in question, without legal barriers to entry, but there must be *de facto* competition in the market.[31]

Following a broad consultation with the industry,[32] the Commission has acknowledged that effective competition now exists in most Member States for all public telecommunications services, including the provision of public telecommunications networks. As a result, the Commission has decided to exclude practically all telecommunications services from the scope of EU procurement rules, with their continued application only for a limited number of services in Greece and Portugal.[33] The Commission has indicated that the exemption of most telecommunications services through an Article 8 exemption is only the prelude to the exclusion of the telecommunications sector altogether from the scope of the Utilities Directives.[34] Accordingly, a list was agreed on May 12, 1999 by the Commission specifying which telecommunications services, in which Member State, are considered to be exempted from public procurement rules.[35]

1–265 The whole European public procurement legislation is currently being reviewed. The Commission has submitted *inter alia* a proposal for a new "Utilities Directive" which no longer

---

[29] *British Telecom (Leased Lines)* case, para.1–263, n.27 above.

[30] Council Directive 92/13 of February 25, 1992 co-ordinating the laws, regulations and administrative provisions relating to the application of Community rules on the procurement procedures of entities in the water, energy, transport and telecommunications sectors: O.J. 1992 L76/14.

[31] *British Telecom (Leased Lines)* case, para.1–263, n.27, above. The Court stated that the determination of whether a contracting entity is exposed to competition such that it falls within the exemption should be made on an individual basis. Such analysis should focus on the characteristics of the services at issue, the existence of alternative providers of these services, price factors, the market position of the contracting entity and the existence of any legal constraints on market entry.

[32] Commission Communication, Public Procurement in the European Union, COM(98) 143.

[33] Communication from the Commission pursuant to Art.8 of Directive 93/38, O.J. 1999 C129/11. Procurement in relation to public fixed telephony and the transmission of data/value-added services (telephone cards, internet and call-back connection) are still subject to the Utilities Directive in Portugal and Greece, as are procurement contracts relating to satellite services in Greece.

[34] Commission Communication, Public Procurement in the European Union, COM(98) 143, above, para.1–263, n.27.

[35] For the complete list of telecommunications services exempted from public procurement rules, see *www.europa.eu.int/comm/internal_market/en/publproc/general/util.htm*.

includes the telecommunications sector.[36] If the proposal is adopted and implemented into the national laws of the Member States, purchases by entities operating in this sector will no longer be subject to the rules and procedures of the new Utilities Directive. However, if such entities fulfil the criteria of a so-called "body governed by public law" they would fall within the scope of the proposed new "Public Sector Directive".[37] This does not necessarily mean that their purchases would be subject to the more stringent rules of the Public Sector Directive. It is explicitly inapplicable to public contracts

> "for the principal purpose of permitting the contracting authorities to provide or exploit public telecommunications networks or to provide to the public one or more telecommunications services".[38]

As far as other utilities and contracting authorities are concerned the exclusion of the telecommunications sector brings about an increased tendering obligation. The current Public Service Directive[39] and Utilities Directive exclude from their scope purchases of voice telephony, telex, mobile telephone, paging and satellite services.[40] If the Proposals for a new Public Sector Directive and a new Utilities Directive are adopted and once they have been implemented by the Member States, all contracting authorities and all utilities will have to tender contracts for the purchase of such services.[41]

L. Telecommunications Equipment

1–266 Liberalisation of the telecommunications sector started by removing national restrictions on the supply of telecommunications equipment. With the adoption of the Telecommunications Terminal Equipment Directive in 1988, only the incumbent telecommunications operators were authorised to supply and market the telecommunications equipment to be connected to public switched telephone networks. The Commission therefore acted to promote competition in this sector, whilst preserving the integrity of networks against inadequate equipment. The Commission's

---

[36] Proposal for a Directive of the European Parliament and of the Council co-ordinating the procurement procedures of entities operating in the water, energy and transport sectors, COM(2000) 276 final, O.J. 2001 C29/112. The proposal has been modified in the meantime to include postal services; see Amended proposal for European Parliament and Council Directive co-ordinating the procurement procedures of entities operating in the water, energy, transport and postal services sectors, COM(2002) 235 final, O.J. 2002 C203/183.

[37] Proposal for a Directive of the European Parliament and of the Council on the co-ordination of procedures for the award of public works contracts, public supply contracts and public service contracts COM(2000) 275 final, O.J. 2001 C29/11.

[38] *ibid.*, Art.13.

[39] Council Directive 92/50 of 18 June 1992 relating to the co-ordination of procedures for the award of public service contracts, O.J. 1992 L209/1, as amended by Commission Directive 2001/78 of September 13, 2001, amending Annex IV to Council Directive 93/36, Annexes IV, V and VI to Council Directive 93/37, Annexes III and IV to Council Directive 92/50, as amended by Directive 97/52, and Annexes XII to XV, XVII and XVIII to Council Directive 93/38, as amended by Directive 98/4, O.J. 2001 L285/1.

[40] *ibid.*, Annex IA; Utilities Directive, para.1–262, n.24, Annex XVIA.

[41] Proposal for a new Public Sector Directive, para.1–263, n.27, Annex IIA; Proposal for a new Utilities Directive, para.1–263, n.26, Recital (8) and Annex XVIIA.

action in the equipment sector has been threefold: (i) abolition of the monopoly rights of incumbent telecommunications operators to manufacture, market and maintain terminal equipment and satellite earth equipment; (ii) the harmonisation and mutual recognition of conformity assessment procedures; and (iii) the harmonisation of technical standards.

1. Liberalisation of Terminal Equipment and Satellite Earth Equipment

1–267   The liberalisation of the telecommunications terminal equipment market was achieved by the Commission adopting the Telecoms Equipment Directive[42] pursuant to Article 86(3) (*ex* Article 90(3)) of the EC Treaty. In the preamble to the Telecoms Equipment Directive, the Commission indicated that its policy in this area was based largely on the freedom to supply goods across borders, as provided for in Article 28 (*ex* Article 30) of the EC Treaty. The Directive's adoption was also motivated by the need to prevent incumbent telecommunications operators abusing their dominant position as network operators, in violation of Article 82 (*ex* 86) of the EC Treaty,[43] by limiting, through their monopoly network rights, the sources of supply for users of and the potential for technical progress in terminal equipment.

The scope of the Terminal Equipment Directive was extended to cover satellite equipment with the adoption in 1994 of the Satellite Directive.[44] Satellite equipment benefits from the provisions of the RTTE Directive.[45] The RTTE Directive does not apply however to receive-only radio equipment intended to be used solely for the reception of sound and TV broadcasting (*e.g.* DTH equipment). The RTTE Directive abolishes Community-wide or national type approval regimes for radio and telecommunications terminal equipment, removes *a priori* market controls by introducing a system based on manufacturers' declarations and surveillance, and relaxes the regulatory requirements for the free movement and putting into use of telecommunications terminal equipment, including satellite equipment. In particular, when equipment has been manufactured according to harmonised standards and/or the manufacturer has followed one of the conformity assessment procedures contained in the RTTE Directive, this equipment is presumed to comply with the essential requirements standard and may thus be freely marketed across the EU.[46] ETSI has been mandated to develop such harmonised standards.[47]

1–268   Abolition of monopoly rights and freedom to market terminal equipment — The Telecoms Equipment Directive required Member States to withdraw all exclusive or special rights granted to businesses in relation to terminal equipment,[48] including satellite earth equipment.

---

[42] Commission Directive 88/301 of May 16, 1988 on competition in the markets in telecommunications terminal equipment (Telecoms Terminal Equipment Directive), O.J. 1988 L131/73.

[43] On Art.82, see para.6–014 *et seq.*

[44] See, above, para.1–004, n.10.

[45] Directive 99/5 of March 9, 1999 on radio equipment and telecommunications terminal equipment and the mutual regulation of their conformity (RTTE Directive), O.J. 1999 L91/10. See, below, para.1–274 *et seq.*

[46] *ibid.*, Art.5(1).

[47] The lack of harmonised pan-European standards has been identified as a key problem for the cross-border marketing of satellite equipment such as VSATs: see "Market Access: Problems and Solutions", Report of the Satellite Action Plan Regulatory Working Group, available at: *www.ispo.cecbe/infosoc/telecompolicy/en/saprep13.doc.*

[48] Telecommunications Terminal Equipment Directive, para.1–267, n.42, Art.2.

Exclusive or special rights are monopoly rights granted by a Member State to one or a limited number of (public or private) undertakings, otherwise than according to objective, proportional and non-discriminatory criteria, to import, market, connect and maintain terminal equipment.[49] As a result, all undertakings have the right, across the EU, to import, market, connect, bring into service and maintain terminal equipment that meet certain harmonised technical standards.

1–269 Types of equipment covered — The Telecoms Equipment Directive applies to equipment connected, directly or indirectly, to the termination of a public telecommunications network for the purposes of sending, processing or receiving information.[50] This includes telephone sets, modems, telex terminals, data transmission terminals, mobile telephones, private automatic branch exchanges (PABXs) and routers. It also includes satellite earth station equipment, *i.e.* equipment capable of being used for the transmission and/or the reception of radio-communication signals by means of satellites or other space-based systems.[51]

1–270 Essential requirements — Member States may refuse to allow equipment to be placed on the market and brought into service on their territory when the equipment does not satisfy relevant common technical standards or, in their absence, certain safety and technical standards, known as "essential requirements" (*e.g.* protection of the health and safety of users and any other person, electro-magnetic compatibility, the protection of network integrity, and, in certain cases, the inter-working of terminal equipment and the protection of personal data and privacy).[52] Moreover, Member States may require businesses to have appropriate technical qualifications to connect, bring into service and maintain terminal equipment, provided such qualifications are based upon objective, non-discriminatory and published criteria.[53]

1–271 Access to network termination points — Users of terminal equipment must be given access to public network termination points and Member States are required to publish the technical characteristics of these points.[54]

1–272 Publication of national technical specifications and type-approval procedures — Member States are required to disclose technical specifications and type-approval procedures to the Commission in draft form and publish them.[55]

---

[49] *ibid.*, Art.3.

[50] *ibid.*, Art.1. A connection is "indirect" if other equipment is placed between the terminal and the termination point of the network. A connection may be made via optical fibre or electro-magnetic means.

[51] *ibid.* This includes transmit-only, receive-only and transmission and receiving equipment.

[52] *ibid.*, Art.3. It must be noted that the "essential requirements" referred to in the Telecommunications Terminal Equipment Directive, para.1–267, n.42, were generally the same as the "essential requirements" referred to in the previous ONP Framework Directive, Art.3(2). Under the ONP Framework Directive, access to the public telephone network would have been refused on the ground that this was necessary to protect "essential requirements", see, above, para.1–052, n.30. The Access Directive makes clear that access, once mandated, cannot be refused for any reason (Access Directive, para.1–011, n.29, Art.12) and, therefore, the reference to the "essential requirements" in the interconnection context is no longer pertinent. On the issue of grounds upon which access may be legitimately refused, see para.1–159, above.

[53] Telecommunications Terminal Equipment Directive, para.1–267, n.42, Art.3.

[54] *ibid.*, Art.4.

[55] *ibid.*, Art.5.

1–273 Independent bodies for granting type-approval — Member States are required to entrust the responsibility for drawing up technical specifications and for type-approval to an independent body unconnected with any undertaking offering goods or services in the telecommunications sector.[56] It was essential for the success of the liberalisation process to take away this regulatory function from incumbent operators, to avoid any risk of discrimination (*e.g.* undue delay in granting, or refusal to grant, a type-approval) against suppliers of equipment competing with the incumbents' own equipment. In fact, this was the first step towards the creation of independent NRAs with broad jurisdiction over the various aspects of telecommunications.[57]

2. Harmonisation and Mutual Recognition of Conformity of Equipment

1–274 The establishment of a competitive Community market in telecoms equipment is dependent to a large extent on the mutual recognition of national type-approvals between Member States. Indeed, the marketing of new equipment throughout the EU was slowed down considerably by the requirement to obtain type-approval in every Member State in which the product was placed on the market. The introduction of an efficient system of mutual recognition of conformity in the telecommunications sector took considerable effort and time, in large part owing to the reluctance of certain Member States to accept third-country type-approvals in this sector on the stated ground that network safety and integrity were greatly at risk from the connection of equipment which was not efficiently controlled. The RTTE Directive constitutes the last step in the establishment of a single market in terminal equipment. It is the fourth directive adopted on this subject since 1986.[58]

The RTTE Directive provides the regulatory framework for the placing on the market, free movement and putting into service in the EU of radio equipment and telecommunications terminal

---

[56] *ibid.*, Art.6. Joined cases C–46/90 and C–93/91 *Procureur du Roi v Jean-Marie Lagauche* [1993] E.C.R. 5267, the Court of Justice held that a Belgian regulation prohibiting the marketing of terminal equipment without the prior type-approval by a public company (*i.e.* the Belgian RTT, the incumbent operator) offering telecommunications services, was contrary to Art.6 of the Telecommunications Terminal Equipment Directive. See also Case C–69/91 *Criminal proceedings against Francine Gillon, born Decoster* [1993] I E.C.R. 5335, and Case C–92/91 *Criminal proceedings against Annick Neny, born Taillandier* [1993] I E.C.R. 5383 where the Court of Justice held that a French regulation prohibiting, subject to criminal penalties, the sale of terminal equipment without prior type-approval of the equipment was contrary to Art.6 of the Directive, when the independence of the authority delivering the type-approval is not ensured.

[57] See para.1–041, above.

[58] See Council Directive 86/361 of July 24, 1986 on the initial stage of the mutual recognition of type-approval for telecommunications terminal equipment, O.J. 1986 L217/21. This was replaced by Council Directive 91/263, O.J. 1991 L184/28, on the approximation of the laws of the Member States concerning telecommunications terminal equipment, including mutual recognition of their conformity (Second Phase Directive), O.J. 1991 L128/1, the scope of which was extended to certain satellite earth station equipment pursuant to Council Directive 93/97, in respect of satellite earth station equipment, O.J. 1993 L290/1. These Directives were subsequently consolidated into Directive 98/13 of the European Parliament and of the Council of February 12, 1998, relating to communications terminal equipment and satellite earth station equipment, including the mutual recognition of their conformity, O.J. 1998 L74/1, which was itself repealed, with effect from April 7, 2000 by the RTTE Directive. For a discussion of the context that led to the adoption of these successive directives, see Higham, Bannister and Gordon, *EC Telecommunications Law* (Wiley & Sons, 1996) sections 3.8–3.15 and Mosteshar, *European Community Telecommunications Regulation* (Graham & Trotman, 1993), pp.24–32.

equipment.[59] Member States were required to transpose the RTTE Directive into national law no later than April 7, 2000 and apply them from April 8, 2000.[60] Equipment that was placed on the market in accordance with the rules applicable prior to the entry into force of RTTE Directive on April 8, 2000 or within two years after that date may still be freely placed on the market and brought into service, notwithstanding that it may not comply fully with the RTTE Directive.[61]

1–275 Types of equipment covered — In addition to telecommunications terminal equipment,[62] the RTTE Directive also applies to radio equipment,[63] which was not covered by the previous directives concerning type-approval. The RTTE Directive does not apply to certain types of equipment, including receive-only radio equipment intended solely for the reception of sound and TV broadcasting, as well as cabling and wiring.[64]

1–276 Conformity based on self-certification — The RTTE Directive is based upon the principle of declarations by equipment manufacturers that their equipment conforms to the essential requirements identified in Article 3 of the Directive, *i.e.* that it respects certain safety requirements and satisfies the protection requirements with regard to electro-magnetic compatibility.[65] Radio equipment must also use the allocated spectrum so as to avoid harmful interference.[66] Following consultation with the Telecommunications Conformity Assessment and Market Surveillance Committee, in accordance with Article 15 of the RTTE Directive, the Commission may decide that specified apparatus must meet additional requirements concerning: (i) interworking via networks with other apparatus, so that it may be connected to the interface of the appropriate type throughout the Community; (ii) avoidance of harm to the network or its functioning and misuse of network resources, to avoid unacceptable degradation of service; (iii) incorporating safeguards concerning the protection of personal data and privacy of subscribers; (iv) supporting features for the avoidance of fraud; (v) supporting features ensuring access to the emergency services; (vi) supporting features to facilitate use by disabled users.[67] This self-certification system is similar to that used for products such as television sets and personal computers. It replaces the regime of official public

---

[59] RTTE Directive, para.1–267, n.45, Art.1(1).

[60] France has obtained an exemption from the application of the directive, as regards the maintenance of the national requirements for telecommunications terminal equipment intended for connection to the analogue public switched telephone network of France Telecom. See Commission Decision of May 26, 2000, in O.J. 2000 L135/25. Such exemption should however expire at the beginning of 2004.

[61] The Commission published a communication in the framework of the implementation of the RTTE Directive, listing each standard and the date of the cessation of the presumption of conformity with the suspended standard. See O.J. 2002 C190/19.

[62] "Telecommunications terminal equipment" is defined as "a product enabling communication or a relevant component thereof, which is intended to be connected directly or indirectly by any means whatsoever to interfaces of public telecommunications networks (that is to say, telecommunications networks used wholly or partly for the provision of publicly available telecommunications services)": see RTTE Directive, para.1–267, n.45, Art.2(1).

[63] "Radio equipment" is defined as "a product, or relevant component thereof, capable of communication by means of the emission and/or reception of radio waves utilising the spectrum allocated to terrestrial/space radio-communication": RTTE Directive, para.1–267, n.45, Art.2(1).

[64] *ibid.*, Art.1(4) and Annex I.

[65] *ibid.*, Arts 10 and 3(1).

[66] *ibid.*, Art.3(2).

[67] *ibid.*, Art.3(3).

type-approval on the basis of official testing that was previously in place, which was perceived as imposing unduly long assessment and approval procedures in comparison with the average lifetime of telecommunications and radio equipment.

1–277 Manufacturers can choose between several procedures for assessing compliance of equipment with the essential requirements laid down in the Directive.[68] Conformity for terminal equipment can be made following a purely internal production control mechanism, without the intervention of an independent testing body (Annex II procedure). However, manufacturers can elect to follow other procedures that provide for varying levels of intervention by an independent testing body, which can review the manufacturer's tests and issue an opinion on conformity and, for full quality assurance procedures, compliance with the requirements for such procedures. Radio equipment operating in the spectrum allocated to terrestrial/space radio communications must be subject to conformity assessment procedures involving an independent testing body.[69] When equipment meets standards harmonised at EU level, there is a presumption of compliance with the essential requirements laid down by the Directive,[70] although the RTTE Directive contains procedures to be applied in circumstances where a Member State or the Commission considers that conformity with a harmonised standard does not ensure compliance with essential requirements, which shall be brought before the Telecommunications Conformity Assessment and Market Surveillance Committee.[71]

Equipment that has satisfied one of the conformity assessment procedures and complies with all relevant essential requirements bears the "CE" conformity marking, which shall be affixed under the responsibility of the manufacturer or importer.[72]

1–278 Equipment complying with the essential requirements can be freely traded across Europe — Member States must ensure that equipment complying with the essential requirements laid down in Article 3 of the RTTE Directive can be placed on the market, imported into the EU, put into service and connected to the network without any further national restrictions.[73] Member States must also ensure that operators of public telecommunications networks do not refuse to connect telecommunications terminal equipment to appropriate interfaces on technical grounds when the equipment complies with the essential requirements.[74] Manufacturers and importers of equipment are required to provide information to the user on the intended use of the apparatus and provide a declaration of conformity.[75] As regards radio equipment making use of frequency bands not harmonised throughout the EU, the manufacturer or importer must notify the national

[68] *ibid.*, Art.10 and Annexes II (conformity to type), III (production quality assurance), IV (full quality assurance) and V (minimum criteria to be taken into account by Member States when designating notified bodies in accordance with Art.11(1)).
[69] *ibid.*, Art.10(3) and (4).
[70] *ibid.*, Art.5.
[71] *ibid.*, Art.5(2).
[72] *ibid.*, Art.12(1) and Annex VIII.
[73] *ibid.*, Arts 6, 7 and 8.
[74] *ibid.*, Art.7(3).
[75] *ibid.*, Art.6(3).

authority responsible for spectrum management of the intention to place such equipment on the market four weeks before the start of the placing on the market.[76]

1–279 Safeguard measures — Member States are allowed to take appropriate measures to withdraw an apparatus from the market or from service, prohibit it from being further placed on the market and restrict its free movement if they ascertain that this apparatus does not comply with harmonised standards or any of the essential requirements laid down by the RTTE Directive.[77] Member States may also take similar measures in relation to radio equipment that has caused or is likely to cause harmful interference on nationally allocated frequency bands.[78] Likewise, if a Member State considers that a certain type of equipment is causing serious damage to a network or harmful radio interference, the operator of the network may be authorised to refuse connection, to disconnect such apparatus or to withdraw it from service.[79] In case of emergency, the operator may disconnect the equipment if the protection of the network requires the equipment to be disconnected without delay and if the user can be offered an alternative solution, without delay and without incurring costs. The operator must then immediately inform the NRA.[80]

The RTTE Directive requires the Member State to inform the Commission of any such measures indicating the reasons for its decision.[81] The Commission will then consult the parties concerned (*i.e.* the competent NRA, the manufacturer and/or importer of the equipment and other Member States) and inform the Member State within two months of its opinion as to whether the measures are justified. If it considers that the measure is not justified, the Commission will request the Member State to withdraw the measure.[82]

1–280 Placing equipment manufactured outside the EU on the European market — Equipment manufactured outside the EU can be freely placed on the market, traded and put into service across the EU provided that it meets the essential requirement standards set down by the RTTE Directive. In this respect, compliance with the conformity assessment procedures set forth by the Directive and technical standards harmonised at the EU level should ensure the benefit of such freedom to third countries' manufacturers. The self-certification conformity procedure introduced by RTTE Directive should greatly facilitate the entry of third country manufacturers on the EU market. The main obstacles will, however, remain the diverging standards across the world for certain types of equipment. The RTTE Directive provides for a mechanism that can allow for the adoption of measures against third countries that do not allow similar access to their national markets of equipment manufactured in the EU.[83]

[76] *ibid.*, Art.6(4).
[77] *ibid.*, Art.9(1).
[78] *ibid.*, Art.9(5).
[79] *ibid.*, Art.7(4).
[80] *ibid.*, Art.7(5).
[81] *ibid.*, Art.9(2).
[82] *ibid.*, Art.9(6).
[83] *ibid.*, Art.16.

3. Harmonisation of Standards

1–281   Under the EC Treaty's rules on the free movement of goods, which prohibit national rules that restrict trade in imported goods, Member States may nevertheless rely on national standards to protect essential mandatory requirements, such as safety and consumer protection.[84] As a result, where national standards differ or are incompatible, the marketing across Europe of equipment manufactured according to the national standards of one Member State can be seriously impeded even if the principle of mutual recognition should be applicable. Mutual recognition of conformity assessment procedures and national standards would thus have little impact on the equipment market within the EU, if Member States were to continue at the same time to apply different standards to the concept of "mandatory requirements". Early on, it was thus perceived that, to ensure integration of a liberalised common market for telecommunications equipment, the harmonisation of standards should go hand in hand with mutual recognition requirements. The EU has therefore taken a number of initiatives to promote the adoption of harmonised European standards that would be recognised in all Member States and replace national standards. Initially, in the 1960s and 1970s, such standards were promulgated by EC Council Directives that set out exhaustive lists of performance objectives and design specifications. However, this approach was abandoned as being too cumbersome.

1–282   Therefore, in 1983 the Community adopted general legislation on technical standards. Under Directive 83/189,[85] Member States were required to notify the Commission before adopting new technical standards. If national measures are not notified, they are unenforceable.[86] The Directive allowed the Commission to challenge measures that it considers incompatible with the EC Treaty. However, it did not in itself result in harmonised technical standards nor mutual recognition of the conformity with essential or mandatory requirements recognised at the Community level. Directive 93/189 was repealed and consolidated by Directive 98/34.[87] Member States must now inform the Commission and the European Standardisation bodies (CEN, CENELEC and ETSI) of any draft national standard (*i.e.* a technical specification approved by a recognised standardisation body and with which compliance is not compulsory) or technical regulation (*i.e.* a technical specification, the observance of which is compulsory) that they are contemplating introducing unless they are identical to or a fully equivalent transposition of an international or European standard.[88] The Commission, after consultation with other Member States, may then decide, within three months following notification of the draft technical regulation or standard, that the adoption of a European standard may be preferable. Member States are then obliged to postpone adoption of the draft national standard or technical regulation until a European standard (drawn up by the European Standardisation bodies) or common technical regulation has been adopted on this subject or

---

[84] See Art.30 (*ex* Art.36) of the EC Treaty and the case law of the Court of Justice following Case 120/78 *Rewe-Zentrale AG v Bundesmonopolverwaltung für Branntwein ("Cassis de Dijon")* [1979] E.C.R. 649.

[85] Council Directive of March 28, 1983 laying down a procedure for the provision of information in the field of technical standards and regulation, O.J. 1983 L109/8. See generally Weatherill, "Compulsory Notification of Draft Technical Regulation: The Contribution of Directive 83/189 to the management of the Internal Market" (1996) 16 Y.E.L. 129–204.

[86] Case C–194/94 *CIA Security International SA v Signalson SA ns Securitel Sprl* [1996] I E.C.R. 2201.

[87] Directive 98/34 of June 22, 1998 as amended by the Transparency Directive, see, above, para.1–015, n.43.

[88] *ibid.*, Arts 2 and 8.

if the Commission intends to propose Community legislation on the subject.[89] Such a system enables EU action where adoption of national standards or technical regulations could raise barriers to trade between Member States. The task of developing harmonised technical specifications is entrusted to specialised bodies, the European Telecommunications Standards Institute (ETSI), the European Standards Committee (CEN), or the European Electronical Standards Committee (CENELEC). Once the technical specification is agreed upon within a specialised body, it can be made compulsory in the form of a common technical regulation (CTR) following the adoption of a decision by Commission.[90]

1–283   Terminal equipment which has been manufactured and approved according to harmonised standards adopted by a recognised body under a mandate from the Commission is presumed to comply with the essential requirements set forth in the RTTE Directive and may therefore be placed on the market, freely circulated within the Common Market and put into service throughout the EU.[91]

M. Remedies for Infringement of Directives and National Implementing Measures

1–284   This section briefly describes various types of remedy that may be available should a Member State fail to comply with its obligations under Community directives, or should undertakings fail to comply with measures to implement them.

1. Remedies in Case of Infringement of Directives by Member States

1–285   Proceedings by the Commission under Article 226 of the EC Treaty — Liberalisation and harmonisation directives bind Member States as to the result to be achieved, but leave to the Member States the choice of form and methods to achieve that objective.[92] Implementing legislative measures must be taken by national authorities by the deadline specified in the directive. Although the details of the national legislation may vary, the result must be the same in all Member States.

In the event that a Member State fails to fully implement a directive into national law in a timely or in an appropriate fashion, the Commission, on its own initiative[93] or, in most cases, following a

---

[89] *ibid.*, Art.9.

[90] See, *e.g.* Commission Decision 97/751 of October 31, 1997 on a common technical regulation for the attachment requirements for terminal equipment interface to 140 Mbit/s digital unstructured and structured leased lines, O.J. 1997 L305/66; Commission Decision 97/545 of July 9, 1997 on a common technical regulation for the general attachment requirements for Data Terminal Equipment (DTE) to connect to Packet Switched Public Data Networks (PSPDNs) offering CCITT Recommendation X.25 interfaces, O.J. 1997 L223/21; and Commission Decision 94/821 of December 9, 1994 on a common technical regulation for attachment requirements of terminal equipment interface for ONP 64 kbit/s digital unstructured leased lines, O.J. 1994 L339/81.

[91] RTTE Directive, para.1–267, n.45, Art.5. See, above, para.1–274 *et seq.*

[92] Art.249 (*ex* 189) of the EC Treaty, third para. See generally Hartley, *The Foundations of European Community Law* (Oxford University Press, 4th ed., 1998) p.99; and Weatherill & Beaumont (para.1–006, n.18).

[93] In the telecommunications sector, the Commission closely monitors the implementation of directives by Member States and has so far issued eight reports assessing the level of implementation of the liberalisation and harmonisation directives by Member States: see para.1–216, n.87, where a link to the latest report is provided. Member States are generally also required to notify implementing measure to the Commission, which assists in this monitoring process.

complaint by an injured party, can initiate proceedings against the Member State under Article 226 (*ex* 169) of the EC Treaty.[94] Infringement proceedings under Article 226 involve several phases. First, whether acting on its own initiative or after having received a complaint, the Commission will consult informally with the Member State concerned and attempt to bring the infringement to an end. This informal stage, which may last from a few months to years, results in a large proportion of infringements being terminated by Member States without further steps by the Commission: the Member State in question will then adopt measures to properly implement the relevant directive. If the matter is not resolved at the informal stage, the Commission will send to the Member State a formal letter of notice setting out its case against the Member State. If no settlement is reached, the Commission will send a "reasoned opinion" to the Member State establishing the legal arguments on which the Commission is relying. As a last resort, the Commission will refer the matter to the Court of Justice, which in appropriate cases will eventually adopt a judgment establishing the infringement and requiring the Member State to take the necessary measures to comply with the judgment.[95] In the case of a continued failure to comply with the Treaty provisions, the Commission may refer the matter back to the Court of Justice, which may impose a fine upon the Member State in question. Article 226 proceedings can last several years, which undermines substantially their effectiveness in resolving disputes in a sector like telecommunications. Nevertheless, the Commission has brought numerous cases before the Court of Justice for failure to implement a liberalisation or harmonisation directive in the telecommunications sector. Such cases have been concerned with how NRAs have interpreted and implemented specific provisions.[96]

1–286 Review by the Commission under Article 86(3) — Article 86(1) (*ex* 90(1)) of the EC Treaty obliges Member States neither to enact nor maintain measures that are contrary to the EC Treaty to the benefit of public undertakings or undertakings with exclusive or special rights. Article 86(3) gives the Commission the power to address decisions or directives to Member States to ensure the application of Article 86(1).[97] Article 86(3) proceedings are initiated by the Commission either following a complaint or on its own initiative. In contrast to Article 226 proceedings, Article 86(3) proceedings are a much more efficient enforcement tool, as the Commission alone is involved in the process and it takes the final decision. However, the Commission can only adopt an Article 86(3) decision if the Member State's conduct constitutes a violation of another Treaty provision, normally Article 82 (*ex* 86) of the EC Treaty that prohibits the abuse of a dominant former incumbent operator in a situation where it could abuse its dominant position. As a result, a failure to implement, either at all or properly, a telecommunications directive would not ordinarily as such give the Commission a cause of action under Article 86(3). However, in some instances this could be the

---

[94] For a comprehensive review of the procedure under Art.226 of the EC Treaty, see Schermers & Waelbroeck, *Judicial Protection in the European Communities* (Kluwer, 1992), p.277 *et seq.* and Weatherill & Beaumont (para.1–006, n.18), p.192 *et seq.* A Member State may also initiate an infringement proceeding against another Member State pursuant to Art.227 (*ex* Art.170). In practice, Member States are very reluctant to use this possibility and there have been very few precedents. For a review of the case law of the European Courts in relation to infringement proceedings for failure to transpose EU telecom directives properly, see the Commission's *Guide to the Case Law of the European Courts in the field of Telecommunications*, which is available at: *http://www.europa.eu.int/information_society/topics/telecoms/implementation/infringement/doc/guidecaselaw.pdf*.

[95] Art.229(1) of the EC Treaty.

[96] Art.228(2) of the EC Treaty.

[97] The conditions of application of Art.86 of the EC Treaty are discussed in more details in Pt II; see para.6–054 *et seq.*

case. For example, should the conditions for a licence favour the incumbent operator to the detriment of a new entrant in violation of the non-discrimination requirement embodied in the Authorisation Directive, a complaint before the Commission could result in an Article 86(3) decision concerning an infringement by the Member State in question of Article 86(1) in conjunction with the EC Treaty's competition rules (Articles 81 and/or 82),[98] the rules on the freedom to provide cross-border services (Article 49) or the freedom of establishment (Article 43).[99] When a Member State fails to implement an Article 86(3) decision, the Commission may bring the matter before the Court of Justice under Article 226.[1]

1–287 Enforcement of directives by private parties — Although directives are addressed to Member States, individuals may rely on provisions of directives having direct effect, *i.e.* domestic courts have a duty to enforce the rights that private parties derive from those provisions.[2] Individuals may rely on directives in actions against Member States if (i) the deadline for implementation has passed and the Member State has failed to implement the directive or has implemented it in an incorrect manner; and (ii) the provisions are sufficiently clear and precise; (iii) leaving little or no discretionary power to the Member State.[3] Directives may have direct effect with respect to publicly owned telecommunications operators on the basis that they are "emanations of the State" and this may remain the case even after they have been privatised.[4] As any action by the Commission against a Member State is likely to take a considerable time (and until recently had no effective sanctions), private action before national courts may bring more immediate results, given the availability of interlocutory proceedings at national level, although proceedings could be lengthened by the need for a preliminary ruling from the Court of Justice under Article 224 of the EC Treaty, regardless of whether the directive has direct effect. Directives can only have vertical direct effects: they do not have horizontal direct effects. This means that, once their implementation date has passed, they may be relied on against the State and any "emanation" of it (including nationalised industries and NRAs), but not against private individuals and undertakings.[5] Nevertheless, national courts should seek to interpret national law in accordance with the provisions of a directive, so far as this is possible, even against private undertakings.[6] Injured parties can also seek damages against Member States before national courts for failure to implement a directive in question so as to deny them the rights afforded by the directive.[7]

---

[98] See, for instance, the Commission's decisions in *Omnitel* and *Second GSM Licence in Spain* discussed in paras 6–060 and 6–061, below.

[99] See, for instance, the Commission's decision in *VTM* discussed in para.2–013, below.

[1] Case 226/87 *Commission v Greece* [1988] E.C.R. 3611.

[2] See Case 41/74 *Yvonne van Duyn v Home Office* [1974] E.C.R. 1337. See also Hartley (para.1–285, n.92, above), p.195; and Weatherill & Beaumont (para.1–006, n.18), p.341. For instance, Art.2 of the Services Directive was found to have direct effect in *Telsystem v Telecom Italia* (Italian Antitrust Authority, decision of January 10, 1995) and *3C Communications v SIP* (Italian Antitrust Authority, decision of March 4, 1992).

[3] Case 148/78 Pubblico *Ministero v Ratti* [1979] E.C.R. 1629.

[4] Case 188/89 *A Foster v British Gas plc* [1990] E.C.R. 3313.

[5] Case 152/84 *M. H. Marshall v Southampton and South-West Hampshire AHA (Teaching)* [1986] E.C.R. 723; and Case 80/86 *Kolpinghuis Nijmeyen BV* [1987] E.C.R. 3969. Despite arguments that directives should have "horizontal direct effect", the Court of Justice has confirmed that they do not: Case C–91/92 *Paola Faccini Dori v Recreb Srl.* [1994] I E.C.R. 3325.

[6] Case C–106/89 *Marleasing SA v La Comercial Internacional de Alimentacion SA* [1990] I E.C.R. 4135.

[7] See Joined Cases C–6/90 and C–9/90 *Andrea Francovich and Daniela Bonifaci v Italian Republic* [1991] I E.C.R. 5357. A Member State may be liable to third parties in connection with the implementation of a

2. Remedies for Infringement of National Implementing Measures

1–288 Enforcement by NRAs — NRAs have the primary responsibility for enforcing national rules implementing EU communications directives. The specific conditions under which the competent NRA may act, as well as the procedural rules for action by it (*e.g.* the possibility of imposing penalties) are determined by national legislation. It is beyond the scope of this book to describe the various national regimes. However, the directives of the New Regulatory Framework set out a number of principles that national procedural rules must take account of.

1–289 NRAs' own intervention in relation to access and interconnection — NRAs may intervene at their own initiative in any matter concerning access and interconnection, in order to ensure that operators respect the provisions of the communications directives. They may force a party to negotiate access and interconnection and set the conditions for the conclusion of an access and interconnection agreement.[8]

1–290 Dispute resolution between private parties — Member States must ensure that any party (such as users, service providers and consumers) that has an unresolved dispute with an organisation providing electronic communications networks or services, has a right to bring the matter before the competent NRA or another independent body.[9] Easily accessible and inexpensive out-of-court procedures must be available at a national level to resolve such disputes in a fair, transparent and timely manner. Where warranted, this may involve the payment of compensation. These procedures must provide for a transparent decision-making process in which due respect is given to the rights of the parties, which must be given the opportunity to state their case. NRAs must issue a binding decision in the shortest possible timeframe and in any case within four months of submission. NRAs may decline jurisdiction to resolve a dispute if other mechanisms (such as mediation) are more suitable to resolving the dispute. Any such decision must be reasoned and made available to the parties and be published, and decisions by NRAs must be subject to appeal to a court. The availability of dispute resolution by an NRA is without prejudice to either party's right to bring an action before the courts.[10] Whilst NRAs may be able to resolve disputes, it is unlikely (save perhaps in the context of consumer groups) that they would be able to award damages.

1–291 Resolution by NRAs of cross-border disputes between operators and between operators and consumers — In case of disputes between operators in different Member States, or between parties active in different Member States,[11] NRAs must co-ordinate their efforts to bring to an end the

---

directive where: (i) the directive in question was intended to confer rights on individuals and the content of those rights may be determined from the provisions of the directive in question; (ii) the failure to implement the directive was sufficiently serious; and (iii) there was a direct causal link between the breach of the obligation to implement and the damage sustained by the third party.

[8] Access Directive, para.1–011, n.29, Art.5(4): see para.1–181, above.

[9] Universal Service Directive, para.1–011, n.30, Art.34.

[10] Framework Directive, para.1–009, n.25, Art.20; Universal Service Directive, Art.34(4).

[11] A party is free to enter into an access and/or interconnection agreement in any Member State, regardless of whether it is authorised or not to provide its services within that territory: Access Directive, para.1–011, n.29, Art.3(1).

dispute. However, no time limit is set in this case.[12] In cross-border disputes involving consumers, Member States must co-ordinate their efforts to resolve the dispute.[13]

1–292   Other mechanisms — Member States may adopt other mechanisms to resolve a dispute that has arisen between parties, even in cases of cross-border disputes, including mediation. Where such measures are available, NRAs may decline to resolve a dispute. In the case of unresolved disputes involving consumers, relating to issues covered by the Universal Service Directive, transparent, simple and inexpensive out-of-court procedures must be made available to the concerned consumers.[14] In appropriate cases, systems of compensation and/or reimbursement may be put in place. These provisions also cover online out-of-court dispute resolution mechanisms available for consumers involved in online transactions.[15] In particular, national legislation should not hamper the establishment of such complaint offices.[16]

1–293   Court action — Aside from any action before NRAs, injured parties may also initiate court action if an undertaking infringes national implementing measures or if an NRA fails to apply them properly. The Framework Directive provides that Member States must provide rights of appeal against decisions of NRAs to an independent body, which may be a court. The body must have "appropriate expertise". Appeals must take into account the merits of the case. Where the review body is judicial in character, its decision must be subject to review by a court or tribunal.[17] Although the availability of interlocutory proceedings and remedies such as damages and mandatory injunctions may provide the businesses concerned with the opportunity of rapid and efficient remedies, national courts may not be in the best position to settle all types of dispute. Despite the complexity and specificity of the required technical assessment that some cases raise, in many Member States, appeal of NRAs' decisions must be brought before a court. The question arises whether it would not be appropriate, given the specificity of the disputes, to create expert tribunals at the national level to decide on those appeal proceedings similar to those set up in some Member States for hearing appeals against decisions of national competition authorities. This may also raise an issue of correct implementation of the Framework Directive, to the extent that it requires an appeal being available not only on the procedure but also on the merits of the case,[18] as not all administrative courts review the facts of cases, but only the law.

1–294   Transparency procedure — The Framework Directive provides for a transparency procedure, pursuant to which any draft national measure imposing (or amending or withdrawing) *ex ante* obligations on operators with SMP (and in exceptional cases, all operators) must first be submitted to other NRAs and the Commission, which may comment on it.[19] The Commission, after consultation with the Communications Committee, may adopt a decision to require the NRA to amend or withdraw its proposed measure.[20] As the Commission's decision would have legal

---

[12] Framework Directive, para.1–009, n.25, Art.21.
[13] Universal Service Directive, para.1–011, n.30, Art.34(3).
[14] *ibid.*, Art.34.
[15] *ibid.*, Art.34(2).
[16] *ibid.*
[17] Framework Directive, para.1–009, n.25, Art.4.
[18] *ibid.*, Art.4.
[19] *ibid.*, Art.7(3).
[20] *ibid.*, Art.7(4).

effects, any operator, user or provider that might be injured by such decision would be entitled to challenge it before the Court of First Instance, provided that it can be shown that it (or he) is individually and directly concerned by the decision.[21] If the Commission does not adopt a decision requiring the amendment or withdrawal of the NRA's proposed measure, an aggrieved party would still be entitled to bring an action against the NRA's final measure, according to general remedies available for infringement of national implementing measures or relevant directive, and provided that certain conditions are met.[22]

1–295 Communications Committee — The Framework Directive[23] established a Communications Committee to replace the ONP Committee, established under the previous ONP regulatory framework.[24] Arguably, the conciliation procedure that was available before the ONP Committee under the 1998 regulatory framework would still be available before the new Communications Committee, to the extent that the Communications Committee will function as interface between the Commission and the operators as regards matters relating to the implementation of the New Regulatory Framework's directives. Hence, any user complaining that he has been or may be injured by an infringement of the directives comprising the New Regulatory Framework may, where no agreement has been reached at national level (for instance, by use of the procedures to be made available according to Article 20 of the Framework Directive),[25] request the Commission and/or the competent NRA to refer the matter to the Communications Committee. Under the previous ONP procedure, a working group had to be convened including two members of the ONP Committee, one representative of the NRA concerned, the chairman of the Committee or another official of the Commission. After hearing the NRA, the injured party and the communications operator, the working group would endeavour to reach an agreement between the parties involved. It remains to be seen how the new Communications Committee will work in this regard.

N. Access to the EU Telecommunications Market for Non-EU Businesses

1–296 Background — Some preliminary steps for the liberalisation of the telecommunications sector at the international level were taken within the World Trade Organisation (WTO) when 69 members concluded[26] the Agreement on Basic Telecommunications Services on February 15,

---

[21] Art.230 of the EC Treaty, fourth paragraph. On the issue of "direct concern", see Case C–50/00P, *Union de Pequeños Agricultores v Council* [2002] I E.C.R. 6677, judgment of July 25, 2002; confirming that a natural or legal person can bring an action for annulment against a regulation only if its provisions are of direct and individual concern to that person, if *i.e.* the applicant's legal position is affected by reason of certain attributes peculiar to him or by reason of a factual situation which differentiates him from all other persons, and makes him the equivalent of the addressee. In doing so, the Court overruled the Court of First Instance's recent judgment in Case T–177/01 *Jégo-Quéré & Cie SA v Commission* [2002] II E.C.R. 2365, judgment of May 3, 2002, which had the effect of extending the concept to any person whose rights or obligations would be affected by the Community measure.

[22] See, above, para.1–288 *et seq.*

[23] Framework Directive, para.1–009, n.25, Art.22.

[24] ONP Interconnection Directive, para.1–006, n.23, Art.15.

[25] See above, para.1–290 *et seq.*

[26] The WTO members which are signatories to the Fourth Protocol are: Argentina, Antigua and Barbuda, Australia, Bangladesh, Belize, Bolivia, Brazil, Brunei Darussalam, Bulgaria, Canada, Chile, Colombia, Côte

1997.[27] This Agreement is the "Fourth Protocol" to the General Agreement on Trade and Services (GATS),[28] an agreement on the liberalisation of services that was concluded in 1994 within the framework of the Uruguay Round of trade negotiations.[29] The Fourth Protocol entered into force on February 5, 1998. The GATS and the Agreement on Basic Telecommunications Services contains provisions that are relevant to cross-border trade in the telecommunications sector and also contains certain market liberalisation measures regarding telecommunications.

1–297   GATS obligations — The Fourth Protocol is an integral part of the GATS. The obligations laid down in the GATS therefore apply fully to telecommunications activities. The GATS lays down three main principles: most favoured nation (MFN),[30] "national treatment",[31] and market access.[32] Under the MFN principle, WTO members must treat services and service suppliers from other WTO members no less favourably than like services and service suppliers from any other member.[33] Although they do not have to be reasoned, any exceptions that WTO members make by way of a "reservation" from the MFN clause must respect a list of criteria.[34] Under the national treatment principle, foreign suppliers must be given treatment no less favourable than that accorded to local services and service suppliers.[35] WTO members may make exceptions to this principle, provided they do so in a written declaration that specifies the extent of their obligations on market access. Each WTO member that is signatory to the Fourth Protocol to the GATS has set out binding commitments on providing access to its telecommunications market. These are contained in a so-called "schedule of commitments". WTO members may impose restrictions on their market access in their schedules of commitments. For example, such restrictions may involve limitations on the number of operators that may be given access to the domestic market. A large number of WTO members, including the European Communities (on behalf of its Member States) and the United States, submitted specific schedules of commitments as part of the adoption of the GATS in 1994 in relation to market access and national treatment in the telecommunications sectors.

d'Ivoire, Czech Republic, Dominica, Dominican Republic, Ecuador, El Salvador, the European Communities (on behalf of its Member States), Ghana, Grenada, Guatemala, Hong Kong, Hungary, Iceland, India, Indonesia, Israel, Jamaica, Japan, Korea, Malaysia, Mauritius, Mexico, Morocco, New Zealand, Norway, Pakistan, Papua New Guinea, Peru, Philippines, Poland, Romania, Senegal, Singapore, Slovak Republic, South Africa, Sri Lanka, Switzerland, Thailand, Trinidad and Tobago, Tunisia, Turkey, United States of America and Venezuela.

[27] See *www.wto.org/english/tratop_e/serv_e/telecom_e/telecom_commit_exempt_list_e.htm*.

[28] See *www.wto.org/english/tratop_e/serv_e/gatsintr_e.htm*.

[29] For a comprehensive review of the impact of the GATS in the telecommunications sector, see Bronckers & Larouche, "Telecommunications Services and the World Trade Organisation" (1997) 31(3) *Journal of World Trade* 5–48; Ryan, "Trade in Telecommunications Services: A Guide to the GATS" (1997) 3 C.T.L.R. 95; and Mavroidis & Neven, "The WTO Agreement on Telecommunications: It's Never too Late" in *State Monopolies in the European Union and Beyond*, (D. Géradin, Kluwer, 1997).

[30] GATS, Art.II.

[31] *ibid.*, Art.XVII.

[32] *ibid.*, Art.XVI.

[33] As a result, WTO Members that have not signed the Fourth Protocol can still benefit from the market opening commitments made by signatories mandated by this agreement without having to offer access to their own market in return.

[34] An agreement on a list of reservations from the MFN principle can be found in the Annex of Exemption from Art.II of the GATS.

[35] GATS, Art.XVII.

These commitments are, however, generally limited essentially to value-added services (*e.g.* email, voice mail, online information and databases services, electronic data interchange (EDI), enhanced facsimile services, code and protocol conversion, online information and data processing), which account only for a minor part of the overall telecommunications market.[36] The market access commitments in respect of these services took effect with the entry into force of the GATS on January 1, 1995. No agreement was reached regarding basic telecommunications services. However, it was agreed to continue the negotiations, which led eventually to the adoption of the Fourth Protocol, in 1997.

1–298   GATS obligations that are specific to telecommunications — An Annex on Telecommunications is attached to the GATS, providing specific rules regarding public telecommunications networks and services. Although it was concluded as part of the GATS in 1994, the entry into force of the Annex on Telecommunications was subject to the entry into force of the WTO members' schedules of commitments on February 5, 1998. The Annex on Telecommunications imposes two main obligations on WTO members: (i) an obligation to ensure transparency as regards information on access to and use of public telecommunications networks and services (*e.g.* tariffs, specifications of technical interface, conditions on attachment of terminal equipment); and (ii) the obligation to guarantee access to and use of public telecommunications networks and services on reasonable and non-discriminatory terms and conditions. Accordingly, foreign suppliers of telecommunications must (i) be given access to, and be able to use, public telecommunications networks or services, including private leased lines; (ii) have the right to purchase or lease and attach terminal or other equipment to the network; and (iii) be able to interconnect private leased or owned circuits with public networks or services, or with circuits leased or owned by another service supplier.[37] Their obligations are without prejudice to the right of the network owner to impose access or usage conditions with a view to safeguarding public service duties (*e.g.* universal service), to protect network or service integrity and to restrict network use. These obligations benefit service suppliers in sectors other than telecommunications[38] and providers of telecommunications services competing with incumbent network operators.[39] WTO members may also take measures to ensure the security and confidentiality of messages, provided that such measures do not amount to arbitrary or unjustifiable discrimination or a disguised restriction on trade in services.

1–299   Commitments under the Fourth Protocol — The Fourth Protocol covers "basic telecommunications services", on which WTO members had been unable to reach agreement before the GATS was concluded in 1994. Basic telecommunications services comprise voice telephony, packet-switched and circuit-switched data transmission, telex, telegraph, facsimile and private leased circuit services.[40] These services still account for the bulk of the telecommunications market.

1–300   Market-access and national treatment commitments — Sixty-nine WTO members have attached schedules of specific commitments to the Fourth Protocol. The extent of these commitments

[36] Bronckers & Larouche (para.1–296, n.29), p.19.
[37] Mavroidis & Neven (para.1–296, n.29), pp.6–7.
[38] This is however limited to those sectors where WTO members have accepted commitments in relation to market access and national treatment.
[39] Mavroidis & Neven (para.1–296, n.29), p.7.
[40] See *www.wto.org/english/tratop_e/serv_e/telecom_e/telecom_coverage_e.htm#Top*.

varies from one WTO member to another, but most industrialised countries have committed to liberalise fully their markets for voice telephony and data transmission services.[41] In particular, at the initiative of the United States, a larger number of countries have committed to permit foreign ownership or control of all telecommunications services and facilities. However, the privatisation of publicly owned telecommunications operators falls outside the scope of the GATS, with the result that foreign investment in the local incumbent operator may not be possible until the State decides to privatise it.[42]

1–301 Specific commitments on regulatory principles reference paper — As part of the Fourth Protocol, a large number of WTO members agreed to apply six principles to telecommunications regulatory regimes. These principles are contained in a so-called "Regulatory Principles Reference Paper". They cover: (i) the introduction of competitive safeguards to prevent anti-competitive practices in the telecommunications sector; (ii) interconnection; (iii) universal service; (iv) the public availability of licensing criteria; (v) the establishment of independent regulatory bodies; and (vi) the use of objective, transparent and non-discriminatory procedures for the allocation of scarce resources such as frequencies, numbers and rights of way.[43] The purpose of these "reference principles" is to ensure that incumbent operators, who remain the dominant players in the market, are prevented from using their market position to the detriment of new entrants.[44] These principles are expressed in very basic terms and do not contain the same level of detail as the equivalent principles of the EU regulatory framework.

1–302 Specific remedies and dispute settlement mechanism — The GATS contains a specific remedies and dispute settlement mechanism that can be used when a WTO member does not respect its obligations.[45] The GATS dispute mechanism can only be used by States that are WTO members; private parties (*e.g.* a supplier having difficulties entering a foreign market) have no right to use the mechanism. Some WTO members, such as the EU and the United States, have domestic legal mechanisms that allow private parties to petition their government to take appropriate action when a foreign government fails to comply with its WTO obligations, including recourse to the WTO dispute settlement mechanism.[46] In a sector like telecommunications where markets continue to evolve rapidly, recourse to the WTO dispute settlement mechanism may be inappropriate for obtaining a rapid resolution of a dispute, although the WTO dispute resolution mechanism is still effective. It would be preferable for a foreign operator to be able to seek market access by being able to enforce WTO obligations in domestic courts by relying on these regulatory principles as implemented into national law.[47] However, this may not always be possible. In the EU, it is doubtful

---

[41] Mavroidis & Neven (para.1–296, n.29), pp.11–12; the authors explain that WTO members considered it necessary to produce specific schedules specifying the extent of their commitments, mainly because the provisions of the Annex on Telecommunications were not precise enough and left too much room for interpretation.

[42] Bronckers & Larouche (para.1–296, n.29), p.22.

[43] For a comprehensive review of these principles, see *ibid.*, pp.22–32.

[44] *ibid.*, p.23.

[45] For a review of these remedies, see *ibid.*, pp.37–42.

[46] In the EU, Council Regulation 3286/94 of December 22, 1994, O.J. 1994 L349/71. See Bronckers, "Private Participation in the Enforcement of WTO Law: The New EC Trade Barriers Regulation" (1996) 33 C.M.L.R. 299.

[47] See Eeckhout, "The Domestic Legal Status of the WTO Agreement: Interconnecting Legal Systems" (1997) 34 C.M.L.R. pp.11–58.

that GATS, its Annexes and Protocols would have direct effect so as to be capable of being enforceable by national courts.

1–303 Schedule of the EU's commitments — In its schedule of commitments, the EU has undertaken to apply to service suppliers from WTO countries the EU telecommunications regulatory package in the same manner as it is applied to EU service providers, with a few exceptions. Accordingly, non-EU undertakings must in principle have unrestricted access to and use of public telecommunications networks and services across the EU, including access to and use of private leased circuits. The EU's obligations under GATS are limited to ensuring access to existing services and networks, and there is no obligation for a WTO member to authorise a foreign supplier to establish, acquire, lease, operate or supply new public or private telecommunications networks. The EU has, nevertheless, elected as part of its specific commitments to abolish nearly all restrictions in this respect, with a few exceptions. This means that market entry by non-EU undertakings offering fixed and mobile voice services is allowed on the same terms as those applicable to EU undertakings. While the national law of a number of WTO members (*e.g.* the United States and Australia) continues to limit the level of foreign ownership of telecommunications companies, the EU has abandoned any such limitations, except in the case of France. In France, non-EU individuals or companies may not own more than 20 per cent of the shares or voting rights of companies authorised to establish and operate radio-based infrastructure for the provision of telecommunications services to the general public. Portugal and Finland also had restrictions, which were enshrined in their national regimes until recently, but they have now expired. As regards interconnection, non-EU undertakings benefit, in principle, from the same rights and obligations under the Access Directive as EU undertakings.

1–304 GATS 2000 — A new round of negotiations for the liberalisation of trade in services within the territories of the WTO members started in January 2000; this round is known as GATS 2000. As regards telecommunications, negotiations are based on the WTO members' current commitments made in 1997 and the WTO Agreement on Basic Telecommunications Services. The new round of negotiations provides an opportunity to extend these commitments and adopt new commitments that will cover all electronic communications services.[48] Participants in these negotiations submitted their initial proposals for specific commitments by June 30, 2002 and initial formal offers were scheduled to be made by March 31, 2003. The EU's position is based on the New Regulatory Framework, adopted in March 2002.

1–305 The EU's schedule of commitments expressly excludes audio-visual content, which is defined as the exercise of editorial control over broadcasts. As a result, non-EU content providers may still be subject to market access restrictions in the EU.[49]

1–306 The European Economic Area (EEA) — On January 1, 1994, the Agreement creating the European Economic Area (EEA) between the EU Member States and five Member States of the European Free Trade Association (EFTA), *i.e.* at the time Austria, Finland, Iceland, Liechtenstein,

---

[48] See David Luff, "International Trade Law and Broadband Regulation: Towards Convergence" (2002) 3 *J.N.I.* 240–270.

[49] See para.2–036, below.

Norway and Sweden, entered into effect.[50] The EEA aims at creating a homogeneous European Economic Area.[51] To this end, it creates an association which provides for the same four freedoms as are found in the EC Treaty, as well as for its competition provisions and provisions on state aid. The EEA partners also took on board almost the entire *acquis communautaire*. For this purpose, Protocols and Annexes to the Agreement contain a long list of references to Community secondary legislation in many areas, including telecommunications services[52] and certain information society services,[53] which have been transposed in the EEA partner states. An EFTA Surveillance Authority (ESA) was created in order to ensure that the EFTA States correctly implement these provisions. EC competition and state aid rules in the EEA are enforced by the ESA and the European Commission.[54] This means in practice that undertakings or users and customers in the non-EU EEA countries (*i.e.* Iceland, Liechtenstein and Norway) are subject to, or benefit from, the same rules in the communications sector as those applying in the EU.

[50] For more information, see *http://secretariat.efta.int/*. Austria, Finland and Sweden have since joined the EU.
[51] EEA, Art.1.
[52] *ibid.*, Annex XI.
[53] *ibid.*, Annex XVII.
[54] A more detailed discussion of the ESA and EEA falls outside the scope of this book. For general background information on the EEA, see, for example, Sven Norberg, "The Agreement on a European Economic Area" (1992) C.M.L.R. 1171–1198; Toledano Laredo, "The EEA: an overall view" (1992) C.M.L.R. 1199–1231; Helmut Tichy, "Securing a smooth shift between the two EEA pillars: prolonged competence of EFTA institutions with respect to former EFTA States after their accession to the European Union" (1995) C.M.L.R. 131–156; Sven Norberg, "The Dynamic and Homogeneous EEA — Challenges for the EFTA Court" (1994) E.B.L.R. pp.191–200.

Chapter II
The EU Regulatory Framework Applicable to Broadcasting

2–001 Regulation of the broadcasting sector in Europe is largely national, although some measures have been adopted at the EU level to create a single market in broadcasting.[1] However, a number of Member States continue to have legislation that preserves State or regional public monopolies, restricts the ownership and control of broadcasters, imposes requirements on political impartiality and local content, and limits media cross-ownership.[2] In contrast to the telecommunications sector, the EU audio-visual sector is still to a significant extent regulated by unharmonised national legislation that covers a much wider scope than the limited aspects dealt with by Community directives on television. For example, the licensing of broadcasting services is still a matter of national law. National broadcasting laws must, however, comply with the provisions of the EC Treaty as interpreted by the European Court of Justice and the Court of First Instance.[3]

A. Limitations on Member States: Action as a Result of the EC Treaty's Rules on Free Movement

2–002 To the extent that it is a cultural activity, broadcasting remains largely a matter of national law.[4] However, broadcasting is also an economic activity and as such is subject to the EC Treaty, in particular its provisions concerning the freedom to provide services (Article 49 of the EC

---

[1] See generally, Winn, *European Community and International Media Law* (European Business Law & Practice Series, 1994); Barendt, *Broadcasting Law* (Clarendon, 1995). See also Nihoul, *Telecommunications and broadcasting networks under EC law* (Academy of European Law, 2000); Walden and Angel, *Telecommunications law* (Blackstone Press, 2000); Larouche, *Competition Law and Regulation in European Telecommunications* (Hart, 2000).

[2] See Cavallin, "European Policies and Regulations on Media Concentration" (1998) *International Journal of Communications Law and Policy* 1–18.

[3] As regards the application of the EC Treaty's competition rules in the broadcasting section, see para.6–073 *et seq.*, para.7–011 and para.8–170 *et seq.*

[4] Art.151 of the EC Treaty provides for the possibility of limited Community action in the field of culture.

Treaty (*ex* 59)), the freedom of establishment (Article 43 of EC Treaty (*ex* 52)), the free movement of goods (Article 28 of the EC Treaty (*ex* 30)) and the competition and state aid rules (Articles 81 to 86 of the EC Treaty (*ex* 85 to 90)). Furthermore, any matter that is not specifically regulated by secondary Community law, such as the TWF Directive,[5] remains subject to the provisions of the EC Treaty. Because broadcasting to the public is a service, the most relevant freedom is that of providing services; the free movement of goods and the freedom of establishment are of less relevance. The application of the EC competition rules to the broadcasting sector is examined in Part II.[6]

1. Freedom to Provide Services (Article 49 of the EC Treaty)

2–003   Types of activities covered — Article 49 of the EC Treaty prohibits national restrictions on the freedom to provide services within the EU by nationals of Member States who are established in a Member State other than that of the intended recipient of the services. Television and radio transmissions are considered as services and therefore subject to Article 49 *et seq.* of the EC Treaty.[7] Television services include terrestrial broadcasts, retransmissions by cable and transmissions by satellite. Public performances of films and musical recordings are also considered as services within the meaning of Article 49 of the EC Treaty.[8]

2–004   Prohibition of discriminatory national restrictions — Article 49 of the EC Treaty prohibits all restrictions on the freedom to provide services within the Community. This clearly covers any national legislation (whether national, regional or local) that discriminates against providers of broadcasting services established in another Member State. Examples of discrimination found in the case law of the Court of Justice include: a prohibition of foreign programmes containing advertisements directed at local viewers[9]; the granting to a broadcaster of the monopoly

---

[5] TWF Directive, para.1–015, n.42.

[6] See para.6–073 *et seq.*; para.7–011 *et seq.*; para.8–170 *et seq.*

[7] As regards television services, see Case C–17/00 *François De Coster v Collège des bourgmestre et échevins de Watermael-Boitsfort* [2001] I E.C.R. 9445; Case C–260/89 *Elliniki Radiophonia Tileorassi Anonimi Etairia ("ERT") v Dimitiki Etairia Pliroforissis* [1991] I E.C.R. 2925; and Case C–155/73 *Sacchi* [1974] E.C.R. 409. As regards radio transmission, see Case C–288/89 *Stichting Collectieve Antennevoorziening Gouda v Commissariaat voor de Media* [1991] I E.C.R. 4007 and Case C–353/89 *Commission v The Netherlands* [1991] I E.C.R. 4069.

[8] Winn, para.2–001, n.1, p.68.

[9] Case C–352/85 *Bond van Adverteerders v The Netherlands ("Dutch Advertisers")* [1988] E.C.R. 2085. A Dutch law prohibited the retransmission by cable networks of foreign programmes originally transmitted by satellite that contained advertisements directed at Dutch viewers. The justification for the prohibition was the need to preserve the non-commercial character of television in the Netherlands, where advertising was permitted only through a public agency. The Court of Justice held that the national regulation in question was discriminatory and infringed Article 49 of the EC Treaty since it deprived broadcasters established in other Member States of any possibility of broadcasting on their stations advertisements intended especially for Dutch viewers. It would also have made broadcasting such channels more difficult; as such adverts would have had to be removed prior to retransmission in the Netherlands. See Case C–6/98 *Arbeitsgemeinschaft Deutscher Rundfunkanstalten (ARD) v PRO Sieben Media AG, supported by SAT 1 Satellitenfernsehen GmbH, Kabel 1, K 1 Fernsehen GmbH* [1999] I E.C.R. 7599, and Case T–266/97 *Vlaamse Televisie Maatschapij NV v Commission* [1999] II E.C.R. 2329. See also Case C–318/00 *Bacardi-Martini and Cellier des Dauphins* [2003] E.C.R., not yet reported. Even if the reasons for a preliminary ruling were found inadmissible, the case illustrates well the range of issues dealt with in this kind of case.

right to broadcast both domestic and foreign programmes[10]; the obligation for domestic broad-casters to commission their productions from domestic producers[11]; the obligation for operators of conditional access services to obtain prior authorisation for the marketing of apparatus, equipment, decoders or digital transmission and reception systems, where the prior authorisation scheme is not based on objective, non-discriminatory and published criteria[12]; and the imposition by a Member State of an annual tax on satellite receiving equipment used for the reception of television programmes transmitted by satellite as opposed to cable.[13] Any measure that may make the provision of cross-border broadcasting services more difficult or expensive will infringe Article 49 of the EC Treaty. For example, in *De Coster*,[14] the tax on satellite dishes did not actively prevent the reception of foreign services. It did, however, make them more difficult. Broadcasters established in Belgium enjoyed unlimited access to cable distribution (which covered virtually all the population) for their programmes, unlike foreign broadcasters, which had to transmit most of their programmes via satellite.

2–005 Permissible restrictions justified on public policy grounds — Article 46 of the EC Treaty permits discrimination against foreign providers of services ("public policy" exception) on grounds of public policy, public security or public health. Because this is an exception to a fundamental freedom enshrined in the EC Treaty, it must be interpreted strictly and in such a way that its effects are limited to what is necessary in order to protect the interest it seeks to safeguard (*i.e.* it must satisfy a proportionality test).[15] Moreover, economic aims cannot fall within the public policy exception.[16]

2–006 Prohibition of non-discriminatory restrictions — Article 49 of the EC Treaty prohibits any national restriction on the freedom to provide services, even if applied without distinction to

[10] In *ERT*, para.2–003, n.7, the Court of Justice held that, because the monopoly rights of the national broadcaster (ERT) extended to the right to broadcast both its own programmes and those from other Member States, ERT had the ability to favour its own programmes to the detriment of foreign programmes.

[11] *Commission v The Netherlands*, para.2–003, n.7. The Court of Justice considered that the obligation for Dutch broadcasters to procure productions only from Dutch producers infringed Art.49 of the EC Treaty, since it prevented foreign programme producers from providing services to Dutch broadcasters.

[12] Case C–390/99 *Canal Satélite Digital SL v Administración General del Estado, and Distribution de Television Digital SA (DIS)* [2002] I E.C.R. 607. The Court of Justice examined this restriction simultaneously under both Art.28 of the EC Treaty (free movement of goods) and Art.49 of the EC Treaty. It considered that the national legislation imposing this restriction restricted both fundamental freedoms, that in order for it to be justified, it must pursue a public interest objective recognised by EC law and comply with the principle of proportionality.

[13] *ibid.*

[14] See above, para.2–003, n.7.

[15] *ERT*, para.2–003, n.7, and *Dutch Advertisers*, para.2–004, n.9, at para.36.

[16] *Dutch Advertisers*, para.2–004, n.9 at para.34. The Dutch government argued that the provision of television advertising exclusively by a public agency and the prohibition on advertising contained in foreign broadcasts were justified on grounds of public policy under Art.46, in so far as they were necessary to maintain the non-commercial and, thereby, pluralistic nature of Dutch television. The Court held that the purpose of the system was to secure all advertising revenues to Dutch broadcasters, which was an economic goal. It was therefore not a permissible restriction justified by the "public policy" exception of Art.46. See also Case C–17/92 *Federación de Distribuidores Cinematográficos v Estado Español et Unión de Productores de Cine y Televisión* [1993] I E.C.R. 2239.

both domestic and foreign providers of services, if it is liable to prohibit or impede the activities of providers of services established in other Member States.[17]

2–007 Non-discriminatory restrictions permitted in the general interest — In *Debauve*,[18] the Court of Justice held that, in the absence of harmonisation of national broadcasting laws, non-discriminatory national restrictions could be justified on considerations of general interest. To be justified in the general interest, non-discriminatory restrictions must, however, be proportionate to the general interests protected and there must be no other measures less restrictive of intra-Community trade in services that could be adopted as alternatives.[19] Justifications based on protection of the general interest that have been accepted by the Court of Justice to justify non-discriminatory restrictions are: (i) the maintenance of social order[20]; (ii) the protection of consumers' rights[21]; (iii) the preservation of the national and artistic heritage of a Member State[22]; and (iv) the need to guarantee the freedom of speech and the plurality of the media in a Member State.[23]

2–008 Exclusive broadcasting rights are permitted in copyright licences — The issue of the interaction between national copyright laws and the freedom to provide services under Article 49 of the EC Treaty in the broadcasting sector has been considered by the Court of Justice. It is normal practice for the owner of the copyright in a film or a television programme to grant exclusive licenses to broadcast his film or programme for a specific geographic area (*e.g.* a country or linguistic region of a country).[24] The Court of Justice had to consider whether the owner of the copyright in a film or programme could rely on that copyright to object to the broadcast or

---

[17] Case C–76/90 *Manfred Säger v Dennemeyer & Co. Ltd.* [1991] I E.C.R. 4221.

[18] Case 52/79 *Procureur du Roi v Marc J.V.C. Debauve* [1980] I E.C.R. 833, at para.12. See also Case 279/80 *Criminal proceedings against Alfred John Webb* [1981] I E.C.R. 3305 at paras 16 and 17.

[19] Case 39/75 *Robert-Gerardus Coenen v Sociaal-Economische Raad* [1975] E.C.R. 1547; *Procureur du Roi v Marc J.V.C. Debauve*, para.2–007, n.18. Case 205/84 *Commission v Germany* [1986] E.C.R. 3755; *Dutch Advertisers*, para.2–004, n.9; Case C–154/89 *Commission v France* [1991] I E.C.R. 659; Case C–180/89 *Commission v Italy* [1991] I E.C.R. 709; Case C–198/89 *Commission v Greece* [1991] I E.C.R. 727; *Commission v The Netherlands*, para.2–003, n.7; and *Manfred Säger v Dennemeyer & Co. Ltd.*, para.2–006, n.17.

[20] Case 15/78 *Société Générale alsacienne de Banque SA v Koestler* [1978] E.C.R. 1971.

[21] Case 154/89 *Commission v France* [1991] E.C.R. 659; Case 220/83 *Commission v France* [1986] E.C.R. 3663, para.2–007, n.19; Case C180/89 *Commission v Italy* [1991] E.C.R. 709; *Commission v Greece* [1991] I E.C.R. 727, para.2–007, n.19. See also, Joined Cases C–34/95 *Konsumentombudsmannen v De Agostini (Svenska) Förlag AB* and C–35 and 36/95 *Konsumentombudsmannen v TV-Shop i Sverige AB* [1997] I E.C.R. 3843.

[22] *Commission v Italy* [1991] I E.C.R. 709, para.2–007, n.19.

[23] *ibid.* See also Case C–288/89 *Stichting Collectieve Antennevoorziening Gouda v Commissariaat voor de Media* [1991] I E.C.R. 4007, and Case C–148/91 *Vereniging Veronica Omroep Organisatie v Commissariaat voor de Media* [1992] I E.C.R. 487. Neither the Court of Justice nor the Commission have had yet the opportunity to take a position on the lawfulness under Art.49 of national rules obliging cable operators to carry certain channels, the so-called "*must carry*" obligation. To the extent that domestic channels are often the only ones to benefit from "*must carry*" provisions, these rules are arguably discriminatory within the meaning of Art.49 and, in any event, would restrict the ability of foreign broadcasters to obtain cable carriage. It seems doubtful that they could be justified on "public policy" grounds under Art.46. Moreover, whatever general interest consideration is put forward to justify those rules (*e.g.* protection of consumers or plurality of the media through guaranteed access to certain public domestic channels), it can be questioned whether the imposition of a "*must carry*" obligation is proportionate to the objective to be achieved. While it does not take away the validity of this argument, it must be conceded that national "*must carry*" obligations have now been somewhat acknowledged and confirmed by the EU legislation in the Universal Service Directive (see para.2–047, below).

[24] See para.6–073 *et seq.* for the application of the EC Treaty's competition rules to this practice.

retransmission of a programme containing that film or programme in a Member State once the film or programme had been broadcast in another Member State with his consent. In *Coditel*,[25] the Court of Justice considered that Article 49 of the EC Treaty does not prohibit a copyright owner from relying on rights under national copyright law to object to the broadcasting or retransmission of a film or a programme that has been exhibited in another Member State with the copyright owner's consent. As a result, the author or his assignees may continue to rely on their copyright and other rights in respect of a film, a television programme or a sound recording to prevent unauthorised exhibition to the public across the EU[26]: the rights are not exhausted by the broadcast in the first Member State. In *Coditel*, the Court of Justice also affirmed the legality of the practice of copyright owners imposing a "window" (*i.e.* a set period of time) between the showing of the film in the cinema and its subsequent broadcasting on television or distribution on videotapes.[27]

2–009 Prior authorisation schemes must comply with the proportionality test — In *Canal Satélite Digital*[28] the national legislation in question imposed a prior authorisation scheme for the marketing of apparatus, equipment, decoders or digital transmission and reception systems. This was held to be a restriction on both the free movement of goods (the equipment itself) and services (the broadcast that would have been received using the equipment). The Court of Justice laid down a series of elements the referring court had to take into account in order to assess whether the measure was justifiable under EC law:

(i) a prior administrative authorisation scheme must be based on objective, non-discriminatory and published criteria;

(ii) the national measure must not essentially duplicate controls which have already been carried out in the context of other procedures, either in the same or another Member State;

---

[25] Case 62/79 *SA Compagnie générale pour la diffusion de la télévision, Coditel v Ciné Vog Films* [1980] E.C.R. 881. This case arose out of a breach of Belgian copyright by cable companies that restransmitted, in the Liège area, a programme that had been broadcast in Germany with the consent of the owner of the copyright in a film included in the retransmitted programme. The cable companies argued that the application of national copyright law to the retransmission of a broadcast emanating from another Member State infringed the freedom to provide services guaranteed by Art.49. The Court considered that Art.49 did not prohibit the exercise of copyright, to prevent such retransmission provided that this did not constitute a means of arbitrary discrimination or a disguised restriction on trade between Member States. According to the Court, this would be the case if the copyright owner was able to create artificial barriers to trade between Member States. The judgment of the Court is based on the so-called "essential function" or "specific subject matter" of copyright, which is to guarantee that the author is remunerated for his/her efforts. In contrast to books or records (which are goods and therefore subject to the free movement of goods principle enshrined in Art.28 of the EC Treaty), television programmes or films are exploited in a non-material form to a paying audience. Therefore, if the copyright owner is to be properly remunerated, it is necessary to be able to impose a fee for each exhibition of the film or programme: if the cable operators had been able to retransmit the broadcast containing the film, the copyright owner would not have been properly remunerated in respect of his Belgian copyright.

[26] Public showing of a film may be prohibited whether the film is shown on television or in cinemas.

[27] See also Joined Cases 60 and 61/84 *Cinéthèque SA v Fédération nationale des cinémas français* [1985] E.C.R. 2605. Art.7 of the TWF Directive (above, para.1–015, n.42) requires Member States to ensure that broadcasters under their jurisdiction do not broadcast cinematographic works outside periods agreed with the rights holders.

[28] See *Canal Satélite Digital* above, para.2–004, n.12.

(iii) a prior authorisation procedure will be necessary only where subsequent control must be regarded as being too late to be genuinely effective and to enable the Member State to achieve the aim pursued by the national legislation; and

(iv) a prior authorisation procedure is not a justifiable restriction on the fundamental principles of the free movement of goods and the freedom to provide services if, on account of its duration and the disproportionate costs to which it gives rise, it will deter undertakings from pursuing their business plan.

2. Free Movement of Goods (Article 28 of the EC Treaty)

2–010   Article 28 of the EC Treaty applies to goods and not to services — The broadcasting of films or television programmes to the public is a service and thus falls within the scope of Article 49 of the EC Treaty and not Article 28 of the EC Treaty, which covers restrictions on the free movement of goods. However, Article 28 of the EC Treaty is relevant to the extent that it governs trade in material, sound recordings, films, apparatus and other products used for the transmission of television signals. Likewise, the production, sale and rental of videocassettes are subject to Article 28 of the EC Treaty.[29]

2–011   Scope of Article 28 of the EC Treaty — Article 28 of the EC Treaty prohibits national measures that are capable of hindering intra-Community trade.[30] This covers both discriminatory national measures and also measures that apply without distinction to domestic and imported goods, if they have or may have a restrictive effect on the free movement of goods between Member States. National measures infringing Article 28 of the EC Treaty may in certain cases be justified on the grounds set out in Article 30 of the EC Treaty, including public policy, public health, public morality and security and the protection of industrial and commercial property. In *Cassis de Dijon*, the Court of Justice held that non-discriminatory measures restricting inter-state trade may also be justified by reference to "mandatory requirements", including the effectiveness of fiscal supervision, the protection of public health, the fairness of commercial transactions, the defence of the consumer and the protection of culture and in particular cinematographic production.[31] A national measure that restricts trade in goods is, however, only justified if it is proportionate to its purpose and that purpose cannot be attained by measures less restrictive of intra-Community trade. For

---

[29] *Cinéthèque*, above, para.2–008, n.27.

[30] Case 229/83 *Association des Centres distributeurs Édouard Leclerc v SARL "Au blé vert"* [1985] I E.C.R. 1, and Case 8/74 *Procureur du Roi v Benoît and Gustave Dassonville* [1974] E.C.R. 837.

[31] Case 120/78 *Rewe-Zentral AG v Bundesmonopolsverwaltung für Branntwein (Cassis de Dijon)* [1979] E.C.R. 649. On *Cassis de Dijon* and the subsequent case law under Art.28 of the EC Treaty, see Weatherill & Beaumont (para.1–006, n.18), p.492 *et seq.* In Case C–267/91 *Keck & Mithouard* ("*Keck*") [1993] I E.C.R. 6097, the Court departed from *Cassis de Dijon* by deciding that the application of national provisions restricting or prohibiting "selling arrangements" (such as a prohibition on selling goods below costs) that applies to both domestic and imported goods did not hinder trade between Member States. Therefore indistinctly applicable national provisions fall outside the scope of Art.28 of the EC Treaty, provided that they apply to all traders operating within the national territory and that they affect in the same manner, in law and in fact, the marketing of domestic products and of those from other Member States. In *De Agostini*, para.2–007, n.21, the Court of Justice qualified national legislation affecting cross-border television advertising as a "selling arrangement" within the meaning of *Keck*.

instance, in *Cinéthèque*,[32] a French law imposing a "window" between the showing of the film in the cinema and its subsequent distribution on videotapes was justifiable under Article 28 of the EC Treaty in so far it applied indiscriminately to national and foreign suppliers of videotapes and was necessary to protect cinematographic production.

2–012 Exhaustion of copyright — National copyright laws may be invoked to prevent the retransmission of television programme recordings, even when the original broadcast was authorised by the copyright owner in another Member State, of the copyright in the programme or any part of it (such as a film or musical work).[33] However, the owner of copyright in a film, television programme or sound recording may not rely on national copyright law to prevent imports of material copies (*e.g.* videocassettes or records) of the protected item if such copies have been put on the market in another Member State with the copyright owner's consent,[34] under the so-called "exhaustion of rights" doctrine. According to this doctrine, the copyright owner has the exclusive right to put the goods on the market in the Community for the first time. This allows him/her to be appropriately remunerated for his/her endeavour, which is the "specific subject matter" of a copyright. Once the copyright owner has exercised that right and obtained the appropriate remuneration for that first sale of the product, he/she may no longer rely on national legislation to prevent that product from being imported into another Member State.

3. Freedom of Establishment (Article 43 of the EC Treaty)

2–013 Article 43 of the EC Treaty (*ex* 52) guarantees the right of EC citizens and companies to establish businesses in other Member States.[35] Article 43 of the EC Treaty prohibits not only discriminatory national rules, but also any other barrier to the establishment of a business in another Member State. As with restrictions on the freedom to provide services, restrictions on the freedom of establishment may be justified on grounds of public policy, public security or public health (Article 46 of the EC Treaty) or for reasons of public interest.[36] For example, in *VTM*,[37] the monopoly granted to VTM to broadcast television advertising aimed at the Flemish Community in Belgium was held to infringe Article 43 of the EC Treaty, as it reserved to a domestic operator a specific portion of the Flemish broadcasting market. This made it impossible for a competing broadcaster from another Member State to establish itself in Belgium to broadcast television programmes containing advertising aimed at the Flemish public. The Commission and the Court of First Instance both considered that there was no necessary relationship between the objective of preserving media pluralism, which was put forward by the Belgian state as the justification for the restriction of the freedom of establishment, and the grant of the monopoly to VTM.

---

[32] *Cinéthèque*, above, para.2–008, n.27.
[33] See above, para.2–008.
[34] Case 78/70 *Deutsche Grammophon Gesellschaft mbH v Metro-SB-Großmärkte GmbH & Co. KG.* [1971] E.C.R. 487.
[35] Case C–2/74 *Reyners* [1974] E.C.R. 631.
[36] See paras 2–005 and 2–007.
[37] See *Vlaamse Televisie Maatschappij*, O.J. 1997 L244/18. This Commission decision, which was based on Art.82 of the EC Treaty (*ex* 86), was upheld by the Court of First Instance, Case T–266/97 *VTM v Commission* [1999] I E.C.R. 2329.

4. Remedies for Infringement of the EC Treaty's Rules on Free Movement

2–014   Should a Member State maintain national rules that infringe Articles 28, 49 or 43 of the EC Treaty, the Commission, on its own initiative or upon complaint from an injured party, may initiate proceedings against that Member State under Article 226 of the EC Treaty for failure to fulfil its obligation under the EC Treaty and bring the matter before the Court of Justice. In the case of continued failure to comply with provisions of the EC Treaty, the Court of Justice may, upon application by the Commission, impose a fine on the Member State in question. Most Article 226 EC proceedings are settled without a formal decision of the Court, upon the Member State voluntarily terminating the infringement.[38]

When a Member State infringes the EC Treaty by granting rights in favour of a public undertaking or an undertaking enjoying special or exclusive rights, the Commission may initiate proceedings under Article 86(3) of the EC Treaty (*ex* 90(3)) and itself adopt a decision ordering the Member State to terminate the infringement. This does not involve the Commission bringing the matter before the Court of Justice, as is the case in proceedings under Article 226 of the EC Treaty.[39] Proceedings under Article 86 of the EC Treaty are therefore likely to proceed much faster than those brought under Article 226 of the EC Treaty.

Moreover, in so far as Articles 28, 43 and 49 of the EC Treaty have direct effect,[40] injured parties could rely on these provisions before national courts, in order to obtain judgments that the national rules in question infringe the provisions of Articles 28, 43 or 49 of the EC Treaty. In some cases, this may involve a reference to the European Court of Justice for a preliminary ruling. National courts are also entitled to award damages against a Member State for a breach of Articles 28, 43 or 49 of the EC Treaty.[41]

B. Community Legislation in the Broadcasting Sector

2–015   The Community has adopted legislation covering a number of different aspects of broadcasting relevant to the creation of an internal market in television and radio broadcasting. These include aspects of the licensing regulation of broadcasters, the regulation of associated services (such as conditional access services), technical standards for digital broadcasting and intellectual property matters.

1. Television Without Frontiers Directive

2–016   In its case law, the Court of Justice has recognised that certain national broadcasting laws that protect the general interest (*e.g.* protection of consumers, plurality of media, etc.) may

---

[38] See para.1–285.

[39] On Art.86 of the EC Treaty, see para.4–013 *et seq.*

[40] See, in relation to Art.49 of the EC Treaty, Case C–33/74 *Van Binsbergen* [1974] E.C.R. 1299; in relation to Art.43, *Reyners* (above, para.2–013, n.35); in relation to Art.28, Case C–13/68 *SpA Salgoil v Italian Ministry of Foreign Trade, Rome* [1968] E.C.R. 453. On the concept of direct effect, see above, para.1–287 and para.1–294, n.20.

[41] See para.1–287.

justify restrictions on the movement of goods and services or on the freedom of establishment.[42] Although lawful under the EC Treaty, the disparities existing between different national broadcasting laws were, however, obstacles to the creation of an internal market in broadcasting within the Community and involved at least an element of distortion of competition. There was, therefore, a need for a certain degree of harmonisation and co-ordination of national broadcasting laws at the Community level to achieve an internal market in broadcasting. For these reasons, the Community adopted the TWF Directive in 1989.[43] The TWF Directive was subsequently substantially revised in 1997.[44] The purpose of the TWF Directive is to produce a harmonised system for the licensing and regulation of television broadcasters in the Community. A body of case law of the European Court of Justice has also developed under the TWF Directive. More recently, the Commission has considered it necessary to initiate a period of reflection and consultation on the possible future reform of the TWF Directive.[45] However, the contents of the TWF Directive are still considered to be well suited to the changing audio-visual industry in Europe.[46] The Fourth Report from the Commission on the application of the TWF Directive has proposed a work programme to determine whether there is a need for new legislation in this area.[47]

2–017 Scope of the TWF Directive: television services — The TWF Directive applies to television broadcasting services, *i.e.* all services that consist of pre-determined programme schedules broadcast simultaneously to more than one receiver. Although the term "television programmes" is not defined by the TWF Directive, the term "television broadcasting" is defined as

[42] See Section A, para.1–001, above.

[43] See para.1–015, n.42, for full citation.

[44] *ibid.* The revised TWF Directive has now been implemented in all Member States. Nevertheless, Italy and Luxembourg were condemned by the Court of Justice for failing to implement it by the implementation date of December 31, 1998 — see Case C–119/00 *Commission v Luxembourg*, [2001] I. E.C.R. 4795 and Case C–207/00 *Commission v Italy* [2001] I E.C.R. 4571.

[45] See Speech by Viviane Reding (Member of the European Commission responsible for Education and Culture): "TWF: amending the directive", RTL Group Management Conference, Venice, June 22, 2001 (*http://europa.eu.int/rapid/start*), and Speech by Viviane Reding at the European Voice Conference on TWF: "The Review of the TVWF", Brussels, March 21, 2002 (*http://europa.eu.int/comm/avpolicy/legis/speech_en.htm*). See also *http://europa.eu.int/comm/avpolicy/regul/regul_en.htm*.

[46] See Council meeting on Education, Youth and Culture, November 11–12, 2002, Council Press Release of December 19, 2002, 15691/02 (Presse 404), pp.16–18.

[47] See Fourth Report from the Commission to the Council, the European Parliament, the European Economic and Social Committee and the Committee of the Regions on the application of Directive 89/552 "Television without Frontiers", COM(2002) 778 final, of January 6, 2003. The main issues for review are the following: (i) the scope for regulation under the TWF Directive; (ii) the links with other Community legal instruments; (iii) the regulation of events of major importance; (iv) the promotion of European works; (v) the proportionality of the rules on advertising; (vi) the effectiveness of the current rules for the protection of minors; (vii) the means of exercising the right of reply; (viii) the adequacy of the current criteria to define jurisdiction; and as a new theme (ix) the possibility of including a right to short extracts to events subject to exclusive rights. See also Commission Press Release IP/03/6 of January 7, 2003, "What changes will be made to the Community's audiovisual policy? Work programme for reviewing the 'Television without Frontiers' Directive". In essence, the work programme envisages a review of the legislation to be terminated with: (i) the adoption of an assessment report on the implementation of the Recommendation on the protection of minors and human dignity in the third quarter of 2003; and (ii) the adoption of a Communication on the results of the public consultations and possible proposals in late 2003–early 2004.

"the initial transmission by wire or over the air, including that by satellite, in unencoded or encoded form, of television programmes intended for reception by the public, including the communication of programmes between undertakings with a view to their being relayed to the public".[48] The TWF Directive applies to television services regardless of whether they are broadcast terrestrially, via satellite or by cable and includes the cable retransmission of programmes broadcast terrestrially or by satellite.[49] Expressly excluded from the scope of the TWF Directive are telecommunications services providing items of information or other messages on individual demand, *i.e.* telephone, telecopying, electronic data banks and other services.[50] In the framework of the revision of the TWF Directive, consideration was given to extending its scope to include other services such as video-on-demand.[51] However, it was decided not to include these services in the scope of the Directive because of the specificity of the technological and regulatory issues raised by these services. This raises the possibility that competition between services that are largely substitutable from a consumer's perspective may be distorted if the services are regulated differently (for example, in relation to rules governing television content) according to the mode of transmission.[52] The TWF Directive does not cover matters such as the responsibility of the Member States and their authorities with regard to the organisation (including the systems of licensing, administrative authorisation or taxation) or financing of broadcasters, nor the content of programmes. The TWF Directive applies only to broadcasts intended for reception in the EU: it does not apply to broadcasts from Member States that are intended exclusively for third countries and which are not received directly or indirectly by the public in any Member State.[53] The regulation of such broadcasts remains within the competence of the Member State. In view of the process of technological convergence in the area of telecommunications, the scope of the TWF Directive is currently under consideration.[54]

2–018   *Jurisdiction over a broadcaster* — As originally drafted, Article 2 of the TWF Directive did not lay down any criteria for determining which Member State had jurisdiction over

---

[48] TWF Directive, para.1–015, n.42, Art.1(a).

[49] Case C–11/95 *Commission v Belgium* [1996] I E.C.R. 4115 where the Court of Justice confirmed that the TWF Directive applies to cable retransmission of television programmes.

[50] TWF Directive, para.1–015, n.42, Art.1(a).

[51] Near-video-on-demand consists of a pre-determined programme schedule broadcast at regular intervals, from which the viewer can select a specific programme. In contrast, video-on-demand does not involve the broadcasting of a pre-determined programme schedule to the public, but consists of a catalogue of programmes which the receiver can choose to access at any time on a "one-to-one" basis using a telecommunications link.

[52] Drijber, "The Revised TWF Directive: Is It Fit for the Next century?" (1999) 36 C.M.L.R. 87–122, at p.88.

[53] TWF Directive, para.1–015, n.42, Art.2(b).

[54] During the year 2002 the Commission reviewed three different studies on different aspects related to the TWF Directive: (i) the production of European television programmes; (ii) technological and market developments; and (iii) new forms of advertising techniques: See Carat Crystal and Bird & Bird, Rapport Final "Étude sur le développement des nouvelles techniques publicitaires", April 2002, and Arthur Andersen, "Outlook of development of the market for European audiovisual content and of the regulatory framework concerning production and distribution of this content", June 2002, available at: *http://europa.eu.int/comm/ avpolicy/stat/studi_en.htm*. As shown above, in n.46 and in view of the results of these studies, the Commission has decided, however, to delay the actual reform of the TWF Directive until further analysis of the circumstances in the sector has been undertaken.

Community broadcasters.[55] This led to extensive case law from the Court of Justice on the issue, where it held that a broadcaster comes under the jurisdiction of the Member State in which it is established.[56] The amendments to the TWF Directive included the insertion of a new Article 2, which includes specific criteria to determine which Member State has jurisdiction over a broadcaster.[57] These criteria take into account judgments of the Court of Justice, but go further. A "broadcaster" is defined in the TWF Directive as the natural or legal person who has editorial responsibility for the composition of schedules of television programmes and who transmits them or has them transmitted by third parties.[58] Jurisdiction is now based on the following criteria:

(i) the Member State in which the broadcaster is "established"; or

(ii) if a broadcaster is not established in any Member State, on the basis of use of a national frequency, national satellite capacity or a national satellite up-link; or

(iii) if neither (i) nor (ii) is applicable, on the basis of Article 43 of the EC Treaty (*ex* 52).[59]

2–019 *Place of establishment* — The primary jurisdictional test under the TWF Directive is the Member State in which the broadcast is established.[60] Article 2(3) sets out a number of principles to determine the broadcaster's Member State of establishment. A broadcaster is deemed to be established in a Member State if it has its head office in that Member State and the editorial decisions about programme schedules are taken in that Member State.[61] If a broadcaster has its head office in one Member State but editorial decisions on programme schedules are taken in another Member State, it is deemed to be established in the Member State where a significant part of the workforce involved in the pursuit of the television broadcasting activity operates.[62] If a significant part of the workforce involved in the pursuit of the television broadcasting activity operates in each of those Member States, the broadcaster is deemed to be established in the Member State where it has its head office.[63] If a significant part of the workforce involved in the pursuit of the television broadcasting activity operates in neither of those Member States, the broadcaster is deemed to be established in the Member State where it first began broadcasting in accordance with the system of law of that Member State, provided that it maintains a stable and effective link with the economy of that Member State.[64] When a broadcaster has its head office in a Member State but decisions on programme schedules are taken in a third country outside the EU, or *vice versa*, it is

---

[55] As originally noted, Art.2(1) simply required each Member State to ensure that (i) broadcasters under its jurisdiction and (ii) broadcasters that were not under the jurisdiction of any Member State but which made use of a frequency or satellite capacity granted by, or a satellite up-link located in that Member State, comply with the law applicable to broadcasts intended for the public in that Member State.

[56] Case C–222/94 *Commission v United Kingdom* [1996] I E.C.R. 4025; *Commission v Belgium*, above, para.2–016, n.49; Case C–56/96 *VT4 Ltd v Vlaamse Gemeenschap* [1997] I E.C.R. 3143; *De Agostini*, above, para.2–007, n.21.

[57] TWF Directive, para.1–015, n.42, Art.2(2).

[58] *ibid.*, Art.1(b).

[59] *ibid.*, Art.2(2) to 2(5).

[60] *ibid.*, Art.2(2), first indent.

[61] *ibid.*, Art.2(3)(a).

[62] *ibid.*, Art.2(3)(b).

[63] *ibid.*

[64] *ibid.*, Art.2(3)(b).

deemed to be established in that Member State, provided that a significant part of the workforce involved in the pursuit of the television broadcasting activity operates in that Member State.[65] If none of these criteria result in a broadcaster falling under the jurisdiction of a Member State, the additional criteria laid down in Articles 2(4) and 2(5) must be applied. In *VT4*,[66] which was considered under the TWF Directive in its original form, the Court of Justice considered the issue of determining the Member State having jurisdiction over a broadcaster when the latter is established in more than one Member State. In this case, the Flemish Government had refused to authorise the Flemish cable operators to retransmit the programmes of VT4, because it considered that this broadcaster (which was incorporated in the UK and operated under a UK licence), was in fact established in Belgium, where it could not be licensed because of the existing monopoly of VTM.[67] The Court of Justice held that when a broadcaster is established in more than one Member State, it falls under the jurisdiction of the Member State in the territory of which it has its centre of activities, taking into consideration in particular the place where decisions concerning programme policy are taken and the programmes to be broadcast are finally put together. In the case of VT4, that was the United Kingdom.

2–020 *Additional jurisdictional criteria* — Article 2(4) establishes additional jurisdictional criteria that are applicable when a broadcaster cannot be deemed to be established in a Member State by applying the principles set out in Article 2(3). A broadcaster is deemed to be under the jurisdiction of a Member State when: (i) it uses a frequency granted by that Member State; or, (ii) if it does not use such a frequency, it uses a satellite capacity relating to that Member State; or (iii) if it uses neither such a frequency nor such a capacity, it uses a satellite up-link situated in that Member State.[68]

When the question of which Member State has jurisdiction over a broadcaster cannot be solved by applying the criteria laid down by either Article 2(3) or Article 2(4), Article 2(5) provides that the competent Member State will be that in which the broadcaster is established within the meaning of Article 43 of the EC Treaty. The concept of "establishment" within the context of Article 43 has been defined by the Court of Justice as involving the actual pursuit of an economic activity through a fixed establishment in another Member State for an indefinite period.[69]

2–021 **Responsibility of the transmitting State to check compliance by broadcasters** — A Member State must ensure that all television broadcasts transmitted by broadcasters under its jurisdiction (as determined according to Articles 2(2) to 2(5) of the TWF Directive) comply with the rules of the system of law applicable to broadcasts intended for the public in that Member State (including, in particular, national provisions implementing the Directive).[70]

---

[65] *ibid.*, Art.2(3)(c).

[66] See above, para.2–018, n.56.

[67] As discussed above in para.2–013, the Commission has adopted a decision, upheld by the Court of First Instance, that the monopoly of VTM was contrary to Art.82 of the EC Treaty (*ex* 86), in combination with Art.43 of the EC Treaty.

[68] TWF Directive, para.1–015, n.42, Art.2(4)(a)–(c).

[69] Case C–221/89 *R. v Secretary of State for Transport Ex p. Factortame Ltd* [1991] I E.C.R. 3905, at para.20.

[70] TWF Directive, para.1–015, n.42, Art.2(1).

2–022   Free movement for broadcasts — A television broadcast made by a broadcaster established in a Member State and broadcasting in compliance with the laws of that Member State, including provisions to implement the standards determined by the TWF Directive, shall be freely received and retransmitted in every other Member State under the so-called "transmitting state" principle.[71] This principle has also been used in other economic sectors to achieve the internal market. The rationale behind the "transmitting State principle" is that once the transmitting state has verified compliance with the law applicable to broadcasting in that Member State, there is no need for any secondary control in the receiving Member State. Accordingly, secondary control by the receiving Member States is unlawful unless one of a number of exceptions is applicable.[72] Recent developments at national level have demonstrated, however, that certain Member States have failed to respect this principle.[73] In so far as the freedom of reception and retransmission under the TWF Directive only applies to Community broadcasters under the jurisdiction of a Member State, the receiving state may, however, seek confirmation that a broadcaster is indeed a Community broadcaster under the terms of the TWF Directive. Member States must ensure that broadcasters under that jurisdiction comply with the provisions of the TWF Directive[74] and provide appropriate procedures for third parties directly affected, including nationals of other Member States, to apply, in accordance with the applicable national law, to the competent judicial or other authorities to seek effective compliance with the provisions of the Directive.[75]

2–023   The transmitting state principle applies only to the fields co-ordinated by the TWF Directive — The obligation of the receiving State not to restrict the free movement of Community broadcast only applies in relation to the fields co-ordinated by the TWF Directive.[76] These fields, which will be described in detail below, include the promotion, distribution and production of European television programmes, television advertising, sponsorship and teleshopping, the protection of minors, the right of reply and the accessibility of events of major importance for society on free-to-air television. This means that the receiving state may continue to restrict the transmission and retransmission of broadcasts by broadcasters under the jurisdiction of another

---

[71] *ibid.*, Art.2(a)(1).

[72] In *Commission v Belgium*, above, para.2–017, n.49, the Court of Justice found that a system of prior authorisation for the retransmission by cable of television programmes coming from other Member States was incompatible with the TWF Directive. This judgment confirms that it is only for the transmitting state to monitor compliance with the standards laid down by the TWF Directive. The Court also stated that, even when there is indication that the laws of the transmitting state do not properly implement the terms of the TWF Directive, it is not permissible for the receiving state to set up a general authorisation system to ensure the broadcaster's compliance with the provisions of the TWF Directive. If the receiving state considers that the transmitting state has not complied with its obligation under the TWF Directive, the only option open to it is to invoke the procedures under Arts 226, 227 or 243 of the EC Treaty against the transmitting State. This was confirmed in Case C–14/96, *Criminal proceedings against Paul Denuit* [1997] I E.C.R. 2729.

[73] As reported by the Commission in the Third Report from the Commission to the Council, the European Parliament and the Economic and Social Committee on the application of Directive 89/552 "Television without Frontiers", COM(2001) 0009 final, the Commission was informed of the Dutch authorities' decision to prohibit the distribution of the RTL 4 and RTL 5 channels (which are broadcast from Luxembourg) in the Netherlands unless the broadcasters RTL/Veronica De Holland Media Groep SA obtained Dutch licences for these television channels.

[74] TWF Directive, para.1–015, n.42, Art.3(2).

[75] *ibid.*, Art.3(3).

[76] *ibid.*, Art.2(a)(1).

Member State, on the basis of national broadcasting laws that regulate matters which have not been harmonised by the TWF Directive. Any such national measures must, nevertheless, be compatible with the general provisions of the EC Treaty on the free provision of services and the free movement of goods and the freedom of establishment.[77]

This issue of the extent to which Member States may continue to regulate broadcasters under national laws that are inconsistent with the TWF Directive was considered by the Court of Justice in the *De Agostini* case.[78] This preliminary ruling concerned an action brought by the Swedish Consumer Ombudsman against two Swedish advertisers for respectively misleading advertising and infringement of a Swedish law prohibiting all television advertising designed to attract the attention of children under the age of 12. The Court of Justice was asked whether the TWF Directive (as well as Articles 28 and 49 of the EC Treaty) (i) prevented a Member State from taking action against television advertisements contained in a programme broadcast from another Member State; and (ii) precluded the application of a national law prohibiting advertisements directed at children. As regards the first question, the Court of Justice noted that the TWF Directive only partly covered the regulation of the content of television advertising and, therefore, did not exclude the application of national rules other than those specifically concerning broadcasting and programmes. In particular, it did not preclude the application of national rules aimed at consumer protection against an advertiser in relation to advertising contained in programmes broadcast from another Member State, provided that these measures did not involve a secondary control on television broadcasts in addition to the control which the transmitting state exercised under the TWF Directive.

With respect to the second question, the Court noted that the Directive contains a set of provisions specifically devoted to the protection of minors, compliance with which shall be ensured by the transmitting state. This is, thus, a field specifically co-ordinated by the TWF Directive. Consequently, the receiving state could not apply provisions of national law specifically designed to control the content of television advertising with regard to minors, since this would involve the secondary control of television broadcasts in addition to the control which the transmitting state exercises under the TWF Directive. In contrast, a Member State would not be precluded from applying legislation designed to protect consumers or minors *in general*, provided that its application would not prevent the retransmission, as such, in its territory of broadcasts from another Member State. In practice, it would seem that a national authority could require an advertiser to make corrections to an advertisement or to refrain from using certain misleading expressions, provided that the application of general consumer protection law does not lead to a systematic supervision of advertisements contained in television broadcasts from other Member States.[79]

2–024 Specific exceptions to the transmitting state principle — protection of minors and avoidance of incitement to racial, sexual, religious or national hatred — The TWF Directive permits a Member State to derogate provisionally from its obligation to ensure the freedom of reception

---

[77] See para.2–003 *et seq.*; para.2–010 *et seq.*; para.2–013 *et seq.*
[78] See Joined Cases C–34/95 to 36/95, *Konsumentombudsmannen (KO) v De Agostini (Svenska) Förlag AB and TV-Shop i Sverige AB* [1997] I E.C.R. 3843. See also C–412/93 *Société d'importation Edouard Leclerc-Siplec v TF1 Publicité SA and M6 Publicité SA* [1995] I E.C.R. 179.
[79] See *Stuyck* [1998] 34 C.M.L.R. 1445.

(including retransmission) of a television broadcast transmitted from another Member State if this broadcast manifestly, seriously and gravely infringes one of the rules on protection of minors contained in Articles 22 and 22a of the TWF Directive.[80] Article 22 requires Member States to ensure that television broadcasts made by broadcasters under their jurisdiction do not include any programmes which might seriously impair the physical, mental or moral development of minors, in particular those that involve gratuitous violence or pornography.[81] This obligation also covers other programmes which are likely to impair the physical, mental or moral development of minors, except where it is ensured, by selecting the time of the broadcast or by any technical measure (such as conditional access), that minors in the area of transmission will not normally hear or see such broadcasts.[82] When such programmes are broadcast in unencoded form, Member States must ensure that they are preceded by an acoustic warning or are identified by the presence of a visual symbol throughout the duration of the transmission.[83] In the framework of the revision of the TWF Directive, consideration was given to requiring the use of a "V-chip", an electronic device designed to filter harmful content.[84] Although the amendments to the TWF Directive do not include such provisions, the amended Directive does require the Commission to carry out a study on the possible advantages and drawbacks of imposing further measures to facilitate the control exercised by parents or guardians over programmes that minors may watch.[85]

The receiving state may only take measures to prevent reception of a broadcast that is considered to be harmful to minors or incite hatred on the grounds of race, sex, religion or nationality if the broadcaster has previously infringed these provisions at least twice in the previous 12 months.[86] The receiving state must also notify the broadcaster concerned and the Commission in writing of the alleged infringements and the measures it intends to take should there be further infringements. The receiving state may adopt corrective measures only if consultations with the transmitting state and the Commission have not produced an amicable settlement within 15 days of the notification and the infringement persists. The Commission must adopt, within two months following

---

[80] TWF Directive, para.1–015, n.42, Art.2a(2). Even if the Court of First Instance did not consider Art.2a(2) in its judgments, the facts of Case T–69/99 *Danish Satellite TV A/S (Eurotica Rendez-Vous Television) v Commission* [2000] II E.C.R. 4039 illustrate the application of Art.2a(2). In this case, the Commission took the view that the measures adopted by the Member State concerned (the United Kingdom) in respect of an "adult" programme broadcast from Denmark were not discriminatory, were appropriate for the purpose of protecting minors and compatible with Community law. The Court of First Instance dismissed an action for annulment of the Commission's decision, as the applicant was not directly concerned by it and therefore did not have *locus standi* to seek annulment. See also *R. v Secretary of State for the National Heritage Continental Television BV* [1993] 3 C.M.L.R. 387, dealing with the effect of Art.2(2) of the TWF Directive.

[81] TWF Directive, para.1–015, n.42, Art.22(1). In Case E–8/97, *TV 1000 Sverige AB v The Norwegian Government* [1998] *EFTA Court Report* 70, the EFTA Court held that pornography is not automatically prohibited pursuant to Art.22(1), such that it must be shown that the broadcast in question may have the effect of impairing the development of minors. This assessment (which is essentially a moral one) must be undertaken by the national authorities of the receiving state.

[82] TWF Directive, para.1–015, n.42, Art.22(2).

[83] *ibid.*, Art.22.

[84] Drijber (para.2–017, n.52), pp.102–103.

[85] TWF Directive, para.1–015, n.42, Art.22(b). See also Study on "Parental Control of Television Broadcasting" P.C.M.L.P. (University of Oxford, 1999), and follow-up study "Parental Control in a Converged Communications Environment" (2000).

[86] TWF Directive, para.1–015, n.42, Art.2a(2)(b).

notification of the measures taken by the receiving state, a decision on whether the measures are compatible with Community law.[87] If the Commission considers that the measures are not compatible with Community law, the receiving state must withdraw them as a matter of urgency.[88] The transmitting state may impose its own remedies or sanctions for any infringement of Articles 22 and 22a.[89]

2–025 Rules applicable to domestic broadcasters — Member States must ensure that all television broadcasts transmitted by broadcasters under their jurisdiction comply with the rules applicable to broadcasts intended for the public in that Member State.[90] This provision prevents a Member State from applying less stringent rules to broadcasters under their jurisdiction whose programmes are intended for foreign audiences.[91]

Article 3(1) permits Member States to impose on broadcasters under their jurisdiction more detailed or stricter rules in the areas covered by the Directive. This provision has been used by the French authorities to require French broadcasters to broadcast a minimum of 60 per cent of European content during the hours of the day when there is a significant audience,[92] as opposed to a majority of airtime required by the TWF Directive. Sweden has also used that provision to prohibit all television advertising aimed at children less than 12 years old.[93] The case law of the Court of Justice under Article 49 of the EC Treaty confirms that a Member State can enforce stricter measures against broadcasters whose activities are all or mostly directed towards its territory when these broadcasters have been established in another Member State for the sole purpose of avoiding the rules that would be applicable to them if they were established in that Member State.[94] It

[87] *ibid.*, Art.2a(2).
[88] *ibid.*
[89] *ibid.*, Art.2a(3).
[90] *ibid.*, Art.3(2).
[91] *Commission v United Kingdom*, above, para.2–018, n.56. In this case the Commission claimed that UK legislation: (i) applied criteria other than that of establishment for determining which broadcasters fall within the jurisdiction of the United Kingdom; (ii) also applied a criterion which is not relevant for the purposes of such jurisdiction, namely the criterion of reception; (iii) failed to make third-country broadcasts falling under the United Kingdom's jurisdiction subject to UK law; and (iv) applied different regimes to domestic and non-domestic satellite services. The Court held that the Commission's objections were well founded, and that the United Kingdom had failed to fulfil its obligations.
[92] The legal basis for broadcasting requirements is Art.27 of Law No.86-1067 of September 30, 1986 as amended, and Arts 13 and 14 of Decree No.90-66 of January 17, 1990 (as amended by Decree No.2001-1330 of December 8, 2001).
[93] See Chap.7, s.4 of the Swedish Television and Radio 1996 Act.
[94] Case C–148/91 *Veronica Omroep Organisatie v Commissariaat voor de Media* [1993] I E.C.R. 487. The body responsible for overseeing broadcasting in the Netherlands (the Commissariaat) sought to enforce certain restrictions contained in Dutch law against Veronica, a Dutch public broadcaster. Veronica had helped set up a commercial station in Luxembourg that could be relayed to the Netherlands by cable, and this station did not fulfil the public service remit for which Veronica was funded by the Commissariaat. The national court asked the European Court whether or not such restrictions were compatible with Community law. In particular, it asked whether the restrictions infringed the free movement of capital (Art.67 of the EC Treaty) or alternatively the free movement of services (Art.59 of the EC Treaty); whether the specific activities carried out by Veronica should be subject to such restrictions; and whether those restrictions were justifiable and proportionate. The Court held that the free movement of capital and the freedom to provide services must be interpreted as not precluding national legislation which prohibits a broadcasting organisation established in that State (i) from

would appear that this case law can still be relied on following the amendment of the TWF Directive.[95]

2–026 Transmission of major events on free-to-air television — There is considerable concern that many important events (in particular major sporting events) could be broadcast only on pay-television, thereby depriving the majority of the population of the possibility of watching them. Pay-television operators have increasingly acquired exclusive rights to important sports events, in particular for leading domestic football competitions. Article 3(a) therefore permits Member States to take measures to ensure wide access by the public to free-to-air television coverage of major sports events that are regarded in that Member State as being of "major importance" for society. This covers both events of national importance (for example, the Tour de France in France or international cricket matches in the United Kingdom), as well as events of international importance such as the Olympic Games or the Football World Cup.[96] The system operates in three phases, to ensure that the Commission can control national measures.

investing in a broadcasting company established or to be established in another Member State, and (ii) from providing that company with a bank guarantee or drawing up a business plan, and (iii) giving legal advice to a television company to be set up in another Member State, where those activities are directed towards the establishment of a commercial television station whose broadcasts are intended to be received, in particular, in the territory of the first Member State and those prohibitions are necessary in order to ensure the pluralistic and non-commercial character of the audio-visual system introduced by that legislation. See also Case C–23/93, *TV10 SA v Commissariaat voor de Media* [1994] I E.C.R. 4795. TV10 was a commercial station set up by Dutch nationals in Luxembourg aimed at the Dutch domestic market. The Dutch Commissariaat denied it access to the Dutch cable on the grounds that it was neither a public nor foreign broadcaster, but a domestic broadcaster trying to appear foreign to circumvent restrictive Dutch broadcasting legislation. TV10 appealed to the national court, which then asked the European Court if intention to circumvent national law with an artificial cross-border set-up justified treating the situation as a purely internal one, and if not, could it still restrict the freedom to provide (broadcasting) services in the light of that intent to evade national law? The Court held (i) that broadcasting constituted the cross-border provision of a service under the EC Treaty, so the matter could not be viewed purely as an internal matter by the Member State, and (ii) that the freedom to provide services does not preclude a Member State from treating as a domestic broadcaster a broadcasting body constituted under the law of another Member State and established in that State but whose activities are wholly or principally directed towards the territory of the first Member State, if that broadcasting body was established there in order to enable it to avoid the rules which would be applicable to it if it were established within the first State. In *Commission v Belgium* above, para.2–017, n.49, the Court of Justice had left the issue open of whether a Member State could still rely on the precedent originally laid down in Case 33/74; *Van Binsbergen* [1974] E.C.R. 1299 to prevent circumvention of national rules.

[95] Recital 14 of Directive 97/36 amending the TWF Directive, para.1–015, n.42, specifically refers to the *Van Binsbergen* precedent. Drijber, above, para.2–017, n.52, at p.95, considers that the "*Van Binsbergen* defence" could only be invoked successfully by a Member State in exceptional circumstances: (i) circumvention cannot be presumed by imposing an *a priori* authorisation system (see *Commission v Belgium*, above, para.2–017, n.49); (ii) an element of abuse, *i.e.* an improper or wrongful conduct, must be demonstrated (see *TV10 SA v Commissariaat voor de Media*, above para.2–025, n.94); and (iii) the rules that have allegedly been circumvented must be compatible with Community law (see *VT4*, above, para.2–018, n.56). See also Communication from the Commission on the application of the general principles of free movement of goods and services in Arts 28 and 49 of the EC Treaty, concerning the use of satellite dishes, COM(01) 351, at n.18 where *Van Binsbergen* is confirmed.

[96] The legality of Art.3(a) has been challenged before the Court of First Instance by Kirch Group, a major German broadcaster and rights trader, which holds the rights to, *inter alia*, the FIFA World Cup in the context of action brought in Case T–33/01 *Kirch Media GmbH & Co KgaA and Kirchmedia WM AG v Commission*, O.J. 2001 C134/24.

2–027 *Drawing up a list of major events* — Member States may take measures to ensure that broadcasters under their jurisdiction do not broadcast on an exclusive basis events which are regarded by that Member State as being of major importance for society in such a way as to deprive a substantial proportion of the public in that Member State of the possibility of following such events via live coverage or deferred coverage on free television. If it intends to take such measures, the Member State must draw up, in a clear and transparent manner, in due and effective time, a list of designated events, which may be national or non-national, that it considers to be of major importance for society.[97] The Member State must consider whether these events should be broadcast in full or in part, whether on free television and whether live or in deferred coverage. The events that are designated will vary from one Member State to another depending on the national traditions. Member States may, however, only designate events that are of general interest to the general public in the EU or in a given Member State or in an important component part of a given Member State.[98]

2–028 *Notification of listed major events to the Commission* — Member States must immediately notify to the Commission any measures they intend to take in relation to "listed events". The Commission then has three months to verify that the proposed measures are compatible with Community law and communicate them to the other Member States. Notification of the measures does not have suspensive effect. It must also seek an opinion from the Content Committee established under Article 23(a) of the TWF Directive, which is comprised of representatives of the Member States under the chairmanship of the Commission. The Commission must verify that such measures are compatible with Community law,[99] particularly in relation to Article 49 of the EC Treaty (freedom to provide services) and ensure that the restrictive effect of the proposed measure on the free marketing of broadcasting rights is proportionate to the objective of ensuring public access to certain events.[1]

2–029 *Obligation to prevent circumvention* — Member States must ensure that broadcasters under their jurisdiction do not exercise their exclusive broadcasting rights to circumvent the lists of events drawn up by other Member States.[2] As a result, transmitting broadcasters are obliged to respect the list of the receiving state. The implementation of this provision could raise a number of practical issues. For example, it is not clear how the regulatory authorities of the transmitting state would be systematically informed of the broadcasting rights purchased by broadcasters under their jurisdiction.

2–030 Promotion of the distribution and production of European works — Concerns had been expressed that non-European programmes, especially of United States origin, would dominate the European television market without regulatory intervention to require "local content in television programmes". As a result, the TWF Directive contains two specific provisions to promote the European audio-visual production industry.

---

[97] See publication of consolidated measures in accordance with Art.3a(2) of the TWF Directive, para.1–015, n.42, in O.J. 2002 C189/2.

[98] TWF Directive, para.1–015, n.42, Recital 21.

[99] *ibid.*, Art.3a(2).

[1] Drijber, above, para.2–017, n.52, p.96.

[2] TWF Directive, para.1–015, n.42, Art.3a(3).

2–031 *Reservation for European works* — Member States must ensure, where practicable and by appropriate means, that broadcasters reserve a majority proportion of their transmission time (excluding the time appointed to news, sports events, games, advertising, teletext services and teleshopping) for "European works".[3] Recognising that many television channels in the community did not include such a level of European works at the time of the adoption of the TWF Directive in 1982, this proportion must be achieved progressively on the basis of suitable criteria having regard to the broadcaster's informational, educational, cultural and entertainment responsibilities to its viewing public.[4] Where the requirement for a majority of programming to be of European origin cannot be attained by a particular channel, it must not be lower than the average for 1988[5] in the Member State concerned.[6]

2–032 *Reservation of transmission time or programming budgets for European works created by independent producers* — In an attempt to stimulate television production by small and medium-sized businesses, the TWF Directive requires Member States to ensure, where practicable and by appropriate means, that broadcasters under their jurisdiction reserve at least 10 per cent of their transmission time (excluding the time allocated to news, sports events, games, advertising, teletext services and teleshopping) for European works created by producers who are independent of broadcasters. Alternatively, Member States may decide to impose requirements that at least 10 per cent of a broadcaster's programming budget be devoted to such works.[7] The term "independent producer" is not defined by the TWF Directive and is thus left to the discretion of Member States, but clearly covers programmes produced by companies which are not "in-house" production units or subsidiaries of the relevant broadcaster. Appropriate account should also be taken of the amount of programmes supplied to the same broadcaster and the ownership of secondary rights.[8] This proportion is also to be achieved progressively on the basis of suitable criteria, having regard to the broadcaster's informational, educational, cultural and entertainment responsibilities to its viewing public. Moreover, this objective must be achieved by earmarking an adequate proportion for recent works, *i.e.* works transmitted within five years of their production.[9]

2–033 *Definition of "European works"* — Article 6 of the TWF Directives defines as "European works" those works that (i) originate from a Member State[10]; and (ii) originate in European

---

[3] *ibid.*, Art.4. See Fifth Communication from the Commission to the Council and the European Parliament on the application of Arts 4 and 5 of Directive 89/552 "Television without Frontiers", as amended by Directive 97/36, for the period 1999–2000, COM(02) 612 final, November 8, 2002. See also Fourth Report from the Commission to the Council, the European Parliament, the European Economic and Social Committee and the Committee of the Regions on the application of Directive 89/552 "Television without Frontiers", above, para.2–016, n.47.

[4] TWF Directive, para.1–015, n.42, Art.4(1).

[5] Greece and Portugal were considered separately and the reference year for the calculation of the proportion laid down in Art.4(1) for these two Member States is 1990.

[6] TWF Directive, para.1–015, n.42, Art.4(2). See also Drijber, para.2–017, n.52, who stresses the inadequacy of maintaining the reference to the 1988 level, in light of the current difficulties for commercial broadcasters in meeting a standard set at a time when the audio-visual context was still very much dominated by public broadcasters who could more easily meet the proportion required by the TWF Directive.

[7] TWF Directive, para.1–015, n.42, Art.5.

[8] *ibid.*, Recital 31.

[9] *ibid.*

[10] *ibid.*, Art.6(1)(b).

countries other than EU Member States that are signatories to the Council of Europe Convention on Transfrontier Television or certain other European Countries, provided certain conditions, described below, are met, in particular that works originating from Member States are not subject to discriminatory measures in the third countries concerned.[11] The TWF Directive includes such works as "European" in order to meet the obligations of the Member States under the Convention on Transfrontier Television, to which they are all signatories and which also includes European content rules. Works from non-European countries are European works if they are made mainly with authors and workers residing in one or more of those States and meet one of the following conditions: (i) they are made by one or more producers established in one or more of those States; (ii) production of the works is supervised and actually controlled by one or more producers established in one or more of those States or (iii) the contribution of co-producers of those States to the total co-production costs is preponderant and the co-production is not controlled by one or more producers established outside those States.[12]

If the European third country is not a party to the European Convention on Transfrontier Television, the works will be considered as being "European works" if they are made exclusively, or in co-production with producers established in one or more Member States, by producers established in one or more European third countries with which the EU has concluded agreements relating to the audio-visual sector, provided that those works are mainly made with authors and workers residing in one or more European states.[13] Works that are not considered to be "European" by virtue of the above criteria may nevertheless be deemed to be "European works" if they are produced within the framework of bilateral co-production treaties between EU Member States and third countries, provided that the EU co-producers supply a majority share of the total cost of the production and the production is not controlled by one or more producers established outside the territory of the Member States.[14] Finally, works that are not "European works" under the above criteria, but are made mainly with authors and workers residing in one or more Member States, shall be considered as "European works" to an extent corresponding to the proportion of the contribution of EU co-producers to the total production costs, such that a proportion of their broadcast time can be counted towards the 10 per cent of airtime that must be reserved for independent European producers.[15]

2–034 *Broadcasts of cinematographic works* — Member States must ensure that broadcasters under their jurisdiction do not broadcast cinematographic works outside periods agreed with the right holders.[16] This provides a certain degree of protection for the cinema industry.

2–035 *Exclusion of "local television" from European content requirements* — The European content requirements do not apply to television broadcasts that are intended for local audiences and do not form part of a national network.[17]

---

[11] *ibid.*, Art.6(1)(b) and (c).
[12] *ibid.*, Art.6(2).
[13] *ibid.*, Art.6(3).
[14] *ibid.*, Art.6(4).
[15] *ibid.*, Art.6(5).
[16] *ibid.*, Art.7.
[17] *ibid.*, Art.9.

2–036 *Compatibility of European content rules with the EU's international obligations* — The European content requirements imposed by the TWF Directive have given rise to substantial controversy both within and outside the EU. The EU has made a reservation from its obligations under the Most Favoured Nation (MFN) principle[18] under the General Agreement on Trade and Services, pursuant to which a WTO member must grant treatment to service and service providers from other WTO members on no less favourable terms than the treatment accorded to services and service providers from any other state.[19] When the amendment of the TWF Directive was being undertaken, consideration was given to substantially amending its provisions imposing European content requirements, in particular by removing the rather ambiguous wording "where practicable" (which has proved to be a loophole for those Member States that are unenthusiastic about local content requirements), or to imposing a ten-year deadline on the rules. However, no agreement could be reached and these provisions remained substantially unamended.[20] The legality of these provisions has been questioned, in particular as regards the compliance of the European content requirements with the EU's obligations under the GATS.[21]

2–037 **Regulation of television advertising, sponsorship and teleshopping** — The TWF Directive contains a number of measures regarding the regulation of advertising, sponsorship and teleshopping. These are intended to protect viewers against excessive advertising (in particular certain types of advertising) and ensure media pluralism, including the press.

2–038 *Advertising and teleshopping* — Television advertising is defined as

"any form of announcement broadcast in return for payment or for similar consideration or broadcast in connection with a trade, business, craft or profession in order to promote the supply of goods or services, including immovable property, rights and obligations, in return for payment".[22]

As a result of the 1997 amendment to the TWF Directive, the scope of the TWF Directive was extended to teleshopping, which consists of direct offers broadcast to the public with a view to the supply of goods or services, including immovable property, rights and obligations, in return for payment.[23] Television advertising and advertising techniques have been the subject of a study

---

[18] See para.1–297, above.

[19] See Flint, "GATS 2000 and the European Audiovisual Industry" (1999) *International Media Law* 41–45; Pietrantonio, "European Audiovisual Policy Towards The Year 2000 — A Strategy For The Next GATS Negotiations", (CCH Editions Ltd, 1999), pp.13–15; and Deselaers and König, "The WTO Millenium Round and the Audiovisual Sector" (1999) *International Trade Law Review* 147–154.

[20] Drijber, para.2–017, n.52, pp.89–90.

[21] *ibid.*, pp.108–133; see also De Witte, "The European Content Requirements in the EC Television Directive — Five years after", (*Yearbook of Media and Entertainment Law*, 1995) p.101; Donaldson, "TWF: Continuing Tension Between Liberal Free Trade and European Cultural Integrity" (1996) 20(1) *Fordham International Law Journal* 90–180; and Dolmans, "Quotas Without Content: The Questionable Legality of European Contents Quotas Under the TVWF Directive" (1995) E.L.R. 329 *et seq.*

[22] TWF Directive, para.1–015, n.42, Art.1(c).

[23] *ibid.*, Art.1(f).

undertaken on behalf of the Commission in the light of the evolution of new technologies and a possible review of the TWF Directive.[24]

2–039 *Format of advertising and teleshopping* — Member States are required to ensure that television advertising and teleshopping are readily recognisable as such and are kept separate from other parts of the programme service by optical and/or acoustic means.[25] Isolated advertising and teleshopping spots are permitted but they must remain the exception. Subliminal techniques may not be used and surreptitious advertising is prohibited.[26]

2–040 *Timing of advertising and teleshopping* — Advertising and teleshopping spots must be inserted between programmes.[27] They may also be inserted during programmes provided that the integrity and value of the programme (taking into account natural breaks in and the duration and nature of the programme) and the rights of the rights holders are not prejudiced, and a number of other conditions, summarised below, are met. A study commissioned by the European Commission has recommended the review of the rules governing advertising and teleshopping, in particular in relation to rules governing its timing.[28]

2–041 *Sports programmes and programmes with autonomous parts* — As regards programmes consisting of autonomous parts or sports programmes and similarly structured events and performances containing intervals, advertising and teleshopping spots may only be inserted between the parts or in the intervals.[29]

2–042 *Films and other audio-visual works* — Advertising and teleshopping may be placed during the transmission of audio-visual works (such as feature films and films made for television) once for each period of 45 minutes, provided that their scheduled duration is more than 45 minutes. A further break for advertising or teleshopping is permitted if the scheduled duration of the film is at least 20 minutes longer than two or more complete periods of 45 minutes. These rules are not applicable to series, serials, light entertainment programmes and documentaries.[30] In *ARD v PRO*

---

[24] Carat Crystal and Bird & Bird, Rapport Final "Étude sur le développement des nouvelles techniques publicitaires", April 2002, available at: *http://europa.eu.int/comm/avpolicy/stat/studpdf/pub_rapportfinal.pdf*. New advertising techniques that were considered in this study were: (i) interactive advertising; (ii) advertising on "split screen"; and (iii) virtual publicity. The study considered whether there was any need to reform the TWF Directive to adapt it to new advertising techniques. For more details on this study, see above, para.2–017, n.54.

[25] TWF Directive, para.1–015, n.42, Art.10(1).

[26] *ibid.*, Art.10(3) and (4). Surreptitious advertising means the representation in words or pictures of goods, services, the name, the trademark or the activities of a producer of goods or a provider of services in programmes when such representation is intended by the broadcaster to serve as advertising and might mislead the public as to its nature. Such representation is considered to be intentional in particular if it is done in return for payment or for similar consideration. See Art.1(c).

[27] *ibid.*, Art.11(1).

[28] See above, para.2–017, n.54.

[29] TWF Directive, para.1–015, n.42, Art.11(2).

[30] *ibid.*, Art.11(3). See, concerning the scope of Art.11(3) and the definition of "television series", Opinion of the AG in Case C–245/01, *RTL Television GmbH v Niedersächsische Landesmedienanstalt für privaten Rundfunk* (not yet reported) of May 22, 2003. Advocate General Jacobs concluded that (i) Art.11(3) applies irrespective of whether films made for television have from the outset been produced for television and

Sieben Media AG,[31] the Court of Justice held that Article 11 must be interpreted as meaning that the duration of advertisements must be included in the period of time in relation to which the permissible number of interruptions is calculated (as opposed to not including the duration of the advertisements and basing the calculation only on the duration of the film itself). However, the Court also held that Article 11(3), in conjunction with Article 3(1) of the TWF Directive, authorises Member States to prescribe stricter rules for domestic broadcasters and, in particular, that they may prescribe that the duration of advertisements may not be included when calculating the permissible number of interruptions. The Court further held that such prescription was not caught by Article 28 of the EC Treaty (*ex* 30) and that, although caught by Article 49 of the EC Treaty (*ex* 59), it was a justifiable derogation from Article 49 of the EC Treaty on grounds of general interest, and was proportional.

2–043 *Light entertainment* — The regime applicable to advertisements broadcast during light entertainment programmes, such as series or serials, is more liberal. The only restriction is that a period of at least 20 minutes should elapse between each successive advertising break in the programme.[32]

2–044 *Religious services* — Advertising and teleshopping may not be inserted in any broadcast of a religious service.[33]

2–045 *News, documentaries, religious and children's programmes* — Advertising and teleshopping may not be broadcast during any news and current affairs programmes, documentaries, religious programmes or children's programmes with a duration of less than 30 minutes. If the programme's duration is 30 minutes or longer, advertisements and teleshopping are permitted, provided that a period of at least 20 minutes elapses between each successive advertising break.[34]

2–046 *Possibility to provide for different rules for local broadcasts* — Member States are entitled (with due regard for Community law) to lay down different conditions from those contained in the TWF Directive in relation to the timing of advertising and teleshopping services broadcast on television channels that are broadcast solely within their national territory, and which cannot be received, directly or indirectly, by the public in one or more other Member States.[35]

2–047 *Content of advertising and teleshopping* — As a general matter, television advertising and teleshopping must not: (i) prejudice respect for human dignity; (ii) include any discrimination on grounds of race, sex or nationality; (iii) be offensive to religious or political beliefs; (iv) encourage

---

provided with breaks designed for the insertion of advertising spots, and (ii) several audio-visual works constitute a *series* within the meaning of that provision where either they share a continuing dramatic narrative or have characters (*dramatis personae*) in common.

[31] Case C–6/98 *ARD v PRO Sieben Media AG* [1999] I E.C.R. 7599.
[32] TWF Directive, para.1–015, n.42, Art.11(4).
[33] *ibid.*, Art.11(5).
[34] *ibid.*, Art.11(5).
[35] *ibid.*, Art.20. The study commissioned by the Commission on advertising contains references to national laws in this field, above, para.2–017, n.54, referred to in particular at p.35 in relation to definitions, pp.40–41 in relation to publicity breaks, pp.44–45 in relation to average publicity volumes, and p.48 in relation to regulation of publicity on alcoholic beverages.

behaviour prejudicial to health or to safety; or (v) encourage behaviour prejudicial to the protection of the environment.[36] Specific additional rules are set out for certain types of product.

2–048 *Tobacco products* — All forms of television advertising and teleshopping for cigarettes and other tobacco products are prohibited.[37] This covers indirect forms of advertising, which, without directly mentioning the tobacco product, seek to circumvent the prohibition by using brand names, symbols or other distinctive features of tobacco products or of undertakings whose known or main activities include the production and sale of tobacco.[38]

2–049 *Medicinal products* — Television advertising for medicinal products and medical treatments that are available only on prescription in the Member State within whose jurisdiction the broadcaster falls is prohibited.[39] The TWF Directive regulates teleshopping for medicinal products. Teleshopping for medicinal products which are subject to a marketing authorisation as well as teleshopping for medical treatment are prohibited.[40]

2–050 *Alcohol* — Television advertising and teleshopping for alcoholic beverages must comply with the following conditions: (i) it may not be aimed specifically at minors or, in particular, depict minors consuming these beverages; (ii) it must not link the consumption of alcohol to enhanced physical performance or to driving; (iii) it must not create the impression that the consumption of alcohol contributes towards social or sexual success; (iv) it must not claim that alcohol has therapeutic qualities or that it is a stimulant, a sedative or a means of resolving personal conflicts; (v) it must not encourage immoderate (*i.e.* excessive) consumption of alcohol or present abstinence or moderation in a negative light; and (vi) it must not place emphasis on high alcoholic content as being a positive quality of the beverages.[41]

2–051 *Protection of minors* — Television advertising must not cause moral or physical detriment to minors.[42] In particular, for that purpose, advertising must comply with the following conditions: (i) it must not directly exhort minors to buy a product or a service by exploiting their inexperience or credulity; (ii) it must not encourage minors to persuade their parents or others to purchase the goods or services being advertised; (iii) it must not exploit the special trust minors place in parents, teachers or other persons; and (iv) it must not unreasonably show minors in dangerous situations. Teleshopping must also satisfy these conditions and, in addition, it must not exhort minors to contract for the sale or rental of goods and services.[43]

---

[36] TWF Directive, para.1–015, n.42, Art.12.

[37] *ibid.*, Art.13.

[38] *ibid.*, Preamble.

[39] *ibid.*, Art.14(1).

[40] *ibid.*, Art.14(2). The question of whether a medicinal product requires a marketing authorisation is dealt with in Council Directive 65/65 of January 26, 1965 on the approximation of provisions laid down by law, regulative or administrative action relating to medicinal products, O.J. 1965 L22/369, as last amended by Directive 93/39, O.J. 1993 L214/22.

[41] TWF Directive, para.1–015, n.42, Art.15.

[42] *ibid.*, Art.16(1).

[43] *ibid.*, Art.16(2).

2–052 *Sponsorship* — The TWF Directive contains provisions regulating sponsorship, which is increasingly important for commercial television. Sponsorship is defined as

> "any contribution made by a public or private undertaking not engaged in television broadcasting activities or in the production of audio-visual works, to the financing of television programmes with a view to promoting its name, its trade mark, its image, its activities or its products".[44]

It is permissible for non-broadcasting undertakings to sponsor all types of programmes, except news and current affairs programmes.[45] Sponsored television programme must meet the following requirements: (i) the sponsor may not influence the content and scheduling of sponsored programmes in such a way as to affect the responsibility and editorial independence of the broadcaster in respect of sponsored programmes; (ii) sponsored programmes must be clearly identified as such by the name and/or logo of the sponsor at the beginning and/or the end of the programmes; and (iii) they must not encourage the purchase or rental of the products or services of the sponsor or a third party, in particular by making special promotional references to those products or services.[46] In *RTI*,[47] the Court of Justice held that the TWF Directive does not prohibit references to the name and/or logo of the sponsor at moments other than the beginning and/or the end of the sponsored programme. The mention of the sponsor's name during the programme must not amount, however, to circumventing of the prohibition on surreptitious advertising contained in Article 10(4) of the TWF Directive.

2–053 *Tobacco* — Television programmes may not be sponsored by undertakings whose principal activity is the manufacture or sale of cigarettes and other tobacco products.[48]

2–054 *Medical products* — As a result of the 1997 amendment of the TWF Directive, companies whose principal activity is the manufacture or sale of medicinal products or medical treatment may promote the name or the image of the undertaking but may not promote specific medicinal products or medical treatments available only on prescription in the Member State within whose jurisdiction the broadcaster falls.[49]

2–055 *Advertising quotas* — The TWF Directive lays down limits on the proportion of transmission time that can be devoted to teleshopping spots, advertising spots and other forms of advertising (*i.e.* telepromotions). With the exception of teleshopping windows, advertising and teleshopping must not exceed 20 per cent of a channel's daily transmission time.[50] The transmission time for advertising spots must not exceed 15 per cent of a channel's daily transmission time.[51] In

---

[44] *ibid.*, Art.1(e).
[45] *ibid.*, Art.17(4).
[46] *ibid.*, Art.17(1).
[47] Joined Cases C–320/94, C–328/94, C–329/94, C–337/94, C–338/94 and C–339/94 *Reti Televisive Italiane SpA (RTI)* [1996] I E.C.R. 6471. See Drijber, above, para.2–017, n.52, p.116.
[48] TWF Directive, para.1–015, n.42, Art.17(2).
[49] *ibid.*, Art.17(3).
[50] *ibid.*, Art.18(1).
[51] *ibid.*

RTI,[52] the Court of Justice held the position that telepromotions (*i.e.* television promotions of products or services by means of games or studio shows) should be considered as "other forms of advertising" for the purpose of extending from 15 per cent to 20 per cent the daily limit on advertising. Moreover, the proportion of advertising spots and teleshopping spots within a given clock hour may not exceed 20 per cent (*i.e.* 12 minutes).[53] Self-promotional activities by broadcasters (*e.g.* trailers with extracts of programmes on the promotion of products that are ancillary to such programmes) in connection with their own programmes and ancillary products are not subject to these limits, nor are public service announcements and charity appeals broadcast free of charge.[54]

2–056 *Teleshopping* — Teleshopping consists of the broadcast of direct offers for the sale of goods and/or services.[55] Teleshopping is becoming increasingly popular, with entire television channels being devoted to it. The TWF Directive distinguishes between three forms of teleshopping: (i) teleshopping spots, which are similar to short advertising breaks[56]; (ii) teleshopping windows on generalist channels which are essentially short programmes[57]; and (iii) channels exclusively devoted to teleshopping.[58] The proportion of daily broadcasting time that may be devoted to teleshopping spots is cumulated within the same limits as advertising spots, *i.e.* advertising spots and teleshopping spots combined may not exceed 20 per cent of the channel's daily broadcasting time.[59] The number of windows devoted to teleshopping broadcast by a channel not exclusively devoted to teleshopping may not exceed eight per day and each window must be of an uninterrupted duration of at least 15 minutes[60] subject to an overall maximum duration of three hours.[61] Teleshopping windows must be clearly identified as such by optical and acoustic means.[62] Channels that are exclusively devoted to teleshopping are now permitted under the TWF Directive[63] and are subject *mutatis mutandis* to the rules applicable to other channels, with the exception of the rules on teleshopping quotas.[64]

2–057 *Possibility for Member States to impose stricter rules* — Member States may impose different regulations on advertising and teleshopping on broadcasters under their jurisdiction.[65] Member States may impose stricter or less strict advertising rules in respect to programmes that are intended for reception only for their national territory and which may not be received, directly or indirectly, in one or more Member States.[66] In *RTI*,[67] the Court of Justice confirmed that the

[52] *RTI*, above, para.2–052, n.47.
[53] TWF Directive, para.1–015, n.42, Art.18(2).
[54] *ibid.*, Art.18(3).
[55] *ibid.*, Art.1(f).
[56] *ibid.*, Art.18(1).
[57] *ibid.*, Art.18(a).
[58] *ibid.*, Art.19.
[59] *ibid.*, Art.18(2).
[60] *ibid.*, Art.18(a)(1).
[61] *ibid.*, Art.18(a)(2).
[62] *ibid.*
[63] In its initial form, Art.18(3) of the TWF Directive imposed a daily limit of one hour on teleshopping.
[64] *ibid.*, Art.19. However, advertising on such channels must be limited to the daily maximum limits laid down by Art.18(1).
[65] *ibid.*, Art.20.
[66] *ibid.*, Art.20.
[67] *RTI*, above, para.2–052, n.47.

possibility of increasing the daily limit on advertising from 15 to 20 per cent of the daily total transmission time under Article 18 was only an option for Member States, with the result that Member States may continue to impose stricter rules (*i.e.* a 15 per cent daily limit) on broadcasters under their jurisdiction. In *Leclerc-Siplec*,[68] the Court of Justice upheld the lawfulness under the TWF Directive of a French law prohibiting the broadcast of advertising concerning the distribution of fuel.

2–058   *Right of reply* — The TWF Directive requires broadcasters to provide a right of reply to any natural or legal person whose legitimate interests, in particular reputation and good name, have been damaged by an assertion of incorrect facts in a television programme. Alternatively, Member States can provide for equivalent remedies which presumably would include broadcasting a full apology. Such remedies are without prejudice to any other remedies that may be imposed by national law.[69] The right of reply must exist in relation to all broadcasters under the jurisdiction of a Member State.[70] Member States must adopt measures needed to establish the right of reply or the equivalent remedies and determine the procedure to be followed for its exercise by an affected person. In particular, the procedures must allow the person concerned to exercise the right of reply (or equivalent remedies) appropriately, within a reasonable time of the request for a right of reply being substantiated and at an appropriate time and in an appropriate manner without imposing unreasonable terms or conditions.[71] Member States must ensure that the right to reply (or equivalent remedy) be available to persons resident or established in other Member States.[72] An application for a right of reply may be rejected if it is not justified to protect the complainant's legitimate interests (*e.g.* reputation and good name), would involve the broadcaster in committing a criminal offence, would render the broadcaster liable to civil law proceedings, or would transgress standards of public decency.[73] Disputes as to the exercise of the right of reply must be subject to judicial review.[74]

2–059   Application of the TWF Directive to non-EU broadcasters — The GATS, in particular the MFN principle and national treatment, applies in principle to cable or broadcast distribution of radio or television programmes.[75] However, the application of the GATS to broadcasting services is not yet effective in the EU as the EU has notified to the WTO an exemption of unlimited duration (pursuant to Article II(2) of the GATS) concerning the European content requirements imposed by Articles 4 and 5 of the TWF Directive. Moreover, the EU has not yet made any commitment in relation to the obligation to accord national treatment to broadcasters from other WTO Member States, either in relation to market access or the conditions governing the provision of services in the broadcasting sector.[76] As a result, non-EU broadcasters may, in principle, not benefit from the

---

[68] Case C–412/93, *Société d'Importation Edouard Leclerc-Siplec v TF1 Publicité SA and M6 Publicité SA* [1995] I E.C.R. 179.

[69] TWF Directive, para.1–015, n.42, Art.23(1).

[70] *ibid.*, Art.23(2).

[71] *ibid.*, Art.23(1).

[72] *ibid.*, Art.23(3).

[73] *ibid.*, Art.23(4).

[74] *ibid.*, Art.23(5).

[75] See above, para.1–297 *et seq.*

[76] See Drijber, para.2–017, n.52, p.122.

liberalisation measures contained in the TWF Directive and therefore remain fully subject to national media restrictions. Nevertheless, this has not been a significant handicap, as third country broadcasters can easily obtain broadcasting licences in certain Member States, such as the UK, which impose relatively few restrictions on non-EEA broadcasters, save in relation to terrestrial broadcasters. The TWF Directive specifically states that it does not apply to broadcasts intended exclusively for reception in third countries, and which are not received directly or indirectly by the public in one or more Member States.[77] For example, the transmission of television signals from a Member State directly to the United States is not subject to the provisions of the TWF Directive and therefore remains fully subject to national broadcasting restrictions. In the case of broadcasts to third countries that are signatories to the Council of Europe Convention on Transfrontier Television,[78] the provisions of that convention will be applicable. The Convention imposes a number of provisions that are similar to those imposed by the TWF Directive.

2. Broadcasting Aspects of the New Regulatory Framework

2–060   The New Regulatory Framework has been examined in Chapter I. Certain parts of the New Regulatory Framework directly or indirectly concern broadcasting, although broadcasting is only covered to a limited extent by the directives comprising the New Regulatory Framework.

(a) Access to Cable Television Networks

2–061   **Distinction between transmission and content** — The question of whether open access to cable television networks within the scope of Article 12 of the Access Directive[79] can be requested by television broadcasters is closely linked to the question of whether broadcasters offer transmission services or content. Whilst the scope of "electronic communications networks" includes cable television networks, satellite networks and other networks used for radio and television broadcasting,[80] and the scope of "electronic communications services" includes transmission services in networks used for broadcasting, this latter term excludes services providing, or exercising editorial control over, content transmitted using electronic communications networks and services.[81] This is confirmed by the Access Directive, where Recital 2 explicitly states that services providing content (such as radio and television broadcasting services) are excluded from the scope of the New Regulatory Framework. The New Regulatory Framework accordingly makes a clear distinction between broadcasting services and services for their transmission.

2–062   **No right under the New Regulatory Framework for broadcasters to demand access to cable television networks** — The exclusion of broadcasters from the scope of "electronic communications services" means that a broadcaster cannot rely on Article 12 of the Access Directive to seek access to a cable television network, because it is a provider of content. As a result, broadcasters will have

---

[77] TWF Directive, para.1–015, n.42, Art.2(b).
[78] See European Convention on Transfrontier Television (STE No.132), Strasbourg, May 5, 1989, amended by the Protocol amending the European Convention on Transfrontier Television (STE No.171), adopted on October 1, 1998 and entering into force on March 1, 2002.
[79] See above, para.1–044 *et seq.*, on Art.12 of the Access Directive, para.1–011, n.29.
[80] Framework Directive, para.1–009, n.25, Art.2(a).
[81] *ibid.*, Art.2(c).

to rely on general competition law provisions[82] to seek such access, unless they can benefit from national rules that impose "must carry" obligations on cable television network operators.[83] In contrast, cable operators, who are providers of electronic communications services under Article 2(c) of the Framework Directive, can rely on the Access Directive to access another cable network having SMP.

2–063 **"Must carry" obligations** — Article 31(1) of the Universal Service Directive permits Member States to impose proportionate and transparent "must carry" obligations on cable television network operators. "Must carry" obligations must be necessary to meet clearly defined public interest objectives and must be transparent and proportionate. They may be imposed where a significant number of end users use cable networks to receive radio and television broadcasts. "Must carry" obligations must also specify the radio and televisions broadcast channels and services that benefit from the "must carry" obligations.[84] It follows that although broadcasters cannot rely on the Access Directive, some may benefit from national "must carry" measures. "Must carry" obligations can therefore be imposed by Member States to require cable networks to distribute certain radio and television broadcasts to the public.[85] "Must carry" obligations may also include the transmission of services specifically designed to enable appropriate access by disabled users.[86] "Must carry" obligations can also be imposed on terrestrial and satellite networks.[87] Member States may determine the appropriate remuneration to be paid by broadcasters who benefit from "must carry" obligations, provided these are applied in a proportionate, non-discriminatory and transparent manner.[88]

(b) Access to Conditional Access Systems

2–064   Article 6 of and Annex I to the Access Directive concern the regulation of conditional access systems and associated facilities. They lay down a framework of rules applicable to conditional access and maintain the approach set out in the now repealed Advanced Television Standards Directive,[89] in particular with respect to the obligation to provide conditional access

---

[82] In particular, rules prohibiting the abuse of a dominant position. See, above, para.1–147.

[83] See para.2–063, below.

[84] Access Directive, para.1–011, Art.31(1).

[85] Two examples of "must carry" obligations currently in force in Member States are to be found in Belgium and France. In Belgium, the law of March 30, 1995 concerning cable distribution and broadcasting activities in the Brussels region (MB February 22, 1996) imposes "must carry" obligations on operators of televisual radio transmission services and two ministerial decrees dated January 17, 2001 and January 24, 2002 designate those broadcasting companies whose television channels must be transmitted by operators authorised to operate cable networks in Brussels. Similar provisions are in force in the Flemish and Walloon regions under regional decrees. In France, Art.34-I of the Law (no.86-1067) of September 30, 1986 on freedom of communication (as amended by the Law (no.2000-719) of August 1, 2000) imposes "must carry" obligations on all cable network operators which require a wide range of channels, both public and commercial to be carried. For an overview of national "must carry" regulations in each Member State, see Ovum and Squire Sanders "An Inventory of EU 'Must Carry' Regulations — A Report to the European Commission, Information Society Directorate", February 2001, *http://europa.eu.int/ISPO/infosoc/telecompolicy/en/OVUM-mustcarry.pdf.*

[86] Universal Service Directive, para.1–011, n.30, Recital 43.

[87] *ibid.*, Recital 44.

[88] *ibid.*, Art.31(2).

[89] Directive 95/47, O.J. 1995 L281/51, repealed by Art.26 of the Framework Directive, para.1–009, n.25.

systems on fair, reasonable and non-discriminatory terms. The Access Directive takes a technology-neutral approach to such regulation. However, given the need to take into account recent technological developments in regulating digital television gateways, the new Access Directive permits NRAs to extend conditional access obligations to new technological and market developments such as electronic programme guides (EPGs) and application program interfaces (APIs).[90]

2–065   Definition of conditional access system — The concept of "conditional access system" as defined by the Framework Directive covers any system by which a service provider controls viewer access to different programmes and channels, so that only those authorised to watch (for example by paying the appropriate fee) can access the programmes or services.[91] From a technical perspective, conditional access is achieved by the broadcaster (or its own contractor, such as a satellite or cable network operator) scrambling the broadcast signal whilst providing subscribers or other authorised recipients with a decoder (or "set-top box") that allows them to unscramble the signal.

2–066   Right of access to conditional access systems — Subscribers using a specific conditional access system are unlikely to invest in a second set-top box or dish to watch broadcasts that use a different system. Accordingly, the operator of a conditional access system that is used by a large proportion of the viewing population may constitute a "gatekeeper" for television broadcasters to reach viewers particularly if it is part of a vertically integrated broadcaster. Therefore, there is a risk that the operator of the conditional access system could abuse its position and prevent market entry by broadcasters, particularly those competing with its own channels. Therefore, specific *ex ante* regulation is needed beyond the application of competition rules to prevent dominant providers of conditional access systems from abusing their market power. Accordingly, in 1995, the Advanced Television Standards Directive[92] was adopted, which laid down rules for the regulation of conditional access services. These rules have been consolidated in the Access Directive and ensure that broadcasters can obtain conditional access services on fair, reasonable and non-discriminatory terms.

The Access Directive therefore requires Member States to ensure that specific conditions are applied by them in relation to conditional access to digital television and radio services broadcast to

---

[90] Access Directive, para.1–011, n.29, Recital 10, Art.5(1)(b) and Annex I Pt II.

[91] The term "conditional access system" is defined by Art.2(f) of the Framework Directive, para.1–011, n.25, as "any technical measure and/or arrangement whereby access to a protected radio or television broadcasting service in intelligible form is made conditional upon subscription or other form of prior authorisation". A "conditional access device" is defined by Art.2(b) of the Conditional Access Directive (Directive 98/84 of the European Parliament and of the Council of November 20, 1998 on the legal protection of services based on, or consisting of, conditional access, O.J. 1998 L320/54) as "any equipment or software designed or adapted to give access to a protected service in an intelligible form", and the term "protected services" covers any "television broadcasting, radio broadcasting and on-line services provided on the basis of conditional access, as well as provision of conditional access to these services". It should be noted that conditional access systems do not include pay-television services. Some free television services broadcast by satellite are encrypted for copyright reasons and this definition also covers new activities such as interactive services that extend beyond the traditional pay-television market.

[92] See above, para.2–064, n.89.

viewers and listeners in the Community, irrespective of the means of transmission.[93] These conditions include the requirement that all operators of conditional access services, irrespective of the means of transmission, who provide access services to digital television and radio services and on whose access services broadcasters depend to reach any group of potential viewers or listeners must:

(i) offer to all broadcasters, on a fair, reasonable and non-discriminatory basis compatible with Community competition law, technical services enabling the broadcasters' digitally transmitted services to be received by viewers or listeners authorised by means of decoders administered by the service operators;

(ii) comply with Community competition law; and

(iii) keep separate financial accounts regarding their activity as conditional access providers.[94]

Member States have some discretion on how to implement this. For example, in the United Kingdom, the responsibility for regulating conditional access providers has been given to OFTEL, the telecommunications regulator. OFTEL has taken the position that regulatory intervention in relation to conditional access regulation under the Advanced Television Standards Directive should take place as a last resort, when commercial negotiations fail to produce an agreement, in accordance with the rules governing interconnection and access generally. Despite the requirement of non-discrimination, OFTEL has allowed different prices to be charged to different operators on the basis of objective criteria, for example whether those seeking access are free-to-air, pay-television or interactive service operators.

2–067 The Access Directive foresees a regular review of the regulatory regime for conditional access to be carried out by the NRAs for their respective national markets and by the Commission for the Community as a whole to take account of market and technological developments.[95] NRAs may also review the conditions applied to conditional access operations to determine if they should be maintained, amended or withdrawn in the light of market developments, in particular whether the market is effectively competitive or still has operators with SMP.[96]

If the NRAs should find that one or more operators of conditional access systems does not have SMP, it may amend or withdraw regulatory conditions on such operators, provided that this does not adversely affect end-users' access to radio and television broadcasts and broadcasting channels and services for which "must carry" obligations have been imposed[97] and this would not adversely

---

[93] Access Directive, para.1–011, n.29, Art.6(1) and Annex I, Pt I. Cowie and Marsden, "Convergence, Competition and Regulation" (1998) *International Journal of Communications Law and Policy* 12–13, available at: *www.digital-law.net/IJCLP/11998/ijclp_webdoc_6_1_1998.htm.*

[94] Access Directive, para.1–011, n.29, Annex I, Pt I(b).

[95] *ibid.*, Arts 6(2) and 17.

[96] *ibid.*, Art.6(3). This involves a market analysis in accordance with Art.16 of the Framework Directive. See above para.1–031 *et seq.*

[97] Art.31 of the Universal Service Directive, para.1–011, n.30.

affect the prospects for effective competition for retail digital television and radio broadcasting services and conditional access by associated facilities.[98] Appropriate notice must be given to parties that would be affected by any such amendment or withdrawal.[99]

It therefore follows that Member States may be required to continue to impose *ex ante* regulation on operators of conditional access systems even if they do not have SMP. Member States may also impose regulations on the presentational aspects of EPGs and similar listing and navigational facilities.[1] Member States may also impose *ex ante* regulation on providers of EPGs and APIs, regardless of any finding of SMP, where that is necessary to ensure end users' access to digital radio and television broadcasting services. Such *ex ante* regulation shall require access to EPGs and APIs to be provided on fair, reasonable and non-discriminatory terms.[2]

The regulation of conditional access system is limited to the extent that it benefits digital television and radio broadcasters to the exclusion of the providers of non-broadcast services, such as video-on-demand, audio-on-demand, electronic publishing, online services offered to the public on a subscription or usage-related basis and analogue broadcasters whose only course of action under Community law to gain access to such systems would be to rely on Article 82 EC. As the regulation on conditional access for services other than digital television and radio services is not harmonised by the Access Directive, Member States may impose their own regulatory regimes for conditional access for other services. Such regulatory regimes must be compatible with general principles of Community law.

2–068 Licensing of intellectual property rights in conditional access systems — The Access Directive re-enacts the provisions of the now repealed Advanced Television Standards Directive, in so far as it does not impose compulsory licences on owners of conditional access technology. However, it does impose obligations on the holders of industrial property rights to conditional access products and systems, when granting licences to manufacturers of consumer equipment, to do so on fair, reasonable and non-discriminatory terms.[3] In particular, rights holders may not make the granting of licences subject to conditions that prohibit, deter or discourage the inclusion in the same product of: (i) a common interface, that allows connection of the licensed system with several other access systems; or (ii) means specific to another access system, provided that the licensee complies with relevant and reasonable conditions ensuring, as far as it is concerned, the security of trans-actions of conditional access system operators.[4] These provisions should ensure that consumer equipment (such as set-top boxes and integrated television sets) can be used to access programmes processed by different conditional access systems, and irrespective of the means of transmission used.

2–069 Technical standards for the interoperability of analogue and digital television sets — The Advanced Television Standards Directive contained a number of provisions designed to ensure the

---

[98] Access Directive, para.1–011, n.29, Art.6(3), second para.
[99] *ibid.*, third para.
[1] *ibid.*, Art.6(4).
[2] *ibid.*, Art.5(1), second para.; sub-para.(b). On the application of Art.5 generally, see above, paras 1–150 and 1–170.
[3] Access Directive, para.1–011, n.29, Annex I, Pt I, (c).
[4] *ibid.*

interoperability of television transmission systems and receivers.[5] These provisions have been consolidated into the Universal Service Directive, which requires Member States to ensure the interoperability of consumer digital television equipment.[6]

Any analogue television set with an integral screen with a visible diagonal measurement greater than 42cm which is put on the market for sale or rent in the Community must be fitted with at least one open interface socket, as standardised by a recognised European standards organisation (for example CENELEC's EN 50 049-1:1997 standard) permitting the simple connection of peripherals, especially additional decoders and digital receivers.[7]

In addition, and extending the scope of the former Advanced Television Standards Directive, any digital television set with an integral screen with a visible diagonal measurement greater than 30cm which is put on the market for sale or rent in the Community is to be fitted with at least one open interface socket permitting the simple connection of peripherals and able to pass all the elements of a digital television signal, including information relating to interactive and conditionally accessed services. This open interface socket must either be standardised by, or conform to, a standard adopted by a recognised European standards organisation (such as CEN, CENELEC or ETSI), or conform to an industry-wide specification, for example, the DVB common interface connector.[8]

Article 17 of the Framework Directive enables the Commission to make the implementation of technical standards and/or specifications compulsory in certain circumstances in order to encourage the harmonised provision of electronic communications networks and services, and associated facilities and services. In addition, under Article 18(1) of the Framework Directive, Member States must encourage (i) providers of digital interactive television services, for distribution to the public in the EU on digital interactive television platforms, and (ii) providers of enhanced digital television equipment, for the reception of such services (*i.e.* set-top boxes), to use a single open standard for API. Member States are also under an obligation (under Article 18(2) of the Framework Directive) to encourage all prioprietors of APIs to make available on fair, reasonable and non-discriminatory terms (for appropriate remuneration) all such information that is necessary to enable suppliers of digital interactive television services to provide all services supported by the API in a fully functional form.

The Directive therefore leaves it to market players in the first instance to achieve full interoperability of set-top boxes, without imposing any specific standard. Member States may, however, intervene to impose a specific open standard, where commercial negotiation alone is not sufficient to achieve the objective of full interoperability, under national rules. In doing so, Member States may in principle choose any open standard. In practice, the Commission considers Multi Home Platform (MHP) as the preferred standard to achieve the objectives of the New Regulatory

---

[5] See Advanced Television Standards Directive, para.2–064, n.89, Arts 4 and 5.
[6] Universal Service, para.1–011, n.30, Art.24 and Annex VI.
[7] *ibid.*, Annex VI(2), first para. (consolidating Art.3 of the Advanced Television Standards Directive).
[8] *ibid.*, second para.

Framework, and may require a Member State to use the MHP standard when enacting regulations imposing an open API.[9]

2–070 Common scrambling algorithm — In order to ensure that all consumer equipment intended for the reception of digital television signals, for sale or rent or otherwise made available in the Community, can in principle enable consumers in the EU to access all broadcasts of digital television services, the Universal Service Directive makes compulsory the inclusion of the common European scrambling algorithm in all consumer equipment capable of receiving digital television signals. The common scrambling algorithm must be administered by a recognised European standards organisation, currently ETSI. Moreover, such equipment must be capable of displaying signals transmitted in clear (*i.e.* transmitted without being scrambled or otherwise protected by a conditional access system), provided that, in the event that such equipment is rented, the rentee is in compliance with the relevant rental agreement.[10]

2–071 Transcontrol of conditional access — Many pay-television services broadcast by satellite are also retransmitted to consumers via cable or terrestrial networks. The operators of these networks will need to control their subscribers' access to such programmes. This involves a process known as "transcontrol" whereby control over access to protected programmes is transferred to the cable or terrestrial network operator. Accordingly, under the Access Directive, Member States are required to ensure that conditional access systems operated on the market in the Community have the necessary technical capability for cost-effective transcontrol, allowing the possibility for full control by network operators at local or regional level of the services using such conditional access systems.[11] Unlike the Advanced Television Standards Directive (Article 4(b)) previously in force, the regime under the Access Directive is not limited to cable television operators; it is applicable to all network operators, thereby ensuring regulation on a technologically neutral basis. Therefore, operators of digital networks and ADSL-enabled networks could also rely upon this.

2–072 Protection from piracy — The primary purpose of conditional access systems is to prevent unauthorised access to pay-television and other services, so that broadcasters and other service providers can collect their remuneration. However, there is an active market in the production and distribution of devices (such as pirated or counterfeited smart cards) that enable programmes to be viewed without payment. The Community therefore adopted the Conditional Access Directive[12] to impose a harmonised regime to control the placing on the market of such

---

[9] Framework Directive, para.1–009, n.25, Arts 17 and 18, and Official Statement by EU Commissioner for Information Society Erkki Liikanen, of December 21, 2001, in Information Note by the Council 2001/1324 (COD), where the Commission indicates MHP as the preferred open standard for API. This interpretation of the provision of the Framework Directive is furthermore confirmed by Commission Communication on "Barriers to widespread access to new services and applications of the information society through open platforms in digital television and third generation mobile communications", COM(2003) 410 of July 9, 2003, published on *www.europa.eu.int/information_society/topics/telecoms/regulatory/maindocs/documents/acte_en.pdf*. See also further on the issue of the interoperability of digital television sets, paras 1–174 and 2–066 above and para.6–089 below.

[10] Universal Service Directive, para.1–011, n.30, Annex VI. This consolidates Art.4(6) of the Advanced Television Standards Directive, para.2–064, n.89.

[11] Access Directive, para.1–011, n.29, Annex I, Pt 1(a).

[12] See para.2–065, n.91.

illicit devices, which give unauthorised access to television and radio broadcasts and information society services (such as online services) that are provided against remuneration and on the basis of conditional access.

Accordingly, Member States must prohibit, in their territory, the manufacture, import, distribution, sale, possession, rental, installation, maintenance, replacement and promotion (advertising, marketing, sponsorship, sales, promotion, etc.) for commercial purposes of illicit devices, *i.e.* any equipment or software designed or adapted to give access to a protected service, in an intelligible form, without the authorisation of the service provider.[13]

2–073 Sanctions and remedies — Member States are also required to provide for effective, dissuasive and proportionate remedies and sanctions in respect of any prohibited activities concerning illicit devices.[14] Member States must take necessary measures to ensure that service providers whose activities are damaged by infringing activities on their territory have access to appropriate remedies, including bringing an action for damages, obtaining an injunction or other preventive measures and, where appropriate, applying for the disposal of illicit devices.[15] Whilst such sanctions and remedies are a matter of national law, they must ensure that Community law is applied with the same effectiveness and thoroughness as provisions of national law.[16] Member States are not obliged to impose criminal sanctions for infringing activities, but may do so.[17] Remedies under the Conditional Access Directive are also without prejudice to other sanctions or remedies that may be available under national law, such as general preventive measures and powers of seizure of illicit devices or under intellectual property laws.[18]

2–074 Internal market principles — Member States must refrain from restricting the provision of protected (and associated) services originating in another Member State and the free movement of conditional access devices, for reasons relating to the prevention against unauthorised access to protected services, save where the restriction relates to action taken to prevent the placing on the market of illicit devices.[19]

3. Copyright Directives

2–075 Works such as films, and television and radio programmes are protected under national law by copyright or neighbouring rights (such as fixation, reproduction and distribution rights). Differences in the legal protection provided by the laws of the Member States for copyright works created barriers to trade and distorted competition, thereby impeding the creation and functioning of an internal market in broadcasting services. As a result, the EU has adopted legislation intended

---

[13] *ibid.*, Arts 3(1) and 4.
[14] *ibid.*, Arts 3(1) and 5(1).
[15] *ibid.*, Arts 3(1) and 5(2).
[16] *ibid.*, Recitals 17 and 18 referring to Art.5 of the EC Treaty and to Council Resolution of June 29, 1995 on the effective uniform application of Community law and on the penalties applicable for breaches of Community law in the internal market, O.J. 1995 C188/1.
[17] *ibid.*, Recital 23.
[18] *ibid.*, Recitals 21 and 23.
[19] *ibid.*, Art.3(2).

to harmonise national laws on copyright and related rights. The most recent Community legislation to be adopted was the Copyright Directive,[20] which was adopted in 2001 to introduce a series of provisions applicable to all fields of the Information Society. However, there remains other relevant Community legislation relating to particular segments of the Information Society, including rental rights, lending rights and copyright protection for the broadcasting of programmes by satellite and cable retransmission.[21]

2–076 Fixation, reproduction and broadcasting Rights — The Rental Right Directive introduced a rental and lending right for authors of certain copyright works and owners of neighbouring rights in such works.[22] The Rental Right Directive applies to the lending or rental of copyright works, including films, *i.e.* of cinematographic or audio-visual works or moving images, whether or not accompanied by sound.[23] The provisions of the Rental Right Directive on rental and lending rights in works other than films and sound recordings are beyond the scope of this book.[24] The Rental Right Directive also confers certain neighbouring rights on authorised copyright works being fixation, reproduction, broadcasting and communication to the public, and distribution rights.

2–077 Fixation right — Member States must provide broadcasting organisations with the exclusive right to authorise or prohibit the fixation of their broadcasts (*i.e.* physical recording of the production), whether these broadcasts are transmitted by wire or over the air, including by cable or satellite.[25] Cable network operators do not enjoy a fixation right where they merely retransmit by cable the broadcast of broadcasting organisations.[26]

2–078 Reproduction right — Article 7 of the Rental Right Directive introduced a right giving owners of copyright works the right to authorise or prohibit the reproduction of their works. The Copyright Directive repealed Article 7 and introduced a general reproduction right covering the reproduction of all works in the Information Society. Member States must provide for the exclusive right to authorise or prohibit direct or indirect, temporary or permanent reproduction by any means and in any form, in whole or in part for (i) performers, of fixation of their performances[27]; (ii) producers of the first fixation of films, in respect of the original and copies of their films[28]; and (iii) broadcasting organisations, of fixations of their broadcasts, whether those broadcasts are transmitted by wire or over the air, including by cable or satellite.[29]

2–079 Broadcasting and communication to the public — Member States must grant to performers the exclusive right to authorise or prohibit the broadcasting by wireless means (including by

---

[20] See above, para.1–252, n.85, and below, para.2–090.
[21] *ibid.*, Art.2.
[22] Council Directive 92/1 of November 19, 1992 on rental right and lending right and on certain rights related to copyright in the field of intellectual property, O.J. 1992 L346/61.
[23] *ibid.*, Arts 1 and 2(1).
[24] See Winn, para.2–001, n.1, pp.240–244.
[25] Rental Right Directive, para.2–076, n.22, Art.6(2).
[26] *ibid.*, Art.6(3).
[27] Copyight Directive, above, para.1–252, n.85, Art.2(b).
[28] *ibid.*, Art.2(d).
[29] *ibid.*, Art.2(e).

satellite) and the communication to the public of their performances, except where the performance is itself already a broadcast performance or is made from a fixation.[30] Member States must set up a system ensuring that the user pays an equitable remuneration, if a phonogram is used for broadcasting by wireless means or for any communication to the public.[31] Finally, broadcasting organisations must have the exclusive right to authorise the rebroadcasting of their broadcasts by wireless means, as well as the communication to the public of their broadcasts if the communication is made in places accessible to the public against payment of an entrance fee.[32]

2–080 Distribution right — Broadcasting organisations must have the exclusive right (known as a "distribution right") to make available the fixation of their broadcasts, as well as copies thereof, to the public by sale or otherwise.[33] Performers, phonogram producers, and the producers of the fixation of a film have the same right in relation to, respectively, the performances, the phonograms, and the original and copies of the films.[34] The distribution right is only exhausted by the first sale of a tangible copy of the work in the EU by the right-holder or with his consent[35]; however, this does not arise in relation to online services allowing access to the work, or in relation to material copy of the work made by a user of such an online service.[36] The distribution right may be transferred, assigned or subject to the granting of contractual licence.[37]

2–081 Limitations to related rights — Member States may provide for limitations from the exclusive rights granted to owners of fixation, reproduction, broadcasting and distribution rights in respect of: private use,[38] use of short excerpts in connection with the reporting of current events, the making of ephemeral fixation by a broadcasting organisation by means of its own facilities and for its own broadcasts, and uses solely for the purposes of teaching or scientific research.[39] Member States may also provide additional limitations with regard to the protection of performers, producers of phonograms, broadcasting organisations and of producers of the first fixations of films, which shall be of the same kind as provided in relation to copyright in literary and artistic works. However, compulsory licences may be provided only to the extent that they are compatible with the Rome Convention.[40] However, these limitations shall only be applied in certain special cases which do not conflict with the normal exploitation of the subject-matter and do not unreasonably prejudice the legitimate interests of the right-holder.[41]

2–082 Duration of the related rights — The term of copyright protection of audio-visual works expires 70 years after the death of the last of the following persons to survive: (i) the principal

---

[30] Rental Right Directive, above, para.2–076, n.22, Art.8(1).

[31] *ibid.*, Art.8(2).

[32] *ibid.*, Art.8(3).

[33] *ibid.*, Art.9(1).

[34] *ibid.*

[35] *ibid.*, Art.9(2). See also Copyright Directive, above, para.1–252, n.85, Art.4.

[36] See Copyright Directive, above, para.1–252, n.85, Recital 29.

[37] Rental Right Directive, above, para.2–076, n.22, Art.9(3). This exception is subject to any existing or future legislation on remuneration for reproduction for private use. *ibid.*, Art.10(3).

[38] This exception is subject to any existing or future legislation on remuneration for reproduction for private use. *ibid.*, Art.10(3).

[39] *ibid.*, Art.10.

[40] *ibid.*, Art.10(3).

[41] *ibid.*, as inserted by Art.11(1)(b) of the Copyright Directive, above, para.1–252, n.85.

director; (ii) the author of the screenplay; and (iii) the author of the dialogue and the composer of music specifically created for use in the audio-visual work.[42] As regards related rights, the duration of the rights is (i) 50 years after the date of the performance in the case of the rights of performers; (ii) 50 years after the fixation is made in the case of the rights of producers in the first fixation of a film; and (iii) 50 years after the fixation or transmission of a broadcast whether this broadcast is transmitted by wire or over the air, including by cable or satellite in the case of the rights of broadcasting organisations.[43]

2–083 Copyright and related rights applicable to satellite broadcasting and cable retransmission — The Satellite and Cable Directive introduced a harmonised level of copyright protection for broadcasts made in the Community.[44] The Satellite and Cable Directive was adopted to remove barriers to cross-border broadcasting and the retransmission by cable networks of programmes from other Member States that were caused by the application of divergent national copyright systems. It facilitates the licensing of copyright works for inclusion in cross-border satellite broadcasts and their immediate retransmission by cable. It will also ensure appropriate remuneration for rights holders. It complements the TWF Directive, which did not address copyright issues.[45] As with the latter, the Cable and Satellite Directive is presently subject to review in the context of a major technological change in the provision of audio-visual services[46]; it is, however, still too early to determine what changes might be justified in order to extend the scope of the Satellite and Cable Directive.

2–084 Exclusive rights for works to be broadcast via satellite — The Satellite and Cable Directive requires Member States to provide authors with the exclusive right to authorise the communication to the public by satellite of copyright works.[47] This covers broadcasts using only satellites operating on frequency bands reserved for the broadcast of signals for reception by the public or for closed (point-to-point) communication with individual users, provided that the broadcasting organisation has control of and responsibility for the signals in an uninterrupted chain of communication reaching from the up-link station to the satellite and back to the down-link station.[48] This covers encrypted broadcasts if the recipient is provided with the means to decrypt it.[49] Authorisation may only be obtained from the author by agreement, whether directly or through a collecting society acting on behalf of the author.[50] This agreement needs only to be obtained in the Member State where the broadcasting originates rather than in all Member States where the broadcast is received, as the act of communication to the public by satellite is deemed to

---

[42] Council Directive 93/98 of October 29, 1993 harmonising the term of protection of copyright and certain related rights, O.J. 1993 L290/9, Art.2.

[43] *ibid.*, Art.3.

[44] Council Directive 93/83 of September 27, 1993 on the co-ordination of certain rules concerning copyright and rights related to copyright applicable to satellite broadcasting and cable retransmission, O.J. 1993 L248/15. See also Report from the European Commission on the application of Council Directive 93/83 on the co-ordination of certain rules concerning copyright and rights related to copyright applicable to satellite broadcasting and cable retransmission, COM(2002) 430 final, July 26, 2002.

[45] *ibid.*, Recital 12.

[46] See Report from the European Commission above, para.2–083, n.44, p.16.

[47] Satellite and Cable Directive, para.2–083, n.43, Art.2.

[48] *ibid.*, Arts 1(1) and 1(2)(a), defining "satellite" and "communications to the public by satellite."

[49] *ibid.*, Art.1(2)(c).

[50] *ibid.*, Art.3(1).

occur solely in the Member State where, under the control and responsibility of the broadcasting organisation, the programme-carrying signals are introduced into an interrupted chain of communication leading to the satellite and down towards the earth.[51] Given the definition of broadcaster and the regulation of broadcasters under the TWF Directive,[52] this need not necessarily be the Member State in which the satellite up-link is located. It is the law of the country where the signal is "introduced" by the broadcasting organisation that applies in considering if the rights granted by the Satellite and Cable Directive have been infringed. The licence may cover the entire area covered by the satellite footprint.

The Court of Justice has been asked to interpret the Satellite and Cable Directive, in particular the concepts of an "act of communication to the public" and "reception by the public" in the context of distributing a broadcast within a hotel to the various rooms. The Court held that the circumstances in which a broadcast is a communication to and received by the public is a question that should be decided in accordance with national law as the Satellite and Cable Directive provides only for a minimum degree of harmonisation.[53]

2–085 Collective agreement with collecting societies — Many copyright works contain a bundle of different copyrights owned by different persons. Negotiating with each different copyright owner would be inefficient, and also entails a risk that the smooth operation of contractual arrangements could be prevented by the owner of copyright in individual parts of the programme refusing to enter into an agreement.[54] This process would also be burdensome for copyright owners. Therefore, the Satellite and Cable Directive permits Member States to extend (except as regards cinematographic works)[55] collective agreements between collecting societies and broadcasting organisations covering a given category of works to include right-holders of the same category that are not represented by the collecting society, provided that the communication by satellite is a simulcast of a terrestrial broadcast by the same broadcaster and the unrepresented right-holder has the right to exclude the extension of the collective agreement to his works so that he can exercise his rights either individually or collectively.[56] These provisions apply from January 1, 2000 to any agreements, concerning the exploitation of works, in force on or before January 1, 1995 and expiring after January 1, 2000.[57]

2–086 No distinction between direct broadcast satellites and communications satellites — The Satellite and Cable Directive does not distinguish between communication to the public via direct

---

[51] *ibid.*, Art.1(2)(b).
[52] See above, para.2–016.
[53] See Case C–293/98, *Entidad de Gestión de Derechos de los Productores Audiovisuales (Egeda) v Hostelera Asturiana SA (Hoasa)* [2000] I E.C.R. 629. See also Report from the European Commission above, para.2–083, n.44, p.13.
[54] In relation to this type of right, see Commission Decision of October 8, 2002, Case COMP/C2/38.014, *IFPI "Simulcasting"*, O.J. 2002 L107/58. The Commission granted exemption from Art.81(1) of the EC Treaty to the "Agreement on reciprocal representation to license simulcasts". The Commission recognised the interest of this agreement as a collective management system ("one-stop shop" system) for the granting of rights, traditionally granted on a national basis.
[55] Satellite and Cable Directive, para.2–083, n.44, Art.3(3).
[56] *ibid.*, Art.3(2).
[57] *ibid.*, Art.7(2).

broadcast satellites and via communication satellites.[58] This is because of the technical progress that by 1993 had allowed the individual reception of transmissions from both types of satellite.[59]

2–087 Application of the directive to communications by satellite from non-EU countries — The Cable and Satellite Directive applies principally to programmes up-linked within the Community for reception by viewers located in it. However, it can have a certain extra-territorial effect because communications by satellite to viewers in the Community from non-EU countries can, under certain conditions, be deemed to occur within a Member State and therefore be subject to it.[60] Where an act of communication to the public by satellite occurs in a non-EU country which does not provide authors with an equivalent exclusive right to authorise broadcasting of the work by satellite, the act of communication to the public will be deemed to occur in the Member States if either: (i) the programme-carrying signals are transmitted to the satellite from an up-link station situated in a Member State, in which case the exclusive broadcasting right is exercisable against the person operating the up-link station[61]; or (ii) if there is no use of an up-link station situated in a Member State but a broadcasting organisation established in a Member State has commissioned the act of communication to the public by satellite, the act will be deemed to have occurred in the Member State in which the broadcasting organisation has its principal establish-ment in the EU and the exclusive broadcasting right will be exercisable against that broadcasting organisation.[62]

2–088 Cable retransmission right — Many television channels broadcast by satellite or terres-trial means are also retransmitted over cable networks. The Satellite and Cable Directive also provides authors of copyright with rights concerning cable retransmission, *i.e.* the simultaneous, unaltered and unabridged retransmission by a cable or microwave system of an initial transmission from another Member State of television and radio programmes intended for reception by the public.[63] Accordingly, Member States must give holders of copyright and related rights the right to authorise or prohibit the cable retransmission of programmes broadcast from other Member States and containing their works.[64] Retransmission must take place on the basis of individual or collective contractual arrangements between copyright owners, holders of related rights and cable operators.[65] To facilitate negotiations, a grant or refusal of authorisation by the copyright owner for immediate cable retransmission may only be exercised through a collecting society.[66] If a right-holder has not transferred the management of his rights to a collecting society, he will be deemed to have mandated a collecting society that manages similar rights, under the same rights and conditions as those right-holders that have expressly entered into an agreement with the collecting society.[67] The right-holder shall have at least three years (or such longer period fixed by

---

[58] *ibid.*, Art.1(1).
[59] *ibid.*, Recital 6.
[60] *ibid.*, Art.1(2)(d).
[61] *ibid.*, Art.1(2)(d)(i).
[62] *ibid.*, Art.1(2)(d)(ii).
[63] *ibid.*, Art.1(3).
[64] *ibid.*, Art.8(1).
[65] *ibid.*
[66] *ibid.*, Art.9(1).
[67] *ibid.*, Art.9(2). If there is more than one such society, the right-holder may choose which society is mandated to manage his rights.

the relevant Member State) from the date of the cable retransmission to claim his rights. All national statutory licence systems were to be abolished. Member States may provide that where a right-holder has authorised the initial transmission within its territory of a work or other protected subject-matter, he shall be deemed not to exercise his cable transmission rights on an individual basis.[68] The cable retransmission rights provisions of the Satellite and Cable Directive are presently under review.[69]

2–089 Remedies — The Satellite and Cable Directive provides that, where no agreement is reached regarding the authorisation of the cable retransmission of a broadcast, either party must be able to call upon the assistance of one or two independent and impartial mediators[70] whose task is to assist in the negotiations, including by submitting proposals to the parties.[71] The parties will be deemed to have accepted such a proposal if it is not rejected by one of them within three months.[72] Member States must also ensure, by means of civil or administrative law, that the parties enter and conduct negotiations regarding authorisations for cable retransmissions in good faith and do not prevent or hinder negotiation without valid justification.[73]

2–090 Protection of copyright in the Information Society — As a result of the impact of new technologies on copyright and related rights, in 2001 the European Parliament and the Council adopted the Copyright Directive to ensure an adequate level of legal protection for all works distributed to the public within the so-called "Information Society".[74] The Directive includes provisions related to broadcasting, which are analysed in detail in the following chapter.[75]

---

[68] *ibid.*, Art.9(3).
[69] See the Report from the European Commission, above, para.2–083, n.44, pp.8–9 and 16.
[70] Satellite and Cable Directive, para.2–084, n.44, Arts 11(1) and 11(4).
[71] *ibid.*, Art.11(2). According to the Report from the European Commission above, para.2–083, n.44, the provisions of the Satellite and Cable Directive related to mediation are likely to be reviewed, pp.9–10 and 16.
[72] Satellite and Cable Directive, Art.11(3).
[73] *ibid.*, Art.12(1).
[74] See above, para.1–252, n.85.
[75] See para.3–021 *et seq.*

Chapter III

The EU Regulatory Framework
for the Internet

A. Introduction

3–001 What is the internet? — The internet is generally described as a "network of networks".[1] In fact, it consists of a global network interconnecting computers around the world, through the use of an open protocol, the Internet Protocol (IP).[2] The internet was initially developed at the end of the 1960s by the US military. It was subsequently adopted by universities in the 1970s and 1980s as a means to link the scientific community together and to provide easy and speedy access to information resources. It was only during the second half of the 1990s that commercial use of the internet developed, as private businesses perceived the potential benefits of the internet. The use of an open protocol such as IP allows the interoperability of various types of networks and facilities (*e.g.* copper and fibre optic circuits, coaxial cable and wireless connections) and the provision of various types of services over the same network. The internet is a decentralised network without any central point of control or access, with the result that any "host" computer (*i.e.* server) can be accessed from any connected computer anywhere in the world. The internet is also a packet-switched network, which means that information is broken down into small packets of data, each of which is transmitted separately through the system. Each data packet bears routing information enabling the switching equipment (*i.e.* the router) through which it passes to know to which computer it should be sent. The data packets are reassembled in the correct order upon arrival at their intended destination (another computer), so that the message can be read by the computer user. Packet-switched networks must be distinguished from circuit-switched networks, such as the public switched telephone network, where a dedicated transmission path (*i.e.* a circuit) must be opened for each transmission. Packet-switched systems enable network resources (*i.e.* the available

---

[1] On the technical aspects of the internet, see Werbach, "Digital Tornado: The Internet and Tele-communications Policy" (1997) 3 *OPP Working Paper Series*, available at: *www.fcc.gov/Bureaus/Wireless/OPP/working_papers/oppwp29pdf.html*; Hance, *Business and Law on the Internet*, (McGraw-Hill, 1997), p.41; and Wilde, *Wilde's WWW: Technical Foundations of the Worldwide Web* (Springer-Verlag, 1999).

[2] See Werbach, para.3–001, n.1, pp.13–16; and Hance, para.3–001, n.1, p.40.

bandwidth) to be used more efficiently, as they enable a greater volume of data to be carried on the same transmission facilities.[3]

Viewed simplistically, the technical operation of the internet involves four different players: end-users, content providers, internet access service providers (ISPs) and backbone or "top-level network" providers. End-users access the internet through dial-up or dedicated (*i.e.* "always on") connections to access information or purchase services supplied by content and service providers.[4] ISPs connect end-users to internet backbone networks, while backbone providers route traffic between ISPs and interconnect with other backbone providers. Interconnection between ISPs and backbone providers has been traditionally effected through so-called "peering" agreements, *i.e.* barter arrangements between ISPs for the exchange of traffic between themselves without payment.[5] The reality is more complex, as certain backbone operators also act as ISPs, and some large end-users connect directly to backbone providers.

3–002   The internet is a prime driver of convergence — The internet's distinctive feature is its technical architecture. This has been a primary factor behind the process of convergence. The use of an open protocol enables network interconnectivity and, with any necessary technical adjustments, the provision of any type of information (*i.e.* voice, images and data) on any type of network (*e.g.* cable, public telephone networks and wireless systems). Internet-based services are therefore separate from the underlying infrastructure on which they are transmitted. Accordingly, the internet competes with traditional transmission networks (such as broadcasting, telecommunications and other data communications services) by providing an alternative means of distributing services and content. For example, the internet can now be used to distribute television or radio programmes, voice telephony and software, in competition with the traditional channels of distribution. In this way, the internet has greatly contributed to bringing together the telecommunications, broadcasting and IT sectors, which were historically separate because they used different delivery vehicles.[6] In this context, the convergence brought about by the internet has raised the question, discussed below, whether the regulatory regime applicable to traditional media (*i.e.* telecommunications and broadcast) should be extended to internet-based services.

---

[3] This may raise a quality problem for services such as voice telephony or video that require a constant level of transmission, as some packets can be lost or delayed. However, improvements in IP networks technology are now permitting speech and video to be successfully transmitted.

[4] The primary internet services include electronic mail (or email), the World Wide Web (WWW), Telnet, File Transfer Protocol (FTP), Gopher and newsgroups: see Hance, above, para.3–001, n.1, pp.42–46. The world wide web is the principal factor in the exponential growth of internet use for the purpose of electronic commerce ("e-commerce").

[5] The decision of the European Commission in *WorldCom/MCI* contains a detailed description of the working of interconnection arrangements between ISPs and backbone providers. The European Commission's subsequent decision in *MCI WorldCom/Sprint* noted that while there had been a number of technical developments, these developments had not had any significant impact on the structure of the market or on interconnection agreements between backbone providers of universal connectivity and other ISPs. See, below, para.8–088 *et seq.* and para.8–101 *et seq.*

[6] Werbach, para.3–001, n.1, pp.1–8. For an analysis of the impact of the internet on the telecommunications sector, see Gilhooly, "Towards the Global Internet Infrastructure" (1999) 3 *International Journal of Communications and Policy* 1.

3–003   Legal issues raised by the internet — The emergence of the internet as a major vehicle for cross-border communications raises a number of complex legal issues. Indeed, the novelty and uniqueness of the phenomenon are challenging the application of existing laws in many areas.[7] It has even been claimed that the evolving internet faced a legal vacuum and that there was a need to urgently develop a new regulatory framework specifically for it. Although, as discussed below, specific regulatory intervention is clearly needed in certain respects, many of the legal questions raised by the use of the internet may be solved to a large extent by the application of existing rules. However, a review of all legal questions raised by the use of the internet, many of which (*e.g.* liability on the internet, conflict of laws, rules of evidence, contractual issues and crime on the internet) continue to fall largely within the ambit of national laws, is beyond the scope of this work.[8] This chapter focuses on a number of specific regulatory issues raised by the internet and reviews how these issues have been addressed, if at all, by EU regulation.

B. Internet Governance: Naming and Addressing

3–004   The domain name system — The issue of internet governance and regulation is a subject of controversy and intense debate among the different actors of the internet community.[9] Some take the position that the internet should not be regulated at any level, whether national or international, whilst others consider that a minimum degree of regulation is necessary to address certain issues that cannot be left exclusively to competitive forces and self-regulation.[10] This section gives a brief overview of the organisations responsible for the management of the domain name system (DNS).

Every computer connected to the internet has a unique IP address, which is a number that identifies it to other computers. The DNS maps user-friendly names onto these numbers, which are difficult to remember. The domain name space is constructed as a hierarchy. It is divided into top-level domains (TLDs), with each TLD then divided into second-level domains (SLDs). A number of TLDs carry a country code (ccTLD), while a small set of top-level domains (gTLDs) do not carry any national identifier, but denote the intended function of the domain space (*e.g.* ".com" for commercial organisations, ".org" for non-profit organisations and ".int" for international organisations).

---

[7] See Gardrat, "Another Look at European Internet Law" (1998) 7(1) *Media Law & Policy* 27.

[8] Reference should be made to specific commentaries, which have extensively reviewed these matters. These include: Hance, para.3–001, n.1, above; Rosenoer, *Cyberlaw: the Law of the Internet* (Springer-Verlag, 1996); Johnston, Handa & Morgan, *Cyberlaw: What You Need to Know about Doing Business Online* (Stoddart Publications, 1997); and Chissick & Kelman, *Electronic Commerce: Law and Practice* (Sweet & Maxwell, 2002). For a review of the treatment of these issues in the national laws of various European, Asian and North American countries, see Smith, *Internet Law and Regulation* (Sweet & Maxwell, 2002).

[9] See Issgon, Grewlich & Di Pietrantonio, "Competing Telecommunications and Cyber Regulation: Is there a Need for Transatlantic Regulatory Framework?" (1999) 3 *International Journal of Communications Law and Policy* 1.

[10] See Kelleher, "Generic Domain Names on the Internet" (1998) 20(2) E.I.P.R. 62; and Mathiason & Kuhlman, "International Public Regulation of the Internet: Who Will Give You Your Domain Name?", March 1998 in *International Studies Associations Panel on Cyberhype or the Deterritorialization of Politics?*, available at: *www.intlmgt.com/domain.html.*

To register a domain name, a registrant (*i.e.* a person or company desiring a domain name) must first provide a registrar with the contact and technical information that makes up the registration and enter into a registration contract with it. The registrar keeps records of the contact information and submits the technical information to a central directory known as a registry. A registry is an entity that receives domain name service information from domain name registrars, inserts that information into a centralised database and propagates the information in internet zone files on the internet so that domain names can be found by users around the world.

3–005   Background of the domain management structure — Historically, the internet developed as a result of the efforts of the US government to set up an advanced data communications infrastructure for the purposes of national security and research. As a result of this legacy, management of the internet has traditionally been based in the United States, with major components of the domain name system performed by or subject to agreements with US government agencies, including the Defence Advanced Research Project Agency (DARPA) and the National Science Foundation (NSF). Until 1998, the registration and allocation of gTLDs was managed by the internet Assigned Numbers Authority (IANA), and Network Solutions, Inc. (NSI), under contract from the US government. Under this arrangement, IANA/NSI acted as a monopolistic registry and registrar of .com, .net and .org domains worldwide.

3–006   Recent amendments to the domain management structure — As the international use of the internet grew and became more commercialised, a general consensus emerged in the internet community that the IANA/NSI registration and allocation system was inadequate to ensure the smooth operation of the internet. In particular, there was widespread dissatisfaction about the absence of competition in domain name registration. In addition, existing mechanisms for resolving conflicts between trademark owners and domain name holders were considered to be both cumbersome and expensive. Finally, as the internet became more and more international, there was dissatisfaction outside the United States, especially in Europe, that internet domains and new top-level domains were allocated by US-based entities that were neither representative of, nor accountable to, the general internet community. As a result, several initiatives were launched in order to identify the most appropriate structure for regulating the DNS.[11]

These initiatives resulted in the US administration initiating a public consultation in the course of 1997, which resulted in the publication of a Green Paper on Internet Governance in January 1998.[12] In essence, the US Green Paper proposed to remove, after a transition period, the United States government from any role in internet governance and to replace IANA with a US-based private, non-profit corporation. The EU was very critical of the proposals contained in the US Green Paper, because they did not ensure an appropriate representation of non-US interests at the

---

[11] In particular, a Memorandum of Understanding was signed in 1997 within the framework of the International Ad-Hoc Committee (IAHC), a committee composed of representatives of different organisations including IANA, the International Telecommunications Union (ITU) and the World Intellectual Property Organisation (WIPO). The Memorandum of Understanding recommended a new structure for the management and administration of the DNS, based on a self-regulating market: see Kelleher, para.3–004, n.10, above, and Mathiason and Kulhman, para.3–004, n.10, above.

[12] US Green Paper on Internet Governance, "A Proposal to Improve Technical Management of Internet Names and Addresses", January 30, 1998.

board level of the new entity to be entrusted with the management of domain names. The US government amended its initial proposals to accommodate these objections. In June 1998, it issued a policy statement in the form of a White Paper, setting out the different steps for the reform of the organisation and management of the DNS.[13]

3–007   Creation of new managing entity for the domain name system — The Internet Corporation for Assigned Names and Numbers (ICANN), a private non-profit corporation, was incorporated in the United States on October 1, 1998 to succeed IANA in administering the DNS. Representation at the board level of ICANN is organised so as to ensure balanced and representative participation from the various actors of the internet community, both on a functional and geographic level.[14]

3–008   Competitive registrars and registries — ICANN is currently managing the transition of the DNS from a government-sanctioned monopoly to a competitive market in which the DNS is operated by private businesses. The key element of this liberalisation process is the accreditation by ICANN of a potentially unlimited number of competitive, market-driven registries and registrars for the gTLDs. In order to implement this system and allow for competing registrars, NSI (now called Verisign) developed the Shared Registration System (SRS) protocol and associated hardware and software to permit multiple registrars to provide registration services for the existing gTLDs. Verisign licenses this protocol and software to registrars by way of a standard licensing agreement.[15]

The first phase of this process, the "test-bed" phase, ran from March to November 1999. In April 1999, Verisign accredited five registrars (America Online, CORE, France Telecom, Melbourne IT, and register.com) to take registrations in the .com, .net and .org gTLDs. These registrars began live operations in June 1999.[16] Shortly thereafter, ICANN began accepting applications from a potentially unlimited number of registrars. Currently there are over 100 accredited registrars.[17]

---

[13] US Department of Commerce, "Management of Internet Names and Addresses", Statement of Policy, June 5, 1998, Docket Number: 980212036-8146-02. The changes in policy brought about by the White Paper were largely welcomed by the European Commission: Commission Communication, "Management of Internet Names and Addresses: Analysis and Assessment from the European Commission of the U.S. Department of Commerce White Paper", COM(1998) 476 final.

[14] ICANN's board is made up of 19 members: nine "at large" directors, five of whom are chosen by individual members in an online direct election; nine directors representing the technical- and policy-oriented Supporting Organisations (which are the Domain Name Supporting Organisation (DNSO), the Address Supporting Organisation (ASO), the Protocol Supporting Organisation (PSO)); and the President and CEO of ICANN, Dr Paul Twomey. The "at large" directors represent the world's internet users as individuals, though in practice, the electorate for such directors is limited to individual domain name holders: see "Final Report on ICANN At-Large Membership", available at: *www.atlargestudy.org/final_report.shtml.*

[15] The European Commission has initiated an investigation under the EC Treaty's competition rules into the conditions of this standard licensing agreement. It has not yet rendered a decision on this matter: see para.6–093, below.

[16] Information on the accreditation guidelines and process is available at: *www.icann.org/registrars/accreditation.htm.*

[17] A list of accredited registrars is available at: *www.internic.net/alpha.html.* Information on the accreditation process can be obtained at: *www.icann.org/registrars/accreditation.htm.*

3–009   Creation of new gTLDs — In November 2000, ICANN adopted seven new gTLDs: .aero, a restricted gTLD for the air transport industry; .biz, an open gTLD for businesses; .coop, a restricted gTLD for use by co-operatives; .info, an open gTLD that will compete with .com; .museum, a restricted gTLD for use by museums; .name, a gTLD restricted to individuals; and .pro, a restricted gTLD for the legal, medical and accounting professions. All of these gTLDs, except for .pro, are currently operational and .biz, .info and .name are currently accepting registrations.[18]

3–010   Creation of the .eu gTLD — One of the key elements of the eEurope 2002 Action Plan launched at the Lisbon Summit of 2000 was the establishment of the .eu gTLD to supplement existing ccTLDs and gTLDs. After a lengthy consultation process with Member States, on April 22, 2002, the European Parliament and the Council adopted the Regulation on the implementation of the .eu top-level domain.[19] This Regulation provides for the designation of a registry that will manage the .eu gTLD, the obligations of the registry and the general public policy framework for the implementation and functions of the .eu gTLD, for example, on extra-judicial dispute settlement and the treatment of intellectual property rights.[20] On May 22, 2003, the Commission designated EURID—the European Registry for Internet Domains — as the registry for the .eu gTLD.[21] The Commission expects that the .eu gTLD will become fully operational by the end of 2003.

C. Licensing and Other Market Entry Restrictions for Internet Services

1. Licensing of Internet-Based Services

3–011   Introduction — Any undertaking wishing to provide services on the internet is faced with the issue of whether its proposed activity is subject to any licensing or market entry conditions in the country where its services will be provided. The answer to this question essentially depends on the nature of the activity undertaken. In the EU, the regulatory regime applicable to the internet varies according to the nature of the undertaking's activities.

3–012   Internet service providers under the New Regulatory Framework — The New Regulatory Framework explicitly divides internet services into two categories, namely electronic communications services and information society services.

3–013   *Electronic communications services* — The first category, "electronic communications services", is defined in the Framework Directive as services normally provided for remuneration which consist wholly or mainly in the conveyance of signals on electronic communications

---

[18] For information on the status of these gTLDs and links to the relevant registries, see *www.internic.net/faqs/new-tlds.html*.

[19] Regulation No.733/2002 of the European Parliament and of the Council of April 22, 2002 on the implementation of the .eu Top Level Domain, O.J. 2002 113/1.

[20] *ibid.*, Arts 3–5.

[21] Commission Decision 2003/375 of May 21, 2003 on the designation of the .eu Top Level Domain Registry, O.J. 2003 L128/29.

networks. However, this excludes services providing or exercising editorial control over content using electronic communications networks and services, and information society services which do not consist wholly or mainly in the conveyance of signals on electronic communications networks (*i.e.* most information society services).[22] This category of services includes internet access services and the conveyance of email.[23] The same undertaking can provide services that are electronic communication services (such as internet access) and information society services (such as web-based content).[24] The provision of electronic communications services is normally subject only to a general authorisation, in accordance with the provisions of the Authorisation Directive.[25] ISPs that provide their services over fixed line networks or over satellite networks may also avail themselves of the European Radiocommunications Office's (ERO) "one-stop shopping" procedure, which enables them to obtain a general authorisation in multiple Member States by virtue of submitting a single application to the ERO.[26] Member States may require ISPs to obtain individual rights of use in order to use radio frequencies (*e.g.* provision of internet access over wireless networks) or numbers (*e.g.* for providing dial-up or broadband internet access over their own networks), where this is necessary to allow efficient access to, and use of, radio frequencies and/or numbers.[27] However, these provisions are unlikely to be relevant to most ISPs, as they generally do not use their own networks to provide internet access services and thus do not require their own frequencies or numbers.

3–014 *Information society services* — As noted above, most information society services are not regulated under the New Regulatory Framework, as they do not involve the conveyance of signals on electronic communications networks. "Information society services" are defined in the Transparency Directive as any service normally provided for remuneration, at a distance (*i.e.* without the parties being simultaneously present), by electronic means (*i.e.* by means of electronic equipment for the processing, including digital compression, and storage of data and entirely transmitted, conveyed and received by wire, radio, optical or other electro-magnetic means) and at the individual request of the recipient of services.[28] This category includes the provision of web-based content and e-commerce services. The New Regulatory Framework does not apply to the provision of internet content[29] or other information society services, which are regulated by the

---

[22] Framework Directive, para.1–009, n.25, Art.2(c).

[23] *ibid.*, Recital 10.

[24] *ibid.*

[25] Authorisation Directive, para.1–011, n.28, Art.3. See also para.1–060 *et seq.*

[26] For details of the ERO's "one-stop shopping" procedure, go to *www.eto.dk/oss.htm*. With respect to satellite networks, the one-stop shopping procedure for satellite telecommunications authorisations and rights of use applies to a variety of networks and services, whether provided over fixed or mobile networks or by means of satellite broadcasting. The one-stop shopping procedure applies to all of the services covered by the Framework Directive, para.1–009, n.25, including data transmission and internet access services. See paras 1–013 and 1–137.

[27] Authorisation Directive, para.1–011, n.28, Art.5. See also para.1–082 *et seq.* An illustrative list of services that are not considered to be information society services can be found in Annex V of Directive 98/34 of the European Parliament and of the Council of June 22, 1998 laying down a procedure for the provision of information in the field of technical standards and regulations, O.J. 1998 L204/37, Art.1(2), above cited at para.1–015, n.43, which includes voice telephony, telephone consultations with a lawyer or doctor, and radio and television broadcasting services.

[28] Access Directive, para.1–011, n.29, Recital 2.

[29] E-Commerce Directive, para.1–015, n.44. See para.3–062 *et seq.*, below.

E-Commerce Directive.[30] ISPs and other undertakings that provide content and other information society services as well as electronic communications services will be subject to both the New Regulatory Framework and the E-Commerce Directive.[31]

3–015 Internet backbone providers — Internet backbone providers operate high capacity broadband networks. These qualify as electronic communications networks under the New Regulatory Framework.[32] Therefore, the provision of internet backbone services, or universal or top-level connectivity, is subject to the general authorisation regime described in the Authorisation Directive[33] and, if radio frequencies or numbers are used, potentially also to the individual rights of use regime.[34]

The question can be raised whether internet backbone providers could also be considered as public communications networks within the meaning of the Framework Directive,[35] in which case they would additionally have the rights and the obligations on access and interconnection contained in the Access Directive.[36] Generally, it is unlikely that internet backbone providers would be subject to the *ex ante* regulatory regime for operators that have been designated as possessing SMP under the terms of the Framework Directive.[37] This is because internet backbone providers' services should not be considered "publicly available", since their customers are ISPs and large businesses, rather than the public at large. Similarly, internet backbone providers would not be subject to universal service obligations because they do not operate public telephone networks or provide publicly available telephone services.[38]

3–016 Content providers — The internet can be used to provide a great variety of services, including content services. The licensing regime applicable to services or information provided over the internet thus depends on the nature of the service or content in question. Information society services (other than those that consist wholly or primarily in the conveyance of signals on electronic communication networks) such as web-based content, e-commerce and web-hosting, are covered by the E-Commerce Directive. These services are subject to regulation only by the Member State in

---

[30] Framework Directive, para.1–009, n.25, Recital 10.

[31] Authorisation Directive, para.1–011, n.28, Art.3.

[32] Framework Directive, para.1–009, n.25, Art.2(a).

[33] Authorisation Directive, para.1–011, n.28, Art.3.

[34] *ibid.*, Art.5.

[35] Framework Directive, para.1–009, n.25, Art.2(d).

[36] Access Directive, para.1–011, n.29, Art.4. The Access Directive does not specifically define the term "public" or "publicly available". In any case, Recital 1 of the Access Directive states that operators of non-public networks do not have obligations under the Access Directive except where, in benefiting from access to public electronic communications networks, they may be subject to conditions laid down by Member States.

[37] Framework Directive, para.1–009, n.25, Art.16 and Annex I. Annex I does not include the provision of internet backbone services, or "wholesale internet connectivity", in the list of markets for which NRAs are required to conduct a market analysis for the purposes of identifying operators with SMP, although the Commission and NRAs could possibly identify additional such markets for internet backbone services. See Commission Recommendation on Relevant Markets (Explanatory Memorandum), para.1–012, n.36, at p.27, where the Commission offers its rationale for not subjecting markets for wholesale internet connectivity to *ex ante* regulation by NRAs.

[38] Universal Service Directive, para.1–011, n.30, Art.2(b) and (c).

which the service provider is established[39] (the "country of origin" principle), and the provider of such services may not be subject to any prior authorisation regime specifically aimed at information society services as such.[40] This does not mean that providers of services over the internet are exempted from generally applicable rules simply by virtue of using the internet. For example, a lawyer providing legal advice over the internet is still subject to generally applicable national rules requiring him to be a member of the relevant Bar, but Member States may not impose any additional obligations over and above those applicable to lawyers in general for him to provide his services by means of the internet. Similarly, services that are generally prohibited or regulated in a given Member State, *e.g.* gambling, would be similarly prohibited or regulated online.[41] Certain services are excluded from the scope of the E-Commerce Directive.[42] Other types of service that are not provided by electronic means do not come within the scope of the E-Commerce Directive and remain subject to existing regulatory regimes under national and/or Community law.

Member States may derogate from the "country of origin" principle, *i.e.* they may continue to apply national laws to providers of information society services established in other Member States, in the following areas: copyrights, neighbouring rights and other intellectual and industrial property rights; the issue of electronic money; the freedom of parties to choose the applicable law of their contract; contractual obligations concerning consumer contracts; rules on the formal validity of contracts creating or transferring interests in land; the possibility of unsolicited commercial communications by email; measures necessary for public policy reasons (in particular the prevention, investigation, detection and prosecution of criminal offences; the protection of minors; the prevention of incitement on the grounds of sex, race, religion and nationality; and the protection of human dignity); measures for the protection of human health; measures for the protection of public security; and measures for the protection of consumers, including investors.[43]

3–017   Web-casting and internet protocol voice telephony — In the context of convergence, it is interesting to review the status of web-casting, which straddles the line between internet and broadcasting services, and of IP voice telephony, which straddles the line between internet and telecommunications services. Web-casting services, which consist of the provision of real-time radio or video services over the internet, are readily available. Although real-time video broadcasting is still limited at the moment to users with high-speed connections, it is expected that new internet technologies, such as multi-casting will soon permit the widespread use of the internet as a major means of transmitting audio and video. This raises the question of whether the strict licensing conditions and other regulatory restrictions applicable to the broadcasting sector (*e.g.* regarding licensing, programming, European content quotas and levels of advertising)[44] should apply to

---

[39] E-Commerce Directive, para.1–015, n.44, Art.3(1) and (2).

[40] *ibid.*, Art.4(1).

[41] *ibid.*, Art.1(5)(d) (gambling is explicitly excluded from the coverage of this Directive).

[42] *ibid.*, Art.1(5)(d). The E-Commerce Directive does not apply to: (i) the activities of notaries and other professions to the extent that they involve a direct and specific connection with the exercise of public authority; (ii) the representation of a client and reference of his interests before the courts; and (iii) gambling activities (including lotteries and betting transactions).

[43] *ibid.*, Arts 3(3) and 3(4).

[44] See para.2–016 *et seq.* on the application of the TWF Directive to television broadcasting in the Community.

analogous internet-based services, or whether web-casting should be treated as an information society service for which prior authorisation is excluded by the E-Commerce Directive.

Depending on the format used, the web-casting of audio-visual content may fall under either the E-Commerce Directive or the TWF Directive.[45] Web-cast content that is provided to users on demand, *i.e.* where transmission is initiated upon the individual user's request (such as with video-on-demand), would fall under the E-Commerce Directive as an information society service. Such transmission, even if it includes video content, does not fall within the scope of the TWF Directive because it does not involve the broadcasting of a pre-determined programme schedule to the public. Although both Directives adopt the "country of origin" principle, the regulatory requirements for broadcasters are much more onerous.[46] By contrast, web-cast content that is transmitted simultaneously to multiple users who have not made an individual request, *e.g.* where the film, song, etc., is broadcast automatically at regular intervals (as in pay-per-view systems) or where a web-caster continually broadcasts a selection of content in the same way as a terrestrial radio station, is not an information society service and would thus be subject to the provisions of the TWF Directive.[47]

With respect to web-casting services that do not qualify as information society services, there are two policy considerations that weigh against regulating them in the same way as traditional (*i.e.* terrestrial, satellite or cable) broadcasting services. First, the rationale for strict broadcasting regulation (*i.e.* spectrum scarcity and general accessibility to broadcasts) does not necessarily apply to equivalent internet-based services.[48] For instance, the technical architecture of the internet permits the implementation of filtering techniques that allow users, such as parents, to block access to certain sites, thereby achieving the objective of traditional rules on protection of minors that regulate the broadcasting sector. It may therefore be disproportionate to impose such rules on internet broadcasters. Second, the decentralised nature of the internet may limit substantially the ability of local regulators to enforce regulatory restrictions upon content providers that supply services over the internet from foreign countries. The desirability of regulatory intervention should thus be carefully weighed. In this context, the continued reliance on self-regulation, which has been a specific feature of the success of the internet since its inception, may offer the best alternative to address abuses in this context. The alternative argument in favour of regulating internet broadcasting in accordance with the rules applicable to "traditional" radio and television is the need to ensure an appropriate level of protection for an essential public interest, while regulating all service providers in a uniform, but technologically neutral manner.

With respect to IP voice telephony (or "voice over IP"), as technology improves its quality and makes it equivalent functionally to traditional voice telephony services, the question arises as to whether IP voice telephony should be subject to the same licensing and regulatory requirements applicable to traditional voice telephony.[49] Following broad public consultation in 1998, the

---

[45] See para.1–015, n.42; see, also, for the definition of broadcasting services under the TWF Directive, para.2–017, n.51, above.

[46] See, above, para.2–018 *et seq.*

[47] E-Commerce Directive, para.1–015, n.44, Recital 18.

[48] See Werbach, para.3–001, n.1, p.44.

[49] Internet voice telephony is made possible through the use of specific software enabling the coding, compression and transmission of voice signals between internet subscribers using the same and interoperable

Commission took the position that telephony should not be subjected, for the time being, to the regulatory regime applicable to traditional voice telephony services.[50] As a result, in contrast to traditional voice telephony services, Member States may subject the provision of voice communication services on the internet only to a general authorisation or a declaration procedure[51] and may not require internet access and/or service providers to contribute to the costs of providing universal service under the Universal Service Directive.[52]

2. Free Movement of Internet Services Across the EU

3–018   Free movement of services — Under Article 49 of the EC Treaty, service providers established in a Member State are free to provide services across the EU.[53] This provision is fully applicable to internet-based services. As a result, ISPs established in one Member State are free to provide services to customers located in another Member State. Article 49 of the EC Treaty requires Member States to refrain from introducing or maintaining any rule that restricts this freedom. In particular, this provision prohibits any national regulation that discriminates against providers of internet services established in other Member States. An obvious example of discrimination would be a requirement for internet users to gain access to the internet only through ISPs established in a given Member State. Article 49 of the EC Treaty also prohibits national rules that apply without distinction to national service providers and service providers established in other Member States, when the effect of the national rules is to render more costly or to discourage the activities of foreign service providers.[54]

3–019   Possible exceptions to the free movement of services — Restrictions on the free movement of services may be permissible if they are justified on the grounds of public policy, public security or public health (Article 46 of the EC Treaty). Moreover, non-discriminatory restrictions in the general interest may be lawful, even if their effect is to restrict the activities of foreign service providers.[55] Considerations of the general interest that the Court of Justice has accepted as justifying restrictions on the free movement of services have included: (i) the maintenance of social order[56]; (ii) the protection of consumers and workers[57]; and (iii) the supervision of compliance with professional ethics rules.[58] As a result, it would in principle be permissible for a Member State to rely on national rules prohibiting, for instance, the distribution of child

---

software. Three categories of internet voice telephony may be distinguished: (i) commercial services provided from PC to PC; (ii) commercial services provided between PCs and telephone handsets connected to the public switched telecommunications network (PSTN); and (iii) the provision of calls between two telephone handsets connected to the PSTN.

[50] For the status of voice communications on the internet under Community law, see above, para.1–084.

[51] Authorisation Directive, para.1–011, n.28, Art.3.

[52] On universal service, see para.1–202 *et seq.*

[53] See para.2–003 *et seq.*

[54] See para.2–006.

[55] Case C–52/79, *Procureur du Roi v Marc J.V.C. Debauve* [1980] E.C.R. 883. See also, above para.2–007.

[56] See para.2–007, n.20.

[57] *ibid.*, n.21.

[58] See Joined Cases C–110/78 and C–111/78, *Ministère public and "Chambre syndicale des agents artistiques et impresarii de Belgique" ASBL v Willy van Wesemael* [1979] E.C.R. 35; Case C–76/90, *Manfred Säger v Dennemeyer & Co. Ltd* [1991] I E.C.R. 4221; Case C–106/91, *Claus Ramrath v Ministre de la Justice, and l'Institut des réviseurs d'entreprises* [1992] I E.C.R. 3351.

pornography or the incitement of violence or racism, to prevent the distribution on the internet of such content. Likewise, Member States could in principle rely on national consumer protection rules (*e.g.* national laws prohibiting sales at loss) to object to the distribution over the internet of services that infringe such rules.

There are, however, limitations on the ability of Member States to rely upon such exceptions to the principle of free movement of services. First, exceptions to a fundamental principle of Community law must be interpreted strictly. For example, it is an established principle that the "public policy" exception can only be successfully relied upon by Member States where there is a "real and sufficiently serious threat, affecting a basic interest of society".[59] Second, the national measures must be proportionate to the public interest considerations that they seek to protect and must be the least restrictive measures for attaining such objectives.[60] Third, these exceptions may not be relied upon when they are effectively protecting an economic interest. Fourth, by analogy with the situation in the broadcasting sector, the application of non-discriminatory restrictions to foreign services is only justified in the absence of legislation at the Community level, unless such legislation permits Member States to impose restrictions. For example, the E-Commerce Directive permits Member States to impose restrictions on ISPs from other Member States under certain specified conditions.[61]

3–020 Notification of national restrictions — A specific mechanism has been set up at the Community level in order to ensure that national technical standards and regulations do not unduly restrict the free provision of information society services, including internet services, across the EU. This mechanism, which is the result of the Transparency Directive,[62] extends to information society services a system of prior notification of technical standards and regulations, which was previously applicable only to goods.[63] The Transparency Directive requires any draft national rule which is specifically (and not implicitly or incidentally) aimed at regulating information society services to be notified to the European Commission (and effectively to the other Member States) before implementation and at a time when it is still possible to amend it according to the applicable national legislative procedure.[64] Failure to notify in accordance with the Transparency Directive may cause the national measures in question to be unenforceable.[65] The adoption of the draft national rule must be suspended for three months following its notification to the Commission.[66]

---

[59] Case C–30/77, *Régina v Pierre Bouchereau* [1977] E.C.R. 1999.

[60] See, above, para.2–007, n.19. For example, it is doubtful that a national law could lawfully prohibit the diffusion over the internet of certain types of content directed at minors when technical devices would permit filtering of such content by parents.

[61] See Section G.1, para.3–062, below.

[62] Transparency Directive, para.1–015, n.43.

[63] For a discussion of the Transparency Directive and its background, see D'Acunto, "Le Mécanisme de Transparence Réglementaire en Matière de Services de la Société de l'Information Instauré par la Directive 98/48/CE" (1998) 4 *Revue du Marché Unique Européen* 59.

[64] The Commission's Enterprise DG maintains a searchable database of all notified national measures: see *http://europa.eu.int/comm/enterprise/tris/*.

[65] See Case C–194/94, *CIA Security International SA v Signalson SA and Securitel SPRL* [1996] I E.C.R. 2201.

[66] Member States may immediately adopt the national measure without complying with the suspension obligation for urgent reasons related to the protection of public health, public safety, public policy or the protection of the security and the integrity of the financial system: Transparency Directive, para.1–015, n.43, Art.1(2). Such measures must still, however, be notified to the European Commission.

This suspension period provides an opportunity for the Commission and the other Member States to take a position on whether the proposed national measure could create obstacles to the free movement of services between Member States and whether co-ordinated action at EU level would be preferable. If this is the case, the three-month suspension period may be extended for up to an additional 15 months, until the adoption of Community legislation on the subject. National rules concerning broadcasting and telecommunications are not subject to this notification requirement.[67]

D. Intellectual Property Rights and the Internet

1. Copyright

3–021 Introduction — The ready availability on the internet of works protected by copyright constitutes a real challenge to the enforcement of copyright law. The open network nature of the internet, combined with digitalisation, enables the production at low cost of copies of equivalent quality to the original of the work. In particular, the possibility for users to access and copy works placed on the internet from anywhere in the world makes enforcement of national copyright laws, whose territorial scope is limited, against infringers (both domestic and foreign) very difficult. The protection of copyright on the internet therefore raises many legal issues,[68] such as: the determination of the types of work that can be protected by copyright (*e.g.* email, websites, computer programs, databases), the scope of copyright protection (*i.e.* moral and economic rights), and the exceptions to copyright protection (*e.g.* the ability to reproduce copyright works). This section will examine the regulatory initiatives taken by the EU to address these issues.[69]

Legislative action at the EU level has been motivated by the perception that the maintenance of divergent national copyright rules in the Member States gave rise to legal uncertainty, thereby jeopardising the proper development of the information society, especially e-commerce, in Europe. In particular, the lack of adequate protection for works in digital form in certain Member States was considered an obstacle to the development of new products and services. The European Commission therefore recognised the need to ensure an appropriate level of copyright protection across Europe for works on the internet, which has to be achieved by the harmonisation of national provisions.

3–022 Scope of the Copyright Directive — The Information Society Copyright Directive[70] focuses on four aspects of copyright protection in respect of information society activities within

---

[67] *ibid.*, Annex V. In contrast to rules applying to traditional broadcasting services, national rules on video-on-demand would fall within the regime established by the Transparency Directive in so far as video-on-demand would qualify as an information society service.

[68] For a detailed review of these issues, see, *e.g.* Hance para.3–001, n.1, pp.81–100; and Köhler & Burmeister, "Copyright Liability on the Internet Today in Europe (Germany, France, Italy and the EU)" (1999) 21(10) E.I.P.R. 485.

[69] For a discussion of other copyright Directives, see para.2–075 *et seq.*

[70] Copyright Directive, para.1–252, n.6. The Information Society Copyright Directive also serves to implement the Community's and the Member States' obligation under the WIPO Copyright Treaty (available at: *www.wipo.org/eng/diplconf/distrib/94dc.htm*) and the WIPO Performances and Phonogram Treaty, which deal with the protection of authors and the protection of performers and phonogram producers, respectively.

the internal market: the reproduction right, the right of communication to the public, the distribution right and the protection of technical measures and rights-management information. The Information Society Copyright Directive[71] does not affect, but rather complements, existing Community copyright directives relating to: (i) the legal protection of computer programmes[72]; (ii) rental rights, lending rights and certain rights related to copyright in the field of intellectual property[73]; (iii) copyright and related rights applicable to broadcasting of programmes by satellite and cable retransmission[74]; (iv) the term of protection of copyright and certain related rights[75]; and (v) the legal protection of databases.[76] The Information Society Copyright Directive is without prejudice to other legal provisions, including patent rights, trade marks, design rights, utility models, semi-conductor topographies, type faces, conditional access, access of broadcasters to networks, the protection of national measures, competition and unfair competition laws, trade secrets, security, confidentiality, data protection and privacy, access to public documents and the law of contract.[77] To the extent it has a horizontal dimension, the issue of liability for copyright infringement is not addressed in the Information Society Copyright Directive but rather in the E-Commerce Directive.[78]

3–023 *Exclusive reproduction right* — Member States must provide for a copyright owner to have an exclusive right to authorise or prohibit the reproduction of his copyright work (whether a literary work, a fixation of a performance, a phonogram, a film or a broadcast). The reproduction right covers any "direct or indirect, temporary or permanent reproduction by any means or in any

In particular, the WIPO Copyright Treaty improves the means to fight worldwide piracy by providing authors with a cause of action against unauthorised circumvention of technical protection and the alteration of copyright management information. For a discussion of the WIPO Treaties, see Ficsor, *The Law of Copyright and the Internet: The 1996 WIPO Treaties, Their Interpretation and Implementation* (Oxford University Press, 2002).

[71] Copyright Directive, Art.1(2).

[72] Computer programmes obtain legal protection under Council Directive 91/250 of May 14, 1991 on the legal protection of computer programmes, O.J. 1991 L122/42, as amended by Directive 93/98: see, above, para.1–250 *et seq.* and see also von Lewinski, "Proposed EC Directive on Copyright and Related Rights in the Information Society as It Progresses" (1999) 30 I.C.C. 767. Computer programmes that are available on the internet are already protected by copyright, pursuant to the Computer Programmes Directive, provided that they are original in the sense that they are the author's own intellectual creation. As a result, the copyright owner of a computer programme has the exclusive right to authorise the permanent or temporary reproduction of a computer programme by any means and in any form, in part or in whole. Unless provided otherwise by contract, authorisation of the author would not be required for the reproduction of a computer programme, where this reproduction is necessary for the use of the computer programme by the lawful acquirer in accordance with its intended purpose, including error correction. This would cover permanent or temporary storage of a computer programme on the user's computer hard disk if this is necessary to use the computer programme acquired online. As discussed below, the Directive extends a similar principle beyond computer programmes to cover any type of copyrightable work.

[73] See para.2–077 *et seq.*

[74] See para.2–089 *et seq.*

[75] See para.2–084 *et seq.*

[76] See para.1–250 *et seq.*

[77] Copyright Directive, para.1–252, n.85, Art.9.

[78] An example of this would be an ISP's potential liability for contributory infringement of copyrights by permitting users to use their services or their network for the unauthorised transmission of copyrighted content.

form, in whole or in part of the copyright work".[79] This definition would cover temporary copies made by the user's computer in order to enable use of the work. However, an exception to the exclusive reproduction right is provided for temporary acts of reproduction; that are transient or incidental; that are an integral and essential part of a technological process; whose sole purpose is to enable either the transmission of a work by an intermediary or the lawful use of a work or other subject-matter; and that have no independent economic significance or value.[80] This exception covers acts of caching and browsing.[81] This exception has been criticised as being unprecedented in any copyright legislation, and completely unclear.[82] Its purpose appears to be to exclude from liability for copyright infringement online service providers and other intermediaries who may unknowingly cache, host or transmit material that would otherwise infringe the reproduction right. It is, however, only available in certain specific cases that do not conflict with the normal exploitation of the work or other subject-matters, and that do not unreasonably prejudice the legitimate interests of the right-holder.[83]

The Information Society Copyright Directive contains a long list of other exceptions to the reproduction right, which Member States may choose (but are not required) to provide in their national copyright law.[84] These exceptions include: reproduction (*i.e.* photocopying) on paper (except for sheet music); private copying on any medium by natural persons for non-commercial purposes[85]; reproduction for the sole purpose of illustration for teaching or scientific research; and reproductions of broadcasts by social institutions pursuing non-commercial purposes, in each case provided that the right-holder receives fair remuneration.[86] Other exceptions, which are not specifically subject to the requirement that the right-holders receive fair remuneration, include: reproduction by public institutions such as libraries, educational establishments and museums for non-commercial purposes; quotations from works that have already been made legally available; ephemeral recordings of works by broadcasters by means of their own facilities and further broadcasts; use for teaching or scientific research; use for the benefit of people with disabilities for

---

[79] Copyright Directive, para.1–252, n.85, Art.2.

[80] *ibid.*, Art.5(1).

[81] *ibid.*, Recital 33. "Caching" refers to the storage of frequently used information in areas more easily accessible to the user. ISPs may store cached material on servers that are in closer proximity to users' computers or on ones that receive less traffic, or even on users' hard disks. Caching involves copying all, or a substantial part, of the contents of a given web page: see Kelman & Chissick, para.3–003, n.8. "Browsing" is the act of searching the internet to locate or acquire information without knowing of the existence or format of the information sought: see *www.atis.org/tg2k/_browsing.html*.

[82] The EU Committee of the American Chamber of Commerce in Belgium, *EU Information Society Guide* (1998), p.25; Ross, "The Future of E.U. Copyright Law: the Amended Proposal for a Directive on Copyright and Related Rights in the Information Society" (1999) 4(4) *Communications Law* 128.

[83] Copright Directive, para.1–252, n.85, Art.5(3).

[84] *ibid.*, Art.5(2) to 5(5).

[85] This exception covers reproduction by natural persons on both analogue and digital recording media but provides, in the case of digital copying, that the exception to the exclusive reproduction right is without prejudice to operational, reliable and effective technical means capable of protecting the interest of the copyright holder (*i.e.* technical means allowing copies to be tracked in order to ensure fair remuneration of the right-holder). It would thus seem that, where operational and reliable copyright protection and royalty systems are in place, the exception would not apply; see Ross, para.3–023, n.82, p.131.

[86] Copyright Directive para.1–252, n.85, Art.5(2) and (3).

non-commercial purposes; reproduction by the press for reporting on current events; and for public security or for use in administrative and judicial proceedings.[87]

The Information Society Copyright Directive contains a general limitation on the application of these exceptions and limitations. These exceptions only apply to specific cases and cannot be interpreted in such a way as to allow their application to be used in a manner that unreasonably prejudices the right-holders' legitimate interests or that conflicts with the normal exploitation of their works or other subject-matter.[88]

3–024 *Exclusive right of communication of a work to the public* — Member States must provide authors with the exclusive right to authorise (or prohibit) any communication or making available to the public, by wire or wireless means.[89] The Information Society Copyright Directive provides for the right of communication to the public for holders of neighbouring rights as well (*i.e.* performers, phonogram producers, film producers and broadcasters), but only with respect to communications to members of the public that were not present at the time of the original performance, filming, etc., *e.g.* performers are ensured the right to control the subsequent, recorded communication of their performance, but this Directive does not affect their rights in the original performance to the public.[90] This seems to introduce an element of discrimination between copyright owners, *i.e.* authors of literary works (whose rights are protected regardless of the media) and holders of neighbouring rights.[91]

The "making available" right covers broadcasts, cable transmissions and the downloading of copyright works. It is also specifies that the right of communication to the public includes the making available of works in such a way that members of the public may access them from a place and at a time individually chosen by them, *i.e.* when using online interactive services (including the internet and interactive digital television). The term "public" is not defined by the Directive, which may lead to differences in the implementation of this provision in different Member States.[92]

The communication of works to the public covers the transmission or retransmission to the public by wire or wireless means, including broadcasting. However, the mere provision of physical facilities for enabling or making a communication does not amount in itself to an act of communicating a work to the public.[93] This excludes from the scope of the right of communication to the public activities such as those of operators of telecommunications networks that are performed only in preparation of an act of communication of works and the making available of subject-matter to the public. Exceptions to the right of communication to the public include communication of works and the making available of other subject-matter to the public for: teaching or scientific research; current

---

[87] *ibid.*

[88] *ibid.*, Art.5(5).

[89] *ibid.*, Art.3.

[90] *ibid.*, Art.3(2), Recital 24.

[91] Ross, para.3–023, n.82, also points out that the Rental Rights Directive, para.2–059, n.22, and the Satellite and Cable Retransmission Copyright Directive, para.2–066, n.44, do not provide holders of neighbouring rights with a right of communication to the public in non-interactive media to the same extent as that provided by the Directive to authors.

[92] See Ross, para.3–023, n.82, p.131.

[93] Copyright Directive, para.1–252, n.85, Recital 27.

economic, political or religious reporting; quotations; the benefit of people with disabilities; public security or use in administrative and judicial proceedings; and private research or study, to individual members of the public by dedicated terminals on the premises of libraries, education establishments or museums of works and other subject-matter not subject to purchase or licensing terms that are contained in collections.[94]

3–025 *Exclusive distribution right* — The Information Society Copyright Directive also requires Member States to provide authors with an exclusive distribution right, in respect of the works or copies thereof, to authorise (or prohibit) any form of distribution to the public by sale or otherwise.[95] The distribution right is made available only for authors' works.[96] The distribution right is only exhausted by the first sale or other transfer of ownership of the original of the work or a copy thereof in the Community by the right-holder or with his consent.[97] Exhaustion of the distribution right does not occur when the first sale takes place without the consent of the right-holder, regardless of whether this occurs outside or within the EU, for example, as a result of a compulsory licence. Likewise, exhaustion does not arise in relation to works made available online, since the distribution of a work through online access alone should be analysed as the provision of a service rather than as the distribution of a copyright work.[98] The same applies to a material copy of a work or other subject-matter made by a user of such an online service with the consent of the right-holder. Accordingly, every online service may be subject to authorisation where the copyright or related right so provides.[99] Member States may provide exceptions to the distribution right in those cases where they provide for exceptions to the reproduction right, so long as it is justified by the purpose of the authorised act of reproduction.[1]

3–026 *Protection of technical measures to prevent copying* — Technological developments have allowed right-holders to make use of technological measures to prevent and inhibit the infringement of copyright and neighbouring rights.[2] According to the Information Society Copyright Directive,[3] Member States must also provide adequate legal protection against the unauthorised circumvention of any effective technological measures designed to protect any copyright and

[94] *ibid.*, Art.5(3).
[95] *ibid.*, Art.4(1).
[96] Distribution rights for related rights (fixations of performance, phonograms, films and broadcasts) were already provided for by Art.9 of the Rental Rights Directive, para.2–059, n.22: see above, para.2–063 *et seq.*
[97] On the exhaustion of rights doctrine as developed by the Court of Justice, see above, para.1–250, n.86.
[98] Copyright Directive, para.1–252, n.83, Recital 29.
[99] *ibid.*
[1] *ibid.*, Art.8(4).
[2] For a discussion of the different types of technological measures that can prevent unauthorised copying, see Marks & Turnbull, "Technical Protection Measures: The Intersection of Technology, Law and Commercial Practices" (2000) 22(5) E.I.P.R. 198. The two main forms of technological protection measures are access control and copy protection. Access control includes measures such as encryption. Access control devices can be installed on computer hardware. Copy protection devices control the copying of content, by incorporating flags in digital signals that must be recognised by hardware installations. Examples of copy control measures include serial copyright management system (SCMS), which allows users to make an unlimited number of copies from the original, while preventing them from making copies of the copies, and the contents scramble system ('CSS'), which was designed to prevent the copying of DVD films.
[3] Copyright Directive, para.1–252, n.85, Art.6(1).

related rights (including the *sui generis* right provided by the Database Directive[4]) that the person concerned carries out in the knowledge, or with reasonable grounds to know, that he or she pursues that objective.[5] In particular, Member States must also provide adequate legal protection against the manufacture, distribution, sale, rental, advertisement for sale or rental, or possession for commercial use of devices, products or components or the provision of services, which are promoted, advertised or marketed for the purpose of circumvention, having only a limited commercially significant purpose or use other than to circumvent, or primarily designed, produced, adapted or performed for the purpose of facilitating the circumvention of any effective technological measures designed to protect copyright and related rights.[6] A technological measure includes any technology, device or component that is designed to prevent or restrict unauthorised acts and is deemed to be effective where the access to or the use of a protected work or other subject-matter is controlled through the application of an access code or any other type of protection process that achieves the protection objective in an operational and reliable manner with the authority of the right-holder.[7] Such processes may include encryption, scrambling or other transformation of the work or other subject-matter. These provisions are without prejudice to the right to decompile a computer programme in order to ensure interoperability with other computer programmes as provided for by the Computer Program Directive.[8]

According to Article 6(4) of the Information Society Copyright Directive, notwithstanding the prohibitions on circumvention of technical measures to prevent unauthorised copying, Member States must take appropriate measures to ensure that right-holders make available to the beneficiaries of certain exceptions and limitations the means of benefiting from these exceptions and limitations.[9] The covered exceptions and limitations are those applying to: (i) photocopies; (ii) copies made by libraries, educational establishments or museums; (iii) ephemeral recordings made by broadcasting organisations; (iv) reproduction of broadcasts by social institutions;

---

[4] *ibid.*, Art.6(3).

[5] Some commentators have argued that this provision may limit the ability of consumers to protect themselves from privacy-invasive technological measures. See, for example, Bygrave, "The Technologisation of Copyright: Implications for Privacy and Related Interests" (2002) 24(2) E.I.P.R. 51. Bygrave argues that devices such as cookies that are used to monitor private usage of copyrighted works for the purpose of detecting copyright infringements can be considered protected technological measures. Therefore, consumers' use of technological devices or software that interferes with their operation could violate this Directive.

[6] Copyright Directive, para.1–252, n.85, Art.6(2). This implies in practice that systems which have lawful purposes as their main function, but that incidentally enable circumvention of technological measures to prevent copying, fall outside of the scope of this provision: see Ross, para.3–023, n.82, p.132. The European Commission has recently proposed a similar measure to combat fraud and counterfeiting that would apply to all forms of intellectual property rights. The proposed Directive would require Member States to forbid the manufacture, import, distribution and use of "illegal technical devices", *i.e.* any device that is designed to circumvent technical devices used to protect and authenticate products or services, *e.g.* security holograms, optical devices, smart cards, magnetic systems, special inks, microscopic labels, etc. See Commission Communication, "Proposal for a Directive of the European Parliament and of the Council on measures and procedures to ensure the enforcement of intellectual property rights", available at: *http://europa.eu.int/comm/internal_market/en/indprop/piracy/com2003-46/com2003-46_en.pdf.*

[7] Copyright Directive, para.1–252, n.85, Art.6(3).

[8] *ibid.*, Art.6(4), fifth para. and Recital 50. See also Computer Programme Directive, para.1–249, n.76, Art.6.

[9] Copyright Directive, para.1–252, n.85, Art.6(4). For a general discussion of Art.6(4), and its interpretation, see Casellati, "The Evolution of Art.6(4) of the European Information Society Copyright Directive" (2001) 24 *Columbia — VLA Journal of Law and the Arts* 369.

(v) reproductions or communication to the public for the sole purpose of teaching or scientific research; (vi) reproductions or communication to the public for people with disabilities; and (vii) reproductions or communication to the public for public security or official use.[10] Right-holders may make available such means by voluntarily adopting the necessary technological measures (which shall themselves enjoy protection from circumvention in order to prevent their abuse) or by entering into any necessary agreements; or, if voluntary measures or agreements are not put in place in a reasonable period of time, Member States may put in place measures to modify technological measures taken by right-holders to the extent that their technological measures do not allow for the enjoyment of these exceptions or limitations.[11] Member States may also take such measures to ensure the benefits of the private copying limitation, unless right-holders have made reproduction possible to the extent necessary to benefit from this limitation.[12]

Member States' power to require right-holders to permit authorised copying is subject to three important limitations. First, it can only be exercised in respect of beneficiaries that already enjoy legal access to the protected work or subject-matter. Second, Member States can only do so in the absence of voluntary technical measures or voluntary agreements by right-holders; technological measures applied voluntarily by right-holders, including those applied in implementation of a voluntary agreement, must enjoy legal protection.[13] Finally, the above listed exceptions and limitations do not apply to interactive, on-demand content that is made available to the public on agreed contractual terms.[14] Some commentators have argued that the impact of these provisions is to elevate contract law over copyright law because they allow right-holders to contract out of these exceptions and limitations.[15]

3–027 *Protection of rights management information* — Member States must also provide for adequate legal sanctions against any person who knowingly and without authority removes or alters any electronic rights-management information, or who distributes, imports for distribution, broadcasting communication or making available to the public works or other subject-matter protected under the Information Society Copyright Directive or the Database Directive from which electronic rights-management information has been removed or altered without authority.[16] The expression "rights-management information" means any information provided by right-holders that identifies the protected work or subject-matter, the author or other right-holders, or information about the terms and conditions of use of the work or other subject-matter, and any

---

[10] *ibid.*, Art.6(4), first para. These exceptions are contained in Arts 5(2)(a), 2(c), 2(d), 2(e), 3(a), 3(b), and 3(e). The first four exceptions and/or limitations apply only to reproduction rights, while the remaining three apply to both reproduction and communication rights.

[11] *ibid.*, Recital 51.

[12] *ibid.*, Art.6(4), second para. This measure does not prevent right-holders from adopting adequate measures to limit the number of private copies. Furthermore, the technological measures used to ensure the benefits of these exceptions and limitations must also enjoy the legal protection provided for in Art.6(1). See *ibid.*, Art.6(4), third para.

[13] *ibid.*, Art.6(4), third para. Thus circumvention tools provided by right-holders to consumers for the purpose of accessing copyrighted works must enjoy legal protection.

[14] *ibid.*, Art.6(4), fourth para. By contrast, non-interactive provision of online content remains subject to these exceptions and limitations. See *ibid.*, Recital 53.

[15] See Casellati, para.3–026, n.9, pp.392–393.

[16] Copyright Directive, para.1–252, n.85, Art.7.

numbers or codes that represent such information.[17] Examples of such information include digital watermarking (which places a unique piece of code in the content that cannot be removed without damaging the content); digital fingerprinting (which creates a digital trail as pieces of content are copied each time); and encryption.[18]

3–028 *Sanctions and remedies* — Member States must provide appropriate sanctions and remedies in respect of infringements of the rights and obligations set out in the Information Society Copyright Directive and must take all measures necessary to ensure that those sanctions and remedies are applied.[19] Sanctions and remedies must be effective, proportionate and dissuasive. Member States must take measures necessary to ensure that right-holders whose interests are affected by an infringing activity carried out on its territory can bring an action for damages and/or apply for an injunction and, where appropriate, for the seizure of infringing material.[20] Injunctions should be obtainable against intermediaries (such as ISPs) that carry a third party's infringement of a protected work or other subject-matter on their networks, even if the intermediary benefits from an exception under Article 5 of the Information Society Copyright Directive.[21]

3–029 *Implementation of the Information Society Copyright Directive* — Member States were required to implement the Information Society Copyright Directive by December 22, 2002. However, it does not apply to any act concluded or rights acquired prior to that date.[22] Also, it will not affect any contracts concluded or rights acquired prior to its entry into force, but will apply to such contracts if those contracts have not expired before that date.

2. Trademarks – Domain Name Disputes

3–030 Cybersquatting and cybercloning — As the commercialisation of the internet in general, and e-commerce in particular, has expanded, internet addresses and domain names have become increasingly valuable. This has led to the development of practices such as cybersquatting, which occurs when a third party, in bad faith, registers as a domain name the business name or trademark of an existing company. A similar practice is cybercloning, whereby a foreign company appropriates the brand name and business model of a competitor in a given country and then registers an identical or a similar domain name with that country's ccTLD in order to establish a copycat business in the local market. Many large, international companies have found themselves the victims of these practices and have sought redress in national courts or through the arbitration system established by ICANN and the WIPO, which is described below.[23]

---

[17] *ibid.*, Art.6(3).

[18] See Owen, "Digital Rights Management — Controlling Electronic Copying" (2002) 99 *In-House Lawyer* 28.

[19] *ibid.*, Art.8(1).

[20] *ibid.*, Art.8(2).

[21] *ibid.*, Recital 59.

[22] *ibid.*, Arts 10 and 13.

[23] See Lemanski-Valente & Majka, "Trademarks and ccTLDs in the European Union: What US Trademark Owners Should Know" (2001) 136 Supp. (*Domain Names*) *Trademark World* 4. The authors discuss French and Greek cases involving cybersquatting. In France, Ibazar, a competitor of eBay, registered ebay.fr first. The French court permitted the domain name ebay.fr to be retained by Ibazar, which eBay subsequently acquired in a deal worth over $100 million. In another case, a small Greek firm had registered the domain names

3–031 Domain name dispute settlement system — In order to resolve the rapidly growing number of domain name disputes, ICANN and the WIPO jointly developed the Uniform Domain Name Dispute Resolution Procedure (UDRP),[24] which was formally adopted on August 26, 1999. The UDRP has been adopted by all registrars in the .com, .net, and .org gTLDs, all seven of the new gTLDs and a limited number of ccTLDs.[25] The UDRP has been included, retrospectively, in the registration contract for all those TLDs, so that every registrant under these TLDs is subject to the UDRP. The UDRP provides an expedited administrative procedure for disputes involving allegations of abusive registration, under which trademark owners have to submit their complaints to an approved dispute resolution provider. Panels are empowered to require registries either to cancel improperly obtained domain names or to require the transfer of the domain name in dispute to a successful complainant. This procedure has proven to be very popular and has already resolved disputes concerning over 10,000 domain names.[26]

Unfortunately, most ccTLDs in the EU have not yet adopted the UDRP. For domain names registered under these ccTLDs, the only recourse against cybersquatting or other trademark violations is to bring legal proceedings for trademark infringement in a national court.

3. Hypertext Linking Liability

3–032 Hypertext linking — Hypertext linking is the process whereby the user of one website is able to, by the click of the mouse, move between pages in the same site or to pages in another site. Hypertext links to other sites may either be initial links (which link to the home page of the second site) or deep links (which by-pass the home page of the second site and take users directly to internal pages). While the use of initial links between websites appears to be permissible, website owners are increasingly challenging the practice of deep linking, alleging that this practice violates copyrights, trademarks and database rights.[27] This issue is of particular relevance to search engines,

amazon.gr and amazon.com.gr. A Greek court subsequently found that this firm had intentionally misled consumers into believing that they were operated by Amazon.com. See also Kitterman, "Strategies for Preventing International Trademark Disputes: What Every Business Doing E-commerce Should Know" (2002) 2(2) *World E-Commerce & IP Report* 12.

[24] See: *www.icann.org/dndr/udrp/policy.htm*.

[25] See Bettink, "Domain Name Dispute Resolution under the UDRP: The First Two Years" (2002) 24(5) E.I.P.R. 244. For a more critical review of the UDRP, see Thornburg, "Fast, Cheap, and Out of Control: Lessons from the ICANN Dispute Resolution Process" (2002) 6 *Computer Law Review and Technology Journal* 89.

[26] The ICANN website provides a full-text, searchable database for all disputes resolved by a decision: see *www.icann.org/udrp/udrpdec.htm*.

[27] Website owners have also put forward a number of other theories to object to hypertext linking, including: cable retransmission rights (UK) *Shetland Times Ltd v Dr Jonathan Wills* 1997 F.S.R. 604 (newspaper obtained injunction preventing another newspaper from linking to its news articles because the articles were found to be a cable transmission); trespass (US) *eBay v Bidders Edge* (2001) E.C.L.R. 12 (use of spiders by defendant to gather information on bids and displaying them on its website constituted a trespass because spiders used up so much of eBay's computers' capacity that it could not perform essential functions); and tortious interference with prospective business advantage (US), *Ticketmaster v Tickets.com* (2001) E.C.L.R. 14 (Ticketmaster alleged that deep linking deprived it of advertising revenue; settled out of court). For a thorough review of the relevant cases, see Sableman, "Link Law Revisited: Internet Linking at Five Years" (2001) 16 *Berkeley Technology Law Journal* 1273.

which may be guilty of infringement by deep linking to the part of the website most relevant to the search, rather than the home page,[28] arguably depriving website owners of advertising revenue.

A practice closely related to deep linking is "framing", which occurs when a click on the link from one site to another site brings up the second page "framed" within the original site. Some website owners have successfully argued that "framing" obscures the origin of the information contained in the second website and thus constitutes trademark infringement and/or unfair competition.[29]

3–033 Websites and database rights — The Database Directive defines a database to be "a collection of independent works, data or other materials arranged in a systematic or methodical way and individually accessible by electronic or other means."[30] The Database Directive grants to the maker of a database that has made a substantial investment in either the obtaining, verification or presentation of the contents the right to prevent the extraction and/or re-utilisation of the whole or a substantial part of the contents of the database.[31]

Websites consist of a number of data files (which are themselves often copyright works), stored in a systematic way, and they are generally considered to be within the scope of the definition of a "database"[32] contained in the Database Directive. Some recent judgments in national courts have confirmed this interpretation and found that deep linking to another website can be a violation of qualitatively substantial parts of database rights in the linked website.[33] To succeed, plaintiffs must establish that they have made a substantial investment in the creation of the database and that the defendant unfairly extracted a quantitatively substantial part of the database[34] or repeatedly unfairly extracted qualitatively substantial parts.[35]

---

[28] See Greenwood & Davis, "Database Right — Developing IP Protection for the Internet Age" (2002) 100 *In House Lawyer* 2.

[29] For a survey of these cases, see Paeman & Aalto, "Hyperlinking Liability in Europe: Precedent and Future" (2001) 1(8) *World E-Commerce & IP Report* 6.

[30] Databases Directive, para.1–249, n.71, Art.1(2); see also, above, para.1–252.

[31] *ibid.*, Art.6(1).

[32] See Auld, "The Legal Classification of Websites and Liability for Hypertext Links" (2001) 17(4) C.L.S.R. 254.

[33] See, in the United Kingdom, *British Horseracing Board v William Hill*, February 9, 2001, (2002) E.C.C. 24 (issues referred to the Court of Justice by the UK Court of Appeals), where it was held that a "database" covers nearly all collections of data in searchable form, including the plaintiff's database containing information on racehorses, jockeys and trainers that was required by bookmakers. See also in Germany, *Stepstone v Ofir.de*, Landegerichtheit Köln, Judgment 28 O.J. C692/00 of February 28, 2001, where it was held that the defendant's job-search engine violated Stepstone's database rights by deep linking to its job listings, which in the process obliterated Stepstone's advertising banners. But see also *Stepstone France v Ofir France*, Commercial Court of Nanterre, Judgment of November 8, 2000, which held that deep links to Stepstone France's job listings was not a violation of Stepstone's database rights because Ofir France did not provide any information about jobs except hyperlinks and because it did not obliterate Stepstone France's advertising banners.

[34] In the Netherlands, see *Algemeen Dagblad BV v Eureka Internetdiensten*, Judgment of August 22, 2000, where the Rechtbank Rotterdam held that a newspaper's website was not a database because no substantial investment was made to obtain the information.

[35] In the United Kingdom, see *British Horseracing Board v William Hill*, above, para.3–033, n.33, where it was held that the defendant's repeatedly taking substantial amounts of data on a daily basis was qualitatively substantial because this was the most commercially valuable information.

3–034 Hypertext linking and copyright — Hypertext links can also be classified as either "normal links" or "embedded links".[36] A normal link is simply a reference to other documents already available on the web, *i.e.* a shortcut so that users do not have to type out the document's URL. Normal links do not create an extra copy of the work other than the one created in the user's computer's random access memory (RAM). An embedded link is an electronic process that is automatically activated when the web page is loaded. It is often used to call up images, text or video that are part of another website, but which appear on the screen as an embedded part of the first website.

Normal links, which make temporary copies, fall within the scope of the exclusive reproduction right, but such copies are permitted under the Information Society Copyright Directive and do not constitute an infringement.[37] Similarly, use of embedded links does not involve making copies on the part of the linking site. A temporary copy is made on the user's computer, so while there is no infringement of the reproduction right, this practice may still violate the exclusive right of communication to the public.[38]

E. Protection of Privacy and Security

3–035 Introduction — One of the main technical challenges in ensuring the commercial development of the internet is preserving the confidentiality and security of commercial transactions taking place over the internet. For example, the possibility of electronic messages being intercepted continues to hinder the public acceptance of private banking activities on the internet. Techniques such as encryption technologies are constantly undergoing further development to respond to this challenge. This section reviews the EU regulatory framework on network security and the protection of privacy in relation to communications on the internet.

1. Protection of the Privacy of Internet Communications

3–036 The internet potentially represents a serious threat to privacy, as it is an open network. This means that private communications on the internet can be intercepted and that confidential files stored in computers connected to the internet can be accessed and copied from anywhere in the world. Moreover, many activities on the internet, often unnoticed by internet users, leave tracks that reveal personal data that may be collected, analysed and used in a different context. For example, visiting a website reveals information on users' habits and tastes, which may be useful for marketing purposes. The expanding use of the internet therefore raises a number of legal issues in relation to the protection of privacy, including the right of public authorities to monitor communications on the internet to prevent crime, and the right of employers to monitor the electronic correspondence of employees.

---

[36] For a comparison of the treatment of potential copyright liability for hypertext linking in the US, the EU and various EU Member States, see Garrote, "Linking and Framing: A Comparative Law Approach" (2002) 24(4) E.I.P.R. 184.
[37] Copyright Directive, para.1–252, n.85, Arts 2 and 5(1).
[38] *ibid.*, Art.3.

In all Member States, the protection of privacy and the confidentiality of correspondence are protected as an essential right by way of general laws (very often of a constitutional nature) or as a result of similar principles developed by court precedents.[39] Article 8 of the European Convention on Human Rights, which forms part of the legal order of all Member States, as well as that of the EU, and which can be relied upon by private parties in all Member States, protects privacy and the confidentiality of correspondence between internet users. Article 8 would thus, in principle, prohibit any governmental authority (subject to limited exceptions permitted by Article 8, *e.g.* the prevention of crime and the protection of public security) or private parties such as employers or ISPs from monitoring or intercepting communications on the internet. Moreover, self-regulation principles applicable to internet activities ("good cybermanners" or "netiquette") prescribe that internet users may not disclose confidential information about other users without their consent.[40]

3–037 EU Framework Data Protection Directive — The Framework Data Protection Directive harmonises national laws on the processing of personal data and the free movement of such data.[41] It is fully applicable to internet-based activities.[42] For example, the creation of files from data collected over the internet or the transfer of such data over the internet are subject to the provisions of the Framework Data Protection Directive. "Data" is defined very broadly and covers not only text but also digitised images and sounds. As a result, the processing of data on the internet can only be done for explicit and legitimate purposes that must be determined at the time of collection of the data.[43] Moreover, prior to the data processor carrying out any processing operations, its processing activities must be notified to a national supervisory authority, which must check compliance with the provisions of national law implementing the Directive.[44] Personal data may only be processed if the user has given his consent or when the processing is necessary for a limited number of reasons, such as the performance of contracts and compliance with legal obligations.[45] The person responsible for the processing (the "data controller") must also provide certain information to the person on whom it is collecting data (the "data subject"), such as indicating the purpose for which the data is being collected.[46] The data subject has the right of access to his personal data held by the data processor, is entitled to know where the data originates and to have it corrected or erased if it is incomplete or inaccurate.[47] The data controller must implement appropriate technical and organisational measures to protect personal data against destruction, loss, alteration, dissemination or unauthorised access, particularly when the processing involves transmitting data via a network.[48]

The Commission's Article 29 Data Protection Working Party has determined that the provisions of the Framework Data Protection Directive, as well as those of the European Convention on

---

[39] For a description of the applicable national rules in France and the United Kingdom, see Hance, para.3–001, n.1, p.124.

[40] See Hance, para.3–001, n.1, p.126.

[41] Framework Date Protection Directive, para.1–233, n.24.

[42] See para.1–233 *et seq.*

[43] Framework Data Protection Directive, para.1–233, n.24, Arts 6 and 7.

[44] *ibid.*, Arts 18–21.

[45] *ibid.*, Art.7.

[46] *ibid.*, Art.10.

[47] *ibid.*, Arts 10–12 and 14.

[48] *ibid.*, Art.17.

Human Rights,[49] apply to limit the ability of employers to monitor the email and internet usage of employees.[50] The Commission has therefore recommended that employers comply with the "Transparency Principle" in developing their policies on employee email and internet monitoring. Under this principle, employers must inform employees of: (i) the extent to which communication facilities owned by the company may be used for personal/private communications by employees; (ii) the reasons and purposes for which surveillance, if any, is being carried out; (iii) the details of any surveillance measures; and (iv) the details of any enforcement procedures.[51] Where employers permit the use of their facilities for private purposes, surveillance should only be carried out for very limited purposes, *e.g.* to ensure network security or to scan for viruses. With respect to monitoring employees' use of internet access, the Transparency Principle requires employers to specify: (i) material, if any, which cannot be viewed or copied; (ii) where it may be necessary to prevent access to certain sites or to prohibit misuse, whether such monitoring relates to individuals, specific sections of the company or whether the content of the sites visited is viewed or recorded by the employer; and (iii) the use, if any, that will be made of data collected concerning which employees visited which websites. Furthermore, employers must inform workers and their representatives about the implementation of their monitoring policy and the investigation of alleged breaches.

Personal data may only be transferred to countries outside the EU if the non-EU country ensures an "adequate level of protection".[52] This provision has given rise to substantial controversy between the United States and the EU, which had taken the position that the United States did not offer an adequate level of protection (discussed below).[53]

3–038 E-Privacy Directive — The E-Privacy Directive[54] was adopted as part of the New Regulatory Framework and elaborates the general principles set out in the Framework Data Protection Directive, in a technologically neutral fashion, so that they can be applied in the specific context of electronic communications, including to the internet. Member States had to transpose the E-Privacy Directive into national law by October 31, 2003. Its requirement that the consent of users and subscribers be given for the use of their personal data will have an important impact on a number of common business practices used on the internet, such as "spamming", electronic marketing and the use of "cookies".[55]

---

[49] See *Halford v United Kingdom*, November 23, 1992, Series A No.251/B, para.29, where the European Court of Human Rights held that Art.8 of the European Convention on Human Rights, which protects against intrusions into individual's "private life" and "correspondence", applies to communications made from business premises.

[50] Art.29 Data Protection Working Party, "Working document on the surveillance of electronic communications in the workplace", WP 55, available at: *http://europa.eu.int/comm/internal_market/en/dataprot/wpdocs/wp55_en.pdf*. This Working Party is an independent European advisory body that was established under Art.29 of the Framework Data Protection Directive, para.1–233, n.24, to advise the Commission on matters relating to national measures adopted under this Directive, the level of protection offered by third countries, amendments to the Directive or other specific data protection measures and codes of conduct drawn up at Community level: see Framework Data Protection Directive, Arts 29 and 30.

[51] *ibid.*, paras 3.1.3, 4.3.

[52] Framework Data Protection Directive, para.1–233, n.24, Arts 25 and 26; see also para.1–246 *et seq.*

[53] See above para.1–246.

[54] See para.1–234 *et seq.*

[55] An internet "cookie" is a computer record of information that is sent from a web server to a user's computer for the purpose of identifying that computer on the occasion of future visits to the same website.

"Spamming" is the use of unsolicited email for direct marketing purposes, without the consent of the recipient. The Telecommunications Data Protection Directive, which the E-Privacy Directive repealed and replaced, included a consent requirement for "unsolicited calls".[56] Many Member States interpreted this narrowly when transposing the Telecommunications Data Protection Directive, only granting protection against unsolicited voice telephony direct marketing.[57] This was at least in part because, at the time of its adoption in 1997, internet use and the use of the internet for direct marketing were relatively limited. The E-Privacy Directive explicitly expands the rules governing unsolicited communications to cover the use of automated calling systems, fax machines and electronic mail for the purposes of direct marketing. Such use is permitted only if the subscriber has given his or her prior consent.[58] If a supplier obtains a customer's email address in the context of the sale of a good or service, it may use this address for the direct marketing of its own similar goods or services, provided that the consumer is given the opportunity to object, free of charge, when the address is first given and each time a message is sent.[59] Other types of unsolicited communications shall not be allowed either without the consent of the subscriber, or in respect of subscribers who have indicated that they do not want to receive such communications. Member States must choose between these two options.[60] Furthermore, direct marketing by email that disguises or conceals the identity of the sender is prohibited altogether, as are communications that do not include an address to which the recipient may send a request that such communications cease.[61] Member States may also extend these protections to subscribers other than natural persons.[62]

The E-Privacy Directive similarly requires the providers of electronic communications services to obtain users' and subscribers' consent in order to install cookies or similar devices (such as Javascript) that can enter a user's terminal in order to gain access to information, to store hidden information or to trace the activities of the user, as some or all of these types of information may qualify as location data or traffic data.[63] Furthermore, cookies and similar devices are permissible only so long as they are used for a legitimate purpose, *e.g.* to analyse the effectiveness of advertising or to verify the identity of users engaged in online transactions.[64] Users must also be provided with clear and precise information on the purposes for which a cookie is to be installed and used and have the opportunity to refuse to have a cookie installed on their terminal equipment. However, service providers may still condition access to specific website content on the well-informed acceptance of a cookie or similar device, provided it is for a legitimate purpose.

They may collect and store data on search requests, websites visited and information input into websites. When the user revisits the website, the website may retrieve this information from the cookie, unless it has been deleted by the user in the meantime. See Szafran, "Data Protection and Privacy on the Internet: Technical Considerations and European Legal Framework" (2001) 7(3) C.T.L.R. 56.
[56] Telecommunications Data Protection Directive, para.1–232, n.22.
[57] Commission Communication, "Proposal for a Directive concerning the processing of personal data and the protection of privacy in the electronic communications sector", COM(2000) 385, p.5.
[58] E-Privacy Directive, para.1–011, n.31, Art.13(1).
[59] *ibid.*, Art.13(2).
[60] *ibid.*, Art.13(3).
[61] *ibid.*, Art.13(4).
[62] *ibid.*, Art.13(5).
[63] *ibid.*, Arts 6 and 9. See also para.1–244 for the definitions of "location data" and "traffic data".
[64] *ibid.*, Recitals 24 and 25.

3–039 Applicability of EU data protection legislation to non-EU undertakings — Undertakings that are not established in the EU are nevertheless subject to the EU data protection and privacy directives if they make use of equipment for data processing, automated or otherwise, situated in the EU, unless such equipment is used only for purposes of transit through the territory of the EU. This provision has far-reaching consequences for internet-based activities. For example, if the operator of a website located in the US deposited a cookie or Javascript onto the PC of a user located in the UK without the user's consent and then reviewed the data collected by the cookie when the user revisited the US website, this would probably violate the EC's data protection directives.[65] This is because the website operator is making use of equipment located in the EU, *i.e.* the hard drive of the user's PC.

A prominent example of the application of the EU data protection rules to non-EU undertakings is Microsoft's .NET Passport system. This is an online authentication system, closely connected with Microsoft's Hotmail email service, that permits subscribers to use a single user ID and password to access a wide range of participating websites. The system raised a number of data protection issues concerning the lack of adequate information about the transfer of personal data to third countries.[66] The Article 29 Data Protection Working Party was concerned about, first, the value and quality of subscriber's consent, particularly with respect to the fact that subscribers were not given a sufficiently clear indication that by opening a Hotmail account, they were consenting for Microsoft to share their personal data with businesses for the purpose of targeted advertising. The second main issue was the link between Hotmail and .NET Passport, *e.g.* it was not made sufficiently clear to subscribers that by signing up for Hotmail, they were simultaneously getting a Passport account and that personal information entered for either account would be shared with the other. The Commission accepted a number of commitments from Microsoft to resolve these data protection issues, including the following: (i) ensuring that users from the EU received sufficient information on their data protection rights, and about those third countries which offered an adequate level of protection during the application process; (ii) informing users that they must get a .NET Passport account to sign up for Hotmail and that by signing up for Hotmail they are opting in to receive targeted advertising; (iii) providing users with the option of providing personal information to Hotmail only and not having it stored in their .NET Passport account; and (iv) establishing new controls so that users can choose, on an opt-in basis, whether or not to store information they choose to communicate to a participating website in their .NET Passport profile. Finally, the Commission here made clear that all websites participating in the .NET Passport system are themselves data controllers, and they are all therefore responsible for complying with EU data protection legislation.

[65] See Art.29 Data Protection Working Party, "Working Document on determining the international application of EU data protection law to personal data processing on the Internet by non-EU based websites," WP 56 available at: *http://europa.eu.int/comm/internal_market/en/data prot/wpdocs/wp56_en.pdf.*
[66] See Article 29 Data Protection Working Party, "Working Document on on-line authentication services", WP 68, available at: *http://europa.eu.int/comm/internal_market/en/dataprot/wpdocs/wp68_en.pdf.* This document also discusses the Liberty Alliance, which is an association of over 100 companies that wish to offer similar online authentication services. It concluded that this project was still in the development stages and had not yet been implemented and that therefore it was too early to offer an assessment of its compliance with EU data protection legislation.

3–040 *Safe Harbour Decision* — As discussed in Chapter I,[67] the Framework Data Protection Directive requires Member States to ensure that personal data may only be transferred to non-EU countries that ensure an "adequate level of protection".[68] The United States follows a different approach regarding data protection, relying on a mix of sectoral legislation, regulation and self-regulation, rather than comprehensive legislation administered by specialised government agencies. In order to bridge these different privacy approaches and to ensure that US organisations can receive data from the European Community in compliance with the Framework Data Protection Directive, the US Department of Commerce, in consultation with industry and the European Commission, developed a self-certification system based on a set of "safe harbour principles".

On July 26, 2000, the European Commission determined that these "safe harbour" principles offered adequate protection of personal data and adopted its Safe Harbour Decision.[69] This Decision allows the transfer of personal data from the EU to US organisations that adopt self-regulatory privacy policies that comply with the following principles:

(i)   notice (an organisation must inform individuals about the purposes for which it collects and uses information about them);

(ii) choice (an organisation must offer individuals the opportunity to opt out, or, in the case of sensitive information (*e.g.* medical data, race and political opinions) to opt in, if the data is to be disclosed to a third party or if it will be used for a purpose other than that for which it was originally collected);

(iii) onward transfer (to disclose information to a third party, the organisation must apply the above notice and choice principles);

(iv) security (organisations must take reasonable measures to prevent the loss, misuse, unauthorised access, disclosure, alteration and destruction of personal data);

(v)   data integrity (personal information must be relevant for the purposes for which it is to be used);

(vi) access (individuals must have access to the personal information held by an organisation and be able to correct, amend or delete inaccurate information);

(vii) enforcement (individuals must have effective recourse to remedy violations of these principles).[70]

3–041 *Contractual means for ensuring an "adequate level of protection"* — The Contractual Clauses Decision[71] lays out a set of contractual conditions that, if complied with, allow non-EU entities to satisfy the requirement that they provide an adequate level of protection for personal

---

[67] See above, para.1–246.

[68] Framework Data Protection Directive, para.1–233, n.24, Arts 25 and 26.

[69] Commission Decision 2000/52 of July 26, 2000 pursuant to Directive 95/46 of the European Parliament and of the Council on the adequacy of the protection provided by the safe harbour privacy principles and related frequently asked questions issued by the US Department of Commerce, O.J. 2000 L215/7.

[70] *ibid.*, Annex 1.

[71] Commission Decision 2002/16 of December 27, 2001 on standard contractual clauses for the transfer of personal data to processors established in third countries, under Directive 95/46, O.J. 2002 L6/52.

data, thereby allowing personal data to be exported from the EU, notwithstanding that they are established in non-EU countries that do not provide an adequate level of protection for personal data. The data exporter must agree and warrant that the processing of personal data is in accordance with the data protection rules of the Member State from which the data is exported, including those contained in the European Convention on Human Rights. Furthermore, the Contractual Clauses Decision imposes strict standards for liability. The data importer (*i.e.* the data processor established in a third country) and the data exporter (*i.e.* the data controller transferring the data from the EU) must agree to be held jointly and severally liable for any damage suffered by a data subject resulting from any violation of the data protection rules, unless they are able to prove that neither one of them is responsible for the damages caused due to the violation.[72] Furthermore, a data subject may sue either the data importer or data exporter to enforce any of the obligations under the contract as a third party beneficiary, where this is permitted by national law.[73]

2. Security of Internet Communications

3–042   Technical aspects of internet security — Cryptographic technologies are widely recognised as essential tools for ensuring the security of, and trust in, electronic communications. Two important applications of cryptography are digital encryption and signatures.[74]

3–043   *Encryption* — Encryption is the transformation of data into a form that is unreadable by anyone without a decryption key. The process of transforming data back into a readable form is called "decryption". The purpose of encryption is to ensure confidentiality by keeping the information hidden from anyone for whom it is not intended. There are two types of encryption systems: symmetric and asymmetric systems. In a symmetric encryption system (also called a "private key cryptography system"), one single key is used both to encrypt and decrypt data. In order for symmetric encryption systems to remain secure, the parties involved must keep the private key secret after they have communicated it to each other. The level of security may be improved by changing the private key regularly. An example of this system is the Data Encryption Standard (DES) developed by the US government.

An asymmetric encryption system (also called a "public key cryptography system") involves the use of two keys, a private key and a public key, which are related in a complex way. The sender encrypts a message with his private key and communicates his public key to all those with whom he wants to communicate encrypted messages. By using the sender's public key, the receiver can then decrypt the message. The public key can also be used to encrypt messages that only the holder of the private key can decrypt. Public keys are published and accessible to everyone. The use of two

---

[72] Contractual Clauses Decision, Art.6. This may exceed the scope of Art.23(2) of the Framework Data Protection Directive, para.1–233, n.24, which exempts data exporters from liability if they can prove that they are not responsible for the event causing the damage. See Bond & Knyrim, "Data Transfer to Third Countries: Standard Contractual Clauses of the European Commission" (2002) 18(3) C.L.S.R. 187.

[73] Contractual Clauses Decision, Art.3.

[74] See Commission Communication, "Ensuring Security and Trust in Electronic Communication: Towards a European Framework for Digital Signatures and Encryption" COM(97) 503, Annexes 1–3; Brazell, "Electronic Security: Encryption in the Real World" (1999) 24(3) E.I.P.R. 17; and Baker, "International Developments Affecting Digital Signatures" (1998) 32(4) *The International Lawyer* 963.

different keys makes this system more secure than a symmetric encryption system. An example of this system is RSA (Rivest, Shamir and Adleman). The only security problem raised by asymmetric encryption systems is ensuring the authenticity of the public key and guaranteeing that a public key indeed comes from the user to whom it is purported to belong. For that purpose, certification authorities have been created that issue and monitor public keys and can therefore guarantee, or authenticate, that they originate from a specific user. The leading certification authority is Verisign.

3–044 *Digital signatures* — Digital signatures are used to prove the origin of data (authentication) and verify whether data has been altered (integrity). A digital signature is a string of data created by using the sender's private key. It is obtained by computing, with the help of software, a digest of the message to be signed containing its essential characteristics (the so-called "hash function"). The digital signature, like a hand-written signature, is unique and different every time because the result of the computation will depend on the contents of the message. This digest will then be encrypted using the sender's private key. Thus, the key is not usually used to encrypt the message (although that can be the case), but only to encrypt the digital signature. The receiver will then use the sender's public key to decrypt the digital signature and user software to compute the digest and compare both computed digests. Even the smallest change in the data would result in two diverging digests and would be discovered immediately. This system therefore permits the origin of a message (through the complementarity of the key-pair) and its integrity (through the hashing function) to be ascertained.

3–045 EU regulation of cryptography — The use of cryptography is essential in solving a number of legal issues raised by the use of the internet and is therefore an important factor in its development.[75] First, encryption can ensure the confidentiality of communications disseminated on what is essentially an open network. In that sense, encryption may contribute to preventing the unauthorised interception of messages sent over the internet. Second, the use of techniques such as digital signatures can greatly reduce the legal uncertainty regarding the use of the internet for trade purposes because they guarantee the origin and integrity of data. Finally, cryptography also permits the enforcement of copyright and other intellectual property rights and conditional access to broadcasting services, which otherwise would be substantially undermined by the use of digital technology on open networks. For these reasons, it was considered at the EU level that the use of cryptography should be encouraged in order to ensure a more secure environment and thereby contribute to the development of the internet for commercial purposes.[76] Moreover, whilst some Member States had already adopted legislation or intended to do so, action at the EU level was perceived as being necessary in order to avoid divergent national regulatory systems that would have restricted intra-Community trade in encryption products.[77]

3–046 *EU restrictions on the use of cryptography* — Historically, law enforcement agencies and national security services have been concerned that cryptography could be used to transmit illegal

---

[75] For a review of the legal issues raised by cryptography, see Brazell, para.3–042, n.72, p.17; Szafran, "Regulatory Issues Raised by Cryptography on the Internet" (1998) 3(2) *Communications Law* 38; and Berhhard, "How to Secure the Network: Mutual Trust and Encryption" [1998] 3 *International Business Law Journal* 317.

[76] Commission Cryptography Communication, above, para.3–042, n.75, p.1.

[77] *ibid.*

messages and help perpetuate criminal or terrorist activities. As a result, under the Wassenaar Arrangement on export controls for conventional arms and dual-use goods and technologies,[78] a group of 28 countries apply export controls to encryption products. Under the Wassenaar Agreement, cryptography is considered as a "dual-use" good, *i.e.* a good that can be used both for military and civilian purposes. The Dual-Use Regulation,[79] which replaces an earlier regulation that contained substantial limits on both intra-EU trade and exports, entirely liberalises intra-EU trade in information security products, including encryption, except for certain specialised products. Furthermore, undertakings may obtain a Community General Export Authorisation for exports of such products to 10 countries; for exports to other countries, exporters must apply for General National Licences, which are valid only for exports to a particular country.

In this area, governments are faced with a dilemma. On the one hand, they want to promote the use of techniques ensuring the security and the confidentiality of the internet, while on the other hand, they want to ensure that these techniques are not used to pursue illegal activities. A compromise may be found by encouraging the use of key escrow and key recovery systems, which are encryption systems providing a backup decryption capability allowing authorised institutions, under certain conditions, to decrypt data using archived keys that are under the control of Trusted Third Parties (TTPs). In a key escrow system, a copy of the secret key is deposited with an authorised TTP. The key can also be split into two or more parts that are deposited with different TTPs. In a key recovery system, the private key would not be immediately placed into escrow and the encryption system would allow authorised organisations, such as licensed TTPs, to rebuild the private key on request. After considering the adoption of specific measures regulating key escrow and key recovery schemes, the Commission has moved away from its initial plan to prepare Community legislation on this subject, out of concerns for the protection of privacy raised by such systems.[80] Proposals to enact similar regulation in the United States have been dropped.

3–047 EU Directive on electronic signatures — On November 30, 1999, the Council and the European Parliament adopted the Electronic Signatures Directive in order to facilitate the use of electronic signatures and certain certification services in the internal market.[81] The Electronic Signatures Directive has two objectives: (i) to remove obstacles to the legal recognition of digital signatures by laying down harmonised criteria on the legal effects of digital signatures; and (ii) to avoid regulatory disparities within the EU concerning the use of cryptographic technologies. Member States were required to have implemented the provisions of the Electronic Signatures Directive into national law by July 19, 2001.

---

[78] The Wassenaar Arrangement, which was signed in July 1996, replaced the Treaty of the Co-ordinating Committee for Multilateral Export Controls (COCOM), an international organisation for the control of the export of strategic products and technologies to proscribed destinations. Member States were to a large extent NATO members but also included other countries such as Japan and Australia. The Wassenaar Arrangement contains essentially the same provisions as the COCOM Treaty. See Szafran, para.3–045, n.75, p.44.

[79] Council Regulation 1334/2000 of June 22, 2000 setting up a Community regime for the control of exports of dual-use items and technologies, O.J. 2000 L159/1.

[80] See Szafran, para.3–045, n.75, p.47.

[81] Directive 1999/93 of the European Parliament and of the Council of December 13, 1999 on a Community framework for electronic signatures, O.J. 2000 L13/12.

3–048 *Provision of certification services* — Certification services involve the verification of electronic signatures, so that recipients can be assured that an electronic signature belongs to the purported sender. Member States must ensure that certification service providers are allowed to offer services without being required to obtain prior authorisation.[82] Member States may nevertheless introduce or maintain voluntary accreditation schemes aimed at enhancing levels of certification-service provision, provided that the conditions related to such schemes are objective, transparent, proportionate and non-discriminatory.[83] Such schemes will promote the levels of trust, security and quality demanded by the market and should encourage best practice; however, adherence to such a scheme cannot be made mandatory by a Member State. Member States must ensure the establishment of a system that allows for effective supervision of certification-service providers, including determination of conformity of secure devices used to create electronic signatures with the requirements of this Directive.[84] A Member State may not restrict the provision of certification services originating in another Member State in the fields covered by the Electronic Signatures Directive.[85] In addition, Member States must ensure that equipment used for the creation or verification of electronic signatures or electronic signature certification services can circulate freely within the EU.[86]

Electronic signatures in the public sector (in fields such as public procurement, taxation, social security, health and legal matters) may be made subject to additional requirements, where this is justified by the specific characteristics of the application concerned. Any new, additional criteria must be proportionate, non-discriminatory, transparent and objective and must not constitute obstacles to cross-border provision of services.[87]

3–049 *Common criteria for certificates authenticating electronic signatures* — Although certificates may be used for a variety of functions and contain different pieces of information, the Electronic Signatures Directive focuses on the regulatory framework applying to advanced electronic signatures based on "qualified certificates". A qualified certificate must meet certain

[82] *ibid.*, Art.3(1). "Certification-service provider" means "any entity or a legal or natural person who issues certificates or provides other services related to electronic signatures": *ibid.*, Art.2(12).
[83] *ibid.*, Art.3(2).
[84] The conformity of secure signature-creation devices is to be checked against the criteria in Annex III. Such devices must ensure that, first, signature-creation data used to guarantee electronic signatures can occur only once, are kept secret, and cannot be derived, *ibid.*, Arts 3(3) and 3(4). These tasks may be undertaken by public or private bodies. Secondly, signatures must be protected against forgery. Thirdly, the signature-creation devices must be able to protect reliably against unauthorised use. In addition, devices must not alter the data to be signed or prevent such data being presented to the signatory prior to the signature. The Commission may publish generally recognised standards for electronic signature creation devices (*i.e.* hardware or software intended for use by certification-service providers for the provision of electronic signature services, or for the creation or verification of electronic signatures). Compliance with Annex III shall be presumed if these standards are used, *ibid.*, Art.3(5). "Certificate" is defined "as an electronic attestation which links signature-verification data to a person and confirms the identity of that person." *ibid.*, Art.2(9). "Electronic signature" is defined as "data in electronic form which is attached to or logically associated with other electronic data and which serves as a method of authentication." *ibid.*, Art.2(1).
[85] *ibid.*, Art.4(1).
[86] *ibid.*, Art.4(2).
[87] *ibid.*, Art.3(7).

defined requirements specified by Annex I of the Electronic Signatures Directive[88] and be issued by a qualified certification service provider. Only advanced electronic signatures need to be given legal recognition under the Electronic Signatures Directive.[89]

3–050 *Legal effects of electronic signatures* — Member States must ensure that advanced electronic signatures based on a qualified certificate and that are created by a secure signature-creation device satisfy the legal requirements of a signature in relation to data in electronic form in the same manner as a hand-written signature satisfies those requirements in relation to paper-based data.[90] Member States must also ensure that such electronic signatures are admissible as evidence in legal proceedings.[91] This means that electronic signatures must be accepted in the same way as hand-written signatures, thereby promoting the conclusion of contracts and other documents online. Member States must also respect the legal effectiveness of any private agreements between participants in a closed system under which they will accept electronic signatures from each other.[92]

3–051 *Liability of certification service providers* — The Electronic Signatures Directive lays down minimum rules for the liability of certification service providers in relation to electronic signatures that are based on qualified certificates that they issue that are created by a secure-signature-creation devices. In particular, Member States must ensure that, under their national laws, certification service providers are liable for damages caused to any person who has reasonably relied on that certificate as regards the accuracy of the information contained in the qualified certificate and for assurance that the signatory held the private key corresponding to the public key mentioned in the certificate and that both keys were complementary.[93] The certification service provider will not be liable if it can prove that it has not acted negligently. Member States must also impose liability on certification service providers for damages suffered by any person who reasonably relies upon a qualified certificate for failure to register revocation of the certificate, so long as the certification service provider has not acted negligently.[94] Certification service providers must be given the option of limiting the use of a certificate or providing for a limit on the value of transactions for which the certificate can be used, provided that these limitations are recognisable to third parties.[95] The certification service provider shall incur no liability for damages arising from

---

[88] *ibid.*, Annex 1. These requirements include, among others: the identification of the certification service provider and the Member State in which it is established; the name of the signatory (or a pseudonym, which must be identified as such); the codes or public keys used for purposes of verifying an electronic signature; an indication of the beginning and end of the period of validity of the certificate; and limitations on the use of the certificate, including any limitations as to the value of transactions for which it may be used. A "qualified" certificate must also clearly indicate that it is being issued as a qualified certificate.

[89] *ibid.*, Annex II. Annex II sets out detailed requirements to be met by certification service providers, which guarantee their ability to effectively run a secure and safe certification system that is used for issuing qualified certificates. "Advanced electronic signature" means an electronic signature which meets the following requirements: (a) it is uniquely linked to the signatory; (b) it is capable of identifying the signatory; (c) it is created using means that the signatory can maintain under his control; and (d) it is linked to the data to which it relates in such a manner that any subsequent change of the data is detectable: *ibid.*, Art.2(2).

[90] *ibid.*, Art.5(1)(a).

[91] *ibid.*, Art.5(1).

[92] *ibid.*, Recital 16.

[93] *ibid.*, Art.6(1).

[94] *ibid.*, Art.6(2).

[95] *ibid.*, Arts 6(3) and 6(4).

use of a certificate that exceeds the usage limitations placed upon it. The provisions of Article 6 on the liability of certification service providers are without prejudice to Community law on unfair terms in consumer contracts,[96] such that any evaluation of liability imposed by a service provider in a contract with a consumer must meet the requirements of reasonableness in order to be enforceable.

3–052 *Non-EU certification service providers* — Certificates issued by certification service providers established outside the EU must be recognised as legally equivalent to certificates issued by certification service providers established in the EU if: (i) the non-EU provider fulfils the requirements of the Electronic Signatures Directive and has been accredited under a voluntary accreditation scheme of a Member State; (ii) an EU certification service provider in compliance with the Directive guarantees the certificate issued by the non-EU provider; or (iii) the non-EU provider or the certificate it has created is recognised under a bilateral or multilateral agreement between the EU and third countries or international organisations.[97] In order to facilitate cross-border certification services with non-EU countries and legal recognition of advanced digital signatures, the Commission may propose measures for the implementation of international standards and agreements, and may, if mandated by the Council (acting by qualified majority) negotiate bilateral and multilateral agreements with non-EU countries and international organisations.[98] If EU companies experience market access difficulties in third countries, the Council may (again acting by qualified majority) mandate that the Commission negotiate comparable rights for EU undertakings in those third countries.[99]

3–053 Attacks against information systems — Information systems have been subject to an exponentially increasing number of attacks in recent years. The most common forms of attack include: hackers trying to gain unauthorised access to systems in order to copy, modify or destroy data; "denial of service attacks", which attempt to overload web servers or ISPs by bombarding them with a large number of automatically generated messages; viruses; the use of "sniffers", which intercept communications; and "spoofing", *i.e.* identity theft for the purpose of misrepresentation or fraud.[1] In response, the European Commission has published a proposal for a Framework Decision on attacks against information systems.[2]

The primary provision of this proposal concerns the approximation of Member States' criminal laws regarding serious attacks against information systems through illegal access to them, or by illegal interference with them or by aiding, abetting or attempting such acts.[3] If the Framework Decision is adopted, Member States would be required to ensure that serious attacks against information systems (such as those of the types listed above) are punishable by effective, proportionate and dissuasive penalties, including a maximum term of imprisonment of at least

---

[96] Council Directive 93/15 of April 5, 1993 on unfair terms in consumer contracts, O.J. 1993 L95/29.
[97] Electronic Signatures Directive, para.3–047, n.81, Art.7(1).
[98] *ibid.*, Art.7(2).
[99] *ibid.*, Art.8(3).
[1] See Commission Communication, "Network and Information Security: Proposal for a European Policy Approach", COM(01) 298 (Information Security Proposal).
[2] Commission Proposal for a Council Framework Decision on attacks against information systems, COM(02) 173.
[3] *ibid.*, Arts 3–5.

one year or more,[4] in order to bring these offences within the scope of the European arrest warrant[5] and other instruments such as the Decision on money laundering.[6] Furthermore, Member States would be required to increase the maximum term of imprisonment to not less than four years if there are aggravating circumstances, *i.e.* if: (i) the offence is committed within the framework of a criminal organisation; (ii) the offence causes or results in substantial economic losses, physical harm to a person or substantial damage to critical infrastructure; or (iii) the offence results in substantial proceeds for the perpetrators.[7] Penalties must be imposed upon any individuals or organisations that commit these offences.[8] The proposed Framework Decision also includes provisions requiring the Member States to establish their jurisdiction to prosecute offences that are: committed on that Member State's territory; committed by their nationals and that affect individuals or groups in that Member State; or where the offence is committed for the benefit of a legal person established in the territory of another Member State.[9] These will be particularly important given the international nature of "cyber attacks", which enable one country to attack information systems in another. The Commission's proposal envisages that the Framework Decision should enter into force no later than December 31, 2003.[10]

The Commission has also proposed to establish a European Network and Information Security Agency.[11] The proposed agency's function would be to advise and co-ordinate the activities of different actors in the information security field, both private and public. Specific tasks would include: ensuring the interoperability of networks and information systems; provision of opinions and support for harmonised processes and procedures in the Member States; identification of the relevant standardisation needs; enabling the exchange of information on network and information security, including best practices, between all users; promotion of security standards and certification schemes; and contributing to co-operation between the Community and third countries on information security issues.[12] In order to ensure that all relevant interests are represented, the Management Board of this agency would consist of representatives appointed

---

[4] *ibid.*, Art.6.

[5] Council Framework Decision of June 17, 2001 on the European arrest warrant and the surrender procedures between Member States: money laundering, the identification, tracing, freezing, seizing and confiscation of the intermediaries of and the proceeds of crime, O.J. 2002 L190/1. Under this Decision, Member States' courts will issue European arrest warrants with a view to the arrest or surrender by the Member States of a person suspected of committing a criminal offence, for the purpose of conducting a criminal prosecution or executing a custodial sentence or detention order, Art.1(1). Warrants may be issued in respect of offences punishable by the law of the issuing state by a maximum period of at least 12 months' imprisonment or detention, *ibid.*, Art.2(1). By requiring a maximum penalty of at least 12 months' imprisonment, Member States will be able to use a European arrest warrant to more easily detain and prosecute those suspected of attacking or misusing information systems. The European arrest warrant must be operational by December 31, 2003.

[6] Council Framework Decision of June 26, 2001 on money laundering, the identification, tracing, freezing, seizing and confiscation of the intermediaries of and the proceeds of crime, O.J. 2001 L182/1.

[7] Information Security Proposal, para.3–053, n.1, Art.7.

[8] *ibid.*, Art.10.

[9] *ibid.*, Art.11.

[10] *ibid.*, Art.13.

[11] See Commission Communication, "Proposal for a Regulation of the European Parliament and of the Council Establishing the European Network and Information Security Agency", COM(03) 63.

[12] *ibid.*, Arts 1–2.

by, on the one hand, the Council and the Commission, and, on the other, by industry and consumer groups, who, along with the Executive Director and Advisory Boards chosen by the Management Board, would be charged to act independently in the public interest in carrying out these tasks.[13]

F. Regulation of Illegal and Harmful Content

3–054   EU action plan on the safer use of the internet — One of the main benefits of the internet is that it permits greater and easier access to a wide variety of content. However, the internet can also be used to carry a considerable amount of harmful or illegal content and as a vehicle for criminal activities. While the benefits of the internet far outweigh its potential drawbacks, the use of the internet to distribute illegal or harmful content could hamper its development by creating resistance to its use, especially by children. Although prevention of crime on the internet is still essentially a matter of national law, a consensus has developed among Member States that, in view of the international character and the complexity of the challenges encountered, action at the EU level was needed in order to ensure the co-ordination and convergence of measures between Member States, to control harmful and illegal use of the internet in order to avoid distortions of competition and legal uncertainty and to stimulate co-operation in a number of areas. As a result, a Community action plan on promoting the safer use of the internet (the "Action Plan") was adopted in 1999 for the period until 2002.[14] The Action Plan had four main lines of action: (i) the promotion of self-regulation as a tool for creating a safer internet environment; (ii) the development of filtering and rating systems; (iii) the encouragement of awareness actions; and (iv) the adoption of support actions.[15] The Commission has subsequently amended the Action Plan, extending the Action Plan until 2004 and adapting its scope and implementation to take account of the lessons learned from the original Action Plan and of the development of new technologies such as interactive services.[15a] Furthermore, the Action Plan is opened up to participation by the candidate and accession

---

[13] *ibid.*, Arts 4–7 and 11.

[14] Decision 276/1999 of the European Parliament and of the Council of January 25, 1999 adopting a multi-annual Community action plan on promoting safer use of the internet by combating illegal and harmful content on global networks, O.J. 1999 L33/1. For background on Community actions in this area, see the Commission Communication on illegal and harmful content on the internet, COM(96) 487; the two reports of the Working Party, "Illegal and Harmful Content on the Internet", available at *www.echo.lu/legal/en/internet*; Commission Communication, "Green Paper on the Protection of Minors and Human Dignity in Audio-visual and Information Services", COM(96) 483; Commission Communication, "Action Plan on promoting safe use of the Internet", COM(97) 582; Council Resolution on illegal and harmful content on the Internet, O.J. 1997 C70/1.

[15] See Commission Communication, "Follow-up to the Multiannual Community Action Plan on Promoting Safer Use of the Internet by combating illegal and harmful content on global networks", COM(02) 152. The Commission released a report evaluating the results of the eEurope Action Plan in February, 2002, in which it concluded that the Action Plan had been very successful in meeting the goals set at the Feira European Council of June 2002, for example: dramatic increases in the proportion of Community citizens connected to the internet (from 18.3 per cent in March 2000 to 42.6 per cent in November 2002); the successful adoption of several of the legislative measures described in this chapter such as the E-Commerce and Digital Signatures Directive; increasing competition and lowering prices of internet access; increasing use of e-commerce; and increasing level of internet security. See Commission Communication, "eEurope 2002 Final Report", COM(03) 66.

[15a] Decision 1151/2003 of the European Parliament and of the Council of June 16, 2003, amending Decision 276/1999 adopting a Multiannual Community Action Plan on promoting safer use of the internet by combatting illegal and harmful content on global networks.

countries. The follow-up Action Plan does not contain any new regulatory initiatives and generally seeks to increase the effectiveness of the existing policy framework.

3–055 *Promotion of self-regulation* — The Action Plan acknowledges the importance of self-regulation and co-operation from the internet industry in creating a safer environment on the internet. The Action Plan favours the creation of a European network of centres (known as hot-lines) which would allow users to report content that they come across in the course of their use of the internet that could be harmful or illegal. This system should work in close co-operation with law enforcement authorities, which remain fully responsible for prosecuting and punishing those responsible for distributing illegal content. The Action Plan encourages self-regulation and adherence to codes of conduct, through systems of visible "quality-site labels".

3–056 *Development of filtering and rating systems* — The use of rating and filtering systems is an important aspect of providing safer use of the internet. Rating systems enable a content provider or an independent third party to rate content on a scale according to the nature of the content in question (*e.g.* whether it contains violence or pornography and thus should be made inaccessible to persons under a certain age). Filtering systems enable the user to select the content he/she wishes to receive. Through the Action Plan, the Commission intended to stimulate the adoption of inter-nationally compatible filtering and rating systems. The Commission also favours the adoption of third-party rating systems over self-rating systems.

3–057 *Encouragement of awareness actions* — The Action Plan calls for the implementation of a European campaign and an information and awareness action programme, in order to inform parents and all people working with children (such as teachers and social workers) of the benefits and drawbacks of internet use and of the best way (including technical aspects) to protect children against exposure to content that could be harmful to their development. The Action Plan implements these awareness actions in two phases. During the first phase, the most appropriate channels, media and content to reach the target audience are to be identified. Consumer organisations play a key role in this regard. In the second phase, a selection is to be made to determine the most appropriate channels to qualify for Community support.

3–058 *Adoption of support actions* — The Action Plan acknowledges the need, given the international dimension of the internet, to co-ordinate action in this field at the international level. The Action Plan proposed a number of initiatives, including the organisation of international conferences on the subject.

3–059 *Implementation of the Action Plan* — The Commission was responsible for the imple-mentation of the Action Plan. It was therefore for the Commission (with the assistance of an advisory committee of representatives of the Member States) to decide whether a specific project should qualify for European financial support. The financial contribution of the EU in a specific project was not to exceed 50 per cent of the cost of the project, except in duly justified cases. The total budget allocated to the Action Plan, as amended, amounts to €38.3 million.

3–060 Proposal for a Framework Decision on child pornography — In order to address the issue of child pornography on the internet, the Commission has proposed a Framework Decision on combating the sexual exploitation of children and child pornography.[16] If adopted, this proposal would require Member States to ensure that the following intentional acts involving child pornography are punishable by a term of imprisonment of not less than four years when these acts, in part or in whole, are committed through the use of a computer: (i) production; (ii) distribution, dissemination or transmission; (iii) offering or otherwise making available; and (iv) acquisition or possession of child pornography. This would cover not only sexually explicit visual representations of children (*i.e.* a person under 18 years of age), but also images of persons whose age is unknown but who appear to be a child (though there is an exemption from liability where it can be established that the person is not a child), and images that are altered or even entirely generated by a computer in order to appear to be images of children. It is proposed that the minimum punishment should be increased to eight years if certain aggravating circumstances are present.

G. Electronic Commerce

3–061   The use of the internet for commercial activities raises a number of very challenging legal issues, including issues of contract law (*e.g.* contract formation, determination of payment timing and location, and the application of the rules of evidence to internet transactions),[17] liability, conflict of laws[18] and taxation.[19] It is beyond the scope of this book to provide a comprehensive and exhaustive review of these issues and reference is made to specialised publications on this subject.[20] This section will focus on the specific regulatory initiatives at the EU level to address the issues resulting from the expansion of the internet.

1. E-Commerce Directive

3–062   Country of origin principle — The European Parliament and the Council adopted the E-Commerce Directive on June 8, 2000.[21] The E-Commerce Directive was adopted to remove a number of obstacles that had been encountered by undertakings in providing online services, in particular as a result of the need for providers of online services to comply with divergent national regulations. Uncertainty as to which Member State's rules applied to e-commerce activities was

---

[16] COM(2000) 854 final, available at: *http://europa.eu.int/eur-lex/en/com/pdf/2000/en_500PC0854_01.pdf.*

[17] For a comparative review of the treatment of these issues in the national laws of the US and a number of European countries, see Spindler & Börner, *E-Commerce Law in Europe and the USA* (Springer, 2002).

[18] See, *e.g.* Van Overstraeten, "Surfing through Governing Laws on the Internet" (1998) *International Business Law Journal*; Dutson, "The Internet, the Conflict of Laws, Litigation and Intellectual Property: the Implications of the International Scope of the Internet on Intellectual Property Infringements" (1997) *Journal of Business Law* 495; Burnstein, "Conflict on the Net: Choice of law in Transnational Cyberspace" (1996) 29 *Vanderbilt Journal of Transnational Law* 75.

[19] For a review of the tax issues raised by the use of the internet, see Le Gall, "Trading on Internet, Tax Aspects" (1998) *International Business Law Journal* 357. For a comparative study of the taxation of e-commerce in the EU, the US, Japan and a number of other countries, see Doernberg, Hinnekins, Hellerstein and Li, *Electronic Commerce and Multijurisdictional Taxation* (Kluwer Law International, 2001).

[20] See generally, Chissick and Kelman, para.3–003, n.8; Hance, para.3–001, n.1; and Hoedl, "How to Market Services: Advertising, Consumer Protection and Personal Data" (1998) *International Business Law Journal* 285. See also Long, "European Initiatives for On-line Financial Services—Part 1—Financial Services and the Electronic Commerce Directive" (1999) 18(1) *Butterworths Journal of International Banking and Financial Law* 324; Thornton, "Electronic Commerce: Key Issues" (1999) 1(1) *Perspectives on European Business Law* 14.

[21] E-Commerce Directive, para.1–015, n.44.

also a difficulty, in particular as regards Member States' ability to regulate the provision of services originating in other Member States. These obstacles were preventing the development of informtion society services in the EU and the creation of an internal market in these services. As an internal market initiative based on the principle of free movement enshrined in the EC Treaty (in particular, in Articles 47, 55 and 95 of the EC Treaty), the E-Commerce Directive adopts the "country of origin" principle, which allows undertakings providing information society services which are authorised in one Member State to provide services throughout the EU. An information society service provider will, under the "country of origin" principle, be subject only to the laws of the Member State in which it is established.[22] Therefore, Member States may not restrict, within the fields co-ordinated by the E-Commerce Directive, the provision of information society services by undertakings established in other Member States.[23]

3–063 Scope — The objective of the E-Commerce Directive is to ensure the free movement of information society services in the internal market by harmonising national laws on information society services.[24] It does this by establishing specific harmonised rules only in a limited number of areas necessary to ensure the functioning of the internal market. These include national laws on the establishment of service providers, commercial communications, electronic contracts, the liability of intermediaries, codes of conduct, out-of-court dispute settlement, court actions and co-operation between Member States.[25] However, it does not establish additional rules on private international law and the jurisdiction of the courts.[26] The E-Commerce Directive does not affect the application of existing laws in the fields of taxation, data protection, competition law, the activities of notaries and lawyers, and gambling activities,[27] nor does it affect Community or national laws that promote cultural and linguistic diversity and the defence of pluralism.[28] It complements Community law, including on the protection of public health and the protection of consumers, all of which continues to be applicable to electronic commerce.[29] A number of fields are explicitly excluded from the scope of the "country of origin" principle, so that Member States may continue to apply national legislation to information society service providers established in other Member States. The excluded fields are: copyright and neighbouring rights; electronic money; insurance; the freedom of parties to choose the law applicable to the contract; consumer contracts; and certain real estate contracts and unsolicited commercial communications by email.[30] This means that, in these fields, information society services will continue to be subject to regulation by any Member State in which they do business, as well as by the Member State of establishment. Furthermore, by way of derogation from Article 2(2), Member States may, under certain conditions, restrict the freedom to provide information society services for reasons of public policy, public health, public security and

---

[22] *ibid.*, Art.3(2). The "co-ordinated fields" are requirements of national law applicable to providers of information society services and to information society services, whether of a general or specific nature, concerning the taking up of the activity of an information society service (*e.g.* qualifications, authorisations and notifications) and the pursuit of an information society service (*e.g.* quality or content of the service, advertising, contracts and the liability of the service provider); *ibid.*, 2(h).

[23] *ibid.*, Art.3(2).

[24] *ibid.*, Art.1(1) and 1(2).

[25] *ibid.*, Art.1(2).

[26] *ibid.*, Art.1(4).

[27] *ibid.*, Art.1(5).

[28] *ibid.*, Art.1(6).

[29] *ibid.*, Art.1(3).

[30] *ibid.*, Art.3(3) and Annex.

consumer/investor protection, provided there is a serious and grave risk of prejudice to those objectives and that the restrictions are proportionate to the objective to be achieved.[31] However, Member States may only act if the Member State of establishment has been requested to take appropriate measures and has either taken no measures, or inadequate measures, and the Commission and the Member State of establishment have been informed that such measures will be taken,[32] save in situations of urgency.[33] The Commission must then examine whether such measures are compatible with Community law; if not, it must ask the Member State in question to refrain from taking such measures.[34]

3–064 **Place of establishment of information society service providers** — A provider of information society services is deemed to have its establishment in the Member State where it pursues an economic activity using a fixed establishment for an indeterminate duration.[35] Accordingly, the place of establishment of an undertaking providing services via an internet website is not necessarily the country where the server and technology supporting its website are located,[36] nor the countries in which its website are accessible. Likewise, the place of establishment does not depend on the fact that a service provider established in one Member State offers services targeted at the territory of another Member State. In the event that a supplier is established in two or more Member States, the supplier will, for the purposes of the E-Commerce Directive, be considered to be established in the Member State where it has the centre of its activities in accordance with the Court's case law.[37]

3–065 **No prior authorisation** — Member States may not make the provision of information society services subject to prior authorisation or any procedure having equivalent effect.[38] However, Member States may require information society service providers to comply with authorisation schemes not specifically targeted at information society services. For example, if Community or national legislation requires professional qualifications or authorisation by a professional body in order to carry on a particular professional activity, this requirement will apply in full to any undertaking wishing to carry on such professional or business activities by means of the internet. In addition, information society services that constitute electronic communications services (*e.g.* internet access services) remain subject to the general authorisation requirements or individual rights of use under the New Regulatory Framework.[39]

3–066 **General information to be provided by providers of information society services** — Member States must ensure that each information society service provider provides certain information to recipients and national authorities. Thus, information society service providers

---

[31] *ibid.*, Art.3(4).

[32] *ibid.*

[33] *ibid.*, Art.3(5).

[34] *ibid.*, Art.3(6).

[35] *ibid.*, Art.2(c). See also Joined Cases C–213/89 & 46/93, *R. v Secretary of State for Transport Ex p. Factortame Ltd* [1991] I E.C.R. 3905 and *Brasserie du Pêcheur SA v Bundesrepublik Deutschland and R. v Secretary of State for Transport Ex p. Factortame Ltd* [1996] I E.C.R. 1029.

[36] E-Commerce Directive, Art.6(b).

[37] Case C–56/96, *VT4 Ltd v Vlaamse Gemeenschap* [1997] I E.C.R. 3143. See also E-Commerce Directive, para.1–015, n.44, Recital 19.

[38] E-Commerce Directive, Art.4(1).

[39] On the requirements of the Authorisation Directive, see para.1–060.

must provide to the recipients of such services and the competent authorities, in an easily, directly and permanently accessible form, at least: their name, and, where relevant, trade register and registration number (if any), geographical address, contact details (including an email address), relevant supervisory or professional authorisations (if any) and VAT number.[40] In addition, where information society services refer to prices, these must indicate whether they are inclusive of taxes and delivery costs.[41] This obligation supplements existing information requirements laid down in the Distance Contracts Directive.[42] Thus, even if no contract is concluded, the information society services provider will have to make available these elements of information, for example, on its website.

The E-Commerce Directive also establishes the principle that commercial communications must be clearly identifiable as such.[43] In particular, the natural or legal person on whose behalf the commercial communication is made must be clearly identifiable.[44] Likewise, promotional competitions, games or offers, such as discounts, premiums and gifts, where authorised by the Member State in which the service provider is established, must be clearly identifiable, and the conditions for participation or qualification must be easily accessible and be presented accurately and unequivocally.[45] Unsolicited commercial communications by email should also be clearly identifiable, so that the recipient can instantly identify such emails as being a commercial communication without having to open them.[46] In this regard, Member States must take measures to ensure that service providers undertaking unsolicited commercial communications by email consult regularly and respect the opt-out registers in which natural persons not wishing to receive such commercial communications can register themselves.[47] These provisions are without prejudice to Community data protection legislation concerning unsolicited marketing.

The E-Commerce Directive contains specific rules on e-commerce activities conducted by members of regulated professions. Commercial communications that are part of an information society service provided by a member of a regulated profession must comply with the relevant professional rules, including those on the independence, dignity and honour of the profession, professional secrecy and fairness towards clients and the members of the profession.[48] The Member States and Commission shall encourage professional associations and bodies to establish codes of

---

[40] *ibid.*, Art.5(1).

[41] *ibid.*, Art.5(2).

[42] Directive 97/71 of the European Parliament and of the Council of May 20, 1997 on the protection of consumers in respect of distance contracts, O.J. 1997 L144/19. See para.3–075 *et seq.*, below.

[43] E-Commerce Directive, para.1–015, n.44, Art.6(a). This obligation is in addition to any other information requirements imposed by Community law. Commercial communication is defined as any form of communication designed to promote, directly or indirectly, the goods, services or image of a company, organisation or person, pursuing a commercial, industrial or craft activity or exercising a liberal profession. The following do not in themselves constitute commercial communications: (i) information allowing direct access to the activity of the company, organisation or person, in particular a domain name or an email address; and (ii) communications relating to the goods, services or images of the company, organisation or person compiled in an independent manner, in particular without financial consideration.

[44] *ibid.*, Art.6(b).

[45] *ibid.*, Arts 6(c) and 6(d).

[46] *ibid.*, Art.7(1).

[47] *ibid.*, Art.7(b).

[48] *ibid.*, Art.8(1).

conduct to govern the information society service activities of their members.[49] The Commission may also draw up proposals for Community initiatives to ensure the cross-border provision of professional services via the internet, and must take account of such codes of conduct.[50]

3–067 Electronic contracts — Member States must ensure that their legal systems allow contracts to be concluded electronically. Member States must also ensure that the legal requirements applicable to contracts neither prevent the effective use of electronic contracts nor result in such contracts being deprived of legal effect and validity on account of having been made electronically.[51] However, Member States may declare that contracts falling into the following categories can be excluded from that obligation: contracts creating or transferring rights in real property (other than rental rights); contracts that by law require the involvement of courts, public authorities or professionals exercising public authority (such as notaries); contracts of suretyship guaranteed by collateral securities furnished by private individuals; and contracts governed by family law and the laws of succession.[52] Member States must provide an explanation to the Commission for any derogation that they make in respect of contracts falling within these categories.[53] The E-Commerce Directive accordingly places a positive obligation on Member States to identify and amend any national law that might prevent, limit or deter the use of electronic contracts. Examples of legal requirements which the Member States must examine and, where appropriate, amend are: (i) requirements as to the medium used for the contract, such as requirements that contracts be "on paper", "written" or "signed in writing", that there be an original copy or that there be a certain number of originals; (ii) requirements as to human presence (for example, that contracts be negotiated or concluded by natural persons or in the physical presence of both parties); and (iii) requirements as to the involvement of third parties (for example, that the contract be concluded in the presence of witnesses).

Providers of information society services must explain clearly, comprehensively and unambiguously, and prior to the conclusion of the contract, the manner of formation of a contract by electronic means.[54] In particular, the information to be provided to the recipient of the services must include: (i) the different technical steps to follow to conclude the contract (though contracting parties who are not consumers can agree otherwise); (ii) whether or not the concluded contract will be filed by the service provider and whether it will be accessible; (iii) the technical means for correcting input errors prior to the conclusion of the contracts; and (iv) the languages offered for the conclusion of the contract.[55] The service provider must also provide details of any relevant codes of conduct to which he subscribes and how these can be consulted electronically.[56] These obligations do not apply to contracts concluded exclusively by an exchange of emails or by equivalent individual communication.[57]

---

[49] *ibid.*, Art.8(2).
[50] *ibid.*, Art.8(3).
[51] *ibid.*, Art.9(1).
[52] *ibid.*, Art.9(2).
[53] *ibid.*, Art.9(3).
[54] *ibid.*, Art.10(1).
[55] *ibid.*
[56] *ibid.*, Art.10(2).
[57] *ibid.*, Art.10(4).

3–068 Liability of intermediary service providers — The E-Commerce Directive exempts information society service providers from liability for unlawful acts in three cases. These are available only when the information society service provider's activities are limited to the technical process of opening and giving access to a communication network over which information made available by third parties is transmitted and temporarily stored (or cached), *i.e.* for technical, automatic and passive activities.[58] These exemptions from the liability of service providers do not affect the ability of Member States' courts or administrative authorities to require service providers to terminate or prevent infringements.[59] These limitations cover situations where a service provider acts as a "mere conduit" or performs caching and hosting activities. Information society service providers act as a "mere conduit" where they play a passive role in transmitting on or providing access to a communication network information provided by third parties, provided that the information society service provider: (i) does not initiate the transmission; (ii) does not select the receiver of the transmission; and (iii) does not select or modify the information contained in the transmission.[60] The acts of transmission and providing access include the automatic, immediate and transient storage of the information transmitted provided that this is done solely for the purpose of carrying out the transmission and that the information is not stored any longer than reasonably necessary for the transmission.[61] Limitations on the liability of service providers cover liability for all types of unlawful activities initiated by third parties online (*e.g.* copyright infringement, unfair competition practices, misleading advertising and defamation). The E-Commerce Directive also exempts information society service providers from liability for unlawful acts, subject to certain conditions, when they act as caching[62] or hosting[63] agents for their customers. However, to benefit from this exemption from liability, the service provider must not have deliberately collaborated with a recipient of its services in order to undertake illegal activities. Member States are prohibited from imposing general obligations on information society service providers to screen or to actively monitor third party content while providing transmission, network access, caching and hosting activities, or to actively seek facts or circumstances indicating illegal activity.[64] However, Member States may oblige service providers to inform the public authorities of illegal activities undertaken or information provided by recipients of their service or to identify recipients of their service with whom they have storage agreements.[65] This does not affect orders made in accordance with national law to monitor specific activity or prevent Member

---

[58] *ibid.*, Recital 42.

[59] *ibid.*, Arts 12(3), 13(2) and 14(3).

[60] *ibid.*, Art.12(1).

[61] *ibid.*, Art.12(2).

[62] See above, para.3–023, n.81. E-Commerce Directive, para.1–015, n.44, Art.13(1).

[63] E-Commerce Directive, para.1–015, n.44, Art.14(1). Hosting occurs where the service provider stores information provided by a recipient of the service at its request, such as the provision of server space for a company's website.

[64] *ibid.*, Arts 15(1) and 16. An important condition in both cases is that, in order to benefit from this limitation of liability, service providers must act expeditiously to remove or disable access to information upon obtaining actual or constructive knowledge of illegal activities or information stored. Furthermore, because, unlike the US Digital Copyright Millennium Act, the E-Commerce Directive does not contain "Notice and Takedown" procedures, Member States are free to develop their own specific requirements that must be fulfilled for the removal or disabling of information to take place expeditiously. Nevertheless, the intention is that industry should develop voluntary codes of conduct, *ibid.*, Art.16. See also McEvedy, "The DMCA and the E-Commerce Directive" (2002) 24(2) E.I.P.R. 65.

[65] E-Commerce Directive, Art.15(2).

States from imposing duties of care on service providers to detect and to prevent certain types of illegal activities.[66] Member States and the Commission shall also encourage the development of codes of conduct designed to contribute to the proper implementation of the terms of the E-Commerce Directive.[67] Member States must also not discourage out-of-court settlements of disputes between service providers and recipients of their services, in particular for consumer disputes,[68] and they are to ensure that court actions are available under national law to allow for the quick adoption of interim measures to terminate alleged infringements of the national legislation implementing the provisions of the E-Commerce Directive.[69] Member States must also determine appropriate sanctions for infringements of national law implementing the E-Commerce Directive that are effective, appropriate and dissuasive.[70]

3–069 Implementation and review — Member States were required to have implemented the E-Commerce Directive by January 17, 2002. The Commission is to review the application of the E-Commerce Directive and propose any changes needed to adapt it to legal, technical and economic developments in the field of information society services, in particular with respect to the prevention of crime, the protection of children and consumers and the proper functioning of the internal market.[71] The Commission shall, in particular, analyse the need for proposals concerning the liability of providers of hyperlinks and location tool services, notice and take-down procedures and the liability of information society service providers following the taking down of content, as well as the need for additional conditions for the exemption from liability in the light of technical developments.[72] The E-Commerce Directive does not apply to information society services supplied by service providers established in third countries. However, in view of the global dimension of electronic commerce, the Community's rules should be consistent with international rules and the E-Commerce Directive, and are therefore without prejudice to the results of discussions within international organisations such as the WTO, OECD, and UNCITRAL on legal issues.[73] Therefore, further changes to the E-Commerce Directive may be required to take account of international developments.

3–070 Consumer e-commerce contracts relating to the harmonisation of national law — The E-Commerce Directive does not cover consumer contracts.[74] Instead, they are governed by other Community legislation on the jurisdiction of the courts in civil and commercial matters, the applicable law of contracts, distance selling, unfair contract terms in consumer contracts, indication of prices, sales of timeshares, injunctions to protect consumers' interests, liability for defective products and advertising of medical products.

---

[66] *ibid.*, Recitals 47 and 48.
[67] *ibid.*, Art.16.
[68] *ibid.*, Art.17.
[69] *ibid.*, Art.18.
[70] *ibid.*, Art.20.
[71] *ibid.*, Art.21(1).
[72] *ibid.*, Art.21(2).
[73] *ibid.*, Recital 158.
[74] *ibid.*, Arts 1(3), 3(3) and Annex.

3–071 Jurisdiction — Jurisdiction in non-domestic matters is governed by the Brussels Regulation.[75] Under the Brussels Regulation (and the Brussels and Lugano Conventions), the general principle of jurisdiction is that an individual or a business may be sued in the Member State where it is domiciled. The Brussels Regulation contains a number of exceptions to this general rule, which are to be construed narrowly.[76] The Brussels Regulation gives consumers (*i.e.* persons acting outside their trade or profession) the choice to bring proceedings related to contracts concluded by them either in the Member State in which the consumer is domiciled or in the Member State where the other party to the contract, whether a person or an undertaking, is domiciled[77] if: (i) the contract is for the sale of goods on instalment credit terms; (ii) the contract is a contract for a loan repayable by instalments (or any other form of credit) made to finance the sale of goods; or (iii) the contract is made with a commercial or professional person or undertaking pursuing activities in the consumer's Member State or who otherwise "direct" their activities to the consumer's Member State.[78] That is to say, the Brussels Regulation adopts both "country of origin" and "country of destination" principles in relation to jurisdiction. Although the Brussels Regulation does not specifically address the e-commerce context, this means that because a business-to-consumer (B2C) e-commerce website may be accessible to consumers located throughout the EU, undertakings doing business over the internet are in principle subject to the jurisdiction of all Member States in which their customers reside.[79]

Service providers, however, may bring a claim against a consumer only in the Member State in which the consumer is domiciled.[80] These rules may be departed from only by an agreement: (i) that is entered into after a dispute has arisen; (ii) that allows the consumer to sue in courts other than those of the Member State where either the consumer or the service provider are domiciled; or (iii) that confers jurisdiction on the Member State where both parties are domiciled or habitually resident.[81] Special rules apply in the event of matters relating to tort, delict or quasi-delict, which may be relevant to claims of defective or dangerous goods or service supplied over the internet. In

---

[75] Council Regulation 44/2001 on jurisdiction and the recognition and enforcement of judgments in civil and commercial matters, O.J. 2001 L12/1. As the EU's most important trading partners are not subject to the Brussels Regulation and the Rome Convention, the EU, its Member States, and 46 other countries, including the US, China and Japan, are working on the Draft Hague Convention on jurisdiction and foreign judgments in civil and commercial matters. In its present form, if adopted, the Draft Hague Convention would also allow consumers to sue information society service providers in the courts of the country where the consumer is domiciled under the same conditions as those in the Brussels Regulation. However, there is still a great deal of debate as to whether choice of forum clauses in consumer contracts (under which the courts of another country are given exclusive jurisdiction) will be enforceable. The current draft also includes provisions relating to industrial and intellectual property. Information on this convention is available at *http://www.hcch.net/e/ workprog/jdgm.html.*

[76] Case C–220/88, *Dumez France SA and Tracoba SARL v Hessische Landesbank* [1990] E.C.R. 49.

[77] Brussels Regulation, para.3–071, n.75, Art.16(1).

[78] *ibid.*, Arts 15(1) and 16.

[79] See, generally, Motion, "The Brussels Regulation and E-Commerce — A Premature Solution to a Fictional Problem" (2001) 7(8) C.T.L.R. 209. The Commission's original proposal for a draft Regulation contained a Recital that specifically stated that websites were deemed to be directed at all Member States in which they were accessible. See COM(99) 348, O.J. 1999 C376/1.

[80] Brussels Regulation, para.3–071, n.75, Art.16(2).

[81] *ibid.*, Art.17.

such cases, the courts of either the Member State where the harmful event occurred or may have occurred also have jurisdiction, in addition to those of the Member State in which the defendant is domiciled.[82]

3–072 Applicable law of the contract — The applicable law is governed by the so-called Rome Convention.[83] This Convention applies both to contracts that contain a choice of law clause and to those that do not. It generally permits choice of law provisions in consumer contracts,[84] but it does not set aside mandatory national consumer protection laws applicable to consumer contracts for: (i) the sale, hire or pledge of moveables; (ii) insurance contracts (to the extent that these fall within the scope of the Convention); (iii) banking contracts; (iv) wagering contracts; and (v) package holidays. Specifically excluded from these mandatory provisions are transport contracts (other than for package holidays) and contracts for the supply of services in countries other than the Member State where the consumer resides. Consumers are protected by these mandatory provisions so long as: (i) they have taken all steps to conclude the contract in their country of residence, *e.g.* by mouse-click; and (ii) the contract was preceded by a specific proposal or publicity of the offeror.[85] Whilst there is general agreement that advertising by email is a specific proposal, opinions vary on whether web advertising constitutes a specific proposal.[86]

3–073 Other matters on consumer contracts — The Community has adopted a wide range of other legislation which, although not specifically directed at e-commerce, will have an effect upon it. These include measures dealing with the following topics: unfair terms in consumer contracts,[87]

---

[82] *ibid.*, Art.5(3). See Case C–21/76, *Handelskwekerij G. J. Bier BV v Mines de potasse d'Alsace SA* [1976] E.C.R. 1735, confirming that the plaintiff has a choice of jurisdictions in which to bring his case. This provision covers ostensibly all matters of non-contractual liability. See also Case C–189/87 *Athanasios Kalfelis v Bankhaus Schröder, Münchmeyer, Hengst and Co* [1987] E.C.R. 1472.

[83] 1980 Rome Convention on the law applicable to contractual obligations, O.J. 1991 C52/1. The Commission has also recently proposed a draft Regulation (the "Rome II Regulation") that would govern the applicable law in cases of non-contractual liability such as product liability. Under this proposal, the general rule is that the applicable law is that of the country in which the damage is sustained would apply, which would usually be the consumer's country of residence. In the case of product liability, the applicable law would be that of the consumer's habitual residence, unless the manufacturer can prove that the product was manufactured there without its consent. There are also special rules for torts such as unfair competition, defamation, environmental torts and infringement of intellectual property rights. See Commission Communication, "Proposal for a Regulation of the European Parliament and of the Council on the law applicable to non-contractual obligations ("Rome II")", COM (2003) 427.

[84] *ibid.*, Art.3. If no choice of law clause is included in a contract, the contract should be governed by the laws of the Member State with which it is most closely connected. *ibid.*, Art.4.

[85] *ibid.*, Arts 3 and 5(2).

[86] See, for example, Niemann, "Webvertisements Covered by Art.5(2) Rome Convention?" (2000) 5(3) *Communications Law* 99; Moerel, "The Country-of-Origin Principle in the E-Commerce Directive: The Expected 'One-Stop' Shop" (2001) 7(7) C.T.L.R. 184. Moerel concludes that whether a choice of law clause will override mandatory consumer protection laws in the Member State of the consumer's domicile will depend on the circumstances of the individual case. For example, some e-commerce sites attempt to ensure the applicability of their choice of law clauses by: including a disclaimer ("only intended for consumers from"); asking for the consumer's place of residence; refusing to supply consumers resident outside a certain territory; setting up the site in a national language or using a local currency; and using a national internet address and contact address. It remains to be seen whether such measures would be upheld by courts, including the Court of Justice.

[87] Council Directive 93/13 of April 5, 1993 on unfair terms in consumer contracts, O.J. 1993 L95/29.

distance contracts with consumers,[88] misleading and comparative advertising,[89] consumer credit contracts,[90] package holidays,[91] the indication of prices,[92] product safety,[93] timeshare contracts,[94] injunctions to protect consumers' interests,[95] liability for defective products,[96] the sale of consumer goods and associated guarantees,[97] the advertising of medical products,[98] and the advertising of tobacco products.[99]

3–074 E-Commerce Taxation Directive — Prior to the entry into force of the E-Commerce Taxation Directive,[1] the imposition of VAT on e-commerce activities was governed by the Sixth VAT Directive.[2] Under the Sixth VAT Directive, EU suppliers were obliged to charge VAT when selling their products to customers located outside the EU, while non-EU suppliers were not required to pay VAT on sales within the EU. This system distorted competition and hampered the functioning of the internal market. The E-Commerce Taxation Directive was therefore adopted in order to eliminate these distortions of competition in the supply of e-commerce services to

[88] Directive 97/7 of the European Parliament and of the Council of May 20, 1997 on the protection of consumers in respect of distance contracts, O.J. 1997 L144/19 and Directive 2002/65 of the European Parliament and of the Council of September 23, 2002 concerning the distance marketing of financial services and amending Council Directive 90/619 and Directive 97/7 and 98/27, O.J. 2002 L271/16; see para.3–076, below.

[89] Council Directive 94/45 of September 10, 1984 concerning misleading and comparative advertising, O.J. 1984 L251/17, as amended by Directive 97/55 of the European Parliament and of the Council, O.J. 1997 L290/18.

[90] Council Directive 87/102 of December 22, 1986 for the approximation of the laws, regulations and administrative provisions of the Member States concerning consumer credit, O.J. 1987 L42/48, as last amended by Directive 98/7 of the European Parliament and of the Council, O.J. 1998 L107/17.

[91] Council Directive 90/314 of June 13, 1990 on package travel, package holidays and package tours, O.J. 1990 L158/59.

[92] Directive 98/6 of the European Parliament and of the Council of February 16, 1998 on consumer protection in the indication of prices of products offered to consumers, O.J. 1998 L80/27.

[93] Council Directive 92/59 of June 29, 1992 on general product safety, O.J. 1992 L228/24.

[94] Directive 94/47 of the European Parliament and of the Council of October 26, 1994 on the protection of purchasers in respect of certain aspects of contracts relating to the purchase of the right to use immovable properties on a timeshare basis, O.J. 1994 L286/83.

[95] Directive 98/27 of the European Parliament and of the Council of May 19, 1998 on injunctions for the protection of consumers' interests, O.J. 1978 L164/51, as amended by Directive 1999/44, O.J. 1999 L171/12.

[96] Council Directive 85/347 of July 25, 1985 on the approximation of the laws, regulations and administrative provisions concerning liability for defective products, O.J. 1985 L210/29, as amended by Directive 1999/34, O.J. 1999 L141/20.

[97] Directive 99/44 of the European Parliament and of the Council of May 25, 1999 on certain aspects of the sale of consumer goods and associated guarantees, O.J. 1999 L171/12.

[98] Council Directive 92/28 of March 31, 1992 on the advertising of medical products, O.J. 1990 L113/13.

[99] Directive 98/43 of the European Parliament and of the Council of July 6, 1998 on the approximation of laws, regulations and administrative proceedings of the Member States relating to the advertising and sponsorship of tobacco products, O.J. 1998 L213/9.

[1] Council Directive 2002/38 of May 7, 2002 amending temporarily Directive 77/388 as regards the value added tax arrangements applicable to radio and television broadcasting services and certain electronically supplied services, O.J. 2002 Ll28/41. At the same time, the Council also adopted Regulation 792/2002 of May 7, 2002 amending temporarily Regulation (EC) 218/92 on administrative cooperation in the field of indirect taxation (VAT) as regards additional measures regarding e-commerce, O.J. 2002 L128/1.

[2] Council Directive 77/388 of May 17, 1977 on the harmonisation of the laws of the Member States relating to turnover taxes — Common system of value added tax: uniform basis of assessment, O.J. 1997 L145/1.

consumers; the VAT regime applicable to e-commerce between businesses remains unchanged. The central provision of the E-Commerce Taxation Directive is the establishment of a special scheme for the taxation of electronically supplied services provided to consumers within the Community by service providers that are not established in the Community. The general principle for the taxation of such services is that they should be taxed in the Member State where the recipient of these services is located.

Such providers are required to choose a particular Member State — the "Member State of identification" — from which it is to receive a VAT identification number.[3] Service providers must then submit, on a quarterly basis, to the Member State of identification a VAT return that sets forth the identification number and, for each individual Member State of consumption where tax has become due, the total value, less VAT, of the electronic services supplied and the total amount of the corresponding tax.[4] Member States had to implement the E-Commerce Taxation Directive by July 1, 2003.

The E-Commerce Taxation Directive should provide a coherent system for levying VAT on electronically supplied services, including: (i) website supply, web-hosting and distance main-tenance of programmes and equipment; (ii) supply of software and updating thereof; (iii) supply of music, films and games, including games of chance and gambling games, and of political, cultural, artistic, sporting, scientific and entertainment broadcasts and events; and (iv) supply of distance teaching. However, the mere fact that a supplier of a service and a customer communicate by email does not necessarily mean that the service provided is an electronic service.[5]

2. Regulatory Framework for Distance Selling and Marketing

3–075 The EU has adopted three legislative measures on consumer protection that are particularly relevant to e-commerce: the Distance Contracts Directive,[6] the Financial Services Distance Marketing Directive,[7] and the Framework Decision on Combating Fraud and Counter-feiting.[8] The Commission has also issued a Communication on e-commerce and financial services,[9] in which it lays out its policy framework for completing the internal market in financial services.

---

[3] E-Commerce Taxation Directive, para.3–074, n.1, Art.1. The service provider must provide the Member State of identification with the following information: name, postal address, electronic addresses (including websites), national tax number, if any, and a statement that the person is not identified for value added tax purposes within the Community.

[4] *ibid.*, (which will be incorporated as Art.26(c) of the Sixth VAT Directive, para.3–074, n.2).

[5] *ibid.*, Annex, inserting a new Annex L into the Sixth VAT Directive.

[6] Distance Contracts Directive, para.3–073, n.90. For a comprehensive review of the Distance Contracts Directive, see Chissick and Kelman, para.3–003, n.8.

[7] Directive 2002/65 of the European Parliament and of the Council of September 23, 2002 concerning the distance marketing of consumer financial services and amending Council Directive 90/619 and Directives 97/7 and 98/27, O.J. 2002 L271/16.

[8] Council Framework Decision 2001/413 of May 28, 2001 on combating fraud and counterfeiting of non-cash means of payment, O.J. 2001 L149/1.

[9] Commission Communication, "E-commerce and Financial Services", available at: *http://europa.eu.int/ comm/internal_market/en/finances/general/ecom.htm.*

3–076   The Distance Contracts Directive — Many consumer contracts are concluded without the consumer and the supplier ever coming into physical contact with one another, *i.e.* at a "distance". Harmonisation of national laws on distance selling was an important and necessary step in completing the internal market in goods and services, as different and/or diverging national rules affected competition and the cross-border provision of goods and services. It was also necessary to ensure a harmonised level of consumer protection throughout the EU. For the purposes of the Distance Contracts Directive, distance selling is defined as the conclusion of a contract regarding goods or services whereby the contact between the consumer and the supplier takes place by means of technology for communication at a distance.[10] The use of distance communication means that the two parties are not simultaneously physically present.[11] This form of selling goods and services covers a wide range of trade activities including traditional forms such as telephone press advertising, mail-order catalogues and personal mailing, but also modern techniques of distance selling such as the internet, email or automated telephone calls and faxes.[12]

3–077   Information to be provided to the consumer — The service supplier must provide certain information to the consumer prior to the conclusion of the contract. The information to be provided includes: the identity of the supplier; his address (in the case of payment in advance); the main characteristics of the goods or services; the price, including taxes and delivery costs; the arrangements for payment, delivery or performance; the existence of a right of withdrawal; the costs of using the means of communication at a distance (if other than at the basic rate); the period for which the offer or the price remains valid; and the minimum duration of the contract.[13] This information must be provided in a clear, comprehensive and appropriate way, respecting the principles of good faith in commercial transactions and the principles governing the protection of those who are unable under national law to give their consent, such as minors.[14]

3–078   *Written confirmation of information* — The consumer must receive written confirmation (or confirmation in another durable medium) of the following information: the identity of the supplier; his address (in the case of payment in advance); the main characteristics of the goods or services; the price, including taxes and delivery costs; the arrangements for payment, delivery or performance; the existence of a right of withdrawal, after-sales services and guarantees; and the conditions for cancelling the contract, if it is of unspecified duration or for more than one year.[15] This information must be provided in good time during the performance of the contract or, at the latest, at the time of delivery. This provision does not apply to the performance of services that are supplied on only one occasion and are invoiced by the operator of the communication network (*e.g.* premium rate telephone services), although consumers must always be able to obtain the geographical address of the service provider, where complaints may be addressed.[16] In the case of

---

[10] Distance Contracts Directive, para.3–073, n.88, Arts 2(1) and 2(4).

[11] *ibid.*

[12] *ibid.*, Annex I. Some of these forms of direct marketing are regulated under Community law: see paras 3–067 and 3–070.

[13] *ibid.*, Art.4.

[14] *ibid.*, Art.4(2).

[15] *ibid.*

[16] *ibid.*, Art.5(2).

telephone communications, the identity of the supplier and the commercial purpose of the call must be made explicitly clear at the beginning of the conversation.[17]

3–079 *Right of withdrawal* — The consumer must be given a right to withdraw from the contract, which can be exercised for at least seven working days after conclusion of the contract, with a limited number of exceptions (*e.g.* where performance of the contract for services has begun with the consumer's agreement; contracts for personalised goods; the sale of audio or video recordings; computer software that has been unsealed by the consumer; and/or magazines and newspapers).[18] Withdrawal must be free of charge for the consumer, except in relation to any direct costs for returning goods already delivered. Any reimbursement of sums already paid by the consumer must be done within three days of withdrawal.[19]

3–080 *Performance* — Any order must be executed by the supplier within 30 days from the day following that on which the consumer forwarded his order to the supplier.[20] Where the supplier fails to perform his obligations under the contract on the ground that the goods or services ordered are unavailable, the consumer must be informed of this situation and must be able to obtain a refund of any sums he has paid as soon as possible and in any case within 30 days.[21] The consumer may be provided with goods or services of equivalent quality and price, provided the consumer was properly informed of this possibility before or during the conclusion of the contract. If such alternative goods are not acceptable to the consumer, the supplier must bear the costs of returning them and the consumer must be informed of this.

3–081 *Payment by card* — Member States must ensure that in the case of fraudulent use of a payment card (*e.g.* access card or a debit card), the consumer is able to request cancellation of the order and reimbursement of the sums paid.[22] This provision has been criticised in so far as it is limited to payment by card and does not apply to new payment methods such as electronic money, and because this provision is not applicable in case of defective execution, non-execution or negligence by the issuer of the card.[23]

3–082 *Inertia selling* — Member States must take measures to prohibit the supply of goods or services for remuneration to a consumer without their being ordered by the consumer beforehand where such supply involves a demand for payment (so-called "inertia selling"). The absence of a response by the consumer must not constitute consent and must not expose the consumer to liability to pay for the goods.[24]

3–083 *Mandatory nature of the Distance Contracts Directive* — The consumer may not waive the rights conferred on him by national laws implementing the Distance Contracts Directive.[25]

---

[17] *ibid.*, Art.4(3).
[18] *ibid.*, Arts 6(1) and 6(3).
[19] *ibid.*, Art.6(2).
[20] *ibid.*, Art.7(1).
[21] *ibid.*, Art.7(2).
[22] *ibid.*, Art.8.
[23] See Salaün, "Electronic Payments and Contracts negotiated through the Internet" (1999) 5(2) C.T.L.R. 26.
[24] Distance Contracts Directive, para.3–073, n.88, Art.9.
[25] *ibid.*, Art.12.

Simultaneously, Member States must ensure that consumers do not lose the benefits of consumer protection laws by virtue of the choice of the law of a non-member country as the law applicable to the contract, if the contract has a close connection with the territory of one or more Member States.[26]

3–084 *Minimum level of guaranteed protection* — The Distance Contracts Directive represents only the minimum level of harmonised consumer protection. Therefore, Member States may introduce or maintain more stringent provisions that are compatible with the EC Treaty, in order to ensure a higher level of consumer protection. In particular, the marketing of certain goods and services (*e.g.* medicinal products) may be prohibited within their territory.

3–085 *Goods and services to which the Distance Contracts Directive is not applicable* — The Distance Contracts Directive does not apply to: contracts relating to financial services[27]; contracts concluded by means of automatic vending machines or automated commercial premises; contracts concluded with telecommunications operators through the use of public pay-phones; and contracts concluded for the construction and sale of immovable property or other property rights, except rentals.[28] Moreover, contracts relating to foodstuffs, beverages or other goods intended for everyday consumption, accommodation, transport, catering and leisure are exempted from a number of obligations imposed by the Directive (*i.e.* prior information, written confirmation, right of withdrawal, performance).[29]

3–086 *Implementation* — Member States were required to implement the Distance Contracts Directive no later than June 4, 2000.

3–087 **Financial Services Distance Marketing Directive** — The provision of consumer financial services (such as investment services, insurance and reinsurance, banking and operations related to dealings in futures and options) was exempted from the scope of the Distance Contracts Directive.[30] Following a broad consultation, the Commission concluded that there was a need to complete the internal market in financial services and to strengthen consumer protection in this field in light of the growing importance of distance selling in the marketing of financial products and the specific issues raised by distance trading of this type of product. It was therefore justified in this sector, which is already regulated by a number of financial services directives (which overlap somewhat with the information obligations under the Distance Contracts Directive), to adopt specific legislation for financial services.[31] Different and divergent national laws had also created serious obstacles to the cross-border provision of financial services by means of distance communications.

---

[26] *ibid.*, Art.12(2).
[27] *ibid.*, Art.3(1) and Annex II.
[28] *ibid.*, Art.3(1).
[29] *ibid.*, Art.3.
[30] *ibid.*
[31] Commission Green Paper, "Financial Services — Meeting Consumers' Expectations", COM(96) 209; Commission Communication, "Financial Services — Enhancing Consumer Confidence", COM(97) 309.

Following a number of Commission proposals,[32] on September 23, 2002 the Council and the European Parliament adopted the Financial Services Distance Marketing Directive.[33] The purpose of this Directive is to establish a clear regulatory framework for the cross-border marketing of financial services at a distance, by approximating Member States' rules on the distance marketing of consumer financial services.[34] As a result, suppliers of financial services will be able to offer their products throughout the EU, without the hindrance of having to comply with different national laws on the distance selling of consumer financial services.

3–088 *Consumer protection provisions* — The Financial Services Distance Marketing Directive closely follows the approach of the Distance Contracts Directive. The definition of a "distance contract" is identical to that contained in Article 2 of the Distance Contracts Directive, except that it applies only to financial services rather than to goods and services generally.[35] It also provides that certain information must be supplied to consumers before the conclusion of the contract.[36] This information includes: the supplier (including representatives in the Member State of the consumer's residence and any professional intermediary); the financial service involved (including its characteristics, the total price or a method for calculating it, notice of any special risks related to the financial service and details of relevant taxes); the distance contract (including the existence, or otherwise, of a right of withdrawal, the minimum duration of the contract, right to early termination, and clauses on applicable law and jurisdiction); and redress (including out-of-court complaint and redress procedures, and the existence of guarantee funds and other compensation arrangements).[37] This information is more extensive than that required under the Distance Contracts Directive and reflects the specific nature of financial services products. As with the Distance Contracts Directive, this information must be provided in a clear, comprehensible and appropriate manner, having due regard to principles of good faith and the protection of those who may lack contractual capacity, such as children.[38] Furthermore, if Community law imposes additional information requests on providers of financial services, these shall continue to apply, and, pending further harmonisation, Member States may retain stringent requirements on the prior provision of information, provided that they are in compliance with Community law.[39] Contractual terms and conditions and information must be communicated to the consumer on paper or on another durable media (such as floppy disks, CD-ROMs, DVDs and the hard drive of the consumer's computer, but not on an internet website) in good time before the consumer is bound by any distance contract or offer,[40] or, if the contract is concluded at the customer's request before that is done, immediately after the conclusion of the contract.[41] The consumer may at any time request a paper copy of the contract or change the means of distance communication.[42]

---

[32] For the Commission's initial proposals, see COM(98) 468, available at: *http://europa.eu.int/eur-lex/pri/en/oj/dat/1998/c_385/c_38519981211en00100017.pdf* and COM(99) 385, available at: *http://europa.eu.int/eur-lex/en/com/pdf/1999/en_599PC0385.pdf*.

[33] Financial Services Distance Marketing Directive, para.3–075, n.7.

[34] *ibid.*, Art.1(1).

[35] *ibid.*, Art.2.

[36] *ibid.*, Art.3.

[37] *ibid.*, Art.3(1).

[38] *ibid.*, Art.3(2).

[39] *ibid.*, Arts 4(1) and 4(2).

[40] *ibid.*, Art.5(1).

[41] *ibid.*, Art.5(2).

[42] *ibid.*, Art.5(3).

3–089 *Right of withdrawal* — Consumers must have a period of at least 14 days to withdraw from the contract (which is extended to 30 days for life insurance and personal pension operations) without having to indicate grounds for withdrawal and without penalty.[43] The supplier may not begin to perform the contract before expiry of the time limit for the exercise of the right of withdrawal without the consumer's express consent.[44] When the consumer exercises his right of withdrawal, he may be required to pay a sum compensating the supplier for the costs incurred and/or the services rendered prior to the exercise of the withdrawal.[45]

3–090 *Other provisions* — As with the Distance Contracts Directive, Member States must ensure that, in the case of fraudulent use of a payment card, the consumer can request the cancellation of the payment and that any sums paid be reimbursed.[46] Member States must prohibit the supply of financial services without prior request on the part of the consumer and exempt the customer from obligations to pay for such unsolicited services.[47] With respect to unsolicited communications, Member States must ensure that suppliers can only use distance communications if they have either obtained the consumer's consent or if the consumer has not manifestly expressed an objection.[48] The consumer may not waive the rights conferred on him by national laws that transpose the Financial Services Distance Marketing Directive into national law, and Member States must ensure that the consumer does not lose the protection granted by this Directive by virtue of the law of a non-member country as the law applicable to the contract, if the contract has a close connection with the territory of one or more Member States.[49] Member States must provide for appropriate, effective, proportional and dissuasive sanctions for a supplier's failure to comply with national implementing legislation.[50] Adequate and effective judicial and administrative redress must be available to protect consumers' interests, including actions by public bodies, consumer organisations and professional organisations.[51] Member States must also put in place schemes for out-of-court complaints and redress concerning consumer disputes.[52] Finally, Member States may place the burden of proof on the supplier to show that it has complied with its obligations to inform the consumer, to obtain the consumer's consent and to perform the contract.[53]

3–091 *Implementation* — Member States must implement this Directive by October 9, 2004.[54]

---

[43] *ibid.*, Art.6.
[44] *ibid.*, Art.7(1).
[45] *ibid.* Member States may render withdrawal from an insurance contract free of charge to the consumer: *ibid.*, Art.7(2).
[46] *ibid.*, Art.8.
[47] *ibid.*, Art.9. This is without prejudice to the renewal of an existing contract, where that is permitted by national law.
[48] *ibid.*, Art.10. Communications by automatic calling machines and fax always require the prior consent of the consumer: *ibid.*, Art.10(1).
[49] *ibid.*, Art.12.
[50] *ibid.*, Art.11.
[51] *ibid.*, Art.13.
[52] *ibid.*, Art.14.
[53] *ibid.*, Art.15.
[54] *ibid.*, Art.21(1).

3–092 Framework Decision on Fraud and Counterfeiting[55] — This Framework Decision requires Member States to ensure that a number of means of fraud and counterfeiting using non-cash means of payment are treated as criminal offences. It covers the following misuses of "payment instruments" (*i.e.* credit cards or other cards issued by financial institutions, eurocheques and travellers' cheques): (i) theft; (ii) counterfeiting or falsification for fraudulent use; (iii) receiving, transporting or selling stolen or counterfeit payment instruments; and (iv) fraudulent use of stolen or counterfeit payment instruments. It also requires Member States to criminalise any theft or other property loss that is committed by means of using a computer to alter, delete or suppress computer data or otherwise interfering with the operation of a computer system. Finally, Member States must criminalise the fraudulent making, receiving, obtaining, sale or transfer of devices that are peculiarly adapted to the commission of the criminal offences listed above.

3–093 E-Commerce and Financial Services Communication[56] — This Communication sets out a wide range of legislative and non-legislative measures the Commission intends to adopt in order to complete the internal market in financial services. First, the Commission will develop a programme of convergence covering contractual and non-contractual rules that will pave the way for a country of origin approach covering all financial services sectors and forms of distance selling. This will involve: (i) legislation guaranteeing high levels of harmonised consumer protection relating to advertising, marketing and sales promotions (the Financial Service Distance Marketing Directive being the implementation step of this first initiative); (ii) legislation ensuring the convergence of sector-specific (*e.g.* banking, insurance, etc.) and service-specific (*e.g.* mortgage credit, consumer credit, etc.) national rules on information requirements to facilitate the easy comparison of prices and conditions; and (iii) an ongoing review of national rules on retail financial services contracts. Second, the Commission intends to take a number of non-legislative measures designed to increase consumer confidence in cross-border transactions and internet payments by creating a Community-wide network to handle financial services complaints through third-party and alternative dispute resolution systems. With respect to internet payments, this Communication also supports legislation granting consumers the right to a refund in the event of unauthorised transactions or non-delivery of goods or services.

3. Electronic Money

3–094 Background — Initially, payment for goods and services obtained over the internet was made by traditional bank transfer. However, the development of e-commerce required faster means of payment and, as a result, credit cards and debit cards are now widely used as a means of payment on the internet. However, the use of credit cards on an open network like the internet raises issues of security (*e.g.* the interception of card numbers) and privacy (*e.g.* the tracking of customers' purchasing patterns). Although encryption can resolve some of these issues, these concerns have led to the creation of alternative means of payment that are specific to the internet.

3–095 Electronic accounts — Banks have developed electronic accounts ("e-accounts") for internet transactions. The user opens an e-account with a financial institution (*e.g.* First Virtual

---

[55] Council Framework Decision 2001/413 of May 28, 2001 combating fraud and counterfeiting of non-cash means of payment, O.J. 2001 L149/1.
[56] E-Commerce and Financial Services Communication, para.3–075, n.9.

Holdings Inc., Netchèque, Netchex and I-Pay in the Netherlands) and receives an encrypted code, which identifies him in his internet transactions. The user transfers funds from his bank account to his e-account. When he wants to purchase an item on the internet, the user informs the seller of his code, which enables the seller to check the validity of the account with the relevant financial institution. The financial institution, which acts as an intermediary, then pays the seller and debits the buyer's e-account. The use of e-accounts thus avoids confidential information such as credit card numbers being communicated over the internet.

3–096 Electronic money — An innovative method of payment for transactions conducted on the internet is electronic money. Electronic money is digital data representing a certain monetary value. This monetary value is stored either on chips on bank cards or cards that are similar to phone-cards (*e.g.* the Proton system in Belgium and the Mondec system in the United Kingdom), or on computer software stored on a customer's PC that can be used to buy products or services over the internet. Customers wishing to use e-money must open an e-cash account with their bank in addition to their regular account. They will then be able to transfer amounts from their regular accounts to their e-cash accounts. Customers withdraw e-cash coins from their e-account and store them on their PC. Users can then pay with e-cash coins when purchasing goods or services over the internet. When the seller is paid with e-cash coins, he sends them to the bank for verification. The bank will then credit the amount on the e-cash account of the seller with the bank. For the time being, the e-cash system can only be used if the seller and the buyer have a bank account with the same bank.

Electronic money has many characteristics of cash. The primary similarity is that no authorisation is required from a bank or third party to use electronic money (unlike with debit or credit cards). Another major similarity with cash is anonymity. Electronic money uses a system of blind signatures to avoid the bank being able to track the customer's spending. E-cash coins are not created at the bank but by the software installed on the customer's PC. Each e-cash coin has its own serial number and is sent to the bank in an encrypted digital envelope at the time the customer wishes to withdraw electronic money from his account. The bank validates the e-cash coins with digital stamps (without opening the digital envelope) and sends the e-cash coins back to the seller and debits the e-cash account of the customer. The bank is thus not able to recognise the e-cash coins it has stamped.[57]

The use of these new payment techniques raises a number of legal issues, such as: the legal status of electronic money and of the relationship between the customer, the seller and the issuing bank; the issues of liability in the event of fraudulent use; consumer protection issues; and the question of the legal status and supervision of users of electronic money. This section reviews the EU regulatory initiatives that have been taken to address these issues.

3–097 Commission's Recommendation on Electronic Payment — In 1997, the Commission adopted a recommendation concerning electronic payment instruments with a view to promoting

---

[57] See Abels, "Paying on the Net Means and Associated Risks" (1998) 3 *International Business Law Journal* 349; see also Hance, para.3–001, n.1.

customer confidence and retailer acceptance of these instruments (the "Electronic Payment Recommendation").[58] The Electronic Payment Recommendation is not binding on Member States, but the Commission has indicated that it would propose appropriate binding legislation covering the issues dealt with in the Recommendation, if its implementation by the Member States was unsatisfactory. Member States were invited to take the necessary measures to implement the Electronic Payment Recommendation by December 31, 1998.

The Electronic Payment Recommendation basically applies to all transactions effected by means of an electronic payment instrument.[59] The term electronic payment covers "remote access payment instruments" of the e-account type, which allow payment at a distance through access, by way of a personal identification code, to funds held with an institution. It also covers electronic money instruments, which are defined as reloadable payment instruments, consisting of a stored-value card or computer memory on which value units are stored electronically.[60] The term "issuer" is defined broadly to cover not only financial institutions but also any other institutions such as supermarkets, which, in the course of their business, make available to their customers an electronic payment instrument pursuant to contracts concluded with them. The Electronic Payment Recommendation provides for minimum requirements regarding the information to be provided to customers on the terms and conditions governing the issuance and use of electronic payment instruments. It also specifies the respective obligations and liabilities of the holder and of the issuer of electronic payment instruments.[61]

3-098 Electronic Money Institutions Directive — In order to promote confidence and trust among businesses and consumers regarding the use of electronic money, the European Parliament and the Council have adopted the Electronic Money Institutions Directive.[62] This introduces a separate prudential supervisory regime for electronic money institutions, in order to secure the mutual recognition, authorisation and supervision of electronic money institutions on the basis of a single licence recognised throughout the Community. An "electronic money institution" is defined as any institution, other than a credit institution as defined in Directive 2000/12, which issues means of payment in the form of electronic money.[63] The business activities of such electronic money institutions must be limited to the issuance of electronic money and the provision of closely related financial and non-financial services, such as administering electronic money and means of payment (excluding the granting of any form of credit).[64] Second, undertakings that issue electronic

---

[58] Commission Recommendation of July 30, 1997 concerning transactions by electronic payment instruments and in particular the relationship between the issuer and holder, O.J. 1997 L208/52.

[59] *ibid.*, Art.1.

[60] *ibid.*, Art.2.

[61] For more details, see Salaün, para.3–081, n.23, pp.19–31.

[62] Directive 2000/46 of the European Parliament and of the Council of September 18, 2000 on the taking up, pursuit of and prudential supervision of the business of electronic money institutions, O.J. 2000 L275/39.

[63] *ibid.*, Art.1(3)(a). See also Directive 2000/12 of the European Parliament and of the Council of March 20, 2000 relating to the taking up and pursuit of the business of credit institutions, O.J. 2000 L126/1. "Electronic money" is defined as monetary value as represented by a claim on the issuer which is: (i) stored on an electronic device; (ii) issued on receipt of funds of an amount not less than the monetary value issued; and (iii) accepted as means of payment by undertakings other than the issuer. *ibid.*, Art.1(3)(b).

[64] Electronic Money Institutions Directive, para.3–098, n.62, Art.1(5).

money but which do not wish to undertake the full range of banking activities nevertheless enjoy the benefits of being able to operate throughout the EU on the basis of authorisation in one Member State (the so-called "single passport") and so be on an equal footing with credit institutions.[65] Third, an alternative system of prudential regulation to that contained in Directive 2000/12 is provided for electronic money institutions, which includes requirements covering initial capital and ongoing own funds requirements, limitations on investments and sound and prudent operation.[66] The bearer of e-money may require the issuer to redeem it in coins and bank notes or by a transfer to a bank account free of charges other than those strictly necessary to carry out that operation. A minimum threshold for redemption may be stipulated, under the contract between the issuer and the bearer, but threshold may not exceed €10.[67] Electronic money institutions that were operational before the implementation of the Electronic Money Institutions Directive (which was required by April 29, 2002) benefit from "grand-fathering" provisions and were presumed to be authorised in accordance with the Directive (and thus benefit from mutual recognition). They then had six months to demonstrate compliance.[68]

---

[65] *ibid.*, Art.2.

[66] *ibid.*, Arts 4, 5 and 7. These requirements are, however, lower than those applicable to credit institutions under Directive 2000/12, para.3–098, n.63. Member States' regulatory authorities must verify compliance at least twice per year. *ibid.*, Art.6.

[67] *ibid.*, Art.3.

[68] *ibid.*, Arts 9 and 10.

Part II: Application of EU Competition Rules to Telecommunications, Broadcasting and the Internet

Introduction — The competition rules of the EC Treaty and secondary EU legislation are not specific to the communications sector and apply in principle to any business (whether public or private) that carries on an economic activity, regardless of the industry in which it is active.[1] Accordingly, many principles of competition law discussed in the following chapters are derived from the case law of the European Courts and the Commission in cases involving a broad array of sectors, unrelated to communications. The special conditions of the communications sector, however, warrant specific consideration when applying the EU's competition rules. The sudden and rapid pace of liberalisation of the telecommunications sector combined with the existence on most national markets of large, powerful players inherited from the era of state monopolies makes the context of the telecommunications business unique in many respects. Furthermore, the broadcasting and electronic communications sectors raise different issues, such as the interface between economic, technological and other policy considerations (such as culture, linguistic diversity and media plurality) that must be considered when applying the EU's competition rules.

The application of the EU's competition rules to the communications sector is the indispensable complement to the sector-specific regulation discussed in Part I. The continued presence of incumbents with strong market power and control of essential network assets raises many competition issues. Although some of them are addressed by specific regulation (*e.g.* interconnection), there is a need to supplement this regulatory framework by the application of competition rules in those many areas (*e.g.* access) where issue-specific regulation alone would not achieve full liberalisation. Effective implementation of competition rules should also ensure that the benefits of liberalisation are not undermined by collusion between operators or inefficient consolidation through mergers and acquisitions. Furthermore, the New Regulatory Framework is predicated upon the "rolling back" of sector-specific regulation in favour of the application of competition law. As a result, NRAs are increasingly acting as competition authorities. The ongoing convergence of telecommunications, media and information technology sectors is also a significant factor in applying competition law in these sectors.

Issues considered in Part II — Part II will firstly provide a brief overview of the main provisions of EU competition law as well as the most common enforcement and procedural issues for businesses (Chapter IV). In so far as it is an essential tool for the application of competition rules, the issue of market definition in the communications sector will then be examined (Chapter V). The specific application of competition rules to the market conduct of communications operators

---

[1] Certain sectors of the economy, such as transport or agriculture, mainly due to their strategic importance for state governments are, however, subject to specific regimes which provide for deferred and gradual application of competition rules in these sectors.

will then be reviewed in light of the Commission's 1991 Competition Guidelines[2] and Access Notice[3] and the decision-making practice of the Commission and the case law of the European Court of Justice and the Court of First Instance (Chapter VI). A section will then be devoted to examining the application of the EC Treaty's State aid rules in the communications sector (Chapter VII). As restructuring has been, and will continue to be, a major feature of the communications industry, the application of the EU's competition rules to the most common mechanisms for reorganisation in the sector (mergers and acquisitions, joint ventures and strategic alliances) will be considered (Chapter VIII). Finally, current and possible future trends in the interaction between competition rules and sector-specific regulation applying to the communications sector will be reviewed (Chapter IX).

[2] 1991 Competition Guidelines on the Application of EEC Competition Rules in the Telecommunications Sector, O.J. 1991 C233/2.
[3] Notice on the Application of the Competition Rules to Access Agreements in the Telecommunications Sector, O.J. 1998 C265/2.

Chapter IV
Overview of EU Competition Rules

A. Article 81 (*ex* 85) of the EC Treaty: Prohibition of Anti-Competitive Agreements, Decisions and Concerted Practices

4–001 Scope — Article 81(1) of the EC Treaty prohibits agreements[1] between undertakings,[2] decisions by associations of undertakings,[3] and concerted practices[4] that have the object or effect of

---

[1] An agreement involves the expression of a joint intention by the undertakings involved to conduct themselves on the market in a specific way, the object or effect of the conduct being the prevention, restriction or distortion of competition: Case T–7/89 *Hercules v Commission* [1991] II E.C.R. 1711, on appeal Case C–51/92P [1999] I E.C.R. 4235 (appeal dismissed). An agreement need not be legally binding. Informal agreements and "gentlemen's agreements" are within Art.81(1) (Case 41/69 *ACF Chemiefarma v Commission* [1970] E.C.R. 661), as well as agreements made under duress (Case T–141/89 *Tréfileurope Sales v Commission* [1995] II E.C.R. 791). All that is required is that the undertakings involved reach a consensus to regulate their future competitive conduct, thereby restraining their autonomy and independence by taking account of the interests of the other participants: Case T–1/89 *Rhône-Poulenc v Commission* [1991] II E.C.R. 867. However, there is no agreement if the parties are still in negotiations (Case E–3/97 *Jaeger v Opel Norge* [1998] Rep. EFTA Ct I (EFTA Court)), nor if the conduct is in fact unilateral (Case T–41/96 *Bayer v Commission* (ADALAT) [2000] II E.C.R. 3383, appeal pending: Cases C–2 and 3/01).

[2] The concept of "undertaking" is not defined in the EC Treaty. According to the case law of the European courts, it includes any entity that is engaged in an economic or commercial activity (whether or not with a view to making a profit), regardless of its legal form (*i.e.* limited company, partnership, sole trader, trade association, co-operative, self-employed professionals, publicly owned companies and state trading businesses) and the way in which it is financed: Case C–41/90 *Höfner & Elser v Macrotron* [1991] I E.C.R. 1979. However, tasks undertaken in the public interest which form part of the essential interests of the State, are not undertakings for the purpose of EC competition law, even if financed by users: Case 364/92 *SAT Fluggesellschaft v Eurocontrol* [1994] I E.C.R. 43.

[3] The concept of "decisions by association of undertakings" are typical measures laid down by trade associations, co-operatives and professional bodies such as their statutes, by-laws, rules and codes of conduct and recommendations issued by them. However, these fall only within the scope of Art.81(1) to the extent that they co-ordinate or restrict their members' behaviour: Case T–136/94 *Eurofer v Commission* [1999] II E.C.R. 263, and further appeal Case C–179/99P, pending at May 9, 2003.

[4] A concerted practice has been defined by the European Court of Justice as "a form of co-ordination between undertakings which, without having reached the stage where an agreement properly so called has been concluded, knowingly substitute practical co-operation between them for the risks of competition": Cases 48/69, etc., *ICI v Commission* [1972] E.C.R. 619. For a detailed review of the concept, see Bellamy and Child, *European*

preventing, restricting or distorting competition appreciably[5] and come within EC jurisdiction[6] because they have, or are likely to have, an appreciable effect on trade between EU Member States.[7] Particularly serious restrictions on competition by Article 81(1) include agreements and

Community Law of Competition (Sweet & Maxwell, 5th ed., 2001), Chap.2. In most cases, the distinction between an agreement and a concerted practice is of little practical consequence as the Commission may categorise arrangements as constituting an agreement and/or a concerted practice: C–49/92P *Commission v Anic Partecipazioni* [1999] I E.C.R. 4125 (*polypropylene cartel*). However, mere parallel behaviour in an oligopolistic market does not constitute a concerted practice, unless concertation constitutes the only plausible explanation for the parallel conduct: Cases C–89/85, etc., *Åhlström OY v Commission* [1993] I E.C.R. 1307 (*Woodpulp II*).

[5] As a result of the case law of the Court of Justice, it is established that, to fall within the scope of the prohibition contained in Art.81(1), an agreement must affect trade between EU Member States and restrict competition to an appreciable extent: Case C–22/71 *Béguelin Import v GL Import Export* [1971] E.C.R. 949. The presence or lack of appreciable effect is a question of fact and degree that will generally depend on the market shares and importance of the businesses on the market. There is a presumption of appreciable effect when the parties concerned have a combined market share exceeding 5 per cent of the market for the product concerned: Case 107/82 *AEG v Commission* [1978] E.C.R. 3151. Nevertheless, the Commission and any national court applying Art.81(1) must do a full and proper market analysis to determine whether the agreement or concerted practice does in fact have an appreciable effect on both competition and inter-state trade, given the relevant economic context: Cases T–374/94, etc., *European Night Services v Commission* [1998] II E.C.R. 3141.

[6] Most EU Member States have now adopted national competition rules which apply to anti-competitive agreements and conduct affecting essentially national or regional markets. A review of national competition laws is beyond the scope of this book. However, as these national rules generally mirror EC competition rules, the principles of EC competition law will generally be valid also in the framework of the application of Member States' competition laws. Council Regulation 1/2003 of December 16, 2002 on the implementation of the rules on competition laid down in Arts 81 and 82 of the EC Treaty, O.J. 2003 L1/1, will change the enforcement of Arts 81 and 82 when it enters into force on May 1, 2004. In particular, when national courts and competition authorities apply national competition law to an agreement, practice or conduct, they must also apply Arts 81 and 82 (as appropriate) if the agreement, practice or conduct may affect trade between Member States: *ibid.*, Art.3(1). Furthermore, the application of national competition laws to agreements, decisions or concerted practices within the meaning of Art.81(1) may not result in the prohibition of such agreements, decisions and concerted practices which affect or may affect trade between Member States, when these agreements, decisions or concerted practices do not restrict competition within the common market (so fall outside of Art.81(1)) or meet the conditions of Art.81(3) (for individual exemptions) or are covered by a block exemption regulation: *ibid.*, Art.3(2). Member States, however, are not precluded from adopting and applying on their territory stricter national competition laws which prohibit or sanction unilateral conduct engaged in by undertakings (*e.g.* abusive behaviour toward economically dependent undertakings): *ibid.*, Art.3(2). These provisions do not apply when national merger control laws are applied, nor to the application of national laws with an objective other than prohibiting anti-competitive agreements, practices and conduct: *ibid.*, Art.3(3).

[7] The requirement of effect on trade between Member States is a jurisdictional criterion determining the boundaries of the application of Community competition rules in contrast to national competition rules. Trade is "affected" where an economic activity (whether the supply of goods or services) is capable of being altered, thereby leading to an alteration in trade flows or patterns between Member States from that which would normally be expected in the absence of the agreement or concerted practice, and thereby leading to distortions in competition, provided that this can be foreseen with a sufficient degree of probability. The effects on trade may be direct or indirect, actual or potential: Case 56/65 *Société Technique Minière v Commission* [1966] E.C.R. 235 and Case 322/81 *Michelin v Commission* [1983] E.C.R. 3461. In addition, trade between Member States will be regarded as being affected if the agreement or practice alters the competitive structure within the common market to an appreciable extent: Cases 6 and 7/73 *Commercial Solvents v Commission* [1974] E.C.R. 223. The European Court of Justice has given a very broad interpretation to this concept, with the result that co-operation between companies that are all located, and the conduct takes place, in one Member State falls within the scope of Art.81(1) on the basis that the agreement could partition markets and prevent imports: Case 8/72

concerted practices between undertakings to fix prices, production or sales quotas; share markets or sources of supply; exchange confidential market information; jointly sell products; or adopt a policy of resale price maintenance. Such agreements involve so-called "hard-core" restrictions on competition which are presumed to have an anti-competitive effect, even if the market shares of the parties involved are below the thresholds of the *De Minimis* Notice.[8] In all other cases, the Commission or the court must demonstrate that the agreement or practice has an effect upon actual or potential competition, whether due to horizontal and/or vertical restrictions.[9] Finally, if an agreement is pro-competitive, any restrictions within the agreement that are objectively justified in order to obtain the pro-competitive outcome will fall outside Article 81(1).[10]

4–002 Consequences of infringement of Article 81(1) of the EC Treaty — The restrictions on competition contained in an agreement violating Article 81(1) are void and unenforceable[11] unless they are exempted under Article 81(3).[12] Whether or not the agreement as a whole is void and unenforceable is a matter of national law and will depend upon the extent to which the infringing provisions can be "severed" from the remainder of the agreement.[13] The infringing parts of the agreement (or all of it if the infringing parts are not severable) are unenforceable both between the parties and against third parties. Furthermore, the parties to a prohibited agreement, decision or concerted practice may be subject to substantial fines imposed by the Commission.[14] In addition,

Cementhandelaren v Commission [1972] E.C.R. 977. However, a national agreement that has effects only within one Member State and has no appreciable effect upon imports or exports falls outside of Art.81(1) and may only be assessed under national competition law: Cases 215 and 216/96 *Bagnasco v BPN and Carige* [1999] I E.C.R. 135. In the framework of the implementation of Regulation 1/2003, para.4–001, n.6, above, the Commission intends to adopt a Notice on the concept of "effect on trade between Member States", which will reflect current case law. For a detailed analysis of the constituent elements of Art.81(1) and the applicable case law, see Bellamy and Child (para.4–001, n.4), Chap.2.

[8] Commission Notice on agreements of minor importance which do not appreciably restrict competition under Art.81(1) of the Treaty establishing the European Community (*de minimis*), O.J. 2001 C368/13. The *De Minimis Notice* quantifies, with the help of market share thresholds, what is not an appreciable restriction on competition under Art.81(1). The Notice provides that agreements between undertakings which affect trade between Member States do not fall within Art.81(1) if (i) the aggregate market share of the participating undertakings does not exceed 10 per cent on any of the relevant markets in the case of horizontal agreements; or (ii) the market share of each of the participating undertakings does not exceed 15 per cent on any of the relevant markets in the case of vertical agreements. If the agreement is difficult to classify as a horizontal or vertical agreement, the 10 per cent threshold is applicable. In addition, the Notice introduces a special *de minimis* market share threshold of 5 per cent for markets where competition is restricted by the cumulative effect of parallel networks of agreements having similar effects on the market. The Notice also states that agreements between small and medium-sized enterprises (SMEs) are rarely capable of appreciably affecting trade between Member States and accordingly generally fall outside the scope of Art.81(1).

[9] *European Night Services*, above, para.4–001, n.5.

[10] This is the so-called "Ancillary Restraints Doctrine". See, *e.g.* Case 26/76 *Metro v Commission* (No.1) [1977] E.C.R. 1875 and Case 250/92 *Gøttrup-Klim v Dansk Landbrugs* [1994] I E.C.R. 5641.

[11] Art.81(2) of the EC Treaty.

[12] Council Regulation 17/62 implementing Arts 85 and 86 [now 81 and 82] of the EC Treaty (O.J. 1962 L13/204) sets out the rules of procedure for the application of Arts 81 and 82.

[13] Case 56/65 *Société Technique Minière v Maschinenbau Ulm* [1966] E.C.R. 235 and Case 319/82 *Soc. de Vente de Ciments et Bétons de l'Est v Kerpen & Kerpen* [1983] E.C.R. 4173.

[14] Under Regulation 17/62, para.4–002, n.12, as amended by Council Regulation 1216/1999 amending Regulation 17/62, O.J. 1999 L148/5, the Commission may impose fines of up to 10 per cent of an undertakings' worldwide turnover in the preceding business year, or which range from €1,000 up to a maximum of €1 million, whichever is the greater, for an intentional or negligent infringement of Arts 81 or 82, with the level

they may also be exposed to third-party claims for damages in national courts, as Article 81(1) has direct effect.[15] In certain circumstances, contracting counterparties may be entitled to damages for losses suffered by their performance of an agreement that is in breach of Article 81(1).[16] Agreements that fall within the scope of the Article 81(1) prohibition will nevertheless be valid and enforceable if either they are notified to and exempted by the Commission pursuant to Article 81(3), or if they meet the criteria laid down in one of the "block exemption" regulations.

4–003   Territorial scope of Article 81(1) of the EC Treaty — Article 81(1) applies to any agreement or concerted practice which has an effect, actual or potential, upon trade between Member States, and which has the object or effect of preventing, restricting or distorting competition in the common market. It is now well established that Article 81 applies to an agreement between undertakings that are located outside the EU provided the agreement or concerted practice has the requisite effects on competition and inter-State trade within the EU.[17] An undertaking's country of incorporation and the location of its management are therefore irrelevant.

4–004   Negative clearances and exemptions under Article 81(3) of the EC Treaty versus direct effect and applicability of Article 81(3) of the EC Treaty — Article 81(3) provides that the prohibition on anti-competitive agreements and practices contained in Article 81(1) be declared inapplicable if the agreement or practice in question: (i) contributes to improving the distribution of goods or services or promotes technical or economic progress; (ii) allows consumers a fair share of the resulting benefits; (iii) does not impose restrictions on the undertakings concerned which are not indispensable to achieving these objectives; and (iv) does not afford the parties the possibility of limiting competition with respect to a substantial part of the products in question.[18] Notification of an agreement to the Commission ensures protection against fines that might otherwise have resulted from the implementation of the agreement,[19] but it does not in itself have any effect on the

---

depending on both the gravity and duration of the infringement. See also Commission Notice of February 19, 2002 on immunity from fines and reduction in fines in cartel cases, O.J. 2002 C45/3 and Commission Guidelines on the method of setting fines imposed pursuant to Art.15(2) of Regulation No.17/62 and Art.65(5) of the ECSC Treaty, O.J. 1998 C9/3.

[15] Community law does not impose a harmonised system of reparation for breaches of it, which are matters for national law. However, remedies must be equivalent to those for national law and be sufficient to ensure the effective protection of EC law rights: see, *e.g.* Case 242/95 *GT-Link v DSB* [1997] I E.C.R. 4449 (concerning Art.82) and Case 128/92 *HJ Banks & Co v British Coal Corporation* [1994] I E.C.R. 1209 (concerning competition provisions of the ECSC Treaty).

[16] Case 453/99 *Courage Ltd v Crehan* [2001] I E.C.R. 6297: a party may recover damages from the other party to an agreement in breach of Art.81(1) where that other party is in a markedly stronger position, such that the party seeking damages had either a seriously compromised ability, or no ability, to freely negotiate the terms of the agreement and the other party accordingly bears a significant responsibility for the breach of competition law.

[17] Cases 89/85, etc. *Ahlström v Commission* (*Woodpulp I*) [1988] E.C.R. 5193 (Art.81: unlawful agreement implemented in the common market); and Case T–102/96 *Gencor v Commission* [1999] II E.C.R. 753 (Merger Regulation: merger would have had anti-competitive effects within the EU). A separate question is that of enforcing Community competition law against undertakings established outside the EU, although bilateral treaties between the EU and countries such as the United States and Canada can minimise the difficulties in enforcing EU law.

[18] For a detailed review of the application of Art.81(3), see Bellamy and Child (para.4–001, n.4), Chap.3.

[19] Regulation 17/62, para.4–002, n.12, Art.15(5). Immunity from fines may, however, be withdrawn under Art.15(6) if the agreement involves a manifestly serious infringement of Art.81(1): Case T–19/91 *Vichy v Commission* [1992] II E.C.R. 415. In such cases, an individual exemption is unlikely to be granted.

enforceability of the notified agreement.[20] Exemption guarantees the enforceability of the agreement for the period of the exemption (which will be determined by the Commission) and thereby prevents private legal actions by third parties or a counterparty.[21] The Commission has also adopted so-called "block exemption" regulations[22] that automatically exempt, without the need to notify,[23] a specific agreement that meets the conditions set forth in the block exemption regulation in question.

Undertakings may also notify agreements or practices with a view to obtaining a declaration from the Commission that they do not infringe Article 81(1). This is called a "negative clearance". An application for negative clearance alone does not give protection from fines. Notification for exemption and application for negative clearance can be made on the same form, the so-called Form A/B. Generally, undertakings make a combined application for negative clearance and/or individual exemption. The Commission is not subject to any deadline upon receiving a notification and proceedings can last for several years.

The existing notification and exemption regime under Regulation 17/62 will cease to apply from May 1, 2004, when Regulation 1/2003[24] comes into force. Under Regulation 1/2003, the inapplicability of Article 81(1) will no longer be conditional upon having made a notification to the Commission and on obtaining an exemption/negative clearance decision from the Commission.

---

[20] Case 48/72 *Brasserie de Haecht v Wilkin II* [1973] E.C.R. 77 (notification does not suspend the direct effect of Art.81(2)). However, if the Commission has not given a final decision yet as to whether or not an agreement infringes Art.81(1) and falls within the scope of Art.81(3), or the Commission's decision is under appeal before the Community courts, the national courts should not give a final judgment on whether or not Art.81(1) is infringed but rather should stay the proceedings or take interim measures: Case 344/98 *Masterfoods v HB Ice Cream* [2000] I E.C.R. 11369.

[21] The Commission only adopts formal exemption decisions in cases of particular significance given the importance of the market or parties concerned or the legal issues involved. Most of the time, in order to expedite proceedings and given its limited resources, the Commission issues so-called "comfort letters" signed by a senior official of the Commission indicating that the Commission is closing the file and that no further action is intended. Although such comfort letters do not have the same legal effect as a formal exemption decision, in practice, they very often provide businesses with a satisfactory level of protection from the application of Art.81(1). Comfort letters may indicate either that Art.81(1) is not infringed, or that the Commission would, if so minded, adopt an individual exemption decision under Art.81(3). Comfort letters have no formal legal status, but can be taken into account by national courts: Case 99/79 *Lancôme v Etos* [1980] E.C.R. 2511.

[22] Regulation 240/96 on the application of Art.81(3) to certain categories of technology transfer agreements, O.J. 1996 L31/2; Regulation 2790/1999 of December 22, 1999 on the application of Art.81(3) to categories of vertical agreements and concerted practices, O.J. 1999 L336/21; Regulation 2658/2000 of November 29, 2000 on the application of Art.81(3) to categories of specialisation agreements, O.J. 2000 L304/3; Regulation 2659/2000 of November 29, 2000 on the application of Art.81(3) to categories of research and development agreements, O.J. 2000 L304/7; and Regulation 1400/2002 of July 31, 2002, on the application of Art.81(3) to categories of vertical agreements and concerted practices in the motor vehicle sector, O.J. 2002 L203/30. See also the Commission's Guidelines on Vertical Restraints, O.J. 2000 C291/1 and the Commission's Guidelines on the applicability of Art.81 to horizontal co-operation agreements, O.J. 2001 C3/2.

[23] Certain block exemption regulations contain an "opposition procedure" under which an agreement can be notified and if the Commission does not object to it within a specified period, the agreement automatically benefits from the block exemption. Agreements that fall outside the terms of a block exemption regulation can, in appropriate cases, be notified to the Commission for an individual exemption under Art.81(3).

[24] Regulation 1/2003, above, para.4–001, n.6.

Instead, the prohibition contained in Article 81(1) is automatically inapplicable *ab initio* to agreements and concerted practices that satisfy the conditions set out in Article 81(3).[25] As a result of the direct applicability of Article 81(3) from May 1, 2004, national competition authorities and courts will be able to carry out a full assessment of agreements and practices by examining both their restrictive effects under Article 81(1) and their potential benefits that may justify the application of Article 81(3). As notifications will no longer be possible, companies and their legal advisers will need to consider whether their agreements fall within the scope of Article 81(1) and, if so, whether the requirements for the application of Article 81(3) are met. This is particularly important bearing in mind that under Regulation 1/2003, agreements and concerted practices that fall within Article 81(1) shall be prohibited automatically (unless they meet the conditions of Article 81(3)), without requiring any prior decision to that effect.[26]

In order to give guidance to national competition authorities and courts as well as to companies and ensure a consistent application of Community competition law, the Commission will still adopt block exemption regulations, notices and guidelines and is also empowered, on its own initiative and in the Community public interest,[27] to adopt decisions finding that Article 81(1) is inapplicable for a particular agreement, decision or concerted practice either because Article 81(1) is not infringed or because the conditions of Article 81(3) are complied with.[28] In general, the Commission will henceforth deal principally with the investigation of cartels and other serious infringements of Article 81(1) and only occasionally consider agreements and practices that raise wider Community interests, justifying a decision to be taken by it. The Commission will also have the right to intervene in proceedings before national competition authorities and courts in order to ensure the consistent application of EC competition law.

B. Article 82 (*ex* 86) of the EC Treaty: Prohibition of the Abuse of a Dominant Position

4–005 Scope — Article 82 prohibits conduct by dominant firms that amounts to an abuse of their dominant position, provided that this has, or is likely to have, an appreciable effect on trade between EU Member States.[29] A dominant position exists when an undertaking has the economic

---

[25] *ibid.*, Art.1(2).

[26] *ibid.*, Art.1(1).

[27] The Community public interest should be interpreted in the light of Recital 14 of Regulation 1/2003 which aims to restrict these types of decision to situations where orientation is needed in the case of incoherent application of Arts 81 and 82 or a policy is needed with regard to new types of cases that have not been settled in the existing case law and administrative practice.

[28] Recital 14 and Art.10 of Regulation 1/2003. These decisions are of a declaratory nature, cannot be obtained on demand by undertakings and, provided the facts underlying the decision do not change, create rights *erga omnes* (*i.e.* these decisions have an effect on national competition authorities and national courts) for the duration of the decision (contrary to individual exemptions under Art.81(3) which have an effect only between the parties).

[29] For a complete review of the constituent elements of Art.82, see Bellamy and Child, para.4–001, n.4, Chap 9. It must be appreciated that Art.82 does not prohibit dominance, only the abuse of it: Case 322/81 *Michelin v Commission* [1983] E.C.R. 3461. Similarly, it does not prohibit the achievement or strengthening of a sole or collective dominant position: Case T–17/93 *Matra Hachette v Commission* [1994] II E.C.R. 595 (although this would be prohibited under the Merger Regulation, if the transaction in question is a

power to act with relative disregard for other participants in a specific market.[30] The existence of dominance therefore presupposes the definition of relevant product and geographic markets in relation to which the market position of the undertaking in question may be assessed.[31] A number of criteria need to be considered in assessing dominance. Market shares are a key indicator of dominance,[32] but other important criteria include the existence of barriers to entry, the overall size and strength of the undertaking in relation to its competitors, ownership of intellectual property or control of an "essential facility" and vertical integration. The presumption of dominance may be rebutted by other factors that demonstrate the existence of competitive constraints, *e.g.* the countervailing power of purchasers, the existence of potential competition, and the dynamic nature of the market. Examples of possible abuses of a dominant position include: excessive pricing, predatory (or unfairly low) pricing, price discrimination, refusal to supply, abuse of intellectual property rights, refusal to grant access to an "essential facility", and bundling or tying practices. An abuse of a dominant position can result either from an agreement or from unilateral conduct.

4–006 Consequences of an infringement of Article 82 of the EC Treaty — As with infringements of Article 81(1), provisions of agreements entered into by a dominant undertaking that result in an abuse of its dominant position, thereby infringing Article 82, are void and unenforceable, as Article 82 has direct effect.[33] The abuse of its dominant position exposes the dominant company to fines[34] and third-party claims for damages in national courts.

4–007 No exemption possible for breach of Article 82 of the EC Treaty — No exemption from the prohibition in Article 82 is possible. However, businesses have the possibility of applying to the Commission for negative clearance regarding the application of Article 82 to a specific market

---

concentration). Furthermore, in the absence of dominance, abusive conduct is not prohibited by Art.82: Case 247/86 *Alsatel v Novasam* [1988] E.C.R. 5987.

[30] The Court of Justice has defined a dominant position under Art.82 as: ". . . a position of economic strength enjoyed by an undertaking which enables it to hinder the maintenance of effective competition on the relevant market by allowing it to behave to an appreciable extent independently of its competitors and customers and ultimately of consumers": *Michelin*, above, para.4–005, n.29, at p.3503.

[31] Market definition is an essential tool for the application of EC competition rules. It is however one of the most challenging and controversial issues in the application of competition policy. The issue is discussed in detail in Chap.6. The Commission has published guidelines on this issue: the Commission Notice on the Definition of Relevant Market for the Purposes of Community Competition Law, O.J. 1997 C372/5.

[32] A market share of over 75 per cent held over time will in itself be very strong evidence of dominance: Case 85/76 *Hoffmann-La Roche v Commission* [1979] E.C.R. 461. A market share of over 50 per cent will give rise to a rebuttable presumption of dominance: Case 62/86 *AKZO v Commission* [1991] I E.C.R. 3359. Market shares of between 40 per cent and 50 per cent will give rise to dominance only if other factors also enable the undertaking to exercise strong market power: Case 27/76 *United Brands v Commission* [1978] E.C.R. 207. Below 25–30 per cent dominance is highly unlikely save in exceptional circumstances.

[33] Case 127/73 *BRT v SABAM* [1974] E.C.R. 51. Agreements that involve an abuse of a dominant position cannot benefit from an individual exemption under Art.81(3) or a block exemption under a block exemption regulation: Cases 395/96P and 396/96P *Compagnie Maritime Belge Transports v Commission* [2000] I E.C.R. 1365. See para.4–002, n.13, above, on the application of the principle of severance.

[34] Regulation 17/62, para.4–002, n.12, Art.15(2)(a). Fines for the intentional or negligent breach of Art.82 may be up to a maximum of €1 million or 10 per cent of the undertaking's turnover in the previous year, whichever is the greater, with the level depending on both the gravity and duration of the infringement. From May 1, 2004, the Commission's power to levy fines for breaches of Art.82 will be contained in Art.23 of Regulation 1/2003, para.4–001, n.6.

conduct, but this is rarely used and will be withdrawn from May 1, 2004 with the entry into force of Regulation 1/2003.[35] Such an application does not provide immunity from fines. Under Regulation 1/2003, the Commission, at its own initiative and in the Community public interest, can adopt a decision declaring that Article 82 is not applicable to a certain type of agreement or conduct.[36]

C. Enforcement of Articles 81 and 82 of the EC Treaty

4–008 Member States as well as natural and legal persons claiming a "legitimate interest" and that consider that they have been prejudiced by anti-competitive agreements and practices and/or the abuse of a dominant position may file complaints with the Commission alleging an infringement of Article 81(1) and/or Article 82.[37] They may request the Commission to adopt interim measures pending its investigation.[38] If the Commission should finally determine that Article 81 and/or 82 have been infringed, in order to bring the infringements to an end, it may order positive action to be taken, as well as require the termination of certain conduct. It will normally also order that no similar agreements be entered into and no similar conduct be committed in the future.[39] Under Regulation 1/2003, the Commission will be able to impose any remedy, whether behavioural or structural, which is necessary to bring the infringement effectively to an end, having regard to the principle of proportionality.[40] The Commission can also impose periodic penalties (*i.e.* fines that are imposed on a daily basis until the undertaking complies with an order of the Commission)[41] and substantial fines if the Commission decides that Articles 81 or 82 have been infringed.[42]

---

[35] Regulation 17/62, para.4–002, n.12, Art.2.

[36] Recital 14 and Art.10 of Regulation 1/2003, para.4–001, n.6.

[37] Regulation 17/62, para.4–002, n.12, Art.3(2). The Commission must consider whether an infringement has occurred and whether there is a Community interest in investigating it. If it considers that the case raises no Community interest (whether legal, economic or political), it is under no duty to investigate further: Case T–24/90 *Automec v Commission II* [1992] II E.C.R. 2223.

[38] The Commission will only impose interim measures, pursuant to Art.3(1) of Regulation 17/62 (para.4–002, n.12) on its own initiative or at the request of complainants, in cases of *prima facie* violations of Art.81(1) and of proven urgency in order to remedy a situation likely to cause serious and irreparable damage to the complainant, or damage which would be intolerable for the public interest: Case T–44/90 *La Cinq v Commission* [1992] II E.C.R. 1. Under Regulation 1/2003, para.4–001, n.6, Art.8 explicitly gives the Commission power to adopt decisions ordering interim measures. In particular, Art.8(1) provides that "in cases of urgency due to the risk of serious or irreparable damage to competition, the Commission, acting on its own initiative may by decision, on the basis of a *prima facie* finding of infringement, order interim measures".

[39] Regulation 17/62, para.4–002, n.12, Art.3.

[40] Recital 12 and Art.7(1) of Regulation 1/2003, para.4–001, n.6. Art.7(1) also provides that "structural remedies can only be imposed either where there is no equally effective behavioural remedy or where any equally effective behavioural remedy would be more burdensome for the undertaking concerned than the structural remedy". According to this provision, the Commission may also find that an infringement has been committed in the past if it has a legitimate interest in doing so.

[41] Regulation 17/62, para.4–002, n.12, Art.16; from May 1, 2004, Art.24 of Regulation 1/2003, para.4–001, n.6.

[42] According to Art.15(2) of Regulation 17/62, para.4–002, n.12, fines for breaches of Arts 81 and 82 may range from €1,000 up to a maximum of €1 million or up to 10 per cent of the worldwide turnover for the preceding year of the group of companies to which the business concerned belongs, whichever is greater. Art.23(2) of Regulation 1/2003, para.4–001, n.6, enables the Commission to impose fines of up to 10 per cent of

Under Regulation 17/62, only Articles 81(1) and 81(2) have so-called "direct effect".[43] Regulation 1/2003 will, from May 1, 2004, extend the direct effect of Article 81 to include Article 81(3).[44] Direct effect means that domestic courts have the power and duty to enforce both prohibitions contained in, and the rights that private parties derive from, these provisions of the EC Treaty.[45] Accordingly, private parties may seek injunctions (both interim and permanent) and/or claim damages before national courts as an alternative to, or in parallel with, a complaint to the Commission.[46] They may also complain to national competition authorities.[47]

D. The Reform of the Enforcement of EC Competition Law

4–009   Regulation 1/2003 — Since the adoption of Regulation 17/62 in 1962 the Community has significantly expanded and Community competition policy is now set against a different socio-economic background. The enforcement of Community competition law has fallen principally upon the Commission, which in recent years has received many more notifications and complaints than it can handle, leading to delays and many cases never being considered in any detail. The current enforcement regime therefore no longer ensures the effective protection of competition. In addition, the notification and exemption regime applicable under Regulation 17/62 imposes an excessive burden on companies. In 2000, the Commission adopted a proposal for a new Regulation,[48] to introduce three major changes to the current enforcement regime:

(i)   the discontinuation of the prior notification and exemption system;

(ii) the replacement of the Commission's exclusive right to exempt agreements under Article 81(3) with a so-called "directly applicable exemption system", whereby the Commission,

the total turnover in the preceding business year of each undertaking participating in the infringement of Arts 81 and/or 82. In addition, it provides that, where the infringement of an association relates to the activities of its members, the fine must not exceed 10 per cent of the sum of the total turnover of each member active on the market affected by the infringement of the association. Art.23(4) of Regulation 1/2003 also provides that, in cases of infringements committed by associations of undertakings, the Commission may recover the fine from the members of the association in case of default on the part of that association. For breaches of procedural rules, Art.15(1) of Regulation 17/62 provides that the Commission may impose a fine from €100 to €5,000, whereas Art.23(1) of Regulation 1/2003 allows fines for breaches of procedural rules of up to 1 per cent of the total annual turnover.

[43] Case 127/73, *BRT v SABAM*, above, para.4–006, n.33.

[44] Regulation 1/2003, para.4–002, n.6, Art.1(2).

[45] Case 127/73, *BRT v SABAM*, above, para.4–006, n.33.

[46] The Court of Justice has clearly established the need for consistency in the application of EC competition rules as a result of the concurrent jurisdiction of the Commission and national courts to apply Arts 81(1), 81(2) and 82: Case 234/89 *Delimitis* [1991] I E.C.R. 935. See also Commission Notice on Co-operation between National Courts and the Commission in applying Arts 81 and 82 of the EC Treaty, O.J. 1993 C39/6.

[47] See Commission Notice on co-operation between national competition authorities and the Commission in handling cases falling within the scope of Arts 85 and 86 of the EC Treaty, O.J. 1997 C313/3.

[48] Proposal for a Council Regulation on the implementation of the rules on competition laid down in Arts 81 and 82 of the EC Treaty and amending Regulations No.1017/68, No.2988/74, No.4056/86 and No.3975/87, COM(2000) 582, September 27, 2000.

national competition authorities and national courts would be able to apply Article 81(3) directly in all proceedings in which they are called upon to apply Article 81(1); and

(iii) increased powers of investigation for the Commission.

Regulation 1/2003 was adopted by the Council on December 16, 2002 to give effect to these proposals. It will enter into force on May 1, 2004 and will be directly applicable and binding in its entirety in all Member States.[49]

4–010   Objectives of Regulation 1/2003 — By adopting Regulation 1/2003, the Council intended to increase the protection of competition in three ways. First, the direct applicability of Article 81(3) will enable not only the Commission but also national competition authorities and courts to apply Articles 81 and 82 in their entirety and thus enhance the protection of competition.[50] Second, the discontinuation of the notification system will free up valuable resources at the Commission enabling it to focus on the detection and punishment of the more serious infringements of Community competition law, such as hard-core horizontal cartels, agreements that result in market foreclosure and serious abuses of a dominant position. Finally, the increase in the investigative powers of the Commission will ensure a more effective application of Articles 81 and 82.[51]

4–011   Core elements of Regulation 1/2003 — Regulation 1/2003 requires national competition authorities and courts additionally to apply Articles 81 and 82 where they apply national competition law to cases which may affect trade between Member States[52] and provides that the application of national competition laws to agreements and practices within the meaning of Article 81(1) may not lead to the prohibition of such agreements and practices if they are not also prohibited under Community competition law either because they fall outside Article 81(1) or meet the conditions of Article 81(3).[53] It is clearly intended that the application of these provisions should ensure a uniform application of Articles 81 and 82 throughout the Community.

The Commission and the national competition authorities shall apply Community competition rules in close co-operation.[54] In particular, national competition authorities must inform the Commission before, or without delay after, commencing proceedings involving the application of Articles 81 and 82 and before adopting a final decision requiring an infringement to be ended,

---

[49] Regulation 1/2003, para.4–001, n.6, Art.45.

[50] National competition authorities will, on their own initiative or following a complaint, require infringements to be ended, impose interim measures, accept commitments and impose fines, periodic penalty payments and other penalties provided for by national law. Regulation 1/2003, para.4–001, n.6, Art.5. National courts shall have the power to apply Arts 81 and 82: *ibid.*, Art.6.

[51] Regulation 1/2003, para.4–001, n.6: codifies the rules governing: the obtaining of judicial orders at national level in order to ensure that companies fully collaborate with on-site investigations (Arts 20 and 21: see also Case C–94/00 *Roquette Frères* [2002] I E.C.R. 9011, available at: *www.curia.eu.int*); increases the powers vested in Commission officials during inspections (power to search private homes of staff of the undertakings concerned; the power to seal any premises or business records; and the power to ask oral questions: Arts 20, 21 and 22); and increases the fines for breaches of procedural rules and the periodic penalty payments fines (Arts 23 and 24).

[52] *ibid.*, Recital 8 and Art.3(1).

[53] *ibid.*, Recital 8 and Art.3(2).

[54] *ibid.*, Art.11(1).

accepting commitments or withdrawing the benefit of a block exemption regulation.[55] In each case, information may also be provided to other national competition authorities. National authorities may also consult the Commission in any other circumstances when applying Community law.[56] If the Commission should itself bring proceedings under Regulation 1/2003, national competition authorities cannot apply Articles 81 or 82 to the same case.[57] The Commission and national competition authorities can exchange and use in evidence any information (whether of fact or law), including confidential information, provided that it is used only for applying Articles 81 or 82, that its use is in accordance with rules protecting the rights of defence and that it is not used by the receiving authority to impose custodial sanctions.[58] If two or more national competition authorities are investigating the same agreement, decision or concerted practice, authorities or the Commission may suspend their proceedings (or reject a complaint) on the basis that another authority is dealing with the case.[59] They may also reject a complaint if another national competition authority has already dealt with the same agreement, decision or concerted practice.[60] Regulation 1/2003 maintains the role of the Advisory Committee on Restrictive Practices and Dominant Positions,[61] which the Commission must consult before finding and requiring the termination of an infringement, adopting interim measures, accepting commitments in order to terminate proceedings, adopt a decision of inapplicability under Article 10 of Regulation 1/2003, impose fines or periodic penalty payments, or withdraw the benefit of a block exemption regulation[62] and it must take the utmost account of the Committee's opinion.[63] The Advisory Committee shall be composed of representatives of national competition authorities[64] and may also consider cases being brought by national competition authorities under Articles 81 or 82, although in these cases it may not issue an opinion.[65]

4–012   Regulation 1/2003 also contains provisions to ensure co-operation between the Commission and national courts. National courts may request the Commission to provide them with information in its possession or to give an opinion on questions concerning the application of Articles 81 or 82.[66] The Commission must also be provided with a copy of any judgment of national courts that applies Articles 81 or 82.[67] The Commission and national competition authorities may make written and, with the court's permission, oral submissions to national courts that are hearing cases involving Articles 81 and 82.[68] Finally, national courts may not take a different decision to

---

[55] *ibid.*, Art.11(3) and 11(4).

[56] *ibid.*, Art.11(5).

[57] *ibid.*, Art.11(6). If a national competition authority has already started its own investigation, the Commission must first consult with it.

[58] *ibid.*, Art.12. If national competition law is also being applied to the same case by the receiving authority, exchanged information may also be used to apply national competition law, provided the same outcome is reached: Art.12(2).

[59] *ibid.*, Art.13(1).

[60] *ibid.*, Art.13(2).

[61] This Advisory Committee was originally established under Regulation 17/62, para.4–002, n.12.

[62] *ibid.*, Art.14(1).

[63] *ibid.*, Art.14(5). Opinions may be published: *ibid.*, Art.14(6).

[64] *ibid.*, Art.14(2).

[65] *ibid.*, Art.14(7).

[66] *ibid.*, Art.15(1).

[67] *ibid.*, Art.15(2).

[68] *ibid.*, Art.15(3). National competition authorities can only make observations to the national courts of their Member State.

that already reached by the Commission in relation to the same agreement, decision or practice.[69] They must also not give decisions that would conflict with a decision contemplated by the Commission and, if necessary, should stay their proceedings.[70] Similarly, national competition authorities may not adopt decisions that would run counter to an existing decision of the Commission.[71]

The proposals leading to the adoption of Regulation 1/2003 were subject to some criticism.[72] In particular, concern was expressed that decentralisation of the enforcement of Community competition law to Member States could lead to inconsistent implementation, depending on the willingness and/or ability of national competition authorities and courts to ensure an effective application of Community competition law.[73] This could be a particular problem following enlargement of the EU in May 2004, when 10 new Member States[74] will join the EU, as most of the new Members States have limited experience of applying competition law. In addition, Regulation 1/2003 may contain several lacunae that could jeopardise an effective decentralised implementation system.[75]

E. Article 86 (*ex* 90) of the EC Treaty

4–013 Introduction — Article 86[76] has been the main tool relied upon by the Commission to liberalise hitherto "monopolised" markets such as telecommunications, and to expose them to competition, in order to ensure compliance with the Community's competition rules and the unity of the internal market. With the liberalisation of the telecommunications sector and the privatisation of incumbent operators, Article 86 may be of limited future application in this sector, save for cases concerning government measures in relation to partially privatised companies and in relation to telecommunications operators with special and/or exclusive rights in other sectors. However, it will remain relevant to the broadcasting sector, where there remain publicly owned and/or publicly funded broadcasters in many Member States and private broadcasters with specific or exclusive rights.

---

[69] *ibid.*, Art.16(1).

[70] *ibid.*

[71] *ibid.*, Art.16(2).

[72] See, *e.g.*, EU Committee of American Chamber of Commerce, "EU Committee Final Draft Position Paper on the White Paper on the Modernisation of the Rules Implementing Arts 81 and 82", September 7, 1999: *www.eucommittee.be*. The EU Committee also expressed concern at the increase in legal uncertainty and the administrative burden for companies, who might also face parallel proceedings in several Member States.

[73] For an assessment of the impact of the modernisation on the role and function of the EC Courts, see Ehlermann and Atanasiu, "The Modernisation of EC Antitrust Law: Consequences for the Future Role and Function of the EC Courts", (2002) 3 E.C.L.R. 72–80.

[74] The new Member States will be Cyprus, the Czech Republic, Estonia, Hungary, Lithuania, Latvia, Malta, Poland, Slovenia, and Slovakia.

[75] See, *e.g.*, Bourgeois and Humpe, "The Commission's Draft 'New Regulation 17'", (2002) 2 E.C.L.R. 43–51, who argue that the draft Regulation lacked clear rules on the allocation of cases between different national competition authorities and on the legal effect of decisions of national competition authorities.

[76] For a complete review of the constituent elements of Art.86, see Blum and Logue, *State Monopolies under EC Law* (Wiley & Sons, 1998).

4–014   Article 86(1) of the EC Treaty: Prohibition on Government Induced Restrictions on Competition — Article 86(1) requires Member States not to enact or maintain any measure contrary to the rules of the EC Treaty, in particular the competition rules, in relation to public undertakings[77] to which it has granted special or exclusive rights.[78] Article 86(1) can therefore be applied in relation to public companies, as well as to any body forming part of the public administration[79] and to private companies. A private undertaking will not have special or exclusive rights if it is licensed according to objective, proportional and non-discriminatory criteria that do not limit the number of potential licensees, even if it is granted special privileges (such as rights to acquire land and lay cables under land), provided these are made available to all licensees and therefore do not confer an advantage over competitors.[80] State "measures" include legislative acts, administrative directions, the exercise of shareholder rights and non-binding recommendations, as well as the grant of special and exclusive rights.[81] Thus maintaining a State monopoly could fall within Article 86(1), but the Court of Justice does allow the Member States a margin of appreciation in determining if this is the case.[82] Although Article 86(1) is addressed only to Member States, it has direct effect and can therefore be invoked by a private business against a Member State in a national court.[83] However, Article 86(1) is only infringed if it is shown that another provision of the EC Treaty having direct effect is also infringed.[84] Therefore, the mere creation of a dominant position by granting an exclusive right is not as such incompatible with Article 82, so it is not an infringement of Article 86. Article 86 will be infringed only if the undertaking is placed in a position where it will inevitably infringe Article 82 (or cannot avoid doing so) by abusing its dominant position by exercising the exclusive rights granted to it by the State.[85] Thus, it was an infringement of Article 86 for Belgium to reserve to its incumbent monopoly telecommunications operator, the RTT, the right to lay down specifications for terminal equipment

---

[77] A "public undertaking" is not defined in the Treaty but is defined in secondary legislation as "any undertaking over which the public authorities may exercise directly or indirectly a dominant influence by virtue of their ownership of it, their financial participation therein, or the rules which govern it": see Commission Directive 80/723 on the transparency of financial relations between Member States and public undertakings, Art.2, O.J. 1980 L195/35.

[78] "Special rights" are defined as rights that are granted by a Member State to a limited number of undertakings, through any legislative, regulatory or administrative instrument, which, within a given geographical area: (i) limits to two or more the number of such undertakings, otherwise than according to objective, proportional and non-discriminatory criteria; or (ii) designates, otherwise than according to such criteria, several competing undertakings; or (iii) confers on any undertaking or undertakings, otherwise than according to such criteria, any legal or regulatory advantages which substantially affect the ability of any other undertaking to import, market, connect, bring into service and/or maintain telecommunications terminal equipment in the same geographical area under substantially equivalent conditions: Art.1, Satellite Directive, para.1–004, n.10.

[79] Case C–118/85 *Italy v Commission* [1987] E.C.R. 2599.

[80] Case C–302/94 *R. v Secretary of State for Trade and Industry Ex p. British Telecommunications plc (Leased Lines)* [1996] I E.C.R. 6417.

[81] Case C–202/88 *France v Commission (Terminal equipment for telecommunications)* [1991] I E.C.R. 1223; Cases C–271/90, etc. *Spain v Commission ("Telecommunications services")* [1992] I E.C.R. 5833.

[82] Case 67/96 *Albany* [1999] I E.C.R. 5751.

[83] Case C–13/77 *GB-Inno v ATAB* [1977] E.C.R. 2115; Case C–242/95 *GT Link v DSB* [1997] I E.C.R. 4449. Note also that Arts 81 and 82 continue to apply directly to all undertakings with special or exclusive rights, even if in public ownership: Case C–179/90 *Porto di Genova* [1991] I E.C.R. 5889.

[84] Case C–18/88 *RTT v GB-Inno-BM* [1991] E.C.R. 5941.

[85] Case C–323/93 *Centre d'Insémination de la Crespelle v Coopérative de la Mayenne* [1994] I E.C.R. 5077.

and to grant approvals to competing suppliers, as this enabled the RTT to reserve for itself, without objective justification, the ancillary equipment market, thereby eliminating competition in that market.[86] Similarly, Article 86 will be infringed if a Member State sets or confirms tariffs for undertakings with special or exclusive rights and such tariffs are excessive and thereby infringe Article 82.[87]

4–015 Article 86(2) of the EC Treaty: Services of General Economic Interest — Article 86(2) provides that the rules of the EC Treaty, including Articles 81, 82 and 87, apply to undertakings entrusted with the operation of services of general economic interest[88] or to revenue-producing monopolies, provided that the application of those rules does not obstruct the performance of the tasks entrusted to them. In essence, this means that such undertakings remain subject to the EC Treaty's competition rules, save where their application would prevent the performance of the public interest tasks assigned to them. However, this in turn is subject to the provision that the non-application of the EC Treaty's competition rules would not affect the development of trade to such an extent as to be contrary to the Community interest.[89] Article 86(2) may therefore be invoked to justify the grant of special or exclusive rights, provided that they have been granted by an act of public authority, such as legislation or a concession granted by public law.[90] In *Corbeau*, the Court of Justice held that Article 86(2) permits Member States to confer exclusive rights on undertakings to which they entrust the operation of a service of general economic interest (in this case, the postal service) that involves both profitable and loss-making operations, provided that restrictions on, or even the exclusion of, competition by other undertakings are necessary to ensure the performance of the particular tasks assigned to the business in question under economically acceptable conditions (*i.e.* by cross-subsidising unprofitable services with revenues from profitable services).[91]

---

[86] Case C–18/88 *RTT v GB-Inno-BM* [1991] I E.C.R. 5941.

[87] Case C–242/95 *GT Link v DSB* [1997] I E.C.R. 4449.

[88] The concept of services of general economic interest is defined in the Commission Communication on Services of General Economic Interest, COM 2000/9 O580, Annex II, O.J. 2001 C17/4, as "market services which the Member States subject to specific public service obligations by virtue of a general interest criterion". According to the case law of the Court of Justice, services of general economic interest must be generally available (Case 10/71, *Ministère public luxembourgeois v Muller* [1971] E.C.R. 723), and not be concerned with purely private interests (Case 127/73, *BRT v SABAM* [1974] E.C.R. 54). It has been held to include services such as the operation of the public telephone network (*British Telecommunications*, O.J. 1982 L360/36, upheld in Case 41/83 *Commission v Italy* [1985] E.C.R. 873) and television broadcasting (Case C–260/89 *ERT v DEP* [1991] I E.C.R. 2925). However, with liberalisation at Community level, it would appear that these older cases no longer represent the law. Thus, the Court of First Instance has held that an exclusive right to broadcast television advertising does not fall within Art.86(2): Case T–266/97, *Vlaamse Televisie Maatschappij v Commission* [1999] II E.C.R. 2329. See for the current developments: Green Paper on Services of general economic interest, below, para.7–022, n.4.

[89] Art.86(2), final sentence.

[90] Case 127/73, *BRT v SABAM* [1974] E.C.R. 313; Case C–159/94, *Commission v France* [1997] I E.C.R. 5815.

[91] Case C–320/91 *Procureur du Roi v Corbeau* [1993] I E.C.R. 2533. In this case, however, the Court considered that the application of Art.86(2) was not justified as regards specific services that would be separated from the service of general interest, which offer certain additional features not offered by the traditional postal service (*i.e.* a special "home collection" service in the city of Liège) and which, by their nature and the conditions in which they are offered, such as the geographical area in which they are provided, do not compromise the economic equilibrium of the service of general economic interest performed by the holder of the exclusive right. However, if competition in these services would adversely affect the service of general economic interest, it may be justifiable to restrict competition in the other services. See Blum and Logue, para.4–013, n.76, p.28 *et seq.*

This could be the case where the entry by a competitor exclusively into the more profitable sectors would obstruct the provision of the service of general economic interest, for example by damaging the financial equilibrium of the entrusted undertakings, such that the service could not be provided under economically acceptable conditions. For a discussion of the *Altmark Trans* case which concerns the issue of compensation payments for costs incurred for the provision of services of general economic interest and if such compensation falls under the prohibition of state aid according to Article 87(1), see Chapter VII, below.[91a] Article 86(2) has direct effect, such that national courts may apply it and decide whether an undertaking has indeed been entrusted with the operation of a service of general economic interest, and whether the requirements for the application of the derogation are met.[92] While national courts are indisputably competent to assess whether the derogation contained in Article 86(2) does not apply, the Commission has taken the position that it has exclusive jurisdiction to determine whether the "tailpiece" exception to the derogation afforded by Article 86(2) applies[93] with the result that, in case of doubt, national courts should suspend the proceeding and refer the matter to the Commission. However, in *Rendo*, the Court of First Instance settled the matter by holding that the national courts equally have the power to decide whether the Article 86(2) derogation applies in any given case.[94] It is, however, for the undertaking (or Member State) seeking to rely upon Article 86(2) to demonstrate that it satisfies the criteria laid down by Article 86(2), which will be interpreted narrowly.[95]

4–016   Article 86(3) of the EC Treaty: Enforcement of Article 86(1) of the EC Treaty — Article 86(3) requires the Commission to ensure Member States' compliance with Article 86 and empowers the Commission to adopt decisions or directives to that effect.[96] Article 86(3) is unusual under the EC Treaty in that the Commission may directly adopt legislative provisions without the need for the Council to have first adopted implementing legislation, including legislation to ensure that Member States comply with the Treaty.[97] The Court of Justice has expressly upheld the rights of the Commission to adopt legislation under Article 86(3) to require the liberalisation of the telecommunications sector,[98] provided that the Commission could withdraw special or exclusive rights only to the extent that they were specifically defined and that it could demonstrate that such rights were contrary to the EC Treaty.[99] In the case of infringements of Articles 81 or 82 by public undertakings or undertakings with special or exclusive rights, within the scope of Articles 86(1) or 86(2), Article 86(3) enables the Commission to proceed against the relevant Member State, in parallel with, or as an alternative to, a separate action against the business concerned.[1] Article 86(3)

[91a] See paras 7–021 to 7–023.

[92] Case C–393/92, *Almelo* [1994] I E.C.R. 1477.

[93] 1991 Competition Guidelines on the Application of EEC Competition Rules in the Telecommunications Sector, O.J. 1991 C233/2. This is on the basis that the Commission is the guardian of determining and protecting the Community interest.

[94] Case T–16/91, *Rendo v Commission* [1992] II E.C.R. 2417.

[95] See, *e.g., BRT v SABAM*, above, para.4–015, n.90; Case T–260/94 *Air Inter v Commission* [1997] II E.C.R. 997.

[96] In contrast with a directive, a decision addresses a specific violation by a Member State of Art.86(1) and the consequences thereof: see, *e.g., Omnitel Pronto Italia*, O.J. 1995 L280/49.

[97] Cases 188/80, etc., *France, Italy and the United Kingdom v Commission* [1982] E.C.R. 2545.

[98] Case C–202/88, *France v Commission (Terminal Equipment for Telecommunications)* [1991] I E.C.R. 1223.

[99] Cases C–271/90, etc., *Spain, Belgium and Italy v Commission (Services Directive)* [1992] I E.C.R. 5833.

[1] For example, in the telecommunications sector, the Commission's decisions in *Omnitel Pronto Italia*, above, para.4–016, n.96, and *Second GSM Licence in Spain*, O.J. 1997 L76/19; see further paras 6–060, and 6–061 *et seq.*

was the basis for the adoption by the Commission of the directives that were adopted from 1988 to 1996 to progressively open up the telecommunications sector to full competition by 1998.[2]

F. State Aid

4–017 Introduction — Articles 87–89 (*ex* Articles 92–94) lay down the rules to regulate the granting of aid to undertakings by Member States, including the circumstances in which state aid shall be prohibited and when it may be permitted or approved.[3]

4–018 Article 87(1) of the EC Treaty: General Prohibition on State Aid — Article 87(1) prohibits any aid granted by a Member State or through state resources in any form whatsoever which distorts or threatens to distort competition by favouring certain undertakings or the production of certain goods, and affects trade between Member States. The term "aid" is a broad concept. It has been applied to cover measures going beyond traditional cash injection and has been found to include investment grants, subsidies to cover operating losses, interest-free loans or loans at reduced rates of interest, preferential discount rates in respect of export credit guarantees, preferential reductions of public charges such as social security payments, preferential energy tariffs on non-commercial terms, the deferment or write-off of payment of taxes or selective tax benefits or exemptions, debt write-offs, and the provision of capital.[4] In certain circumstances, discriminatory business taxation (or other taxation, such as VAT or insurance taxes), the provision of infrastructure, the provision of land at below-market rates and guarantees may also be aid measures.[5] The funding of television channels by licence fees (a form of tax revenue) has been held to constitute state aid, assuming that all other necessary criteria are also met.[6] A measure is only state aid if it is granted by a Member State or from state resources, *i.e.* if it results in a burden on public finances from increased expenditure or reduced revenue. This covers aid granted by a government, government departments, local or regional governments, publicly-owned or controlled companies, and public or private bodies designated or established by the state.[7] No resources need actually be transferred from the state for aid to exist.[8] However, a statutory obligation imposed on undertakings to acquire goods from other undertakings at a price above the market price or above the real economic value of those goods does not involve state aid.[9]

---

[2] See, for example, Telecommunications Terminal Equipment Directive, para.1–004, n.8, and Services Directive, para.1–004, n.9.

[3] For a comprehensive review, see Evans, *EC Law of State Aid* (Clarendon Press, Oxford, 1997); Hancher, Ottervanger and Slot, *EC State Aids* (Sweet & Maxwell, 2nd ed., 1999); and Bellamy and Child, para.4–001, n.4, Chap.19.

[4] Bellamy and Child, para.4–001, n.4, para.19–023, citing the relevant case law of the Court of Justice.

[5] *ibid.*, paras 19–024 to 19–028.

[6] Case 70/98, *Kinderkanal and Phoenix*, XXIXth Report on Competition Policy (1999), at point 226 and Case 88/98 *BBC News 24 (TV Licence fees)*, available at *http://europa.eu.int/comm/secretariat_general/sgb/state_aids/industrie/nno88-98.pdf*.

[7] Cases C–72 and 73/91, *Sloman Neptun v Bodo Ziesemer* [1993] I E.C.R. 887 and Case T–358/94, *Air France v Commission (Caisse des Dépôts et Consignations)* [1996] II E.C.R. 2109.

[8] Case C–387/92, *Banco Exterior de España v Ayuntamiento de Valencia* [1994] I E.C.R. 887.

[9] Case C–379/98, *PreussenElektra v Schleswag* [2001] I E.C.R. 2099 (statutory obligation to purchase electricity from renewable sources at above market prices).

4–019 It is not always easy to determine whether a certain state measure or intervention constitutes state aid. The overriding principle is that the measure or intervention will be assessed by reference to its effects, rather than its legal form. State aid exists when an undertaking receives a benefit that mitigates the charges that would normally be included in its budget,[10] by which it is able to improve its financial position and/or reduce its costs of operation.[11] The key is whether the funds provided go beyond a normal commercial transaction. Accordingly, for capital transfers or the provision of loans to or the acquisition of shares in an undertaking, for example, the Commission and the Court of Justice apply the so-called "market economy investor principle".[12] According to this principle, whenever state resources are contributed in a manner which would be acceptable to a private investor operating under normal market economy conditions and making funds available to a private undertaking, no advantage is conferred, and therefore, there is no state aid. In applying the market economy investor principle, regard must be had to the information available and foreseeable developments at the time, and it must be considered whether the state will receive an acceptable return on the funds provided by it within a reasonable time, although this can take account of investors' long-term views of making an adequate return.[13] In view of the still significant involvement of the Member States in the communications and broadcasting sectors, and considering the very recent liberalisation of these markets and the financial difficulties of many operators, this principle is particularly relevant.[14]

4–020 Assuming that a specific state measure or intervention constitutes aid within the meaning of Article 87(1), it would be unlawful only if it distorts competition (or threatens to do so) by favouring certain undertakings or the production of certain goods, *i.e.* the act must be "specific" to a specific undertaking, or to a group of undertakings in a specific industry or region. Accordingly, an aid that applies to all undertakings without any restriction would not be prohibited by

[10] Case C–30/59, *Steenkolenmijnen v High Authority* [1961] E.C.R. 95.

[11] Case C–39/94, *SFEI v La Poste* [1996] I E.C.R. 3547. The benefit may be permanent or of a limited duration: Case T–67/94, *Ladbroke Racing v Commission* [1998] II E.C.R. 1.

[12] See in particular the Commission Communication to the Member States on the application of Arts 92 and 93 of the EC Treaty and of Art.5 of Commission Directive 80/723 to public undertakings in the manufacturing sector, O.J. 1993 C307/3. Although this Communication is limited to the manufacturing sector and public undertakings, the market economy principle itself is applied more broadly, as the Communication itself states in para.3. Some of the most recent cases confirming and explaining the scope of the market economy principle include: Case C–482/99, *France v Commission (Stardust Marine)* [2002] I E.C.R. 4397 (the Commission must consider the measures in the context of the period in which they were granted) and Case T–323/99 *Industrie Navali Meccaniche Affini SpA (INMA) and Italia Investimenti SpA (Itainvest) v Commission (Itainvest)* [2002] II E.C.R. 545.

[13] Case T–296/97, *Alitalia v Commission* [2000] II E.C.R. 3871.

[14] See, for example, the rescue aid granted to the German operator, MobilCom. The Commission had approved €50 million of rescue aid to MobilCom and opened an investigation into a further €112 million of funding provided by the German Government: Commission Press Release IP/03/92 of January 21, 2003 and O.J. 2003 C210/4. The Commission has also announced an in-depth investigation into possible state aid in relation to the French Government's provision of up to €9 billion of funding to France Télécom to cover its debts: Commission Press Release IP/03/150 of January 30, 2003. The Commission has also investigated or is investigating a number of cases of state aid in the broadcasting sector, for example the funding of the BBC's new digital television and radio channels by way of a licence fee (which was held not to involve state aid) decision of May 22, 2002, available at *http://europa.eu.int/comm/secretariat_general/sgb/state_aids/industrie_2002.htm* and state funding of TV2 in Denmark (proceedings were opened on January 21, 2003, see Commission Press Release IP/03/91).

Article 87(1). Determining whether a state intervention constitutes a general measure or favours certain undertakings or sectors is difficult; valuable guidance on where to draw this distinction can be found in the Commission's notice on business taxation.[15]

To be within the scope of Article 87(1), an aid measure must also affect trade between Member States.[16] This means that the aid measure must be "capable" of affecting inter-state trade, including potential effects upon future trade patterns.[17] Trade will be affected for the purposes of Article 87(1) if an aid measure would make it more difficult for imported products to compete with the recipient's own products or services.[18] Therefore, also a non-appreciable effect on trade is caught by Article 87(1), as even small amounts of aid given to small producers can distort or threaten to distort competition and thereby affect inter-state trade.[19]

4–021   Articles 87(2) and 87(3) of the EC Treaty: Aid That Is or May Be Compatible — Article 87 lists types of aid that are compatible as such with the common market or that may be declared compatible by the Commission or the Council. Article 87(2) lists three types of aid that are deemed compatible with the common market:

(i)   aid having a social character, granted to individual consumers, provided that such aid is granted without discrimination in relation to the origin of the products concerned;

(ii) aid to make good the damage caused by natural disasters or exceptional occurrences; and

(iii) aid granted to the economy of certain areas of the former East Germany affected by the former division of Germany.

Article 87(3) sets out a number of types of aid that may be compatible with the common market, provided that this is justified in each case. The Commission may authorise four types of aid:

(i)   aid for very depressed regions;

(ii) aid to promote an important European project or to remedy a serious disturbance in a Member State;

(iii) sectoral and regional aids which do not adversely affect trading conditions to an extent contrary to the common interest; and

(iv) aid to promote culture and heritage conservation where such aid does not affect trading conditions and competition in the Community to an extent contrary to the common interest.[20]

---

[15] Commission notice on the application of the state aid rules to measures relating to direct business taxation, O.J. 1998 C384/3, para.13–27.

[16] On the concept of effect on trade between Member States, see above, para.4–003, n.17.

[17] Case T–447/93 *AITEC v Commission* [1995] II E.C.R. 1971.

[18] Case 102/87, *France v Commission (FIM)* [1988] E.C.R. 4067.

[19] Case 259/85, *France v Commission* [1987] E.C.R. 4393. See however, Commission Regulation 69/2001 of January 12, 2001 on *de minimis* rule for state aid, O.J. 2001 L10/30: aid measures granted to an undertaking that are less than €100,000 over a three-year period fall outside of Art.87(1).

[20] Art.87(3)(a)–(d).

As these are derogations from Article 87(1), they must be interpreted strictly. The Council (acting by qualified majority following a proposal by the Commission) may specify other categories of aid that may be considered compatible with the common market.[21] The Council may, upon application by a Member State, also authorise aid in exceptional circumstances, provided it acts unanimously.[22] The Commission has issued several notices, communications, guidelines and regulations on how it applies the exemptions contained in Article 87(3). In the communications sector the guidelines for rescuing and restructuring firms in difficulty may also be relevant.[23] Article 86(2) may be applicable in such a way that state aid provided to an undertaking entrusted with services of general economic interest in order to fund such services falls outside the scope of Article 87(1).[24]

4–022   Article 88 of the EC Treaty: Procedural Aspects of State Aid Law — Article 88 and Regulation 659/1999[25] contain rules relating to the review and notification of state aids. The Commission is obliged to keep under constant review all systems of aid existing in the Member States,[26] *i.e.* aid measures in operation as at the date on which the EC Treaty came into operation in the relevant Member State or aid which has been approved by the Commission or the Council.[27] Such aid is not subject to notification to the Commission, but may still be reviewed by it. New aid measures and alterations to existing aid measures that are contemplated by a Member State must be notified to the Commission and may not be implemented until the Commission has authorised them.[28] The Member States themselves need to assess whether a specific measure constitutes or may constitute aid, which will include an assessment of whether it can be regarded as normal economic conduct in light of the market economy investor principle or as a measure of general application. If a Member State concludes that a proposed measure does not constitute state aid, a notification is not required, although it is common for Member States to make "failsafe" notifications. However, the Commission may investigate on its own initiative whether a state measure constitutes state aid and if the Commission, and ultimately the Court of Justice, find that it does, the measure will be considered to constitute a state aid measure that was unlawfully granted if it has not previously been notified.

---

[21] Art.87(3)(e).

[22] Art.88(2), third sub-para. This can include overruling a decision by the Commission to prohibit aid.

[23] Community guidelines on state aid for rescuing and restructuring firms in difficulty (notice to Member States including proposals for appropriate measures), O.J. 1999 C288/2. Other administrative acts that might be applicable: state aid and risk capital, O.J. 2001 C235/3; Commission Regulation 70/2001 of January 12, 2001 on the application of Arts 87 and 88 of the EC Treaty to state aid to small and medium-sized enterprises, O.J. 2001 L10/33; Commission Regulation 68/2001 of January 12, 2001 on the application of Arts 87 and 88 of the EC Treaty to training aid, O.J. 2001 L10/20; Community framework for state aid for research and development, O.J. 1996 C45/6; Guidelines on aid to employment, O.J. 1995 C334/4.

[24] Case T–106/95, *FFSA v Commission* [1997] II E.C.R. 229 (tax concessions to French post office justified by need to offset additional costs of performing its public service obligations). See also Commission Discussion Paper of November 12, 2002, "Services of general economic interest and State aid", available at: *http://europa.eu.int/comm/competition/state_aid/others/1759_sieg_en.pdf*. See also Case C–280/00, *Altmark Trans* [2003] (not yet reported in the E.C.R.), discussed below, paras 7–021 to 7–023.

[25] Council Regulation 659/1999 of March 22, 1999 laying down detailed rules for the application of Art.93 of the EC Treaty, O.J. 1999 L83/1.

[26] Art.88(1) of the EC Treaty.

[27] Regulation 659/1999, Art.1.

[28] Art.88(3) of the EC Treaty and Art.2 of Regulation 659/1999.

The Commission has a period of two months to conduct a preliminary investigation and deter-mine whether to close the procedure or to open formal investigation proceedings under Article 88(2), if it considers that the aid is *prima facie* incompatible with the common market or if the Commission has not been able to take a position after its preliminary review.[29] The formal investigation should be completed within a maximum duration of 18 months, although the Commission may exceed this limit in certain circumstances.[30] These deadlines do not apply if the aid measure was applied unlawfully, *i.e.* without having been first notified and either cleared or approved by the Commission. In addition, unlawfully implemented aid can be restrained by the Commission adopting interim measures,[31] or by national courts, as Article 88 has direct effect. National courts may also award damages to competitors who suffer loss due to an unlawful implementation of state aid.[32]

4–023 Article 88(1) requires the Commission to keep existing aid — *i.e.* aid which was already in place when the EC Treaty entered into force or which has been approved by the Commission or the Council — under review. If, after giving notice to the Member State concerned to submit its comments, the Commission finds that an existing aid is no longer compatible with the common market, or misuses existing aid, it must adopt a recommendation proposing appropriate measures for the Member State to abolish or alter the aid scheme within a time period determined by the Commission.[33] If the Member State does not implement the Commission's recommendation, or misuses existing aid, the Commission may initiate a formal investigation under Article 88(2).[34] Existing aid measures may be implemented provided the Commission has not found them to be incompatible with the common market. The Commission must close a formal investigation (whether into existing or new aid) by adopting a decision: that there is no aid; that the measure is compatible with the common market (taking account of any modifications); or that the measure is incompatible with the common market and should not be implemented.[35] Approval decisions may be made subject to conditions.

4–024 Specific rules applying to state aid to the broadcasting sector — Apart from the general rules on state aid, there are some specific rules that apply to state aid in the broadcasting sector. Protocol 32 to the Amsterdam Treaty refers to the specific role of public broadcasting.[36] Protocol 32 is appended to the EC Treaty, and provides that the provisions of the EC Treaty (including Articles 87 to 90 on state aid) are without prejudice to the Member States' ability to fund public service broadcasting. In addition, the Commission issued a "Communication on the application of State aid rules to public service broadcasting" on November 15, 2001,[37] which sets out how the

[29] *ibid.*, Art.4(4). Many cases are subject to a formal review, owing to their complexity making it impossible for the Commission to reach a final view on whether a measure is not aid, is compatible aid or is aid which raises serious doubts.
[30] *ibid.*, Art.7.
[31] *ibid.*, Arts 10 and 11.
[32] Case C–39/94, *SFEI* [1996] I E.C.R. 3547, *per* Jacobs AG.
[33] Regulation 659/1999, para.4–022, n.25, Arts 17 and 18.
[34] *ibid.*, Arts 16 and 19(2).
[35] *ibid.*, Art.7.
[36] Protocol on the system of public broadcasting in the Member States, attached to the Treaty of Amsterdam, amending the Treaty on European Union, the Treaties establishing the European Communities and certain acts, signed in Amsterdam on October 2, 1997, O.J. 1997 C340/109.
[37] O.J. 2001 C320/5.

Commission will apply the EC Treaty's state aid rules to the state financing of public service broadcasters and their compatibility with the EC Treaty under Article 86(2). These specific instruments are considered in more detail in Chapter VII, below.[38]

G. Merger Control Regulation

4–025 Pursuant to the "Merger Control Regulation",[39] concentrations that meet certain worldwide and Community-wide turnover thresholds (the so-called "Community dimension") must be notified to the Commission and may not, without a derogation, be implemented before receiving Commission approval.[40] Failure to notify a concentration when required to do so and infringement of such suspension obligations may result in the imposition of fines upon the undertakings concerned.[41] With a view to accommodating business concerns for the rapid approval and implementation of concentrations, the Commission is subject to strict deadlines to complete its investigation and adopt a decision. The Commission has an initial period (known as "Phase I") of one month to adopt one of the following decisions: (i) the transaction is not within the scope of the Merger Control Regulation; (ii) approval of the concentration, with or without commitments (remedies); or (iii) indicating that it has serious doubts about the concentration, thereby opening a four-month formal investigation (known as "Phase II").[42] At the end of Phase II, the Commission must either approve (with or without commitments) or prohibit the concentration.[43]

The Merger Control Regulation applies to so-called "concentrations", a concept that covers mergers and acquisitions as well as the formation of joint ventures that are autonomous economic entities.[44] The Commission is required to assess whether the concentration will create or strengthen a dominant position as a result of which effective competition would be significantly impeded within the common market or a substantial part of it. This involves the definition of the relevant product and geographic market, on which to assess the effects of the concentration on competition. A dominant position may be created or strengthened due to horizontal, vertical or conglomerate effects. Dominance may be enjoyed by an undertaking (single-firm dominance) or by two or more undertakings together (joint or collective dominance). When the Commission considers that the concentration will lead to the creation or strengthening of a dominant position, it must prohibit it, unless the parties offer commitments to enable the Commission to approve it subject to certain conditions (*e.g.* divestiture of certain assets).[45]

4–026 In the case of joint ventures reviewed under the Merger Control Regulation, the Commission must also consider the risk of co-ordination of the independent activities of the

---

[38] See para.7–020 *et seq.*
[39] Council Regulation 4064/89 of December 21, 1989 on the control of concentrations between undertakings, O.J. 1989 L395/1, as amended by Council Regulation 1310/97 of June 30, 1997, O.J. 1997 L180/1.
[40] *ibid.*, Arts 4 and 7.
[41] Up to a maximum of €50,000 for failure to notify (Art.14(1) of the Merger Control Regulation, *ibid.*) and up to a maximum of 10 per cent of the aggregate worldwide turnover of the undertakings concerned in the case of implementation of a concentration before receipt of Commission approval (Art.14(2), *ibid.*).
[42] *ibid.*, Arts 6(1) and 10(1).
[43] *ibid.*, Arts 8 and 10.
[44] *ibid.*, Art.3.
[45] *ibid.*, Art.8.

parent companies and the joint venture, according to the principles of Article 81(1) and 81(3) of the EC Treaty.[46] The Merger Control Regulation created a "one-stop shop" for the review of concentrations with a Community dimension. Subject to certain limited exceptions,[47] Member States may not apply national competition laws to a concentration with a Community dimension.[48] The application of the Merger Control Regulation in the telecommunications, internet and broadcasting sectors is considered in detail in Chapter VIII.[49]

[46] *ibid.*, Art.2(4).

[47] *ibid.*, Art.4 (reference back in full or in part to the national competition authorities of one or more Member States for them to review the transaction under national competition law) and Art.21(3) (ability of Member States to take measures to protect legitimate interests other than those protected under the Merger Control Regulation).

[48] *ibid.*, Art.21(1) and (2).

[49] For a detailed review of the Merger Control Regulation, see Hawk and Huser, *European Community Merger Control: A Practitioner's Guide* (Kluwer Law International, 1996); Cook and Kerse, *EC Merger Control* (Sweet and Maxwell, 1996); Briones, Folguera, Font and Navarro, *Merger Control in the EU* (Oxford University Press, 2002).

Chapter V

Market Definition in the Telecommunications Sector

A. Introduction

5–001 Market definition is key to the application of competition rules. Indeed, in order to assess the effects of an agreement or concerted practice on competition for the purposes of Article 81 of the EC Treaty, and to assess whether there is a dominant position and if so an abuse of it within the meaning of Article 82 of the EC Treaty or whether a concentration could lead to the creation or strengthening of a dominant position for the purposes of the Merger Control Regulation, it is essential to first define the relevant product and geographic market(s) on which these actions may have an impact. The main purpose of market definition is to identify the competitive constraints faced by the undertakings involved, in particular their actual competitors that are capable of constraining their conduct and thus of preventing them from behaving independently of effective competitive pressure.[1] This is why an accurate market definition is the cornerstone for the correct assessment of the competitive impact of an agreement, practice, market conduct or a concentration. The broader the market definition, the less likely competition concerns will be identified. The methodology of the Commission in defining the relevant market does not substantially differ depending on whether it is applying Article 81, Article 82 or the Merger Control Regulation or other Community Competition law.[2] Accordingly, the content of this section will be equally valid in the

---

[1] Commission Notice on the definition of the recent market for the purposes of Community Competition law, O.J. 1997 C372/5, para.2.

[2] *ibid.*, para.1. In Case T–29/92, *SPO v Commission* [1995] II E.C.R. 289, the Court of First Instance stated (para.74) that the approach to defining the relevant market differs according to whether Art.81 or Art.82 of the EC Treaty is to be applied. In the Court's view, when applying Art.81, the purpose of market definition is to determine whether the agreement, decision or concerted practice under review is likely to affect trade between Member States and appreciably prevent, restrict or distort competition in the Common Market. By contrast, in Art.82 cases, market definition is a necessary precondition to determining the effects of allegedly anti-competitive behaviour; before this analysis can be undertaken, it must first be ascertained that a dominant position exists, which requires the relevant market to be identified. However Bellamy and Child, *European Community Law of Competition* (5th ed., Sweet & Maxwell, 2001) at 6–093 *et seq.*, state that although the purpose of market definition is different as between the two provisions, it is not clear how it is suggested that

framework of the assessment of market conduct, alliances and mergers and acquisitions under Articles 81 and 82, and the Merger Control Regulation reviewed in Chapters VI, VII and VIII, respectively. If the Commission fails to define properly the relevant market, its decisions may be annulled,[3] except if this does not substantially affect the analysis of the agreement, practice, conduct or concentration under review,[4] or (in Article 81 cases) if it is self-evident that an agreement that contains a "hard-core" restriction will have an appreciable effect upon competition and inter-state trade.[5] Market definition is also relevant for regulatory purposes, as it is key to determining which undertakings are dominant and which have SMP, as only undertakings with SMP can have *ex ante* regulatory obligations imposed on them by NRAs under the New Regulatory Framework.[6]

B. Guidelines on the Definition of the Relevant Product Market

5–002 The relevant market within which to assess a given competition issue is established by a combination of the product and geographic markets. A relevant product market comprises all the products or services that are considered by users as substitutes given their characteristics, prices and uses.[7] A relevant geographic market is a specific geographic area where businesses are competing in the supply of products or services to users.[8] Undertakings are subject to three types of competitive constraint, which are analysed in determining the relevant product and geographic markets: demand substitutability, supply substitutability and potential competition.

Demand-side substitutability (*i.e.* the ability of consumers to switch to substitute products that they consider sufficiently similar in function, price and attributes in case of a small non-transitory price increase) is the primary criterion used by the Commission in defining the relevant product market when applying EU competition law. Demand-side substitution is the most immediate and effective competitive force on the supplier of a given product.[9]

---

the definition itself should be different. It is interesting to note that the Commission Notice on Market Definition, n.1, above, makes the methodology for defining the relevant market equally relevant to the application of Arts 81 and 82 and the Merger Control Regulation. The Commission notes, however (*ibid.*, para.12), that the methodology may lead to different results, depending on the competition issue being examined. For example, the scope of the geographic market might be different when analysing a concentration where the analysis is essentially prospective, from an analysis of past behaviour under Arts 81 or 82. For a criticism of the Commission's position on this point, see Baker and Wu, "Applying the Market Definition Guidelines of the European Commission" (1998) E.C.L.R. 273.

[3] Case 6/72, *Europemballage and Continental Car v Commission* [1973] E.C.R. 215; Cases T–68/89, etc., *Società Italiano Ventro v Commission (Italian Flat Glass)* [1992] II E.C.R. 1403.

[4] Case T–7/93, *Langnese-Iglo v Commission* [1995] II E.C.R. 1533 and Case T–9/93 *Schöller v Commission* [1995] II E.C.R. 1611.

[5] Case T–62 *Volkswagen v Commission* [2000] II E.C.R. 2707.

[6] See para.1–040 *et seq.*

[7] The Commission defines the relevant product market as comprising "all those products and/or services which are regarded as interchangeable or substitutable by the consumer, by reason of the products' characteristics, their prices and their intended use": Commission Notice on Market Definition, para.5–001, n.1, para.7.

[8] The Commission defines the relevant geographic market as "the area in which the undertakings concerned are involved in the supply and demand of products or services, in which the conditions of competition are sufficiently homogeneous and which can be distinguished from neighbouring areas because the conditions of competition are appreciably different in those areas": *ibid.*, para.8.

[9] *ibid.*, para.13.

Supply-side substitutability (*i.e.* the ability of suppliers of products that are not demand substitutes to adjust their production resources to produce the products that are demand substitutes and to market them in the short term without incurring significant additional costs or risks in response to small and permanent changes in relative prices) is rarely taken into consideration when defining the relevant market. Rather, it is used at a later stage to assess the impact of the agreement or market conduct on the competitive structure of the market concerned.[10] Supply-side substitutability will only be taken into account where its effects are equivalent to those of demand-side substitutability.

5–003 The standard test to measure the demand-side substitutability of products, to assess whether they can be considered as substitutes for the users, and the geographic dimension of the market is the analysis of customers' responses to a hypothetical small (in the range of 5–10%) but permanent price increase in the product to be considered. If a sufficient number of customers would switch to alternative products or other suppliers of the same product located elsewhere to make the price increase unprofitable because of the resulting loss of sales, these alternative products or geographic areas must be included in the relevant market. This analysis is repeated until alternative substitutes or additional geographic areas are such that a permanent increase in prices would be profitable.[11] For example, in the beverage sector, the analysis could start with mineral water and be extended gradually to the different types of soft drinks, carbonated beverages and other types of beverage. In addition to the standard hypothetical price increase test defined above, the Commission will also rely on other types of evidence in defining the relevant product market: (i) evidence of substitution in the recent past; (ii) the views of customers and competitors; (iii) consumer preferences; (iv) barriers to entry and switching, and the costs associated with switching to potential substitutes; (v) different categories of customers and price discrimination between them.[12] The geographic product market will generally be defined on the basis of the following elements: (i) past evidence of orders to other areas; (ii) basic demand characteristics (*i.e.* national preferences, preferences for national brands, language, culture and life style, need for local presence); (iii) views of customers and competitors; (iv) current geographic pattern of purchases; (v) barriers to entry and the costs associated with switching to companies located in other areas (such as the need for a local presence, the costs of distribution networks, and regulatory and other barriers to trade).[13]

---

[10] *ibid.*, para.14. Supply-side substitution will be taken into account when defining the market only when suppliers can switch production and start supplying the relevant products in the short term without incurring significant additional costs or risks in response to small and permanent changes in relative prices. This may be the case when companies manufacture a wide range of qualities or grades of one type of product; even if, for a given final customer or group of consumers, the different qualities or grades are not substitutable, the different qualities or grades will form a single product market, provided that most suppliers are able to offer and sell the various qualities or grades immediately. For instance, the Commission has taken the position that different grades and qualities of paper formed part of the same product market, as manufacturers would use their paper mills to manufacture a wide range of grades and qualities, and were in fact able to readily switch production between them: Case M.166, *Torras/Sarrio*, Commission Decision of February 24, 1992. The same was true of still and sparkling water: Case M.1065, *Nestlé/San Pellegrino*, Commission Decision of February 16, 1998. However, supply-sided substitutability does not necessarily exist between similar products. For example, there is not supply-side substitutability between car and truck tyres, owing to the differences in the production techniques and the machinery needed: Case 322/81, *Michelin v Commission* [1983] E.C.R. 3461.

[11] *ibid.*, para.17.

[12] *ibid.*, para.36 *et seq.*

[13] *ibid.*, para.44 *et seq.*

Although different products may have some demand-side and/or supply-side substitutability, they may nevertheless be in distinct product markets, due to specific characteristics of the products that justify finding of distinct (narrow) product markets. Thus, auditing services for large companies constituted a separate product market from other auditing services, owing to the special skills needed to audit big companies.[14] Similarly, as the provision of internet services at different levels had different characteristics (such as the number and size of suppliers and barriers to entry), the Commission found a number of distinct product markets for internet access, including for "top-level" internet access.[15] Even if there are substitutable products, a narrow market definition may be appropriate; for example, cellular digital mobile services were considered to be part of a separate market from both fixed network services and analogue mobile services.[16]

C. The Definition of the Relevant Market in the Telecommunications Sector

5–004 Market definition is a highly contextual exercise and it can only be undertaken with precision in the framework of specific cases. This is particularly true in the telecommunications sector, given the rapid development and the constant evolution of new products and services. The Commission provided some guidance on its approach to market definition in the sector in its 1991 Competition Guidelines on the Application of EC Competition Rules in the Telecommunications Sector (the "1991 Competition Guidelines")[17] and in its Notice on the Application of the Competition Rules to Access Agreements in the Telecommunications Sector (the "Access Notice").[18] With the convergence of sector-specific rules and competition law, in particular as regards the definition and the assessment of the relevant markets under the New Regulatory Framework for electronic communications, the Commission's SMP Guidelines[19] provide an important source of reference, as does the Commission Recommendation on relevant product and service markets.[20] The Commission, the Court of Justice and the Court of First Instance's case law on market definition in the telecommunications sector also provides important guidance.

5–005 Convergence between sector-specific regulation and competition law in the definition of the relevant market — The Framework Directive requires the NRAs to define the relevant markets for the application of *ex ante* regulation according to the concepts of competition law.[21] The use of the same market definition methodologies for both regulatory and competition law purposes will ensure that the relevant market defined for the purpose of sector-specific regulation will generally

---

[14] Case M.1016, *Price Waterhouse/Coopers & Lybrand*, O.J. 1999 L50/27.
[15] Case M.1069, *WorldCom/MCI*, O.J. 1999 L116/1.
[16] *GSM, Radio telephony services in Italy*, O.J. 1995 L280/49.
[17] O.J. 1991 C233/2.
[18] O.J. 1998 C265/2.
[19] SMP Guidelines, para.1–012, n.35.
[20] Recommendation on Relevant Markets, para.1–012, n.36.
[21] See para.1–021 *et seq.* In this regard, it should be recalled that the services in respect of which *ex ante* regulation was imposed under the 1998 Regulatory Framework were not necessarily markets for competition law purposes, since they were based on certain specific aspects of end-to-end communications rather than on the demand- and supply-side criteria used in competition law analysis.

correspond to the relevant market defined for the purposes of competition law.[22] In some cases, however, markets defined by the Commission and the national competition authorities in applying competition law proceedings may differ from those identified by the NRAs for the purposes of the New Regulatory Framework, and in particular from the list of markets included in the Commission Recommendation on the Relevant Markets.[23] Indeed, the latter identifies those product services in respect of which *ex ante* regulation may be imposed, *i.e.* those that meet the three criteria set by the Commission, namely: (i) the existence of high and non-transitory barriers to entry (whether structural, legal or regulatory); (ii) the continuing lack of effective competion over time, taking into consideration the dynamic aspects of the concerned markets; and (iii) the inadequacy of competition law (absent *ex ante* regulation) to remedy enduring situations of market failure.[24] Market definition for the purposes of *ex ante* regulation is discussed in Chapter I.[25]

The Commission's SMP Guidelines (which will be updated regularly by the Commission) for the application of sector-specific regulation also constitute a document of practical relevance to the definition of relevant markets for the purposes of applying competition law, at least in so far as they are explicitly based on the prior decision-making practice of the Commission and the case law of the Court of Justice and the Court of First Instance.

5–006 1991 Competition Guidelines and Access Notice — In the 1991 Competition Guidelines, the Commission indicated that distinct product or service markets could exist at least for terrestrial network (facilities) provision, voice communication services, data communication services and satellites.[26] In this respect, the 1991 Competition Guidelines are already considerably outdated. For example, although the Commission was essentially targeting the public switched telephone networks (PSTNs) of incumbent telecommunications operators, the market for terrestrial networks should be extended to include cable networks as they have been technically adjusted to provide point-to-point telecommunication services (*e.g.* voice telephony). Likewise, the distinction made in the 1991 Competition Guidelines and the Access Notice between voice and data communications has become somewhat blurred, as technology now permits voice communication to be made in packet-switched mode (*e.g.* internet voice telephony). The SMP Guidelines, which were adopted in 2003, are based on the principle of technology neutrality and take into account the convergence process between telecommunications and media communications.

5–007 Market definition in the context of convergence — The rapid and complex technological and market developments taking place in the communications sector are making market definition an extremely complicated exercise. The implementation of new, in particular digital, technologies has completely transformed the telecommunications and broadcasting industries, which until

---

[22] See SMP Guidelines, para.1–012, n.35, para.37, where the Commission encourages NRAs to ensure consistency between the definition of the markets in sector-specific regulation and competition law.

[23] Art.15(1) of the Framework Directive, para.1–009, n.25, which makes clear that the markets defined by NRAs for the purposes of that Directive are without prejudice to those defined by the national competition authorities and by the Commission in the exercise of their respective powers under competition law in specific cases.

[24] Commission's Recommendation on the Relevant Markets, para.1–012, n.36, para.9.

[25] See para.1–021 *et seq.*

[26] 1991 Competition Guidelines, para.5–004, n.17.

recently were characterised by a rather stable environment. These developments have placed an enormous strain on the capacity of competition and regulatory authorities to assess adequately the structure of emerging markets. This is particularly true as regards the assessment of mergers and joint ventures under the Merger Control Regulation, where the Commission has to undertake a dynamic and prospective (*i.e.* forward-looking) definition and analysis of markets which are very new and constantly changing. This is an important challenge for competition authorities, as erroneous market definitions inevitably lead to mistakes in the competitive assessment of transactions and possibly to unwarranted prohibition decisions.[27] In this respect, it has been suggested that the complexity of the convergence process will require competition authorities to possess expertise not only in the application of competition rules, but also in the sectors concerned.[28]

5–008 Market definition is evolving with technological developments — In the Access Notice and the SMP Guidelines, the Commission acknowledges that, given the pace of technological change in the communications sector, any attempt to define particular product markets in its Notices and Guidelines would involve the risk of the definitions rapidly becoming inaccurate and irrelevant.[29] The decision-making practice of the Commission reflects the impact of the rapid technological evolution on market definition. For example, although the Commission had initially considered that each type of mobile communications system (*i.e.* analogue and digital) formed a separate product market,[30] it has subsequently found that at least analogue and digital mobile systems belong to the same product market in light of the technological evolution towards the integration of all these systems into one single product.[31] It has also indicated that it is ready to identify

[27] Larouche, para.1–001, n.1, p.230, suggests that, in *MSG*, O.J. 1996 L364/1, the Commission defined the relevant product market (for cable television networks in Germany) according to short-term rather than long-term considerations, by deciding that cable TV networks in Germany belonged to a separate market or were distinct from other technical means of delivering broadcasting to the consumer such as satellite and terrestrial transmission networks. According to Larouche, such a market definition according to technology is inherently unstable, especially if it is considered that the introduction of digital technology is likely to result in a complete renewal of customer equipment in the medium to long term. By wrongly defining the relevant market, the Commission wrongly prohibited the merger. For a review of the *MSG* decision, see para.8–171 *et seq.*

[28] Bazanella and Gerard, "Enjeux et conséquences juridiques de la convergence technologique entre les télécommunications et l'audiovisuel", in *Télécommunications et Audiovisuel: convergence de vues?* (Poullet and Queck, Dirs, 1996), pp.13–33; KPMG "*Public Issues Arising from Telecommunications and Audiovisual Convergence*" (1996), report for the European Commission.

[29] SMP Guidelines para.1–012, n.35, para.47; and Access Notice, para.5–004, n.18.

[30] 1991 Competition Guidelines, para.5–004, n.17. See also *GSM Radiotelephony services in Italy*, above, para.5–003, n.16.

[31] See Case M.1055, *Cégétel/Vodafone/SFR*, Commission Decision of December 19, 1997; Case M.1177, *Belgacom/TeleDanmark/Tulip*, Commission Decision of May 19, 1998; Case JV.2, *Enel/FT/DT*, Decision of June 22, 1998; Case M.1430, *Vodafone/AirTouch*, Commission Decision of May 21, 1999; and Case M.1669, *Deutsche Telekom/One2One*, Commission Decision of September 27, 1999. See, by contrast, the position of the Commission in *Omnitel*, Decision of April 10, 1995, O.J. 1995 L280/49, where the Commission took the position that analogue mobile was probably a separate market from that of digital cellular because: (i) GSM is pan-European; (ii) it permits transmission of large quantities of data; and (iii) it is more secure. The decision of the Commission in *BiB*, O.J. 1998 C322/6, provides another illustration of the impact of the technological evolution on market definition. In this case, the Commission distinguished between online services delivered via television sets from those delivered via PCs because of the different market penetration between TVs and

separate markets for international wholesale roaming services,[32] seamless pan-European mobile communications services (in particular to large corporate customers),[33] wholesale access for short messages services (SMS) to mobile telephony infrastructure,[34] and, lastly, wireless local area networks (WLAN).[35] The continuing convergence of networks (*i.e.* the ability of different network platforms to carry similar kinds of services) and equipment (*i.e.* the amalgamation of consumer devices such as the telephone, television and personal computer) has a great impact on market definition. For example, the Commission's platform-dependent definition of telecommunications services as those transmitted over the public telecommunications network has become obsolete, given that existing services (*e.g.* voice telephony) are now supplied over different types of established network (PSTNs, cable and utilities networks). A packet-switched network, such as the internet, may be used to transit digitised voice signals in competition with traditional voice telephony. Likewise, according to the Commission, it cannot be excluded that in the future xDSL (different variations of Digital Subscriber Line) technology and multi-point video distribution services based on wireless local loops may be used for the transmission of broadcast material in direct competition with other existing television transmission systems, such as delivery systems cable, direct-to-home (DTH) satellite transmission and terrestrial analogue or digital transmission platforms.[36]

5–009 Criteria most commonly used by the Commission to define the relevant market — In line with the methodology set out in its Notice on Market Definition, the Commission relies primarily on demand-side substitutability to defining the relevant product market. For example, in *Omnitel*,[37] the Commission based its market definition on the fact that fixed and mobile telephony belonged to different product markets as there was no demand-substitution between them.[38] Evidence showed that customers do not generally cancel a fixed telephone subscription when they buy a mobile telephone. Other criteria taken into consideration by the Commission are: (i) price differentials between products (*e.g.* fixed and mobile telephony)[39]; (ii) different payment structures (*e.g.* cable

PCs and the different prices, characteristics and uses of TVs and PCs with a resulting consumer demand for TV-based services and PC-based services. The Commission, however, noted that its position may change over time as internet access via television will become more widely available in the short to medium term. Likewise, in Case M.1263, *Nortel/Bay*, Commission Decision of August 21, 1998, the Commission noted that, given the evolutionary nature of the information technology business, data networking products change rapidly as new technologies could offer potential benefits resulting in new data networking products.

[32] See Case M.2726, *KPN/E-Plus*, Commission Decision of March 7, 2000; Case M.1863, *Vodafone/BT/Airtel*, decision of December 18, 2000; Case M.2469, *Vodafone/Airtel*, Commission Decision of June 26, 2001; and Case M.2803, *Telia/Sonera*, Commission Decision of May 28, 2002.
[33] See Case M.1795, *Vodafone/Mannesmann*, Commission Decision of April 12, 2000; Case M.2016, *FranceTélécom/Orange*, decision of August 11, 2000; Case M.2305, *Vodafone/Eircell*, decision of March 2, 2001; and Case M.2469, *Vodafone/Airtel*, decision of June 26, 2001.
[34] See Case M.2598, *TDC/CMG/MIGway/JV*, decision of October 4, 2000, where the Commission indicated that such a market is pan-European in scope.
[35] See Case M.2803, *Telia/Sonera*, Commission Decision of May 28, 2002, where the Commission left open the question of whether WLAN can be considered as a separate market. WLAN is a technology used to provide two functionalities: (a) network access at public locations for broadband internet access; and (b) network access in buildings to avoid cabling. It is used for data communication, not for voice.
[36] SMP Guidelines, para.1–012, n.35, n.35.
[37] Commission Decision of October 4, 1995, O.J. 1995 L280/49.
[38] The same conclusion has been confirmed in a number of subsequent decisions, such as in Case M.2803, *Telia/Sonera*, Commission Decision of May 28, 2002.
[39] See SMP Guidelines, para.1–012, n.35, nn.60–61.

and satellite television)[40]; (iii) different product characteristics (*e.g.* pay-television and free access television)[41]; and (iv) the existence of specific customer groups (*e.g.* enhanced telecommunications for international corporations, and telecommunications for travelling customers).[42] Since its decision in *Hermes*,[43] where the Commission defined a separate market for carrier services based on the specificity of customers (*i.e.* telecommunications operators and not end-users), it is now settled practice for the Commission to distinguish separate markets depending on the level of trade (*i.e.* wholesale or retail).

5–010 Precedents on market definition — Appendices 2 and 3 contain a table with the relevant product and geographic market definitions adopted by the Commission and the Court of Justice (including the Court of First Instance) in their respective case law under Articles 81 and 82 and the Merger Control Regulation in the telecommunications, broadcasting and internet sectors. Some of these decisions are reviewed in detail in the subsequent chapters. The following observations are pertinent regarding these precedents on market definition.

5–011 Market definition is case specific — The definition of the relevant market depends to a large extent on the facts of the particular case and the competition measures that are being applied.[44] For example, the Commission may wish to define the relevant market differently if it is examining existing market dominance and past abuses of such dominance under Article 82 of the EC Treaty (which is essentially a retrospective exercise) or the possible creation of a dominant position as a result of a concentration being assessed under the Merger Control Regulation (which is essentially a forward-looking exercise). In the latter case, the Commission must use a forward-looking approach to market definition and will need to take into consideration matters such as upcoming technological developments and possible new competing products that would result in increased competition and thus justify a wider product market. This obviously is not always relevant when the Commission is called to review past practices on a specific product market. Similarly, the removal of trade and regulatory barriers to the cross-border provision of services may justify a wider definition of the geographic market than that taken in previous cases. Accordingly, as market definition will evolve with technological progress and liberalisation, businesses should not rely blindly on previous decisions being precedents for market definition, although the

---

[40] See, *e.g.*, *MSG*, O.J. 1996 L364/1, at para.41.

[41] See, *e.g.*, *MSG*, *ibid.* For a detailed review of the market definition in the pay-television sector, see McCallum, "EC Competition Law and Digital Pay Television" (February 1999) *Competition Policy Newsletter*, at pp.14–16.

[42] See, *e.g.*, *Phoenix/Global One*, Commission Decision of July 17, 1996, O.J. 1996 L239/57.

[43] Case M.683, *GTS Hermes/HIT Rail BV*, Commission Decision of March 25, 1996, O.J. 1996 C157/13.

[44] In fact, in merger cases reviewed under the Merger Control Regulation, the Commission often leaves open the issue of the precise market definition as, regardless of how the market is defined, the concentration would not raise any competitive concerns. In the Access Notice, para.5–004, n.18, the Commission indicated that the "definition of particular product markets — for example, the determination of whether call origination and call termination facilities are part of the same facilities market — is best done in the light of a detailed examination of an individual case", at para.47. For a discussion on the extent to which call termination services provided on each individual fixed or mobile network constitute a separate product market, see, respectively, Case M.1439, *Telia/Telenor*, Commission Decision of June 15, 1999, and Case M.2803, *Telia/Sonera*, Commission Decision of May 28, 2002. See also, Crowther, "Market Definition in EC Mobile Telephony" (December 1998/January 1999) *Global Competition Review* 29–30.

Commission will usually only depart from a previous market definition where it is justified in light of its market analysis.[45] However, this does not detract from the value of previous decisions on market definition when assessing the position that the Commission may take, at least initially, when confronted with a new case in a market that it has already analysed in the past.

5–012   Access to facilities — In order to supply services to end-users, a service provider needs access to one or more facilities (*e.g.* the termination points of the telecommunications networks to which these end-users are connected, or customer information such as directory services). Consequently, the Commission must consider at least two types of relevant market in the telecommunications sector, following its liberalisation: markets for liberalised services provided to end-users (the service market) and markets for access to those facilities necessary to provide liberalised services to end-users such as information and the physical network (the access market). For example, in the context of a particular case, it will be necessary to define the relevant access market (such as interconnection to the public telecommunications network), and the relevant service markets (such as the provision of public voice telephony services).[46]

As regards the access market, the question of whether it should be divided into as many separate product markets as there are existing categories of network infrastructure, depends clearly on the degree of substitutability between such (alternative) networks, given the technological changes and the classes of user to which access is provided.[47] Access to networks (whether fixed or mobile) may also be defined by reference to two potentially separate product markets, one for call origination and another for call termination. In respect of mobile networks, the question has arisen as to whether the market for access to mobile infrastructure relates to access to an individual mobile network or to all mobile networks; in general, this question should be decided on the basis of an analysis of the structure and functioning of the market.[48]

5–013   Equipment markets — With regard to manufacturers for telecommunications equipment, the Commission considers that separate equipment markets could exist for: (i) public switches; (ii) private switches; (iii) transmission systems; (iv) telephone sets; (v) modems; (vi) telex terminals; (vii) data transmission terminals; and (viii) mobile phones.[49] As internet voice telephony becomes operational on a commercial basis, the distinction between telephone sets and data transmission terminals will become increasingly blurred; this will result in the need to revisit the market definitions suggested by the Commission.

---

[45] See Joined Cases T–125 and 127/97, *The Coca-Cola Company v Commission* [2000] II E.C.R. 1733, paras 81 and 82, where the Court of First Instance held that markets defined in previous cases are not binding on the Commission, so would not be of decisive relevance for the market definition in subsequent cases, even if involving the same parties; a new analysis is always required.

[46] Access Notice, para.5–004, n.18, para.45.

[47] See SMP Guidelines, para.1–012, n.35, paras 67 and 68, where the Commission indicates that a distinction should be made between the provision of infrastructure to other operators (the wholesale market) and the provision of network access to end-users (the retail market). At the retail level, a further segmentation may be justified between business and residential customers, given their different demand characteristics.

[48] *ibid.*, para.69. See also Commission Press Release IP/02/483 of March 27, 2002, where the Commission announced that it had sent a Statement of Objections to KPN, upon complaint by WorldCom, now MCI, for an alleged abuse of its dominant position on the market for fixed-to-mobile termination calls.

[49] Access Notice, para.5–004, n.18, para.27.

5–014 Satellite market — Regarding the provision of satellite services, the Commission considers that, although there is a high degree of substitutability between the satellite and terrestrial networks for long distance voice and data transmission services, the two are not substantially interchangeable, but rather complementary, for certain specific voice and data transmission services such as: (i) services to peripheral or less-developed regions; (ii) links between non-contiguous countries; (iii) the reconfiguration of capacity; and (iv) the provision of routing for traffic restoration. In addition, satellites are not substantially interchangeable with fixed networks for the provision of direct broadcasting[50] and with multi-point private networks for the provision of value-added services. As a consequence, the Commission has taken the view that for all these uses, satellite networks constitute distinct product markets.[51]

5–015 Fixed network services — The Commission has distinguished between subscriber (retail) access to switched voice telephony services (local, long distance and international), and business data communications services. In respect of fixed telephony retail services, the Commission has also distinguished between the initial connection and the monthly rental, and between residential and business users, the latter possibly being broken down further into separate markets for professional, small and medium-sized corporate customers and for large businesses.[52]

5–016 Mobile network services — In the mobile sector, the Commission has identified distinct markets for each of cellular phones, paging, telepoint, cordless voice and cordless data communication services.[53] In its *Eirpage* decision, the Commission held that paging services constituted a distinct product market because they are cheaper than other forms of mobile communications in terms of price and running costs and less unwieldy than mobile telephones.[54] The Commission noted that, although these differences were expected to diminish in the future, paging would continue to exist as a separate option in the mobile communications sector because it offers one-way communications, a distinct advantage in keeping down subscribers' billing costs. The Commission's position on this point is likely to continue to change in the future since, as the Commission itself noted in the 1991 Competition Guidelines,[55] the evolution of technology is moving towards the integration of the different wireless communications systems into one single product with enhanced features. As a result, for certain or all uses, several of these systems will in the future form part of a single product market.[56]

5–017 Relevant geographic market — A geographic market is an area in which: (i) businesses enter into competition with each other; and (ii) the objective conditions of competition applying to the

---

[50] In *Nordic Satellite Distribution*, the Commission considered that "[d]istribution of TV signals via satellite (transponders) is a market distinct from TV distribution by terrestrial links, since considerable differences exist between the two modes of distribution both technically and financially", O.J. 1995 L53/20, at para.53. See also *MSG* decision, O.J. 1996 L364/1, at para.141. In contrast, in *BiB (Open)*, O.J. 1999 L312/1, the Commission took the position that cable and satellite retail pay-TV belong to the same product market.
[51] Access Notice para.5–004, n.18, para.29.
[52] SMP Guidelines, para.1–012, n.35, para.65.
[53] *ibid.*, para.45.
[54] *Eirpage*, O.J. 1991 L306/22, para.10.
[55] 1991 Competition Guidelines, para.5–004, n.17, at para.30.
[56] For instance, certain types of cordless phone may become cellular telephones depending on the distance that they roam from their base stations.

products or services in question are similar for all traders.[57] In the electronic communications sector, the geographical scope of the relevant product market has traditionally been determined by reference to two main criteria: (i) the area covered by a network; and (ii) the existence of legal and other regulatory instruments that could prevent the cross-border provision of services or networks.[58] On the basis of these two main criteria, geographic markets may be local, regional, national or covering territories of two or more countries (for instance, pan-European, EEA-wide or global markets). In the 1991 Competition Guidelines, the Commission took the view that each national territory within the EU would very often constitute a distinct geographic market, where: (i) the customer's needs could not be satisfied by using services provided by foreign service providers; (ii) there were different regulatory conditions governing the provision of, and access to, services, in particular special or exclusive rights which were apt to isolate national territories; and (iii) with respect to equipment and networks, there were no common standards applicable throughout the EU with the result that national markets could be isolated.[59] However, with the complete liberalisation of the Community telecommunications market (and the resulting abolition of all exclusive and special rights) and the process of the harmonisation of national laws (*i.e.* licensing regimes, technical standards and regulatory laws), the relevant geographic market, in appropriate cases, progressively extends to, at least, the EU territory. This tendency has been acknowledged by the Commission in its practice.[60] As regards the market for satellite up-linking, the geographic market may cover the whole Community to the extent that up-links could be provided for any of several countries.[61] With respect to space segment capacity, the scope of the geographic market will depend on the footprint of the satellite and its ability to compete with other satellites for transmission to a given area.[62] Despite this, the geographic scope of certain markets will remain local or at the widest national level, due to regulatory or physical constraints; for example, local loop and mobile networks are national in scope.[63]

[57] 1991 Competition Guidelines, para.5–004, n.17, n.31; Case 27/76, *United Brands v Commission* [1978] E.C.R. 207, para.44.

[58] SMP Guidelines, para.1–012, n.35, para.59.

[59] *ibid.*, para.32.

[60] See, *e.g.*, in the mobile sector, Case M.1177, *Belgacom/TeleDanmark/Tulip*, Commission Decision of May 19, 1998 (where the parties argued that the market for mobile telephony is increasingly European due to the compatibility between different systems, the diminishing gap between international and national prices, and the increasing conclusion of interconnection agreements); Case M.1795, *Vodafone/Mannesmann*, Commission Decision of April 12, 2000 (where the Commission indicated that there was demand for advanced, seamless pan-European services from international mobile customers and large corporations); Case M.2016, *FT/Orange*, decision of August 11, 2000; Case M.2305, *Vodafone/Eircell*, Commission Decision of March 2, 2001 (where the Commission confirmed the findings of its previous Commission Decision, *Vodafone/Mannesmann*); Case M.2469, *Vodafone/Airtel*, Commission Decision of June 26, 2001 (provision for advanced, seamless pan-European mobile telecommunications services); and in the equipment sector, Case M.1226, *GEC/GPTH*, Commission Decision of July 27, 1998.

[61] The Commission followed the same approach in *Astra* where it held that the geographic market for up-link services is Community-wide since programme providers are not bound by national boundaries and can transmit their programmes either by conventional or other means to another territory for up-linking or establish studios in the locality where the conditions are the most favourable: O.J. 1993 L20/23, para.17.

[62] The Commission took a similar position in *Nordic Satellite Distribution*, where it considered that the geographic market for the provision of satellite transponder capacity to broadcasters consisted of those transponders with a footprint (*i.e.* the geographic area where the television signals distributed by a satellite can be received by direct-to-home households having standard receiving equipment) that covers the Nordic region (*i.e.* Norway, Sweden, Denmark and Finland): O.J. 1995 L53/20, para.62; see also *International Private Satellite Partners*, O.J. 1994 L354/75, para.34.

[63] See para.5–018, below.

5–018 The geographic dimension of certain markets is expanding — Telecommunications markets have traditionally been considered as national or regional markets. They were characterised by regulatory and technical restrictions on the provision of cross-border services, networks and equipment with the result that telecommunications services, networks and equipment were marketed at the national level only. The geographic scope of the market was thus frequently determined by the scope of the special or exclusive rights of the incumbent telecommunications operator.[64] As a consequence of the harmonisation of technical standards and licensing procedures across the EU and the liberalisation of telecommunications services and networks, increasingly telecommunications services and equipment can be provided or sold and networks operated across national borders without restrictions. Increasingly customers are no longer limited to local suppliers but may turn to alternative suppliers located abroad. As a result, the Commission has started gradually to extend the geographic dimension of the relevant markets. For example, the Commission has held on numerous occasions that the provision of value-added services is a global market, given the liberalisation of markets and the resulting disappearance of barriers to the cross-border provision of services.[65] Likewise, the Commission has recently acknowledged that in the mobile telecommunications sector, there is an increasing trend towards the creation of a pan-European market for mobile services provided to business customers.[66] However, in *Vodafone/AirTouch*, the Commission considered that subscriptions with foreign mobile operators were not yet an economically sensible alternative for consumers, given the additional costs of permanent roaming.[67]

5–019 Some geographic markets will remain national at their widest — Despite the removal of legal, regulatory and technical barriers to cross-border trade, the Commission continues to define product markets nationally (or more narrowly) when regulatory or physical restrictions and/or diverging technical standards still restrict cross-border entry to the geographic market.[68] The

---

[64] See, *e.g.*, Case 247/86, *Alsatel v Novasam* [1988] E.C.R. 5987. This was an equipment case, but as the incumbent operator could at that time (before liberalisation) impose technical standards for equipment to be connected to its network, technical standards varied by Member State, thus isolating each Member State's territory.

[65] See, *e.g.*, Case M.353, *BT/MCI*, Commission Decision of July 27, 1994, O.J. 1994 L223/36; Case M.532, *Cable & Wireless/Schlumberger*, Commission Decision of December 22, 1994; Case M.618, *Cable & Wireless/Veba*, Commission Decision of August 16, 1995; Case M.689, *ADSB/Belgacom*, Commission Decision of February 29, 1996; Case M.856, *British Telecom/MCI (II)*, Commission Decision of May 14, 1997; Case M.951, *Cable & Wireless/Maersk Data-Nautec*, Commission Decision of July 10, 1997; Case M.927, *STET/GET/Union Fenosa*, Commission Decision of August 20, 1997; *Unisource*, Commission Decision of October 29, 1997, O.J. 1997 L318/1; Case M.1046, *Ameritech/TeleDanmark*, Commission Decision of December 5, 1997; Case JV.15, *BT/AT&T*, Commission Decision of March 30, 1999; Case M.1741, *MCI WorldCom*Sprint, Commission Decision of June 28, 2000; Case M.2257, *FT/Equant*, Commission Decision of March 21, 2001; and Case M.2648, *KPNQwest/Ebone/GTS*, Commission Decision of January 16, 2002.

[66] See Case M.1795, *Vodafone/Mannesmann*, Decision of April 12, 2000; Case M.2016, *FT/Orange*, Commission Decision of August 11, 2000; Case M.2305, *Vodafone/Eircell*, Commission Decision of March 2, 2001; Case M.2469, *Vodafone/Airtel*, Commission Decision of June 26, 2001. See also previously *Cegetel*, O.J. 1998 C238/3, and Case M.1465, *Deutsche Telekom/Max Mobil*, Commission Decision of April 22, 1999.

[67] Case M.1430, *Vodafone/Airtouch*, Commission Decision of May 21, 1999.

[68] In *Telecom Eireann*, the Commission defined the geographic market for basic telecommunications services (*i.e.* voice telephony, leased lines, mobile telephony and telex) as limited to Ireland on the ground that public telephony continued to be reserved to the incumbent operator until January 1, 2000: Case M.802, Commission Decision of December 18, 1996.

Licensing Directive, and its replacement, the Authorisation Directive, have harmonised and simplified licensing procedures in the electronic communications sector, with the result that only a limited number of services are subject to individual licences or, under the Authorisation Directive, "rights of use".[69] Under the Authorisation Directive, national regulatory authorities have to comply with tight deadlines and may only refuse individual rights of use for a limited number of objective and non-discriminatory reasons. The number of individual rights of use may be limited solely for concerns relating to access to radio frequencies and numbers. In this context, to the extent that licensing procedures are no longer substantial obstacles to cross-border provision of services or networks, regulatory restrictions might no longer justify defining a market on a national basis except where a limited number of businesses are licensed to provide services or networks or where there are other barriers that cause markets to be isolated from one another.

For instance, certain electronic communications markets may be considered to be national for reasons relating to the physical characteristics or capacity of a network (*i.e.* the area covered by the network): for example, local loop; retail internet access; and call termination onto mobile networks.

5-020 By contrast, the broadcasting sector, at least as far as the control of editorial content is concerned, is still characterised by unharmonised national or regional restrictions on the cross-border provision of services (*e.g.* ownership restrictions and local content obligations in the audio-visual sector, national licensing procedures). Moreover, cultural and language differences continue to segregate markets. Consequently, the Commission has consistently defined the relevant geographic market in the media sector along national borders and/or linguistic regions.[70]

---

[69] See para.1–083 *et seq.*

[70] See Case M.110, *ABC/Générale des Eaux/Canal+/W.H.Smith*, Commission Decision of September 10, 1991; Case M.410, *Kirsch/Richemont/Telepiú*, Commission Decision of August 2, 1994; Case M.489, *Bertelsmann/News International/Vox*, Commission Decision of September 6, 1994; Case M.469, *MSG*, Commission Decision of November 9, 1994, O.J. 1994 L364/1; Case M.584, *Kirsch/Richemont/Multichoice/ Telepiú*, Commission Decision of May 5, 1995; Case M.566, *CLT/Disney/SuperRTL*, Commission Decision of May 17, 1995; Case M.490, *Nordic Satellite Distribution*, Commission Decision of July 19, 1995, O.J. 1995 L53/20; Case IV/M.553, *RTL/Veronica/Endemol*, Commission Decision of September 20, 1995, O.J. 1996 L134/ 32; Case M.655, *Canal+/UFA/MDO*, Commission Decision of November 13, 1995; Case M.810, *n-TV*, Commission Decision of September 16, 1996; Case M.779, *Bertelsmann/CLT*, Commission Decision of October 7, 1996; Cases M.853 and M.865, *Bell CableMedia/Cable & Wireless/Videotron* and *Cable & Wireless/Nynex/ Bell Canada*, Commission Decision of December 11, 1996; Case M.878, *RTL7*, Commission Decision of February 14, 1997; Case M.939, *Bank America/General Electric/Cableuropa*, Commission Decision of June 19, 1997; Case M.1022, *Cable i Televisió de Catalunya*, Commission Decision of January 28, 1998; Case M.1091, *Cableuropa/SpainCom/CTC*, Commission Decision of January 28, 1998; Case M.1251, *Particel International/ Cableuropa*, Commission Decision of July 30, 1998; Case 36.539, *BiB*, Commission Notice under Art.19(3) of Council Regulation 17/62, O.J. 1998 C322/6; Case M.1574, *Kirsch/Mediaset*, Commission Decision of August 3, 1999; Case JV.30, *BVI Television (Europe)/SPE Euromovies Investments/Europe Movie CoPartners*, Commission Decision of February 3, 2000; Case M.1889, *CLT-UFA/Canal+/Vox*, Commission Decision of March 21, 2000; Case M.1943, *Telefonica/Endemol*, Commission Decision of July 11, 2000; Case M.2050, *Vivendi/Canal+/ Seagram*, Commission Decision of October 13, 2000; Case M.2137, *SLDE/NTL/MSCP/NOOS*, Commission Decision of October 16, 2000; Case JV.57, *TPS*, Commission Decision of April 30, 2002.

Chapter VI

Market Conduct

A. Outline of the Section

6–001 Introduction — This Chapter focuses on the application of the EC Treaty's competition rules (Articles 81, 82 and 86) to the market conduct of telecommunications operators in light of the case law of the Community courts and the Commission's decision-making practice. It will review the type of co-operation between businesses that is permitted or prohibited, the circumstances under which a telecommunications operator may lawfully refuse to deal with another operator and other competition-related issues. Specific attention will be given to the application of EC competition rules to the provision of satellite, broadcasting and online services, with a special emphasis on the internet. This chapter does not consider the application of Articles 81 and 82 to joint ventures, alliances and similar arrangements: these are dealt with in Chapter VIII.

B. Control of Market Conduct under Article 81 of the EC Treaty

6–002 Many types of agreements between telecommunications operators are not specific to the telecommunications sector. The general conditions for the application of Article 81 to these agreements have been described above.[1] This section will focus on the specific application of Articles 81(1) (which prohibits agreements between undertakings, decisions of associations and concerted practices that have as their object or effect the prevention, restriction or distortion of competition within the common market and which affect inter-state trade) and 81(3) (pursuant to which agreements that infringe Article 81(1) may be exempted if they fulfil certain criteria) of the EC Treaty to the communications sector. Guidance in this respect may be gained from the 1991 Competition Guidelines and the 1998 Access Notice. Although some of the concepts and principles referred to in the 1991 Competition Guidelines are no longer relevant given the full liberalisation of the Community markets for telecommunications networks and services, they remain a useful guide to the Commission's approach to applying Article 81 to agreements between communications

---

[1] See para.4–001, *et seq.*

operators. The decision-making practice of the Commission and the case law of the Court of Justice and Court of First Instance will also be analysed.

1. Agreements between Competitors in the Telecommunications Sector

6–003 The telecommunications industry is a network-based industry. This means that it is necessary for operators to enter into various agreements with each other in order to provide end-to-end connectivity and services. Such agreements can be vertical (between suppliers and customers, or between operators at different levels of the supply chain) or horizontal (between competitors). Individual agreements between competitors in the telecommunications sector can have varying degrees of either detrimental or beneficial effects on competition. Indeed, one agreement can have both kinds of effect. Interconnection agreements are a prerequisite for competition between network operators, although their terms might be restrictive of competition. The existence of infrastructure-sharing agreements can help to maintain a higher number of competing mobile operators, although it can also facilitate collusion between them by means of sharing infrastructure costs. Operators of broadcast transmission networks have to enter into agreements with content providers in order to provide their transmission services. On the other hand, the fixing of mobile roaming tariffs between various competing operators or the joint marketing of media rights by sports bodies may infringe Article 81 of the EC Treaty by limiting competition. In the following section, various specific types of agreement are considered in the light of their effect on competition.

2. Specific Agreements

6–004 Pricing — Agreements between telecommunications operators on pricing, discounts, collection charges for services, or customer or geographic market sharing are generally considered to be restrictive of competition. They therefore will almost certainly fall within Article 81(1) and are unlikely to be approved or exempted by the Commission. Price competition is considered a crucial element of the competition process, as it gives customers choice and is apt to stimulate technical progress.[2]

With this in mind, the Commission therefore objected to a recommendation from the European Conference of Postal and Telecommunications Administrations (CEPT) to its members (*i.e.* all the then incumbent monopoly operators in 1990) which fixed the terms for leasing international telecommunications circuits.[3] The CEPT recommendation suggested that operators should impose a 30 per cent surcharge where the capacity of the circuits was to be used for third-party traffic or if such a circuit was interconnected to the public telecommunications network. The recommendation also provided for the application of uniform tariff coefficients for the determination of the price of international telecommunications leased circuits. This recommendation represented the incumbent operators' reaction to the use of leased lines by companies such as Swift to provide value-added services to third parties and therefore compete with the incumbents' traditional services such as telexes. The Commission considered that the CEPT recommendation constituted an illegal

---

[2] See 1991 Competition Guidelines, para.5–004, n.17, para.45.
[3] See Commission Press Release IP/90/188, March 6, 1990.

price-fixing agreement between the members of CEPT and infringed Article 81(1). The recommendation was therefore subsequently abandoned by CEPT. The Commission considered that the risk of price co-ordination was particularly acute in the case of interconnection agreements, given the high proportion (50 per cent) of the new entrant's total costs represented by interconnection charges and the resulting limited scope for price competition if such rules were maintained. Similarly, in *Global European Network*,[4] the Commission only permitted the creation of a pan-European high quality, heavy capacity optical fibre network once provisions relating to the setting of prices by the operators involved had been deleted. The Commission also objected to provisions that restricted third party access to the optical fibre network.

Following its sector inquiry into the mobile telecommunications sector between 1999 and 2001, which was carried out pursuant to Article 12 of Regulation 17, the Commission found indications of price fixing in the mobile telephony markets. In the Commission's view, the inquiry showed that in a number of Member States, a group of operators applied the same or very similar per minute inter-operator tariffs in respect of roamed calls that they carried on their networks.[5] According to the Commission, the similarities in price and the convergence of inbound roaming tariffs across the EU could not be fully explained by the high degree of oligopolistic interdependence of mobile operators in the roaming markets (which might have provided an explanation for tariff parallelism). Rather, the Commission considered that the operators' pricing similarities were explained by collusive behaviour, which was facilitated by the exchange of confidential information through the platform of the GSM Association.[6] In July 2001, the Commission carried out on-site investigations at nine different mobile operators in Germany and the UK in order to find evidence of an infringement of Article 81(1) of the EC Treaty.[7]

The Commission is also reviewing the Vodafone Eurocall scheme, which has been notified to it for negative clearance under Article 81(1) or exemption under Article 81(3). Eurocall is a preferential roaming scheme, which enables Vodafone subscribers to make and receive calls at uniform prices throughout Vodafone-affiliated networks in Europe. The Commission may find that such a scheme infringes competition on the mobile roaming markets and has issued a "Carlsberg Notice" stating that the agreements might fall under Regulation 17/62.[8]

Generally, the Commission may be prepared to exempt under Article 81(3) agreements that set up common tariff structures or principles, without containing an agreement to fix prices, provided that they have the effect of making tariffs more cost-related and transparent so as to benefit users.[9]

6–005 Access to facilities and leased lines — The Commission is usually quite reluctant to find in accordance with Art.81 agreements between telecommunications operators that restrict third party access to networks where such arrangements have the effect of foreclosing third parties from

---

[4] See Commission, XXVIIth Report on Competition Policy (1997), point 73.
[5] See Commission Working Document on the Initial Findings of the Sector Inquiry into Mobile Roaming Charges, December 13, 2000, cited at para.1–037, n.3, p.20. See further para.6–012, below.
[6] See below, para.6–009.
[7] See Commission Press Memo, MEMO/01/262, July 11, 2001.
[8] See Carlsberg Notice O.J. 2001 C42/13.
[9] See 1991 Competition Guidelines, para.5–004, n.17, para.45.

the service market for which access to the facility concerned is required. In this regard, in the framework of its investigation of CEPT,[10] the Commission objected to a CEPT recommendation (which involved a ban on subleasing or making the use of leased circuits subject to the condition that the communications related exclusively to the activity for which the circuit was granted) that would have led to restrictions on the use of leased lines by third parties wishing to provide competitive services.

Access agreements, such as interconnection agreements, are essential to the interoperability of services and infrastructure and thereby increase competition in downstream markets for services.[11] However, they can have anti-competitive and exclusionary effects on third parties. In its Access Notice, the Commission indicated in this respect that exclusive access agreements that allow access by a limited number of companies or only through the telecommunications network of one party (to the exclusion of third party networks) are restrictive of competition to the extent they limit third party access to the network. The Commission will normally see the conditions of Article 81(3) met only if there is an objective reason to justify the special access conditions, for example if the special access conditions for a particular facility are indispensable in order to ensure its financial viability and its development.[12] In doing so, the Commission will nevertheless seek to ensure that third parties are not completely foreclosed (or are only foreclosed for a limited duration) from access to the facility.[13] On occasion, the Commission has imposed third party access obligations on the parties to a merger to remedy the effects on competition of a concentration reviewed by it in the context of the Merger Control Regulation.[14]

6–006 Infrastructure sharing — Operators that obtained licences for the provision of third generation mobile services (3G) increasingly identified a need to co-operate with their competitors in setting up their 3G infrastructure, given the high cost of the licences, the investments needed to roll out this infrastructure and the downturn in expected 3G revenues. Operators have argued that without a sharing of their radio network infrastructures, they would not be able to meet their roll-out obligations and remain financially viable. Network infrastructure sharing agreements can therefore promote a timely network roll-out, thereby facilitating the commencement of competition on the downstream services markets. However, it could also lead to anti-competitive co-ordination,

[10] Above, para.6–004.

[11] See Access Notice, para.5–003, n.18, para.133.

[12] The Commission also referred to the need to increase the competitiveness of European industry structures in the 1991 Competition Guidelines, para.5–004, n.17, para.47.

[13] See, *e.g. Eurotunnel*, Commission Decision of 13, 1994, O.J. 1994 L354/66. In this case, the Commission granted an individual exemption to a track access agreement that contained restrictions on the use of the Channel Tunnel by third parties to offer rail transport services in competition with SNCF and British Rail on the ground that SNCF and British Rail needed a privileged position to recoup the large investments committed by them to ensure the viability of the project. In order to reduce the risk of foreclosure of third parties, British Rail and SNCF were required to make available, at any hour of the day, to any interested party, 25% of the 50% of the tunnel's capacity that had been reserved to them. The decision, including the conditions imposed upon the parties to provide third party access, was subsequently annulled by the Court of First Instance. The Court considered, among other things, that the Commission had not established that infrastructure that the Commission required to be made available was an essential facility to which third parties must have access in order to compete on the downstream markets: Joined Cases T–374, 375, 384 and 388/94, *European Night Services* [1998] II E.C.R. 3141.

[14] See below, para.9–016 *et seq.*

depending on the precise parts of the infrastructure that are shared. The Commission has therefore announced that it will carefully scrutinise "arrangements whereby companies coordinate their services through the sharing of infrastructure and the specific modalities envisaged. If customers do not suffer because of these types of arrangements, [the Commission] will not oppose them. However, the contrary also applies: the Commission will not authorise forms of co-ordination which would lead to co-ordinated behaviour that would damage consumers."[15]

The Commission considered the question of 3G infrastructure sharing in the case *T-Mobile/ VIAG Interkom*.[16] In February 2002, both companies notified to the Commission a framework agreement concerning infrastructure sharing and reciprocal national roaming for 3G mobile telephony company in Germany and the UK. In April 2003, the Commission issued a decision with respect to the agreements relating to the UK. It concluded that the site sharing agreement did not restrict competition and thus did not fall under Article 81(1). The national roaming agreement was exempted from the competition rules under Article 81(3) after the parties had undertaken that they would no longer be roaming in the ten biggest cities in the UK. The exemption will run until the end of 2007 for national roaming in small cities and until the end of 2008 for rural areas. The Commission views this decision as a model for similar future cases.[17] Subsequently, the Commission issued a similar decision in respect to the agreement to be implemented in Germany.[17a]

Many NRAs in the EU have already developed a position on network infrastructure sharing. Although the approaches taken vary considerably, it can be said that the sharing of masts and passive network elements are generally permissible, while the sharing of core network components or frequencies will generally not be authorised. Regarding co-operation on a geographical basis, NRAs and the Commission will generally allow national roaming agreements between licensed network operators to the extent that it benefits consumers by allowing the operators involved to offer better and quicker coverage, especially in less built-up and more remote areas.[18] Any agreement amounting to customer or geographic market sharing would most certainly be considered to infringe Article 81(1).[19]

6–007 Market sharing — Agreements between telecommunications operators amounting to market sharing at the product, geographic or customer levels are generally considered *per se* infringements of Article 81(1) and are unlikely to be capable of exemption under Article 81(3). In the Access Notice, the Commission stressed that, in certain cases, interconnection agreements may be an instrument of market sharing between the network operator providing access and the network operator seeking access, rather than an element of network competition between them.[20]

6–008 Choice of telecommunications routes — The Commission considers that agreements between telecommunications network operators on telecommunications routes set up to provide

---

[15] See Monti, "Defining the Boundaries of Competition Policies in High-Tech sectors", SPEECH/01/375, p.6.
[16] O.J. 2002 C189/2.
[17] See Commission Press Release IP/03/589 of April 30, 2003.
[17a] See Commission Press Release IP/03/1026 of July 16, 2003.
[18] *ibid.*
[19] See below, para.6–007.
[20] See Access Notice, para.5–004, n.18, para.136.

international services may have the effect of restricting "hub" competition, *i.e.* the competition between telecommunications operators to provide international communications services to global companies.[21] Such agreements are capable of exemption under Article 81(3) if common route designation is necessary to ensure the interconnection of networks and therefore the establishment of European-wide networks.

6–009 Technical and quality standards — Agreements on technical and quality standards between telecommunications operators and manufacturers of equipment are generally viewed favourably by the Commission, as they facilitate the promotion of pan-European telecommunications services.[22] The Commission has promoted co-operation on standards between equipment manufacturers and operators within the framework of European standardisation bodies such as the European Telecommunications Standards Institute (ETSI), European Committee for Standardisation (CEN) and the European Committee for Electrotechnical Standardisation (CENELEC). One important benefit of standardisation agreements from a competition perspective is that they prevent dominant network operators (generally the incumbent former monopoly operators) from dictating standards in order to restrict access by new entrants to their markets.

Standardisation agreements can, however have restrictive effects on competition, in particular when they restrict access by third parties to a specific market. For example, in *X-Open*, the Commission found that arrangements among computer manufacturers to develop open industry standards infringed Article 81(1) and it was prepared to grant an exemption under Article 81(3) on the condition that wide and quick access by non-members to the standards was guaranteed.[23] The balance between the economic benefits of standardisation agreements and their restrictive effects on competition is particularly complex. The Commission will view these agreements favourably under Article 81(3) only if it is convinced that their benefits (such as increased openness and facilitating easier market entry) outweigh the restrictions on competition that result from them.[24] It would appear that a standards organisation such as ETSI, which was set up to promote the adoption of European-wide standards, could not oblige its members to share technology as a condition for membership.[25] Such an obligation would be excessive and could hinder innovation.

The Commission will also ensure that the benefits of standardisation accrue to end-users. In this context, the Commission has objected to the use by manufacturers and mobile network operators of the "SIM lock" feature of mobile handsets (which prevents a different SIM card being used with a mobile handset) and the standardisation of this feature within ETSI. Indeed, this anti-theft feature

---

[21] See 1991 Competition Guidelines, para.5–004, n.17, para.48.

[22] *ibid.*, para.49; see Dolmans, *International Computer Law*, (Bender, New York, 1988–1999), para.4–7.

[23] *X-Open Group*, O.J. 1987 L35/36.

[24] See, *e.g.*, *Global European Network*, O.J. 1994 C55/3, which concerned a technical co-operation agreement between telecommunications network operators with the purpose of improving the quality and availability of international leased lines.

[25] See *ETSI IPR Undertaking*, O.J. 1995 C76/5. In this case, a proposed arrangement between ETSI members to reduce the risk of infringing the intellectual property rights of members in the course of the development of standards, was only approved following the removal of a requirement for all ETSI members to undertake to cross-licence all their intellectual property rights (including future intellectual property rights) for use in ETSI standards, except intellectual property rights that were expressly withheld.

of mobile phone handsets allegedly has the effect of locking a particular handset to a particular service provider, with the result that subscribers were restricted in their freedom to switch to another service provider.[26] A European industry standard that has been identified as being very helpful for the development of a uniform European mobile market is the GSM Standard. Second generation mobile telecommunications operators in Europe use the GSM Standard on either or both of the 900 or 1800 MHz frequency sales (GSM 900 and DCS/GSM 1800 respectively). Meanwhile, the GSM Standard has also become the industry standard in many parts of the world outside Europe. However, the Commission is increasingly concerned about the extent of co-operation between market players in the framework of the GSM Association, which administers the GSM Standard. The level of co-operation within this organisation goes beyond the setting of technical standards and increasingly encompasses commercial issues. GSM Association members have agreed to a Standard International Roaming Agreement (STIRA), which has been notified to the Commission under Article 81(1). The Commission's review of this agreement will take into account the allegations of the anti-competitive co-ordination of roaming tariffs.[27]

6–010 Preferential arrangements — The Commission has also objected to agreements that give certain equipment manufacturers privileged access to an operator's network, particularly if the operator in question is dominant in the relevant network or services market; this is because competing equipment manufacturers are foreclosed from all or a significant part of the market for equipment used by the relevant type of network.[28] Similar questions have arisen in relation to exclusive or preferential arrangements between joint ventures and their parent companies under which the joint venture will purchase all or a proportion of its requirements of certain services.[29] Pricing access to land or other rights of way may also fall within Article 81(1) if such access would be essential for competing operators wishing to construct their own networks.[30]

6–011 Exchange of confidential information — Agreements between telecommunications operators to exchange information will be viewed favourably by the Commission to the extent that they are necessary to ensure the proper functioning of the provision of telecommunications services, interconnectivity between networks or to allow one-stop shopping and billing. Such agreements, however, will infringe Article 81(1) if they extend to sharing commercially confidential data such as tariffs, discounts and commercial strategies and are unlikely to be capable of exemption under Article 81(3). In addition, when assessing co-operative joint ventures between

[26] See Commission Press Release IP/96/791 of August 8, 1996. "SIM locking" has also been an issue of interest to national regulatory authorities.
[27] See Commission Memo, MEMO/01/262 of July 7, 2001.
[28] In *STET/Haltel/AT&T/AT&T-NSI*, O.J. 1992 C333/03, the Commission required STET's subsidiary, Telecom Italia, not to discriminate in favour of Italtel. See also *Eirpage*, O.J. 1991 L306/22, where the Commission required the Eirpage joint venture not to discriminate in favour of equipment manufactured by Motorola, a shareholder in Eirpage.
[29] See *Astra*, O.J. 1993 L20/23: obligation for customers to purchase BT's up-linking services if they wished to use Astra satellite capacity provided by SES; see also para.8–300, below; *Cégétel + 4*, O.J. 1999 L218/14 (Corr. L237/10): provisions under which Cégétel would, in France, only distribute BT's "Concept" international services for corporate customers fell within Art.81(1), but were exempted under Art.81(3). See, below, para.8–278 *et seq.*
[30] See *Télécom Développement*, O.J. 1999 L218/272; see also, under the Merger Control Regulation, Case M.827, *DBKom*, Commission Decision of October 23, 1996: exclusive access to DB's land was not ancillary to the formation of the DBKom joint venture.

telecommunications network operators for the provision of global value-added network services, the Commission has generally required the parties involved not to discriminate against other service providers by providing the joint venture with customer information that is not readily available and obtainable elsewhere by the joint venture's competitors.[31] Furthermore, the exchange of information between competitors on a regular basis by way of an online portal may fall within the scope of Article 81(1). The Commission has, in particular, identified concerns about the GSM Association Infocentre, which collects tariff information from various GSM operators.[32]

In its Access Notice, the Commission acknowledged that telecommunications network operators may obtain certain customer and traffic information relating to their competitors in the framework of interconnection arrangements.[33] In this context, the Commission has recommended that network operators adopt safeguards to ensure that confidential information is only disclosed to those parts of the company that are responsible for interconnection and that those parts of its business responsible for service provision do not have access to it. The freedom of operators to exchange information on customer and usage-related data is further restricted by the E-Privacy Directive, which forms part of the New Regulatory Framework.[34]

6–012   Roaming agreements between mobile network operators — Operators of mobile networks and providers of mobile services have entered into so-called "roaming agreements". These enable users of mobile services to use their handsets on different networks whether in countries other than that in which their service provider is established or in the same country.[35] Roaming agreements regulate the way in which the costs of a roamed call are allocated at the wholesale level. If a subscriber is roaming on another network and originates a call, the visited network operator bills the home network operator for this call. With the increase of both the penetration of mobile telephony and European travel, roaming is becoming a growing source of revenue for mobile operators. In general, the Commission considers that roaming arrangements could have the effect of restricting competition in the provision of international mobile services and could thus infringe Article 81(1). The Commission is particularly concerned that such arrangements result in price fixing or market sharing and involve an unjustified exchange of information between competitors, thereby discouraging the provision of cross-border mobile services. The Commission, however, has also acknowledged the benefits of such agreements, in particular a reduction in the costs of negotiating individual agreements and the fact that they enable speedy availability of roaming

---

[31] See *Infonet*, O.J. 1992 C7/3, para.9(1)(d); *Atlas*, Commission Decision of September 19, 1996, O.J. 1996 L239/23, para.28(4); and *Unisource*, Commission Decision of October 29, 1997, O.J. 1997 L318/24, para.47.
[32] See European Commission, Findings of the Sector Inquiry into Mobile Roaming Charges, cited at para.1–037, n.3, p.21.
[33] See Access Notice, para.5–004, n.18, para.139.
[34] E-Privacy Directive, para.1–011, n.31, Art.3.
[35] Roaming is defined in the Mobile Green Paper, COM(94) 145 of April 1994, as "the facility supported by commercial arrangements between operators and/or service providers, which enables a subscriber to use his/her radio telephone equipment on any other network which has entered into a roaming agreement in the same or another country for both outgoing and incoming calls". Roaming agreements therefore allow both call origination (where the roaming customer's handset is recognised as being able to make calls in the roaming area) and call termination (where the location of the roaming customer's handset is known and where calls can be passed to the roaming customer in the roaming area). Both of these facilities make use of the network of a mobile operator in the roaming area.

services. Most roaming agreements follow the terms of the GSM Association's Standard roaming agreement, known as STIRA. Pursuant to this agreement, the visited network operator can charge the home network operators of subscribers roaming within its network a uniform inter-operator tariff ("IOT"). Individual discounts from the IOT are possible. In 1996 and 1998, the Commission approved the STIRA agreement by way of a conditional comfort letter after it had received reassurances that: (i) roaming charges would be cost-based; (ii) exchanges of information would be kept to a minimum; and (iii) the agreement would not prevent providers of mobile services from by-passing the roaming agreements and undertaking active sales in another operator's area. After the initial stage of the Sector Inquiry into Mobile Roaming Charges, which the Commission completed in December 2000,[36] the Commission now seems more concerned with the system of STIRA and IOT. According to the Commission's initial findings, this system has led to collusion and sharing of confidential information between competitors on the wholesale roaming markets, as well as to collusive behaviour in the retail markets where identical mark-ups on the IOT are charged to customers in many European countries.

It remains to be seen how the Commission will react to the technical and commercial developments which are expected with respect to roaming. These developments may well include greater flexibility in roaming charges, higher penetration rates of flat rate roaming and preferential roaming schemes, the emergence of roaming brokerage and a technology that will allow operators to increase their control of roaming activity and promote offerings of pre-paid roaming and closed-user group features (CAMEL).

C. Application of Article 82 of the EC Treaty to Market Conduct

6–013 Article 82 of the EC Treaty prohibits the abuse of a dominant position held within the EU or a substantial part of it.[37] The application of Article 82 presupposes that the existence of a dominant position and an abuse of it be established by the Commission.

1. Dominance

6–014 Concept of dominance — The Court of Justice has defined a dominant position under Article 82 as:

"... a position of economic strength enjoyed by an undertaking which enables it to hinder the maintenance of effective competition on the relevant market by allowing it to behave to an appreciable extent independently of its competitors and customers and ultimately of its consumers."[38]

6–015 Market definition — To establish whether an undertaking possesses a dominant position, it is first necessary to define the relevant product and geographic market on which to assess the

---

[36] See Findings of the Sector Inquiry into Mobile Roaming Charges, para.1–037, n.3, above.

[37] See para.4–005 *et seq.*

[38] See Case 322/81, *Michelin v Commission* [1983] E.C.R. 3461. See also Case 311/84, *Télémarketing* [1985] E.C.R. 3261, Case 27/76, *United Brands v Commission* [1978] E.C.R. 207, and Case 85/76, *Hoffmann-La Roche v Commission* [1979] E.C.R. 461.

conditions of competition and the market power of the firm under investigation. The methods and criteria to define the relevant product and geographic market, as well as the Commission's decision-making practice and the case law of the Court of Justice and the Court of First Instance in this respect, have been described in a previous chapter.[39] The Commission's approach with respect to market definition in the telecommunications sector is explained in the SMP Guidelines.[40] Markets defined for the purposes of Article 82 may differ from markets defined for the purposes of reviewing a concentration under the Merger Control Regulation or for the purposes of applying *ex ante* sector-specific regulation, as market definition in certain situations will have to take probable future developments into account. However, market definition for the purposes of assessing dominance under Article 82 is determined only on the basis of the competitive situation at the relevant time period, which will be in the past.[41]

As far as the definition of the telecommunications markets is concerned, under the New Regulatory Framework market definition for the purposes of *ex ante* regulation will be carried out by the NRAs,[42] whilst in the context of Article 82 the Commission or a national competition authority is the authority competent for defining markets.[43] However, NRAs, the Commission and national competition authorities will wish to ensure consistent market definition.

6–016 Elements indicating dominance — The existence of a dominant position may derive from the combination of several factors which, taken separately, are not necessarily conclusive. Among these factors, the most important one is the existence of a very large market share, normally of over 40 per cent.[44]

In the SMP Guidelines, the Commission identified several criteria which can be used to measure the ability of an undertaking to behave to an appreciable extent independently of its competitors, customers and consumers, and thereby be dominant. These criteria are the following:

- the overall size of the undertaking;

- control of infrastructure that cannot easily be duplicated;

- technological advantages or superiority;

- the absence of, or only low, countervailing buying power;

- easy or privileged access to capital markets and other financial resources;

- product and/or services diversification (*e.g.* the ability to provide bundled products or services);

---

[39] See para.5–001 *et seq.*

[40] See SMP Guidelines, para.1–012, n.35, para.33 *et seq.*

[41] See para.5–011, above.

[42] See Framework Directive, Art.15(3); see para.1–009, n.25, above.

[43] National competition authorities and/or NRAs may also apply Art.82 and/or national equivalents in certain cases, in particular with the entry into force of Regulation 1/2003, which will introduce significant changes to the enforcement of Community competition law: see para.4–001, n.6, above.

[44] See *Hoffmann-La Roche*, para.6–014, n.38, para.42.

- economies of scale;

- economies of scope;

- vertical integration;

- a highly developed distribution and sales network;

- the absence of potential competition; and

- barriers to expansion by competitors.

According to the SMP Guidelines,[45] a dominant position can be found as the result of a combination of the above criteria; a number of these are explained below in further detail.

6–017   *Legal monopoly* — Where a business has a legal monopoly to supply a product or to provide a service, this business by definition does not face competition and consequently automatically enjoys a dominant position on the market.[46] Accordingly, prior to 1998 and the full liberalisation of telecommunications, the Commission took the position[47] that incumbent telecommunications operators (in markets that had not been liberalised) held a dominant position for the operation and exploitation of telecommunications networks and the provision of telecommunications in the relevant market services (*e.g.* voice telephony) to the extent that they held exclusive or special rights granted by Member States to operate such networks or provide such services.[48] Statutory monopoly rights (*i.e.* exclusive rights) and special rights have now been abolished in all Member States. However, as discussed below, the ending of legal monopolies has not put an end to the dominant position of incumbent telecommunications operators to the extent that they have retained a strong market position on their national markets, particularly for the operation of local loop networks and for the provision of voice telephony services.

6–018   *High market shares* — The existence of a large market share is generally considered as the principal indicator of the existence of a dominant position, particularly if it persists over time. It is also the most commonly used criterion in this respect. But as the market share does not provide any indication of the competitive processes of the relevant market, this factor alone cannot be determinative, save if the share is extremely high. A market share of over 50 per cent is rebuttably presumed to be evidence of dominance,[49] *i.e.* that competitors are unable to expand their output by a sufficient volume to meet the shifting demand resulting from the undertaking's price increase. By contrast, undertakings with market shares of less than 25 per cent can be presumed not to enjoy a (single) dominant position on the market concerned.[50] Market shares of between 30 and 40 per

---

[45] See para.1–012, n.35, at paras 78 and 79.

[46] See, *e.g.* Case C–41/90 *Höfner and Elser v Macrotron* [1991] I E.C.R. 1979 and Case T–229/94 *Deutsche Bahn* [1997] II E.C.R. p.1689.

[47] See *e.g.* Case C–18/88 *RTT v GB-Inno-BM* [1991] I E.C.R. 5941, para.17.

[48] See 1991 Competition Guidelines, para.5–004, n.17, para.79.

[49] See Access Notice, para.5–004, n.18, para.73 and SMP Guidelines, para.1–012, n.35, para.75; see also Case C–62/86, *AKZO v Commission* [1991] I E.C.R. 3359, para.60; Case T–228/97, *Irish Sugar v Commission* [1999] II E.C.R. 2969, para.70, *Hoffmann-La Roche v Commission*, para.6–014, n.38, above, para.42; and Case T–139/98, *Amministrazione Autonoma dei Monopoli di Stato (AAMS) v Commission* [2001] II E.C.R. 3413, para.51.

[50] See SMP Guidelines, para.1–012, n.35, para.75; see also Recital 15 of Merger Control Regulation, n.89, which sets out a rebuttable presumption that such a market position does not confer dominance.

cent are generally not indicative of dominance, although in appropriate cases they may be.[51] Market shares of between 40 and 50 per cent are evidence of dominance, depending on: (i) the evolution of the market share level over time; (ii) the size of the market shares of the nearest competitors, and (iii) the presence of other factors that may indicate dominance.[52]

The Commission has indicated that, in relation to markets for access to facilities (such as a network), the economic significance of obtaining access to a specific network depends on the coverage of the network with which interconnection is sought. Accordingly, the market power of a given company controlling a facility will be measured partly by the number of subscribers who are connected to termination points of the communications networks of that company as a percentage of the total number of subscribers connected to termination points in the relevant geographic area.[53] In order to determine dominance in cases involving access to facilities, it is necessary to define the relevant market narrowly: ownership of a network or facility (such as an up-linking station or cable landing station) that forms its own relevant market will usually imply dominance.[54]

In order to constitute reliable indicators of dominance, high market shares must persist over time, normally for at least three to five years,[55] although a decline over that period does not necessarily rebut the existence of a dominant position, particularly if the market shares are very high to start with.[56]

6–019 ***Barriers to entry*** — In assessing the existence of dominance, the Commission examines whether the market is characterised by certain factors that may restrict the ability of new entrants to enter the market as effective competitors, the so-called "barriers to entry". Such factors include large start-up (or sunk) costs, economies of scale, technical resources, control by the incumbent operator of strategic infrastructure or intellectual property rights, or the need for a large distribution system. Regulatory requirements (such as licences, and rights to frequencies) can also form barriers to entry, if they are limited and thus not readily available to newcomers. The overall size and strength of the undertaking alleged to be dominant may in itself be a barrier to entry, as it could dissuade competitors.[57] Some of the barriers to entry specific to the communications sector are reviewed below.

6–020 ***Technical resources*** — The possession of technological advantages may be a barrier to entry and constitute an indication of dominance.[58] In the communications sector, the possession of information concerning access protocols or interfaces necessary to ensure the interoperability of

---

[51] Case C–250/92, *Gøttrup-Klim v Dansk Landsbrugs Grovvareselskab Amba* [1994] I E.C.R. 5641.

[52] See Bellamy and Child, para.4–001, n.4, para.9–039 *et seq.*

[53] See Access Notice, para.5–004, n.18, para.72.

[54] See para.6–023, below.

[55] See *Hoffmann La-Roche*, para.6–014, n.38, above.

[56] See Joined Cases T–24/93, etc. *Compagnie Maritime Belge Transports v Commission* [1996] II E.C.R. 1201, on appeal cases C–395 and 396/969, [2000] I E.C.R. 1365 (shares of 90%); *British Airways/Virgin*, O.J. 2000 L244/56 (shares of 40%, having declined over eight years from 48%).

[57] See *Michelin*, para.6–014, n.38, above; *Hoffmann-La Roche*, para.6–014, n.38.

[58] See *Hoffmann-La Roche*, para.6–014, n.38, above; Case T–51/89, *Tetra Pak Rausing v Commission* [1990] II E.C.R. 307; Case T–83/91 *Tetra Pak International v Commission* [1994] II E.C.R. 755.

software and hardware may constitute a barrier to entry.[59] The possession of technical resources may also facilitate the introduction of proprietary technology and can thus foreclose third party entry into the market.[60]

6–021 *Licences and other regulatory barriers* — In the telecommunications sector, barriers to entry are often high because of legislative and other regulatory requirements, in particular the need to hold a licence, and to obtain rights to scarce resources such as frequencies or numbers. These requirements may in particular limit the number of available licences and — in connection with this — the provision of certain services. While licences for the operation of a fixed telephony network or to provide services on fixed networks can be obtained easily from the relevant authority, the number of mobile telephony licences is restricted in all Member States due to the scarcity of the available spectrum. Once all available licences are allocated, new entrants are unable to enter the mobile market in question, unless they can come to a commercial agreement with an existing licensee. This could be a roaming agreement or a mobile virtual network operator agreement.[61] The same rationale applies to frequency rights, which are required for communication services that involve the transmission of signals by wireless means. Rights over land may also be indicative of dominance, if access to the land is needed by competitors.[62]

6–022 *Intellectual property rights* — When technical information is protected by intellectual property rights which grant a legal monopoly over the protected information, this may be a further indication of dominance.[63] Although it may be a factor contributing to the establishment of dominance, ownership of an intellectual property right does not in itself establish dominance.[64] The question is whether the holding of such an intellectual property right enables the owner to impede competition to an appreciable extent on the relevant market.[65]

6–023 *Control of access to "essential facilities"* — Despite the liberalisation of the telecommunications sector, control of access to facilities (*e.g.* leased lines and networks) is still likely to be considered as a strong indicator of the continuing dominance of incumbent telecommunications network operators in their respective national infrastructure markets. This will be the case until effective alternative infrastructures to the incumbent's network (*i.e.* networks of new entrants and of cable television and utility companies) become available and can provide effective competition to the incumbent. A facility would be deemed "essential" when access to it cannot be reasonably duplicated for technical, legal or economic reasons. A company owning or

---

[59] See 1991 Competition Guidelines, para.5–004, n.17, para.81.

[60] See concerns of the German Cable Office in its decision prohibiting the acquisition of German cable networks by Liberty Media, Case B7-168/01 of February 22, 2002, para.68 *et seq.*, *www.bundeskartellamt.de/B7-168-01.pdf*.

[61] The New Regulatory Framework offers Member States the possibility of allowing spectrum trading, which would enable third party entry into mobile markets after the licensing process is over. It remains to be seen how and to what extent this possibility will be used.

[62] See *Flughafen Frankfurt/Main*, O.J. 1998 L72/30.

[63] See *Tetra Pak International*, para.6–020, n.58.

[64] See Case 238/87 *Volvo v Veng* [1988] E.C.R. 6211; Joined Cases C–241 and 242/91P, *RTE and ITP v Commission ("Magill")* [1995] I E.C.R. 743.

[65] In *Magill*, n.64, above, the Court of Justice considered that television stations, because they were the only source of the information needed to publish a weekly television listing magazine, enjoyed a monopoly over this information owing to it being protected by copyright, and were therefore dominant in the market for listings magazines, as they were able to use their copyright to prevent effective competition on that market.

controlling access to such an essential facility will be deemed to enjoy a dominant position in the market for access provision to that facility within the meaning of Article 82.[66]

Even if a facility is not considered to be "essential", Article 82 may still apply and may oblige dominant operators to provide access to their facilities, or change the conditions under which access is granted and/or other services are provided. In the course of the sectoral inquiries into the telecommunications sector, the Commission found several indications that competition is restricted by the behaviour of incumbent operators with respect to their control of the local loop and of leased lines.[67] Access to facilities can be refused outright or be effectively refused by excessive prices, imposing discriminatory conditions or by simply delaying the process of providing access to a competitor.

6–024 Dominance as a purchaser — Because they are still dominant in the markets for operating networks and providing certain telecommunications services (*e.g.* voice telephony and leased lines), incumbent telecommunications network operators will continue to purchase a very high share of some communications equipment, works or software services. Accordingly, to the extent that there are no alternative buyers for a substantial part of a supplier's output on a specific equipment market, network operators may be considered to be dominant with respect to the demand for these products or services, with the result that suppliers of such services or products are dependent on them.[68] The dependence of suppliers on communications network operators must be examined on a case-by-case basis. In *Alcatel/Telettra*, a concentration between equipment suppliers in Spain, the Commission found that, although the merged entity would have accounted for a very high market share for line transmission equipment and microwave equipment in Spain, the concentration did not create a dominant position because on the relevant markets Telefonica, as the incumbent telecommunications network operator, was the unique buyer of this equipment, and had the ability to source equipment from alternative suppliers, thereby countervailing any market power that the merged entity might have had.[69] When prohibiting the acquisition by Liberty Media of a substantial part of Deutsche Telekom's broadband cable network, the German Federal Cartel Office was concerned with Liberty's high purchasing power on the market for set-top boxes.[70] If the transaction had been completed, Liberty would have been in a position to purchase up to 10 million set-top boxes, and could have been a dominant purchaser of such boxes.

6–025 Joint or collective dominance — Article 82 also applies when two or more companies together abuse a dominant position. Any individual or collective abuse by one or more undertakings of a joint or collective dominant position will infringe Article 82.[71] For two or more

---

[66] See Access Notice, para.5–004, n.18, para.74; for a review of the concept of essential facility, see para.6–043 *et seq.*

[67] See Squire Sanders, Legal Study on Part II of the Local Loop Sectoral Inquiry, February 2002; European Commission, Working Document on the Initial Results of the Leased Lines Sector Inquiry, September 8, 2002, available at: *http://europa.eu.int/comm/competition/antitrust/others/sector_inquiries/local_loop.*

[68] See 1991 Competition Guidelines, para.5–004, n.17, para.82.

[69] Case M.42, *Alcatel/Telettra*, O.J. 1991 L122/48.

[70] See *BKartA*, Case No.B7-168/01, decision of February 22, 2002, para.6–020, n.6, above, para.84.

[71] Case C–30/87, *Bodson* [1988] E.C.R. 2479; Case T–6877 and 78/89 *Società Italiana Vetro v Commission* (*Italian Flat Glass*) [1992] II E.C.R. 1403; Case C–393/92, *Almelo* [1994] I E.C.R. 1477; *Compagnie Maritime Belge*, para.6–017, n.56, above [2000] I E.C.R. 1365; and Case T–228/97 *Irish Sugar v Commission* [1999] II E.C.R. 2975.

companies to be considered jointly (or collectively) dominant, the following conditions must be met: (i) the companies must have substantially the same position *vis-à-vis* customers and competitors that a single company would have if it had a dominant position (*e.g.* two telecommunications network operators covering the same geographic area)[72]; (ii) "even in the absence of structural or other links between them, they operate in a market the structure of which is considered to be conducive to co-ordinated effects"[73]; and (iii) they adopt common conduct on the market.[74] It is not entirely clear to what extent the assessment of joint or collective dominance in the context of Article 82 differs from the assessment of joint or collective dominance in the context of the Merger Control Regulation and — after the entry into force of the New Regulatory Framework — of *ex ante* regulation under Article 14 of the Framework Directive. The Commission has taken the position that the analysis of joint or collective dominance under Article 82 is the same as the analysis of this concept under the Merger Control Regulation.[75] The judgment of the Court of First Instance in the *Airtours* case[76] suggests that there cannot be a finding of collective dominance unless the Commission can demonstrate a situation of "co-ordinated oligopoly" or "tacit collusion".[77]

Annex II of the Framework Directive contains a "checklist" for market characteristics and provides — for the first time ever — statutory guidance on the characteristics that must be present if a market can be considered as being collectively dominated. This checklist is also relevant for the analysis under Article 82. It is not impossible that competition and/or regulatory authorities will raise collective dominance concerns in various telecommunications markets, where a small number of strong players offer or demand fairly uniform products and services. Examples could include: mobile markets (including roaming); cable transmission markets; markets for the provision of

---

[72] See *Compagnie Maritime Belge*, para.6–018, n.56, above, para.36.

[73] See Framework Directive, para.1–009, n.25, Annex II. For a review of the case law on collective dominance, see the Opinion of Advocate General Fenelly in *Compagnie Maritime Belge*, para.6–018, n.56, above, para.19–35.

[74] Cases C–140 to 142/94, *DIP v Comune di Bassano del Grappa* [1995] I E.C.R. 3257. The Commission does not consider that the existence of agreements between the companies is necessary for a finding of joint dominance. The kind of interdependence that is characteristic of oligopolistic markets would be deemed to constitute a sufficient economic link for that purpose.

[75] See Gonzalez-Diaz, "Recent Developments in EC Merger Control Law The Gencor Judgment" (1999) 3 *World Competition* 22. For the development of the Community Court's case law on the Merger Control Regulation, see Cases C–68/94 and C–30/95, *French Republic v Commission (Kali & Salz)* [1998] I E.C.R. 1375 and Case T–102/96 *Gencor v Commission* [1999] II E.C.R. 753. In *Gencor*, the Court rejected Gencor's assertion that the existence of structural links between the allegedly dominant companies is a prerequisite for a finding of joint or collective dominance. In *Gencor*, the Court took into consideration the following additional factors in establishing collective dominance: product homogeneity, similar cost structures, high market transparency, price-inelastic demand, slow demand growth, mature production technology, high entry barriers, high levels of market concentration, a lack of buyer power and a low level of competition. See Korah, "Gencor v Commission: Collective Dominance" (1999) E.C.L.R. 336 and Gonzalez-Diaz, above.

[76] In *Airtours*, the Commission had applied the concept of joint dominance to prohibit the acquisition by Airtours of First Choice, two operators in the UK foreign package holiday market, despite the UK foreign package holiday market apparently not having all the characteristics of an oligopolistic market (there was no product homogeneity, volatile market shares, rather low barriers to entry). The prohibition decision was annulled by the Court of First Instance: Case T–342/99, *Airtours v Commission* [2002] II E.C.R. 2585.

[77] *Airtours, ibid.*, para.60 *et seq.*

leased lines; and markets for media content rights. Although mobile operators apparently compete intensively at the retail level in most national markets, the Commission has indicated that the market for wholesale roaming was a market conducive to a finding of collective dominance.[78] Moreover, the other markets mentioned above could also be subject to similar findings as few suppliers hold large shares in the market for leased lines, the level of concentration in most European cable markets has increased significantly in recent years and attractive rights for television content (*e.g.* sport and movies) are supplied by only few sellers.

6–026 Dominance on closely related markets — In the *Tetra Pak* case, the Court of Justice held that, when a company is dominant on a specific product market, it may commit an abuse of that dominance on other product markets (where it is not dominant) that are closely related to the dominated market. In other words, a finding of dominance on a specific market may be extended to closely related markets.[79] This rationale can be applied to closely related horizontal and vertical markets. To the extent that incumbent telecommunications network operators have a strong position on infrastructure markets and on the services markets downstream of that infrastructure, the Commission may well find, based on the *Tetra Pak* precedent, that such telecommunications network operators hold a dominant position on these related markets as a whole, by relying on evidence of dominance on only one of these markets.

This competition law concept of the "leveraging" of market power from one market to another has also been included in the New Regulatory Framework. Pursuant to Article 14(3) of the Framework Directive, an undertaking with SMP on market A may under some conditions be deemed to have SMP also on a closely related market B and would thus be subject to *ex ante* regulation on that market as well. It therefore remains to be seen whether Article 82 will still play a major role in the future as far as leveraging problems in the communications sector are concerned, because leveraging issues may instead be addressed by way of *ex ante* regulation.

2. Abuse of a Dominant Position

6–027 Introduction — Dominance is not in itself prohibited by Article 82 and there is no restriction on a dominant undertaking with reasonable and normal commercial conduct.[80] However, the difference between what is permissible and prohibited conduct for a dominant company is often difficult to establish. The Court of Justice has held that

> "[t]he concept of abuse is an objective concept relating to the behaviour of an undertaking in a dominant position which is such as to influence the structure of the market where, as a result of the very presence of the undertaking in question, the degree of competition is weakened

---

[78] See Initial Findings of the Sector Inquiry into Mobile Roaming Charges, para.1–037, n.3, p.3.

[79] See *Tetra Pak International* para.6–020, n.58, above. Access Notice, para.5–004, n.18, para.65. The adequacy of the Court's reasoning has been criticised, as it may have the effect of punishing legitimate competition by dominant companies on those markets where they are not dominant: Naftel, "Does the European Commission's Telecommunications Access Notice Send the Correct Economic Signals to the Market?" (1999) 5 *Phoenix Center for Advanced Legal & Economic Policy Studies Paper Series*, No.5, January 1999 10–13, and Korah, "Tetra Pak II — Lack of Reasoning in Court's Judgment" (1997) II E.C.L.R. 98.

[80] See Commission, XXIVth Report on Competition Policy (1994), point 207.

and which, through recourse to methods different from those which condition normal competition in products or services on the basis of the transactions of commercial operators, has the effect of hindering the maintenance of the degree of competition still existing in the market or the growth of that competition".[81]

Therefore, as a general guideline, any conduct by a dominant firm which seriously and unjustifiably distorts competition within a properly defined market will be prohibited by Article 82 if it affects trade between Member States. The concept of abuse of a dominant position is based on the assumption that dominant companies have a "special responsibility" towards competitors, suppliers and customers, because of their strong position on the market, not to engage in certain conduct that may distort competition that would be permissible if undertaken by non-dominant firms.[82] Specific market conduct is not abusive if it is objectively justified.

In the communications sector, the application of a "special responsibility" *rationale* has traditionally been applied to incumbent telecommunications operators, which are former monopolists. The activities of these companies were mostly developed from public services, which by definition had been subject to general interest obligations. Following the complete liberalisation of the sector, telecommunications companies, which were privately owned and run from the outset, have grown to become global players. Consequently, Article 82 may increasingly be found to apply to companies that do not have any roots in the public sector.

(a) Price-Related Abuses

6–028 Introduction — Article 82(a) expressly identifies unfair selling prices as abusive. Therefore, dominant communications operators can infringe Article 82 by charging prices that are either too high or too low. In the first case, the infringement lies in the fact that either consumers or competitors are charged higher prices than are justified by the value of the service or product received. The anti-competitive behaviour by the dominant operator is based on the exploitation of its ability to charge such prices due to the lack of effective competition that it faces. In the second case, the dominant operator is able to use its financial resources or other economic possibilities, which stem from its dominance, in order to charge unfairly low prices, which cannot be met by its competitors in the market, thereby effectively blocking competitors' access to the market or forcing them from it. The following paragraphs will review a number of pricing-related abuses that have commonly appeared in the communications sector.

6–029 Excessive pricing — A communications operator may not charge excessive prices for the services offered by it on the market in which it holds a dominant position.[83] In *General Motors*, the Court of Justice adopted a test of "fairness" based on the relationship between the price charged and the economic value of the good or service in question provided by the dominant firm.[84] A price

---

[81] *Hoffmann-La Roche*, para.6–014, n.38, above, para.541.
[82] *Michelin*, para.6–014, n.38, above.
[83] Case T–228/97, *Irish Sugar plc v Commission* [1999] II E.C.R. 2975.
[84] Case 26/75, *General Motors Continental v Commission* [1975] E.C.R. 1367 para.12; see also *United Brands*, para.6–014, n.38, above.

is excessive if it has no reasonable relationship to the economic value of the good or service.[85] In order to determine whether a price is "excessive", the cost of the product or service in question must be analysed.[86] This is a difficult analysis to undertake, particularly if intellectual property rights are involved, as an analysis of the dominant firm's cost structure is required. In this context, it would be acceptable to include in the "fair" price a significant profit margin to compensate for the risk associated with the development of a new network. This is essential if the incentives for communications operators to invest in research and development and product development are to be maintained.[87]

When following a cost-based approach, appropriate cost allocation is fundamental to determining whether a price is excessive. For instance, when a company is engaged in a number of activities, it will be necessary to allocate the relevant costs to the various activities, together with an appropriate contribution towards common costs.[88] Appropriate cost allocation may be difficult in the communications sector, as many dominant incumbent operators have until recently operated as government departments under public budget rules and do not prepare accounts by activity. However, the New Regulatory Framework will oblige dominant undertakings to prepare proper accounts by separate business activity.[89] The Commission adopted a cost-based approach in its investigation of Belgacom's prices for access to subscriber data required for the publication of telephone directories.[90]

6–030 If a cost-based analysis is not feasible, alternative costing methods may be used, for example comparing prices with those of comparable goods or services supplied by other undertakings[91] or the prices for the same goods or services in different Member States.[92] The Commission

[85] A price based on the subjective value of the good or service for the user (because, for instance, of the intended use) and which bears no reasonable relationship to the costs incurred in supplying it would thus be deemed abusive: see 1991 Competition Guidelines, para.5–004, n.17, para.96.
[86] For the cost allocation rules under the New Regulatory Framework, see para.1–183 *et seq.*, above.
[87] See Dolmans, para.6–009 above, n.22, para.4–87. The author also refers to the extent to which a share of the telecommunications network operator's fixed network costs may be charged to a competing value-added service provider using the network. This question is also addressed in the Commission's communication on interconnection pricing, which describes the Commission's intended use of forward-looking long-run average incremental costs ("FL-LRAIC") to assess the appropriateness of operators' interconnection prices. This method allows the network operator to include in its interconnection charges a proportion of the capital investment needed to adjust network capacity in the long term. See also para.1–185.
[88] See Access Notice, para.5–004, n.18, para.107.
[89] Access Directive, para.1–011, n.29, Art.11(1), second para. at Art.13. See also, above, para.1–155 *et seq.*
[90] See *ITT Promedia/Belgacom*, XXVIIth Report on Competition Policy (1997), point 67. This investigation was triggered by a complaint from ITT Promedia arguing that the prices charged by Belgacom for subscriber data (based upon a proportion of ITT Promedia's revenue) were excessive and discriminatory within the meaning of Art.82. The Commission carried out an investigation with the support of an expert auditing firm. The proceeding was terminated following a settlement with Belgacom which agreed to a substantial reduction (by more than 90%) of its prices by dropping any variable component in relation to the turnover or profits of directory publishers; Commission Press Release IP/97/292 of April 11, 1997. See also Haag and Klotz, "Commission Practice concerning excessive pricing in telecommunications" 2 (1998) *Competition Policy Newsletter*.
[91] See Case 30/87, *Bodson* [1988] E.C.R. 2479 and Joined Cases 110/88, 241/88 *François Lucazeau v SACEM* [1989] E.C.R. 2811.
[92] See *United Brands*, para.6–014, n.38, above. This "benchmarking" approach has been used for general (*i.e.* fixed-to-fixed) interconnection prices, as well as in investigations into fixed-to-mobile prices and international accounting rates: see Naftel, para.6–026, n.79, above, p.32.

used this method in its investigations into Deutsche Telekom's pricing for network access[93] and the provision of carrier pre-selection and number portability.[94] An inter-country comparison approach has also been taken by the Commission in its sectoral inquiries into mobile roaming and leased lines, in order to identify possible excessive pricing in the area of wholesale roaming tariffs[95] and in the area of leased line prices in the bandwidths of 2 Mbps, 34 Mbps and 155 Mbps.[96] In both cases, the results from the sector inquiry have led to the opening of individual cases under Article 82. With respect to leased lines, two *ex officio* cases have been closed after significant price reductions have occurred.[97]

The Court of Justice has held that, in determining whether a price is excessive, account may be taken of Community legislation setting out prices in a particular sector.[98] The Commission would thus not be prevented from referring to pricing decisions taken by NRAs in the framework of *ex ante* regulation under the Access Directive.[99]

6-031 *Price squeeze* — The second form of abuse involving unfairly (and thus anti-competitively) high charges is called "price squeeze" (or "margin squeeze"). It can only be committed by vertically integrated companies, which at the same time use the services of their upstream businesses to provide the services of their own downstream businesses and sell those upstream services to third parties that compete with their downstream businesses. A price squeeze by a dominant network operator occurs when it is shown that the dominant company's own downstream operations could not (given their own retail prices) operate profitably on the basis of the price charged to its competitors by the upstream business of the dominant company.[1] In other words, the dominant undertaking will increase its wholesale (upstream) prices and reduce its retail (downstream) prices, making it impossible for downstream competitors to compete profitably.[1a] A

[93] See Commission Press Release IP/96/975, November 4, 1996. In this case the Commission considered that Deutsche Telekom was charging excessive tariffs for access by competitors to its network. The Commission based its finding on a comparison between access prices in Germany and in similar Member States. The Commission concluded that a difference of more than 100% between Deutsche Telekom's prices and the price levels in comparable markets was unacceptable and was evidence of excessive pricing. As a result, Deutsche Telekom agreed to reduce its prices from 38% in the case of local network access to 78% for access to the long-distance network.

[94] See Commission Press Release IP 98/430 of May 13, 1998. The Commission adopted a similar comparative (or "benchmarking") approach in its assessment of Deutsche Telekom's charges for the provision of carrier pre-selection and number portability. In particular, the Commission used its investigative powers under Art.11 of Regulation 17/62 to request information from businesses and industry associations in other Member States. The Commission terminated its investigation in light of parallel proceedings before the German NRA, Reg TP. Deutsche Telekom subsequently agreed to reduce its prices, notably for carrier pre-selection, by almost 50%.

[95] See Initial Findings of the Sector Inquiry into Mobile Roaming Charges, para.6-004, n.5, above.

[96] See Initial Results of the Leased Lines Sector Inquiry, para.6-023, n.67, above.

[97] See Commission Explanatory Memorandum — Leased Lines, where the Commission indicated that it closed the leased line sector inquiry and two *ex officio* cases in Belgium and Italy, on December 10, 2002 *http:// europa.eu.int/comm/competition/antitrust/others/sector_inquiries/leased_lines/exmemonovember2002.pdf.*

[98] See Case 66/86, *Ahmed Saeed* [1989] E.C.R. 838.

[99] See, above, para.1-011, n.29.

[1] See Access Notice, para.5-004, n.18, paras 117-119. See also *Napier Brown-British Sugar*, O.J. 1998 L284/41. For a criticism of the Commission's approach to price squeeze in the Access Notice, see Naftel, para.6-026, n.79, above, pp.333-334.

[1a] See Commission decision in the *Deutsche Telekom* case, imposing fines of €12.6 million for price-squeezing new entrants in the local-loop market, Press Release IP/023/717 of May 21, 2003; O.J. 2003 L263/9.

dominant operator will support the loss-making operation of its downstream operations either by allocating to its upstream operations costs that should normally be allocated to its downstream operations, by improperly determining the transfer prices between its businesses or by cross-subsidising the downstream business with the excessive revenues of the upstream business. Sometimes, a situation susceptible to price-squeeze occurs as a consequence of historic particularities of certain national markets.[1b] In order to address this issue, the Commission has recommended that already early on vertically integrated dominant operators produce separate regulatory accounts for each of their different business areas.[2]

A price squeeze is basically a combination of excessive pricing at the upstream level and predatory pricing on the downstream level. The Commission does not always pursue price squeeze cases as such, but sometimes prefers to open a case on the basis of predatory pricing alone.[3] The Commission investigated Wanadoo's ADSL internet access service pricing on this basis. It believed that the retail prices charged by Wanadoo for various retail products were below cost. In its reasoning, the Commission stated, however, that the alleged predation could be remedied either by raising Wanadoo's retail prices, or by an increase in the wholesale prices charged to Wanadoo by its parent, France Télécom.

6–032 *Predatory pricing* — Predatory pricing takes place where a dominant firm sells a good or service for a sustained period of time below cost with the intention of eliminating or weakening a competitor or deterring entry to the market. Predatory pricing must not be confused with normal price competition that is the result of the competitive process. Pricing will be deemed predatory and thus abusive if it is: (i) below the dominant company's average variable cost (which is presumed to have a predatory intent); or (ii) below its average total cost and a predatory intent on the part of the dominant firm can be shown.[4] In the Access Notice, the Commission indicated that a test based upon concepts of variable and total costs may not be appropriate in the communications sector, because the sunk costs of the network represent a significant part of the costs of offering a service and because of the fact that the marginal or variable cost is a negligible proportion of costs.[5] Instead, the Commission has recommended examining the total incremental costs of offering a service over an appropriate time frame, generally in excess of one year.[6] However, in a recent case,[7] the Commission initiated an investigation alleging predatory pricing on the basis of prices being below average variable costs during an initial period and in a subsequent period, pricing below total cost, together with an intention to predate. In earlier cases, the Commission took the position that predatory pricing could also occur when a dominant firm undertakes selectively targeted price reductions aimed at certain customers in order to eliminate competitors, while retaining its prices

[1b] See, *e.g.* the pending *KPN* case, Commission Press Release IP/02/483 of March 27, 2002.
[2] See Commission Recommendation on interconnection in a liberalised telecommunications market — Part 2: Accounting Separation and Cost Accounting, O.J. 1998 L141/6. See also, above, para.1–155 *et seq.*
[3] See *Wanadoo Interactive*, Commission Press Release IP/01/1899, of December 21, 2001 and IP/03/1025 of July 16, 2003.
[4] See Case C–62/86 *Akzo v Commission* [1991] I E.C.R. 3359. See also *Tetra Pak*, para.6–020, n.58, above.
[5] Likewise, in the broadcasting sector, the marginal cost, and thus the average variable cost of broadcasting to an additional viewer, is negligible when the transmitter is in operation.
[6] See Access Notice, para.5–004, n.18, paras 110–116.
[7] See *Wanadoo Interactive*, para.6–031, n.3, above. Wanadoo was fined €10.35 million.

above its total costs.[8] This suggests an evolution from a test of predation based on the relationship between cost and price to a test where price discrimination is the main criterion in identifying predatory pricing.[9]

6–033 *Cross-subsidisation* — Cross-subsidisation occurs when a business allocates all or part of the costs of its activities in one product or geographic market to its activities in another product or geographic market, or uses revenues from one activity to cover losses made in another activity.[10] Cross-subsidisation by a dominant communications operator could distort competition and therefore infringe Article 82 when it cross-subsidises operations where it faces competition (*e.g.* value-added downstream services) with the revenues derived from a market on which it is dominant (*e.g.* network provision).[11] The dominant operator would then be in a position to offer better prices, terms and conditions than its competitors on the competitive market, not as a result of efficiency or performance, but rather by artificial and unfair means such as using monopoly revenues earned on a different market. In the long term, this would affect the position of value-added service providers and discourage new entrants. In such a case, cross-subsidisation may give rise to predatory pricing on the downstream level, or could be the source of a price-squeeze situation, although it can exist even if the downstream operation is profitable. Cross-subsidisation can be the result of the direct allocation of costs between activities, or of funding the subsidised operations with low-interest loans or capital, or provision of premises, equipment, experts or other services at a cost substantially lower than market price.[12] In this context, the costs involved in setting up the new activity should be borne by the new activity alone and not by profits from the dominant business.[13]

6–034 Following the full liberalisation of the telecommunications market in January 1998, the question arose as to whether cross-subsidisation would continue to raise competition concerns. Indeed, it could be argued that cross-subsidisation should only be considered anti-competitive (and thus infringe Article 82) when revenue generated by activities conducted pursuant to an exclusive or

---

[8] See *Irish Sugar*, O.J. 1997 L258/1. Advocate General Fenelly took the same position in *Compagnie Maritime Belge*, para.6–018, n.56, above. He suggested that the Court of Justice did not define exhaustively the categories of predatory pricing in *Akzo* but only identified two types of predatory pricing. The issue of predatory pricing was not examined in substance by the Court of Justice. See also Andrews, "Is Meeting Competition a Defence to Predatory Pricing — The *Irish Sugar* Decision Suggests a New Approach" (1998) E.C.L.R. 49–57.

[9] Many economists consider that predation is an exceptional phenomenon unlikely to occur in practice, as in most cases a predator would not be able to recoup its losses and predation is thus an implausible strategy: see, *e.g.*, MacGee, "Predatory Pricing Cutting: the *Standard Oil* Case" (1958) *Journal of Law and Economics*. Other economists consider that predation is likely only in markets with high barriers to entry: see Elzinga & Mills, "Testing for Predation: Is Recoupment Feasible?" (1989) 34 *Antitrust Bulletin* 869.

[10] See 1991 Competition Guidelines, para.5–004, n.17, paras 102–108. For a detailed analysis of the concept of cross-subsidisation, see Hancher and Buendia Sierra, "Cross-subsidization and EC Law" (1998) 35 C.M.L.R. 901 and Abbamonte, "Cross-subsidization and Community Competition Rules: Efficient Pricing Versus Equity" (1998) E.L.R. 1998 414.

[11] For an analysis of the conditions under which cross-subsidisation may constitute a state aid prohibited by Art.87(1) of the EC Treaty, see Hancher and Buendia Sierra, para.6–033, n.10, pp.927–938 and Abbamonte, para.6–033, n.10, pp.430–433. See Case C–39/94 *SFEI v La Poste* [1996] I E.C.R. 3547 and the Commission decision in *SFMI-Chronopost*, O.J. 1998 C164/37.

[12] See, *e.g. SFEI v La Poste, ibid.*

[13] See XVI Report on Competition Policy (1986), points 334–336, that contains the finding of a study carried out on behalf of the Commission on predatory pricing.

special right granted by the state are used to subsidise other competitive activities; if so, as exclusive and special rights have been abolished, cross-subsidisation would no longer be an issue. However, the Commission addressed this question in its *Unisource* and *Uniworld* decisions and took the view that cross-subsidisation by a dominant operator remained an abuse, despite the abolition of exclusive or special rights.[14] The Commission's position in this respect may be considered deplorable. Indeed, preventing a business from subsidising its activities with income generated from activities in markets in which it enjoys a dominant position would seem to be an unjustified extension of the principles established by the Court of First Instance in *Tetra Pak II*.[15] The Court of First Instance held in that case that an abuse may be committed in markets which are distinct from, but neighbouring, those in which a dominant position exists when the markets are closely associated. The close association between the markets means that the economic power deriving from the dominance in one market may be exploited in an abusive fashion in the other, competitive market. The Court's judgment would not appear to have been intended to be so wide as to restrain a company from using income generated from activities in a market in which it enjoys a dominant position to subsidise activities in other markets.

Cross-subsidisation is not easy to establish. Most of the time, it will be necessary to show that cross-subsidisation amounts to a predatory practice, on the basis that the price of the product or service in question is below its average variable costs. This will not often be the case in the telecommunications sector since, as discussed above, fixed costs, *i.e.* the sunk costs of the network, may be very high and marginal or variable operating costs very low. Alternatively the Commission will have to show that the service's price is set below its average total cost and the dominant undertaking has a predatory intent.[16] In order to facilitate a cost-based analysis, the Commission and the Council have adopted several measures aiming at improving the transparency of the accounting practices of dominant operators and facilitating the detection of cross-subsidisation practices.[17] The New Regulatory Framework permits NRAs to impose price controls and accounting separation obligations "in situations where the lack of effective competition means that any operator concerned is capable of sustaining prices at an extensively high level, to the detriment of end users".[18] Unlike the 1998 Regulatory Framework, this will also cover the situation

---

[14] See *Unisource* and *Uniworld*, Commission Decisions of October 29, 1997, O.J. 1997 L318/24 and L318/1 respectively. For a detailed review of these decisions, see paras 8–274 *et seq.*

[15] *Tetra Pak II*, para.6–020, n.58, above.

[16] See para.6–032, above.

[17] Under the so-called "Faulhaber" rule, it is accepted in economic theory that there is no cross-subsidy when the price of a product or service is greater than or equal to its incremental cost (*i.e.* the cost associated with producing a second product or service) and less than or equal to its stand alone cost (*i.e.* the hypothetical cost of producing a specific product or service in isolation from any other product or service). Another method is the fully distributed cost method under which all costs, including common costs, are allocated to all the different products or services of the company in question. Optimal pricing rules can also be used to detect cross-subsidisation: see Abbamonte, para.6–033 n.10, pp.416–417, citing Faulhaber, "Cross-Subsidisation: Pricing in Public Enterprises" (1975) *American Economic Review* 966. The Commission seems to prefer a cost-based analysis of cross-subsidisation. The Commission has recommended that interconnection costs be calculated on the basis of forward-looking long-run average incremental costs (FL-LRAIC) rather than on the basis of the fully distributed costs method, despite the clear preference of incumbent operators for the fully distributed costs method, as this would have allowed them to include in their costs of providing interconnection the historical cost of developing their networks: see para.1–185.

[18] See Access Directive, para.1–011, n.29, Art.13.

of price-squeezing by a dominant network operator. Other than this, the Access Directive does not mandate the use of a specific cost allocation methodology (*e.g.* forward-looking long-run average incremental costs (FL-LRAIC)), and only provides limited guidance to NRAs as to how they should calculate operators' costs.

6–035   Moreover, in the context of its review of joint ventures, the Commission has, in certain cases, as part of its approval required certain undertakings from the parties to establish separate and transparent accounting in order to guarantee that no cross-subsidisation would result between reserved and competitive activities.[19] In these cases, the Commission seems to have considered that the prices of the joint ventures should be fixed at a level above their total costs, including an appropriate proportion of the costs that are common both to the operation of the joint venture's business and those of the parent companies. This standard seems rather strict to the extent that it goes beyond the standard adopted by the Court of Justice in *Akzo*, *i.e.* prices above average total cost are presumed to be lawful.[20]

(b) Non-Price-Related Abuses

6–036   *Extension of dominance into neighbouring markets* — Prior to 1998 and the full liberalisation of the Community's telecommunications sector, the Court of Justice had already established the principle that incumbent telecommunications operators could not take advantage of their dominant positions in the markets for reserved services (*e.g.* voice telephony services and public network provision) to extend, without objective reasons, their dominance into markets where they did not have exclusive or special rights and therefore faced competition. In *RTT v GB-Inno-BM*, the Court of Justice held:

> "[if] an undertaking holding a monopoly in the market for the establishment and operation of the network, without objective necessity reserves to itself a neighbouring but separate market . . . [this] constitutes an infringement of Art. 8[2] of the Treaty".

Similarly, in *Telemarketing*[21] it held that

> "an abuse within the meaning of Art. 8[2] is committed where, without an objective necessity, an undertaking holding a dominant position on a particular market reserves to itself or to an

---

[19] See *Eirpage*, O.J. 1991 L306/22, discussed at para.8–284 *et seq.*, *Atlas*, O.J. 1996 L239/23, discussed at para.8–269 *et seq.*, and *Unisource/Uniworld*, para.6–039, n.14, above, discussed at para.8–274 *et seq.* These cases concerned co-operative joint ventures reviewed by the Commission under Art.81. The Commission has however also addressed the issue of cross-subsidisation under the Merger Control Regulation in *PTT Post/ TNT/GD Express Worldwide*, Case M.843, Commission Decision of November 8, 1996.

[20] See Hancher and Buendia Sierra, para.6–033, n.10, above, pp.920–921. The authors consider that, in industries such as telecommunications where common costs are important, it is reasonable to require that prices be fixed at a level above average total costs. The severity of the test is, according to them, somehow balanced by the operator's discretion in the choice of the cost allocation method. For a discussion of the extent to which Art.86(2) can be relied upon to justify cross-subsidisation to finance public service obligations, see para.6–054 *et seq.*

[21] Case 311/84 [1985] E.C.R. 3261, paras 26 and 27. See also Case 41/83 *Italian Republic v Commission* [1985] E.C.R. 873.

undertaking belonging to the same group an ancillary activity which might be carried out by another undertaking as part of its activities on a neighbouring but separate market, with the possibility of eliminating competition from such undertaking."

Despite the full liberalisation of the communications markets and the abolition of all exclusive and special rights, the prohibition on the unjustified extension of dominance into neighbouring markets will continue to apply in so far as incumbent telecommunications operators remain in a dominant position in those markets that were formerly reserved to them, or in any other markets that have since developed (such as internet service provision). As mentioned above,[22] the Commission has indicated that it will rely on the *Tetra Pak* precedent to control any extension of dominance on a facility market to those services markets that are dependent on that facility. Accordingly, any unjustified extension of its upstream dominance onto a downstream service market by a dominant network access provider (*e.g.* through a denial of access to its network) is likely to be prohibited by Article 82 unless this extension has already been dealt with by *ex ante* regulation. This could also apply in other circumstances, such as the adoption by a dominant network operator of conditions for network configuration (*e.g.* adoption of proprietary network architecture as sole standard for the provision of value-added services) that make access (and ultimately service provision to end-users) objectively more difficult for non-integrated competing service providers.[23]

This principle should not, however, prevent dominant network operators from entering new services markets, provided that they do not exploit their dominant position on their traditional markets in order to gain an unfair advantage on these new services markets.[24]

6–037 Refusal to deal and usage restrictions — A dominant firm cannot refuse to supply an existing customer unless it can show an objective justification for doing so.[25] It is not clear what constitutes an "objective justification". However, the wish of the dominant firm to enter the market of the customer,[26] or to retaliate disproportionately against the customer's trading policies,[27] do not constitute acceptable "objective justifications". Furthermore, it is not in itself an objective justification for an undertaking holding a dominant position on a particular market to reserve to itself or to an undertaking belonging to the same group an ancillary activity which might be carried out by another undertaking as part of its activities on a neighbouring but separate market, with the

---

[22] See para.6–026.

[23] See Access Notice, para.5–004, n.18, para.102.

[24] In Case JV.2, *ENEL/France Telecom/Deutsche Telekom*, where the Commission examined, under Art.2(4) of the Merger Control Regulation, the possible "spill-over" effects of a joint venture, which was to operate on the Italian fixed and mobile voice telephony and data communications market, on competition on the French and German markets on which France Telecom and Deutsche Telekom were, respectively, dominant.

[25] In *Commercial Solvents*, the Court of Justice held that "an undertaking which has a dominant position on the market in raw materials and which, with the object of reserving such raw material for manufacturing its own derivatives, refuses to supply a customer, which is itself a manufacturer of these derivatives, and therefore risks eliminating all competition on the part of this customer, is abusing its dominant position within the meaning of Art.8[2]", Cases 6 and 7/73, *Commercial Solvents v Commission* [1974] E.C.R. 223.

[26] *Commercial Solvents, ibid.*

[27] See *United Brands*, para.6–014, n.38.

possibility of eliminating all competition from such undertaking.[28] In *Telemarketing*, a Luxembourg television station, RTL, refused to broadcast telemarketing advertisements unless the telephone number referred to in the advertisement was that of its telemarketing subsidiary. The Court of Justice upheld the Commission's decision that the conduct of RTL, which held a dominant position on the market for advertisements directed at the French speaking community in Belgium, was an abuse of its dominant position. Usage restrictions imposed by a dominant business on its existing customers would also be deemed to be abusive. In the *Belgian RTT* case, the Commission held that a dominant firm in a market for telecommunications services may not impose any restrictions on the use of such services unless they "are necessary to the task of providing the service of general economic interest with which it has been entrusted".[29] In this case, the Commission objected to a practice of RTT which consisted of subjecting the lease of telecommunications circuits to a restriction that the circuits not be used for the transmission of third-party data traffic. Although this case relates to a period where network operation was still a reserved service, it would seem that these principles will be applicable in the liberalised environment as long as telecommunications network operators are still dominant in network provision. Other examples of usage restrictions include the prohibition imposed by a telecommunications network operator on third parties: (i) to connect private leased circuits by means of concentrator, multiplexer or other equipment to the public switched network; and (ii) to use private leased circuits for providing certain services in competition with the telecommunications network operator.[30]

Another example of an abuse would arguably be the refusal of a dominant incumbent telecommunications operator to supply to internet service providers a flat rate wholesale tariff to allow them to offer unmetered internet access. In Germany, the NRA (RegTP) ordered Deutsche Telekom to offer such a flat rate wholesale product to ISPs, which it had refused to do.[31] It cannot be excluded that the refusal by an incumbent operator to supply such a product or even an unjustified delay in the supply of wholesale services can constitute an abuse of a dominant position.[32]

6–038 In principle, a dominant undertaking can refuse to grant third parties licences to its intellectual property rights.[33] It is only in exceptional circumstances that the exercise of an exclusive

---

[28] Case 311/84, *Centre Belge d'Études de Marché-Télémarketing (CBEM) v SA Compagnie Luxembourgeoise de Télédiffusion (CLT)* [1985] E.C.R. 3261 (*Telemarketing*). See also *RTT v GB-INNO*, para.6–017, n.47, above.

[29] See Commission Press Release IP/90/67 of January 29, 1990. For a review of the conditions under which a dominant firm can derogate from Art.82 of the EC Treaty based on its "general interest" duties under Art.86(2) of the EC Treaty, see para.6–054 *et seq.*

[30] See 1991 Competition Guidelines, para.5–004, n.17, para.89.

[31] See RegTP Press Release, available at: *www.regtp.de/en/aktuelles/pm/02290/*. On October 10, 2002, the Administrative Court in Cologne annulled RegTP's decision. In its reasoning, the Court held that Deutsche Telekom was not obliged (under German rules) to provide services to a competitor, which it (formally) does not provide to its own subsidiaries or downstream operations: see decision VG Köln Az.1 L1617/02, not yet published.

[32] In its sector inquiry into the leased lines market, the Commission observed that some incumbent operators used unjustified delays in supplying leased lines to competitors: see Commission Working Document on the Initial Results of the Leased Lines Sector Inquiry, 2000, para.6–023, n.67, above, p.19.

[33] See *Volvo v Veng*, para.6–021, n.64, above, where the Court of Justice held that "the right of the proprietor of a protected design to prevent third parties from manufacturing and selling or importing, without

right arising from an intellectual property right, such as a refusal by a dominant undertaking to grant a licence, would be deemed abusive. The Court of Justice defined these circumstances in the *Magill* case, which concerned a refusal by three British and Irish broadcasters to license their programme schedules (which were protected by copyright under applicable national law) to a third party that wished to launch its own "listings" magazine in competition with the broadcasters' own magazines. The circumstances in which a dominant undertaking may not refuse to grant a licence are[34]:

(i) the licence to the intellectual property right in question must be necessary for access to a downstream market from that on which the undertaking is dominant;

(ii) the refusal to grant a licence must have the effect of either

   (a) limiting product innovation to the detriment of customers, taking into account that "a specific, constant, and regular pattern of potential demand" for a new product was not being met by the dominant firm itself, or

   (b) excluding all competition from the downstream products or services market; and

(iii) there should be no objective and proportionate justification for the refusal to grant a licence.

It is not clear from the decision what would constitute an objective and proportionate justification. If these circumstances are met, the dominant undertaking must license its intellectual property rights to third parties on terms, including royalties, that are reasonable. Thus, competition law can impose compulsory licensing obligations on dominant undertakings, although only in exceptional circumstances. However, compulsory licensing obligations will not exist where the intellectual property rights in question are not essential for competitors to compete on the downstream market.[35] In practice, a balance of interests will have to be drawn between the improved competition on the downstream market and the possibility of reduced incentives on dominant firms to innovate that may be the result of the compulsory licence. It would seem, however, that the fact that licensing of a competitor may result in lost revenue is not a legitimate justification for a refusal to grant a licence.[36]

---

its consent, products incorporating the design constitutes the very subject-matter of this exclusive right. It follows that an obligation imposed upon the proprietor of a protected design to grant to third parties, even in return for a reasonable royalty, a licence for the supply of products incorporating the design would lead to the proprietor thereof being deprived of the substance of the exclusive right, and that a refusal to grant such a licence cannot in itself constitute an abuse of a dominant position".

[34] See *RTE and ITP v Commission*, para.6–022, n.64, above.

[35] See Case T–504/93, *Tiercé Ladbroke v Commission* [1997] II E.C.R. 923.

[36] See *British Midland/Aer Lingus*, O.J. 1992 L96/34 and *Sea Containers/Stena Sealink*, O.J. 1994 L15/8. The *Magill* judgment has been widely criticised in so far as it jeopardises the substance of intellectual property rights and therefore might undermine the incentive to invest in research and development, to the longer-term detriment of consumers. See, *e.g.* Walbroeck, "L'arrêt Magill: quel avenir pour le droit d'auteur?" in *Questions de Droit de l'Audiovisuel Européen* (Bruylant, 1997), pp.7–16 and Van Liederkerke, "Access to Infrastructure, Networks and Services under EC Competition Law. Interconnection in Telecommunications and Precedents in other sectors", in *The Law of Information Super-Highways and Multimedia: A New Challenge* (Bruylant, 1997), pp.136–137. See also *IMS Health*, in which the Commission ordered an allegedly dominant company to grant licences to third party competitors: Case C481/01 PR, *NDC Health v Commission (Application for interim measures)*, Order of the President of the Court, April 11, 2002 [2002] I E.C.R. 3401. See also, below, para.6–050 *et seq.*

6–039 *Discriminatory practices* — Article 82(c) states that an abuse may consist of applying similar conditions to equivalent transactions with other trading parties, thereby putting them at a competitive disadvantage. Accordingly, a dominant firm may not discriminate with regard to the price or quality of the service provided to different customers or service providers. Discrimination consists of not treating like cases alike, or of treating different cases in the same way. However, there is no discrimination if there is an objective justification for the difference.[37] For instance, it is perfectly legitimate for a supplier to charge a customer a lower price based on objective factors such as cost savings and technical considerations specific to supplying that customer or because the customer is operating at a different level of trade (wholesale or retail).[38] Discriminatory pricing may also be justified in order to "meet competition", in the framework of a defence strategy by a dominant firm which aims at preserving its existing customer base from being won by competitors,[39] although there may be limits to this if the discrimination has an exclusionary object or effect aimed at competitors. This defence would only justify purely defensive acts and would not excuse a strategy aimed at eliminating competition by undercutting the prices of competitors or other aggressive strategies with a view to gaining new customers.[40] Discrimination may relate to elements such as tariffs, restrictions or delays in making network connections, the provision of maintenance or repair services or information about network programming, signalling protocols, technical standards or any other facilities necessary for proper interconnection and interoperability, numbering and routing.[41] Discrimination may also arise in respect of the technical configuration of the network access, in relation to, *e.g.*:

(i) the degree of technical sophistication of the access (*i.e.* restrictions on the type or level in the network hierarchy of exchange involved in the access or the technical capabilities of this exchange);

(ii) the number and/or location of connection points (*i.e.* the requirement to collect and distribute traffic for particular areas at the switch which directly serves that area rather than at a higher level of the network hierarchy may have a significant impact on the cost of the company seeking access); and

(iii) equal access (*i.e.* the possibility for customers of the party requesting access to obtain the services provided by the access provider using the same number of dialled digits used by the customers of the latter).[42]

Discrimination in the conditions for access to certain facilities will restrict competition on the downstream market on which the company requesting access is operating or is planning to operate.[43] In particular, incumbent telecommunications operators may not grant other operators

---

[37] See Bellamy and Child, para.4–001, n.4, para.9–083.

[38] See Access Notice, para.5–004, n.18, paras 120 and 128.

[39] See Waelbroeck "Price Discrimination and Rebate Policies Under EC Competition Law" (Fordham Corporate Law Institute), Chap.10, pp.147–160; Springer, "Meeting Competition: Justification of Price Discrimination under EC and US Law" (1997) E.C.L.R. pp.251–258.

[40] See Case T–65/89, *BPB Industries and British Gypsum v Commission* [1993] II E.C.R. 389.

[41] See 1991 Competition Guidelines, para.5–004, n.17, para.98.

[42] See Access Notice, para.5–003, n.18, para.127.

[43] See 1991 Competition Guidelines, para.5–004, n.18, para.121. The Commission notes that discrimination can also have an effect on competition if it operates between closely related downstream markets. For instance, mobile and fixed telephony, despite a certain convergence, still constitute separate product markets, largely due

less favourable access conditions (including in terms of interconnection capacity, access pricing and quality of lines) than those granted to their own services businesses.[44]

6–040 To a large extent, discrimination by dominant undertakings in the communications sector is already prohibited or controlled by way of *ex ante* regulation. In so far as an operator has been designated as having SMP, which will be possible only if it has an individual or collective dominant position on a specified market, that operator will be subject to non-discrimination obligations regarding access and prices.[45] Consequently, it would not be surprising if many future cases arising under Article 82 did not predominantly involve discriminatory practices in the core area of application of the New Regulatory Framework, but increasingly concern other activities, outside the scope of *ex ante* regulation. These potential cases could include, for instance, cable operators discriminating between affiliated and non-affiliated broadcasters and producers of set-top box middleware discriminating between various content and services providers as to the way in which their offerings are displayed by EPGs.[46]

6–041 Bundling and tying practices — Article 82(d) states that an abuse may consist in making the conclusion of contracts subject to acceptance by the other parties of supplementary obligations which, by their nature or according to commercial usage, have no connection with the subject of such contracts. Accordingly, it may be an abusive practice for a dominant firm to subject the supply of products or services in respect of which it holds a dominant position (the "tying product") to an undertaking from the customer to purchase other products (the "tied products") from it or a third party. In so far as the former incumbent telecommunications network operators are still the dominant providers of the services that were reserved to them until full liberalisation (*e.g.* voice telephony), it would be abusive for them to bundle those services with other services, through contractual provisions, commercial pressure or through discounts.[47] The tying or bundling of services would not be considered abusive if it was objectively justified by technical considerations, if the two products are components of a single wider system[48] or if they are supplied together by nature or by custom.

---

to the significant price difference between the two services. In such a case, charging higher interconnection prices to mobile operators by comparison with fixed operators would have the effect of hampering the convergence of fixed and mobile services and therefore reducing competition to fixed services from mobile operators.

[44] The issue of non-discriminatory treatment between third parties and dominant undertakings' own business divisions, subsidiaries or joint ventures has been addressed by the Commission in a number of cases. See, *e.g.*, *Unisource/Uniworld*, O.J. 1997 L318/24 and *Iridium*, O.J. 1997 L16/87. See also Case T–229/94 *Deutsche Bahn v Commission* [1997] II E.C.R. 1689, where the Court of First Instance confirmed that discrimination between a third party and the dominant firm's own subsidiary or division constituted an infringement of Art.82. For a discussion of this case, see Kallaugher and Völcker, "Art. 8[2], Essential Facilities and Telecommunications" in *IBC Telecommunications and EC Competition Law Conference* (1998), pp.11–12. For a criticism of the requirement that the dominant firm provide non-discriminatory access to competitors at the prices it charges its own businesses, see Naftel, para.6–026, n.79, p.14, who stressed that under US anti-trust law's "essential facilities" doctrine, even a successful claimant wins no more than the right to access the facilities at commercial (retail) prices.
[45] See Access Directive, para.1–011, n.29, Art.10.
[46] See, *e.g.* the commitments given by the parties in Case JV.37, *BSkyB/Kirch PayTV*, O.J. 2000 C110/45, discussed below at para.8–189.
[47] See Access Notice, para.5–004, n.18. para.103.
[48] See Case T–30/89, *Hilti v Commission* [1991] II E.C.R. 1439, confirmed on appeal, Case C–53/92P [1994] I E.C.R. 667; and Case T–83/91, *Tetra Pak v Commission* [1994] II E.C.R. 755, confirmed on appeal in Case C–33/94P, *Tetra Pak v Commission* [1996] II E.C.R. 5951.

This may be increasingly difficult to assess in the context of the telecommunications sector (and in related IT sectors[49]), as the products manufactured and marketed in these sectors are technologically very complex.

6–042   Abuse of a dominant purchasing position as a purchaser — Despite the liberalisation of the Community telecommunications market, incumbent communications operators will generally still be considered to hold a dominant position on their national market in respect of the purchase of equipment and services. Accordingly, Article 82 prevents such dominant communications operators from imposing on their suppliers, as a condition for purchasing goods from them: (i) excessively favourable prices or other trading conditions; (ii) a requirement to be appointed as the exclusive distributor for the purchased product; (iii) the granting of a licence on the standards for the products purchased or other products. It would also be an abuse for a dominant operator to systematically exclude a supplier from the possibility of supplying it, without economic necessity (*e.g.* on nationality grounds).[50]

3. A specific Type of Abuse: Restricting or Refusing Access to Essential Facilities

6–043   Introduction — Despite the full liberalisation of the telecommunications sector in 1998 and the significant growth of competition in communications markets since then, the Community's communications markets have remained relatively concentrated by conventional competition standards.[51] In several Member States, incumbent operators continue to control the only nation-wide fixed-line telecommunications infrastructure. In the local loop market, even strong *ex ante* access regulation has not resulted in significant competition.[52]

The essential facilities doctrine has traditionally served as the conceptual underpinning of the Commission's policy of promoting competition in services by obliging dominant incumbent operators to grant third parties access to their networks and other facilities. However, after the judgment of the Court of Justice in *Bronner*,[53] expectations as to the regulatory importance of the essential facilities doctrine have suffered a setback.

[49] See the *Microsoft* cases in the US (87 F Supp. 2d 30 (DDC 2000)) and before the European Commission, Commission Press Release IP/01/1232 of August 30, 2001. 10 months after the US Department of Justice settled its decade-long anti-trust investigation of Microsoft, the Commission has sent Microsoft another Statement of Objections to give it a final opportunity to comment before concluding its anti-trust probe, see Press Release IP/03/1150 of August 6, 2003.

[50] See 1991 Competition Guidelines, para.5–004, n.17, paras 116–120.

[51] See the Commission's Seventh Report on the Implementation of the Telecommunications Regulatory Package (2001); see also OECD, Competition and Regulation Issues in Telecommunications, February 1, 2002, (DAFFE/COMP, 2002) 6. In 2002, the total number of authorised voice telephony operators decreased by 9% and for public network operators by 1.5%: see the Commission's Eighth Report on the Implementation of the Telecommunications Regulatory Package, para.1–108, n.52, p.15.

[52] See Council Regulation 2887/2000 of December 18, 2000 on Unbundled Access to the Local Loop, O.J. 2000 L336/6; see Nikolinakos, "Promoting Competition in the Local Access Network: Local Loop Unbundling" (2001) E.C.L.R. 266; Michalis and Ruhle, "Local Access Competition and Local Loop Unbundling — A Comparative Analysis" M.M.R. 23; Monti, *Getting Competition in Local Access*, speech made in the context of a public hearing sector inquiry on local loop unbundling in Brussels on July 8, 2002 (SPEECH/02/323); and Buigues, *Benefits for consumers from Competition in the "New Economy"*, speech of February 26, 2002 in Madrid, p.11: *http://europa.eu.int/comm/competition/speeches/text/sp2002_004_en.pdf*.

[53] Case C–7/97, *Oscar Bronner v Media Print* [1998] I E.C.R. 7791.

(a) The Origin and Scope of the Essential Facilities Doctrine

6–044 The term "essential facilities doctrine" finds its origins in commentaries on United States antitrust case law and is based on applying and interpreting Section 2 of the Sherman Act.[54] In applying Article 82 of the EC Treaty, the European Commission and the European Courts have adopted many of the criteria that have been developed in US antitrust law applying the essential facilities doctrine. Thus, the Commission and the Community courts perceive the essential facilities doctrine as a subset of abuse cases under Article 82.[55]

Initially, the Commission applied a very broad interpretation of the essential facilities doctrine. Generally, it defined an "essential facility" as "a facility or infrastructure, without access to which competitors cannot provide services to their customers".[56] According to the Commission, a dominant undertaking owning or operating an essential facility was obliged to grant access to either its competitors or customers if a refusal to do so would have had a significant effect on competition and could not be legitimately justified.[57] This very broad application of Article 82 to "essential facilities" by the Commission has been heavily criticised by commentators[58] and has been subject to controls by the Court of Justice in recent case law.

6–045 The Court of Justice has not explicitly accepted or rejected the essential facilities theory, but has significantly limited its scope. In *Magill*[59] and *Bronner*[60] the Court held that a refusal by a dominant firm to supply a product or service can only be regarded as an abuse of its dominance and thus infringe Article 82 if the following conditions are met[61]:

- the product or service is indispensable for carrying on the business as there is no actual or potential substitute;

[54] Section 1 of the Sherman Act, 15 USC, reads as follows: "every person who shall monopolize, or combine or conspire with any other person or persons, to monopolize any part of the trade or commerce among several States, or with foreign nations, shall be deemed guilty of a felony, and, on conviction thereof, shall be punished by fine not exceeding $10,000,000 if a corporation, or, if any other person, $350,000, or by imprisonment not exceeding three years, or by both said punishments, in the discretion of the court".

[55] See OECD, The Essential Facilities Concept (Paris 1996), p.93; and Capobianco, "The Essential Facility Doctrine: Similarities and Differences Between the American and the European Approach" [2001] 26 E.L.R. 548.

[56] *B&I plc/Sealink Harbours* [1992] 5 C.M.L.R. 255, para.41, in which the Commission referred in a note to former decisions, such as *Commercial Solvents, Télémarketing, Renault, Volvo, ERT, Magill* and *Inno*; see furthermore *Sea Container/Stena Sealink* O.J. 1994 L5/8, para.66. A broad overview of the Commission's case law is presented by Temple Lang, "Defining Legitimate Competition: Companies' Duties to Supply Competitors, and Access to Essential Facilities" (1994) 18 *Fordham International Law Journal* 437, at pp.455–467.

[57] The Commission referred for the first time to the term "essential facilities" in *Sea Containers/Stena Sealink*, and ruled that an undertaking which occupies a dominant position in the provision of an essential facility, and which refuses other companies access to that facility without objective justification, or grants access to competitors only on terms less favourable than those which it gives to its own services, infringes Art.82.

[58] Capobianco, para.6–044, n.55; Martenczuk, "Die "essential" facilities-Doktrin im Europäischen Wettbewerbsrecht und der Zugang zu Vertriebsnetzen" EuR 565; Koenig/Loetz, "Bedeutung der Essential facilities-Doktrin für den Zugang zu Netzinfrastrukturen in europäischen Telekommunikationsrecht" (2000) E.W.S. 377.

[59] *RTE and ITP v Commission*, para.6–022, n.64, above.

[60] *Oscar Bronner v Media Print*, para.6–043, n.53, above.

[61] The Court of First Instance has taken the same position; see *Tiercé Ladbroke SA v Commission*, para.6–038, n.35, above.

- the refusal is likely to eliminate all competition in the market on the part of the business requesting the product or services; and

- there is no objective justification for the refusal.[62]

With the first condition, the Court limits the application of the essential facilities doctrine to those cases where it is physically, legally or economically impossible for any competitor to duplicate the facility and excludes its application where it is simply economically unattractive (but not impossible) to replicate it.[63] After *Bronner*, the duplication of a facility is only deemed as economically impossible if it is not viable even assuming the same usage rate and capacity as for the facility in question. In *Bronner*, the court held that

> "[f]or such access to be capable of being regarded as indispensable, it would be necessary at the very least to establish [. . .] that it is not economically viable to create a second home-delivery scheme for the distribution of daily newspapers *with a circulation comparable to that of the daily newspapers distributed by the existing scheme*". (emphasis added)[64]

As to the second condition, which requires that the refusal is likely to eliminate all competition on the relevant downstream market, it is important that by denying a competitor access to an essential facility operated by it, the dominant undertaking is preserving its own dominance on the downstream market.[65] The mere fact that, by retaining a facility for its own use, a dominant undertaking retains an advantage over a competitor cannot justify requiring access to be made available to it. The Court already stated in *Tiercé Ladbroke*[66] that a refusal to sell is not abusive if the refusing supplier is not present on the market where the requesting party wishes to operate. Therefore, a refusal to sell should only be abusive when the refusal aims at protecting the dominant undertaking's market power. That is why in the port cases, a port operator, who is not active in the downstream market for ferries, can refuse to deal with a ferry operator without infringing Article 82.[67]

---

[62] See *Bronner* case, para.6–043, n.53, para.41. The first criterion is new in so far as it has never before been a condition elaborated by the Commission in its decisions relating to refusals to deal or to grant access. See Doherty, "Just What Are Essential Facilities?" 2001 38 C.M.L.R. 397, at pp.419–422, who examines the previous case law, respectively applying the criteria set out by the Court in *Bronner*. In *Magill*, the Court of Justice set out a fourth condition, *i.e.* the refusal prevents the appearance of a new product for which there was a potential consumer demand. This is clearly a circumstance specific to the licensing of intellectual property rights (with which *Magill* was concerned) and the absence of which would not preclude the application of Art.82 to a refusal to supply goods or services not protected by intellectual property rights. See the discussion of the IMS case below at para.6–051, where the existence of this fourth condition, where the essential facility is an intellectual property right, is an issue of contention in the framework of the appeal of the Court of First Instance.

[63] See *Bronner*, para.6–043, n.53, above, paras 44–45. See also The Opinion of Advocate General Jacobs in *Bronner*, paras 65–66 and Capobianco, para.6–044, n.55, above.

[64] *Bronner* case, para.6–043, n.53, above, para.46.

[65] See *Tiercé Ladbroke SA v Commission*, para.6–038, n.35, para.130. See also the Opinion of Advocate General Jacobs in *Bronner* who pointed out that the dominant undertaking has to have at least a "genuine stranglehold on the related market".

[66] See para.6–038, n.35, above.

[67] *Irish Intercontinental Group v CCI Morlaix (Port of Roscoff)* [1995] 5 C.M.L.R. 77.

(b) Overlaps Between the Essential Facilities Doctrine and Sector-Specific Regulation

6–046   Essential facilities in the Access Notice — In the 1998 Access Notice, which remains in effect in parallel with the New Regulatory Framework,[68] the Commission described three different kinds of scenario in which a refusal to grant access to telecommunications facilities to third parties might trigger the application of Article 82[69]:

   (i) a refusal to grant access for the purposes of providing a service where another operator has been given access by the facility provider to allow it to provide such services;

   (ii) a refusal to grant access for the purposes of a providing service where no other operator has been given access by the facility provider to allow it to provide such services market; and

   (iii) a withdrawal of access from an existing customer.

Only the second case relates to the concept of essential facilities because the first and third constellations do not reach beyond the traditional concepts of non-discrimination and refusal to deal. According to the Commission, a dominant undertaking will infringe Article 82 by refusing access to its (essential) facilities if:

   (i) access to the facility in question is generally essential in order for third parties to compete on the related market;

   (ii) there is sufficient capacity available to provide access;

   (iii) the facility owner fails to satisfy demand for an existing service or product, blocks the emergence of a potential new service or product, and/or impedes competition on an existing or potential service or product market;

   (iv) the undertaking seeking access is prepared to pay a reasonable and non-discriminatory price for such access and to accept non-discriminatory terms and conditions for access; and

   (v) there is no objective justification for refusing to provide access.[70]

6–047   Essential facilities under the New Regulatory Framework — General competition law is applicable in parallel with *ex ante* regulation under the New Regulatory Framework. The crucial question is, what scope *ex ante* regulation will leave for the application of the essential facilities doctrine in practice. The regulation of the communications sector under the New Regulatory Framework addresses most of the issues of access and market entry that have hitherto been addressed using the essential facilities doctrine. The concept of access[71] has been broadened to bring

---

[68] See the reference, which is taken to the Access Notice in the SMP Guidelines, para.1–012, n.35, para.24.
[69] See Access Notice, para.5–004, n.18, para.84 *et seq.*
[70] See *ibid.*, para.91; see also, above, para.6–037.
[71] Garzaniti and von Bonin, "The Impact of the New SMP concept Telecommunications Operators in the EU" *Global Competition Review* 54 (June 2002).

additional facilities within the scope of the regulatory access regime.[72] Under Article 12 of the Access Directive, NRAs will be able to require access to be granted to specific network elements and associated facilities when the following conditions are fulfilled:

(i) a dominant undertaking owns specified network elements and/or facilities;

(ii) it denies access or proposes unreasonable terms or conditions having a similar effect;

(iii) the denial of access will hinder the emergence of a sustainable competitive market at the retail level; and

(iv) providing access is feasible.[73]

6–048 Notwithstanding the provisions of the Access Directive, the essential facilities doctrine may still apply in appropriate cases to other facilities in the communications sector,[74] *e.g.* in relation to set-top boxes,[75] satellite transponder capacity,[76] EPGs,[77] internet navigator software and internet backbone networks.[78] In such an event, an NRA may refrain from using the provisions of the Access Directive to mandate access to a specific facility. The essential facilities doctrine may also provide undertakings with additional grounds for seeking access in cases falling outside of the New Regulatory Framework, which only applies to electronic communications services, electronic communications networks, associated facilities and associated services,[79] but excludes content services. Cases on the borderline of the "regulation of transmission" and the "regulation of content" (including radio or television broadcasting content, financial services, information society services and web-based content[80]) may still fall within the scope of the essential facilities doctrine. In addition, as Article 82 has direct effect (unlike the provisions of the New Regulatory Framework

---

[72] An example is the right of mobile operators to install microwave links on their competitors' base station, which has traditionally been viewed as an essential facilities problem and may today fall under the regulatory regime: see Kallaugher and Völcker, para.6–039, n.44, above, citing a judgment of the OLG Düsseldorf of September 2, 1997 (M.M.R. 1998, pp.258–261), where the German court considered that mobile base stations were essential facilities that could not be reproduced by competitors and that a refusal to grant access was an abuse of dominant position under the provisions of the German Act Against Restraints of Competition that corresponds to Art.82.

[73] In addition, the NRAs are obliged to take into account the initial investment of the facility owner, the need to safeguard competition in the long term, and any relevant intellectual property rights: see Access Directive, para.1–011, n.29, Art.12(2).

[74] See the Access Notice, para.5–004, n.17, paras 6 and 7.

[75] See below, para.6–088.

[76] If all viewers' satellite reception dishes in a specific area are directed at a given satellite, new broadcasters that wish to reach those viewers may be forced to use that satellite, such that it could be an essential facility if there is no other suitable satellite available.

[77] This issue is whether the owner of an electronic programme guide could be required to give access to competitors and display the latter's programmes on its EPG.

[78] See the Commission's decision in *WorldCom/MCI*, where it took the position that WorldCom/MCI's internet backbone network would constitute an essential facility; see para.6–091, below.

[79] See Framework Directive, para.1–009, n.25, Art.1(1).

[80] See Framework Directive, para.1–009, n.25, Recital 5 and Art.2(c), and Access Directive, para.1–011, n.29, Recital 2, as a result of which services providing, or exercising editorial control over, content transmitted using electronic communications networks and services are excluded from the application of the New Regulatory Framework.

Directives), third parties may continue to use Article 82 and the essential facilities doctrine to seek access in private litigation and through complaints to the Commission.

6–049 In the future, broadcasters and ISPs could use the essential facilities doctrine when seeking access to electronic communication services and platforms in order to provide content to end-users. Even if ISPs' technical access to the economically important sector of broadband services[81] falls within the New Regulatory Framework,[82] it has to be noted that "web-based content" falls outside the access regime of the framework.[83]

4. The Use and Abuse of Intellectual Property Rights in the Light of Article 82 and the Essential Facilities Doctrine

6–050 Abuses of intellectual property rights — The mere ownership of an intellectual property right is not itself sufficient to establish dominance. Likewise, the exercise of an intellectual property right by a dominant firm is not in itself abusive.[84] However, the exercise by dominant firms of their intellectual property rights has been found to be abusive in the following cases: the registration of trademarks to divide markets; the imposition of unfair licensing terms; the bringing of infringement actions to force the defendant to enter into restrictive licensing arrangements; the acquisition by a dominant undertaking of an exclusive licence; and the charging of an excessive price for a product or service protected by an intellectual property right.[85] In *Ladbroke*, the Court of First Instance considered that it would be discriminatory and thus abusive behaviour for the holder of an intellectual property right to refuse to grant a licence to a third party if a licence had already been granted for the same product and geographic market to another company, unless there are objective reasons justifying the discrimination.[86] However, in *Magill*, the Court of Justice upheld a Commission decision which had the effect of ordering the compulsory licensing of television programme listings (which enjoy copyright protection under Irish and UK law) to an independent publisher. The product that the independent publisher wished to offer, a comprehensive TV listing of various channels, had not been provided by the broadcasters themselves.[87] A review of this jurisprudence by the European Courts is expected in the main proceedings of the appeal against the Commission's decision in *IMS Health*.[88]

6–051 In *IMS*,[89] the very broad application of the principles of the essential facilities doctrine by the Commission led to a conflict between competition and intellectual property law. In its decision,

---

[81] As to the "open access debate", see Wagner, Die "Open Access Debate" in den USA — Zugangsansprüche von Internet Service Providern zum Breitbandkabel" (2001) M.M.R. 659; and Robinson, "On Refusing to Deal With Rivals" (2002) 87 *Cornell Law Rev.* 1177, at pp.1223–1228.

[82] See Framework Directive, para.1–009, n.25, Recital 10.

[83] See Rosenthal, "Neue Antworten auf Fragen der Konvergenz — Entwicklungen des Kommunikationsrechts in Europa und den USA" (2002) *T.M.R.* 181, at p.186.

[84] See Case 107/76, *Hoffmann-La Roche v Centrafarm* [1978] I E.C.R. 1139.

[85] See Bellamy & Child, para.4–001, n.4, citing the relevant case law at paras 9–105 to 9–110.

[86] *Tiercé Ladbroke v Commission*, para.6–038, n.35, above.

[87] *RTE and ITP v Commission*, para.6–022, n.64, above.

[88] See Commission Decision of July 3, 2001, *NDC Health/IMS Health — Interim measures*, O.J. 2002 L59/18.

[89] Case T–184/01 *IMS Health Inc. v Commission* (2001) II E.C.R. 3193 and 2349. On August 10 and October 26, 2001 the Court of First Instance made orders suspending the Commission's decision in so far as it

the Commission held that it is unlawful for a dominant undertaking to refuse to license to its competitors its intellectual property rights that give it a competitive advantage on the very market on which that intellectual property is exploited and on which its competitors wish to use it. In *IMS*, the Commission granted interim measures in favour of competitors of IMS Health and required IMS Health to license its intellectual property rights to them, based on the principles of the essential facilities doctrine. IMS produces reports to pharmaceutical companies about the geographical development of the sales of pharmaceuticals in Germany. In order to produce these reports, IMS has developed, over many years, a structure to group raw sales data from pharmacies and wholesalers to show sales in small geographic areas — known as "bricks" — covering all of Germany. Each of the 1,860 "bricks" is made up of one or more postcode areas and contains at least four pharmacies. Once formatted in this structure, the data from pharmacies and wholesalers can be analysed according to the customer's needs. According to the Commission, IMS's refusal to share with competitors its intellectual property rights in the "brick structure" was an abuse of its dominant position because: (a) the 1,860 brick structure was indispensable for the competitors to carry on their business in competition with IMS, in so far as there was no actual or potential substitute for it; (b) IMS's refusal to license was not objectively justified; and (c) the refusal was likely to foreclose the market to potential new entrants and eliminate all prospects of competition in Germany, thereby resulting in IMS abusing its dominant position in Germany. The enforcement of the interim measures imposed by the Commission was suspended by the President of the Court of First Instance. The President of the Court noted that the Commission was relying on a very broad interpretation of the "exceptional circumstances" in which, according to *Magill*, Article 82 may require the licensing of intellectual property rights to third parties. Accordingly, there was an arguable case, to be determined in the main proceedings, that the Commission had wrongly applied *Magill*. In particular, the President took the position that there was a serious dispute regarding the correctness of the Commission's legal conclusion, that it was not required for the essential facilty doctrine to apply, that the refusal to license intellectual property rights by a dominant undertaking must prevent the appearance of a new product on a market separate from that on which the undertaking is dominant. He then found that the requirements for the granting of interim measures under Article 82 were not met and that the interim measures could have caused IMS serious and irreparable harm such that the balance of interests between those of IMS and its competitors was in favour of discharging the interim measures pending the Court's judgment in the substantive proceedings.

Accordingly, the exercise of intellectual property rights might be subject to restrictions imposed under Article 82 only in exceptional cases.[90] Such an exceptional case would require the following conditions to be cumulatively fulfilled:

- a licence to the intellectual property right is indispensable for the third party seeking access to it to carry on its business as there is no actual or potential substitute;

---

impaired interim measures requiring IMS Health to license its intellectual property rights to competitors. These orders were upheld by the Court of Justice on appeal: Case C–481/01 P (R), *NDC Health Corporation and NDC Health GmbH & Co. KG*, Order of April 11, 2002. The Commission later withdrew its interim decision, see Press Release IP/03/1159 of August 13, 2003.

[90] Case T–184/01, *IMS Health Inc. v Commission*, para.6–051, n.89, Order of October 26, 2001, para.94; upheld on appeal in Case C–481/01, *NDC Health v IMS Health*, Order of April 11, 2002, para.64, where the Court made reference to *Volvo v Veng, RTE and ITP v Commission*; see Schmidt, "Art.82's "Exceptional Circumstances" that Restrict Intellectual Property Rights" (2002) E.C.L.R. 210–216.

- the right owner's conduct must have the effect of reserving to itself the secondary market by excluding all competition on that market;

- the reliance on national copyright provisions must prevent the appearance of a new product, which the right owner does not offer and for which there is a potential consumer demand; and

- there must be no objective justification for the refusal.[91]

While the Commission is of the opinion that Article 82 may be infringed even if these conditions are not fulfilled,[92] the President of the Court of First Instance in *IMS* relied on *Magill* and *Bronner* to find that it was at least arguable that the Commission had wrongly extended the essential facilities doctrine by requiring IMS Health to license its competitors. The President of the Court of First Instance left open to the main proceedings the legal question as to (i) whether, for the essential facilities doctrine to apply to intellectual property rights, a refusal to license by a dominant undertaking must prevent the appearance of a new product on a market separate from that on which the undertaking in question is dominant; or (ii) whether it is sufficient that the refusal to license the IPR would eliminate all competition on the very market on which the holder of the IPR is actually itself in competition with the entity, seeking access to the IPR.[92a]

5. Access Rights and Infrastructure Competition

6–052 A general issue in telecommunications policy (though common to other liberalised sectors) is whether to promote the development of alternative infrastructure that would compete with the incumbent's network or promote the access by competitors to existing infrastructures. In the Access Notice, which remains in effect in parallel to the New Regulatory Framework, the Commission clearly elected to favour immediate access to existing infrastructures over the promotion of competition in the provision of networks. This is in line with the policy choice made in the New Regulatory Framework and with even more far-reaching initiatives in some Member States.[93] This strategy is also in line with specific public policy considerations such as the protection of the environment and planning a policy of sharing of facilities. Although this approach may foster competition in the provision of services in the short term, it can be questioned whether it would act against consumers'

---

[91] *IMS Health Inc. v Commission*, para.6–051, n.89, above, paras 96–98.

[92] In the opinion of the Commission, the sole exercise of copyright-related right may amount to an abuse of a dominant position, even in the absence of additional abusive conduct, when it prevents the appearance of a new product: *NDC Health v IMS Health — Interim measures*, para. 6–051, n.90, above, para.67.

[92a] In *IMS Health v NDC*, Advocate General Tizzano has taken the position that there is no abuse of dominant position where the company seeking access to the license wishes to exploit the IPR so as to compete in the same market as the owner of the IPR; Case C–481/01, *IMS Health v NDC*, not yet published.

[93] See German Telecommunications Act (TKG), s.33 and German Act Against Restraints of Competition (GWB) 1998, s.19(4)(4), which prohibits an incumbent company from refusing to grant access to its facilities or infrastructure to another company when it is factually or legally impossible for the company seeking access to compete on the upstream or downstream market without sharing the facilities or infrastructure in Germany. TKG, s.33(1) obliges an incumbent operator to grant access to competitors to its essential facilities. See also the judgment of the German Federal Administrative Court (BVerwG) of April 4, 2001 (6 C 6/00) rejecting an appeal by Deutsche Telekom AG against a decision of the German Regulatory Authority to grant third party access to its local loop, (2001) NVwZ p.1399. See further OVG Münster, judgment of February 15, 2002 (13 A 4075/00), (2002) M.M.R., at p.408.

interests in the long run by removing economic incentives for both incumbents and alternative infrastructure providers to invest in the enlargement and modernisation of their networks.[94] To the extent that new entrants can obtain access to the dominant incumbent's networks at the same price charged by the dominant operator to its own downstream services, new entrants may be less inclined to develop their own infrastructure, with the result that they remain dependent on the incumbent's network, which will in turn remain an actual or quasi monopoly in the longer term. This may ultimately reduce consumer choice and perpetuate the need for *ex ante* regulation. The regulation of access pricing and conditions also requires continuous monitoring by NRAs with inevitable shortcomings. It is thus arguable that competition and consumer interests would be better served in the long run by a regulatory policy that promotes infrastructure competition between various networks.

D. Restrictions on Market Conduct under Article 86 of the EC Treaty

6–053 This section reviews how the various provisions of Article 86 of the EC Treaty can apply to the market conduct of communications firms.[95]

1. Article 86(1) of the EC Treaty: The Prohibition of Monopoly Rights

6–054 Introduction — Article 86 is a very complex provision which has made a significant contribution to the process of liberalising markets in Europe that were originally monopolies, in particular in "utility sectors" such as telecommunications.[96] Article 86(1) of the EC Treaty contains an obligation on the Member States not to enact or maintain measures, which are contrary to the Treaty's rules, in particular (but not only) to the competition rules, with respect to certain undertakings. Article 86(2) of the EC Treaty provides for a limited exemption from the competition rules for such undertakings to the extent that they are "entrusted with the operation of services of general economic interest". Finally, Article 86(3) of the EC Treaty gives the Commission important legislative and executive powers to ensure compliance with these provisions by adopting directives and decisions to bring infringements of the Treaty to an end.

6–055 Article 86(1) and the liberalisation of the telecommunications sector — Article 86 applies to "public" undertakings and to undertakings to which "special or exclusive rights" have been granted. Many incumbent telecommunications operators in Europe are still "public" undertakings, because the Member States exercise, directly or indirectly, a dominant influence by virtue of their continued shareholdings in them.[97] With respect to "public" undertakings, Article 86(1) prohibits

[94] See the Opinion of Advocate General Jacobs in *Bronner*, para.6–043, n.53, above, para.94, stating in substance that compelling a competitor to grant access to its facilities created only with substantial investment and effort may undermine the incentives to undertake such investment in the future. The Access Notice has been criticised by commentators otherwise favourable to the "essential facilities" doctrine as an "over-zealous and over-interventionist approach": see Nikolanikos, "Access Agreements in the Telecommunications Sector — Refusal to Supply and the Essential Facilities Doctrine under EC Competition Law" (1999) E.C.L.R. 399, at p.410.
[95] For a brief description of the constituent elements of Art.86, see above, para.4–005 *et seq.* For a detailed analysis, see Bellamy and Child, para.4–002, n.4,, para.13–001 *et seq.*, and Whish, *Competition Law* (Butterworths, 4th ed., 2001) p.189 *et seq.*
[96] Whish, *ibid.*, p.190.
[97] See Transparency Directive, para.1–015, n.43, Art.2(1)(b), as amended by O.J. 2000 L193/75.

Member States from doing anything that would cause such undertakings to infringe other Treaty provisions, notably Articles 81 and 82.

6–056 With respect to private undertakings providing telecommunications services or networks, it would seem that, in so far as a Member State has fully implemented the sector-specific directives of the 1998 regulatory package and the New Regulatory Framework and abolished all "special or exclusive" rights to provide telecommunications services and networks, the Commission can no longer rely on Article 86(1) to object to the action of a Member State in favour of such private businesses. "Special or exclusive rights" are defined in the New Regulatory Framework's Liberalisation Directive.[98] Article 2(1) of the Liberalisation Directive requires Member States not to grant or maintain in force exclusive or special rights in the electronic communications sector. Therefore, the Authorisation Directive requires Member States to make the operation of all telecommunications networks and the provision of all telecommunications services subject to a general authorisation. This general authorisation can only be made subject to conditions that are objectively justified, non-discriminatory, proportionate and transparent.[99] Consequently, if a Member State has fully implemented these provisions, there can no longer be any private undertaking with exclusive or special rights within the meaning of Article 86(1).[1] In such a case, if a Member State were to infringe certain Treaty provisions in favour of a specific business or to take action that caused an undertaking to itself infringe the Treaty, the Commission would have to rely on Article 226 to initiate infringement action.

2. Article 86(2): Derogation from the Competition Rules for Public Undertakings Providing Services of General Economic Interest

6–057 **The concept of services of general economic interest** — Article 86(2) exempts from the EC competition rules undertakings that have been entrusted with providing services of general

---

[98] Liberalisation Directive, para.1–011, n.31, Art.1(5), according to which "exclusive rights" shall mean the rights that are granted by a Member State to one undertaking through any legislative, regulatory or administrative instrument, reserving it the right to provide an electronic communications activity within a given geographical area. According to Art.1(6), "special rights" shall mean the rights that are granted by a Member State to a limited number of undertakings through any legislative, regulatory or administrative instrument, which within a given geographical area: (a) designates or limits to two or more the number of such undertakings authorised to provide an electronic communications service or undertake an electronic communications activity, otherwise than according to objective, proportional and non-discriminatory criteria; or (b) confers on undertakings, otherwise than according to such criteria, legal or regulatory advantages which substantially affect the ability of any other undertaking to provide the same electronic communications service or to undertake the same electronic communications activity in the same geographical area under substantially equivalent conditions.

[99] This also applies to the rights of use for radio frequencies and for numbers (Art.6(1) of the Authorisation Directive, para.1–011, n.28).

[1] This conclusion is supposed by the judgment of December 12, 1996 of the Court of Justice in Case C–302/94, *R. v Secretary of State for Trade and Industry Ex p. British Telecommunications* [1996] I E.C.R. 6417, where the Court considered that, prior to the full liberalisation of the UK's telecommunications markets, BT and Mercury still enjoyed "special rights" within the meaning of the ONP Leased Lines Directive because they had been granted according to criteria which appeared to be neither objective, proportionate, nor free from discrimination, and gave a substantial competitive advantage to them over other network operators. However, when such a competitive advantage has been granted according to objective, proportionate and non-discriminatory criteria, there is no granting of a special right.

economic interest, to the extent that their application would obstruct the performance of those services. The Court of Justice held in *Corbeau* that there was justification within Article 86(2) for restricting competition to a business entrusted with the operation of a service of general economic interest (in this case, the postal monopoly) that involved more and less profitable operations, where the entry by a competitor into only the more profitable sectors would undermine the economic balance of the service on which the business depended.[2] This seems to suggest that Article 86(2) can be relied on in the context of the competition rules, to justify cross-subsidisation from a profitable service to a public interest service if it is the only means of ensuring the necessary economic conditions for the firm entrusted with public service obligations.[3] In *Commission v The Netherlands*,[4] the Court of Justice seems to have established that, for the derogation of competition rules under Article 86(2) to apply, it is not necessary to show that the financial equilibrium of the company would be threatened without the derogation, but that the company could not perform the public interest service in question under acceptable economic conditions if it were exposed to competition.

Community legislation, under the 1998 regulatory framework and the New Regulatory Framework has made it clear that Article 86(2) cannot be applied in the telecommunications sector, because it would arguably have prevented both the full liberalisation and the introduction of a fully competitive environment in this sector[5] and because Community law has laid down "universal service" obligations to ensure that the public interest in maintaining the provision of essential telecommunications services throughout the Community is maintained.

6–058   The concept of universal service — In order to ensure the availability of essential telecommunications services to subscribers throughout the Community under acceptable conditions, NRAs may impose on telecommunications undertakings certain universal service obligations. The conditions under which universal service is to be organised and funded, and under which undertakings may be made subject to universal service obligations, are subject to sophisticated regulation contained in the Universal Service Directive.[6]

3. Commission Action under Article 86(3) of the EC Treaty

6–059   Introduction — Article 86(3) obliges the Commission to ensure compliance with Article 86(1) and empowers it to adopt decisions or directives (addressed to the Member States) to that effect. Aside from being the legal basis for the series of liberalisation directives described in Chapter I, Article 86(3) enables the Commission, in case of an infringement of Articles 81 or 82 by a public undertaking or by an undertaking with special or exclusive rights, to proceed against the relevant Member State, in parallel with, or as an alternative to, a separate action against the

---

[2] Case C–320/91, *Procureur du Roi v Corbeau* [1993] I. E.C.R. 2533. See also above, Case C–393/92, *Almelo* [1994] I E.C.R. 1477 (concerning exclusive supply and purchasing contracts of electricity between Dutch regional and local distributors, challenged under Arts 86 and 81) and Cases C–157 and 160/94 *Commission v Netherlands etc.* [1997] I E.C.R. 5699 (concerning the legality of various statutory monopolies to import and export electricity and gas).

[3] Hancher and Buendia Sierra, para.6–033, n.10, pp.939–942.

[4] See above, n.2.

[5] See Commission Full Competition Directive, para.1–004, n.13.

[6] See above, para.1–011, n.30.

undertaking concerned.[7] The Commission has used its powers under Article 86(3) to ensure a "level playing field" for new entrants by taking action against Member States that discriminate in favour of the existing public operator in determining the conditions under which new entrants may provide services in competition with the public operator.[8]

6–060 **_Omnitel_** — In *Omnitel*, the Commission adopted a decision under Article 86(3) to ensure equal treatment between Telecom Italia Mobile (TIM) and Omnitel, by requiring TIM, a (then) state-controlled company that provided mobile services in Italy, to ensure fair competition.[9] Omnitel was a privately owned company, which had been required to pay a substantial licence fee to provide GSM mobile services in Italy. TIM had not paid a comparable licence fee. The Commission found that TIM enjoyed a monopoly on the Italian analogue mobile market and had special rights to operate a GSM mobile network. Its parent company, Telecom Italia, simultaneously enjoyed a monopoly in the telecommunications networks and voice telephony services at that time. The Commission further found that GSM mobile services should probably be regarded as belonging to a different market than analogue mobile services. The Commission identified a number of advantages that had been afforded to TIM that, in the Commission's view, would have allowed it to gain a dominant position in the Italian market for GSM mobile services.

The Commission found that Telecom Italia could infringe Article 82 by abusing its dominant position on the market for voice telephony on fixed networks and analogue mobile telephony by entering the GSM market and, for example, imposing interconnection charges that were not justified by the costs involved. The Commission also found that under Article 86(1), Italy was obliged to refrain from enacting measures that would, by increasing the access costs of the sole rival of a public undertaking, significantly distort competition. The Commission reasoned that as a result of the licence fee and other conditions imposed on Omnitel, TIM and Telecom Italia could adopt either of the two following commercial strategies, each of which would result in them infringing Article 82, and thus Italy infringing Article 86(1): (i) TIM could have decreased its GSM tariffs to a level so low that it would have resulted in Omnitel, burdened by the payment of the licence fee, not being able to compete profitably; or (ii) TIM could have exploited Omnitel's inability to make investments following the payment of the licence fee by, for example, limiting the provision of its GSM service and maintaining high tariffs for that service in order to divert customers to its analogue mobile services. In order to rectify the situation, the Commission adopted a decision requiring Italy either to refund the licence fee paid by Omnitel or to take other equivalent steps to remove the discriminatory burden imposed upon Omnitel, such that Italy no longer discriminated in favour of TIM.

6–061 **_Second GSM licence in Spain_** — This case has a similar background to the *Omnitel* case. It concerned a decision of the Commission regarding the initial licence fee imposed on Airtel Mobil

---

[7] A third party, even a competitor of the undertaking favoured by the Member State in question, may not compel the Commission to act under Art.86(3): see Case T–32/93, *Ladbroke Racing Ltd v Commission* [1994] II E.C.R. 1015. The Commission has thus a wide margin of discretion in deciding whether or not to take action under Art.86(3).

[8] See Bellamy and Child, para.4–001, n.4, para.13–017.

[9] O.J. 1995 L280/49.

("Airtel") for the granting of a second licence for providing GSM mobile services in Spain.[10] Airtel, which commenced services in October 1995, was selected on the basis of a tendering process that resulted in it having to pay a licence fee of Pta 85 billion. However, the public telecommunications operator, Telefonica de Espana ("Telefonica"), was granted its GSM licence without having to pay an initial licence fee. The Commission decided that the imposition of the licence fee on Airtel only was discriminatory and thereby constituted an infringement of Article 86(1) of the EC Treaty in conjunction with Article 82 of the EC Treaty.

The Commission found that, given the financial burden imposed on Airtel, Telefonica would have had the choice between two commercial strategies, each of which would have resulted in it infringing Article 82. First, the initial payment made by Airtel would necessarily have to be covered by it from its income, so that it would have difficulties in competing with Telefonica through lower tariffs. Telefonica would therefore have been able to extend its dominant position on the fixed voice telephony market and the analogue mobile telephony market into the market in GSM services by reducing its tariffs, extending its distribution network, and/or conducting intensive advertising campaigns. Second, the need to finance the initial licence fee would delay Airtel's investments in its network, thereby restricting its ability to compete with Telefonica. This could have encouraged Telefonica to retain higher tariffs for its GSM services and to limit production, markets or technical development as regards GSM services to the benefit of its older analogue services.

The Commission consequently considered that the competitive advantage granted to Telefonica would have led to Telefonica infringing Article 82. As this was the result of acts of the Spanish government, Spain thereby infringed Article 86. The Commission therefore ordered Spain to: (i) reimburse the initial licence fee imposed on Airtel, or (ii) adopt corrective measures equivalent in economic terms to the licence fee paid by Airtel.

6–062 *max.mobil Telekommunikation GmbH v Commission* — In a largely similar case in Austria, the first GSM licence was granted under — allegedly — privileged conditions to Mobilkom, a subsidiary of the incumbent telecommunications operator. max.mobil, a competitor of Mobilkom in the mobile market, had claimed that less favourable conditions were applied to it when it was granted a GSM licence. Although both Mobilkom and max.mobil were charged the same concession fees for their licences, max.mobil claimed that its licence was worth less due to its later market entry. Therefore, it should have paid less for a second licence. Because of this difference to the earlier cases (see above), the Commission rejected max.mobil's complaint under Article 86 against Austria.[11] max.mobil appealed this and brought an action for annulment before the Court of First Instance. Although the Court of First Instance declared this action for annulment admissible, it dismissed max.mobil's action on the merits, because the Commission had observed its duty to properly investigate a complaint and had given sufficient reasoning for its decision not to open proceedings.[12]

---

[10] O.J. 1997 L76/19.
[11] See Letter by the Commission to max.mobil from December 11, 1998 as cited by the Court of First Instance, see below.
[12] Case T–54/99, *max.mobil Telekommunikation Service GmbH v Commission* [2002] II E.C.R. 313.

E. Specific Restrictions on Market Conduct Related to Transmission Infrastructure

6–063 As far as transmission infrastructure is concerned, many behavioural rules applicable to operators with SMP are included in the *ex ante* regulation of the New Regulatory Framework for the communications sector. However, some specific problems are not within the scope of the New Regulatory Framework, where the Treaty's competition rules alone will continue to apply with respect to communications infrastructure.

1. Frequencies

6–064 The control of and access to radio spectrum and frequencies is an important competitive advantage for transmission providers or integrated media companies and could enable them to exercise dominance on services markets. Therefore, radio spectrum policy forms an important part of the New Regulatory Framework.[13] Beyond this regulation, many EU Member States have complex rules on frequencies allocation and spectrum policy,[14] which sometimes give rise to criticism by the Commission.[14a]

2. Satellite Services

6–065 Articles 81 and 82 are fully applicable to the market conduct of undertakings active in the satellite sector. Agreements between communications network operators concerning the operation of satellite systems may fall within the scope of Article 81(1). In the *Astra* case, the Commission refused to exempt under Article 81(3) of the EC Treaty a joint venture between British Telecom (BT) and Société Européenne de Satellites (SES) for the provision of broadcasting satellite services.[15] In particular, the Commission objected to a requirement for customers that wished to lease SES's satellite capacity to use exclusively BT for up-link services to transmit signals to the satellites.

Moreover, agreements between communications network operators concluded under international conventions (*e.g.* Eutelsat, Intelsat) to pool space segment capacity are not immune from the application of the EC Treaty's competition rules. The Commission on several occasions indicated its willingness to see competition law principles fully implemented within the framework of international satellite organisations.[16] In the 1991 Competition Guidelines, the Commission provided

[13] See Radio Spectrum Decision, para.1–011, n.32.
[14] See, *e.g.* the detailed German regulation on the allocation of frequency areas, frequency plans, fees for frequency use and single frequency allocation, available at: *www.regtp.de/tech_reg_tele/start/fs_06.html*.
[14a] On July 24, 2003, the Commission referred Germany to the European Court of Justice over the spectrum allocation rules contained in the media law for the Land Rheinland-Pfalz, see Press Release IP/03/1103 of July 24, 2003.
[15] See O.J. 1993 L20/23.
[16] In its 1990 Satellite Green Paper and again in its 1994 "Direct Access" paper, the Commission insisted on unrestricted access for service providers to space segment capacity: "Towards Europe-wide Systems and Services. Green Paper on a Common Approach in the Field of Satellite Communications in the European Community, Communications from the Commission", (COM(90) 490, Brussels, November 20, 1990) and Communication from the Commission to the Council and the European Parliament on Satellite Communications: the Provision of Direct Access to Space Segment Capacity (COM(94) 210), Brussels, June 10, 1994). See further, above, para.1–128 *et seq.*

examples of situations where arrangements between communications network operators concluded within international satellite organisations could be deemed to infringe the EC Treaty's competition rules: (i) agreements restricting competition between the operators in the supply of space segment capacity (*e.g.* agreements on price or customer sharing); (ii) agreements between operators to limit the quality and quantity of supplies to third parties; (iii) the bundling of satellite capacity and up-link services[17]; and (iv) agreements between operators providing that member operators are to be the exclusive distributors of the space segment capacity provided by the international organisations. Such restrictions of competition are unlikely to be exempted under Article 81(3) as they limit competition between satellite providers, to the detriment of customer choice. Moreover, such provisions could also be deemed to infringe Article 82 in so far as the telecommunications network providers that are members of the relevant international organisation still hold a dominant position on their national markets in the provision of satellite capacity or up-link services.[18] Although enforcement action by the Commission against such international organisations or their members is possible, the Commission has so far refrained from initiating any infringement proceedings, probably because it feared the political implications of such action.[19] The Commission also had the opportunity to review arrangements for the restructuring of international satellite organisations into commercial entities.[20]

Satellite is an attractive transmission infrastructure for the (exclusive) provision of (pay)TV content. The Commission accepts exclusive distribution and non-compete clauses within certain limits.[20a]

3. Cable

6–066 Although the digitalisation of cable networks will eventually reduce shortages of transmission capacity for broadcasting and other services, this is not likely to happen in the short to medium term in all EU Member States.[21] Accordingly, operators of cable networks are still in a position of being able to prevent or restrict competition in the broadcasting sector, especially on the pay-TV segment, by refusing to carry certain channels or by doing so only on unfair and/or discriminatory terms.

[17] See *Astra*, para.8–300, below.

[18] *ibid.*

[19] The Commission stated in the "Direct Access" paper, para.6–065, n.16, above, that Intelsat, given its substantial assets and the stable character of its market, held a dominant position in the provision of satellite capacity.

[20] *Inmarsat*, O.J. 1997 C137/5. In this case, the Commission approved under Art.81(1) the transformation of Inmarsat into a public company with the existing signatories (*i.e.* the incumbent telecommunications operators) as shareholders, on the assumption that an initial public offering would take place within three years to dilute such shareholders' interests.

[20a] See case *Telenor/Canal+/Canal Digital*, Art.19(3) notice, O.J. 2003 C 149/16.

[21] Cable penetration and the technical status of the existing cable networks differ significantly in the various Member States. For example, while cable penetration rates in Spain are relatively low, the existing networks are digital and technically very modern. In contrast, the penetration rate in Germany is comparatively high, but the systems are somewhat technically outdated and lack the necessary upgrading to carry broadband services.

(a) The Competitive Approach Towards Cable — EU Commission and Selected Member States

6–067 The Commission has constantly expressed its concerns regarding the competition issues raised by the dual ownership by telecommunications operators of both cable and tele-communications infrastructures, as this prevented the use of cable networks as a competitor to the incumbents' own telecommunications networks. Stopping short of mandating the end of common ownership by way of a legislative measure, the Commission has so far only required the legal separation of the cable and telecommunications businesses of telecoms operators.[22] However, in the course of its review of concentrations and joint ventures under the competition rules, the Commission has repeatedly attempted to pursue its goals of the separation of ownership of cable and telecommunications networks and of breaking up competitive bottlenecks in the cable industry by requiring legal separation or even divestment as a condition for clearance.[23]

6–068 At the Member State level, the competitive situation of cable operators differs to a great extent. While, for example, in the UK cable networks are "closed" systems, in which the operator is not obliged by law to grant access to third party content providers, countries such as the Netherlands and Germany (which have much greater cable penetration rates) have extensive regulations imposing must-carry and non-discrimination obligations upon cable operators. In Germany, operators have virtually no discretion with respect to the allocation of analogue cable spectrum and only limited freedom to choose the content that they carry on the digital portion of their cable capacity.[24] While in some Member States significant concentration of cable operators has taken place (*e.g.* the UK), the cable market in other Member States remains very fragmented (*e.g.* Germany).

(b) The Struggle for Competition in Cable

6–069 All over Europe, cable is generally perceived as the only viable infrastructure to compete with the incumbent operators' telephone networks at the local loop level. Therefore, the New Regulatory Framework for the telecommunications industry includes cable networks in the system of *ex ante* regulation. However, it remains to be seen what pro-competitive impact this will have on competition in services provided over cable and on infrastructure competition between cable and telecommunications networks. This is because the provision of broadcasting and other content services over cable is, to a large extent, excluded from the scope of the New Regulatory Framework.[25]

---

[22] See Separation Directive 95/51, O.J. 1996 L308/59.

[23] See *NSD*, O.J. 1995 L53/20 and *MSG Media Service*, O.J. 1994 L364/1, discussed at paras 8–164 and 8–168. See also *British Interactive Broadcasting (BiB)*, O.J. 1998 C322/6, where the Commission required BT to divest its interests in cable operations in the United Kingdom as a condition for granting an exemption to a joint venture to operate digital TV-based interactive services; discussed at para.8–342, below. Under the Merger Control Regulation, see Case M.2803 *Telia/Sonera*, discussed at para.8–129, below.

[24] Furthermore, the Bundeskartellamt uses a very narrow market definition, separating the cable network vertically into a backbone and a local access network (network levels 3 and 4). This market definition makes it very difficult for cable operators to establish end-to-end customer relationships and to market new, digital services. See, *e.g. Liberty Media/Deutsche Telekom* discussed at para.6–024, above.

[25] See Garzaniti and von Bonin, para.6–047, n.70, above, and von Bonin, "Kabelnetze und europäische Regulierung" (2002) K&R 565. See also, above, para.1–013.

4. Alternative Broadband Infrastructures

6–070 In so far as alternative broadband infrastructures are already technically and economically marketable, they raise very different competition problems. The market for wholesale and retail DSL (digital subscriber line) technology is, in many Member States, dominated by the incumbent telecommunications operators.[26] Consequently in the area of broadband networks and services, the Commission has to deal with the "typical" problems of price and non-price abuses by dominant operators.[27] As regards wireless local loop (WLL), UMTS and Fibre-to-the-Home (FTTH), the Commission and the Member States have struggled to assist operators develop a viable business model for the introduction of these services. The technology of broadband communication via electrical power lines (powerline communication) has been abandoned almost everywhere for technical and commercial reasons.

F. Restrictions on Market Conduct Related to Content and Services

6–071 Introduction — Market conduct in the electronic communications services sector no longer relates to the regulation of businesses active in the telecommunications field only. What is often described as "convergence" is a process in which the businesses of signal transmission, content provision and IT services are increasingly interlinked. All of these areas are subject to the EC's competition rules. To the extent that the provision of content and services is not perceived as a commercial or economic activity, but as the exercise of cultural functions, the Member States have significantly reserved their power to regulate these non-economic activities at the national level. This section will review specific issues raised by the application of competition rules to media content and the provision of such services.[28]

1. Restrictions on Market Conduct in Relation to Content

6–072 Application of the competition rules — In general, EC competition rules (including the rules on state aid) apply to all forms of anti-competitive behaviour in the area of content provision. Wherever conflicts arise between competition law and the power of the Member States to regulate cultural affairs, a reasonable compromise must be found between the interest of preserving viable competition in the broadcasting sector and the Member States' cultural interests. Article 86 provides useful guidance on how to arrive at such compromise. Consequently, Member States have agreed that the provisions of the EC Treaty do not prevent Member States from financing public broadcasting, as long as this does not restrict the conditions of trade and competition within the

---

[26] In the EU, 56,000 new DSL customers are acquired by incumbent telecommunications operators each week, while only 6,000 unbundled local loop lines per week are being acquired by competing service providers under the Local Loop Unbundling Regulation with a view to providing competing DSL services.

[27] See *Wanadoo/France Telecom*, in which the Commission is applying Art.82 to practices of the France Telecom group in the broadband sectors: see para.6–031, n.3, above.

[28] For a detailed review of the principles and precedents of EC competition rules in this sector, see Temple-Lang, "Media, Multimedia and European Community Antitrust Law" in *Annual Proceedings of the Fordham Law Institute: International Antitrust Law & Policy*, (Hawk ed., Fordham Corporate Law Institute, 1998), pp.377–448.

Community to the extent that it counters the common interest.[29] The Commission will have an opportunity to review this subject again following a complaint filed by the Association of German Private Broadcasters in April 2003. The association asks the Commission to find elements of illegal state aid in the German licence fee system for public broadcasters.[30]

(a) Content Agreements

6–073 Exclusivity — Programming rights for films and sports events are generally sold exclusively and in respect of distinct national territories or common language areas. However, the competitive analysis of exclusivity in media rights agreements differs slightly for films and sports events, the two key "drivers" of broadcasting, whether free-to-air or pay-television.

6–074 *Exclusive rights to films or television programmes* — When no rational investor would acquire attractive content without having the exclusive right to exploit it in the relevant territory, such exclusivity would, in principle, not infringe Article 81(1).[31] This will have to be examined on a case-by-case basis and the Commission is likely to scrutinise closely any claim that Article 81(1) is not applicable to exclusive programming rights to films. In fact, it would be unwise for businesses to rely on Article 81(1) being inapplicable to (a series of) exclusive programming arrangements, and a better course of action may be to structure the respective agreements in a way that they qualify for exemption under Article 81(3).

The question of whether exclusive programming rights are permissible under Article 81 will depend, to a large extent, on the duration and scope of the exclusivity and its foreclosure effect on other broadcasters.[32] An agreement giving the exclusive right to broadcast the entire catalogue and output of a film studio will fall within Article 81(1). However, such an arrangement could be exempted by the Commission under Article 81(3) of the EC Treaty provided that the duration and the scope of the exclusivity rights are limited on a geographic and language basis and in terms of number of films, and that third party access to the programmes is not substantially foreclosed.[33] The Commission will also take into consideration the cumulative effect of similar exclusive arrangements between a broadcaster and different content producers, particularly the "major" studios. A possible remedy to the risk of other broadcasters being foreclosed from access to the

---

[29] See Protocol no.23 to the Treaty of Amsterdam on public broadcasting in the Member States, which is considered in detail, below, in para.7–030 *et seq.*

[30] See Press Release available at: *www.vprt.de/dateien/09_03_Beschwerde_EU.pdf.*

[31] Case C–262/82, *Coditel v Ciné-Vog Films (No.2)* [1982] E.C.R. 3381. See also Case C–258/78, *Nungesser v Commission* [1982] E.C.R. 2015.

[32] With respect to exclusive distribution agreements via DTH sattelite, see case *Telenor/Canal+/Canal Digital*, Art.19(3) notice, O.J. 2003 C 149/16.

[33] In *ARD*, the Commission exempted an arrangement giving the German television channel exclusive rights to broadcast on the catalogue of films of Metro Goldwin Mayer. The Commission agreed to exempt the arrangement after the duration of the agreement had been reduced from 15 to 10 years and a sub-licensing system giving third party access to the films covered by the arrangement had been set up.The Commission also specified that the exemption had been granted because the exclusivity was limited to the German language. By contrast, the Commission indicated that an exclusivity relating to all languages would substantially restrict inter-state broadcasting and could therefore not be exempted: *ARD*, O.J. 1989 L284/36.

broadcasting rights subject to the agreement will be for the Commission to require sub-licensing on transparent, reasonable and non-discriminatory terms.[34]

6–075 *Exclusive rights to sports events* — The application of competition law is slightly different in relation to the broadcasting of sports events. For most sports events, the right to televise is valuable for only a very short time (*i.e.* whilst the event is taking place and, for deferred rights, for a short time thereafter). For sports organisers, the sale of exclusive rights is a way of ensuring the maximum short-term profitability of the event organised, as the price paid for exclusivity by one broadcaster will probably be higher than the sum of the amounts which would be paid by several broadcasters for non-exclusive rights.[35] Exclusivity is also important to the broadcaster, because it protects the value of its sports programmes, increases the value of the rights to it, through the possibility of sub-licensing, and increases its audience and therefore revenues from advertising. Exclusivity is also essential for pay-television broadcasters, as viewers are more likely to subscribe if it is the only way to get access to a particular sports event. It is considered that exclusivity, according to these conditions, is objectively justified and does not itself infringe Article 81(1) unless the exclusivity is for too long a period or has other detrimental effects on competition.[36] Those effects may be found, for example, as a result of the cumulative effects of a series of exclusive contracts or where the exclusivity results in significant rights not being exploited by any broadcaster.[37] Generally, the exclusivity is limited to the duration of a specific event (live, deferred transmission or for short clips) but a longer period of exclusivity may be justified, for example to assist a new entrant becoming established in the market and, in particular, a new entrant introducing new and expensive technology which needs exclusivity of a certain duration to recover the large investment costs.[38]

6–076 Collective purchasing of programming rights by broadcasting companies — The joining together of broadcasters to purchase programming rights is in principle not prohibited by

---

[34] See Temple-Lang, para.6–071, n.28, p.411, indicating however that the Commission is unlikely to get involved in determining the terms of sub-licensing as a condition for an exemption, but would rather leave such a task to national authorities.

[35] Wachtmeister, "Broadcasting of Sport Events and Competition Law" in (1998) 2 *Competition Policy Newsletter* 6.

[36] See UEFA Champions League, see O.J. 2002 C196/3. On July 23, 2003, the Commission took a formal decision to exempt the new UEFA joint selling agreements for the media rights for the Champions League. UEFA will be allowed to continue selling the rights to the Champions League brand while involving more broadcasters and service providers in the distribution of football content. See Press Release IP/03/1105 of July 24, 2003. See also the decision in the *Telenor/Canal+/Canal Digital* case, para.6–065 above. See also para.6–078 below.

[37] See Temple-Lang, para.6–071, n.28, pp.410–411, referring to a case where the Commission allowed an agreement between BSkyB, the BBC and the English Football Association under which the first two companies shared exclusive rights to broadcast FA matches: draft notice pursuant to Art.19(3) of Council Regulation 17 concerning a notification in Cases *ITVA/Football Authorities* and *BBC, BSB and Football Association*, O.J. 1993 C94/6. The Commission generally accepts exclusive rights for one season, but in this case permitted a longer period because BSkyB was entering a new market for direct-to-home satellite television.

[38] See Wachtmeister, para.6–075, n.35, p.8. Under Art.3(a) of the Television Without Frontiers Directive, Member States must also take measures to ensure that broadcasters under their jurisdiction do not broadcast on an exclusive basis major sports events such as the Olympic Games and the Football World Cup; see para.1–015, n.42, discussed at para.2–016 *et seq.*

Article 81(1) if the broadcasters would not have the resources to individually buy the rights in question. Otherwise, collective purchasing arrangements will normally fall under Article 81(1) to the extent that such arrangements restrict competition between broadcasters in bidding for programming rights and an exemption under Article 81(3) would thus be required. In *European Broadcasting Union (EBU)*,[39] the Commission exempted, from 1993 to 2005, the joint acquisition by the EBU, an association of European broadcasters, of sports television rights and the rules for sub-licensing of such rights on pay-TV channels. The collective acquisition of sports rights was exempted subject to the condition that the EBU and its members grant access to such rights to third parties. On appeal by several commercial broadcasters, the Court of First Instance again[40] annulled the Commission's exemption decision.[41] It held that whilst the joint purchasing of televised transmission rights for an event does not in itself fall within the scope of Article 81(1), the particular facts of the case led to the conclusion that competition would be eliminated on certain markets. The following facts therefore brought the revised EBU/Eurovision arrangements within Article 81(1): (i) the market structure; (ii) the position of the EBU on the market for certain international sporting events (for example, the Olympic Games have always been sold to EBU members in Europe); and (iii) the degree of vertical integration of the EBU and its members. In order to be capable of exemption, the severe restriction of competition resulting from this arrangement would need to be compensated by an effective system of third party access to the rights on a sub-licensing basis. However, a substantial review of the actual operation of the EBU's third party access system revealed that competitors to EBU members did not have the possibility of obtaining access to unused live broadcasting rights, nor an adequate access to deferred transmissions. Accordingly, the revised EBU arrangements did not meet the requirement for an exemption under Article 81(3) and the Court concluded that the Commission had wrongly granted an individual exemption.

As broadcasting entities grow larger and extend their operations beyond national markets, group-wide purchasing of rights on an international basis becomes increasingly attractive. Companies like News Corporation and Canal+, which each directly or through affiliates reach millions of households worldwide, seek to minimise their programme acquisition costs by purchasing rights on a global scale. If joint purchasing occurs between competitors, the Commission will apply Article 81(1). Intra-group arrangements between undertakings forming part of a single economic entity cannot be caught under Article 81, but Article 82 could be applied if a dominant group acts as a global purchaser.

---

[39] *EBU/Eurovision System*, O.J. 2000 L151/18.

[40] An earlier Commission exemption decision relating to the same matter, O.J. 1993, L179/23, had already been annulled by the Court of First Instance: Joined Cases T–528/93, etc. *Métropole Television v Commission* [1996] II E.C.R. 649. The Court found that the Commission had not considered whether membership requirements of the EBU were objective and sufficiently precise, so that they could be applied uniformly and without discrimination to all actual or potential members, with the result that it was impossible to tell whether these membership criteria were indispensable for the purpose of granting an Art.81(3) exemption. As a result, the EBU clarified the rules of interpretation of the criteria to become a member and re-notified its arrangements to the Commission, which granted a further exemption under Art.81(3).

[41] See Judgment of October 8, 2002 in Joined Cases T–185, 216, 299, 300/00, *M6 v Commission*, not yet reported.

6–077   Collective selling of programming rights — Broadcasting rights to sports events are very often sold by a league or association representing the clubs or participants. Competition authorities in the Netherlands, the United Kingdom and Germany have considered that joint selling by clubs amounts to anti-competitive price-fixing and does not warrant an exemption.[42] To the extent they would affect trade between Member States, such arrangements would be likely to infringe Article 81(1) in so far as they create price transparency between rights owners, restrict output and bundle the products offered. The availability of an exemption under Article 81(3) has to be assessed on a case-by-case basis, taking into consideration the specific characteristics of the sport in question, including the need to ensure "solidarity" between weaker and stronger participants or the training of young players, which could only be achieved through redistribution of revenues from the sale of broadcasting rights that have been sold collectively.[43] The Commission has recently reviewed the following case in this area.

6–078   *UEFA Champions League* — In a notice published on August 17, 2002,[44] the Commission expressed a favourable view on the revised arrangements of Union des Associations Européennes de Football (UEFA) for the joint selling of the commercial rights of the Champions League. The agreements were exempted by a formal decision on July 23, 2003.[44a] In the Commission's view, the rules concerning the sale of broadcasting rights to the Champions League restricted competition on a horizontal level, because joint selling prevented participating clubs from taking independent commercial action in respect of their rights. Competition was furthermore restricted on a vertical level because exclusive licences were granted to a single broadcaster in each Member State, covering all television rights.[45] UEFA therefore modified its rules.

The revised selling agreement still provides for a joint selling of the broadcasting rights to the Champions League, but instead of selling all the rights as a bundle to only one broadcaster per country, UEFA will sell the rights in several packages for shorter periods of time. The revised agreement will also allow individual football clubs to exploit some of the rights with their fan base, for example by showing Champions League matches on a deferred basis on their website or own television channel. Even though UEFA will retain the exclusive right to sell the rights to the live transmission of the main matches, clubs will have the opportunity, with respect to other matches, to

---

[42] The issue arises regardless of whether the rights belong to the clubs or to the league. For a review of a decision of the German Federal Supreme Court holding that the central marketing of broadcasting rights of German clubs' home matches in the European cups is anti-competitive under German antitrust rules, see Deeg and Ringel, "Central Marketing of Television Broadcasting Rights by the German Football Association" (1999) 4(2) *Communications Law* 55–69.

[43] See Wachtmeister, para.6–075, n.35, p.10. The Commission is still investigating under EC competition rules the German centralised system for the broadcasting of football matches under the auspices of the German football league, O.J. 1999 C6/10. On the basis of newly liberalised marketing rules, the German Football League (DFL) and the Commission have reached a settlement in principle, which still needs to be market-tested by way of an official publication according to Art.19(3) of Regulation 17/62, see Press Release IP/03/1106 of July 24, 2003. The Commission is also investigating the selling of rights to the UK's F.A. Premier League: see Commission Press Release IP/02/1951 of December 20, 2002.

[44] Notice published pursuant to Art.19(3) of Council Regulation 17 concerning *Joint selling of the media rights of the UEFA Champions League on an exclusive basis*, O.J. 2002 C169/3. See also Commission Press Release, IP/02/860 of June 3, 2002.

[44a] See Press Release IP/03/1105 of July 24, 2003.

[45] *ibid.*, para.5.

sell their matches individually provided that UEFA has not managed to sell them. The Commission has exempted the UEFA agreements until July 31, 2009, *i.e.* for two contract periods of three years each.

(b) Agreements Related to the Exploitation of Media Rights

6–079 Introduction — To an increasing extent, holders of broadcasting rights to sports events do not only enter into agreements for the marketing of the sports rights they possess, but also regulate in detail the way in which broadcasters can exploit these rights. Two examples of recent Commission practice are reviewed below.

6–080 *UEFA broadcasting regulations* — UEFA has rules regulating the broadcasting of football matches.[46] The object of the regulations was to provide national football associations with a limited opportunity to schedule domestic football during times when no football could be broadcast on television in their country. The purpose of this rule was to protect stadium attendances and amateur participation in the sport. The original broadcasting rules notified to the Commission had been the subject of complaints from a number of broadcasters, who argued that the rules unduly restricted not only their freedom to show the matches they had paid for but also competition. This concern was shared by the Commission, which found that the original UEFA broadcasting regulations infringed Article 81(1) and did not meet the requirements for an exemption unless modified.[47] The Commission therefore invited UEFA to alter its regulations by clearly defining the main domestic fixture schedule and introducing a rule that the hours blocked should correspond to this schedule.

UEFA's new broadcasting rules, as amended in July 2000, allow national football associations to prevent broadcasting of football within their territory for two-and-a half hours either on Saturday or on Sunday at hours that corresponded to their main domestic fixture schedule. Even though these regulations still have the effect that at times broadcasters may be deprived of the possibility of broadcasting football events live, the Commission reached the conclusion that this effect could not be qualified as constituting an appreciable restriction of competition within the meaning of Article 81(1).[48]

6–081 *FIA Formula One World Championship* — In a notice of June 13, 2001,[49] the Commission expressed its intention to approve the new Formula One broadcasting agreements. Under the original broadcasting agreements, which were concluded by Formula One Administration Limited (FOA) with 60 broadcasters worldwide, FOA used to contract with a broadcasting company in the host country to serve as the host broadcaster for each Grand Prix. The host broadcaster was granted limited exclusivity. Some of the agreements provided for a discount of 33 per cent on the price paid by the broadcaster if the broadcaster agreed not to broadcast any open wheeler racing other than

---

[46] *UEFA's Broadcasting Regulations*, O.J. 2001 L171/12.
[47] *ibid.*, para.4
[48] *ibid.*, para.51.
[49] See Notice published pursuant to Art.19(3) of Council Regulation 17 concerning Cases *Notification of FIA Regulations*, COMP/36.638 — *Notification by FIA/FOA of agreements relating to the FIA Formula One World Championship* and *GTR/FIA*, O.J. 2001 C169/5.

Formula One. The duration of the broadcasting agreements was between one and five years for free-access television and up to 11 years for contracts with certain pay-television broadcasters.

The Commission issued a Statement of Objections in June 2000 in relation to the original agreements. It made the preliminary assessment that certain agreements between FOA and broadcasters granting the latter exclusivity in their territories for excessive periods of time restricted competition within the meaning of Article 81.[50] In reply to the Statement of Objections, FOA removed from its standard form contract the provision whereby broadcasters were offered a discount on the fee payable if they did not broadcast any other form of open wheeler racing. Furthermore, FOA limited the duration of contracts where exclusive rights had been granted to a maximum of five years in the case of host broadcasters and to a maximum of three years in all other cases. When broadcasting agreements for a given territory with free-to-air broadcasters were due to expire, FOA undertook to notify comparable rival broadcasters beforehand to facilitate competitive bidding.

(c) The Reaction of the Commission and Member States to Dominance in Broadcasting

6–082 A new challenge — Broadcasting, which traditionally has come within the domain of the cultural policy of each Member State, is becoming a major business. Moreover, it increasingly shows signs of concentration on an international level. While the Member States have historically relied on sector-specific, national broadcasting regulation, the Commission's only means to intervene in this sector are the competition rules, save to the limited extent that it has powers under the Television Without Frontiers Directive.[51]

Dominance may occur at the content level or in the provision of broadcasting capacity (the "carrier" level), or at both levels for some companies. Beyond simple market shares, the following factors may be relevant in the broadcasting sector in assessing market power: (i) the control of a large portfolio of programmes; (ii) the control of conditional access technology; (iii) the control of EPGs; (iv) know-how in subscriber management services; (v) the control of broadcasting transmission facilities or capacity (*i.e.* terrestrial transmission stations, satellite transponder capacity, radio frequency spectrum and cable bandwidth); (vi) a large customer base; (vii) control of a number of existing channels; and (viii) vertical integration (*i.e.* activities at both the content and carrier level).[52] The market power of an operator in the broadcasting sector may be increased as a result of the so-called "tipping effect". This effect occurs when one company obtains a market share which is substantially greater than its competitors, and when this in itself causes it to attract more customers, thereby "tipping" the market to it.[53] For example, advertisers will contract with the leading broadcaster only on the assumption that they will reach a larger audience and will therefore get better value for their advertising expenditure. Similarly, subscribers will choose to join the largest broadcaster on the assumption that it will have better resources and thus provide better and more interesting programming. This effect will have to be taken into account when investigating dominance in broadcasting.

[50] *ibid.,* p.8.
[51] See above, para.2–016 *et seq.*
[52] See Temple Lang, para.6–071, n.28, pp.399–401.
[53] *ibid.,* pp.401–402.

6–083   The impact of convergence — Although the telecommunications and broadcasting sectors still constitute separate product markets, the convergence brought about by digital technology is bringing these markets closer together with the result that the market position of a company active on one of these markets is relevant in assessing its conduct on the other.[54] For example, interactive services can be provided on both broadcasting and telecommunications networks. Cable operators and telecommunications network operators that may be dominant in the supply of their respective traditional services, are thus in a position to extend their activities into these new markets.[54a] Likewise, dominant telecommunications undertakings may be able to offer feature films and other visual information over their upgraded telephone networks, in addition to traditional telecommunications and other interactive services. In short, the broadcasting and telecommunications markets are now sufficiently related for dominance in one market to potentially be used to gain market power in the other.[55] The Commission will scrutinise carefully any such extension of dominance through restrictive agreements, abusive conduct, or the control of "bottlenecks" such as conditional access systems.[56] In this regard, the Commission will express concerns and raise objections when such an extension of market power has the effect of substantially raising barriers to entry to third parties that would be required to enter several markets at once.[57]

6–084   "Must-carry" rules — Convergence is also the reason for the Council and Parliament for having included "must-carry" rules with respect to content in the New Regulatory Framework for electronic communications services, despite it generally excluding content-related services from its scope of application. Article 31 of the Universal Services Directive allows (but does not oblige) Member States to impose "must-carry" obligations on undertakings providing electronic communications networks where those networks are used by a significant number of end-users for receiving television and radio programmes. The imposition of such obligations must be in accordance with a strict proportionality test.[58]

6–085   The role of Article 86 and the Member States — Regulation of the broadcasting sector remains largely national and has not been harmonised at the European level to the same extent as the telecommunications sector. There remains a large amount of national legislation which maintains state or regional public monopolies, rules on the diversity of ownership and control, and local content rules. State intervention in the broadcasting sector remains very important, through the financing and control of public service broadcasters.[59] The sector is, in many Member States, still characterised by the maintenance of special or exclusive rights to the benefit of specific broadcasters. Therefore there remains ample scope for the application of Article 86 in the broadcasting sector. The Commission has used this provision to ensure equality between broadcasters. In

[54] *ibid.*, pp.402–404.
[54a] On April 24, 2003, an association of German private broadcasters (VPRT) filed a complaint with the EU Commission alleging unfair cross-subsidisation of the German public broadcasters' online and e-commerce activities by the traditional TV business financed by statutory license fees.
[55] See the discussion regarding dominance as a basis for SMP in the context of sector-specific regulation, above, para.1–018.
[56] See below, para.6–088 *et seq.*
[57] See Temple-Lang, para.6–071, n.28, p.404.
[58] See above, para.2–063 *et seq.*
[59] See above, para.4–018 *et seq.* See also von Bonin, *Die Kontrolle digitaler Kommunikationsinhalte* (2000), p.129 *et seq.*

VTM,[60] the Commission objected to a monopoly right granted by the Flemish Community of Belgium to a private Flemish broadcaster, VTM, that gave VTM the sole right to broadcast television advertising aimed at the Flemish Community as a whole. Although the regulatory measure applied equally to Belgian and foreign broadcasters, the Commission considered that the measure was discriminatory and therefore infringed Article 86(1) in conjunction with Article 43 (*ex* Article 52) of the EC Treaty (the right of establishment), in so far as it reserved to a domestic operator a specific portion of the Flemish broadcasting market.

Furthermore, in the United Kingdom, the Independent Television Commission (ITC) refused to issue new licences for the operation of digital terrestrial television multiplexes to British Digital Broadcasting (BDB), a joint venture involving BSkyB, the dominant pay-television broadcaster in the United Kingdom, on the basis of advice from the Commission that the granting of such a licence (amounting to a special right) to the joint venture would strengthen the existing dominant position of BSkyB on the UK pay-television market in violation of Article 86(1), in conjunction with Article 82.[61]

6–086 In addition to the provisions of the Television Without Frontiers Directive,[62] broadcasters are subject to various national rules aiming at, among other things, preserving the quality of programmes, pluralism and local content.[63] Accordingly, broadcasters may argue that the EC Treaty's competition rules are not applicable to them, pursuant to Article 86(2), in so far as such an application would obstruct the operation of their public duties under national law. Public broadcasting qualifies as a service of general economic interest within the meaning of Article 86(2) of the EC Treaty,

> "in so far as it involves the obligation to provide varied programming including cultural, educational, scientific and minority programmes without any commercial appeal and to cover the entire population irrespective of the costs".[64]

Moreover, public broadcasters have special rights within the meaning of Article 86(2) of the EC Treaty in so far as they are entitled to receive public funding to finance their public service remit and that such a right has been granted to them otherwise than according to objective and non-discriminatory criteria. The availability of a derogation would thus depend on the extent to which the application of competition rules would obstruct the performance of the public duties of the broadcaster. No doubt the Commission (as well as national authorities or courts) would adopt a narrow interpretation of such an exception and very convincing elements would have to be brought forward to make a case in this respect.[65]

[60] See *VTM*, upheld on appeal, *VTM v Commission*, para.2–013, n.37.
[61] Temple-Lang para.6–071, n.28, pp.405–406. The ITC agreed to grant the licence to BDB only on condition that BSkyB withdrew from the joint venture.
[62] See para.2–016 *et seq.*
[63] In Germany, broadcasting regulation is under the jurisdiction of the various Länder. A "Media Concentration" Law contains special provisions, which *inter alia* provide that broadcasters can be obliged to broadcast third-party content when they reach a certain audience share (25% or 30%): German Broadcasting State Treaty, s.26(2).
[64] See Joined Cases T–528, 542 and 546/93 *Métropole Télévision SA, Reti Televisie Italiane SpA, Gestevision Telecinco SA and Antena 3 de Television v Commission* [1996] I E.C.R. 649; see also Case C–320/91, *Corbeau* [1993] I E.C.R. 2533.
[65] Art.16 of the EC Treaty, as introduced by the Amsterdam Treaty, stresses the role of the Member States in guaranteeing certain services of general economic interest for citizens, and a specific Protocol to the

2. Restrictions of Competition in Relation to Technical Services

6–087 The use of decoding systems ("set-top boxes" and related systems) raises two main competition issues. The first concerns the access of competing pay-television operators to existing installed bases of set-top boxes. The second concerns the interoperability of proprietary digital set-top boxes.

6–088 Access to set-top boxes: provision of conditional access services — The question arises whether the emergence of new technologies has created new "bottlenecks", consisting of facilities such as set-top boxes in the pay-television sector. Given the scale of investment required to launch a new set-top box population, new entrants in the pay-television market may very often have no option but to provide their pay-television services using the set-top boxes of incumbent operators.[66] There are three essential components of a set-top box to which broadcasters require access: conditional access services, EPGs and API interfaces. When these components are proprietary, new entrants are dependent on the incumbent operator for access to the market place. It is not clear whether these facilities could be treated as essential facilities, such that third party access to them could be required under Article 82. This is a complex issue that has yet to be addressed in the decision-making practice of the Commission.[67] OFTEL, the UK telecommunications regulator, which has responsibility for conditional access issues in the United Kingdom, has taken the position that a conditional access system for digital satellite broadcasting services could constitute an essential facility for broadcasters wishing to compete on the digital satellite broadcasting market.[68]

Amsterdam Treaty links public service television and radio services to democratic, social and cultural requirements as well as the requirement of safeguarding pluralism and information. There have been several attempts to use this Protocol as a sort of exemption from the Treaty's competition rules, but the Commission does not share this interpretation and considers that public service television must be considered on the same level as the other services of general interest within the meaning of Art.86(2): see para.6–057 *et seq*. In Case 155/73, *Sacchi* [1974] E.C.R. 409, the Court held that television companies, in so far as in some Member States they are entrusted with services of general economic interest, must comply with the competition rules, provided that to do so is not demonstrably incompatible with the accomplishment of their tasks. The Commission has recently launched an investigation into the funding of public service television broadcasters to verify compliance with state aid rules of the public financing of broadcasting activities: see para.4–018, n.14.

[66] This is also an issue for free-to-air broadcasters which may need to encode their signal for copyright reasons in order that only viewers within a certain territory can receive their signal.

[67] Although the concept of essential facilities was not discussed as such, it seems that the Commission considered in the *BiB* case that set-top boxes constituted an essential facility, since it imposed, as a condition for clearance of the joint venture, third party access to set-top boxes on fair, reasonable and non-discriminatory terms; *BiB*, para.6–067, n.23, above; see also para.8–346 *et seq*.; see also merger prohibition decision in Case M.467, *MSG-Media Service*, para.68 *et seq*., where the Commission concluded that even full third party access to set-top boxes would not prevent the creation of a dominant position. See further below, para.8–171 *et seq*.

[68] This case concerned a conditional access system to be developed in the United Kingdom by BSkyB, the leading pay-television broadcaster and the only operator of a DTH satellite platform in the United Kingdom. OFTEL stated that "[t]here is therefore a substantial risk that the first conditional access system to be adopted will be a bottleneck. Other service providers wishing to use conditional access to sell subscription services into the market would have to use this system": OFTEL, "The Pricing of Conditional Access Services for Digital Television", October 1997, para.2.5. For an analysis of this case, see Overd and Bishop, "Essential Facilities: The Rising Tide" (1998) E.C.L.R. 183–185.

Under the New Regulatory Framework, Articles 5 and 6 of the Access Directive (in connection with Annex I to this Directive) provide, by way of *ex ante* regulation, that NRAs can oblige providers of conditional access services to grant access on fair, reasonable and non-discriminatory terms to technical services, EPGs and APIs.

Access issues do not only arise in relation to alleged abuses of dominant position under Article 82, but also have to be considered under Article 81 in so far as conditional access systems are set up by joint ventures or consortia. In such cases, the Commission could very well impose an obligation to give non-discriminatory access to the system to third parties as a condition for any exemption under Article 81(3).[69]

6–089   Interoperability of set-top boxes and MHP — In some Member States, for example in the United Kingdom, set-top boxes are generally operated on a proprietary basis. However, the Commission and certain other Member States are in favour of facilitating the interoperability of decoders through the use of open standards. Several initiatives by the European Parliament, to make MHP (an open middleware standard agreed to by the DVB industry association) mandatory for all set-top box operators, have failed. So far, there are only recommendations for MHP at the Member State[70] and Commission levels.[71] However, the EC Treaty's competition rules could be used, even without a mandatory MHP requirement, to ensure that a proprietary digital set-top box is not tied to a single provider of digital broadcasting services. The Commission has required suppliers of conditional access services based on proprietary set-top box technology to enter into simulcrypt agreements as a condition for approval of a joint venture.[72]

G. Restrictions on Market Conduct in the Online and Internet Sectors

6–090   There have been an increasing number of cases concerning the application of the EC Treaty's competition rules to online services and the internet.[73] This section reviews some competition issues that are particularly pertinent to these sectors.

---

[69] See *BiB*, para.6–067, n.23, above.

[70] See, *e.g.* s.13(2), No.2 of the By-laws to s.53 of the German Broadcasting State Treaty.

[71] Framework Directive, para.1–009, n.25, Art.18(1) requires Member States to encourage the use of a single open standard for API. As discussed above at para.2–070, sector-specific regulation however does not require the adoption of a specific open standard, such as MHP, for API. See Liikanen, Speech to EBU Conference, March 27, 2001: "the Commission considers that this voluntary, industry led standardisation is the best process to reach interoperability, and to guarantee widespread implementation of the standard." EU Member States are also under an obligation to encourage all proprietors of APIs to make available on fair, reasonable and non-discriminatory terms (for appropriate remuneration) all such information as is necessary to enable providers of digital interactive television services to provide all services supported by the API in a fully functional form: see Framework Directive, Art.18(2). This obligation is without prejudice to the ability of NRAs to impose open access to such information, under the provisions of the Access Directive, regardless of any SMP designation: see Access Directive, para.1–011, n.29, Art.5(1)(b), discussed above at para.2–066.

[72] *BiB*, para.6–067, n.23. Simulcrypt involves a commercial agreement between the suppliers of different proprietary conditional access systems to synchronise the different systems so that populations of digital set-top boxes embedding each system are able to scramble signals that have been encoded using either conditional system.

[73] See Coates, "Competing for the Internet" (1998) 2 *Competition Newsletter*; Rutley, "EC Competition Law in Cyberspace: An Overview of Recent Developments" [1998] E.C.L.R. 186–203; and Nordemann, Czychowski and Grüter, "The Internet, the Name Server and Antitrust Law" (1998) E.C.L.R. 99–105.

6–091   Access to online and internet networks and services — Given the sheer scale of the investment required to set up and develop networks to carry online and internet services, most service providers will continue to rely on incumbent operators' networks to enter those markets. The principles discussed above regarding network access, and in particular the Access Notice, are particularly relevant in this sector. In *WorldCom/MCI*, the Commission expressed concerns that WorldCom, as a result of its acquisition of MCI, would have controlled a large share of the market for top-level internet services, *i.e.* the market for the provision of a network capable of connecting directly to any other network on the internet (through peering agreements) without relying on a third party network to relay traffic.[74] The Commission considered that this would have enabled WorldCom to favour its own internet services and degrade the quality of competing internet services providers that relied on WorldCom's internet top-level services to relay portions of their traffic. The Commission only approved the concentration subject to WorldCom's commitment to divest MCI's entire internet business.

Another example of typical competition issues in the internet and online sector is *Vodafone/ Vivendi/Canal+*, a joint venture to form a multi-platform portal called Vizzavi. In its decision to approve the joint venture, the Commission insisted on undertakings which were supposed to ensure that rivals' internet portals had equal access to the parent company's set-top boxes and mobile handsets.[75]

The essential facilities doctrine can also play an important role in this sector. The Commission relied on the doctrine in an investigation concerning SWIFT's rejection of La Poste's application for membership of SWIFT's interbanking payment system.[76] The Commission alleged that SWIFT, a co-operative society owned by a large number of banks around the world, was in a quasi-monopolistic position on the market for "international payment message transfer networks" and that its payment infrastructure was an essential facility. SWIFT had abused its dominant position on this market by excluding La Poste (which provided banking services) from SWIFT membership without justification. The case was settled following an undertaking given by SWIFT to give access to its network to those institutions, such as La Poste, that satisfied objective criteria proportional to the need to avoid systemic risks to the security of its network.

6–092   Extension of dominance — The internet symbolises the convergence of the information technology and telecommunications sectors. Both sectors require a high level of investment and are therefore conducive to being concentrated markets. Accordingly, as major players on the tele-communications or information technology markets extend their activities into the internet sector, the issue of an abusive extension of dominance inevitably arises as the risk of discriminatory or tying practices increases.[77] A good illustration is provided by the ongoing Commission investigation concerning Microsoft's practice of bundling its internet browser, Explorer, with Microsoft's

---

[74] Case M.1069, *WorldCom/MCI*, Commission Decision of March 3, 1998; O.J. 1999 L116/1. For a review of this case, see para.8–088 *et seq.*

[75] Case JV.48, *Vodafone/Vivendi/Canal+*, Commission Decision of July 20, 2000, Commission Press Release IP/00/821 of July 20, 2000. For a review of the case, see para.8–138.

[76] *La Poste/SWIFT*, O.J. 1997 C335/3.

[77] See Coates, para.6–091, n.73, pp.8–9.

operating software.[78] Computer manufacturers are required to install Microsoft's Explorer browser as a condition for the licensing to them of Microsoft's operating system software.[79] Such a practice could be found by the Commission to be an abusive extension of Microsoft's dominant position on the market for operating software into the related market for browser software. In the United States, the US Federal District Court ordered Microsoft to desist from the bundling practice, following Microsoft's threat to terminate Compaq's licence to Windows 95 when Compaq tried to sell computers without Microsoft's Internet Explorer.[80] The European Commission's investigation is ongoing.[81]

6–093   Trade associations and other self-regulated bodies — So far, the internet has not been centrally regulated by public authorities, but rather by self-regulating private bodies such as ICANN, which regulates the allocation of domain names, currently operated by VeriSign.[82] The conditions of membership and the decisions of these associations or bodies, whose membership often includes competing businesses, must comply with Article 81. Accordingly, their membership rules must be based on clear, objective and non-discriminatory criteria, the application of which can be effectively reviewed.[83] Furthermore, the decisions of these bodies and associations must not

[78] Commission Press Release IP/01/1232 of August 30, 2001.

[79] See Rutley, para.6–091, n.73, who indicates that, because Microsoft has had its web browser placed on the hard drives of computers, independent software developers have complained that software developed to run on Microsoft's operating system also needs the browser to start the computer operating, although these programmes have nothing to do with the internet.

[80] The US Department of Justice (DoJ) initiated court action against Microsoft alleging that Microsoft's agreements with computer manufacturers in the United States violated a consent decree concluded in 1995 between Microsoft and the DoJ which prohibited Microsoft from "entering into any operating system license agreement that is expressly or impliedly conditioned upon the licensing of any . . . other product". The consent decree also provided that "this provision . . . shall not be construed to prohibit Microsoft from developing integrated products". Microsoft argued that the combination of Windows 95 and Internet Explorer that it licensed to computer OEMs was such an integrated product, while the DoJ argued that Microsoft's practices amounted to an illegal bundling. In its initial finding of facts delivered on November 5, 1999, the Court upheld the DoJ's allegation that Microsoft had abused its monopoly position, in particular by binding the licensing of its operating software (Windows) to its internet navigation system (Explorer). A consent decree has recently been upheld by the competent US Court.

[81] The Commission has approved licensing and distribution agreements between Microsoft and European internet service providers for products using Microsoft Explorer. This decision follows from a commitment by Microsoft to remove from these agreements an exclusivity clause preventing service providers from promoting internet browser software not written by Microsoft. The Commission has specified that this decision was without prejudice to its position on Microsoft's global behaviour concerning a possible abuse of dominant position. In August 2003, the Commission sent Microsoft another statement of objections to give it a final opportunity to comment before concluding its antitrust probe; see para.6–041, n.49, above.

[82] See Rutley, para.6–090, n.73, citing bodies such as the Internet Policy Advisory Centre (IPAC), which is concerned with domain name proposals; the Internet Engineering Task Force (IETF) and the World Wide Web consortium, which has a policy-making role, developing and filtering software standards and internet Protocols.

[83] This means that admission to membership must not be entirely at the discretion of the board of directors, and decisions impairing the right of members must be reasoned and be subject to the right of appeal to properly constituted tribunals: *Cauliflowers*, O.J. 1978 L21/23 and *London Sugar Market Ltd*, O.J. 1985 L369/25. For a review of the case law on trade associations under Art.81, see Riesenkampff and Lehr, "Membership of Professional Associations and Art.81 of the EC Treaty" (1996) 19(4) *World Competition*, 57–68; and Temple Lang, "Trade Associations and Self Regulation under EEC Antitrust Law" (Hawk ed., Fordham Corporate Law Institute, 1998), pp.605–671.

lead to restrictions of competition among the members, such as price-fixing and market sharing.[84] The implementation of technical standards (*e.g.* software standards and internet protocols) by a self-regulatory body could restrict competition between members if the members are prevented from dealing with products that do not meet such standards. However, arrangements of this kind could qualify for an exemption under Article 81(3) since they enhance product compatibility and therefore benefit consumers.[85] In so far as they have the exclusive right to allocate domain names, it could be argued that these organisations are dominant on the market for the allocation of domain names and that, as a result, they may not engage in any practices constituting an abuse of such a dominant position.[86]

6–094 Specific issues in relation to online services — Competition in online services is based on the range of services made available to the customer. In this regard, it is expected that the initial package of online services (such as electronic shopping, email, access to bulletin boards and access to specialised databases) will over time be broadened to include more complex audio-visual communications, such as video-conferencing and "virtual" shopping malls. As the range of services available online is broadened and the subscription becomes more attractive to subscribers, the online service will attract an increase in customer revenues (that are based on a flat monthly subscription charge). As the customer base increases, the online service provider will attract extra revenue from advertisers and from telecommunications network operators (in the form of a percentage of the price paid by the customer to its telephone operator for making internet calls). This has served as the *rationale* behind recent alliances in this sector between online service providers, telecommunications operators and content providers.[87]

[84] See Coates, para.6–090, n.73, pp.3–4, where the author stressed the concerns raised by the participation of incumbent dominant telecommunications operators in domain name registration activities. The Commission has reviewed the practices of Network Solutions, Inc. (NSI) in the registration of internet generic domain names in the .com, .org and .net domains. NSI, in co-operation with ICANN, had until recently been acting as a monopolistic registrar of top-level domain names worldwide, pursuant to a contract with the US government. This contract was amended in October 1998 to initiate a stepwise liberalisation of the registration system for top-level domain names. The liberalisation process involves the accreditation by ICANN of a number of competing registrars, through a so-called "Shared Registration System". To implement this system and allow for competing registrars, NSI developed a protocol and associated software supporting a system that allowed multiple registrars to provide registration services for the registry of the existing generic top-level domain names. Following a number of complaints from third parties, the Commission initiated proceedings to investigate a number of concerns identified in relation to the licensing conditions imposed by NSI upon registrars for the use of the protocol and software. In particular, the Commission's concerns related to: (i) the lack of safeguards to prevent NSI from discriminating against competing registrars in favour of NSI's affiliated registrar; (ii) the fact that NSI as a registrar was not subject to the conditions and obligations imposed by ICANN as part of the accreditation process; (iii) certain requirements to enter the market, *e.g.* a performance bond of $100,000 which could constitute a barrier to market entry; and (iv) the domain names portability rules and NSI's related policy, which the Commission believed could act as strong deterrents to domain owners transferring from one registrar to another. The Commission has indicated that these contractual clauses could infringe Art.81 and also put NSI in a dominant position contrary to Art.82: see Commission Press Release IP/99/596 , July 29, 1999.

[85] See *X/Open Group*, Commission Decision of December 15, 1986, O.J. 1987 L35/36.

[86] Nordemann, Czychowski and Grüter, "The Internet, the Name Server and Antitrust Law" (1998) E.C.L.R. 99.

[87] See, *e.g.*, *America OnLine/Bertelsmann/Deutsche Telekom, Microsoft Network (MSN), Europe On-Line; AOL/Time Warner*, as discussed, below, at para.8–223 *et seq.*

While the Commission has regarded the emergence of online services as a positive innovation, it nevertheless monitors this sector closely. For instance, the Commission launched an investigation regarding the online services joint venture between the major publishers, Matra-Hachette, Pearson and Burda.[88] The Commission expressed concerns on the issues of: (i) whether the publications controlled by the partners would be available on fair conditions to other online service providers; and (ii) whether content providers not associated with the joint venture would have access to the customer base on conditions similar to those of the partners.[89]

6–095 German internet bookselling case — Several book wholesalers, who intended to sell books at discount prices to German consumers via the internet, complained to the Commission against the German book retail price maintenance system. The Commission issued a Statement of Objections, arguing *inter alia* that several publishers and booksellers applied the system, which it considered fixed retail prices, in a way which appreciably affected trade between Member States and therefore infringed Article 81(1). The case was settled after the defendants submitted an undertaking, pursuant to which the retail price maintenance system would not be applied to transborder sales (including internet sales), unless such sales were made in order to circumvent the national retail price maintenance system.[90]

H. Enforcement of the Market Conduct Rules of the EC Treaty

6–096 Businesses that are prejudiced by the anti-competitive conduct of other market players have a choice of possible remedies under the EC Treaty's competition rules.

6–097 Complaint to the Commission — Businesses may file complaints with the Commission alleging an infringement of Article 81 and/or Article 82.[91] No particular form is required for a complaint.[92] Companies may request the Commission to adopt interim measures pending the completion of its investigation if the case is urgent and they would otherwise suffer serious and irreparable harm.[93] The Commission may order positive action to be taken, as well as prohibit

---

[88] See Commission Press Release IP/95/1354 of December 6, 1995. The JV company, Europe Online, filed for bankruptcy in 1996 after the three initial investors withdrew their investments. Today, Europe Online is a different company with different business objectives.

[89] See also *BiB*, para.6–067, n.23, above, where the Commission required, as a condition for granting an exemption, that the parties provide non-discriminatory access to the set-top box population of the joint venture to other providers of interactive online services.

[90] See Commission Press Release IP/02/461 of March 22, 2002.

[91] See Bellamy and Child, para.4–001, n.4, para.12–019 *et seq.*

[92] *ibid.*, para.12–020. For convenience, the Commission has made Form C available for the purpose of lodging a complaint, although there is no obligation to use it. The complaint will normally identify the nature of the complainant's interest, the facts alleged, the complainant's reasons for concluding that a *prima facie* case of infringement exists and a request that the Commission act on the matters disclosed.

[93] The Commission will only grant interim measures, pursuant to Art.3(1) of Regulation 17/62, in case of *prima facie* violation of Arts 81 or 82 and of proven urgency in order to remedy a situation likely to cause serious and irreparable damage to the complainant, or damage which would be intolerable for the public interest: see Case T–44/90, *La Cinq v Commission* [1992] II E.C.R. 1. See also the *IMS Health* cases, para.6–051, n.89, above. The Commission will keep the possibility to grant interim measures under the modernised enforcement system, see Regulation 1/2003, Art.8.

certain conduct. The Commission can also impose periodic penalties (*i.e.* fines that are imposed on a daily basis) until the company complies with an order of the Commission, and large fines if it decides that Articles 81 or 82 have been infringed.[94]

6–098   Enforcement action before the national courts — Articles 81(1), 81(2) and 82 of the EC Treaty have always had so-called "direct effect". This means that domestic courts have a duty to enforce the rights that private parties derive from those provisions.[95] Accordingly, private parties may seek interlocutory and permanent injunctions (whether of a prohibiting or mandatory nature) and/ or claim damages before national courts as an alternative to, or in parallel with, a complaint to the Commission.[96] In comparison with a complaint before the Commission, procedures before national courts offer the following advantages: (i) national courts can award damages for infringements of the EC Treaty's competition rules; (ii) national courts can usually adopt interim measures and order termination of an infringement more quickly than the Commission is able to do; (iii) it is possible before a national court to combine a claim under Community law with a claim under national law; and (iv) in certain Member States, legal costs can be awarded to the successful applicant.[97]

As of 1 May 2004, the role of national courts in the enforcement of EU competition rules will be strengthened. Pursuant to the new Regulation 1/2003 on the implementation of the rules on competition laid down in Articles 81 and 82 of the Treaty, Article 81(3) will then be understood as a directly applicable legal exemption to Article 81(1). National courts will have jurisdiction to decide whether a certain agreement falls under this exemption or not.[98]

6–099   Enforcement action before national competition authorities — Member States have domestic competition rules that generally mirror the EC Treaty's competition rules. Implementation of national competition law is generally entrusted to an administrative body, separate from the NRA, regulating the telecommunications sector.[99] Moreover, national competition authorities are also (subject to having powers under national law) empowered to apply Articles 81(1), 81(2) and 82 as long as the Commission has not initiated its own procedures.[1] From May 1, 2004, national

---

[94] The fines imposed by the Commission may range from €1,000–1,000,000 or 10% of the worldwide turnover for the preceding year of the group of companies to which the parties concerned belong: Art.15(2) of Regulation 17/62 (Art.23 of Regulation 1/2003).

[95] Case C–127/73, *BRT v Sabam* [1973] E.C.R. 51.

[96] The Court of Justice has clearly established the need for consistency in the application of EC competition rules as a result of the concurrent jurisdiction of the Commission and national courts to apply those rules; see Case C–234/89, *Delimitis* [1991] I E.C.R. 935. See the Commission Notice on Co-operation between National Courts and the Commission in Applying Arts 85 and 86 of the EC Treaty, O.J. 1993 C39/6. For a review of the application of Arts 81 and 82 in the Member States, see also the Access Notice, para.25, and Bellamy and Child, para.4–001, n.4, para.10–001 *et seq.*

[97] See Access Notice, para.5–004, n.18, para.25.

[98] See para.4–004 *et seq.*

[99] In the United Kingdom, OFTEL — the telecommunication regulator — has the power to apply UK competition law (the Competition Act, 1998) to agreements and practices within the telecommunications sector. In the Netherlands the competition and regulatory authorities (Nma and OPTA) are planned to merge into a single authority.

[1] Regulation 17/62, Art.9(3). However, the Commission has the sole power to declare Art.81(1) inapplicable pursuant to Art.81(3), although this will change from May 1, 2004 with the entry into force of Regulation 1/2003: see above, para.6–098.

competition authorities will be the primary enforcers of both Art.81 (including Art.81(3)) and Art.82 pursuant to Regulation 1/2003. In principle, national competition law can then still apply in parallel to any given situation notwithstanding that Articles 81 and/or 82 also apply. Companies can thus file a complaint before national competition authorities under national competition law and at the same time initiate an action before the Commission under Community competition law. However, pursuant to Art.3(2) of Regulation 1/2003, the application of national law may not lead to different results than the application of Community law.[2] As a result, a national competition authority cannot, for example, authorise under national competition rules an agreement that has been prohibited under the Community competition rules.[3] In order to reduce the risk of parallel investigations yielding conflicting results, the Commission has adopted a notice setting forth guidelines to be followed by national competition authorities in case of parallel proceedings before them and the Commission.[4]

6–100   Enforcement action before national regulatory authorities (NRAs) — To the extent that a specific practice infringes an operator's obligations under telecommunications sector-specific regulation, national rules implementing the telecommunications directives have established specific procedures empowering NRAs to intervene to punish such practices. For example, NRAs have jurisdiction, within the New Regulatory Framework, over certain access agreements which must be notified to them.[5] Those agreements or practices may thus fall within the scope of both the competition rules and sector-specific regulation.

6–101   Enforcement action against businesses established outside the EU — Companies located outside the EU are not immune from the EC Treaty's competition rules. Articles 81 and 82 of the EC Treaty apply to market conduct having an effect, actual or potential, upon trade between Member States, whatever the nationality or territorial location of the businesses concerned. Thus, these rules apply to the practices of businesses established outside the EU, provided these practices have an appreciable effect within the EU.[6]

---

[2] As far as Art.82 is concerned, Art.3(2), cl.2 of Regulation 1/2003 permits stricter treatment of unilateral conduct under national law.

[3] Likewise, a national competition authority cannot prohibit an agreement exempted under Art.81(3). See already under the current regime: the Opinions of Advocate General Tesauro in Case C–70/93, *BMW v ALD* [1995] I E.C.R. 3439 and Case C–266/93, *Bundeskartellamt v Volkswagen and VAG Leasing* [1995] I E.C.R. 3477.

[4] See Commission Notice on Cooperation Between National Competition Authorities and the Commission in Handling Cases Falling Within the Scope of Arts 85 or 86 of the EC Treaty, O.J. 1997 C313/3. The Commission will publish a notice on the same issue regarding the situation under Regulation 1/2003. See also, Access Notice, para.17 *et seq.*

[5] Access Directive, para.1–011, n.29, Art.9; see also, above, para.1–148 *et seq.*

[6] Joined cases C–89/85, C–104/85, C–114/85, C–116/85, C–117/85, C–125/85, *Ahlström v Commission* [1993] I E.C.R. 1307, and Case T–102/96, *Gencor v Commission* [1999] II E.C.R. 753.

Chapter VII
Application of State Aid Rules

7–001 Introduction — The EC Treaty's rules on state aids (Articles 87 and 88 of the EC Treaty) are fully applicable to the telecommunications and broadcasting sectors.[1] Accordingly, under Article 87(1), Member States may not, in principle, grant any aids that would distort competition by favouring certain telecommunications or broadcasting operators. Any aid that a Member State contemplates granting must be notified to the Commission and must not be implemented prior to the Commission having given its approval in accordance with Article 88(3) of the EC Treaty.

Before assessing the aspects of the EC Treaty's State aid rules that are of particular importance to the broadcasting and telecommunications sectors, the concept of state aid will first be examined. Often, there is room for argument as to whether a certain measure constitutes aid at all, or whether it is a new aid or an existing aid (*i.e.* aid that was in existence at the time that the EC Treaty became applicable in a particular Member State or has been approved previously by the Commission and/or is now being modified).

The application of Article 86 of the EC Treaty to the granting of aid in the broadcasting sector is then considered, together with a review of the question of whether rescue and restructuring aid may gain more importance in the near future. Finally, an overview is given of the remedies that are available to Member States, beneficiaries of aid, and competitors of beneficiaries.

A. State Aid in the Broadcasting and Telecommunications Sectors

7–002 For a measure to constitute state aid, Article 87(1) requires that four cumulative criteria be fulfilled:

(i) it must be granted by a Member State or through state resources;

(ii) it must confer an economic advantage;

(iii) it must favour certain undertakings or specific sectors; and

---

[1] For a description of these provisions, see para.4–017 *et seq.*

(iv) it must distort or threaten to distort competition and affect trade between Member States.

7–003 Use of state resources — The use of state resources is particularly important in the broadcasting and communications sectors. After the liberalisation of the telecommunications sector, many Member States have retained significant shareholder interests in communications operators, and, therefore, potentially have a tendency to continue supporting these companies. Furthermore, the Universal Service Directive explicitly allows Member States to set up funding mechanisms to raise the funds that are necessary to finance the provision of universal service (*e.g.* the provision of access at fixed locations, directory inquiry services, ensuring nationwide coverage of public pay-phones, and ensuring access and affordability of publicly available telephone services for disabled users).[2]

In the broadcasting sector, most Member States have broadcasters that are owned by the state, and/or which are financed wholly or partly from public funds. For example, some Member States have established funds (*e.g.* the German fee for public broadcasters[3] and the UK BBC licence fee[4]) or oblige users of broadcasting services to pay certain fees to a fund or organisation, which are then used to provide public service broadcasting companies with the necessary funds to provide their services.[5]

7–004 Article 87(1) of the EC Treaty applies to all funds that are either publicly held or financed. Revenue that a state obtains from taxation and other compulsory levies is clearly a state resource.[6] Furthermore, so too is revenue from so-called "parafiscal charges". These are charges that are levied on private persons and businesses and are paid into a fund or account, which might be held by a public or by a private entity, where national laws provide for the existence of, and mandatory payments into, such fund or account,[7] which is then used to finance an activity.[8] The redistribution of these monies to certain beneficiaries will constitute state aid (assuming all other criteria are met), because these funds are considered to be "state resources", as they are

[2] Universal Service Directive, para.1–011, n.30, Art.13(1)(a) and Annex IV, Pt B.

[3] *Kinderkanal and Phoenix*, XXIXth Report on Competition Policy (1999), at point 226.

[4] Case NN88/98, *BBC News 24* (funding of BBC News 24 Channel from licence fee revenues), decision of December 14, 1999, available at: *http://europa.eu.int/comm/secretariat_general/sgb/state_aids/industrie/nno88-98.pdf* and Case N–631/2001, *BBC Licence Fee* (use of increased licence fee to fund nine new BBC digital channels), decision of May 22, 2002, available at: *http://europa.eu.int/comm/secretariat_general/sgb/state_aids/industrie_2002.htm*, paras 18–20.

[5] Marton, "The Impact of EU Competition Law on the Financing of Public Service Broadcasters" in *Communications Law* (2001), p.56, referring to the Commission decisions in the *Kinderkanal/Phoenix*, *BBC News 24* and *BBC licence fee* cases, where the Commission considered the use of reserves from compulsory licence fees to constitute state aid.

[6] Case 173/73, *Italy v Commission* [1974] E.C.R. 709.

[7] Private funds at the disposal of the state may also, for the purposes of Art.87(1), be considered as state resources: Case T–358/94, *Air France v Commission (CDC-P)* [1996] II E.C.R. 2109 (private funds deposited with a public body established by public law were state resources); and Case T–67/94, *Ladbroke Racing v Commission* [1998] II E.C.R. 1 (unclaimed winnings held by a bookmaking body controlled by the French state were state resources, and the state governed their use).

[8] Case C–78/76, *Steinike und Weinlig v Germany* [1977] E.C.R. 595; Case C–290/83 *Commission v France* [1985] E.C.R. 439.

either collected under compulsory conditions or are resources available to funds governed by public law or passing through the hands of a public entity. In its most recent decision concerning the BBC licence fee collected in the UK (under legal compulsion from all owners of a television set) for funding the BBC's services, the Commission confirmed that the collection of the licence fee by the BBC directly from private individuals (rather than by the state, which would then pass the revenues to the BBC) did not affect the character of the funds as "state resources".[9] Provided that the revenue stays under public control, and is therefore available to the competent national authorities, the funds must be considered as state resources.

The Universal Service Directive permits Member States to establish financing mechanisms to fund the additional net costs of operators with universal service obligations that they incur in providing universal service.[10] The funds can constitute parafiscal charges, as they will be collected from either other operators or subscribers under compulsory conditions. The Directive explicitly refers to the possibility for Member States to provide a mechanism for the financing of the services that the undertakings with universal service obligations are required to provide. Where the provision of universal service represents an unfair burden, *i.e.* causes extra net costs to be incurred by the designated undertaking, the Member States are entitled either to set up mechanisms to compensate the undertaking for these additional net costs or to share the net cost of universal service obligations between all providers of electronic communications networks and services.[11] For the purposes of analysing whether a financing mechanism set up by the Member States to raise funds for compensation for the extra net cost of universal communication services, or the collection of contributions from other operators, results in the use of "state resources" in the sense of Article 87(1), Recitals 18, 22 and 24 of the Universal Service Directive are of assistance. These recitals state that such mechanisms need to be compatible with Articles 87 and 88 of the EC Treaty, and explicitly mention the compensation of net costs of universal service provision from "public funds" (such as funding from general government budgets and other public financing sources), and that funding must only be for the actual net costs incurred and no more. Recital 24 states:

> "Member States' schemes for the costing and financing of universal service obligations should be communicated to the Commission for verification of compatibility with the Treaty."

These recitals reflect the case law of the Court of Justice in relation to parafiscal funds.[12] It is therefore clear that mechanisms set up to fund the net costs of universal service provision would *prima facie* amount to the use of "state resources" for the purposes of Article 87(1).

7–005 However, it is not always clear where to draw the line between state resources and the transfer of private monies from one undertaking to another undertaking. The analysis of whether a certain measure includes the transfer of state resources or merely constitutes a redistribution of funds directly between undertakings pursuant to law, without these monies going through "the state's hands", depends as much on the origin of the funds (*i.e.* directly from the state budget or

---

[9] *BBC News 24* and *BBC licence fee*, para.7–003, n.4, above.
[10] Universal Service Directive, para.1–011, n.30, Arts 12 and 13; discussed at para.1–202 *et seq.*
[11] *ibid.*, Art.13(1).
[12] Para.7–004, nn.6–8, above.

from a fund set up by the state to which individuals and businesses are required to contribute, whether compulsory or voluntarily) as on the level of state intervention.[13] Well-established Court of Justice case law provides that no state resources are used when a state fixes the conditions under which undertakings deal with each other or consumers,[14] although the state use of resources collected from private individuals to fund other private undertakings or public undertakings does qualify as a state aid if the other conditions are met.[15] The Court of Justice has recently confirmed these principles in *Preussen Elektra*.[16] In *Preussen Elektra*, the German state had adopted regulations requiring electricity suppliers to purchase electricity from generators using renewable energy sources (such as wind power), at prices higher than market prices. These costs were partially financed by other generators through elevated minimum prices as fixed in the German law. The German law therefore required private undertakings to provide financial advantages to other private undertakings. The Court of Justice held that this scheme for financing renewable sources of electricity did not involve state resources and simply regulated the terms upon which undertakings contracted with each other.

A case is currently pending before the Court of Justice which concerns a fund set up to finance so-called "stranded costs" of electricity producers, *i.e.* investments made before market liberalisation that cannot be recovered in a liberalised market.[17] As a result of the liberalisation of the electricity market, the Commission agreed that some of the costs electricity producers had incurred before market liberalisation, and that could not be recovered by increasing prices in a competitive market, should be reimbursed. Spain (as well as other Member States in similar cases) provided for systems of obligatory contributions by private consumers into a fund (in the form of a current account) from which sums were to be paid out to the electricity generators or distributors who had incurred stranded costs. Neither the Member State nor the entity administering the funds had a discretion on how to administer and distribute the funds. In the light of the *Preussen Elektra* judgment, it could be argued that these contributions from end-consumers never became state resources, so fall outside Article 87(1). However, this would depend upon the nature of the funding mechanism. The imposition of compulsory levies that are administerd by the state would tend to suggest that they should be considered as state resources. Arguably, a similar question could arise with regard to funding mechanisms set up under national law (licence fees for public broadcasters, financing schemes for communications operators) for the benefit of communications operators and broadcasters providing services in the public interest.

7–006 For the purposes of defining whether a certain state measure constitutes state aid, where funds are directly distributed by the state or indirectly by a state-owned or governed entity, these

---

[13] See the opinion of Advocate General Fenelly in Case C–200/97, *Ecotrade/AFS* [1998] I E.C.R. 7907; Case C–379/98, *Preussen Elektra* [2001] I E.C.R. 2099, para.58 *et seq.*

[14] Case C–82/77, *Openbare Ministerie v van Tiggele* [1978] E.C.R. 25 (minimum price for alcoholic spirits was not considered to constitute state aid).

[15] *E.g.* Case C–290/83, *Commission v France (Caisse Nationale de Crédit Agricole)* [1985] E.C.R. 439.

[16] Case C–379/98, *Preussen Elektra v Schleswag* [2001] I E.C.R. 2099.

[17] Case C–40/99, *Spain v Commission*, pending. See also Commission Decisions concerning state aid: Cases N 6/A/2001, *Ireland*; N661/99, *UK*; N 34/99, *Austria*; N 597/1998, *the Netherlands*; and NN 49/99, *Spain*; all of these decisions are published on website: *http://europa.eu.int/comm/secretariat_general/sgb/state_aids/*. See also Commission Decision in Case C–31/2002 (*ex* N 149/2000), *Belgium*, O.J. 2002 C222/2.

transfers would be considered as involving the use of state resources.[18] A separate question is whether and to what extent such financing schemes, or the use of funds collected under them, are compatible with Articles 87 and 86(2) of the EC Treaty.[19]

It was recently decided by the Court of Justice that funds provided by a public company or a state-owned bank (following long-standing case law) could involve the use of state resources, where this was *"imputable to the State".*[20] It is, therefore, not sufficient that a publicly owned or controlled company[21] has transferred resources to a subsidiary or another company. It has to be further examined whether the state or the public authorities owning or otherwise controlling the public company or bank have in fact influenced the decision to grant the funds by being involved in one way or another in the decision to grant the funds. This can be inferred from the state body, the company or the bank being required to take account of the requirements of the public authorities, its legal status (*i.e.* whether governed by public or private law), the nature of its activities and the degree of state supervision of any activity in its functions. This issue will be of relevance, where a publicly owned or controlled broadcasting or communications company grants capital injections, loans or other advantages to its subsidiaries, as is frequently the case with public broadcasters owning production and/or advertising companies.[22]

7–007   Conferral of an "economic advantage" — This criterion is often crucial and many cases of public financing are not within the scope of Article 87(1) on the basis that the so-called "market economy investor test" is satisfied. Alternatively, no advantage might be conferred because the resources made available are consideration for services performed by the recipient undertaking.

The "market economy investor" test has been developed by the Commission and the Court of Justice in considering state aid generally, as well as more specifically in the broadcasting sector.[23] It can be applied to financial transactions between a Member State or a state-owned company and another company, whether or not wholly or partly owned by the state, for example the granting of loans or guarantees or the making of capital injections. Under this test, where a diligent and reasonable private investor, expecting a return on its investment within a reasonable period of time,

---

[18] *e.g.* Case NN88/98, *BBC News 24* and Case N 631/2001, *BBC licence fee*, para.7–003, n.4, above.

[19] See below, para.7–020 *et seq.*

[20] Case C–482/99, *France v Commission (Stardust Marine)* [2002] I E.C.R. 4397, para.50 *et seq.*

[21] See Commission Regulation on the Transparency of Financial Relations between Member States and Public Undertakings, last amended in 2000, O.J. 2000 L193/75, Art.2(2) for guidance on the definition of "public undertaking". It has been argued that a company, even if it is 100% owned by the state is not a public undertaking due to the constitutional guarantee of independence from influence by the state, Storr, "Grundversorgung in Rundfunk und Binnenmarkt" *Kommunikation & Recht* (2002), pp.464–466.

[22] See, *e.g.* C–39/94, *SFEI v La Poste* [1996] I E.C.R. 3547.

[23] Case C–40/85, *Belgium v Commission (Boch (No.2))* [1986] E.C.R. 2321. The principle has been applied by the Commission and the Court of Justice in many subsequent cases, most recently in Case C–482/99, *France v Commission (Stardust Marine)* [2002] I E.C.R. 4397. In the broadcasting sector see: Case C–60/99, capital increases and other ad hoc subsidies in favour of France2 and France3, O.J. 1999 C340; and Case C–62/99, capital increases and other measures in favour of RAI, O.J. 1999 C351/20. See also Commission Communication to the Member States, O.J. 1993 C307/3, and Commission Communication on the application of state aid rules to public service broadcasting, O.J. 2001 C320/5, para.17. See also Bartosch, "The Financing of Public Broadcasting and EC State Aid Law: An Interim Balance" (1999) E.C.L.R. 197–200; and Marton, para.7–003, n.5, pp.56–60.

would have undertaken the financial transaction under the same conditions, the transaction is considered to represent reasonable economic conduct and does not involve any state aid, since no advantage is conferred on the recipient of the loan, guarantee or capital injection.[24]

7–008 The private investor principle is of particular importance in the broadcasting and telecommunications sectors, due to the recent liberalisation. Where the state remains a shareholder in a company, as it is often the case with many privatised companies, it is not easy to assess whether further financial support from the state would be made by a reasonable private investor, for example because it would help the company to survive and generate profits in the future. This question has explicitly arisen in the context of the French government's decision to provide over €9 billion of financing to France Télécom, which the Commission is now formally investigating under Article 88(2). Determining whether such financing involves state aid requires an economic analysis of the financing in the context of the prevailing circumstances, in particular whether the state can expect that its investment will lead to the profitability of the company and thus a reasonable return for the investor within a reasonable period of time. If an investment could only at best be based on profitability in the long term, it will not be easy to convince the Commission that such an investment constitutes the conduct of a private sector investor.[25]

It is clear from Court judgments and Commission decisions that the market economy investor test applies in the communications and broadcasting sectors. Thus, in *BBC News 24*, which concerned the use of BBC licence fee revenues to fund a new news-based channel, the Commission considered that the licence fee provided an advantage for the BBC, as it did not have to compete for revenue in the advertising market. The market economy investor test was not met, as a private sector investor would not have invested in a channel such as BBC News 24, which could not make a profit, being a "public service" channel.[26] Similarly, in *SIC*, the Portuguese state had granted various financial advantages to RTP, the Portuguese public broadcaster. The Court of First Instance confirmed that such funding could involve state aid.[27] The Commission has also analysed whether public broadcasters made economically justifiable investments when granted loans or receiving capital injections.[28] The financial situation of the undertaking that receives the funds is often the most decisive factor.

7–009 **Aid to a specific undertaking or sector** — The third criterion of the concept of state aid requires that the measure be "specific", in that it favours particular undertakings or the production of particular goods or services. Thus, excluded from the scope of Article 87(1) EC are general measures that do not confer an advantage on certain companies or a certain sector.

This condition is not easy to apply and is particularly important where state measures impose a burden, such as social security levies or taxes, but provide exemptions from these taxes or levies to

---

[24] See also para.4–018 *et seq.*

[25] See, *e.g.* Case C–305/89, *Italy v Commission (Alpha Romeo (No.1))* [1991] I E.C.R. 1603 (capital injection into a persistently loss-making enterprise was considered state aid, as no private sector company would have invested in a comparable private sector company).

[26] See *BBC News 24*, para.7–003, n.4, above.

[27] Case T–46/97, *SIC v Commission* [2000] II E.C.R. 2125.

[28] Case NN 2/2002, *ZDF Medienpark*, published at: *http://europa.eu.int/comm/competition/state_aidregister/ii/*.

certain companies or to certain (sub-)sectors of the economy. The Commission's notice on business taxation[29] gives indications as to when a tax exemption constitutes a general measure and not an advantage granted selectively to certain undertakings. Usually, a tax exemption granted only to one sector or sub-sector of the economy constitutes an aid measure within the scope of Article 87(1), as undertakings in that sector are placed in a more favourable position than other taxpayers.[30] It is only where the logic of the tax system requires specific rules for a certain (sub-)sector — for example due to the nature of the business in the sector in question or a specific regime applying to it — that a tax exemption will be considered of a general nature, and, therefore, not within the scope of Article 87(1).[31] For example, tax exemptions for the agriculture and fisheries sectors may not constitute aid, because these sectors are governed by complex regulatory schemes. The Commission has found, however, that an exemption from corporate taxes for the whole manufacturing sector has to be regarded as a state aid.[32]

Although the Commission has not yet adopted any decisions regarding exemptions from tax laws and/or social insurance schemes in the communications and broadcasting sectors, some complaints in the broadcasting sector (involving the state funding of RAI and RTP, the Italian and Portuguese state broadcasters respectively) have raised the issue and it can be expected that the Commission will adopt decisions in the future that will probably follow the existing general practice outlined above.[33] In the investigation concerning the financing of RAI, the Commission has been called upon to assess whether the following measures involved state aid: (i) the exemption from all taxes of the revaluation of RAI's assets; and (ii) a 75 per cent reduction of the concession fee payable by RAI to the Italian state. The Commission's preliminary finding is that the tax exemption relating to the revaluation of RAI's assets constituted an aid measure, because an undertaking would normally have paid the applicable tax rate on the net revaluation of its assets, and would, therefore, have incurred a cash outflow to pay such taxes to the state. The exemption conferred an economic advantage on RAI, as it was able to avoid making such a payment. Interestingly, the Commission considers that the 75 per cent reduction in the concession fee did not involve state aid.[34]

In the investigation concerning state measures in respect of RTP (Radio Television Portugal), the Commission is examining whether the exemption of RTP from duties and expenses relating to the

---

[29] Commission Notice on the Application of the State Aid Rules to Measures Relating to Direct Business Taxation, O.J. 1998 C384/3.

[30] Case C–387/92, *Banco Exterior de Espana v Commission* [1994] I E.C.R. 877. See also *R. v Commissioner of Customs and Excise Ex p. Lunn Poly* [1999] 1 C.M.L.R. 1357 (English Court of Appeal): differential taxation of travel insurance depending on the supplier was a state aid measure in favour of those undertakings subject to tax at the lower rate.

[31] See Case C–173/73, *Italy v Commission* [1974] E.C.R. 709.

[32] Commission Notice on Business Taxation (see n.29, above), para.18, nn.12–13.

[33] Case C–85/2001 (*ex* NN 133/B/01, NN 85/B/2001 and NN 94/B/99), *State financing to RTP*, O.J. 2002 C85/9. The Commission is also investigating various other measures for financing RTP, including debt rescheduling, waivers of interest on outstanding social security contributions, loans, guarantees for bonds issued by RTP and capital injections; and Case C–62/99 (*ex* NN 140/98), *Capital increase and other support measures in favour of RAI*, O.J. 1999 C351/20. The Commission is also investigating various other measures for financing RAI, including loans and converting RAI's debts into long-term loans.

[34] *Capital increase and other support measures in favour of RAI*, ibid.

registration of the document creating RTP as a company governed by private law in 1992 constituted state aid. The Commission's preliminary finding is that this exemption did not constitute aid, because the exemption from registration duties is inherent in the tax system, as the conditions for imposing the registration tax do not exist where a public undertaking is transformed into a commercial entity by a legislative act.[35]

7–010 Distortion or risk of distortion of competition, affecting trade between Member States — The last condition for a state measure to constitute state aid is that it must be capable of distorting or threatening to distort competition, thereby affecting trade between Member States contrary to the Community interest. This criterion is interpreted very broadly: the Commission need only to show that the measure is capable of affecting trade between Member States, whether at the present time or in the future.[36] An aid measure will clearly affect trade if the beneficiary is able to compete in international markets[37] and competition will be affected if the recipient is active on markets already characterised by (strong) competition.[38]

The Commission's practice, confirmed by the case law of the Court of Justice and Court of First Instance, shows that only in very limited circumstances will a state measure be excluded from the scope of Article 87(1) on the basis that it does not affect competition and trade between Member States.[39] An example of such a case would be the funding by the state of a kindergarten or local public swimming pool operating only at the local level and serving exclusively local residents and businesses.[40] However, measures benefiting local broadcasters are usually not exempt from the scope of Article 87(1), since their broadcasting activities, even though they are local, will nevertheless reduce the number of consumers watching other national and international programmes and thereby affect the competitive position of other broadcasters, for example in competing for advertising revenues. This would presumably still be the case if the beneficiary did not carry out advertising, as it would reduce the number of viewers or listeners of commercially funded channels, thereby making them less attractive to advertisers.[41] The reason for this wide interpretation of an effect on competition and trade is that in almost every case a state measure will either distort or threaten to distort competition, even if there is only potential competition. State

---

[35] *State financing to RTP* n.33, above. The Commission considers that various of the other measures under investigation (capital injection and loans) involve state aid, as no market economy investor would at that time have invested in RTP, due to its weak financial position.

[36] Case C–107/87, *France v Commission* [1989] E.C.R. 4067; Cases T–447/94, etc. *AITEC v Commission* [1995] II E.C.R. 1971.

[37] Case C–730/79, *Philip Morris v Commission* [1980] E.C.R. 2871.

[38] Case T–214/95, *Het Vlaamse Gewest v Commission* [1998] E.C.R. 717 (interest-free loan of €0.5 million was likely to distort or threaten to distort competition given that the air transport market was highly competitive); but see also the Commission's Regulation 69/2001 of January 12, 2001 on *de minimis* rule for state aid, O.J. 2001 L10/30: aid measures granted to an undertaking that are less than €100,000 over a three year period fall outside of Art.87(1).

[39] Case C–47/69, *France v Commission* [1970] E.C.R. 487, applied in *Het Vlaamse Gewest v Commission* n.38, above. See also Marton, para.7–003, n.5, above, pp.56–61.

[40] See, for example Commission guidelines on state aid for undertakings in deprived urban areas, O.J. 1997 C146/8: aid to small firms in deprived urban areas which carry out only local activities falls outside of Art.87(1) (has now become redundant and expired).

[41] Case N 548/2001, *Belgian aid in favour of local television in the French Community*, p.4, published at: *http://europa.eu.int/comm/secretariat_general/sgb/state_aids/industrie_2002.htm*.

funding of undertakings operating only within the territory of the granting state involves the danger of preventing companies from other Member States from offering their goods or services at the same prices as the aided undertaking in the Member State that is granting the financial or other assistance.

Therefore, wherever a good or service is provided or could be provided by undertakings other than the beneficiary of the aid, the prohibition contained in Article 87(1) will normally apply. It is not necessary for the Commission to engage in the same type of analysis of the potential effect of the aid measure on the market in the same way as it does when it applies Articles 81 and 82 of the EC Treaty.[42] Nevertheless, despite this wide interpretation of Article 87(1), the Commission must give reasons in its decisions as to why in any given particular case a state measure distorts or threatens to distort competition, including identifying the relevant market, the place of the beneficiary on that market, and the pattern of competition and inter-state trade on that market.[43]

7–011 Application of the state aid rules in the broadcasting sector and possible derogations — In its recent Communication on the Financing of Public Service Broadcasters (the "Communication on public service broadcasting"), the Commission gave some guidance as to which state measures in the broadcasting sector may constitute state aid and whether the derogations contained in Articles 87(2) or (3) of the EC Treaty apply.[44] In this Communication, the Commission states that the following measures may constitute state aid provided that all the other requirements of Article 87(1) for a measure to qualify as state aid are fulfilled:

(i)   the financing of public service broadcasters out of the state budget or through a levy on owners of television sets; and

(ii) capital injections or debt write-offs in favour of public service broadcasters that fail to satisfy the market economy investor test.[45]

The Communication on public service broadcasting states that the acquisition and sale of programme rights, as well as advertising, take place at an international level, in particular in homogeneous linguistic areas. Therefore, state financing of public broadcasters enabling these activities may affect trade between Member States and favour the public broadcasters over competing commercial broadcasters.[46]

---

[42] *Philip Morris*, para.7–010, n.37, above, and *Het Vlaamse Gewest*, para.7–010, n.38, above.

[43] Cases C–296 and C–318/82, *Netherlands and Leeuwarder Papierwarenfabriek v Commission* [1985] E.C.R. 817, at p.824.

[44] Communication from the Commission on the Application of State Aid Rules to Public Service Broadcasting, O.J. 2001 C320/5.

[45] See, for example, *State financing to RTP*, para.7–009, n.33, above; and *Capital increase and other support measures in favour of RAI*, para.7–009, n.33, above. Case C–60/99 (*ex* NN 167/95), *Capital increases and other ad hoc subsidies in favour of France2 and France3*, O.J. 1999 C340/57; and the Commission's opening of an investigation into the plans of the French government to solve France Télécom's financial difficulties by way of a substantial capital injection or a loan, para.7–008, n.25, above.

[46] Communication on public service broadcasting, n.44, above, para.17. See Cases T–106/95, *FFSA v Commission* [1997] II E.C.R. 229, *SIC v Commission*, para.7–008, n.27, above, and Case C–332/98, *France v Commission* [2000] I E.C.R. 4833.

7–012 Once a state measure in the broadcasting sector is found to constitute state aid, the next step is to examine whether one of the derogations under Article 87(2) or (3) of the EC Treaty apply, under which an aid measure is deemed or can be declared to be compatible with the common market. The only derogation likely to be applicable is that in Article 87(3)(d), for state aid granted in order to promote culture. In *BBC News 24*[47] the United Kingdom did not rely upon Article 87(3)(d), presumably because the provision of a 24-hour news channel could not be regarded as a "cultural" activity. However, in *BBC Licence Fee*[48] the Commission considered that some of the new BBC digital channels that would be financed by the licence fee were of a cultural nature. As an exception from a prohibition laid down in the EC Treaty, Article 87(3) has to be interpreted restrictively.[49] An aid measure only qualifies for an exemption under Article 87(3)(d) if its purpose is exclusively to promote culture. Most public broadcasters are vested with a very general public service obligation not only referring to culture, but also to educational, as well as democratic and informative, needs. Hence, most aid to broadcasters cannot be approved under Article 87(3)(d) unless it is provided exclusively for funding cultural aspects of broadcasting.[50] The Commission did consider the application of Article 87(3)(d) in its *Kinderkanal/Phoenix* decision.[51] The Commission considered that the exception contained in Article 87(3)(d) was not applicable, as the channels in question seemed to be aimed at the democratic and educational, rather than cultural, needs of German society. This has been criticised on the basis that under Community law it should be for the Member State to determine what falls within its cultural policy (including media pluralism) and that the Commission should simply consider if the aid measure in question affects trade and competition to an extent that is contrary to the Community interest.[52] The Commission has a wide discretion in determining if an aid measure is contrary to the common interest, thereby falling outside of the scope of the exception contained in Article 87(3)(d), where this could adversely affect trading conditions to an extent contrary to the public interest.

Most Member States offer special funding for the production of certain types of films or to young producers that would otherwise be unable to pursue their activities. The Commission has found that any aid measures in such schemes are compatible with the common market by virtue of the cultural exception in Article 87(3)(d).[53] The Commission has determined special criteria that it applies in assessing aid to the audio-visual (cinema and television production) sector.[54]

---

[47] See para.7–003, n.4, above.

[48] *ibid.*

[49] *Philip Morris*, para.7–010, n.37, above. See also Bavasso, "Public service broadcasting and State aid rules: between a rock and a hard place" (2002) E.C.L.R. 340, at p.342.

[50] *Belgian aid in favour of local television in the French Community*, above, n.41; see also Bavasso (above, n.49).

[51] See para.7–003, n.3, above.

[52] See Koenig, *EC Competition and Telecommunications Law* (Kluwer, 2002, The Hague), p.203, referring to Case C–288/89, *Collectieve Antennevoorziening Gouda v Commissariat voor de Media* [1991] I E.C.R. 4007; Case C–148/91, *Veronica* [1993] I E.C.R. 487, and Case C–23/93, *TVIO* [1994] I E.C.R. 4795, which — in the context of proceedings under Art.49 of the EC Treaty (freedom to provide services) — stated that it was for the Netherlands to decide the scope of its cultural and broadcasting policy, which could be relied upon to restrict the freedom to provide broadcasting services.

[53] A recent example is Case N237/2000, *Extension of the Irish aid scheme to film and TV production*, published at: *http://europa.eu.int/comm/secretariat_general/sgb/state_aids/industrie_2002.htm.*

[54] These were first laid down in the Commission's decision of June 1998 in the Case concerning *French scheme of automatic aid to film production* (Commission Communication to the Council, the European Parliament, the

If the requirements of Article 87(3)(d) are not met, as will be likely in many cases, then in order to be permitted as state aid, a measure must fall within the scope of the derogation from the Treaty's competition rules (including those on state aid) contained in Article 86(2) EC. This allows in certain circumstances the granting of state resources for the provision of public services by telecommunications and broadcasting companies that have been entrusted with providing such services in the general interest.[55]

B. State Aid Investigation

7–013 The procedure applicable to the Commission's investigations into state aid under Article 88(2) was governed until 1999 by the case law of the Court of Justice and the Court of First Instance, and the Commission's practice. In 1999, a Regulation laying down detailed rules for the application of Article 87 (*ex* Article 93) of the EC Treaty ("Procedural Regulation") entered into force and codified then existing case law and practice.[56] As a preliminary remark, it should be noted that unlike investigation procedures under Articles 81 and 82, a state aid investigation takes place exclusively between the Commission and the Member State. This is because Article 87 is addressed not to undertakings but to Member States. The beneficiary of the aid, and third parties, can only influence the procedure in an informal way and/or via the Member State.

7–014 Lawful aid and unlawful aid — The Commission begins its investigation either on the basis of a notification of an ad hoc aid or aid scheme submitted by the Member State (this is known as "lawful aid") or, in the absence of a notification, on the basis of information it receives through the press or from complainants, usually competitors (this is known as "unlawful aid").

According to Article 88(3) Member States may not grant state aid without prior authorisation by the Commission, unless one of the limited exemptions in Article 87(2) applies or the aid falls within the scope of a block exemption regulation. The Procedural Regulation codifies the so-called standstill clause, prohibiting the implementation of the aid measure during the Commission's investigation procedure.[57]

Where an aid measure is notified to the Commission, it has to take an initial decision within a period of two months.[58] This period, however, starts running only when the Commission has

---

Economic and Social Committee and the Committee of the Regions on certain legal aspects relating to cinematographic and other audiovisual works, COM(01) 534, in O.J. 2002 C43/6, s.2.4). These special criteria are: the grantor of the aid must ensure the cultural nature of the films (in order to avoid the subsidisation of commercial productions that do not contribute to culture); the aid intensity must be limited to 50%, presumably of the production costs (this is not specified), with the exception of aid for "low-budget" films; the state cannot grant additional aid that would affect the neutrality of the aid in terms of the cultural objective (neutral incentive effect); and lastly, the producer must be free to spend at least 20% of the film budget in other Member States so that exchange (presumably this refers to trade) within the European Union is favoured.

[55] See below, Sections C and D.

[56] Regulation 659/99 of March 22, 1999 laying down detailed rules for the application of Art.93 of the EC Treaty, O.J. 1999 L83/1.

[57] *ibid.*, Art.3.

[58] *ibid.*, Art.4(5).

received all information necessary for it to take its decision. Frequently, the preliminary investigation period takes between six months and a year or even longer, because the information submitted by the Member State is insufficient and the Commission is obliged to ask for additional information. Where a speedy approval decision is sought, the Member State must submit complete and accurate information as quickly as possible.

The limitation of the Commission's initial investigation to two months applies only when the aid measure has been notified pursuant to Article 88(3) and the Procedural Regulation. In case of an investigation concerning an unlawful aid measure (*i.e.* that has not been notified by the Member State) *ex officio*, the Commission is not bound by this two-month period. However, the European Courts have limited the Commission's discretion to prolong the preliminary investigation period indefinitely in several cases concerning the broadcasting sector, where the Commission had to determine if financing schemes in Spain, France and Portugal involved state aid.[59] In each case, the Commission failed to take a decision several years after having received complaints from competing broadcasters and conducting an investigation. It was held to have infringed Article 88(3), in conjunction with Article 88(2), for not having taken a timely decision on whether to open a formal investigation. Where the Commission has doubts as to the compatibility of a measure with the common market, it must open a formal investigation within a reasonable time, which will depend on the circumstances of the particular case.

7–015   The two stages of the Commission's investigation — Pursuant to Article 4 of the Procedural Regulation, at the end of the preliminary investigation period of two months, the Commission will either: (i) find that the measure does not constitute state aid at all; (ii) find that the measure constitutes state aid, but is compatible with the common market; or (iii) find that it has serious doubts as to whether the measure is state aid or as to the compatibility of an aid measure with the common market.

In the first two situations, the Commission will close its investigation at the end of the preliminary procedure. However, if the Commission has serious doubts about whether the measure is an aid measure or about the compatibility of an aid measure with the common market, it will open a formal investigation procedure according to Article 88(2) EC and Articles 4(4) and 6 of the Procedural Regulation. If the Commission finds that it has serious doubts only about some aspects of a state measure, it can adopt a "hybrid" decision to investigate only those aspects and approve the remainder.[60] This formal investigation procedure can be terminated by the Commission adopting one of three possible decisions: (i) a decision that the measure does not constitute aid; (ii) a decision that the measure constitutes aid, but that it is compatible with the common market (positive decision) — in which case the provision of the aid may be made subject to certain conditions (conditional positive decision); or (iii) a decision that the aid is not compatible with the

---

[59] Case T–95/96, *Gestevision Telecinco* [1998] II E.C.R. 3407, at para.73 *et seq.* (the Commission had failed to adopt a decision four years after Gestevision's complaint that Spanish public broadcasters were receiving state aid); Case T–17/96, *Télévision Française 1* [1999] II E.C.R. 1757, at para.74 *et seq.* (the Commission had failed to adopt a decision two-and-a-half years after TF1's complaint that competing French broadcasters were receiving state aid); *SIC*, above, para.7–008, n.27, at para.70 *et seq.* (the Commission had failed to adopt a decision 39 months after SIC's complaint that public broadcasters in Portugal were receiving state aid).

[60] Case T–107/96, *Pantochim v Commission* [1998] II E.C.R. 311.

common market and is prohibited (negative decision).[61] Ordinarily, this final decision must be taken within 18 months of opening the formal investigation, although this can be extended.[62] In the case of a negative decision, the Commission will order the recovery of the aid if it had been (unlawfully) granted despite the lack of prior authorisation by the Commission.[63] If a recovery decision is adopted following a negative decision, the Member State must take all measures to recover the aid from the beneficiary, including interest at a commercial rate.[64] Recovery of aid is intended to re-establish the previously existing situation and is to be effected in accordance with the provisions of national law, provided that national law does not render recovery practically impossible.[65] If the recipient cannot repay the aid, the Member State must institute winding-up proceedings and pursue the recipient as an unsecured creditor.[66] The only defence open to the Member State is that recovery is absolutely impossible.[67] Therefore, recipients of unlawfully granted aid assume a risk if they accept unapproved aid.

During the investigation procedure the Commission may adopt decisions imposing so-called information,[68] suspension[69] or provisional recovery injunctions.[70] An information injunction obliges the Member State to supply information specified by the Commission, where it has failed to do so following a request by the Commission. Failure to comply with an information injunction will result in the Commission taking a final decision on the basis of the best information available to it.[71] Suspension and provisional recovery injunctions are very rarely adopted. A suspension injunction requires the Member State to require the suspension of unlawfully granted or misused aid pending the outcome of the investigation.[72] A provisional recovery injunction requires the provisional recovery of unlawfully granted aid pending the outcome of the investigation.[73] Usually, the Commission will order recovery only when it has taken a final negative decision.

7–016 New aid and existing aid — The Commission's power to investigate state aid measures under Article 88(2) and the Procedural Regulation is not as far reaching in so far as existing aid is concerned. According to Article 1(b) of the Procedural Regulation, an existing aid is (i) aid which was put into effect prior to, and is still applicable after, the entry into force of the EC Treaty in respect of the Member State concerned; (ii) aid which has been authorised (whether by decision or because it is deemed to be approved by operation of law) by the Commission or by the Council; and (iii) aid measures that initially were not considered to be aid and only subsequently became aid measures because of the evolution of the common market, including the liberalisation of an activity by

---

[61] Procedural Regulation, above, para.7–013, n.56, Art.7(2)–7(5).

[62] *ibid.*, Art.7(6).

[63] *ibid.*, Art.14(1).

[64] *ibid.*, Art.14. This is subject to a limitation period, such that aid may not be recovered more than 10 years after it was awarded: *ibid.*, Art.15.

[65] Case C–24/95, *Land Rheinland-Pfalz v Alcan Deutschland (No. 2)* [1997] I E.C.R. 1591.

[66] Case C–52/84, *Commission v Belgium (Boch (No. 1))* [1986] E.C.R. 89.

[67] *ibid.*

[68] Procedural Regulation, above, para.7–013, n.56, Art.10.

[69] *ibid.*, Art.11(1).

[70] *ibid.*, Art.11(2).

[71] *ibid.*, Art.13.

[72] *ibid.*, Art.11(1).

[73] *ibid.*, Art.11(2).

Community law. The latter definition of existing aid is of relevance to the telecommunications and broadcasting sectors where, pursuant to liberalisation under Community law and national law that has introduced competition, financing mechanisms and other aid measures will now fall under the Commission's scrutiny, for example the German and UK licence fees for public broadcasters that had been in existence for a long time before this market started being liberalised in the 1980s.[74]

When examining existing aid schemes, the Commission may request information from the Member States[75] and may, if it is of the opinion that the aid is not or is no longer compatible with the common market, adopt a recommendation proposing "appropriate measures" to Member States to amend or abolish the aid or to introduce procedural requirements.[76] If the Member State does not accept proposed appropriate measures, the Commission can open a formal investigation procedure under Article 88(2), leading to the adoption of a clearance (no aid), a positive decision, a conditional positive decision or a negative decision. The Commission may not order recovery of existing aids. Adjustments to an aid scheme that are suggested to make the aid scheme compatible with the common market may only apply to the future granting of the aid but not retroactively.[77]

Minor changes to existing aid are not required to be notified, but substantive changes to an existing state aid measure are considered to be new aid and must be notified to the Commission and be authorised before the aid can be granted.[78]

Owing to the relatively recent liberalisation of the broadcasting market, the Commission has had to assess existing national financing schemes for public service broadcasters, in order to establish whether these constitute new or existing aid.[79] Some of these financing schemes for public broadcasters were in place before the broadcasting markets were liberalised. These schemes could be subject to the state aid rules on existing aid, as competition and cross-border trade in broadcasting services and associated services (such as the sale of advertising and programme rights) could take place with the liberalisation of that market. Existing aid measures remain legitimate and may continue to be implemented provided that the financing schemes are not substantially amended after liberalisation unless and until the Commission has adopted a final decision that they are incompatible with the common market under Article 88(2). Changes to existing aid schemes may be considered as new aid if they extend the beneficiaries, the duration of the scheme and/or the amount of aid and therefore will need to be notified and approved prior to implementation.

---

[74] See also Commission's Communication on public service broadcasting, above, para.7–011, n.44, para.20.

[75] Procedural Regulation, above, para.7–013, n.56, Art.17.

[76] *ibid.*, Arts 17, 18.

[77] Hancher, Ottervanger, Slot, *E.C. State Aids* (Sweet & Maxwell, 2nd ed., 1999), para.19–061. See also for aid schemes: Case C–292/95, *Spain v Commission (No. 2)* [1997] I E.C.R. 1931 (it was held that the Commission was not entitled to adopt a decision to apply an appropriate measure in the motor vehicle sector retroactively without the Member State concerned having agreed to it).

[78] Procedural Regulation, para.7–013, n.56, Art.1(c); see also Case NN 133/A/01 and NN 94/A/99, *Compensation indemnities to public service broadcaster RTP*, O.J. 2002 C98/2.

[79] Communication on public service broadcasting, above, para.7–011, n.44, para.20.

C. Impact of the State Aid Rules on Public Companies and Companies Benefiting from Exclusive or Special Rights — Article 86(1) of the EC Treaty

7–017 — Article 86(1) of the EC Treaty requires Member States not to adopt or maintain, in relation to public undertakings or undertakings for which exclusive or special rights have been granted, any measure that is contrary to the rules of the EC Treaty: this includes the Treaty's competition and state aid rules.[80] Although exclusive and special rights have been abolished in the communications sector,[81] incumbent operators in several Member States are still wholly or partly publicly owned or controlled. Likewise, in the broadcasting sector, there remain a large number of publicly owned broadcasting companies, as well as a number of private broadcasters that continue to benefit from exclusive or special rights under national law. In this context, the question has arisen as to whether a transfer of resources between the different activities of publicly owned companies or companies enjoying exclusive or special rights could constitute an aid measure within the meaning of Article 87(1) of the EC Treaty.[82] For example, could the financing of new added-value activities by a public operator through the use of income from its public service or reserved activities operations be caught by Article 87 of the EC Treaty?

7–018 It is established law that the transfer of financial resources (*e.g.* in the form of capital injections or non-commercial loans) between publicly owned companies that operate under the structure of a public holding company, or between a parent public company and its subsidiary, involve the use of state resources and to the extent that they involve any cross-subsidy of the recipient, are subject to the state aid rules.[83] This principle also applies to internal financial transfers between different activities of the same undertaking, for example, where the profits generated by a specific activity that is legally reserved to the public undertaking or for which it is dominant on the relevant market, are used to fund its activities in a market where it faces competition. This principle is not limited to financial contributions but also applies to the provision of goods, services, personnel or other resources that are provided on preferential, non-market terms.[84] It has been argued that the state aid rules would also apply to cross-subsidies between different product markets by a firm which is not publicly owned or controlled, but which enjoys exclusive or special rights within the meaning of Article 86(1) of the EC Treaty.[85]

---

[80] See above, para.4–013 *et seq.*

[81] See above, para.1–003 *et seq.*

[82] Hancher & Buendia Sierra, "Cross-subsidisation and EC Law" [1998] C.M.L.R. 901–945, at pp.927–942; Hancher, Ottervanger & Slot, *E.C. State Aids*, para.7–016, n.77, above, para.7–045 *et seq.*

[83] Case C–303/88, *Italy v Commission (ENI-Lanerossi)* [1991] I E.C.R. 1433, and Case C–305/88, *Italy v Commission (Alfa Romeo)*, para.7–008, n.25, above.

[84] See *SFEI v La Poste*, above, para.7–006, n.22; Case T–613/97, *Ufex* [2000] II E.C.R. 4055.

[85] Hancher & Buendia Sierra, n.82, above, pp.931–933. The Court of First Instance has held that the use of profits from a reserved monopoly activity to finance an activity subject to competition can, in certain circumstances, amount to the abuse of a dominant position; Case T–613/97, *Ufex*, n.84, above. Accordingly, where such excess profits derive from the granting or maintaining of exclusive or special rights, Art.86(1) would also be infringed. In the state aid context, this principle could also be applied, although it may be difficult to show any use of state resources in such circumstances from the mere grant of an exclusive or special right: the undertaking would presumably need to have received state resources to fund the reserved activities.

In order to be able to identify the transfer of funds from the part of an undertaking that provides the services for which it has been granted exclusive or special rights to its other commercial activities in respect of which it faces competition, the Commission has amended the so-called Transparency Directive.[86] Article 3(a) of the Transparency Directive obliges undertakings that benefit from special or exclusive rights (or who perform a public service obligation in the sense of Article 86(2)[87]) to keep separate accounts for each of their activities. As amended, the Transparency Directive allows the Commission to examine and control the provision, and use by public undertakings, of public funds made available to them, as well as the allocation, using proper accounting principles, of costs and revenues between different activities, thereby ensuring respect for the state aid rules. However, the Transparency Directive does not presuppose that every transfer of resources necessarily amounts to state aid or that such state aid is incompatible with Article 87(1) of the EC Treaty. The Commission is still required to demonstrate that the conditions for the application of Article 87(1) are satisfied, in particular, that the market investor test is not met.[88] In determining whether there is any cross-subsidisation and thus state aid, the Commission must consider whether, without a monopoly activity to which common costs could be allocated, a private investor would be prepared to subsidise its other activities on a competitive market over the same period of time and what the cost would be to a private investor for providing the same services; in other words, has the subsidiary paid a price that it would not have obtained under normal market conditions?[89] In the Commission's decision concerning the French *La Poste*,[90] the Commission considered the application of the market investor test to the provision of logistical and commercial assistance by the French postal monopoly to a subsidiary, SFMI-Chronopost, which pursued private courier activities in competition with other undertakings, in order to determine if this involved cross-subsidisation (and thus state aid) in favour of the subsidiary. This decision was annulled by the Court of First Instance.[91] The Court accepted that the market economy investor test must be applied in order to determine if there is any cross-subsidisation and thus aid, but found that the Commission had wrongly applied it by not taking into account all factors that a private investor would have taken into consideration in fixing the price for the intra-group supply. The fact that the French post office had covered all of its costs (including a reasonable return on capital) in providing assistance to its subsidiary was not determinative. The correct test was whether a parent company acting in a competitive market and pursuing a profit-making strategy would have charged the same, or a higher price, given that La Poste's monopoly position may have enabled it to provide assistance at a lower cost than a parent company not benefiting from exclusive or special rights.

7–019 Companies that benefit from special and/or exclusive rights, and at the same time have other commercial activities, will be subject to an ever increasing scrutiny, not only by the

---

[86] Commission Directive 80/723 of June 25, 1980 on the transparency of financial relations between Member States and public undertakings, O.J. 1980 L195/35, as last amended by Commission Directive 2000/52 of July 26, 2000 amending Directive 80/723, O.J. 2000 L193/75. Directive 80/723 is now known as "Directive 80/723 of June 25, 1980 on the transparency of financial relations between Member States and public undertakings as well as financial transparency within certain undertakings".

[87] See para.4–015, above.

[88] See para.7–007, above.

[89] Hancher and Buendia Sierra, para.7–017, n.82, above, pp.936–938.

[90] Case *Chronopost*, O.J. 1998 L164/37.

[91] Case T–613/97, *Ufex*, para.7–018, n.84, above.

Commission, but also by competitors who monitor the pricing and commercial behaviour of these companies.

The rules which have to be applied for identifying the costs and revenues of the reserved activities of a public undertaking (which receive state funds to meet the cost of providing services of general economic interest within the scope of Article 86(2) of the EC Treaty) from its commercial activities, apply equally when identifying activities carried on under special and exclusive rights from commercial activities.[92]

D. State Aid Rules and the Financing of Public Broadcasting — Article 86(2) of the EC Treaty

7–020   The application of the state aid rules to the financing of publicly owned broadcasters through public funds is a subject of intense controversy.[93] Determining if such financing involves state aid is a two-step process. The first issue to examine in this respect is whether the state funding of a public broadcaster amounts to a state aid within the meaning of Article 87(1).[94] It is then necessary to consider whether, if the funding amounts to a state aid measure under Article 87(1) of the EC Treaty, a derogation from the state aid rules is available pursuant to Article 86(2).[95]

7–021   **Existence of a state aid measure** — In order for state financing to be an aid measure, it must favour certain undertakings or sectors.[96] The Court of Justice has held that the provision of financing to an undertaking does not "favour" that undertaking if it constitutes a consideration for the services performed by the recipient.[97] The same principle could apply to situations where the state provides an undertaking with compensation for providing services of general economic interest, under a public service obligation. The Court of Justice has held that where an undertaking provides a service of general economic interest within the scope of Article 86(2) and compensation is granted to cover the costs of the fulfilment of the undertaking's public service obligations, no advantage is granted and, therefore, there is no state aid.[98] The Court reached this decision in the *Ferring* case, which concerned public service obligations imposed on certain pharmaceutical wholesalers in France. Ferring, a pharmaceutical manufacturer, objected to the payment of a sales levy on drugs that it supplied directly to pharmacies, without using a wholesaler. Ferring considered that the sales tax amounted to state aid in favour of the wholesaler, as it was only levied on manufacturers that sold directly to pharmacies. The Court of Justice considered that direct sales were treated differently,

---

[92] See also Transparency Directive, para.7–018, n.86, Art.2(1)(d) and (e).

[93] For a comprehensive review of the issue, see Bartosch, para.7–007, n.23, pp.197–204.

[94] See generally, above, para.7–003 to 7–010.

[95] See generally, above, para.4–015 *et seq.*

[96] See above, para.7–007 *et seq.*

[97] The Court considered that indemnity paid to companies collecting waste oils did not constitute an aid measure, because the indemnity was a remuneration for the services performed by them for performing this task in the general interest; Case C–240/83, *Association de défense des brûleurs d'huiles usagées* [1985] E.C.R. 531: Bartosch, para.7–007, n.23, above, p.200, rightly points out that application of the market investor test is not appropriate to assess the lawfulness of public funding of specific public services remits.

[98] Case C–53/00, *Ferring v Agence Centrale des Organismes de Sécurité Sociale (ACOSS)* [2001] E.C.R. 9067, para.27.

thereby *prima facie* conferring an advantage on the wholesalers (who were exempt from the tax). However, the public service obligations imposed on wholesalers imposed higher costs on them. Accordingly, no state aid existed to the extent that the tax exemption compensated the wholesalers for their extra costs and put them on an equal footing with manufacturers that sold directly to pharmacies.[99] Only compensation in excess of the costs incurred from meeting the public service obligation would amount to state aid, which would not be within the scope of Article 86(2).[1] This finding of the Court of Justice has been criticised for undermining the Commission's exclusive authority to examine the state aid content of state measures and the obligation of prior notification of state aid under Article 88(3) of the EC Treaty, in particular given that any financial measures in excess of the costs of meeting public service obligations will amount to an aid measure.[2] Accordingly, the Advocates General in two subsequent cases have asked the Court of Justice to overrule its judgment in *Ferring* and to find that compensation for the costs of public service obligations constitutes state aid, but can be justified under Article 86(2).[3]

On July 24, 2003 the Court of Justice gave judgment in the *Altmark Trans* case[3a] in which it generally confirmed its approach in *Ferring*, but gave guidance on how to calculate the appropriate compensation for providing a public service. According to the Court, if the compensation paid to an undertaking for fulfilling a public service obligation imposed on it simply meets the costs of providing the public service (plus a reasonable profit margin). These payments constitute a *quid pro quo* and do not constitute a state[3b] measure in the sense of Article 87(1)[3b]; therefore, there is no requirement to apply an exemption from competition under Article 86(2). It can be expected that the Court of Justice will follow the approach it took in *Altmark Trans* on the other relevant cases that are still pending, in order to achieve legal certainty with regard to applying the state aid rules to compensation payments for providing public services.

---

[99] *Ferring*, above, n.98, para.27.

[1] *ibid.*, para.33.

[2] Nicolaides, "Distortive effects of compensatory aid measures: a note on the economics of the Ferring judgment" (2002) E.C.L.R 313; Alexis, "Services publics et aides d'État" (2002) *Revue du droit de L'Union européenne* 63; Gundel, "Staatliche Ausgleichszahlungen für Dienstleistungen von allgemeinem wirtschaftlichem Interesse: Zum Verhältnis zwischen Artikel 86 Absatz 2 EGV und dem EG-Beihilfenrecht" (2002) R.I.W. 222.

[3] Case C–280/00, *Altmark Trans and Regierungspräsidium Magdeburg*, Second Opinion of Advocate General Léger of January 14, 2003. Advocate General Léger has advised the Court the *Ferring* judgment should be overruled in its entirety. See also Opinion of Advocate General Jacobs in Case C–126/01, *GEMO*, of April 30, 2002, para.110 *et seq.*, where he suggests that the *Ferring* precedent should only be applied when the public service obligation and the financing mechanism are clearly defined and explicitly conferred on a designated undertaking (the "*quid pro quo*" argument). In cases where the public service obligation and financing mechanism are not clear, Advocate General Jacobs suggests that the measure would need to be considered under Art.87(1), which implies in practice the obligation to notify this measure to the Commission. See also the Opinion of Advocate General Stix-Hackl of November 7, 2002 in Joined Cases C–34 to C–38/01, *Enirisorse v Ministero delle Finanze*, who considers that the *Ferring* principle can only be applied where the general interest duties have been clearly defined and the compensation is clearly identifiable, as only then can analysis of the costs incurred and the compensation paid be undertaken to ensure that there is a "direct and manifest" link between the two.

[3a] Case C–280/00, *Altmark Trans and Regierungspräsidium Magdeburg v Nahverkehrsgesellschaft Altmark GmbH* [2003] E.C.R. I-0000 (not yet published), judgment of July 24, 2003 para.88 *et seq.*

[3b] See para.7–023 below.

7–022   This issue has direct relevance to the broadcasting sector, where a strong regime of public service obligations is in place in all Member States. The future application of the state aid rules to the financing of public broadcasters will be determined by the outcome of the *Altmark Trans*, and also of the cases *GEMO* and *Enirisorse* still pending before the Court of Justice. This is clear from the statement of the Commission in its Report to the Seville European Council, where it stated that it will refrain from finalising the Community position on how to determine the compensation for the costs incurred for meeting public service obligations until the Court of Justice has handed down its judgments in these cases.[4] It could well be that the Commission will set out its framework on the basis of the *Altmark Trans* case, without awaiting the judgments in the other pending cases.

The main consequence of the *Altmark Trans* judgment is that compensation paid to cover costs incurred in meeting public service obligations is not *prima facie* state aid within the scope of Article 87(1) if certain conditions are met. Accordingly, the making of compensation payments does not have to be notified to the Commission under the state aid rules, provided they do not exceed the amount necessary to meet the costs of providing the public service (plus a reasonable profit margin),[4a] if the compensation exceeds this level, the payment *prima facie* constitutes state aid and must be notified to the Commission under Article 88(3) prior to being paid. The Commission has announced that it will issue a text (*e.g.* guidelines or a framework) setting out the principles for calculating the appropriate level of compensation.[4b] This text will have to take account of the principles laid down by the Court of Justice for determining whether compensation payments may constitute state aid.

7–023   The *Altmark Trans* judgment has considerable practical relevance, including in the broadcasting sector. Member States may, according to the Court, grant funding to public service broadcasters without needing to await the Commission's authorisation, provided certain criteria are met. This will result in the granting of such payments being accomplished more quickly and with fewer administrative steps. Nevertheless, Member States and recipients of compensation payments will only achieve legal certainty with regard to compensation payments if they strictly abide by the conditions that the Court has formulated for determining the appropriateness of such compensation payments.

---

[4] Report to the Seville European Council on the Status of Work on the Guidelines for State Aid and Services of General Economic Interest of May 30, 2002, published on: *http://europa.eu.int/comm/competition/state_aid/others/seville_en.doc*. See also Report of the Commission of June 16, 2002 on the status of work on the guidelines for state aid and services of general economic interest, COM(02) 280 final; and Report of the Commission of November 27, 2002 on the state of play in the work on the guidelines for state aid and services of general economic interest, COM(02) 336 final.

[4a] If the Court of Justice had reached the opposite conclusion, and thereby overruled its judgment in *Ferring*, any compensation payment would have been *prima facie* state aid, and consequently, would have had to have been notified to the Commission, and could only have been granted after the Commission's authorisation.

[4b] Presidency conclusions of the Barcelona European Council (March 15–16, 2002), at 19, point 42, available at: *http://ue.eu.int/en/Info/eurocouncil/index.htm*; and Presidency conclusions of the Seville European Council (June 21–22, 2002), at p.18, point 54, available at: *http://ue.eu.int/en/Info/eurocouncil/index.htm*. See also the Green Paper on Services of general economic interest, COM(2003)0270, of May, 21, 2003, available at: *http://europa.eu.int/prelex/rech_simple.cfm?CL=en*.

Altmark Trans concerned a challenge (submitted to the Court for preliminary ruling) by a competitor to the award of a licence for providing local and regional bus services in Germany, for which the licensee (Altmark Trans) had in the past received state funds. Altmark Trans required public subsidies in order to provide the transport services that it was entrusted with providing, as its operations were not profitable.

The Court examined first whether the measure in favour of Altmark Trans met the conditions for a state measure to constitute aid, in particular, the question of whether an *"economic advantage"* was conferred on the undertaking.[5] It concluded that state funding that is compensation for the services provided by the recipient undertaking in order to discharge a public service obligation, such that it does not enjoy any real financial advantage and is not put in a more favourable position than the undertakings competing with it, does not confer a "financial advantage" in the sense of Article 87(1).[5a] The Court thereby confirmed its earlier judgments in *ABDHU* and *Ferring*.[5b]

7–023/1 The Court specified that such compensation payments may only be considered not to be state aid if four conditions are each met[5c]:

(i) The undertaking must be *entrusted* with the public service obligation,[5d] which must be *clearly defined*.

(ii) The parameters for calculating the compensation payment must be established in advance *in an objective and transparent manner*, to prevent an economic advantage being granted to the undertaking concerned. A Member State cannot, therefore, justify a payment to cover losses after they were incurred on the basis that it is a "compensation payment" if these parameters had not been established beforehand: such funding will *prima facie* be a state aid measure.

(iii) The compensation paid from public funds *may not exceed* the sum *necessary* to totally or partly cover the costs incurred in fulfilling the public service obligations *and a reasonable profit margin*, taking into account the *revenues* received by the undertaking concerned in providing the services of public economic interest.

(iv) The costs that may be reimbursed from public funds may be established either: (a) by awarding the service by way of an *open and transparent tender* to the tenderer that requires the lowest public subsidy; or, alternatively, (b) on the basis of an analysis of the

---

[5] *Altmark Trans*, para.7–021, n.3a above, para.82 *et seq.* In view of the merely local or regional scope of the bus transport services, the Court also analysed whether *"trade between Member States"* could be affected by the subsidies in question, which it confirmed was possible, given the possibility for companies from other Member States to offer transport services in the region, which could have been adversely affected by the measure (if it were an aid measure): see paras 77 to 79.

[5a] *Altmark Trans*, para.7–021, n.3a above, para.87.

[5b] Case C-240/83, *Procureur de la République v Association de défense des brûleurs d'huiles usagées (ADBHU)*, [1985] E.C.R. 531; and Case C-53/00, *Ferring SA v Agence centrale des organismes de sécurité sociale (ACOSS)*, [2001] I E.C.R. 9067.

[5c] *Altmark Trans*, para.7–021, n.3a above, paras 89 to 98.

[5d] On the concept of "entrusting" of public services, see para.7–030, below.

costs that a *typical undertaking*[5e] *that is well run and adequately provided* with the resources required to provide the service in question in order to meet the public service obligations, would have incurred when providing those services (again taking into account the revenues and a reasonable profit margin).

The Court of Justice very clearly states that non-fulfilment of any one of these four conditions will lead to compensation payments being considered *prima facie* to be state aid.[5f] In view of the fact that in some cases there may be doubts over the appropriateness of the amount of, and methods of calculating, the costs for which compensation may be paid, precautionary notifications to the Commission may be advisable in such cases, not least because the *Altmark Trans* judgment bears some ambiguities in its application. For example, private competitors and others will argue, with regard to these conditions, that the Court chose as a point of reference for determining whether payments are appropriate, a *"typical undertaking, well run"* and not necessarily an undertaking that is economically efficient. This could enable undertakings entrusted with public service obligations to continue operating at losses (as long as they fulfil the non-economic aspects of their public service obligations well), which will then be covered by state resources. Therefore, the Member States and the recipient undertaking will need to be satisfied that the recipient operates efficiently and indeed has incurred the costs for which it claims compensation. Detailed cost accounting records will therefore be required to demonstrate compliance with the *Altmark Trans* criteria. The concept of a "reasonable profit margin" will also potentially raise questions: many public sector broadcasters are not profit-making concerns. Furthermore, the calculation of a reasonable profit margin raises difficult questions, both in determining what is "reasonable" and in the method to be used, for example if the margin should be a simple percentage of revenues or a sum that allows a reasonable return on capital employed to be made. Because of these uncertainties, and the likely actions of the Commission (and third parties) in reviewing compensation payments, precautionary notifications may well become the norm.

In this sense, recital 24 of the Universal Service Directive suggests that Member States that wish to set up a financing mechanism for covering the net costs of providing universal electronic communications services provided by communications operators with universal service obligations, should permit the Commission to verify that the proposed mechanism is compatible with the Treaty (*i.e.* that the financing is limited to the net extra costs, as permitted by the Directive). The Universal Service Directive could be interpreted as a statutory example of the principles laid down by the Court of Justice in *Ferring* and *Altmark Trans*, as it only allows for compensation of the net

---

[5e] The German version refers to an "average" undertaking.

[5f] *Altmark Trans*, para.7–021, n.3a above, para.94. It is worthwhile noting, that the Court of Justice at no point refers to the criteria that must be met for Art.86(2) to be applicable, although the conditions it laid down are materially the same as those of Art.86(2) (entrustment, definition and proportionality). According to AG Léger it could be concluded that Art.86(2) has become irrelevant with regard to compensating the costs incurred in meeting public service obligations where the requirements of *Altmark Trans* are met. However, Art.86(2) will remain applicable where the criteria laid down by the Court, in particular that of *"setting out the parameters **prior** to granting the funding"* is not fulfilled. Since all other criteria are materially the same as the ones of Article 86(2) an exemption from the competition rules under Art.86(2) should in principle not be available to and exempt state funding of broadcasters where the conditions set out by the Court are not complied with.

costs incurred in meeting universal service obligations, and hence no over-compensation, and requires that compensation is compatible with the Treaty's state aid rules.[6]

It can be expected, that following the *Altmark Trans* judgment, some Member States will need to clarify the definition of the public service obligations of public broadcasters, since often the public service obligations of public service broadcasters are set out quite vaguely, if at all. Also the parameters for calculating the compensation that is payable before the payments are made might lead to some adjustments of the rules governing compensation payments to public service broadcasters.

7–024 The nature of public broadcasting as a public service within the scope of Article 86(2) and its financing by state resources was confirmed by the Member States in a protocol on public broadcasting as part of the Amsterdam Treaty.[7] This protocol states that the provisions of the EC Treaty

> "are without prejudice to the competence of Member States to provide for the funding of public service broadcasting insofar as such funding is granted to broadcasting organisations for the fulfilment of the public service remit as conferred, defined and organised by each Member State and insofar as such funding does not affect trading conditions and competition in the Community to an extent which would be contrary to the common interest, while the realisation of the remit of that public service shall be taken into account."

At the end of 2001, the Commission issued its Communication on public service broadcasting in order to give guidance for the preconditions and assessment of the appropriate level of compensation for the net costs incurred by public service broadcasters in fulfilling their public broadcasting obligations.[8] The conditions set out in the Communication and the relevant case law are discussed in detail below.

7–025 **The role and legal context of public service broadcasting** — Before assessing to what extent the financing of public broadcasters falls outside of the scope of the prohibition of state aid contained in Article 87(1), it is necessary to consider the acknowledged role and legal context of public service broadcasting.

Public service broadcasting is, under certain conditions, to be regarded as a service of general interest subject to specific regulation by the Member States.[9] National legislation governing broadcasting will typically aim to protect common values such as freedom of expression, the right of reply, pluralism, cultural and linguistic diversity, and the protection of minors and of human dignity, and consumer protection.[10] In its Communication on public service broadcasting,

---

[6] Universal Service Directive, para.1–011, n.30 above, Recitals 18–24.
[7] Protocol annexed to the Treaty of the European Community — Protocol on the system of public broadcasting in the Member States, O.J. 1997 C340/109.
[8] Communication on public service broadcasting, para.7–011, n.44.
[9] See para.6–085 *et seq.*
[10] Communication on public service broadcasting, above, para.7–011, n.44, paras 5 and 14; and Commission Communication on services of general interest in Europe, COM(2000) 580 final, p.35.

the Commission acknowledges the central role of broadcasting in the functioning of democratic societies and of public service broadcasting in pursuing cultural diversity and providing, free of charge, information to allow all citizens to participate in public life, providing educational programming, and high quality entertainment and to guarantee pluralism.[11] The Commission also pointed out that not only public service broadcasters but also commercial broadcasters, some of whom also have public service obligations, play a role in contributing to pluralism, enriching the cultural and political debate and widening the choice of programmes.[12] The Communication also observes that public service broadcasting is, for a not inconsiderable proportion of the population, the main source of information.[13] For all these reasons, the Commission states that "broadcasting, although having a clear economic relevance, is not comparable to a public service in any other economic sector", due to its broad access to the population and its impact upon individual and public opinion.[14]

7–026 The Council has also stated its views on public service broadcasting and has reaffirmed the importance of public service broadcasting in the social, democratic and cultural life of the European Union and that public service broadcasting needs to benefit from technological progress, including the provision of new audio-visual and information services to diversify its activities in the light of the digital age. The Council also stated that public service broadcasting must be able to continue to offer a wide range of programming, in accordance with its remit as defined by the Member States, and that it is legitimate in this context that public service broadcasting seeks to reach wide audiences.[15] The Council's Resolution also sets out that public service broadcasters must provide broad public access to their various channels and services, without discrimination and on the basis of equal opportunities.

The provision of public service broadcasting and the fulfilment of its special obligations must remain within the limits of Articles 87(1) and 86(2), as well as all other relevant provisions of the Treaty. Article 87(3)(d) provides for a specific justification for state aid where the exclusive aim of an aid measure is to promote culture, although the broad range of objectives of public service broadcasting may make it difficult for Article 87(3)(d) to be successfully invoked by a Member State.[16] In addition, Article 16 of the EC Treaty obliges the Community and the Member States to ensure that public services operate on the basis of principles and conditions which enable them to fulfil their mission. Article 16 is explicitly without prejudice to the application of Articles 86 and 87. Therefore, the provision of public services must respect the prohibition of state aid imposed by Article 87(1). The provisions of the Transparency Directive, which governs the financing and accounting practices of public undertakings and undertakings with exclusive or special rights, is applicable to publicly owned broadcasters and telecommunications companies (and certain private

[11] Communication on public service broadcasting, para.7–011, n.44, paras 5–14. See also *BBC News 24*, above, para.7–003, n.4, paras 49–61.
[12] Communication on public service broadcasting, above para.7–011, n.44, para.14.
[13] *ibid.*, para.5.
[14] *ibid.*, para.6.
[15] Resolution of the Council and of the Representatives of the Governments of the Member States, meeting within the Council of January 25, 1999 concerning public service broadcasting, O.J. 1999 C30/1.
[16] See, *e.g. Kinderkanal and Phoenix*, para.7–003, n.3, and also above, para. 7–012.

broadcasters) and obliges them to keep separate accounts for their commercial and public service activities.[17-18]

7–027 Conditions for the application of Article 86(2) of the EC Treaty — The provision of services of general economic interest must comply with the rules of the Treaty, including the competition and state aid rules. However, under Article 86(2), a derogation from the application of the Treaty (including the competition and state aid rules) may be applicable if the application of those rules would prevent the performance of the relevant public interest tasks assigned to the undertaking providing those services.[19] The provision of public service broadcasting services may fall within the scope of Article 86(2), if the relevant requirements of Article 86(2) are met. As Article 86(2) is a derogation from the Treaty, it must be interpreted restrictively.[20] The Commission has stated that its assessment of whether a state aid measure granted to a broadcaster falls within the scope of Article 86(2) will be based on three conditions[21]:

   (i) the service must be a service of general economic interest and be clearly defined as such by the Member State ("definition condition");

   (ii) the undertaking in question must be explicitly entrusted by an act of the Member State with the provision of that service ("entrustment condition"); and

   (iii) the application of the competition rules (*i.e.* the prohibition of state aid) must obstruct the performance of the tasks assigned to the undertaking and the derogation must not affect the development of trade to the extent that it would be contrary to the interests of the Community ("proportionality condition").

The Protocol on the system of public broadcasting in the Member States annexed to the EC Treaty under the Amsterdam Treaty provides interpretative guidance on the application of Article 86(2) to the funding of public service broadcasting.[22] The Protocol requires the Commission to take into account the need for Member States to fund public service broadcasters in order for them to fulfil their public service remit when considering whether the "proportionality" condition is met.

7–028 Definition of the service as one of general economic interest — The Commission's first task is to consider if the undertaking concerned is providing a service of general economic interest. The Court of Justice has previously held that public broadcasting services can be services of general economic interest and thereby fall within Article 86(2),[23] although this will not always necessarily be

---

[17-18] See para.7–018, above.

[19] *ibid.*

[20] See para.7–012, above.

[21] Communication on public service broadcasting, para.7–011, n.44, paras 28–31. See also para.7–023 for the conditions the Court of Justice set out in its *Altmark Trans* judgment for compensation payments to be considered appropriate, and hence no state aid in the sense of Art.87(1).

[22] Above, para.7–024 and, in particular, para.7–030 *et seq.*, below.

[23] Case C–260/89, *ERT v Dimotiki* [1991] I E.C.R. 2925; see also Case T–69/89, *RTE v Commission* [1991] II E.C.R. 485.

the case.[24] In establishing if a broadcasting service falls within Article 86(2), the Commission must first identify its public service remit. In its Communication on public service broadcasting, the Commission stressed the important role of public service broadcasters and that public service broadcasters may take advantage of new technologies to extend their public service activities in the digital age (*e.g.* to provide online news services) and provide a broader range of programming using digital transmission technology (*e.g.* special interest programmes), provided that they also address the democratic, social and cultural needs of society. It is for the Member States to define the public service remit, provided that they take account of the Community law concept of "services of general economic interest", which will have a wide definition in this case, given the specific and unique characteristics of the broadcasting sector. The Commission will verify that the public service remit has been clearly and precisely defined and that no manifest errors have been made in defining the public service obligation, such as including e-commerce services and other services that cannot be reasonably regarded as meeting society's democratic, social and cultural needs. In the Commission's view, commercial activities carried on by public service broadcasters will not normally be part of a public service remit.[25] In this context the Commission, in its recent decision in respect of the use of the BBC licence fee to fund nine new digital television and radio services to be provided by the BBC, decided that a public service broadcaster is entitled to extend and diversify its activities so that it can provide programmes via digital networks, provided that it is addressing the same democratic, social and cultural needs of society.[26] This is the case where the same range of programmes, such as information, education and entertainment programmes provided for in the original public service remit, are broadcast by means of digital, terrestrial, cable and satellite networks, or using the internet. The fact that digital services may or may not be capable of reception by the entire population does not affect this conclusion, provided that this is only due to temporary technical constraints and that this is justified by the wider goal of promoting digital services so that the entire population will in due course switch over to digital channels.[27]

7–029 Doubts have been expressed as to whether it will be possible to distinguish between services that will not fall within a public service remit (such as e-commerce services) and services that are part of the public service obligations of public service broadcasters (such as online news services).[28] The recent case concerning the use of the BBC licence fee shows and confirms that the distinction will largely depend on the *content* of the services provided and whether they meet the democratic, social and cultural interests of society. Whereas e-commerce in the sense of trading via the internet (*e.g.* the sale and purchase of film rights or advertising space) clearly constitutes a commercial activity,[29] the provision of news and information via the internet may very well

---

[24] Case T–266/97, *Vlaamse Televisie Maatschappij v Commission* [1999] II E.C.R. 2329: exclusive rights to broadcast television advertisements in the Flanders region of Belgium not within Art.86(2), so could not justify restrictions on the freedom of establishment contrary to Art.52 of the EC Treaty.

[25] Communication on public service broadcasting, para.7–011, n.44, paras 33–39; see also *BBC News 24*, para.7–003, n.4, at paras 49–61.

[26] *BBC licence fee*, above, para.7–003, n.4, at paras 27–30. See also *BBC News 24*, above, para.7–003, n.4, at paras 59–60.

[27] *BBC licence fee*, above, para.7–003, n.4, para.30.

[28] Bavasso, para.7–012, n.49, p.340 *et seq.*, at p.345.

[29] See, in this regard, the judgment of the Court of First Instance in *Vlaamse Televisie Maatschappij (VTM)*, above, para.7–028, n.24.

constitute a public service, being simply an extension of services provided using "traditional" transmission networks. It is for the Member States to define the remit of public broadcasters given that the Protocol on public broadcasters to the EC Treaty explicitly allows for the Member States to define and arrange the obligations of public broadcasters, but also because of the principle of subsidiarity. The Commission's power is limited to examining whether Member States have made manifest errors by including services that do not meet the democratic, social and cultural needs and are purely of a commercial nature (*e.g.* sales of advertising, e-commerce, sales of programme rights to other broadcasters).

Furthermore, the Commission's practice shows that special interest channels devoted to a particular audience — such as children's channels (see *Kinderkanal*), news channels, documentary channels (see *Phoenix*), sports channels, and channels for minority audiences — may fall within a public service remit even though they are targeted at only a limited group of persons: there is no requirement for a specific channel to be targeted at and be of interest to the entire community or even all of a Member State's territory (for example, channels broadcast in regional languages in Wales or in the regions of Belgium).[30] The Commission decided in *Kinderkanal and Phoenix* that it was also in view of the fact that private broadcasters do not provide the same combination of a violence-free and advertisement-free special interest channel for children and a special interest channel giving background information for topics related to the society and culture, that Germany had manifestly not abused its power to define the public service remit of public service broadcasting.

The Member States must be precise when defining a broadcaster's public service remit and use precise terms, in order that the Commission can efficiently examine that the remit and financing falls within Article 86(2) and in order to allow the Member States to monitor compliance with the public service obligations.[31] Thus, in *BBC News 24*, the Commission considered that it is for the Member State concerned (the United Kingdom) to determine whether a particular programme or service should be provided under a public service remit or be left to the market to provide on a commercial basis: thus, the United Kingdom was free to decide that a channel devoted entirely to news and carrying no advertising could be provided as a service of general economic interest, even though other broadcasters (such as BSkyB) provided news channels funded by advertising.[32] Member States often define the public service remit very widely and in a general manner, for example by obliging public service broadcasters to provide a wide range of programmes for information, entertainment, cultural and educational development.[33] However, this degree of latitude does not necessarily mean that the definition condition is not met; it is sufficient that the definition used by the Member State does not include commercial activities[34] and enables the Commission to monitor compliance with the conditions of Article 86(2).[35] A clear definition of the

---

[30] *BBC licence fee*, above, para.7–003, n.4, para.33; *Kinderkanal & Phoenix*, above, para.7–003, n.3. See also Simboeck, *Public Service Broadcasting and state aids: an EC Commission decision*, (Communications Law, 1999) pp.187–188.

[31] Communication on public service broadcasting, para.7–011, n.44, paras 37–39. See also *BBC News 24*, above, para.7–003, n.4, para.47 *et seq.*, and Case C–280/00, *Altmark Trans*, above para.7–021, n.3a.

[32] *BBC News 24*, above, para.7–003, n.4, para.52.

[33] *Belgian aid in favour of local television in the French Community*, above, para.7–010, n.41, p.7.

[34] *ibid.*

[35] *BBC News 24*, above, para.7–003, n.4, para.71.

public service remit is also required for competitors to be able to monitor the conduct of public service broadcasters on the commercial market (sale of advertising space, trading film rights) and clear and more detailed provisions would be desirable, also with regard to the recent case law in the *Altmark Trans* case, which requires a clear definition of public service obligations and adequate compensation payments in the context of Article 87(1).[35a]

7–030 Entrusting a broadcaster with its public service remit and supervision by the Member State — In order for Article 86(2) of the EC Treaty to apply, the public broadcaster must have been formally entrusted with public service obligations by means of an official act, *e.g.* a legislative or administrative act, or a contract. In *BBC News 24*, the Commission accepted that the description of the tasks assigned to the BBC and the setting-up of a certain mechanism, under which the BBC would initially propose which activities it would undertake and then seek the UK government's consent to provide them, constituted an "entrustment" with public services, as only with that consent could the BBC provide the service in question under its public service remit.[36] This requirement generally poses no problem, because in most cases specific laws, administrative acts and/or contracts exist that set out the obligations of public broadcasters. However, in *BBC licence fee*, the Commission found that there was no clear legal documentation showing that the BBC had been entrusted with the provision of nine new digital channels. Nevertheless, this was not an impediment to the Commission being satisfied that the BBC would supply the new digital services in accordance with the UK government's wishes, as it was effectively supervised by an independent authority whose members were appointed by the government.

Supervision of public service broadcasters has to take place on two levels. First, it must be monitored whether the public broadcasters fulfil their public service remit correctly. Second, it must be established that no public funds are being misused for financing the commercial activities of public service broadcasters and that they are not being over-compensated for fulfilling their public service remit.[37] The Commission is only responsible and competent for the second type of monitoring, as the qualitative and quantitative control of the performance by public service broadcasters of their public service remit is a matter for the relevant Member State. The Commission will, however, verify whether adequate control mechanisms have been put in place by the relevant Member State to monitor if public sector broadcasters are performing their tasks in accordance with the criteria laid down by the state when entrusting them with their public service obligations.[38]

7–031 Proportionality of compensation and monitoring — The "proportionality" test has two elements. First, the funding provided from state resources must not exceed the costs of meeting public service remits, so that there is no risk of cross-subsidisation. Second, the funding must not affect competition in a disproportionate manner. The proportionality of the compensation

---

[35a] See above, para.7–023.

[36] *BBC News 24*, above, para.7–003, n.4, para.62 *et seq*. See also *Kinderkanal and Phoenix* where the situation was very similar, since the funding for the two special interest channels could only be granted after the Prime Minister of each of the German Länder had approved its programme, above, para.7–003, n.3, s.6.3. See also *Belgian aid in favour of local television in the French Community*, para.7–010, n.41, para.40 *et seq*.

[37] With regard to the risk of over-compensation, see below, para.7–031.

[38] *Belgian aid in favour of local television in the French Community*, para.7–010, n.41, p.8. *BBC licence fee*, above, para.7–003, n.4, paras 37–38.

provided to public service broadcasters for the net costs of meeting their public service obligations is at the core of the problem of cross-subsidies and the application of the state aid rules. In its Communication on public service broadcasting, the Commission does not give any specific indication as to precisely which costs may be justified, but states that the state aid must not exceed the net costs incurred by the broadcasters, taking into account any direct or indirect revenues derived from providing services with its public service remit. This will include taking into account the net benefit that its commercial activities obtain due to its public service activities.[39] In its recent judgment in *Altmark Trans* the Court of Justice made express reference to the "revenues and a reasonable profit margin" that must be taken into account when calculating the net costs to be compensated. It also specified that the point of reference for assessing the costs is a "typical undertaking, well run".[39a] The Court of Justice's judgment in *Ferring* is also instructive in this regard: only the net costs of fulfilling a public service mandate will be justified, and any compensation in excess of this amount will not be justified and will result in the derogation in Article 86(2) being inapplicable[40] and the compensation payment constituting a state aid in the sense of Article 87(1).[40a] Accordingly, compensation will only be proportionate if it does not exceed the net costs that the broadcaster incurs due to its public service obligation.[41]

For the derogation provided by Article 86(2) of the EC Treaty to be applicable, it is not necessary that it must be impossible to fulfil the service of general economic interest mission if the Treaty's competition rules are applied. Article 86(2) may also be applied to grant an exemption from the competition rules if their application would obstruct in law or in fact the performance of the services of general economic interest.[42] The Commission points out that financial transparency (in the form of separate accounts for the public service and commercial activities of the broadcasters) is essential if it is to be able to apply the proportionality test, as it can only be applied if there is a proper allocation of costs and revenues. However, a proper allocation of costs between different activities may be difficult, as public service and commercial activities may share the same inputs.[43]

The Commission will consider that there is over-compensation if a public service broadcaster is able to reduce the price of its commercial activities (such as sales of advertising and commercially-operated channels) below a price that is necessary to allow it to recover the stand-alone costs of such services that an efficient commercial operator in a similar situation would have to recover. In such case, the Commission will normally consider both that the funding is disproportionate and that it affects trading conditions and competition to an extent that is contrary to the public interest, such that it falls outside the scope of the Protocol on public service broadcasting and Article 86(2) is not applicable.[44]

---

[39] Communication on public service broadcasting, para.7–011, n.44, para.57.
[39a] See above, para.7–023.
[40] *Altmark Trans* above, para.7–021, n.3a.
[40a] *Ferring*, para.7–021, n.98, para.27.
[41] *BBC licence fee*, above, para.7–003, n.4, para.44; *BBC News 24*, above, para.7–003, n.4, para. 72 *et seq.*
[42] Case C–159/94, *France v Commission (Import and Export Monopoly for gas and electricity)* [1997] I E.C.R. 5815; see also Bartosch, para.7–007, n.23, para.202; and *BBC News 24*, above, para.7–003, n.4, para.72.
[43] Communication on public service broadcasting, above, para.7–011, n.44, paras 49–55.
[44] *ibid.*, para.58.

7–032 It is for the Member States to choose how to fund public service broadcasters. Funding schemes can fall into two categories: "single funding" schemes (where all funds come from public sources) and "dual funding" schemes (where public service broadcasting is funded from both state sources and from commercial revenues, such as advertising sales). However, the Commission will assess all funding schemes for compatibility with the Treaty's rules.[45] As funding schemes in Member States are different from each other, the Commission will continue to assess the proportionality of compensation on a case-by-case basis, as it is obliged to do in all cases of state aid.

To be able to assess the proportionality of compensation, broadcasters that provide public services and commercial services need to have separate accounts for these two activities, in accordance with the Transparency Directive.[46] The costs and revenues for both types of activity must be separated and allocated to the appropriate service.[47]

With regard to revenues, the revenues that are derived from services provided under the broadcaster's public service obligation must take into account and should be used for covering the costs of providing public service broadcasting. Furthermore, where public service resources (*e.g.* programmes, personnel) are used to provide both public service and commercial broadcasts, or are commercially exploited (*e.g.* by selling programmes abroad), these revenues also have to be treated as revenues from providing the public services.[48]

7–033 With regard to costs, the Commission accepts that costs incurred to provide both public service and commercial broadcasts (*e.g.* personnel, equipment and fixed installations) may be allocated on the basis of the difference in the broadcaster's total costs with and without its commercial activities, *i.e.* by hypothetically assuming that all commercial activities are discontinued and calculating the avoidable costs of doing so.[49] Consequently, where the costs of the broadcaster's public activities exceed the costs of its commercial activities (as is often the case for public broadcasters producing programmes primarily for broadcasting under their public service obligations), such common costs can be considered entirely as costs incurred in providing public services.[50] The Commission acknowledges that this approach is more generous than that usually imposed on utility providers, which are obliged to allocate the costs proportionately to the accounts of all activities. The Commission explains that this is justified by the fact that a separation of these costs in the broadcasting sector is generally not feasible and would be arbitrary, since the same resources and inputs are used for both the public service and commercial activities, for example when a programme that has been broadcast as part of the public service is then sold to another broadcaster.[51]

In *BBC News 24*, the Commission considered — on the basis of the BBC's own internal accounting (as certified by its auditors) — whether the state aid provided by the UK for running a 24-hour news service without advertising or subscription revenues exceeded the actual costs of

[45] *ibid.*, paras 44–48.
[46] *ibid.*, at para.49, and Transparency Directive, above, para.7–018, n.86.
[47] Transparency Directive, above, para.7–018, n.86, Art.3(a).
[48] *Belgian aid in favour of local television in the French Community*, above, para.7–010, n.41, p.8.
[49] Communication on public service broadcasting, above, para.7–011, n.44, para.55.
[50] *ibid.*, paras 55–56.
[51] *ibid.*, para.56.

providing the service. Most costs were payable to other BBC departments (such as news bureaux) and were charged at full cost. Furthermore, as the news channel had to be provided from within the BBC's existing licence fee reserves, the BBC could only fund the news channel by cost savings and efficiency gains elsewhere in its organisation. Accordingly, the Commission was satisfied both that only the net costs of providing the news channel were funded by the state aid and that this was proportionate to its costs. The fact that the costs of BBC News 24 were higher than commercial alternatives was irrelevant, given that it paid the full costs incurred in using the BBC's news-gathering network, which was much more extensive than those of CNN and BSkyB.[52]

In *BBC licence fee*, the Commission was obliged to conduct an *ex ante* analysis of the funding of new channels not yet in operation. The Commission considered that it was satisfied that cross-subsidisation and abuses of the additional licence fee funding that was to be made available, could not take place due to various mechanisms imposed upon BBC by its regulatory regime under UK law. These mechanisms included requirements for its commercial activities to be undertaken by separate legal entities within the BBC Group, for the BBC's accounts to be independently audited and published, for the BBC to take into account commercial revenues from exploiting its public service activities, and for the BBC's commercial subsidiaries to pay a fair charge for inputs (such as programme rights, facilities and resources, presentation and promotion services, and accommodation) received from the public service activities of the BBC on a normal market basis.[53] As a result, the Commission concluded that the funding of the BBC's new digital services from licence fee reserves did not involve state aid, as the funding was not disproportionate to the net public service costs of the BBC, such that no advantage was enjoyed by it. In the alternative, the requirements of Article 86(2) were met.[54]

7–034 In *Kinderkanal and Phoenix*, the Commission had to examine the German funding mechanism. In Germany, an independent and pluralistic body, the "Commission for the calculation of the finance requirements of broadcasters" (KEF), examines the finance requirements that are submitted to it *ex ante* for the period of the following two years. The KEF is obliged to examine the finance requirements in the light of the public service broadcasting obligations of the public service broadcasters. It will suggest an increase or decrease of the broadcasting fees payable by the viewers if this is necessary in view of the finance requirements of the public service broadcasters in order to fulfil their public service obligations. The KEF had examined the finance requirements for the two advertisement-free special interest channels *Kinderkanal* and *Phoenix* and concluded that financial means of DEM 100 million yearly for *Kinderkanal* and DEM 5 million yearly for *Phoenix*, plus DEM 240 million for the years 1997 to 2000 for *Phoenix*, were appropriate to fulfil the finance requirements for those channels.[55] The KEF had reduced the finance requirements for *Kinderkanal*, for which DEM 120 million were notified, because it considered that the programme could be performed at less costs. It suggested that a reduction of the daily broadcasting time and use of existing programmes should reduce the financing requirements and were necessary for the *Kinderkanal* programme to be economically justified. The Commission regarded the role of the

---

[52] *BBC News 24*, above, para.7–003, n.4, paras 75–85.
[53] *BBC licence fee*, above, para.7–003, n.4, paras 42–53.
[54] *ibid.*, para.55.
[55] *Kinderkanal and Phoenix*, above, para.7–003, n.3, para.6.3.

KEF to be essential for determining the costs that were necessary to provide the public services of *Kinderkanal* and *Phoenix*.[56] It found that the KEF did not merely take notice of the financing requirements, but played an essential role for ensuring that the appropriateness of the costs was examined in the light of providing cost-effective public broadcasting services. The Commission concluded that the examination of the KEF was sufficient to ensure that the funding of the special interest channels was appropriate and limited to the actual costs of *Kinderkanal* and *Phoenix*, and the requirements of Article 86(2) EC were met.[57]

In the case *Belgian aid in favour of local television in the French Community*, the Commission also had to make an *ex ante* assessment of the proportionality of the aid granted to the local television broadcasters. It stressed specifically (i) that the funding must be limited to the net costs of the public service broadcasting obligations so that no cross-subsidisation is possible and (ii) that the local broadcasters' conduct must conform with the conduct of a commercial broadcaster in order to ensure cost efficiency and the appropriateness of revenues (referring also to point 58 of the Communication on public service broadcasting).[58] The Commission decided that the control mechanism was adequate to ensure that the local television broadcasting services would not be over-compensated.[59] The local broadcasters had to report yearly about their expenses and revenues and the Belgian authorities had assured the Commission that they were going to apply the principle of proportionality when examining the appropriateness of the funding of local television broadcasters.

In early January 2003, the Commission announced that it was launching a formal investigation into the state funding of TV2, a Danish public service broadcaster. It was concerned that TV2 could have been over-compensated for the additional net costs of meeting its public service obligation between 1995 and 2002, and that TV2 had used the over-compensation to cross-subsidise its advertising and other commercial services, such as its loss-making internet business. The Commission would, in particular, be considering if TV2 had been able to cut its advertising rates to below a level that an efficient commercial operator would have to charge to cover its costs.[60] It has also published its preliminary findings in relation to state funding for RTP, the Portuguese public service broadcaster. This follows the Court of First Instance's judgment in the *SIC* case.[61] The Commission is of the view that annual compensation indemnities paid by the Portuguese state to RTP in respect of its public service obligations could amount to state aid, and has requested further information from the Portuguese authorities.[62]

7–035 Conclusion — The fact that the Commission has recently investigated the financing of certain public broadcasters and is continuing investigations into others[63] demonstrates the increased importance of state aid rules in the broadcasting sector.

---

[56] *ibid*. See also Communication on public service broadcasting, above, para.7–011, n.44, paras 41 and 42.
[57] *Kinderkanal and Phoenix*, above, para.7–003, n.3, para.6.3.
[58] *Belgian aid in favour of local television in the French Community*, above, para.7–010, n.41, p.8.
[59] *ibid*. See also Communication on public service broadcasting, above, para.7–011, n.44, para.57 *et seq*.
[60] *TV2/Denmark*, Decision of January 21, 2003, Commission Press Release, IP/03/91.
[61] Above, para.7–008, n.27.
[62] *Compensation indemnities to public service broadcaster RTP*, Invitation to submit comments, O.J. 2002 C98/2.
[63] See investigation into *TV2* in Denmark, above, para.7–034, n.60. See also continuing investigation into *RTP*, above, para.7–034, n.62.

When assessing notified aid schemes *ex ante*, the Commission does not undertake a very detailed assessment of the costs and revenues involved and the possibility of cross-subsidies, as little financial information is available in such cases. Rather, so long as national legal provisions provide that public funds may not be used for commercial purposes and as long as an efficient monitoring system is in place, the Commission will find that it is unlikely that cross-subsidies will arise.[64] However, the Commission's recent decision in *Deutsche Post*,[65] shows that it will examine in great detail the costs incurred, the revenues obtained and their respective allocation to the public service and commercial activities of an undertaking with a public service remit when dealing with the financing of public services on an *ex post* basis (*i.e.* when the Commission is reviewing a possible aid measure in the form of compensation payments for the costs of providing public services that has not been notified and has already been granted). A stricter *ex post* analysis is appropriate, once the Commission has received indications (presumably by competitors) that a public undertaking is engaging in anti-competitive practices (such as price cutting) and the necessary data and other materials are available to examine these allegations. An examination of this nature is clearly not possible where the Commission examines an aid or financing mechanism *ex ante*, *i.e.* before the measure has been implemented and costs have been incurred.

It is clear from the *Deutsche Post* case (in which the Commission found that *Deutsche Post*, the monopoly provider of the basic postal service in Germany, had received state funding in excess of the net costs of providing a universal public postal service and was using this to unfairly reduce costs in competitive sectors) that the Commission will order the reimbursement of state funds received by a public service broadcaster as compensation for meeting its public service obligations, if they exceed the net costs of providing services under its public service remit. Public broadcasters must, therefore, carefully allocate their costs and revenues between their activities, and Member States must ensure that the resources they make available do not exceed the net costs incurred in providing public service broadcasting services.

7–036 The final part of the "proportionality" test is that the state funding of public services must not have a disproportionate impact upon trading conditions and competition in the common market to an extent that is contrary to the Community interest. This part of the "proportionality" test is required by the Protocol on public service broadcasting.[66] The proportionality test will not be met if the state funding results in market distortions that are not necessary for the fulfilment of the broadcasters' public service mission, for example if it is used to cross-subsidise activities (*e.g.* by allowing it to decrease prices) on competitive markets, thereby affecting competition.[67] This assessment can only be undertaken on a case-by-case basis: the central question is whether the distortion on competition can be justified by the need to perform the public service as defined by the Member State concerned and for it to be funded from state resources.[68] In *BBC News 24*, the Commission considered that the adverse effects on competing suppliers of news channels (such as CNN, BSkyB and Bloomberg), who generally lost market shares due to reduced cable penetration

---

[64] *BBC licence fee*, above, para.7–003, n.4, at para.39 *et seq.*
[65] *Deutsche Post AG*, O.J. 2002 L247/27, at para.86 *et seq.*
[66] See above, para.7–024.
[67] Communication on public service broadcasting, above, para.7–011, n.44, paras 47, 48 and 58.
[68] *ibid.*, paras 59–61.

rates, was not excessive (so was not disproportionate) to the benefits of the new BBC News 24 channel. Furthermore, some damage to competitors must be accepted from the provision of a service of general economic interest, provided it does not make it impossible for them to do business or preclude prospective competitors from entering the market.[69]

A very similar reasoning was given in the *Kinderkanal and Phoenix* case, where the Commission found that the financial difficulties of a competing broadcaster also providing a children's channel did not result from the funding of *Kinderkanal* but rather from a lack of access to the cable network. The state funding of *Kinderkanal* did not render it impossible for the competitor to make sufficient earnings by advertising in order to finance its own children's channel. The difficulties of the private broadcaster were caused by a lack of network penetration, which was not examined under Articles 87, 88 and 86(2) of the EC Treaty. The Commission found that the access to the cable network was not a state aid measure, because the price at which access was granted was not influenced by the state. The access to cable was to be examined in another investigation, examining whether Germany had infringed Article 2(1) and (2) of Directive 89/522/EC concerning the rules for access to the network and Article 59 (now Article 49 of the EC Treaty).[70]

In the case of *Belgian aid in favour of local television in the French Community* the Commission had found that there was only very limited effect on trade between Member States considering that the television broadcasters acted only on a local level. The content of these broadcasters would concern regional and local events and it was unlikely that such programmes would be shown on a national or international level. Also advertising rights would be sold on a merely local level, reaching only a limited audience and at substantially inferior advertising tariffs. Therefore, the Commission did not consider that the distortion of competition caused by the funding went beyond what was necessary for the local broadcasters to be able to fulfil their public service obligation.[71]

7–037 Universal Service Directive and Article 86(2) of the EC Treaty — The general principles on financing of services of general economic interest explained above apply to telecommunications operators that have been designated with obligations to provide public services under the Universal Service Directive[72] and receive funds from state resources for the net costs incurred in meeting those obligations. In addition, the financing of universal service obligations must comply with the requirements of the Universal Service Directive.[73]

Articles 12 and 13 of the Universal Service Directive permit Member States to compensate telecommunications operators that have been designated with universal service obligations for the net costs of meeting those obligations, where the national regulatory authority has determined that these net costs impose an unfair obligation on the designated undertakings.[74] The national

---

[69] *BBC News 24*, above, para.7–003, n.4, paras 87–101.
[70] *Kinderkanal and Phoenix*, above, para.7–003, n.3, s.6.3.
[71] *Belgian aid in favour of local television in the French Community*, above, para.7–010, n.41, p.9.
[72] Universal Service Directive, above, para.1–011, n.30.
[73] In the event that it does not do so, the Member State in question will have failed to comply with its obligations under that Directive and the funding mechanism will be unlawful: See Case C–146/00, *Commission v France* [2001] I E.C.R. 9767.
[74] See generally, para.1–214 *et seq.* and para.7–004, above.

regulatory authority must calculate the net costs of the universal service obligation, taking account of the benefits accruing to the designated undertaking in accordance with Annex IV of the Universal Service Directive[75] and using independently audited or verified accounts.[76] The net costs may be provided from public funds[77] or be shared between all providers of electronic communications networks and services on a transparent, non-discriminatory, proportionate and unbundled basis that causes the least distortion to the functioning of the market.[78] In this way, the Universal Service Directive ensures that a harmonised minimum telephone service (including access to the fixed network, directory inquiry services, public pay-phones and special measures for disabled users), available at affordable prices and at a minimum level of quality, is provided throughout the Community and is financed with the minimum of market distortion.[79]

Provided any funding mechanism for the net costs of universal service complies with the requirements of the Universal Service Directive, it would — since the *Altmark Trans* has upheld and confirmed the *Ferring* judgment[80] — not constitute state aid, as the funding would amount only to compensating the operator for providing a public interest service. Indeed, it has been argued that Article 86(2) has no applicability in the telecommunications sector given that Community legislation has harmonised and provided exhaustively for how universal service is to be provided and financed in the telecommunications field, given that Member States may not fund any services other than those permitted under the Universal Service Directive.[81] In this regard, it is instructive that the Commission's challenge to France's funding mechanism (under the ONP Interconnection Directive[82]) for France Télécom's universal service obligations was brought on the basis of an incorrect implementation of the ONP Interconnection Directive, rather than as a case of state aid, even though France Télécom would clearly have received more than the net costs of meeting its universal service obligations.[83]

7–038 However, the financing mechanisms that Member States may set up to compensate operators with universal service obligations for the net costs incurred can constitute state aid within Article 87(1) of the EC Treaty if the compensation exceeds the net costs of complying with the public service obligations, thereby constituting over-compensation, and consequently a state aid measure that cannot be justified. Annex IV of the Universal Service Directive gives guidance on calculating the net costs of universal service provisions by national regulatory authorities[84]:

- the net cost of meeting the universal service obligation is to be calculated as the difference between the net cost for the designated undertaking of operating with the universal

---

[75] Universal Service Directive, para.1–011, n.30, Art.12(1).

[76] *ibid.*, Art.12(2).

[77] *ibid.*, Art.13(1)(a).

[78] *ibid.*, Arts 13(1)(b), (2)–(4) and 14.

[79] *ibid.*, Arts 3–10; see para.1–202 *et seq.*, above.

[80] *Ferring*, above, para.7–021, n.98; *Altmark Trans*, above, para.7–021, n.3a.

[81] See Bartosch, "EC Telecommunications Law: What Aid does Article 90(2) offer to the former Monopolists?" [1999] C.T.L.R. 12–15.

[82] ONP Interconnection Directive, para.1–006, n.23, Art.5.

[83] *Commission v France*, above, para.7–037, n.73. France did not raise Art.86(2) in its defence.

[84] See also para.1–214 *et seq.*, above.

service obligation and operating without the universal service obligations, taking account of the costs that would have been avoided had there been no universal service obligation;

- the net cost calculation should assess the benefit, including intangible benefits, to the undertaking designated with universal service obligations — these could, for example, include additional customers that the undertaking attracts through operating nationwide;

- the net cost calculation can take account only of the costs for providing designated services that can only be provided at a loss or provided under cost conditions falling outside normal commercial standards; this may include the provision of the emergency telephone service, certain public pay-phones (*e.g.* in remote areas) and the provision of certain services and/or equipment for disabled users;

- the net costs of providing designated services to end-users or groups of end-users who can only be served at a loss or under cost conditions falling outside normal commercial standards — taking account of the costs of providing the network and services, the revenue generated and the impact of any geographical averaging of prices imposed by the Member States. This includes end-users or groups of end-users that would not be served by a commercial operator which did not have an obligation to provide universal service; and

- separate calculations must be made for each aspect of a universal service obligation, in order to ensure that there is no double counting of costs of any direct or indirect benefits.

7–039 In *Commission v France*,[85] the Commission challenged the system put in place by the French government to compensate France Télécom for its universal service mechanism. The Court of Justice held that by not following the requirements of the Interconnection Directive, which set out the mechanism for financing universal service under the 1998 regulatory framework, France had implemented an unlawful recovery system. Of particular relevance was that the French government had imposed cost-sharing obligations on operators that were not, under the Directive, required to contribute to the financing of universal service; that account have been taken of the costs of servicing profitable customers (rather than just the costs of supplying unprofitable customers), leading to the costs of France Télécom in providing universal service being inflated; and that costs had not been calculated on a transparent basis and certain cost elements had been calculated on a flat-rate basis rather than by reference to the actual costs incurred in serving unprofitable customers; and no account was taken of the benefits of providing a universal service. In summary, the methods of calculating net costs resulted in over-compensation to France Télécom, owing to the inflation of its net costs above the proper level. The Court of Justice affirmed that establishing a level playing field for telecommunications providers requires an objective and transparent costs structure, which requires specific calculations to be made on the basis of the actual costs and benefits of providing universal service. Costs should be calculated on a forward-looking basis, rather than by using historic costs. *Commission v France* provides useful guidance on how the new provisions of the Universal Service Directive will be interpreted.

---

[85] See above, para.7–037, n.73.

E. Rescue and Restructuring Aid

7–040 The telecommunications and broadcasting sectors have experienced economic difficulties as a result of companies that borrowed heavily to build networks or expand their businesses and that have been unable to meet their debt repayments. Some companies, such as Energis, NTL and Global Crossing, have successfully emerged from insolvency or near insolvency through refinancing and restructuring themselves on the capital markets. Others, such as KPN QWest, have been liquidated. Finally, some undertakings (notably MobilCom in Germany and France Télécom) have received financial assistance from the state to resolve their financial difficulties and the question has arisen as to whether this involved state aid.

The injection of capital, the granting of loans and the provision of guarantees to a company in financial difficulties from a public company or public bank may constitute an aid measure. In this case, the Community Guidelines on rescue and restructuring aid must be applied and their special requirements must be respected.[86]

The provision of equity capital, loans or guarantees to a company by a Member State, a public authority or a state-owned bank or company, does not necessarily involve state aid on the basis that the "market economy investor" test is met (*i.e.* because the provision of financial assistance represents reasonable commercial conduct and is provided at the same conditions as those that a private investor would accept, and if the state could reasonably expect to make a reasonable return on its investment within a reasonable period of time).[87] However, where the recipient is in financial difficulties, it may be difficult if not impossible to demonstrate that financial assistance is being provided in accordance with the market economy investor principle. It is, therefore, first necessary to examine whether the proposed state measure constitutes a state aid measure, taking account of the market economy investor principle. In making this assessment, it has to be taken into account that a private investor would normally only make further capital available or provide loans to a company in financial difficulties if it was already a shareholder or major creditor and if it could expect a reasonable return on both its existing investment and the new funds being provided in due course. The seriousness of the financial difficulties of the recipient is, therefore, of particular relevance. Accordingly, if it is unlikely that the recipient would be able to raise the necessary capital from private investors, the provision of state funds to a firm in difficulty will amount to an aid measure.[88] Account will be taken of the undertaking's likely future profitability: unless its prospects are such as to attract private financial investors, the provision of capital by the state, for example for a restructuring and modernisation programme, will amount to an aid measure.[89]

---

[86] Community Guidelines on State aid for Rescuing and Restructuring Firms in Difficulty, O.J. 1999 C288/2, corrigendum O.J. 2000 C121/29.

[87] See Communication to the Member States on public undertakings in the manufacturing sector, O.J. 1993 C307/3, paras 17 and 27. See also *Stardust Marine*, above, para.7–006, n.20; Case T–323/99, *INMA & Itainvest* [2002] II E.C.R. 545, at paras 76 and 94. See generally, above, para.7–007.

[88] *Netherlands and Leeuwarder Papierwarenfabriek v Commission*, above, para.7–010, n.43. See also *Air France v Commission (CDC–P)*, above, para.7–004, n.7, where the subscription by the French state for virtually all of the securities of Air France, which was in a critical financial position, amounted to an aid measure.

[89] Case C–142/87, *Belgium v Commission (Tubemeuse)* [1990] I E.C.R. 959.

7–041 When it has been established that the financial support constitutes aid, this aid might be justified according to Article 87(3)(c) of the EC Treaty under the conditions set out in the Guidelines for Rescue and Restructuring Aid.[90] These guidelines require that the recipient company must be in financial difficulties. A firm in difficulty is one that is unable, through its own resources or with funds from its shareholders or creditors, to stem losses that — without intervention by the public authorities — would cause it to go out of business in the short to medium term, in particular if it has lost more than half of its capital or meets the requirements of national law for insolvency proceedings.[91] Rescue aid, in the form of a loan or loan guarantee at an interest rate at least comparable to those for healthy firms, may be granted to a firm in difficulty, for a maximum period of six months, which may only be extended in exceptional circumstances, provided the loan is for no more than a sum needed to keep the firm in business during that period, pending the development of a restructuring plan.[92] Aid for the restructuring of the company may subsequently be granted, if approved by the Commission. Restructuring aid will only be approved if the restructuring plan will restore the firm to long-term viability in a reasonable period of time without it needing further state aid.[93] Restructuring aid must be proportional to the needs of the company and to the market situation and competitors. Restructuring aid will only be authorised if competition is not seriously affected by the provision of the aid and, in order to counter-balance the adverse effect of the aid on competition, the beneficiary of the aid must normally reduce its production capacity, abandon all structurally loss-making activities and fully implement the restructuring plan.[94] Restructuring aid may be granted to a company only once under the "one time, last time" condition.[95]

A recent example of rescue aid granted in the communications sector was the rescue aid granted by Germany to the mobile operator MobilCom. The Commission approved aid of €50 million granted in the form of a state-guaranteed loan, which it considered was necessary to keep MobilCom afloat pending the development of a restructuring plan following the withdrawal of support from its major shareholder, France Télécom.[96] The Commission has opened a formal investigation into a later state guarantee, as it had serious doubts as to whether this further provision of state support met the rescue and restructuring aid guidelines, as it appeared to be used by MobilCom for financing restructuring measures, even though no restructuring plan had been submitted to the Commission.[97] A recent example of a possible restructuring aid is the shareholders' advance provided by the French state to France Télécom. France Télécom was facing financial difficulties owing to the size of its debts and planned to undertake a rights issue in which public and private shareholders would subscribe for new shares. However, owing to adverse market conditions, this recapitalisation could not take place immediately and France provided a loan of up to €9 billion ahead of its participation in the planned rights issue. The Commission has announced

---

[90] See above, para.7–040, n.87.
[91] *ibid.*, paras 4–5.
[92] *ibid.*, paras 23–26.
[93] *ibid.*, paras 31–32.
[94] *ibid.*, paras 29–43.
[95] *ibid.*, para.48.
[96] *Rescue Aid in favour of MobilCom*, Decision of January 21, 2003, Commission Press Release, IP/03/92.
[97] *Restructuring aid in favour of MobilCom*, Decision of July 9, 2003, O.J. 2003 C 210/4.

a formal investigation, as it is possible that the shareholder advance did not meet the requirements of the market economy investor test.[98]

An example of restructuring aid is the aid granted by France to Société Française de Production, a film production company.[99] Société Française de Production was a company in financial difficulties and France granted industrial and financial restructuring aid to ensure the survival of the company. The aid was approved subject to conditions, in particular the implementation of the restructuring plan (which the Commission examined closely), which included a significant reduction in its workforce, the implementation of measures to improve its efficiency and reducing its costs and a reduction in its capacity.[1]

F. Procedural Rights and Remedies

7–042   In this section the procedural rights and remedies that may be available to Member States, beneficiaries of state aid and competitors in the field of state aid are considered.[2]

1. Procedural Rights and Remedies During the Commission's Investigation

7–043   Competitors — Competitors may bring to the Commission's attention, by way of a complaint, any measure that they consider to be state aid with a view to triggering a preliminary investigation by the Commission under Article 88(2) EC.[3] The Commission must then investigate the matter raised by the complaint, and open a formal investigation procedure under Article 88(2) where it has serious doubts either as to whether a particular measure is a state aid measure or whether an aid measure is compatible with the common market.[4] The investigations that the Commission undertook in relation to the financing schemes of public broadcasters in the United Kingdom,[5] France,[6] Portugal,[7] Spain,[8] and Denmark[9] were initiated as a result of such informal complaints from competitors. In cases brought by the complainants in the French, Spanish and Portuguese cases, the Court of First Instance held that the Commission must take a decision on whether to open a formal investigation under Article 88(2) within a reasonable period of time after receiving a complaint: delays of between two and four years were not acceptable, even when the Commission

---

[98] *Aid to France Télécom*, Decision of January 30, 2003, Commission Press Release, IP/03/150.

[99] *Société Française de Production*, O.J. 1998 L205/68.

[1] *ibid.*

[2] For a general description, see Hancher, Ottervanger and Slot, *E.C. State Aids*, above, para.7–016, n.77, Pt IV, Chaps 19–21.

[3] Procedural Regulation, above, para.7–013, n.56, Art.20.

[4] *SIC*, above, para.7–008, n.27, para.70 *et seq.* (concerning RTP); *Gestevision*, above, para.7–014, n.59, para.74.

[5] *BBC News 24* and *BBC licence fee*, both above, para.7–003, n.4.

[6] *TF1*, above, para.7–014, n.59. See also *Capital increase in favour of France2 and France3*, above, para.7–011, n.45.

[7] *SIC*, above, para.7–008, n.27. See also *RTP*, above, para.7–009, n.33.

[8] *Gestevision*, above, para.7–014, n.59.

[9] *TV2*, above, para.7–034, n.60.

faces difficulties in assessing the aid content of financing schemes.[10] When faced with delays due to a lack of information from the Member State concerned, the Commission should either use its formal powers to obtain information or initiate formal investigations under Article 88(2).

7–044 Competitors have very limited rights during the Commission's investigation. Competitors have no right to be heard or involved during the Commission's initial two-month preliminary investigation under Article 88(3),[11] such that the Commission is under no obligation to give complainants the opportunity to state their views at this stage.[12] When the Commission has opened a formal investigation procedure under Article 88(2), competitors, as interested parties,[13] may submit comments and observations; hence, during a formal investigation they have a right to be heard,[14] although this does not extend to a right to access the Commission's file, or other rights of defence available to those against whom proceedings have been initiated.[15] Nevertheless, the Commission must, in the interests of sound administration, conduct a diligent and impartial investigation of a complaint, including where necessary matters not expressly raised by the complainant.[16] Furthermore, competitors are entitled to receive copies of the Commission's decisions adopted at the termination of the formal investigation[17] or any other decision.[18] Competitors can informally ask, but have no right to require, the Commission to make a suspension and/or a provisional recovery order pending completion of the investigation procedure.[19] These orders are made very rarely and are within the sole discretion of the Commission, and can therefore only be contested by competitors if there is a manifest error. The Commission will order the provisional recovery of state aid if there is no doubt that the measure constitutes state aid, where there is an urgency to act, and where a competitor will suffer substantial and irreparable damage because of the unlawful granting of the aid.[20]

7–045 Member States — Member States safeguard their rights by following the notification procedure laid down in the Procedural Regulation. The Commission is obliged to take its preliminary decision within a period of two months after receipt of a complete notification[21] only if the aid has been notified before being granted.[22] In almost all cases, the Commission sends lists of questions and requests for more information to the Member State that has made the notification, if, as is usually the case, the information submitted with the notification is not sufficient for the Commission to take its decision. In order to make it possible to obtain an

[10] *Gestevision*, above, para.7–014, n.59, para.74; *TF1*, above, para.7–014, n.59, para.74; *SIC*, above, para.7–008, n.27, para.70.
[11] Case T–266/94, *Foreningen af Jernskibs — og Maskinbyggerier i Danmark Skibsvaerftsforeningen v Commission* [1996] I E.C.R. 1399.
[12] Case C–317/95 P, *Commission v Sytravel* [1997] I E.C.R. 4681.
[13] Procedural Regulation, above, para.7–013, n.56, Art.1(h).
[14] *ibid.*, Art.20.
[15] *Ufex*, above, para.7–018, n.84.
[16] *Sytravel*, above, para.7–044, n.12.
[17] Procedural Regulation, above, para.7–013, n.56, Art.20(1).
[18] *ibid.*, Art.20(3).
[19] *ibid.*, Art.11; see also above, para.7–015.
[20] *ibid.*, Art.11.
[21] *ibid.*, Art.4.
[22] *ibid.*, Art.13(2).

approval decision quickly at the end of the preliminary investigation phase, it is advisable for the Member State to submit, as much and as quickly as possible, the information needed to assess the compatibility of the aid.

According to the principle of the right to be heard, the Member State that has granted the aid measure under investigation has the right of access to the documents on which the Commission's decision is based.[23] Such right to access refers mainly to the formal investigation procedure under Article 88(2), whereas during the preliminary investigation these rights are limited and often, the Commission does not have much or any additional information than that submitted by the Member State. Furthermore, the Member State has the right to effectively make known its view on the observations provided by interested third parties and on which the Commission proposes to base its decision,[24] although a failure by the Commission in this respect will result in the decision being annulled only if, absent the irregularity, the outcome might have been different.[25]

7–046 Beneficiaries of state aid — Beneficiaries have no formal rights during the preliminary investigation procedure, as it is the Member State that is the notifying party. At the preliminary stage, the beneficiaries may, therefore, be limited to informal meetings with the Commission and trying to influence the Member State's submissions.

When a formal investigation procedure has been opened under Article 88(2), the beneficiary is an interested party,[26] and therefore has the same rights as competitors and other interested parties (such as other Member States and trade associations).[27] So far the Community courts have not held that beneficiaries have a right to access the files and documents that have been the basis of the Commission's decision to provide observations on the comments of other interested parties.[28]

2. Procedural Rights and Remedies Before the Community Courts

7–047 Appeal against a decision — Once a final decision has been taken by the Commission under Article 7 of the Procedural Regulation, beneficiaries as well as competitors and Member States may be entitled to challenge the decision pursuant to Article 230 of the EC Treaty. According to Article 230,[29] Member States may challenge any decision adopted by the Commission as they are "privileged applicants" and have automatic *locus standi* to do so and do not need to show any interest in order to bring proceedings. Any action by a Member State is heard by the Court of Justice. Non-privileged applicants may only challenge decisions addressed to them or if the decision is of direct and individual concern to them. Challenges brought by non-privileged applicants (including regional bodies) are heard in the Court of First Instance, with an appeal on

---

[23] Case C–234/84, *Belgium v Commission (Meura)* [1986] E.C.R. 2263, para.27; Case C–301/87, *France v Commission (Boussac)* [1990] I E.C.R. 307, para.29.

[24] *Boussac*, above, para.7–045, n.23.

[25] *ibid.*

[26] Procedural Regulation, above, para.7–013, n.56, Art.1(h).

[27] Case C–294/90, *British Aerospace plc v Commission* [1992] I E.C.R. 493.

[28] Case T–371 and 394/94, *British Airways* [1998] II E.C.R. 2405, paras 57 and 64.

[29] See generally, Weatherill and Beaumont, *EC Law* (Penguin, 3rd ed., 1999), Chap.8.

grounds of law to the Court of Justice. In all cases only decisions that are intended to have binding legal effects can be reviewed under Article 230.

The Member State that is the addressee of the Commission's decision is entitled to challenge a decision of the Commission concerning state aid granted by it. Another Member State may also challenge the decision, for example because it objects to a Commission decision to approve a state aid measure. Regional bodies that have granted aid may also be entitled to challenge a Commission decision, provided they can show that the decision is of direct and individual concern to them.[30] Beneficiaries and competitors may challenge a Commission decision under Article 230(4) if they can show that they are directly and individually concerned by it. A beneficiary of aid is normally directly and individually concerned by a decision, including a conditional approval of aid,[31] although this will not be the case where the Commission has prohibited a state aid measure applicable to all operators in a sector, as then each beneficiary is in no different position to any other potential beneficiary of the aid, so that the decision is of general application.[32] Third parties will have *locus standi* to bring on appeal if they are either the complainant[33] or have participated in a formal investigation as an interested party if their position on the market would be affected by the granting of the aid.[34] The Court of First Instance has acknowledged the admissibility of a challenge by competitors if it is clear that the Member State will go ahead with the granting of an approved aid.[35] The decisions that may be challenged under Article 230 include decisions to open (or not to open) a formal investigation procedure under Article 88(2), decisions to approve or not to approve aid (whether at the end of the preliminary investigation or at the end of the formal investigation), decisions requiring aid to be repaid, and conditional decisions to approve aid.

The grounds for challenging a decision under Article 230 are: lack of competence; the infringement of essential procedural requirements (violation of the right to be heard, failure to open a formal investigation procedure, and other procedural irregularities); an infringement of the Treaty or other rules of Community law relating to its application (usually an incorrect interpretation of Articles 87, 88 or 86(2), *e.g.* the market economy investor principle, or Article 253, which imposes a duty for decisions to be adequately reasoned); or a misuse of powers. Most challenges are based upon procedural irregularities, a lack of reasoning in the contested decision, manifest error on the part of the Commission, or other errors of law.[36]

---

[30] *Vlaamse Gewest*, above, para.7–010, n.38: an autonomous regional body had *locus standi* as the decision prevented it from exercising its own competence under national law.

[31] *Philip Morris*, above, para.7–010, n.37.

[32] Case T–88/96, *Arbeitsgemeinschaft Deutscher Luftfahrt-Unternehmen and Hapag-Lloyd Fluggesellschaft v Commission* [1999] II E.C.R. 179: challenge to the decision to prohibit a tax advantage made available to all airlines in Germany was inadmissible.

[33] Case C–198/91, *Cook v Commission* [1993] II E.C.R. 2487: complainant had *locus standi* to challenge a decision not to open a formal investigation procedure, as this was the only way of safeguarding its procedural rights.

[34] Case C–169/84, *COFAZ v Commission* [1986] E.C.R. 391, and Case C–169/94, *CdF Chemie AZF v Commission* [1990] I E.C.R. 3083.

[35] Case T–435/93, *ASPEC* [1995] II E.C.R. 1281, para.60.

[36] See Bellamy and Child, above para.4–001, n.4, paras 19–091 to 19–095.

7–048   There has been only one challenge to a Commission decision concerning a state aid in the broadcasting sector. In *SIC*[37] the complainant, SIC (a private broadcaster), objected to the state financing of the Portuguese public broadcaster, RTP. The Commission decided not to open a formal investigation procedure. The Court of First Instance found, however, that documents in the Commission's file indicated that it had serious doubts that the Portuguese measures in favour of RTP involved state aid. These measures included compensation for complying with public service obligations between 1992 and 1995; certain tax exemptions; debt waivers; an excessively high price paid by the state for RTP's cable network; late payments by RTP of the licence fee for using its cable network; and certain investment aids. The decision not to open a formal investigation procedure was, therefore, substantially annulled, leading to the Commission recommencing its investigation.[38]

7–049   Action for failure to act — Article 232 EC entitles Member States and others to bring an action before the Court of Justice (in the case of a Member State) or the Court of First Instance (in the case of other applicants) if the Commission has failed to act (by way of adopting a decision or otherwise defining its position) within two months of being requested to do so. In the state aid field, competitors who have made complaints regarding the alleged provision of state aid to public broadcasters have brought actions under Article 232 where the Commission has failed to act by not investigating the complaint and failing to decide whether or not to open formal proceedings under Article 88(2).[39] They also challenged the Commission's failure to take a decision in due time on possible state aid measures which they had brought to the Commission's attention. In all three cases, the Court of First Instance found that the time period for the Commission's preliminary investigation had exceeded the limit of what was reasonable (between 27 and 47 months)[40] and that the Commission should have opened a formal investigation procedure in view of the difficulties the Commission had encountered in assessing the alleged aid measures. In *Gestevision* the Court of First Instance held that, although the Commission had had difficulties in assessing the extent of the state aid included in the compensation for the provision of services under a public service obligation, this could not justify the duration of the preliminary investigation: a formal investigation should have been initiated.

The procedural requirements of Article 232 must be observed, in particular, the time-limits (*i.e.* the making of a formal demand on the Commission to adopt its position; a time period of two months for the Commission to adopt its position; a time period of an additional two months to

---

[37] *SIC*, above, para.7–008, n.27, paras 75–109.

[38] *ibid.*

[39] *ibid.* The appeal in *SIC* was withdrawn when the Commission adopted a decision not to open an investigation procedure; *Gestevision*, above, para.7–014, n.59; *TF1*, above, para.7–014, n.59, para.28, where the Court of First Instance also held that a claim against the Commission's failure to act pursuant to Art.86(3) (Art.90(3)) by competitors was admissible.

[40] *TF1*, above, para.7–014, n.59, paras 76, 80 (31 months); *Gestevision*, above, para.7–014, n.59, para.79 *et seq.* (26 and 47 months). See also *SIC*, above, para.7–008, n.27, para.102, concerning an appeal against a decision of the Commission not to open a formal investigation. The Court based its finding — that the Commission had substantial difficulties in assessing the aid character of the measure — amongst others on the fact that investigation took 33, and 39 months, hence, far longer than is necessary for a preliminary investigation.

lodge the action with the Court of Justice or the Court of First Instance); and the need for the non-privileged applicant to show that it is individually and directly concerned by the decision or action that was requested.[41]

3. Remedies before National Courts

7–050   Action before the national courts for interim relief and damages — Another possibility for competitors to seek protection against an unlawful granting of aid is to challenge the decision of the Member State to grant the aid before national courts.

The Commission has exclusive authority (subject to the Council's powers) for the examination of state aid measures under Articles 87, 88 and 86 EC,[42] which means that national courts cannot prohibit existing or approve new aid. However, in relation to new aid, national courts have the power (and indeed the duty) to decide if a measure is an aid (if this can be easily established), and if it has been implemented by a Member State prior to notification and approval by the Commission. If aid has been granted in breach of Article 88(3) (a provision which is directly applicable, and can therefore be invoked by competitors), national courts must take all necessary measures to give effect to individuals' rights under Article 88(3) and restrain the unlawfully granted aid.[43] National courts must grant all appropriate remedies to competitors who would be damaged by the Member State's failure to comply with the "standstill" provision of Article 88(3); this includes orders for repayment of the illegal aid, interim relief and damages.[44] The fact that the aid may subsequently be approved by the Commission is immaterial, as it is the breach of the "standstill" obligation imposed by Article 88(3) that national courts must restrain.[45]

7–051   The Commission has issued a communication to the Member States indicating when and to what extent the courts of a Member State may deal with a case where a state aid is concerned.[46] The Commission provides a procedure for national courts to seek assistance of a procedural nature from the Commission; the Commission must respond to such requests promptly.[47] The Notice also summarises the powers of the Commission and the national courts under state aid rules.

If the Commission has adopted a decision requiring a Member State to recover illegally paid aid, the Member State must do so promptly under the provisions of national law, including by bringing debt recovery proceedings or, if the recipient cannot repay the aid, insolvency proceedings.[48]

---

[41] See Case *TF1*, above, para.7–014, n.59, para.76.

[42] Case 74/76, *Ianelli v Meroni* [1977] E.C.R. 557.

[43] *SFEI v La Poste*, above, para.7–006, n.22; Case 120/73, *Lorenz v Germany* [1973] E.C.R. 1471.

[44] See Advocate General Tesauro in *Tubemeuse*, above, para.7–040, n.89, and Advocate General Jacobs in *SFEI v La Poste*, above, para.7–006, n.22.

[45] *SFEI v La Poste*, above, para.7–006, n.22.

[46] Note on Cooperation between the Commission and the Courts of the Member States in the Area of State aid, O.J. 1995 C312/8.

[47] *SFEI v La Poste*, above, para.7–006, n.22.

[48] *Land Rheinland-Pfalz v Alcan Deutschland (Alcan No. 2)*, above, para.7–015, n.65: the Member State must re-establish the previously existing situation. See also *Tubemeuse* above, para.7–040, n.89, where the Court of Justice held that it is sufficient for the implementation of a recovery order to register the repayment claim in the insolvency proceedings actual repayment need not have taken place.

National law must not render the recovery of illegally paid aid impossible[49] and the Member State must effect recovery except if it is absolutely impossible to do so, which is likely to occur only very rarely if at all. The Commission may bring enforcement proceedings before the Court of Justice if a Member State fails to recover illegally paid aid. Beneficiaries of illegally paid aid cannot challenge the validity of the original recovery decision in national court proceedings for the recovery of the aid (by way of an Article 234 reference to the Court of Justice for a preliminary ruling), if the time period for bringing an annulment action under Article 230 has expired.[50] Presumably, competitors could, if they have standing under national law, bring proceedings in a national court if a Member State fails to comply with a recovery decision, under general principles of Community law concerning effective judicial protection and the enforcement of Member State's obligations to comply with their Treaty obligations.

---

[49] Case C–94/87, *Commission v Germany (Alcan No. 1)* [1989] E.C.R. 175.
[50] Case C–188/92, *TWD Textilwerke Deggendorf (No. 1)* [1994] I E.C.R. 833.

Chapter VIII

Mergers and Acquisitions, Joint Ventures and Other Alliances

A. Outline of the Chapter

8–001 This chapter reviews the main substantive and procedural rules of EU competition law that are applicable to mergers and acquisitions and the formation of joint ventures, strategic alliances and other forms of collaboration and co-operation in the communications and broadcasting sectors. First, the application of the Merger Control Regulation to transactions that are concentrations is reviewed. Second, there is a review of the competition rules of the EC Treaty that are applicable to joint ventures and other transactions (such as strategic alliances, minority share holdings and other forms of co-operation between undertakings) that do not constitute a concentration and fall outside of the scope of the Merger Control Regulation. Third, the principal decisions of the Commission and the judgments of the Court of First Instance and the Court of Justice in the communications and broadcasting sectors are explained and assessed.

B. Concentrations: Mergers, Acquisitions and Full-Function Joint Ventures

8–002 **Introduction** — In its 1991 Competition Guidelines,[1] the Commission acknowledged that transactions leading to the restructuring of the communications industry can be beneficial, if they enable companies to rationalise and achieve the economies of scale that are necessary for them to make the investments in research and development that are required in order to remain competitive in a worldwide market. However, it also states that not all mergers and acquisitions have positive economic benefits and some will result in the creation or strengthening of a dominant player, thereby jeopardising the maintenance of effective competition on a specific market.

Prior to the adoption and entry into force of the Merger Control Regulation, the Commission had only limited powers to review mergers, even though they had lasting structural effects upon the

---

[1] Guidelines on the Application of EEC Competition Rules in the Telecommunications Sector, O.J. 1991 C233/2.

markets concerned. It was entitled to apply Article 82 (*ex* Article 86) of the EC Treaty to mergers that would have strengthened an existing dominant position, on the basis that if an already dominant undertaking acquires an actual or potential competitor, it reduces competition, thereby committing a "structural" abuse.[2] The *Continental Can* doctrine was applied only to a few mergers, given that it could only be applied when an already dominant undertaking was a party to a merger. Article 81 (*ex* Article 85) of the EC Treaty could be applied to the acquisition of a minority shareholding in a competitor, where this led to an acquisition of influence over the competitor, thereby appreciably restricting competition.[3] However, it was doubtful that Article 81 of the EC Treaty could be applied to a transaction where a controlling interest was acquired. National merger control could also be applicable to mergers, leading to uncertainty for both companies and regulators. The need for an assessment of the effects on competition of mergers and acquisitions prior to their implementation finally persuaded the Council to adopt the Merger Control Regulation in 1989.[4]

8–003   Reform of the Merger Control Regulation — On December 11, 2002, the Commission adopted a proposal for a package of measures for a comprehensive reform of the review of mergers under the Merger Control Regulation. This package[5] consisted of: (i) a proposal for the revision of the Merger Control Regulation[6]; (ii) draft guidelines on the appraisal of horizontal mergers (*i.e.* mergers between competitors)[7]; and (iii) a series of non-legislative "best practice" measures intended to improve the decision-making process.[8] It is unlikely that the new rules will come into force before May 2004. However, appropriate references are made in this chapter to the Commission's proposal.

1. Scope of the Application of the Merger Control Regulation: Concentrations

8–004   The Merger Control Regulation applies to "concentrations", which is a broad concept covering transactions that bring about a lasting change in the structure of the undertakings concerned. A concentration arises when two or more previously independent businesses merge, or when a business acquires, through the purchase of shares or assets, by contract or by other means (*e.g.* a public bid) direct or indirect control of the whole or part of another business.[9] "Control" is defined as the ability to exercise "decisive influence" over another undertaking by rights, contracts or other

---

[2] Case C–6/72, *Europemballage and Continental Can v Commission* [1973] E.C.R. 215.

[3] Case C–142 and 156/84, *BAT Reynolds v Commission (Philip Morris)* [1987] E.C.R. 4487. In the telecommunications sector, the "Philip Morris" doctrine was applied to the joint venture between BT and MCI, which involved them taking cross-minority shareholdings: Case *BT/MCI*, see below, para.8–264 *et seq.*

[4] Council Regulation 4064/89 on the control of concentrations between undertakings, O.J. 1989 L395/1, as amended by Council Regulation 1310/97, O.J. 1997 L180/1.

[5] The texts are available on the Commission's competition website: *http://europa.eu.int/comm/competition/index_en.html*. This proposed package followed an earlier Green Paper on the review of Council Regulation (EEC) No.4064/89, available at: *http://www.europa.eu.int/comm/competition/mergers/review/green_paper.pdf*.

[6] Proposal for a Council Regulation on the control of concentrations between undertakings, O.J. 2003 C20/4.

[7] Draft Commission Notice on the appraisal of horizontal mergers, available at: *www.europa.eu.int/comm/competition/mergers/review/final_draft_en.pdf*.

[8] DG Competition Draft Best Practices on the conduct of EC Merger Control proceedings, available at: *www.europa.eu.int/comm/competition/mergers/other/best_practices_public_cons.pdf*.

[9] Merger Control Regulation, above, para.8–002, n.4, Art.3(1).

means. Decisive influence can be acquired in various ways, including share ownership, shareholders' agreements and other economic relationships that may give *de facto* control. Control may be acquired and exercised by one undertaking or by two or more undertakings jointly.[10] A concentration may also occur where a transaction results in a change in the nature of control over an undertaking, *i.e.* from joint to sole control or *vice versa* or even a change in the nature of joint control.[11] The question whether sole or joint control is acquired has sometimes proved to be a difficult issue to resolve, especially in the case of joint ventures. As the concept of control is an objective concept, control may be acquired even if it is not the intention of the parties.[12]

8–005 Acquisition of sole control — Transactions that involve the acquisition of the control over another undertaking typically involve the acquisition of all or a majority of the voting shares in a company. A majority shareholder would, nevertheless, not be considered to have "sole" control if the consent of one or more minority shareholders is required for decisions regarding the company's strategic commercial behaviour, which would then result in a situation of joint control.[13] In cases involving minority shareholders, the Commission distinguishes between shareholders' rights to determine the strategic commercial behaviour of an entity (*e.g.* prior approval or veto rights over budgets, business and strategy plans or hiring and firing of senior management) and rights that enable a minority shareholder to protect the value of its investment (*e.g.* corporate decisions affecting incorporation, changes in legal headquarters, dissolution or winding-up).[14]

A shareholder with a 50 per cent shareholding or even a lesser interest may thus be found to have sole control if it has rights that enable it alone to determine the strategic commercial behaviour of a company, for example, a casting vote to break deadlocks, the right to appoint more than half the members of the joint venture's decision-making body or preferential voting rights.[15] A shareholding

---

[10] *ibid.*, Art.3(3). See also Commission Notice on the concept of a concentration under Council Regulation (EEC) 4064/89 on the control of concentrations between undertakings (the "Concentration Notice"), O.J. 1998 C66/5.

[11] See, for example, Case M.452, *Avesta (II)*, Commission Decision of June 9, 1994 (change in nature of joint control following sale of its interest by one of four jointly controlling shareholders: joint control now enjoyed by three shareholders); Case M.1911, *Dow/BSL*, Commission Decision of April 27, 2000 (exit of shareholder resulting in change from joint to sole control); Case M.23, *ICI/Tioxide*, Commission Decision of November 28, 1990 (acquisition of 50% interest of other joint venture partner resulted in a change from joint to sole control); and Case M.560, *EADS/Lufthansa*, Commission Decision of May 11, 1995 (acquisition of 25% interest in Lufthansa subsidiary, involved a change from sole to joint control).

[12] Case M.157, *Air France/Sabena*, Commission Decision of October 5, 1992.

[13] See for example, Case M.827, *DB Kom*, Commission Decision of October 23, 1996; Case M.853, *Bell CableMedia/Cable & Wireless/Videotron*, Commission Decision of December 11, 1996; Case M.1911, *Dow/BSL*, Commission Decision of April 27, 2000; Case M.0046, *Blackstone/CDPQ/Kabel Nordrhein-Westfalen*, Commission Decision of June 19, 2000; Case M.2437, *NEC/Toshiba*, Commission Decision of June 6, 2001; Case M.2550, *Mezzo/Muzzik*, Commission Decision of December 6, 2001. In each case, the Commission considered that despite the majority shareholding of one of the partners in a joint venture company, the majority shareholder did not have sole control due to the minority shareholders' veto rights on the commercial policy and strategy of the venture company.

[14] See, for example, Case M.232, *PepsiCo/General Mills*, Commission Decision of August 5, 1992; Case M.353, *BT/MCI (I)*, Commission Decision of September 13, 1993; Case M.2665, *Johnson Professional Holdings/ DiverseyLever*, Commission Decision of March 4, 2002.

[15] See Case M.794, *Coca-Cola/Amalgamated Beverages GB*, O.J. 1997 L218/15.

of less than 50 per cent can confer sole control on a *de facto* basis if the other shares are held by a large number of small shareholders with dispersed interests, where the largest shareholder can achieve a majority of the votes at shareholders' meetings. This is usually assessed on the basis of voting patterns at past shareholders' meetings.[16]

8–006 *Asset acquisitions* — Asset acquisitions may also be concentrations, if the assets form an "undertaking" within the meaning of the Merger Control Regulation. The Commission considers that assets comprise an "undertaking" if market turnover can be clearly attributed to the assets in question.[17] Thus, the transfer of all the tangible and intangible assets used in a business operation would be a concentration. The Commission has suggested that acquisition of individual brands or licences only may constitute a concentration.[18] Asset swaps and the division of assets upon termination of a joint venture may also constitute concentrations: each part of the transaction will be assessed separately.[19]

8–007 *Temporary joint control treated as an acquisition of sole control* — When joint control is held only during a limited period after conclusion of the transaction, the transaction will be analysed as an immediate acquisition of sole control by the party that will have sole control after the initial period has ended. This temporary transitional period of joint control should not exceed three years.[20] For example, in *Banco Santander/British Telecom*,[21] the Commission considered that BT acquired sole control over the acquired entity, as the rights that Banco Santander enjoyed that gave it control expired three years after the transaction, such that there was no lasting change in control. Similarly, in *Albacom*,[22] the veto rights of BNL were limited to an initial three-year period, such that BT had acquired sole control of the new joint venture.

[16] For cases where the Commission found that a minority shareholding was sufficient to confer sole control given the dispersion of shareholding, see, *e.g.*, Case M.25, *Arjomari-Prioux/Wiggins Teape Appleton*, Commission Decision of December 10, 1990 (acquisition of 39% shareholding as acquisition of sole control); Case M.159, *Mediobanca/Generali*, Commission Decision of December 19, 1991 (12.84% shareholding did not give sole control); Case M.343, *Société Générale de Belgique/Générale de Banque*, Commission Decision of August 3, 1993 (25.96% shareholding gave sole control); Case M.504, *Avesta (III)*, Commission Decision of December 20, 1994 (49.9% shareholding gave sole control); Case M.613, *Jefferson Smurfit Plc/Munksjo AB*, Commission Decision of July 31, 1995 (29.04% shareholding gave sole control). See also Case M.558, *La Rinascente/Cedis Migliarini*, Commission Decision of March 15, 1995 (35.85% shareholding gave sole control); Case M.557, *Alfred C Topfer/Champagne Céréales*, Commission Decision of April 6, 1995 (36% shareholding gave sole control); Case M.1046, *Ameritech/Tele Danmark*, Commission Decision of December 5, 1997 (42% shareholding gave sole control).

[17] Concentration Notice, para.8–004, n.10, para.11. See, for example, Case M.286, *Zürich/MMI*, Commission Decision of April 2, 1993: acquisition of goodwill, premises and the benefit of employment contracts.

[18] *ibid.*

[19] See, *e.g.* Case M.1056, *Stinnes/BTL*, Commission Decision of February 4, 1998 (asset swap) and Case M.197, *Solvay/Laporte*, Commission Decision of March 26, 1992 (dissolution of joint venture by division of assets).

[20] Concentration Notice, para.8–004, n.10, para.38.

[21] Case M.425, *Banco Santander/British Telecom*, Commission Decision of March 28, 1994 and Case M.604, *Albacom*, Commission Decision of September 15, 1995.

[22] Case M.604, *Albacom*, Commission Decision of September 15, 1995.

8–008   Stock options — A stock option does not confer sole control unless it is certain that it will be exercised in the near future: if it is unclear that the option will be exercised, it will not be taken into account until it is actually exercised.[23]

8–009   Acquisition of joint control — Two or more shareholders have joint control if each has the right to veto the strategic commercial behaviour of the joint venture, thereby requiring them to co-operate on major decisions in order to avoid a deadlock situation. Joint control would normally be found if shareholders have a veto right over one or more of the following decisions: (i) approval of the appointment of senior management (*i.e.* CEO, managing director or general manager) and approval of day-to-day management decisions; (ii) approval of the annual budget; (iii) approval of detailed business plans (as opposed to general business plans describing the aims of the joint venture); (iv) investment decisions, except if the level above which consent is required is high or where investment is not an essential feature of the market on which the joint venture is active; and (v) certain decisions that are important given the nature of the market on which the joint venture is active (*e.g.* in relation to the choice of technology or product development in markets on which technology and product innovations are important features).[24]

The levels of individual shareholding are not significant; what is important is that the minority shareholders have veto rights over such matters. Veto rights may be set out in the joint venture's articles of association, in the joint venture agreement, in a shareholders' agreement or due to provisions of national law[25] that give the minority shareholder a blocking minority. Joint control may also exist in the absence of veto rights, if the shareholders agree to vote in the same way[26] or, exceptionally, if the strong common interests of the minority shareholders mean that they would not act against each other in relation to the joint venture.[27] There is no joint control if there are no veto rights, such that any majority of shareholders is sufficient for decisions to be taken. In these cases, the identity of the majority shareholders will vary from time to time, such that there are only "shifting alliances".

By contrast, veto rights that are accorded to minority shareholders in order to protect their financial interest as investors in the joint venture are normally not sufficient to confer joint control on them, as they do not relate to key commercial matters. Such veto rights include: (i) decisions on the scope of activities of the joint venture; (ii) changes to the articles of association or by-laws of the joint venture; (iii) decisions to increase or decrease the joint venture's capital; (iv) decisions on

[23] Case M.259, *British Airways/TAT*, Commission Decision of November 27, 1992; upheld on appeal in Case T–2/93, *Air France v Commission* [1994] II E.C.R. 323.

[24] Concentration Notice, para.8–004, n.10, paras 21–29; see Case M.1875, *Reuters/Equant-Project Proton*, Commission Decision of April 17, 2000.

[25] For example, Case M.70, *BHF-Bank/Crédit Commercial de France*, Commission Decision of May 2, 1996, where the two main shareholders each had 30%, which gave them a blocking minority, such that decisions required both to agree.

[26] Case M.331, *Fletcher Challenge/Methanex*, Commission Decision of March 31, 1993.

[27] Case M.553, *RTL/Veronica/Endemol*, O.J. 1996 L134/21: each parent contributed a different essential element of the joint venture's business, so none would wish it to fail; upheld on appeal in Case T–221/95, *Endemol Entertainment/Commission* [1999] II E.C.R. 1299. Compare with *Television par Satellite*, O.J. 1999 L90/6, where no joint control was found in a strategic joint venture where only a majority vote of four equal shareholders was required, so no joint control was present.

the liquidation, reorganisation or voluntary bankruptcy of the joint venture; (v) approvals of investment that could have an effect on the financial position of the company, the sale or purchase of interests in other businesses, agreements between the joint venture and other shareholders or its management, or other large transactions that do not arise in the ordinary course of business; (vi) decisions on litigation and dispute settlement other than in the ordinary course of business; and (vii) any other decisions that do not relate to the commercial policy and strategy of the joint venture, its budget, or its business plan.[28]

8–010 Operations that are not concentrations — Certain operations are not concentrations, even if they confer control: (i) temporary holdings by financial institutions, acquired with a view to resale; (ii) acquisition of control by a liquidator or similar office holder; and (iii) acquisitions by financial holding companies that will not be involved in the day-to-day management of the under-taking and will vote their shares only to maintain the value of their investment.[29]

8–011 Concentrative and co-operative joint ventures — As originally worded, the Merger Control Regulation made a distinction between "concentrative" joint ventures (*i.e.* ventures that performed on a lasting basis all of the functions of an autonomous economic entity without giving rise to the co-ordination of competitive behaviour of the parents) and "co-operative" joint ventures (*i.e.* ventures that lacked a full-function character, or full-function ventures that gave rise to co-ordination between two or more parents that remained active in the joint venture market or on upstream, downstream or neighbouring markets). As a result, only concentrative joint ventures were concentrations for the purposes of the original Merger Control Regulation. Other joint ventures had to be reviewed under Article 81(1) of the EC Treaty, which led to a degree of legal uncertainty. For example, the "strategic alliance" between BT and MCI, which involved the creation of a joint venture, known as "Concert", to develop and supply new value-added inter-national telecommunications services and the parties taking minority shareholdings in each other, was reviewed under Article 81(1) of the EC Treaty even though the joint venture was a concen-tration. This was because the joint venture led to the co-ordination of the activities of BT and MCI, such that it was co-operative.[30] An individual exemption was subsequently granted under Article 81(3) of the EC Treaty, as the joint venture restricted competition between BT and MCI, but had benefits in that it allowed new services to be developed more quickly than would otherwise have been the case.[31]

The formation of a full-function joint venture such as the Concert joint venture between BT and MCI would now be reviewed under the Merger Control Regulation, as it now applies to all full-function joint ventures. Thus, following its unsuccessful bid for MCI and the dissolution of the BT/MCI joint venture, BT entered into a joint venture with AT&T to provide international services. This was approved under the Merger Control Regulation, following an in-depth investigation

---

[28] Concentration Notice, para.8–004, n.10, paras 21–24.

[29] Merger Control Regulation, para.8–004, n.10, Art.3(5).

[30] Case M.353, *BT/MCI (I)*, Commission Decision of September 13, 1993; the Commission also held that the acquisition of the minority shareholdings in the other party did not confer control, so were also not concentrations.

[31] Case *BT/MCI*, below, para.8–264 *et seq.*

under Article 2(4) of the Merger Control Regulation into the co-operative effects of the formation of the joint venture in markets where BT, AT&T and the joint venture were all present.[32]

The Merger Control Regulation was amended as of March 1, 1998[33] with the result that all full-function joint ventures are now concentrations for the purposes of European merger control, regardless of whether they may lead to co-ordination of competitive behaviour between the parents, which is now assessed under Article 2(4) of the Merger Control Regulation. The question of whether a full-function joint venture is co-operative or concentrative remains relevant to the substantive analysis of the formation of the joint venture.

8–012   Criteria for a joint venture to be full-function — A joint venture will be "full-function" if it performs on a lasting basis all the functions of an autonomous economic entity, *i.e.* if it is an independent player on the market. Three principal elements determine whether a joint venture will be autonomous: (i) the scope of activities and resources contributed to the joint venture; (ii) the extent of vertical relationships between the parents; and (iii) the duration of the joint venture. As shown below, the concept of autonomy is interpreted very broadly by the Commission.

The concept is applied objectively, without reference to the legal form of the joint venture. Although most full-function joint ventures will be legal entities with their own legal personality, a contractual joint venture can be full-function if it meets the necessary criteria and the parent companies effectively withdraw from the market in favour of the joint venture.[34] Finally, as an autonomous entity, a full-function joint venture must act on the market as an independent supplier and purchaser under its own commercial pricing, so that "it will interface directly with its customers and suppliers on the market".[35]

8–013   *Scope of activities and resources contributed to the joint venture* — A joint venture is "full-function" if it performs on a lasting basis all the usual activities or functions performed by other entities operating on the same market. Accordingly, joint ventures that are limited to a single activity (*e.g.* sales and marketing or R&D) are generally not considered to meet this condition, as they only perform one specification within their parents' commercial activities, without access to the market place. To the extent that a joint venture would encompass the production and sale of products (albeit through the parents), it will normally satisfy this criterion.[36]

[32] Case JV.15, *BT/AT&T*, Commission Decision of March 30, 1999.
[33] Regulation 1310/97, O.J. 1997 L180/1.
[34] Case JV.19, *KLM/Alitalia*, Commission Decision of August 11, 1999: although KLM and Alitalia would remain separate legal entities, their contractual joint venture would have effectively taken over and integrated their scheduled passenger and cargo services, which would be jointly operated and marketed.
[35] Case M.1785, *Reuters/Equant-Project Proton*, Commission Decision of April 17, 2000 (full-function joint venture); see also Case *BT/MCI*, below, para.8–264 *et seq.* (joint venture not full-function, as parents would decide its prices and conditions of supply).
[36] Commission Notice on the concept of full-function joint ventures under Council Regulation 4064/89 on the control of concentrations between undertakings, O.J. 1998 C66/1 (the "Full-function Joint Ventures Notice"), para.13.

To be full-function, a joint venture must have its own day-to-day management and access[37] to sufficient financial and other resources, including staff and assets (both tangible and intangible) in order to operate as an independent business on a lasting basis.[38] In a number of cases, the Commission has considered that a joint venture was "full-function" even though only very limited assets and operations were contributed to the joint venture, although this will depend upon the nature of the joint venture's business and will need to be objectively justified. For example, with respect to intellectual property rights, it is not necessary that the rights be assigned to the joint venture but an irrevocable licence to the joint venture for its duration is sufficient.[39] Likewise, in *Cable & Wireless/Schlumberger*, the Commission concluded that a joint venture was full-function despite the fact that: (i) the joint venture would be dependent on the parents' retained employees for technical and sales support services (although the joint venture would eventually recruit its own technical and sales staff); and (ii) the joint venture would have been reliant on its parents for ongoing financing, until it had attained sufficient cash flow to be self-financing.[40] However, a joint venture will not be full-function if it remains heavily dependent on its parents for finance, staff (for example under secondment arrangements), assets and services such as marketing and information technology.[41]

8–014 Vertical relationships between the parents and the joint venture — The Commission does not generally regard a heavy reliance of the joint venture on its parents during the start-up period (*i.e.* a maximum of three years, although occasionally longer) as an obstacle to a finding of autonomy and thus full functionality.[42] Furthermore, long-term or indefinite parent-to-joint-venture vertical relationships are unlikely to raise a significant risk of the joint venture not being full-function unless: (i) they represent most or all of the joint venture's input or output requirements; (ii) to the extent the arrangements involve inputs supplied by the parents, the joint venture adds little or no value before reselling these inputs; (iii) the purchase–supply arrangements involve exclusivity elements that "lock in" the joint venture for a long-term or indefinite duration; and (iv) these "locked-in" arrangements do not reflect normal commercial conditions in the relevant industry.[43] Likewise, a finding of full functionality would not be refused when certain activities of the joint venture (*e.g.* production, distribution of products or purchase of raw materials) are performed by one or more parents on behalf of the joint venture under an agency agreement

---

[37] "Access" does not necessarily mean ownership: see *KLM/Alitalia*: Commission Decision of August 11, 1999.

[38] Full-function Joint Ventures Notice, above, n.36, para.12.

[39] See, for example Case M.149, *Lucas/Eaton*, Commission Decision of December 9, 1991; Case M.360, *Arvin/Sogefi*, Commission Decision of September 23, 1993; M.394, *Mannesmann/RWE /Deutsche Bank*, Commission Decision of December 22, 1993, and Case M.1969, *UTC/Honeywell /i2/My Aircraft.com*, Commission Decision of August 4, 2000.

[40] Case M.532, *Cable & Wireless/Schlumberger*, Commission Decision of December 22, 1994.

[41] Case M.1315, *ENW/Eastern*, Commission Decision of October 15, 1998; see also Case M.722, *Téneo/Merrill Lynch/Bankers Trust*, Commission Decision of April 15, 1996 (inadequate financial resources in relation to its financial needs, insufficient personnel and reliance on parents for technical resources).

[42] Full-function Joint Ventures Notice, para.8–013, n.36, para.14. See Case M.788, *AgrEvo/Maruberi*, Commission Decision of September 13, 1996.

[43] See Hawk and Huser, *European Community Merger Control: A Practitioner's Guide* (Kluwer Law International, 1996), citing a number of Commission decisions applying these principles.

negotiated at arm's length.[44] An important consideration will be whether the joint venture could obtain the requested services from a third party or carry out such activities itself.[45]

In *Telefónica/Terra/Amadeus*, the joint venture was full-function even though 40 per cent of its business came from one parent company.[46] In *Callahan Invest/Kabel Nordrhein Westfalen*,[47] KNW was a joint venture shell company set up to acquire Deutsche Telekom's cable television network in Nordrhein Westfalen in Germany. Although Deutsche Telekom remained a minority non-controlling shareholder in KNW, and KNW had significant commercial links with Deutsche Telekom (for services related to the operation of its cable network, the provision of network infrastructure (such as fibre-optic circuits), and provision of broadcasting service), KNW was regarded as being full-function.

8–015 Duration of the joint venture — To be full-function, a joint venture must operate on a "lasting basis". A fixed minimum term of 5–7 years (subject only to early termination or dissolution in exceptional circumstances, such as a fundamental and irretrievable disagreement between the shareholders) is considered sufficient for the joint venture to be an autonomous economic entity.[48]

2. Jurisdiction Turnover Thresholds

8–016 The Merger Control Regulation only applies to concentrations that have a "Community dimension", *i.e.* those that are of a significance to be reviewed by the Commission, rather than by national competition authorities. The Community dimension of a concentration is calculated on the basis of turnover thresholds laid down in Article 1 of the Merger Control Regulation. Turnover is calculated on the basis of the previous financial year of each participant to the concentration which are referred to as "undertaking concerned".[49] There are two alternative methods of determining a Community dimension:

8–017 First jurisdictional test — Concentrations have a Community dimension and fall within the scope of the Merger Control Regulation if all of the following three conditions are met:

  (i) the combined aggregate worldwide turnover of all the undertakings concerned exceeds €5 billion;

[44] In *BT/MCI* below, para.8–264 *et seq.*, the Commission expressed serious doubts as to whether the joint venture was autonomous of the parties, in particular in light of the fact that the joint venture was required to sell all of its output to its parents, who would not be acting as agents of the joint venture but would instead independently determine the sales terms at which they would each resell the joint venture's output. See, however, Case M.1964, *Planet Internet/Fortis Bank/Mine JV*, Commission Decision of July 10, 2000, where the Commission held that joint venture was full-function despite one of the parent companies being designated as the provider of all operational services of the joint venture, on the basis of arm's length commercial terms.
[45] Case M.686, *Nokia/Autoliv*, Commission Decision of February 5, 1996.
[46] Case M.1812, *Telefónica/Terra/Amadeus*, Commission Decision of April 27, 2000.
[47] Case JV.46, *Callahan Invest/Kabel Nordrhein Westfalen*, Commission Decision of June 19, 2000.
[48] See, *e.g.* Case M.090, *BSN-Nestlé/Cokoladovny*, Commission Decision of February 2, 1992; Case M.152, *Volvo/Atlas*, Commission Decision of January 14, 1992; Case M.293, *British Airways/TAT*, Commission Decision of January 18, 1993; Case M.791, *British Gas Trading/Group 4 Utility Services Ltd*, Commission Decision of October 7, 1996; *Planet Internet/Fortis Bank/Mine JV*, see para.8–014, n.44, above.
[49] See Commission Notice on calculation of turnover under Council Regulation No.4064/89 on the control of concentrations between undertakings (the "Turnover Notice"), O.J. 1998 C/25.

    (ii) the aggregate EU-wide turnover of each of at least two of the undertakings concerned exceeds €250 million; and

   (iii) each of the undertakings concerned did not achieve more than two-thirds of its aggregate EU-wide turnover within one and the same Member State.[50]

The worldwide turnover threshold gives an indication of the overall size of the transaction whilst the EU-wide turnover ensures that the transaction will have a connection with the EU. The "two-thirds" rule ensures that transactions that nevertheless have a mainly national effect are not reviewed by the Commission.

8–018   Second jurisdictional test — The scope of application of the Merger Control Regulation was extended as of March 1, 1998 to apply to concentrations that do not meet the thresholds contained in the first turnover test but meet the following conditions:

    (i) the combined aggregate worldwide turnover of the undertakings concerned exceeds €2.5 billion;

   (ii) the aggregate EU-wide turnover of each of at least two of the undertakings concerned exceeds €100 million;

  (iii) in each of at least three Member States, (a) the combined turnover of all the undertakings concerned exceeds €100 million, and (b) the turnover of each of at least two of the undertakings concerned exceeds €25 million; and

  (iv) each of the undertakings concerned did not achieve more than two-thirds of its aggregate EU-wide turnover within one and the same Member State.[51]

8–019   Calculation of turnover — The concept of "turnover" refers to the amounts derived by the companies involved in the concentration in the preceding financial year from the sale of products and the provision of services falling within their ordinary activities, after deduction of sales rebates and of value added tax and other taxes directly related to turnover.[52] This excludes intra-group transactions. The aggregate turnover of an undertaking concerned is calculated by adding the respective turnovers of the following:

    (i) the undertaking concerned;

   (ii) any undertaking controlled, directly or indirectly, by the undertaking concerned;

  (iii) any undertaking which controls, directly or indirectly, the undertaking concerned; and

---

[50] Merger Control Regulation, para.8–002, n.4, Art.1(2).

[51] *ibid.*, Art.1(3).

[52] *ibid.*, Art.5(1). Special rules apply to calculating the turnover of banks, credit and other financial institutions and insurance undertakings, O.J. 1998 C66/25: Merger Control Regulation, Art.5(3). See also "Turnover Notice", cited at para.8–016, n.49, above.

(iv) any undertaking controlled by undertakings that control, directly or indirectly, the undertaking concerned.[53]

However, in the case of an acquisition of sole control of parts of a business, only the turnover related to the acquired parts of the seller are taken into account with regard to the seller.[54]

8–020 Geographic allocation of turnover — The application of the jurisdictional thresholds requires the turnover of the undertakings concerned to be allocated geographically, in particular between the EEA Member States. As a general principle, turnover must be attributed to the place where the customer is located.[55] This is in most cases the place where the deal was made, where the turnover for the supplier in question was generated and where competition with alternative suppliers took place. This is the so-called "point of delivery" rule. The application of this rule in the telecommunications sector is problematic in relation to the allocation of revenues from long-distance calls and the supply of other cross-border services. Should the turnover be allocated totally to the country where the call originates, totally to the country where the call terminates or allocated between both countries? Likewise, the same issue arises in relation to payments received by national telecommunications operators from other telecommunications operators for terminating long-distance calls originating in other countries. In 1994, in a draft notice on the calculation of turnover, the Commission generally considered that two different approaches could be taken in the context of a specific transaction. First, the allocation of turnover could focus on where competition takes place, rather than on where the service is provided or consumed by the consumer. Under this approach, turnover earned from customers would be allocated according to where the service is ordered, which is: (i) for services with a variable tariff (*e.g.* standard voice telephony, mobile telephony and calling cards), the caller's location when making the call regardless of to where the call is being made or where that call is subsequently billed to a customer; (ii) for services with a fixed tariff (*e.g.* line rental, subscription charges for mobile telephones, leased lines and corporate direct services), in case of individual subscribers their private residence and in case of businesses the location of the relevant decision-making entity within the enterprise. Alternatively, the allocation of turnover could focus on where the service is provided. Under this approach, turnover earned from customers would be allocated: (i) for services with a variable tariff, according to the location of the person being called; and (ii) for services with a fixed tariff, in case of individual subscribers according to their private residence and in case of businesses according to the location of the relevant decision-making entity within the enterprise.[56]

---

[53] Merger Control Regulation, para.8–002, n.4, Art.5(4).

[54] *ibid.*, Art.5(2).

[55] *ibid.*, Art.5(2); see also Turnover Notice, para.8–016, n.49, paras 45–48.

[56] In Case M.1741, *WorldCom/MCI*, below, para.8–088 *et seq.*, the Commission acknowledged these various possible methods of geographically allocating revenue earned by telephone companies but failed to take a definitive position as to the most appropriate method, as the concentration satisfied the turnover thresholds of the Merger Control Regulation under all the different methods considered. In Case M.1767, *AT&T/IBM/ INTESA*, Commission Decision of December 20, 1999, the Commission adopted exactly the same approach. See also Case M.366, *Alcatel/STC*, Commission Decision of September 13, 1993, where the Commission determined that the turnover of a submarine telecommunications systems operator was to be allocated to the place at which its investors were established.

3. Procedural Aspects

The procedural aspects of EC merger control law are to be found both in the Merger Control Regulation itself and in the Implementing Regulation.[57]

8–021 Filing obligation — Concentrations with a Community dimension must be notified to the Commission within one week after the conclusion of the agreement, the announcement of a public bid, or the acquisition of a controlling interest, whichever occurs first.[58] Only the conclusion of legally binding agreements triggers the obligation to notify.[59] An agreement is considered to be legally binding if it cannot be unilaterally rescinded by either party. An agreement would be considered sufficiently binding even though it is subject to conditions, provided that such conditions do not entirely depend on the willingness of the parties. Agreements, the closing of which is subject to customary conditions (*e.g.* shareholder, court or regulatory approvals), satisfy this test.

If the reform of the Merger Control Regulation as proposed by the Commission is adopted,[60] it will be possible to make a notification prior to the conclusion of a legally binding agreement and the requirement that concentrations be notified to the Commission within a week of the conclusion of such an agreement would be abolished.

The filing obligation falls upon the party (or parties) that acquire control (or joint control) under the concentration, *i.e.* all parties to a merger or joint venture, all bidders in a joint bid situation and in other cases the acquiring party.[61]

8–022 Notification form — Notifications of concentrations must be made on Form CO.[62] This form requires the parties to furnish information on the transaction and the affected markets. A "short form" notification, requiring substantially less information, may be made for joint ventures where the EEA turnover and assets of the joint venture are each below €100 million.[63] Even when these conditions are not met, where a concentration does not raise any competition concerns,

---

[57] Commission Regulation (EC) No.447/98 of March 1, 1998 on the notifications, time limits and hearings provided for in Council Regulation (EEC) No.4064/89 on the control of concentrations between undertakings, O.J. 1998 L61/1.

[58] Merger Control Regulation, para.8–002, n.4, Art.4(1).

[59] Case M.23, *ICI/Tioxide*, Commission Decision of November 28, 1991.

[60] See above, para.8–003.

[61] Merger Control Regulation, para.8–002, n.4, Art.4(2).

[62] Regulation 447/98 cited, above, at n.57, Art.2.

[63] Commission Notice on a simplified procedure for treatment of certain concentrations under Council Regulation (EEC) No.4084/89, O.J. 2000 C217/32. The Commission has introduced a simplified procedure which applies to certain concentrations that do not raise competition concerns. Under this procedure, when all necessary conditions are met, the Commission will adopt a short-form clearance decision within one month from the date of the notification without carrying out a detailed initial investigation. Pursuant to the Commission's Notice on a simplified procedure for treatment of certain concentrations, eligible concentrations include:

> (i) the acquisition of joint control over a joint venture, provided that the joint venture has no or negligible activities within the EEA (*i.e.* the EEA turnover of the joint venture and/or the activities contributed is less than €100 million and the total value of assets transferred to the joint venture is less than €100 million);

the Commission may waive the parties' obligations to submit detailed information in response to specific sections of Form CO.

8–023 Suspension obligation — The implementation of a concentration with a Community dimension may not take place until it has been notified and clearance has been received from the Commission.[64] Nevertheless, in the case of public bids, shares in the target company may be acquired, provided that prior to approval by the Commission the bidder does not exercise the voting rights, except where necessary to maintain the value of the investments and with the permission of the Commission.[65] In other situations, the Commission may, upon a reasoned request, grant a derogation from the suspension obligation, where this is necessary to prevent serious damage to one or more of the parties or a third party, thereby taking account of the effect on competition. The Commission takes a restrictive approach in granting derogations and generally requires a strong degree of potential damage.[66] A failure to comply with the suspension obligation can be punished with fines of up to 10 per cent of the turnover of the undertakings concerned, and the transaction is void unless subsequently notified and approved.[67]

8–024 Commission investigation — The Commission has an initial one-month period (Phase I)[68] to decide either to approve the transaction (either unconditionally or subject to conditions following an offer of remedies made by the parties)[69] or to open an in-depth (Phase II) investigation

(ii) a merger or an acquisition of sole or joint control, provided that none of the parties to the concentration are engaged in business activities in the same product market and/or in the same geographic market, or in a product market which is upstream or downstream of a product market in which another party is engaged;

(iii) a merger or an acquisition of sole or joint control, and two or more of the parties to the concentration are engaged in business activities:

(a) in the same product and geographic market;

(b) in a product market upstream or downstream of a product market;

provided that their combined market share does not exceed 15% for horizontal relationships and 25% for vertical relationships.

[64] Merger Control Regulation, para.8–002, n.4, Art.7(1).

[65] *ibid.*, Art.7(3).

[66] In Case M.042, *Alcatel/Telettra*, Commission Decision of April 12, 1991, O.J. 1991 L122/48, the Commission granted an Art.7(4) derogation soon after the opening of a Phase II investigation on the grounds that the parties had offered satisfactory remedies to address the Commission's concerns. In Case JV.2, *ENEL/ FT/DT (Wind)*, Commission Decision of June 22, 1998 the Commission granted a derogation in order to enable the joint venture to meet the deadlines and obligations imposed as a result of the licences granted by the Italian authorities and to enable it to start building its network. Similar derogations were granted in Case M.1822, *Mobil/JV Dissolution*, Commission Decision, February 2, 2000, and Case M.2008, *AOM/Air Liberté/ Air Littoral*, Commission Decision of March 24, 2000, where the Commission refused to grant the derogation requested by France Télécom, which wanted to acquire full control of Global One by acquiring Deutsche Telekom's shareholding in the joint venture prior to approval, on the grounds that Deutsche Telekom's continued representation at various levels of Global One management was hindering France Télécom's ability to properly manage Global One, the shareholders being in dispute. The Commission refused the derogation on the basis that France Télécom had not shown to what extent its situation was different from the situation of any other party acquiring a new business and who wanted control over it as soon as practicable.

[67] Merger Control Regulation, para.8–002, n.4, Arts 7(5) and 14(2)(b).

[68] *ibid.*, Art.10(1); Implementing Regulation, Art.6(4).

[69] *ibid.*, Art.6(1)(b) and (2). If the Commission considers that the notified transaction is not a concentration and/or does not have a Community dimension it will adopt a decision to this effect: *ibid.*, Art.6(1)(a).

if it has serious doubt regarding the competitive impact of the transaction.[70] The initial one-month period is extended to six weeks if the parties offer undertakings, if they modify the notified transaction in order to obtain clearance, or if a Member State requests a reference back under Article 9 of the Merger Control Regulation.[71] When the Commission decides to open an in-depth (Phase II) investigation, it must take a final decision within a maximum four months of the decision to initiate the Phase II.[72]

4. Substantive Assessment

All concentrations, including full-function joint ventures, are appraised by the Commission under Article 2 of the Merger Control Regulation. In the cases of joint ventures, this includes an appraisal of the co-ordination effects of the joint venture as well as its concentrative effects.

8–025 All concentrations: creation or strengthening of a dominant position — Concentrations will be prohibited if they create or strengthen a dominant position as a result of which competition would be significantly impeded in the common market or a substantial part of it.[73] The Commission can apply this test to determine not only whether the concentration would result in the creation or strengthening of single-firm dominance but also whether it would create or strengthen a joint or collective dominant position jointly held by two or more undertakings in duopolistic or oligopolistic markets.[74]

However, in order to establish the creation or strengthening of a joint or collective dominant position, the Commission must produce cogent evidence that this would be the direct, immediate and lasting effect of the concentration.[75] According to the Court of First Instance, it is necessary to show that members of the oligopoly are able to adopt the same policy, that they will be deterred from departing from that policy (due to identified "retaliation" mechanisms) and that competitors and customers cannot constrain this parallel behaviour.[76] Adverse effects on competition may

---

[70] *ibid.*, Art.6(1)(c).

[71] *ibid.*, Art.10(1).

[72] If the reform of the Merger Control Regulation as proposed by the Commission is adopted (see above, para.8–003), three weeks would be added to the timetable of an in-depth (Phase II) investigation following the submission of an offer of commitments by the parties. Furthermore, with the agreement of the parties, up to four weeks could be added for the purpose of ensuring a thorough investigation.

[73] Merger Control Regulation, para.8–002, n.4, Art.2(3).

[74] Cases C–68/94 and C–30/95, *France v Commission (Kali & Salz)* [1998] I E.C.R. 1375; Case T–102/96, *Gencor v Commission* [1999] II E.C.R. 879 and Case T–342/99, *Airtours v Commission* [2002] II E.C.R. 2585. See recently, Case M.2810, *Deloitte & Touche/Andersen UK*, Commission Decision of May 29, 2002; Case M.2816, *Ernst & Young France/Andersen France*, Commission Decision of August 5, 2002. See also above, para.6–025. The proposal for a revision of the Merger Control Regulation adopted by the Commission in December 2002 (see above, para.8–003) will clarify the substantive standard, by making it clear, in particular, that the Merger Control Regulation applies to concentrations leading to a joint or collective dominant position in oligopolistic markets, and to situations where a concentration results in "unilateral effects" on competition, owing to the relevant market in question being oligopolistic. The draft Commission Notice on horizontal mergers (see above, para.8–003) aims to give further guidance on to how the Commission will apply the dominance test in oligopolistic markets.

[75] Case T–342/99, *Airtours/Commission* [2002] II E.C.R. 2585.

[76] *ibid.*

result from horizontal, vertical or conglomerate effects upon competition, although conglomerate mergers will only rarely be anti-competitive.[77]

The issue of whether a concentration would result in the creation or strengthening of a dominant position will depend to a large extent on the product and geographic market definition adopted by the Commission.[78] As with the assessment of dominance under Article 82 of the EC Treaty,[79] the combined market shares of the parties following implementation of the concentration play a central role in determining the competitive impact of a transaction. There is a presumption that market shares below 25 per cent cannot give rise to a single-firm dominant position.[80] Combined market shares in excess of 40 per cent will normally raise concerns that a single-firm dominance is created and often lead to an in-depth (Phase II) investigation, especially if competitors and customers strongly object to the transaction, as the views of competitors and customers play an important role in the Commission's assessment. Nevertheless, high market shares post-merger do not necessarily result in the prohibition of the concentration if other factors indicate the existence of continued significant competitive pressure,[81-82] as market shares are only one factor in analysing if a concentration would create or strengthen a dominant position. Other relevant factors include the extent of the increase in market share, the extent of competition from other players and whether there is likely to be competition from potential market entrants.

8-026   Full-function joint ventures must be assessed to see not only if they lead to the creation or strengthening of a dominant position but also if they have the object or effect of co-ordinating the competitive behaviour of the undertakings that remain independent.[83] This assessment is made using the criteria of Article 81(1) and (3) of the EC Treaty.[84] This test was introduced as part of the 1998 reform of the Merger Control Regulation, which brought all full-function joint ventures under its scope, including those that had co-operative effects and had hitherto been excluded from it. It applies to the co-ordination of the competitive behaviour of the parents, either with each other and/or with the joint venture. Even if the formation of the joint venture raises no dominance concerns, the concentration will be prohibited if it has such anti-competitive effects and they are appreciable unless the exemption criteria laid down in Article 81(3) of the EC Treaty are applicable.

Many of the co-operative full-function joint ventures notified under the Merger Control Regulation since its amendment concern the communications sector.[85] As the Commission is now

[77] Cases T–5 and 80/02, *Tetra Laval/Commission*, judgment of October 25, 2002, not yet reported.
[78] On market definition, see Chap.V.
[79] See para.6–013 *et seq.*
[80] Merger Control Regulation, para.8–002, n.4, Recital 15.
[81-82] For example, Case M.222, *Mannesmann/Hoesch*, Commission Decision of November 12, 1993 (no dominance with a 70% market share, owing to significant potential competition); Case M.781, *Schering/Gene-Jenapharm* (no dominance with a 60% market share, owing to the innovative nature of the products and demand mobility).
[83] Merger Control Regulation, para.8–002, n.4, Art.2(4).
[84] *ibid.*, on Art.81(1) and (3) of the EC Treaty, see para.4–001 *et seq.* and 4–004 *et seq.*
[85] As of December 31, 2002, out of the 35 decisions taken by the Commission regarding co-operative full-function joint ventures reviewed under the Merger Control Regulation, 18 were telecommunications or broadcasting-related transactions. Case JV.1, *Telia/Telenor/Schibsted*, Commission Decision of May 27, 1998; Case JV.5, *Cegetel/Canal + /AOL/Bertelsmann*, Commission Decision of May 27, 1998; Case JV.2, *Enel/FT/*

required to review the elements of co-operation within the strict deadlines laid down by the Merger Control Regulation, the Commission has tended to review the effects of the contemplated co-operation under criteria laid down by Article 81(1) of the EC Treaty, rather than consider whether it complies with the criteria for an exemption under Article 81(3) of the EC Treaty. From this practice, it results that a co-operation would be caught by Article 81(1) of the EC Treaty if three conditions are fulfilled: (i) there is a sufficient probability of co-ordination[86]; (ii) there is a causal link between the creation of the joint venture and the co-ordination of independent competitive behaviour[87];

DT (Wind), Commission Decision of June 22, 1998; Case JV.3, *BT/Airtel*, Commission Decision of July 8, 1998; Case JV.6, *Ericsson/Nokia/Psion*, Commission Decision of August 11, 1998; Case JV.4, *Viag/Orange UK*, Commission Decision of August 11, 1998; Case JV.7, *Telia/Sonera/Lietuvos Telekomas*, Commission Decision of August 14, 1998; Case JV.9, *Telia/Sonera/Motorola/Omnitel*, Commission Decision of August 18, 1998; Case JV.11, *@Home Benelux*, Commission Decision of September 15, 1998; Case JV.8, *Deutsche Telekom/Springer/Holtzbrink/Infoseek*, Commission Decision of September 28, 1998; Case JV.12, *Ericsson/ Nokia/Psion/Motorola*, Commission Decision of December 22, 1998; Case JV.15, *BT/AT&T*, Commission Decision of March 30, 1999; Case JV.16, *Bertelsmann/Viag/Game Channel*, Commission Decision of May 5, 1999; Case JV.17, *Mannesmann/Bell Atlantic/OPI*, Commission Decision of May 21, 1999; Case JV.26, *Freecom/Dangaard*, Commission Decision of December 1, 1999; Case JV.24, *Bertelsmann/Planeta/BOL Spain*, Commission Decision of December 3, 1999; Case M.1883, *NEC/Mitsubishi*, Commission Decision of April 3, 2000; Case JV.37, *BSkyB/KirchPayTV*, Commission Decision of March 21, 2000; Case M.1741, *WorldCom/ Sprint*, Commission Decision of June 28, 2000; Case M.2025, *GE Capital/BTPS/MEPC*, Commission Decision of July 27, 2000; Case M.2053, *Telenor/Bell South/Sonofon*, Commission Decision of August 4, 2000; Case M.1863, *Vodafone/BT/Airtel/JV*, Commission Decision of December 18, 2000; Case M.2211, *Universal Studio Networks/De Facto 829 (NTL)/Studio Cannel Ltd*, Commission Decision of December 20, 2000; Case M.2565, *PPC/WIND/JV*, Commission Decision of November 28, 2001; Case M.2250, *Mezzo/ Muzzik*, Commission Decision of December 6, 2001, and Case M.2851, *Intracom/Siemens/STI*, Commission Decision of February 10, 2003.

[86] See Case M.1863, *Vodafone/BT/Airtel/JV*, Commission Decision of December 18, 2000: it was not possible to determine "with the required degree of certainty" that Vodafone and BT (which acquired joint control of the Spanish mobile operator Airtel under the concentration) would have co-ordinated their activities in other markets, *e.g.* mobile markets outside of Spain, given that they had not done so in the past despite their existing shareholdings in Airtel.

[87] In Case *ENEL/FT/DT (Wind)*, below, para.8–083 *et seq.*, the Commission considered that there was no clear evidence that the joint venture had the object of restricting competition and that it was not possible to demonstrate that the formation of Wind would have resulted in the co-ordination of the behaviour of France Télécom and Deutsche Telekom. Indeed, FT and DT already operated a joint venture, Global One, through which they co-operated. Accordingly, the creation of a joint venture in Italy did not have a causal link to their co-operation in other markets that led to a restriction of competition between them. Likewise, in Case JV.4, *Viag/Orange UK*, Commission Decision of August 11, 1998, the Commission found that there was no causal link between the formation of a joint venture to provide fixed and mobile telephony services in Switzerland and a risk of co-ordination between the parents in Austria, because they were already co-operating in that manner through another joint venture. In Case *Universal Studio Networks/De Facto 829 (NTL)/Studio Cannel Ltd*, below, para.8–233 *et seq.*, the Commission concluded that co-ordination between Universal and NTL (the joint venture parents) was unlikely, given that they did not have significant activities on the same market as the joint venture and were not active on the same upstream, downstream or neighbouring markets. Furthermore, any attempt by Universal to leverage its presence in the upstream market for the supply of programming would not result from any co-ordination of its activities with NTL, but would be the result of the vertical integration arising from its entry into the downstream market for the wholesale supply of pay-TV channels to pay-TV operators, which in any event would not have been appreciable. However, in Case *BT/AT&T*, below, para.8–092 *et seq.*, the Commission considered that the formation of the joint venture would have resulted in the co-ordination of the activities of BT (the dominant UK telecommunications operator) and AT&T (which had a UK subsidiary, ACC, exercising, indirectly, joint control in Telewest, a UK cable television operator and

(iii) the effects of the co-ordination are sufficiently appreciable.[88] The co-ordination may be horizontal[89] or vertical.[90]

8–027 From the Commission's existing decision practice under Article 2(4) of the Merger Control Regulation, the risk of co-ordination of independent activities can arise if both parents have significant competing activities in the joint venture's markets or in upstream or downstream or neighbouring markets or if the joint venture's parents retain independent competitive activities in non-related markets.

If the parents both remain active in neighbouring, upstream or downstream markets an appreciable effect on competition from co-operation may arise if: (i) the joint venture's market and the markets in which the parents are active are technically or commercially related, with the result that co-ordination via the joint venture could be expected to provide the parents with technical or marketing information relevant to the markets on which they remain competitors; (ii) the joint venture's activities are not peripheral to the parents' core business[91]; and (iii) the parents' combined market shares in the markets on which they are independently active is not insignificant.[92]

a principal competitor to BT). Even though the joint venture itself raised no dominance concerns, a Phase II investigation was launched and the joint venture was approved only after AT&T agreed to sell ACC and create "firewalls" to prevent it from influencing Telewest. This was required because the effects of co-ordination would have been appreciable, given the market share of BT. See also Case *BSkyB/KirchPayTV*, below, para.8–196 *et seq.*, and Case JV.57, *TPS*, Commission Decision of April 30, 2002, O.J. 2002 C137/28.

[88] In Case *Telia/Telenor/Schibsted*, below, para.8–078 *et seq.*, the Commission considered that, given the low market shares of the parents on the market for website production, the effects of any co-ordination of the competitive behaviour of the parents would not be appreciable. In Case M.1327, *NC/Canal+/CDPQ/Bank America*, Commission Decision of December 3, 1998, a joint venture (Numericable) between Canal+, CDPQ and Bank America in France and Spain, the Commission considered that there was a risk that Canal+, a pay-TV operator and owner of a larger number of programme rights, would discriminate in favour of a Spanish cable operator (Cableuropa) controlled by its partners in Numericable and that this would have had an adverse effect upon competing cable operators, who would have been denied access to Canal+ content. Accordingly, the joint venture had to be modified with undertakings by Canal+ to negotiate, in a fair and non-discriminatory fashion, licensing agreements and film distribution rights with other Spanish cable operators in order for the Commission to approve it. See also Case M.2025, *GE Capital/BTPS/MEP*, Commission Decision of July 27, 2000; Case M.2053, *Telenor/Bell South/Sonofon*, Commission Decision of August 4, 2000; and Case M.2565, *PPC/WIND/JV*, Commission Decision of November 28, 2001.

[89] *e.g. NC/BT/AT&T*, below, para.8–092 *et seq.*

[90] *e.g. Canal+/CDPQ/Bank America*, below, para.8–191 *et seq.*

[91] See Case JV.7, *Telia/Sonera/Lietuvos Telekomas*, Commission Decision of August 14, 1998 and Case JV.9, *Telia/Sonera/Motorola/UAB Omnitel*, Commission Decision of August 18, 1998; where the parents retained a significant share of their home fixed telephony markets, but the Lithuanian fixed line and mobile telecommunications markets on which the two joint ventures were active were too small to raise a risk of co-ordination in the Swedish and Finnish markets.

[92] Based on the Commission's decision practice, this test would likely be satisfied if the parents' combined market share is more than 15%; see Case JV.7, *Telia/Sonera/Lietuvos Telekomas*, Commission Decision of August 14, 1998; Case JV.9, *Telia/Sonera/Motorola/UAB Omnitel*, Commission Decision of August 18, 1998; Case *ENEL/FT/DT (Wind)*, below, para.8–079 *et seq.*; *Mezzo/Muzzik*, below, para.8–246 *et seq.*, and Case M.2565, *PPC/WIND/JV*, Commission Decision of November 28, 2001.

5. Enforcement

8–028 **Prohibition** — If, after a Phase II investigation, the Commission finds that a concentration does not meet the above-mentioned compatibility standard, it may prohibit its consummation.[93] If the transaction has already been implemented (whether in contravention of the suspension obligation, or pursuant to a derogation), the Commission must order the divestment of assets, legal entities or operations, cessation of joint control or "any other action that may be appropriate in order to restore conditions of effective competition".[94] As of March 1, 2003, out of the 18 prohibition decisions adopted since the entry into force of the Merger Control Regulation on September 21, 1990, five have concerned the broadcasting sector[95] and one the telecommunications sector.[96]

8–029 **Approval subject to conditions** — In many cases, the Commission has approved concentrations subject to conditions and obligations that give effect to commitments that the parties have offered to address the competition concerns identified by the Commission. Normally, remedies will be of a structural nature (*e.g.* divestiture of assets/operations).[97] In certain cases, however, the Commission has also accepted behavioural remedies, sometimes alone and otherwise in combination with structural remedies.[98] The Commission's stated preference is for structural remedies given

[93] Merger Control Regulation, para.8–002, n.4, Art.8(3).

[94] *ibid.*, Art.8(4).

[95] Case M.469, *MSG*, Commission Decision of November 9, 1994, O.J. 1994 L364/1; Case M.490, *Nordic Satellite Distribution*, Commission Decision of July 19, 1995, O.J. 1995 L53/20; Case M.553, *RTL/Veronica/Endemol*, Commission Decision of September 20, 1995, O.J. 1996 L134/32; Case M.1027, *Deutsche Telekom/BetaResearch*, Commission Decision of May 27, 1998, O.J. 1999 L53/31; and Case M.993, *Bertelsmann/Kirch/Premiere*, Commission Decision of May 27, 1998, O.J. 1999 L53/1.

[96] Case M.1741, *WorldCom/Sprint*, Commission Decision of June 28, 2000, O.J. 2000 C355/35.

[97] See *WorldCom/MCI*, below, para.8–088 *et seq.*, where the Commission required that MCI divest its internet business as a condition of approval. See also Case M.1795, *Vodafone Airtouch/Mannesmann*, Commission Decision of April 12, 2000, O.J. 2000 C141/19 (divestment of Mannesmann's UK mobile operation, Orange); Case M.2016, *France Télécom/Orange*, Commission Decision of August 11, 2000, O.J. 2000 C261/6 (divestment of Orange's interests in a Belgian mobile operator); Case M.2050, *Vivendi/Canal+/Seagram*, Commission Decision of October 13, 2000, O.J. 2000 C311/3 (divestment of Vivendi's shareholding in BSkyB, which had links with competing studios, plus various behavioural obligations); Case M.2300, *YLE/TDF/Digita/JV*, Commission Decision of June 26, 2001, O.J. 2001 C272/15 (divestment of TDF's existing subsidiary that was the principal competitor to Digita on the Finnish markets for the distribution and transmission of radio programmes); Case M.2574, *Pirelli/Olivetti/Telecom Italia*, Commission Decision of September 20, 2001, O.J. 2001 C325/12 (divestment by Edizione of its interests in Blu (a competitor to Telecom Italia in the Italian mobile market) and Autostrade (a competitor to Telecom Italia in the Italian fixed network transmission capacity market)); Case M.2803, *Telia/Sonera*, Commission Decision of July 10, 2002, O.J. 2002 C201/19 (divestment of Telia's mobile operations in Finland and its cable television operations in Sweden, the latter to remedy the vertical effects on competition in Finland by combining Sonera with the principal alternative fixed network in Sweden for terminating calls from Finland). The Commission has adopted a Notice on commitments setting out general principles for determining commitments appropriate to resolve competitive concerns in proceedings under the Merger Control Regulation: Commission Notice on remedies acceptable under Council Regulation (EEC) No.4064/89 and under Commission Regulation (EC) No.447/98 (the "Remedies Notice"), O.J. 2001 C68/3.

[98] Case M.190, *Nestlé/Perrier*, Commission Decision of July 22, 1992, O.J. 1992 L356/1, where the Commission, in addition to requiring the divestiture of a number of bottled water brands, required Nestlé to refrain

that concentrations have a structural effect on competition.[99] Remedies may be proposed by the parties and conditions and obligations may be imposed by the Commission, as a condition for clearance, in both of Phase I and/or Phase II proceedings.

8–030 Fines — The Commission may impose fines from €1,000 to €50,000 on an undertaking that, intentionally or negligently: (i) fails to notify a concentration with a Community dimension; (ii) supplies incorrect or misleading information in a notification or in response to a request for information from the Commission; and (iii) produces incomplete documents or refuses to submit to an investigation ordered by the Commission.[1] In addition, an undertaking may be fined up to 10 per cent of the aggregate worldwide turnover of the group to which it belongs, if it intentionally or negligently: (i) fails to comply with any conditions or commitments imposed by the Commission as a condition for clearance; (ii) consummates a transaction before the expiry of the suspension obligation; and (iii) consummates a concentration that has been prohibited by the Commission or, having done so, fails to take measures ordered by the Commission to restore effective competition.[2] Periodic penalty payments of up to €25,000 per day may be imposed for failures to provide information requested by the Commission or to submit to an investigation ordered by the Commission.[3] Periodic penalty payments of up to €100,000 may be imposed for each day of delay in complying with conditions attached to a derogation decision, an approval decision taken at the end of Phase II or a decision taken to restore effective competition.[4] Fines and penalty payments imposed to date have generally been modest.[5]

from directly or indirectly providing any information less than one year old regarding its sales volumes to any trade association or other entity which would be likely to make it available to other competitors, in order to reduce the possibility of joint dominance. See also Case *NC/Canal+/CDPQ/BankAmerica*, below, para.8–191 *et seq.* (obligation of Canal+ to license content to all Spanish cable television networks on a fair and non-discriminatory basis in accordance with Spanish and EC Competition law); Case M.1838, *BT/Esat*, Commission Decision of March 27, 2000, O.J. 2000 C341/3 (obligation to allow a contractual conterparty (Global One) to terminate a distribution agreement with Esat and for BT not to renew certain distribution agreements); Case *BSkyB/KirchPay TV*, below, para.8–196 *et seq.* (obligations on the parties to allow providers of competing digital interactive television platforms access to KirchPayTV's digital pay-TV services and to negotiate simulcrypt agreements); Case M.1747, *Telekom Austria/Libro*, Commission Decision of February 28, 2000, O.J. 2000 C108/8; and Case *Telia/Sonera*, below, para.8–129 *et seq.* (commitment to effect legal separation of the parties' fixed and mobile networks and services businesses in Finland and Sweden).

[99] See Remedies Notice, para.8–029, n.97, at para.13. See also Case T–102/96, *Gencor/Commission* [1997] II E.C.R. 753. The Commission must also consider behavioural and other non-structural commitments where they would resolve the competition concerns raised by a concentration. See Cases T–5 and 80/02, *Tetra Laval/Commission*, CFI Judgment of October 25, 2002, not yet reported.

[1] Merger Control Regulation, para.8–002, n.4, Art.14(1).

[2] *ibid.*, Art.14(2).

[3] *ibid.*, Art.15(1).

[4] *ibid.*, Art.15(2).

[5] For example, €33,000 on Samsung for a failure to notify a concentration (*Samsung*, DGIV Newsletter 1998–2, p.71); periodic penalty payments of €6,000 per month on AP Møller for a failure to notify three concentrations (Case M.969, *AP Møller*, O.J. 1999 L183/29); a fine of €50,000 on each of Sanofi and Synthélabo for failure to disclose a material overlap that was brought to the Commission's attention by third parties after approval had initially been given (Case M.1397, *Sanofi-Synthélabo*, O.J. 2000 L95/34: the approval decision was also revoked); and two fines on Deutsche Post of €50,000 each for the deliberate supply of incorrect and misleading information (*Deutsche Post*, XXIXth Report on Competition Policy (1991), p.75).

6. Ancillary Restrictions

8–031 Introduction — The contractual arrangements giving effect to most concentrations, except for most public bids, will contain contractual provisions that impose restrictions on the parties, for example non-compete and non-solicitation obligations. Separate contracts may also be entered into, for example supply and purchase agreements and distribution agreements and intellectual property licences. These agreements may restrict the commercial freedom of the parties and, therefore, in principle fall within Article 81(1) and/or Article 82 of the EC Treaty. However, if they are directly related to and necessary for the implementation of the concentration, they will fall outside of Article 81(1) and/or Article 82 of the EC Treaty on the basis that without them the concentration could not have been implemented at all, or only at substantially higher cost, with greater uncertainty and/or with greater difficulty.[6] Such restrictions are known as "ancillary restrictions".

The Commission has recently changed its policy in respect to ancillary restrictions.[7] Under the previous policy,[8] the Commission would approve ancillary restrictions (if they met the relevant criteria) at the same time as approving the concentration under the Merger Control Regulation, with the result that such restrictions did not need to be subsequently notified under Article 81 of the EC Treaty or national competition rules. Under the 2001 Ancillary Restraints Notice, the Commission stated that it would no longer take a position, as part of its review of concentrations, on whether a restriction was ancillary. It considered that if a restraint is ancillary, it falls outside of the scope of Article 81(1) of the EC Treaty without the need for an action on its part and that the assessment of whether restraints are ancillary to the concentration (or are covered by a relevant block exemption or fall under Article 81 of the EC Treaty) is the sole responsibility of the parties to the concentration, and disputes as to whether restrictions are ancillary fall under the jurisdiction of national courts.[9] The 2001 Notice reflects the Commission's existing practice on the interpretation of the ancillary restraints doctrine and provides the parties with guidance. However, the Court of First Instance has ruled that the Commission's new practice was incorrect. According to the Court, the Merger Control Regulation applies to restraints that were directly related to, and necessary for, a concentration, such that the Commission is obliged as part of its decision to state whether a restraint was ancillary (or not) to a concentration when these restraints are notified as part of the concentration.[10] Furthermore, the Court ruled that the Commission has exclusive competence to rule on whether restraints are ancillary.

8–032 Non-compete and non-solicitation obligations — With respect to concentrations involving an acquisition of sole control, a non-compete obligation accepted by the seller of up to three years' duration is ancillary if there is a transfer of goodwill and know-how. In the case of a transfer of goodwill, only a two-year maximum duration is accepted, unless special circumstances justify a

---

[6] Case 42/84, *Remia/Commission* (1985) E.C.R. 2545 (decided under Art.81(1) of the EC Treaty, as pre-dates the Merger Control Regulation).

[7] Commission Notice on restrictions directly related and necessary to concentrations, O.J. 2001, C188/05.

[8] Commission Notice regarding restrictions ancillary to concentrations, O.J. 1990 C203/5.

[9] *ibid.*

[10] Case T–251/00, *Lagardère and Canal+ v Commission*, Judgment of November 20, 2002, not yet reported.

longer period.[11] In the case of full-function joint ventures, non-compete clauses imposed on the parents are regarded as ancillary restraints if their duration is up to five years, although when they exceed three years this must be justified by the particular circumstances of the case.[12] Non-compete clauses that continue to apply after the termination of the joint venture are never considered to be directly related and necessary to the implementation of the concentration. Non-solicitation obligations and confidentiality clauses are dealt with in the same way as non-compete obligations.[13] Non-compete obligations accepted by the purchaser or the target business are not ancillary.[14] Any non-compete obligation must be limited to the products or services acquired and the territories in which the target business is active or would shortly have become so.[15]

8–033 Purchase or supply obligations — Supply and purchase agreements may be considered as ancillary to a concentration where they are necessary to ensure the continued supply of the products for the transferred or retained activities. Such arrangements should be limited to the duration necessary for a transitional period within which to develop alternative sources of supply or demand. This period will not normally exceed three years and must always be justified by the particular circumstances of the case.[16] Exclusive contracts and contracts for unlimited volumes are not normally ancillary to a concentration.[17] Transitional service agreements are assessed in the same way as contracts for the supply of goods.[18]

8–034 Intellectual property licences — Exclusive licences or field of use restrictions in intellectual property agreements entered into as part of a concentration are generally accepted as ancillary to the concentration, as they ensure that the acquirer (or joint venture) will have full use of the assets transferred.[19] However, if they are not ancillary, Article 81(1) of the EC Treaty will apply in which case there only remains the possibility of an exemption under Article 81(3) of the EC Treaty. This exemption may be a block exemption under the technology transfer block exemption Regulation[20] or, if this Regulation does not apply, an individual exemption by the Commission following application to it as Form A/B.[21]

7. One-Stop Shopping: Exclusive Jurisdiction Under the Merger Control Regulation

8–035 Introduction — Concentrations with a Community dimension are subject to the exclusive jurisdiction of the Commission under the Merger Control Regulation, to the exclusion of

---

[11] Ancillary Restrictions Notice, para.8–031, n.7, para.15. By contrast, the former Ancillary Restraints Notice accepted a five-year non-compete clause in the case of the transfer of goodwill and know-how.

[12] *ibid.*, para.30. Under the previous Notice, para.8–031, n.8, there was no limit in the duration of these types of change.

[13] *ibid.*, para.20.

[14] *ibid.*, para.12.

[15] *ibid.*, paras 16–17.

[16] *ibid.*, paras 25–30.

[17] *ibid.*, paras 28–29.

[18] *ibid.*, para.31.

[19] *ibid.*, para.III.B.22.

[20] Regulation 240/96 on the application of Art.81(3) of the EC Treaty to certain categories of technology transfer agreements, O.J. 1996 L31/2.

[21] See above, para.4–008 *et seq.*

national merger control rules.[22] This is the so-called "one-stop shopping" principle, which gives businesses engaged in international transactions the advantage of dealing with one single authority, thereby avoiding the need to make filings with potentially several national competition authorities, reducing the risk of conflicting decisions and promoting legal certainty.

8–036 Reference back to national authorities — However, the Merger Control Regulation contains several exceptions to the "one-stop shopping" principle.[23] Article 21(3) of the Merger Control Regulation permits Member States to take appropriate measures to protect legitimate interests other than those protected by the Merger Control Regulation. The plurality of the media is expressly stated to be a legitimate interest. Other legitimate interests that have been recognised by the Commission include the application of national sector-specific regulation aimed at regulating licensed undertakings generally and not mergers.[24-25] Pursuant to Article 21(3) of the Merger Control Regulation, a Member State could prohibit or approve subject to conditions a concentration that had been approved by the Commission under the Merger Control Regulation in order to protect the plurality of the media within its territory. However, a Member State could not use this exception to permit a concentration prohibited under the Merger Control Regulation.

Furthermore, under Article 9 of the Merger Control Regulation, a Member State may request that jurisdiction over a merger be referred to its competition authorities, where it threatens to create or strengthen a dominant position on a distinct national market or to affect competition on a distinct local market within that Member State that does not constitute a substantial part of the common market.[26] A decision to make a reference back to a Member State is at the discretion of the Commission: it may decide to keep jurisdiction. A reference back can relate to a part only of a concentration, and different parts may be referred to different Member States.[27] In the communications sector, two mergers have been referred back to national authorities: one in the Spanish satellite pay-TV sector[28] and the other in the Italian telecommunications market.[29]

[22] Merger Control Regulation, para.8–002, n.4, Art.21(2).
[23] *ibid.*, Art.21(3). See Case M.423, *Newspaper Publishing*, Commission Decision of March 14, 1994 (concerning application of UK rules on mergers in the newspaper sector designed to protect plurality in that sector).
[24-25] Case M.567, *Lyonnaise des Eaux/Northumbrian Water*, Commission Decision of December 21, 1995; Case M.1346, *EDF/London Electricity*, Commission Decision of January 27, 1999.
[26] Merger Control Regulation, para.8–002, n.4, Art.9(2).
[27] In Case M.2898, *Leroy Merlin/Brico*, Commission Decision of December 13, 2002, different aspects of the merger were referred to the French, Spanish and Portuguese authorities and the Commission approved the remainder.
[28] Case M.2845, *Sogecable/CanalsatéliteDigital/Vía Digital*, Commission Decision of August 16, 2002. This merger was subsequently approved, subject to commitments, by the Spanish authorities. The Commission decision to make the reference back under Art.9 has been challenged before the Court of First Instance by competitors (Case T–346 and 347/02).
[29] Case M.2216, *ENEL/Wind/Infostrada*, Commission Decision of January 19, 2001. This merger was partially referred to the Italian authority on the grounds that the acquisition of Infostrada by ENEL and France Télécom (which controlled Wind) could have enabled ENEL to protect or strengthen its dominant position in the Italian electricity market by bundling energy and telecommunications services.

8–037 References by Member States to the Commission — Under Article 22(3) of the Merger Control Regulation, the Member States may, individually or jointly,[30] refer a concentration without a Community dimension to the Commission if it has an effect on trade between Member States. The Commission will then investigate it under the Merger Control Regulation in the same manner as concentrations with a Community dimension. The proposed joint venture in the Dutch broadcasting sector between RTL, Veronica and Endemol (Holland Media Group) was referred by the Dutch authorities to the Commission under Article 22(3) of the Merger Control Regulation, as at that time the Netherlands had no effective merger control regime. The Commission prohibited the joint venture, as it would have had a dominant position on the Dutch television broadcasting, television advertising and independent television production markets. This included having to adopt a decision requiring the joint venture to be unwound, as the suspension obligation does not apply in Article 22(3) cases.[31] Following the withdrawal of Endemol from the joint venture, the Commission approved the revised structure.[32]

8. Concentrations Without a Community Dimension

8–038 Concentrations that fall below the above-mentioned thresholds do not have a Community dimension and are not subject to approval by the Commission under the Merger Control Regulation.[33] Rather, they may be reviewable under national merger control rules if they meet the relevant provisions of national law. Co-operative full-function joint ventures falling below the thresholds nevertheless remain subject to review by the Commission under Articles 81 and 82 of the EC Treaty. Most EU Member States have national merger control regimes providing for either mandatory or voluntary pre-merger filings. The types of transaction that are subject to mandatory or voluntary filings under national merger law vary from Member State to Member State, as do the jurisdictional thresholds.

8–039 Mandatory filings — Austria, Belgium, Denmark, Finland, France, Germany, Greece, Ireland, Italy, the Netherlands, Portugal, Spain and Sweden have mandatory pre-merger filing requirements in respect of mergers, that are triggered by turnover thresholds, asset thresholds, and/or market share tests.

8–040 Voluntary filings — In the United Kingdom, the Office of Fair Trading has jurisdiction to review transactions meeting certain thresholds (relating to either the target's UK turnover and/or the parties' combined market share), although notification of those transactions is not mandatory. However, when a transaction meeting these thresholds is not notified to it, the Office of Fair Trading can and usually will investigate the merger even after the transaction has been completed.

---

[30] Case M.2698, *Promatech/Sulzer Textil*, Commission Decision of July 24, 2002 (referral by several Member States: conditional approval after Phase II investigation); Case M.2738, *GEES/Unison*, Commission Decision of April 17, 2002 (referral by several Member States: unconditional approval at end of Phase I investigation).

[31] Case *RTL/Veronica/Endemol*, below, para.8–179 *et seq.*

[32] Commission Decision of July 17, 1996, O.J. 1996 L294/4. See also Case T–221/85, *Endemol Entertainment v Commission* [1999] II E.C.R. 1299, in which Endemol's appeal was dismissed.

[33] The only exception to this is where a merger filing to be reviewed by national competition authorities is referred to the Commission under Art.22(3).

A voluntary pre-merger filing will normally be made in relation to transactions that may raise competition concerns.[34]

8–041   No national merger control — Luxembourg does not have a merger control law requiring the mandatory or voluntary filing of concentrations.

C. Transactions That Do Not Amount to a Concentration

8–042   The Merger Control Regulation does not apply to transactions that are not concentrations, either because they do not involve the acquisition of control or because, in the case of a joint venture, it is not full-function. Accordingly, two types of transaction that fall outside of the Merger Control Regulation can be distinguished: (i) the acquisition of a minority shareholding; (ii) the creation of a joint venture that is not full-function. Such transactions cannot be notified under the Merger Control Regulation. However, they may be subject to Articles 81 and 82 of the EC Treaty (and the equivalent provisions of national competition law).

8–043   Acquisition of a minority shareholding — Articles 81 and 82 of the EC Treaty may apply to agreements involving the acquisition of a minority shareholding that is not sufficient to confer control for the purposes of the Merger Control Regulation, but nevertheless is significant enough: (i) to allow the acquirer the ability and the incentive to influence the behaviour of the other company (if it is a competitor); or (ii) to allow co-ordination between it and the other shareholders.[35] The Commission may apply Article 81(1) of the EC Treaty to an acquisition of a minority shareholding if it would raise concerns that the acquiring party would be able to exercise direct or indirect influence over the target company's market conduct so as to appreciably restrict or distort competition.[36] This would be the case, for example, if the minority shareholding allowed the firms to take into consideration each other's interests when determining their independent commercial policy. Typically, Article 81(1) of the EC Treaty will apply only if a shareholding of over 25 per cent is acquired; acquisitions of 25 per cent or less will ordinarily not raise competition concerns, except in specific circumstances.[37] Thus, when BT and MCI acquired minority shareholdings of 20 per cent in each other, the Commission found that Article 81(1) of the EC Treaty was not infringed. However, non-controlling minority shareholdings may constitute mergers for the purposes of national merger control legislation.[38]

---

[34] United Kingdom merger control underwent radical changes from the summer of 2003, with the entry into force of the Enterprise Act 2002. However, notification will remain voluntary.

[35] See Hawk and Huser, para.8–014, n.43.

[36] Case 142 and 156/84, *BAT Reynolds/Commission (Philip Morris)* [1987] E.C.R. 4487.

[37] In *Wilkinson/Gillette*, O.J. 1993 L116/21, the Commission considered that the acquisition of a 22% shareholding by an already dominant undertaking (Gillette) in a competitor (Eemland) infringed Art.82 of the EC Treaty, because of co-operation arrangements (trademark separation and supply arrangements), the existence of an oligopolistic market structure with high entry barriers, the financial dependence of Eemland on its minority shareholder Gillette, and Gillette's preemption and conversion rights that prevented third parties from taking over Eemland and influencing certain business decisions.

[38] For example, Vivendi's acquisition of a 24% shareholding in BSkyB was considered to be a merger under the UK Fair Trading Act 1973 (even though another shareholder had a shareholding of nearly 40%) and was

8–044   Non full-function joint ventures as instruments of co-operation — Since March 1, 1998, only joint ventures that are not full-function fall outside the scope of the Merger Control Regulation. Accordingly, they are subject to review under Articles 81 and 82 of the EC Treaty. In so far as restructuring in the telecommunications sector often takes the form of co-operative arrangements between operators, many joint ventures and alliances that would have been examined previously under Articles 81 and 82 of the EC Treaty pursuant to Regulation 17/62 now fall within the scope of the Merger Control Regulation. Following this change, a large number of full-function autonomous joint ventures with a co-operative object or effect, and therefore examined under the Merger Control Regulation, have involved communications companies.

8–045   Procedural aspects — If the parties wish to exclude the risk of fines or the unenforceability of restrictive provisions (or even the entire transaction) in relation to the acquisition of a minority shareholding or the formation of a non-full-function joint venture, a voluntary notification under Form A/B pursuant to Regulation 17/62 should be considered, with a view to obtaining a negative clearance (*i.e.* a Commission decision that Article 81(1) of the EC Treaty is not infringed) or an individual exemption (*i.e.* a Commission decision that Article 81(1) of the EC Treaty is infringed but that the transaction meets the requirements for exemption under Article 81(3) of the EC Treaty). In contrast with the strict deadlines under the Merger Control Regulation, review proceedings by the Commission following a notification made under Regulation 17/62 are not subject to any deadline. The Commission has adopted a notice on agreements of minor importance, stating that agreements among actual or potential competitors do not infringe Article 81(1) of the EC Treaty if the parties have a combined market share on any relevant market(s) not exceeding 10 per cent. The same applies to agreements among undertakings that are not actual or potential competitors if the parties have a combined market share on any relevant market(s) not exceeding 15 per cent.[39]

D. Major Commission Decisions in Relation to Joint Ventures and Concentrations in the Communications Sector

8–046   This section will first review the major concentrations (mergers and full-function joint ventures) in the telecommunications, broadcasting and internet sectors examined by the Commission under the Merger Control Regulation. Second, it will analyse the main co-operative (or non-full-function) joint ventures, strategic alliances and other transactions in these sectors that have been reviewed by the Commission under Articles 81 and 82 of the EC Treaty. Finally, the decisions of the Commission in these cases is assessed and commented on.

1. Major Decisions under the Merger Control Regulation

8–047   Since the early 1990s, the rapid pace of liberalisation, the globalisation of trade and the need for restructuring, mergers and alliances has resulted in a considerable number of mergers, acquisitions and joint ventures in the telecommunications sector being notified to the Commission.

---

referred to the Monopolies and Mergers Commission (as it then was), but was subsequently approved: *Vivendi SA/British Sky Broadcasting Group plc*, Cm.4691 (2000).
[39] O.J. 2001 C368/07.

This section will focus on the main merger cases reviewed by the Commission so far. These transactions have covered telecommunications equipment, fixed telecommunications networks and services, mobile networks and services, television broadcasting and the internet. Some transactions covered two or more of these sectors.

(a) Concentrations in the Telecommunications Equipment Sector

8–048 Introduction — The Commission has examined a large number of concentrations involving companies active in the telecommunications equipment sector. Most of these concentrations did not raise any serious competition issues and were approved by the Commission at the end of its Phase I investigation. Telecommunications equipment markets are increasingly competitive as a result of the liberalisation of the sector and the increased harmonisation of standards at the European level within the framework of the European Telecommunications Standards Institute ("ETSI") and other European standardisation bodies. Markets are no longer restricted to individual Member States, such that competition is no longer restricted to the national level, as it is now easier for customers to purchase and for manufacturers to supply equipment across borders. Moreover, the Utilities Procurement Directive has contributed to the breaking down of the traditional nationality-based buying policies of the incumbent telecommunications operators.[40]

Alcatel/Telettra[41]

8–049 The transaction — This transaction involved the acquisition by Alcatel of a controlling interest in Telettra, a subsidiary of Fiat that was active in the telecommunications systems and equipment sector. Upon completion of the transaction, Fiat retained a minority shareholding in Telettra.

8–050 The relevant product markets — The Commission identified four relevant product markets: (i) public switching equipment; (ii) line transmission equipment; (iii) microwave equipment; and (iv) private switching equipment.

8–051 The relevant geographic markets — The Commission defined the relevant geographic market as Spain on the following grounds: (i) the incumbent Spanish telecommunications operator, Telefónica (which at that time had a monopoly over public networks and most services), was the main purchaser of telecommunications equipment in Spain and traditionally purchased equipment from locally established suppliers; (ii) at the time of the transaction there was no legal obligation in Spain for Telefónica to comply with the procedures established by the Utilities Procurement Directive for the next five years; and (iii) there were vertical links between Telefónica and its major equipment suppliers (including Telettra), by means of minority shareholdings with the result that these suppliers were in a privileged position on the equipment market.

8–052 Competitive analysis — The Commission considered that the transaction would have lead to the combination of the two principal suppliers of equipment to Telefónica, the Spanish

---

[40] See App.7.
[41] Case M.042, *Alcatel/Telettra*, Commission Decision of April 12, 1991, O.J. 1991 L122/48.

incumbent operator and principal buyer of this type of equipment, with the merged entity having very high market shares on the Spanish markets for line transmission equipment (81 per cent) and microwave equipment (83 per cent). After completion of its in-depth Phase II investigation, the Commission found that, despite its very high market shares in these markets, the merged entity did not have a dominant position, given the buying power of a monopsonic purchaser such as Telefónica. In fact, Alcatel and Telettra's high market shares were the result of Telefónica's choice of the two companies as its principal equipment suppliers. Consequently, following the merger of these two entities, Telefónica was able to maintain a diversified purchasing policy by increasing its purchases from other suppliers such as AT&T and Ericsson, as a result of which the combined market share of Alcatel/Telettra would diminish. The Commission also considered that there were no substantial barriers to other European suppliers entering, or increasing their presence on, the Spanish market, except for the existing structural links between Telefónica and Alcatel/Telettra. Accordingly, the Commission approved the concentration subject to the condition that Alcatel fulfil its undertaking to purchase Telefónica's shareholdings in Telettra, one of Telettra's subsidiaries and one of Alcatel's subsidiaries.

Siemens/Italtel[42]

8–053 The transaction — This concentration involved the creation of a concentrative joint venture between Siemens and STET (the then parent company of Telecom Italia, the Italian incumbent operator) for the purpose of manufacturing telecommunications systems and equipment. The transaction took place within the framework of the reorganisation of the state-owned STET group and the separation within that group of the subsidiary providing telecommunications services (Telecom Italia) and the subsidiary active in equipment manufacturing (Italtel). This operation was also motivated by the need for Italtel to find a strategic partner in order to develop its equipment manufacturing activities. The transaction involved STET and Siemens contributing their respective subsidiaries (Italtel and Siemens Telecomunicazioni) into a joint venture company that was to be jointly controlled by them. The Commission considered that the joint venture was a full-function entity and therefore a concentration subject to the Merger Control Regulation, despite the fact that for the foreseeable future after completion, the joint venture would have made the bulk of its sales to Telecom Italia, a subsidiary of STET. The Commission found that this did not affect the autonomy of the joint venture since this was the inevitable result of the then infrastructure monopoly in favour of Telecom Italia and was not due to the manufacture of telecommunications equipment being an ancillary activity to the provision of telecommunications services.

8–054 The relevant product markets — The Commission identified the following relevant product markets for telecommunications equipment: (i) public switching systems; (ii) transmission; (iii) radio systems; (iv) mobile radio networks; (v) private switching and key telephone systems (KTS); and (vi) communications terminals. It is interesting that the Commission did not define separate product markets based on the type of technology (*e.g.* analogue, digital, SDH, ATM, GSM) used by the equipment in question. The Commission left the issue open as to whether — within the

---

[42] Case M.468, *Siemens/Italtel*, Commission Decision of February 17, 1995, O.J. 1995 L161/27.

market for telecommunications terminal equipment telephones, fax machines, and mobile telephone handsets formed separate markets.

8–055 The relevant geographic markets — The Commission indicated that the geographic scope of each of the product markets that it had identified was probably at least Europe-wide. The Commission based its findings on the following factors: (i) technological developments; (ii) international standards and national-/type-approval of equipment; (iii) the application of the Utilities Procurement Directive; and (iv) the liberalisation of public voice telephony and telecommunications infrastructure and services. In particular, the Commission distinguished the present case from its decision in *Alcatel/Telettra*,[43] where it held that the geographic market for public switching systems equipment was national — on the grounds that none of the characteristics that it had identified in its earlier decision that justified a specific Spanish market (*i.e.* that the Spanish telecommunications operator had traditionally purchased from local suppliers, the deferred application of the Utilities Procurement Directive in Spain, vertical links between the incumbent telecommunications operator and its main suppliers) applied fully to the situation in Italy.

8–056 Competitive analysis — The Commission found that the joint venture resulted in Siemens, through the joint venture, sharing the pre-existing shareholder link between the Italian incumbent telecommunications operator, Telecom Italia, and the equipment manufacturer, Italtel. The concentration could have had a negative impact upon public procurement opportunities for competitors and on the opening up of national equipment markets to EU-wide competition. Nevertheless, at the end of its Phase II investigation, the Commission found that, despite the new entity's high market share in Italy (about 55–60 per cent), the concentration would not have led to the creation of a dominant position on the relevant markets. The Commission based its decision on the following factors: (i) the high degree of concentration in the supply of public switching systems was normal because telecommunications operators normally limited the number of different technologies or systems coexisting in a network to a maximum of two or three; (ii) standardisation and public procurement rules at the EU-level would contribute increasingly to open national markets; and (iii) progress towards liberalisation of the markets for telecommunications services and infrastructure would lead increasingly to the creation of a worldwide market for public telecommunications equipment in which the joint venture would have had a smaller market share. The Commission recognised that any benefits of any privileged treatment to the joint venture imposed on Telecom Italia due to the shareholder link between the new joint venture and Telecom Italia, would have to be shared with Siemens. Accordingly, by comparison with the situation existing prior to the concentration where STET alone controlled Italtel, the concentration reduced the incentives for STET or Telecom Italia (at that time still controlled by STET) to favour the joint venture at the expense of Telecom Italia, for instance by accepting higher prices for equipment. This element helped to convince the Commission that STET's interests in the joint venture would not conflict with its interests in Telecom Italia.

---

[43] See above, para.8–049 *et seq.*

Marconi/Bosch Public Network[44]

8-057 The transaction — The transaction consisted of the acquisition of Bosch Public Network Telecommunications (BPN) by Marconi by way of purchase of assets. BPN comprised the public network activities of the telecommunications equipment business of Robert Bosch GmbH.

8-058 The relevant product markets — The Commission identified two relevant product markets: (i) the cable/wireline transmission equipment market; and (ii) the access networks equipment market. The cable/wireline transmission equipment market comprised the equipment needed for the transport of traffic between local and transit central exchanges and on leased lines between business customers. The access networks equipment market comprised a wide range of electronic products used to connect the homes of subscribers and the premises of businesses to the public local telephone exchange network that have traditionally been based on copper or fibre cables. The Commission did not, however, identify a separate market for support services offered by telecommunications equipment suppliers.

8-059 The relevant geographic markets — The Commission considered the geographic scope of both markets to be at least EEA-wide, if not worldwide.

8-060 Competitive analysis — The Commission found that the market share of Marconi on the EEA transmission equipment market would have been only slightly increased by the transaction. The parties' 1998 overall EEA market shares were estimated to be between 20–25 per cent for Marconi, and between 2–5 per cent for BPN. Their main competitors were Alcatel, Lucent, Nortel and Siemens. On the EEA market for access networks equipment, the parties' market shares in the EEA were estimated to be even less (Marconi, 5–10 per cent; and BPN, 2–5 per cent), with Alcatel, Ericsson, Lucent, Nortel and Siemens being the most important competitors. Therefore, the concentration did not raise any dominance concerns.

Alcatel/Thomson Multimedia[45]

8-061 The transaction — This concentration involved the creation of a joint venture by the French undertakings Alcatel and Thomson Multimedia (TMM). The joint venture was set up by the parties in order to merge their respective activities in MPEG (Moving Picture Experts Group) transmission, and cable access. It was intended that the joint venture would supply equipment used for the emerging sector of interactive video services offered by its customers (telecommunications operators, broadcasters and cable-based multi-service operators).

8-062 The relevant product markets — The Commission indicated that the relevant market for interactive video networks, as suggested by the parties, could be further broken down into different segments for MPEG network products and for cable access network products. A further

---

[44] Case M.1800, *Marconi/Bosch Public Network*, Commission Decision of January 19, 2000, O.J. 2000 C144/08.
[45] Case M.2048, *Alcatel/Thomson Multimedia*, Commission Decision of October 26, 2000, O.J. 2000 C348/15.

segmentation by the different products manufactured by the parties was also potentially possible. However, ultimately the Commission left the precise market definition open.

8–063 The relevant geographic markets — The Commission indicated that the geographic market was worldwide, as customers tended to buy interactive video network products from multiple sources on a global basis and the parties were also active on this basis. However, the geographic definition was ultimately left open.

8–064 Competitive analysis — In view of the parties' relatively low market shares and the existence of a number of strong incumbent or potential competitors in the evolving market for interactive video networks, the Commission concluded that the proposed concentration did not raise any dominance concerns.

Schneider/Thomson Multimedia[46]

8–065 The transaction — Schneider Electric Industries S.A. (Schneider) and Thomson Multimedia S.A. (TMM) created a full-function joint venture to design, develop, manufacture and sell powerline communications products. These products allow the transmission of data through normal electric cables at the same time as electricity.

8–066 The relevant product markets — The parties had identified the market of "no-new-wiring home networking products and technologies" as the relevant product market. A "home network" may be defined as the establishment of communications capabilities between two or more devices enabling the mutual transfer of data. This includes the products and technologies of phoneline networking, wireless networking, powerline networking and future no-new-wiring networking. However, it was not necessary for the Commission to define the precise scope of the relevant product market, because even on the basis of the narrowest possible product market definition (powerline products), the operation would not have led to the creation or strengthening of a dominant position.

8–067 The relevant geographic markets — The Commission did not decide on the geographic scope of the market. However, the Commission indicated that due to different regulatory conditions in individual Member States, and the lack of uniform European standards, the relevant geographic market could have been national in scope.

8–068 Competitive analysis — The Commission's investigation confirmed that the formation of the joint venture would not lead to the creation or strengthening of a dominant position on the wider market for all no-new-wiring home networking products and technologies, nor on the narrower markets of phoneline, wireless, powerline and future no-new-wiring networking products and technologies. This was because the Commission's market investigation had shown that many large multinational companies were at that time active in manufacturing these products and technologies and there seemed to be significant actual and potential competition.

---

[46] Case M.2403, *Schneider/Thomson Multimedia*, Commission Decision of June 16, 2001, O.J. 2001 C251/3.

(b) Concentrations in Telecommunications Networks and Services Sector

8–069 Introduction — The liberalisation and globalisation of telecommunications markets has obliged many telecommunications operators to join forces in order to offer large corporate customers global "one-stop" telecommunications services, whereby these customers can obtain all their worldwide telecommunications from one single operator.[47] Likewise, the development of satellite and mobile services have very often necessitated that telecommunications operators enter into alliances and joint ventures in order to exploit new opportunities (such as new mobile licences and internet services). In other cases, large operators have acquired others in order to expand their service offerings and/or geographic reach. Although many such restructuring operations have taken the form of strategic alliances and co-operative joint ventures that have fallen outside the scope of the Merger Control Regulation,[48] a number of mergers and joint ventures between telecommunications operators have been concentrations reviewed under the Merger Control Regulation. Some of the most important of the more than 80 decisions in this sector are reviewed in this section.

Hermes[49]

8–070 The transaction — Hermes Europe Railtel BV was a concentrative joint venture between a number of European railway companies, GTS, a company providing a broad range of telecommunications services, and Racal, a company formed from the former telecommunications activities of British Rail in the United Kingdom. Hermes was established to build a pan-European telecommunications network dedicated to the cross-border transmission of telecommunications traffic exploiting the rights of way of the participating railway companies and Racal. In 2000, Hermes was renamed Global TeleSystems Europe BV. It has since sold most of its business, as a result of a restructuring undertaken in order to enhance its position as a pan-European data and internet service-only provider.

8–071 The relevant product markets — Although the Commission did not take a definitive position on market definition, it suggested that the relevant market was the market for carriers' carrier services, *i.e.* the wholesale transport of traffic over permanent dedicated facilities through the network of the transit carrier, using a high bandwidth digital circuit for both voice and data services. The Commission failed to take a position on a distinction proposed by the parties between two separate markets for: (i) point-to-point connections; and (ii) provision of pan-European transport networks.

8–072 The relevant geographic markets — Because Hermes would provide its services across borders, the Commission concluded that the market was at least EEA-wide.

8–073 Competitive analysis — The Commission considered that the transaction did not raise any dominance concerns and cleared it without opening an in-depth investigation. With respect to

---

[47] These services are also known as Managed Data Network Services ("MDNS").

[48] See App.7.

[49] Case M.683, *GTS Hermes/HIT Rail BV*, Commission Decision of March 25, 1996, O.J. 1996 C157/13.

the provision of point-to-point connections, Hermes would compete with a number of incumbent telecommunications operators with significant market shares. As regards the operation of pan-European transport networks (carriers' carrier services), the Commission concluded that, even if such a market were to be considered as a distinct market of which Hermes, as the first entrant, would have a 100 per cent market share, Hermes would have had no opportunity to foreclose the market because of the possibility for incumbent telecommunications operators to combine their (much larger) networks to compete with Hermes. Moreover, utility suppliers' networks could also be used to create competing pan-European networks. In addition, telecommunications consortia such as Unisource or Atlas had the resources to compete with Hermes. Finally, the Commission took into account that the potential customers of Hermes were strong and well-informed companies with considerable buying power. It is interesting to note that the Commission found an obligation imposed upon Hermes not to provide telecommunications network facilities services at a national level to be an ancillary restraint, since it reflected the decision of the parents to limit the business of the joint venture to international services. However, the Commission refused to treat as an ancillary restraint the possibility of an exception from this restriction when, on the application of a customer, the relevant national railways consented to the provision of services at the national level by Hermes.

BT/MCI (II)[50]

8–074   The transaction — The transaction consisted of the proposed merger between British Telecommunications and MCI Communications Corporation. The transaction followed the parties' formation of the Concert joint venture and went a step further in integrating the two companies.[51] Following the rejection of the transaction by BT's shareholders and WorldCom's successful takeover bid for MCI, the transaction was abandoned.

8–075   The relevant product markets — The Commission identified the following relevant product markets: (i) international voice telephony services (including international direct dials (IDD) and international private leased circuits (IPLCs)); and (ii) audio-conferencing. With respect to international voice telephony services, the Commission indicated that satellite and cable could not be considered as substitute transmission media in providing international voice services, given the technical deficiencies of satellites (*i.e.* greater signal propagation delay time, echo effects and susceptibility to environmental or climatic conditions such as heavy rains) as compared with cable.

8–076   The relevant geographic markets — The geographic scope of international voice telephony services affected by the concentration was related to specific call traffic routes between any country pair (in this case, the United Kingdom–United States route). Two distinct geographic markets could be identified with any specific international route, each comprised of the originating bilateral traffic from the countries concerned. The possibility of hubbing, *i.e.* re-routing United Kingdom–United States traffic through third countries, did not appear to be a viable commercial possibility at the time, since under the then prevailing international accounting rates system, it would have been more expensive than using direct routes. As regards audio-conferencing, the

---

[50] Case M.856, *British Telecom/MCI (II)*, Commission Decision of May 14, 1997, O.J. 1997 L336/1.
[51] See below, para.8–264 *et seq.*

geographic scope of the market was national, as customers generally purchased audio-conferencing services at the national, rather than global or international, level.

8–077 Competitive analysis — The Commission concluded that the merger, as originally notified, would have created or reinforced a dominant position in the markets for international voice telephony services between the United Kingdom and the United States, and for audio-conferencing services in the United Kingdom. In the markets for international voice telephony services between the United Kingdom and the United States, the Commission focused on the parties' significant capacity entitlements on transatlantic cables and the lack of satisfactory substitutes (*e.g.* satellite communications). As a result of the merger, BT/MCI would have been able to carry United Kingdom–United States traffic over its own end-to-end international transmission facilities, thereby avoiding fees typically charged to originating operators by foreign correspondent carriers that deliver calls to the destination country. In the short and medium term, no competitors could have matched BT/MCI's cost advantages, first because competitors carrying calls to or from the United Kingdom would have continued to be required to pay fees to BT to obtain capacity ("half circuits") on BT's United Kingdom network, and second, because BT's and MCI's combined cable capacity (combining BT's "half circuit" at the United Kingdom end and MCI's "half-circuit" at the United States end into a "full circuit") would have enabled them to restrict market entry by prospective new UK operators.

To address the Commission's concerns relating to these markets, BT and MCI offered the following commitments: (i) to make available, at cost, to new international facilities operators in the United Kingdom, BT's and MCI's current and prospective overlapping capacity on the United Kingdom–United States route on submarine transatlantic cable TAT 12/13; (ii) to sell to other UK operators, upon their request and at cost, the capacity BT leased to them; and (iii) to sell to other operators, upon their request, the capacity necessary to have calls carried over BT's UK network in order to allow these operators to set up their own end-to-end facilities.

In the UK audio-conferencing market, the Commission found that owing to BT's and MCI's very high combined market share (over 80 per cent) and the high barriers to entry in the market caused by a relatively static customer base, the merger would have created a dominant position. To address the Commission's concerns, the parties committed to divest MCI's UK audio-conferencing business. As a result of these commitments, the Commission gave conditional approval to the merger.

Telia/Telenor/Schibsted[52]

8–078 The transaction — This transaction was the first co-operative full-function joint venture to be reviewed by the Commission following the entry into force of the revised Merger Control Regulation on March 1, 1998. It involved the formation of a joint venture (Scandinavia OnLine) between Schibsted Multimedia AS, Telenor Nextel AS and Telia AB for the provision of certain internet services to consumers and business customers, mainly in Sweden.

[52] Case JV.1, *Telia/Telenor/Schibsted*, Commission Decision of May 27, 1998, O.J. 1999 C220/28.

8–079 The relevant product markets — The Commission distinguished the following relevant product markets to assess the competitive effects of the concentration: (i) the provision of content on the internet; (ii) internet advertising; and (iii) website production. The basis for the distinction was that content and advertising generate revenues in different ways and from different sources and the activities are carried out by different players and require different inputs. As regards website production, the Commission took into consideration that it demands both specific design and computer skills. In assessing the risk of co-ordination as a result of the joint venture, the Commission also identified the market for dial-up internet access as a candidate market for co-ordination, in so far as Telenor and Telia were both active on this product market.

8–080 The relevant geographic markets — The Commission defined the relevant geographic market to be national, possibly on a linguistic basis, *i.e.* the market for internet content services in Swedish including in Sweden and in the Swedish language communities in other Nordic countries.

8–081 Competitive analysis: dominance — The Commission found that the transaction would not have raised any issues of dominance on the market for internet advertising, despite the parties' and joint venture's high market shares, because the market was a rapidly growing market with many players. Moreover, the transaction raised no concerns on the market for website production, given the parties' and joint venture's low market shares.

8–082 Competitive analysis: co-ordination of competitive behaviour — The Commission also had to assess the risk of co-ordination of the competitive behaviour of the joint venture's parents under Article 2(4) of the Merger Control Regulation. The Commission indicated that, in order to establish a restriction of competition in the sense of Article 81(1) of the EC Treaty, it was necessary that the co-ordination of the parent companies' competitive behaviour was: (i) likely; (ii) appreciable; and (iii) the result of the creation of the joint venture. The Commission identified two candidate markets for possible co-ordination: (i) website production; and (ii) dial-up internet access. With respect to website production, the Commission considered that, given the parents' low market shares, any restriction of competition as a result of the co-ordination of competitive conduct of the parents on this market would not have been appreciable. As regards dial-up internet access, the Commission concluded that the market was characterised by high price-sensitivity, low barriers to entry and a high number of players so that co-ordination of market behaviour was not likely, despite the relatively high combined market shares of the parties on this market.

ENEL/FT/DT (Wind)[53]

8–083 The transaction — This transaction consisted of the creation of a co-operative joint venture company, Wind, between ENEL, the principal electricity provider in Italy, France Télécom (FT), and Deutsche Telekom (DT). The purpose of Wind was to offer a full range of domestic and international telecommunications services to business and residential customers located in Italy, in competition with the incumbent telecommunications operator, Telecom Italia. It was intended that Wind would use the existing telecommunications network of ENEL, which would be extended,

---

[53] Case JV.2, *ENEL/FT/DT (Wind)*, Commission Decision of June 22, 1998.

upgraded and leased to Wind. This transaction is interesting as a concrete illustration of the entry of utility companies into the telecommunications markets and the creation of "multi-utility companies".

8–084   The relevant product markets — The Commission considered that a number of product markets would be affected by the transaction:

   (i) fixed line telephony, which could be divided into a number of segments:

      (a) international voice telecommunications services;

      (b) domestic voice telecommunications services;

      (c) international data telecommunications services; and

      (d) domestic data telecommunications services;

   (ii) *mobile telephony.*

The Commission did not specify whether each segment of the fixed line telephony market constituted a separate product market. Regarding mobile telephony, the Commission indicated (although it did not take a firm position) that it might have been no longer appropriate to consider that DCS 1800 and GSM constituted separate product markets on the grounds that dual mode handsets allowed users to use both frequencies and GSM, analogue, DCS 1800 and DECT networks competed at the local level.

8–085   The relevant geographic markets — The Commission defined the markets for domestic and international voice telephony, data services and mobile telephony in Italy to be national, and that for enhanced services to be international. In relation to mobile telephony, the Commission indicated that the market was national owing to significant price differences between local and international mobile telephony that reduced the incentive for subscribers to seek subscriptions from foreign operators.

8–086   Competitive analysis: dominance — The Commission approved the transaction at the end of Phase I. The Commission considered that the concentration could not have led to the creation or strengthening of a dominant position on any of the affected markets, because of the presence of larger competitors, in particular Telecom Italia, on all of these markets. The Commission considered that, if mobile DCS 1800 services were considered to constitute a separate product market, Wind would have had 100 per cent of the market, since it was the only licensee authorised to provide such mobile services using the DCS 1800 standard in Italy. However, in such a case, Wind's dominant position would not have been the result of the concentration but of the decision of the Italian authorities to award only one licence for the provision of DCS 1800 services in Italy.

8–087   Competitive analysis: co-ordination of competitive behaviour — The Commission considered that it was not likely that the creation of the joint venture would have resulted in the co-ordination of the competitive behaviour of the parents on the markets on which the joint venture would be active or on other closely related markets. For the Commission, any risk of the co-ordination of the competitive behaviour of FT and DT would have been the result of the

Atlas/Global One strategic alliance and not of the creation of Wind. The Commission cleared, as ancillary to the concentration, a non-compete clause (with some limitations as to its geographic scope and duration), the lease of ENEL's networks to Wind for a period of 15 years, and exclusive consultancy agreements between Wind and DT and FT until 2000.

WorldCom/MCI[54]

8–088   The transaction — The transaction was a merger between WorldCom and MCI. WorldCom provided services to businesses and private consumers, such as switched and dedicated international, long-distance and local voice and data communications services and internet services. MCI offered businesses and private customers a portfolio of integrated services, including long-distance, wireless, local paging, messaging, information, outsourcing and advanced global communications services, including internet services. This transaction was based in the United States, but had a significant impact in the EU, where both companies were active.

8–089   The relevant product markets — The Commission distinguished the following relevant product markets: (i) host to point of presence access services (*i.e.* the provision of connection services between the host computer of the internet user and the nearest point of presence of his internet service provider via the public switched network or a dedicated private line); (ii) internet access services, which had to be distinguished from other forms of data transmission services using different protocols; and (iii) "top-level" or "universal" internet connectivity services, provided by a network capable of connecting directly to any other network on the internet through so-called "peering" agreements (*i.e.* barter arrangements between top-level internet services providers (ISPs) which allow traffic to be exchanged between them without payments) without relying on a third network to relay the traffic (the so-called internet "backbone").

8–090   The relevant geographic markets — The Commission defined the relevant geographic markets as follows: (i) as the physical connection from the final user to the ISP, whether by dial-up or dedicated access, could only be provided locally, the market for host to point of presence access services was regional or national, depending on the scope of the supplier's network; (ii) the market for the provision of internet access services to final users was local or international depending on the nature of the customer (*i.e.* large corporations or individuals); and (iii) the market for top-level internet connectivity was global by nature.

8–091   Competitive analysis — The Commission considered that the parties' combined position in the market for internet backbone services would have created network effects rendering their service more attractive than those of their rivals.[55] The ability of competitors with existing peering

---

[54] Case M.1069, *WorldCom/MCI*, Commission Decision of July 8, 1998, O.J. 1999, L166/1.

[55] The Commission used different methodologies and criteria (*i.e.* revenues, traffic flow, number of reachable addresses, numbers of points of presence and actual bandwidth used for traffic exchange) to assess the parties' market shares. The Commission concluded that, regardless of the criterion used, the combined entity would have held a market share in the market for top-level internet services of over 50%. Its network would have been significantly larger than that of its nearest competitor, Sprint, whether by revenue or traffic flow, with the next largest competitor, GTE Group, being about half the size of Sprint.

relations with MCI and/or WorldCom to continue to provide backbone internet services would have depended on their being able to continue offering their customers connectivity to the MCI/WorldCom network. MCI/WorldCom would have been able to exploit such a dependency to its advantage.[56] For example, the parties would have been in a position to degrade the service quality of internet service providers that relied on MCI/WorldCom's top-level services to relay portions of their traffic, by deciding not to upgrade the capacity at private peering points (*i.e.* private interconnection points for direct bilateral connections between ISPs). The Commission based its reasoning in this case on the concept of "network externalities", a phenomenon whereby the attraction of a network to its customers is a function of the number of other customers connected to the network. The Commission argued that once a network reaches a certain size, or if there is a marked disparity in size between it and other networks, it will grow further because it offers its customers a better and more varied service.[57] The Commission rejected the parties' initial offer of a commitment to divest the physical assets of MCI's internet business but not the customers associated with it. The Commission then approved the merger after the parties expanded their divestiture commitment to include MCI's entire internet business.

BT/AT&T[58]

8–092 The transaction — The transaction involved the creation of a joint venture between British Telecommunications plc and AT&T Corp. to provide global telecommunications services to multinational companies and international carrier services to other telecommunications companies. This transaction was the first decision to involve a Phase II investigation concerning the assessment of the co-ordinative effects of a joint venture since the entry into force of the revised Merger Control Regulation on March 1, 1998.

8–093 The relevant product markets — The Commission identified the following product markets as being affected by the transaction: (i) the market for global telecommunications services (GTS) to multinational corporate customers; (ii) international carrier services; (iii) international voice telephony services on the United Kingdom–United States route; and (iv) certain telecommunications services in the United Kingdom (business and retail basic voice services, wholesale carrier services, domestic value-added services, teleconferencing, telex, domestic data services, internet access, outsourcing services and mobile services). As regards the market for GTS services, the Commission considered that there was one single product market for all GTS services and that there was no need to break it down into narrower product markets for individual services, because these services were priced and supplied as a package by all global suppliers. With respect to international carrier services, the Commission left open the issue of whether the market should be defined on a global basis (as it was decided in the *Unisource* decision[59]) or in terms of individual

---

[56] The Commission argued (at para.126 of its Decision) that as a result of the merger, the MCI WorldCom network would have constituted, either immediately or in a relatively short time thereafter, an essential facility to which all other ISPs would have no choice but to interconnect (directly or indirectly) in order to offer a credible internet access service.

[57] For a critical comment on the Commission's application of this concept in this case, see Veljanovski, "Internet v MCI WorldCom Merger, The Misuse of Network Effects Again" (1999) *International Review of Competition Law* 11–12.

[58] Case JV.15, *BT/AT&T*, Commission Decision of March 30, 1999.

[59] Case *Unisource*, Commission Decision of October 29, 1997, O.J. 1997 L318/1.

country pair routes. As it had done in *BT/MCI*,[60] the Commission took the position that, because of technical factors such as the delay inherent in satellite circuits, cable and satellite were still not substitutable for the provision of international voice traffic, for reasons of both quality and reliability.

8–094   The relevant geographic markets — The Commission defined the relevant geographic markets as follows:

    (i)   GTS services to multinational corporate customers: worldwide;

   (ii)   international carrier services: at least European and possibly global;

  (iii)   international voice telephony services on the United Kingdom–United States route: national (United Kingdom); and

  (iv)   certain UK services: national.

8–095   Competitive analysis: dominance — With regard to GTS services, the parties would have had a market share of between 35 and 50 per cent, depending on the method used to calculate market shares. Despite this high market share, the Commission did not consider that the transaction would have created a dominant position, owing to the strength of the competitors (*i.e.* Global One, MCI/WorldCom, Equant and Cable & Wireless). The Commission also considered that there was potential competition from local operators (who could form strategic alliances, or joint ventures or merge to provide GTS services) and also from IT/computing companies. The Commission also took into consideration that capacity costs were decreasing fast, with the result that new operators would have a competitive cost base, at least in the long term. The Commission noted the concerns of third parties that BT's strong market position in the United Kingdom could have allowed the joint venture and its parents to consolidate their position against competitors. However, the Commission found no evidence that BT's dominant position in the local loop in the United Kingdom would have led to the creation of a dominant position in the market for GTS services. In particular, this was because the customers that would be targeted by the joint venture would usually not rely on the local loop network but use dedicated (leased) lines. In addition, alternative infrastructure to the local loop (*e.g.* cable television networks) existed in many parts of the United Kingdom, and the regulator, OFTEL, was at that time engaged in a consultation process on the options for improving local loop access.

With respect to international carrier services, the Commission found that the joint venture would not have created or strengthened a dominant position in this market, owing to a number of factors:

- the emergence of a number of new competitors;

- the combined volumes of international traffic carried by both parties and the volumes of international traffic carried by their main competitors being comparable;

- there was no lack of capacity either in the Community or on transatlantic routes, due to the existence of alternative pan-European networks and new and planned high-capacity submarine transatlantic cables;

---

[60] See above, para.8–064 *et seq.*

- there was no significant overlap in capacity ownership, except on the transatlantic routes; and, finally

- the cost of capacity was decreasing fast, thereby facilitating increased competition.

With regard to the UK market for the provision of international voice telephony services on the United Kingdom–United States route, the Commission considered (following *BT/MCI (II)*[61]) whether there were constraining factors that could have prevented the joint venture's competitors from competing with it on a level playing field. Important factors in the Commission's analysis were access to transatlantic transmission capacity, domestic interconnection with transatlantic cable capacity, local loop access in the United Kingdom, and the possibility on the part of competitors to self-correspond on the United Kingdom–United States route (*i.e.* have networks in both countries). The joint venture would have accounted for approximately half of the two-way bilateral traffic between the United States and the United Kingdom. However, this would not give it a dominant position. The Commission found that increased competition from Cable & Wireless, WorldCom/MCI and Energis, the increased availability of transatlantic cables since the *BT/MCI (II)* decision, and more competition in the operation of cable landing stations and backhaul circuits since that decision meant that, while BT still enjoyed a very strong position in the United Kingdom, the UK regulatory regime would have prevented BT using its market position to underpin the joint venture's position on the United Kingdom–United States route. The Commission concluded that the joint venture would not have had a dominant position in this market.

8–096 Competitive analysis: co-ordination of competitive behaviour — The Commission had concerns that the joint venture would have resulted in the co-ordination of the independent activities of BT and AT&T within the meaning of Article 2(4) of the Merger Control Regulation. It was concerned that the joint venture would have been active on neighbouring and closely related markets on which both parents (or related companies) were also active, so that there would be an incentive for the parents to compete less with each other on the UK markets for local, national, international voice telephony, wholesale carrier services, internet services, local loop access and global telecommunications services for multinational customers. As a result, the Commission initiated Phase II proceedings into the effect of the joint venture.

The Commission considered that there was a real likelihood of co-ordination between BT and AT&T (and its affiliates) and that this would have appreciably affected competition within the common market, thereby infringing Article 81(1) of the EC Treaty. However, AT&T offered various commitments, which removed the possibility of co-ordination, so that no Article 81(3) of the EC Treaty analysis was necessary. AT&T undertook: (i) to divest ACC UK (a wholly owned subsidiary that provided long-distance telecommunications services in the United Kingdom); (ii) to increase structural separation ("firewalls") between AT&T and Telewest (a UK cable operator and a principal competitor to BT in the UK retail telecommunications markets) in which AT&T had an indirect 22-per-cent participation that gave it joint control of Telewest; and (iii) to permit another distributor to be appointed to distribute the communications services of the AT&T-Unisource joint venture, in addition to AT&T (that had hitherto been the exclusive distributor of Unisource services in the United Kingdom).

---

[61] See above, para.8–074 *et seq.*

Telia/Telenor[62]

8–097   The transaction — This landmark decision rendered by the Commission concerned the acquisition of joint control by the Swedish and Norwegian governments of a new company that was to be created to hold the shares of Telia and Telenor, the incumbent telecommunications operators in Sweden and Norway, respectively. Both companies were active in providing the full range of telephony and related services, as well as the retail distribution of television services and related services. This was the first transaction reviewed under the Merger Control Regulation which involved the merger of two incumbent telecommunications operators in Europe. As a result of disagreements between the parties, the transaction was abandoned after the Commission had approved the merger subject to far-reaching undertakings of the parties. The case was also unusual in that, because of the involvement of Telenor, it was a case that was handled by the Commission in co-operation with the EFTA Surveillance Authority under the provision of Article 57 of the EEA Agreement.

8–098   The relevant product markets — Before identifying the product markets affected by the transaction, the Commission gave an introductory description of the telecommunications industry. In particular, the Commission explained the structure and operation of telephone networks, as well as the significance of access to the local loop and interconnection. It also briefly summarised the internet and broadband services.

Addressing the markets affected by the transaction, the Commission identified the following relevant product markets related to *telephony and related services*: (i) the provision of local loop infrastructure; (ii) the provision of long-distance and international network infrastructure; (iii) the provision of subscriber access to telephone services (with sub-markets for subscriber access to local, long-distance and international services); (iv) the provision of mobile telephony services; (v) operator access to networks (with sub-markets for operator access to local loop, long-distance and international networks); (vi) the provision of business data communications services; (vii) the provision of ISP services (retail and wholesale); (viii) the provision of internet advertising services; and (ix) the sale of advertising space in telephone directories (local and business telephone directories).

In relation to *television services*, the Commission identified the following relevant product markets: (i) the provision of satellite transmission capacity; (ii) the acquisition and distribution (via cable and DTH (direct-to-home satellite)) of television signals; (iii) the buying of content; (iv) the wholesale supply of content rights; and (v) the technology for technical services relating to pay-TV. Also in the television services context, the Commission concluded that there were a number of factors indicating that a certain degree of substitutability already existed between cable, DTH satellite and SMATV (Satellite Mast Antenna Television) distribution platforms. It did not contest third parties' submissions that, with the introduction of digital services, cable and DTH offerings could become less homogeneous, thereby increasing the incentive for customers to switch between different platforms. However, the Commission did not find that there were separate markets for the different television distribution infrastructures and left the market definition open in this respect.[63]

---

[62] Case M.1439, *Telia/Telenor*, Commission Decision of October 13, 1999.
[63] See, however, Case *MSG*, below, para.8–171 *et seq.*, and Case *Nordic Satellite Distribution*, below, para.8–175 *et seq.*, where the Commission found that the distribution of television services by cable was a distinct market from satellite and terrestrial transmission.

With regard to pay-TV services, the Commission followed its previous practice of not subdividing pay-TV services into distinct markets for analogue and digital transmission services, stating that digital services were an emerging market which would gradually replace analogue services.[64]

8–099   The relevant geographic markets — The product markets for *telephony and related services* were found to be national in scope, except for international calls (*i.e.* access to international call services), where the Commission considered that there were separate geographic markets for specific "country pair" relationships,[65] meaning the routes over which traffic can be exchanged between two given countries, for calls from Norway to Sweden, and Norway or Sweden to Denmark and Finland. Regarding the market for business data communications services, the Commission noted that in previous decisions it had found the market to be wider than national, possibly European or even worldwide.

Regarding *television services*, the Commission found the markets for DTH distribution, cable television, the wholesale supply of rights to content and technical services relating to pay-TV to be national in scope. It left open the question of whether the markets for content buying and retail television distribution were national, Scandinavian (Norway, Sweden and Denmark) or Nordic (Norway, Sweden, Denmark and Finland). Finally, it decided, in line with its *Nordic Satellite Distribution* decision,[66] that the market for satellite transponder capacity was Nordic.

8–100   Competitive analysis — The Commission had a number of concerns in relation to this transaction. In general, the Commission was concerned that the merger would have eliminated potential competition between the parties (who were each other's most likely potential competitor) and would have increased the ability and incentives of the merged entity to: (i) eliminate actual competition from third parties, in particular by raising rivals' costs by increasing interconnection tariffs and/or decreasing interconnection quality; (ii) bundle products across a wider geographic area; and (iii) protect its home markets from other operators active in the Nordic region. On a market-by-market basis, the Commission's concerns related to the Swedish and Norwegian markets for fixed switch telephony services (local, long-distance and international), mobile telephony, business data communications, internet access, PABX distribution and local telephone directories. In addition, on the Irish mobile telephony market, the merged entity would have had control over both of the operators active on the Irish mobile market. Finally, as a result of the strengthened vertical integration of the merged entity and the increased number of households connected to its distribution systems, the concentration would have created a dominant position on the markets for retail distribution of television services, content buying, the wholesale supply of content rights, satellite transponder capacity and the technology for scrambling and unscrambling of television signals.

---

[64] See also Case *TPS*, below, para.8–250 *et seq.*, a decision under Art.81 of the EC Treaty; Case *BSkyB/KirchPayTV*, below, para.8–196 *et seq.*, and Cases *Bertelsmann/Kirch Premiere* and *Deutsche Telekom/Beta Research*, below, para.8–187 *et seq.*

[65] The Commission adopted this bilateral routes approach in a number of other cases, including *BT/MCI (II)*, above, para.8–074 *et seq.*; *BT/AT&T*, above, para.8–092 *et seq.*; M.2257, *France Télécom/Equant*, Commission Decision of March 21, 2001, O.J. 2001 C187/08; and *Nordic Satellite Distribution*, below, para.8–175.

[66] Case *Nordic Satellite Distribution*, below, para.8–175 *et seq.*

The Commission approved the concentration only after the parties made the following, extensive commitments: (i) the divestiture of all existing overlaps in the fields of telecommunications services (*i.e.* the sale of Swedish businesses owned by Telenor, and the Norwegian businesses owned by Telia); (ii) either Telia or Telenor selling their shareholdings in one of the two existing Irish mobile telephony operators; and (iii) the divestiture of the parties' interests in cable television networks in Sweden and Norway. Moreover, the Swedish and Norwegian governments (as shareholders in Telia and Telenor) committed to implementing a set of regulatory measures to introduce local loop unbundling in both countries.

This was the first case in which the Commission approved a concentration subject to conditions requiring the parties to provide unbundled access to their local loop networks. The Commission noted that the shortcomings of the regulatory regimes in Sweden and Norway (including no mandatory local loop unbundling and *ex post*, instead of *ex ante*, price regulation of interconnection charges) contributed to the strengthening of the parties' dominant position in their home markets. The Commission also underlined that even if the regulatory systems had been effective, regulation could not have been expected to control or prevent the structural competition problems raised by the merger, *i.e.* it would not have prevented the creation and/or strengthening of a dominant position.[67]

MCI WorldCom/Sprint[68]

8–101   The transaction — The notified concentration consisted of the merger between the two US-based global telecommunications companies, MCI WorldCom and Sprint. The Commission prohibited the transaction despite the parties' offer of commitments, including the divestment of Sprint's internet business.

8–102   The relevant product markets — The Commission defined the following product markets: (i) the provision of top-level (or universal) internet connectivity; (ii) GTS services; and (iii) international voice telephony services.

In its decision, the Commission started its analysis by giving a fairly detailed description of the internet and of the internet access markets. In order to be able to provide end-users with access to the internet, ISPs need to enter into agreements with backbone network providers, so-called connectivity or top-level providers, to reach the whole of the internet. Such arrangements are made either by peering arrangements (*i.e.* an agreement between two network operators to accept traffic from each other's customers for termination on their respective networks, without payment of a fee) or transit arrangements (*i.e.* commercial agreements granting access to the backbone operator's network for a fee). In line with its decision in *WorldCom/MCI*,[69] the Commission identified three different internet access markets: (i) the provision of host to point of presence connectivity; (ii) the provision of internet access services; and (iii) the provision of top-level (or universal) connectivity. The Commission's definition of a distinct product market for the provision of top-level (or universal)

---

[67] On the interaction between competition law and regulation, see Chap.X, below.
[68] Case M.1741, *MCIWorldCom/Sprint*, Commission Decision of June 28, 2000, O.J. 2000 C14/6.
[69] See above, para.8–088 *et seq.*

connectivity was based on a distinction between wholesale and retail internet access services. According to the Commission, only organisations which are capable of delivering complete internet connections using only their own network could be top-level internet connectivity providers. Top-level connectivity must be supplied entirely by peering agreements (or use of their own networks) and not by transit agreements. By contrast, secondary (or second-tier) internet connectivity providers could deliver only some of their own peering-band connectivity and were forced to supplement it through transit services obtained from top-level connectivity providers. The second-tier providers required transit agreements and could not avoid buying transit services from the top-level internet connectivity providers in order to provide universal connectivity. Furthermore, resellers could only supply connectivity acquired from the providers. Therefore, the Commission concluded that neither second-tier providers nor resellers were capable of significantly constraining the behaviour of the operators of the top-level networks or preventing them from acting independently of the other providers.

According to the Commission, GTS services were

> "telecommunications services linking a number of different customer locations, generally in at least two different continents and across a large number of different countries. They are generally purchased by multinational companies or organisations with presence in many countries and a number of continents. The services provided are enhanced services — going beyond the provision of simple services such as basic voice and fax — to provide customers with package solutions including virtual private networks for both voice and data services and advanced functionalities".

GTS services are a basket of telecommunications services on the basis of which companies offer a tailored, customised package of global telecommunications services to their large international corporate customers. This basket includes value-added voice services (virtual private network services, calling cards, freephone services, etc.), domestic and international data communications services using *inter alia* the X.25, frame relay, ATM (Asynchronous Transfer Mode) and IP protocols, dedicated transmission circuits for voice and data services (managed bandwidth, VSAT (Very Small Aperture Terminal) and private virtual circuits), custom network solutions (systems/equipment procurement, tailored and managed services and outsourcing) and platform-based enhanced services (messaging including access to local area network (LAN) interconnection, electronic data interchange (EDI), video-conferencing, audio-conferencing and electronic mail). As in *BT/AT&T*,[70] the Commission investigated whether certain or all of the individual services included in the basket of GTS services could be isolated from other services forming the basket and be considered as separate relevant product markets. On the basis of a detailed market investigation, the Commission concluded that this was not the case and that the relevant product market was GTS services.

8–103 The relevant geographic markets — Following its earlier decision in *WorldCom/MCI*,[71] the Commission defined the market for internet connectivity as being global. As regards the GTS market, the Commission confirmed that it had a global scope, as it had already found in *BT/AT&T*.[72]

---

[70] See above, para.8–092 *et seq.*
[71] See above, para.8–088 *et seq.*
[72] See above, para.8–092 *et seq.*

8–104 Competitive analysis — The Commission concluded that the concentration would have led either to the creation of a dominant position in favour of the merged entity or the strengthening of an existing dominant position in favour of MCI WorldCom on the market for the provision of top-level (or universal) internet connectivity. The Commission identified five operators of top-level networks (MCI WorldCom, Sprint, AT&T, Cable & Wireless and GTE) as having a particularly strong position and was concerned that the merger would have lead to the formation of a powerful top-level network provider that through its size[73] would have been able to behave independently of its competitors and customers, *i.e.* to control the prices of its competitors and customers, to control technical developments, and to discipline the market. Given the global scope of the market for top-level connectivity, the Commission saw a likely impact on consumers in Europe. Furthermore, potential competitors entering the market would need to match the scale and scope of the existing top-level networks in order to qualify for peering with them, thereby deterring market entry. The merged entity's network would have had a much higher percentage of "on-net" traffic than those of its competitors, generating network externalities.[74] This would have allowed the entity to be less dependent on other networks and to have become an unavoidable trading partner for competitors and customers in order for them to stay competitive. Accordingly, the merged entity would have been dominant. The parties had offered to divest Sprint's internet business, but subsequently withdrew both it and the notification (without formally abandoning the merger). The Commission considered that the offered commitment was inadequate to remedy the anti-competitive effects of the concentration, as it would not have re-established, with sufficient certainty, immediate and effective competition in the market for top-level internet connectivity. This was because Sprint's internet business was completely intertwined with its traditional telecommunications businesses, the divested business would have had little power to retain its customer base and would have continued to be dependent on MCI WorldCom/Sprint for its future operations, and the remedies would have been complex to structure, implement and monitor. In part, the Commission appeared to be influenced by the difficulties encountered by Cable & Wireless when it acquired MCI's internet business following conditional approval of the prior WorldCom/MCI merger.

In analysing the concentration's impact on the GTS market, the Commission first found that owing to the important role of the Concert Alliance (BT/AT&T) in global bidding contests for GTS customers, a merged MCI WorldCom/Sprint could not have been expected to have enjoyed a single dominant position. The Commission also examined whether the two largest players (MCI WorldCom/Sprint and the Concert Alliance) would have had a joint dominant position on the

---

[73] The Commission's investigation showed that the merged entity's market share would have been between 37 and 51% (based on traffic exchanged) and 30 and 65% (based on revenue). In its decision in *WorldCom/MCI*, the Commission has already expressed concerns about the level of concentration in this market, because, at that time, MCI and WorldCom were the market leaders in wholesale internet connectivity, with market shares of around 30–40% (WorldCom) and 10–20% (MCI), with Sprint being the second largest universal internet connectivity provider with a market share of around 10–15%. The approval of the WorldCom/MCI transaction was, therefore, at the time conditional upon the divestment of MCI's internet business, which was sold to Cable & Wireless. See above, para.8–088 *et seq.*

[74] Network externalities exist when the amount that one party is willing to pay for access to a network depends on who and how many other parties are connected to it: see Abbamonte and Rabassa, "Foreclosure and Vertical Mergers — The Commission's Review of Vertical Effects in the Last Wave of Media and Internet Mergers" (2001) E.C.L.R. 214.

GTS market following the concentration. The Commission found, however, that the existence of competitive constraints from competitors such as Equant and Cable & Wireless would have prevented parallel behaviour by the two leading players. Therefore, one of the elements necessary for a finding of joint collective dominance was absent.[75]

Telia/Oracle/Drutt[76]

8–105   The transaction — The transaction involved the acquisition of joint control by Swedish incumbent Telia and Oracle of Drutt Corporation, a full-function joint venture, which was originally solely controlled by the software company Oracle. The Swedish operating subsidiary of Drutt was active in developing and marketing the open wireless portal *www.halebop.com*, and it provided internet access via mobile networks, particularly WAP-enabled handsets, in Sweden.

8–106   The relevant product markets — The Commission identified three relevant product markets, namely the provision of: (i) internet advertising space; (ii) dial-up internet access; and (iii) internet portal services.

As Drutt would have been financed by advertising revenues rather than subscription fees, the Commission considered that a separate market for the provision of internet advertising space was relevant. It indicated that there could be a further, narrower market for selling advertising on mobile platforms, but ultimately left this question open. The Commission noted that owing to the increase in the number of ways to access the internet, its competition analysis needed to look beyond the traditional dial-up and dedicated internet access using fixed line and PC as access tools. However, as already indicated in *Vodafone/Vivendi/Canal+*,[77] the Commission found that internet access via mobile phones was unlikely to be a substitute for the traditional means of internet access, owing to the differences in the sizes of the screens and the format of the material that can be obtained through the different platforms. Ultimately, the Commission did not decide whether dial-up internet access via mobile phones represented a distinct product market from internet access via PCs. Finally, the Commission found that the market for internet portals could be divided into vertical portals (with a focus on particular content categories) and horizontal portals (with a comprehensive internet offering), and that vertical portals could be further broken down according to the type of platform used. The Commission also considered distinguishing the mobile platform market by the type of handset used (*i.e.* WAP-enabled or second generation handsets), but since Drutt's number of registered users of the portal services was greater than the number of WAP phones in circulation, it doubted that the market would be this narrow.

8–107   The relevant geographic markets — The market for internet advertising was considered to be national in geographic scope, although the Commission suggested that it might also be wider

---

[75] In Case T–342/99, *Airtours/Commission* [2002] II E.C.R. 2585, the Court of First Instance confirmed that the Commission may prohibit a merger if it would lead to the creation or strengthening of a dominant position and set out the relevant criteria that must be met. See above, para.8–025, n.74.

[76] Case M.1982, *Telia/Oracle/Drutt*, Commission Decision of September 11, 2000, O.J. 2000 C374/10.

[77] Case COMP/JV.48, *Vodafone/Vivendi/Canal+*, Commission Decision of July 17, 2000; O.J. 2003 C118/25.

based on common language areas. The Commission furthermore restated its position that internet-related markets may be considered to be national due to the need for local loop services.[78] It was suggested that this (internet-related) market was national, but could be increasingly European.

8–108   Competitive analysis — The Commission found that there was no overlap between Oracle or Telia on the one hand and Drutt on the other, on either the internet advertising or dial-up internet access markets. In particular, the Commission held that Telia's position on the Swedish market for dial-up internet access would not have been strengthened by the transaction, because Drutt's services existed and would have continued to exist separately from Telia's dial-up internet access services. In relation to the provision of internet portal services, whether general or specifically for mobile customers, the Commission found that the combination of Drutt's services with those of Telia would not have threatened to create or strengthen a dominant market position, regardless of how that market was defined, due to Drutt's low reach, the number of significant competitors active in Sweden and the low barriers to entry into the market.

France Télécom/Equant[79]

8–109   The transaction — The transaction concerned the acquisition by France Télécom of sole control of Equant by way of a purchase of the majority of Equant's share capital. The transaction resulted in a merger of the networks of Equant and Global One, a wholly owned subsidiary of France Télécom.

8–110   The relevant product markets — The Commission identified the following relevant product markets: (i) bilateral international routes; (ii) global telecommunications services; (iii) the provision of managed data network services (MDNS); (iv) the provision of global telecommunications services/MDNS to French companies; and (v) the provision of telecommunications services to French companies.

In line with previous decisions,[80] the Commission found that there were distinct markets for the provision of telecommunications services on bilateral routes (country pairs). It suggested, furthermore, that the provision of carrier services between any pair of countries or territories could have constituted a separate relevant product market, but ultimately left the market definition open. With respect to GTS services, the Commission referred to its previous decisions,[81] but drew a further distinction between: (i) "*managed solutions*", consisting of higher level end-to-end services meeting the client's specific requirements and combining the management of the network and equipment and the provision of related services (such as MDNS); and (ii) "*unmanaged solutions*", consisting of basic services with a lower degree of management and customisation (such as the provision of bandwidth, basic VPN, frame relay, and ATM services). The Commission's investigation had shown that the provision of cross-border MDNS services could be a discrete market

---

[78] See Case *Telia/Telenor*, above, para.8–097 *et seq.*
[79] Case M.2257, *France Télécom/Equant*, Commission Decision of March 21, 2001, O.J. 2001 C187/08.
[80] Cases *BT/MCI (II)*, above, para.8–074 *et seq.*; and *BT/AT&T*, above, para.8–092 *et seq.*
[81] Cases *BT/MCI (II)*, above, para.8–074 *et seq.*; *BT/AT&T*, above, para.8–092 *et seq.*; and *MCI WorldCom/Sprint*, above, para.8–101 *et seq.*

within the wider categories of data communications services or global telecommunications services because of different demand- and supply-side considerations.

8–111   The relevant geographic markets — In *BT/MCI (II)*, the Commission identified two distinct geographic markets within any international route, each comprised of the originating bilateral traffic from the countries concerned.[82] The Commission followed this approach to market definitions for bilateral international routes. The market for GTS services was considered to be global in scope. With respect to the provision of MDNS services to multinational corporations, it was recognised that these services could be provided on a national, pan-European or global level, and that the geographic market was at least pan-European, if not global in scope.

8–112   Competitive assessment — Since France Télécom did not have any significant interests on the routes linking France to the countries to which Equant had privileged access, the concentration did not involve any significant overlaps on any bilateral international routes. As to the market(s) for GTS services, irrespective of whether an assessment was made on the basis of a market for global telecommunications services to multinational corporations or the narrowest market for MDNS services to French customers, the transaction did not lead to the creation or strengthening of a dominant position. The Commission found that even if the merged entity would have generated half of the total market revenues from the provision of MDNS services to corporate customers, this would not have prevented its competitors from bidding successfully for new contracts on what was principally a "bidding market". In reaching this conclusion, the Commission analysed a list of the main GTS providers that customers would consider using. This analysis showed that, besides Global One and Equant, Concert, WorldCom and Infonet had taken part in a significant number of bids in the past and had won a significant number of new contracts. This demonstrated the ability of several competitors to credibly take part in future bids. Therefore, the Commission concluded that there was no indication that the merged entity would have been able to use its existing market position to prevent future competition in the market for GTS services, irrespective of the geographic scope of the market.

Speedy Tomato/Olivetti [83]

8–113   The transaction — The transaction involved the creation of a joint venture in Italy, Speedy Tomato S.p.A., by Speedy Tomato AB, a subsidiary of Telia, the Swedish telecommunications group and Olivetti Tecnost, a subsidiary of the Italian Olivetti Group. The joint venture was formed to launch the Italian version of the Speedy Tomato internet portal.

8–114   The relevant product markets — The aim of the joint venture was to offer internet portal services in Italy such as email, SMS, chat and calendar, news, weather, sport, financial services, games and horoscopes as well as paid-for content services provided by third party providers. The Commission considered in detail the possible existence of separate product markets for the provision of internet advertising space and the provision of internet portal services. Previously,[84]

---

[82] Case *BT/MCI (II)*, above, para.8–074 *et seq.*
[83] Case M.2463, *Speedy Tomato/Olivetti*, Commission Decision of June 14, 2001, O.J. 2001 C279/7.
[84] Case JV.11, *@Home Benelux*, Commission Decision of September 15, 1998, O.J. 1999 C178/17; and Case *Vodafone/Vivendi/Canal+*, below, para.8–138 *et seq.*

the Commission had defined internet advertising as being a market in its own right and noted, without taking a definitive position, that this market could be divided further into advertising for fixed and mobile platforms. In respect of internet portal services, the Commission also referred to its decision in *Vodafone/Vivendi/Canal+*,[85] in which it had recognised the possibility that there is a distinct market for different types of internet portal. For horizontal portals the market could be divided according to which platform is used to access the internet (*i.e.* PC, mobile phone, digital television). Vertical portals were seen as those that focus on providing relatively narrow access to a particular content category.

8–115   The relevant geographic markets — The market for internet advertising was considered by the Commission as likely to be national in scope, although it could have been wider if the same language is spoken in more than one country. It took the same approach with respect to internet portal services.

8–116   Competitive assessment — The concentration did not threaten to create or strengthen a dominant position on the Italian markets for internet advertising space or internet portals. This was because Telia was not active in the Italian portal market and although Olivetti had a 30–50 per cent market share of the internet dial-up access in Italy (through its Telecom Italia subsidiary), there were no indications that the vertical relationship would have given rise to any competition concerns.

Pirelli/Edizione/Olivetti/Telecom Italia[86]

8–117   The transaction — The transaction consisted of the acquisition of joint control of Olivetti (and indirectly of its subsidiary Telecom Italia) by Pirelli and Edizione.

8–118   *The relevant product markets* — The Commission identified the following relevant markets: (i) telecommunications infrastructure; (ii) telecommunications services; (iii) mobile telecommunications services; and (iv) transmission capacity (including capacity on local access (or local loop), incumbent national and international backbone networks).

8–119   The relevant geographic markets — The Commission defined the geographic scope of the market for telecommunications infrastructure as being EU-wide; and as national for fixed and mobile telecommunications services and the provision of transmission capacity.

8–120   Competitive assessment — The Commission concluded that the transaction did not raise any issues of dominance on the markets for telecommunications infrastructure and services, because the concentration would not have changed the position of the parties on these markets. However, in the market for mobile telephony, the concentration would have reduced the number of licensed operators from four to three, because Blu was jointly controlled by Edizione, Autostrade and Sitech and Telecom Italia Mobile was controlled by Olivetti. The Commission further noted

---

[85] *ibid.*
[86] Case M.2574, *Pirelli/Edizione/Olivetti/Telecom Italia*, Commission Decision of September 20, 2001, O.J. 2001 C325/12.

that the Italian mobile market also had high barriers to entry. The transaction therefore raised serious competition concerns in the Italian mobile market, on which Telecom Italia Mobile had a dominant position. Moreover, the transaction would have reinforced the existing dominant position of Telecom Italia in the Italian transmission capacity market, because of the participation of Edizione in Autostrade, which was a competitor to Telecom Italia in the same market for long-distance connections. Although other operators were installing their own networks, the market still presented high barriers to entry owing to the timing, costs and difficulties of building networks (including obtaining rights of way and the topography of Italy).

To address the Commission's concerns, the parties committed to divest Edizione's participation in both Autostrade and Blu to a suitable purchaser possessing the necessary technical and financial resources for developing their respective activities. This undertaking was designed to promote the development of UMTS services and prevent any strengthening of the dominant position held by Telecom Italia Mobile on the Italian mobile market. However, Edizione failed to find a suitable purchaser for its participation in Blu and owing to its weak financial position, Blu risked liquidation, which could have caused anti-competitive effects. Therefore, in August 2002, Edizione received the Commission's authorisation for the separate sale of the business assets of Blu to the other mobile operators.[87] The new measures involve transferring Blu's sites and employees to each of the operators in the sector (Telecom Italia Mobile, Omnitel, Wind and H3G), its brand name and customer base to Wind, and the whole of its share capital to Telecom Italia Mobile. Blu's frequencies will be reallocated by the competent national regulatory authorities in a non-discriminatory manner as part of the forthcoming "re-farming" process in which the entire frequency spectrum is to be reallocated. The Commission also required the operators concerned to enter into agreements to ensure fair and non-discriminatory use of site and facilities, in order to ensure both that Telecom Italia Mobile's existing dominant position on the Italian GSM market could not be strengthened, and that future UMTS operators could roll out their networks.

BT/Concert[88]

8–121   The transaction — This transaction concerned the break-up of Concert, a joint venture originally created and jointly controlled by AT&T and British Telecommunications (BT) for the provision of global telecommunication services.[89] The transaction was intended to return to BT and AT&T assets initially contributed to the joint venture. Certain of Concert's assets were transferred to AT&T. BT then acquired AT&T's 50 per cent share in Concert.

8–122   The relevant product markets — The relevant product markets for the assessment of the concentration were identified as the provision of: (i) GTS to multinational customers; (ii) international carrier services (ICS) to carriers worldwide; (iii) advanced mobile telecommunications

---

[87] Commission Press Release, IP/02/1183 of August 6, 2002. See also Case M.2958, *Wind/Blu*, Commission Decision of September 12, 2002, O.J. 2002 C239/20, which concerned Wind's acquisition of certain assets of Blu.

[88] Case M.2642, *BT/Concert*, Commission Decision of December 17, 2001, O.J. 2002 C079/11. See also Case M.2651, *AT&T/Concert*, Commission Decision of December 17, 2001, O.J. 2002 C16/15, concerning AT&T's acquisition of assets originally contributed by it to Concert. This was dealt with under the simplified procedure.

[89] See Case *BT/AT&T*, above, para.8–092 *et seq.*

services to business customers and mobile telecommunications services in the United Kingdom and Ireland; and (iv) certain telecommunications services in the United Kingdom and Ireland.

8–123 The relevant geographic markets — The Commission considered that the geographic scope of the product markets was global for GTS and ICS services, regional for the provision of mobile services to business customers, and national in relation to the provision of mobile and other services in the UK and Ireland. However, the Commission ultimately left the precise definition open, given that even on the narrowest product and geographic market definitions, the transaction raised no competition concerns.

8–124 Competitive assessment — The transaction did not lead to the creation or strengthening of a dominant position on any relevant market. With regard to horizontal aspects, the only potential area of overlap was the market for tele-conferencing services where both BT and Concert were present; however, BT had already withdrawn from this market prior to the transaction. The Commission, therefore, was able to focus on the assessment of whether the disappearance of Concert, and the acquisition of part of its assets by BT, might allow BT to create or strengthen a dominant position on any affected upstream and downstream telecommunications market in the United Kingdom or Ireland.

The following markets were found to be vertically affected because BT had market shares greater than 25 per cent: (i) the UK market for business and residential retail basic voice services; (ii) the UK backhaul market; (iii) the UK domestic value-added data services market; (iv) the UK tele-conferencing market; and (v) the market for the national distribution of GTS services in Ireland. BT claimed that there would be no strengthening of its position on these markets because the transaction did not significantly affect its already existing vertical relationship with Concert and the markets were dynamic and competitive owing to the existence of a number of competitors, low barriers to entry thereby facilitating entry by newcomers and the fact that price is the main factor for customers in choosing a supplier. The Commission agreed with BT's assertions and concluded that the UK and Irish markets where BT was present, as well as the markets where Concert was active, appeared to be competitive in terms of the number of players and choice for customers and end-users, the level of prices, and the possibility for customers to change suppliers. Finally, the transaction would not increase barriers to entry. Therefore, the Commission concluded that the de-concentration and BT's acquisition of part of Concert would have had no appreciable impact either on the competitive structure of the UK and Irish markets or on the businesses of Concert's customers.

KPNQwest/Ebone/Global TeleSystems[90]

8–125 The transaction — The transaction, effected through bankruptcy proceedings in the Netherlands and the United States, led to the acquisition by KPNQwest of control over the Ebone and Central European operations of Global TeleSystems (GTS), a US-based telecommunications operator. KPNQwest was a joint venture between the Dutch incumbent operator KPN Telecom and US-based Qwest Communications International, and provided international data services.

---

[90] Case M.2648, *KPNQwest/Ebone/GTS*, Commission Decision of January 16, 2002, O.J. 2002 C034/10.

8–126   The relevant product markets — In its decision, the Commission left open the precise definition of the relevant product and geographic markets for all market segments that could have been affected, because no competition concerns arose as a result of the transaction. However, there was for the first time since the burst of the new economy "bubble" a discussion of the Commission's previous approach to market definition. The Commission identified the following markets: (i) carriers' carrier services; (ii) internet connectivity (wholesale); (iii) dedicated internet access (retail); (iv) global corporate telecommunications services (GCTS); and (v) web-hosting.

The Commission had found in previous decisions that the traditional model of telecommunications carriers entering into separate arrangements with other individual carriers was increasingly being challenged by players with global network infrastructure that offer other carriers a wide range of services. As a result, there was a distinct market for *carriers' carrier services*, consisting of the leasing of transmission capacity and the provision of related services to third party telecommunications carriers and service providers.[91] The most relevant related services included:

(i) *switched transit*, that is the transport of traffic over bilateral facilities between the originating carrier, the transit carrier and the terminating carrier: neither the originating carrier nor the terminating carrier need bilateral facilities between themselves, but need facilities only with the transit carrier;

(ii) *traffic hubbing offerings*, where the provider takes care of all or part of the international connections required by the carrier: these offerings are typically designed for new entrant carriers, which are interconnected with the provider over bilateral facilities and whose international traffic is merged with other traffic on the provider's global network;

(iii) *reseller services* for providing capacity to service providers without international telecommunications facilities of their own; and

(iv) *dedicated transit services*, that is leased line offerings for the transport of traffic through the domestic network of the transit carrier[92] which the Commission considered were part of the carriers' carrier market.

The Commission, in line with previous decisions, found several distinct product markets for the provision of internet access services. In relation to the wholesale internet connectivity market, the Commission referred to the definitions adopted in its *WorldCom/MCI* and *MCI WorldCom/Sprint* decisions, *i.e.* that there are distinct products markets for top-level interconnectivity, second-tier interconnectivity and retail internet access.[93] Furthermore, it suggested that there might be separate markets for dial-up access and dedicated ("always on") connections. The market investigation also confirmed the Commission's findings in previous decisions, distinguishing between internet access

[91] See also Case *Unisource*, Commission Decision of October 29, 1997, O.J. 1997 L318/1; and Case *BT/AT&T*, above, para.8–092 *et seq.*
[92] Leased line facilities used for this purpose may include discrete voice circuits or a high-bandwidth digital circuits that can be used for both voice and data services.
[93] Case *WorldCom/MCI*, above, para.8–088 *et seq.*; and Case *MCI WorldCom/Sprint*, above, para.8–101 *et seq.*

services to residential and to commercial customers, since commercial customers generally required dedicated internet access, while residential end-users preferred dial-up.[94] However, the investigation showed that the demands of residential and corporate customers are converging, with the introduction of xDSL broadband services and broadband ("always on") internet access via cable networks.

As in *France Télécom/Equant*,[95] the Commission again considered whether there were separate markets for the supply of managed and unmanaged data services to corporate customers or whether they were part of the wider market for GCTS services, *i.e.* packaged enhanced cross-border telecommunications solutions supplied to large national and international corporate customers.[96] At least four market segments were identified within the market for web-hosting services: (i) the local supply of basic co-location services such as connectivity, power and the physical facilities; (ii) the national supply of shared and dedicated hosting, *i.e.* hosting a customer's website on the host's servers and providing necessary support applications; (iii) the national and possibly cross-border, regional supply of managed services to permit the outsourcing of complex enterprise applications and support infrastructure, including "front-end" and "back-office" applications hosted on the providers' platforms (so-called "ASP"); and (iv) the national supply of content delivery services (CDS) such as streaming content delivery services and static content delivery products.

8–127 The relevant geographic markets — The Commission suggested the following geographic markets (but did not take a final position): (i) the market for carriers' carrier services was at least Europe-wide and possibly global, in line with its decision in *BT/AT&T*; (ii) the scope of internet connectivity services was global, as it had found in *MCI WorldCom/Sprint*; (iii) the market for retail internet access services was national in scope, as found in *Telia/Telenor* and confirmed in *UGC/Liberty Media*; (iv) the scope of GCTS services was at least EEA-wide and possibly world-wide, in line with *FT/Equant* and *MCI WorldCom/Sprint*; (v) the market for co-location services was local; and (vi) the market for shared and dedicated hosting, ASP and CDS services was national, even though some of these services might be provided on a cross-border basis.

8–128 Competitive assessment — The Commission's market investigation did not identify any competition concerns in any of the relevant markets and demonstrated that the merged entity would have continued to face strong competition and competitive constraints from a number of large competitors both at the European and world levels in all areas, including internet connectivity services in Europe, where the merged entity would be a significant (but not dominant) provider.

Telia/Sonera[97]

8–129 The transaction — This transaction concerned the acquisition by Telia, the incumbent telecommunications and the largest cable TV operator in Sweden, of sole control over Sonera, the

---

[94] See Case *BT/Esat Digifone*, below, para.8–154 *et seq.*; and Case M.2222, *UGC/Liberty Media*, Commission Decision of April 24, 2001, O.J. 2001 C172/20.

[95] See above, para.8–109 *et seq.*

[96] See Cases *BT/AT&T*, above, para.8–092 *et seq.*; *MCI WorldCom/Sprint*, above, para.8–101 *et seq.*; and *British Telecom/MCI II*, above, para.8–074 *et seq.*

[97] Case M.2803, *Telia/Sonera*, Commission Decision of July 10, 2002, O.J. 2002 C201/19.

largest provider of long-distance national and international network services in Finland. Both companies also had other activities, including in the mobile and internet sectors.

8–130   The relevant product markets — The Commission distinguished the following relevant markets, namely the provision of: (i) mobile telephony services; (ii) wholesale international roaming services; (iii) Wireless Local Area Network (WLAN) services; (iv) operator access to networks, *i.e.* interconnection and call termination regarding mobile and fixed networks; (v) corporate communications services; and (vi) internet access services. Referring to previous decisions,[98] the Commission confirmed the existence of a separate market for the operation of mobile communications networks, which are not substitutable for fixed line services. In line with previous decisions,[99] the Commission also defined separate markets for international roaming services (as distinct from national roaming), the provision of airtime on mobile networks, and the provision of indirect access through carrier pre-selection (*i.e.* call origination) or pre-selection. The Commission left open, however, the question of whether the provision of WLAN[1] services formed a separate product market distinct from a wider mobile communications services and/or a wider corporate communications services market.

The Commission identified a separate product market for call termination, further distinguishing between markets for call termination on mobile networks and termination on fixed networks. This finding was in line with the general approach taken by the Commission in the context of defining markets for the purpose of the New Regulatory Framework[2] and the (preliminary) conclusions reached by the Commission in its Statement of Objections of March 27, 2002 addressed to KPN for the alleged abuse of a dominant position regarding the termination of telephone calls on the KPN network.[3] The precise definition of the markets for corporate communications services was left open, as was the definition of the market for internet access services.

8–131   The relevant geographic markets — The Commission did not decide whether the market for the provision of mobile telephony networks was wider than national. In *Telia/Telenor*, *Vodafone/Airtouch* and *Vodafone Airtouch/Mannesmann*,[4] the Commission had found this market to be national. The geographic markets for wholesale international roaming, WLAN services, call termination and call origination services and internet access services were considered to be national in scope. The Commission did not take a final decision on the geographic scope of the markets for corporate communications services.

8–132   Competitive assessment — The transaction was only approved subject to far-reaching conditions that reflected commitments made by the parties. The Commission found that the

[98] Cases *Telia/Telenor*, above, para.8–097 *et seq.*; and *Vodafone Airtouch/Mannesmann*, Commission Decision of April 12, 2000, O.J. 2000 C141/19.

[99] Case M.2726, *KPN/E-Plus*, Commission Decision of March 7, 2002, O.J. 2002 C079/12; and Case M.1863, *Vodafone/BT/Airtel JV*, Commission Decision of December 18, 2000, O.J. 2001 C042/11.

[1] WLAN technology is used to enable data (but not voice) communication in buildings by avoiding cabling, and in public locations to provide broadband internet access.

[2] See Commission on the Relevant Markets for the purpose of *ex ante* regulation, para.1–020 *et seq.*

[3] Commission Press Release, IP/02/483 of March 27, 2002.

[4] Case *Telia/Telenor*, above, para.8–097 *et seq.*; Case M.1430, *Vodafone/AirTouch*, Commission Decision of May 21, 1999, O.J. 1999 C295/2; and Case *Vodafone Airtouch/Mannesmann*, below, para.8–142 *et seq.*

transaction would have led to direct horizontal overlaps in the parties' activities in Finland for mobile communications services. The combined market share of the parties would have increased to between 55 and 70 per cent, twice the size of their closest competitor. To remedy this concern, Telia committed to divest its mobile communications businesses in Finland, including equipment for the provision of WLAN services. This also addressed concerns raised by the overlaps in the parties' businesses for wholesale international roaming and WLAN services in Finland.

The Commission identified Telia as an actual or potential competitor that could have exercised competitive pressure on Sonera in Finland. Therefore, the Commission concluded that Sonera's existing dominant position in a number of fixed and mobile telecommunications markets would have been strengthened by the elimination of Telia as an actual or, in some cases, potential competitor for a wide range of telecommunications services in Finland. Finally, the Commission was concerned about the vertical integration of: (i) the parties' activities in certain retail markets, such as corporate communications and mobile communications services, in both Sweden and Finland, where the parties had strong market positions; (ii) the parties' activities for the provision of wholesale call termination services on their respective fixed and mobile telephony networks, where the parties had monopoly positions; and (iii) the parties' activities for the provision of wholesale international roaming in Sweden and Finland, where the parties had strong market positions. The Commission concluded that there were vertical links, which would have given the merged entity the opportunity to foreclose competitors from the retail services markets in both countries, thereby creating, or strengthening existing dominant positions.

In order to remedy the Commission's concerns of market foreclosure, Telia committed to divest its cable network in Sweden and to create separate legal entities for each of the parties' fixed and mobile networks and services in both Sweden and Finland. The Commission considered cable as being the most credible substitute to the local loop infrastructure of the incumbents. The acquirer of Telia's cable television network could thus — upon the upgrade of the cable network — offer "triple play" services, *i.e.* the provision of high speed internet access, television and telephony services, in competition with the merged entity's services provided over the traditional telephone lines. The parties further committed to grant third parties non-discriminatory access to their fixed and mobile network services as well as to their international wholesale roaming services in Sweden and Finland. The open access obligations (which were behavioural in nature) were considered by the Commission as sufficient to remedy its competition concern, since they were backed by a structural remedy leading to the legal separation of the merged entity's activities, which would assist in monitoring the behavioural remedies.

(c) Concentrations in the Mobile Sector

8–133 Over the last few years, the number of acquisitions, mergers, joint ventures and other transactions in the mobile sector has dramatically increased reflecting the growing importance of these services.[5] With the introduction of UMTS services throughout Europe, the number of mergers in this sector may increase further, although a major difficulty remains the regulatory issues

[5] See below, App.7.

surrounding the sale or surrender of a UMTS licence. Already under the current GSM system, three operators, UK-based Vodafone, the French-based France Télécom group and the German-based Deutsche Telekom, have in particular been very active in acquiring (mainly majority) interests in mobile operators all over Europe to build up a pan-European mobile network providing seamless services to mobile customers, particularly business users. In *Vodafone AirTouch/ Mannesmann*, the geographic scope of the merged entity's networks made the Commission fear that the transaction would have created network effects and gatekeeper issues that would have given the merged entity a unique position on a pan-European basis, thereby detrimentally affecting competition, and led to Vodafone offering open access remedies to guarantee that its competitors were also able to offer the same seamless pan-European services of the same quality. As a result of these open access remedies, Vodafone was subsequently able to make further acquisitions of European mobile operators which were also cleared by the Commission subject to the same conditions.[6] The Commission also imposed an open access condition on Vodafone in the *Vizzavi* case.[7] Again owing to network effects and gatekeeper concerns, the Commission obliged the parties to the *Vizzavi* joint venture to grant third parties access to Vodafone's mobile web portal.

In addition to concentrations that have specifically concerned the mobile market, a number of others have had an impact upon the mobile sector as well as on the fixed sector.[8]

Vodafone/AirTouch[9]

8–134   The transaction — This transaction consisted of the acquisition of AirTouch by Vodafone. Both companies were involved in the operation of mobile telecommunications networks and the *rationale* for the transaction was to enable the merged group to provide seamless mobile communications worldwide.

8–135   The relevant product markets — Although it did not take a definitive position on the definition of the relevant product market, the Commission seemed to agree with the parties that there was a single market for mobile telecommunications services, regardless of the technical standard used to provide such services (*i.e.* analogue, GSM 900 or DCS 1800). Whilst analogue networks were in the process of being entirely replaced by second generation digital platforms (GSM 900 and DCS 1800), the two digital standards were readily substitutable for one another from a consumer's perspective. Moreover, dual-mode handsets rendered the distinction between the two standards less of an issue for the consumer.

8–136   The relevant geographic markets — The Commission considered that the relevant geographic market was national, despite the increased availability of roaming facilities that enabled subscribers to use their existing handset on a foreign network. A subscription with a mobile

---

[6] Case M.2305, *Vodafone Group Plc/Eircell*, Commission Decision of March 2, 2001, O.J. 2001 C128/3; and Case M.2469, *Vodafone/Airtel*, Commission Decision of June 26, 2001, O.J. 2001 C207/9.

[7] See Case *Vodafone/Vivendi/Canal+*, below, para.8–138 *et seq.*

[8] In particular, Case *Telia/Sonera*, above, para.8–129 *et seq.*; and Case *Pirelli/Edizione/Olivetti/Telecom Italia*, above, para.8–117 *et seq.*

[9] Case M.1430, *Vodafone/AirTouch*, Commission Decision of May 21, 1999, O.J. 1999 C295/2.

operator established in another Member State was not an economically sensible alternative for a customer, given the significant additional costs associated with permanent international roaming.

8–137 Competitive analysis — Based on national markets, the activities of the parties only overlapped in Sweden and Germany. In Sweden, AirTouch and Vodafone had holdings in Europolitan (51.1 per cent and 20 per cent respectively). However, this did not lead to any increase in market share, nor to any modification in the nature of control of Europolitan. The combined entity remained in third place behind the two leading players, Telia Mobitel and Comviq, hence the transaction did not give rise to any competition concerns in Sweden.

In Germany, AirTouch had a joint venture with Mannesmann, Mannesmann Mobilfunk, which, through its subsidiary D2, was the market leader in the German mobile market. AirTouch had joint control of Mannesmann Mobilfunk. Vodafone had a joint venture, E-Plus, with o.tel.o and Bell South, the third largest operator on the German market. Vodafone had joint control of E-Plus. The Commission noted that, given the presence of T-Mobile (the second largest player on the German mobile market and a subsidiary of Deutsche Telekom, the incumbent German fixed operator), the concentration was not likely to lead to the creation of single dominance on the market. However, the transaction, by creating a structural link between two of the three main mobile operators in Germany (E-Plus and D2) would have created a duopolistic market situation (between E-Plus and D2 on the one hand and T-Mobile on the other), accounting for almost 100 per cent of a market which had considerable barriers to entry (*i.e.* the need to obtain regulatory licences, which were unlikely) and in which information was readily available to customers and competitors who wish to make pricing comparisons. According to the Commission, these factors could have resulted in anti-competitive parallel behaviour and, absent commitments from the parties, it could have opened a Phase II investigation. In order to address these concerns, the Commission approved the transaction subject to Vodafone's commitment to sell its entire shareholding in E-Plus, thereby eliminating any overlap between the parties in the German mobile telecommunications market.

Vodafone/Vivendi/Canal+ (Vizzavi) [10]

8–138 The transaction — The operation concerned the creation of a full-function joint venture, "Vizzavi", by Vodafone, Vivendi and Canal+. Vizzavi was set up by the parties to provide a multi-access internet portal in Europe, providing customers with a seamless environment for web-based interactive services, across a variety of platforms, such as fixed and mobile telephone networks, PCs, palm-top computers and television sets.

8–139 The relevant product markets — The Commission found the following product markets to be relevant: (i) market for internet access; (ii) internet content and services markets (with further segments for internet advertising and provision of paid-for content); (iii) market for portals, distinguishing portals with a broad focus (horizontal portals) or a narrow focus (vertical portals); and (iv) market for digital interactive television services. Furthermore, the Commission identified the following closely related upstream markets: (i) market for mobile telecommunications services; and (ii) market for pay-television.

---

[10] Case COMP/JV.48, *Vodafone/Vivendi/Canal+*, Commission Decision of July 17, 2000 O.J. 2003 C118/25.

For the first time, the Commission defined a separate market for portals based on the existence of a specific consumer demand for particular intermediation services. In line with its *BiB* decision, the Commission confirmed that end-user substitutability for a package of interactive services was distinguishable from demand substitutability of the individual services that form part of the package. Therefore, a market for portals could clearly be distinguished from the market for internet access as well as from the markets for internet content and services.

8–140 The relevant geographic markets — The Commission found the markets for internet access as well as for internet content and services to be national in scope. In the view of the Commission, the same was true for the markets for digital interactive television services and for mobile telecommunications services. The market for portals was considered to be pan-European. Finally, the Commission found it possible to define a Nordic pay-TV market, owing to language characteristics and largely uniform programming of pay-TV in the Nordic countries (Denmark, Norway and Sweden, as regards language and programming, Finland as regards programming).

8–141 Competitive assessment — The Commission was concerned that the creation of Vizzavi could have had an anti-competitive effect on: (i) the developing national markets for television-based internet portals; and (ii) the developing national and pan-European markets for mobile phone-based internet portals. These concerns arose owing to the range of the parties' activities in mobile networks, content and television platforms, which could have foreclosed competing content providers and portal providers.

In order to address these concerns, the Commission approved the joint venture only after the parties committed to permit third party access to their pay-TV and mobile platforms on a non-discriminatory basis, whereby consumers could choose their content provider, independently of their access provider, by allowing them to access third party portals, change the default portal themselves, and authorise a third party portal operator to change the default setting for them.

The undertakings ensured that the then current competitive model of internet services pursuant to which consumers could choose their content provider regardless of their access provider would be carried over into the emerging market of internet provision via mobile phones and digital television.

Vodafone Airtouch/Mannesmann[11]

8–142 The transaction — The transaction concerned the takeover of Mannesmann by Vodafone. Following an unsolicited public bid (which Mannesmann ultimately agreed to), Vodafone acquired sole control over Mannesmann in March 2000.

8–143 The relevant product markets — As in previous decisions,[12] the Commission based its assessment of the concentration on the definition of a product market for mobile telecommunications services encompassing both GSM 900 and GSM 1800 and possibly also analogue

[11] Case M.1795, *Vodafone Airtouch/Mannesmann*, Commission Decision of April 12, 2000, O.J. 2000 C141/19.
[12] Case *Vodafone/AirTouch*, above, para.8–134 *et seq.*

platforms, although the exact market definition was ultimately left open. The Commission also suggested that a further segmentation could be made between markets for network operators and service providers and/or between business and residential customers, but that this was premature. A distinct market was, however, identified for the provision of the emerging advanced seamless pan-European mobile telecommunication services to internationally mobile customers. These services, which would be provided using enhanced GSM networks equipped with technologies such as GPRS, EDGE and CAMEL,[13] included mobile internet services, mobile video, wireless location services and other data-based services for mobile users. Finally, the Commission concluded that there were distinct markets for mobile telephony handsets and for mobile telecommunications network equipment.

8–144 The relevant geographic markets — The Commission considered that the market for mobile telephony services was national. It left, however, the definition of the geographic market open for the product markets for advanced mobile telecommunication services, mobile telephony handsets and mobile network equipment.

8–145 Competitive analysis — Taking into account the national dimension of the product market, the activities of the parties as providers of mobile telecommunications services overlapped only in the United Kingdom and Belgium. In the United Kingdom, the merger would have resulted in the merged entity having sole control over two of the four existing operators with a combined market share of 53.6 per cent (Vodafone 33.2 per cent, and Mannesmann 20.4 per cent, via Orange). The high market shares and the limited amount of available spectrum in the United Kingdom, which acted as a barrier to the granting of a new licence, raised serious doubts as to the transaction's compatibility with the common market.[14] The same conclusion was reached as regards the Belgian market, where Vodafone and Mannesmann had joint control of Belgacom Mobile and KPN Orange respectively. The merger would have resulted in the merged entity having a market share of nearly 70 per cent. To remove the concerns raised in the United Kingdom and in Belgium, the parties committed to the de-merger of Orange, the Mannesmann subsidiary that operated in the United Kingdom and had a 50 per cent shareholding in KPN Orange. Orange was subsequently sold to France Télécom.[15]

With regard to the market for seamless pan-European mobile telephony services, the Commission found that the merged entity (which would at the time have had controlling interests in mobile operators in eight Member States and joint control of operators in three more, with a total subscriber base of over 40 million, equal to 30 per cent of all mobile subscribers in Europe) would have been in a unique position to build an integrated network of advanced telecommunications

---

[13] The acronyms stand for General Packet Radio Service, Enhanced Data GSM Environment (or Enhanced Data Rates for Global Evolution), and Customised Application of Mobile Enhanced Logic, respectively. These technologies enable data services to be provided over existing second generation GSM networks.
[14] The Commission's decision does not state whether this was due to the creation or strengthening of a sole or joint/collective dominant position.
[15] Case *France Télécom/Orange*, below, para.8–146 *et seq.* Unusually for transactions implementing commitments under the Merger Control Regulation, this necessitated a further divestment of Orange's 50% shareholding in KPN Orange as France Télécom already had control of the second largest Belgian mobile operator, Mobistar.

services across the common market, as it had unrivalled scale and geographic coverage as compared to competitors such as BT, France Télécom, Deutsche Telekom and Telecom Italia. This would have enabled the merged entity to overcome the technical and commercial barriers to providing advanced seamless services on a large scale, while it would be highly unlikely for third parties to replicate, by agreement or merger, a similar network in the short or medium term (3–5 years). The Commission considered that other mobile operators simply could not have offered similar technologically advanced services because of the segmentation of their existing networks and the difficulties in integrating them into a seamless integrated network. Network effects would have drawn customers towards the Vodafone/Mannesmann network and, to provide competing pan-European services, competitors would have needed access to that network. Therefore, competitors would, if they were allowed access to the merged entity's network at all, have had to face significant costs and performance/quality disadvantages, given their dependency on Vodafone/Mannesmann in order to offer equivalent pan-European services. Third parties would also have needed to have access to the merged entity's network in order to locate their own customers and to provide their advanced services to their subscribers when they were roaming on the merged entity's network. The merged entity would therefore have the ability either to refuse competitors access to its network or to allow access only on terms which would make it impossible for its competitors to compete in the provision of pan-European mobile services. The Commission, therefore, had serious doubts that the concentration would have led to a dominant position for Vodafone/Mannesmann on the market for seamless pan-European mobile services.

To remedy this concern, Vodafone submitted a set of undertakings that would give other operators non-discriminatory access to the merged entity's integrated network, thereby allowing other mobile operators the possibility of providing pan-European advanced seamless services to their customers by using the integrated network of the merged entity. These undertakings included a commitment not to enter into exclusive roaming agreements; to give third parties open access to roaming agreements, wholesale arrangements and open access to standards; and the provision of SIM cards to enable subscribers to override preferred roaming arrangements. Owing to the fast development of the mobile telecommunications sector, the access undertakings were limited to a period of three years until April 2003, when it was anticipated that UMTS networks would be rolled out in Europe. By limiting these commitments to three years, other operators were given the incentive to roll out their own networks to provide advanced mobile services.

These conditions were subsequently applied by the Commission in subsequent proceedings and played an important part in the approval of Vodafone's subsequent acquisitions of European mobile operators in Ireland and Spain, by which Vodafone aimed to enlarge its "footprint" for the provision of seamless pan-European mobile services.[16]

With regard to the mobile handset and mobile network equipment markets, the Commission found that although the merged entity would be a strong buyer in these markets, this buying power

---

[16] Case *Vodafone Group Plc/Eircell*, below, para.8–150 *et seq.*; and Case *Vodafone/Airtel*, below, para.8–158 *et seq.* The only EEA States in which Vodafone does not presently have a subsidiary or joint venture are Luxembourg, Norway, Denmark, Finland and Liechtenstein although it has co-operation agreements with Danish and Finnish operators. It also has interests in a number of other countries: Hungary, Malta, Poland and Romania, as well as in Albania and Switzerland.

did not raise any competition concerns, owing to the existence of other powerful buyers in the market.

France Télécom/Orange[17]

8–146 The transaction — The transaction involved the acquisition of Orange by France Télécom. The sale of Orange by Vodafone was undertaken to comply with the conditions imposed by the Commission in approving its acquisition of Mannesmann.[18]

8–147 The relevant product markets — The Commission, in line with its *Vodafone Airtouch/ Mannesmann*[19] decision, identified the following relevant product markets: (i) mobile telecommunication services, encompassing both GSM 900 and DCS 1800 networks and possibly also analogue networks; (ii) the provision of seamless pan-European mobile telecommunication services to internationally mobile customers; (iii) mobile handsets; and (iv) mobile telecommunications network equipment. The Commission again left open the question of whether the mobile telecommunications services market could be further segmented between network operators and service providers and/or between business and residential customers.

8–148 The relevant geographic markets — The Commission suggested (but did not take a definitive decision), again in line with its decision in *Vodafone Airtouch/Mannesmann*,[20] that: (i) the market for mobile telecommunications services was national; (ii) the market for the provision of seamless pan-European mobile telecommunication services to internationally mobile customers was at least pan-European; and (iii) the markets for mobile handsets and mobile telephony network equipment were global in scope.

8–149 Competitive analysis — The Commission was principally concerned about the concentration's impact on the Belgian market for mobile telecommunications services. No competitive concerns were identified in other Member States where France Télécom and/or Orange were active, other than France, where Orange was a reseller of mobile services. The transaction would have resulted in the merged entity having a combined market share of over 30 per cent and would have enabled France Télécom, which already had sole control over the second largest Belgian mobile telecommunications provider, Mobistar, to jointly control (together with KPN) the third mobile operator, KPN Orange Belgium. The merger would thus reduce the number of independent players on the Belgian mobile market from three to two. This reduction of players was even more problematic because of the crucial role played by Orange (the smallest player, but the newest entrant) in breaking the duopolistic pricing behaviour of Proximus (the market leader and joint venture of the incumbent operator Belgacom and Vodafone) and Mobistar. Prices in the Belgian mobile market had fallen by 33–50 per cent from 1997 to 2000 as a clear result of Orange's market entry and demonstrated the competitive nature of the market since Orange's entry. The Commission, therefore, concluded that the concentration raised serious doubts as to its compatibility with the common

---

[17] Case M.2016, *France Télécom/Orange*, Commission Decision of August 11, 2000, O.J. 2000 C261/6.
[18] Case *Vodafone Airtouch/Mannesman*, above, para.8–142 *et seq.*
[19] *ibid.*
[20] *ibid.*

market, owing to the creation of a joint dominant position. The parties removed this concern by committing to divest Orange's 50 per cent shareholding in KPN Orange Belgium to KPN.

In France, France Télécom had a market share of over 40 per cent. Orange was active in France as a reseller of mobile services provided by another network operator. The Commission had serious doubts that the acquisition of Orange would have strengthened France Télécom's ability to dominate the French mobile market. France Télécom therefore committed to divesting Orange's French reseller business.

Given that France Télécom was not yet active on the market for seamless pan-European mobile telecommunications services (but planned to be so, through the launch of services under the "Orange" brand) and this emerging market was characterised by increasing demand on the many types of different services on offer and on price, the Commission found it unlikely that the transaction would have led to the creation of a joint dominant position between France Télécom and Vodafone, who would have been the two largest mobile groups in Europe after the transactions, as the two companies were of different sizes and the market for pan-European services was still emerging. The concentration raised no competition concerns on the markets for mobile handsets and mobile telecommunications network equipment markets.

As Vodafone received part of the consideration for selling Orange in the form of France Télécom shares (giving it 9.9 per cent of France Télécom), the Commission considered whether this raised any competition concerns. It found that it did not so, owing to Vodafone transferring all of its shareholder rights to a voting trustee, which ensured that Vodafone did not obtain any influence over, or confidential information about, the France Télécom group.

Vodafone Group Plc/Eircell[21]

8–150 The transaction — The transaction involved the acquisition by Vodafone of sole control of Eircell, the mobile subsidiary of the Irish incumbent operator Eircom.

8–151 The relevant product markets — The Commission used the market definitions adopted in its *Vodafone AirTouch/Mannesmann* decision[22] including an emerging market for the provision of advanced seamless pan-European mobile telecommunications services to internationally mobile customers (in particular large corporate customers), and a market for mobile telephony services that included both analogue and digital networks. The Commission also considered the wholesale provision of roaming services as a possible relevant market, but did not adopt a decision in this regard.[23]

---

[21] Case M.2305, *Vodafone Group Plc/Eircell*, Commission Decision of March 2, 2001, O.J. 2001 C128/3.

[22] See above, para.8–142 *et seq.*

[23] The Commission made reference to the initial findings of its sector inquiry under Arts 81 and 82 of the EC Treaty into mobile roaming charges (available at: *http://europa.eu.int/wmm/competition/antitrust/others/sector_inquiries/roaming/working_document_en_initial_results.pdf*; and see above para.6–012); and Case M.1863, *Vodafone/BT/Airtel JV*, Commission Decision of November 16, 2000, O.J. 2000 C332/06.

8–152 The relevant geographic markets — For the advanced seamless pan-European mobile telecommunications services market, the geographic scope was defined as being pan-European. The geographic scope of the market for mobile telephony services was found to be national.

8–153 Competitive assessment — The transaction was approved without conditions. For the provision of advanced seamless pan-European mobile telecommunications services, the small size of Eircell's customer base would not have significantly enhanced Vodafone's ability to offer advanced seamless pan-European mobile services and even if competition concerns had arisen, the open access commitments given by Vodafone in *Vodafone AirTouch/Mannesmann*[24] remained in effect and would have removed, also in this case, all potential competition concerns. These existing undertakings meant that, upon consummation of the transaction, Eircell would have been obliged to provide third party operators with non-discriminatory access to its network and services. In considering whether to extend the duration of the commitment (which would have expired in April 2003), the Commission considered that the current deadline for the expiry of the commitments given in *Vodafone AirTouch/Mannesman* gave operators interested in providing advanced pan-European services sufficient time to set up arrangements with other operators, and start providing seamless pan-European services.

For mobile telephony services on a national level, the Commission was not concerned about the possible elimination of Vodafone as a possible future 3G competitor to Eircell, because there were a number of other potential entrants into the Irish mobile market, such as the other two UK mobile operators not already active in 2G in Ireland, Orange and One2One, that could have competed against the incumbent GSM operators in the forthcoming UMTS auction. On the wholesale roaming market, the Commission considered the transaction to have as its main effect the vertical integration of Vodafone and Eircell in the provision of wholesale roaming services in the United Kingdom and Ireland. However, the Commission found that although the United Kingdom was the principal source of inbound roaming traffic for Irish operators, the parties would be prevented from pursuing a roaming policy that would have foreclosed other operators because of the presence of other mobile operators in Ireland and the United Kingdom constituting valid alternatives to the Vodafone group for both inbound and outbound roaming. In addition, the open access commitments given to the Commission in *Vodafone AirTouch/Mannesmann* would become applicable to Eircell once it became part of the Vodafone group, thereby preventing Eircell from entering into exclusive roaming agreements.

BT/Esat Digifone[25]

8–154 The transaction — The transaction consisted of British Telecommunications (BT) acquiring Telenor's stake in, and thereby sole control of, the Irish mobile operator Esat Digifone.

8–155 The relevant product markets — The Commission considered two relevant product markets: (i) the emerging market for the provision of horizontal portals providing WAP-based

---

[24] See above, para.8–142 *et seq.*
[25] Case M.2282, *BT/Esat Digifone*, Commission Decision of March 16, 2001, O.J. 2001 C66/13.

internet access, which it had first identified in *Vodafone/Vivendi/Canal+*[26]; and (ii) the wholesale roaming services market. Owing to a lack of competition concerns on these markets, the Commission ultimately left the market definition open.

8–156   The relevant geographic markets — As in *Vodafone/Vivendi/Canal+*, the Commission left open the question of whether the market for the provision of horizontal portals providing WAP-based internet services should be considered national, regional, pan-European or wider in geographic scope. The geographic market for wholesale roaming services was left open.

8–157   Competitive assessment — The Commission identified a horizontal overlap in the activities of BT and Digifone for the provision of fixed/mobile WAP portal services. However, irrespectively of the precise geographic market definition, the Commission's investigation showed that there was a number of competitors of the parties active in the provison of English language content in Ireland and the United Kingdom (Vodafone/Eircell in Ireland, and Vodafone, Orange and One2One offering WAP in the United Kingdom), and even more in a pan-European or even wider market (with competitors such as Deutsche Telekom in Germany, Telecom Italia in Italy and Telefónica in Spain). Accordingly, the transaction was not found to lead to the creation or strengthening of a dominant position.

There was also a vertical link between the parties concerning the provision of international wholesale roaming services. BT Cellnet (BT's then mobile subsidiary) and Esat Digifone already had a preferential, but non-exclusive roaming relationship. However, the Commission concluded that owing to the presence of a number of competitors in both Ireland and the United Kingdom, the transaction would not have lead to any significant foreclosure effects either in Ireland or in any other country where BT was active as mobile operator.

Vodafone/Airtel[27]

8–158   The transaction — The transaction consisted of Vodafone acquiring sole control over the Spanish mobile telecommunications operator Airtel Movil, which had, prior to the transaction, been jointly controlled by Vodafone and BT.[28] Through the transaction, Vodafone acquired BT's entire shareholding in Airtel.

8–159   The relevant product markets — In line with previous decisions, the Commission identified the following relevant product markets: (i) the operation of mobile telecommunications networks[29]; (ii) internet portals accessed via mobile phones and separate related services markets for internet advertising and the provision of paid-for content offered through such portals[30]; (iii) the emerging market for the provision of advanced seamless pan-European mobile telecommunications

---

[26] See above, para.8–138 *et seq.*

[27] Case M.2469, *Vodafone/Airtel*, Commission Decision of June 26, 2001, O.J. 2001 C207/9.

[28] See, for the prior notification of the jointly controlled joint venture, Case M.1863, *Vodafone/BT/Airtel JV*, Commission Decision of November 16, 2000, O.J. 2000 C332/06.

[29] Case *Vodafone/Airtouch*, above, para.8–134 *et seq.*; and Case *Telia/Telenor*, above, para.8–097 *et seq.*

[30] Case *Vodafone/Vivendi/Canal+*, above, para.8–138 *et seq.*

services to international mobile customers and multinational corporations[31]; and (iv) the market for wholesale international roaming.[32] International roaming agreements are bilateral agreements between mobile operators in different countries. Most operators have more than one "outbound" international roaming agreement per country and normally have "inbound" roaming agreements with more than one operator per originating country. The provision of international wholesale roaming to foreign mobile network operators satisfies primarily a demand by foreign mobile network operators who wish to offer their own subscribers a "seamless service", not limited to the territory in which they have their own physical networks.

8–160 The relevant geographic markets — The relevant geographic market for the provision of mobile telephony networks was considered to be national. The definition of the geographic market for internet portals and related services was left open, but the Commission suggested that the market was national in scope. The Commission also left open the definition of the geographic market for pan-European mobile telecommunications services, but indicated that it was pan-European. For wholesale international roaming services, the Commission confirmed that the market is national in scope.

8–161 Competitive assessment — The transaction was declared to be compatible with the common market and thus approved. The Commission found no overlap in the activities of Airtel and Vodafone in the mobile services market. For internet portals and related services market the Commission found that no competition concerns arose even if Vodafone decided to have the portal of Vizzavi (its joint venture with Vivendi and Canal+) as the default portal on the Airtel network. Airtel would have been subject to the conditions imposed on Vodafone in the *Vodafone/Vivendi/Canal+ (Vizzavi)* case, such that Airtel would have been obliged to ensure that its customers were able to change to competing portals.

The Commission also found that the transaction had no significant impact on Vodafone's ability to offer advanced seamless pan-European mobile telecommunications services. As with the *Vodafone/Eircell* case, any possible competition concerns in this market were addressed and removed by the application of the undertakings given by Vodafone in *Vodafone AirTouch/ Mannesmann*.[33] Under these undertakings Airtel would have been required to provide third parties non-discriminatory access to certain wholesale services necessary for the provision of competing pan-European services.

As in *Vodafone/Eircell*, the Commission examined whether the transaction gave Vodafone incentives to impair other operators' access to the international wholesale roaming services market, and in particular to foreclose access to Airtel's network. In line with *Vodafone/Eircell*, the Commission found that this would not have been the case. First, Vodafone would not gain any benefits from refusing access to Airtel's network in Spain, since foreign operators requiring roaming services in Spain could have turned to a number of alternative actual and potential competitors to Vodafone. Secondly, Airtel, as part of the Vodafone group, would have become bound by the

[31] Case *Vodafone Airtouch/Mannesmann*, above, para.8–142 *et seq.*
[32] Case M.1863, *Vodafone/BT/Airtel JV*, Commission Decision of November 16, 2000, O.J. 2000 C332/06.
[33] See above, para.8–142 *et seq.*

conditions imposed in *Vodafone AirTouch/Mannesmann* not to discriminate against third parties regarding access to its networks.

KPN/E-Plus[34]

8–162   The transaction — The transaction consisted of a change from joint to sole control by KPN (the Dutch incumbent operator) over the German mobile operator, E-Plus Mobilfunk. E-Plus had originally been jointly controlled by KPN and US-based BellSouth Corporation.

8–163   The relevant product markets — The concentration concerned the markets for the provision of retail and wholesale mobile telephony network operator services. However, the Commission concentrated its analysis on the market for international wholesale roaming services (as defined in previous decisions[35]), as the only affected market.

8–164   The relevant geographic markets — The Commission analysed the impact of the concentration on the (national) market for international wholesale roaming services in the Netherlands.

8–165   Competitive analysis — The Commission, as it had done in previous cases in which it had considered the wholesale roaming services market, analysed whether there was a risk of market foreclosure due to the possibility of the parties entering into exclusive roaming agreements after completion. KPN had a very strong market position and was the market leader in the Dutch wholesale market for international roaming, with a market share between 50 and 60 per cent.[36] However, given E-Plus's market share of less than 15 per cent on the German market, the Commission found it unlikely that KPN Mobile would choose E-Plus as its exclusive roaming partner in Germany. Even if KPN and E-Plus were to enter into exclusivity arrangements, any resulting foreclosure effects in Germany and in the Netherlands would have been insignificant. Furthermore, even if KPN were to have received all of E-Plus's outbound traffic to the Netherlands on KPN Mobile's Dutch network, this would not have had any significant impact on KPN Mobile's position in the Dutch market, as it would have added less than 10 per cent to its current market share. Therefore, the Commission found that the transactions raised no concerns and was compatible with the common market.

TDC/CMG/MIGway JV[37]

8–166   The transaction — TDC Mobile International and CMG Wireless Data Solutions set up MIGway, a full-function joint venture that was intended to be active as a provider of wireless application infrastructure services for internet content and service providers that will distribute

---

[34] Case M.2726, *KPN/E-Plus*, Commission Decision of March 7, 2002, O.J. 2002 C79/12.

[35] Case M.1863, *Vodafone/BT/Airtel JV*, Commission Decision of November 16, 2000, O.J. 2000 C332/06; Case *BT/Esat Digifone*, above, para.8–154 *et seq.*; and Case *Vodafone/Airtel*, above, para.8–158 *et seq.*

[36] Subsequently, in March 2002, the Commission announced that it had reached a preliminary view that KPN Mobile had abused its dominant position for the termination of calls on its mobile network through discriminating or otherwise unfair behaviour, and served a Statement of Objections on the company. See Commission Press Release, IP/02/483 of 27 March 2002.

[37] Case M.2598, *TDC/CMG/Migway JV*, Commission Decision of October 4, 2001, O.J. 2002 C16/16.

their content and services for Short Messages Services (SMS) to mobile network operators in Europe. TDC mobile is a wholly owned subsidiary of TDC (formerly TeleDenmark), which is a shareholder in (and has joint control of) Belgacom, the incumbent operator in Belgium.

8–167   The relevant product markets — The Commission confirmed the parties' view that the relevant product market was the market for wholesale access for SMS to mobile telephony infrastructure on a pan-European-level. The Commission also identified a number of vertically related markets. Upstream it identified markets for: (i) SMS platforms (which are used for conveying SMS messages on the mobile networks); (ii) connectivity to the international signalling networks (in order to ensure the necessary connections with the national mobile network operators); and (iii) call centre services. It also identified the following downstream product markets: (i) the provision of content and services for electronic media; and (ii) mobile telecommunications services.

8–168   The relevant geographic markets — The Commission left the geographic market definitions mainly open, but suggested, however, that the geographic scope of most of the relevant markets was European — with the exception of the market for mobile telecommunications services which (in line with previous decisions[38]) was held to be national.

8–169   Competitive assessment — The transaction was found to be compatible with the common market and was thus approved by the Commission. The joint venture was about to enter the emerging market for wholesale access for SMS to the mobile telephony infrastructure. Potential competitors, such as the existing mobile operators with an SMS platform, would not have faced any major barriers to entering this new market. In addition, the Commission did not find any horizontal overlaps between the parties. Except for the market for mobile telecommunications services, the Commission also found no vertical market on which there would be adverse effects on competition. However, even in relation to the national markets for mobile telecommunications services, where TDC Mobile had a 44 per cent market share in Denmark and Belgacom Mobile (which was indirectly jointly controlled by TDC) accounted for 55 per cent in Belgium, the Commission found no competition concerns, as third parties had not raised competition concerns with regard to the effect of the formation of the joint venture on this market.

(d)   Concentrations in Television Broadcasting

8–170   Introduction — The emergence of new technologies, in particular digital technologies, has changed dramatically the context of the audio-visual sector in Europe. Digitalisation permits a larger offering of channels and the development of interactive services. In light of the considerable investment required by new technologies and the increasingly high purchase price of programming rights, there has been a natural tendency towards consolidation in this sector, and there has been a large number of concentrations notified under the Merger Control Regime in this area. Broadcasting markets are still national in scope, owing to the persistence of divergent regulatory environments and different linguistic and cultural contexts.[39] These markets are also characterised by significant barriers to entry, although with the introduction of digital platforms, some barriers to

---

[38] See above, para.8–171 *et seq.*
[39] See above, para.5–017 *et seq.*

entry may be reduced. The Commission has been particularly vigilant in its assessment of concentrations in this sector, to ensure that mergers and acquisitions do not lead to the creation or strengthening of bottlenecks and "gatekeeper" positions that could hinder the entry of new operators. As a result, the Commission has prohibited five concentrations in this sector, which are reviewed below. Others have been approved only after the imposition of far-reaching conditions.[40]

MSG Media Service[41]

8–171   The transaction — This case concerned the setting up of a joint venture, Media Service GmbH (MSG), between the German media group Bertelsmann, Deutsche Telekom (DT) and the leading German supplier of rights to feature films, Kirch. The purpose of the joint venture was to supply services for the technical, business and administrative handling of pay-TV and other communications services. If implemented, this transaction would have resulted in a situation where a public telecommunications operator, holding (at that time) a monopoly for the supply of telephone network services and owning nearly all cable-TV networks in Germany, would have combined its future activities in the joint venture's market with those of the leading pay-TV suppliers.

8–172   The relevant product markets — The Commission distinguished the following relevant product markets: (i) administrative and technical services for pay-TV; (ii) pay-TV services; and (iii) the operation of cable television networks. The Commission considered that pay-TV was a separate market from free access television because of the following factors: (i) the different types of funding for free and pay-TV resulted in different programme mixes; and (ii) pay-TV offered a greater quantity of channels, more special interest channels, and interactive services such as home banking and near-video-on-demand. Pay-TV in the form of pay-per-channel, pay-per-view and near-video-on-demand services constituted therefore a single product market. The Commission implied that video-on-demand and interactive services such as home banking or home shopping may form separate markets, but did not determine this point. With respect to the market for cable television networks, the Commission noted that cable was a market distinguishable from satellite and terrestrial transmission for the following reasons: (i) different payment structures for connection (one-off fee for installation of satellite and relatively small, regular payments for cable subscription fees); (ii) many households could not receive cable, whilst some landlords and owners' associations prohibited the installation of satellite dishes; and (iii) differences in the costs of programming.[42]

8–173   The relevant geographic markets — The Commission took the position that the relevant geographic market for each identified product market was Germany. As regards pay-TV, the

---

[40] See below, App.7.

[41] Case M.469, *MSG*, Commission Decision of November 9, 1994, O.J. 1994 L364/1.

[42] Larouche considers that the Commission took a short-term approach in deciding that cable television networks belonged to a separate product market distinct from that of other technical means of delivery to the consumer such as satellite and terrestrial; Larouche, *Competition Law and Regulation in European Telecommunications* (Hart Publishing, 2000), p.230. In contrast, in Case *BiB*, below, para.8–346 *et seq.*, the Commission took the position that cable and satellite retail pay-TV form part of a single product market, which it has followed in subsequent cases, including *BSkyB/KirchPayTV*, below, para.8–196 *et seq.*, and *UGC/Liberty Media*, below, para.8–238 *et seq.*

market was national because of: (i) regulatory differences between Member States; (ii) the fact that the broadcast of television programmes was largely restricted (to specific Member States); and (iii) language and cultural barriers. As to administrative and technical services for pay-TV, the market was national owing to the necessity to have transmission capacity with the respective national network owners, but was geared towards a European dimension given the absence of obstacles to the cross-border supply of decoders (set-top boxes) and smart-cards. The market for cable networks also had a national scope, due to DT's (at the time) statutory monopoly on the laying and operating of cable networks on public roads in Germany.

8–174 Competitive analysis — The Commission considered that the concentration would have led to the creation or strengthening of a dominant position on the three affected markets.

With respect to the market for administrative and technical services for pay-TV, MSG would have been the first and only supplier of such services in Germany. The Commission took the position that this initial monopoly would have persisted over time and sealed off the market from competition in its starting phase. Market entry by a third party would have been very unlikely, given that DT owned most of the cable networks in Germany and controlled its development, and because Bertelsmann and Kirch both had very substantial programming resources.[43]

As regards the pay-TV market, the dominant position of Kirch and Bertelsmann, through their Premiere joint venture on the German pay-TV market, would have been considerably strengthened as a result of MSG's long-lasting monopoly on the market for technical and administrative services. According to the Commission, all pay-TV suppliers entering the German market would have been forced to take the services underlying pay-TV from an enterprise (MSG) controlled by the dominant pay-TV suppliers. This would have given Bertelsmann and Kirch the possibility of influencing the competitiveness of future pay-TV operators by directing the terms and conditions on which MSG made its services available to those competitors. MSG would thus have served as a "gate-keeper" to the German pay-TV market. Moreover, MSG would have served as the vehicle for information gathering by Bertelsmann and Kirch regarding the activities of their competitors.

Finally, the Commission considered that the concentration would have strengthened DT's dominant position on the market for cable television networks, because private operators would not have been able to easily compete with DT if it controlled MSG. The undertakings proposed by the parties (including the adoption by MSG of a decoder base with a common interface, a non-discrimination policy towards other pay-TV suppliers and a commitment by MSG not to disclose to its parents any of the competitive information gathered by it about competing pay-TV suppliers) were rejected by the Commission as being insufficient to prevent the creation or strengthening of a dominant position or because they were only behavioural (rather than structural) and therefore difficult to monitor. The Commission therefore prohibited the transaction.

---

[43] As this market was still in its infancy, this case illustrates the difficulty for a competition authority in undertaking a prospective analysis of emerging markets on how they will develop and how a concentration would affect that development. In this connection, Larouche stresses that "when the Commission concludes that the transaction is likely to lead to the creation of a dominant position on a market which does not yet exist, it must be kept in mind that this is no more than a guess on future developments, however it may be"; Larouche, above, para.8–172, n.42, 232.

Nordic Satellite Distribution[44]

8–175   The transaction — The operation consisted of the formation of a joint venture, Nordic Satellite Distribution (NSD), between TeleDanmark, Norsk Telekom and Kinnevik. Norsk Telecom was the largest cable operator in Norway with approximately 30 per cent of all connections. Furthermore, it controlled the satellite capacity of one of the two satellites allocated for broadcasting to the Nordic region and was an important pay-TV operator. TeleDanmark was the incumbent telecommunications operator in Denmark and was also the largest cable television operator in Denmark with about 50 per cent of household connections. In addition, TeleDanmark, together with Kinnevik, controlled most of the satellite capacity of the second Nordic satellite. Kinnevik was a Swedish conglomerate with interests in television programming, magazines and newspapers as well as in steel, paper, packaging and telecommunications. Kinnevik was the main provider of satellite television programmes in the Nordic region, had the most popular channels and was the largest pay-TV distributor in the Nordic countries through its Viasat companies. The purpose of the joint venture was to transmit satellite television programmes to cable operators and to households that could receive satellite television on their own dish (the "direct-to-home" market).

8–176   The relevant product markets — The Commission identified three affected product markets: (i) the provision of satellite television transponder capacity and related services to broadcasters; (ii) the distribution of satellite pay-TV and other encrypted television channels to DTH households; and (iii) the operation of cable networks. Following its decision in *MSG*, the Commission took the position that the distribution of television signals via satellite (using transponders) was a market distinct from television distribution by terrestrial and cable networks, since considerable technical and financial differences existed between the different modes of distribution.

8–177   The relevant geographic markets — As regards the provision of satellite television transponder capacity for television broadcasting, the Commission found that the relevant geographic market was the market for those transponders with a footprint (*i.e.* the geographical area where the television signals distributed by a satellite could be received by DTH households with standard receiving equipment) that covered the Nordic region (*i.e.* Norway, Sweden, Denmark and Finland). With respect to the distribution of satellite pay-TV and other encrypted television channels to DTH households, the Commission indicated that DTH distribution was a retail operation, with marketing at the local level. Finally, according to the Commission, the market for the operation of cable networks was national because cable operators are faced with different market conditions in different countries in terms of geography, marketing and legislation.

8–178   Competitive analysis — As regards the market for the provision of satellite television transponder capacity for television broadcasting to the Nordic region, the Commission found that the joint venture would have acquired a dominant position in so far as it would have been able to control a large majority of the transponder capacity available for broadcasting to the Nordic region. Through its control of transponder capacity, its links to Kinnevik as an important broadcaster of Nordic television channels and distributor of satellite television channels to DTH households

---

[44] Case M.490, *Nordic Satellite Distribution*, Commission Decision of July 19, 1995, O.J. 1995 L53/20.

and its links to its parents as cable operators, the joint venture would have been in a position to foreclose other satellite operators from leasing transponders to broadcasters.

With respect to the Danish market for operation of cable networks, the creation of NSD would have resulted in the strengthening of TeleDanmark's dominant position. NSD would have been able to discriminate in favour of TeleDanmark (which already controlled approximately 50 per cent of cable connections in Denmark) when offering channels to other Danish cable operators.

Finally, the transaction would have resulted in Viasat, Kinnevik's distribution company, acquiring a dominant position on the market for the distribution of satellite pay-TV and other encrypted television channels to DTH households because of its structural links with the dominant provider of transponder capacity for the Nordic region (NSD) and very large cable operators (TeleDanmark and Norsk Telekom).

For these reasons, the Commission considered that the transaction would have resulted in the creation of a highly vertically integrated operation extending from the production of television programmes to retail distribution services for pay-TV and other encrypted channels through operation of satellites and cable networks. The parties would have achieved such strong market positions that they would have been able to foreclose the Nordic satellite market to competitors. NSD would thus have obtained a "gatekeeper" function for the Nordic market for satellite television broadcasting. The transaction was thus prohibited.

Holland Media Group[45]

8–179   The transaction — The operation consisted of the creation of a joint venture, Holland Media Group (HMG), between RTL4 (a Dutch broadcasting subsidiary of the Luxembourg television group CLT and the Dutch publishing group VNU), Veronica (a Dutch commercial broadcaster) and Endemol (the largest independent producer of television programmes in the Netherlands). HMG was to be a new company that would have packaged and supplied television and radio programmes that it would broadcast itself. This transaction did not meet the then applicable turnover thresholds of the Merger Control Regulation and was therefore not required to be notified to the Commission. However, on the basis of Article 22(3) of the Merger Control Regulation, the Dutch government referred the concentration to the Commission on the grounds that the concentration would have materially impeded competition in the Netherlands. Concentrations referred to the Commission pursuant to Article 22(3) are not subject to the standstill obligation imposed by Article 7(1) of the Merger Control Regulation and may be implemented without waiting for the decision of the Commission.

8–180   The relevant product markets — The Commission considered that the following product markets were affected by the concentration: (i) television broadcasting (with a distinction between free and pay-TV); (ii) television advertising; and (iii) independently produced Dutch language television programmes. With respect to the market for television broadcasting, the Commission indicated that, in terms of trade relationships between broadcasters on the supply side and viewers

[45] Case M.553, *RTL/Veronica/Endemol*, Commission Decision of September 20, 1995, O.J. 1996 L134/32.

and advertisers on the demand side, a distinction had to be drawn between the market for television advertising (where broadcasters compete for advertising revenue) and the market for pay-TV, where pay-TV suppliers principally compete for subscriptions. Moreover, the Commission indicated that the market for television advertising must be distinguished from advertising through other media because of differences in the types of customer, advertising techniques and prices.

8–181   The relevant geographic markets — The Commission defined the scope of the geographic market as being limited to the Netherlands. The Commission excluded the Flemish region of Belgium from the relevant geographic market, despite the commonality of language, on the basis of cultural differences and national preferences of viewers.

8–182   Competitive analysis — As regards the market for free-to-air broadcasting, the Commission found that HMG would have achieved a dominant position for the following reasons: (i) the HMG channels would have been able to co-ordinate their programming; (ii) the vertical structural link to Endemol (the leading independent supplier of Dutch language programming) would have ensured preferential access for HMG to Endemol's portfolio of successful entertainment programmes; (iii) HMG's structural link with VNU, an important Dutch media group, would have ensured the promotion of HMG's programmes in Dutch newspapers; and (iv) there were, at that time, no channels able to compete on the same footing as HMG.

Moreover, HMG's strong position on the market for free TV would have permitted HMG to dominate the market for television advertising. According to the Commission, the existence of HMG was in itself dissuasive to market entry by any potential newcomer. Indeed, any new player on the Dutch free TV market would have had difficulties in building up a programme schedule for the Dutch market which would be attractive for advertisers, since the main targets for advertising were already covered by HMG. Moreover, any newcomer would have to face the power of the three combined HMG channels and HMG's ability to react immediately to new entrants.

With respect to the market for Dutch independent television production, the Commission considered that Endemol already held a dominant position on this market because of: (i) its high market share (approximately 50 per cent); and (ii) the lack of substitutability of competitors' programmes for those of Endemol, which were among the most popular and were presented by the best known Dutch television personalities. The creation of HMG would only have strengthened Endemol's existing dominant position, as HMG would have given Endemol a further outlet for its programmes and foreclosed access to HMG by other programme producers.

For these reasons, the Commission prohibited the concentration. Because the concentration had already been implemented at the time of the Commission's prohibition decision, the Commission invited the parties to propose appropriate measures to restore effective competition on the relevant markets. The Commission approved a modified version of the transaction following the withdrawal of Endemol from the joint venture.[46] The Commission considered that Endemol's decision not to participate in the joint venture would remedy the concerns resulting from the vertical links between

---

[46] See above, para.8–179 *et seq.*

HMG and Endemol (*i.e.* privileged access to Endemol's production and foreclosure of other programme producers). Moreover, HMG undertook to transform its channel, RTL5, that had been operated as a general interest channel, into a news channel to be operated over time as a pay-TV channel. The Commission also found that there had been a number of changes in the Dutch television and television advertising markets since its prohibition decision which, together with the commitments offered by the parties, removed the Commission's competition concerns.

Bertelsmann/CLT[47]

8–183   The transaction — The transaction concerned the creation of a joint venture, CLT-UFA, between Bertelsmann (the largest media group in Germany) and Audiofina (the holding company of Compagnie Luxembourgeoise de Télévision (CLT), a company active in the radio and television sectors). It was intended that the joint venture would operate the broadcasting activities of its parent companies.

8–184   The relevant product markets — The Commission distinguished the following relevant markets: (i) free access television; (ii) pay-TV; (iii) production of television programming; (iv) rights or licences to content for television broadcasting; and (v) free access radio. Interestingly, the Commission noted that, within the market for television rights, distinct product markets may have existed for films and other fiction rights and sports rights because of the specific features of sport events (*e.g.* rights must be acquired in advance of the event, and their attractiveness is highly dependent on national or regional audiences).

8–185   The relevant geographic markets — The Commission determined that the geographic scope of the relevant markets was either national, regional or language-based, owing to the existence of different regulatory regimes, language barriers, cultural factors and different conditions of competition (*e.g.* the structure of national markets for cable networks).

8–186   Competitive analysis — The Commission found that the activities of the two parties overlapped in Germany only. On the market for free-access television, the joint venture would have had a market share of 26 per cent, whilst public broadcasters would have had a market share of 39 per cent and Kirch a 29 per cent market share. CLT-UFA would have had a 38 per cent market share for television advertising, compared to a 50 per cent market share for Kirch. Owing to the existence of effective competition between operators on this market, the Commission considered that there was no risk of the creation or strengthening of a joint dominant position on this market. The Commission took the same position with respect to the markets for the production of television programming and the sale of rights or licences to television content, since both markets would continue to have been dominated by Kirch. To the extent CLT was not present on the pay-TV market in Germany and could not be expected to enter it on its own, the Commission took the position that the concentration would not have resulted in the creation of a dominant position on this market. With respect to the other countries in which CLT was active, the Commission considered that CLT did not have a dominant position and that the concentration could not have been expected to affect the competitive situation of those markets where Bertelsmann was not

---

[47] Case M.779, *Bertelsmann/CLT*, Commission Decision of October 7, 1996, O.J. 1996 C364/3.

active. Some competitors had argued that the proposed concentration, which would have resulted in the creation of a joint venture that would have been the leading European television broadcaster in terms of television channels, would have led over time to CLT-UFA having a strong or even dominant position throughout Europe, in particular in light of the combined entity's increased buying power for television rights. The Commission rejected this argument, as the television broadcasting market, and in particular the market for the acquisition of television rights, was a national rather than a European market.

Bertelsmann/Kirch/Premiere and Deutsche Telekom/BetaResearch[48]

8–187 The transaction — Despite the prohibition of the *MSG* joint venture in 1994,[49] the same parties entered into a new transaction at the end of 1997, with a view to developing jointly their pay-TV activities in Germany. This time, the joint venture was not limited to the provision of the administrative and technical services needed for pay-TV, but extended to the pay-TV market itself. This operation consisted of forming two closely-related joint ventures, each of which was a concentration, that were reviewed simultaneously by the Commission: (i) the acquisition of joint control of the German pay-TV channel, Premiere, by CLT-UFA (a joint venture between Bertelsmann and Audiofina) and Kirch, upon Canal+'s withdrawal from Premiere; and (ii) the acquisition of joint control by CLT-UFA, Deutsche Telekom and Kirch of BetaResearch, a company that had been solely controlled by Kirch and which held exclusive licences for Germany, Austria and the German-speaking part of Switzerland to the Beta access technology incorporated into the "d-box" decoder. As part of the transaction, Kirch was to transfer its own pay-TV channels and pay-TV broadcasting rights to Premiere. The aim of the transaction was to develop Premiere into a joint digital pay-TV channel and marketing platform incorporating Kirch's current digital television activities and operating on the basis of the "d-box" technology provided to Premiere by Kirch. In the context of the transaction, it was intended that Deutsche Telekom would build a technical platform for the digital distribution of pay-TV programmes over its cable television networks and supply the technical services required for the provision and broadcasting of digital pay-TV in Germany.

8–188 The relevant product markets — The Commission distinguished three affected product markets: (i) pay-TV; (ii) technical services for pay-TV; and (iii) cable television networks. Regarding pay-TV, the Commission based its finding on the reasons developed by it in the *MSG* case (*i.e.* (i) the different types of funding of free and pay-TV resulted in different programme mixes; and (ii) pay-TV offered a greater quantity of channels, more special interest channels, and interactive services).[50] The Commission acknowledged that, as the process of digitalisation continued to develop, there would be in the future a certain convergence between pay-TV and free television, particularly if free-TV channels were largely supplied in digital "bouquets" by pay-TV operators. The Commission considered that this potential development was not sufficient to justify the definition of a single product market for free television and pay-TV. Moreover, the Commission took the position that no distinction should be made between analogue and digital pay-TV. It

---

[48] Case M.993, *Bertelsmann/Kirch/Premiere*, Commission Decision of May 27, 1998, O.J. 1999 L53/1; and Case M.1027, *Deutsche Telékom/BetaResearch*, Commission Decision of May 27, 1998, O.J. 1999 L53/31.
[49] Case *MSG*, above, para.8–171 *et seq.*
[50] Case *MSG*, above, para.8–171 *et seq.*

considered that digital pay-TV was only a further development of analogue pay-TV and would have completely superseded analogue pay-TV in a few years after the transaction. As regards the market for technical services, the Commission did not seem to consider that the use of different transmissions technologies for cable and satellite transmission justified distinguishing separate markets for technical services for cable and satellite pay-TV. Along the lines of the *MSG* case, the Commission maintained that cable and satellite television transmission systems constituted separate markets, due to different payment structures for connection, the fact that many households could not receive cable, some landlords and owners' associations prohibited the installation of satellite dishes and differences in the costs of programming. In particular, the Commission took into consideration that, in Germany, the operation of cable networks is much more profitable than satellite platforms.

8–189 The relevant geographic markets — The Commission considered that the relevant geographic market was Germany or, at its widest, the German-speaking area comprised of Germany, Austria, Luxembourg and the German-speaking parts of Belgium and Switzerland. The Commission based its findings on the reasons it had developed in its *MSG* and *HMG* decisions (*i.e.* different regulatory regimes, language barriers, cultural factors and other competition conditions prevailing in individual Member States). In contrast to *MSG*, the Commission appeared more open to accepting that the relevant geographic market should not have been limited to Germany, but extended to the whole German-speaking area. As regards cable networks, the Commission considered that, despite the abolition of Deutsche Telekom's monopoly on laying and operating cable networks in public roads, Deutsche Telekom still had a predominant position on that market (in particular in relation to "backbone" or "level 3" cable-television networks) and the conditions of competition in Germany were thus still very different from the conditions of competition in other countries.

8–190 Competitive analysis — The Commission concluded that the transaction would have resulted in the creation or strengthening of a dominant position on the affected markets.

With respect to the market for pay-TV, Premiere would have become the only pay-TV operator in Germany and in the entire German-speaking area. According to the Commission, such a monopoly could have been expected to be durable because of the combination of the important programme resources of Kirch and CLT-UFA, and the existing subscription base of Premiere would have prevented the development of any additional broadcasting and marketing platform in the German pay-TV market. Given its position as the only marketing platform in Germany for pay-TV services, Premiere would have been in a position to determine the conditions under which other broadcasters could enter the German pay-TV market.

As regards the market for technical services for pay-TV, BetaResearch would have attained a lasting dominant position on this market. The Beta access technology and the d-box decoder, which operated with a self-contained (proprietary) encryption system, would have become the standard decoder technology. Indeed, as the development of an alternative decoder infrastructure was not very likely given the strong position of Premiere, other service providers would have had to use the d-box decoder and the Beta access technology and would therefore have been dependent on obtaining a licence for this technology from BetaResearch. BetaResearch could thus prevent, through its licensing policy, other service providers from entering the German pay-TV market.

With respect to the market for cable networks in Germany, the Commission considered that after the transaction, Deutsche Telekom would have emerged as the only supplier of technical services for pay-TV distributed through cable networks and would therefore be able to strengthen its existing dominant position on this market to the detriment of other cable operators.

It is worth noting that the Commission rejected the parties' argument that the concentration should have been approved because Kirch was a failing firm. The Commission considered that the conditions for the application of the failing firm defence that it has set out in its *Kali and Salz* decision were not established.[51] In particular, the Commission considered that the termination of Kirch's pay-TV activities would have had less of a negative impact on competition than the concentration would have had, since assets and all pay-TV distribution rights of DF1 (Kirch's digital pay-TV subsidiary) would not have been transferred to Premiere and could have been acquired by competing pay-TV organisations.

The Commission considered that the remedies proposed by the parties (such as third party access to a certain proportion of the parties' pay-TV programming rights, unbundling of Premiere's offer of various channels, an undertaking to purchase only pay-TV rights to the exclusion of free-TV rights, co-operation with cable operators for the distribution of Premiere's channels and an undertaking to grant licences to BetaResearch's access technology) were insufficient. Whilst Kirch and Deutsche Telekom were willing to provide the Commission with the minimum undertakings required by it to ensure future competition on the pay-TV market (in particular, by ceding programming rights and allowing private cable operators to independently market Premiere in

---

[51] Case M.308, *Kali and Salz/MdK/Treuhand*, Commission Decision of December 14, 1993, O.J. 1994 L186/38. In *Kali and Salz*, the Commission held that a merger which should normally be prohibited, because it leads to the creation or strengthening of a dominant position, could nevertheless be authorised if, even in the event of the merger being prohibited, the acquirer would inevitably have achieved or reinforced an existing dominant position as a result of the target company's withdrawal from the market. According to the Commission, for the failing firm defence to apply, three conditions must be met: (i) the acquired firm would in the near future be forced out of the market if not taken over by another firm; (ii) the acquiring firm would take over the market share of the acquired firm if it were forced out of the market; and (iii) there is no less anti-competitive alternative purchaser. In Joined Cases C–68/94 and C–30/95, *France v Commission* [1998] E.C.R. 1375, the Court of Justice upheld this test, but held that the criteria to be applied are wider, since for the Court a merger can be regarded as a rescue merger if "the competitive structure resulting from the concentration would deteriorate in similar fashion even if the concentration did not proceed". For a detailed review of the Commission's decision practice in relation to the failing firm defence, see Monti and Rousseva, "Failing Firms in the Framework of the EC Merger Control Regulation" [1999] 24 E.L.R. 38–55. In Case M.2314, *BASF/Pantochim/Eurodial*, Commission Decision of July 11, 2001, O.J. 2002 132/45, the Commission was of the view that there would still be the possibility of third parties acquiring the business or assets of the target undertaking in the event of its subsequent insolvency. If these assets were taken over by competitors in the course of bankruptcy proceedings, the economic effects would be similar to a takeover of the failing firms themselves by an alternative purchaser. Therefore, it needs to be established, in addition to the first three criteria, that the business or assets to be purchased would inevitably disappear from the market in the absence of the merger. In any event, the application of the concept of the "rescue merger" principle requires that the deterioration in the competitive structure of the market due to the merger is less than would be the case in the absence of the merger. In Case M.2314, *BASF/Pantochim/Eurodiol*, Commission Decision of July 11, 2001, the Commission concluded that the deterioration in the competitive structure of the market as a result of the notified merger would have been less significant than in the absence of the merger and thus applied the "rescue merger" principle, as the bankruptcy of the target companies would have resulted in capacity shortages and price increases.

combination with their own channels), Bertelsmann was not. The Commission therefore prohibited the two concentrations in two decisions adopted on the same day.

NC/Canal+/CDPQ/BankAmerica[52]

8–191 The transaction — The transaction concerned the acquisition of joint control by Canal+, Capital Communications CDPQ and BankAmerica (the last two via an acquisition vehicle, Exante) of NumériCâble, a company operating cable television networks in France and which was, prior to the transaction, a wholly-owned subsidiary of Canal+.

8–192 The relevant product markets — Based on previous decisions, the Commission defined the relevant product market as the market for pay-TV, distinct from free-access television financed by advertising or state contributions.

8–193 The relevant geographic markets — The Commission found that the relevant geographic market was national, in particular for cultural reasons. The Commission assessed the effect of the transaction on the pay-TV market in France as well as in the French-speaking areas of Europe. The Commission also assessed the impact of the transaction on the pay-TV market (as well as on the market for wholesale supply of films and sports channels for retail pay-TV) in Spain for the purposes of its assessment of possible anti-competitive co-ordination between the parent companies, as Canal+ had a Spanish pay-TV subsidiary, and CDPQ and BankAmerica had shareholdings in a Spanish cable operator.

8–194 Competitive analysis: dominance — The Commission found that there was no risk of the joint venture resulting in a dominant position, given the relatively low market share of NumériCâble in France and the fact that BankAmerica and CDPQ were not present on the pay-TV market in France.

8–195 Competitive analysis: co-ordination of independent activities — The Commission then examined whether there was a risk of co-ordination of the competitive behaviour of the parent companies under Article 2(4) of the Merger Control Regulation, applying the principles of Article 81(1) and 81(3) of the EC Treaty. A joint venture will have anti-competitive co-ordination effects if co-ordination of the parent companies' competitive behaviour is likely, appreciable and the result of the creation of the joint venture. The Commission, when making such an appraisal, must take into account in particular whether two or more parent companies retain to a significant extent activities in the same market as the joint venture or in a market which is downstream or upstream from that of the joint venture or in a neighbouring market closely related to this market. In this case, BankAmerica and CDPQ had a controlling interest in Cableuropa, a cable network operator in Spain and a future significant competitor of Sogecable, Canal+'s pay-TV subsidiary in Spain, on the Spanish pay-TV market. Cableuropa was also a buyer of pay-TV rights from Sogecable. In so far as the parent companies were active in the same product market (*i.e.* pay-TV) or in vertically related markets (*i.e.* the wholesale supply of films and sports channels for retail pay-TV), the

---

[52] Case M.1327, *NC/Canal+/CDPQ/BankAmerica*, Commission Decision of December 3, 1998, O.J. 1999 C233/21.

Commission found that the effect of the transaction could have given rise to the co-ordination of the independent competitive behaviour of Sogecable and Cableuropa, as a result of their vertical relationship, *i.e.* with regard to the supply of content rights needed to operate in the pay-TV market.

The Commission was concerned that this co-ordination could have resulted in discrimination *vis-à-vis* other market players in their access to Sogecable's content thereby putting them at a competitive disadvantage. As a result, the Commission approved the transaction only after Canal + and Sogecable had undertaken not to discriminate in favour of Cableuropa and had committed to ensure fair and equal treatment in supplying Canal + /Sogecable's content to third party broadcasters in Spain.

BSkyB/KirchPayTV[53]

8–196 The transaction — The concentration consisted in the acquisition by British Sky Broadcasting Group ("BSkyB") of a shareholding in KirchPayTV that gave it joint control of KirchPayTV together with Kirch Vermögensverwaltung, which prior to the transaction had exercised sole control over KirchPayTV.

8–197 The relevant product markets — The Commission discussed in some detail the markets relating to the provision of pay-TV and related services. It distinguished the following markets: (i) the market for pay-TV; (ii) the market for interactive digital TV services (iDTV); and (iii) the market for the acquisition of broadcasting rights. The Commission noted, in line with its previous decisions, that the market for pay-TV was a distinct market, separate from that for free TV. First, the trade relationships in the two markets were different because in the case of pay-TV there was a relationship between the provider and its subscribers, whilst in the case of advertising-financed free TV there was a trade relationship between the provider and the advertising industry. Secondly, the fact that subscribers were prepared to pay considerable subscription fees for pay-TV indicated that pay-TV was a distinguishable product with specific extra utility. However, the Commission, in line with previous decisions, saw no reason to distinguish between markets for analogue and digital pay-TV, because digital pay-TV was only a further development of analogue pay-TV. The market for iDTV was found to be an emerging market separate from that for pay-TV. However, whilst being a separate market, the market for pay-TV was seen as "complementary" to, and likely to be the "driver" for, digital interactive television services. Whilst pay-TV was perceived as being "entertainment based", iDTV was perceived as being "transactional" or a source of information for the consumer. The Commission further found that the market for digital interactive TV services was separate from that for high-street retailing.[54] The Commission also distinguished between markets for digital interactive services made available via television sets and those made available via personal computers. Finally, the Commission addressed the market for the acquisition of broadcasting rights, in particular for films and sports events, although the Commission (again) left open the question of whether the two segments constituted separate markets.

---

[53] Case JV.37, *BSkyB/KirchPayTV*, Commission Decision of March 21, 2000, O.J. 2000 C110/45.

[54] It should be noted, however, that in Case M.1812, *Telefónica/Terra/Amadeus*, Commission Decision of April 27, 2000, O.J. 2000 C235/6 and in Case M.2627, *Otto Versand/Sabre/Travelocity*, Commission Decision of December 19, 2001, O.J. 2001 C21/29, the Commission held that the provision of online travel agency services was not a different market from the provision of travel agency services by traditional travel agencies.

8–198 The relevant geographic markets — Owing to different regulatory regimes, language barriers, cultural factors and other different conditions of competition, the geographic scope of the market for pay-TV was found to be national. The Commission left open the question of whether it could be extended beyond Germany to the entire German-speaking area. The market for digital interactive TV services was also found to be national. Based on the fact that film broadcasting rights are normally granted for a specific language version and broadcasting area, the Commission found that the geographic markets for the acquisition of broadcasting rights, in this case, were those for the United Kingdom, Ireland and Germany. As regards some sporting events, the Commission noted that the rights are sometimes acquired for the entire European territory and that, therefore, there could be a separate market for pan-European sports rights, although the Commission ultimately left this question open.

8–199 Competitive assessment — The Commission expressed serious doubts about the compatibility of the concentration with the common market, as it considered that it could have strengthened KirchPayTV's existing dominant position on the pay-TV market in Germany and led to the creation of a dominant position on the emerging market for digital interactive TV services in Germany. First, the Commission found that KirchPayTV had, through Premiere, a monopoly in the provision of pay-TV services in Germany. It agreed with third parties that the operation would have strengthened KirchPayTV's existing dominant position by providing it with an influx of financial resources and know-how. However, contrary to third party allegations that the concentration would have eliminated BSkyB and/or News Corp (BSkyB's largest shareholder) as potential competitors in the German pay-TV market, the Commission concluded that neither BSkyB nor any other company was likely to enter the German pay-TV market in the short to medium term owing to:

(i) the strong position of free TV in Germany;

(ii) Kirch's control of the d-box decoder and BetaResearch's encryption technology used by Deutsche Telekom in Germany for the provision of technical services for the transmission of digital signals over cable networks.[55] In order to try to avoid the need to use BetaResearch's technology, any new entrant in the German pay-TV market would have had to enter the market through satellite transmission, which was not a viable alternative in Germany owing to its limited reach;

(iii) Kirch's leading position as a content provider in Germany; and

(iv) the need for BSkyB or any other company to invest considerable financial resources in order to enter the German market.

With regard to the market for digital interactive TV services, the Commission noted that the installation of a technical infrastructure for the transmission of digital interactive TV services required major investment. Given these enormous costs, market entry by third parties was only possible if there was a realistic opportunity for successful market penetration. Against this background, the

---

[55] Deutsche Telekom, as the largest cable network operator in Germany, exclusively used BetaResearch access technology, which was only decipherable by the d-box decoder.

Commission was concerned that the concentration was likely to have significantly reduced third parties' options, because it would have enabled KirchPayTV to enter the market before, or at the same time as, any other operator. This early entry would most likely have resulted in Kirch's decoder, the d-box, becoming the standard decoder in Germany. Given the proprietary technology developed by BetaResearch on which the d-box was based, such first mover advantage was likely to raise barriers to entry and to create a dominant position. The Commission found furthermore that Kirch would have been able to leverage its dominant position in the German pay-TV market into the digital interactive TV services market, as it would have been the only undertaking in Germany offering both services. Any third party provider of digital interactive services that wished to reach customers using the d-box would have encountered difficulties obtaining a licence from Beta-Research, as it would have been regarded (and treated) as a competitor to the affiliated KirchPayTV. Therefore, the Commission found that the concentration would have created a dominant position in the market for digital interactive TV services.

Assessing the concentration's effects on the market for the acquisition of broadcasting rights, the Commission did not agree with third parties as to the possibilities for KirchPayTV or BSkyB — owing to their dominant positions in the pay-TV markets in Germany and the United Kingdom, respectively — to tie the acquisition of pay-TV rights for Germany to those for other broadcasting windows (*e.g.* free-to-air, internet, or pay-per-view) and/or to other territories (*e.g.* the United Kingdom, Ireland or Italy). Kirch already had the power to engage in tied buying for different windows and the addition of BSkyB would not have significantly strengthened this position. As regards the concern that Kirch and BSkyB's added resources as a result of the concentration would have enabled them to outbid other purchasers, the Commission found that there was no indication that in buying rights jointly they would have offered more than they would have offered had they bid separately for the individual rights. Finally, any tying arrangement for different territories would face a number of practical obstacles, because the output deals for film or sports rights were usually concluded under exclusive contracts for long periods, and the chances of these contracts ending at a similar time for two or more territories was low, making such activities difficult to co-ordinate.

8–200 The parties offered two sets of undertakings to remedy the Commission's concerns. These were accepted by the Commission. The first set of undertakings related to the acquisition of broadcasting rights and included a commitment not to engage in tied purchasing arrangements, which the Commission, based on its competition assessment of the market for programme rights, did not deem to be necessary. The second set of commitments offered by the parties related to the technical platform for pay-TV and thereby addressed the Commission's concerns in relation to the markets for pay-TV and interactive digital TV services. In particular, Kirch committed to implementing the Multimedia Home Platform (MHP) interface, an API developed by the Digital Video Broadcasting Project (DVB) and standardised by the ETSI, in the d-box. However, the Commission fell short of requiring KirchPayTV to also include a Common Interface (CI) in the d-box. Instead, the Commission tried to achieve the interoperability of different technical platforms through a commitment from Kirch to enter into simulcrypt agreements with other conditional access providers. The undertakings provided for a dispute resolution system to ensure that these agreements were entered into on fair and non-discriminatory terms. However, the obligation on Kirch to enter into simulcrypt agreements did not subsequently work in practice, because the licensing system proved to be too burdensome. First of all, the licensing regime created additional costs for competing pay-TV providers, who would have needed to pay licence fees in order to receive access to the Kirch conditional access system. But even more importantly, this licensing regime would have forced competing pay-TV providers to rely on BetaResearch, which in return was controlled by their competitor Kirch and therefore had an incentive to abuse its position and prevent or make difficult market entry by competing broadcasters. Only a neutral and independent licensor could have guaranteed that the licensing conditions were fair and non-discriminatory. For these reasons, no simulcrypt agreement was ever concluded between Kirch and any other broadcaster.[56]

Canal + /Lagardère/CanalSatellite and Canal + /Lagardère/Liberty Media/Multi thematiques[57]

8–201 The transaction — The transaction consisted of two linked concentrations that were reviewed together by the Commission. The first concentration concerned (i) the acquisition of joint control by Lagardère (together with Canal +) over CanalSatellite, a provider of pay-TV services; (ii) the acquisition of joint control by Canal + (together with Lagardère) over EuroMusique MCM, a producer of thematic channels; and (iii) the creation of an interactive services joint venture between CanalSatellite and Lagardère (JV2). The second concentration consisted of: (i) the acquisition of joint control by Lagardère (together with Canal + and Liberty Media) over Multi-thematiques; and (ii) the creation by Lagardère (Hachette) and Multithematiques of a special interest channels provider.

8–202 The relevant product markets — The Commission distinguished the following relevant product markets: (i) the market for the distribution and operation of special interest channels (with a possible further division into distinct sub-segments based on the different channel "themes"); (ii) the market for pay-TV (with a possible distinct market for the provision of multichannel bouquets); (iii) the market for interactive digital TV services; and (iv) the market for the acquisition of broadcasting rights.

8–203 The relevant geographic markets — All the relevant product markets were deemed to be mainly national in geographic scope.

8–204 Competitive assessment: dominance — As regards the co-operation between Lagardère and Canal +, relating to the French market for the distribution and operation of special interest channels, the Commission concluded that the new entity would not have had a dominant position, owing to the presence of competitors of a similar size on the market and the restricted scope of the relevant joint venture (the key drivers for pay-TV subscriptions — sport, cinema and information — were expressly excluded from its scope).

---

[56] This can be compared with Case *Vodafone Airtouch/Mannesmann*, above, para.8–142 *et seq.*, where the roaming agreements that Vodafone committed to enter into with other operators were published with the decision and the Commission was therefore able to verify that they were appropriate, fair and non-discriminatory.

[57] Case JV.40, *Canal + /Lagardère/CanalSatellite*, Commission Decision of June 22, 2000, O.J. 2000 C110/45; and Case JV.47., *Canal + /Lagardère/Liberty Media/Multithematiques*. See Case T–251/00, *Lagardère and Canal + /Commission*, Judgment of November 20, 2002, [2002] II E.C.R. 4825, concerning the Commission's approach to the issue of ancillary restraints in this case. See above, para.8–031.

The Commission considered the market for digital interactive TV services was an emerging market on which Lagardère was not yet active. Moreover, there was sufficient competition and no risk of market foreclosure due to the "open decoder technology" adopted by CanalSatellite that allowed third party access to the CanalSatellite digital platform.

As regards the market for the acquisition of broadcasting rights, the incremental increase in the buying power of Lagardère and Canal+ as a result of the transaction *vis-à-vis* the general interest channels was considered to be too small to have had a major impact on general interest channel providers, as the combined value of the broadcasting rights acquired by both Lagardère and Canal+ for their special interest channels did not represent more than 10 per cent of the rights acquired by the general interest channels.

8–205 Competitive assessment: co-ordination of independent activities — The Commission also concluded that there was no risk of co-ordination under Article 2(4) of the Merger Control Regulation. First, there was no risk of co-ordination of the independent activities of the parent companies because their respective channels belonged to different segments of the market. Moreover, the competitive situation of the market would have rendered co-ordination ineffective. In relation to the market for the distribution of pay-TV services between the parents, there was no overlap, as Lagardère was not active in this market. Moreover, the operation would not have altered the distribution of Lagardère's channels, all of which were already distributed exclusively on CanalSatellite. Secondly, there was no risk of co-ordination as a result of the concentrations on the neighbouring market for the sale of broadcasting rights. The segments where both Lagardère and Canal+ were active (documentaries and animation) had an international dimension, were characterised by a high degree of competition and the parties' presence on these market segments was weak. The Commission reached the same conclusion as regards the neighbouring markets for audio-visual production, cinema production, television advertising and the production of internet websites.

Bertelsmann/GBL/Pearson TV[58]

8–206 The transaction — This operation concerned the acquisition of joint control by Bertelsmann and Group Bruxelles Lambert (GBL) of Pearson TV, which was active in TV production and transmission in the United Kingdom.

8–207 The relevant product markets — The Commission identified the following relevant markets: (i) television advertising; (ii) television productions which, as in previous decisions,[59] was limited to independent productions that are not for captive use but are offered for sale on the market; and (iii) the sale of TV rights/licences. As regards television advertising, the Commission had previously distinguished between the markets for free TV and pay-TV, but in this case it indicated that since in the United Kingdom there was advertising not only on free TV but also on pay-TV, there might be a wider market for all television advertising in the United Kingdom.

---

[58] Case M.1958, *Bertelsmann/GBL/Pearson TV*, Commission Decision of June 29, 2000, O.J. 2000 C180/14.
[59] Case *RTL/Veronica/Endemol*, above, para.8–179 *et seq.*, and Case M.1943, *Telefónica/Endemol*, Commission Decision of July 11, 2000, O.J. 2000 C235/6.

However, it ultimately left this market definition open. As regards the sale of rights and licences, although the Commission discussed the possible existence of separate segments for film and other fiction rights on the one hand, and sports rights on the other, this question was ultimately left open.

8–208   The relevant geographic markets — The Commission took the position that the markets for television advertising were national, since television advertising is directed to the geographic area in which the television broadcasters have their main audience. The market for television productions was found to be national, in some cases comprising a broader region sharing the same language. With respect to the markets for television rights and licences, the Commission noted that film and sports rights were normally granted for one country or language region, although the demand is sometimes Europe-wide or even worldwide. However, the geographic delineation of the markets for both television productions and television rights and licences was left open.

8–209   Competitive analysis — The concentration did not raise any significant competition concerns. The parties' activities only overlapped to a negligible extent on the UK television advertising market, the German market for independent television productions and the German market for the sale of television rights. Addressing the vertical integration in Germany following the transaction, the Commission noted that the addition of the market shares in the upstream markets for television programmes and television rights was insignificant as Pearson's activities in Germany were negligible. The Commission, therefore, concluded that the transaction did not significantly reinforce the already existing vertical integration of CLT-UFA. Furthermore, CLT-UFA's main competitor, the Kirch Group, was also vertically integrated and had access to a comprehensive library of television programmes and rights.

Telecom Italia/News TV/Stream[60]

8–210   The transaction — The transaction concerned the emerging pay-TV market in Italy and consisted of the acquisition of joint control by the incumbent telecommunications operator Telecom Italia and News TV, a subsidiary of News International (which in turn is controlled by News Corporation Ltd, a shareholder in BSkyB, itself a shareholder in KirchPayTV) of Stream, a satellite and cable digital pay-TV operator in Italy.

8–211   The relevant product markets — The Commission identified the following relevant markets: (i) pay-TV[61]; (ii) transmission capacity (indicating that the market could be further subdivided into separate markets for cable capacity and satellite capacity); (iii) set-top boxes and conditional access technology, although the Commission left open the question of whether the sale of set-top boxes was, in fact, a separate market or formed part of the market for technical and administrative services for pay-TV; and (iv) the acquisition of broadcasting rights for pay-TV channels.

[60] Case M.1978, *Telecom Italia/News TV/Stream*, Commission Decision of June 29, 2000, O.J. 2002 C66/14.
[61] As defined in Case *Bertelsmann/Kirch/Premiere*, above, para.8–187 *et seq.*

8–212 The relevant geographic markets — The Commission found that the pay-TV market was still national in scope, due to language and cultural differences.[62] It found that the market for transmission capacity was also national, given the prevailing market conditions in Italy. The same approach was taken in relation to the market for set-top boxes, which the Commission concluded was national in scope.

8–213 Competitive analysis — The increase of the shareholdings of the parties in Stream as a result of the concentration to 50 per cent each (by purchasing the interests of other existing shareholders and participation in a capital increase) did not lead to any addition of their market shares on the pay-TV market. However, the Commission noted that the concentration would have vertical effects in relation to the parents' activities in upstream markets, for example the Italian transmission capacity market, in which Telecom Italia was the main supplier of capacity, *i.e.* cable or satellite capacity. Telecom Italia owned all of Italy's cable television networks, and its subsidiary Telespazio provided approximately 80 per cent of all satellite capacity available to television broadcasters. The Commission was concerned that Telepiù (the only other pay-TV operator active in Italy) would, as a consequence of the transaction, have been obliged to acquire the necessary transmission capacity (whether cable or satellite) from a parent of its competitor Stream. However, it decided that under the existing market conditions there was insufficient evidence of foreclosure effects. First, it noted that mainly owing to the existence of long-term satellite capacity transmission contracts (only some of which were with Telespazio), Telepiù's ability to acquire sufficient satellite capacity (whether from Telespazio or other providers) would not be worsened as a consequence of the merger. Secondly, because of its low penetration rate (around 1 million homes), the cable network in Italy was considered by the Commission as being of minor importance to the pay-TV market. Any future development of the cable network was hard to predict and, in any event, it was not clear that it would be carried out by Telecom Italia alone, owing to the high costs of this development. The Commission did not impose any open access conditions in respect of Telecom Italia's satellite and cable platforms as a condition for clearance of the concentration and observed that the future regulatory framework for electronic communications networks and services would ensure fair and non-discriminatory access to cable networks where the operator had significant market power.[63]

As regards the markets for set-top boxes and conditional access technology, the Commission considered that there was no risk of foreclosure effects to the detriment of Stream's competitors (such as Telepiù) as a result of News TV providing Stream with open conditional access technology via NDS (a supplier of open conditional access software in which it held an 80 per cent stake). This was because neither NDS, in the market for conditional access technology, nor Stream, in the market for pay-TV, had a dominant position in Italy. Moreover, Stream was subject to the requirements under the Advanced TV Standards Directive[64] and thereby was obliged to implement simulcrypt technology to ensure that viewers can receive digital services of different service providers by means of a single decoder. The Advanced TV Standards Directive required providers

---

[62] See also Case M.410, *Kirch/Piemont/Telepiù*, Commission Decision of August 2, 1994, O.J. 1994 C225/3.
[63] See above, para.1–145 *et seq.*
[64] This has now been repealed and replaced by the Access Directive, in particular Art.6: see above, para.1–171.

of conditional access systems for digital television to offer access to their platforms on fair, reasonable and non-discriminatory terms. Article 6 of the new Access Directive reconfirms this obligation. The national regulatory authorities must undertake a regular review of this regime and, as a result, may decide to extend the existing obligations to new gateways, such as electronic programme guides ("EPGs") and application programme interfaces ("APIs").

Finally, in relation to broadcasting rights, owing to the broad range of suppliers of content, it did not appear that the vertical integration between Stream and the companies belonging to the NewsCorp group would have prospectively foreclosed the acquisition of broadcasting rights by Telepiù (the market leader in the Italian pay-TV market) and hinder competition in this sector.

Telefónica/Endemol[65]

8–214 The transaction — The transaction consisted in the acquisition of sole control by Telefónica, the Spanish incumbent telecommunications operator (and a shareholder in Sogecable, a cable television operator) over the Dutch company Endemol, which was active in the production and sale of TV programmes.

8–215 The relevant product markets — The Commission distinguished the following relevant product markets: (i) the production of TV programmes; (ii) free access TV; and (iii) pay-TV, which was found to be a separate market in line with *Bertelsmann/Kirch/Premiere*.[66] With regard to the market for the production of television programmes, the Commission found that in-house production by broadcasters for their own use should be excluded from the market, whereas production that was sold to third parties by broadcasters had to be included in the market, since it competed with independent productions.

8–216 The relevant geographic markets — Despite its decision in *RTL/Veronica/Endemol*,[67] where the geographical scope of the market for the production of television programmes was defined as national, the Commission considered a wider definition in this case, given that one third of the programmes bought by Spanish broadcasters were imported from American programme producers. However, for linguistic, cultural, licensing and copyright reasons, the Commission continued to consider that the pay- and free TV markets were national in scope.

8–217 Competitive analysis — The Commission found that the merger did not bring about any material change in the structure of the market for the production of TV programmes, given the insignificant role of Telefónica as a producer of TV programmes for third parties. Even considering a narrower market definition for "content for pay-TV", where Telefónica played an important, but, compared to the market leader Sogecable, limited role as buyer of content for pay-TV, the Commission found that the merger did not raise any issues and rejected third party concerns of a collective dominant position of Endemol and Sogecable, given that the two companies' productions were asymmetric and Endemol's production output was not suitable for pay-TV.

---

[65] Case M.1943, *Telefónica/Endemol*, Commission Decision of July 11, 2000, O.J. 2000 C235/6.
[66] Case *Bertelsmann/Kirch/Premiere*, above, para.8–187 *et seq.*
[67] See above, para.8–179 *et seq.*

The backwards vertical integration of Telefónica into the upstream market of TV production as a result of the merger was not considered by the Commission to raise competition concerns, owing to Telefónica's small market shares in free TV (between 25 and 30 per cent) and pay-TV (15–25 per cent), and the absence of Endemol in these markets. Supplies of TV programmes to TV broadcasters would have remained available owing to the significant number of competing Spanish producers and imported TV programmes. The possible elimination of Telefónica as a customer for Endemol's competitors would not have had a significant impact, given the number of other TV broadcasters that were potential buyers of TV programmes from independent producers.

Blackstone/CDPQ/Kabel Baden-Württemberg[68]

8–218   The transaction — The concentration involved the acquisition of joint control by US-based Blackstone Group and Canada's Capital Communications (CDPQ) through the investment vehicle Callahan InvestCo, which had been formed by Callahan Associates International and a group of European and North American investors, including Blackstone and CDPQ, over Kabel Baden-Württemberg (Kabel BW). Kabel BW was a new company and had been an indirect subsidiary of Deutsche Telekom (DT). At closing, DT transferred its regional cable network business in Baden-Württemberg to Kabel BW. Callahan had already acquired DT's cable network in Nordrhein-Westfalen, whilst DT had also sold a 65 per cent interest in its cable TV operations in Hessen to US-based NTL.

8–219   The relevant product markets — The Commission noted that the parties intended to upgrade Kabel BW's cable network in order to be able to offer a wide array of services in addition to the traditional TV transmission services. It therefore needed to base its assessment of the concentration on a number of markets that were relevant to Kabel BW's future intended activities. The following markets were identified as being relevant for the assessment of the transaction: (i) transmission capacity for pay-TV, but leaving open the question of whether there were separate markets for the distribution of pay-TV via cable and via satellite; (ii) technical and administrative services for pay-TV, including the provision of conditional access systems, the software for both subscriber and operator premises and subscriber management systems; (iii) telecommunications services, distinguishing between the markets for domestic and international voice and data telecommunications services, with a further segmentation between the voice market (for residential and business customers) and the data market (mainly for business customers) and making a further segmentation between domestic and international markets; and (iv) internet access services, with a possible further division between the low-bandwidth services (*e.g.* dial-up service) offered mainly to residential customers and high-bandwidth services (*e.g.* dedicated high-speed connections) offered mainly to business customers.

8–220   The relevant geographic markets — As in previous decisions, the Commission found that the markets for pay-TV, telecommunications services and internet access services were mainly national in scope, *i.e.* in this case Germany. However, the Commission left open the question of the possible existence of a regional market for transmission capacity for pay-TV. The Commission

---

[68] Case JV.50, *Blackstone/CDPQ/Kabel Baden-Württemberg*, Commission Decision of August 8, 2000, O.J. 2000 C323/4.

noted that the market for technical and administrative services for pay-TV could be wider than Germany and cover the entire German-speaking area.

8–221 Competitive assessment — The Commission noted that even though Kabel BW would continue to have a *de facto* monopoly in the cable pay-TV market in Baden-Württemberg, this position was not the result of the transaction, but reflected the fact that Kabel BW would simply take over DT's existing market position following the transaction. With regard to the other relevant markets, the Commission simply found that the transaction would not have led to the creation of a dominant position, because none of the parties were active on these markets.

In Germany, the cable television networks are, because of their historical development, divided into four levels. "Level 1" corresponds to the studio instalments and is owned and operated by the relevant broadcasting station. "Level 2" is the backbone network including the cable head end. "Level 3" corresponds to the cables running from the cable head end to the boundary of a given plot of land (such as an apartment building or a private house). "Level 4" is the network infrastructure between this boundary and the junction boxes of individual TV households, and involves the in-house wiring and the cable connecting various households located on one property, for example in an apartment building. For the supply of cable television, network levels 3 and 4 are of particular importance. In the past, level 3 networks were installed and operated almost exclusively by Deutsche Telekom, whilst level 4 networks were built and operated by small independent private cable operators, such as building management companies or other private service providers. Blackstone and CDPQ were already active in the cable sector in Baden-Württemberg through the joint venture Kabel BW. In Baden-Württemberg approximately 3.2 million households could be reached via the cable network and 2.3 million households were connected to the cable network. Kabel BW served approximately 2–2.3 million households on the level 3 network and some 0.8–1 million households on the network level 4 which corresponded to a share of 35–44 per cent.

While the parties to this transaction received clearance for their joint acquisition of DT's level 3 cable network assets in Baden-Württemberg, one year later, in *Blackstone/CDPQ/DeTeKS BW*,[69] the parties' acquisition of DT's remaining level 4 cable network in Baden-Württemberg was itself subject to Commission approval under the Merger Control Regulation. In that case, the operation consisted of the acquisition of joint control by Blackstone and CDPQ (through Kabel BW) of Deutsche Telekom's network level 4 cable unit DeTeKabelService Baden-Württemberg (DeTeKS BW). For market definition purposes, the Commission referred to the product markets defined in its earlier decision,[70] namely: (i) transmission capacity for TV; (ii) telecommunications services; and (iii) internet access, which it had found to be regional or national in scope. However, given the absence of any competition issues as a result of the transaction, the Commission did not find it necessary to further delineate the relevant markets. The Commission noted that the operation did not have any impact on competition in the EEA, since, although the parties were already active through Kabel BW as level 4 network operators, the acquisition would have allowed Kabel BW to serve directly an increment of less than 5 per cent of the cable households in Baden-Württemberg.

[69] Case M.2643, *Blackstone/CDPQ/DeTeKS BW*, Commission Decision of November 23, 2001, O.J. 2001 C358/12.
[70] Case JV.46, *Callahan Invest/Kabel Nordrhein Westfalen*, Commission Decision of June 19, 2000.

On a national level, Kabel BW's market share would have risen by less than 1 per cent and would have remained below 5 per cent.

8–222 In this context, it is interesting to note that, in January 2002, the German Bundeskar-tellamt[71] prohibited Liberty Media's ("Liberty") proposed acquisition of six other regional cable networks. The target level 3 network accounted for 60 per cent of the total German cable network. The Bundeskartellamt, following an in-depth Phase II investigation, concluded that the transaction would have given Liberty a dominant position in the German market for cable-TV, one of the European cable markets with the highest penetration rate. The Bundeskartellamt decided that the merger would have: (i) considerably worsened the competitive structure of the German cable markets by combining Liberty's existing content business with DT's cable distribution networks, thereby strengthening the existing market position of each, thereby disadvantaging competing broadcasters and preventing "open access" to the network in question; (ii) strengthened Liberty's market position without creating improvements to or efficiency gains in other markets (such as the pay-TV and telephony markets) which could outweigh the restrictions of competition in the cable television markets[72]; and (iii) made the situation worse for consumers than if Deutsche Telekom had retained its cable networks for the time being. In an attempt to gain clearance, Liberty had committed to making significant investments to modernise the Deutsche Telekom cable networks that it sought to acquire, but could not satisfy the Bundeskartellamt, which wanted to see a more rapid upgrade of the networks used to distribute television signals (so-called "one way" networks). The Bundeskartellamt, in particular, questioned Liberty's willingness to complete the planned upgrade and feared that Liberty could have concentrated on supplying television services. The Bundeskartellamt insisted on having the offering of "triple-play" services, and in particular of internet telephony,[73] available much faster than Liberty's roll-out plan provided for. However, Liberty, in response, insisted on its original roll-out plan pointing to the need for sound financing of the cable upgrade. Finally, the Bundeskartellamt was concerned about the proprietary design of the set-top box Liberty intended to use, which it considered could have foreclosed access to the networks for competing broadcasters.

AOL/Time Warner[74]

8–223 The transaction — This transaction involved the merger of America Online (AOL) with Time Warner to create AOL Time Warner, the first vertically integrated internet service provider that would distribute Time Warner's content on AOL's distribution networks.

---

[71] *Liberty/KDG*, BKartA Decision of February 22, 2002 (Case B7-168/01), available at: *www.bkarta.de/ 137_168_01.pdf*. See also Bundeskartellamt press release of February 26, 2002 (in English), available at *www. bundeskartellamt.de/26_02_2002.englisch.html*.

[72] The Bundeskartellamt, however, noted that the concentration would have led to improvements in competition in the high-speed internet access market.

[73] The Bundeskartellamt was particularly interested in having cable telephony introduced as soon as possible, because access to the local loop is still regarded as the weak point of telecommunications liberalisation in Germany. By trying to open an alternative infrastructure, the Bundeskartellamt intended to remedy the shortcomings of German telecommunications regulation.

[74] Case M.1845, *AOL/Time Warner*, Commission Decision of October 11, 2000, O.J. 2001 L268/28.

8–224 The relevant product markets — The Commission identified a number of product markets as being relevant for the analysis of the transaction.

First, the Commission identified an emerging market for the online distribution of music (narrowband content). The market for online music was found to have a different business model from the distribution of recorded music through "bricks and mortar" shops or e-commerce channels and different pricing. The Commission considered whether this market should be further divided into separate product markets for music downloading (the electronic transfer of an entire music file to a user's computer before playback is allowed, as a result of which the file remains as a permanent copy on the recipient's computer) and streaming audio (the temporary transmission of audio files over the internet to the user's computer, without file storage taking place). However, the Commission finally left this question open.

Secondly, the Commission identified a distinct product market for the supply of music player software. This software needs to be compatible with the compression technology of the music file and, if used, the Digital Rights Management (DRM) technology[75] and the encryption technology.

Thirdly, in line with previous decisions,[76] the Commission identified a market for dial-up (narrowband) internet access services (*i.e.* the provision of internet access through a normal telephone line) which were mainly used by residential and small and medium-sized business customers. This product market was distinct from that for dedicated internet access (*i.e.* access through a dedicated fixed-line cable link) which was mainly used by large business customers. The Commission did not determine whether residential and business dial-up access constituted two separate sub-segments.

Fourthly, the Commission discussed the existence of a market for the provision of a "one-stop" integrated supply of broadband content (both audio and video) via the internet. Such a market for broadband content appeared to the Commission to be distinguishable from the market for the traditional distribution of content through pay-per-view or video-on-demand services or video or DVD rentals. However, the Commission ultimately left this question open.

Finally, the Commission considered the existence of a distinct product market for residential broadband internet access. The Commission noted that broadband access (through telephone lines equipped with digital subscriber line (DSL) technology or through a cable modem) enabled customers to receive greater audio/video functionality and new services (such as voice email, video-conferencing, and video and audio streaming) which could not be offered effectively via narrowband access. Broadband access was also generally more expensive. The Commission left open the question of whether broadband access in general should be considered as a separate market, or whether DSL and cable modem access belonged to the same or to separate broadband access markets.

---

[75] See further on the Commission's approach with respect to DRM-related markets, Case M.3042, *Sony/Philips/Intertrust*, Commission Decision of December 20, 2002, O.J. 2003 C23/8.
[76] Case *Telia/Telenor*, above, para.8–097 *et seq.*

8–225 The relevant geographic markets — Although language barriers have often caused the Commission to define markets as being national in scope, this was not the case in this concentration. The fact that the language of music players software could be changed easily led the Commission to determine that the market for music players was global. Similarly, because US films and other content delivered over the internet had an international appeal and were popular in all EEA countries, the Commission considered whether the geographic market for the supply of broadband content via the internet should have been wider than national. Referring to its *Telia/ Telenor* decision,[77] the Commission concluded that the internet dial-up access market could not have been wider than national, given the need to use the local loop infrastructure, and therefore the relevant market was found to be national, with separate geographic markets for each of the nine Member States in which AOL operated. Similarly, with regard to a potential market for broadband internet access, the Commission concluded that the need for the use of a physical infrastructure connection was the reason to ultimately define this (potential) market as being probably national in scope. Finally, the Commission noted that the possibilities offered by digital technologies (*i.e.* to buy and receive music immediately, no matter the location, without using national distribution channels) implied that the market for online music was at least EEA-wide.

8–226 Competitive analysis — The Commission's principal concerns were related to the links between AOL and Bertelsmann (another major provider of both video and audio content), especially the 50/50 joint venture between AOL and Bertelsmann, AOL Europe. This raised competition concerns on some of the relevant affected markets.

Analysing the impact of the transaction on the market for the online distribution of music, the Commission found that, owing to the structural and contractual links between AOL and Bertelsmann resulting from AOL Europe, the merged entity would have controlled Time Warner's and Bertelsmann's music catalogues, which were two of the largest music libraries in the world. This concern was exacerbated because of the then still pending merger between EMI and Time Warner,[78] a transaction which, if implemented, would have resulted in the merged entity having control of the catalogues of three of the then five major record companies. As a result, by controlling such a sizable music catalogue, the merged entity would have been able to refuse to license these catalogues to competing online music distributiors or impose unfair licence conditions. The sheer size of the music catalogues of Time Warner and Bertelsmann (and, if the EMI Time Warner transaction had proceeded, of EMI) when combined with AOL's internet distribution strength would have compelled competing music labels to distribute their music via AOL in order to achieve the maximum penetration rate for their content. In the view of the Commission, this unique market position could have been used by the merged entity to charge excessive prices for the carriage of third party content or to restrict (or degrade the quality of) third party access, thereby favouring the content of Time Warner and Bertelsmann. Finally, the Commission was concerned that the transaction would have enabled the merged entity to dictate the technical standards for music delivery over the internet. By adopting a proprietary formatting technology for the downloading

---

[77] See above, para.8–097 *et seq.*
[78] Case M.1852, *Time Warner/EMI*, which was abandoned on October 5, 2000, during Phase II proceedings. On the opening of Phase II proceedings (Decision of June 14, 2000), see Commission Press Release IP/00/617 of June 14, 2000.

and streaming of its content, the new entity would have been able to prevent its content from being downloaded through competing technologies, thereby imposing its proprietary technology. Competing record companies wishing to distribute music online would therefore have been obliged to format their content using the merged entity's new technology, thus giving the new entity both control over the downloading and streaming of music over the internet and the ability to raise competitors' costs through excessive carriage fees. The Commission concluded that the new entity would, therefore, have become dominant in the market for the online distribution of music.

The Commission's concern in respect of the new entity's "gatekeeper" role, arising from its ability to dictate the technical standards for online music delivery, was also key to its assessment of the impact of the merger on the market for music players. The Commission noted that the new entity could have formatted its music to make it compatible only with its own player software, Winamp, but at the same time Winamp could have played different file formats used by other companies. Winamp would thereby have become the only music player that was able to play virtually all the music available on the internet, as no other music player would be able to decode the proprietary format used by the merged entity. Moreover, the merged entity would have been able to charge excessive prices to third party content providers. The Commission considered that this would have led to the new entity holding a dominant position on the music player market.

8–227 The Commission's competition concerns were partly removed as a result of the abandonment of the EMI/Time Warner merger. The parties furthermore committed to ensuring Bertelsmann's exit from AOL Europe and AOL Compuserve France and committed, in the interim, to maintaining an arm's length relationship between Bertelsmann and AOL prior to Bertelsmann's exit from AOL Europe. In this context, the parties committed that they would not take any action that would mean that Bertelsmann's music catalogue would only be made available online through AOL Time Warner or playable only through AOL Time Warner's music players, nor would Bertelsmann exclusively promote AOL's internet access services in Europe.

In order to address the Commission's concerns related to the broadband content market, where the vertically integrated merged entity would have arguably enjoyed a considerable competitive advantage over non-integrated competitors, the parties committed that for three years following the completion of the merger, AOL, as a condition of entering into content delivery deals for its US online service, would not require content providers to enter into agreements for the provision of content to its affiliated internet service providers (ISPs) in the EEA.

With regard to the internet dial-up access market(s), the Commission was concerned that subscribers would have less of an incentive to abandon AOL (and its affiliated joint ventures) and more new customers would be attracted to AOL's services than to those of competitors because of the large AOL community of users that they could communicate with. This would have increased the number of content providers wishing to have their content distributed via AOL. The merged entity would therefore have become a "one-stop shop", combining attractive content with its internet distribution strength in the USA. This would have resulted in the creation of network effects: the more content acquired, the less the reason for a subscriber to abandon AOL and the greater the reason for a potential new customer to subscribe to AOL. More subscribers would bring more content and *vice versa*.

8–228 Whilst the Commission was concerned about the vertical integration leading the merged entity to be able to set excessive access prices to unaffiliated content providers, it did not raise concerns in relation to the internet broadband access market and the availability of open access of unaffiliated internet service providers to the new entity's distribution facilities, since neither AOL nor Time Warner owned transmission infrastructure in Europe (unlike in the United States).

The latter issue, however, was the major concern of the regulatory authorities in the United States. Against the background of a national regulatory debate on the question of whether cable companies should be required to give unaffiliated ISPs open access to their broadband platforms,[79] the Federal Trade Commission (FTC) and the Federal Communications Commission (FCC) imposed far-reaching open access requirements on the parties as a condition of their approval of the merger. This prevented the merged entity from providing internet access in the United States only through AOL. After the European Commission's clearance decision in October 2000, the FTC, on December 14, 2000, entered into a consent decree that outlined the terms of its approval of the merger to which AOL and Time Warner agreed. Under the terms of the consent decree, AOL Time Warner was: (i) required to open its cable system to competing ISPs; (ii) prohibited from interfering with content transmitted on the bandwidth contracted for by unaffiliated ISPs and from interfering with the ability of unaffiliated providers of interactive television services to interact with interactive signals, triggers or content that AOL Time Warner had agreed to carry; (iii) prevented from discriminating on the basis of affiliation in the transmission of content, or from entering into exclusive arrangements with other cable companies with respect to ISP services or interactive television services; and (iv) required to market and offer AOL's services to DSL subscribers in Time Warner cable areas where affiliated cable broadband service was available in the same manner and at the same retail pricing as they did in those areas where affiliated cable broadband ISP services were not available.[80]

The FCC approved the merger on January 11, 2001, but required the companies to comply with several additional conditions.[81] Under these conditions, AOL Time Warner was required to: (i) allow competing ISPs on Time Warner's cable systems to have an unimpeded "first-screen" relationship with their subscribers, a direct billing relationship with customers, to benefit equally from the technical features, such as caching, of the high-speed internet platform, and to be afforded fair carriage contracts; (ii) open its "advanced" instant-messaging network to one competitor immediately and to two others within 180 days from the launch of the service; and (iii) avoid any agreement with AT&T that would make AOL Time Warner the exclusive ISP on AT&T's high-speed cable-modem platform. In addition, the FCC reaffirmed its decision of December 2000 to

---

[79] See further, Rosenthal, "Open Access of Internet Service Providers to the Cable Operators' Facilities in the United States" (2001/01) 6 *International Journal of Communications Law and Policy*, available at: *www.ijclp.org*. For an update on this issue (in German) see Rosenthal, "Neue Antworten auf Fragen der Konvergenz–Entwicklungen des Kommunikationsrechts in Europa und den USA" (2002) T.M.R. 181.

[80] See *"In the matter of America Online, Inc. and Time Warner, Inc., Agreement Containing Consent Orders"*, File No.0010105, Docket No.C–3989, December 14, 2000.

[81] See *"Subject to Conditions, Commission Approves Merger Between America Online, Inc. and Time Warner, Inc."*, Public Notice FCC 01-11 (January 11, 2001), available at: *www.fcc.gov*. FCC chairman William E. Kennard has seen the measure as going "a little bit further" in "plugging the holes" left after the FTC's AOL/Time Warner merger decision. See "FCC Clears Way for AOL Time Warner Inc.", *Washington Post* (January 12, 2001), at p.A01.

require AT&T to sell its 25 per cent stake in Time Warner Entertainment. However, the FCC fell short of imposing merger conditions relating to interactive television, but instead launched a new proceeding on the issue.

Vivendi/Canal + /Seagram[82]

8–229 The transaction — This transaction involved the acquisition by French-based communications and utilities conglomerate Vivendi, and its listed subsidiary Canal + (in which it had a 49 per cent shareholding giving it sole control) of sole control over Seagram, the Canadian beverages and entertainment company. Following the consummation of the transaction, the merged entity was called "Vivendi Universal", with the shareholding in the new entity held by Vivendi (59 per cent), Seagram (29 per cent) and Canal + (12 per cent). Seagram's entertainment assets included Universal Studios (film), Universal Music Group (music) and United International Pictures, a joint venture between Universal, MGM and Paramount (distribution of motion pictures to cinemas, etc.). Vivendi was the ultimate parent company of a group of companies that was active in France and internationally, particularly in the provision of telecommunications networks and related services (through Cégétel). It was also active in cinema and television, most importantly through its listed subsidiary Canal +. Canal + is active in the production of pay-TV channels, the distribution and marketing of bouquets of television services by cable and satellite, the production and distribution of feature films and audio-visual works, and the licensing of broadcasting rights for films, audio-visual works and sports events.

8–230 The relevant product markets — Given the breadth of the activities of both Vivendi and Seagram, the Commission identified several horizontally and vertically affected markets.

Among the horizontally affected markets, the Commission distinguished: (i) the market for the distribution of films to theatres and cinemas; and (ii) the market for the licensing of broadcasting rights (which could be further broken down into separate markets for broadcasting rights to sports events, for feature films and for made-for-TV programmes).

The following vertically affected relevant markets were identified by the Commission: (iii) the pay-TV market[83] (which was separate from the free TV market[84]); (iv) the emerging market for portals, distinguishing, in line with its *Vodafone/Vivendi/Canal +* decision,[85] between portals having a broad focus ("horizontal portals") and portals with a narrow focus ("vertical portals"), but leaving open the question of whether there was a narrower segment for portals accessible via mobile phones; and (v) the market for online music distribution, without further distinguishing between music downloading and music streaming.[86] With regard to the latter market, the Commission

---

[82] Case M.2050, *Vivendi/Canal + /Seagram*, Commission Decision of October 13, 2000, O.J. 2000 C311/3.

[83] Case *MSG Media Service*, above, para.8–171 *et seq.*; and Case *BSkyB/KirchPayTV*, above, para.8–196 *et seq.*

[84] The Commission, in this context, discussed the different exhibition windows for films and, in this context, stressed the importance for pay-TV operators of having "first-window" films.

[85] See above, para.8–138 *et seq.*

[86] Such a distinction had already been considered by the Commission in Case *AOL/Time Warner*, above, para.8–223 *et seq.*

found that the identification of a further sub-market for online music delivery to mobile customers was premature.

8–231   The relevant geographic markets — The Commission found that the markets for film distribution to theatres and cinemas, and the licensing of broadcasting rights were national; and that the market for pay-TV was national or regional in scope because of cultural or linguistic differences. In line with previous decisions[87] the market for portals was found to be pan-European. It was suggested that the geographic scope of the market for online music distribution extended beyond national borders and was at least EEA-wide, owing to the possibilities offered by digital technology. However, the Commission ultimately left the geographic definition of this product market open.

8–232   Competitive analysis — Owing to the low combined market shares of the parties, the Commission found that the transaction did not raise any competition concerns on the horizontally affected markets for film distribution to theatres and for the licensing of broadcasting rights.

With regard to the pay-TV markets, the Commission found that Canal+'s existing dominant positions in France, Spain, Italy, Belgium and the Netherlands would have been strengthened by the transaction and that in addition, Canal+ would have become dominant in the Nordic countries as a result of the transaction. Prior to the merger, Canal+ already had a *de facto* near-monopoly position in these countries in relation to "first window" rights for premium films.[88] In addition, Canal+ was "ideally placed" to renew its existing contracts with major content and film providers. The merger would have created the world's largest film library and the second largest library of TV-programming in the EEA. Therefore, the Commission considered that Canal+'s vertical integration with Seagram/Universal (through Vivendi) would have led not only to the elimination of Universal as a source of supply for competing pay-TV operators, but also to Canal+ being able to permanently renew its contracts for content with Universal, as well as with the other studio majors owing to its own and Universal's co-financing of films and Universal's links to Paramount and MGM through UIP. Accordingly, the transaction would have strengthened Canal+'s bargaining power *vis-à-vis* the US studios, which in return would have strengthened Canal+'s position on the "first window premium film segment", which would most likely have led to the foreclosure of competing providers on the pay-TV market and to the strengthening of Canal+'s existing dominant position.

In relation to the emerging markets for portals and online delivery of music, the Commission found that the position of Vizzavi (a multi-access portal, jointly controlled by Vodafone, Vivendi, and Canal+, which provides seamless access to the internet from various devices[89]) on the market for portals was likely to be strengthened by the merger owing to the addition of Universal's music content. In the Commission's view, the vertical integration of Universal and Vizzavi would have denied competing portals access to Universal's music catalogues. Further, the addition of

---

[87] See *Vodafone/Vivendi/Canal+*, above, para.8–138 *et seq.*
[88] The "first window" is the first period (usually three months) of the availability of premium films on pay-TV following their theatrical (usually up to 8 months), video rental (usually 6 months) and pay-per-view (usually 3 months) releases.
[89] Case *Vodafone/Vivendi/Canal+*, above, para.8–138 *et seq.*

Universal's broad music content to the large distribution channels that Vivendi and Canal+ already had in place (internet access via mobile phone handsets and PCs, and via TV set-top boxes respectively) would have created a highly attractive portal for customers and other content providers, who would be attracted by Vizzavi's high penetration rate. The Commission found that this could have given rise to network effects, to the detriment of both competitors and customers. The latter would have been "walled in" to Vizzavi and would have been forced to pay higher prices, owing to the lack of competition between parties. The conditions imposed in *Vodafone/Vivendi/Canal+* [90] were found to be insufficient to resolve these concerns, as they only required Vizzavi and its parents to allow other portal operators to access Vodafone's mobile customers' handsets and Vivendi's set-top boxes. These open access obligations for distribution purposes did not address, however, the concern of the foreclosure of content providers that would have resulted from the transaction. Accordingly, the parties were obliged to submit specific undertakings to resolve the Commission's concerns as to content foreclosure.

The initial undertakings proposed by the parties to remedy the Commission's competition concerns (including the possibility for third parties to bid for Universal's films on a non-discriminatory basis in Spain and France, and an undertaking not to discriminate in favour of Vizzavi in the supply of music on the internet for two years) were behavioural. As such, the Commission rejected them, as they were found to be inadequate to remedy the transaction's adverse effects on competition. However, the Commission accepted revised undertakings offered by the parties. These included a commitment by Universal not to grant Canal+ more than 50 per cent of the "first-window" rights to all films produced or co-produced by Universal for a period of five years, unless there were no competing offers at a fair market value [91] (before the merger, it had licensed 100 per cent of its films to Canal+). Secondly, Vivendi agreed to divest its shareholding in BSkyB, the largest pay-TV operator in the United Kingdom. BSkyB's largest shareholder, News Corp., controlled Fox studios. This divestment eliminated the parties' links with a potential competitor in the pay-TV market as well as with another studio and potential source of output deals. Thirdly, in response to the Commission's concerns in relation to the dominant position of Vizzavi on the emerging markets for portals and music distribution, Universal undertook to make its music catalogue available to third parties on a non-discriminatory basis for a period of five years, with a possible revision after three years. In addition, the parties proposed an arbitration procedure in case of disputes. The degree of regulation resulting from the undertakings in this case is remarkable, particularly owing to Universal not having a dominant position in music rights, where it was only one of the main five players. In a way, this decision supplements the decision in *Vodafone/Vivendi/Canal+*. [92] Whilst in *Vodafone/Vivendi/Canal+*, the Commission focused on open access to distribution platforms, it added, in this case, an open access obligation regarding content as a condition for clearance of a merger that resulted in the vertical integration of content providers and distributors.

---

[90] Above, para.8–138 *et seq.*

[91] Concerns have been raised as to how this commitment will be implemented in practice; see *e.g.* Shang, *Butterworths Merger Control Devices 2001*, 10(1), pp.18–21.

[92] See above, para.8–138 *et seq.*

Universal Studio Networks/De Facto 829 (NTL)/Studio Channel Limited[93]

8–233   The transaction — Studio Channel was a joint venture jointly controlled by Universal Studio Networks and De Facto 829. Universal Studio Networks was ultimately owned by Vivendi and Canal+, whilst De Facto 829 was a wholly-owned subsidiary of NTL. Studio Channel was formed in order to create and commercialise a film channel to be supplied to, and distributed by, retail pay-TV operators in the United Kingdom and Ireland distributing "second window" and library films, *i.e.* films which have already been previously shown on pay-TV.

8–234   The relevant product markets — The Commission defined the relevant product markets as being: (i) the production and supply of TV programmes for TV (the "content market"); (ii) the wholesale supply of basic-tier pay-TV channels to pay-TV operators (the "wholesale market"); and (iii) the retail distribution of pay-TV channels to end customers via cable, satellite or digital terrestrial television (the "retail market"). The Commission considered that it was not necessary to decide whether there were separate markets for basic-tier and premium pay-TV channels respectively, nor for the provision of "pay-per-view" films and/or channels as distinct from premium channels, at either the wholesale or retail levels.

8–235   The relevant geographic markets — The Commission left open the question of whether the market for the production and supply of programming for pay-TV was global, despite the fact that the licensing of the rights in question was done on a national basis. The Commission, in line with its decision in *Kirch Richemont/Telepiù*,[94] decided that the market for the wholesale supply of pay-TV channels to pay-TV operators was national in scope (*i.e.* the UK and Ireland), as the conditions of competition varied considerably from one country to another. Likewise, the market for the retail distribution of pay-TV channels to the final consumer was considered to be national, as found by the United Kingdom Competition Commission in the *NTL/CWC Consumer* case.[95]

8–236   Competitive analysis: dominance — The Commission based its assessment on the assumption that Studio Channel would not operate in France, as it was clear from the notification and from the Shareholders' Agreement that the channel would not be sold outside the United Kingdom and Ireland.

As regards the content market, the formation of the joint venture would not have led to the creation or strengthening of a dominant position as, in light of historical market information on the UK market, the market share of Studio Channel was likely to be *de minimis* in the medium term. The joint venture would provide content providers with an additional outlet and it would not have been in its commercial interest to purchase content exclusively from Universal.

---

[93] Case M.2211, *Universal Studio Networks/De Facto 829 (NTL)/Studio Channel Limited*, Commission Decision of December 20, 2000, O.J. 2001 C363/31.

[94] Case M.410, *Kirch Richemont/Telepiù*, Commission Decision of August 2, 1994.

[95] Competition Commission, *NTL Incorporated and Cable & Wireless Communications plc*, February 24, 2000, Cm.4666. The Competition Commission had to consider whether the relevant geographic market was limited to each cable operator's "franchise area" (*i.e.* the area for which it was licensed to build and operate a cable network) or extended to the entire territory of the United Kingdom.

As regards the wholesale market, although Universal was also active in the United Kingdom and Ireland through the supply of the Sci-Fi channel, and NTL had a stake in Front Row and in Onrequest (two pay-per-view film channels), the Commission found that the joint venture, even in the narrowest possible market definition, would have had only a low market share and would not have led to the creation or strengthening of a dominant position. Finally, the Commission noted that, in the retail market, it was unlikely for a channel focusing on second-window and library films to become a key factor in driving pay-TV subscriptions. As a result, the channel would need to be offered to all pay-TV platforms in the United Kingdom in order to be commercially successful. Moreover, even if the joint venture were to have been distributed exclusively via NTL's cable networks, the increase in NTL's market shares in the distribution market was likely to be *de minimis* in the medium term. The Commission, therefore, concluded that the concentration did not raise any dominance concerns.

8–237 Competitive analysis: co-ordination of independent competitive behaviour — The Commission finally considered whether the formation of the joint venture could possibly have resulted in the co-ordination of competitive behaviour on the UK market for pay-TV. However, the Commission found, in applying Article 2(4) of the Merger Control Regulation, that even if the parents were to co-ordinate their activities with a view to bundling Studio Channel with some of their pre-existing channels, this would not have restricted competition to an appreciable extent, since the market shares of the channels were small.

UGC/Liberty Media[96]

8–238 The transaction — The transaction involved the acquisition by the US-based cable and media company Liberty Media Corporation (Liberty) of an 81 per cent voting shareholding (but 43 per cent economic shareholding) in UnitedGlobalCom Inc. (UGC), which in return controlled United Pan-Europe Communications (UPC). Liberty thereby acquired joint control of UGC and thus UPC, together with its founding shareholders. In Europe, Liberty had interests in companies active in content production, cable television networks in the United Kingdom and Ireland, and the operation of pay-TV channels. UGC owned UPC, which was active in Europe in providing cable television, telephony and internet services in Austria, Belgium, France, Germany, the Netherlands, Norway and Sweden. UPC also had interests in certain pay-TV channels.

8–239 The relevant product markets — The Commission, revisiting earlier decisions that it has taken in the communications sector, identified the following relevant markets: (i) voice telephony services, which could be sub-divided further into distinct markets for local, long-distance/national and international services[97]; (ii) internet access, where it was possible to further distinguish between dial-up and dedicated access and perhaps between the provision of dial-up services to residential and business customers or even between dial-up narrowband access provided over normal telephony lines and high-speed, broadband/always-on access. Following the approach that it had taken in *Vizzavi*,[98] the Commission also distinguished the market for (iii) internet portals; (iv) internet

---

[96] Case M.2222, *UGC/Liberty Media*, Commission Decision of April 24, 2001, O.J. 2001 C172/20.
[97] Case *Telia/Telenor*, above, para.8–097 *et seq.*
[98] Case *Vodafone/Vivendi/Canal+*, above, para.8–138 *et seq.*

advertising; and (v) content. The Commission further identified markets for (vi) pay-TV and related services (with a further sub-segmentation into three separate markets for: (a) the production and supply of TV programming; (b) the wholesale supply of pay-TV channels to pay-TV operators; and (c) the retail distribution of pay-TV channels to final consumers[99]). Another market identified, based on *Telia/Telenor*,[1] was (vii) the market for the TV distribution infrastructure, *i.e.* cable, satellite and digital terrestrial and telecommunications networks. Finally the Commission discussed (viii) a possible market for the provision of broadband/"triple-play" services, *i.e.* a combined service provided over cable networks, consisting of telephony, high-speed internet access and interactive TV services. The Commission ultimately left open the question of the existence of such a product market, but indicated that while the technical capabilities of an upgraded two-way cable network suggested that a separate market for "triple-play" services existed, it was questionable whether there was a distinct consumer demand for the provision of such a combination of services.

8–240 The relevant geographic markets — The Commission found that the markets for voice telephony and internet access were national in scope. It further indicated that the relevant markets for portals, internet advertising and content were to be mainly considered as national, except for certain products where pan-European markets were emerging. As regards the markets for pay-TV and related services, the Commission did not adopt a definitive position but underlined that it had found in previous decisions[2] that the geographic scope of the markets for the production and supply of TV programming could be divided linguistically or nationally. As for the wholesale supply of pay-TV channels to pay-TV operators, the Commission found that the product market could be considered as being national in scope, owing to national variations in terms of language and culture. Finally, it left open the question as to whether the market for the retail distribution of pay-TV channels to the final consumer was national or more local.

8–241 Competitive assessment — The transaction was held to be compatible with the common market, as no dominant position would have been created or strengthened in any of the relevant markets.

In voice telephony, the parties had a low combined market share and there existed several significant competitors. As regards the market for internet access, broadband and "triple-play" services, there was no horizontal overlap in the activities of the parties, since their services were offered in different geographic markets. For internet portals, internet content and internet advertising, the Commission noted that the operation would not have resulted in any horizontally affected markets and, furthermore, that the parties' ability to foreclose access to their portal, internet advertising and content services was not significantly altered by the transaction. With regard to the market for the production and supply of TV programming, the Commission concluded that the combination of the parties' activities in this market would not have created or strengthened a dominant position, because the majority of UGC's programming was not sold to third parties and SBS Broadcasting (in which UGC held a minority stake) had very little content of its own.

---

[99] See Case *Universal Studio Networks/De Facto 829 (NTL)/Studio Channel Limited*, above, para.8–233 *et seq.*

[1] See above, para.8–097 *et seq.*

[2] Case *Universal Studio Networks/De Facto 829 (NTL)/Studio Channel Limited*, above, para.8–233 *et seq.*

In relation to the wholesale supply of pay-TV channels to pay-TV operators, the Commission found no horizontal overlaps in the parties' activities as a result of the transaction, except in Portugal where the overlap was not, however, appreciable. There was also no overlap in the markets for retail distribution of pay-TV channels to the viewer, because the parties were active in different geographic markets. The Commission, finally, noted that the transaction's vertical effects with respect to the markets for the wholesale supply of pay-TV channels to pay-TV operators and the retail distribution of pay-TV channels to the final consumer, did not raise any competition concerns since the vertical relationship was not significant in each of the countries concerned.

YLE/TDF/Digita/JV[3]

8–242 The transaction — This transaction concerned the acquisition by France Télécom's subsidiary Télédiffusion de France (TDF) of joint control over the Finnish undertaking Digita Oy. Prior to the transaction, Digita had been solely controlled by Finland's national public broadcaster, Yleisradio (YLE). Digita provided distribution and terrestrial transmission services for radio and TV programmes, data distribution services, leasing of space for antennae and equipment, and technical, construction, maintenance and support services in Finland. TDF, via its subsidiary Telemast Nordic Oy, provided terrestrial transmission and distribution services for radio programmes in Finland.

8–243 The relevant product markets — The Commission identified two horizontally affected markets: (i) the distribution of radio programmes; and (ii) the terrestrial transmission of radio programmes by low-power frequencies. The Commission suggested that there could have been a distinct product market for the digital transmission of radio programmes, but ultimately left this question open. The following vertically affected markets were also identified: (iii) transmission equipment for low-power-frequency radio customers; and (iv) distribution equipment for radio customers. Finally, the following conglomerate markets were identified: (v) the terrestrial transmission of radio programmes by high-power frequencies; (vi) the distribution of TV programmes; and (vii) the terrestrial transmission of TV-programmes. The Commission indicated that the terrestrial transmission of radio and TV programmes using high- and low-power frequencies constituted distinct product markets from cable and satellite transmission in Finland. This was due to the specific topography of Finland, which favoured terrestrial transmission, which was the only distribution platform providing national coverage.

8–244 The relevant geographic markets — The relevant geographic market for horizontally affected markets (i) and (ii) and for conglomerate markets (v), (vi) and (vii) was found to be Finland. With regard to the vertically affected markets, the parties submitted that the geographic market was at least EEA-wide, owing to product standard harmonisation, and may even have been worldwide, owing to uniform international standards and the lack of barriers to entry. The Commission did not come to a conclusive decision on this point but noted, however, that even if this geographic definition was correct for the larger radio stations with an international presence, a

---

[3] Case M.2300, *YLE/TDF/Digita JV*, Commission Decision of June 26, 2001, O.J. 2001 C272/15.

local presence was still necessary for the smaller local radio stations, for reasons of language and to ensure after-sales services.

8–245 Competitive assessment — The Commission was mainly concerned about the high combined market share of TDF/Telemast and Digita in the Finnish markets for the distribution of radio programmes (75–85 per cent) and the terrestrial transmission of radio programmes by low-power frequencies (60–70 per cent). The investigation had shown, furthermore, that high barriers to entry existed in these markets owing to their limited size, their highly concentrated nature, the absence of legislation imposing co-location or site-sharing obligations on either TDF/Telemast or Digita, and the fact that local radio stations preferred to outsource their distribution and transmission requirements to the same service provider as a "one-stop-shop" provider. Therefore, the elimination of TDF/Telemast as an actual competitor to Digita was considered by the Commission to create the risk of creating a dominant position in relation to both transmission equipment for low-power-frequency radio customers and the distribution of radio programmes. As to the vertically affected markets, the Commission found that the parties' position on the market for the supply and procurement of radio- and TV-distribution and transmission equipment in Finland was quite large, and that the creation of a vertically integrated group would have reduced the already limited number of independent sources for the supply of such equipment in Finland. The parties offered to divest Telemast in order to address the Commission's competition concerns relating to the horizontally and vertically affected markets which were removed by the divestment. The divestment also resolved the concerns expressed by third parties that the transaction would eliminate TDF/Telemast as a potential competitor to Digita in the conglomerate markets. Finally, the Commission found that the transaction would not have strengthened YLE's dominant position on the market for the acquisition of broadcasting programmes because, by reducing the vertical link between YLE and Digita from 100 per cent to 51 per cent, the proposed transaction reduced the incidence of price discrimination in favour of YLE, and it would not have altered the *de facto* monopoly position of Digita that existed before the transaction.

Mezzo/Muzzik[4]

8–246 The transaction — This transaction consisted of the formation of a newly created joint venture company that would provide a digital music channel (broadcasting classical, jazz and world music programmes) that would be distributed in digital format via cable networks and by satellite in France and Belgium. Under the transaction, three French companies that were active in the production and distribution of cable and satellite channel markets, Lagardère Thematiques (jointly controlled by Canal+ and Lagardère), France Télémusique (controlled by France Télévision) and Wanadoo Audiovisuel (controlled by France Télécom's internet subsidiary, Wanadoo), would acquire joint control over the new company, that was to be created by merging Mezzo (previously controlled by France Télévision and France Télécom) and MCM Classique Jazz-Muzzik (previously controlled by Lagardère Thematiques). These two pay-TV channels were wholly dedicated to music.

[4] Case M.2550, *Mezzo/Muzzik*, Commission Decision of December 6, 2001, O.J. 2001 C 21/29.

8–247   The relevant product markets — The Commission considered, but did not take a final position on, the following markets that had been identified in the view of the parties as being relevant for the assessment of the transaction: (i) the distribution and operation of special interest channels, with a possible further division on a case-by-case basis into further sub-segments based on the different musical themes to be delivered; (ii) pay-TV; (iii) the acquisition of broadcasting rights; and (iv) the production of TV programming for pay-TV.

8–248   The relevant geographic markets — The parties submitted, in line with *Universal Studio Network/NTL*,[5] that the market for the distribution and operation of special interest channels was national in scope. The same geographic delineation was suggested for the markets for pay-TV, the acquisition of broadcasting rights and the market for the production of TV-programming. The Commission questioned whether the latter market should have been defined as being regional, based on common language areas. Finally, it was considered whether a market for classical music channels, if it existed as a separate product market, should have had a Europe-wide dimension, as the content of the channels was of a transnational nature and the distribution rights were obtained on a multinational basis.

8–249   Competitive assessment — The Commission found that the transaction did not raise any competition concerns. It noted that due to the negligible turnover of the proposed joint venture and the fact that the classical music services presently offered by Mezzo and Muzzik were not drivers for pay-TV subscriptions, the formation of the joint venture would not have raised any competition concerns or led to any co-ordinated behaviour by the parent companies in the French and Belgian markets for the distribution and operation of special interest channels. Even on the basis of the narrowest definition of a market for the distribution of classical music channels, the Commission found that the new entity would have been only one of many players facing fierce competition from a number of classical music channels. The same rationale was followed by the Commission as regards the possibility of co-ordination between the parties on the French market for pay-TV and the market for the acquisition of broadcasting rights. As to the possibility of vertical effects being caused by the transaction, the Commission noted that the parent companies were active on markets upstream and downstream of the joint venture's activities but that there was no risk of market foreclosure, given that the turnover of the joint venture was small (compared with that of its parent companies) and the parent companies would not enter into exclusive distribution agreements for Mezzo and Muzzik's content. Even if exclusivity arrangements were to have been entered into between the parent companies and the joint venture, these would not have led to foreclosure effects because many other channels offered the same content as Mezzo and Muzzik, and music, in general, was not a driver for pay-TV subscriptions.

TPS[6]

8–250   The transaction — This transaction concerned the increase by Télévision Française 1 (TF1) of its shareholding in the digital satellite television provider Télévision par Satellite (TPS)[7]

---

[5] See above, para.8–233 *et seq.*

[6] Case JV.57, *TPS*, Commission Decision of April 30, 2002, O.J. 2002 C137/28.

[7] The creation of TPS was approved by the Commission under Art.81(3) of the EC Treaty in its Decision of March 3, 1999, O.J. 1999 L90/6; see below, para.8–342 *et seq.*

through the acquisition of the 25 per cent shareholding of France Télévision Enterprise (which was owned by France Télévision and France Télécom). As a result of the transaction, TPS would henceforth have been jointly controlled by TF1, Métropole Télévision (M6) and the Suez group.

8–251 The relevant product markets — As in its previous decisions,[8] the Commission found that the market for pay TV was separate from that for free TV.[9] The Commission, however, declined to further subdivide the market for pay-TV into separate markets for analogue and digital pay-TV, as at the time digital pay-TV was an emerging market and a further development of analogue pay-TV.[10] The market for the distribution and operation of special interest channels was also considered to be relevant to the proposed transaction, as was a separate market for the acquisition of broadcasting rights.

8–252 The relevant geographic markets — The Commission left open the question of whether the geographic market for pay-TV was France or the French-speaking area of Europe (France, Luxembourg and parts of Belgium and Switzerland). The market for the distribution and operation of special interest channels had, however, a national dimension.

8–253 Competitive assessment: dominance — The Commission briefly stated that the concentration would not have led to the creation or strengthening of a dominant position on any of the relevant markets.

8–254 Competitive assessment: co-ordination of independent competitive behaviour — Having found that the transaction raised no dominance issues, the Commission went on to analyse in more depth whether there was a risk of the co-ordination of the independent behaviour of the parent companies of TPS, under Article 2(4) of the Merger Control Regulation. On the market for the distribution and operation of special interest channels, the Commission identified a risk that the parent companies could have incentives to share the market amongst themselves or to impose common conditions on the other pay-TV distributors. However, the Commission found that this risk did not result from the transaction and that, in any event, such behaviour would have had no significant effect, given the high number of special interest channels in France and the corresponding strong bargaining power of the distributors. The Commission also dismissed the risk of market foreclosure as a result of any future exclusive dealing arrangements that could have been entered into between TPS and its parent companies, because distributors such as TPS would always have the economic incentive to distribute not only the content of affiliated content providers but also the content of third party content providers, in order to make their offering attractive to subscribers.

Newscorp/Telepiù[11]

8–255 The transaction — The transaction concerned the acquisition by the Australian-based international media group Newscorp of the Italian satellite pay-television provider Telepiù from

---

[8] Case *MSG Media Service*, above, para.8–171 *et seq.*; and Case *Bertelsmann/Kirch/Premiere*, above, para.8–187 *et seq.*

[9] See also Case M.2996, *RTL/CNN/N-TV*, Commission Decision of November 5, 2002, O.J. 2002 C310/23.

[10] Case *TPS*, Commission Decision of March 3, 1999, O.J. 1999, L90/6; see below, para.8–342 *et seq.*

[11] Case M.2876, *Newscorp/Telepiù*, Commission Decision of April 2, 2003. See also Commission Press Release IP/03/478 of April 2, 2003.

Vivendi Universal by way of purchase of shares. Telepiù was then to be merged with Stream, the second provider of satellite pay-television services in Italy which, prior to the transaction, was a 50/50 joint venture between Newscorp and Telecom Italia, to form a combined Direct-to-Home satellite pay-television platform. Telecom Italia would hold a minority stake in the new entity. Except for the participation of Telecom Italia, the transaction mirrored a previous deal pursuant to which Vivendi would have acquired Stream and merged it into Telepiù. This transaction was reviewed under Italian merger control laws and, after having received clearance from the Italian competition authorities on May 13, 2002, was then abandoned by Vivendi.

8–256 The relevant product markets — The Commission found that the following markets were affected by the concentration: (i) the market for pay-television; and (ii) the upstream markets for the acquisition of audio-visual television content, namely the rights to premium films, football events, and other sports events, and the acquisition of television channels.[12] It is interesting to note that the Commission, in line with previous decisions,[13] refused to adopt a broad market definition for television broadcasting including both pay-TV and free TV services. In their notification, the parties had argued that, at least in Italy where free TV was particularly strong, the strength of free TV broadcasters amounted to an effective competitive constraint on pay-TV operators. The Commission's investigation, however, did not confirm this view but instead led it to conclude that in Italy there was a clear distinction, from the perspective of both customers and suppliers, between free-to-air TV and pay-TV, such that the conditions of competition were different. Whereas in the case of free-to-air TV the relationship between audience share and advertising rates was crucial, in the case of pay-TV, the key factor was the relationship between the profile of programmes and the number of subscriptions. The fact that pay-TV subscribers were prepared to pay considerable sums for pay-TV services clearly indicated that pay-TV constituted a different product market distinct from that for free-to-air TV. In the context of the upstream markets for the acquisition of audio-visual television content, the Commission found that the acquisition of broadcasting rights for feature films constituted a separate market from made-for-television programmes.[14]

8–257 The relevant geographic markets — Owing to different regulatory regimes, language barriers, cultural factors and other different conditions of competition prevailing in the different Member States, the geographic scope of the market for pay-TV was found by the Commission, in line with previous decisions,[15] to be either national or a wider area that is linguistically homogenous. Similar considerations led the Commission to conclude that the market for the acquisition of audio-visual television content was also national in scope.

8–258 Competitive assessment — The Commission concluded, after an in-depth Phase II investigation, that the transaction would have resulted in the merged entity having a near monopoly in

---

[12] For a discussion of the case, see also Mendes Pereira, "Vertical and horizontal integration in the media sector and EU competition law", paper delivered at the conference "The ICT and Media Sectors within the EU Policy Framework" held in Brussels on April 7, 2003.

[13] See, for example, *BSkyB/Kirch Pay TV*, above, para.8–196 *et seq.*; and *Bertelsmann/Kirch/Premiere*, above, para.8–187 *et seq.*

[14] See also *Vivendi/Canal+/Seagram*, above, para.8–229 *et seq.*

[15] See, for example, *BSkyB/KirchPayTV*, above, para.8–196 *et seq.*

the Italian pay-TV market. Prior to the transaction, Telepiù already had a market share of more than two-thirds of the Italian pay-TV market and the Commission found that this dominant position would have been further strengthened by the merger with Stream, which had a market share of over 30 per cent. In 2001, Telepiù had a 60–70 per cent market share of the Italian pay-TV subscribers, and 65–75 per cent of the market in terms of value, whereas Stream's shares were 30–40 per cent and 25–35 per cent respectively. The Commission's market investigation showed further that the Italian pay-TV market was essentially limited to DTH satellite transmission, where both Stream and Telepiù were active. The competitive constraint that the combined pay-TV platform would have to face upon consummation of the transaction was considered as "minimal". Neither cable (which is only marginally developed in Italy through e.Biscom), nor DTT (which is still in its experimental phase) could, in the view of the Commission, have exercised more than a "minimal" amount of competitive pressure on the merged entity. The same was true for free-to-air TV.

Furthermore, the Commission was concerned about the vertical effects on competition that would have resulted from the transaction. It found that the vertical integration of NDS, a supplier of conditional access systems that is controlled by Newscorp, with the merged entity would have raised the already high barriers to entry in the Italian pay-TV market thereby further contributing to the strengthening of the combined entity's dominant position. The Commission found it highly likely that the transaction would have resulted in the merged entity using a single conditional access technology, namely that developed by NDS. This would have made NDS's conditional access system the standard technology in Italy, and access to this conditional access system would be dependent on Newscorp. The deployment of any alternative conditional access system would also be dependent on Newscorp's willingness to enter into simulcrypt arrangements to enable set-top box interoperability. According to the Commission, not only would Newscorp have had the incentive to foreclose the Italian pay-TV market by pursuing exclusionary strategies or raising rivals' costs but it would also have had the ability to do so. Existing sector-specific regulation, in particular open access requirements, were, in the view of the Commission, only able to mitigate the anti-competitive effects of the transaction, but were not sufficient to prevent potential new DTH entrants from being technically dependent on the merged entity for conditional access services.

In regard to the vertical effects of the transaction on the upstream markets (for the acquisition of programming rights and channels), the Commission found that the transaction would have resulted in the creation of a near-monopsony in the Italian markets for the acquisition of audio-visual content. As a result of the merged entity's increased bargaining power, the quasi-monopolist pay-TV provider would have been able to "tailor" its contractual relations with content providers so as to foreclose third party access to content by imposing long-term contracts, exclusivity arrangements and/or provisions to protect its rights (holdback rights) from transmission by other means.

The Commission, finally, examined under Article 2(4) of the EC Merger Regulation whether the minority shareholding of Telecom Italia in the merged entity would have created co-ordination (or spill-over) concerns in relation to the parties' independent activities, given Telecom Italia's strength in xDSL broadband access, which was considered by the Commission to be suitable "to a certain extent" for the distribution of pay-TV services. However, the Commission concluded, on the evidence before it, that there was no risk of co-ordination taking place, as (i) the merged entity did not have strong incentives to select its minority shareholder Telecom Italia as its privileged partner; and (ii) the mere existence of a link between the Telepiù/Stream platform and Telecom Italia (without Telecom Italia having *de facto* decisive influence over the merged entity) did not provide the parties with an incentive to align their conduct so as to limit the remaining scope for competition between them. Finally, there was no evidence that the merger would have strengthened Telecom Italia's existing dominant position in the Italian markets for broadband internet access and fixed telephony. In this context, Newscorp offered an undertaking not to make joint offers with Telecom Italia that combined pay-TV services and internet broadband services, and not to discriminate in favour of Telecom Italia. The Commission took note of these undertakings but added that they did not constitute conditions or obligations for the clearance decision.

8–259 Given the serious competition concerns raised by the Commission, it is not surprising that the parties invoked the "failing firm" defence and argued that Stream would inevitably have exited the market absent the transaction. The Commission did not share this view, and found that the formal requirements for the "failing firm" defence were not met.[16] In the Commission's view, the parties failed to prove that Stream would have been forced out of the market if not taken over by Newscorp and that there were no less anti-competitive purchasers for Stream. However, in its assessment of the effects of the transaction on competition, the Commission did take into account the serious financial difficulties of both Italian pay-TV providers (both were loss-making and had never made a profit) and the specific features of the Italian television markets (where pay-television providers were struggling owing to heavy competition from the 12 national free-to-air broadcasters). As a result, the Commission concluded that the approval of the merger, subject to appropriate conditions, would have been more beneficial to consumers than a disruption caused by a potential closure of Stream. The resulting approval of the transaction was a remarkable departure from the well established approach taken so far by the Commission in the communications field, namely to preserve inter-platform competition.[17] For the first time, the Commission cleared a "merger to monopoly" by trying to achieve the desired future inter- and intra-platform competition not by prohibiting a concentration, but instead using far-reaching behavioural undertakings that amount to a comprehensive regulatory regime applicable to the merged entity.

8–260 Under the conditions and obligations to which the Commission's approval decision is subject, Newscorp committed to (i) grant third parties access to its pay-TV platform; (ii) grant third parties access to content; and (iii) withdraw from terrestrial broadcasting activities in Italy. The commitments will remain in force until December 31, 2011. With regard to infrastructure, Newscorp committed to grant open access to its digital satellite platform, as well as access to the application program interface on the basis of a cost-oriented non-discriminatory formula (which would allow it to recover its directly attributable costs of providing the services, a share of the relevant technical fixed and common costs, and a reasonable return over an appropriate period). Newscorp further committed to procure that NDS would grant third parties fair and non-discriminatory licences for its conditional access system technology. However, the Commission again[18] failed to achieve the

---

[16] The "failing firm" defence was also rejected by the Commission in *Bertelsmann/Kirch/Premiere*, above, para.8–187 *et seq*. Since the entry into force of the EC Merger Regulation, this defence has been accepted only twice by the Commission, in Case M.308, *Kali + Salz/MDK/Treuhand*, Commission Decision of December 14, 1993, and in Case M.2314, *BASF/Pantochim/Eurodiol*, Commission Decision of July 11, 2001; see above, para.8–190, n.51.

[17] See, for example, *BSkyB/KirchPayTV*, above, para.8–196 *et seq*.

[18] *ibid*.

interoperability of different technical platforms by imposing a common interface but instead agreed to accept Newscorp's commitment to enter into simulcrypt agreements within nine months of a request by competitors wishing to use a conditional access technology other than the one operated by Newscorp. This is even more surprising, given that the Commission, in its competitive assessment of the vertical effects resulting from the concentration, noted that simulcrypt agreements, in the past, had proven to be difficult to implement.

As regards access to content, Newscorp entered into a commitment: whereby (i) the maximum duration of the period of exclusivity in agreements with premium content providers would be reduced to two years for contracts with football clubs and three years for contracts with film producers; (ii) to obtain exclusivity only with respect to DTH transmission; and (iii) to insert into existing exclusive content agreements of the parties a unilateral termination right in favour of football clubs and film producers. Finally, Newscorp committed to establish a sub-licensing scheme, whereby it would supply content, through a wholesale offer to be made pursuant to the retail minus principle to third parties, on an unbundled and non-exclusive basis, thereby giving them the right to distribute premium content on platforms other than DTH, if and for so long as the merged entity's satellite platform offers such content to its subscribers. Under this scheme, the new entity would keep separate accounting records for its wholesale and retail operations.

Finally, Newscorp committed to divest Telepiù's digital and analogue terrestrial transmission assets and not to engage in future DTT activities, either as a network or as a retail operator. The Commission, in this context, required the merged entity to sell the frequencies to a suitable buyer who committed to offer pay-TV services after the switchover from analogue to digital terrestrial broadcasting in Italy.

2. Major Co-operative Joint Ventures and Strategic Alliances Reviewed Under Articles 81 and 82 of the EC Treaty

8–261 Introduction — A number of co-operative arrangements, joint ventures and strategic alliances in the telecommunications and broadcasting sectors have been reviewed by the Commission under Articles 81 and 82 of the EC Treaty. Such co-operation agreements may restrict competition between telecommunications operators to the extent that they lead to the co-ordination of commercial behaviour of the undertakings involved on the market (*e.g.* in terms of their pricing, product specifications and development, or by sharing markets or sources of supply). In addition, such agreements may restrict the entry of third parties on the market, in so far as those third parties need access to the partners' networks in order to compete. Entry may be restricted as a result of unfair discriminatory practices by telecommunications operators against third parties competing with their own value-added services, for example by refusing access to their networks, imposing usage restrictions or other unfavourable access or pricing conditions and cross-subsidisation of different activities.[19]

The Commission has, however, acknowledged that co-operation agreements may bring overall economic benefits that outweigh their restrictive effect on competition. In this context, the

---

[19] 1991 Guidelines para.8–002, n.1, para.59.

Commission has indicated that, on a case-by-case basis, it may be possible to grant an individual exemption under Article 81(3) of the EC Treaty if the agreement contributes, *inter alia*, to the development of Europe-wide services and standardisation, lower costs to users, and general improvements in infrastructure. However, restrictions on third party access or unjustified discrimination against third parties are unlikely to be exempted.[20] The Commission's practice and guidelines in reviewing co-operative joint ventures and strategic alliances between telecommunications operators under Article 81(3) of the EC Treaty are analysed in this section.

Before March 1, 1998, joint ventures that involved co-operation between the parties were reviewed by the Commission within the framework of Regulation 17/62 (*i.e.* voluntary notification for negative clearance or individual exemption with no deadline for a Commission decision) and not under the Merger Control Regulation even if they were full-function. However, as from March 1, 1998, arrangements resulting in the formation of a full-function joint venture are subject to review under the Merger Control Regulation (*i.e.* compulsory notification if certain turnover thresholds are met and strict deadlines for a Commission decision), even if they have co-operative objects or effects. To the extent that such full-function joint ventures involve a risk of co-ordination of the parties' independent behaviour, they continue to be reviewed under the principles of Article 81(1) and (3) of the EC Treaty within the framework of the investigation timetable applicable under the Merger Control Regulation.[21] Therefore, the Commission's decision-making practice regarding co-operative joint ventures and strategic alliances that pre-dates the 1997 amendment of the Merger Control Regulation remains relevant.

(a) Co-operative Joint Ventures and Strategic Alliances for the Provision of Global Advanced Services

Infonet[22]

8–262 The transaction — The transaction concerned the formation of a joint venture, Infonet, between five European telecommunications operators (France Télécom, Deutsche Telekom, Telefónica of Spain, RTT of Belgium, and PTT Telecom of the Netherlands) and various non-EU telecommunications operators (MCI, Telecom Australia, Singapore Telecom, Swedish Telecom, the Swiss PTT and Kokusai Denshin Denwa of Japan). The purpose of Infonet was to provide global value-added network services (commonly known as VANS), including data and voice communications services, on a "one-stop shopping" basis. Under the "one-stop shop" principle, a customer would have a single point of contact with a supplier of an international service, notably for ordering and billing purposes, instead of contacts with different suppliers in each of the various countries involved. Infonet operated its data communications services, the largest part of its business, on the basis of an international packet-switched network, constructed with lines leased from telecommunications operators around the world.

---

[20] *ibid.*, para.61.
[21] Merger Control Regulation, para.8–002, n.4, Art.2(4).
[22] *Infonet*, Commission Notice pursuant to Art.19(3) of Regulation 17/62, O.J. 1992 C7/3.

8-263 Competitive analysis — The Commission considered that, as notified, the joint venture created the risk of cross-subsidisation by the Community operators involved in favour of Infonet and discrimination by them against other service suppliers. The Commission announced its intention to take a favourable decision under Article 81(3) of the EC Treaty subject to a number of conditions that addressed these concerns. In relation to the risk of discrimination, the Community operators involved in the joint venture undertook to offer third party suppliers the same terms and conditions for network access as those granted to Infonet. With respect to the risk of cross-subsidisation, the Community operators involved in Infonet agreed with Infonet that all services that were to be provided by the telecommunications operators to Infonet would be provided on an arm's length basis. In order to ensure compliance with these undertakings, the Community operators also agreed to keep specific records of their dealings with Infonet, and Infonet undertook to submit yearly reports on its dealings with the Community operators.

BT/MCI[23]

8-264 The transaction — This was the first major strategic alliance in the telecommunications sector to be reviewed by the Commission. The operation was twofold: (i) BT was to take a 20 per cent shareholding in MCI; and (ii) the creation of a joint venture, Concert, for the provision of enhanced and value-added global telecommunications services to multinational (or large regional) companies. This was found not to be a concentration under the Merger Control Regulation and was then subsequently notified under Regulation 17/62. The transaction was the first step of a process that led subsequently to the proposed merger between MCI and BT,[24] a transaction that was never implemented following WorldCom's successful takeover bid on MCI.[25] As a result, BT acquired MCI's minority ownership in Concert. Concert services were later sold by AT&T as part of the joint venture between BT and AT&T.[26] The Concert joint venture was dissolved at the beginning of 2002 as a result of the BT/Concert transaction pursuant to which BT acquired AT&T's 50 per cent interest in Concert.[27]

8-265 The relevant product markets — The Commission defined the relevant markets as value-added and enhanced services to large multinational corporations including: (i) data services; (ii) value-added application services; (iii) traveller services; (iv) intelligent network services; (v) integrated VSAT network services; and (vi) global outsourcing services. These services have specific features that have been adjusted to the needs of corporate customers, such as a single point of contact, seamless end-to-end global services and customised billing. They were different from those services that had previously been offered by national telecommunications operators, which could not provide one-stop shop, end-to-end (or seamless) services to customers' premises located abroad.

---

[23] Case M.353, *BT/MCI*, Commission Decision of July 27, 1994, O.J. 1994 L223/36.
[24] Case *BT/MCI(II)*, above, para.8–074 *et seq.*
[25] Case *WorldCom/MCI*, above, para.8–088 *et seq.*
[26] Case *BT/AT&T*, above, para.8–092 *et seq.*
[27] Case *BT/Concert*, above, para.8–121 *et seq.*; and Case M.2651, *AT&T/Concert*, Commission Decision of December 17, 2001, O.J. 2002 C16/15.

8–266 The relevant geographic markets — The Commission considered that the scope of the market for value–added and enhanced services for corporate customers was global by nature, owing to the liberalisation of markets and the disappearance of national borders.

8–267 Competitive analysis — The Commission considered that BT's acquisition of a minority shareholding in MCI fell outside the scope of Article 81(1) of the EC Treaty. Given the way in which the transaction had been constructed and the market context of the case, there was no risk that the competitive behaviour of the parties would have been co-ordinated or influenced as a result of the minority shareholding, as BT had undertaken in the purchase agreement not to increase its shareholding for 10 years and not to seek to control or influence MCI. Likewise, the Commission considered that those parts of the transaction affecting only the United States were not caught by Article 81(1) of the EC Treaty, as they were unlikely to affect trade within the EEA.

The creation of the Concert joint venture was found to infringe Article 81(1) of the EC Treaty because BT and MCI were, and for the foreseeable future would have continued to be, potential competitors on the overall market for telecommunications services, and in particular in the supply of enhanced and value-added global telecommunications services that were to be offered by Concert. Furthermore, Concert was considered to be a vehicle for the parents to pool their respective intellectual property rights and to cross-license these to each other and the joint venture on an exclusive basis. The formation of the joint venture and the restrictions of competition resulting from it were nevertheless granted an individual exemption by the Commission pursuant to Article 81(3) of the EC Treaty for a seven-year period. The Commission considered that Concert would have been in a position to offer a set of services of a global nature to corporate customers more quickly, cheaply and of a more advanced nature than either BT or MCI could have done on their own. The Commission also took into consideration the extent of third party competition from a number of strong players at the time, including AT&T's Worldsource, Atlas, Unisource and International Private Satellite Partners.

8–268 Applying the ancillary restraints doctrine,[28] the Commission concluded that the obligations of BT and MCI not to compete with Concert were ancillary to the joint venture's creation and successful operation, and thereby fell outside the scope of Article 81(1) of the EC Treaty. The Commission reached the same conclusion in relation to obligations accepted by the parent companies to obtain all their requirements of global value-added and enhanced services for corporate customers from the joint venture. However, by contrast, the Commission considered that two other provisions were caught by Article 81(1) of the EC Treaty as they appreciably restricted competition and were not necessary for the formation of the joint venture: (i) the appointment of BT as the exclusive distributor of Concert's services within the EEA; and (ii) a provision intended to dissuade MCI from using its technology to enter the EEA market (in competition with BT) in certain telecommunications sectors that were not supplied by Concert. The Commission only agreed to exempt these provisions under Article 81(3) of the EC Treaty for a limited period (until November 16, 2000 and for five years from the date of adoption of the decision respectively). These individual exemptions were granted only after the Commission had received reassurances that, despite the appointment of BT as Concert's exclusive distributor in the EEA, a user in the EEA

---

[28] See para.8–031 *et seq.*

that did not have any significant presence in the United States could nevertheless approach MCI to obtain Concert's services without first having to approach BT which meant that passive sales in the EEA by MCI remained a possibility.

Interestingly, in relation to the risk of discrimination by BT against third parties and cross-subsidisation in favour of Concert, the Commission considered that the regulatory constraints to which BT and MCI were subject in the United Kingdom under the supervision of OFTEL ensured that no undue discrimination or cross-subsidisation would occur. The Commission subsequently adopted a different position in relation to the Atlas joint venture, given the different regulatory position in France and Germany at that time.[29]

Atlas and Phoenix/Global One[30]

8–269 The transaction — This transaction provided the framework for co-operation between France Télécom (FT), Deutsche Telekom (DT) and Sprint Corporation (Sprint) for the provision of value-added services to corporate users at a global level. The operation consisted of two transactions: (i) the creation of a 50/50 joint venture (Atlas) between DT and FT to provide end-to-end services to corporate customers; and (ii) FT and DT participating, through Atlas, in a second alliance, Phoenix (subsequently renamed Global One), with Sprint. The services that were to be provided by Atlas were principally customised packages of extensive telecommunications services in combination with enhanced features, provided over extensive networks of high-speed large-capacity leased lines linking sophisticated equipment on customer premises to the providers' nodes. Atlas provided advanced telecommunications services to corporate users both Europe-wide and, outside of France and Germany, on a national basis. In France and Germany, Atlas provided sales support to the sales forces of FT and DT in relation to all services in the Atlas portfolio. Through Phoenix, advanced telecommunications services offered by Atlas also had the capacity to link customers' premises worldwide over the Phoenix backbone network.

As part of the Phoenix agreements, FT and DT each acquired a 10 per cent shareholding in Sprint, with appropriate board representation and investor protection as minority shareholders. Special provisions prevented FT and DT from acquiring control of, or exercising (either jointly or individually) influence on, Sprint. Phoenix was established to provide global value-added telecommunications networks services to corporate users, traveller services and carriers' carrier services. Although the two transactions were closely related, they were subject to two separate but parallel proceedings under Article 81(1) and (3) of the EC Treaty, and separate decisions were adopted on the same day.

In January 2000, FT purchased DT's and Sprint's stakes in Global One[31] and the cross-shareholdings were unwound, in order for FT to be able to provide integrated voice and data communications, including applications hosting and network integration. In November 2000, FT

[29] See above, para.8–267 *et seq.*
[30] *Atlas*, Commission Decision of July 17, 1996, O.J. 1996 L239/23; *Phoenix/Global One*, Commission Decision of July 17, 1996, O.J. 1996 L239/57.
[31] Case M.18656, *France Télécom/Global One*, Commission Decision of March 24, 2000, O.J. 2001 C–43/3.

announced a transaction by which Equant would acquire Global One's data business and FT would acquire SITA Foundation's controlling interest in Equant as a result of which FT acquired sole control over Equant, and the networks of Equant and Global One were merged.[32]

8–270   The relevant product markets — In both its *Atlas* and *Phoenix/Global One* decisions, the Commission distinguished the following affected markets: (i) customised packages of corporate telecommunications services; and (ii) packet-switched data communications services. Moreover, the Commission considered that the following two product markets were also affected by the Phoenix transaction: (i) traveller services; and (ii) carriers' carrier services. The Commission considered that packet-switched data communications constituted a separate market from customised packages of corporate telecommunications services because most existing customers for these packet-switched data communications were small enterprises and were not potential customers for customised packages of corporate telecommunications services.

8–271   The relevant geographic markets — The Commission considered that separate geographic markets for customised packages of telecommunications services and packet-switched data communications services existed at the global, cross-border regional and national levels, based on cost and price differences for network provision (*e.g.* leased lines) and services.

8–272   Competitive analysis — The Commission considered that the Atlas and Phoenix ventures were both within the scope of Article 81(1) of the EC Treaty to the extent that the joint ventures eliminated or at least substantially reduced competition between the parties, who were actual or potential competitors to each other. The Commission considered that the non-competition obligations of the parents as regards the activities of Atlas and Phoenix and the parents' obligations to buy from Atlas and Phoenix all of their requirements were ancillary to the formation of the joint ventures, in so far as they were necessary to ensure their success and viability. The Commission took the position that the acquisition by both FT and DT of minority shareholdings in Sprint fell outside the scope of Article 81(1) of the EC Treaty, since these shareholdings would not have afforded DT and FT the possibility of exercising a controlling influence over Sprint. In this respect, the Commission took into consideration both that United States corporate and antitrust laws would have prevented access to and misuse of Sprint's confidential information by DT and FT, and that the parties had given a specific commitment in this regard in the joint venture agreements.

The Commission considered that both joint ventures satisfied the conditions applicable for the granting of an individual exemption under Article 81(3) of the EC Treaty. In particular, the Commission considered that the transactions enabled the parties to offer seamless added-value services, at the European level (through Atlas) and at the global level (through Phoenix) to the benefit of business customers. With respect to Atlas, the Commission noted that by combining their R&D within the framework of the joint venture, DT and FT would have enabled Atlas to provide more advanced features and services of a better quality than either parent would have been capable of providing independently within the same time frame. The Commission also noted that the harmonised joint DT and FT network would have also improved the level of telecommunications

---

[32] Case *France Télécom/Equant*, above, para.8–109 *et seq.*

services provided by competitors of Atlas that interconnected to these networks. Likewise, in relation to Sprint, the Commission indicated that it would have taken much longer for Sprint alone to become a global supplier to the ever increasing number of multinational companies that needed a comprehensive range of customised global non-reserved corporate telecommunications services.

The Commission therefore granted individual exemptions for a five-year period in respect of Atlas and for a seven-year period in respect of Phoenix. The Commission also granted an individual exemption to a provision to appoint DT and FT as the exclusive distributors of Atlas and Sprint services in their home markets. The Commission considered that, because it protected DT and FT against the use by third parties of the intellectual property rights (IPRs) contributed by them to the joint venture, the exclusivity was an incentive for the parents to contribute valuable IPRs to the joint ventures. It must be noted, however, that the distribution agreements did not prevent passive sales, *i.e.* the possibility for a customer in Germany to solicit services from FT and a customer in France to solicit services from DT.

8–273 To meet its concerns about the effect of the joint ventures on competition, at a time when neither the French nor German markets had been fully liberalised, the Commission made the granting of the individual exemptions subject to a number of conditions and to the receipt of undertakings by the national telecommunications ministers of France and Germany and the parties to the Atlas and Phoenix alliances. First, the French and the German governments made a firm political commitment to liberalise (by granting licences to third parties) their respective countries' alternative telecommunications infrastructures for the provision of liberalised telecommunications services by July 1, 1996, and to liberalise fully all telecommunications services, including public voice telephony services and the provision of infrastructure, by January 1, 1998.[33] The Commission considered that it was only from the moment that alternative infrastructures would become available in France and Germany that other telecommunications services providers would have been able to compete with Atlas without being dependent on Atlas' parents for their leased-line requirements in those Member States. Accordingly, the Commission specified in the decision that the individual exemption would only be applicable from the date on which two or more licences for the operation of alternative infrastructures were granted in both Germany and France.

The same concern of the Commission, to prevent Atlas gaining a strong and unassailable foothold in the market prior to full market liberalisation in France and Germany, explained the condition that FT and DT had to keep their domestic public-switched data networks in France and Germany (Transpac and Datex-P, respectively) separate from the Atlas joint venture until January 1, 1998, the date on which full liberalisation was introduced both under the commitments given by the

---

[33] The Commission's strategy of involving national governments in the regulatory process and granting approvals or exemptions only where the governments make binding commitments to liberalise their national markets was an unprecedented and quite remarkable step. The Commission adopted the same strategy more recently in Case *Telia/Telenor*, above, para.8–097 *et seq.*, where it made its approval of a merger between the two incumbent operators in Sweden and Norway subject to a commitment from the Swedish and Norwegian Governments to introduce local loop unbundling in the countries. This was possible because both companies were state controlled. The conditions in both *Atlas/Phoenix-Global One* and *Telia/Telenor* also reflected the Commission's perception of inadequacies in the relevant Member States' regulatory regimes and the weak state of competition in their markets.

French and German governments and under the Full Competition Directive.[34] FT and DT were also required to establish and maintain access to their domestic public switched data networks in France and Germany respectively on a non-discriminatory, open, and transparent basis for all providers of low-level data services (the so-called X.25 services). The parties' obligations extended to any generally applied, standardised interconnection protocol that may subsequently have modified, replaced, or co-existed with the current standard. Moreover, FT and DT were obliged not to engage in the cross-subsidisation of Atlas or Phoenix. All entities formed pursuant to the Atlas and Phoenix ventures were required to be distinct entities, legally separate from the parent companies, and would be subject to regular auditing to ensure that dealings between such entities and FT and DT took place on an arm's length basis. The imposition of obligations on FT and DT to prevent any undue discrimination or cross-subsidisation contrasts with the position of the Commission in *BT/MCI*, where it considered that it was appropriate to rely exclusively on the efficiency of the United Kingdom regulatory regime to prevent such anti-competitive conduct. However, at that time the regulatory regimes in both France and Germany were inadequate to prevent such conduct, unlike the situation in the United Kingdom, where OFTEL had been an independent regulator with several years of experience in such matters. Finally, FT was required to sell its interest in INFO AG, an important competitor of Datex-P on the German data network services market, in order to address the Commission's concern to preserve competition in packet-switched data communications networks.

Unisource/Uniworld[35]

8–274 The transaction — The Unisource and Uniworld joint ventures had a similar structure to those of Atlas and Phoenix-Global One. The operation comprised two separate transactions: (i) the formation of Unisource, a joint venture composed of Telia of Sweden, KPN of the Netherlands and Swisscom of Switzerland to provide pan-European value-added telecommunications services to corporate customers; and (ii) the formation of Uniworld, a joint venture between Unisource and AT&T to provide similar services with global connectivity. Although closely related, the two joint ventures constituted separate transactions and were subject to separate Commission proceedings and decisions. Following the formation of the Concert joint venture between British Telecommunications and AT&T,[36] AT&T sold its interest in Uniworld (now AUCS) to Unisource.[37] Three years later, the parties decided to reduce the scope of Unisource, so that it would be merely a holding company for the parents' joint ownership of AUCS,[38] which continued to offer value-added services to multinational companies in Europe.

[34] See above, para.1–003 *et seq.*

[35] *Unisource*, Commission Decision of October 29, 1997, O.J. 1997 L318/1; and *Uniworld*, Commission Decision of October 29, 1997, O.J. 1997 L318/24.

[36] Case *BT/AT&T*, above, para.8–092 *et seq.*

[37] Case M.1581, *AT&T/Unisource/AUCS*, Commission Decision of July 8, 1999, O.J. 1999 C238/7.

[38] Case *Unisource*, Commission Decision of December 29, 2000, O.J. 2001 L52/30. This decision repealed the decision in the original *Unisource* case, because the remaining activity of Unisource did not fall within Art.81(1) of the EC Treaty, as the parents were free to compete with AUCS and with each other in the provision of global telecommunications services.

8–275   The relevant product markets — The Commission distinguished the following affected markets: (i) non-reserved corporate telecommunications services; (ii) traveller services; and (iii) carriers' carrier services. In contrast with the *Atlas* decision, the Commission no longer considered that data communications services constituted a market distinct from other customised corporate telecommunications services. Moreover, the Commission noted that as pan-European mobile services extended to corporate customers' fixed private or virtual networks, they might have to be included in the market for corporate telecommunications services.

8–276   The relevant geographic markets — The Commission took the position that separate geographic markets existed for customised packages of telecommunications services at the global, cross-border regional and national levels. With respect to traveller services, the market was increasingly global, whilst the market for carriers' carrier services was at least cross-border regional (*i.e.* pan-European).

8–277   Competitive analysis — The competitive analysis was very similar to that of the Commission in the *BT/MCI* and *Atlas* cases. Because the parent companies were at least potential competitors on the relevant markets, the joint ventures fell within the scope of Article 81(1) of the EC Treaty. The Commission nevertheless exempted the joint ventures pursuant to Article 81(3) of the EC Treaty on the grounds that they would enable the parties, through Unisource/Uniworld, to satisfy customers' demands for pan-European added-value services earlier than they could each have done acting separately. Moreover, the parties' harmonised networks would also improve the level of services provided by competitors of Unisource interconnecting to these networks.

The Commission considered that the non-competition obligations accepted by the parents as regards the scope of the activities of the joint ventures were ancillary to the formation of the joint venture because they expressed the firm commitment of the shareholders towards Unisource. By contrast, the Commission considered that the exclusive distribution arrangements between the parents and the joint ventures regarding the home countries of the Unisource shareholders infringed Article 81(1) of the EC Treaty and could not be considered as ancillary to the formation of the joint ventures. However, after having received commitments that these exclusive agreements would not prevent passive sales by other distributors (including the parents), the Commission individually exempted the distribution agreements on the grounds that they would improve distribution by ensuring that distributors concentrated their marketing efforts on their respective territories.

The Commission imposed a number of conditions and required certain contractual changes to the transactions before it would grant the individual exemptions. Contractual changes required by the Commission related to agency arrangements and transit negotiations concerning agency arrangements. The joint ventures were obliged not to act as exclusive agents for their shareholders in the fields of basic services and/or the provision of leased lines until full liberalisation had taken place in all of the countries of the joint ventures' shareholders regarding transit negotiations. Moreover, the joint ventures undertook not to act as exclusive representatives for their shareholders in negotiations of transit tariffs with licensed operators in or through the shareholders' countries, until full liberalisation had taken place in all of the countries of the joint ventures' shareholders. The Commission also required the parties not to discriminate in the provision of leased lines and interconnection services, not to misuse confidential information, and not to engage in tying or the cross-subsidisation of the joint ventures' activities with income generated from activities in markets where the parties held a dominant position.

In a subsequent transaction by which the European parties decided to reduce the scope of Unisource so that it would be merely a holding company for their joint ownership of Uniworld (in which AT&T was no longer a shareholder),[39] the Commission noted that since its 1997 decision the telecommunications markets in the Community had been liberalised and competition was taking place in the countries where KPN, Telia and Swisscom were active. Therefore, even though the parent companies continued to hold high market shares in their respective home markets, they faced competition from various companies and were even competing against Unisource (by now known as AUCS and managed by Infonet) in the supply of global communications services. Furthermore, Unisource represented less than 3 per cent of the revenues of any of its parents. For these reasons the Commission held that the revised Unisource agreements did not appreciably restrict competition in the relevant market and fell outside of Article 81(1) of the EC Treaty. It therefore decided to repeal its 1997 decision.

Cégétel + 4 and Télécom Développement[40]

8–278 The transaction — This operation comprised two related joint ventures. The first transaction (Cégétel + 4) concerned the acquisition of shareholdings in Cégétel, previously a wholly-owned subsidiary of Vivendi (formerly named Compagnie Générale des Eaux), by BT, Mannesmann (the then second-largest operator in Germany) and SBC (a regional telecommunications operator in the United States). As a result of the transaction, the parties had the following shareholdings in Cégétel: Vivendi (44 per cent), BT (26 per cent), Mannesmann (15 per cent) and SBC (15 per cent). The second transaction involved setting up a joint venture, Télécom Développement (TD), between SNCF (the French national railways company) and Cégétel. The purpose of TD was to develop and operate a national long-distance telecommunications network using the surplus capacity on SNCF's internal optical fibre network, capacity made available by Cégétel on its own network and new capacity to be installed by TD. Through this arrangement, Cégétel's goal was to become the second full-service telecommunications operator in France after France Télécom. Although Cégétel and Télécom Développement were both full-function joint ventures, they were notified to the European Commission in 1997, *i.e.* before the reform of the Merger Control Regulation. As the joint ventures had co-operative aspects, they fell outside of the Merger Control Regulation and were instead reviewed under Article 81 of the EC Treaty.

8–279 The relevant product markets — The Commission considered that the telecommunications markets affected by the Cégétel arrangements were the following: (i) voice telephony services, both long-distance and local; (ii) mobile telephony; (iii) data services; (iv) internet services and access provisions; (v) the outsourcing of telecommunications services; (vi) managed network services and leased lines; and (vii) directories. As regards the TD joint venture, the Commission stated that the following product markets were affected by the transaction: (i) the provision of

[39] *ibid.*
[40] Case 36.592, *Cégétel + 4*, Commission Decision of May 20, 1999, O.J. 1999 L218/14; and Case 36.581, *Télécom Développement*, Commission Decision of July 27, 1999, O.J. 1999 L218/24.

long-distance voice-telephony services; (ii) the supply of long-distance transmission capacity; and (iii) the provision of interconnection services, including access to international services.

8–280   The relevant geographic markets — For most of the relevant product markets, the geographic market was considered to be national, except those for corporate telecommunications services, for which there existed at least three distinct geographic markets, namely at the global, cross-border regional and national levels. As regards GSM mobile services, the geographic market was increasingly European due to the increased substitutability throughout Europe of networks operators' subscriptions through the use of "roaming" agreements. To the extent that TD's network would be limited to France, the Commission considered that the relevant geographic market for the services supplied by TD was France.

8–281   Competitive analysis — The Commission found that the two joint ventures were not caught by Article 81(1) of the EC Treaty. The Commission based its decision on the negligible market share of Cégétel in France on most of the relevant telecommunications markets (except for mobile telephony where its subsidiary, SFR, had a 38 per cent market share) and the presence of a dominant operator, France Télécom, in nearly all segments of the French telecommunications market.

In relation to the Cégétel + 4 arrangements, the Commission considered as ancillary to the joint venture the following clauses:

(i)   "preferred supplier" clauses, pursuant to which Cégétel would select one of the shareholders as a supplier in preference to third parties, when the terms offered by the shareholder in question matched or were more favourable than those offered by third parties. Conversely, the shareholders would choose Cégétel as their preferred supplier under the same conditions;

(ii) "preferred customer" clauses, pursuant to which BT would offer Cégétel terms and conditions in relation to the provision of international traffic services that were at least as favourable to Cégétel as those conditions that BT offered to other licensed operators in France and conversely, Cégétel would offer to BT terms and conditions that were at least as favourable to BT as those conditions that Cégétel offered to any other operator in the United Kingdom; and

(iii) non-compete obligations, pursuant to which the shareholders agreed that Cégétel would be the sole entity through which they would carry out telecommunications activities in France.

In relation to the non-compete obligation, the Commission required the parties to remove the marketing and sale of GSM services from the scope of this provision, with the result that Cégétel's shareholders were each free to sell GSM services to end-users in France. Cégétel was also free to sell GSM services outside of France. The Commission considered, nevertheless, that the appointment of Cégétel as the exclusive French distributor of Concert's value-added international services for corporate costumers infringed Article 81(1) of the EC Treaty and was not ancillary to the joint venture. However, it granted an individual exemption for this agreement for 10 years under

Article 81(3) of the EC Treaty, as it benefited Cégétel's customers and assisted in the development of Concert's products.

As regards the TD project, the Commission considered that it fell outside of Article 81(1) of the EC Treaty, as SNCF and Cégétel were not actual or potential competitors. In addition the following clauses were found to be ancillary to the joint venture: (i) TD's exclusive right to the use of SNCF's surplus optical fibre capacity; (ii) TD's non-exclusive right to occupy public railway land for a period of 30 years allowing it to deploy a telecommunications network (the Commission had objected to the original clause, which would have granted TD a "priority" right of access, as this could have hindered competing operators that also needed to use SNCF's land to build their networks); (iii) an exclusive distribution agreement with a TD subsidiary to distribute TD's long-distance telephony services to the public; (iv) an exclusive supply agreement under which Cégétel and its subsidiaries would provide all their long-distance traffic in France to TD, provided that TD's prices were at market price; and (v) an undertaking by SNCF not to compete with TD or Cégétel in so far as Cégétel abstained from any other investment in long-distance telecommunications networks.

(b) Joint Ventures and Strategic Alliances for Paging and Mobile Services

Konsortium ECR 900[41]

8–282   The transaction — The transaction consisted of a co-operative arrangement between Nokia, AEG and Alcatel for the formation of Konsortium ECR 900, a joint venture formed to jointly develop, manufacture and distribute a new pan-European digital cellular mobile telephone system, the so-called Groupe Speciale Mobile (GSM, also known as Global System for Mobile). In so far as the only buyers of such equipment at that time were the national incumbent operators and that demand was channelled through invitations to tender, the consortium was also used for the purpose of submitting bids in response to calls for tender.

8–283   Competitive analysis — The Commission found that the formation of the joint venture did not have as its object or effect the prevention, restriction or distortion of competition within Article 81(1) of the EC Treaty and therefore granted a negative clearance. The Commission followed a three-step approach. First, the Commission considered that the joint development and manufacture of the GSM system did not restrict competition, since none of the companies alone was able to undertake such activities given: that the GSM system had not previously existed; the high costs and financial risks involved; the tight time schedule to complete the tenders; the shortage of qualified staff; the limited demand in the market; and the fact that the invitations for tender called for joint bidding. For the same reasons, the Commission granted negative clearance to the joint distribution of the GSM system. The Commission also considered that the following provisions of the joint venture agreement did not infringe Article 81(1) of the EC Treaty: (i) the parties were prevented from submitting tenders or concluding contracts for GSM systems outside the scope of the joint venture; (ii) in the case of common development activities, technical documentation was to be freely exchanged, but was not to be exchanged if only one of the parties

---

[41] Case 32.688, *Konsortium E.C.R. 900*, Commission Decision of August 22, 1990, O.J. 1990 L228/31.

was involved; and (iii) in the case of the termination of the joint venture, the parties were restricted during a certain period from exploiting and licensing the technical information jointly obtained from the joint development work within Konsortium ECR 900. The Commission also granted negative clearance to a provision providing that where a party is excluded from the joint venture because of an infringement of the joint venture agreements, that party was to lose the right to use the jointly developed technical documentation supplied to it. For the Commission, if the firm in breach of the agreement were free to use the technical information, it would receive unjustified benefits which would lead to an undeserved competitive advantage *vis-à-vis* the other parties. According to the Commission, competition that is not based on performance is not protected by Article 81 of the EC Treaty.

Eirpage[42]

8–284 The transaction — This case concerned a joint venture, Eirpage, between Bord Telecom Eireann (BTE), the Irish incumbent telecommunications operator, and Motorola, an equipment manufacturer, for the setting-up, promotion and operation of a nationwide paging system interconnected to the public telecommunications network.

8–285 The relevant product markets — The Commission considered that paging formed a distinct product market from other forms of mobile communications for the following reasons: (i) it was cheaper in terms of the price of the equipment and running costs; (ii) at the time, mobile telephones were larger in size than paging units and thus more unwieldy; and (iii) paging offered one-way communications, which was a distinct advantage in keeping down billing costs.

8–286 The relevant geographic markets — The Commission considered that the relevant geographic market was national, *i.e.* Ireland.

8–287 Competitive analysis — The Commission considered that BTE and Motorola were potential competitors on the market for paging services. Therefore, the joint venture fell within the scope of Article 81(1) of the EC Treaty, in so far as it restricted competition between the parties as potential competitors. As an illustration of the Commission's broad interpretation of the concept of "effect on trade between Member States" when applying Article 81(1) of the EC Treaty, it is interesting to note that, although the paging services to be operated by the Eirpage joint venture were to be restricted to the territory of Ireland, the Commission considered that the joint venture had an effect on trade between Member States. The Commission based this finding on the following grounds: (i) the joint venture would have had a dissuasive effect on market entry by competitors from other Member States; (ii) the promotion of the concept of paging as such by the joint venture company could be expected to attract other providers of paging services from other Member States; (iii) the stimulation of sales brought about by the joint venture was likely to attract further imports or investments; and (iv) the joint venture formed part of the Motorola group's broader EC and worldwide strategy.

[42] Case 32.737, *Eirpage*, Commission Decision of October 18, 1991, O.J. 1991 L306/22.

The Commission granted an individual exemption under Article 81(3) of the EC Treaty in respect of the joint venture, because it would bring substantial benefits to consumers of paging services, more rapidly and to a greater extent than could have been achieved by the parties without the joint venture. In particular, the joint venture would have brought enhanced paging services with a larger geographic coverage. The exemption was granted by the Commission after a number of amendments were made to the contractual arrangements between BTE, Motorola and Eirpage and the parties had provided certain undertakings. First, in order to prevent any risk of the foreclosure of third parties, BTE and the relevant administration had to give the Commission reassurances that the granting of licences for paging services did not constitute a barrier to entry and that third parties would be treated on an equal footing with Eirpage. Secondly, the parties amended the agreements to allow Eirpage's sales agents for paging services to promote their own complementary paging services (but not those of Eirpage's competitors) and to compete with Eirpage upon termination of the agency agreement. Thirdly, BTE gave assurances that it would not cross-subsidise the activities of Eirpage from its other operations, nor grant more favourable conditions to Eirpage. Accordingly, transactions with Eirpage would be at arm's length. Fourthly, Eirpage undertook to co-operate with paging equipment manufacturers to ensure that their products could be used on the Eirpage system, in order to prevent Motorola obtaining an undue advantage on this market. Finally, the Commission required that the obligations of the parents not to compete with the joint venture be limited to the duration of the joint venture and therefore rejected the initial three-year post-termination ban on competition.

(c) Joint Ventures and Strategic Alliances for Telecommunications Equipment

STET/Italtel/AT&T-NSI[43]

8–288 The transaction — The transaction involved the creation of a joint venture between STET (the holding company of what is now Telecom Italia), Italtel, AT&T and NSI for the development, production and marketing of telecommunications equipment for public and private switching systems, operating systems, public transmission systems, and certain private terminal equipment. Technical co-operation between the parties took the form of the exchange of technical and commercial information for the joint development of products, with the granting of exclusive licences and patents on a reciprocal basis. The commercial co-operation between the parties consisted of exclusive cross-distribution and purchasing agreements, with each party being the exclusive distributor of the jointly developed products for the countries in which it was already present. It was also foreseen that each party would have acquired a minority holding in the other parties' capital. Subsequently, STET terminated the arrangements and substituted them by a joint venture with Siemens in 1994.[44]

8–289 The relevant product markets — The Commission considered that the product markets affected by the agreement were the markets for telecommunications equipment for public and private switching systems, operating systems, public transmission systems and certain private

---

[43] *STET, Italtel, AT&T and AT&T-NSI*, Commission Notice pursuant to Art.19(3) of Regulation 17/62, O.J. 1992 C333/3.
[44] Case *Siemens/Italtel*, above, para.8–053 *et seq.*

terminal equipment. The Commission distinguished between the markets for public and private network equipment, because of their different demand structures. The main users of public network equipment were operators of public networks with exclusive or special rights, whilst private network equipment was sold to a wide range of customers. With the liberalisation of the telecommunications sector, this distinction is becoming irrelevant, as public network switching equipment is sold to an increasingly wider range of customers.

8–290   The relevant geographic markets — The Commission considered that each Member State constituted a separate relevant geographic market, despite the ongoing standardisation of technical standards, the liberalisation of services and equipment markets and the adoption of transparent procurement rules. In particular, the Commission found that the Italian market had specific structural characteristics as the telecommunications industry was vertically integrated under STET, which controlled the network operator (then SIP, the predecessor to Telecom Italia) and the main equipment manufacturer (Italtel). Now that liberalisation and standardisation have advanced further, the Commission has broadened the scope of the geographic market for telecommunications equipment.[45]

8–291   Competitive analysis — The Commission found that the joint venture fell within Article 81(1) of the EC Treaty, but took a favourable view of the transaction under Article 81(3) of the EC Treaty. The Commission was concerned initially by certain aspects of the arrangements, including the territorial protection covering the distribution of public network products and the potential restrictions on competition resulting from the vertical integration of the parties in their respective markets. As a result, the parties agreed to abandon all territorial restrictions, except where the scale of investment necessary to place a licensed product on the market could justify protection against active competition from other parties for a limited time period. With respect to the issue of vertical integration, the Commission was concerned that the parties would have been in a position to obtain favourable terms for the equipment supplied by the joint venture (the Commission was particularly concerned that AT&T would benefit from prices that did not reflect costs) and that vertical integration could have resulted in the creation of undue barriers to entry (in particular in relation to STET). AT&T provided assurances to address the Commission's concerns, whilst STET demonstrated that the position of Italtel was not so strong as to prevent the entry of competitors and also undertook to sell its products only at prices that reflected costs.

[45] In 1995, in Case *Siemens/Italtel*, above, para.8–053 *et seq.*, the Commission considered that Italy was no longer a separate geographic market due to: (i) technological developments; (ii) international standards and national/type-approval of equipment; (iii) the application of public procurement directives; and (iv) the liberalisation of the public voice telephony and telecommunications infrastructure. See also Case M.651, *AT&T/Philips*, Commission Decision of February 5, 1996, in which the Commission indicated that the scope of the geographic market for public switching and transmission systems was at least Europe.

(d) Joint Ventures and Strategic Alliances in the Satellite Sector

Alcatel Espace/ANT Nachrichtentechnik[46]

8–292 The transaction — This transaction concerned a joint venture between Alcatel (a French supplier of telecommunications equipment) and ANT (a German supplier of telecommunications equipment and technology), for the research and development of space electronic equipment in the field of civil radio communications and broadcasting satellites and data transmission to satellites and space vehicles. The joint venture would extend to the joint exploitation of the results through the rationalisation of the manufacturing, servicing and testing of such equipment, as well as through co-operation in the bidding and negotiation of contracts. The joint venture set forth a framework for co-operation involving: (i) consultations and the exchange of information before starting R&D activities relating to space equipment; (ii) the development of R&D and production by one party with the understanding that the results would be made available to the other party; and (iii) co-ordination regarding commercial exploitation of the results of the R&D.

8–293 The relevant product markets — The Commission defined the relevant product market as that for the manufacture of satellites and components, owing to the specific structure of demand (*i.e.* unique projects requiring newly developed components and R&D, that was specific to the particular requirements of the customer).

8–294 The relevant geographic markets — The market was, in principle, worldwide in so far as transport costs were negligible, given the high price of final products. However, legal restrictions and national preferences (especially in the military sector) could have restricted the scope of the geographic market.

8–295 Competitive analysis — The Commission exempted the joint venture under Article 81(3) of the EC Treaty. The parties considered that the arrangement was not restrictive of competition within the meaning of Article 81(1) of the EC Treaty. However, the Commission found that the arrangement altered the previously autonomous position of the parties with respect to the planning, financing, research and development, production and marketing of the equipment within the scope of the joint venture, as the parties were no longer able to act independently. The Commission held that Commission Regulation 418/85, which provided a block exemption for certain categories of research and development agreements,[47] was not applicable, to the extent that co-operation extended to marketing of products. The Commission nevertheless decided to grant an individual exemption. The Commission considered that the arrangement would have promoted technical and economic progress. The co-operation would have allowed the development of sophisticated and very costly equipment more rapidly than if the parties had undertaken the investment independently. The co-operation also enabled the development of a wider and higher quality range of products, as well as substantial cost savings. Given the number and size of the parties' competitors, the Commission considered that it was unlikely that the reduction in competition

---

[46] Case 32.006, *Alcatel Espace/ANT Nachrichtentechnik*, Commission Decision of February 3, 1990, O.J. 1990 L32/19.

[47] O.J. 1985 L53/5, as amended by Commission Regulation 151/93.

between the parties would have allowed them to increase their prices significantly. The Commission also took into consideration the fact that the agreement allowed for independent action by the parties. In addition, competitive conditions were required by and between the parties to allow the consideration of competing proposals from third parties and to purchase from them.

Intrax[48]

8–296 The transaction — Intrax was a joint venture between PTT Telecom (now KPN Telecom BV), the Dutch incumbent operator, and Nederlandse Omroepproduktie Bedrijf (NOB), the main Dutch television facilities house, for the provision of Satellite News Gathering (SNG) services. SNG services are based on two complementary services: (i) the provision by facilities houses such as NOB of technical services and activities required to prepare and broadcast television programmes; and (ii) the up-linking (*i.e.* transmission) of signals to satellites from ground stations, which was traditionally an activity undertaken by telecommunications operators. SNG facilities have been developed to allow the rapid on-the-spot collection and transmission of audio-visual news and data at remote locations that are not normally served by terrestrial networks, *e.g.* at disaster scenes, sports events and other events which require immediate live coverage and conveyance to the general public. Intrax was acquired by BT in February 1999 and is currently fully owned by British Telecom Broadcast Services.

8–297 The relevant product markets — Although the Commission did not take a position specifically in this respect, it defined implicitly the relevant product market as being the market for SNG services.

8–298 The relevant geographic markets — Likewise, the Commission did not take a definitive position, but implicitly defined the relevant geographic market as being the Netherlands.

8–299 Competitive analysis — The Commission cleared the arrangement under Article 81(1) of the EC Treaty by way of a comfort letter. The Commission considered that there were no barriers to entry on the Dutch market for foreign suppliers of SNG services. In this regard, the Commission took into consideration that the arrangements were not exclusive: (i) PTT Telecom was free to provide up-linking services to parties other than Intrax; (ii) NOB was free to provide technical facilities to parties other than Intrax; and (iii) both PTT Telecom and NOB were free to compete directly with Intrax for the provision of SNG services. Of particular importance in the Commission's analysis was the fact that the Dutch market for satellite up-linking had already been liberalised, so that up-linking services could be obtained from parties other than PTT Telecom. The Commission was also satisfied that companies competing with Intrax in the Netherlands would have had access to Eutelsat and Intelsat transponder capacity through PTT Telecom on a non-discriminatory basis (*i.e.* on the same terms as those granted to Intrax), or through other national signatories of the Eutelsat and/or Intelsat conventions or via independent satellites.

[48] *Intrax*, Commission Notice pursuant to Art.19(3) of Regulation 17/62, O.J. 1993 C117/3.

Astra[49]

8–300   The transaction — Astra was a joint venture between British Telecommunications (BT) and Société Européenne des Satellites (SES), a Luxembourg-based private satellite operator, for the marketing and provision of television broadcasting programmes originating in the United Kingdom using the Astra IA satellite. The joint venture would have offered suppliers of televisions programmes originating in the United Kingdom a package service, consisting of satellite up-linking in the United Kingdom by BT to the Astra IA satellite and the provision of satellite transponder capacity by SES on the Astra IA satellite for receiving the signals and beaming them back for reception by earth stations (whether cable network head-ends or individual DTH customer's dishes).

8–301   The relevant product markets — The Commission distinguished the following relevant product markets: (i) space segment capacity for the distribution of television channels; and (ii) satellite up-linking services. The Commission refused to distinguish between two separate product markets for capacity on low-powered and medium-powered satellites. The Commission considered that both offered customers the same possibilities in terms of geographic coverage and transmission to cable head-ends. The fact that only medium-powered satellites enabled DTH reception by individual customers' small dishes was not deemed to be sufficient by the Commission to consider it as a separate product market, since the use of one or other type of satellite capacity would not have made any difference in countries with well-developed cable systems.

8–302   The relevant geographic markets — The Commission considered that the geographic scope of both product markets was Europe.

8–303   Competitive analysis — In a rather unusual step, the Commission refused to clear or exempt the proposed joint venture. The Commission took the position that the proposed arrangements restricted competition on the markets both for the provision of satellite transponder capacity and for up-link services and thereby infringed Article 81(1) of the EC Treaty. As regards the market for space segment capacity, the joint venture would have restricted competition between competitors on this market, in so far as BT was also offering satellite transponder capacity as a signatory of the Intelsat and Eutelsat conventions. In this context, the Commission rejected BT's argument that it could not be regarded as a competitor to SES to the extent it could only provide low-powered satellite capacity and not medium-powered capacity such as that offered by SES. The Commission considered that low-powered and medium-powered satellites offered the same possibilities to customers, with the exception of DTH, and were therefore part of the same product market. Moreover, the Commission found that BT had sufficient financial and technical resources to enter independently the market for the operation of satellites. Finally, SES was precluded from marketing transponder capacity in the United Kingdom outside of the scope of the joint venture and was obliged to consult with BT in setting the price charged to UK customers for the use of transponder capacity on the Astra IA satellite. The Commission found that these arrangements involved far-reaching price co-ordination between the two parties and deprived customers of a new, alternative source of supply for transponder capacity in the United Kingdom.

---

[49] *Astra*, Commission Decision of January 28, 1993, O.J. 1994 L20/23.

As regards the up-link market, the Commission found that the parties were direct competitors, in so far as it was technically and commercially feasible for programme providers in the United Kingdom to transmit their programmes to Luxembourg (whether by satellite link or by a tele-communications link) for up-linking in Luxembourg. However, various clauses of the joint venture agreements eliminated competition between the parties, as BT was obliged to consult with SES in setting the price for its supply of up-linking services, whilst SES was prohibited from offering commercially preferential terms to programme providers for the use of its up-link facility in Luxembourg. Moreover, the tying of BT's up-link services with the provision by SES of satellite capacity on the Astra IA satellite would have limited customer choice in relation to up-linking services. Furthermore, the duration of customers' contracts (10 years) had the effect of foreclosing access to those customers by competitors.

The Commission refused to grant an exemption pursuant to Article 81(3) of the EC Treaty. The Commission found that the benefits of improved competition resulting from the availability of the Astra satellite to broadcasters in the United Kingdom in competition with the Intelsat and Eutelsat satellites was not the result of the joint venture, but arose independently from the existence of these satellites as such. Moreover, it was not demonstrated that co-operation with BT was indispensable in permitting the entry of SES into the UK market for transponder capacity. The Commission considered that the efficiencies resulting from customers negotiating only one contract for both up-linking and satellite capacity did not compensate for the disadvantages that this tying entailed both for customers (who were faced with bundled services) and competitors, who were thereby foreclosed.

The parties had already terminated the joint venture prior to the Commission's decision. However, existing contracts with customers were unaffected by the termination of the joint venture. The Commission argued that the survival of these contracts with customers perpetuated the restrictive effects of the joint venture, since these customers did not have access to unbundled up-link and transponder capacity on the Astra IA satellite. The Commission therefore required the parties to allow existing customers of the joint venture the opportunity to terminate their contracts, or to renegotiate them under different terms. In doing so, the Commission itself determined the legal effect of anti-competitive provisions on the joint venture agreement, instead of leaving this task to national courts under national law as mandated by the practice of the Court of Justice.[50]

Aérospatiale/Alcatel Espace[51]

8–304 The transaction — This case concerned a co-operation arrangement between Aérospatiale and Alcatel Espace relating to civilian and military satellites, with the possibility of extending their co-operation to other areas, such as earth observation. The arrangement provided for business co-operation between the parties, coupled with technical and industrial specialisation. The parties intended to rationalise their activities but without the integration of their production

---

[50] Long, *Telecommunications Law and Practice* (Sweet & Maxwell, 2nd ed., 1995), p.289.
[51] *Aérospatiale/Alcatel Espace*, Commission Notice pursuant to Art.19(3) of Regulation 17/62, O.J. 1994 C47/6.

lines. The parties thus remained separate entities as regards their "space" activities, with their own research and production facilities. The arrangement set forth co-operation procedures based on the exchange of information and consultation in all areas covered by the alliance, as well as on joint commercial action.

8–305   The relevant product markets — The Commission defined the relevant product market as that for the provision of telecommunications satellites, both civilian and military. This definition was based on specific features of supply (*i.e.* the complexity of the product, the specificity of environment and high quality requirements, and customised products with specific research & development) and demand (*i.e.* well informed customers with considerable purchasing power).

8–306   The relevant geographic markets — The Commission considered that the relevant geographic market was at least Community-wide, except for certain customers that adopted national preferences. The Commission based this finding on the following elements: (i) the low level of transport costs; (ii) increased cross-border commercialisation of satellite-based services; (iii) the rapid deregulation and technological developments with increased access to satellites; and (iv) the fact that the Utilities Procurement Directive would have diminished the importance of national preferences.

8–307   Competitive analysis — In approving the arrangement, the Commission took into consideration the context of the transaction. Owing to the historical compartmentalisation of national markets in Europe, the supply side of the satellite market in Europe was highly fragmented and involved a very large number of firms. This situation contrasted with the situation in the United States, where the market was dominated by a small number of companies, which were very large and vertically integrated. Moreover, the American companies had the benefit of a large, deregulated and unified domestic market and of large government space programmes. With barriers to entry falling, it was expected that American companies would increase their activities in Europe. The response of European companies to market entry by American companies would be to increase in size and become vertically integrated, through mergers and large-scale strategic alliances. This operation was an example of such strategy. In adopting a favourable attitude towards the arrangement, the Commission also took into account that the co-operation and joint commercial strategy contemplated by the agreements left the parties a substantial margin for independent action.

International Private Satellite Partners[52]

8–308   The transaction — This case relates to a joint venture, International Private Satellite Partners (IPSP), in the form of a United States limited partnership, between eight companies that were active in the telecommunications and aerospace sectors.[53] The purpose of IPSP was: (i) to provide international business telecommunications services to businesses in Europe and North America using its own satellite system on a one-stop shop basis; and (ii) to offer bulk transmission

---

[52] *International Private Satellite Partners*, Commission Notice pursuant to Art.19(3) of Regulation 17/62, O.J. 1994 L354/75.
[53] Orion Satellite, British Aerospace, COM DEC Satellite, General Dynamics, Kingston, MCN Sat. US, STET and Nissho.

capacity to third parties to the extent that its capacity was not fully used by IPSP or its partners. The services to be offered by IPSP were intended to address the growing need of multinational companies for end-to-end communications between geographically dispersed locations around the world and between their customers or suppliers. To support its operations, IPSP intended to launch and operate high-power Ku-band telecommunications satellites with a footprint covering much of North America, much of the EEA and portions of Central and Eastern Europe.

8–309 The relevant product markets — The Commission considered that the following product markets were affected by the transaction: (i) the supply of international value-added services to large corporations, *i.e.* voice calling, high-speed fax, data storage and transport, and video-conferencing; and (ii) the supply of bulk satellite transmission capacity.

8–310 The relevant geographic markets — The geographic scope of the relevant product market was determined by the geographic reach of the satellites, in this case, North America, much of the EEA, and portions of Central and Eastern Europe.

8–311 Competitive analysis — The Commission granted negative clearance to the arrangement under Article 81(1) of the EC Treaty. The Commission considered that none of the partners could have been considered actual or potential competitors for the following reasons: (i) only the joint venture company had the necessary authorisations and licences to launch and operate satellites; (ii) none of the partners held the necessary authorisations and licences to provide international telecommunications services in all countries inside the footprint of the satellites; and (iii) none of the partners individually would have had the financial resources to make the investments necessary to enter the market. Moreover, the Commission indicated that IPSP, as a new competitor, may have been expected to increase the level of competition in a fast-growing segment of the overall telecommunications market, that had until recently been reserved to companies holding exclusive rights. It appears that the Commission viewed favourably the entry of this new joint venture, which comprised mostly operators other than incumbent telecommunications operators on the market for international added-value services.

As regards specific contractual restrictions, the Commission made distinctions between the following categories of restriction: (i) those clauses that fell outside the scope of Article 81(1) of the EC Treaty, *e.g.* the appointment of STET as IPSP's exclusive representative agent in Eastern Europe; (ii) those clauses that were non-appreciable restrictions of competition, *e.g.* granting STET the exclusive right to promote the sale of IPSP's services in Italy; and (iii) those provisions that were ancillary to the joint venture as they were necessary for the creation and operation of IPSP, *e.g.* non-compete obligations or "most favoured nation" clauses which ensured that IPSP treated each partner on an equal basis with other customers. In particular, it is worth noting that the Commission cleared a provision that the prices for IPSP's services would be established by the joint venture company although the sale of its services would have been undertaken by representative agents chosen by the joint venture company. In this regard, the Commission noted that the principle of uniform prices and other conditions in different territories was appropriate in fulfilling the demands for worldwide telecommunications services, on a one-stop shopping and billing basis, from customers with branches or subsidiaries dispersed in different territories.

Inmarsat-P[54]

8–312   The transaction — This case concerned the "Inmarsat-P Project" of the International Mobile Satellite Organisation (Inmarsat). This project was established to set up an affiliate, I-CO Global Communications (ICO) to finance, construct, and operate a worldwide satellite personal communications system (S-PCS). Inmarsat was an intergovernmental organisation providing mobile satellite communications worldwide to the maritime community. It was constituted as an intergovernmental treaty organisation of which 80 countries were members. The signatory in each country (typically the incumbent national telecommunications provider) owned shares in Inmarsat corresponding to its usage of the system. The signatory also distributed Inmarsat services to users or sub-distributors within this territory. ICO was established for the provision of space segment and associated ground infrastructures for the delivery of S-PCS services. Members of Inmarsat who invested a minimum amount in ICO had an option to become service wholesalers to distribute ICO's S-PCS services in their own country. The services that were to be supplied by Inmarsat to ICO as part of the Inmarsat-P project were to have been negotiated at arm's length. Payment for Inmarsat's services was to be made on a fully allocated costs basis, plus a reasonable fee of 6.5 per cent of the actual costs incurred by Inmarsat in fulfilling the specific task. Since 1999, Inmarsat has been a limited company, rather than an international treaty organisation.[55] It now supports satellite links for phone, fax and data communications to ship, vehicle, aircraft and portable terminals.

8–313   The relevant product markets — The Commission considered that S-PCS services constituted a separate product market. In this respect, the Commission noted that S-PCS services were expected to act as a complement to and even a substitute for public switched fixed telephone networks and cellular mobile telephony in remote areas with low population density and/or where the terrestrial network infrastructure was very poor.

8–314   The relevant geographic markets — The geographic scope of the market was worldwide, because S-PCS services had a global coverage.

8–315   Competitive analysis — The Commission took a favourable approach to the Inmarsat-P project. The Commission took into account that there were already, at that time, a number of other initiatives to develop and operate similar S-PCS systems (*i.e.* Iridium, Globalstar and Odyssey). The Commission also indicated that owing to the scarcity of available frequencies, the heavy financial burden involved in launching and operating the large number of satellites needed for S-PCS systems, and the high level of market uncertainty, it was unlikely that there would have been more than a few players worldwide in the S-PCS services market. The Commission only took a favourable position regarding the creation of ICO and the relationship between Inmarsat and ICO.

---

[54] *Inmarsat-P*, Commission Notice pursuant to Art.19(3) of Regulation 17/62, O.J. 1995 C304/6.

[55] The Commission subsequently approved the transformation of Inmarsat into a public limited company in which existing signatories became shareholders. This approval was conditional on a public offering having taken place within three years of Inmarsat's restructuring, in order to dilute the shareholdings of the current signatories and to reduce the potential for conflicts of interest between the signatories' roles as shareholders and as distributors of Inmarsat's services. The approval was granted by way of a negative clearance comfort letter. See Commission Press Release IP/98/923 of October 22, 1998. The approach of the Commission in this case was a reflection of a trend towards separating infrastructure provision from service provision.

It did not take a position on the terms and conditions for the distribution of ICO's services, as the relevant contracts in this respect had not been submitted to the Commission for clearance.

Iridium[56]

8–316 The transaction — Iridium was a company owned by Motorola and 16 strategic investors (including STET and Vebacom), which was established to provide satellite personal communications services on a worldwide basis. Iridium's services included voice, paging and basic data services such as facsimile, that were provided via portable hand-held telephones, vehicle-mounted telephones, pagers and other subscriber equipment. Regarding the distribution of Iridium's services, each investor in Iridium had designated a gateway[57] operator which would have had exclusive rights to provide Iridium services within a certain geographic area. Service providers designated by the gateway operators would have been responsible for the marketing and retail sale of services and terminals. Iridium later faced severe financial difficulties and in December 2000, its operating assets, including the satellite constellation and its terrestrial network, real property and intellectual property capital, were purchased by Iridium Satellite LLC, a privately held corporation.

8–317 The relevant product markets — In line with the *Inmarsat* precedent,[58] the Commission defined the relevant product as that for S-PCS services. The Commission noted that S-PCS systems were expected to act as a complement to both GSM and DECT wireless terrestrial mobile technologies, in particular in areas with low penetration of terrestrial mobile systems. However, even in urban areas or densely populated areas, S-PCS services would not have been a substitute to cellular and paging systems, because of the cellular and paging systems' advantages in terms of cost, voice quality and signal strength. Customers of Iridium and other S-PCS providers would have been international travellers with dual terminals that would operate in the terrestrial (GSM/DECT) mode within a given network, and switch to satellite in areas outside of terrestrial networks' coverage.

8–318 The relevant geographic markets — The market was likely to be worldwide in so far as, from a technical point of view, the Iridium system would have been able to provide global coverage. However, the Commission left the issue open as the outcome of its assessment of the case would not have been affected by how narrowly the geographic market was defined.

8–319 Competitive analysis — The Commission granted negative clearance under Article 81(1) of the EC Treaty. The Commission considered that the shareholders of Iridium were not actual or potential competitors in the S-PCS services market for the following reasons: (i) the provision of S-PCS services was a complex and risky business with an uncertain future[59]; (ii) no investor in Iridium would have been in a position to assume independently the risks of technical failure inherent in space operations or of the commercial failure of the project; (iii) given the global reach of S-PCS

---

[56] *Iridium*, Commission Decision of January 18, 1997, O.J. 1997 L16/87.
[57] Gateways are switches which communicate with subscribers' units and other satellites via the systems control segment and the constellation.
[58] See above, para.8–312 *et seq.*
[59] The financial difficulties subsequently encountered by Iridium confirmed the significant risks associated with launching such a business.

systems, no investor held the necessary authorisations and licences to provide S-PCS services on a worldwide basis; and (iv) the array of technologies required for an S-PCS system was outside the individual capability of the investors in Iridium.

The Commission found a number of potentially restrictive contractual provisions to be ancillary to the joint venture, thereby falling outside of Article 81(1) of the EC Treaty. In particular, Iridium's pricing policy provided that regional gateway operators could set freely the prices for S-PCS services but only within certain ranges determined by Iridium. In line with its decision in *IPSP*,[60] the Commission considered that this policy ensured the maintenance of the coherence and the integrity of the worldwide service that Iridium was to provide. Such coherence was particularly important for potential users of the system, which would be moving around the world, but would have expected to receive a single bill in a single currency. The principle of uniform prices and other conditions in different countries, together with the implementation of marketing practices in a decentralised manner, seemed appropriate to fulfil customers' needs. As regards the exclusive right of the investors in Iridium to provide Iridium's services within a specified territory, the Commission considered that exclusivity was necessary in order to give investors the incentive to undertake the high costs and investment required to operate Iridium services, given the inherent risks of the system. In this regard, the Commission took into account that there was no restriction for gateway operators or service providers on dealing with competing S-PCS systems or on selling services to customers not located in the same area or country. The Commission also emphasised that Iridium services could be expected to face intense competition from other S-PCS systems and other terrestrial mobile telecommunications systems.

Eutelsat[61]

8–320 The transaction — This transaction concerned the restructuring of Eutelsat. Originally, Eutelsat was an intergovernmental treaty organisation with 48 member countries. As a result of the restructuring, Eutelsat was transformed into a company incorporated in France, with the 48 signatories (who act as distributors of Eutelsat services to sub-distributors or users) becoming shareholders of Eutelsat. The shareholding of each signatory shareholder was proportional to its usage of the system. The signatories' shareholdings were to be diluted by way of an initial public offering of 30 per cent of the company's shares that was to have been carried out within two years of the restructuring, *i.e.* by July 2003.

8–321 Competitive assessment — The Commission noted that the restructuring of Eutelsat was, in many respects, similar to that of Inmarsat.[62] The Commission found that the public offering would have reduced the possible conflicts of interest between the role of the members as share-holders and their role as distributors of Eutelsat's services. Further, Eutelsat would also have been able to directly distribute its services, so that its customers had the choice of receiving their services from distributors (*i.e.* the shareholders) or direct from Eutelsat itself. For these reasons, the

---

[60] See above, para.8–308 *et seq.*
[61] *Eutelsat*, see Commission Press Release IP/00/1360 of November 27, 2000.
[62] See above, para.8–312 *et seq.*

Commission concluded that the restructuring was not within the scope of Article 81(1) of the EC Treaty.

Nordic Satellite and Modern Times Group[63]

8–322   The transaction — This transaction involved the Swedish satellite operator Nordic Satellite and Modern Times Group, a Swedish group active in broadcasting, the print media and e-commerce. The notified agreement concerned the upgrade of Modern Times' analogue satellite broadcasting operations to digital satellite broadcasting using Nordic Satellite's satellites. Under the agreement, Nordic Satellite would be the exclusive provider of satellite transponder capacity for the digital transmission of television signals to Modern Times until 2005.

8–323   Competitive assessment — The Commission found that although the agreement fell within Article 81(1) of the EC Treaty, it was pro-competitive, as it facilitated the upgrade of Modern Times' broadcasting services from analogue to digital transmission to viewers receiving DTH satellite television services. This benefited consumers, who would have a wider choice of television channels at more competitive prices. Before the co-operation, Canal Digital (a joint venture between Canal+ and Telenor) was the only provider of digital DTH television services in Scandinavia. The Commission also noted that the agreement would allow for the more efficient use of Nordic Satellite's satellite transponders. Therefore, the Commission decided to grant a five-year individual exemption under Article 81(3) of the EC Treaty.

(e) Joint Ventures and Strategic Alliances in Broadcasting and Interactive Services

Screensport/EBU Members[64]

8–324   The transaction — This case concerned a joint venture for the operation of Eurosport, a transnational satellite sports television channel, between the Eurosport Consortium, a group of members of the European Broadcasting Union (EBU), Sky Television and News International, the parent company of Sky. The arrangement extended the EBU system of joint buying and the exchange of programmes to the joint venture, which was granted preferential access to certain sports programmes produced by EBU members. The Commission's decision followed a complaint by Screensport, a similar type of sports channel.

8–325   The relevant product markets — The Commission defined the relevant product market as the market for the broadcasting of sports events. It further implicitly acknowledged the existence of a separate market for transnational satellite sports channels.

8–326   Competitive analysis — The Commission decided that the joint venture infringed Article 81(1) of the EC Treaty and did not warrant an exemption under Article 81(3) of the EC Treaty. The

---

[63] *Modern Times Group AB and Nordiska Satellitaktiebolaget*, Commission Press Release IP/01/1845 of December 20, 2001.
[64] *Screensport/EBU Members*, Commission Decision of March 9, 1991, O.J. 1991 L63/32.

Commission found that the arrangements between the Eurosport Consortium, Sky and News International would have had the effect of limiting or distorting competition. The joint venture would have brought together two potential competitors for sports programmes which would co-operate rather than compete with each other. At the same time, it would have denied third parties access to programmes. The arrangements gave Eurosport preferential access to certain sports programmes, to the detriment of Screensport. The Commission considered the fact that the joint venture created a second transnational sports channel was not sufficient to justify an individual exemption under Article 81(3) of the EC Treaty, as it had not been established that the joint venture was indispensable to achieving such an objective. In fact, Sky had already announced that it would ensure extensive broadcasting of sports events, regardless of whether the joint venture was approved. As a result of the Commission's decision, Sky withdrew from arrangements with various other broadcasting entities. Screensport and Eurosport subsequently merged in order to operate a single sports channel, and this was approved by the Commission in 1993.[65]

European Broadcasting Union[66]

8–327 The transaction — This case concerned a co-operative arrangement, through an association of broadcasters, the European Broadcasting Union (EBU), for the joint buying of television rights to sports events, and for exchanging sports programmes. Membership of the EBU was restricted to public broadcasters subject to public interest obligations to the exclusion of commercial broadcasters.

8–328 The relevant product markets — The Commission considered that the relevant product market was the market for the acquisition of sports rights for television programmes. There was a specific market for such rights because of the specific characteristics of sports programmes: (i) they were very attractive to public and commercial broadcasters, owing to high viewing figures; (ii) they were particularly suited to carrying advertisements; (iii) they transcended cultural and linguistic barriers and were therefore suited to transnational broadcasting and advertising; and (iv) they were expensive programmes to produce because of high risks and costs.

8–329 The relevant geographic markets — The relevant geographic market was generally a given territory, usually a country, as television rights are normally granted on an exclusive basis for a given country.

8–330 Competitive analysis by the Commission — The Commission found that the arrangement infringed Article 81(1) of the EC Treaty, in so far as it restricted competition between public broadcasters in the purchase of programming rights to sports events. The Commission also found that the joint buying arrangement considerably strengthened the market position of the public broadcasters to the disadvantage of their independent competitors. The Commission granted an individual exemption under Article 81(3) of the EC Treaty, because the EBU system reduced transaction costs, benefited smaller member broadcasters and facilitated the exchange of programmes between countries. For example, at the national level, the system permitted better

---

[65] *Eurosport Mark III*, Commission Notice pursuant to Art.19(3) of Regulation 17/62, O.J. 1993 C76/8.
[66] *EBU/Eurovision System*, Commission Decision of June 11, 1993, O.J. 1993 L179/23.

co-ordination between different broadcasters and thus quasi-permanent coverage of major events such as the Olympic Games or the FIFA World Cup. The arrangement also benefited consumers in that they would enjoy more, and higher quality, sports programmes. The Commission, nevertheless, subjected the exemption to the condition that the rules for sub-licensing programmes to non-members be applied in a reasonable and non-discriminatory manner.

8–331   Review by the Court of First Instance — The Commission's decision was annulled by the Court of First Instance following a challenge by various broadcasters that were not EBU members.[67] The Court held that the Commission had not considered whether the membership requirements of EBU were objective and sufficiently precise, so that they could be applied uniformly and without discrimination to all actual or potential members. This meant that it was impossible for the Commission to assess whether these membership criteria were indispensable for the purpose of Article 81(3) of the EC Treaty.

8–332   Further competitive analysis by the Commission — The EBU subsequently, on the Commission's request, changed its membership rules. These were then renotified to the Commission, which adopted a second individual exemption decision covering the period from February 26, 1993 to December 31, 2005.[68] The revised EBU system, as modified, provided non-EBU members with access to Eurovision sport programmes, including on pay-TV, and on both a live and deferred transmission basis. The Commission found that it therefore met the criteria for the granting of an individual exemption under Article 81(3) of the EC Treaty.

8–333   Further review by the Court of First Instance — The exemption decision was again challenged in the Court of First Instance by four free-TV channels that were not EBU members. These parties alleged that the EBU's rules governing the joint acquisition of television rights for sporting events, the exchange of the signal for sports broadcasts under Eurovision, and contractual access for third parties to that system, gave rise to serious restrictions on competition and that the Commission had erred in granting an exemption under Article 81(3) of the EC Treaty. The Court of First Instance agreed with the applicants and annulled the decision.[69] It stated that the sub-licensing system did not guarantee competitors of EBU members sufficient access to the transmission rights for sporting events which EBU members held by virtue of their participation in that purchasing association. Whist it was true that the joint purchasing of television transmission rights for a particular event is not in itself a restriction on competition in breach of Article 81(1) of the EC Treaty and may be justified by the particular characteristics of the product and the market in question, the Court of First Instance pointed out that the exercise of those rights in a specific legal and economic context may nevertheless lead to a restriction on competition. The Court of First

---

[67] Joined Cases T–528, 542, 343 and 546/93, *Metropole Television v Commission* [1998] II E.C.R. 649. For a critical review of the case, see Larouche, para.8–172, n.42, pp.234–238.

[68] *Eurovision*, Commission Decision of May 10, 2000, O.J. 2000 L151/18. In March 2000, M6 (a private French broadcaster) had requested the Commission to find the revised EBU membership rules anti-competitive and not qualifying for exemption under Art.81(3) of the EC Treaty. The Commission rejected this complaint. M6's challenge to this refusal was held by the Court of First Instance to be inadmissible: Case T–354/00, *M6 v Commission* [2001] II E.C.R. 3177.

[69] Joined Cases T–185/00, T–299/00 and T–300/00, *M6, Gestevision, Telecinco, and SIC v Commission*, [2002] II E.C.R. 3805. See also Court Press Release IP/80/02 of October 8, 2002.

Instance also considered whether the scheme for access to the Eurovision system compensated for the restrictions on competition imposed on third parties. In this context, the Court was concerned that the system failed to allow competitors to EBU members to obtain sub-licences for the live broadcast of unused Eurovision rights (*i.e.* rights acquired by Eurovision, but not broadcast by an EBU member in a particular territory). According to the Court, a distinction had to be made between live and deferred transmissions. The Court of First Instance noted that even if it were acceptable for EBU members to reserve live transmissions for themselves, nothing justified their extending that right to all the competitions in a given event when they did not intend to broadcast those events live. The Court concluded that, by reaching a different conclusion, the Commission had committed a manifest error of assessment. It therefore annulled the exemption decision.

Auditel [70]

8–334   The transaction — This case involved the setting-up, by Italian public and private broadcasters, of Auditel, a company whose purpose was to record and disseminate information on audiences for television broadcasts, divided into national, regional and sub-regional areas. The aim of the joint venture was to provide an objective and undisputed basis for calculating audience ratings in view of television advertising. Under this arrangement, the partners undertook to use exclusively the services provided by Auditel and to recognise the validity only of the figures resulting from Auditel's measurements and research. The purpose of this clause was to avoid disagreements on television audience shares.

8–335   The relevant product markets — The Commission defined the relevant product market as that for audience-rating measurements, *i.e.* figures showing the number of people watching a given channel at a given point in time.

8–336   The relevant geographic markets — Although the Commission did not take an explicit position, it was implicit that the Commission considered the relevant market to be national, along the lines of the geographic scope of the broadcasting market.

8–337   Competitive analysis — The Auditel joint venture was the subject of complaints to the Commission by competitors, who argued that the parties' obligation to use Auditel exclusively gave it a dominant position on the audience-rating measurement market, and that Auditel was abusing this position through its pricing policy. The Commission granted a negative clearance to the Auditel joint venture under both Articles 81(1) and 82 of the EC Treaty, but only after the parties had accepted to withdraw the exclusivity clause benefiting Auditel. Despite the withdrawal of this provision prior to the adoption of the Commission's decision, the Commission formally stated that the exclusivity clause infringed Article 81(1) of the EC Treaty and could not be exempted under Article 81(3) of the EC Treaty. In this respect, the Commission considered that the justification provided by the parties for the exclusivity (*i.e.* the desire to avoid disagreements on audience shares) was not acceptable. Indeed, the reliability of all broadcasters should ensure the objectivity of the audience rating and the requirement that members used only Auditel's figures was thus superfluous.

[70] *Auditel*, Commission Decision of November 24, 1993, O.J. 1993 L306/50.

The Commission found that as the exclusivity provision had been eliminated, Auditel would no longer have had a monopoly position and that there was therefore no longer an issue under Article 82 of the EC Treaty. It is interesting to note that the Commission's decision was adopted more than seven years after the original notification of the arrangement.

British Digital Broadcasting[71]

8–338   The transaction — British Digital Broadcasting (BDB) was a joint venture between Carlton, Granada and BSkyB for the operation of a digital terrestrial television platform that would broadcast both free and pay-TV services and, potentially, digital interactive services. BSkyB was the leading pay-TV operator in the United Kingdom, whilst Granada and Carlton both operated free TV channels (including, between them, most of the leading commercially funded free TV channels broadcast terrestrially) with only limited interests in pay-TV operations. Granada also had a minority shareholding in BSkyB. BDB had concluded a supply agreement with BSkyB for the supply of various Sky channels for an initial duration of seven years, which was exclusive as regards digital terrestrial television.

8–339   The relevant product markets — The Commission continued to distinguish between the markets for free TV (financed by state funds and/or advertising) and pay-TV (funded by subscription fees). Within the market for pay-TV, the Commission did not distinguish between analogue and digital systems.

8–340   The relevant geographic markets — The Commission found that the market for pay-TV was national or regional.

8–341   Competitive analysis — The Independent Television Commission (ITC) refused to grant a licence to BDB to operate a new digital terrestrial platform after having received indications from the European Commission and the UK Office of Fair Trading that the participation of BSkyB in BDB as both a shareholder and a supplier of programming raised competition concerns and would have had the effect of strengthening BSkyB's existing dominant position on the pay-TV market in the United Kingdom.[72] The licence was granted by the ITC to BDB only after BSkyB's withdrawal from the joint venture. In the light of this development, the Commission cleared the transaction by way of a comfort letter. The Commission considered that the co-ordination of the competitive conduct of Granada and Carlton on the market for pay-TV as a result of the joint venture did not raise substantial competition concerns in particular in light of the presence of a large competitor, BSkyB. The Commission nevertheless insisted, in order to be able to issue a comfort letter, that the supply agreement with BSkyB for a number of channels be reduced from seven to five years (to prevent the foreclosure of the other programme suppliers) and that Granada undertake not to use its shareholding in BSkyB to prevent BDB from competing with BSkyB. The ITC required BSkyB to continue providing its channels to BDB for this period, given the importance of BSkyB's channels

---

[71] *BDB(ONdigital)*, Commission Notice, O.J. 1997 291/11. See also ITC Press Release of June 24, 1997, available at: *www.itc.org.uk/latest_news/press_releases*.
[72] See para.6–085 *et seq.*

(particularly sport) in the UK pay-TV market. BDB was subsequently renamed ONdigital (and later ITV Digital), but went into administration and ceased operation in 2002.

TPS + 7[73]

8–342   The transaction — This transaction concerned the creation of a joint venture with a view to launching a digital satellite platform for the distribution in France and other French-speaking parts of other countries of pay-TV services via the Eutelsat satellite. The companies involved in this project, each of which had 25 per cent shareholdings, were the broadcasters TF1, France Télévision Enterprises (itself a joint venture between France Télévision, the operator of the France 2 and France 3 channels, and France Télécom, which operated cable and terrestrial transmission networks), the broadcaster M6 Numérique, and Suez Lyonnaise des Eaux, which operated cable networks. This operation was not a concentration for the purposes of the Merger Control Regulation, as the shareholders did not have joint control even though TPS would have been full-function. TF1 subsequently acquired France Télévision Enterprise's 25 per cent shareholding.[74]

8–343   The relevant product markets — In this case, as it had done in the past, the Commission distinguished between the markets for pay-TV, where the joint venture would be active, and free TV, where some of its parents were active. The distinction between pay-TV and free TV was based on the different funding of the two services, *i.e.* advertising for free TV and subscription fees for pay-TV. The Commission did not identify separate product markets for analogue and digital pay-TV, nor for cable, terrestrial and satellite transmission. The Commission also identified a distinct market for technical services for pay-TV, on the basis of the special technical infrastructure needed for encrypting broadcasts and enabling authorised viewers to decode them. As regards the market for the acquisition of broadcasting rights, the Commission left open the issue of whether distinct markets existed for each of films and sporting events or for the different categories of rights: un-encrypted TV broadcasting, pay-TV, pay-per-view, near-video-on-demand and video-on-demand. Finally, the Commission considered that the market for the distribution and operation of special interest channels was a relevant affected market. In this respect, the Commission noted that this category of programmes, which is not specific to pay-TV, was growing rapidly due to the greater number of channels that could be transmitted as a result of digitalisation.

8–344   The relevant geographic markets — The Commission left open the issue of whether the relevant market should be limited to France or be extended to the French-speaking countries in Europe.

8–345   Competitive analysis — The Commission granted negative clearance to the formation of the joint venture under Article 81(1) of the EC Treaty, taking into consideration its overall positive effect on competition. The operation created a new operator on the French market for pay-TV then dominated by Canal+, which had a market share of over 70 per cent. In this respect, the Commission considered that the fact that some of the partners were actual competitors on the free-TV market did not raise material competition concerns, as the joint venture was active on the separate

---

[73] *TPS + 7*, Commission Decision of March 3, 1999, O.J. 1999 L90/6.
[74] See *TPS*, above, para.8–250 *et seq.*

market for pay-TV services. Likewise, the fact that two partners, France Télécom and Suez Lyonnaise des Eaux, were already present on the pay-TV market as cable operators was not considered to raise significant concerns, because cable penetration in France was limited and cable and satellite were not competing to a large extent in France. However, the parties undertook to delete a clause which committed the two cable operators associated with TPS, France Télécom and Suez Lyonnaise des Eaux, to giving the channels broadcast on TPS priority access to their cable networks and to co-ordinate their offerings with that of TPS, as these would have had anti-competitive foreclosure and co-ordination effects. In so far as the parties (TF1, France Télévision and M6) were competitors on the market for unencrypted free TV and suppliers of special interest channels, the joint venture would not have resulted in the co-ordination of their activities.

The Commission cleared as ancillary to the joint venture an obligation on the parents not to compete with the joint venture in the distribution and marketing of digital pay-TV services, as this was considered to be necessary in order to ensure that all the parties concentrated their efforts on this very risky and costly project. However, the Commission limited the ancillary nature of this clause to a three-year post-launch period. The Commission exempted, under Article 81(3) of the EC Treaty for a period of three years from the date of the notification (*i.e.* October 21, 1999), provisions giving TPS: (i) exclusive distribution rights to the parents' general interest channels (*i.e.* TF1, France 2, France 3 and M6); and (ii) first option to special interest channels and services operated, controlled or produced by the parents and terms and conditions equivalent to those granted to third parties. The parties had argued that the non-compete obligation should have been regarded as ancillary for the duration of the joint venture and that the exempted restrictions should have been exempted for their original 10-year duration. However, the Commission considered that these were restricting competition and could only be justified during the post-launch period. The parties challenged the Commission's decision in so far as it limited the ancillary nature of the non-compete obligation to three years and only granted exemptions for the other clauses for three years. The Court of First Instance upheld the Commission's approach.[75]

British Interactive Broadcasting (BiB, now Open)[76]

8–346   The transaction — This case involved the creation of a joint venture, British Interactive Broadcasting (BiB, subsequently renamed Open), for the setting-up and operation of the infrastructure needed to provide digital interactive TV services to consumers in the United Kingdom. The partners involved in this project were BSkyB, the dominant pay-TV operator in the United Kingdom, British Telecommunications (BT), Midland Bank (now HSBC), a banking institution, and Matsushita, a producer of electronic equipment and technology. Digital interactive TV services were internet-like, online services that were to be delivered via television screens. The services were planned to include retailing, information services, game playing, home banking, home shopping, holiday and travel services and "walled garden" internet access. The scope of BiB did not extend to video-on-demand or to pay-TV. BiB's digital interactive TV service would thus allow content

---

[75] Case T–112/99, *Métropole Télévision — (M6) v Commission* [2001] II E.C.R. 2459.
[76] *British Interactive Broadcasting (Open)*, Commission Decision of September 15, 1999, O.J. 1999 L312/1. For a commentary on this decision, see Font, Galarza, "The British Interactive Broadcasting Decision and the Application of Competition Rules to New Digital Interactive Television Services" (1997) 7 *Competition Policy Newsletter* 7–15.

providers to offer their goods and services directly to digital TV viewers and to complete transactions with such viewers. The service would combine content broadcast via digital satellite (broadcast content) with, in some circumstances, content delivered via standard telephone lines (online content). BiB's infrastructure relied mainly on an interactive set-top box. Each customer would have to acquire and install a set-top box and maintain a connection to a telephone line in order to have access to BiB's services, but was not obliged to subscribe to BSkyB's pay-TV services. The set-top boxes, which would be developed by BSkyB for its pay-TV services, would be subsidised by BiB together with satellite dishes and the installation of the interactive receiving equipment at the customer's home. The subsidy recovery mechanism would be regulated by OFTEL as part of the UK telecommunications regulatory regime. Through the set-top boxes, customers would benefit not only from online services but also from the possibility of interacting with television programmes or advertising and therefore be in a position to influence the content.

8–347 The relevant product markets — The Commission distinguished the following relevant product markets: (i) digital interactive services, including retailing, financial services, information, education, internet access, email and games; (ii) technical and administrative services for digital interactive TV services and retail pay-TV; (iii) pay-TV; (iv) the wholesale supply of film and sports channels for retail pay-TV; and (v) the operation of the local loop telecommunications infrastructure.

The Commission found that a distinction had to be made between online services provided via television sets and those provided via PCs, since they had different market penetration, price, characteristics and use. The Commission noted that the situation could, however, change over time as internet access via television became possible. Digital interactive services were also distinct from high-street retailing, because of the different product ranges sold and the fact that they were priced as a package rather than as individual services. Digital interactive services also differed from retail pay-TV services, because of the nature of the services supplied (entertainment *versus* transactional and information services).

As regards technical and administrative services, the Commission took the position that no distinction should be made between technical services for pay-TV and those for interactive services, because of the large overlap between the technical and administrative services necessary for retail pay-TV and digital interactive TV services.

With respect to pay-TV services, in line with its decision in *BDB*,[77] the Commission refused to define separate markets for digital and analogue pay-TV. In addition, the Commission considered that, at least in the United Kingdom, no distinction should be made between cable and satellite retail pay-TV.[78] Owing to the different value and price of film and sports channels in comparison to other channels, the Commission considered that there was a specific product market for the

---

[77] *BDB(ONdigital)*, para.8–338 *et seq.*, above. See also ITC Press Release of June 24, 1997, available at: *www.itc.org.uk/latest_news/press_releases.*

[78] This contrasts with the position taken by the Commission in Case *MSG*, above, para.8–171 *et seq.*; *Bertelsmann/Kirch/Premiere*, above, para.8–187 *et seq.*; and *Telecom Italia/News TV/Stream*, above, para.8–210 *et seq.*

purchase of such rights, in particular given their importance for pay-TV operators as a driver of subscriptions.

8–348   The relevant geographic markets — The relevant geographic market was found to be the United Kingdom, based on the existence of a specific national regulatory framework for each Member State governing the relevant services.

8–349   Competitive analysis — The Commission exempted the joint venture pursuant to Article 81(3) of the EC Treaty, subject to observance of a number of conditions and obligations imposed upon the parties.[79] The Commission considered that the joint venture would have restricted competition, owing to a number of restrictive clauses such as: (i) a provision that BiB would be the exclusive supplier of digital interactive services via BSkyB's EPG (*i.e.* a navigation system which lists channels and services and via which viewers are able to tune to different data signals and thus change channels and services); (ii) a clause providing BiB and BSkyB with veto rights on any licence of the enhanced API (*i.e.* the set-top box that enables the end-user to decode programmes) for a period of two years from the launch of BiB's services; (iii) Midland Bank (now HSBC) enjoying a ten-year exclusive right for the transaction management system (*i.e.* a mechanism for authorising and undertaking financial transactions in a secure environment); and (iv) customers' purchase of the subsidised set-top box being subject to the customer also taking a subscription to the pay-TV services of BSkyB.

The Commission considered that the joint venture, as initially structured, raised substantial competition problems. BT and BSkyB were potential competitors in the provision of digital interactive television services as both had sufficient skills and resources to launch such services and both would have been able to bear the technical risks of doing so alone. There was a risk that third parties, whether providers of pay-TV services or interactive services, would not have been able to obtain easy access to the set-top box if it was subsidised by BiB, thereby increasing the barriers to entry for potential competitors in these markets.

The Commission nevertheless granted an exemption to the joint venture under Article 81(3) of the EC Treaty, because it benefited consumers and retailers of goods and services by offering a new outlet (via television sets) for the purchase and distribution of services that had previously been available only via personal computers and the internet. The joint venture also enabled the parties to provide a better service and to do so more quickly than would have been the case if they had developed these services alone.

8–350   However, the Commission subjected the exemption to a number of conditions, in order to ensure that third parties could access, under fair and non-discriminatory conditions, all proprietary elements of the set-top boxes that would be subsidised by BiB. These conditions were also aimed at preventing BSkyB from abusing, through the joint venture, its existing dominant position on the market for pay-TV in the United Kingdom. These conditions included,

---

[79] The essential difference between a condition and an obligation under Regulation 17/62 is that a failure to comply with a condition means that the exemption is inapplicable (*i.e.* non-existent) without further action by the Commission, whereas a breach of an obligation can lead to a formal Commission decision withdrawing the exemption.

inter alia: (i) the legal separation of BiB's activities with respect to the supply and subsidisation of set-top boxes and those related to providing interactive services; (ii) the removal of all exclusive rights regarding access to the set-top box, (iii) an obligation to inform both end-users and their sales agents for the sale of set-top boxes that end-users were not obliged to subscribe to BSkyB's digital pay-TV service as a condition of purchasing the set-top box subsidised by BiB; (iv) an obligation to supply third parties with the technical specifications of the set-top box, including proposed changes to the specifications; (v) an obligation to conclude simulcrypt agreements with interested parties[80]; and (vi) obligations concerning the supply of conditional access services with respect to digital interactive services. In imposing these conditions and obligations, the Commission was clearly of the view that the set-top boxes in question would have constituted an essential facility to which third party access should be guaranteed, and that BiB would have had a "gate-keeper" role.

Moreover, the Commission insisted that the bundling by BSkyB of the subsidised set-top boxes with its pay-TV services be terminated. The Commission was also concerned that BT's participation in the joint venture may have led, in the short to medium term, to reduced incentives for BT to invest in its local loop infrastructure, a market in which BT was dominant in the United Kingdom. BT, the only nationwide operator of local loop infrastructure, would have had the possibility of modernising this infrastructure to provide broadband services competing with those provided by BiB and the cable networks. As a result, BT agreed to divest its interests in cable television networks in the United Kingdom. Moreover, the Commission indicated that it would monitor closely the development of competition in the UK broadband local loop market to determine whether BT's participation in BiB was impeding the supply of services using broadband local loop infrastructure. The Commission indicated that it could impose, if appropriate, an obligation upon BT to choose between its continued participation in BiB, and the provision of unbundled access to its local loop infrastructure.[81]

3. Analysis of the Commission's Decision-Making Practice

8–351   Introduction — The Commission has stated that, as a general principle, it favours mergers and joint ventures to the extent that they achieve the rationalisation and economies of scale and scope required for businesses to remain competitive in an increasingly liberalised and global market.[82] However, the Commission is vigilant to ensure that structural arrangements neither perpetuate existing dominant positions nor create new ones through integration that would

---

[80] Simulcrypt involves a commercial agreement between the suppliers of different systems such that populations of digital set-top boxes embedding each system are able to descramble signals using both conditional access systems.

[81] On October 10, 2001, BT was directed by OFTEL to meet any request from any operator wishing to take advantage of local loop unbundling in the United Kingdom for co-mingling (a form of physical co-location where the equipment of the operator requesting local loop unbundling is fitted and operated in an area within a BT exchange where BT could or does house its own equipment, without a permanent barrier between them) other than where it would be impracticable on technical grounds, or would directly and necessarily impair the integrity of any telecommunications system run under the BT licence. OFTEL, *Local Loop Unbundling: provision of co-location in the form of co-mingling. Statement and Direction of October 10, 2001*, available at *www.oftel.gov.uk*.

[82] 1991 Guidelines, para.8–002, n.1, para.59.

combine different activities so as to raise barriers to entry. Accordingly, its approach has varied and continues to vary substantially, depending on the nature of the markets involved (*e.g.* broadcasting, telecommunications services, new services such as the internet and online services or separate markets that are converging), the geographic scope of the market (*i.e.* local, national, European or international), the level of liberalisation of the relevant market and competition in it, and the type of transaction involved (*i.e.* merger, full-function joint venture, co-operative joint venture or strategic alliance) and its economic structure (*i.e.* horizontal, vertical or conglomerate).

Over recent years, the Commission has increasingly used its competition authority (whether under Articles 81 and 82 or the Merger Control Regulation) to impose remedies of a regulatory nature, such as granting licences to competitors,[83] open access to networks[84] and content,[85] local loop unbundling,[86] and even legal separation of different businesses,[87] as conditions for clearance or exemption. The Commission has thus used competition policy as a tool for market liberalisation which, in some cases, may have gone beyond the resolution of the competition concerns raised by the particular transaction. The "regulatory" approach to competition policy has mainly been used in cases involving vertical integration, such as the creation of *Vizzavi*,[88] but also in horizontal merger cases creating "powerhouses", such as Vodafone's takeover of Mannesmann.[89] With the continued digitalisation of transmission infrastructure, open access to networks[90] alone is no longer sufficient to enable competitors to reach the end customer and the issue of open standards will become the focus of attention.[91]

(a) The Commission's Practice in Relation to Telecommunications Services

8–352 The Commission's decision-making practice in the telecommunications services sector covers four distinct types of arrangement, which are considered below in turn: (i) strategic alliances and joint ventures between incumbent operators to provide global services; (ii) joint ventures between incumbent operators and other service providers; (iii) joint ventures and other co-operative arrangements not involving incumbent operators; (iv) concentrations between incumbent operators.

8–353 Strategic alliances and joint ventures between incumbent operators to provide global services — The Commission has approved a number of strategic alliances between incumbent operators that were formed so that they could provide global telecommunications services, mostly to corporate users.[92] The Commission has taken a favourable view of this type of restructuring, as it

---

[83] *Atlas/Phoenix-Global One*, above, para.8–269 *et seq.*
[84] *Vodafone Airtouch/Mannesmann*, above, para.8–142 *et seq.*
[85] *Vodafone/Vivendi/Canal+*, above, para.8–138 *et seq.*; and *AOL/Time Warner*, above, para.8–223 *et seq.*
[86] *Telia/Telenor*, above, para.8–097 *et seq.*
[87] *Telia/Sonera*, above, para.8–129 *et seq.*
[88] *Vivendi/Vodafone/Canal+*, above, para.8–138 *et seq.*
[89] *Vodafone Airtouch/Mannesmann*, above, para.8–142 *et seq.*
[90] See above, para.1–154 *et seq.*
[91] See further Rosenthal, "Open Access from the EU Perspective" (2002/03) 7 *International Journal of Communications Law and Policy*, available at: *www.ijclp.org*.
[92] See *e.g. Atlas* and *Phoenix/Global One*, above, para.8–269 *et seq.*; *Unisource* and *Uniworld*, above, para.8–274 *et seq.*; and *BT/MCI*, above, para.8–264 *et seq.*

has enabled telecommunications operators to reach the critical size and breadth of activities required to compete effectively on a worldwide basis by offering, for instance, "one-stop shop" services and private networks for multinational groups. However, the economic benefits resulting from these operations must be demonstrated and the Commission has been particularly vigilant that such transactions could not result in market sharing, the strengthening of dominant positions of incumbent operators on their respective national markets, and the creation of barriers to entry, which could have resulted in the foreclosure of markets to third parties. In cases involving former monopolist operators that have controlled access to infrastructure, the Commission has imposed appropriate undertakings and conditions in order to ensure that: (i) the arrangements could not permit the parent companies to cross-subsidise the activities of the joint venture with revenues from the exploitation of their telecommunications infrastructure or other services in which they were dominant on their respective home markets; and (ii) third parties were able to obtain access to the telecommunications networks on a non-discriminatory basis, *i.e.* under the same conditions as the joint venture. In this context, the Commission has taken a very close look at the conditions for access to local loop infrastructure and cable TV networks when reviewing transactions between incumbent operators, and it has considered it necessary to impose cable TV network divestiture[93] and local loop unbundling[94] as a condition of its approval of a transaction. However, where no effective remedy was possible, the Commission has prohibited joint ventures involving incumbents which aimed to combine the parties' different strengths, but which would have created "gate-keeper" positions.[95] The Commission's willingness to accept remedies further depends upon whether it is applying Article 81 of the EC Treaty or the Merger Control Regulation.[96]

The Commission has also focused on the network effects that may result from the combination of the activities of the parties to the alliance. The Commission considers that a minimum number of independent networks must be maintained in order for effective competition to be preserved. For example, in *WorldCom/MCI*, the Commission concluded that, after completion of the transaction, WorldCom would have controlled too great a share of the internet backbone capacity available worldwide and would have had a dominant position. It therefore approved the transaction subject to a condition that MCI's internet activities be divested; they were later sold to Cable&Wireless.[97] The Commission was also concerned about network effects resulting in the creation of a dominant position in the subsequent *MCIWorldcom/Sprint*[98] case (which it prohibited), as well as in *Vodafone Airtouch/Mannesmann*[99] (which it permitted subject to open access conditions).

8–354 Joint ventures between incumbent operators and other service providers — The Commission has had the opportunity to review a considerable number of structural arrangements and

---

[93] *British Interactive Broadcasting*, above, para.8–346 *et seq.*

[94] *Telia/Telenor*, above, para.8–097 *et seq.* This transaction pre-dated the adoption of the LLU Regulation which entered into force in January 2001.

[95] *Nordic Satellite Distribution*, above, para.8–175 *et seq.*; and *Deutsche Telekom/Beta Research*, above, para.8–187 *et seq.*

[96] *Deutsche Telekom/BetaResearch*, above, para.8–187 *et seq.*; and *British Interactive Broadcasting*, above, para.8–346 *et seq.*

[97] *WorldCom/MCI*, above, para.8–088 *et seq.*

[98] Above, para.8–101 *et seq.*

[99] Above, para.8–142 *et seq.*

various forms of co-operation between incumbent operators and other service providers. These arrangements have generally been undertaken in order to develop new services[1] or to enter the market for existing services in other geographic areas.[2] The Commission considers that such arrangements raise no competition issues if it can be demonstrated that the partners are not actual or potential competitors and would not have had the resources to develop the new services or enter the market alone.[3]

The Commission favours joint ventures and strategic alliances that enable new competition to be introduced in domestic telecommunications services. For example, the Commission has approved a number of joint ventures between incumbent operators, extending their activities abroad, and utility providers (*e.g.* railway companies, electricity providers) to develop the latter's network to provide domestic telecommunications services in competition with the local incumbent former monopolist.[4]

Arrangements to develop existing services or introduce new services are likely to receive a favourable view from the Commission if it can be demonstrated that the economic benefits outweigh any anti-competitive effects that may result from the arrangements. Economic benefits can include *inter alia*: the rationalisation of the production and distribution of telecommunication services; improvements in existing services or the development of new services; and the transfer of technology and increased competitiveness of European industrial structures.[5] In the absence of proven economic benefits, the Commission will take a negative stance, especially if the joint venture is considered to lead to an extension of the existing dominant position of the incumbent operator into a new market. Likewise, the Commission has opposed transactions that would lead to vertical integration resulting in higher or even insurmountable barriers to entry.[6] In order to approve such co-operation, the Commission will seek to ensure, through appropriate conditions (*e.g.* the parties' commitment not to discriminate and cross-subsidise in favour of the joint operations), that competition from third parties is not foreclosed.[7]

8–355 Joint ventures and other co-operative arrangements not involving incumbent operators — As full liberalisation of the Community telecommunications market has now occurred, the sector is witnessing more joint ventures, mergers and alliances not involving the former monopolists, that are taking place to facilitate market entry or to develop new services. The Commission has already

[1] See, *e.g. Eirpage*, above, para.8–284 *et seq.*; *Astra*, above, para.8–300 *et seq.*; *Intrax*, above, para.8–296 *et seq.*; *IPSP*, above, para.8–308 *et seq.*; and *Inmarsat-P*, above, para.8–312 *et seq.*

[2] See, *e.g. ENEL/FT/DT*, above, para.8–083 *et seq.*; *Cégétel+4 and Télécom Développement*, above, para.8–278 *et seq.*; Case M.595, *British Telecommunications/VIAG*, Commission Decision of December 22, 1995; and Case M.927, *STET/GET/Unión Fenosa*, Commission Decision of August 20, 1997.

[3] *IPSP*, above, para.8–308 *et seq.*

[4] See, *e.g. ENEL/FT/DT*, above, para.8–083 *et seq.*; *Cégétel+4 and Télécom Développement*, above, para.8–278 *et seq.*; Case M.595, *British Telecommunications/VIAG*, Commission Decision of December 22, 1995, and Case M.927, *STET/GET/Unión Fenosa*, Commission Decision of August 20, 1997.

[5] 1991 Competition Guidelines, para.8–002, n.1, para.68.

[6] See, under Art.81 of the EC Treaty, *Astra*, above, para.8–300 *et seq.*, where the Commission considered that BT's vertical integration of up-link services and provision of satellite capacity, through the Astra joint venture, would substantially increase the level of barriers to entry on these markets in the United Kingdom.

[7] See, *e.g. Eirpage*, above, para.8–284 *et seq.*

reviewed a number of such transactions. Arrangements involving companies that are not active — or only marginally active — on the telecommunications market are likely to be approved by the Commission without any difficulty, as their effect is normally to increase competition rather than restrict it. For instance, the Commission has approved a number of joint ventures between service providers and owners of alternative infrastructures leading to the creation of new competitors in the markets for international or domestic services.[8] In assessing these arrangements, the Commission will check that they do not lead to undue restrictions of competition (*e.g.* price fixing, market sharing, customer allocation) or have foreclosure effects (for example by granting exclusive access to important rights of way).[9] Moreover, as businesses other than the former monopolists gain a stronger foothold in certain segments of the market, transactions between these new operators might also raise issues of market dominance.[10]

8–356   Concentrations between incumbent operators — The Commission had to assess two proposed mergers of incumbent operators: *Telia/Telenor*[11] and *Telia/Sonera*.[12] Given the fact that in both cases the two parties were both incumbents active in neighbouring countries and exerted competitive pressure on each other (and indeed were either each other's strongest actual competitor or the most likely potential competitor), the Commission identified a number of competition concerns. To remove these concerns, the Commission imposed far-reaching remedies, which were both structural and regulatory in nature. In *Telia/Telenor*, the Commission considered that the national regulatory safeguards in Sweden and Norway were insufficiently developed to guarantee fair, non-discriminatory and efficient competition. It therefore required each operator to unbundle access to its local loop network as a condition for approval, given that local loop unbundling obligations did not at that time exist in Sweden and Norway. By doing so, the Commission wished to maximise the potential for market entry to compete with the already dominant incumbents. In *Telia/Sonera*, the parties were required to grant non-discriminatory access to their fixed and mobile network services, as well as to their international wholesale mobile roaming services in Sweden and Finland. However, the Commission considered that it was also necessary to have these regulatory remedies "backed" by a structural remedy to make anti-competitive behaviour more difficult to carry out and easier to detect. It therefore required each party to place its fixed and mobile network and services businesses in Sweden and Finland into separate legal entities.

(b) The Commission's Practice in Relation to Restructuring of International Satellite Organisations

8–357   Based on the *Inmarsat-P* case,[13] the Commission appears to impose three requirements in order to grant approval for the restructuring of an international satellite organisation. First,

---

[8] *Hermes*, above, para.8–070 *et seq.*; *Iridium*, para.8-301; Case M.618, *Cable and Wireless/Veba*, Commission Decision of August 16, 1995; Case M.827, *DB Kom*, Commission Decision of October 23, 1996; Case M.975, *Albacom/BT/ENI*, Commission Decision of November 13, 1997; and *Cégétel + 4/Télécom Développement*, above, para.8–278 *et seq.*

[9] *DB Kom, ibid.*; *Télécom Développement, ibid.*

[10] This is particularly true in the mobile sector: see *Vodafone/AirTouch*, above, para.8–134 *et seq.*; and *Vodafone Airtouch/Mannesmann*, above, para.8–142 *et seq.*

[11] See above, para.8–097 *et seq.*

[12] See above, para.8–129 *et seq.*

[13] See above, para.8–312 *et seq.*

shareholdings in the commercial entity to which the organisations business has been transferred must be open to companies that have not been signatories to the international organisation. As a condition for clearance, the Commission has required that there should be a public offering of the shares in the new entity. Secondly, the scope of the activities that are retained by the international organisation and enjoying exclusive or special rights must be kept as small as possible and be limited to activities carried out in the public interest and which can only be provided under special or exclusive rights. In fact, the Commission favours the full privatisation of those organisations and the removal of all exclusive or special rights. Thirdly, the Commission will work to ensure that the successor company should have no undue advantages over competitors. Neither the remaining international governmental organisation, nor its commercial subsidiary, should enjoy advantages over their competitors, for example in respect of frequencies used for the provision of its commercial services. The Commission considers that the frequency rights used for the provision of such services should be held by the commercial entity. Moreover, the conditions governing the use of such frequencies by the commercial entity should be non-discriminatory with regard to those applying to private operators.[14]

(c) The Commission's Practice in Relation to Telecommunications and Satellite Equipment

8–358 Telecommunications and satellite — Although it has considered a considerable number of cases,[15] under both Article 81 of the EC Treaty and the Merger Control Regulation, the

---

[14] See Ungerer, "The transformation of the International satellite organisations: some aspects from a European perspective", available on *www.europa.eu.int/comm/competition/speeches/text/sp99008.htm*.

[15] See, under Art.81(3) of the EC Treaty *Alcatel Espace/ANT Nachrichtentechnik*, above, para.8–292 *et seq.*; Case *Korsortium E.C.R.*, above, para.8–282 *et seq.*; Case *STET, Italtel, AT&T-NSI*, above, para.8–288 *et seq.*, Case *Aérospatiale/Alcatel Espace*, above, para.8–304 *et seq.* See under the Merger Control Regulation: Case *Alcatel/Telettra*, above, para.8–049 *et seq.*; Case M.178, *Saab Ericsson Space*, Commission Decision of January 13, 1992; Case M.133, *Ericsson/Kolbe*, Commission Decision of January 22, 1992; Case M.236, *Ericsson/Ascom*, Commission Decision of July 8, 1992; Case M.249, *Northern Telecom/Matra*, Commission Decision of July 17, 1992; Case M.249, *Ericsson/Hewlett-Packard*, Commission Decision of March 12, 1993; Case M.366, *Alcatel/STC*, Commission Decision of September 13, 1993; Case M.496, *Marconi/Finmeccanica*, Commission Decision of September 5, 1994; Case M.519, *Ericsson/Raychem*, Commission Decision of November 21, 1994; Case M.468, *Siemens/Italtel*, Commission Decision of February 17, 1995, O.J. 1995 L161/27; Case M.676, *Ericsson/Ascom II*, Commission Decision of December 22, 1995; Case M.651, *AT&T/Philips*, Commission Decision of February 5, 1996; Case M.668, *Philips/Origin*, Commission Decision of February 22, 1996; Case M.876, *Telia/Ericsson*, Commission Decision of February 20, 1997; Case M.966, *Philips/Lucent Technologies*, Commission Decision of August 20, 1997; Case M.1113, *Nortel/Norweb*, Commission Decision of March 18, 1998; Case M.1226, *GEC/GPTH*, Commission Decision of June 27, 1998; Case M.1263, *Nortel/Bay*, Commission Decision of August 21, 1998; Case JV.12, *Ericsson/Nokia/Psion/Motorola*, Commission Decision of December 22, 1998; Case M.1440, *Lucent Technologies/Ascend Communication*, Commission Decision of April 6, 1999; Case JV.26, *Freecom/Dangaard*, Commission Decision of December 1, 1999; Case *Marconi/Bosch Public Network*, above, para.8–057 *et seq.*; Case M.1841, *Celestica/IBM (EMS)*, Commission Decision of February 25, 2000, O.J. 2000 C341/2; Case M.1883, *NEC/Mitsubishi*, Commission Decision of April 3, 2000, O.J. 2000 C368/6; Case M.2077, *Clayton Dubilier & Rice/Italtel*, Commission Decision of September 1, 2000, O.J. 2000 C352/7; Case M.2116, *Flextronics/Italdata*, Commission Decision of September 25, 2000, O.J. 2000 C354/39; Case M.2135, *NCR/4 Front*, Commission Decision of October 12, 2000, O.J. 2000 C348/13; Case *Alcatel/Thomson Multimedia JV*, above, para.8–061 *et seq.*; Case M.2215, *Techint/Stella/James Jones/Sirti JV*, Commission Decision of November 22, 2000, O.J. 2000 C368/6;

Commission has cleared all transactions in this sector. On a few occasions the Commission has approved transactions that would have led to high combined market shares on specific national markets that were in the process of converging with other national markets to form a European market, owing to the processes of liberalisation and harmonisation of technical standards.[16] The Commission's favourable attitude towards restructuring in the telecommunications equipment sector is explained by a number of factors. The development of telecommunications and satellite equipment requires a high level of investment and technical know-how. Structural arrangements and other lower forms of co-operation between manufacturers are very often the only option to allow them to reach the critical mass needed to undertake the research and development activities to develop new products. When this is the case, joint ventures between operators generally do not raise competitive concerns, although they may require an exemption if they are reviewed under Article 81 of the EC Treaty. If a joint venture is limited to research and development activities (so is not full-function), it may meet the requirements of one of the Commission's block exemption regulations without the need for a notification to the Commission.[17] Alternatively, the Commission has granted negative clearance under Article 81(1) of the EC Treaty or has granted an individual exemption under Article 81(3) of the EC Treaty arrangements involving the joint marketing of equipment.[18] In assessing the economic benefits resulting from joint ventures in these sectors, the Commission has taken into account the fragmented nature of European suppliers in contrast to their US competitors and the need for them to co-operate in order to remain internationally competitive.[19]

Case M.2199, *Quantum/Maxtor*, Commission Decision of December 8, 2000, O.J. 2001 C68/11; Case M.2265, *Ricoh/Lanier World*, Commission Decision of January 24, 2001, O.J. 2001 C159/3; Case M.2324, *Sanmina Corporation/AB Segerström & Svensson*, Commission Decision of February 23, 2001, O.J. 2001 C74/10; Case M.2358, *Flextronics/Ericsson*, Commission Decision of April 6, 2001, O.J. 2001 C159/4; Case M.2263, *Philips/LG Electronics JV*, Commission Decision of April 9, 2001, O.J. 2001 C180/16; Case M.2403, *Schneider/Thomson Multimedia JV*, Commission Decision of June 13, 2001, O.J. 2001 C251/3; Case M.2452, *Belgacom/BAS Holding/Securitas*, Commission Decision of July 5, 2001, O.J. 2001 C238/7; Case M.2534, *SCI Systems/Nokia Networks*, Commission Decision of August 6, 2001, O.J. 2001 C281/11; Case M.2260, *Hitachi/LG Electronics JV*, Commission Decision of September 14, 2001, O.J. 2001 C296/21; Case M.2549, *Sanmina/SCI Systems*, Commission Decision of September 20, 2001, O.J. 2001 C296/23; Case M.2462, *Ericsson/Sony JV*, Commission Decision of September 27, 2001, O.J. 2001 C281/9; Case M.2546, *EADS/Nortel*, Commission Decision of October 1, 2001, O.J. 2001, C296/21; Case M.2528, *Maersk IT/LM Ericsson/WAC*, Commission Decision of October 15, 2001, O.J. 2001 C319/16; Case M.2629, *Flextronics/Xerox*, Commission Decision of November 12, 2001, O.J. 2001 C339/20; Case M.2638, *3i/Consors/100 World*, Commission Decision of December 10, 2001, O.J. 2002 C49/16; Case M.2609, *HP/Compaq*, Commission Decision of January 31, 2002, O.J. 2002 C39/23; Case M.2689, *3i/Dansk Kapitalanlaeg/Ibsen*, Commission Decision of January 31, 2002, O.J. 2002 C43/24; Case M.2734, *Sanmina-SCI/Alcatel*, Commission Decision of March 21, 2002, O.J. 2002 C91/7; Case M.2784, *Jabil/Alcatel*, Commission Decision of April 24, 2002, O.J. 2002 C108/8; and Case M.2790, *Siemens/First Sensor Technology*, Commission Decision of June 14, 2002, O.J. 2002 C147/21.

[16] *Alcatel/Telettra*, above, para.8-049 *et seq.*; Case M.468, *Siemens/Italtel*, Commission Decision of February 17, 1995, O.J. 1995 L161/27; and Case M.1440, *Lucent Technologies/Ascend Communication*, Commission Decision of April 6, 1999.

[17] Regulation 2658/00 of November 29, 2000, on the application of Art.81(3) of the EC Treaty to certain categories of specialization agreements, O.J. 2000 L304/3; and Regulation 2659/00 of November 29, 2000 on the application of Art.81(3) of the EC Treaty to certain categories of research and development agreements, O.J. 2000 L304/7.

[18] *Konsortium ECR 900*, above, para.8-282 *et seq.*; *STET, Italtel, AT&T-NSI*, above, para.8-288 *et seq.* (individual exemption).

[19] *Aérospatiale/Alcatel Espace*, above, para.8-304 *et seq.*

530

The Commission's positive attitude towards restructuring in this sector is also linked to the increasingly competitive nature of the equipment market. Standardisation and the Utilities Procurement Directive have contributed to the opening of national markets to competition, and the liberalisation of the telecommunications sector is leading to a worldwide market for telecommunications equipment. Furthermore, the demand for telecommunications equipment continues to be concentrated in the hands of a handful of operators with substantial bargaining power.

(d) The Commission's Practice in Relation to Broadcasting[20]

8–359 To date (*i.e.* June 2003), the Commission has authorised more than 50 merger joint ventures and alliances[21] in the broadcasting sector whilst it has prohibited six.[22] The Commission's

---

[20] For a comprehensive review of the competition issues raised by mergers and acquisitions in the broadcasting sector in the light of convergence, see OECD, *Regulation and Competition Issues in Broadcasting in the Light of Convergence*, DAFFE/CL(99)1.

[21] See, under Art.81 of the EC Treaty: *Auditel*, above, para.8–334 *et seq.*; *British Digital Broadcasting*, above, para.8–338 *et seq.*; *TPS*, above, para.8–342 *et seq.*; *British Interactive Broadcasting*, above, para.8–346 *et seq.* See, under the Merger Control Regulation, Case M.110, *ABC/Générale des Eaux/Canal+/W.H. Smith*, Commission Decision of September 10, 1991; Case M.176, *Sunrise*, Commission Decision of January 13, 1992; Case M.410, *Kirch/Richemont/Telepiù*, Commission Decision of August 2, 1994; Case M.0489, *Bertelsmann/News International/Vox*, Commission Decision of September 6, 1994; Case M.525, *Vox II*, Commission Decision of January 18, 1995; Case M.584, *Kirch/Richemont, Multichoice/Telepiù*, Commission Decision of May 5, 1995; Case M.566, *CLT/Disney/SuperRTL*, Commission Decision of May 17, 1995; Case M.655, *Canal+/UFA/MDO*, Commission Decision of November 13, 1995; Case M.810, *n-TV*, Commission Decision of September 16, 1996; Case *Bertelsmann/CLT*, above, para.8–183 *et seq.*; Case M.878, *RTL7*, Commission Decision of February 14, 1997; Case M.939, *BankAmerica/General Electric/Cableuropa*, Commission Decision of June 19, 1997; Case M.1022, *Cable i Televisio de Catalunya*, Commission Decision of January 28, 1998; Case M.1091, *Cableuropa/SpainCom/CTC*, Commission Decision of January 28, 1998; Case M.1148, *STET/GET/Madrid Cable*, Commission Decision of May 28, 1998; Case M.1251, *Particel International/Cableuropa*, Commission Decision of July 30, 1998; Case M.1574, *Kirch/Mediaset*, Commission Decision of August 3, 1999; *BSkyB/KirchPayTV*, above, para.8–195 *et seq.*; Case M.1889, *CLT-UFA/Canal+/Vox*, Commission Decision of March 21, 2000, O.J. 2000 C134/13; *Canal+/Lagardère/Canal Satellite*, above, para.8–201 *et seq.*; Case *Bertelsmann/GBL/Pearson TV*, above, para.8–206 *et seq.*; *Telecom Italia/News TV/Stream*, above, para.8–210 *et seq.*; *Telefónica/Endemol*, above, para.8–214 *et seq.*; *Blackstone/CDPQ/Kabel BW*, above, para.8–218 *et seq.*; *AOL/Time Warner*, above, para.8–223 *et seq.*; *Vivendi/Canal+/Seagram*, above, para.8–229 *et seq.*; Case M.2124, *ISP/ESPNS/Globosat - JV*, Commission Decision of December 4, 2000, O.J. 2001 C190/10; *Universal Studio Networks/De Facto 829 (NTL)/Studio Channel Limited*, above, para.8–233 *et seq.*; Case M.2259, *Terra/Amadeus/1Travel.com*, Commission Decision of January 17, 2001, O.J. 2001 C49/7; Case M.2336, *Thomson Multimedia/Technicolor*, Commission Decision of February 28, 2001, O.J. 2001 C206/8; *UGC/Liberty Media*, above, para.8–238 *et seq.*; Case M.2279, *Nortel/Mundinteractivos/Broad Media JV*, Commission Decision of April 25, 2001, O.J. 2001 C190/9; Case M.2407, *Bertelsmann/RTL Group*, Commission Decision of May 11, 2001, O.J. 2001 C291/5; Case M.2303, *Ciaoweb/We Cube*, Commission Decision of June 14, 2001, O.J. 2001 C179/29; *YLE/TDF/Digita JV*, above, para.8–242 *et seq.*; Case M.2471, *Accenture/Lagardere JV*, Commission Decision of July 26, 2001, O.J. 2001 C327/16; Case M.2352, *SWB/Stadtwerke Bielefeld JV*, Commission Decision of July 27, 2001, O.J. 2001 C321/9; Case M.2652, *Blackstone/CDPQ/Deteks NRW*, Commission Decision of November 23, 2001, O.J. 2001 C358/11; *Blackstone/CDPQ/Kabel BW*, above, para.8–218 *et seq.*; *Mezzo/Muzzik*, above, para.8–246 *et seq.*; *TPS*, above, para.8–250 *et seq.*; Case M.2766, *Vivendi Universal/Hachette/Multithematiques*, Commission Decision of May 3, 2002, O.J. 2002 C154/9; Case M.2723, *RTL/ProSiebenSat1/VG Media*, Commission Decision of May 21, 2002, O.J. 2002 C201/20; Case M.2883, *Bertelsmann/Zomba*, Commission Decision of September 2, 2002, O.J. 2002 C223/13; Case M.2876, *Newscorp/Telepiù*, Commission Decision of April 2, 2003.

more restrictive approach in this area is largely explained by the specific characteristics of the broadcasting sector. In contrast to the telecommunications sector, broadcasting is still largely regulated on a national basis, with limited Community legislation. The maintenance of national or regional regulatory restrictions on cross-border broadcasting activities (notwithstanding the Television Without Frontiers Directive), combined with language and cultural differences, continue to ensure that broadcasting markets are national in geographical scope. The lack of liberalisation and integration of the sector has contributed to the preservation of local monopolies, particularly in terrestrial broadcasting. The broadcasting sector is also characterised by technological evolution (*i.e.* digitalisation) which allows increased possibilities for offering programmes and new services (*e.g.* pay-TV, interactive services), but also requires substantial investment by broadcasters. This means that the economic possibilities for competition in some parts of the market, *e.g.* pay-TV, may be limited. In its assessment of co-operative and structural arrangements, the Commission must draw a difficult balance between the need for mergers and joint ventures to permit the emergence of enhanced and new services, and the concern that such transactions could lead to either the creation or strengthening of monopolies or dominant positions or the creation of high barriers to entry, thereby foreclosing market entry in the long term. Two types of transaction may be distinguished in the broadcasting sector: (i) horizontal transactions; and (ii) vertical transactions.

8–360 Horizontal transactions — Horizontal mergers, joint ventures and other co-operation arrangements between competitors on a specific market raise concerns when the parties to the transaction have a large combined market share.[23] When the parties are not yet active on the relevant market, or are so only marginally, the Commission will generally consider that the transaction is pro-competitive in so far as it permits the emergence of a new player that can act as a counterweight to an existing dominant undertaking[24] or facilitate the launching of new services.[25] Nevertheless, the Commission's approval may be conditional either on modifications to the transaction and/or on ongoing obligations to ensure the maintenance of effective competition.[26] Finally, if the transaction involves operators that are active on different geographic markets, the Commission will generally take a favourable view, given the national or regional scope of the

---

[22] Under Art.81 of the EC Treaty, Case *Screensport/EBU Members*, O.J. 1991 L63/32. Under the Merger Control Regulation, *MSG Media Service*, above, para.8–171 *et seq.*; *Nordic Satellite Distribution*, above, para.8–175 *et seq.*; *RTL/Veronica/Endemol (HMG)*, above, para.8–179 *et seq.*; *Bertelsmann/Kirch/Première*, above, para.8–187 *et seq.*; and *Deutsche Telekom/BetaResearch*, above, para.8–187 *et seq.*

[23] See Case *HMG*, above, para.8–179 *et seq.*, where the Commission prohibited a joint venture that involved two Dutch broadcasters, RTL and Veronica, and Endemol, the largest independent programme producer in the Netherlands. It subsequently authorised the transaction only after Endemol's withdrawal from the joint venture. See further Case *Screensport/EBU Members*, O.J. 1991 L63/32, where the Commission prohibited a joint venture involving Sky and Eurosport as it brought together two potential competitors for sports programmes that would have co-operated instead of competing. See also Case *AOL/Time Warner*, above, para.8–223 *et seq.*; and Case *Vivendi/Canal+/Seagram*, above, para.8–229 *et seq.*

[24] Case *British Digital Broadcasting*, above, para.8–338 *et seq.*; and Case *TPS + 7*, above, para.8–342 *et seq.*

[25] Case *British Interactive Broadcasting*, above, para.8–346 *et seq.*; and Case M.1969, *UTC/Honeywell/i2/My Aircraft.com*, Commission Decision of August 4, 2000.

[26] *E.g. British Interactive Broadcasting*, above, para.8–346 *et seq.*; *British Digital Broadcasting*, above, para.8–338 *et seq.*; *Vivendi/Canal+/Seagram*, above, para.8–229 *et seq.*; and *AOL/TimeWarner*, above, para.8–223 *et seq.*

market and the absence of overlap in the activities of the parties on their respective national markets.[27]

8–361 Vertical transactions — Vertical transactions are often more problematic than horizontal mergers in the broadcasting sector given the vertical nature of the supply chain in broadcasting (from programme production through to transmission, distribution and retail supply) and the fact that many leading broadcasters are vertically integrated. All the transactions that have been prohibited by the Commission had vertical aspects. Vertical transactions have generally involved integration between a broadcaster and a content provider,[28] between a broadcaster and an infrastructure provider[29] or between undertakings active at all these levels.[30] The key issue in each case has been the extent to which competitors to the parties involved have been active at both the content and the infrastructure levels, and the barriers to entry that would result if competitors have to enter the market on both levels at once. The Commission has thus analysed the position of the parties on each of the different markets concerned and checked whether there was a risk that the parties, owing to their strong position on the various markets, would have been able to leverage those positions in the entire supply chain so as to foreclose access to the markets by competitors. If the content provider or broadcaster is dominant, a competing broadcaster might be unable to offer a sufficient number of attractive programmes on the market in question. If the transmission operator (cable, terrestrial or satellite) is dominant, a competing broadcaster might be unable to find alternative infrastructure to transmit its programmes to viewers. For these reasons, a number of operations in this sector have been prohibited, or approved only subject to stringent conditions.

The Commission's major concerns regarding vertical mergers and joint ventures that bring together content and delivery systems under single ownership are: (i) ensuring third party access to infrastructure and content, for example as in *Vizzavi*[31] and *Vivendi/Canal + /Seagram*[32]; (ii) avoiding the creation or strengthening of a "gatekeeper" position, for example as in *Vizzavi*,[33] *AOL/Time Warner*[34] and *BSkyB/KirchPayTV*[35]; (iii) avoiding the leveraging of market power in one market into another, especially into new or emerging markets, for example as in *BSkyB/KirchPayTV*,[36] *AOL/Time Warner*[37] and *Vivendi/Canal + /Seagram*[38]; and (iv) avoiding the exploitation of network

---

[27] Case M.410, *Kirch/Richemont/Telepiù*, Commission Decision of August 2, 1994; *Bertelsmann/CLT*, above, para.8–183 *et seq.*; and *Bertelsmann/GBL/Pearson TV*, above, para.8–206 *et seq.*

[28] Cases *HMG*, above, para.8–179 *et seq.*; *Telefónica/Endemol*, above, para.8–214 *et seq.*; *Bertelsmann/GBL/Pearson TV*, above, para.8–206 *et seq.*; *Vivendi/Canal + /Seagram*, above, para.8–229 *et seq.*

[29] Cases *MSG Media Service*, above, para.8–171 *et seq.*; *Nordic Satellite Distribution*, above, para.8–175 *et seq.*; and *UGC/Liberty*, above, para.8–238 *et seq.*

[30] Cases *Bertelsmann/Kirch/Premiere*, above, para.8–187 *et seq.*; and *Deutsche Telekom/BetaResearch*, above, para.8–187 *et seq.*

[31] See above, para.8–138 *et seq.*

[32] See above, para.8–229 *et seq.*

[33] See above, para.8–138 *et seq.*

[34] See above, para.8–223 *et seq.*

[35] See above, para.8–196 *et seq.*

[36] *ibid.*

[37] See above, para.8–223 *et seq.*

[38] See above, para.8–229 *et seq.*

effects to the disadvantage of competitors and consumers, for example as in *Vizzavi*[39] and *AOL/Time Warner*.[40]

(e) The Commission's Practice in Relation to Converging Services, such as Interactive Services and the Internet

8–362 As telecommunications, broadcasting and information technologies have converged, and continue to do so, mergers and joint ventures will increasingly involve companies active in markets which are presently separate, but converging, and are therefore economically and technically linked. A good illustration of this trend was British Interactive Broadcasting, a joint venture for the provision of digital interactive services between BSkyB, a pay-TV supplier, British Telecommunications; a banking institution, Midland Bank and a technology provider, Matsushita.[41] This transaction raised a number of competition issues as a result of the convergence between the respective sectors of the parties involved, which threatened to eliminate competition on the UK markets for pay-TV and digital interactive services.[42] Such arrangements will very often raise issues of extension of market dominance in one market into separate but related markets. For example, the Commission expressed concerns that BSkyB, through the joint venture, would have been able to extend its dominant position on the UK pay-TV market into the emerging market for digital interactive services. Moreover, arrangements of this nature may have the effect of raising barriers to entry to insurmountable levels because new entrants may be forced to enter several markets at once, or at least to provide a broad range of services simultaneously.[43] The Commission is also concerned that mergers and joint ventures involving converging services may result in an ability to perform anti-competitive practices such as the bundling of services, discriminatory practices or cross-subsidisation. The Commission generally addresses these concerns by requiring undertakings from the parties as a condition for approval. In *British Interactive Broadcasting*, the Commission imposed a number of conditions in order to ensure that third party providers or interactive services had access, on fair and non-discriminatory conditions, to BiB's set-top boxes.[44] However, in some cases, the Commission has found that such conditions would not have been sufficient to resolve its "gatekeeper" and leveraging concerns.[45]

In reviewing the impact of transactions that involve converging sectors, the Commission is particularly vigilant in monitoring arrangements that could lead to the joint or co-ordinated provision of telecommunications and cable-TV networks. As indicated in its review under the competition rules of the joint provision of telecommunications and cable-TV networks,[46] the Commission is concerned that joint control or co-ordinated operation of both cable TV and telecommunications networks may prevent competition in services and infrastructure which is

---

[39] See above, para.8–138 *et seq.*
[40] See above, para.8–223 *et seq.*
[41] Case *British Interactive Broadcasting*, above, para.8–346 *et seq.*
[42] See Temple-Lang, "Media-multimedia and European Community Antitrust Law" *Fordham Corporate Law Institute* 1997, pp.439–440.
[43] See, *e.g. Bertelsmann/Kirch/Premiere*, above, para.8–187 *et seq.*
[44] See also *BSkyB/KirchPayTV*, above, para.8–196 *et seq.*
[45] See *Bertelsmann/Kirch/Premiere* and *Deutsche Telekom/BetaResearch*, above, para.8–187 *et seq.*
[46] O.J. 1998 L71/4.

necessary for the development of telecommunications and multi-media operations. For example, in *British Interactive Broadcasting*, the Commission found that BT's participation in the joint venture may have led to a reduced incentive in the short to medium term for it to invest in its local loop infrastructure to provide broadband services competing with those provided by BiB and the cable networks.[47] As a result, the Commission required BT to divest its interests in cable activities in the United Kingdom. Likewise, in *Telia/Telenor*, the Commission's approval of a merger between the incumbent telecommunications operators in Norway and Sweden was conditional on the divestiture of the parties' cable interests.[48]

8–363 When analysing recent mergers and joint ventures affecting emerging markets and innovative services, the Commission has recently taken an increasingly tough position in order to ensure the provision of an open infrastructure and to avoid the creation of bottlenecks, in particular by imposing remedies of a regulatory nature, such as open access obligations. Open access obligations have been applied by the Commission in relation to both networks (for example in *Vizzavi*)[49] and content (for example in *Vivendi/Canal+/Seagram*).[50] From a regulatory perspective, open access obligations are already imposed by Community law on providers of conditional access systems for digital television,[51] but not for conditional access systems for other services, nor on providers of television services with regard to the provision of TV-programming services (such as EPGs and APIs). Open access only results in access to the network capacity by the requesting provider. This capacity is useless in a digital environment, if the requesting provider is not also granted access to the end customer. For this reason, set-top boxes serve as a "gateway" to the customer. Providers of technical platforms are thus gatekeepers with whom third party service providers have to deal when trying to reach viewers.[52] In *BSkyB/KirchPayTV*, as a condition of its merger approval, the Commission required Kirch to implement in its d-box decoders the MHP interface, an API developed by the DVB Project and standardised by ETSI. However, the Commission fell short of also requiring Kirch to adopt a common interface (CI). Instead, it sought to achieve interoperability of the technical platforms through a commitment from Kirch to enter into simulcrypt agreements with other conditional access providers. The commitments given by Kirch provided for a dispute resolution system, to ensure that these agreements were entered into on fair and non-discriminatory terms. However, this condition failed to have its intended effect, since licensing

---

[47] See Case *British Interactive Broadcasting*, above, para.8–346 *et seq.*

[48] Above, para.8–097 *et seq.* See also *Telia/Sonera*, above, para.8–129 *et seq.*, where Telia was required to divest its cable television networks in Sweden in order to increase competition in local network infrastructure, to counteract the anti-competitive aspects of the merger.

[49] See above, para.8–138 *et seq.*

[50] See above, para.8–229 *et seq.*

[51] See Advanced TV Standards Directive and Art.6 of the Access Directive: see above, para.1–171 and 2–048 *et seq.*

[52] The interoperability of applications on set-top boxes can be achieved via common APIs. APIs serve as a binding link (middleware) between the hardware and the internal and external software of the platform. However, a common API does not prevent a platform operator from using proprietary conditional access systems. The interoperability of competing technical platforms can be achieved by using common interfaces (CIs) in conditional access systems. Interoperability (without a common API) between hardware and external software, and interoperability (without a CI) of competing platforms can be achieved only through licensing agreements between the gatekeeper and the requesting party.

proved to be too burdensome for third parties who also remained dependent on Kirch, who operated the conditional access technology but who was also a direct competitor in the pay-TV market of pay-TV operators that requested access to Kirch's d-boxes. No simulcrypt agreement was ever concluded. Because of the Commission's experience in *BSkyB/KirchPayTV*, parties to future transactions in the pay-TV sector may be required to adopt not only open APIs but also a common interface.[53] This is certainly true for the German Bundeskartellamt, which prohibited Liberty Media's attempt to acquire Deutsche Telekom's cable network, expressing concerns about the proprietary technology that Liberty Media intended to use and how it could have foreclosed access to the network for other broadcasters.[54]

[53] However, in *Newscorp/Telepiù*, above para.8–255 *et seq.*, the Commission again fell short of imposing a common interface.

[54] See above, para.8–218 *et seq.* See further Rosenthal, "Open Access from the EU Perspective" (2002/03) 7 *International Journal of Communications Law and Policy*, available at: *www.ijclp.org.*

Chapter IX

Interaction Between the Competition Rules and Sector-Specific Regulation

9–001 **Introduction** — To the extent that communications activities are subject to both specific regulation and competition rules, the issue arises as to the relationship and interaction between these different sets of rules.[1] From a conceptual perspective, the question is whether the two sets of rules have genuinely different purposes or whether they should converge into a single set of rules in light of recent changes in the markets concerned. From a practical point of view, different authorities are often responsible for monitoring compliance with the two types of rules, leading to a risk of unnecessary duplication of procedures and wastage of time and money for both the regulators and businesses concerned, if the activities of the different bodies involved are not appropriately co-ordinated.[2] This chapter reviews the rather complex relationship between sector-specific regulation and competition rules. It looks at the differences in origin and objectives of the two sets of rules, and analyses current trends of convergence and divergence between these rules at the EU and Member State levels. Concrete examples of the interaction between the different bodies of rules are examined.

A. Sector-Specific Regulation and Competition Rules have a Different Origin but Sometimes Complementary Objectives

9–002 The EC competition rules are rules of general application aimed at protecting consumer interests by prohibiting firms from reducing competition through collusion, from creating or strengthening dominant position (which can be equated to market power) or from the abuse of such a dominant position. The application of the competition rules is basically the result of a long, historic process of economic liberalisation. This process has led to the notion that economic

---

[1] See Grewlich, "Cyberspace: sector-specific regulation and competition rules in European Telecommunications" [1999] 36 C.M.L.R. 937–969.

[2] On the issue resulting from the co-existence of sector-specific regulation in the broadcasting and telecommunications sectors in the context of convergence under the previous sector-specific regulatory framework, see Garzaniti, *Telecommunications, Broadcasting and the Internet: E.U. Competition Law and Regulation* (Sweet & Maxwell, 1st ed., 2000), pp.104–106.

freedom is a pre-existing fundamental right, which the state can only limit by way of general laws pursuing legitimate interests in a proportionate way. Therefore, rules protecting competition apply *ex post* to market conduct, with the exception of merger control, where *ex ante* regulation is proportionate, owing to the irreparable harm to competition that certain mergers can cause. Because of their origin and their conceptual basis, competition rules can be characterised as "low-level" or "soft" regulation.

In contrast, sector-specific regulation seeks to implement certain defined policy goals including, but also exceeding to a certain extent, the notion of effective competition. It can therefore, in one respect, be characterised as more interventionist than competition law. However, in regulated markets, a more intensive degree of intervention may be generally desirable because of the specific characteristics of such markets. Typically, sector-specific regulation is applied in sectors of the economy that for many years were considered to be too politically or economically sensitive[3] to be opened to the free market and thus to competition. Telecommunications services were initially monopoly services provided by the state itself under the regime of administrative law. Even after telecommunications markets were liberalised, the notion prevailed that competition law alone would not guarantee either the seamless continuation of all welfare elements connected to the former state service or effective competition whilst former monopolists could exercise market power.[4] Two types of sector-specific regulation may be distinguished, both of which originate from that fact that the communications sector was formerly — and in some respects still is[5] — an area of state administration.

9–003   On the one hand, certain rules aim at protecting specific public interest objectives such as universal service, affordable pricing, protection of privacy, safety, protection of the environment, protection of media pluralism and diversity, and the protection of minors. These rules promote social justice, consumer or environmental interests that are non-economic in nature, *i.e.* typical general public interests. In that sense, because they pursue public policy objectives, these rules have little in common with competition rules and are applied somewhat independently of competition law.[6]

---

[3] In traditional (European) thinking, control over telecommunications meant control over a strategic infrastructure. The internet was only "privatised" once its military use was no longer prevalent (see para.3–001 *et seq.*). Control over (electronic) media implied control over public opinion. Therefore, a regime of economic freedom of private operators was perceived as being inappropriate for these services, leading either to state provision or to state regulation.

[4] Arguments have been made that certain welfare goals are not being delivered by liberalisation (or at least not fast enough), and that they must be positively secured or stimulated at least temporarily. Examples include the protection of the environment, sufficient availability of infrastructure resources at affordable prices, equal access for all members of society to certain services but also effective competition itself.

[5] See, *e.g.* the system of public broadcasting in Germany. Although the public broadcasters are legally free from state influence, their supervisory and management bodies are staffed with politicians and other protectors of the public interest (such as unions and other "socially relevant groups") see von Bonin, "Die Kontrolle digitaler Kommunikationsinhalte" (2000), p.143.

[6] Those public interests may often justify the exemption of an undertaking from the application of competition law rules. For example, Art.86(2) of the EC Treaty declares that the competition rules are inapplicable to the extent that public undertakings and other undertakings with special or exclusive rights carry out services of economic interest and the application of the competition rules would prevent them carrying out their entrusted tasks: see para.4–015; Art.21(3) of the Merger Control Regulation provides that the exclusive jurisdiction of the Commission to review concentrations with a Community dimension is without

On the other hand, another type of sector-specific regulation involves *ex ante* regulation of matters such as price control and network access obligations (*e.g.* interconnection and access to conditional access systems). Whilst they may be based on social policy objectives, these rules have a specific economic nature. They have been adopted on the assumption that market forces alone, even under the threat of *ex post* application of competition rules, would not suffice, at least not in the short term, to achieve a fully competitive market given that at liberalisation, incumbent operators had monopoly or very strong market positions. In this sense, sector-specific rules complement the competition rules.

9–004 Accordingly, sector-specific regulation and competition rules represent different sets of rules which apply independently of each other, with specific objectives and enforcement methods.[7] Operators must observe both sector-specific regulation and competition rules at both the EU and Member State levels. EU sector-specific directives must be implemented into Member States' laws and therefore have a significant impact on the content of the regulation of the telecommunications and broadcasting sectors in the Member States. EU sector-specific regulations have direct applicability in the Member States, so also influence national regulatory systems. This impact, however, is more significant in the telecommunications sector than in the media sector, because of the greater level of EU-wide harmonisation achieved so far in the telecommunications sector. Operators who are active in the media sector often face additional unharmonised national rules of the Member States, which may restrict inter-state trade in services. It must be noted that in a number of Member States, national sector-specific laws implementing the EU (tele)communications directives overlap to a certain extent with truly national media rules. This overlap leads to a considerable degree of uncertainty for businesses operating in the media sector in these countries.[8] This leads to the following structure:

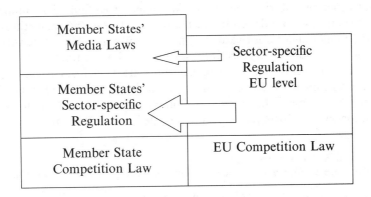

prejudice to the right of the Member States to take measures under national law to protect their legitimate interests, such as the plurality of the media: see para.8–036.

[7] Nihoul, "Convergence in European Telecommunications: A Case Study on the Relationship Between Regulation and Competition (Law)" (1998/99) 2 *International Journal of Communications Law and Policy.* Nihoul takes the view that both sets of rules rely to a large extent on common principles and address identical problems with similar solutions. See also OECD, *Relationship Between Regulators and Competition Authorities*, DAFFE/CLP(99)8, Competition Policy Roundtables.

[8] See von Bonin, "Kabelnetze und Europäische Regulierung" (2002) K&R 565.

The following sections analyse the impact of the adoption of a competition law approach to regulation in the New Regulatory Framework and highlight practical points of interaction between the competition rules and sector-specific regulation, as regards substance, procedure and enforcement.

B. The Adoption of a Competition Law Approach in the New Regulatory Framework

9–005 Substantive issues — The New Regulatory Framework has brought about a new relationship between EU competition rules and EU sector-specific regulation by aligning the regulatory concept of "significant market power", the basic substantive threshold for regulatory intervention in the telecommunications markets, with the competition law concept of "dominance".[9] SMP is the key concept used to identify and designate those operators on whom national regulatory authorities can impose sector-specific obligations to ensure that they cannot unfairly exploit or abuse their market power in the absence of effective competition. The new definition of SMP is based on the competition law concept of market dominance that is applied under Article 82 of the EC Treaty, as interpreted by the Commission and the Community courts.[10] Under Article 14 of the Framework Directive, an undertaking will be deemed to have SMP if, either individually or jointly with others, it enjoys a position equivalent to dominance, that is to say a position of economic strength affording it the power to behave to an appreciable extent independently of competitors, customers and ultimately consumers. This definition encompasses the concepts of single firm and collective dominance, as well as the leveraging of market power on one market onto closely related markets.[11] The consequences of this change are difficult to predict in detail. Certain risks should briefly be mentioned here.

9–006 *Market definition* – Market definition is key in making a finding of dominance on a given market and can in some cases pre-determine such a finding. Under the competition rules, markets may be defined differently under a forward-looking analysis within the framework of the Merger Control Regulation than under a retrospective assessment within the framework of an Article 81 or 82 investigation.[12] It is presently unclear whether the markets defined by NRAs fulfilling their obligations under the Framework Directive and in accordance with the SMP Guidelines[13] will be entirely consistent with those defined by the Commission and the Community courts when applying competition law.[14] Moreover, it is not excluded that NRAs may diverge from market

---

[9] See above, paras 1–018, 1–031 *et seq.*

[10] See, in particular, Case 27/76, *United Brands v Commission* [1978] E.C.R. 207. See generally para.6–013 *et seq.*, above.

[11] Framework Directive, para.1–009, n.25, Art.14(3), states that

> "where an undertaking has significant market power on a specific market, it may also be deemed to have significant market power on a closely related market, where the links between the two markets are such as to allow the market power held in one market to be leveraged into the other market, thereby strengthening the market power of the undertaking".

For a comprehensive analysis of this provision, see para.1–038.

[12] See para.5–001.

[13] Cited at para.1–012, n.35.

[14] According to para.24 *et seq.* of the SMP Guidelines (*ibid.*), the presumption is that markets will be defined for the purposes of an SMP analysis in line with markets defined under the Merger Control Regulation. Both

definitions previously made by national competition authorities.[15] The Commission has published a Recommendation on Relevant Product and Service Markets, setting out 18 relevant markets that NRAs are recommended to use in determining if operators have SMP.[16]

9–007 *Concept of dominance* — Although Article 14(2) of the Framework Directive defines an undertaking with SMP as one which enjoys a "position equivalent to dominance" and uses exactly the same words that the Court of Justice has used when defining "dominance" under Article 82 of the EC Treaty,[17] the SMP Guidelines state that

> "the designation of an undertaking as having SMP [. . .] does not automatically imply that this undertaking is also dominant for the purposes of Article 82 of the EC Treaty [. . .]".[18]

It remains to be seen to what extent this difference will actually materialise. It has been argued[19] that the SMP mechanism introduced by the Framework Directive may lead to the use of narrower market definitions and thereby to more distinct product and services markets and thus to more firms with positions equivalent to dominance for the purposes of regulatory law and dominant positions for the purposes of competition law. This is based on the assumption that NRAs, who use market definition as the basis for future market regulation, will be very cautious and thus have a tendency to define narrower markets. In doing so, regulators would give themselves the possibility of designating more undertakings as having SMP and thus be able to impose specific regulatory obligations on them if they were to deem it necessary. As the designation of SMP involves a finding that a certain undertaking has a position equivalent to dominance, and as there is no substantive difference between the concept of dominance under the regime of SMP under the Framework Directive and under Article 82 of the EC Treaty and the EC merger regulation, it is argued that this approach would have the effect of making more undertakings potentially subject to an infringement of Article 82 of the EC Treaty and could have repercussions on the control of mergers.

9–008 *Collective dominance* — Annex II to the Framework Directive sets out the "check-list" that the Commission uses to determine whether markets have a structure that renders them conducive to co-ordinated effects. The SMP Guidelines address this issue and give guidance on how NRAs must analyse collective dominance.[20] The definition and analysis of collective dominance is

are said to take a forward-looking approach. However, NRAs have commented that, in order to assess whether operators have SMP, they will look rather cautiously at the present structural situation and not adopt too much of a forward-looking approach: see Hocepied, "The New Regulatory Framework for Electronic Communications: From Sector-Specific Regulation to Competition Law", Paper for IBA/ABA Conference "Communications and Competition: Developments at the Crossroads" on May 20, 2002, Washington D.C.

[15] For example, the German NRA (RegTP) has adopted a different market definition with respect to broadband cable networks than the Bundeskartellamt did in its decision B7-168/00, *Liberty Media/Deutsche Telekom*.

[16] Cited at para.1–012, n.36, and discussed at para.1–020 *et seq.* However, NRAs are not required to follow the recommendation, as it does not have binding legal effect, although they will have to justify regulating different markets in the light of national circumstances. See also Framework Directive, para.1–009, n.25, Arts 7(4) and 15(3), discussed at para.1–047 *et seq.*, n.10, above.

[17] Case 27/76, *United Brands v Commission* [1978] E.C.R. 207.

[18] SMP Guidelines, para.1–012, n.35, para.30.

[19] See Case Associates, *Regulating with Competition Law*, October 2001.

[20] SMP Guidelines, para.1–012, n.35, paras 86–106.

one of the most disputed subjects in European competition law, especially with respect to mergers. In its *Airtours* judgment[21] the Court of First Instance has, according to commentators, blocked attempts by the Commission to enlarge the meaning and economic scope of the principle of "collective dominance".[22]

9–009 Procedural issues — Different mechanisms have been put in place to ensure co-operation between the EU Commission and NRAs on the one hand, and between NRAs and national competition authorities on the other hand.[23]

9–010 *The role of NRAs* — The Commission acknowledges that the application of the EC Treaty's competition rules is not sufficient to remedy all the various problems in the telecommunications sector. As a result of sector-specific regulation, NRAs have a wide and far-reaching role in the regulation of the sector. NRAs (or national competition authorities) may not approve any practice or agreement that is contrary to the Community's competition rules.[24] The New Regulatory Framework strengthens the role of NRAs, but at the same time provides the Commission with considerable power to supervise and co-ordinate the activities of the NRAs.[25] There is in fact some scope to argue that NRAs will merely be executing Community law as a network of Commission "outposts" as all deviations from the guiding principles as defined by the Commission must be justified. It remains to be seen whether the consultation and transparency mechanisms set forth in the New Regulatory Framework will have this effect and indeed produce uniform application of the New Regulatory Framework across Europe. However, under the new Regulation 1/2003, national competition authorities will play a much more prominent role in the enforcement of competition rules.

9–011 *Allocation of jurisdiction and co-operation between competition authorities and sector-specific regulators at national level* — The structure of the supervision and regulation of communications and media operators varies between the different Member States. Independent sector-specific regulators have been created in all Member States. In most cases, separate regulatory authorities have responsibility for telecommunications and broadcasting regulation.[26] Competition

---

[21] Case T–342/99, *Airtours v Commission* [2002] E.C.R. 2585. On collective dominance, generally see para.6–025, above.

[22] See Montag and von Bonin, "Collective Dominance in Merger Cases after Airtours", Collection of Papers to the IBA EC Merger Control Conference on November 7 and 8, 2002, to be published.

[23] The enforcement of EC competition law by Member States' competition authorities and national courts will play a more important role after the modernisation of Regulation 17/62 has been implemented with the entry into force of Regulation 1/2003 on May 1, 2004: see above, para.4–011.

[24] Case 66/86, *Ahmeed Saeed Flugreisen* [1989] E.C.R. 803.

[25] See above, para.1–044 *et seq.*

[26] With respect to the regulation of telecommunications and media, there is a trend towards convergence in some Member States as well as a trend towards divergence between different Member States. In Italy and Spain, a single regulatory authority has responsibility for both telecommunications and broadcasting regulation. In the United Kingdom, the government is continuing the process of creating an Office of Communications (OFCOM), which will regulate the converging communications sectors. OFCOM will merge the functions of five existing regulatory bodies: the Independent Television Commission, the Broadcasting Standards Commission, OFTEL, the Radio Authority and the Radio Communications Agency. In a number of federal states (*e.g.* Belgium and Germany), media regulation is a regional or state matter and regulatory competence is thus shared between a number of different regional authorities. In Germany there is one

enforcement is shared between the Commission, national competition authorities, national courts, and in some Member States national regulatory authorities.[27] The necessity of maintaining a wide range of different authorities has been raised, as has the issue of the allocation of responsibility among them. In so far as the application of these different rules requires specific skills, which it would not be easy (or advisable) to centralise in a single body, it is considered that the maintenance of a system of separate sector-specific regulators and competition enforcement agencies is the preferable option, provided that adequate co-operation mechanisms are put in place to ensure the coherent application of both sets of rules.[28] Member States will have to develop mechanisms to ensure effective co-operation between NRAs and national competition authorities in order to ensure consistent market definitions and enforcement action.[29] However, it could also be argued that as regulatory law increasingly uses competition law concepts and as markets become increasingly competitive thereby levering the need for sector-specific legislation, it would be appropriate to have a single body responsible both for competition law enforcement and the enforcement of sector-specific rules.[30]

C. Practical Examples of Interaction Between Competition Law and Sector-Specific Regulation

Sector-specific regulation and competition rules complement each other to attain the objective of market liberalisation and the maintenance of effective competition. Set out below are some examples of circumstances in which sector-specific regulation and competition rules interact and/or overlap and where a coherent interpretation and application of the applicable rules is needed. This interaction takes place at the substantive, procedural and enforcement levels.

9–012 Substantive issues — Competition law and sector-specific regulation interact in a number of substantive matters, including interconnection charges, tariff regulations, access to essential facilities and the use of competition law as an instrument of regulation.

9–013 *Interconnection charges* — Under the competition rules, it is established that discrimination does not amount to the abuse of a dominant position within the meaning of Article 82 if there is an objective reason to justify the difference of treatment.[31] The Access Directive implements

---

telecommunications regulator, RegTP. Owing to the allocation of legislative competences in the federal structure of Germany, there are in addition 15 regional media authorities, which enforce the rules on the regulation of broadcast content, the rules on access to digital services contained in the media laws of the various Länder, as well as the Broadcasting State Treaty between the Länder. Moreover, there is a third type of authority charged with the enforcement of the so-called media concentration rules: the *Kommission zur Ermittlung der Konzentration im Medienbereich* monitors the audience shares of the large broadcasting groups and has the right to impose remedies (such as the broadcasting of third-party content) according to the Broadcasting State Treaty.

[27] For example, in the UK OFTEL, the telecommunications regulator can apply the Competition Act 1998 to companies active in the telecommunications sector.

[28] OECD, above n.7 in this chapter.

[29] See also above, para.9–006, and in particular, n.15.

[30] For example, in the Netherlands, plans have been announced to merge the competition authority, NMa, and the telecommunications and postal services regulator, OPTA.

[31] See above, para.6–038.

this principle in relation to interconnection pricing by stating that NRAs can oblige operators to offer third parties interconnection on the same conditions "in equivalent circumstances" as they provide interconnection to their own businesses or those of affiliates.[32] The Directive therefore requires NRAs to ensure that organisations providing access do not discriminate in favour of services of their own business units or those of subsidiaries or partners. The implementation of sector-specific regulation in the area of interconnection therefore results in the direct application of competition rules principles. NRAs must therefore ensure that they follow an approach that is consistent with that applied by competition authorities. Under competition rules, the Commission has taken up cases involving alleged discrimination of mobile operators refusing to interconnect directly to any fixed line network except the one of their parent companies.[33]

9–014 *Tariff regulation* — The rules of the New Regulatory Framework include a number of specific measures to permit the regulation of the prices of incumbent and other telecommunications operators, should they be designated with SMP. In particular, the tariffs of operators that have been designated with SMP must be non-discriminatory, unbundled, cost-based and transparent.[34] Likewise, Article 6 of the Access Directive requires operators of digital conditional access services to offer their services to all broadcasters on a fair, reasonable and non-discriminatory basis. In certain aspects (*i.e.* cost-orientation, transparency), this pricing regulation is more specific, and may go somewhat further, than the requirements of competition law. However, in other aspects, these specific rules regulate matters that have traditionally fallen within the scope of the competition rules (*i.e.* prohibition on bundling, discrimination and cross-subsidisation). In this respect, sector-specific rules refer specifically to the need for NRAs to interpret these concepts in light of the competition rules.[35] Likewise, national authorities in charge of monitoring compliance with conditional access regulation must apply the rules of the Access Directive in a manner consistent with competition rules.

9–015 *Access to "essential facilities" and sector-specific regulation* — NRAs have the primary responsibility to deal with network access issues under the New Regulatory Framework. Indeed, a number of problems that could be addressed by the application of the competition rules, and in particular the "essential facilities" doctrine applied under Article 82, are governed by sector-specific regulation (*e.g.* interconnection obligations and access to conditional access systems for digital television).[36] This is not to say, however, that the essential facilities doctrine no longer has a role to play in the telecommunications sector. First, as indicated, NRAs are required to apply the competition rules, and their implementation of access regulation must be consistent with the principles established by the Commission and the Court of Justice in relation to access to essential facilities under Article 82 of the EC Treaty. Second, the scope of the application of competition rules is broader than that of the sector-specific rules.[37] Third, in so far as the competition rules

---

[32] Access Directive, para.1–011, n.29, Art.10(2); Liberalisation Directive, para.1–012, n.33: for a discussion of these provisions, see paras 1–058 and 1–153.

[33] See *e.g.* Commission Press Release IP/02/483 of March 27, 2002 concerning the Statement of Objections sent to KPN for an alleged abuse of its dominant position on the fixed-to-mobile termination calls market.

[34] See above, para.1–178 *et seq.*

[35] Access Directive, para.1–011, n.29, Recitals 5 and 6; see also para.1–15, above.

[36] See above, para.6–023.

[37] This has been indicated with respect to the essential facilities doctrine above, see para.6–044 *et seq.*

apply in parallel with sector-specific regulation, companies seeking access may have the possibility of relying on the essential facilities doctrine under competition law in the event of deficient or unsatisfactory implementation of the sector-specific rules by NRAs.

9–016 *Competition rules as an instrument of regulation* — Competition law may be, and in practice has constantly been, used as an instrument to regulate the market, as either an alternative or a complement to sector-specific regulation. In particular, this has been the case when the Commission has made its approval of a concentration under the Merger Control Regulation or the exemption of a transaction reviewed under Article 81 conditional upon implementation of specific conditions or undertakings given by the parties. Often, these measures will have a permanent impact on the structure of the market, which would pre-empt the subsequent adoption of sector-specific regulation.[38] For example, when the Commission made its approval of the British Interactive Broadcasting joint venture conditional on BT divesting its cable interests, the Commission made a clear policy choice in favour of the creation of competition in local network infrastructure.[39] Likewise, the Commission has made the granting of individual exemptions conditional upon accounting separation, non-discrimination and unbundling requirements,[40] which have been subsequently incorporated into sector-specific regulation.

Cases where the Commission has sought the implementation of regulatory goals by way of conditions imposed on clearances of concentrations under the Merger Control Regulation have included: *Telia/Telenor* (divestiture of cable assets, local loop unbundling and granting of access to the local loop),[41] *Vodafone Airtouch/Mannesmann* (third parties' non-discriminatory access to roaming services),[42] and *Vodafone/Vivendi/Canal+* (granting rival internet portals equal access to parent companies' set-top boxes and mobile handsets).[43] Looking at more recent Commission decisions, it is apparent that the Commission has been following a truly regulatory strategy, which goes beyond remedying competition concerns in the individual case at hand. For example, after requiring the parties to grant access to the local loop infrastructure in *Telia/Telenor*, the Commission realised when reviewing *Telia/Sonera*[44] that the adoption of sector-specific regulation requiring local loop unbundling had not produced the desired results for competition in local loop infrastructure and services using that infrastructure. Therefore, it made its approval of the merger conditional upon Telia and Sonera operating their fixed networks (including the local loop) and their retail services businesses using these networks through separate legal entities.[45] The series of merger cases involving Vodafone over the last few years is also interesting in this respect. In *Vodafone Airtouch/Mannesmann*, the Commission made its approval conditional upon non-discriminatory third party access by competitors to Vodafone's pan-European mobile network

---

[38] See Larouche, para.1–001, n.1, pp.240–242.
[39] *British Interactive Broadcasting*, discussed above at para.8–346 *et seq.*
[40] See, *e.g. Atlas*, para.8–255; *Phoenix/GlobalOne*, para.8–269; and *Unisource/Uniworld*, para.8–274 *et seq.*
[41] *Telia/Telenor*, para.8–097 *et seq.*; see para.8–142: see 382 *et seq.*
[42] Case M.1795, *Vodafone Airtouch/Mannesmann*, para.8–142, para.59 and Annex.
[43] Case JV.48, *Vodafone/Vivendi/Canal+* *(Vizzavi)*, above, para.8–138; see also Commission Press Release IP/00/821 of July 24, 2000.
[44] *Telia/Sonera*, above, para.8–129 *et seq.*
[45] *ibid.*, para.119.

for a period of three years in order to protect competition in the emerging market for seamless pan-European mobile services. In both *Vodafone/Eircell*[46] and *Vodafone/Airtel*,[47] the Commission expressly referred to the commitments given by Vodafone in the *Vodafone Airtouch/Mannesmann* case and stated that the continued application of these commitments would remedy the competition concerns that arose in the acquisition of Eircell and the acquisition of sole control of Airtel. This seems a good example of a remedy in a merger case having equivalent effect to general sector-specific regulation. It could be argued that, by using the Merger Control Regulation to regulate the communications markets in the same or a similar manner as general sector-specific directives would, the Commission is short-cutting the lengthy and cumbersome legislative process that must be followed to adopt sector-specific directives on these markets and the involvement of other institutions such as the Council and the Parliament in this process. The question remains open as to whether the Commission's approach could be challenged in this regard as, arguably, exceeding its powers.

9–017 Procedural issues — As well as the substantive interaction between competition law and sector-specific regulation identified above, there are also a number of interactions between them at a procedural level.

9–018 *Complaints* — The Commission has indicated that, in applying its powers under EC competition law, it intends to concentrate only on those cases having political, economic or legal significance for the Community and to leave cases lacking a Community interest to national authorities.[48] In particular, in order to avoid unnecessary parallel proceedings, the Commission has indicated that, once a matter is pending before an NRA, the Commission will normally not pursue any investigation of a complaint under Articles 81 and 82 relating to the same matter.[49] However, if the matter has not been resolved by the NRA within six months, the Commission has stated that it would, in principle, begin an investigation of the case after consultation and in co-operation with the NRA concerned. It remains to be seen how this procedure will be influenced by the consultation and veto mechanisms laid down by Articles 6 and 7 of the Framework Directive.[50]

9–019 *Evidence of pricing abuses* — In order to establish evidence of pricing abuses (*e.g.* cross-subsidisation, excessive or predatory pricing) that may infringe Article 82, competition authorities may base their cost analysis on the sector-specific measures aimed at improving the transparency of the accounting practices of dominant operators, including the relevant method of calculating and

---

[46] Case M.2305, *Vodafone Group plc/Eircell*, above, para.8–150 *et seq.*, para.20.

[47] Case M.2469, *Vodafone/Airtel*, para.8–042 *et seq.*, para.19.

[48] See Access Notice, O.J. 1998 C265/2, para.18; Commission Notice on co-operation between national courts and the Commission in applying Articles 85 and 86 of the EC Treaty, O.J. 1993 C39/6, at para.14; and Commission Notice on co-operation between national competition authorities and the Commission, O.J. 1997 C313/3. The Court of First Instance has upheld this approach: Cases T–24 and 28/90, *Automec v Commission* [1992] II E.C.R. 2223. The new Regulation 1/2003 will fully implement this approach.

[49] For example, the Commission suspended its 1998 investigation of Deutsche Telekom's pricing practices in light of parallel proceedings before the German NRA, Reg.TP. Similarly, in its 1998 investigation of mobile termination charges, it did not proceed with an investigation into two UK operators (Cellnet and Vodafone), as the UK Monopolies and Mergers Commission was already reviewing these charges, following a reference made by the UK regulator OFTEL as part of its tariff review process.

[50] See para.1–044 *et seq.*

allocating work. The implementation of sector-specific regulation thereby becomes a tool for improving enforcement of the competition rules.

9–020 *Fines* — Infringement of the EC Treaty's competition rules can, and usually does, result in the imposition of substantial fines. When agreements have been notified to the Commission pursuant to Regulation 17/62, in principle no fine may be imposed on the businesses concerned for the period after notification, although this immunity can be withdrawn in some cases. This protection will, formally, no longer be available under the new Regulation 1/2003. In principle, notification of an agreement to an NRA does not give immunity from fines for an infringement of the competition rules of the EC Treaty. The Commission has, however, indicated that it does not intend to impose fines in relation to agreements that it ultimately finds to be anti-competitive, if the agreements in question have been notified to an NRA.[51] This policy does not apply to practices or agreements amounting to an abuse of dominant position contrary to Article 82, nor to a serious breach of Article 81 (*e.g.* price-fixing).

9–021 *The competition assessment of transactions in light of sector-specific regulatory framework* — It is interesting to note that in its assessment of strategic alliances and mergers in the telecommunications sector, the Commission has taken into account the efficiency of the national regulatory framework in preventing anti-competitive behaviour that would occur as a result of a joint venture or merger. For example, in *Atlas*[52] the Commission imposed conditions on the parties to prevent undue discrimination and cross-subsidisation between the parent companies and the joint venture as a result of the transaction. By contrast, it found that the efficiency of the UK regulatory regime would have prevented any such risks of anti-competitive conduct in the *BT/MCI* case.[53] In *Telia/Telenor*, the Commission found that the sector-specific regulatory regimes in place in Sweden and Norway at the time were inadequate to prevent anti-competitive conduct by the merged entity, which justified the imposition of remedies of a regulatory nature (*i.e.* local loop unbundling) to compensate for the perceived shortcomings of sector-specific regulation in the two countries.[54] In *Telia/Sonera*, the Commission appeared to take the view that both the *ex post* nature of regulation in Finland and Sweden and the Community's sector-specific regulatory regime (which required accounting separation but not structural separation of undertakings with SMP) were inadequate to prevent anti-competitive conduct that could have arisen due to the vertical effects of the merger. The Commission therefore imposed conditions requiring the legal separation of the different fixed and mobile network and service businesses of the parties in Sweden and Finland, in addition to more "traditional" divestment conditions.[55]

D. Some Considerations Regarding the Relationship Between Sector-Specific Regulation and the Competition Rules

The issue of the relationship between sector-specific regulation and the competition rules in the telecommunications sector and other network industries has been extensively evidenced and

[51] Access Notice, para.9–018, n.48, para.37.
[52] *Atlas*, para.8–269 *et seq.*
[53] *BT/MCI*, para.8–264 *et seq.*
[54] *Telia/Telenor*, para.8–097 *et seq.*
[55] *Telia/Sonera*, para.8–129 *et seq.*

commented on.[56] Only a few thoughts are provided here on this subject, which continues to give rise to intensive debate in the context of convergence, including after the adoption of the New Regulatory Framework.

9–022   *Duality of rules* — In so far as the telecommunications and broadcasting sectors are being liberalised and gradually opened to competition, the question arises whether it is appropriate to maintain sector-specific regulation in addition to a case-by-case application of the competition rules. The issue is particularly relevant in the context of convergence where the telecommunications and broadcasting markets, which historically have been highly regulated, are converging with the information technology sector, which has been largely unregulated. The New Regulatory Framework recognises this question by requiring a periodic review of the market conditions in the sector. When the markets have become competitive, economic regulation must be phased out to the maximum extent possible, with the result that competition rules would be the only remaining tool to regulate competitive markets (the so-called "sunset-clause").[57] However, the New Regulatory Framework does not address the issue of harmonisation of national regulation in the broadcast media. In particular, participants on these markets will continue to find national regulatory traditions onerous when extending their businesses beyond a Member State's borders. This asymmetry in the degree of harmonisation of communications services and activities is politically motivated, as Member States are reluctant to transfer powers to the Community in what they consider to be culturally and politically sensitive media markets.[58]

9–023   *Need to maintain regulation to protect public interest objectives* — Specific regulatory provisions may need to be maintained in so far as they pursue public interest objectives (*e.g.* the protection of minors, media pluralism and diversity, the environment, the security of users, and ensuring affordable pricing of, and universal access to, communications services). As many of these questions are non-economic in nature, their protection cannot be fully achieved by application of the competition rules.[59] In this sense, there is not necessarily a dichotomy between the policies of the development and achievement of open competitive markets and securing public interest objectives, provided that sector-specific regulation is applied in a proportionate manner. For example, in a converging environment, it may be disproportionate to impose on one-to-one communications (*e.g.* video-on-demand) the same level of content regulation that is imposed upon traditional broadcasts. The pervasiveness of the transmission medium should be taken into account and regulation should

---

[56] OECD, para.9–004, n.7; Nihoul, para.9–002, n.7; Blackman and Nihoul, "Convergence Between Telecommunications and Other Media: How Should Regulation Adapt?" *Telecommunications Policy* 22:3 Special issue; Clemens, "The Impact of Convergence on Regulatory Policy in Europe" *Telecommunications Policy* 22:3 Special issue; and Sauter, "The System of Open Network Provision Legislation and the Future of European Telecommunications" in *The Future of EC Telecommunications Law* (Scott and Audéoud ed., Bundesanzeiger, Köln), p.105.

[57] See above, para.9–004, para.1–009 *et seq.*

[58] In some Member States (*e.g.* Germany and Belgium) such transfer would require the consent of regional entities, which is highly unlikely to be obtained.

[59] The extent to which the application of competition rules alone can contribute to the achievement of specific public interest objectives is not easy to determine on an *ex ante* basis. For example, in the telecommunications sector, operators may have an economic incentive to provide universal service, notwithstanding any regulatory obligations to do so, but there is no way of guaranteeing this.

be graduated accordingly.[60] In this context, self-regulation can play an important role in achieving a balance between establishing competitive markets and safeguarding public interest objectives, in particular with regard to content (*e.g.* rules on the protection of minors and human dignity, advertising standards and programme quality).[61] This is very much the approach that has been followed so far in the regulation (or lack of it) of internet-based activities.[62]

9–024 *Need to maintain transitional regulation until effective competition is established* — In the EU, as in many other jurisdictions that have liberalised their telecommunications sector, the peculiar structure of the market (*i.e.* an incumbent dominant operator, high costs of entry and relatively low marginal costs) has required the adoption of specific regulation in order both to foster competition and to constrain the exercise of incumbent operators' market power that could both exploit customers and prevent effective competition from emerging.[63] *Ex ante* rules are therefore considered to be required, at least in the short to medium term, to ensure efficient and timely access to networks or other facilities that would otherwise constitute "bottlenecks" for market entry, and to control tariffs for services that are not subject to effective competition. The application of the competition rules alone, because they essentially apply *ex post* after conduct has taken place, are not adequate to achieve these objectives. Sector-specific regulation provides at least a degree of legal certainty for new entrants and their investors, and provides for a more timely resolution of anti-competitive practice. Without specific *ex ante* rules, anti-competitive conduct could result in incumbents' positions becoming entrenched before any *ex post* application of the competition rules could be effective.[64] The inadequacy of the use of only competition rules to regulate newly liberalised markets in the telecommunications sector is illustrated by the experience in New Zealand, where reliance was placed upon competition rules with only minimalist ("light-handed") application of sector-specific regulation.[65] Indeed, in this country, disputes over the terms of interconnection with the incumbent operator (Telecom New Zealand) led to considerable and seemingly endless competition litigation between the incumbent operator and new entrants. New Zealand therefore had to consider introducing a degree of sector-specific regulation to cover network access and interconnection. As market structures evolve and become more competitive with the market power of incumbent operators being eroded, specific regulation should be gradually phased out in favour of increased reliance on competition rules.[66]

---

[60] See *e.g.* proposals in Germany to extend broadcasting regulation to webcast/internet TV or to impose the traditional TV licence fee (Rundfunkgebühr) to computers with internet capacity.

[61] See von Bonin, para.9–002, n.5, p.201 *et seq.*

[62] However, self-regulation is not without risks for cross-border activities, given the scope for divergent national approaches in developing self-regulation, unless it is co-ordinated to some degree at EU level.

[63] The same approach has been followed in the audio-visual sector as regards access to conditional access systems as a result of the Advanced TV Standards Directive, para.2–064, n.86, discussed at para.2–064 *et seq.*

[64] See Communication on the Results of the Public on the Green Paper, COM(99) 108. According to one commentator on the Convergence Green Paper, regulation also has the effect of creating a national body of expertise in the Member States, which could also be used to apply competition law in the sector, either by the same authorities having responsibility for both regulatory and competition law or by suitable co-operation between different national authorities.

[65] See Webb and Taylor, "Light-Handed Regulation of Telecommunications in New Zealand: Is Generic Competition Law Sufficient?" (1998/99) 2 *International Journal of Communications Law and Policy*.

[66] This is one of the key messages that has emerged from the consultation process initiated by the Commission regarding the adjustments that will be required to the regulatory framework as a result of

9–025 *Need for a long-term viable concept* — A goal of any market liberalisation process must be the creation of long-term, sustainable, effective competition. Therefore, the economic consequences of the adoption of a specific model of sector-specific regulation must be closely monitored. If a preference is given to the (fast) development of service competition by way of imposing on dominant operators far-reaching access obligations combined with wholesale and retail price regulation, the effects in the long run may be negative, as competition in network infrastructure could be undermined. In addition, a price-squeeze may occur, as the result of which neither new entrants nor the incumbent operator will be left with the financial resources necessary to invest in the upgrading and maintenance of existing infrastructures or in the development of alternative infrastructures. As a result, the possibility of creating more sustainable competition in the provision of infrastructure may be jeopardised, thereby leading to prolonged regulation and out-of-date network infrastructure that does not readily respond to the needs of service providers and customers.

In this context, the application of competition law may also have to balance competing policy objectives. For example, by permitting relatively high degrees of co-operation between competitors when sharing 3G infrastructure,[67] it can mitigate somewhat the negative impact of Member States' 3G licensing procedures on the ability of operators to finance the necessary investments needed to meet their roll-out obligations and allow consumers to benefit from new 3G services.

9–026 *National regulatory authorities or a European telecommunications agency?* — In the telecommunications sector, the creation of NRAs at the national level, with varying degrees of independence and competence, has raised the issue of whether there can be effective enforcement of the sector-specific rules across the EU.[68] Even in the light of the various attempts in the New Regulatory Framework to align the enforcement policies of the NRAs, this enforcement system contains an inherent risk of the inconsistent application of a supposedly harmonised system of telecommunications regulation across the EU.[69] A 1997 Commission study on this issue found that, at that time, co-operation between NRAs, national competition authorities and the Commission was very limited and that the independence of certain NRAs was questionable.[70] The study considered several options including the creation of an independent European Telecommunications Authority. The study also found that a majority of market players supported some regulatory functions being performed by an authority acting at the European level, in particular as regards frequency management, numbering, licensing and interconnection. However, the introduction of a

convergence; Convergence Result Communications, above, para.9–024, n.64, p.14. This has considerably influenced the regulatory approach taken in the New Regulatory Framework.

[67] See above, para.6–006.

[68] In so far as non-economic questions such as culture are essentially a state matter, and the Member States have divergent cultural policies, the creation of a single body at the EU level that would be responsible for enforcing content regulation is not presently a realistic option and is not likely to become one in the immediate future.

[69] See, in relation to the old framework for the 1998 liberalisation, Forrester, Norall and Sutton, "The Institutional Framework for the Regulation of Telecommunications and the Application of EC Competition Rules", Report for the Commission, 1995.

[70] Schaub, "Competition Policy in the Telecoms Sector" (1996) 2:1 *Competition Policy Newsletter*. Nera/ Denton Hall, "Issues Associated with the Creation of a European Regulatory Authority for Telecommunications", (1997), available at: *http://europa.eu.int/ISPO/infosoc/telecompolicy/en/nerafin.doc*.

European regulatory authority did not form part of the Commission's proposals that led to acceptance of the New Regulatory Framework. The Commission's consultation on the 1999 Communications Review[71] found broad support for the Commission's proposal for building on the existing regulatory structures with effective communication between the Commission and NRAs,[72] the concept of concentration of regulatory power within the Commission did not find favour with the Member States.[73] In line with this, a more recent study commissioned by the Commission indicated that a majority of participants in the telecommunications sector in Europe were satisfied with the current regulatory structure and the work of NRAs and did not favour the creation of a European regulatory agency.[74] The New Regulatory Framework attempts to introduce better co-operation between the Commission and the NRAs.[75] The outcome of this reform in practice remains to be seen.

[71] Commission Communication, "Towards a New Framework for Electronic Communications Infrastructure and Associated Services: The 1999 Communications Review", COM(99) 539, November 10, 1999, p.51, available at: *www.europa.eu.int/ISPO/infosoc/review99/review99en.pdf.*

[72] Commission Communication on the results of the public consultation on the 1999 Communication Review and Orientation for the New Regulatory Framework, COM(2000) 239 final, April 26, 2000, p.19 available at: *www.europa.eu.int/eur-lex/en/com/cnc/2000/comm2000_0239en02.pdf.*

[73] See, for example, the position of the United Kingdom, which considered that the concentration of decision-making would hamper fast and effective regulation and ignore the market-specific expertise of NRAs, "An initial response from the United Kingdom from the Department of Trade and Industry, the Department of Culture, Media and Sport, the Office of Telecommunications and the Radio Communications Agency", May 2000, available at: *www.oftel.gov.uk/ind_info/international/99re0500.htm.* See also the Independent Regulators Group's Common Position on Commission Working Documents dated 27 April 1999, available at *http://europa.eu.int/ISPO/infosoc/telecompolicy/review99/nrfwd/IRG23e.htm.*

[74] Eurostrategies & Cullen, "Draft Final Report on the Possible Added Value of a European Regulatory Authority for Telecommunications", Report for the EU Commission, September 1999; available at *http://europa.eu.int/ISPO/infosoc/telecompolicy/en/erastudy.pdf.*

[75] See above, para.1–044 *et seq.*

Appendix 1

SMP Table

	1998 Regulatory Framework	2002 New Regulatory Framework
Definition	An operator is rebuttably presumed to have SMP when it has over 25 per cent market share in the relevant interconnection market, but NRAs may use other criteria such as the organisation's ability to influence market conditions (Art.4, ONP Interconnection Directive).	An operator shall be deemed to have SMP when it is individually or jointly dominant in a relevant product or service market, according to the principles of EC competition law (Framework Directive, Art.14).
Objective	To open access markets to new entrants ("assisted" competition) and control market power.	To ensure the development of "effective" competition, and limit the imposition of proportionate regulatory remedies only in cases where markets are not effectively competitive.
Procedure	1. NRA calculates each operator's market shares in the relevant markets for the provision of voice telephony and interconnection. 2. NRA designates operators with SMP on the basis of market share being over 25 per cent (unless no market power above this level). 3. NRA notifies the Commission. 4. Publication in the O.J. 5. NRA imposes regulatory obligations on designated operators.	1. NRA defines the relevant markets according to the SMP Guidelines and the Commission Recommendation on relevant markets. 2. NRA analyses the relevant markets to see whether they are competitive, that is to say there is no operator with a dominant position in accordance with EC competition law principles. 3. If the market is not effectively competitive, NRA proposes to designate SMP operators and impose regulatory obligations on designed operators. It notifies other NRAs and the Commission for a 1-month period of review. 4. If during the 1 month review period, the Commission has serious doubts as to the compatibility with EU law of the NRAs proposed regulatory action, as regards: (i) market definition; (ii) SMP designation; (iii) or imposition of other regulatory obligations than those listed in the Access and Universal Service Directive, it communicates this to the concerned NRA. A further 2-month review period will then follow, after which the Commission can approve, amend or withdraw the market definition, the SMP designation and the proposed regulatory obligations to be imposed.

Procedure for the Designation of SMP — Flow Chart

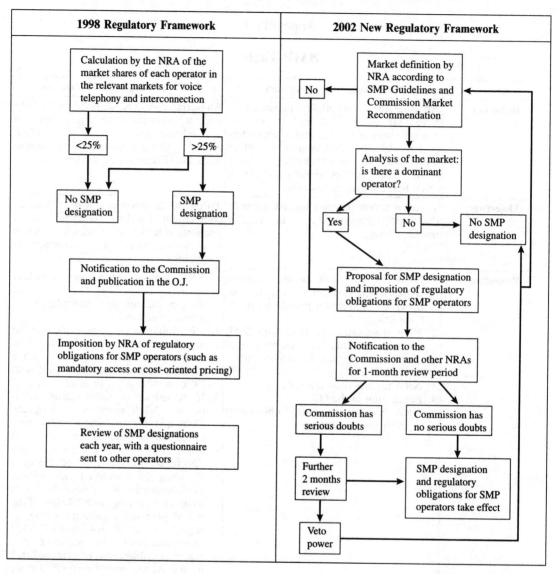

Appendix 2

Market Definition in Telecommunications, Broadcasting and Internet Cases of the Commission and the Court of Justice Under Articles 81, 82 and 86

Case	Reference	Type of Case	Product Markets	Reasons Given for Product Markets	Geographic Markets	Reasons Given for Geographic Markets
British Telecommunications	Commission Decision of December 10, 1982, O.J. 1982 L360/36; on appeal *Italy v Commission* [1985] E.C.R. 873	Abuse of dominant position (Art.82): various practices to eliminate competition from private message-forwarding agencies	Provision of (i) telephone; (ii) telex services; (iii) message forwarding	No reason given	The UK	Implicitly scope of BT's monopoly right
Telemarketing v CLT	Judgment of the Court of Justice of October 3, 1985, [1985] E.C.R. 3270	Abuse of dominant position (Art.82): extension of dominance into separate but related markets to eliminate competition	(i) Television advertising; (ii) telemarketing activities	No reason given	Television advertising aimed at viewers in French-speaking Belgium	No reason given
Alsatel v Novasam	Judgment of the Court of Justice of October 5, 1988, [1988] E.C.R. 5987	Anti-competitive agreements and abuse of dominant position (Arts 81 and 82): contractual provision binding customers to deal exclusively with Alsatel in rental and maintenance of telephone systems	Telephone installation services	The Court did not follow the Commission's suggestion to distinguish between a market for rental and maintenance of telephone systems and that for the purchase of the same equipment. Customers have a clear choice whether to purchase or rent a telephone system	The whole of France (market on which Alsatel is not deemed to be dominant as it is only present on a regional market)	Scope of regulatory licence to sell equipment
Alcatel Espace/ANT Nachrichtentechnik	Commission Decision of January 12, 1990, O.J. 1990 L32/19	R&D co-operation agreement (Art.81)	Manufacture of satellites and components	Specific structure of demand (*i.e.* unique projects requiring newly developed components and R&D, specific to the particular requirements of the customer)	Worldwide market in principle	Given high prices of final products, transport is negligible. Legal restrictions and national preferences may restrict the scope of the market

Case	Reference	Type of Case	Product Markets	Reasons Given for Product Markets	Geographic Markets	Reasons Given for Geographic Markets
Konsortium E.C.R. 900	Commission Decision of July 27, 1990, O.J. 1990 L228/31	Co-operation agreement between AEG, Alcatel and Nokia for joint development and distribution of pan-European digital cellular mobile phone system (GSM) (Art.81)	Provision of GSM system	No reason given	Not specific but implicitly worldwide	No reason given
RTT v GB-Inno-BM	Judgment of December 13, 1991, [1991] E.C.R. 5973	Abuse of dominant position (Art.86 in conjunction with Art.82): Member States cannot grant dominant player on network operation market power to lay standards for equipment to be connected to network and check compliance	(i) Establishment and operation of telecommunications network; (ii) distribution of telecommunications equipment to be connected to public networks	No reason given	Belgium	Geographic scope of monopoly right
Eirpage	Commission Decision of October 18, 1991, O.J. 1991 L306/22	Co-operative joint venture between Motorola and Telecom Eireann in order to establish nationwide paging system (Art.81)	Paging services	Paging forms a distinct product market from other mobile communications because (i) it is cheaper in terms of the price of the equipment and running costs; (ii) mobile telephones are larger in size than mobile units and thus more unwieldy; (iii) paging offers one-way communications, which is a distinct advantage in keeping down billing costs	Ireland	Not specifically motivated (implicitly scope of regulatory licence)
Astra	Commission Decision of December 23, 1992, O.J. 1993 L20/23	Co-operation between BT and SES for the provision of television broadcasting services by satellite (Art.81)	(i) Space segment capacity for distribution of television channels; (ii) up-linking services	The Commission refused to distinguish between two separate product markets: low-powered and medium-powered satellite capacity on the ground. They both offer customers the	(i) Space segment: Europe; (ii) up-link: at least Europe	No reason given

Case	Decision	Agreement	Relevant product market	Relevant geographic market	Comments
			same possibilities as far as geographic coverage is concerned and as regards transmission to cable head-ends. The fact that only medium-powered satellites enable Direct-To-Home (DTH) reception by small dishes was not deemed to be sufficient by the Commission to consider it as a separate product market since the use of one or the other type of satellite capacity will not make any difference in countries with well-developed cable systems (para.13)	Not specified	
Auditel	Commission Decision of November 24, 1993, O.J. 1993 L306/50	Co-operative arrangement between TV broadcasters in the field of audience-relating measurements	The market for audience-rating measurements, *i.e.* the figures showing the number of persons who were watching a given channel at a given point in time	Implicitly Italy	Not specified
BT-MCI	Commission Decision of July 27, 1994, O.J. 1994 L223/36	Co-operative joint venture for provision of enhanced and value-added global telecommunications services (Art.81)	Value-added and enhanced services to large multinational corporations including (i) data services; (ii) value-added application services; (iii) traveller services; (iv) intelligent network services; (vi) global outsourcing services. New services with specific features adjusted to the needs of corporate customers (*e.g.* single point of contact, seamless end-to-end global services, customised billing). Different from services currently offered by national TOs that cannot provide one-stop shop, end-to-end or seamless services to customers' premises located outside the national borders	Global	(i) Liberalisation of markets and disappearance of national borders; (ii) international service by nature

Case	Reference	Type of Case	Product Markets	Reasons Given for Product Markets	Geographic Markets	Reasons Given for Geographic Markets
International Private Satellite Partners (IPSP)	Commission Decision of December 15, 1994, O.J. 1994 L354/75	Co-operative joint venture between Orion, British Aerospace, COM DEV, General Dynamics, Kingston Communications, Matra, Stet and Nissho Iwai in order to offer international private business telecommunications services as well as bulk satellite transmission capacity (Art.81)	(i) international value-added services to large corporations (*i.e.* voice calling, high-speed fax, data storage and transport and video-conferencing); (ii) offering of bulk satellite transmission capacity	Services to be offered by IPSP intended to address the growing need of multinational companies for end-to-end communications between geographically dispersed locations around the world and between their customers or suppliers	North America, much of the EEA, and portions of Central and Eastern Europe	Geographic reach of IPSP satellites
MDNS	Commission Press Release, IP/89/948	Co-operative joint venture between national TOs to provide Europe-wide telecommunications services (Art.81)	Provision of enhanced data communication services	Not specified (no formal decision was taken following the decision to abandon the project)	Europe	Not specified
Belgian Leased Lines	Commission Press Release, IP/90/67	Abuse of dominant position by Belgian RTT (Art.82)	Provision of international leased data transmission circuits	Not specified (no formal decision was taken as a settlement was reached with RTT)	Belgium	Not specified
STET, Italtel, AT&T and AT&T-NSI	Commission Notice pursuant to Art.19(3) of Council Regulation 17/62, O.J. 1992 C333/3	Co-operative joint venture between STET, Italtel, AT&T and NTI for the development and production of telecommunications equipment	Telecommunications equipment for (i) public and (ii) private switching systems; (iii) operations systems (OS); (iv) public transmission systems; (v) private terminal equipment	The Commission distinguished between the markets for public and private network equipment, because of their different demand structures. The main users of public network equipment are public and private network operators with exclusive or special rights, while private network equipment is sold to a wide range of customers	Each Member State constitutes a separate relevant geographic market	The Commission found that the Italian market had specific structural characteristics, the telecommunications industry being then vertically integrated under STET which controlled the network operator (SIP, the predecessor to Telecom Italia) and the main equipment manufacturer (Italtel)

				National	
EBU/Eurovision System	Commission Decision of June 11, 1993, O.J. 1993 L179/23	Co-operative arrangement between broadcasters for buying of television rights	Acquisition of sports programmes	Acquisition of sports rights because of the specific characteristics of these programmes: (i) very attractive to public and commercial broadcasters due to high viewing figures; (ii) particularly suited to carrying advertisements; (iii) transcend cultural and linguistic barriers and therefore suited for transnational broadcasting and advertising; (iv) expensive programmes because huge risks and costs	Television rights are granted on an exclusive basis, for a given country
CEPT Leased Lines	Commission Press Release, IP/90/188	Agreement between TOs within the European Conference of Postal and Telecommunications Administrations (CEPT) on terms for leasing out international telecommunications circuits (Art.81)	Provision of international leased data transmission circuits	Not specified (no formal decision was taken as a settlement was reached with CEPT and its members)	Not specified
Aérospatiolale/Alcatel	Commission Notice pursuant to Art.19(3) of Regulation 17/62, O.J. 1994 C47/6	Co-operation agreement (including specialisation) for development of civilian and military telecommunications satellites (Art.81)	Provision of telecommunications satellites, both civilian and military	Based on specific features of supply (*i.e.* complexity of product, specificity of environment and high requirement for quality, customised products with specific R&D) and demand (*i.e.* well informed customers with considerable purchasing power)	At least Community-wide market except for certain customers with national preference	(i) Low level of transport costs; (ii) increased cross-border commercialisation of satellite-based services; (iii) rapid deregulation and technological developments with increased access to satellite; (iv) Public Procurement Directive should diminish the importance of national preferences

Case	Reference	Type of Case	Product Markets	Reasons Given for Product Markets	Geographic Markets	Reasons Given for Geographic Markets
CMC-Talkline	Commission Notice pursuant to Art.19(3) of Regulation 17/62, O.J. 1994 C221/9	Co-operative joint venture between Matra, Cellcom, Talkline and Norauto for provision of pan-European mobile telephony services (Art.81)	(i) GSM mobile telephony services, in which service providers purchase high volumes of air-time from several operators throughout Europe with a view to bringing a one-stop shop service to individual customers; (ii) access to national GSM networks on a wholesale basis to air-time resellers	Specific services allowing a European one-stop shop GSM service at a lower rate than under current roaming arrangements between national operators	(i) Europe-wide market; (ii) national markets defined by the scope of licences granted to each mobile phone network operator by relevant national authorities	
ETSI Interim IPR Policy	Commission Notice pursuant to Art.19(3) of Regulation 17/62, O.J. 1995 C76/5	Intellectual property rights licensing arrangements within framework of European Telecommunications Standards Institute ("ETSI") (Art.81)	(i) Telecommunications standards; (ii) the downstream markets which use those standards, *i.e.* telecommunications equipment and services markets	Not specified	At least the entire EEA	Not specified
Inmarsat-P	Commission Notice pursuant to Art.19(3) of Regulation 17/62, O.J. 1995 C304/6	Agreement among Inmarsat members for the restructuring of Inmarsat into a commercial entity (Art.81)	Satellite personal communication services (S-PCS)	S-PCS is expected to act as a complement and even a substitute for public switched fixed telephone network and cellular mobile telephony in remote areas of low density and/or where terrestrial infrastructure is very poor	Worldwide	S-PCS has global coverage
Omnitel	Commission Decision of October 4, 1995,O.J. 1995 L280/49	Violation of Art.86 in conjunction with Art.82 by Italy in imposing payment obligation on second mobile operator	Cellular digital mobile radiotelephony services (GSM) a separate market from voice (fixed network) telephony. For the Commission, GSM is likely to be a different market than analogue mobile telephony	No demand substitution between fixed and mobile telephony (consumers do not usually cancel a fixed telephone subscription when they buy a mobile phone). Substantial price differential. By contrast with analogue, GSM is pan-European, permits	Italy	No specific reasons given

			Product markets	Commission analysis	Market definition	Geographic markets
Atlas	Commission Decision of July 17, 1996, O.J. 1996 L239/23	Co-operative joint venture between Deutsche Telekom and France Telecom for provision of value-added telecommunications services to corporate users (Art.81)	(i) Customised packages of corporate telecommunications services; (ii) packet-switched data communications services	transmission of large quantities of data, and is more secure (i) The Commission specifically left open the question of whether each category of product supplied by the joint venture constitutes a separate product market. Given the high cost of service provision, these services can only be viable if provided to multi-national corporations; (ii) the Commission considers that packet-switched data communications constitute a separate market from customised packages from corporate telecommunications services because most existing customers for these packet-switched data communications are small enterprises and are not potential customers for customised packages of corporate telecommunications services	Separate markets for customised packages of telecommunications services and packet-switched data communications services at global, cross-border regional and national levels	Separate geographic markets based on cost and price differences for network provision (*e.g.* leased lines) and services
Phoenix/Global One	Commission Decision of July 17, 1996, O.J. 1996 L239/57	Extension of the Atlas joint venture to Sprint for provision of global telecommunications services to corporate users (Art.81)	(i) Customised packages of corporate telecommunications services; (ii) packet-switched data communications services; (iii) the market for traveller services; (iv) the market for carrier services	(i) and (ii) see *Atlas* decision (above); (iii) traveller telecommunications services comprise offerings that meet the demand of individuals who are away from their normal location, either at work or at home; (iv) specific demand for efficient, high-quality traffic	(i) Separate markets for customised packages of telecommunications services and packet-switched data communications services at global, cross-border regional (*i.e.* pan-European) and national levels; (ii) traveller services: increasingly global (but the Commission left	(i) and (ii) see *Atlas* decision (above); (iii) while technical obstacles (*e.g.* incompatibility of mobile systems, differences in pre-paid cards) still limit the geographic scope, these differences are expected to be overcome in the near future; (iv) international by nature

Case	Reference	Type of Case	Product Markets	Reasons Given for Product Markets	Geographic Markets	Reasons Given for Geographic Markets
Phoenix/Global One— cont.				transportation capacity from established and emerging carriers (*e.g.* providers of services on alternative infrastructure or non-facilities-based carriers seeking an alternative to the local TO for international client traffic)	the issue open); (iii) carrier services: international	
Second Spanish GSM operator	Commission Decision of December 18, 1996, O.J. 1997 L76/20	Violation of Art.86 in conjunction with Art.82 by Spain in imposing payment obligation on second mobile operator	Cellular digital mobile radiotelephony services (GSM) form a separate market from voice (fixed network) telephony. The Commission notes that GSM is also probably a different market from that of analogue mobile telephony	No demand substitution between fixed and mobile (consumers do not usually cancel fixed telephone subscriptions when they buy a mobile phone) and substantial price differential. By contrast with analogue, GSM is pan-European, permits transmission of large quantities of data, is more secure	Spain	No specific reasons given (implicitly scope of licence)
Iridium	Commission Decision of December 18, 1996, O.J. 1997 L16/87	Co-operative joint venture between Motorola and a number of investors (including Stet and Vebacom) to develop and commercialise S-PCS services	The market for satellite personal communication services	S-PCS systems are expected to act as a complement to both GSM and DECT wireless terrestrial mobile technologies, in particular in areas with low penetration of terrestrial systems. However, even in urban areas or densely populated areas, S-PCS will not be a substitute to cellular and paging systems because of the latters advantages in terms of cost, voice quality and signal strength. Customers will be international travellers with dual terminals in the	Probably worldwide (although the Commission left open the issue of narrower geographic markets)	

Unisource	Commission Decision of October 29, 1997, O.J. 1997 L318/1	Co-operative joint venture between PTT Telecom, Swiss PTT and Telia for the provision of value-added telecommunications services to corporate users (Art.81)	(i) Non-reserved corporate telecommunications services; (ii) traveller services; (iii) carrier services	terrestrial mode within a given network and switching to satellites in areas outside terrestrial coverage / (i) By contrast with the *Atlas* decision, the Commission no longer considers that data communications services constitute a market distinct from other customised corporate services; (ii) as pan-European GSM services extended to corporate customers' fixed private or virtual networks they may have to be included in the market for non-reserved corporate telecommunications services; (iii) see *Atlas* decision (above)	(i) Separate markets for customised packages of telecommunications services at global, cross-border regional and national levels; (ii) traveller services: increasingly global (but the Commission left the issue open); (iii) carrier services: at least cross-border regional (*i.e.* pan-European) / See *Atlas* decision (above)
Uniworld	Commission Decision of October 29, 1997, O.J. 1997 L318/24	Extension of the Atlas joint venture to ATT for the provision of global telecommunications services to corporate users (Art.81)	Non-reserved corporate telecommunications services	Specific demand of large multinational corporations for global, seamless services with one-stop shop	Cross-border regional (*i.e.* EEA plus Switzerland) / Need for pan-European services from customers
Télévision Par Satellite (TPS)	Commission Decision of March 3, 1999, O.J. 1999 L90/6	Co-operative joint venture between TF1, France Télévision, France Télécom, CLT-UFA, M6 and Suez Lyonnaise des Eaux for the provision of pay-TV services in France (Art.81)	(i) Pay-TV market; (ii) the market for technical services for pay-TV; (iii) the market in the acquisition of broadcasting rights, in particular for films and sporting events; (iv) xxx	(i) Pay-TV: distinction between pay-TV and free TV and free TV is based on the different funding (advertising for free TV and subscription fees for pay-TV). The Commission did not distinguish separate product markets between analogue and digital pay-TV, nor between cable, terrestrial and satellite transmission; (ii) technical services for pay-TV:	The Commission left the issue open of whether the relevant market should be limited to France or be extended to the French-speaking countries / Most programmes are still purchased on a national or language basis

Case	Reference	Type of Case	Product Markets	Reasons Given for Product Markets	Geographic Markets	Reasons Given for Geographic Markets
Télévision Par Satellite (TPS)—cont.				market definition based on special technical infrastructure for encrypting broadcasters and enabling authorised viewers to decode them; (iii) acquisition of broadcasting rights: the Commission left open the issue whether a distinction was to be made between films and sporting events and within the different categories of rights: unencrypted TV broadcasting, pay-TV, pay-per-view, near-video-on-demand; (iv) distribution and operation of special interest channels this category of pro-grammes which are not specific to pay-TV, is growing rapidly due to the greater offering possibility as a result of digitalisation		
Cégétel+4	Commission Decision of May 20, 1999, O.J. 1999 L218/14	Co-operative joint venture between CGE, BT Mannesmann and SBCI for the provision of telecommunications services	(i) voice telephony services, both long-distance and local; (ii) mobile telephony; (iii) data services; (iv) internet service and access provisions; (v) outsourcing of tele-communications services; (vi) managed network services and leased lines; (vii) directories	Not specified	For most of the seg-ments, the market is national but for corpo-rate telecommunications services, there exist at least three distinct geo-graphic markets, namely at global, cross-border regional and national levels. As regards GSM, the market is increasingly European	(i) Corporate telecom-munications services: based on precedents in *Atlas* and *Phoenix/Global One* (above); (ii) GSM service provi-sion: increased substi-tutability throughout Europe between the various subscriptions allowed by "roaming" agreements

Télécom Développement	Commission Decision of July 27, 1999, O.J. 1999 L218/24	Co-operative joint venture between Cégétel and SNCF for the operation of a national long-distance telecommunications network in France	(i) The provision of long-distance voice telephony services; (ii) the supply of long-distance transmission capacity; (iii) the provision of interconnection services, including access to international services	Not specified	France	The network of the joint venture will be limited to the territory of France
British Interactive Broadcasting (BiB) now renamed Open	Decision of September 15, 1999, O.J. 1999 L312/1	Co-operative joint venture between BSkyB, Midland Bank, BT and Matsushita for the provision of digital interactive TV services	(i) Digital interactive services including retailing, financial services, information education, internet access, email and games; (ii) technical and administrative services for digital interactive TV services and retail pay-TV; (iii) retail pay-TV market; (iv) wholesale supply of film and sports channels for retail pay-TV; (v) local loop infrastructure	(i) Online services via TVs must be distinguished from those services provided via PCs since they have different market penetration, price, characteristics and use. Situation may change over time as internet access via television becomes possible. Digital interactive services are also different from high-street retailing because of different product range and sold and priced as a package rather than as individual service. Also different from retail pay-TV market because of the nature of the product or services supplied (entertainment versus transactional and information services); (ii) because of the large overlap between the technical and administrative services necessary for retail pay-TV and the services necessary for digital interactive TV services; (iii) based on precedents, the Commission refused to distinguish between digital and analogue	UK	Based on the existence of a national regulatory framework

Case	Reference	Type of Case	Product Markets	Reasons Given for Product Markets	Geographic Markets	Reasons Given for Geographic Markets
British Interactive Broadcasting (BiB) now renamed Open—cont.				pay-TV as well as between cable and satellite retail pay-TV; (iv) because of different value and price of film and sports channels by comparison with other channels; (v) specificity of demand for local access		
Telefónica/Sogecable	Press Release, IP/00/372 of April 12, 2000	Pooling agreement between Telefónica and Sogecable for their sports broadcasting rights (in particular to the Spanish Liga and Copa) (Art.81)	(i) Market for the acquisition of rights to broadcasting of football events; (ii) downstream market for the wholesale of such rights with effect on downstream market for pay-TV and pay-per-view		National (Spain)	
Eurovision	Commission Decision of May 10, 2000; O.J. 2000, L151/18	Agreement setting out rules governing the European Broadcasting Union (EBU) in respect of the joint acquisition and sharing of sports TV rights (Art.81)	(i) Market for the acquisition of the broadcasting rights to some major international sporting events; (ii) acquisition of broadcasting rights to national sporting events; (iii) downstream markets for free-to-air and pay-TV broadcasting markets	Whether (i) and (ii) constitute two separate markets was left open; (iii) left open	(i) International; (ii) national; (iii) national	(i) and (ii) were left open; however the Commission took note of the fact that the kind of sporting rights the EBU bids for are major sporting events such as the Olympic Games which have a relevant geographic market extending at least to the whole European territory; (iii) linguistic, cultural, licensing and copyright reasons
UEFA	Commission Decision of April 19, 2001, O.J. 26/6/2001 L171/12	UEFA rules which regulate the broadcasting of football matches (Art.81)	(i) Upstream market for the acquisition of broadcasting rights to football events, which could be further broken down into (a) market for broadcasting rights to regular football events; and (b) separate market	Although the issue of market definition was left open, the Commission noted that: (i) separate programmes have particular characteristics; (ii) they are able to achieve high viewing figures; (iii) they reach an	(i); (ii) and (iii): national	Broadcasting rights on sporting events are generally sold on a national basis, according to national regulations

		for the broadcasting rights to football events which do not take place regularly, *e.g.* World Cup		identifiable audience, which is especially targeted by certain advertisers; (iv) branding encourages audiences to schedule their viewing habits to make appointments to view a particular channel; (v) the Commission's investigation also confirmed that the development of brand image is important for broadcasters in determining whether to acquire football rights	(i) and (ii): services on both relevant product markets are offered on a global basis	
Identrus	Commission Decision of July 31, 2001, O.J. 19/9/2001 L249/12	Agreements concerning the establishment of a network of financial institutions, for Certification Authorities for secure e-commerce transactions (Art.81)	(i) Market for the provision of trust services to Certification Authorities; (ii) downstream market for the provision of trust services by Certification Authorities to end users, initially in the corporate sector	(i) and (ii) are new markets which have not yet been sufficiently developed nor has consumer confidence been tested	(i) and (ii): worldwide markets	
Microsoft	Press Release, IP/01/1232 of August 30, 2001	Abuse of dominant position by Microsoft (Art.82)	(i) Market for personal computer operating systems; (ii) market for low-end server operating systems		n/a	
Opodo Online Travel Portal	Notice pursuant to Art.19(3) of Council Regulation 17/6, O.J. 2001 C323/6	Joint Venture agreement setting up an online travel portal (Art.81)	Market for travel agency services, which comprises the marketing and distribution of airline seats and other travel and travel-related services	Investigated in Case COMP/M 1812 — *Telefonica Terra/Amadeus* of April 27, 2000	National	Based on language barriers and the need to set up national distribution arrangements for tickets. However, the Commission noted that an EU-wide travel agency market may develop with the adoption of the Euro and the growth of online agents

Case	Reference	Type of Case	Product Markets	Reasons Given for Product Markets	Geographic Markets	Reasons Given for Geographic Markets
KPN Mobile	Press Release, IP/02/483 of March 27, 2002	Abuse of dominant position by KPN with respect to the termination of fixed-calls on KPN mobile networks (Art.82)	Calls termination on individual mobile networks	(i) At retail level, users who wish to call a subscriber A of mobile network operator B cannot, at present, choose an alternative mobile operator for terminating calls to subscriber A; (ii) at wholesale level, all public operators are under a regulatory obligation to terminate calls from other networks; (iii) on the supply side, only the individual mobile network operator can offer terminating access, so that there is no substitution between network operators	National (Netherlands)	Based on national regulatory barriers and network coverage
Deutsche Telekom	Commission Decision of May 8, 2002; O.J. 2003 L263/9	Abuse of dominant position by Deutsche Telekom, in particular for predatory pricing as regards access to local loop (Art.82)	Provision of local access to the public fixed telecommunications network (local loop) divided into wholesale and retail local loop access	Deutsche Telekom provides local loop access at two different levels: (i) retail subscription to end customers and (ii) unbundled access to the local loop to competitors allowing direct access to end users. Alternative infrastructure for providing access services, such as fibre-optic networks, wireless local loop, satellite power lines and cable TV networks are not sufficiently developed and cannot be considered as alternative to the DT's local loop network	National (Germany)	Based on nationwide network coverage

T-Mobile/Viag Intercom	Notice pursuant to Art.19(3) of Council Regulation 17/02, O.J. 9/8/2002 C189/22	Framework agreement concerning infrastructure sharing and national roaming (Art.81)	(i) Access to and use of 3G infrastructure; (ii) wholesale access to 3G national roaming	(i) and (ii) left open	National (Germany)	Based on national regulatory barriers and network coverage
BT Cellnet & BT 3G/One to One (UK Agreement)	Notice pursuant to Art.19(3) of Council Regulation 17/62, O.J. 2002 C214/17	Agreement concerning infrastructure sharing and national roaming (Art.81)	(i) Access to and use of 2G, 2.5G and 3G infrastructure; (ii) wholesale access to 3G national roaming	The question whether 3G constitutes a separate product from the 2G and 2.5G market was left open	National (UK)	Regulatory barriers and national network coverage
Wanadoo	Press Release, IP/01/1899 of December 21, 2001	Abuse of dominant position — predatory pricing in the provision of xDSL access (Art.82)	High-speed internet access for residential customers (including access by cable modem)	High-speed internet access available in France allows downstream connections around 10 times faster than conventional internet access	National (France)	Regulatory barriers and national network coverage
IFPI	Case No COMP/C2/38.014, Commission Decision of October 8, 2002 (Press Release, IP/02/1436)	Reciprocal Agreement between record producers' rights administration societies for the licensing of "simulcasting" (Art.81)	(i) Market for multi-territorial simulcasting rights administration services between record producers' collecting societies; (ii) multi-territorial and multi-repertoire licensing of the record producers' simulcasting right	(i) Supply side is characterised by record producers' collecting societies willing and capable of administering on a multi-territorial basis for simulcast use the repertoires of other societies located in territories other than the one where the former's are established. Demand side is characterised by record producers' collecting societies wishing to have their repertoires administered on a multi-territorial basis for simulcast use by another society located in a different territory; (ii) supply side is characterised by the record producers' collecting societies which have been mandated the necessary rights by their record company	(i) At least all EEA-wide, with exclusion of those countries where the local collecting society is not a party to the Reciprocal Agreement, *i.e.* France and Spain; (ii) all EEA countries except France and Spain	(i) The framework resulting from the Reciprocal Agreement renders the conditions of competition in the EEA countries where the local collecting society is a party to the Reciprocal Agreement sufficiently homogeneous to distinguish this area from other areas. Therefore, collecting societies that are party to the Reciprocal Agreement will constitute among each other real alternative sources of provision of this service, at EEA level; (ii) broadcasters whose signal originates in the EEA, even if faced with a hypothetical small permanent relative price increase in multi-territorial/multi-repertoire licences granted by an EEA

Case	Reference	Type of Case	Product Markets	Reasons Given for Product Markets	Geographic Markets	Reasons Given for Geographic Markets
IFPI—cont.				members to grant licences to users. Demand side is characterised by user TV and radio broadcasters who wish to make the conventional radio/TV signal simultaneously available via the internet. Since mono-territorial or mono-repertoire simulcasting licences do not represent a viable alternative service for such users, multi-territorial and multi-repertoire licensing of the simulcasting right constitutes the relevant market		society which is party to the Reciprocal Agreement, will not in principle be able to switch to an alternative source of supply located outside of the EEA. EEA collecting societies which are not party to the Reciprocal Agreement, on the other hand, are not an alternative source of supply either as the provisions of the Agreement will not apply to them

Appendix 3

Market Definition in Telecommunications, Broadcasting and Internet Cases Under the Merger Control Regulation

Case	Reference	Type of Case	Product Markets	Reasons Given for Product Markets	Geographic Markets	Reasons Given for Geographic Markets
Alcatel/Telettra	Case IV/M.042, Commission Decision of April 12, 1991, O.J. 1991 L122/48	Acquisition by Alcatel from Fiat of Telettra, a supplier of telecommunications systems and equipment	(i) Public switching; (ii) line transmission equipment; (iii) microwave equipment; (iv) private switching	No specific reasons given	Spain	The Commission based its definition of the geographic market on the following grounds: (i) the Spanish telecommunications operator, Telefonica, the main purchaser of telecommunications equipment in Spain, traditionally purchases from locally established suppliers; (ii) at the time of the decision there was no legal obligation in Spain for the next five years to apply the procurement procedures established by the Procurement Directives; (iii) there are vertical links between Telefonica and its major equipment suppliers (including Telettra), by means of minority shareholdings with the result that these suppliers are in a privileged position on the market
ABC/Générale des Eaux/Canal+/W.H. Smith	Case IV/M.110, Commission Decision of September 10, 1991	Concentrative joint venture in the television market	Free-access TV broadcasting	Different funding and different programmes support the argument that pay-TV and free TV belong to different markets. The Commission acknowledged that pay-TV remains dependent on the quality and specificity of TV programmes on free-access channels	National or regional	Geographic scope is delimited by language and cultural barriers (can surpass national boundaries)

571

Case	Reference	Type of Case	Product Markets	Reasons Given for Product Markets	Geographic Markets	Reasons Given for Geographic Markets
Sunrise	Case IV/M.176, Commission Decision of January 13, 1992	Concentrative joint venture between Walt Disney, The Guardian, Scottish, LWT and Carlston for the provision of national UK breakfast-time television	Television advertising	Television advertising has different characteristics from other media, and is more expensive. The Commission considered that there was no separate market for breakfast-time television advertising	UK	No specific reasons given
Saab Ericsson Space	Case IV/M.178, Commission Decision of January 13, 1992	Concentrative joint venture between Saab and Ericsson in the area of electronic space equipment	Space equipment including: onboard space computers, data handling systems, separation systems, guidance systems, microwave equipment and microwave antennae	The Commission failed to take a position on whether each of these products represents a separate product market	Europe	No specific reasons given
Ericsson/Kolbe	Case IV/M.133, Commission Decision of January 22, 1992	Concentrative joint venture in the field of public digital transmission technology	Digital cross-connect (DXC) systems	The Commission left open the question of whether DXC systems represented a separate product market within the market for line transmission systems	The Commission left open the question of whether Germany was the relevant geographic market	The Commission acknowledged that the scope of the market was broadening as a result of liberalisation of the telecommunications sector and the adoption of common public procurement rules
Ericsson/Ascom	Case IV/M.236, Commission Decision of July 8, 1992	Concentrative joint venture in the field of public line transmission	Production of public transmission equipment and systems	No specific reasons given	The Commission left the question open of whether the market was pan-European or national	
Northern Telecom/ Matra	Case IV/M.249, Commission Decision of July 17, 1992	Concentrative joint venture in the field of telecommunications equipment	(i) Public switching; (ii) private switching; (iii) telephone sets; (iv) mobile telephony	No specific reasons given (precise market definition not necessary for decision)	The Commission did not take a position on the scope of the geographic market	
Ericsson/Hewlett-Packard	Case IV/M.292, Commission Decision of March 12, 1993	Concentrative joint venture for the supply of telecommunications network management products	Telecommunications networks management (TNM) products serving "multi-vendor network environments", *i.e.* networks comprising equipment from more than one supplier	TNM systems constitute a separate market as, with the ongoing liberalisation and technological advances, there is a need for TNM systems which can support and integrate equipment from a range of manufacturers	At least the Community is not the world	Customers are telecommunications network operators across the globe

JCSAT/SAJAC	Case IV/M.346, Commission Decision of June 30, 1993	Concentrative joint venture between Japanese trading companies in the field of satellite communication business	Operation of satellites and provision of satellite-based services (the Commission left open the question of market definition)	No specific reasons (precise market definition not necessary for decision)	Japan	Implicitly Japan as joint venture is only licensed to provide telecommunications services in Japan
Alcatel/STC	Case IV/M.366, Commission Decision of September 13, 1993	Acquisition by Alcatel from Northern Telecom of STC	Submarine telecommunications systems	No specific reasons (market definition not necessary for decision)	The Commission did not take any decision on the geographic scope	Not specified
Mannesmann/RWE/ Deutsche Bank	Case IV/M.394, Commission Decision of November 27, 1993	Concentrative joint venture for the provision of closed user group corporate telecommunications networks and value-added services	Corporate telecommunications networks and value-added services for corporate customers	No specific reasons (market definition not necessary for decision)	The Commission did not take any decision on the geographic scope	Not specified
Mannesmann/RWE	Case IV/M.408, Commission Decision of February 28, 1994	Concentrative joint venture in the field of mobile data communications services	Mobile data communications services	Mobile packet-switched data communications differ from mobile voice telephony through the conditions of offer (*i.e.* mobile voice telephony networks can only be used effectively for the transmission of voice communication), the customer group (*e.g.* transport and insurance companies) and the prices	The Commission left open the scope of the geographic market (*i.e.* Germany or Europe)	
Kirsch/Richemont/ Telepiù	Case IV/M.410, Commission Decision of August 2, 1994	Concentrative joint venture in the pay-TV sector	Pay-TV	(i) Pay-TV is primarily financed by subscription fees whereas free-access TV is financed by public authorities or by advertising revenue; (ii) pay-TV offers a more specialised programme mix. The Commission left open the question of the precise market definition	National or regional (language-based)	The Commission based its position on the national or regional scope of the market on the following elements: (i) programme rights are purchased on a national or language basis; (ii) rights to broadcast major new films are subject to different national rules regarding the time periods for

Case	Reference	Type of Case	Product Markets	Reasons Given for Product Markets	Geographic Markets	Reasons Given for Geographic Markets
Kirsch/Richemont/ Telepiù—cont.						release; (iii) programme-mix is designed on the basis of the cultural interests of a national or regional audience; (iv) language differences; (v) pay-TV requires the setting-up of subscriber management systems
MSG	Case IV/M.469, Commission Decision of November 9, 1994, O.J. 1994 L364/1	Concentrative joint venture between Bertelsmann, Kirsch and Deutsche Telekom for the provision of pay-TV services	(i) Administrative and technical services for pay-TV; (ii) pay-TV; (iii) cable television networks	(i) Need for specific technical infrastructure (decoders), conditional access technology and subscriber management systems; (ii) pay-TV is a separate market from free-access television: different types of funding lead to different programme-mixes, pay-TV offers a greater quantity of channels, more special interest channels, and interactive services such as home banking and near-video-on-demand; (iii) different payment structures for connection (one-off fee for installation of satellite, relatively small, regular payments for cable fees); many households cannot receive cable, while some landlords and owners' associations prohibit installation of satellite dishes; differential in costs of programming	Germany	(i) Pay-TV: regulatory differences, TV programmes largely nationally restricted, language and cultural barriers; (ii) MSG: national due to the necessity to have transmission capacity with the respective national network owners but geared to European dimension given the absence of obstacles to the supply of decoders and smart-cards; (iii) Cable network: national scope due to DT's statutory monopoly on laying and operating cable networks on public roads

				(i) Civil sector: users are international satellite organisations; increased deregulation and privatisation; (ii) military sector: preference for national suppliers for national security reasons
Matra Marconi Space/ British Aerospace Space Systems	Case IV/M.437, Commission Decision of August 23, 1994	Acquisition by Matra Marconi from British Aerospace of two subsidiaries active in the field of space systems	The space systems market comprises two segments: (i) the space segment (comprising satellites, launchers and manned-flight vehicles); (ii) the ground segment (comprising stations for command and control of spacecraft and stations that provide an interface between communications satellites and users)	The Commission did not take a position on the market definition but indicated that space systems was too broad a definition because each element (*i.e.* satellite, launcher and ground station) is composed of a number of defined sub-systems and equipment that may be purchased separately. Many companies only manufacture sub-systems, equipment or components	Civil sector: worldwide; military sector: the Commission left the issue open
Marconi/Finmeccanica	Case IV/M.496, Commission Decision of September 5, 1994	Concentrative joint venture in the fields of radiocommunications, value-added telecommunications and information technology systems	(i) Military products: high-frequency radio equipment, VHF/UHF equipment, Airborne VHF/UHF radios, global positioning systems equipment, integrated systems and communications electronic warfare; (ii) dual-use products: satellite ground stations (comprising stations for command and control of spacecraft and stations that provide an interface between communications satellite and users). The Commission left open the issue of whether further sub-markets should be distinguished within satellite ground stations; (iii) civilian products: private mobile radio, PTT network traffic management and supervisory systems	Distinction between military and civilian products is based on the special features in order to meet a military specification (*e.g.* resilience of computers under arduous conditions of climate and transport) that increase the price of a product	The Commission did not take a position as to the scope of the markets (*i.e.* national or EEA-wide)

Case	Reference	Type of Case	Product Markets	Reasons Given for Product Markets	Geographic Markets	Reasons Given for Geographic Markets
Bertelsmann/News International/Vox	Case IV/M.0489, Commission Decision of September 6, 1994	Concentrative joint venture in the field of TV channel broadcasting	(i) Advertising in free-access TV broadcasting; (ii) film rights	Although it did not take a firm position in this respect, the Commission indicated that free-access TV and pay-TV belong to different product markets because: (i) free-access television is financed by advertising revenue or other revenues while pay-TV is primarily financed by subscription fees; (ii) free TV presents a different programme-mix from pay-TV that usually offers more specialised programme-mix	National or regional (language-based)	(i) Language differences which influence the purchase of programmes rights; (ii) different rules on time "windows" for release of new films in cinemas, video, pay-TV and free-access TV; (iii) varying programme-mixes on the basis of the cultural interests of a national and regional audience (reference to *Kirsch/Richemont/Telepiù* case)
Matra Marconi Space/Satcomms	Case IV/M.497, Commission Decision of October 14, 1994	Acquisition by Matra Marconi of certain assets of Ferranti International in the field of space segments	(i) Satellite ground stations; (ii) microwave components	Reference to previous case law (*Matra Marconi Space/British Aerospace Space Systems, Marconi/Finmeccanica*)	(i) Satellite ground stations: EEA; (ii) microwave components: not specified	Reference to previous case law (*Marconi/Finmeccanica*)
Ericsson/Raychem	Case IV/M.519, Commission Decision of November 21, 1994	Concentrative joint venture in the field of telecommunications equipment	Telecommunications transmission systems that comprise access transmission systems and equipment and trunk transmission systems	The Commission did not take a firm position on market definition but seemed to consider that the two segments belong to different product markets based on their different characteristics: (i) by contrast with access transmission systems, trunk transmission systems are employed to cover long distances and high capacities; (ii) they have different interface characteristics and are not interchangeable; (iii) interface specifications for both systems also differ	The Commission left open the issue of geographic scope	

						Reference to previous case law (*BT/MCI*)
Cable & Wireless/ Schlumberger	Case IV/M.532, Commission Decision on December 22, 1994	Concentrative joint venture (Omnes) to supply commercial data services, voice services and other added-value services to companies active in certain industries (oil and gas)	International advanced telecommunications services to multinational companies	The supply of these services to the upstream oil and gas sector has no characteristic which distinguishes it from supply to any other sector	Global	
Securicor Datatrak	Case IV/M.561, Commission Decision of April 4, 1995	Concentrative joint venture between Securicor, Central Beheer and Parcom Services in the field of vehicle-tracking systems	Vehicle-tracking services	New service on the market with no competing systems	Not specified	
Vox II	Case IV/M.525, Commission Decision of January 18, 1995	Extension to Vox co-operative joint venture (see above) by entry of Canal+	(i) Advertising in free-access TV broadcasting; (ii) film rights	Reference to previous case law (*MSG* decision)	Germany	No specific reasons given
Siemens/Italtel	Case IV/M.468, Commission Decision of February 17, 1995, O.J. 1995 L161/27	Concentrative joint venture between Siemens and STET in the telecommunications systems and equipment sector	(i) Public switching systems; (ii) transmission; (iii) radio systems; (iv) mobile radio networks; (v) private switching and key telephone systems (KTS); (vi) communications terminals	(i), (ii), (iii) and (iv) based on specific technical features and applications. No separate market depending on technology used (e.g. analogue, digital, SDH, ATM, GSM); (v) data communications equipment is excluded in the present case; (vi) the Commission left the issue open of whether telephones, faxes, and cellular phones form separate markets	The Commission did not take a firm position but indicated that the market is probably at least Europe-wide	Market increasingly international based on: (i) technological developments; (ii) international standards and national/type-approval of equipment; (iii) application of public procurement directives; (iv) liberalisation of public voice telephony and telecommunications infrastructure
TBT/BT/Tele Danmark/ Telenor	Case IV/M.570, Commission Decision of April 24, 1995	Concentrative joint venture to offer voice and data telecommunications services throughout Sweden	(i) International voice telecommunications services; (ii) domestic voice telecommunications services; (iii) international data telecommunications services; (iv) domestic data telecommunications services	No specific reasons given (the Commission did not take a position on the precise market definition)	At least national with the exception of enhanced telecommunications services that are worldwide in scope	Voice and data telecommunications services in Sweden are national given the licensing, regulatory and supervisory framework, current market participants and their market shares as well as the physical interconnection arrangements for telecom operators

Case	Reference	Type of Case	Product Markets	Reasons Given for Product Markets	Geographic Markets	Reasons Given for Geographic Markets
Kirsch/Richemont/Multichoice/Telepiù	Case IV/M.584, Commission Decision of May 5, 1995	Concentrative joint venture in the pay-TV sector	Pay-TV	(i) Pay-TV is financed by subscription fees while free TV is financed by public authorities or advertising revenues; (ii) pay-TV offers a more specialised programme-mix. The Commission acknowledged that some substitutability exists as the value of pay-TV depends on alternative viewing possibilities	National or regional (language-based)	(i) Regulatory differences: programmes are very largely nationally restricted; (ii) language barriers: programmes are generally broadcast only in the relevant national language; (iii) programme rights to broadcast are purchased by television channels on a national basis; (iv) the programme-mix of television channels is designed on the basis of the cultural interests of national or regional audiences
CLT/Disney/Super RTL	Case IV/M.566, Commission Decision of May 17, 1995	Concentrative joint venture in view of the operation of a TV channel	(i) Advertising in television broadcasting; (ii) licensing of film rights	The Commission indicated that a separate market did not appear to exist for advertising in, and licensing of film rights for, children-oriented programmes	National or regional	Due to linguistic cultural and regulatory barriers
Nordic Satellite Distribution	Case IV/M.490, Commission Decision of July 19, 1995, O.J. 1995 L53/20	Concentrative joint venture between Norsk Telecom, Tele Danmark and Kinnevik for the provision of satellite transmission services and distribution services via cable or DTH in the Nordic region	(i) Provision of satellite TV transponder capacity and related services to broadcasters; (ii) distribution of satellite pay-TV and other encrypted TV channels to direct-to-home households; (iii) operation of cable-TV networks	(i) Distribution of TV signals via satellite (transponders) is a market distinct from TV distribution by terrestrial links, since considerable differences exist between the two modes of distribution both technically and financially (see *MSG Media Service*); (ii) cable-TV is a separate market from terrestrial transmission and satellite TV because it is dependent on the maintenance of a	(i) The market of those transponders with a footprint that covers the Nordic region (*i.e.* Norway, Sweden, Denmark and Finland); (ii) national or Nordic (the Commission left the issue open); (iii) cable operation is a national market	(i) Scope of the market is determined by the footprint (*i.e.* the geographical area where the TV signals distributed by a satellite can be received by direct-to-home households with standard receiving equipment); dishes of up to 60 cm in diameter were defined as standard; (ii) DTH distribution is a retail operation with marketing at the local level; (iii) cable TV operators are faced with

			...network (financed by cable fee) and not on the purchase of an antenna. Moreover, cable is not an option to non-cabled households and households subject to aesthetic restrictions on satellite dishes		different market conditions in different countries in terms of geography, marketing and legislation
Cable & Wireless/Veba	Case IV/M.618, Commission Decision of August 16, 1995	Concentrative joint venture in view of the provision of telecommunications services in Germany and the EU	(i) National and international fixed terrestrial networks; (ii) satellite telecommunications services; (iii) managed bandwidth; (iv) Personal Communications Networks (PCNs) mobile telephone networks; (v) mobile radio paging systems; (vi) cable TV networks; (vii) corporate networks; (viii) value-added services	The Commission indicated that mobile PCNs likely form a separate market from that of GSM mobile networks on the grounds that (i) both networks operate on different frequencies; (ii) PCNs aim at local and regional users with no international roaming agreements as is the case for GSM; (iii) both networks cannot be connected	(i) PCN mobile networks: national; (ii) mobile radio paging system: national; (iii) cable-TV networks: national; (iv) corporate networks: international; (v) value-added services: EEA-wide if not worldwide — The presence of regulatory and technical restrictions determines the geographic scope of the market
RTL/Veronica Endemol	Case IV/M.553, Commission Decision of September 20, 1995, O.J. 1996 L134/32	Concentrative joint venture in the TV broadcasting sector	(i) TV broadcasting, (with the distinction between free and pay-TV); (ii) TV advertising; (iii) independently produced Dutch TV programmes	(i) In terms of trade relationships between broadcasters on the supply side and viewers on the demand side, a distinction has to be drawn between on the one hand the market for TV advertising, where broadcasters compete for advertising revenue and on the other hand, the market for pay-TV, where pay-TV suppliers compete for subscriptions; (ii) TV advertising must be distinguished from other media because of different types of customer,	Netherlands — The Commission excluded the Flemish region of Belgium from the relevant geographic market, despite the communality of language, on the basis of cultural differences and national preferences of viewers (paras 26, 28 and 29)

Case	Reference	Type of Case	Product Markets	Reasons Given for Product Markets	Geographic Markets	Reasons Given for Geographic Markets
RTL/Veronica Endemol—cont.				different techniques and prices; (iii) independent production is separate from in-house production		
Canal+/UFA/MDO	Case IV/M.655, Commission Decision of November 13, 1995	Concentrative joint venture in TV broadcasting	(i) TV broadcasting; (ii) TV advertising	The Commission indicated, without taking a firm position, that it is arguable that TV broadcasting is not a market in economic terms since there is no trade relationship between broadcasters of "free TV channels" and viewers	National	Differences in applicable regulatory regime, language barriers, cultural factors
British Telecommunications/VIAG	Case IV/M.595, Commission Decision of December 22, 1995	Concentrative joint venture in the telecommunications sector	(i) Domestic value-added network services; (ii) private switched voice services to large business customers; (iii) domestic corporate network services; (iv) public voice services (the Commission failed to take a position on the issue of whether each of these products form a separate product market)	No specific reasons given (the Commission did not take a position on the precise market definition)	Germany, except for certain value-added and corporate networks services where the relevant market is European or worldwide	The primary area of activity of the joint venture is Germany
Ericsson/Ascom II	Case IV/M.676, Commission Decision of December 22, 1995	Concentrative joint venture in the telecommunications equipment sector	On-site paging equipment and systems (OSP)	No specific reasons given, presumably due to lack of demand-side substitutability	At least EEA-wide	Absence of substantial obstacles (standards, regulation) to cross-border trade. Customers and large companies that negotiate supply at headquarters level
AT&T/Philips	Case IV/M.651, Commission Decision of February 5, 1996	Acquisition by AT&T of certain assets of Philips in the public telecommunications equipment sector	(i) Public switching; (ii) cable transmission; (iii) point-to-point digital radio transmission; (iv) local loop; (v) customer	No specific reasons given (the Commission did not take a position on the precise market definition)	(i) Public switching European market; (ii) cable transmission: tendency towards European dimension; (iii)	(i) Public switching increasingly European with the introduction of new technologies such as ATM; (ii) cable

Case	Transaction	Product market	Reasons	Geographic market	Reasons
		premises equipment (CPE); (vi) wireless access (point-to-multipoint wireless); (vii) cellular infrastructure		point-to-point digital: increasingly European; (iv) local loop: national; (v) customer premises equipment: scope of market is determined by the applicable standard; (vi) wireless access: European, possibly global; (vii) cellular infrastructure: at least European (the Commission did not take a firm position on the issue of market definition)	transmission: increasingly European due to the standardisation of cable transmission equipment; (iv) local loop: still national due to regulatory restrictions; (vii) cellular infrastructure: the GSM standard is used as the EEA standard
Philips/Origin Case IV/M.668, Commission Decision of February 22, 1996	Acquisition by Philips of Origin in the field of information and communication technology services	(i) Information technology services; (ii) information technology software	The Commission based this distinction on the fact that services require a close and constant relationship between the service provider and the client while the software may be sold or licensed to the client	(i) IT services: national; (ii) IT software: trans-border (the Commission did not define precisely the scope of the market)	(i) Due to the requirement for language and local presence; (ii) software can be easily imported/exported from one country to another and distributed after linguistic and regulatory adaptations have been made
ADSB/Belgacom Case IV/M.689, Commission Decision on February 29, 1996	Acquisition of Belgacom by a consortium made of Ameritech, Tele Danmark and Singapore Telecom	The parties proposed the following definition: (i) local telephone services (PSTN and ISDN); (ii) domestic long-distance telephone services; (iii) international telephone services (including VPN); (iv) leased lines; (v) data communications services (inc. Man & Lan, telex, telegraph, EDI); (vi) cellular telephone activities; (vii) non-cellular mobile activities (paging, calling card, pay phones, maritime radio services); (viii) value-added services (including	No specific reasons (the Commission did not take a position on precise market definition)	(i) Basic services (e.g. fixed national and international voice, leased lines, telex): national; (ii) value-added services: at least European and possibly worldwide	(i) Specificity of national legal framework and role of the national telecommunications operators; (ii) no specific reasons (the Commission did not take a position on the precise geographic market definition)

Case	Reference	Type of Case	Product Markets	Reasons Given for Product Markets	Geographic Markets	Reasons Given for Geographic Markets
ADSB/Belgacom—cont.			centre-operator services; (ix) supply and service of CPE; (x) telephone directory publishing; (xi) telephone directory data; (xii) telecommunication and engineering consulting			
GTS Hermes Inc./HIT Rail BV	Case IV/M.683, Commission Decision of March 25, 1996	Concentrative joint venture between ten national railway companies, Racal and GTS for the provision of pan-European telecommunications network	Carriers' carrier services, *i.e.* transport of traffic over permanent dedicated facilities through the network of the transit carrier, using a high-bandwidth digital circuit for both voice and data services. Parties proposed to distinguish two separate markets: (i) point-to-point connections; (ii) provision of pan-European transport networks (the Commission did not take a position on the precise market definition)	Market definition based on specificity of customers, *i.e.* telecommunications operators and not end users	At least EEA	Services will be provided on networks of a number of EEA railway companies
Viacom/Bear Stearns	Case IV/M.717, Commission Decision of March 25, 1996	Concentrative joint venture in TV broadcasting in Germany	Advertiser-supported (free) TV broadcasting	No specific reasons (the Commission did not take a position on precise market definition)	German-speaking area (Germany, Austria and Switzerland)	No specific reasons (the Commission did not take a position on precise market definition)
n-TV	Case IV/M.810, Commission Decision of September 16, 1996	Concentrative joint venture in TV broadcasting in Germany	Television advertising	No specific reasons given	Germany	Specific language, customers and distribution
Bertelsmann/CLT	Case IV/M.779, Commission Decision of October 7, 1996	Concentrative joint venture in TV broadcasting	(i) Free-access TV; (ii) pay-TV; (iii) TV productions; (iv) TV rights/licences; (v) free access radio	(i) Different types of funding (*i.e.* advertising incomes and subscription fees respectively) for free and pay-TV; (iv) distinct product markets may exist for films and other fiction	National or language-based. For free-access radio, possibly regional market (the Commission did not take a position on the precise geographic market)	Due to different regulatory regimes, existing language barriers, cultural factors and different conditions of competition (*e.g.* structure of the market for cable networks)

			Product market definition	Reasons	Geographic market	Reasons
				rights on the one hand and sports rights on the other hand (para.18) because of the specific features of sport events (*e.g.* must be acquired in advance of the event, attractiveness is highly dependent on national or regional audiences)		No specific reasons given (precise definition of geographic market could be left open)
DB Kom	Case IV/M.827, Commission Decision of October 23, 1996	Concentrative joint venture between Mannesman and Deutsche Bahn for the provision of various telecommunications services	The parties proposed the following market definitions: (i) customer-oriented packages of telecommunications services for business purposes; (ii) packet switched data communications services; (iii) transmission services; (iv) voice telephony services; (v) railway-specific telecommunications services; (vi) maintenance of telecommunications systems and equipment (the Commission did not take a position on market definition)	No specific reasons given (the Commission did not take a position on the precise market definition)	The parties considered that all these products must be regarded as national (the Commission did not take a position in this respect)	
Bell Cable Media/Cable & Wireless/Videotron/ *Cable & Wireless/ Nynex/Bell Canada*	Cases IV/M.853 and IV/M.865, Commission Decision of December 11, 1996	Concentrative joint venture in the field of pay-TV broadcasting	The parties proposed the following market definitions: (i) pay-TV; (ii) cable networks; (iii) fixed telecommunications networks; (iv) fixed telecommunications services (with the exception of pay-TV) (the Commission left open the question of market definition)	(i) Definition of pay-TV is based on precedents; (ii) although it did not take a firm position in this respect, the Commission implied that a distinction must be drawn between the provision of cable networks and the provision of services in that capacity, given that competition will occur at different times and in different circumstances (para.27)	(i) Pay-TV: national; (ii) cable networks; national or regional; (iii) fixed telecommunications networks and services: national (with the exception of pay-TV) (the Commission left open the issue of geographic scope)	(i) Pay-TV: different language and cultural barriers, different regulatory systems; (ii) local exclusive franchise may justify the existence of local markets

Case	Reference	Type of Case	Product Markets	Reasons Given for Product Markets	Geographic Markets	Reasons Given for Geographic Markets
Telecom Eireann	Case IV/M.802, Commission Decision of December 18, 1996	Acquisition of joint control of national Irish telecom operator, Telecom Eireann by Dutch PTT telecom and Swedish Telia	(i) Basic telecommunications services (*i.e.* voice telephony, leased lines, mobile telephony and telex); (ii) value-added services (*i.e.* non-public services as well as enhanced services to multinational corporations) with possible distinction between the segment for advanced telecoms services to corporate users and a segment for standardised low-level packet-switched data communications services; (iii) cable-based services	No specific reasons given (the Commission left open the issue of market definition in relation to (i) and (ii). Definition of cable-based services is based on precedents	(i) Basic services have been perceived as being national; (ii) geographic market for added-value services is European and possibly worldwide (the Commission left open the precise geographic scope of these markets)	(i) Public telephony continues to be reserved until January 1, 2000; (ii) as a result of technical change and liberalisation of the regulatory environment
RTL 7	Case IV/M.878, Commission Decision of February 14, 1997	Concentrative joint venture between CLT-UFA and Universal Studios in the field of TV broadcasting in Poland	Free-access commercial television	No specific reasons	Poland	Due to language, specific distribution and customers
Telia/Ericsson	Case IV/M.876, Commission Decision of February 20, 1997	Concentrative joint venture in the field of telecommunications services and systems	The parties proposed the following market definitions: (i) project services (*i.e.* consultancy services to telecommunications network operators, telecommunications equipment suppliers, and IT companies regarding fixed and wireless systems); (ii) SIM personalisation (*i.e.* development and supply of software based SIM-card personalisation systems and applications); (iii) IT security	No specific reasons given (the Commission did not take a position on the precise market definition)	The parties proposed the following geographic market definitions: (i) project services: Sweden; (ii) SIM cards: worldwide; (iii) IT security systems: worldwide; (iv) distribution of modems and similar hardware: Nordic countries	No specific reasons given (precise definition of geographic market could be left open)

Case	Citation	Description	Product market	Commission position	Geographic market	Comments
Castle Tower/TDF/Candover/Berkshire-HSCo	Case IV/M.887, Commission Decision of February 27, 1997	Concentrative joint venture in the field of terrestrial transmission services	systems; (iv) distribution of third party modems, ISDN routers and ATM switches — The parties proposed the following market definitions: (i) terrestrial broadcasting services; (ii) sharing and rental of communications sites; (iii) ancillary services	No specific reasons provided (the Commission left open the issue of market definition)	The parties argued that the markets are national or regional	Although it did not take a firm position, the Commission indicated that the market for terrestrial broadcasting was probably broader than the UK as the BBC is obliged to provide services in both the Channel Islands and the Isle of Man
BT/Tell DK/SBB/ Migros/UBS	Case IV/M.900, Commission Decision of April 16, 1997	Concentrative joint venture to create a second national telecommunications operator in Switzerland	(i) International voice telecommunications services; (ii) domestic voice telecommunications services; (iii) international data telecommunications services; (iv) domestic data telecommunications services	No specific reasons given (the Commission did not take a position as to whether these segments constitute different product markets)	At least national (Switzerland)	Based on Commission precedents
British Telecom/MCI (II)	Case IV/M.856, Commission Decision of May 14, 1997, O.J. 1997 L336/1	Merger between BT and MCI	(i) International voice telephony services (including international direct dials (IDD) and international private leased circuits (IPLCs); (ii) audio-conferencing	(i) The Commission indicated that satellite and cable cannot be considered as substitutes to providing international voice services. This is due to inherently greater signal propagation delay time, echo effects, susceptibility to environmental or climatic conditions such as heavy rains; (ii) possible functional demand substitutes (such as video-conferencing or the organisation of a meeting) are significantly more expensive	(i) Call traffic routes between any country pair (in this case, the UK–US route); two distinct geographic markets can be identified with any international route, each comprised of the originating bilateral traffic from the countries concerned; (ii) audio-conferencing: national	(i) The possibility of hubbing, *i.e.* re-routing US–UK traffic through third countries, does not appear to be a viable commercial possibility at present, since under the current accounting rates system, it would be more expensive than using direct routes; (ii) customers do not generally purchase audio-conferencing globally or internationally but rather at the national level

Case	Reference	Type of Case	Product Markets	Reasons Given for Product Markets	Geographic Markets	Reasons Given for Geographic Markets
PTA/STET/Mobilkom	Case IV/M.908, Commission Decision, June 11, 1997	Concentrative joint venture for the provision of mobile telephony in Austria	The parties proposed to define the relevant product market as that for mobile communication with sub-segments for C-net, D-net, GSM and paging. The Commission left open the issue of market definition		The parties considered that the relevant geographic market for C-net, D-net and paging was national while the market for GSM was of a European dimension. The Commission left the issue open	
BankAmerica/General Electric/Cableeuropa	Case IV/M.939, Commission Decision of June 19, 1997	Concentrative joint venture in the field of CATV broadcasting services	Pay-TV and voice telephony (precise product market definition not necessary for decision)	Definition based on Commission precedents	Spain	(i) Pay-TV: cultural specificity; (ii) voice telephony: as a result of Community and national legal framework
Cable & Wireless/ Maersk Data-Nautec	Case IV/M.951, Commission Decision of July 10, 1997	Concentrative joint venture in the field of telecommunications and IT goods and services to the container transportation market	The parties proposed the following market definitions: (i) telecommunications services; (ii) IT services	The Commission left open the issue of whether there was a separate market for the provision of such services to the international maritime container transportation sector	Global	Based on Commission practice of considering international advanced telecommunications services as global
Daimler Benz/Deutsche Telekom	Case IV/M.962, Commission Decision of July 31, 1997	Concentrative joint venture between Daimler Benz and Deutsche Telekom in the area of telematic services	Telematic services (*i.e.* services designed to improve traffic information and communication through data exchange between a service provider and motor vehicles). (The Commission left open the issue of market definition)		The parties suggested that the market is European-wide (the Commission left the issue open)	
Philips/Lucent Technologies	Case IV/M.966, Commission Decision of August 20, 1997	Concentrative joint venture in the field of telecom equipment	(i) corded phones; (ii) cordless phones; (iii) cellular phones; (iv) answering machines; (v) pagers	Although it did not take a firm position, the Commission indicated that these products, because of their different technologies, characteristics, prices and intended uses, may form separate markets despite a certain tendency towards integration	At least EEA-wide	The products may be used with regard to national boundaries throughout the EEA, due to harmonisation of standards

			No specific reasons given (precise product market definition not necessary for decision)	(i) Basic services: national; (ii) added-value services: European and possibly worldwide (the Commission left open the precise geographic scope of these markets)	Basic services are national due to the legal framework for authorisation and supervision
STET/Get/Union Fenosa	Case IV/M.927, Commission Decision of August 20, 1997	Concentrative joint venture with a view to constituting a second national operator in Spain	(i) Basic telecommunications services; (ii) value-added services (*i.e.* data transmission, email, video-conference, interconnection with local loop (LAN), international global services, customised services)		
Bertelsmann/Burda/ Springer — HOS-MM	Case IV/M.972, Commission Decision of September 15, 1997	Creation of a joint venture jointly controlled by Bertelsmann, Burda and Springer	Medical online services for professional users	Insufficient interchange-ability with other sources of information, such as specialised journals or conferences	Left open
Bertelsmann/Burda — HOS Lifeline	Case IV/M.973, Commission Decision of September 15, 1997	Creation of a joint venture jointly controlled by Bertelsmann and Burda	Advertising on the internet	Not specifically motivated	Left open (tendency: German-speaking area in the EEA)
Albacom/BT/ENI	Case IV/M.975, Commission Decision of November 13, 1997	Concentrative joint venture between BT, ENI and Mediaset	(i) International voice telecommunications services; (ii) domestic voice telecommunications services; (iii) international data telecommunications services; (iv) domestic data telecommunications service; (v) resale of transmission capacity	Definition based on Commission precedents	National, except for enhanced international services provided through global networks (Concert) where the market is worldwide	Scope of geographic market is determined by: (i) extent and coverage of network and customers that can economically be reached; (ii) legal and regulatory system and the right to provide a service. Legal and regulatory framework makes Italy the relevant market, including for resale of capacity. Enhanced international services provided via global networks are worldwide
Siemens/Elektrowatt	Case IV/M.913, Commission Decision of November 18, 1997	Acquisition by Siemens of Elektrowatt	Among various product markets not related to telecommunications, the Commission defined the market for pay-phones as a relevant market. The Commission distinguished between public and private pay-phones	The Commission considered that there was no need to distinguish between the different modes of payment (coin-operated, pre-paid card, credit-card phones). Public pay-phones are owned by telecommunications operators located in public places and available at any time. Private pay-phones are located in private, indoors, accessible at certain times and are	Germany for public pay-phones, EEA-wide market for private pay-phones	As regards, public pay-phones, the Commission considered that the market was Germany because Deutsche Telekom is procuring (and will likely continue to do so) pay-phones exclusively from businesses located in Germany. With respect to private pay-phones, the Commission took into consideration that the sector

587

Case	Reference	Type of Case	Product Markets	Reasons Given for Product Markets	Geographic Markets	Reasons Given for Geographic Markets
Siemens/Elektrowatt — cont.				generally more expensive than public pay-phones. Public pay-phones must also be more robust		has been liberalised and that multinational private suppliers can operate in different countries with the same system
Ameritech/Tele Danmark	Case IV/M.1046, Commission Decision of December 5, 1997	Acquisition of Tele Danmark by Ameritech	The parties proposed the following definition: (i) local telephone services (PSTN and ISDN); (ii) domestic long-distance telephone services; (iii) international telephone services (including VPN); (iv) leased lines; (v) distribution of concert services; (vi) data communications services (inc. Man & Lan, telex, telegraph, EDI); (vii) mobile telephone activities; (viii) value-added services (including centre–operator services); (ix) supply and service of terminal equipment; (x) telephone directory publishing; (xi) telephone directory data; (xii) telecommunication and engineering consulting; (xiii) cable television; (xiv) security monitoring; (xv) submarine cable links in Denmark; (xvi) satellite broadcasting activities	No specific reasons given (precise product market definition not necessary for decision)	(i) Basic services (*i.e.* fixed national and international voice, leased lines, telex) have traditionally been perceived as being national; (ii) geographic market for added-value services is European and possibly worldwide	No specific reasons given (precise geographic market definition not necessary for decision)
Cégétel/Vodafone — *SFR*	Case IV/M.1055, Commission Decision of December 19, 1997	Concentrative joint venture in the field of mobile telephony services in France	Mobile telephony service	The parties argued that, having regard to the likely technological evolution and the characteristics of customer demand, market definition should include all mobile voice services, notwithstanding the standard they use (analogue, GSM, future	The Commission left open the issue of whether the relevant market was France or Europe	The Commission indicated that there is an increasing trend towards a European market for GSM service provision due to a certain degree of substitutability throughout Europe of national subscriptions

			dual-mode mobile handsets). (The Commission left open the issue of whether distinct product markets must be distinguished between analogue and digital mobile telephony)			
Mannesmann/ Olivetti.Infostrada	Case IV/M.1025, Commission Decision of January 15, 1998	Concentrative joint venture for the provision of advanced telecommunications services in Italy	Separate voice and data markets at domestic and international level	Based on Commission practice (precise product market definition not necessary for decision)	Italy	Scope of geographic market is determined by: (i) extent and coverage of network and customers that can economically be reached; (ii) legal and regulatory system and the right to provide a service. Legal and regulatory framework makes Italy the relevant market
Dow Jones/NBC-CNBC Europe	Case IV/M.1081, Commission Decision of January 22, 1998	Concentrative joint venture between Dow Jones and NBC in the field of television services	Broadcasting of news programmes (precise product market definition not necessary for decision)	No specific reasons provided	EEA (precise geographic market definition not necessary for decision)	No specific reasons provided
Cable I Televisio de Catalunya	Case IV/M.1022, Commission Decision of January 28, 1998	Concentrative joint venture between STET, GET, Redesa, Caixa Catalunya and Gas Natural for the provision of multi-media services	The parties proposed the following market definitions: (i) pay-TV; (ii) multi-media services (in particular interactive television); (iii) supply of large bandwidth; (iv) cable services; (v) added-value services; (vi) basic telecom services (the Commission did not take a position on the precise market definition)	(i) Distinction between pay- and free-TV based on Commission precedents; (ii) no specific reasons to distinguish other markets	National (or regional) with the exception of added-value services that are trans-border (the Commission did not take a position on the exact geographic scope)	Specific legal framework, restriction of number of operators and specific national access requirements
Cableuropa/SpainCom/ CTC	Case IV/M.1091, Commission Decision of January 28, 1998	Concentrative joint venture between Bank of America, General Electric in the field of cable services	Pay-TV and voice telephony (precise product market definition not necessary for decision)	Definition based on Commission precedents	Spain	(i) Pay-TV: cultural specificity; (ii) voice telephony: as a result of Community and national legal framework

Case	Reference	Type of Case	Product Markets	Reasons Given for Product Markets	Geographic Markets	Reasons Given for Geographic Markets
Nortel/Norweb	Case IV/M.1113, Commission Decision of March 18, 1998	Concentrative joint venture between Nortel, a subsidiary of Northern Telecom and Norweb, a subsidiary of United Utilities in the field of telecommunications equipment	Digital Power Line Products (DPL Products) (precise product market definition not necessary for decision)	Parties argued that DPL products compete with other internet access technologies such as telephone copper cable, ADSL, fast modems, HDSL (the Commission left the issue open)	EEA (precise geographic market definition not necessary for decision)	Parties argued that standards are similar and DPL products can be easily adapted and are compatible with existing telecommunications networks (the Commission left the issue open)
Belgacom/Tele Danmark/Tulip	Case IV/M.1177, Commission Decision of May 19, 1998	Concentrative joint venture for the provision of mobile telephony in the Netherlands	Mobile telephony market	Parties argued that market definition should include all mobile voice services, notwithstanding the standard they use (analogue, GSM, future dual-mode mobile handsets). (The Commission left the issue open)	The Commission did not take a position as to whether the market is the Netherlands or Europe	Parties argued that the market is increasingly European due to the compatibility between different systems, the diminishing gap between international and national prices, and the increasing conclusion of interconnection agreements
BT/ESB/AIG	Case IV/M.1132, Commission Decision of May 19, 1998	Concentrative joint venture for the provision of telecommunications services to corporations	(i) Telecommunications services to business customers; (ii) the provision of domestic leased circuits; (iii) international private leased circuits; (iv) sophisticated billing	Not specified (the Commission did not have to define the product market specifically)	Not specified (no need to define for the purpose of the decision)	
Bertelsmann/Kirsch Première	Case IV/M.993, Commission Decision of May 27, 1998, O.J. 1999 L53/1	Concentrative joint venture between CLT/UFA and Kirsch in the pay-TV sector	(i) Pay-TV; (ii) technical services for pay-TV	(i) The Commission based its decision on the same reasons developed in the *MSG* precedent (*i.e.* (a) different types of funding lead to different programme-mixes; (b) pay-TV offers a greater quantity of channels, more special interest channels, and interactive services). Despite a certain convergence between pay-TV and free TV, as free-TV	Germany or at most the German-speaking region consisting of Germany, Austria, Luxembourg and the German-speaking parts of Belgium and Switzerland	The Commission based its findings on the same reasons developed in its precedents in *MSG* and *HMG* (*i.e.* different regulatory regimes, language barriers, cultural factors and other competition conditions prevailing in individual Member States). By contrast with *MSG*, the Commission seems more open to accept that the relevant geographic

Case	Reference	Operation	Relevant markets	Commission's comments
			Germany for cable networks	... market should not be limited to Germany but extends to the German-speaking region (i) See *Bertelsmann/Kirsch/Première*, above; (ii) the Commission considered that, despite the abolition of Deutsche Telekom's monopoly on laying and operating cable networks in public roads, Deutsche Telekom still has a predominant position on the market (in particular in relation to level 3 cable TV networks) and the conditions of competition in Germany are thus still very different from conditions of competition in other countries
Deutsche Telekom/Beta Research	Case IV/M.1027, Commission Decision of May 27, 1998, O.J. 1999 L53/31	Concentrative joint venture between CLT/UFA, Kirsch and Deutsche Telekom in order to operate a technical platform for the provision of pay-TV services	(i) Technical services for pay-TV; (ii) cable networks	(i) See in *Bertelsmann/Première*, above; (ii) along the line of the *MSG* precedent, the Commission maintained that television cable and satellite transmissions constitute separate markets (*i.e.* different payment structures for connection, many households cannot receive cable, while some landlords and owners' associations prohibit installation of satellite dishes, differential in costs of programming). In particular, the Commission took into [consideration that] channels too are largely supplied in digital bouquets by pay-TV operators, this is not enough to justify the acceptance of a common market for free TV and pay-TV. No distinction should be made between analogue and digital pay-TV as digital pay-TV is only a further development of analogue pay-TV and will completely supersede analogue pay-TV in the next few years; (ii) the Commission does not consider that the use of different transmission technologies for cable and satellite transmission justifies the distinction of separate markets for technical services for cable and satellite pay-TV

Case	Reference	Type of Case	Product Markets	Reasons Given for Product Markets	Geographic Markets	Reasons Given for Geographic Markets
Deutsche Telekom/Beta Research—cont.				consideration that, in Germany, the operation of cable networks is much more profitable		
Telia/Telenor/Schibsted	Case IV/JV.1, Commission Decision of May 27, 1998[1]	Co-operative joint venture between Telia, Telenor and Schibsted for the provision of internet services	(i) Content provision on the internet; (ii) internet advertising; (iii) website production; (iv) dial-up internet access (the Commission left open the market definition)	(i) and (ii) content and advertising generate revenue in different ways and from different sources and the activities are carried out by different layers and require different inputs; (iii) website production demands both design and computer skills	(i), (ii), (iii) and (iv) national language-based	
STET/GET/Madrid Cable	Case IV/M.1148, Commission Decision of May 28, 1998	Concentrative joint venture between STET, GET and Ufinsa for the provision of multimedia services	Parties proposed the following market definitions; (i) pay-TV; (ii) multi-media services (in particular interactive television); (iii) supply of large bandwidth; (iv) cable services; (v) added-value services; (vi) basic telecom services (the Commission did not take a position on the precise market definition)	(i) Distinction between pay- and free-TV based on Commission precedents; (ii) no specific reasons to distinguish other markets	National (or regional) with the exception of added-value services that are trans-border (the Commission did not take a position on the exact geographic scope)	Specific legal framework, restriction of number of operators and specific national access requirements
Enel/FT/DT	Case IV/JV.2, Commission Decision of June 22, 1998	Fully autonomous co-operative joint venture for the provision of domestic and international telecommunications services to business and residential customers located in Italy	(a) Fixed line telephony: (i) international voice telecommunications services; (ii) domestic voice telecommunications services; (iii) international data telecommunications services; (iv) domestic data telecommunications service; (b) mobile telephony	The Commission did not specify whether each segment of fixed line telephony constituted a separate market. Regarding mobile telephony, the Commission indicated (although it did not take a firm position) that it may no longer be appropriate to consider that DCS 1800 and GSM	(i) Domestic and international voice telephony and data services in Italy: national; (ii) enhanced services: international; (iii) mobile telephony: local	(i) Due to licensing and regulatory regimes; (ii) enhanced international services are global in scope; (iii) mobile telephony is still local due to remaining price differences between local and international mobile telephony that reduces incentive to seek subscription abroad

[1] Following an amendment to the Merger Control Regulation (which entered into force on April 1, 1998) discussed in para.9–008, a certain type of co-operative joint venture is now subject to this Regulation.

are part of separate product markets (see *Cable & Wireless/Veba*, above) on the ground that (i) dual-mode handsets allow users to use both frequencies; (ii) GSM, analogue, DCS 1800 and DECT compete at the local level

Case	Reference	Subject	Product market	Reasons (product)	Geographic market	Reasons (geographic)
GEC/GPTH	Case IV/M.1226, Commission Decision of June 27, 1998	Acquisition by GEC of GPT in the field of public telecommunications equipment	(i) Transmission equipment; (ii) public switching market (the Commission did not take a position on the precise market definition)	No specific reasons given	EEA-wide, if not the world (the Commission did not take a position on the exact geographic scope)	GEC bases the EEA-wide scope of the market on liberalisation, the application of public procurement directives, increased standardisation as well as other factors such as the possibility of price comparison across Europe, facility to transport. For public switching technology, the introduction of ATM technology has also broadened the scope of the market
WorldCom/MCI	Case M.1069, Commission Decision of July 8, 1998, O.J. 1999 L116/1	Merger between WorldCom and MCI	(i) Host to point of presence across services (*i.e.* the provision of connection between the host computer of the internet user and the nearest point of presence of his internet service provider via the public switched network or a private dedicated line); (ii) internet access services; (iii) "top-level" or "universal" internet connectivity services which are those provided by a network capable of connecting directly to any other network on the	(i) Conditions of competition at this level are different from those at the ISP level or further upstream; (ii) internet access services must be distinguished from other forms of data transmission services using different protocols as only internet gives permanent and unfettered access to internet users; (iii) there is no alternative for top-level internet connectivity, in particular secondary peering arrangements do not provide the same level of connectivity	(i) Point to point of presence access services: local; (ii) internet access services: local or international; (iii) top-level internet connectivity: global	(i) The physical connection from the final user to the ISP, whether by dial-up or dedicated access, can only be provided locally with the result that the market is regional or national, depending on the scope of the supplier's cable network; (ii) internet access services to final users may be local or international depending on the nature of the customer (*i.e.* large corporations or individuals); (iii) the market for top-level internet

Case	Reference	Type of Case	Product Markets	Reasons Given for Product Markets	Geographic Markets	Reasons Given for Geographic Markets
WorldCom/MCI—cont.			internet through so-called peering agreements (*i.e.* barter arrangements between top-level internet services providers (ISPs) which allow traffic between them without payments) without relying on a third network to relay the traffic (the so-called internet "backbone")			connectivity is global by nature
BT/Air Touch/Air tel	Case IV/JV.3, Commission Decision of July 8, 1998	Co-operative joint venture in the mobile telephony sector	The parties have proposed to define the relevant product market as the market for mobile telecommunications services, without making a distinction between GSM and DCS 1800. The Commission left the issue of market definition open	The parties based their market definition on the increased availability of GSM/DCS 1800 dual-band handsets	The parties proposed to define the relevant market as national	Although it failed to take a firm position, the Commission suggested that the market may be European given the increase in the number of DCS 1800 licences and roaming agreements between DCS 1800 operators, the availability of dual-band handsets and the reduction of international cellular calling rates during the past few years
UTA/Swisscom	Case IV/M.1199, Commission Decision of July 13, 1998	Acquisition of joint control by Vereinigte Telekom Oesterreich Beteiligungs Gmbh and Swisscom Telekommunikations Holding GmbH over UTA Telekom AG	(i) Public voice telephone services; (ii) leasing of networks; (iii) data transmission through fixed networks	Not specified (the Commission did not have to define the product markets specifically)	Not specified (the Commission did not have to define the geographic market specifically)	Not specified
Particitel International/ Cableuropa	Case IV/M.1251, Commission Decision of July 30, 1998	Extension of joint venture between Bank of America GE to Capital Communications CDPQ	Pay-TV and voice telephony (precise product market definition not necessary for decision)	Definition based on Commission precedents	Spain	No specific reasons given

Orange/Viag	Case IV/JV.4, Commission Decision of August 11, 1998	Co-operative joint venture between Orange and Viag in the sector for mobile services	Although it left the issue of market definition open, the Commission indicated that the relevant product market could be the market for digital mobile telecommunications services	Along the lines of the *Enel* decision, the Commission indicated (although it did not take a firm position) that it may no longer be appropriate to consider that DCS 1800 and GSM are part of separate product markets on the ground (i) that dual-mode handsets allow users to use both frequencies; (ii) of the demand from customers to be able to roam between GSM and DCS 1800	Switzerland	The licence granted to the joint venture is limited to the Swiss territory and access to foreign networks via international roaming agreements do not provide an interchangeable solution notably because of the higher price level
Ericsson/Nokia/Psion	Case No. COMP/JV.6, Commission decision of August 11, 1998	Co-operative joint venture aimed at developing an operating system for use in wireless information devices	(i) Operating systems for wireless information devices; (ii) mobile phones; (iii) wireless information devices (*e.g.* Nokia Communicator); (iv) hand-held computers (*e.g.* Psion products)	(i) Not specified; (ii), (iii) and (iv) the Commission left open the issue of whether or not these should be defined as separate markets in light of the trend towards merging of these products into a single information devices markets	(i) Worldwide; (ii), (iii) and (iv) worldwide, at least, European	(i) The operating system can be used worldwide in various types of wireless information devices; (ii), (iii) and (iv) transport costs are not significant, no barriers to trade, pan-European technical standards, suppliers are active worldwide, prices similar throughout Western Europe
Telia/Sonera/Lietuvos Telekomas	Case IV/JV.7, Commission Decision of August 14, 1998	Acquisition of joint control of a Lithuanian telecommunications operator by Telia and Sonera (formerly Telecom Finland)	The parties proposed the following market definitions: (a) Fixed line telephony: (i) international voice telecommunications services; (ii) domestic voice telecommunications services; (iii) international data telecommunications services; (iv) domestic data telecommunications services; (b) mobile telephony	Not specified	(i) Domestic and international voice telephony and data services: Lithuania; (ii) enhanced services: global; (iii) mobile telephony: the Commission left open the issue of the scope of the market	Along the line of the *Orange/Viag* decision, the Commission noted that there is an increasing trend towards a European market for mobile telephony service provision. The Commission nevertheless failed to take a formal position on the geographic scope of the market

Case	Reference	Type of Case	Product Markets	Reasons Given for Product Markets	Geographic Markets	Reasons Given for Geographic Markets
Telia/Sonera/Motorola/ UAB Omnitel	Case IV/JV.9, Commission Decision of August 18, 1998	Acquisition of joint control of a Lithuanian mobile operator by Telia and Sonera	(i) Mobile telephony; (ii) paging; (iii) data transmission; (iv) internet services (the Commission left the issue of market definition open)	Not specified	The Commission referred to the *Viag/ Orange* precedent	Based on customer tendency to purchase products from multiple sources on a worldwide basis and the fact that all players operate subsidiaries in almost each part of the world. The Commission referred to precedents (*AT&T/Philips, Siemens/Italtel, Compaq/Tandem*) where it held that the market is at least EEA-wide, reasoning that products differ to some extent in the EEA with other regions (the Commission did not take a position on exact definition of relevant market)
Nortel/Bay	Case IV/M.1263, Commission Decision of August 21, 1998	Acquisition of Bay Networks Inc. by Northern Telecom Limited in the sector of data-networking products, systems and services	Parties proposed the following market definitions: (i) Local Network Area (LAN) products; (ii) Wide Area Networks (WAN). Further subcategories can be distinguished (i) Shares media LAN Hub (SMLH); (ii) LAN Switch; (iii) router; (iv) Remote Access Concentrator (RAC); (v) Frame Relay Access Device (FRAD); (vi) Network Switch; (vii) Data-over-cable Model; (viii) X.25 Switch	Distinction between LAN and WAN products based on different customer applications and underlying technologies (*i.e.* LAN products, based on the ethernet protocol, interconnect users and provide shared access to centralised computing resources at fast speed; WAN products interconnect typically LANs or segments of LANs over long-distance, and run over technologies such as ATM or Frame Relay. These technologies offer secure transmission over long distance but at lower speed). Further categories may be distinguished according to standard industry practice and customer purchase patterns. The Commission did not take a position on the relevant product market definition but noted that, given the evolutionary nature of the information technology business, data networking products change	The parties proposed to define the relevant product markets on a worldwide basis	

				rapidly as new technologies could offer potential benefits, and therefore, could result in new data networking products	The relevant geographic market is national, in particular for cultural and language reasons
Home Benelux B.V.	Case IV/JV.11, Commission Decision of September 15, 1998	Co-operative joint venture to provide internet services in the Netherlands	(i) Dial-up internet access for residential and for business customers; (ii) internet advertising; (iii) paid-for content provision	(i) The Commission left open the issue of whether separate markets should be identified for internet access services to residential users and for business customers. The Commission indicated that a single product market could be defined for all alternative means of accessing the internet (*i.e.* electricity lines, cable, telephone lines, wireless access); (ii) and (iii) content and advertising generate revenue in different ways and from different sources	(i), (ii) and (iii) national, regional or language based
WSI Webseek	Case IV/JV.8, Commission Decision of September 28, 1998	Creation of a joint venture between Deutsche Telekom Online Services GmbH, Axel Springer Verlag Ag, Georg von Holtzbrinck GmbH & Co. and Infoseek Corporation	(i) Advertising on the internet; (ii) internet access; (iii) fee-based provision of internet content	Reference to *Telia/Telenor; Cégétel/Canal+; @Home Benelux*	Left open (either Germany or entire German-speaking area in the EEA)
NC/Canal+/CDPQ/ BankAmerica	Case IV/M.1327, Commission Decision of December 3, 1998	Co-operative joint venture between Canal+, Capital Communications CDPQ (CDPQ) and BankAmerica in the fields of cable television networks	(i) Pay-television; (ii) wholesale supply of film and sports channels for retail pay-TV	Based on its decisional practice, pay-TV is distinct from free-access television, which is financed by advertising or state contributions	National
AT&T & TCI	Case IV/M.1252, Commission Decision of December 4, 1998	Merger between AT&T and TCI in the telecommunications and cable sectors	(i) Fixed telecommunications services; (ii) pay-television; (iii) cable networks	Not specified (the Commission did not have to define the product market specifically)	Not specified (the Commission did not have to define the geographic market specifically)

Case	Reference	Type of Case	Product Markets	Reasons Given for Product Markets	Geographic Markets	Reasons Given for Geographic Markets
PTA/Telecom Italia/ Telekom Austria	Case IV/M.1171, Commission Decision on December 16, 1998	Concentrative joint venture between PTA and Telecom Italia whereby Telecom Italia acquires joint control of the Austrian national operator	Parties proposed the following market definitions: (i) voice telephony; (ii) network leasing; (iii) mobile telecommunications; (iv) paging services; (v) consulting and engineering services relating to telephone and other telecommunications means; (vi) data services, including corporate networks and value-added services; (vii) online services and internet access services; (viii) publication of telephone directories. (The Commission did not take a position on the precise market definition)	Not specified (the Commission did not have to define the product market specifically)	The Commission left the question of the relevant geographic market open except for directories where the market was defined as Austria	National scope of directories market based on the existence of specific regulatory constraints
BT/AT&T	Case IV/JV.15, Commission Decision of March 30, 1999	Co-operative joint venture between BT and AT&T in order to provide global telecommunications services to multinational customers and international carrier services	(i) Global telecommunications services; (ii) international carrier services; (iii) international voice telephony services on the UK–US route; (iv) certain UK services (business and retail basic voice services, wholesale carriers services, domestic value-added services, teleconferencing, telex, domestic data services, internet access, out-sourcing services and mobile services)	(i) The Commission considered that this market constituted one single product market because these services are priced as a package and are supplied by the same global suppliers; (ii) the Commission left open the issue of whether the market should be defined on a global basis (as it has decided in the *Unisource* decision) or in terms of country pairs routes. The Commission took, however, the position that, because of factors such as the delay inherent in satellite circuits, cable and satellite	(i) Worldwide; (ii) at least Europe-wide, possibly global; (iii) UK for provision of international voice telephony services on the UK–US route; (iv) national	(i) Services and customers are international; (ii) geographic proximity between purchaser and supplier of switched transit capacity is not relevant; (iv) most of these services require a nationally granted licence, or a certain presence is required within the country concerned

Lucent Technologies/ Ascend Communication	Case IV/M.1440, Commission Decision of April 6, 1999	Acquisition of Ascend by Lucent	Parties proposed the following market definitions: (i) Frame Relay Switches; (ii) ATM WAN switches; (iii) IP Routers; (iv) backbone routers; (v) branch office/small office routers; (vi) personal routers, remote access servers (RAS); (vii) remote access concentrators (RAC). The Commission left the issue of market definition open	The Commission indicated, based on previous practice (*Nortel/Bay*) that some of the segments proposed by the parties could be combined in broader product markets. ATM switches and Frame Relay switches can be considered to form part of a broader product market for WAN switches. Similarly, RAS and RAC might be included into a market for aggregation devices	At least EEA-wide	are currently still not substitutable for the provision of international voice traffic, as far as both quality and reliability are concerned / Not specified
AT&T/IBM Global Network	Case IV/M.1396, Commission Decision of April 22, 1999	Acquisition by AT&T of IBM's Global Network (IGN) business	The parties proposed to distinguish between telecommunications services at the following levels: (i) level 1: basic telecommunications services; (ii) level 2: end-to-end telecommunications services; (iii) level 3: provision of managed solutions; (iv) level 4: services of the highest degree of IT functionality. The Commission considered that the market can be defined in two possible ways: (i) a narrow definition on a service by service basis; (ii) a wide product market covering a broad range of services falling under the "managed solutions" umbrella	The different levels are defined on the basis of the extent of "value-added" components they contain	Worldwide	The conditions of price under which such services are offered do not depend on the geographical location of either the provider or the consumer

Case	Reference	Type of Case	Product Markets	Reasons Given for Product Markets	Geographic Markets	Reasons Given for Geographic Markets
Olivetti/Telecom Italia	Case IV/M.1496, Commission Decision of April 22, 1999	Acquisition of Telecom Italia by Olivetti by way of a public offer	The parties proposed the following market definition. Faxes for (i) private and (ii) professional use; (iii) consulting services in office automation; (iv) computer services to public services, banks, insurance companies and travel agencies; (v) maintenance and management of software and computer services. The Commission left the issue of market definition open	The parties proposed to distinguish between computer services to public services, banks, insurance companies and travel agencies and the same services rendered to other customers because of the need for these customers to connect a central structure with many locations spread across the territory	The parties indicated that the market should be considered as a Community-wide market because of the standard harmonisation and the lack of importance of transport costs. The Commission left the issue open	
Deutsche Telekom/Max Mobil	Case IV/M.1465, Commission Decision of April 22, 1999	Acquisition of Max Mobil by DT	(i) Mobile voice telephony; (ii) fixed voice telephony	(i) The Commission indicated that GSM 900 and DCS 1800 belong to the same product market; (ii) not specified	(i) Mobile: the Commission left the issue open of whether the market was EEA-wide or national; (ii) fixed telephony: national	
Bertelsmann/Havas/Bol	Case IV/M.1459, Commission Decision of May 6, 1999	Concentrative joint venture between Bertelsmann and Havas for the distribution of books via the internet	The parties proposed the following market definitions: (i) all retail consumer book sales; (ii) the narrower market segment for the online sales of consumer books via the internet; (iii) publishing of consumer books; (iv) wholesale distribution of consumer books. The Commission also considered another potential market, *i.e.* that for all forms of "distant sales" of consumer books (including book club sales, mail order and sales via internet). The Commission left the issue of market definition open	The Commission left open the issue of whether the market for sales of books via the internet should be considered wider than France		

Vodafone/AirTouch	Case IV/M.1430, Commission Decision of May 21, 1999	Acquisition of AirTouch by Vodafone in the mobile telecommunications sector.	Mobile telecommunications market (the Commission failed to take a firm position on market definition)	GSM 900 and DCS 1800 are readily substitutable for one another from a consumer's perspective and dual-mode handsets render the distinction between the two standards less of an issue for the consumer	National	Subscription with a mobile operator of another country is not yet an economically sensible alternative for a customer given the additional costs associated with permanent roaming
Wind/Enel STC	Case IV/M.1536, Commission Decision of June 29, 1999	Acquisition by Wind (a joint venture between DT, Enel and FT) of sole control of a subsidiary of Enel in charge of operating Enel's internal telecommunications network	(i) Fixed line telecommunications services; (ii) mobile telephony; (iii) data transmission; (iv) enhanced global services; (v) resale of transmission capacity. The Commission left the issue of market definition open	Not specified	(i) National; (ii) the Commission left open the issue of whether the market was national or European; (iii) national; (iv) global; (v) national	(i), (iii) and (v) due to licensing and regulatory framework for the provision of services in Italy, (iv) because services are provided via global networks
AT&T/Mediaone	Case IV/M.1551, Commission Decision of July 23, 1999	Acquisition by AT&T of Mediaone, a company active in cable services and mobile telephony	(i) Fixed telephony services; (ii) Internet access services; (iii) mobile services; (iv) internet advertising; (v) paid-for content provision	(iii) The Commission indicated that there is an increasing trend towards a European geographic market for mobile service provision, including the different standards; (iv) and (v) the division between dial-up internet access, internet advertising and paid-for content is based on the assumption that these different activities earn revenues in different ways and from different sources and that they are carried out by different undertakings and require substantially different inputs	(ii), (iv) and (v) national or language-based	

Case	Reference	Type of Case	Product Markets	Reasons Given for Product Markets	Geographic Markets	Reasons Given for Geographic Markets
France Telecom/Editel/ Lince	Case IV/M.1553, Commission Decision of July 30, 1999	Concentrative joint venture (Lince) between FT and Editel (a corporate vehicle acting on behalf of Banco Santander, Ferrovial and Multitel) to provide fixed voice telephony services in Spain	The parties have identified the following relevant product markets: (i) local loop telephone services; (ii) operator access to local loop network (interconnection); (iii) business data communication; (iv) ISP services; (v) global telecommunications services. The Commission left the issue of market definition open as the transaction does not raise any competition problems even under the narrowest market definition	Not specified	Not defined	
Kirsch/Mediaset	Case IV/M.1574, Commission Decision of August 3, 1999	Concentrative joint venture between Kirsch and Mediaset for the provision of marketing services for TV advertising	(i) Free-access TV; (ii) marketing of TV advertising; (iii) TV productions; (iv) TV rights/ licences	(i) There is a relevant market for TV advertising where broadcasters compete for advertising revenues. This market must be distinguished from advertising through other media; (ii) the Commission found that there was a separate market for the marketing, as advertising agency, of advertising time and sponsorship for TV broadcasters on an international basis; (iii) the market must be limited to productions commissioned by a broadcaster at the exclusion of captive production; (iv) the Commission left open the issue of whether films and sports form separate markets	(i), (iii), and (iv) the Commission took the position that these markets are still national or language-based; (iii) the Commission left open the issue of whether the market for marketing of TV advertising was national or broader	

Deutsche Telekom One2One	Case IV/M.1669, Commission Decision of September 27, 1999	Acquisition by DT of One2One in the mobile sector in the UK	Mobile telecommunications services encompassing GSM 900 and GSM 1800	Based on *Vodafone/Air Touch* precedent	National	Based on *Vodafone/Air Touch* and *Orange/Viag* precedents
Telexis/EDS	Case IV/M.1654, Commission Decision of September 30, 1999	Concentrative joint venture between EDS and Telexis to provide call centre services	Call centre comprising technology service, manpower management, full service. The Commission left open the issue of whether the various components form separate product markets	Not specified	National	In light of the technical nature of the service
France Telecom/STI/SRD	Case COMP/M.1679, Commission Decision of October 21, 1999	Acquisition of joint control by France Telecom of SRD, a telecommunications company that provides data, internet and voice telephony services to closed-user groups	The parties proposed the following product market definitions: (i) local loop telephone services; (ii) business data communications; (iii) value-added services; (iv) internet services (the Commission left open the issue of product market definition)		The parties proposed the following geographic market definitions: (i) local loop telephone services: national; (ii) business data communications: EEA-wide; (iii) value-added services; worldwide or at least EEA-wide; (iv) internet services: national. The Commission left open the issue of geographic market definition	
Freecom/Dangaard	Case COMP/JV.26, Commission Decision of December 1, 1999	Co-operative joint venture in the sector of sales of handsets of mobile telephones and accessories, and repair services	The parties proposed to define the relevant markets as (i) wholesale of mobile telephones and accessories; (ii) value-added services in connection with these services (hotline services, maintenance and similar services). Although it failed to take a firm position on market definition, the Commission seems to agree with the parties' proposed market definitions	(i) and (ii) mobile handsets and value-added services belong to separate markets because of the existence of independent suppliers of value-added services not present on the market for mobile handsets and the lack of substitutability between the product and the value-added services	The parties proposed to define the relevant geographic market as the EEA plus Switzerland. The Commission failed to take a firm position on the geographic market	The parties based their position on the fact that technical standards are uniform across the EEA and there are no trade barriers. The Commission seems to imply that, as regards wholesale of handsets, the market may be national, as many wholesalers are only active in a specific country and generally there is a need for local presence due, in particular, to linguistic requirements

Case	Reference	Type of Case	Product Markets	Reasons Given for Product Markets	Geographic Markets	Reasons Given for Geographic Markets
Telia/Telenor	Case IV/M.1439, Commission Decision of October 13, 1999	Acquisition of joint control by the Swedish and Norwegian governments of a new company created to hold the shares of Telia AB and Telenor AS	Telephony and related services: (i) provision of local loop infrastructure; (ii) provision of long-distance/international network infrastructure; (iii) subscriber access to telephone services; (iv) provision of mobile telephony; (v) operator access to networks; (vi) provision of business data communications; (vii) ISP services; (viii) internet advertising; (ix) sale of advertising space in telephone directories. Television services: (i) provision of satellite capacity; (ii) acquisition and distribution via cable and DTH (direct-to-home) of television signals; (iii) buying of content; (iv) wholesaling of rights to content; (v) technology for technical services relating to pay-TV	In the television services context, the Commission concluded that there were a number of aspects, which indicated that a certain degree of substitutability already existed between cable, DTH and SMATV (Satellite Mast Antenna Television). It did not contest third parties' submissions that, with the introduction of digital services, cable and DTH offerings could become less homogeneous, thereby increasing the incentive for customers to switch. However, the Commission did not take the position that there were separate markets for the different TV distribution infrastructures and left the market definition open. With regard to pay-TV, the Commission continued not to sub-divide pay-TV services into analogue and digital transmission services, stating that digital services were an emerging market, which would gradually replace analogue services	Telephony and related services: national except for access to international call services (examination on the basis of specific "country pair" relationships) and for business data communications (possibly European or world-wide). Television services: national (left open for content buying and retail TV distribution), market for satellite transponder capacity was considered Nordic	Commission refers to *France Telecom/Equant* and *Nordic Satellite Distribution* decisions
Marconi/Bosch Public Network	Case COMP/M.1800, Commission Decision of January 19, 2000	Acquisition by Marconi of Bosch Public Network	(i) Cable/wireline transmission equipment; (ii) access networks equipment	The Commission referred to previous Commission decisions: *AT&T/ Philips and Siemens/Italtel*	The Commission left open the question whether the market was national or wider	The Commission considered it was not necessary to take a position on geographic market as the operation did not raise any concerns even taking the markets as being national

			Based on earlier decision, *Vodafone/Airtouch*	National	Based on precedents
Bellsouth/Vodafone (E-Plus)	Case COMP/M.1817, Commission Decision of January 26, 2000	Acquisition of E-Plus Mobilfunk (E-Plus) by BellSouth from Vodafone	Analogue mobile voice telephony services and digital voice telephony services using both the GSM 900 and DCS (GSM) 1800 standards	Based on earlier decision, *Vodafone/Airtouch*	National	Based on precedents *Vodafone/Airtouch* and *Deutsche Telekom/One2One*
BVI Television (Europe)/SPE Euromovies Investments/Europe MovieCo Partners	Case COMP/JV.30, Commission Decision of February 3, 2000	Concentration by which BVI Europe and SPE Europe acquired joint control of newly created MovieCo	(i) Acquisition of broadcasting rights, in particular for films and sporting events; (ii) wholesale supply of films and sport channels for pay-TV	(i) Based on TPS decision; (ii) based on *BiB/Open* decision	National	Based on *Kirch/Richemont/Telepiù* precedent
KKR/Bosch Telecom Private Networks	Case COMP/M.1840, Commission Decision of February 29, 2000	Concentration by which KKR acquires BTPN from Bosch	(i) Market for smaller private telecommunications systems which comprised the letting and selling of Telephone Switchboards (Private Automatic branch exchange "PABX"); (ii) larger PABX; (iii) maintenance and installation of PABX	Based on *Telia/Telenor* decision	National	Based on *Telia/Telenor* precedent
MMS/DASA/Astrium	Case COMP/M.1636, Commission Decision of March 21, 2000	Concentration by which MMS and DASA acquired joint control of newly created Astrium	(i) Commercial satellites; (ii) (civil) observation and scientific satellites; (iii) smaller space infrastructures; (iv) larger space infrastructures	The products under (i) and (ii) did not involve the same technological skills and did not address the same customers; as regards (iii) and (iv) the Commission found that the smaller product categories may not have had the capabilities or the financial resources necessary for the production of larger systems, and usually concentrated their prime contractor business in the smaller product categories	(i) Communications satellites and communication satellite equipment: global; (ii) space infrastructures: European	(i) Commercial customers purchased these products without being subjected to geographic considerations, and the conditions of competition in the communication satellite sector were sufficiently homogeneous for the geographic market to be considered worldwide, as customers requested quotations from, and placed orders with, a variety of suppliers in Europe and the USA; (ii) observation and scientific satellites and space probes were primarily purchased by space agencies, and

Case	Reference	Type of Case	Product Markets	Reasons Given for Product Markets	Geographic Markets	Reasons Given for Geographic Markets
MMS/DASA/ Astrium—cont.						competition was usually restricted to domestic satellite prime contractors. Especially, in the case of ESA, procurement of satellites and equipment products was subject to a geographic "juste retour" principle enshrined in the ESA Convention requiring ESA: (i) "to grant preference to the fullest extent possible to industry in all Member States"; and (ii) "to ensure that all Member States participate in an equitable manner, having regard to their financial contribution". The Commission found that there might also be national markets for observation and scientific satellites and space probes in those Member States where national space agencies applied similar procurement procedures at the prime contractor level. In addition there might also be a worldwide market for observation satellites sold to commercial operators or to institutional customers where a domestic producer did not exist (as in Asia), as these customers seemed to obtain these systems through global competitive procurement. But, the issue was left open

CLT-UFA/Canal+/Vox	Case COMP/M.1889, Commission Decision of March 21, 2000	Acquisition of News' 49.9 per cent stake in VOX by CLT-UFA. The creation of Vox as a joint venture between CLT-UFA and News, and the subsequent entry of Canal+ were approved previously by the Commission	Advertising in television broadcasting	Based on previous decisions	National	Based on previous decision, *Bertelsmann/Kirch/Premiere*
BSkyB/KirchPayTV	Case IV/JV.37, Commission Decision of March 21, 2000	Acquisition by British Sky Broadcasting Group plc of joint control over KirchPayTV GmbH & Co. KGaA together with Kirch Vermögensverwaltungs GmbH & Co. KG	(i) Pay-TV; (ii) digital interactive TV services (iDTV); (iii) acquisition of broadcasting rights (the Commission left open the question of whether the markets for the acquisition of broadcasting rights for films and sports events constituted separate markets)	(i) Based on decisions in *MSG Media Service, Bertelsmann/Kirch, Premiere, and Deutsche Telekom/BetaResearch.* (ii) The Commission distinguished (i) from (ii) because the products under (i) are perceived to be "entertainment based" while the products under (ii) are perceived to be "transactional" and a source of information. The Commission also distinguished (ii) from the market for high-street retailing. The Commission made a further distinction between the market for digital interactive services available via television sets and those available via PCs	(i) National, and possibly entire German-speaking area, although question was left open; (ii) national; (iii) UK, Ireland and Germany, with possible separate market for pan-European sports rights, although question was left open	(i) Due to different regulatory regimes, language barriers, cultural factors and other different conditions; (iii) broadcasting rights are normally granted for a given language version and broadcasting area, but sometimes for European territory
Vodafone Airtouch/Mannesmann	Case COMP/M.1795, Commission Decision of April 12, 2000	Acquisition of sole control over Mannesmann by Vodafone Airtouch	(i) Mobile telecommunications services; (ii) provision of seamless pan-European mobile telecommunications services to internationally mobile customers; (iii) mobile handsets; (iv) mobile telephony network equipment	(i) The Commission based its definition on previous *Vodafone/Airtouch* decision, but left open the question whether further segmentation into network operator/service provider and/or into business/residential	(i) National; (ii) at least pan-European, but the conclusion was left open; (iii) and (iv) possibly global in scope	(i) Based on previous *Vodafone/Airtouch* decision; (ii) there was demand for advanced seamless pan-European services from internationally mobile customers, and large corporations, which was

Case	Reference	Type of Case	Product Markets	Reasons Given for Product Markets	Geographic Markets	Reasons Given for Geographic Markets
Vodafone Airtouch/ Mannesmann—cont.				customers was possible; (ii) the Commission found that there was a specific demand by international corporate customers (due to the international scope of their businesses) for seamless pan-European mobile telephony services and that these mobile services would be bought separately and not as a package of mobile and fixed solutions		distinct from the demand for national mobile telecommunications services for smaller companies and private users due to the international scope of the large corporations businesses (cross-border international) and their international customer base — finally, left open; (iii) left open
Reuters/Equant — Project Proton	Case COMP/M.1875, Commission Decision of April 17, 2000	Creation of a joint venture (provisionally named Proton) set up by Reuters and Equant	IP-based extranet services to the financial community	The Commission left open the question of whether the public internet can be considered as a substitute for the IP-based networking services	The geographic scope of the market for the provision of IP-based networking services was considered to be worldwide; but the final decision was left open by the Commission	(i) Strong international characteristics of the market would lead to the conclusion that it was worldwide; but also (ii) cost barriers or practical considerations could prevent a user in Europe from procuring extranet services from a provider abroad
Alcatel/Newbridge Networks	Case COMP/M.1908, Commission Decision of May 10, 2000	Concentration by which Alcatel acquired the control of Newbridge by way of a public bid	(i) DSL (Digital Subscriber Line) equipment; (ii) data switching products such as ATM WAN (Asynchronous Transfer Mode Wide Area Network)	(i) The Commission did not consider xDSL products as part of a separate market from DSL, because although these products had different transmission characteristics, all provided essentially the same service and so were more or less substitutable; (ii) the question of whether data switching products constituted a separate market was left open	Worldwide	Based on Commission's investigation

Case	Decision	Transaction	Product market	Commission comments	Geographic market	Commission comments
Viag Interkom/Telenor Media	Case COMP/M.1957, Commission Decision of June 14, 2000	Acquisition of joint control of a newly formed enterprise "Newco"	Provision of directory assistance services in (i) printed form; (ii) electronic form	The Commission found that telephone directories existed in printed and in electronic form (CD-ROMs, internet) and that those two forms were handled and used differently and had a different pricing structure. They were therefore not considered as being part of the same market	National	The Commission found that it was technically impossible to use the joint venture's telephone numbers abroad, as there was no mechanism to invoice customers calling from abroad. In fact the customer was charged via his telephone bill
Canal+/Lagardère (JV 40) and Canal+/Lagardère/Liberty Media (JV 47)	Case IV/JV.40, Commission Decision of June 22, 2000	JV40: (i) Acquisition of joint control by Lagardère (together with Canal+) over CanalSatellite; (ii) acquisition of joint control by Canal+ (together with Lagardère) over EuroMusique MCM (JV1); and (iii) creation of an interactive services joint venture between CanalSatellite and Largardère (JV2). JV 47: (i) acquisition of joint control by Largardère (together with Canal+ and Liberty) over Multithematiques; (ii) creation of a special interest channels provider Largardère (Hachette)/Multithematiques	(i) Distribution and operation of special interest channels (with possible further division into subsegments based on different themes to be delivered; (ii) pay-TV (with possible sub-segment for provision of multichannel bouquets); (iii) interactive digital TV services; (iv) acquisition of broadcasting rights	The Commission referred to its previous decisions: *TPS* and *BIB/Open*	National	The Commission referred to its previous decisions: *TPS* and *BIB/Open*
MCI WorldCom/Sprint	Case COMP/M.1741, Commission Decision of June 28, 2000	Concentration by which Sprint would have been merged into MCI WorldCom	(i) Market for the provision of top-level or universal internet connectivity; (ii) GTS; (iii) international voice telephony services	(i) hierarchical nature of the internet as discussed in the *WorldCom/MCI* decision; (ii) *BT/AT&T* decision; (iii) left open	Top-level internet connectivity: universal	Based on *MCI WorldCom* decision
Bertelsmann/GBL/Pearson TV	Case IV/M.1958, Commission Decision of June 29, 2000	Acquisition of joint control by Bertelsmann and Group Bruxelles Lambert (GBL) of Pearson TV	(i) TV advertising (although Commission always distinguished between the markets for free TV and pay-TV, it	(ii) The Commission referred to its previous decisions in *RTL/Veronica/Endemol* and *Telefonica/Endemol*	(i) National; (ii) national or regional (region sharing the same language); definition was left open; (iii) national or regional	(i) TV advertising is directed to the area where the TV broadcasters have their main audience

Case	Reference	Type of Case	Product Markets	Reasons Given for Product Markets	Geographic Markets	Reasons Given for Geographic Markets
Bertelsmann/GBL/ Pearson TV—cont.			noted here that there may be a wider market for advertising on free and pay-TV in the UK; ultimately, the question was left open); (ii) TV productions (limited to productions that are not for captive use, but offered on the market); (iii) TV rights/licences (with possible sub-segments of film and other fiction rights, and sports rights; ultimately, definition was left open)		(region sharing the same language), but sometimes EU-wide or even worldwide; definition was left open	
Telecom Italia/News TV/Stream	Case IV/M.1978, Commission Decision of June 29, 2000	Acquisition of joint control by Telecom Italia and British News TV of Stream	(i) Pay-TV; (ii) transmission capacity (with possible sub-segments of cable capacity and satellite capacity); (iii) set-top boxes and conditional access technology (with the question left open whether the sale of set-top boxes was, in fact, a separate market or formed part of the market for technical and administrative services for pay-TV); (iv) acquisition of broadcasting rights for pay-TV channels	(i) The Commission referred to its previous *Bertelsmann/Kirch/ Premiere* decision	National	(i) The Commission referred to its earlier *Kirch/Piemont/Telepiù* decision
Vodafone/Vivendi/ Canal+	Case COMP/JV.48, Commission Decision of July 7, 2002	Acquisition of joint control of Vizzavi by Vodafone, Vivendi and Canal+	(i) Internet access; (ii) internet content and services markets; Sub-markets: internet advertising and provision of paid-for-content; (iii) portals; Sub-markets: vertical portals (having a narrow focus) and	(i) and (ii) The Commission based its decision on previous cases such as *Telia/Telenor/Schibsted* and *Cégetel/Canal+/ AOL/Bertelsmann*; (iii) for the first time, the Commission defined a market for portals based	(i) national; (ii) national (paid-for content tends to be national; (iii) pan-European; (iv) national; (v) national; (vi) Nordic	(i) Due to the necessity for local loop access and the availability of free-phone/local call rate numbers to the nearest point of presence; (ii) due to language and other cultural linguistic and regulatory reasons;

			horizontal portals (having a broad focus); (iv) digital interactive television services; (v) Upstream markets; (v) mobile telecommunication services; (vi) Pay-TV	on consumer demand for particular intermediation services; (iv) in line with its *BiB* decision, the Commission defined digital interactive TV services as a market separate from internet services available via PCs, given the different characteristics and use of PCs compared to televisions; (v) the exact definition of the relevant product market for mobile telecommunications services was left open; (vi) the Commission, as in previous decisions, defined pay-TV as a separate market distinct from free-access TV, financed by advertising or by state contributions	(iii) Commission based its decision on the findings reached in the *Vodafone/Mannesmann* decision; (iv) services offered have to be adapted to national demand and these services are likely to be reliant on retailers with national or regional operations; (v) Commission based its decision on findings in previous cases such as *MSG Media Service* and *Bertelsmann/Kirch/Premiere*; (vi) language characteristics and largely uniform programming of pay-TV in the Nordic countries
Telefonica/Endemol	Case COMP/M.1943, Commission Decision of July 11, 2000	Acquisition of sole control of Endemol by Telefonica	(i) Production of TV programmes; (ii) free-access TV; (iii) pay-TV	(i) Since TV programmes limited to captive users (in-house production) were in some cases sold to third parties (especially in the Spanish market), the latter were in direct competition with programmes produced by independent producers, and were therefore included in the relevant market for TV programme production; (ii) based on *BiB* and *Bertelsmann/Kirch/Premiere* decisions	National — (i) The *RTL Veronica/Endemol* decision was referred to by analogy (but the final conclusion was left open); (ii) in consideration of linguistic, cultural, licensing and copyright reasons, pay-TV and free-access TV are national markets

611

Case	Reference	Type of Case	Product Markets	Reasons Given for Product Markets	Geographic Markets	Reasons Given for Geographic Markets
ACS/Sonera/Vivendi/ Xfera	Case COMP/M.1954, Commission Decision of July 31, 2000	Acquisition of joint control of Xfera by ACS, Sonera and Vivendi. Xfera was granted a 3G (or UMTS) licence in Spain	Mobile telephony services	Commission did not define a separate market for UMTS. A firm definition was left open in this respect, as Xfera was a new entrant in the market for mobile services in Spain	National	Although current technical standards already allow the provision of mobile telephony services Europe-wide (and ultimately even globally), national legal conditions, costs and pricing structure suggested that the market should remain national
Telenor/Bellsouth/ Sonofon	Case COMP/M.2053, Commission Decision of August 4, 2000	Acquisition of joint control with Bellsouth of Sonofon by Telenor	Mobile telecommunications services (encompassing both GSM 900 and DCS 1800 and possibly also analogue platforms)	Based on *Vodafone/ Airtouch* decision	National	Based on *Vodafone/ Airtouch* decision
Telefonica/Tyco/JV	Case COMP/M.1926, Commission Decision August 11, 2000	Acquisition of joint control of the newly created Sam JV by Tyco and Telefonica	(i) Transmission capacity in Latin America; (ii) submarine fibre optic cable network equipment, including manufacture and supply of fibre optic cables, switching systems and its installation	(i) In previous decisions (*Telia/Telenor* and *Acea/ Telefonica*), the Commission found that it is possible to subdivide the markets for network infrastructure into separate submarkets, notably: undersea networks; terrestrial networks; satellite. However, the question was left open in this case; (ii) this market was vertically affected because a subsidiary of Tyco designed, manufactured, supplied and installed submarine fibre optic cable systems, while Tyco competed with other producers for supply contracts for networks	(i) National or, where appropriate, "country pairs", in this case including Central and South America and Florida; (ii) global	Based on *Telia/Telenor* and *Acea/Telefonica* decisions

France Telecom/Orange	Case COMP/M.2016, Commission Decision of August 11, 2000	Acquisition of sole control of Orange by France Telecom	(i) Mobile telecommunications services; (ii) the provision of seamless mobile pan-European mobile telecommunications services to internationally mobile customers; (iii) mobile handsets and mobile telephony network equipment	(i) and (ii) based on *Vodafone Airtouch/Mannesmann* decision; (iii) the Commission also concluded that mobile handsets and mobile telephony network equipment constituted separate markets due to the fact that mobile handsets are used by the final consumer whereas mobile telephony network equipment is used by the network operator to build the mobile telephony infrastructure	(i) National; (ii) left open; (iii) global	(i) Based on *Vodafone Airtouch/Mannesmann* decision; (ii) the competitive assessment of the case would have been the same regardless of whether the market was pan-European or not; (iii) based on *Vodafone Airtouch/Mannesmann* decision
Hutchison/NTT/DoCoMo/KPN Mobile JV	Case COMP/M.2099, Commission Decision of September 5, 2000	Joint control of H3G UK by Hutchison Whampoa, NTT, DoCoMo and KPN. The resulting JV was awarded a 3G (or UMTS) licence in the UK	Mobile telephony services	Given all possible definitions, the concentration did not raise competitive concerns. No separate market for 3G was thus identified	National	Based on *Vodafone Airtouch* decision
Telia/Oracle/Drutt	Case COMP/M.1982, Commission Decision of September 11, 2000	Acquisition of joint control by Telia of Drutt Corporation, a full-function joint venture, originally solely controlled by the software company Oracle	(i) Provision of internet advertising space; (ii) dial-up internet access; (iii) the provision of internet portal services	The Commission considered a separate market for the provision of internet advertising space to be relevant. Also as indicated in *Vodafone/Vivendi/Canal+*, the Commission held that internet access via mobile phones was unlikely to be a substitute for the traditional access tools. The Commission held that the market for internet portals could be divided into vertical portals (with a focus on particular content categories)	National	The Commission considered it to be national in geographic scope although it suggested that it might also be wider based on common language areas. The Commission, furthermore, restated its position that internet-related markets may be considered to be national due to the need for local loop services. It was suggested that this (internet-related) market was national, but could be increasingly European

613

Case	Reference	Type of Case	Product Markets	Reasons Given for Product Markets	Geographic Markets	Reasons Given for Geographic Markets
Telia/Oracle/Drutt— cont.				and horizontal portals (with a comprehensive internet offering), and that vertical portals could be further broken down according to the type of platform used		
AOL/Time Warner	Case COMP/M.1845, Commission Decision of October 11, 2000	Merger of AOL and Time Warner	(i) Online music delivery (both downloading and streaming); (ii) music player software; (iii) dial-up (narrow-band) internet access; (iv) paid-for content other than music (broadband content)	(i) A separate market definition for streaming and downloading was left open; (ii) the more technologies the player software supports, the more music it will be able to play. Therefore there was an interest for player software developers in being licensed as many technologies as possible; (iii) based on *Telia/Telenor*; (iv) based on *Telia/Telenor/Schibsted*	(i) EEA-wide at least; (ii) global; (iii) national; (iv) national or EEA-wide	(i) Left open; (ii) the language of the file menu text on music players could be easily changed to suit a multitude of languages; (iii) on the basis of the need of local loop service; (iv) left open
Vivendi/Canal+/ Seagram	Case COMP/M.2050, Commission Decision of October 13, 2000	Acquisition of sole control of Seagram	(i) Film distribution to theatres; (ii) licensing of broadcasting rights for feature films; (iii) rights for TV programmes; (iv) premium films/first-window/Pay-TV; (v) portals; (vi) online music delivery (both downloading and streaming)	(i) This was the last stage of the cinema entertainment chain; (ii) and (iii) were different from a demand- and supply-side perspective in the light of the different features and pricing structures; (iv) pay-TV films had different timing and windows of exhibition, ranging from theatrical exhibition, to video rentals, to pay-per-view, then first and second windows, until they became available as library programming available for the free TV market; (v) based on	(i) and (ii) national; (iii) pan-European; (iv) pan-European	(i) and (ii) cultural reasons; (iii) based on *Vizzavi*; (iv) left open

Parties	Case/Decision	Transaction	Relevant product market	Product market analysis	Geographic market	Geographic market analysis
				Vizzavi decision, further segmentation of the market into portal market accessible via mobile phones (WAP), via set-top boxes or PCs was left open; (vi) based on *AOL/Time Warner*		
SLDE/NTL/MSCP/ NOOS	Case COMP/M.2137, Commission Decision of October 16, 2000	Acquisition of joint control of the full-function joint venture NOOS by SLDE, NTL and MSCP	The joint venture was active in the provision of (i) retail distribution of pay-TV programmes; (ii) internet access and portal services; (iii) voice telephony services, comprising three separate product markets, including local, long-distance and international telephony services; (iv) supply of cable network infrastructure	(i) Based on *BSkyB/Kirch PayTV* and *Bertelsmann/Kirch/Premiere* decisions; (ii) the Commission recalled that access to internet involved connecting a customer to a network running the IP and that this access could be provided as dial-up access through modems or dedicated ("always on" private line) access, but it left open the question of whether they constituted separate markets; the Commission found in the *Vizzavi* decision that the provision of internet portal services constituted a separate market; (iii) based on *Telia/Telenor* decision; (iv) the Commission confirmed the distinctions made in previous decisions (*BiB* and *Telia/Telenor*) but left open the question of further delimitation of the market	National	(i) For cultural reasons, language barriers and different regulatory regimes, with the possibility of television markets across language zones left open; (ii) due to the necessity of local loop access and the availability of freephone/local call rate numbers to the nearest point of presence (POP) for the former and that licences to operate cable networks are awarded on a national basis for the latter; with respect to internet portal services, the Commission found that national markets may be appropriate for certain internet-related activities; (iii) based on *Telia/Telenor* decision; (iv) based on previous decisions
Alcatel/Thomson Multi- media JV	Case IV/M.2048, Commission Decision of October 26, 2000	Creation of joint venture in order to merge activities in MPEG (Moving Picture Experts Group) transmission and cable access	Market for interactive video networks further broken down into different segments for MPEG network products and for cable access network products	Ultimately Commission left precise market definition open	Worldwide	The Commission considered that customers tend to buy interactive video network products from multiple sources on a global basis and the parties were also active on this basis

615

Case	Reference	Type of Case	Product Markets	Reasons Given for Product Markets	Geographic Markets	Reasons Given for Geographic Markets
Vodafone/BT/Airtel JV	Case COMP/M.1863, Commission Decision of December 18, 2000	Acquisition of Airtel by Vodafone and BT	(i) Mobile telephony services; (ii) wholesale roaming services	(i) The Commission left open the issue of further segmentation of the market; (ii) the Commission believed that the demand from users for international roaming was distinct from national roaming, air-time provision, indirect access through carrier selection or pre-selection and that the provision of wholesale roaming to foreign mobile network operators satisfied primarily a demand by foreign mobile network operators whose main objective was to enable them to offer their own subscribers a seamless service, not limited to the territory in which they had their own physical network	National	Based on *Vodafone Airtouch/Mannesmann* decision
Universal Studio Networks/De Facto 829 (NTL)/Studio Channel Limited	Case COMP/M.2211, Commission Decision of December 20, 2000	Creation of new "Studio Channel"	(i) Production and supply of programming for television (content market); (ii) wholesale supply of basic-tier pay-TV channels to pay-TV operators; (iii) retail distribution of pay-TV channels to the final consumer via cable, DTH or DTT (retail market)	The Commission did not take a firm view on market definition, but it acknowledged the possibility of a separate market for pay-per-view films and/or channels, as distinct from premium film channels, at both wholesale and retail levels, because: (i) on the supply side, pay-per-view films were made available much earlier after theatrical release than films shown on basic-tier or premium pay-TV channels; and	(i) Arguably global even though the licensing of rights in question is done on a national basis; (ii) national or sub-national	(i) Left open; (ii) based on *Kirch/Richemont/ Telepiù*; (iii) based on former findings of the UK Competition Commission; the question of whether the retail market could be further divided into sub-national markets was also left open

				Based on *Telia/Telenor* decision (but question of whether more narrow market definition is possible was left open)
			National	
		(ii) on the demand side, the consumer chose to purchase a given film for an additional fee. By contrast, consumers did not have to pay to view basic-tier films on a per film basis nor did they pay for them on a per channel basis. However, pay-per-view is perceived as being not yet well developed	(i) Based on *Telia/ Telenor* decision (the Commission however left open the question whether the market for transmission capacity should be further divided into dark fibre and optical fibre and/or narrowband and broadband (high speed) networks); (ii) the Commission identified that, in principle, internet access and related services could be divided into services directly related to access on the one hand (residential and business) and portal services on the other (based on e-commerce and online advertising). Furthermore the Commission raised the possibility that the provision of narrowband services was a distinct market from broadband; (iii) referred to the Italian antitrust authority	
		(i) Provision of fixed telecommunications services, which could be divided into: the provision of voice telephony services (local, long-distance and international voice telephony services), business data communications services and transmission capacity (leased lines); (ii) internet access and related services; (iii) supply of electricity		
	Acquisition of joint control of Infostrada by France Télécom and Wind			
	Case COMP/M.2216, Commission Decision of January 19, 2001			
Enel/Wind/Infostrada				

Case	Reference	Type of Case	Product Markets	Reasons Given for Product Markets	Geographic Markets	Reasons Given for Geographic Markets
BT/Viag Intercom	Case COMP/M.2143, Commission Decision of February 19, 2001	Acquisition of sole control of Viag Intercom by BT	(i) Provision and distribution of global telecommunications services (GTS) and related services; (ii) provision of international wholesale roaming	(i) Based on previous decisions (*BT/AT&T*; *AT&T/IBM Global Networks*; *MCI/WorldCom*); (ii) left open	National	Based on *BT/Esat* decision
Vodafone Group Plc/ Eircell	Case COMP/M.2305, Commission Decision of March 2, 2001	Acquisition of sole control of Eircell by Vodafone	(i) Advanced seamless pan-European mobile services to internationally mobile customers; (ii) mobile telephony services (irrespective of whether analogue or digital, GSM 900/1800)	(i) Based on *Vodafone Airtouch/Mannesmann*; (ii) based on *Vodafone/ Airtouch*	(i) Pan-European; (ii) national	(i) Based on *Vodafone Airtouch/Mannesmann* decision; (ii) based on *Vodafone/Airtouch*
BT/Esat Digifone	Case IV/M.2282, Commission Decision of March 16, 2001	Acquisition by BT of sole control of Esat	(i) Emerging market for the provision of horizontal portals providing WAP-based internet access; (ii) wholesale roaming services market	(i) Based on *Vizzavi*; (ii) based on Commission's sector inquiry on roaming	(i) Left open; (ii) left open	
France Télécom/Equant	Case COMP/M.2257, Commission Decision of March 21, 2001	Acquisition by France Télécom of Equant	(i) Carriers' carrier services of telecommunications services between bilateral routes (country pairs); (ii) provision of global telecommunications services (GTS) to multinational corporations; (iii) provision of managed data network services (MDNS); (iv) provision of global telecommunications services/MDNS to French companies; (v) provision of telecommunications services to the airline industry on the basis of proprietary protocols	(i) Based on *BT/MCI*, the Commission agreed that with the availability of satellite telecommunications and transiting through third countries or territories, bilateral routes could be regrouped into wider categories, although in principle the provision of carrier services (*e.g.* through leased lines) between any given pair of countries or territories constituted a separate market; (ii) based on *MCI Worldcom/Sprint*; (iii) the Commission's investigation confirmed that non-managed services could not be	(i) Call traffic routes between any country pair; (ii) global; (iii) global; (iv) France; (v) any international route	Based on previous decisions (*BT/MCI* and *MCI WorldCom/Sprint*)

considered as a substitute for MDNS due to the fact that the running of many large companies required more and more specialised expertise; customers of managed data services were also sophisticated customers with a great knowledge of the different suppliers and these suppliers' capabilities. Therefore the Commission concluded that the provision of cross-border MDNS could be seen as a separate market within the wider categories of data communications services or global telecommunications services because of demand- and supply-side considerations; (iv) the Commission found that the French component of a number of large multinational companies for GTS and MDNS was so significant that it would be possible to price-discriminate between these and other customers, therefore justifying the possibility of identifying a distinct domestic market; (v) the Commission left open the question of whether modern data protocols (*e.g.* IP) were compatible with the specific protocols used by the airline industry (notably, Type A for telecommunications services and Type B for messaging services)

Case	Reference	Type of Case	Product Markets	Reasons Given for Product Markets	Geographic Markets	Reasons Given for Geographic Markets
UGC/Liberty Media	Case COMP/M.2222, Commission Decision of April 24, 2001	Acquisition by Liberty of UGC	(a) Telephony and internet-related services, including: (i) voice telephony; (ii) provision of internet access; (iii) broadband services provided over cable networks/triple-play services; (iv) portals; (v) internet advertising; (vi) content; and (b) pay-television and related services, which could be divided into (i) production and supply of TV programming; (ii) wholesale supply of pay-TV channels to pay-TV operators; (iii) retail distribution of pay-TV digital terrestrial television (DTT)	(i) The Commission found that on the basis of previous decisions there were distinct markets for the provision of voice telephony services to subscribers, which can be divided into local, long-distance/national and international services; (ii) the Commission did not decide on the relevant market definition (dial-up access via PC modem and via dedicated connections; dial-up services to residential and business customers and to smaller businesses; access provided over access mechanisms with different transmission, display and usage characteristics, notably mobile handsets, set-top boxes, and PCs; provision of narrowband and broadband access) for the purposes of the case; (iii) the Commission found that upgraded cable networks were the only networks that would be able to provide triple-play of digital services (broadcast TV, analogue and digital; high-speed data in both directions, including high-speed internet access; interactive TV services; telephony), therefore they were not substitutable	(a) National, except for certain emerging pan-European markets; (b) national or subnational	Based on previous decisions (*Telia/Telenor*; *Universal/NTL*)

Case	Decision	Operation	Product market	Analysis	Geographic market	Comments
				with DSL networks. But this did not address the issue of consumer demand. Therefore the Commission left open the question of whether triple-play services provided over cable network constituted separate markets; (iv)–(vi) based on *Vizzavi* decision; (b) (i) based on *Universal/NTL* decision	National	Market for internet advertising was considered as likely to be national in scope, although possibly wider (language areas). The same approach was taken with respect to internet portal services
Speedy Tomato/Olivetti	Case COMP/M.2463, Commission Decision of June 14, 2001	Creation of a joint venture by Speedy Tomato AB and Olivetti Tecnost S.p.A	(i) Provision of internet advertising space; (ii) provision of internet portal services	Previously the Commission defined internet advertising as a market in its own right and noted, without making a definitive ruling, that the market could be divided further into advertising on a mobile platform. For internet portal services the Commission also referred to its decision in *Vodafone/Vivendi/Canal+* which recognised the possibility of separate markets for internet portals. For horizontal portals, the market could be divided according to which platform is used to access the internet		
Schneider/Thomson Multimedia JV	Case IV/M.2403, Commission Decision of June 16, 2001	Creation of joint venture intended to design, develop, manufacture and sell powerline communications products	Market of no-new-wiring home networking products and technologies as identified by the parties; Commission left precise definition open	Not necessary for Commission to precisely define product market because even on the basis of the narrowest possible product market definition (powerline products) the operation would not lead to creation or strengthening of dominant position	Possibly national	Commission pointed to regulatory conditions which differ for individual Member States and the lack of uniform European Standard

621

Case	Reference	Type of Case	Product Markets	Reasons Given for Product Markets	Geographic Markets	Reasons Given for Geographic Markets
Vodafone/Airtel	Case COMP/M.2469, Commission Decision of June 26, 2001	Acquisition of sole control of Airtel by Vodafone	(i) Operation of mobile telephony networks; (ii) internet portals accessed via mobile phones and related services; (iii) provision of advanced seamless pan-European mobile telecommunications services; (iv) wholesale market for international roaming services	(i) Based on *Vodafone/Airtouch* and *Telia/Telenor* decisions; (ii) based on *Vizzavi*; (iii) based on *Vodafone Airtouch/Mannesmann*; (iv) based on *Vodafone/BT/Airtel*	National	(i) Based on *Vodafone/Airtouch* and *Telia/Telenor* decisions; (ii) based on *Vizzavi*; (iii) based on *Vodafone/Airtouch/Mannesmann*; (iv) based on *Vodafone/BT/Airtel*
YLE/TDF/DigitaJV	Case COMP/M.2300, Commission Decision of June 26, 2001	Acquisition of joint control of Digita, so far solely controlled by YLE, by way of purchase of shares by TDF	(a) Horizontally affected markets: (i) distribution of radio programmes and (ii) terrestrial transmission of radio programmes by low power frequencies; (b) Vertically affected markets: (i) transmission equipment for low-frequency radio customers; (ii) distribution equipment for radio customers; (c) Conglomerate markets: (i) terrestrial transmission of radio programmes by high power frequencies; (ii) distribution of TV programmes; (iii) terrestrial transmission of TV programmes	The markets under (a) referred to the delivery of radio or TV programmes and any related signals from the broadcaster's studio to a transmission station or interface; (b) refers to the delivery from the transmission station or interface to the final consumer over the air. The results of the Commission's investigation suggested that there could be a distinct market for digital transmission programmes from analogue radio equipment, due to differences in their technical characteristics and price. However, the final conclusion was left open	(i) National; (ii) at least EEA-/community-wide and most probably worldwide	Due to the specific topography of Finland, which is a relatively large yet sparsely populated country with very cold climatic conditions, terrestrial transmission of high/low frequency radio programmes and TV programmes constituted distinct product markets which were separate from cable and satellite transmission
Seat Pagine Gialle/Eniro	Case COMP/M.2468, Commission Decision of June 27, 2001	Acquisition by Seat of Eniro	Telephone directories and related markets, which included five separate relevant product markets: (i) sale of advertising space in local telephone directories	The Commission concluded that due to different characteristics of all the proposed markets it was reasonable to consider them as separate, although in some	The Commission found that the geographic extent of all the identified markets was national	The Commission's conclusion was in line with previous decisions, such as *Telia/Telenor*, *Viag Interkom/Telenor Media* and *Telia/Oracle/Drutt*. As regards (iv) the

					Commission considered that it could be wider than national, even though it was acknowledged that linguistic barriers still played an important role. Final decision was left open
		(White pages); (ii) sale of advertising space in business-to-consumer (B2C) telephone directories (Yellow pages); (iii) sale of advertising space in business-to-business (B2B) directories; (iv) internet advertising and, in particular, advertising in online telephone directories; (v) directory assistance services	cases it left the definitive conclusion open		
Flextronics/Alcatel	Case COMP/M.2479, Commission Decision of June 29, 2001	Acquisition by Flextronics of whole of the mobile handset manufacturing operations of Alcatel	The market of Electronic Manufacturing Services (EMS) to Original Equipment Manufacturers (OEMs) in the telecommunications, consumer electronics, computer, medical, and automotive industries	The Commission's investigation showed that EMS providers were normally capable of manufacturing various types of electronic product for OEMs operating in different industries and of switching their production according to orders from time to time received from OEMs. Therefore there were indications that the market was wider than EMS to manufacturers of mobile handsets, but the final conclusion was left open	EEA-wide	Low transport costs, low customs duties and the increased level of sourcing from various countries around the world
TDC/CMG/MIGway JV	Case COMP/M.2598, Commission Decision of October 4, 2001	Full-function joint venture between TDC Mobile and CMG	Wholesale access (SMS) to mobile telephony infrastructure, with the following vertically related upstream markets where one of the parent companies would be present: (i) SMS platforms; (ii) connectivity to the international signalling network; (iii) call-centre services (from	(i) SMS platforms and maintenance was necessary and could not be substituted by other technologies, in order to provide wholesale access (SMS) to mobile infrastructure; (ii) connection to the international signalling system was necessary in order to ensure connections with	The market for wholesale access (SMS) to mobile telephony infrastructure was pan-European; (i) pan-European or global; (ii) at least European; (iii) European or regional; (iv) national or international; (v) national	(i) Platforms were generally provided on a European or even global basis; (ii) connectivity was established through the existing international exchanges typically owned by the incumbent telecommunications operators in the different Member States, thus telecoms

Case	Reference	Type of Case	Product Markets	Reasons Given for Product Markets	Geographic Markets	Reasons Given for Geographic Markets
TDC/CMG/MIGway JV—cont.			customer care services to different types of IT support services). Related downstream markets were: (iv) provision of content and services for electronic media; (v) mobile telecommunications services	national mobile networks operators; (iii) left open; (iv) content and services could be offered by anyone by applying the necessary technology; (v) based on *Vodafone Airtouch/Mannesmann* decision		operators were able to offer these services irrespective of their geographical location; (iii) these services were offered independently of the location of the user of the service; (iv) left open; (v) based on former decisions
Blackstone/CDPQ/Deteks BW	Case COMP/M.2643, Commission Decision of November 23, 2001	Acquisition by Blackstone and CDPQ of joint control of Deteks BW	(i) Transmission capacity for television; (ii) telecommunications services; (iii) internet access; (iv) technical and administrative services for pay-TV	Based on previous case *Blackstone/CDPQ/KBN* (COMP/JV.50)	Either regional or national	Based on case *Blackstone/CDPQ/KBN* (COMP/JV.50)
Flextronics/Xerox	Case COMP/M.2629, Commission Decision of November 23, 2001	Acquisition by Flextronics of Xerox	Electronic manufacturing services (EMS)	Left open	EEA-wide	The market investigation confirmed that the relevant geographic market appeared to be at least EEA-wide if not worldwide. Left open
Blackstone/CPDQ/Deteks NRW	Case COMP/M.2652, Commission Decision of November 23, 2001	Joint acquisition by Blackstone and CDPQ via K-NRW of Deteks NRW	(i) Transmission capacity for television; (ii) telecommunications services; (iii) internet access	Based on case *Blackstone/CDPQ/KBN* (COMP/JV.46)	Either regional or national	The Commission did not find it necessary to further delineate the relevant geographic markets as, considering alternative geographic market definitions, effective competition would not be significantly impeded in the EEA or any substantial part of that area
PPC/Wind/JV	Case COMP/M.2565, Commission Decision of November 28, 2001	Acquisition of joint control by PPC and Wind of NHV	(i) Fixed telephony services; (ii) business data communications; (iii) internet access services; (iv) sale of transmission capacity	Exact scope of the various markets was left open	National	Left open

			Commission left the definition of the product markets open	Either regional or national	Left open
Mezzo/Muzzik	Case COMP/M.2550, Commission Decision of December 6, 2001	Acquisition by Lagardère Télémusique and France Télémusique and Wanadoo Audiovisuel of joint control of the company which stemmed from the merger between *Mezzo* and *Muzzik*	(i) Distribution and operation of special interest channels; (ii) pay-TV; (iii) acquisition of broadcasting rights; (iv) production of TV programming (for pay-TV)		Left open
BT/Concert	Case COMP/M.2642, Commission Decision of December 17, 2001	Acquisition by BT of assets of Concert, jointly controlled by BT and AT&T (de-concentration of Concert)	(i) GTS to multinational business customers; (ii) international carrier services to carriers worldwide; (iii) advanced mobile telecommunications services to business customers and mobile telecommunications services in UK/Ireland; (iv) certain telecommunications services in the UK/Ireland	Commission left the product market definition open since the operation did not give rise to significant competition concerns even on the narrowest possible product market definition	(i) and (ii) global; (iii) and (iv) regional (UK/Ireland)
KPNQwest/Ebone/GTS	Case COMP/M.2648, Commission Decision of January 16, 2002	Concentration by which KPNQwest acquired sole control over Ebone and GTS	(i) Carriers' carrier services; (ii) internet connectivity (wholesale); (iii) dedicated internet access (retail); (iv) Global Corporate Telecommunications Services (GTS); (v) web-hosting	(i) Europe-wide and possibly global; (ii) global; (iii) national; (iv) EEA-wide and possibly worldwide; (v) national	The definitions of the relevant geographic market were left open as, irrespective of geographic market definition, no competition concerns would arise
KPN/E-Plus	Case COMP/M.2726, Commission Decision of March 7, 2002	Acquisition by KPN of sole control of E-Plus	International wholesale roaming services	Based on *Vodafone/Airtel* and *Vodafone/BT/Airtel* decisions	National	Based on *Vodafone/Airtel* and *Vodafone/BT/Airtel* decisions
TPS	Case COMP/JV.57, Commission Decision of April 30, 2002	Acquisition by TF1 of TPS	(i) Pay-TV; (ii) distribution and operation of special-interest channels; (iii) acquisition of broadcasting rights	(i) Based on previous decisions, such as *MSG Media Service*, and *Bertelsmann/Kirch/ Premier*; (ii) based on *Vivendi/Canal+/ Seagram*; (iii) left open	National	Cultural and linguistical reasons
Telia/Sonera	Case COMP/M.2803, Commission Decision of May 28, 2002	Acquisition by Telia of Sonera	(i) Mobile telephony services (including both analogue and digital), with possible further market segmentation	(i) Based on *Telia/ Telenor and Vodafone/ Mannesmann* decisions, with possibility for further segmentation left	(i) National; (ii) national; (iii) national; (iv) national; (v) at least Nordic, if not pan-Baltic; (vi) national	(i) Based on *Telia/ Telenor and Vodafone/ Mannesman*; (ii) based on *KPN/E-Plus* decision; (iii) left open;

Case	Reference	Type of Case	Product Markets	Reasons Given for Product Markets	Geographic Markets	Reasons Given for Geographic Markets
Telia/Sonera—cont.			into corporate vs residential customers and mobile communications services to corporate customers with pan-Nordic needs; (ii) wholesale international roaming; (iii) wireless local area networks (WLAN); (iv) operator access to network (interconnection) and call termination on individual fixed and mobile networks; (v) corporate communications services; (vi) internet access services	open; (ii) based on *KPN/E-Plus* decision; (iii) WLAN is a technology used basically to provide two functionalities: (a) at public locations for broadband internet access; and (b) in buildings to avoid cabling. It is used for data communication, not for voice. However, the final decision on whether WLAN was a separate market was left open; (iv) the market for interconnection and call termination on fixed networks was defined in *Telia/Telenor*. The Commission also examined the markets for call termination onto mobile networks, on the basis of the "calling party pays" principle and the subsequent ability of any operator offering call termination to raise terminating charges without any competitive constraints; (v) based on *Telia/Telenor* and the fact that data business communications services often use different underlying network equipment (ATM and Frametie Delay) than traditional switched voice-related services; (vi) the Commission suggested in previous decisions that there		(iv) based on *Telia/Telenor*; (v) left open; (vi) the necessity for local loop access and availability of free-phone/local call rate number to the nearest point of presence (POP) and the existing regulatory framework

Pirelli/Edizione/Olivetti/ Telecom Italia	Case COMP/M.2574, Commission Decision of September 12, 2002	(i) Telecommunications infrastructure; (ii) telecommunications services; (iii) mobile telephony services; (iv) transmission capacity (including local access network or local loop, incumbent national and international backbone)	could be discrete markets for dial-up access via a PC modem and dedicated (private/ leased lines) connections. It also found that it could be possible to distinguish between the provision of dial-up services to residential and business customers since business customers generally required dedicated internet access, while residential end users preferred dial-up. The need to further separate residential and business customers, as highlighted in previous decisions, was found to be decreasing	National and EU-wide	The Commission defined the market for telecommunications infrastructure as EU-wide; and as national for fixed and mobile telecommunications services and the provision of transmission capacity
RTL/CNN/Time Warner/N-TV	Case COMP/M.2996, Commission Decision of November 5, 2002	Market for free-access television (advertising-financed private television and public television financed through fees or through fees and partly through advertising)	Based on previous decisions	National	The national character of TV broadcasting is mainly due to different regulatory regimes, existing language barriers, cultural factors and other different conditions of competition prevailing in the various markets

Case	Reference	Type of Case	Product Markets	Reasons Given for Product Markets	Geographic Markets	Reasons Given for Geographic Markets
Charterhouse/CDC/ Telediffusion de France SA	Case COMP/M.2925, Commission Decision of November 15, 2002	Acquisition of joint control over TDF by Charterhouse and CDC	(i) Site research and site acquisition for mobile telephony infrastructure; (ii) site installation and upgrade of sites for mobile telephony; (iii) site hosting (namely for mobile telephony equipment and for broadband over-the-air infrastructure)	(i) Consists on the one hand of the identification of suitable sites for the transmission of wireless telephony signals, and the provision of a cost estimate and a site-study setting out the technical specifications, and on the other hand, of the acquisition of the right to use a right by way by leasing or purchasing agreements which is often conducted by construction companies; (ii) a single relevant market exists because both of these activities enable sites to be used for the installation of wireless telephony transmission; (iii) separate relevant product markets for site hosting (may be distinguished according to the type of service hosted)	National	Since the necessary infrastructure was located in France, the Commission confirmed that the geographic market was national in scope
Carlton+Thomson/ Circuit A, RMBI, RMBC	Case COMP/M.2813, Commission Decision of June 21, 2002	Acquisition of joint control over Circuit A, RMBI and RMBC by Carlton and Thomson	Display-advertising services or cinema-screen advertising services	The Commission left open the question of whether the market can be defined as all display advertising services, or the narrower market of cinema screen advertising services	National	Differences in language, tastes and perceptions of customers
Sony/Philips/Intertrust	Case COMP/M3042, Commission Decision of December 20, 2002	Acquisition of joint control by Sony and Philips of Intertrust	(i) Digital rights management (DRM) and Intellectual Property Rights (IPR); (ii) downstream market for DRM solutions based on these IPR; (iii) downstream market for the retail distribution of digitised	Based on previous decisions	Global	Based on previous decisions

			content that is secured by **DRM** technology; (iv) downstream market for content storing, display and playing devices that use DRM technology		The Commission considered it was not necessary to take a position on geographic market as the operation did not raise any concerns
Logica/CMG	Case COMP/M.3014, Commission Decision of December 9, 2002	Acquisition of CMG by Logica	(i) IT services; (ii) mobile messaging services	(i) The Commission based its decision on the previous *IBM/PwC Consulting* decision, but left open the question whether further segmentation was possible; (ii) the Commission left open the question whether SMS and MMS form separate markets, due to the limited present impact of MMS	(i) The Commission left open the question whether the market was national or wider (*e.g.* EEA-wide/global); (ii) EEA-wide/global at least
Newscorp/Telepiù	Case COMP/M2876, Commission Decision of April 2, 2003	Acquisition of Telepiù by Newscorp	(i) Pay-TV; (ii) upstream markets for the acquisition of audio-visual TV content, namely the rights to premium films, football events and to other sports events; and acquisition of TV channels	The Commission, in line with previous decisions such as *BSkyB/Kirch-PayTV*, found that the conditions of competition for pay-TV and free-to-air TV were different. Whereas in the case of free-to-air TV the relationship between audience share and advertising rates was crucial, in the case of pay-TV the key factor was the relationship between the shaping of programmes and the number of subscriptions. With regard to the upstream markets the Commission noted that the acquisition of broadcasting rights for feature films constituted a separate market from made-for-TV programmes	(i) Pay-TV: national; (ii) acquisition of audio-visual TV content: national	The Commission found the markets to be national due to different regulatory regimes, language barriers, cultural factors and other different conditions of competition prevailing in the different Member States

Appendix 4

Useful Internet Addresses

The websites listed below provide up-to-date information on Community and national telecommunications legislation, in English and in other Community languages. This list is not intended to be exhaustive.

European Institutions

EU homepage . . . . *http://europa.eu.int*
DG Competition . . . . *http://europa.eu.int/comm/competition/index_en.html*
DG Information Society. . . . . *http://europa.eu.int/information_society*
New Regulatory Framework. . . . . *http://europa.eu.int/information_society/topics/telecoms/index_en.htm*
Liberalisation Legislation . . . . . . *http://europa.eu.int/comm/competition/liberalization/legislation/*
Speeches on telecoms . . . . *http://europa.eu.int/comm/competition/speeches/index_theme_3.html*
Community R&D Information
    Programme . . . . *http://www.cordis.lu/en/home.html*
Council Press Releases . . . . *http://ue.eu.int/newsroom/NewMain.asp?LANG=1*
Commission Press Releases. . . . . . *http://europa.eu.int/rapid/start/cgi/guesten.ksh*
European Parliament . . . . *http://www.europarl.eu.int/*
European Court of Justice . . . . . . *http://www.curia.eu.int*
CEPT/ECTRA . . . . *http://www.eto.dk/ceptectra/*
European Telecommunications
    Office. . . . . *http://www.eto.dk/*
European Radiocommunications
    Office. . . . . *http://www.ero.dk/*
European Telecommunications
    Standards Institute (ETSI) . . . . *http://www.etsi.org/*
European Regulations Group . . . . *http://www.erg.eu.int/*

Austria

Telekom-Control (*Osterreichische*
    Gesellschaft für
    TeleKommunikations-
    regulierung) Austrian Regulatory
    Authority for
    Telecommunications and
    Broadcasting (RTR-GmbH) . . . *http://www.tkc.at*
Bundesministerium für
    Wirtschaftliche Augelenheiten
    (BMwA) . . . . *http://www.bmwa.gv.at/*
Austrian Government online. . . . . *http://www.austria.gv.at/*
Bundesministerium für
    Wissenschaft und Verkehr. . . . . *http://www.bmbwk.gv.at/start.asp*

Belgium

Federal Internet Site . . . . *http://www.fgov.be/*
Belgian Institute for Postal Services
    and Telecommunications. . . . . . *http://www.bipt.be/taal.htm*

Denmark

KonkurrenceStyrelse . . . .   *http://www.ks.dk/*
National Information Technology
  Agency (NITA) . . . .   *http://www.itst.dk*

Germany

Regulierungsbehörde für
  Telekommunikation und Post
  (Reg TP) . . . .   *http://www.regtp.de/*

Bundeskartellamt (English
  homepage) . . . .   *http://www.bundeskartellamt.de/english_.html*
Federal Office for Post and
  Telecommunications . . . .   *http://www.regtp.de/*

Greece

National Telecommunications
  Commission (NTC) . . . .   *http://www.eett.gr*
Hellenic Ministry of Foreign
  Affairs . . . .   *http://www.mfa.gr/greek/index.html*

Spain

Servicio de Defensa de la
  Competencia . . . .   *http://www.mineco.es/dgdc/sdc*
Tribunal de Defensa de la
  Competencia . . . .   *http://www.tdcompetencia.org*
Comisión del Mercado de las
  Telecomunicaciones (CMT) . . . .   *http://www.cmt.es*
Governmental Information . . . . . .   *http://www.la-moncloa.es/*

Finland

Telecommunication Administration
  Centre (TAC) . . . .   *http://www.ficora.fi/englanti/index.html*
Ministry of Transport and
  Communications . . . .   *http://www.mintc.fi/*

France

L'Autorité de regulation des
  telecommunications (ART) . . . .   *http://www.telecom.gouv.fr/*
Conseil de la Concurrence . . . . . .   *http://www.finances.gouv.fr/conseilconcurrence/*
Direction des postes et
  telecommunications . . . .   *http://www.telecom.gouv.fr/*

Ireland

Office of the Director of
  Telecommunications Regulation   *http://www.odtr.ie*

Department of Enterprise, Trade
and Employment . . . . *http://www.entemp.ie/*

Italy

Autorità garante della Concorrenza
e del Mercato . . . . *http://www.agcm.it/eng/index.htm*
Autorità per le Garanzie nelle
Comunicazioni . . . . *http://www.agcom.it*
Italian National Agency for New
Technology, Energy and the
Environment . . . . *http://www.sede.enea.it/*

Luxembourg

Institut Luxembourgeois de
Régulation (ILR) . . . . *http://www.ilr.lu*
Government and Administrations *http://www.etat.lu/*

The Netherlands

OPTA, Omafhankelijke Post en
Telecommunicatie Autoriteit
(Independent Post and
Telecommunications Regulator) *http://www.opta.nl/*

Portugal

INFOCID – Interdepartmental and
citizen-oriented information
system in Portugal . . . . *http://www.infocid.pt/*
SAPO/Entidades Governamentais *http://www.sapo.pt/culturais/governo/*

Sweden

Swedish National Post and Telecom
Agency . . . . *http://www.pts.se/index_eng.asp?avdelning = hem_english&language = eng*

Konkurrensverket – the Swedish
Competition Authority . . . . *http://www.kkv.se/eng_indexie.htm*

United Kingdom

Office of Telecommunications
(OFTEL) . . . . *http://www.oftel.gov.uk/*
Office of Fair Trading (OFT) . . . . *http://www.oft.gov.uk/*
Competition Commission . . . . . . *http://www.competition-commission.org.uk/*
Department of Trade and Industry *http://www.dti.gov.uk/*
Independent Television
Commission (ITC) . . . . *http://www.itc.org.uk/*
Radio Authority . . . . *http://www.radioauthority.org.uk/*

Iceland

Icelandic Government . . . . *http://www.stjr.is/*

Norway

Official Documentation and
  Information . . . . *http://odin.dep.no/*

Switzerland

Federal Office for Communications *http://www.bakom.ch/*

United States

Federal Communications
  Commission . . . . *http://www.fcc.gov/*
Department of Justice . . . . *http://www.usdoj.gov/*
Federal Trade Commission . . . . . . *http://www.ftc.gov/*

National Telecommunications &
  Information Administration . . . *http://www.ntia.doc.gov/*
Advisory committee on public
  interest obligations of digital
  television broadcasters . . . . *http://www.ntia.doc.gov/pubintadvcom*

Canada

Bureau de la Concurrence/
  Competition Bureau . . . . *http://strategis.ic.gc.ca/*

Japan

Ministry of Posts and
  Telecommunications . . . . *http://www.yusei.go.jp/index-e.html*

Australia

Australian Telecoms Authority
  (Australian Communications
  Authority) . . . . *http://www.austel.gov.au/*

Australian Department of
  Communications, Information
  Technology and the Arts . . . . . . *http://ftp.dca.gov.au/*
Australian Competition and
  Consumer Commission . . . . *http://www.accc.gov.au/*

New Zealand

Ministry of Commerce,
  Competition and Enterprise
  Branch . . . . *http://www.moc.gov.nz/*

International Organisations

International Telecommunication Union	*http://www.itu.int/*
World Telecommunication Policy Forum	*http://www.itu.int/wtpf/*
World Trade Organisation	*http://www.wto.org/*
Organisation for Economic Co-operation and Development . . .	*http://www.oecd.org/*
NAFTA (North American Free Trade Agreement).	*http://www.nafta-sec-alena.org/*
World Bank	*http://www.worldbank.org/*
Intelsat	*http://www.intelsat.int/*
Inmarsat	*http://www.inmarsat.int*

Appendix 5

EC Computing, Telecommunications and Related Measures

This table sets out the principal areas of legislative action in relation to computing and telecommunications.

Subject	Measure	Current Position (as at September 2003)
Telecommunications		
New Regulatory Framework for electronic communications	Directive 2002/21 on a common regulatory framework (2002) O.J. L108/33	Adopted by Council February 14, 2002 Implementation — July 24, 2003
	Recommendation on relevant product and services markets (2003) O.J. L114/45	Adopted by Commission February 11, 2003
	Guidelines on market analysis and assessment of significant market power (2002) O.J. C165/6	Adopted by Commission July 9, 2002
	Recommendation on notifications, time limits and consultations provided for in Article 7 of Directive 2002/21 on a common regulatory framework (2003) O.J. L190/13	Adopted by Commission July 23, 2003
	Directive 2002/19 on access and interconnection (2002) O.J. L108/7	Adopted by Council February 14, 2002 Implementation — July 24, 2003
	Directive 2002/20 on authorisation (2002) O.J. L108/20	Adopted by Council February 14, 2002 Implementation — July 24, 2003
	Directive 2002/22 on Universal service and users' rights (2002) O.J. L108/51	Adopted by Council February 14, 2002 Implementation — July 24, 2003
	Decision 676/2002 on a regulatory framework for radio spectrum policy (2002) O.J. L108/1	Adopted by Council February 14, 2002 Implementation — July 24, 2003
	Commission Directive 2002/77 on competition in the markets for electronic communications services (2002) O.J. L249/21	Adopted September 16, 2002
	Directive 2002/58 on the processing of personal data and the protection of privacy in the electronic communications sector (2002) O.J. L201/37	Adopted by Council July 12, 2002 Implementation—October 31, 2003

Subject	Measure	Current Position (as at September 2003)
New Regulatory Framework for electronic communications—cont.	Decision 2002/622 establishing a Radio Spectrum Policy Group (2002) O.J. L198/49	Adopted by Commission July 26, 2002
	Recommendation on the processing of caller location information for emergency call services (2003) O.J. L189/49	Adopted by Commission July 25, 2003
	Decision 2002/627 establishing the European Regulators Group for Electronic Communications Networks and Services (2002) O.J. L200/38	Adopted by Commission July 29, 2002
Liberalisation of telecommunications services	**Directive 96/19 amending Directive 90/388 on the implementation of full competition in telecommunications markets (the *Full Competition Directive*) (1996) O.J. L74/13	Adopted by Commission March 13, 1996
	Notice on Status of voice communications on Internet under Directive 90/388 (1998) O.J. C6/04	Published by Commission January 10, 1998
	Supplement to the above Notice (2000) O.J. C369/3	Adopted by Commission December 21, 2000
	Communication: Eighth Report on the Implementation of the Telecommunications Regulatory Package COM(2002) 695	Adopted by Commission December 12, 2002
Open Network Provision (ONP)	**Directive 97/51 amending Directive 90/387 (the *ONP Framework Directive*) and Directive 92/44 (the *ONP Leased Lines Directive*) (1997) O.J. L295/23	Adopted by Council October 6, 1997
	Recommendation on leased lines pricing (1999) O.J. C3863	Adopted by Commission November 24, 1999
	**Directive 98/10 replacing Dir95/62 on the application of ONP to voice telephony and on universal service for telecommunications in a competitive environment (1998) O.J. L101/24	Adopted by Council February 26, 1998
Access and interconnection	**Directive 97/33 (the *Interconnection Directive*) (1997) O.J. L199/32	Adopted by Council June 30, 1997
	Note: *amended by Directive 98/61 on numbering (see below)*	
	Notice on the Application of the Competition Rules to Access Agreements in the Telecommunications Sector (1998) O.J. C265/2	Adopted by Commission March 31, 1998

Appendix 5

Subject	Measure	Current Position *(as at September 2003)*
Access and interconnection—cont.	Recommendation 2002/175 amending Recommendation 98/195, as last amended by Recommendation 2000/263 on interconnection in a liberalised telecommunications market (Part 1 — Interconnection pricing) (2002) O.J. L58/56	Adopted by Commission February 22, 2002
	Recommendation 98/322 on interconnection in a liberalised telecommunications market (Part 2 — Accounting separation and cost accounting) (1998) O.J. L141/6	Adopted by Commission April 8, 1998
	Regulation 2887/2000 on unbundled access to the local loop (2000) O.J. L336/4	Adopted by Council December 18, 2000
Licensing	**Directive 97/13 on a common framework for general authorisations and individual licences in the field of telecommunications services (1997) O.J. L117/15	Adopted by Council 10 April, 1997
Numbering	**Directive 98/61 amending Directive 97/33 with regard to operator number portability and carrier pre-selection (1998) O.J. L268/37	Adopted by Council September 24, 1998
Mobile and personal communications	**Directive 96/2 amending Directive 90/388 with regard to mobile and personal communications (1996) O.J. L20/59	Adopted by Commission January 16, 1996
	Communication: The introduction of third generation mobile communications in the European Union: State of play and the way forward COM(2001) 141 final	Adopted by Commission March 20, 2001
	Communication: Towards the Full Roll-Out of Third Generation Mobile Communications COM(2002) 301 final	Adopted by Commission June 12, 2002
	Recommendation on the harmonisation of the provision of public R-LAN access to public electronic communications networks and services in the Community (2003) O.J. L78/12	Adopted by Commission March 20, 2003
Telecommunications equipment	Directive 1999/5 on radio equipment and telecommunications terminal equipment and the mutual recognition of their conformity, replacing Dir 98/13 (1999) O.J. L91/10	Adopted by Council March 9, 1999

Subject	Measure	Current Position (as at September 2003)
Telecommunications equipment—cont.	Communication on the application of the general principles of free movement of goods and services — Articles 28 and 49 EC — concerning the use of satellite dishes COM(2001) 351 final	Adopted by Commission June 27, 2001
Trans-European Telecommunications networks	Decision 1336/97 on a series of Guidelines for trans-European telecommunications networks (1997) O.J. L183/12	Adopted by Council June 17, 1997
	Decision 1376/2002 revising Decision 1336/97 (2002) O.J. L200/1	Adopted by Parliament and Council July 12, 2002
	Regulation 1655/1999 amending Regulation 2236/95 on TENs COM(1999) 0265 (1999) O.J. L197/1	Adopted by Council July 19, 1999
Cable TV	**Directive 95/51 amending Directive 90/388 with regard to Cable TV (1995) O.J. L256/49	Adopted by Commission October 18, 1995
	**Directive 1999/64 amending Directive 90/388 in order to ensure that telecoms and cable TV networks owned by a single operator are separate legal entities (1999) O.J. L175/39	Adopted by Commission June 23, 1999
Satellite communications	**Directive 94/46 amending Directive 90/388 with regard to satellite communications (1994) O.J. L268/15	Adopted by Commission October 13, 1994
Satellite Personal Communications Services	**Decision 710/97/EC on a co-ordinated authorisation approach (1997) O.J. L105/4	Adopted by Council March 24, 1997
	Extended by Decision 1215/2000/EC (2000) O.J. L139/1	Adopted by Parliament and Council May 16, 2000
Satellite Navigation Systems	Resolution on Galileo (satellite navigation) (2001) O.J. C157/1	Adopted by Council April 5, 2001 Adopted by Commission June 6, 2001
	Regulation 876/2002 on the establishment of Galileo Joint Undertaking (2002) O.J. L138/1	Adopted by Council May 21, 2002

Subject	Measure	Current Position (as at September 2003)
Copyright		
	Directive 93/98 harmonizing the term of protection of copyright and certain related rights	Adopted by Council October 29, 1993
Computer programmes	Directive 91/250 on the legal protection of computer programmes (1991) O.J. L122/42	Adopted by Council May 14, 1991
Legal protection of databases	Directive 96/9 (1996) O.J. L77/20	Adopted by Council March 11, 1996
Copyright and related rights relating to satellite broadcasting and cable retransmission	Directive 93/83 on the co-ordination of such rights (1993) O.J. L248/15	Adopted by Council September 27, 1993
Copyright and related rights in the Information Society	Directive 2001/29 on the harmonisation of certain aspects of copyright and related rights in the Information Society (2001) O.J. L167/10	Adopted by Parliament and Council May 22, 2001
Patents		
	Draft directive on the patentability of computer-implemented inventions COM(2002) 92	Adopted by Commission February 20, 2002
Data Protection		
Protection of individuals in relation to processing of personal data	Directive 95/46 (1995) O.J. L281/31	Implementation by October 24, 1998
	Commission Decision 2000/520 pursuant to Dir 95/46 on the adequacy of the Safe Harbor Principles issued by the US Department of Commerce (2000) O.J. L215/7	Adopted by the Commission July 27, 2000
	Commission Decisions 2000/518 & 519 on the adequacy of the data protection laws of Switzerland and Hungary (2000) O.J. L215/1 & 4	Adopted by Commission July 27, 2000
	Commission Decision 2002/2 on the adequacy of the data protection laws of Canada (2002) O.J. L2/13	Adopted by Commission December 20, 2001

Subject	Measure	Current Position (as at September 2003)
Protection of individuals in relation to processing of personal data—cont.	Commission Decision 2001/497 pursuant to Dir 95/46 on Standard Contractual Clauses for the transfer of personal data to third countries (2001) O.J. L181/19	Adopted by Commission June 15, 2001
	Commission Decision 2002/16 on standard contractual clauses for the transfer of personal data to processors established in third countries under Dir 95/46 (2002) O.J. L6/52	Adopted by Commission December 27, 2001
Protection of personal data in relation to telecommunications networks	**Directive 97/66 on the processing of personal data and the protection of privacy in the telecommunications sector (1998) O.J. L24/1	Adopted by Council December 15, 1997
Protection of personal data in relation to electronic communications	Directive 2002/58/EC concerning the processing of personal data and the protection of privacy in the electronic communications sector (2002) O.J. L201/37	Adopted by Council July 12, 2002

Electronic Commerce and the Information Society

Electronic commerce	Directive 2000/31 on electronic commerce (2000) O.J. L178/1	Adopted May 5, 2000
	Directive 2000/46 on the taking up, pursuit of and prudential supervision of e-money institutions (2000) O.J. L275/39	Adopted June 16, 2000
	Regulation 44/2001 on jurisdiction and the recognition and enforcement of judgments in civil and commercial matters ("the Brussels Regulation") (2001) O.J. L12/1	Adopted December 22, 2000
Consumer protection	Directive 93/15 on unfair terms in consumer contracts (1993) O.J. L95/29	Adopted by Council April 5, 1993
	Directive 97/7 on the protection of consumers in respect of distant contracts (1997) O.J. L144/19	Adopted by Council June 4, 1997
	Framework Decision 2001/413/JHA combating fraud and counterfeiting of non-cash means of payment (2001) O.J. L149/1	Adopted by Council May 28, 2001
	Directive 2002/65 on distance selling of consumer financial services (2002) O.J. L271/16	Adopted September 23, 2002

Subject	Measure	Current Position *(as at September 2003)*
Information Society	Communication: eEurope: an information society for all COM(1999) 687	Adopted by Commission December 12, 1999
	Europe 2002 Action Plan	Adopted by Commission June 6, 2000
	Communication: The eEurope 2002 Update COM(2000) 783	Adopted by Commission November 29, 2000
	Communication: eEurope 2002 Impact and Priorities COM(2001) 140 final	Adopted by Commission March 13, 2001
	Communication: eEurope 2002 Final Report COM(2003) 66 final	Adopted by Commission February 11, 2003
	Communication: eEurope 2005: An information society for all COM(2002) 263 final	Adopted by Commission May 28, 2002
	Communication on creating a safer information society (cybercrime) COM(2000) 890 final	Adopted by Commission January 26, 2001
	Communication: Network and Information Security: Proposal for a European Policy Approach COM(2001) 298 final	Adopted by the Commission June 6, 2001 Council Resolution December 6, 2001
	Framework Decision on the European arrest warrant and the surrender procedures between Member States, money laundering, the identification, tracing, freezing, seizing and confiscation of the intermediaries of and the proceeds from crime (2002) O.J. L190/1	Adopted by Council June 17, 2001
	Framework Decision on money laundering, the identification, tracing, freezing, seizing and confiscation of the intermediaries of and the proceeds from crime (2001) O.J. L182/1	Adopted by Council June 26, 2001
	Communication: Action Plan on promoting safe use of the Internet COM(1997) 582	Adopted by Commission February 13, 1998
	Resolution on illegal and harmful content on the Internet (1997) O.J. C70/1	Adopted by Council February 17, 1997

Subject	Measure	Current Position (as at September 2003)
Information Society—cont.	Draft Council Framework Decision on attacks against information systems COM(2002) 173 final	Adopted by Commission April 19, 2002
	Council of Europe Convention on Cybercrime	Open for signature November 23, 2001
Internet	Directive 98/48 amending Directive 98/34 laying down a procedure for the provision of information in the field of technical standards and regulations (1998) O.J. L217/18	Adopted by Council and European Parliament July 20, 1998
	Decision 276/1999 adopting a multiannual Community action plan on promoting safer use of the Internet (1999) O.J. L33/1	Adopted by Council January 25, 1999
	Draft decision amending Decision 276/1999 COM(2002) 152	Adopted by Commission March 22, 2002
	Regulation 733/2002 on the implementation of the Internet Top Level Domain ".EU" (2002) O.J. L113/1	Adopted by Council April 22, 2002
	Communication: Next Generation Internet — priorities for action in migrating to the new internet protocol IPv6 COM(2002) 96	Adopted by Commission February 21, 2002
Encryption/ Conditional access	Regulation 1334/2000 setting up a Community regime for the control of exports of dual-use items and technologies (2000) O.J. L159/1	Adopted by Council June 22, 2000
	Directive 1999/93 on a Community framework for electronic signatures (2000) O.J. L13/12	Adopted by Council December 13, 1999
	Directive 98/84 on the Legal Protection of Services based on, or consisting of, conditional access (1998) O.J. L320/54	Adopted by Council November 20, 1998
	Communication: Ensuring Security and Trust in Electronic Communication — Towards a European Framework for Digital Signatures and Encryption COM(1997) 503 final	Adopted by Commission October 8, 1997

Subject	*Measure*	*Current Position (as at September 2003)*
Media		
Digital TV	**Directive 95/47 on the use of standards for the transmission of television signals (1995) O.J. L281/51	Adopted by Council October 24, 1995
	Report in the context of Directive 95/47: the development of the market for digital television in the EU COM(1999) 540	Adopted by Commission November 9, 1999
	Directive 89/552 on the coordination of certain provisions laid down by law, Regulation on Administrative Action in Member States concerning the pursuit of television broadcasting activities (1989) O.J. L298/23 Amended by Directive 97/36	Adopted by Council October 3, 1989 Adopted by Council June 30, 1997
Taxation		
VAT on the supply of telecommunications services	Directive 1999/59 amending Dir 77/388 (1999) O.J. L162/63	Adopted by Council June 17, 1999
VAT on electronic services	Directive 2002/38 amending Directive 77/388 regarding VAT on certain electronically supplied services (2002) O.J. L128/41 *and* Regulation 792/2002 amending Regulation 218/92 on administrative cooperation in the field of indirect taxation (2002) O.J. L128/1	Adopted by Council May 7, 2002

Appendix 6

The New Regulatory Framework

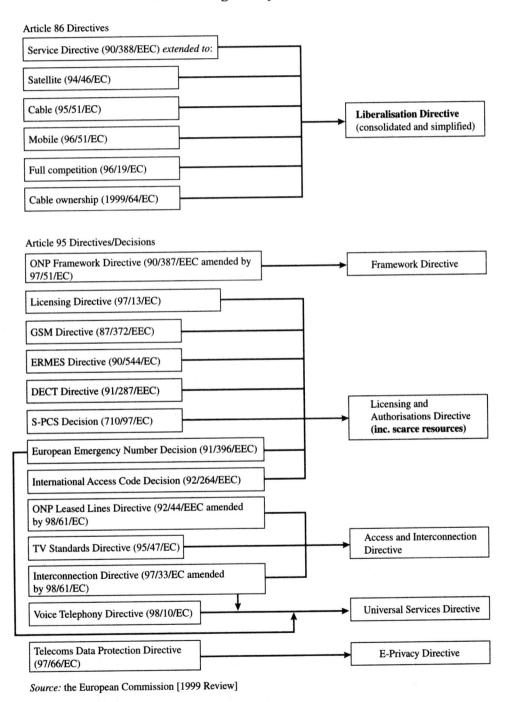

Article 86 Directives

Service Directive (90/388/EEC) *extended to*:

Satellite (94/46/EC)

Cable (95/51/EC)

Mobile (96/51/EC)

Full competition (96/19/EC)

Cable ownership (1999/64/EC)

Liberalisation Directive
(consolidated and simplified)

Article 95 Directives/Decisions

ONP Framework Directive (90/387/EEC amended by 97/51/EC)

Framework Directive

Licensing Directive (97/13/EC)

GSM Directive (87/372/EEC)

ERMES Directive (90/544/EC)

DECT Directive (91/287/EEC)

S-PCS Decision (710/97/EC)

European Emergency Number Decision (91/396/EEC)

International Access Code Decision (92/264/EEC)

Licensing and
Authorisations Directive
(inc. scarce resources)

ONP Leased Lines Directive (92/44/EEC amended by 98/61/EC)

TV Standards Directive (95/47/EC)

Interconnection Directive (97/33/EC amended by 98/61/EC)

Voice Telephony Directive (98/10/EC)

Access and Interconnection
Directive

Universal Services Directive

Telecoms Data Protection Directive (97/66/EC)

E-Privacy Directive

Source: the European Commission [1999 Review]

The New Regulatory Framework

Source: the European Commission, 1999 Review.

Appendix 7

Mergers and Acquisitions, Joint Ventures and Other Alliances

(a) Concentrations in the Telecommunications Equipment Sector

Case M.042 *Alcatel/Telettra*, Commission Decision of April 12, 1991, O.J. (1991) L122/48; Case M.178 *Saab Ericsson Space*, Commission Decision of January 13, 1992; Case M.133 *Ericsson/ Kolbe*, Commission Decision of January 22, 1992; Case M.236 *Ericsson/Ascom*, Commission Decision of July 8, 1992; Case M.249 *Northern Telecom/Matra*, Commission Decision of July 17, 1992; Case M.249 *Ericsson/Hewlett-Packard*, Commission Decision of March 12, 1993; Case M.366 *Alcatel/STC*, Commission Decision of September 13, 1993; Case M.496 *Marconi/Finmeccanica*, Commission Decision of September 5, 1994; Case M.468 *Siemens/Italtel*, Commission Decision of February 17, 1995, O.J. (1995) L161/27; Case M.519 *Ericsson/Raychem*, Commission Decision of November 21, 1994; Case M.676 *Ericsson/Ascom II*, Commission Decision of December 22, 1995; Case M.651 *AT&T/Philips*, Commission Decision of February 5, 1996; Case M.668 *Philips/Origin*, Commission Decision of February 22, 1996; Case M.876 *Telia/Ericsson*, Commission Decision of February 20, 1997; Case M.966 *Philips/Lucent Technologies*, Commission Decision of August 20, 1997; Case M.1113 *Nortel/Norweb*, Commission Decision of March 18, 1998; Case M.1226 *GEC/ GPTH*, Commission Decision of June 27, 1998; Case M.1263 *Nortel/Bay*, Commission Decision of August 21, 1998; Case JV.12 *Ericsson/Nokia/Psion/Motorola*, Commission Decision of December 22, 1998; Case M.1440 *Lucent Technologies/Ascend Communication*, Commission Decision of April 6, 1999; Case JV.26 *Freecom/Dangaard*, Commission Decision of December 1, 1999; Case M.1800 *Marconi/Bosch Public Network*, Commission Decision of January 19, 2000, O.J. (2000) C144/8; Case M.1841 *Celestica/IBM (EMS)*, Commission Decision of February 25, 2000, O.J. (2000) C341/2; Case M.1883 *NEC/Mitsubishi*, Commission Decision of April 3, 2000, O.J. (2000) C368/6; Case M.2077 *Clayton Dubilier & Rice/Italtel*, Commission Decision of September 1, 2000, O.J. (2000) C352/7; Case M.2116 *Flextronics/Italdata*, Commission Decision of September 25, 2000, O.J. (2000) C354/39; Case M.2135 *NCR/4 Front*, Commission Decision of October 12, 2000, O.J. (2000) C348/13; Case M.2048 *Alcatel/Thomson Multimedia/JV*, Commission Decision of October 26, 2000, O.J. (2000) C348/15; Case M.2215 *Techint/Stella/James Jones/Sirti JV*, Commission Decision of November 22, 2000, O.J. (2000) C368/6; Case M.2199 *Quantum/Maxtor*, Commission Decision of December 8, 2000, O.J. (2001) C068/11; Case M.2265 *Ricoh/Lanier World*, Commission Decision of January 24, 2001, O.J. (2001) C159/3; Case M.2324 *Sanmina Corporation/AB Segerström & Svensson*, Commission Decision of February 23, 2001, O.J. (2001) C074/10; Case M.2358 *Flextronics/Ericsson*, Commission Decision of April 6, 2001, O.J. (2001) C159/4; Case M.2263 *Philips/LG Electronics/JV*, Commission Decision of April 9, 2001, O.J. (2001) C180/16; Case M.2403 *Schneider/Thomson Multimedia JV*, Commission Decision of June 13, 2001, O.J. (2001) C251/3; Case M.2452 *Belgacom/BAS Holding/Securitas*, Commission Decision of July 5, 2001, O.J. (2001) C238/7; Case M.2534 *SCI Systems/Nokia Networks*, Commission Decision of August 6, 2001, O.J. (2001) C281/11; Case M.2260 *Hitachi/LG Electronics/JV*, Commission Decision of September 14, 2001, O.J. (2001) C296/21; Case M.2549 *Sanmina/SCI Systems*, Commission Decision of September 20, 2001, O.J. (2001) C296/23; Case M.2462 *Ericsson/Sony/JV*,

Commission Decision of September 27, 2001, O.J. (2001) C281/9; Case M.2546 *EADS/Nortel*, Commission Decision of October 1, 2001, O.J. (2001) C296/21; Case M.2528 *Maersk IT/LM Ericsson/WAC*, Commission Decision of October 15, 2001, O.J. (2001) C319/16; Case M.2629 *Flextronics/Xerox*, Commission Decision of November 12, 2001, O.J. (2001) C339/20; Case M.2638 *3i/Consors/100 World*, Commission Decision of December 10, 2001, O.J. (2002) C049/16; Case M.2609 *HP/Compaq*, Commission Decision of January 31, 2002, O.J. (2002) C039/23; Case M.2689 *3i/Dansk Kapitalanlaeg/Ibsen*, Commission Decision of January 31, 2002, O.J. (2002) C043/24; Case M.2734 *Sanmina-SCI/Alcatel*, Commission Decision of March 21, 2002, O.J. (2002) C091/7; Case M.2784 *Jabil/Alcatel*, Commission Decision of April 24, 2002, O.J. (2002) C108/8; Case M.2790 *Siemens/First Sensor Technology*, Commission Decision of June 14, 2002, O.J. (2002) C147/21; Case M.2925 *Charterhouse/CDC/Telediffusion de France SA*, Commission Decision of November 15, 2002, O.J. (2002) C327/13; Case M.3014 *Logica/CMG*, Commission Decision of December 9, 2002, O.J. (2003) C010/8; Case M.2851 *Intracom/Siemens/STI*, Commission Decision of February 10, 2003, O.J. (2003) C049/3.

(b) Concentrations in Telecommunications Networks and Services

Case M.346 *JCSAT/SAJAC*, Commission Decision of June 30, 1993; Case M.394 *Mannesmann/RWE/Deutsche Bank*, Commission Decision of November 27, 1993; Case M.408 *Mannesman/RWE*, Commission Decision of February 28, 1994; Case M.532 *Cable and Wireless/Schlumberger*, Commission Decision of December 22, 1994; Case M.570 *TBT/TeleDanmark/Telenor*, Commission Decision of April 24, 1995; Case M.618 *Cable and Wireless/Veba*, Commission Decision of August 16, 1995; Case M.595 *British Telecommunications/VIAG*, Commission Decision of December 22, 1995; Case M.689 *ADSB/Belgacom*, Commission Decision of February 29, 1996; Case M.683 *GTS Hermes Inc./HIT Rail BV*, Commission Decision of March 25, 1996; Case M.827 *DB Kom*, Commission Decision of October 23, 1996; Case M.802 *Telecom Eireann*, Commission Decision of December 18, 1996; Case M.900 *BT/Tell DK/SBB/Migros/UBS*, Commission Decision of April 16, 1997; Case M.856 *British Telecom*, Commission Decision of May 14, 1997, O.J. (1997) L336/1; Case M.927 *STET/GET/Union Fenosa*, Commission Decision of August 20, 1997; Case M.925 *Albacom/BT/ENI*, Commission Decision of November 13, 1997; Case M.1046 *Ameritech/TeleDanmark*, Commission Decision of December 5, 1997; Case M.1055 *Cégétel/Vodafone — SFR*, Commission Decision of December 19, 1997; Case M.1025 *Mannesmann/Olivetti/Infostrada*, Commission Decision of January 15, 1998; Case M.1177 *Belgacom/TeleDanmark/Tulip*, Commission Decision of May 19, 1998; Case M.1132 *BT/ESB/AIG*, Commission Decision of May 19, 1998; Case M.1148 *STET/GET/Madrid Cable*, Commission Decision of May 28, 1998; Case JV.2 *Enel/FT/DT/Wind*, Commission Decision of June 22, 1998; Case M.1199 *UTA/Swisscom*, Commission Decision of July 13, 1998; Case JV.4 *Orange/Viag*, Commission Decision of August 11, 1998; Case JV.7 *Telia/Sonera/Lietuvos Telekomas*, Commission Decision of August 14, 1998; Case JV.9 *Telia/Sonera/Motorola/UAB Omnitel*, Commission Decision of August 18, 1998; Case M.1252 *AT&T & TCI*, Commission Decision of December 4, 1998; Case M.1171 *PTA/Telecom Italia/Telekom Austria*, Commission Decision of December 16, 1998; Case M.1496 *Olivetti/Telecom Italia*, Commission Decision of April 22, 1999; Case JV.15 *BT/AT&T*, Commission Decision of March 30, 1999; Case M.1465 *Deutsche Telekom/Max Mobil*, Commission Decision of April 22, 1999; Case JV.17 *Mannesmann/Bell Atlantic/OPI*, Commission Decision of May 21, 1999; Case M.1439 *Telia/Telenor*, Commission Decision of October 13, 1999; Case M.1679 *France Télécom/STI/SRD*, Commission Decision of

October 21, 1999; Case M.1745 *EADS*, Commission Decision of May 11, 2000, O.J. (2000) C307/4; Case M.1926 *Telefónica/Tyco/JV*, Commission Decision of August 11, 2000, O.J. (2000) C255/9; Case M.1875 *Reuters/Equant — Project Proton*, Commission Decision of April 17, 2000; Case M.2191 *BT/Amadeus/JV*, Commission Decision of November 13, 2000, O.J. (2002) C021/31; Case M.1969 *UTC/Honeywell/i2/My Aircraft.com*, Commission Decision of August 4, 2000; Case M.2109 *Reuters/Verlagsgruppe Handelsblatt/Meteor*, Commission Decision of November 20, 2000, O.J. (2000) C361/6; Case M.2204 *Endesa/Telecom Italia/Union Fenosa/Auna*, Commission Decision of December 6, 2000, O.J. (2000) C374/11; Case M.2251 *AOL/Banco Santander/JV*, Commission Decision of December 19, 2000, O.J. (2001) C051/9; Case M.1951 *BT/Japan Telecom/Vodafone Airtouch/JV*, Commission Decision of September 1, 2000, O.J. (2000), C274/10; Case M.1840 *KKR/Bosch Telecom Private Networks*, Commission Decision of February 29, 2000, O.J. (2000) C033/3; Case M.1838 *BT/ESAT*, Commission Decision of March 27, 2000, O.J. (2000) C341/3; Case M.1982 *Telia/Oracle/Drutt*, Commission Decision of September 11, 2000, O.J. (2000) C374/10; Case M.2099 *Hutchison/NTT DoCoMo/KPN Mobile/JV*, Commission Decision of September 5, 2000, O.J. (2000) C328/10; Case M.1747 *Telekom Austria/Libro*, Commission Decision of February 28, 2000, O.J. (2000) C108/8; Case M.1812 *Telefónica/Terra/Amadeus*, Commission Decision of April 27, 2000, O.J. (2000) C235/6; Case M.2195 *Cap Gemini/Vodafone/JV*, Commission Decision of November 29, 2000, O.J. (2000) C273/9; Case M.1741 *MCIWorldCom/Sprint*, Commission Decision of June 28, 2000, O.J. (2000) C014/6; Case M.1938 *BT/Telfort*, Commission Decision of June 21, 2000, O.J. (2000) C55/10; Case M.2053 *Telenor/BellSouth/Sonofon*, Commission Decision of August 4, 2000, O.J. (2000) C295/11; Case M.1964 *Planet Internet/Fortis Bank/Mine JV*, Commission Decision of July 10, 2000; Case M.1880 *Minnesota Mining and Manufacturing/Quante*, Commission Decision of March 31, 2000, O.J. (2000) C255/9; Case M.1973 *Telecom Italia/Endesa/Union Fenosa*, Commission Decision of September 12, 2000, O.J. (2000) C286/6; Case M.2056 *Sonera Systems/ICL Invia Data Info/JV*, Commission Decision of August 28, 2000, O.J. (2000) C322/13; Case M.2217 *Celestica/Nec Technologies UK*, Commission Decision of December 13, 2000, O.J. (2001) C316/14; Case M.1908 *Alcatel/Newbridge Networks*, Commission Decision of May 19, 2000, O.J. (2000) C169/7; Case M.2197 *Hilton/Accor/Forte/Travel Services JV*, Commission Decision of February 16, 2001, O.J. 2001 C127/9; Case M.2216 *Enel/Wind/Infostrada*, Commission Decision of January 19, 2001, O.J. (2001) C039/9; Case M.2143 *BT/VIAG Interkom*, Commission Decision of February 19, 2001, O.J. (2001) C207/10; Case M.2365 *Schlumberger/Sema*, Commission Decision of April 5, 2001, O.J. (2001) C137/9; Case M.2463 *Speedy Tomato/Olivetti*, Commission Decision of June 14, 2001, O.J. (2001) C279/7; Case M.2401 *IndustriKapital/Telia Enterprise*, Commission Decision of May 29, 2001, O.J. (2001) C272/14; Case M.2479 *Flextronics/Alcatel*, Commission Decision of June 29, 2001, O.J. (2001) C278/3; Case M.2513 *RWE/Kärntner Energie Holding*, Commission Decision of August 2, 2001, O.J. (2001) C286/3; Case M.2651 *AT&T/Concert*, Commission Decision of December 17, 2001, O.J. (2002) C016/15; Case M.2642 *BT/Concert*, Commission Decision of December 17, 2001, O.J. (2002) C079/11; Case M.2630 *Siemens/Wiener Stadtwerke/Master Talk*, Commission Decision of November 28, 2001, O.J. (2001) C358/11; Case M.2627 *Otto Versand/Sabre/Travelocity JV*, Commission Decision of December 19, 2001, O.J. (2002) C021/29; Case M.2616 *Deutsche Bank/TDC/JV*, Commission Decision of November 27, 2001, O.J. (2002) C051/28; Case M.2576 *Telefónica/Ericsson/JV*, Commission Decision of September 28, 2001, O.J. (2001) C328/11; Case M.2565 *PPC/Wind/JV*, Commission Decision of November 28, 2001, O.J. (2001) C362/6; Case M.2418 *ORF/Netway/Adworx*, Commission

Decision of May 21, 2001, O.J. (2001) C201/5; Case M.2527 *Telenor Easat/Eco Telecom/Vimpel Communications*, Commission Decision of September 21, 2001, O.J. (2001) C298/11; Case M.2510 *Cendant/Galileo*, Commission Decision of September 24, 2001, O.J. (2001) C321/8; Case M.2494 *Debitel/Debitel Nederland*, Commission Decision of June 29, 2001, O.J. (2001) C198/11; Case M.2477 *Atle/Pricerunner JV*, Commission Decision of October 23, 2001, O.J. (2001) C322/24; Case M.2347 *Mannesmann Arcor/Netcom Kassel*, Commission Decision of January 9, 2001, O.J. (2001) C049/6; Case M.2310 *Hutchison/Investor/HI3G*, Commission Decision of February 19, 2001, O.J. (2001) C029/5; Case M.2257 *France Télécom/Equant*, Commission Decision of March 21, 2001, O.J. (2001) C187/08; Case M.2255 *Telefónica Intercontinental/Sonera 3G Holding/Consortium IPSE 2000*, Commission Decision of January 9, 2001, O.J. (2001) C049/6; Case M.2249 *Marconi/RTS/JV*, Commission Decision of March 23, 2001, O.J. (2001) C107/8; Case M.2648 *KPNQwest/Ebone/GTS*, Commission Decision of January 16, 2002, O.J. (2002) C034/10; Case M.2741 *Vodafone/Arcor*, Commission Decision of March 20, 2002, O.J. (2002) C106/22; Case M.2682 *Credit Suisse/Belgacom/T-Mobile/BEN*, Commission Decision of January 17, 2002, O.J. (2002) C037/25; Case M.2803 *Telia/Sonera*, Commission Decision of July 10, 2002, O.J. (2002) C201/19; Case M.2958 *Wind/Blu*, Commission Decision of September 12, 2002, O.J. (2002) C239/20; Case M.2964 *Global Crossing/Hutchison/ST Telemedia*, Commission Decision of January 16, 2003, O.J. (2003) C016/6.

(c) Concentrations in the Mobile Sector

Case M.1817 *BellSouth/Vodafone (E-Plus)*, Commission Decision of January 26, 2000, O.J. (2000) C258/11; Case M.1821 *BellSouth/VRT (E-Plus)*, Commission Decision of January 31, 2000, O.J. (2000) C258/12; Case M.1795 *Vodafone Airtouch/Mannesmann*, Commission Decision of April 12, 2000, O.J. (2000) C141/19; Case M.1946 *BellSouth/SBC/JV*, Commission Decision of May 26, 2000, O.J. (2000) C202/5; Case M.1957 *VIAG Interkom/Telenor Media*, Commission Decision of June 14, 2000, O.J. (2000) C134/14; Case M.1954 *ACS/Sonera/Vivendi/Xfera*, Commission Decision of July 31, 2000, O.J. (2000) C234/6; Case M.2130 *Belgacom/TeleDanmark/T-Mobile International/BEN Nederland Holding*, Commission Decision of September 25, 2000, O.J. (2001) C362/6; Case M.2137 *SLDE/NTL/MSCP/NOOS*, Commission Decision of October 16, 2000, O.J. (2001) C029/11; Case M.2155 *France Télécom/Schmid/Mobilcom*, Commission Decision of October 24, 2000, O.J. (2001) C130/6; Case M.2144 *Telefónica/Sonera/German UMTS JV*, Commission Decision of November 17, 2000, O.J. (2000) C369/7; Case M.1863 *Vodafone/BT/Airtel*, Commission Decision of December 18, 2000, O.J. (2001) C042/11; Case IV/M.2346 *Telefónica/Portugal Telecom/Brazilian JV*, Commission Decision of March 13, 2001, O.J. (2001) C111/9; Case M.2468 *Seat Pagine Gialle/Eniro*, Commission Decision of June 26, 2001, O.J. (2001) C198/9; Case M.2462 *Ericsson/Sony/JV*, Commission Decision of September 27, 2001, O.J. (2001) C281/9; Case M.2598 *TDC/CMG/Migway JV*, Commission Decision of October 4, 2001, O.J. (2002) C016/16; Case M.2959 *Deutsche Telekom/BEN*, Commission Decision of September 20, 2002.

(d) Concentrations in Television Broadcasting

Case M.110 *ABC/Générale des Eaux/Canal+/W.H. Smith*, Commission Decision of September 10, 1991; Case M.176 *Sunrise*, Commission Decision of January 13, 1992; Case M.410 *Kirch/Richemont/Telepiù*, Commission Decision of August 2, 1994; Case M.0489 *Bertelsmann/News International/Vox*, Commission Decision of September 6, 1994; Case M.469 *MSG*, Commission

Decision of November 9, 1994, O.J. (1994) L364/1; Case M.525 *Vox II*, Commission Decision of January 18, 1995; Case M.584 *Kirch/Richemont, Multichoice/Telpiù*, Commission Decision of May 5, 1995; Case M.566 *CLT/Disney/SuperRTL*, Commission Decision of May 17, 1995; Case M.490 *Nordic Satellite Distribution*, Commission Decision of July 19, 1995, O.J. (1996) L53/20; Case M.810 *n-TV*, Commission Decision of September 16, 1996; Case M.553 *RTL/Veronica/Endemol*, Commission Decision of September 20, 1995, O.J. (1996) L134/32; Case M.779 *Bertelsmann/CLT*, Commission Decision of October 7, 1996; Case M.655 *Canal+/UFA/MDO*, Commission Decision of November 13, 1995; Case M.878 *RTL7*, Commission Decision of February 14, 1997; Case M.939 *BankAmerica/General Electric/Cableuropa*, Commission Decision of June 19, 1997; Case M.1022 *Cable I Televisio de Catalunya*, Commission Decision of January 28, 1998; Case M.1091 *Cableuropa/SpainCom/CTC*, Commission Decision of January 28, 1998; Case M.993 *Bertelsmann/Kirch/Première*, Commission Decision of May 27, 1998, O.J. (1999) L53/1; Case M.1027 *Deutsche Telekom/BetaResearch*, Commission Decision of May 27, 1998, O.J. (1999) L53/31; Case M.1148 *STET/GET/Madrid Cable*, Commission Decision of May 28, 1998; Case M.1251 *Particel International/Cableuropa*, Commission Decision of July 30, 1998; Case M.1327 *C/Canal+/CDPQ/BankAmerica*, Commission Decision of December 3, 1998, O.J. (1999) C233/21; Case M.1574 *Kirch/Mediaset*, Commission Decision of August 3, 1999; Case M.1889 *CLT-UFA/Canal+/Vox*, Commission Decision of March 21, 2000, O.J. (2000) C134/13; Case JV.37 *BSkyB/KirchPayTV*, Commission Decision of March 21, 2000, O.J. (2000) C110/45; Case JV.40 *Canal+/Lagardère/Canal Satellite*, Commission Decision of June 22, 2000, O.J. (2000) C110/45; Case M.1958 *Bertelsmann/GBL/Pearson TV*, Commission Decision of June 29, 2000, O.J. (2000) C180/14; Case M.1978 *Telecom Italia/News TV/Stream*, Commission Decision of June 29, 2000, O.J. (2002) C066/14; Case M.1943 *Telefónica/Endemol*, Commission Decision of July 11, 2000, O.J. (2000) C235/6; Case JV.50 *Blackstone/CDPQ/Kabel Baden-Württemberg*, Commission Decision of August 8, 2000, O.J. (2000) C323/4; Case M.1845 *AOL/Time Warner*, Commission Decision of October 11, 2000, O.J. (2001) L268/28; Case M.2050 *Vivendi/Canal+/Seagram*, Commission Decision of October 13, 2000, O.J. (2000) C311/3; Case M.2124 *ISP/ESPNS/Globosat — JV*, Commission Decision of December 4, 2000, O.J. (2001) C190/10; Case M.2211 *Universal Studio Networks/De Facto 829 (NTL)/Studio Channel Limited*, Commission Decision of December 20, 2000, O.J. (2001) C363/31; Case M.2259 *Terra/Amadeus/1Travel.com*, Commission Decision of January 17, 2001, O.J. (2001) C49/7; Case M.2336 *Thomson Multimedia/Technicolor*, Commission Decision of February 28, 2001, O.J. (2001) C206/8; Case M.2222 *UGC/Liberty Media*, Commission Decision of April 24, 2001, O.J. (2001) C172/20; Case M.2279 *Nortel/Mundinteractivos/Broad Media/JV*, Commission Decision of April 25, 2001, O.J. (2001) C190/9; Case M.2407 *Bertelsmann/RTL Group*, Commission Decision of May 11, 2001, O.J. (2001) C291/5; Case M.2303 *Ciaoweb/We Cube*, Commission Decision of June 14, 2001, O.J. (2001) C179/29; Case M.2300 *YLE/TDF/Digita/JV*, Commission Decision of June 26, 2001, O.J. (2001) C272/15; Case M.2471 *Accenture/Lagardere/JV*, Commission Decision of July 26, 2001, O.J. (2001) C327/16; Case M.2352 *SWB/Stadtwerke Bielefeld/JV*, Commission Decision of July 27, 2001, O.J. (2001) C321/9; Case M.2652 *Blackstone/CDPQ/Deteks NRW*, Commission Decision of November 23, 2001, O.J. (2001) C358/11; Case M.2550 *Mezzo/Muzzik*, Commission Decision of December 6, 2001, O.J. (2001) C021/29; Case JV.57 *TPS*, Commission Decision of April 30, 2002, O.J. (2002) C137/28; Case M.2766 *Vivendi Universal/Hachette/Multithematiques*, Commission Decision of May 3, 2002, O.J. (2002) C154/9; Case M.2723 *RTL/ProSiebenSat1/VG Media*, Commission Decision of May 21, 2002, O.J. (2002) C201/20; Case M.2883 *Bertelsmann/Zomba*, Commission Decision of September 2, 2002, O.J. (2002) C223/13; Case M.2996 *RTL/CNN/N-TV*, Commission Decision of November 5, 2002, O.J. (2002) C310/23; Case M.2876 *NewCorp/Telepiù*, Commission Decision of April 2, 2003.

Index

Fixed voice telephony services
liberalisation of, 1–078—1–081
see also Full Competition Directive
Framework Directive
introduction, 1–011
market reviews, 1–027
regulation covering
broadcasting transmission services, 1–026
fixed location services, 1–025—1–026
leased lines, 1–026
non-fixed location services, 1–025—1–026
voice call termination services, 1–028
Fraud
criminal offences, 3–092
e-commerce, and, 3–092
Free movement of goods (Article 28)
exceptions to, 2–011
exhaustion of copyright, 2–012
proportionality, applying to, 2–011
remedies for infringement, 2–014
scope, 2–011
services, distinguished from, 2–010
transmission goods, 2–010
Freedom of establishment (Article 43)
exceptions to, 2–013
provisions covering, 2–013
setting up businesses, 2–013
Freedom to provide services (Article 49)
activities covered, 2–003
exclusive broadcasting rights, 2–008
internet services, and, 3–018—3–020
national restrictions, 2–004, 2–006—2–007
prior authorisation schemes, 2–009
public policy exception, 2–005
Frequencies
see also Radio frequencies
access to, 1–074, 6–064
allocation of, 1–005, 1–103—1–104
control of, 6–064
convergence, affecting, 1–104
co-ordination of, 1–106
demand for, 1–104—1–105
efficient use of, 1–105
licensing provisions, 1–083
rights of use, 1–073, 1–083, 1–085—1–088, 3–013
spectrum "re-farming", 1–105
and see Radio spectrum
technological advances, affecting, 1–104
Full Competition Directive
voice telephony services
exclusive and special rights, 1–079
new market entrants, 1–080

General Agreement on Trade and Services (GATS)
dispute settlement, 1–301

GATS—*cont.*
EU commitments, 1–303—1–305
Fourth Protocol
obligations, under, 1–297
market access, 1–297, 1–300
MFN principle, 1–297
national treatment principle, 1–297, 1–300
regulatory principles, 1–301
telecommunications services, 1–299, 1–301
GATS 2000
trade liberalisation, and, 1–304
remedies, 1–301
television broadcasts, 2–036, 2–059
General authorisations
electronic communications
authorisation procedures, 1–062
compliance provisions, 1–064
conditions affecting, 1–063
fees and charges, 1–065
"must carry" obligations, 1–063
"one-stop shopping" procedure, 1–066—1–067
General Packaged Radio Service (GPRS)
regulation of, 1–028
Global System for Mobile Communications (GSM)
adoption of, 1–111
allocation of frequencies, 1–104
benefit of, 1–111
development of, 1–111

Harmonisation
Green Paper proposals, 1–002
introduction, 1–006
legislative development, 1–006
liberalisation complementary to, 1–006
national regulatory systems, 1–008
regulatory initiatives, 1–001
technical standards, 1–174
and see Transparency
Horizontal transactions
Commission practice, regarding, 8–360
Human rights
privacy, and, 3–036—3–037, 3–041
Hypertext linking
copyright protection, 3–032, 3–034
database rights, 3–033
deep linking, 3–032
embedded links, 3–034
framing, 3–032
liability for, 3–032
meaning of, 3–032
normal links, 3–034

Information security
  see Data protection, Privacy
Information society
  copyright protection, 2–091, 3–022
    and see Information Society Copyright
      Directive
  technical standards, 1–174
Information Society Copyright Directive
  copyright protection
    authorised copying, 3–026
    products circumventing, 3–026
    rights management information, 3–027
    technical measures enabling, 3–026
  distribution right, 3–025
  implementation, 3–029
  remedies available, 3–028
  reproduction right
    caching and browsing, 3–023
    communication to the public, 3–024
    exceptions to, 3–024
    exclusive rights, 3–023
    fair remuneration, 3–023
    neighbouring rights, and, 3–024
    temporary copies, 3–023
  sanctions, 3–028
  scope, 3–022
Information society service
  definition of, 1–015
Intellectual property rights
  abuse of dominant position, 6–050
  essential facilities doctrine, and, 6–050, 6–051
  excessive pricing, 6–050
  exclusive rights, 6–038
  legal monopoly over, 6–022
  restrictions on use, 8–034
  trademark registration, 6–050
  unfair licensing terms, 6–050
Interconnection
  see also Access
  agreements covering, 1–148
  competition law, and, 9–013
  definition of, 1–146
  dispute resolution, 1–176
  internal market development, 1–177
  mobile termination charges, 1–188—1–191
    and see Fixed-to mobile termination charges
  NRA powers, 1–173, 1–289
  non-discrimination requirements, 1–154
  pricing
    benchmarking, 1–184—1–185
    competition rules, and, 1–180
    cost methodologies, 1–183
    cost-orientated charges, 1–179
    cost-recovery mechanisms, 1–182
    FL-LRAIC, use of, 1–184—1–185

Interconnection—*cont.*
  pricing—*cont.*
    interconnection tariffs, 1–178, 9–013
    international accounting rate, 1–191
    NRA control, 1–181
    reference offers, 1–181
    SMP operators, 1–179
  regulatory framework, 1–143
  rights and obligations, 1–149—1–156
  transparency requirements, 1–154
International telephone services
  accounting rate systems, 1–191
  international settlement rates, 1–191
International trade
  e-commerce, and, 3–069
  telecommunications market, 1–296
    and see GATS, WTO
Internet
  convergence, and, 3–002
  description of, 3–001
  domain names
    see Domain name system
  governance, 3–004—3–010
  Green Paper proposals, 3–006
  legal issues involving, 3–003
  national laws, and, 3–003
  regulatory framework, 3–001, 3–004
  services available, 3–002
    and see Internet services
  USA involvement, 3–005—3–006
  voice telephony services, 1–084
Internet Action Plan
  awareness actions, 3–057
  filtering systems, 3–056
  implementation, 3–059
  launch of, 3–010
  rating systems, 3–056
  self-regulation, and, 3–055
  support actions, 3–057
Internet Assigned Numbers Authority (IANA)
  internet management, and, 3–005—3–006
Internet Corporation for Assigned Names and
    Numbers (ICANN)
  creation of, 3–007
  regulation by, 6–093
  role of, 3–008
Internet Service Providers (ISPs)
  access provisions, 1–147
  confidentiality, and, 3–036
  country of origin principle, 3–016
  essential facilities, access to, 6–049
  free movement provisions, 3–018
  privacy, and, 3–036
  regulation of, 3–012
  rights of use, obtaining, 3–013